Twelfth Edition

Principles of Information Systems

Ralph M. Stair

Professor Emeritus, Florida State University

George W. Reynolds

Instructor, Strayer University

CENGAGE
Learning·

Australia • Brazil • Mexico • Singapore • United Kingdom • United States

Principles of Information Systems, Twelfth Edition

Ralph M. Stair & George W. Reynolds

Product Director: Joe Sabatino

Product Manager: Jason Guyler

Associate Content Developer: Anne Merrill

Sr. Product Assistant: Brad Sullender

Development Editor: Lisa Ruffolo, The Software Resource Publications, Inc.

Sr. Marketing Manager: Eric La Scola

Marketing Coordinator: William Guiliani

Art and Cover Direction, Production Management, and Composition: Lumina Datamatics, Inc.

Manufacturing Planner: Ron Montgomery

Intellectual Property Product Manager: Kathryn Kucharek

Intellectual Property Analysts: Sara Crane and Christina Ciaramella

Cover Credits: © mike.irwin/Shutterstock

For product information and technology assistance, contact us at
Cengage Learning Customer & Sales Support, 1-800-354-9706

For permission to use material from this text or product,
submit all requests online at **www.cengage.com/permissions**

Further permissions questions can be emailed to
permissionrequest@cengage.com

Library of Congress Control Number: 2014951130

Student Edition:

ISBN: 978-1-285-86716-8

Instructor's Edition:

ISBN: 978-1-285-86969-8

Cengage Learning
20 Channel Center Street
Boston, MA 02210
USA

Some of the product names and company names used in this book have been used for identification purposes only and may be trademarks or registered trademarks of their respective manufacturers and sellers.

Any fictional data related to persons or companies or URLs used throughout this book is intended for instructional purposes only. At the time this book was printed, any such data was fictional and not belonging to any real persons or companies.

Cengage Learning reserves the right to revise this publication and make changes from time to time in its content without notice.

Cengage Learning is a leading provider of customized learning solutions with office locations around the globe, including Singapore, the United Kingdom, Australia, Mexico, Brazil, and Japan. Locate your local office at: **www.cengage.com/global**

Cengage Learning products are represented in Canada by Nelson Education, Ltd.

To learn more about Cengage Learning, visit **www.cengage.com**

Purchase any of our products at your local college store or at our preferred online store **www.cengagebrain.com**

Printed in the United States of America
Print Number: 01   Print Year: 2014

Brief Contents

Contents

Preface

As organizations and entrepreneurs continue to operate in an increasingly competitive and global marketplace, workers in all business areas including accounting, customer service, distribution, finance, human resources, information systems, logistics, marketing, manufacturing, research and development, and sales must be well prepared to make the significant contributions required for success. Regardless of your future role, even if you are an entrepreneur, you need to understand what information systems (IS) can and cannot do and be able to use them to help you achieve personal and organizational goals. You will be expected to discover opportunities to use information systems and to participate in the design and implementation of solutions to business problems employing information systems. To be successful, you must be able to view information systems from the perspective of business and organizational needs. For your solutions to be accepted, you must recognize and address their impact on co-workers, customers, suppliers, and other key business partners. For these reasons, a course in information systems is essential for students in today's high-tech world.

Principles of Information Systems, Twelfth Edition, continues the tradition and approach of previous editions. Our primary objective is to provide the best information systems text and accompanying materials for the first information systems course required for all business students. We want you to learn to use information systems to ensure your personal success in your current or future role and to improve the success of your organization. Through surveys, questionnaires, focus groups, and feedback that we have received from current and past adopters, as well as others who teach in the field, we have been able to develop the highest-quality set of teaching materials available to help you achieve these goals.

Principles of Information Systems, Twelfth Edition, stands proudly at the beginning of the IS curriculum and remains unchallenged in its position as the only IS principles text offering basic IS concepts that every business student must learn to be successful. At one time, instructors of the introductory course faced a dilemma. On one hand, experience in business organizations allows students to grasp the complexities underlying important IS concepts. For this reason, many schools delayed presenting these concepts until students completed a large portion of their core business requirements. On the other hand, delaying the presentation of IS concepts until students have matured within the business curriculum often forces the one or two required introductory IS courses to focus only on personal computing software tools and, at best, merely to introduce computer concepts.

This text has been written specifically for the introductory course in the IS curriculum. *Principles of Information Systems, Twelfth Edition*, addresses the appropriate computer and IS concepts while also providing a strong managerial emphasis on meeting business and organizational needs.

APPROACH OF THIS TEXT

Principles of Information Systems, Twelfth Edition, offers the traditional coverage of computer concepts, but places the material within the context of meeting business and organizational needs. Placing information systems concepts within this context and taking a management perspective has always set this text apart from other computer texts, thus making it appealing not only to MIS majors but also to students from other fields of study. The text is not overly technical, but rather deals with the role that information systems play in an organization and the key principles a manager or technology specialist needs to grasp to be successful. The principles of IS are brought together and presented in a way that is understandable, relevant, and interesting. In addition, the text offers an overview of the entire IS discipline, while giving students a solid foundation for further study in more advanced IS courses such as programming, systems analysis and design, project management, database management, data communications, Web site design and development, electronic and mobile commerce, decision support, and informatics. As such, it serves the needs of both general business managers and those who aspire to become IS professionals.

The overall vision, framework, and pedagogy that made the previous editions so popular have been retained in the twelfth edition, offering a number of benefits to students and instructors. While the fundamental vision of this market-leading text remains unchanged, the twelfth edition more clearly highlights established principles and draws on new ones that have emerged as a result of business, organizational, technological, and societal changes.

IS Principles First, Where They Belong

Exposing students to fundamental IS principles is an advantage even for those students who take no IS courses beyond the introductory IS course. Since most functional areas of the business rely on information systems, an understanding of IS principles helps students in their other course work. In addition, introducing students to the principles of information systems helps future business managers and entrepreneurs employ information systems successfully and avoid mishaps that often result in unfortunate consequences. Furthermore, presenting IS concepts at the introductory level creates interest among students who may later choose information systems as their field of concentration.

Author Team

Ralph Stair and George Reynolds have decades of academic and business experience. Ralph Stair brings years of writing, teaching, and academic experience to this text. He wrote numerous books and many articles while at Florida State University. George Reynolds brings a wealth of information systems and business experience to the project, with more than 30 years of experience working in government, institutional, and commercial IS organizations. He has written over two dozen IS texts and has taught the introductory IS course at the University of Cincinnati, Mount St. Joseph University, and Strayer University. The Stair and Reynolds team presents a solid conceptual foundation and practical IS experience to students.

GOALS OF THIS TEXT

Because *Principles of Information Systems, Twelfth Edition*, is written for business majors, we believe that it is important not only to present a realistic perspective on IS in business but also to provide students with the skills they can use to be effective business leaders in their organizations. To that end, *Principles of Information Systems, Twelfth Edition*, has three main goals:

1. To provide a set of core of IS principles that prepares students to function more efficiently and effectively as workers, managers, decision makers, and organizational leaders
2. To provide insights into the challenging and changing role of the IS professional so that students can better appreciate the role of this key individual
3. To show the value of the IS discipline as an attractive field of specialization so that students can evaluate this as a potential career path

IS Principles

Principles of Information Systems, Twelfth Edition, although comprehensive, cannot cover every aspect of the rapidly changing IS discipline. The authors, having recognized this, provide students with an essential core of guiding IS principles to use as they strive to use IS systems in their academic and work environment. Think of principles as basic truths or rules that remain constant regardless of the situation. As such, they provide strong guidance for tough decision making. A set of IS principles is highlighted at the beginning of each chapter. The application of these principles to solve real-world problems is driven home from the opening vignettes to the dozens of real-world examples of organizations applying these principles to the end-of-chapter material. The ultimate goal of *Principles of Information Systems, Twelfth Edition*, is to develop effective, thinking, action-oriented students by instilling them with principles to help guide their decision making and actions.

Survey of the IS Discipline

Principles of Information Systems, Twelfth Edition, not only offers the traditional coverage of computer concepts but also builds a broad framework to provide students with a solid grounding in the business uses of technology, the challenges of successful implementation, the necessity for gaining broad adoption of information systems, and the potential ethical and societal issues that may arise. In addition to serving general business students, this book offers an overview of the entire IS discipline and solidly prepares future IS professionals for advanced IS courses and careers in the rapidly changing IS discipline.

Changing Role of the IS Professional

As business and the IS discipline have changed, so too has the role of the IS professional. Once considered a technical specialist, today the IS professional operates as an internal consultant to all functional areas of the organization, being knowledgeable about their needs and competent in bringing the power of information systems to bear throughout the entire organization. The IS professional must view issues through a global perspective that encompasses the entire enterprise and the broader industry and business environment in which it operates.

The scope of responsibilities of an IS professional today is not confined to just his or her employer but encompasses the entire interconnected network of employees, suppliers, customers, competitors, regulatory agencies, and other entities, no matter where they are located. This broad scope of responsibilities creates a new challenge: how to help an organization survive in a highly interconnected, highly competitive global environment. In accepting that challenge, the IS professional plays a pivotal role in shaping the business itself and ensuring its success. To survive, businesses must strive for the highest level of customer satisfaction and loyalty through innovative products and services, competitive prices, and ever improving product and service quality. The IS professional assumes a critical role in helping the organization to achieve both its overall cost and quality objectives and therefore plays an important role in the ongoing growth of the organization. This new duality in the role of the IS worker—a professional who exercises a specialist's skills with a generalist's perspective—is reflected throughout *Principles of Information Systems, Twelfth Edition.*

IS as a Field of Study

Despite the continuing effects of a slowed economy and outsourcing, business administration/management and computer and information sciences were both listed in the 2014 Princeton Review of top-ten college majors. A 2014 U.S. News & World Report study placed software developer, computer systems analyst, and Web developer as three of the top ten "best jobs for 2014." The U.S. Bureau of Labor Statistics forecasts information security analyst as one of the fastest growing occupations for the period 2013 to 2022. Clearly, the long-term job prospects for skilled and business-savvy information systems professionals are good. Employment of such workers is expected to grow faster than the average for all occupations through the year 2022. Upon graduation, IS graduates at many schools are among the highest paid of all business graduates.

A career in IS can be exciting, challenging, and rewarding! It is important to show the value of the discipline as an appealing field of study and that the IS graduate is no longer a technical recluse. Today, perhaps more than ever before, the IS professional must be able to align IS and organizational goals and to ensure that IS investments are justified from a business perspective. The need to draw bright and interested students into the IS discipline is part of our ongoing responsibility. Throughout this text, the many challenges and opportunities available to IS professionals are highlighted and emphasized.

CHANGES IN THE TWELFTH EDITION

A number of exciting changes have been made to the text based on user feedback on how to align the text even more closely with changing IS needs and capabilities of organizations. Here is a summary of those changes:

- **All new opening vignettes.** All chapter-opening vignettes are new and continue to provide a preview of the issues to be covered from the perspective of national and multinational organizations. The global aspect of information systems continues to be a major theme of the text. Many instructors use these vignettes as the basis for interesting and lively class discussions.

- **All updated Information Systems @Work special interest boxes.** Highlighting current topics and trends in today's headlines, these boxes show how information systems are used in a wide variety of career areas. All boxes have been updated with the latest information available and with new critical thinking and discussion questions. These boxes can be used as the basis for a class discussion or as additional cases that may be assigned as individual or team exercises.

- **All updated Ethical and Societal Issues special interest boxes.** Focusing on ethical issues that today's professional face, these boxes illustrate how information systems professionals confront and react to ethical dilemmas. All boxes have been updated with the latest information available and with new critical thinking and discussion questions. These boxes can also be used as the basis for a class discussion or as additional cases that may be assigned as individual or team exercises.

- **All updated case studies.** Two end-of-chapter case studies for each chapter provide a wealth of practical information for students and instructors. Each case explores a chapter concept or problem that a real-world organization has faced. The cases can be assigned as individual or team homework exercises or serve as the basis for class discussion. Again, all cases have been updated with the latest information available and with new critical thinking and discussion questions.
- **Updated summary linked to objectives.** Each chapter includes a detailed summary, with each section of the summary updated as needed and tied to an associated information system principle.
- **Updated end-of-the chapter questions and exercises.** More than half of all of the extensive end-of-chapter exercises (Self-Assessment Test, Review Questions, Discussion Questions, Problem-Solving Exercises, Team Activities, Web Exercises, and Career Exercises) are new.
- **Extensive changes and updates in each chapter.** This text provides the latest information available on a wide range of IS-related topics including nearly 500 new and current examples of organizations and individuals illustrating the principles presented in the text. In addition, a strong effort was made to update the art work and figures with more than 170 new figures and images. The extensive amount of change makes it impractical to provide a detailed list of all the updates; however, the following table summarizes the changes by chapter:

Chapter	New Company Examples	New Figures	Top Three New or Expanded Topics
1 An Introduction to Information Systems	31	22	• Impact of doubling amount of digital data every two years • 5th generation wireless communications • Information literacy
2 Information Systems in Organizations	28	19	• Types of innovation • Use of several organizational change models to improve the successful implementation of IS • Financial evaluation of projects using IRR and NPV
3 Hardware: Input, Processing, Output, and Storage Devices	41	18	• New solutions for growing storage needs • Infrastructure as a service • Building energy-efficient data centers
4 Software: Systems and Application Software	35	12	• Mobile operating systems • Cloud computing services • Types of software licenses
5 Database Systems and Applications	31	9	• Big data, Hadoop, and NoSQL databases • In-memory databases • ACID properties of SQL databases
6 Telecommunications and Networks	30	5	• Network topologies • Future of municipal Wi-Fi networks and 5G wireless communications • Software defined networking
7 The Internet, Web, Intranets, and Extranets	35	5	• Cloud computing • Web services and Web design framework • Social networking within an organization
8 Electronic and Mobile Commerce	39	5	• Global growth of e-commerce • E-commerce issues and challenges • Two-factor authentication

Chapter	New Company Examples	New Figures	Top Three New or Expanded Topics
9 **Enterprise Systems**	30	5	• Emergence of Tier I, II, and III ERP vendors • Product lifecycle management strategies and systems including CAD, CAE, and CAM • Overcoming the challenges of implementing enterprise systems
10 **Information and Decision Support Systems**	33	8	• Structured, semistructured, and unstructured decisions • Activities supported by marketing MIS • Decision-making approaches including Delphi, brainstorming, group consensus, nominal group, and multivoting
11 **Knowledge Management and Specialized Information Systems**	35	11	• Communities of practice • Assistive technology systems • Informatics
12 **Systems Development: Investigation, Analysis, and Design**	25	18	• Focuses strictly on systems planning, investigation, analysis, and design phases, their tasks, and associated techniques • JAD and functional decomposition • Project steering committee and project sponsor
13 **Systems Development: Construction, Integration and Testing, Implementation, Operation and Maintenance, and Disposal**	29	9	• Leadership required to overcome resistance to change and achieve a successful system introduction • Prototype, Agile, mobile app, end user development • Tips to avoid project failure
14 **The Personal and Social Impact of Computers**	53	15	• Hacking of smartphones • Use of computers to recover stolen property, monitor criminals, and assess crime risk • Current strategies and tools to prevent computer crime including identity theft

ONLINE SOLUTIONS

MindTap™

MindTap for Stair/Reynolds *Principles of Information Systems, 12e*, is a truly innovative and personalized learning experience with assignments that guide students to analyze, apply, and improve thinking! Relevant readings, multimedia, and activities are designed to move students up the levels of learning, from basic knowledge to analysis and application. Embedded within the eReader, **ConceptClips** focus on the challenge of understanding complicated IS terminology and concepts. Student-tested and approved, the videos are quick, entertaining, and memorable visual and auditory representations of challenging topics. Also embedded within the MindTap eReader, animated figures and graphs provide a visual and at times interactive and auditory enhancement to previously static text examples.

MindTap allows instructors to measure skills and outcomes with ease. Personalized teaching becomes yours through a Learning Path built with key student objectives and the ability to control what students see and when they see it. Analytics and reports provide a snapshot of class progress, time in course, engagement, and completion rates.

Aplia™

Engage, prepare, and educate your students with this ideal online learning solution. The original assignments ensure that students grasp the skills and concepts presented in their course. Aplia is an auto-graded solution that improves learning by increasing student effort without additional work from the instructor. Aplia's management solution ensures that students stay on top of their coursework with regularly scheduled homework assignments and automatic grading with detailed, immediate feedback. Instructors can post announcements, upload course materials, email students, and manage the gradebook. Instructors can easily download, save, manipulate, print, and import student grades into a current grading system. Aplia works independently or in conjunction with other course management systems.

STUDENT RESOURCES

Accessible through CengageBrain.com, the student companion Web site contains the following study tools (and more!) to enhance one's learning experience:

PowerPoint Slides

Direct access is offered to PowerPoint presentations that cover the key points of each chapter.

Classic Cases

Adopters frequently request a broader selection of cases to choose from. To meet this need, a set of more than 200 cases from the seventh, eighth, ninth, tenth, and eleventh editions of the text are included here. These are the author's choices of the "best cases" from these editions and span a broad range of profit, nonprofit, small, medium, and large organizations in a broad range of industries.

INSTRUCTOR RESOURCES

The teaching tools that accompany this text offer many options for enhancing a course. And, as always, we are committed to providing the best teaching resource packages available in this market.

Test Bank and Cengage Learning Testing Powered by Cognero

New! Cognero is a full-featured, online-assessment system that allows instructors to manage test bank content; quickly create multiple test versions; deliver tests in several forms including from an LMS; and create test banks anywhere with Internet access!

To access Cognero, log into your Cengage Learning SSO account at http://login.cengage.com. Add this title to the bookshelf. Once the title is properly added to the bookshelf, a link to access Cognero will appear alongside the link to the instructor companion site. Technical questions, guides, and tutorials are hosted on Cengage Learning Technical Support Web site – http://support.cengage.com.

The Teaching Tools that Accompany this Text Offer Many Options for Enhancing a Course

As always, we are committed to providing the best teaching resource packages available in this market. All instructor materials can be found on the password-protected Web site at http://login.cengage.com. Here you will find the following resources:

- **Instructor's Manual** The comprehensive manual provides valuable chapter overviews, highlights key principles and critical concepts; offers sample syllabi, learning objectives, and discussion topics; and features possible essay topics, further readings, cases, and solutions to all of the end-of-chapter questions and problems, as well as suggestions for conducting the team activities.
- **Sample Syllabus** A sample syllabus for both a quarter and semester-length course are provided with sample course outlines to make planning your course that much easier.
- **PowerPoint Presentations** A set of impressive Microsoft PowerPoint slides is available for each chapter. These slides are included to serve as a teaching aid for classroom presentation, to make available to students for chapter review, or to be printed for classroom distribution. The goal of the presentations is to help students focus on the main topics of each chapter, take better notes, and prepare for examinations. Instructors can add their own slides for additional topics they introduce to the class.
- **Figure Files** Figure files allow instructors to create their own presentations using figures taken directly from the text.

ACKNOWLEDGEMENTS

Creation of a text of this scope takes a strong team effort. We would like to thank all of our fellow teammates at Cengage Learning for their dedication and hard work. We would like to thank Joe Sabatino, our product director, for his overall leadership and guidance on this effort. Special thanks to Anne Merrill, our Associate Content Developer, for all her efforts in overseeing and pulling together all the many components of this text and its auxiliary materials. Much credit is due to Lisa Ruffolo of The Software Resource Publications for her tireless effort in editing the text and keeping track of the various revisions and changes. Our appreciation goes out to all the many people who worked behind the scenes to bring this effort to a successful conclusion including art direction, research, manufacturing, and permissions, namely Arul Joseph Raj, Jennifer Feltri-George, and Jennifer Ziegler, our Content Project Managers, who shepherded the text through the production process and kept us on track.

We would also like to thank Kristen Maxwell of Evil Cyborg Productions for creating the ConceptClips videos that so humorously bring many key terms found in the text to life.

We would especially like to thank Naomi Freidman for her outstanding work in writing and revising the opening vignettes, IS @Work, and Ethical & Societal Issues boxes, and the cases for this edition.

We are extremely grateful to Senior Marketing Manager, Eric La Scola, and the salesforce at Cengage Learning whose outstanding effort in marketing this text and supporting our adopters make this all worthwhile.

OUR COMMITMENT

We are committed to listening to our adopters and readers in order to develop creative solutions to meet their needs. The field of IS continually evolves, and we strongly encourage your participation in helping us provide the freshest, most relevant information possible.

We welcome your input and feedback. If you have any questions or comments regarding *Principles of Information Systems, Twelfth Edition,* please contact us through your local representative.

Overview

CHAPTERS

1 An Introduction to Information Systems

Principles	Learning Objectives
• The value of information is directly linked to how it helps decision makers achieve the organization's goals.	• Discuss why it is important to study and understand information systems. • Distinguish data from information and describe the characteristics used to evaluate the quality of data.
• Computers and information systems help make it possible for organizations to improve the way they conduct business.	• Name the components of an information system and describe several system characteristics.
• Knowing the potential impact of information systems and having the ability to put this knowledge to work can result in a successful personal career and in organizations that reach their goals.	• List the components of a computer-based information system. • Identify the basic types of business information systems and discuss who uses them, how they are used, and what kinds of benefits they deliver.
• System users, business managers, and information systems professionals must work together to build a successful information system.	• Identify the major steps of the systems development process and state the goal of each.
• Information systems must be applied thoughtfully and carefully so that society, businesses, and industries around the globe can reap their enormous benefits.	• Describe some of the threats that information systems and the Internet can pose to security and privacy. • Discuss the expanding role and benefits of information systems in business and industry.

Information Systems in the Global Economy
CATERPILLAR, INC.

Advent of Autonomous Vehicles

Reprinted Courtesy of Caterpillar Inc.

Imagine one day that you are driving along a highway, and when you glance at a vehicle passing by, you notice with horror that no one is in the driver seat. Does that seem like a scene from a freaky science fiction movie? Actually, that day is not that far away—and it doesn't look that scary.

Autonomous vehicles, or vehicles that drive on their own, will likely provide many benefits. Ideally, their use will reduce vehicle accidents, thus saving lives and avoiding billions of dollars in repair bills. They will enable the blind and other disabled people to be more mobile. Autonomous vehicles can also decrease manufacturing and shipping costs by reducing the need for truck drivers to deliver supplies, raw materials, and finished products.

In the trucking industry, which suffers from periodic underemployment, autonomous vehicles are already on the roads—in the Australian outback. In 2013, Australia's largest mining companies deployed large fleets of autonomous trucks. Rio Tinto, a world leader in iron ore, aluminum, copper, coal, diamond, and uranium mining, began with a handful of driverless trucks at three mining sites in 2012, and then announced it was increasing its order to 150. Meanwhile, BHP Billiton, a multinational mining and petroleum company, has taken advantage of Caterpillar's line of high-tech autonomous vehicles, ordering both haulers and dozers.

Caterpillar has been working with Carnegie Mellon University for over 20 years to produce the advances in information systems and other technology needed to create autonomous trucks. These trucks have to plan routes, detect obstacles, and avoid them. Timely and correct interpretation of data is critical. Caterpillar's product manager Ed McCord explains, "Any autonomous vehicle has to take in sensor data, then process it fast enough to plan a route and make adjustments."

Like a driver, these trucks need to interpret exceptions. "We must be able to manage exceptions with the software. For example, if an operator hears a strange noise, he'll take preventive action, such as reporting it to maintenance," explains McCord. "Likewise, an operator can see a flat tire on the truck ahead of him, so we are developing technologies that are able to monitor tires."

To meet the need to interpret exceptions, Caterpillar and Carnegie Mellon have developed unique information management systems, robotics, high-precision global position system (GPS) guidance and control systems, machine health monitoring system, and wireless communication systems.

Truck manufacturers are not the only companies moving into this emerging industry. Audi tested its autonomous cars on public roads in Nevada in 2013. It developed miniaturized laser sensor arrays and a single motherboard that controlled the power train, infotainment, traction, and all other electronic systems. Like Volvo, Nissan, and other automobile companies, Audi stresses that self-driving cars won't necessarily be driverless—at least in the near future. Rather, they will be used to relieve drivers during traffic jams and long trips and aid in parallel parking. They will also help avoid accidents by detecting road edges, animals, and pedestrians and by communicating from one vehicle to another. Yet, once governments have created the policy and developed the infrastructure needed to accommodate autonomous vehicles, some or all of the almost 6 million truck drivers, chauffeurs, and cab drivers on the road today may find themselves without work.

The development of information systems to interpret data and respond to it is key to the emergence of the autonomous vehicle industry. Caterpillar has converted what may seem like a futuristic vision into an economic opportunity today.

As you read this chapter, consider the following:

- Why are information systems that can interpret data critical to the development of autonomous vehicles?
- What types of data do autonomous vehicles need to interpret?
- What are the potential advantages and disadvantages of autonomous vehicles?

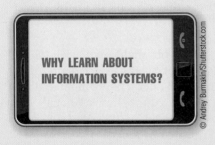

WHY LEARN ABOUT INFORMATION SYSTEMS?

Information systems are used by workers and managers in all lines of business. Entrepreneurs and small business owners use information systems to market their goods and services and to interact with customers around the world. Sales representatives use information systems to advertise products, communicate with customers and suppliers, and forecast sales and inventory levels. Managers use them to make multimillion-dollar decisions, such as whether to build a new manufacturing plant or dedicate more money to research on a new drug. Financial advisors use information systems to advise their clients as they save for retirement or their children's education. From a small neighborhood music store to huge multinational companies, businesses of all sizes cannot survive without information systems to support accounting, marketing, management, finance, production, and similar operations. Regardless of your college major or chosen career, information systems are indispensable tools to help you achieve your career goals. Learning about information systems can help you land your first job, earn promotions, and advance your career.

This chapter presents an overview of information systems, with each section getting full treatment in subsequent chapters. We start by exploring the basics of information systems.

information system (IS): A set of interrelated components that collect, process, store, and disseminate data and information and provide a feedback mechanism to meet an objective.

People and organizations use information systems every day. An **information system (IS)** is a set of interrelated components that collect, process, store, and disseminate data and information and provide a feedback mechanism to meet an objective. The feedback mechanism is critical to help organizations achieve their goals, such as increasing profits or improving customer service. Kohl's considers the effective use of information systems strategic to help drive sales, satisfy customers, and make key business decisions in the extremely competitive and constantly changing retail market. See Figure 1.1. The firm is constantly striving to recruit the most talented information system specialists to keep ahead of its competition.[1]

FIGURE 1.1

Information systems are everywhere

Kohl's department stores offer products and services, and an information system tracks sales to identify popular merchandise. The information system coordinates the suppliers and inventory so that Kohl's can offer enough of the goods customers want to buy.

Today, we live in an information economy. Information itself has value, and commerce often involves the exchange of information rather than tangible goods. Systems based on computers are increasingly being used to create, store, and transfer information. Using information systems, investors make multimillion-dollar decisions, financial institutions transfer billions of dollars around the world electronically, and manufacturers order supplies and distribute goods faster than ever before. Computers and information systems will continue to change businesses and the way we live. To prepare for these innovations, you need to be familiar with fundamental information concepts.

INFORMATION CONCEPTS

Information is a central concept of this book. The term is used in the title of the book, in this section, and in almost every chapter. To be an effective manager in any area of business, you need to understand that information is one of an organization's most valuable resources. This term, however, is often confused with *data*.

Data, Information, and Knowledge

data: Raw facts, such as an employee number, total hours worked in a week, inventory part numbers, or the number of units produced on a production line.

information: A collection of data organized and processed so that it has additional value beyond the value of the individual facts.

Data consists of raw facts, such as an employee number, total hours worked in a week, an inventory part number, or the number of units produced on a production line. As shown in Table 1.1, several types of data can represent these facts. **Information** is a collection of data organized and processed so that it has additional value beyond the value of the individual facts. For example, a sales manager may want individual sales data summarized to see the total sales for the month. Providing information to customers can also help companies increase revenues and profits. For example, social shopping Web site Kaboodle brings shoppers and sellers together electronically so they can share information and make recommendations while shopping online. The free exchange of information stimulates sales and helps ensure shoppers find better values.[2]

TABLE **1.1** Types of data

Data	Represented By
Alphanumeric data	Numbers, letters, and other characters
Audio data	Sounds, noises, or tones
Image data	Graphic images and pictures
Video data	Moving images or pictures

© 2016 Cengage Learning

Data represents real-world things. Hospitals and healthcare organizations, for example, maintain patient medical data, which represents facts about actual patients with specific health situations. Today, hospitals and other healthcare organizations are investing millions of dollars in developing electronic health record programs to store and use the vast amount of medical data generated each year. Medical record systems often store critical health-related data, which can be used to create valuable information capable of saving money and lives. For example, researchers collected data from patient records, hospital discharge forms, and prescription records to study almost 400,000 pregnancies. Using sophisticated data analysis, the researchers determined the key risk factors for blood clots in pregnant women.[3] In addition, integrating information from different sources is an important capability for most organizations. Expedia CruiseShipCenters is a seller of cruise vacations and services, which relies on 60 different email marketing campaigns each month to reach more than 1 million subscribers. It collects, integrates, and analyzes consumer behavioral data from each contact to maximize the revenue potential of future customer interactions. "We wanted to find a way to get a better understanding of the data we were sitting on," said Dave Mossop, manager of interactive marketing, Expedia CruiseShipCenters. Through data integration and analysis, "we gained a holistic view into our customers' interests and are able to apply those insights to match relevant content with the right people at the right time. This has dramatically increased our Web site inquiries and positively impacted sales conversions."[4]

Here is another way to conceive of the difference between data and information. Consider data as pieces of railroad track in a model railroad kit. Each piece of track has limited inherent value as a single object. However, if you define a relationship among the pieces of the track, they gain value. By arranging the pieces in a certain way, a railroad layout begins to emerge. See Figure 1.2a, top. Data and information work the same way. Rules and relationships can be set up to organize data into useful, valuable information.

The type of information created depends on the relationships defined among existing data. For example, you could rearrange the pieces of track to form different layouts. Adding new or different data means you can redefine relationships and create new information. For instance, adding new pieces to the track can greatly increase the value—in this case, variety and fun—of the final product. You can now create a more elaborate railroad layout. See Figure 1.2b, bottom. Likewise, a sales manager could add specific product data to sales data to create monthly sales information organized by product line. The manager could use this information to determine which product lines are the most popular and profitable.

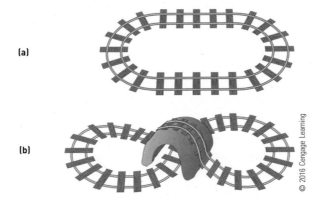

(a)

(b)

© 2016 Cengage Learning

FIGURE 1.2

Data and information

Defining and organizing relationships among data creates information.

process: A set of logically related tasks performed to achieve a defined outcome.

knowledge: The awareness and understanding of a set of information and the ways that information can be made useful to support a specific task or reach a decision.

Turning data into information is a **process**, or a set of logically related tasks performed to achieve a defined outcome. The process of defining relationships among data to create useful information requires knowledge. **Knowledge** is the awareness and understanding of a set of information and the ways that information can be made useful to support a specific task or reach a decision. Having knowledge means understanding relationships in information. Part of the knowledge you need to build a railroad layout, for instance, is the understanding of how much space you have for the layout, how many trains will run on the track, and how fast they will travel. Selecting or rejecting facts according to their relevancy to particular tasks is based on the knowledge used in the process of converting data into information. Therefore, you can also think of information as data made more useful through the application of knowledge. *Knowledge workers (KWs)* are people who create, use, and disseminate knowledge and are usually professionals in science, engineering, business, and other areas. *Knowledge management* is a strategy by which an organization determinedly and systematically gathers, organizes, stores, analyzes, and shares its collective knowledge and experience. The goal is to deal with issues and problems in an effective manner by unleashing the collective value of the organization's best thinking.

In some cases, people organize or process data mentally or manually. In other cases, they use a computer. This transformation process is shown in Figure 1.3.

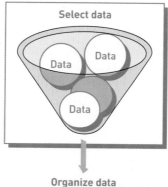

Select data

Data

Data

Data

Data

Organize data

Data (1,1)	Data (1,2)	Data (1,3)
Data (2,1)	Data (2,2)	Data (2,3)
Data (3,1)	Data (3,2)	Data (3,3)
Data (n,1)	Data (n,2)	Data (n,3)

Manipulate data

Total 1	Total 2	Total 3

© 2016 Cengage Learning

FIGURE 1.3

Process of transforming data into information

Transforming data into information starts by selecting data, then organizing it, and finally manipulating the data.

The Value of Information

The value of information is directly linked to how it helps decision makers achieve their organization's goals. Valuable information can help people in their organizations perform tasks more efficiently and effectively. Many businesses assume that reports are based on correct, quality information, but, unfortunately, that is not always true. A recent study of the current state of data management in the United Kingdom found that the average organization believes 17 percent of its total data (from which its information is derived) is inaccurate. Such lack of data quality has serious repercussions. Nearly one-third of the respondents (29 percent) claimed that poor data quality led to the loss of potential new customers, and one-quarter (26 percent) felt it reduced customer satisfaction.[5]

Characteristics of Quality Information

Fundamental to the quality of a decision is the quality of the information used to reach that decision. Any organization that stresses the use of advanced information systems and sophisticated data analysis before information quality is doomed to make many wrong decisions. Table 1.2 lists characteristics that determine the quality of information to decision makers in the organization. Quality information can vary widely in the value of each of these attributes depending on the situation and the kind of decision you are trying to make. For example, with market intelligence data, some inaccuracy and incompleteness is acceptable, but timeliness is essential. Market intelligence data may alert you that a competitor is about to make a major price cut. The exact details and timing of the price cut may not be as important as being warned far enough in advance to plan how to react. On the other hand, accuracy and completeness are critical for data used in accounting for the management of company assets, such as cash, inventory, and equipment.

TABLE **1.2** Characteristics of quality information

Characteristics	Definitions
Accessible	Information should be easily accessible by authorized users so they can obtain it in the right format and at the right time to meet their needs.
Accurate	Accurate information is error free. In some cases, inaccurate information is generated because inaccurate data is fed into the transformation process. This is commonly called garbage in, garbage out (GIGO).
Complete	Complete information contains all the important facts. For example, an investment report that does not include all important costs is not complete.
Economical	Information should also be relatively economical to produce. Decision makers must always balance the value of information with the cost of producing it.
Flexible	Flexible information can be used for a variety of purposes. For example, information on how much inventory is on hand for a particular part can be used by a sales representative in closing a sale, by a production manager to determine whether more inventory is needed, and by a financial executive to determine the total value the company has invested in inventory.
Relevant	Relevant information is important to the decision maker. Information showing that lumber prices might drop might not be relevant to a computer chip manufacturer.
Reliable	Reliable information can be trusted by users. In many cases, the reliability of the information depends on the reliability of the data-collection method. In other instances, reliability depends on the source of the information. A rumor from an unknown source that oil prices might go up might not be reliable.
Secure	Information should be secure from access by unauthorized users.
Simple	Information should be simple, not complex. Sophisticated and detailed information might not be needed. In fact, too much information can cause information overload, whereby a decision maker has too much information and is unable to determine what is really important.
Timely	Timely information is delivered when it is needed. Knowing last week's weather conditions will not help when trying to decide what coat to wear today.
Verifiable	Information should be verifiable. This means that you can check it to make sure it is correct, perhaps by checking many sources for the same information.

© 2016 Cengage Learning

SYSTEM CONCEPTS

system: A set of elements or components that interact to accomplish goals.

Like information, another central concept of this book is that of a system. A system is a set of elements or components that interact to accomplish goals. Systems have inputs, processing mechanisms, outputs, and feedback. See Figure 1.4. For example, consider an automatic car wash. Tangible *inputs* for

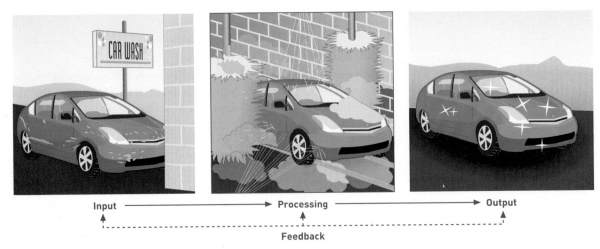

Input ──────▶ Processing ──────▶ Output

Feedback

© 2016 Cengage Learning

FIGURE **1.4**

Components of a system

A system's four components consist of input, processing, output, and feedback.

the process are a dirty car, water, and various cleaning ingredients. Time, energy, skill, and knowledge also serve as inputs to the system because they are needed to operate it. Skill is the ability to successfully operate the liquid sprayer, foaming brush, and air dryer devices. Knowledge is used to define the steps in the car wash operation and the order in which the steps are executed.

The *processing mechanisms* consist of first selecting the cleaning option you want (wash only, wash with wax, wash with wax and hand dry, etc.) and communicating that to the operator of the car wash. A *feedback mechanism* is your assessment of how clean the car is. Liquid sprayers shoot clear water, liquid soap, or car wax depending on where your car is in the process and which options you selected. The *output* is a clean car. As in all systems, independent elements or components (the liquid sprayer, foaming brush, and air dryer) interact to create a clean car.

WHAT IS AN INFORMATION SYSTEM?

As mentioned earlier, an information system is a set of interrelated components that collect, process, store, and disseminate data and information and provide a feedback mechanism to meet an objective. We interact with information systems every day, both in our personal and professional lives. We use automated teller machines at banks, access information over the Internet, select information from kiosks with touch screens, and scan the barcodes on our purchases at self-checkout lanes. At work, we collaborate with project members and coworkers using email. We collect all manner of up-to-the minute corporate data about sales, orders, purchases, and inventory levels for use in decision making via our smartphone or computer. We create business presentations and useful charts using personal computer software. Knowing the potential of information systems and putting this knowledge to work can help you enjoy a successful career and help organizations reach their goals. See Figure 1.5.

FIGURE 1.5

Components of an information system

Feedback is critical to the successful operation of a system.

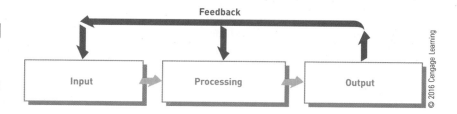

© 2016 Cengage Learning

Input

input: The activity of gathering and capturing raw data.

In information systems, input is the activity of gathering and capturing raw data. In producing paychecks, for example, the number of hours every employee works must be collected before paychecks can be calculated or printed. In a university grading system, instructors must submit student grades before a summary of grades can be compiled and sent to students.

Processing

processing: Converting or transforming data into useful outputs.

In information systems, processing means converting or transforming data into useful outputs. Processing can involve making calculations, comparing data and taking alternative actions, and storing data for future use. Processing data into useful information is critical in business settings.

Processing can be done manually or with computer assistance. In a payroll application, the number of hours each employee worked must be converted into net, or take-home, pay. Other inputs often include employee ID number and rate of pay. The processing can first involve multiplying the number of hours worked by the employee's hourly pay rate to get gross pay. If weekly hours worked exceed 40, overtime pay might also be included.

Then deductions—for example, federal and state taxes or contributions to insurance or savings plans—are subtracted from gross pay to get net pay.

After these calculations and comparisons are performed, the results are typically stored. *Storage* involves keeping data and information available for future use, including output, discussed next.

Output

output: Production of useful information, usually in the form of documents and reports.

In information systems, output involves producing useful information, usually in the form of documents and reports. Outputs can include paychecks for employees, reports for managers, and information supplied to stockholders, banks, government agencies, and other groups. In some cases, output from one system can become input for another. For example, output from a system that processes sales orders can be used as input to a customer billing system. When output is not accurate or not available when needed, it can cause major disruptions in organization work processes. A system-wide computer failure forced Southwest Airlines to ground some 250 flights for one night. The computer glitch impaired the airline's ability to do such things as conduct check-ins, print boarding passes, and monitor the weight of each aircraft.[6]

Feedback

feedback: Information from the system that is used to make changes to input or processing activities.

In information systems, feedback is information from the system that is used to make changes to input or processing activities. For example, errors or problems might make it necessary to correct input data or change a process. Consider a payroll example. Perhaps the number of hours an employee worked was entered as 400 instead of 40. Fortunately, most information systems check to make sure that data falls within certain ranges. For number of hours worked, the range might be from 0 to 100 because it is unlikely that an employee would work more than 100 hours in a week. The information system would determine that 400 hours is out of range and provide feedback. The feedback is used to check and correct the input on the number of hours worked to 40. If undetected, this error would result in a very high net pay!

Ford Motor Company implemented a system that uses feedback data from plant operations to improve production efficiency and reduce downtime. The system collects data on production rates and equipment failure rates to identify those operation bottlenecks that most affect productivity. Maintenance is then planned to eliminate these bottlenecks. Workers are trained and equipped with the necessary tools to solve the problem, and the required spare parts are made available. If something does go wrong, production downtime is held to a minimum.[7]

forecasting: Predicting future events to avoid problems.

In addition to feedback, a computer system can predict future events to avoid problems. This concept, often called forecasting, can be used to estimate future sales and order more inventory before a shortage occurs. Forecasting is also used to predict the weather, the strength and landfall sites of hurricanes, future stock market values, and the winner of a political election. See Figure 1.6.

Computer-Based Information Systems

computer-based information system (CBIS): A single set of hardware, software, databases, telecommunications, people, and procedures that are configured to collect, manipulate, store, and process data into information.

As discussed earlier, an information system can be manual or computerized. A computer-based information system (CBIS) is a single set of hardware, software, databases, telecommunications, people, and procedures that are configured to collect, manipulate, store, and process data into information. Increasingly, companies are incorporating computer-based information systems into their products and services. Fidelity Investments, as well as most other investment companies, offers its customers a wide range of powerful investment tools and access to extensive online research.[8] Automobiles are available with advanced navigation systems that not only guide you to your destination but also incorporate the latest weather and traffic conditions to

FIGURE 1.6

Forecasting

Forecasting systems can help meteorologists predict the strength and path of hurricanes.

technology infrastructure: All the hardware, software, databases, telecommunications, people, and procedures that are configured to collect, manipulate, store, and process data into information.

help you avoid congestion and traffic delays. Digital cameras, mobile phones, music players, and other devices rely on CBIS to bring their users the latest and greatest features.

The components of a CBIS are illustrated in Figure 1.7. "Information technology (IT)" refers to hardware, software, databases, and telecommunications. A business's **technology infrastructure** includes all the hardware, software, databases, telecommunications, people, and procedures that are configured to

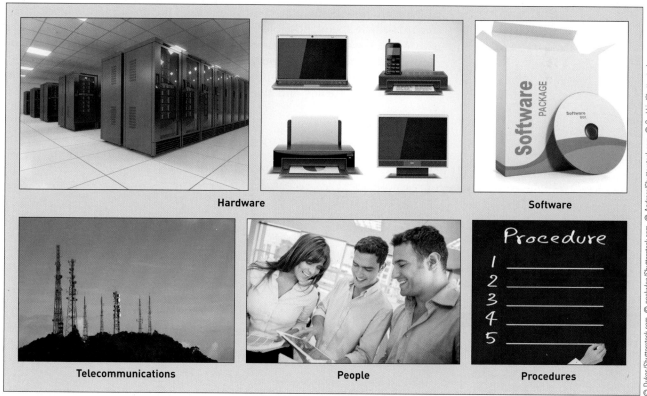

FIGURE 1.7

Components of a computer-based information system

Hardware, software, telecommunications, people, and procedures are part of a business's technology infrastructure.

collect, manipulate, store, and process data into information. The technology infrastructure is a set of shared IS resources that form the foundation of each computer-based information system.

Hardware

Hardware consists of computer equipment used to perform input, processing, storage, and output activities. Input devices include keyboards, mice and other pointing devices, automatic scanning devices, and equipment that can read magnetic ink characters. Processing devices include computer chips that contain the central processing unit and main memory. Advances in chip design allow faster speeds, less power consumption, and larger storage capacity. For example, the Haswell computer chip from Intel will deliver a major improvement in computing performance while using minimal power to extend battery life, features that are critical to laptop computer users.[9]

Processor speed is also important. In June 2013, the supercomputer Tianhe-2, capable of operating at a rate of 33.86 petaflops per second (33.86×10^{15} floating point operations per second), was ranked as the world's fastest computing system. It was developed by China's National University of Defense Technology and cost 100 million U.S. dollars. Li Nan, deputy head of the Tianhe-2 Project, said that complex projects like the design of new autos used to take two to three years; but the use of powerful computers, supercomputers, enable the job to be completed in as little as three months.[10] At the other end of the speed and cost spectrum is the Raspberry Pi computer, which is about the size of a credit card that comes with no monitor or keyboard but costs under $50.[11]

The many types of output devices include printers and computer screens. Some touch-sensitive computer screens, for example, can be used to execute functions or complete programs, such as connecting to the Internet or running a new computer game or word-processing program. Many special-purpose hardware devices have also been developed. Computerized event data recorders (EDRs) are now being placed into vehicles. Like an airplane's black box, EDRs record vehicle speed, possible engine problems, driver performance, and more.

While desktop, laptop, and tablet computers have their own advantages and disadvantages, many people favor the mobility, functionality, and cost associated with tablet computers. See Figure 1.8. This is reflected in the growth of tablet sales and the corresponding decline in desktop and laptop

FIGURE 1.8

Tablet computer

Hardware consists of computer equipment used to perform input, processing, and output activities. The trend in the computer industry is to produce smaller, faster, and more mobile hardware, such as tablet computers.

© iStockphoto.com/Mixmike

sales. Global tablet shipments exceeded laptop computer shipments in 2013. This trend is expected to continue so that by 2017, tablet computers are expected to represent nearly 75 percent of the combined global tablet-laptop market.[12] The new, advanced-capability tablet computers, including iPad and Samsung's Galaxy series, provide computing and communications services whenever and wherever the user wants them.[13] In addition, tens of thousands of applications are designed to run on tablet computers. These applications include games, special-purpose applications to support a wide range of uses, and personal productivity applications (such as word processing, spreadsheet, presentation, and graphics).

Bring your own device (BYOD) is a business policy that permits and, in some cases, encourages employees to use their own mobile devices (smartphones, tablets, or laptops) to access company computing resources and applications, including email, corporate databases, and the Internet. These personal hardware devices are convenient for employees, but can introduce security threats when the organization doesn't completely control its access to corporate data and programs. The Blackstone Group is a New York City–based financial services and investment firm that manages more than $200 million in assets. Employees started bringing iPads to work and soon were connecting some 600 iPads to the corporate network to access confidential documents and email messages. Blackstone implemented mobile device management to enable the Information Systems group to control these devices centrally. The use of passwords is now mandatory, and the Information Systems group can track each device and terminate it from afar if necessary. As a result, concern about lost or stolen devices is minimized, and Blackstone feels confident that no company confidential information will be stolen.[14]

Software

software: The computer programs that govern the operation of the computer.

Software consists of the computer programs that govern the operation of the computer. There are two types of software. System software, such as Microsoft Windows, manages basic computer operations such as start-up, controls access to system resources, and manages computer memory and files. Application software, such as Microsoft Excel, allows you to accomplish specific tasks, including word processing, creating graphs, and playing games. Both system software and application software are needed for all types of computers, from small handheld computers to large supercomputers. The Android operating system by Google, for example, is an operating system mainly for touch screen mobile devices such as smartphones and tablet computers. See Figure 1.9. As of July 2013, 777,094 applications were available for devices that run under the Android operating system.[15] Although most software can be installed from CDs or DVDs, many of today's software packages can be downloaded through the Internet.

Business applications can be categorized by whether they are intended to be used by an individual, a small business, or a large multinational enterprise. For example, Quicken has long been a favorite accounting application for individuals who need money management and budgeting tools to help them watch their spending, increase their savings, and avoid late fees with alerts on upcoming payments.[16] QuickBooks is an accounting application popular with small businesses that enables users to create invoices, track sales and expenses, process credit card payments, run payroll, and generate financial, tax, and sales reports.[17] SAP ERP Financials is an accounting application used by many large, multinational organizations to meet the complexities of global accounting and reporting requirements. The software records all financial transactions into a comprehensive general ledger; supports sophisticated reporting requirements; provides management accounting tools for orders, projects, cost centers, and profit centers; enables the speedy and accurate closing of the firm's books; and helps manage risk and compliance across accounting and treasury.[18]

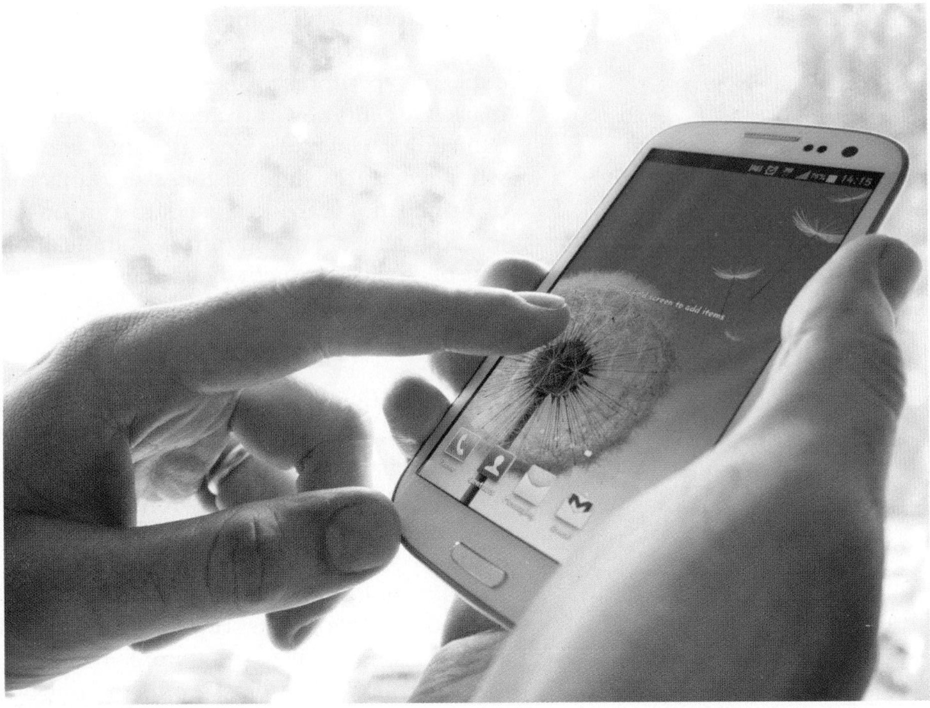

FIGURE 1.9

Smartphone running Android

Android is an operating system designed mainly for touch screen mobile devices such as smartphones and tablet computers.

Databases

database: An organized collection of facts and information, typically consisting of two or more related data files.

A **database** is an organized collection of facts and information, typically consisting of two or more related data files. An organization's database can contain facts and information on customers, employees, inventory, sales, online purchases, and much more. A database is essential to the operation of a computer-based information system.

Carfax maintains an enormous vehicle history database with more than 11 billion vehicle records. Data is gathered from over 75,000 sources across North America, such as U.S. and Canadian motor vehicle departments, service and repair facilities, insurance companies, and police departments. Millions of consumers and 30,000 dealerships use Carfax information every year to help them buy and sell cars with more confidence.[19]

Scientists estimated that in 2011 there was 1.8 zettabytes of digital data in the world and that the amount of data was doubling every two years.[20] See Figure 1.10. (One zettabyte is 10^{21} characters of data, equivalent to the amount of digital information created by every man, woman, and child on earth tweeting continuously for 100 years).[21] The increase in digital data means a huge increase in database storage needs, which will require more storage devices, more space to house the additional storage devices, and additional electricity to operate them. The big question is, how will organizations meet the increased demand for data storage? Another important issue for any organization is how to keep a vast database secure and safe from the prying eyes of outside individuals and groups.

Telecommunications and Networks

telecommunications: The electronic transmission of signals for communications that enables organizations to carry out their processes and tasks through effective computer networks.

Telecommunications is the electronic transmission of signals for communications, which enables organizations to carry out their processes and tasks through effective computer networks. Telecommunications can take place through wired, wireless, and satellite transmissions. The Associated Press was one of the first users of telecommunications in the 1920s, sending news over 103,000 miles of wire in the United States and over almost 10,000 miles of cable across the ocean. In these early days of news gathering, reporters raced to telephones to call in their reports, while cameramen shot footage and then

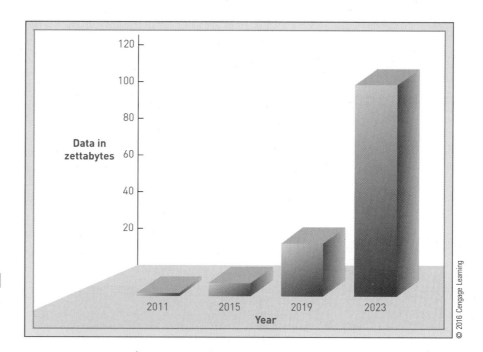

FIGURE 1.10

Growth in data

The amount of digital data is expected to double every two years.

network: Computers and equipment that are connected in a building, around the country, or around the world to enable electronic communications.

Internet: The world's largest computer network, consisting of thousands of interconnected networks, all freely exchanging information.

rushed back to studios to edit their film. Video of what was happening in the world could take several hours, even days to reach the public. Satellite communication networks have eliminated delays in news reporting and made it possible for people to see the news live as it is unfolding. News vans can be deployed quickly to almost anywhere in the world to cover a breaking news event. These vehicles are equipped with audio and video transmitters and antennas that can be aimed accurately at telecommunication satellites providing coverage of the entire earth. Reporters and cameramen can edit and transmit their footage immediately and report live as their signals are relayed from the van to a satellite, and then beamed back to earth from the satellite to a broadcast network control room.[22]

Today, telecommunications is used by people and organizations of all sizes around the world. With telecommunications, people can work at home or while traveling. This approach to work, often called "telework" or "telecommuting," allows someone living in England to send work to the United States, China, or any location with telecommunication capabilities. Telecommunications also enables the use of virtual teams of people working on a project to meet and communicate without ever physically being in the same place.

Networks connect computers and equipment in a building, around the country, or around the world to enable electronic communication. Wireless transmission networks enable the use of mobile devices such as smartphones and portable computers. Samsung and other telecommunication companies are now working on fifth-generation wireless communications that will enable transmission speeds 100 times faster than currently available wireless networks perhaps by the year 2020. Such technology will be needed to support the increased demand for faster transfer of data and video.[23]

The Internet is the world's largest computer network, consisting of thousands of interconnected networks, all freely exchanging information. People use the Internet to research information, buy and sell products and services, make travel arrangements, make investments, conduct banking, download music and videos, read books, and listen to radio programs, among other activities.

More than 2 billion people have access to the Internet. According to predictions, more than 25 billion devices will be connected to the Internet by 2015 and 50 billion by 2020.[24] This Internet of things would consist of a network of billions of wireless identifiable everyday objects that communicate with one another and their human owners. Some objects will be equipped with sensors to measure temperature, pressure, movement, power consumption, and air quality, for example, and to relay that data to a processor for conversion from data to information.[25] Some sensors may be embedded in the roadway to enable computer-driven automobiles.

Workers in many organizations operate in a cloud-computing environment in which software and data storage are provided by the Internet ("the cloud"); the services are run on another organization's computer hardware, and both software and data are easily accessed. See Figure 1.11. This represents a significant change in how data is stored, accessed, and transferred, and it raises many security concerns. The unmanaged employee use of cloud services (e.g., the use of a file-sharing Web site to transfer large documents to clients or suppliers) represents a significant risk. Information systems and business managers should provide employees with a list of validated cloud services to avoid potential issues.[26]

FIGURE **1.11**

Cloud computing

With cloud computing, software and data storage are provided by the Internet ("the cloud") and services are run on another organization's computer hardware; both software and data are easily accessed.

Amazon Web Services offers cloud services that enable an individual or organization to run virtually everything in the cloud: from enterprise applications and research projects to social games and mobile apps. Netflix partners with Amazon Web Services to provide services and delivery of content. Users can stream Netflix shows and movies from anywhere in the world, including on the Web, on tablets, or on small mobile devices such as iPhones.[27]

Internet sites such as Facebook, LinkedIn, Pinterest, and Google+ have become popular places to connect with friends and colleagues. People can also send one another short messages up to 140 characters using Twitter. The Internet has also given rise to citizen journalism, where individuals who are witness to a newsworthy event post their opinions and observations on the Internet for others to read. In the aftermath of the Boston Marathon bombings, citizen journalists broke much of the news and captured unique photos of the events. However, in some cases, they got information wrong, including falsely accusing suspects.[28]

This increased use of the Internet is not without its risks. Some people fear that this increased usage can lead to problems, including loss of privacy and security, with criminals hacking into an organization's data via the Internet to gain access to sensitive company and customer information.

The World Wide Web (WWW), better known as the Web, is a network of links on the Internet to documents containing text, graphics, video, and sound. Information about the documents and access to them are controlled and provided by tens of thousands of special computers called Web servers. The Web is one of many services available over the Internet and provides access to millions of documents. New Internet technologies and increased Internet communications and collaboration are collectively called Web 2.0.

The technology used to create the Internet is also being applied within organizations to create **intranets**, which allow people in an organization to exchange information and work on projects. Accorda is a biotechnology company that develops therapeutic neurological treatments. It launched its Synapse intranet after spending months interviewing employees to discover what their needs were. According to Mike Russo, senior director of corporate digital strategy and innovation, employees had three major needs: quick access to work resources, collaboration, and fun. Russo's team built the new intranet from the ground up, adding in social tools such as one very similar to Twitter.[29]

An **extranet** is a network based on Web technologies that allows selected outsiders, such as business partners and customers, to access authorized resources of a company's intranet. Many people use extranets every day without realizing it—to track shipped goods, order products from their suppliers, or access customer assistance from other companies. Federal Express (FedEx) was one of the first large companies to empower customers to serve themselves at their convenience through the use of a corporate extranet. A fundamental FedEx belief is that the information it provides customers about its services is more important than the services themselves.[30] Customers can access the FedEx extranet to obtain a full range of shipping, billing, and tracking services. See Figure 1.12.

intranet: An internal network based on Web technologies that allows people within an organization to exchange information and work on projects.

extranet: A network based on Web technologies that allows selected outsiders, such as business partners and customers, to access authorized resources of a company's intranet.

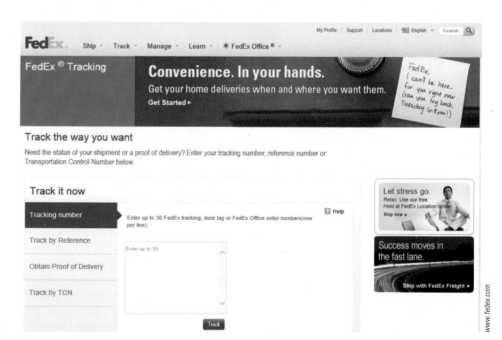

FIGURE 1.12

Extranets

When you sign in to the FedEx site (*www.fedex.com*) to check the status of a package, you are using an extranet.

People

People make the difference between success and failure in all organizations. Jim Collins, in his book *Good to Great*, said, "Those who build great companies understand that the ultimate throttle on growth for any great company is not markets, or technology, or competition, or products. It is one thing above all others: the ability to get and keep enough of the right people."[31] Thus, it comes as no surprise that people are the most important element in computer-based information systems.

Good systems can enable ordinary people to produce extraordinary results. They can also boost job satisfaction and worker productivity.[32] Information systems personnel include all the people who manage, run, program, and maintain the system, including the chief information officer (CIO), who manages the IS department. See Figure 1.13. End users are people who work directly with information systems to get results. They include financial executives, marketing representatives, and manufacturing operators.

FIGURE 1.13

Chief information officer (CIO)

The CIO manages the Information Systems department, which includes all the people who manage, run, program, and maintain a computer-based information system.

procedures: The strategies, policies, methods, and rules for using a CBIS.

Procedures

A **procedure** defines the steps to follow to achieve a specific end result, such as enter a customer order, pay a supplier invoice, or request a current inventory report. Good procedures describe how to achieve the desired end result, who does what and when, and what to do in the event something goes wrong. When people are well trained and follow effective procedures, they can get work done faster, cut costs, make better use of people resources, and enable people to adapt to change. When procedures are well documented, they can greatly reduce training costs and shorten the learning curve.[33]

For example, effective January 1, 2013, the IRS implemented new procedures for issuing individual taxpayer identification numbers (ITINs issued to people who are not eligible to obtain a Social Security number). These new procedures were documented and published on an IRS Web site for viewing by those affected by the new procedures.[34]

Using a CBIS involves setting and following many procedures, including those for the operation, maintenance, and security of the computer. For example, some procedures describe how to gain access to the system through the use of some log-on procedure and a password. Others describe who can access facts in the database or what to do if a disaster, such as a fire, earthquake, or hurricane, renders the CBIS unusable. Good procedures can help companies take advantage of new opportunities and avoid potential disasters. Poorly developed and inadequately implemented procedures, however, can cause people to waste their time on useless rules or result in inadequate responses to disasters.

Now that we have looked at computer-based information systems in general, we will briefly examine the most common types used in business today. These IS types are covered in greater detail in Part 3.

BUSINESS INFORMATION SYSTEMS

Information systems used in business organizations are those for electronic and mobile commerce, transaction processing, management information, and decision support. In addition, some organizations employ special-purpose systems, such as virtual reality, that not every organization uses. Although these systems are discussed in separate sections in this chapter and explained in greater detail later, they are often integrated in one product and delivered by the same software package. See Figure 1.14. For example, some business information systems process transactions, deliver information, and support decisions. Figure 1.15 shows a simple timeline of the development of important business information systems discussed in this section. In addition to owning a complete business information system including hardware, software, databases, telecommunications, and Internet capabilities, companies also can rent business information systems from others. As mentioned before, Amazon Web Services allows people and companies to pay for the business information systems they use. This approach avoids huge outlays of money to purchase expensive equipment and facilities.

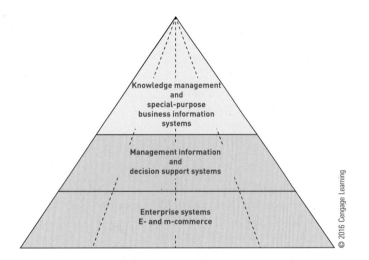

FIGURE 1.14

Business information systems

Business information systems are often integrated into one product and can be delivered by the same software package.

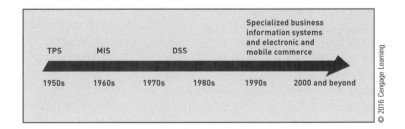

FIGURE 1.15

Business information systems timeline

Business information systems were introduced in the 1950s and changed significantly in most decades after that.

electronic commerce (e-commerce): Any business transaction executed electronically between companies (business-to-business), companies and consumers (business-to-consumer), consumers and other consumers (consumer-to-consumer), business and the public sector, and consumers and the public sector.

Electronic and Mobile Commerce

Electronic commerce (e-commerce) involves any business transaction executed electronically between companies (business-to-business, or B2B), companies and consumers (business-to-consumer, or B2C), consumers and other consumers (consumer-to-consumer, or C2C), business and the public sector, and consumers and the public sector. E-commerce offers opportunities for businesses of all sizes to market and sell at a low cost worldwide, allowing

INFORMATION SYSTEMS @ WORK

With ERP Access, Small Companies Are Reaching for the Skies

You probably don't think of cleaning washrooms and high-tech software at the same time. That means you don't usually think of CIBS.

CIBS, a division of CI (originally Clean Interiors) Business Services, provides a complete range of washroom and pest control services. Founded more than 20 years ago in the United Kingdom, CIBS is now an award-winning cleaning and hygiene services provider.

In its early years, managers at CIBS scheduled services using a combination of spreadsheets, paper files, and small business software. As the company grew, however, the managers reevaluated this method. General Manager Julia Kulinski explains that "Because data was scattered across spreadsheets and paper files, it was difficult for us to get an integrated view of our customers, which we needed to service them properly. For example, when customers called in regarding errors or other service-related issues, service representatives couldn't find the information needed to resolve the issues on the first call."

Other problems affected revenue and expenses. Because invoicing was a manual process, the staff prepared and sent invoices only once a month, and invoices based on paper records often had errors. Management wasn't aware of cost overruns until it was too late to correct them. Further, it wasn't practical to motivate employees by moving to performance-based pay methods, which was a business objective. Finally, and most importantly, CIBS couldn't grow.

CIBS evaluated its options and selected an integrated ERP (enterprise resource planning) system from the German firm SAP. This chapter defines an ERP system as "a set of integrated programs that manages the vital business operations for an entire multisite, global organization." Although most ERP users are large organizations, smaller companies are also taking advantage of ERP systems. With 200 employees, CIBS is a medium-sized company. It too wanted the benefits that an ERP system offers, including a single shared database to store its information and coordinate its operations. As Kulinski puts it, they wouldn't be able to grow otherwise: "For the business to scale, we needed a centralized database, automated processes, and real-time reporting." Small companies need these as much as large ones do.

In fact, ERP use is growing more quickly among small companies than large ones. According to Albert Pang in the *Apps Run the World* blog, total annual revenue of all ERP vendors is growing at 5.6 percent per year for customers with 100 or fewer employees,

dropping steadily to an annual growth rate of 2.4 percent among companies with 5,000 or more employees. The reason is that early ERP systems required expensive hardware, which only the largest organizations could afford.

Today, not only is hardware far less expensive, but many ERP vendors are moving into the cloud. The cloud allows companies that are even smaller than CIBS to "rent" hardware through the vendor and access the ERP software through their vendor's personal computers. Businesses pay as little as $10 per month for ERP cloud-based services.

Kulinski maintains that the move to ERP software solved business problems at CIBS and helped the company grow. She evaluates the financial benefits this way: "I look at the running costs of SAP software—which for us is the equivalent of one full-time employee—and then at the value the software delivers to the business. There's no way one person could deliver this much value to the business."

In the final analysis, delivering value to the business is what information systems are about.

Discussion Questions

1. This case is about an SAP customer and is based in part on SAP materials. However, other software firms also offer ERP software. The two largest vendors in the small company segment are Oracle and Microsoft. Compare their ERP offerings.
2. What advantages did SAP's ERP system offer CIBS?

Critical Thinking Questions

1. List the five problems that CIBS had with its earlier spreadsheet- and paper-based system. Rank them by their importance to CIBS. Justify your rankings. If you disagree with Kulinski's top ranking of limited growth potential, explain why.
2. Consider the challenges of an e-commerce Web site run by one or two people. How would such a small business make use of ERP offerings?

SOURCES: CIBS Web site, *www.ci-bs.co.uk*, and subsidiaries' Web sites, *www.cibshygiene.com* and *www.cibsfacilities.com*, accessed January 17, 2012; SAP, "CIBS: Enabling Growth and Exceptional Service Quality with SAP Software," *www.technologyevaluation.com/research/case-study /CIBS-Enabling-Growth-and-Exceptional-Service-Quality-with-SAP -Software.html*, March 2011, downloaded January 16, 2012; Pang, A., "Infor's Daring Move to Buy Lawson, Shake Up ERP MidMarket," *Apps Run the World* blog, *www.baanboard.com/baanboard/showthread.php? t=60242*, March 13, 2011, accessed January 17, 2012; Gaskin, James E., "How Small Is Too Small a Company for ERP Software?" Inside-ERP, May 9, 2013, *www.inside-erp.com/articles/inside-erp-blog/how-small-is -too-small-a-company-for-erp-software-55821*, accessed July 22, 2013.

them to enter the global market. It also can improve the effectiveness of non-profit organizations. The American Red Cross spent months redesigning its internal processes and converting many of them to e-commerce systems to improve its effectiveness and help more people faster. The new e-commerce platform enables the Red Cross to better support local charters and more quickly recruit volunteers and blood donors. It also began testing to identify changes to Web pages that increase its total site donation revenues.[35]

Mobile commerce (m-commerce) is the use of mobile, wireless devices to place orders and conduct business. M-commerce relies on wireless communications that managers and corporations use to place orders and conduct business with handheld computers, portable cell phones, laptop computers connected to a network, and other mobile devices.

A key aspect of mobile e-commerce that results in conversion of shoppers into buyers is making the mobile site easy and pleasant for customers to use. However, a recent survey reveals that most Web sites are not designed with access by mobile devices in mind and are in need of considerable rework. As a result, 88 percent of mobile shoppers report negative experiences with their shopping and fully one-third of them move on to a competitor's site to complete their shopping.[36]

Two retailers that have recognized the need to improve the mobile shopping experience are makeup retailer Sephora and Amazon.com. Sephora has gone so far as to build two apps for mobile shoppers, one for shoppers with smartphones (see Figure 1.16) and one for shoppers with tablet computers. Each app provides consumers with very different experiences. The strategy seems to be paying off, with mobile orders increasing by 167 percent during the 2012 holiday season. Amazon.com generated about $4 billion in mobile sales last year, about 8 percent of total sales. The company is working on making its mobile shopping app extremely fast and easy. Its goal is to speed

mobile commerce (m-commerce): The use of mobile, wireless devices to place orders and conduct business.

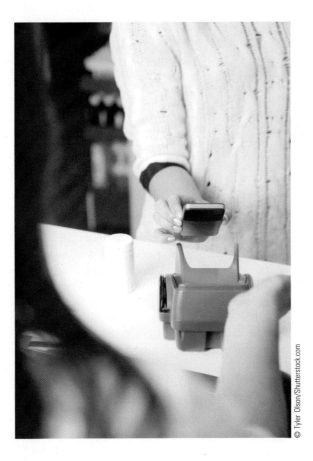

FIGURE 1.16

Mobile commerce (m-commerce)

With m-commerce, people can use smartphones to pay for goods and services anywhere, anytime.

© Tyler Olson/Shutterstock.com

up the buying process so that the time from consumers deciding to buy something until completing their purchase is as short as 30 seconds.[37]

E-commerce offers many advantages for streamlining work activities. Figure 1.17 provides a brief example of how e-commerce can simplify the process of purchasing new office furniture from an office supply company. In the manual system, a corporate office worker must get approval for a purchase that exceeds a certain amount. That request goes to the purchasing department, which generates a formal purchase order to procure the goods from the approved vendor. Business-to-business e-commerce automates the entire process. Employees go directly to the supplier's Web site, find the item in a catalog, and order what they need at a price set by their company. If management approval is required, the manager is notified automatically. As the use of e-commerce systems grows, companies are phasing out their traditional systems. The resulting growth of e-commerce is creating many new business opportunities.

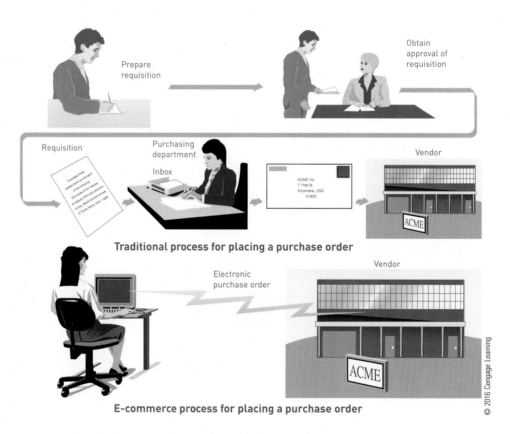

© 2016 Cengage Learning

FIGURE 1.17

Electronic commerce (e-commerce)

E-commerce greatly simplifies purchasing.

electronic business (e-business): Using information systems and the Internet to perform all business-related tasks and functions.

In addition to e-commerce, business information systems use telecommunications and the Internet to perform many related tasks. Electronic procurement (e-procurement), for example, involves using information systems and the Internet to acquire parts and supplies. **Electronic business (e-business)** goes beyond e-commerce and e-procurement by using information systems and the Internet to perform all business-related tasks and functions, such as accounting, finance, marketing, manufacturing, and human resource activities. E-business also includes working with customers, suppliers, strategic partners, and stakeholders. Compared to traditional business strategy, e-business strategy is flexible and adaptable. See Figure 1.18.

Enterprise Systems: Transaction Processing Systems and Enterprise Resource Planning

Enterprise systems that process daily transactions have evolved over the years and offer important solutions for businesses of all sizes. Traditional transaction

Electronic business (e-business)

E-business goes beyond e-commerce to include using information systems and the Internet to perform all business-related tasks and functions, such as accounting, finance, marketing, manufacturing, and human resources activities.

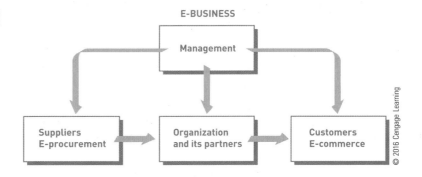

processing systems (TPSs) are still being used today, but increasingly, companies are turning to enterprise resource planning systems.

Transaction Processing Systems

Since the 1950s, computers have been used to perform common business applications. Many of these early systems were designed to reduce costs by automating routine, labor-intensive business transactions. A **transaction** is any business-related exchange such as payments to employees, sales to customers, or payments to suppliers. Processing business transactions was the first computer application developed for most organizations. A **transaction processing system (TPS)** is an organized collection of people, procedures, software, databases, and devices used to perform and record business transactions. If you understand a transaction processing system, you understand basic business operations and functions.

One of the first business systems to be computerized was the payroll system. The primary inputs for a payroll TPS are the number of employee hours worked during the week and the pay rate. The primary output consists of paychecks. Early payroll systems produced employee paychecks and related reports required by state and federal agencies, such as the Internal Revenue Service (IRS). Other routine applications include sales ordering, customer billing and customer relationship management, and inventory control. Airlines and travel agencies use online transaction processing reservation systems to enable travelers to select and book their own flights. These systems enable passengers to choose their destinations and flight dates, compare costs on alternate flight dates, book their seats, and generate electronic tickets. Such online reservation systems are at the center of a whole collection of transaction processing systems employed by airlines. See Figure 1.19.

Enterprise systems help organizations perform and integrate important tasks, such as paying employees and suppliers, controlling inventory, sending invoices, and ordering supplies. In the past, companies accomplished these tasks using traditional transaction processing systems. Today, more companies use enterprise resource planning systems for these tasks.

Enterprise Resource Planning

An **enterprise resource planning (ERP) system** is a set of integrated programs that manages the vital business operations for an entire multisite, global organization. An ERP system can replace many applications with one unified set of programs, making the system easier to use and more effective. Today, using ERP systems and getting timely reports from them can be done using cell phones and other mobile devices.

Although the scope of an ERP system might vary from company to company, most ERP systems provide integrated software to support manufacturing and finance. Many ERP systems also have a purchasing subsystem that orders the needed items. In addition to these core business processes, some

transaction: Any business-related exchange such as payments to employees, sales to customers, and payments to suppliers.

transaction processing system (TPS): An organized collection of people, procedures, software, databases, and devices used to perform and record business transactions.

enterprise resource planning (ERP) system: A set of integrated programs that manages the vital business operations for an entire multisite, global organization.

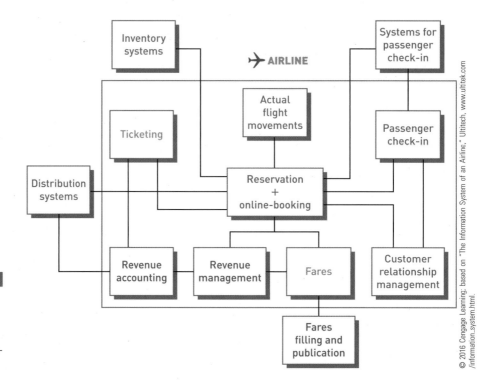

Integrated transaction processing system

The online reservation system is at the center of a collection of information systems used by airlines.

ERP systems can support functions such as customer service, human resources, sales, and distribution. The primary benefits of implementing an ERP system include easing adoption of improved work processes and increasing access to timely data for decision making. See Figure 1.20.

Airfreight 2100 is the exclusive authorized agent of Federal Express in the Philippines and handles all the company's pickup, customs clearance, and delivery needs. Initially, the firm relied on multiple, nonintegrated systems to run its operations. As Airfreight grew, these systems could not provide accurate and current data needed to run the business effectively. Perhaps its most serious problem was that management did not have the data needed to manage its accounts receivables so that too much money was tied up in unpaid accounts. Since the company implemented an ERP system, redesigned its business processes, and tightened its credit policies, it has gained control and reduced the account collection period by 20 percent.[38]

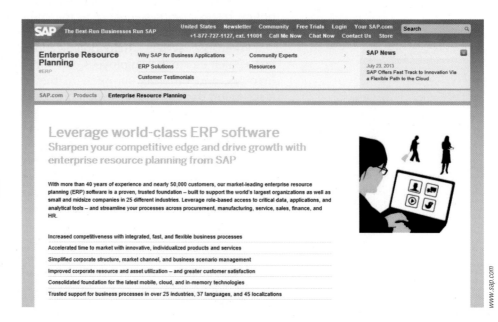

Enterprise resource planning (ERP) software

SAP AG, a German software company, is one of the leading suppliers of ERP software. The company employs more than 50,000 people in more than 130 countries.

Information and Decision Support Systems

The benefits provided by an effective TPS or ERP, including reduced processing costs and required personnel, are substantial and justify their associated costs in computing equipment, computer programs, and specialized personnel and supplies. After adopting an information system, companies soon realize that they can use the data stored in these systems to help managers make better decisions, whether in human resource management, marketing, or administration. Satisfying the needs of managers and decision makers continues to be a major factor in developing information systems.

Management Information Systems

management information system (MIS): An organized collection of people, procedures, software, databases, and devices that provides routine information to managers and decision makers.

A **management information system (MIS)** is an organized collection of people, procedures, software, databases, and devices that provides routine information to managers and decision makers. Manufacturing, marketing, production, finance, and other functional areas of an organization are supported by MISs and share a common database. MISs typically provide standard reports generated with data and information from the TPS or ERP. See Figure 1.21.

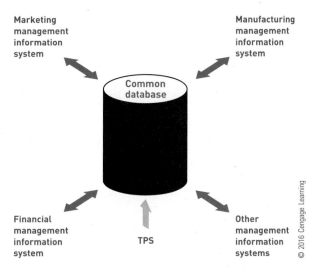

© 2016 Cengage Learning

FIGURE 1.21

Management information system

Functional management information systems draw data from the organization's transaction processing system.

The Scottish Police Authority and Police Scotland are implementing a new management information system to support new standardized national policing processes and daily policing operations and investigations. The system will replace dozens of outdated legacy systems and enable the sharing of operational and case information across Scotland. Deputy Chief Constable Richardson, Police Scotland, said, "Our focus is, and always will be, on keeping people safe and maximizing operational, frontline police activity to allow us to achieve this. There will be efficiencies in terms of streamlining administrative tasks that will free up police officers for frontline activities, allowing them to be more visible and accessible in the communities they serve."[39]

MISs were first developed in the 1960s and typically use information systems to produce managerial reports. In many cases, these early reports were produced periodically—daily, weekly, monthly, or yearly. Because of their value to managers, MISs have proliferated throughout the management ranks.

Decision Support Systems

decision support system (DSS): An organized collection of people, procedures, software, databases, and devices used to support problem-specific decision making.

A **decision support system (DSS)** is an organized collection of people, procedures, software, databases, and devices that support problem-specific decision making. The focus of a DSS is on making effective decisions. Whereas an MIS helps an organization "do things right," a DSS helps a manager "do the right thing."

Many organizations in the travel industry use decision support systems to improve decision making. Airlines now calculate the value of a group of customers who will miss a connection due to a flight delay. They then determine whether it will generate more revenue to delay their connecting flight or book them on the next plane. Hotel chains use decision support systems to analyze how much to spend and where to spend on renovations. (High-end hotels tend to invest in interior renovations, whereas low-end, roadside hotels spend on the exterior to attract drive-by guests.) Hotel chains are also performing dynamic pricing based on the source of the reservation. Orbitz customers, for example, tend to spend more on food and beverage services than do Priceline customers and so are likely to get lower room rates.[40]

A DSS goes beyond a traditional MIS by providing immediate assistance in solving problems. Many of these problems are unique and complex, and key information is often difficult to obtain. For instance, an auto manufacturer might try to determine the best location to build a new manufacturing facility, or a developer of electronic components might need to calculate the risk involved in introducing a new product. See Figure 1.22. A DSS can help by suggesting and evaluating alternatives and assisting in final decision making. A DSS recognizes that different managerial styles and decision types require different systems. The overall emphasis is to support, rather than replace, managerial decision making.

Courtesy of Endeca Technologies, Inc.

FIGURE 1.22

Decision support software

Endeca provides Discovery for Design, decision support software that helps businesspeople assess risk and analyze performance. The data shown here is for electronic component development.

A DSS can include a collection of models used to support a decision maker or user (model base), a collection of facts and information to assist in decision making (database), and systems and procedures (user interface or dialogue manager) that help decision makers and other users interact with the DSS. See Figure 1.23. A type of software called a database management system (DBMS) is often used to manage the database, and a software application called the model management system (MMS) is used to manage the model base. Not all DSSs have all of these components.

Subway uses a DSS to evaluate various initiatives such as implementing bundled meal offers or price promotions. The DSS is able to predict what

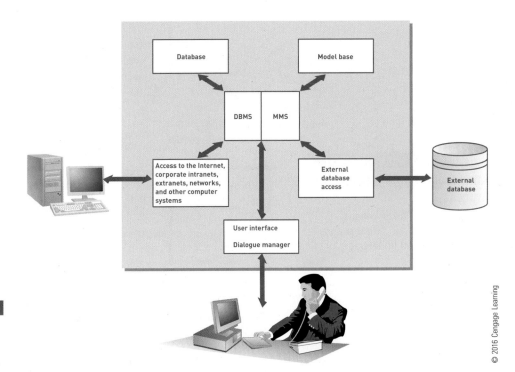

FIGURE 1.23

Essential DSS elements

A DSS typically includes a model base, database, and user interface.

impact the initiative will have on revenues, profits, and market share. It can also help to design a rollout program that maximizes returns. The president and CEO of the Subway Franchisee Advertising Fund Trust says: "It helps us to be maximally creative and risk taking. We can test any exciting but risky idea before we roll it out and rapidly roll out the ones that work."[41]

In addition to DSSs for managers, other systems use the same approach to support groups and executives. A group decision support system includes the DSS elements just described as well as software, called groupware, to help groups make effective decisions. The group may all be located in one place, or it may support a virtual meeting where the members of the group are in multiple locations. An executive support system, also called an executive information system, helps top-level managers, including a firm's president, vice presidents, and members of the board of directors, make better decisions.

Specialized Business Information Systems: Knowledge Management, Artificial Intelligence, Expert Systems, and Virtual Reality

In addition to ERPs, MISs, and DSSs, organizations often rely on specialized systems. A *knowledge management system* (*KMS*) is an organized collection of people, procedures, software, databases, and devices that stores and retrieves knowledge, improves collaboration, locates knowledge sources, captures and uses knowledge, or in some other way enhances the knowledge management process, as shown in Figure 1.24. Consulting firms often use a KMS to capture and provide the collective knowledge of its consultants to one another. This makes each consultant much more valuable and avoids "reinventing the wheel" to solve similar problems for different clients. The workforce at NASA is aging, and it is essential that critical knowledge not be lost as workers retire. Their specialized knowledge must be captured and retained for future reuse. NASA employs knowledge management to document and integrate lessons learned from decades of missions to effectively manage the risk involved in future space exploration and human space flight.[42]

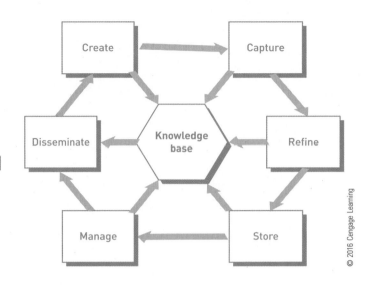

FIGURE 1.24

Knowledge management process

Managing knowledge means an organization can capture and retain specialized knowledge for future use.

artificial intelligence (AI): A field in which the computer system takes on the characteristics of human intelligence.

In addition to knowledge management, companies use other types of specialized systems. Some are based on the notion of artificial intelligence (AI) in which the computer system takes on the characteristics of human intelligence. Artificial intelligence allows computers to beat human champions in games, helps doctors make medical diagnoses, and enables cars to drive hundreds of miles without a human behind the wheel.

The field of artificial intelligence includes several subfields. See Figure 1.25. Some people predict that in the future we will have nanobots, small molecular-sized robots, traveling throughout our bodies and in our bloodstream, monitoring our health. Other nanobots will be embedded in products and services.

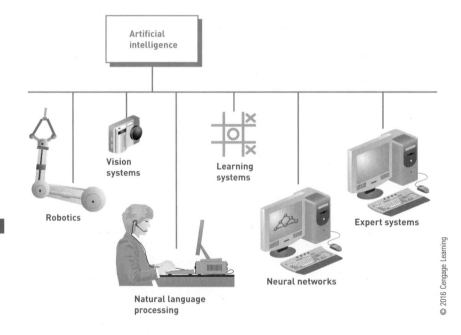

FIGURE 1.25

Major branches of artificial intelligence

The field of AI includes several branches, including robotics and learning systems.

Artificial Intelligence

Robotics is an area of artificial intelligence in which machines take over complex, dangerous, routine, or boring tasks, such as welding car frames or moving pallets of products around in a warehouse. See Figure 1.26. Industries are turning to the use of robots to increase production and quality while

FIGURE 1.26

Robotics

Industrial robots perform complex, dangerous, routine, or boring tasks, such as milling machine tools or assembling automobiles.

decreasing waste and costs. Ford puts all its North American Ford trucks through a strenuous set of durability tests before they are approved for customer use. For health and safety reasons, human drivers are only allowed to drive certain rigorous courses once a day. So to accelerate testing, reduce costs, and increase safety, Ford replaces the human driver with a robot control module that controls vehicle steering, acceleration, and braking on the more dangerous tests. The vehicle's position is monitored by cameras in a central control room and GPS accurate to ±1 inch. This allows Ford to run many more tests per day than with human drivers alone.[43]

Vision systems allow robots and other devices to see, store, and process visual images. Researchers have developed a vision-enabled snake robot that provides a way to view hard-to-reach or radioactively contaminated areas of power plants inaccessible to people. First tested in a nuclear power plant in Austria, the snake can twist and turn as it moves through or over pipes and provide video to a control station. Martin Fries, an engineer for EVN Group (the plant owner) said, "With further development and testing, such a robot could give operators a more complete understanding of a plant's condition and perhaps reduce a plant's downtime by enabling faster, more efficient inspections."[44]

Natural language processing involves the computer understanding, analyzing, manipulating, or generating natural languages. It encompasses three main application areas: (1) computer translation of speech or text from one language to another, (2) dialogue systems that enable a human to communicate with a computer using a natural language, and (3) information extraction that transforms unstructured text into structured data that can be searched and browsed in flexible ways. Natural language processing is opening exciting new possibilities for how humans interact with computers and how we access the vast amount of data available in electronic form.[45]

Learning systems allow computers to learn from past mistakes or experiences, such as playing games or making business decisions. Watson is the artificially intelligent computer system with natural language processing and learning capabilities that first demonstrated its prowess by defeating two former Jeopardy champions in 2011. See Figure 1.27. Now Watson is learning to provide physicians with evidence-based treatment options for lung cancer patients. To do so, Watson was fed a wealth of information about lung cancer, including physician notes, lab results, and clinical research from 1,500 patient cases. In addition, Watson absorbed more than 2 million pages of text from 42 medical journals and clinical trials in the area of oncology research. Oncologists at other cancer treatment centers are testing Watson and providing feedback to IBM, insurer WellPoint, and Memorial Sloan-Kettering Cancer Center (primary developers of Watson) to improve its usability.[46]

FIGURE 1.27

Watson supercomputer

IBM's supercomputer Watson used artificial intelligence to compete with and eventually win against Jeopardy champions.

Another branch of artificial intelligence is neural networks, which allows computers to recognize and act on patterns or trends. Some successful stock, options, and futures traders use neural networks to spot trends and improve the profitability of their investments. Edwin Welch, the director of institutional research and associate registrar at Taylor University, is investigating the use of neural networks in an attempt to identify patterns or trends among students who drop out after their freshman year. From the data that Welch has available, the neural network identified the best predictors of retention for Taylor as high school GPA, SAT and ACT scores, fall-term GPA, percentage of credit hours completed in the freshman fall term, number of midterm grades below a C in the fall term, and the number of credit hours registered for in the spring term. The model has a 78–86 percent accuracy rate in determining whether a given freshman will either leave the university or continue onto sophomore year. Students predicted to be at risk are contacted by the university's Academic Enrichment Center to receive tutoring and are placed on the alert lists of instructors, counselors, and hall directors.[47]

Expert Systems

expert system: A system that gives a computer the ability to make suggestions and function like an expert in a particular field.

Expert systems give the computer the ability to make suggestions and function like an expert in a particular field, helping enhance the performance of the novice user. The unique value of expert systems is that they allow organizations to capture and use the wisdom of experts and specialists. Therefore, years of experience and specific skills are not completely lost when a human expert dies, retires, or leaves for another job. The collection of data, rules,

knowledge base: The collection of data, rules, procedures, and relationships that must be followed to achieve value or the proper outcome.

procedures, and relationships that must be followed to achieve value or the proper outcome is contained in the expert system's knowledge base. Japan Airlines developed an expert system for crew scheduling of its 100 wide-body aircraft and 2,200 flight crew members. The system takes into account crew qualifications for the various planes and routes, restrictions on the allowable number of takeoffs and landings, crew turnaround at various destinations, vacation and meeting needs, and crew preferences. The expert system provided much better schedules in many fewer hours compared to the old manual process, which took 25 people 20 days to complete.[48]

Virtual Reality and Multimedia

Virtual reality and multimedia are specialized systems that are valuable for many businesses and nonprofit organizations. Many imitate or act like real environments. These unique systems are discussed in this section.

virtual reality: An artificial three-dimensional environment created by hardware and software and experienced through sensory stimuli (primarily sight and sound, but sometimes through touch, taste, and smell) and within which an individual can interact to affect what happens in the environment.

Virtual reality is an artificial three-dimensional environment created by hardware and software and experienced through sensory stimuli (primarily sight and sound, but sometimes through touch, taste, and smell) and within which an individual can interact to affect what happens in the environment. Virtual reality has long been used by the military for training pilots. Students have likely encountered virtual reality on gaming boxes such as Xbox 360 or the Wii. Jaguar Land Rover and four of the leading universities in the United Kingdom formed a five-year, £10 million partnership to develop new advanced virtual reality tools including sophisticated computers and processes for use by vehicle manufacturers. The goal is to analyze designs at the component, system, and entire-vehicle levels in a virtual reality environment. Such analysis will enable manufacturers to deliver advanced vehicle designs in less time and at a reduced cost by lessening the need to build physical prototypes.[49]

Augmented reality is a form of virtual reality that has the potential to superimpose digital data over real photos or images. Wikitude is a mobile-based augmented reality application that enables you to overlay many dynamic content sources onto the image captured by a smartphone video camera. See Figure 1.28. For example, you could point your phone camera down a city street and request that the location of any restaurant be displayed on the image. You could then request that the address, phone, directions, and even reviews be overlaid on the image displayed by your phone.[50]

FIGURE 1.28

Wikitude app

You can use Wikitude to augment images displayed on your smartphone with updated content, such as locations of restaurants or transit stations.

www.wikitude.com

A variety of input devices, such as head-mounted displays (see Figure 1.29), data gloves, joysticks, and handheld wands, allow the user to navigate through a virtual environment and interact with virtual objects. Directional sound, tactile and force feedback devices, voice recognition, and other technologies enrich the immersive experience. Because several people can share and interact in the same environment, virtual reality can be a powerful medium for communication, entertainment, and learning.

FIGURE 1.29

Head-mounted display

The head-mounted display (HMD) was the first device to provide the wearer with an immersive experience. A typical HMD houses two miniature display screens and an optical system that channels the images from the screens to the eyes, thereby presenting a stereo view of a virtual world. A motion tracker continuously measures the position and orientation of the user's head and allows the image-generating computer to adjust the scene representation to the current view. As a result, the viewer can look around and walk through the surrounding virtual environment.

Courtesy of 5DT, Inc., www.5dt.com

Multimedia is a natural extension of virtual reality. It can include photos and images, the manipulation of sound, and special 3D effects. Once used primarily in movies, 3D technology can be used by companies to design products, such as motorcycles, jet engines, and bridges. Autodesk, for instance, makes exciting 3D software that companies can use to design large skyscrapers and other buildings. The software can also be used by Hollywood animators to develop action and animated movies.

SYSTEMS DEVELOPMENT

systems development: The activity of creating or modifying information systems.

Systems development is the activity of creating or modifying information systems. Systems development projects can range from small to very large and are conducted in fields as diverse as nuclear science research and video game development. Systems development is initiated for many reasons, including to reduce the cost and effort associated with operating an existing system; to meet a new business need caused by an organizational change such as a merger, acquisition, or formation of a new department; to meet a new government requirement; to provide a new or improved customer service; or to take advantage of new technology development such as the expanding use of smartphones and tablets to replace personal computers. Over the next few years, it is expected that systems developers will concentrate on projects that apply analytics to large amounts of business data, take advantage of cloud computing, and create more mobile applications for their businesses and organizations.[51]

Company employees can develop systems, or companies may hire an outside company (outsource) to perform some or all of a systems development project. Outsourcing allows a company to focus on what it does best and delegate software development to companies that have world-class development capabilities. No matter who does the work, throughout the entire system development process, the project team must constantly strive to gain the support of top-level managers and the people who will actually use the system. The project team must focus on developing a system that achieves significant business goals.

One strategy for improving the results of a systems development project is to divide it into several steps, each with a well-defined goal and a set of tasks to accomplish. See Figure 1.30. These steps are summarized next.

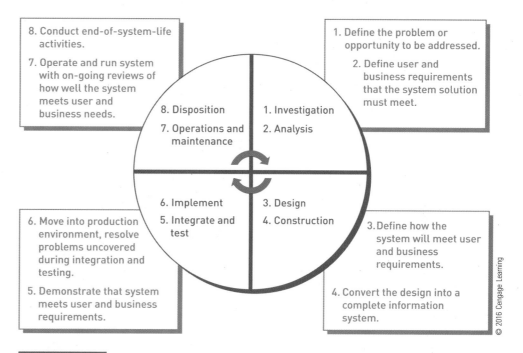

8. Conduct end-of-system-life activities.

7. Operate and run system with on-going reviews of how well the system meets user and business needs.

1. Define the problem or opportunity to be addressed.

2. Define user and business requirements that the system solution must meet.

8. Disposition
7. Operations and maintenance
1. Investigation
2. Analysis
6. Implement
5. Integrate and test
3. Design
4. Construction

6. Move into production environment, resolve problems uncovered during integration and testing.

5. Demonstrate that system meets user and business requirements.

3. Define how the system will meet user and business requirements.

4. Convert the design into a complete information system.

© 2016 Cengage Learning

FIGURE 1.30

Systems development life cycle

Systems development involves several well-defined stages.

Investigation, Analysis, and Design

The first steps of systems development are systems investigation, analysis, and design. The goal of the systems investigation is to gain a clear understanding of the specifics of the problem to be solved or the opportunity to be addressed. What is the scope of the problem? Who is affected and how? How often does this occur? After an organization understands the problem, the next question is, "Is the problem worth addressing?" Given that organizations have limited resources—people and money—this question deserves careful consideration. If the decision is to continue addressing the problem, the next step, systems analysis, involves studying the existing system to uncover its strengths and weaknesses and interviewing those who will use the new system to identify what the system must do to meet their needs and the needs of the organization. This is called defining the system requirements. Systems design determines how the new system must work, what inputs are required, and what outputs must be produced to meet the business needs defined during systems analysis.

Construction, Integration and Testing, Implementation, Operation and Maintenance, and Disposition

Construction involves converting the system design into an operational information system. Tasks include acquiring and installing hardware and software, coding and testing software programs, creating and loading data into databases, and performing initial program testing. Integration and testing is a process of linking together all the components of the system to demonstrate that the system as a whole does indeed meet the user and business requirements. Testing is done both by the technical members of the project team and by trained end users. Implementation involves installing the new system into the actual production computer environment in which it is expected to run and resolving any problems uncovered in integration and testing. Operation and maintenance involves the ongoing running of the system and identifying and making necessary changes to the system due to errors or new user or business requirements. Disposition involves those activities at the end of the useful life of the system. Often, this requires that data from the system's database be extracted and converted into a new format for use in the replacement system. Companies often hire outside companies to do their development, integration and testing, implementation, and operation and maintenance work.

INFORMATION SYSTEMS IN BUSINESS AND SOCIETY

Information systems have been developed to meet the needs of all types of organizations and people. The speed and widespread use of information systems, however, opens users to a variety of threats from unethical people. Computer criminals and terrorists, for example, have used the Internet to steal millions of dollars or promote terrorism and violence. Some studies report that most of corporate security attacks come from people inside the company. Computer-related attacks can come from individuals, groups, companies, and even countries.

Security, Privacy, and Ethical Issues in Information Systems and the Internet

Although information systems can provide enormous benefits, they do raise many security, privacy, and ethical issues. A survey of security breaches in the United Kingdom found that 93 percent of large organizations and 87 percent of small organizations had a security breach in 2012. The average cost of a security breach is increasing, and several individual breaches cost more than £1 million.[52] Edward Snowden, an employee of defense contractor Booz Allen Hamilton working at the National Security Agency (NSA), is responsible for perhaps the most significant leak of classified information in U.S. history. In June 2013, Snowden admitted to passing classified documents to reporters at *The Guardian* and *The Washington Post*—revealing details of NSA surveillance programs that collect and perform data mining on hundreds of millions of U.S. phone and Internet traffic records to identify possible links to known terrorists.[53] This revelation has caused people around the world to wonder if such invasion of privacy is justified. Ethical issues concern what is generally considered right or wrong. Many believe that our use of computers has created new opportunities for unethical behavior. For example, millions of people worldwide engage in what some would consider unethical behavior by viewing pornography, accessing copyrighted videos and music without paying, and making and using illegal copies of software.

You can install firewalls (software and hardware that protect a computer system or network from outside attacks) to avoid viruses and prevent unauthorized people from gaining access to your computer system. You can also use identification numbers and passwords. In response to possible abuses, a number of laws have been passed to protect people from invasion of their privacy, including The Privacy Act, enacted in the 1970s.

Use of information systems also raises work concerns, including job loss through increased efficiency and potential health problems from making

Facebook Has User Privacy Problems

On Christmas 2012, Randi Zuckerberg posted a photo of her family on her private Facebook page. Unfortunately, the privacy settings on Facebook can confuse even the company's top executives. Randi, the sister of Facebook founder Mark Zuckerberg and a former senior Facebook executive, soon found that her photo had leaked to the general public and been tweeted to thousands of people. Randi tweeted Callie Schweitzer, director of marketing at VOX Media, who had first posted the photo to Twitter: "Not sure where you got this photo. I posted it to friends only on FB. You reposting it to Twitter is way uncool."

This incident came only 11 days after Facebook had released new privacy controls meant to help Facebook users understand who can see the content they post. A new shortcuts toolbar allowed users to control "Who can see my stuff" without having to go to a different page. The new release also offered in-product education. Messages explained how content that users hide in their timelines could still appear in their news feed and on other pages. Evidently, these controls did not go far enough to protect Randi Zuckerberg's privacy.

In fact, since it was launched, Facebook has had to address the privacy concerns of its users. In late 2011, Facebook settled a suit by the Federal Trade Commission (FTC) that charged Facebook with deceiving its customers about privacy issues since 2009. (The FTC regulates companies that take credit card information from consumers.) Facebook claimed that it would not share personal information with advertisers, that third-party applications would be given only the information they needed to function properly, that no one could access photos or videos from deleted accounts, and—perhaps most relevant to Randi Zuckerberg's experience—that information posted to an individual's Friends List would remain private. The FTC found that the company had not delivered on any of these claims. As part of the settlement, Facebook agreed to stop these practices until it had a better disclaimer and opt-out procedure. Mark Zuckerberg also issued a statement saying that, over the course of the previous 18 months, Facebook had introduced 20 new tools to address these and other privacy-related concerns.

However, by August 2012, the FTC launched a new investigation into Facebook privacy practices. Facebook partnered with Datalogix—a company that collects credit card purchasing information, such as where users are shopping and what they buy. Facebook users were included in Datalogix advertising research although they were not informed of this. Moreover, if Facebook users did, in fact, find out about the use of their private data, they could only opt out of the research by going to the Datalogix homepage.

Facebook subsidiaries have also experienced privacy controversy. In September 2012, Facebook acquired Instagram, a social media application that allows users to upload photos to the Instagram site for long-term storage and sharing. The product boasted a user-base of 100 million users. On December 17, 2012, Instagram posted a privacy notice claiming the right to sell all photographs posted to its site without compensation to the user. The company further claimed that it could sell any other metadata associated with the photo, such as usernames, gender, addresses, mobile phone number, and email addresses—all information users had to provide when setting up an account. Instagram asked users who did not agree with the notice to remove their accounts within a few weeks. The new policy would go into effect for all users who accessed their accounts after January 19, 2013.

The announcement garnered a great deal of public resentment. On December 18, 2012, Instagram cofounder Kevin Systrom clarified that, despite the notice, the company had no current plans to sell users' photos.

He explained that the company would be redrafting the privacy notice. In the meantime, competitors such as Flickr have picked up a larger market share as a result of Instagram's privacy misstep.

Facebook is a powerful tool for communicating and reconnecting with friends and family. The service it provides is so valuable that users continue to flock to it. However, with every step forward, Facebook seems to take one or two steps backward in its protection of user privacy. Whether at the hands of the FTC or the competition, Facebook will no doubt continue to face repercussions for its decisions.

Although Randi Zuckerberg may have blamed Callie Schweitzer for poor online manners, it is likely that most of the billion Facebook users would prefer to rely on some mechanism beyond social media etiquette to protect their photographs and private information.

Discussion Questions

1. Do you think that Facebook or careless, uninformed users should be held responsible for privacy issues related to using Facebook? Explain.
2. What additional measures should Facebook take to protect user privacy? What additional actions are required on the part of Facebook users to maintain adequate privacy?

Critical Thinking Questions

1. Describe a privacy issue so serious that it would cause you to stop using Facebook.
2. Develop a privacy policy for a student musical organization with roughly 50 members. This Web site stores members' contact information and information about their musical training, abilities, and interests. Who outside the organization might want to use that information and for what purposes? Should the organization allow them to use the information?

SOURCES: Schwartz, Terri, "Randi Zuckerberg's Family Photo Leaks Because of Confusing Facebook Settings," *Zap2it*, December 27, 2012, *http://blog.zap2it.com/pop2it/2012/12/randi-zuckerbergs-family-photo-leaks-because-of-confusing-facebook-settings.html*; Donston-Miller, Debra, "Facebook's New Privacy Policies: The Good News," *InformationWeek*, December 14, 2012, *www.informationweek.com/thebrainyard/news/social_networking_consumer/240144443/facebooks-new-privacy-policies-the-good-news*; Claburn, Thomas, "Facebook Settles FTC Charges, Admits Mistakes," *InformationWeek*, November 29, 2011, *www.informationweek.com/security/privacy/facebook-settles-ftc-charges-admits-mist/232200385*; Goldman, Jeff, "Privacy Concerns Raised over Facebook-Datalogix Partnership," *eSecurity Planet*, September 25, 2012, *www.esecurityplanet.com/network-security/privacy-concerns-raised-over-facebook-datalogix-partnership.html*; Arthur, Charles, "Facebook Forces Instagram Users to Allow It to Sell Their Uploaded Photos," *The Guardian*, December 18, 2012, *www.guardian.co.uk/technology/2012/dec/18/facebook-instagram-sell-uploaded-photos*; "Humbled Instagram Backs Down on Controversial Changes to Serve User Photos as Ads," *Independent.ie*, December 21, 2012, *www.independent.ie/business/technology/humbled-instagram-backs-down-on-controversial-changes-to-serve-user-photos-as-ads-3333391.html*.

repetitive motions. Ergonomics, the study of designing and positioning workplace equipment, can help you avoid health-related problems of using computer systems.

Computer and Information Systems Literacy

Whatever your college major or career path, understanding computers and information systems will help you cope, adapt, and prosper in this challenging environment. Some colleges are requiring a certain level of computer and information systems literacy before students are admitted or accepted into the college.

computer literacy: The knowledge and ability to use computers and related technology effectively.

Computer literacy is defined as the knowledge and ability to use computers and related technology effectively. People may possess varying degrees of computer literacy from simply knowing how to use the computer to obtain news and information from the Internet or sign on to Facebook; to possessing proficiency in using various software productivity tools to create documents, spreadsheets, graphs, and presentations; to being able to write simple programs. See Figure 1.31. Another useful component of computer literacy is knowing how computers operate and how they can connect to networks and other hardware devices. At least a minimal level of computer literacy is mandatory for people to be successful in both their careers and education. Raising your computer skills is a way to expand your job qualifications and be successful in today's information society.

© iStockphoto.com/hocus-focus

FIGURE 1.31

Computer literacy

People can gain computer literacy from knowing how to use the computer to connect with friends and other contacts with a social networking site, such as Facebook (*www.facebook.com*) or Twitter (*www.twitter.com*).

Information systems literacy goes beyond knowing the fundamentals of computer systems and equipment. Information systems literacy is the knowledge of how data and information are used by individuals, groups, and organizations. It includes knowledge of computer technology and the broader range of information systems. Most important, however, it encompasses *how* and *why* this technology is applied in business. Knowing about various types of hardware and software is an example of computer literacy. Knowing how to use hardware and software to increase profits, cut costs, improve productivity, and increase customer satisfaction is an example of information systems literacy. Information systems literacy will help you make a significant contribution on the job. It will also help you advance in your chosen career or field.

information systems literacy: Knowledge of how data and information are used by individuals, groups, and organizations.

Information literacy is the ability to recognize a need for additional information, and then to find, access, evaluate, and effectively use that information to deal with the issue or problem at hand. Because of the abundance of information systems, information literacy is also needed to deal with the problem of "data overload," too many diverse and sometimes conflicting sources of data. Here the challenge is to evaluate the source for authenticity, validity, reliability, and relevance of that data. An employee with good information literacy skills knows the organization's various information systems, databases, and other sources of information available and can access that information to incorporate it into effective decision making.

information literacy: The ability to recognize a need for additional information, and then to find, access, evaluate, and effectively use that information to deal with the issue or problem at hand.

Employees must be able to use computers effectively to accomplish business results. They are expected to identify opportunities to implement information systems to improve their business. They are also expected to lead IS projects in their areas of expertise. They must recognize when additional information is needed and where to get it. To meet these personal and organizational goals, you must acquire computer literacy, information systems literacy, and information literacy. See Figure 1.32.

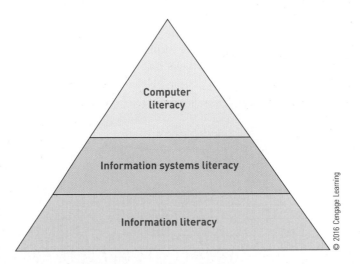

FIGURE 1.32

Three levels of literacy needed for success

To meet personal and organizational goals, you must acquire computer literacy, information systems literacy, and information literacy.

Information Systems in Business

Information systems are used in all functional areas of business organizations and most industries. The following are a few examples.

In finance and accounting, information systems forecast revenues and business activity, determine the best sources and uses of funds, manage cash and other financial resources, analyze investments, and perform audits to make sure that the organization is financially sound and that all financial reports and documents are accurate.

Organizations employ information systems to develop customer demand forecasts to help them plan production and manage inventory levels. J.D. Powers offers a global auto forecasting service to its client base of manufacturers and financial and government institutions around the world. This forecast is extremely valuable to those clients in making capacity planning, production, staffing, and inventory-related decisions.[54]

Sales and marketing professionals use information systems to develop new goods and services (product analysis), select the best location for production and distribution facilities (place or site analysis), determine the best advertising and sales approaches (promotion analysis), and set product prices to get the highest total revenues (price analysis).

Organizations invest heavily in information systems to improve customer service. Kia Motors America, Inc., uses a Web-based information system to aid repair technicians in servicing Kia automobiles properly the first time, which reduces warranty costs and increases customer satisfaction ratings significantly.[55]

Information systems help design products (computer-assisted design, or CAD), manufacture items (computer-assisted manufacturing, or CAM), and integrate machines or pieces of equipment (computer-integrated manufacturing, or CIM).

The agriculture industry is not usually thought of as high tech, but has used information systems to support precision farming for years. See Figure 1.33. Farmers attach a yield monitor and a global positioning unit to their combines

FIGURE 1.33

Information systems in agriculture

Farmers and others in the agriculture industry use information systems to support precision farming.

to indicate how much grain should be harvested in each field. This data is entered in the system that produces a color-coded map predicting the expected yield. From this, farmers can determine in which fields and where they should add lime or fertilizer, for example, to increase the yield.[56]

Human resource management uses information systems to screen applicants, administer performance tests to employees, monitor employee productivity, and generate required government reports.

In manufacturing, information systems process customer orders, develop production schedules, control inventory levels, and monitor product quality. Unilever sells over 400 food, soap, shampoo, and household care products to over 2 billion people worldwide. The firm uses an integrated supply management information system to enable local, regional, and global supply managers to collate and analyze information quickly and easily to assist them in making sourcing decisions.[57]

Retail companies are using the Web to take orders and provide customer service support. Retail companies also use information systems to help market products and services, manage inventory levels, control the supply chain, and forecast demand.

Global positioning systems are also used in the mining industry to identify and evaluate promising areas for mineral exploration, model mine construction, and display geochemical and hydrological data. These systems also help when applying for mining permits, assessing environmental impact, and designing closure and reclamation plans.[58]

Healthcare organizations use information systems to diagnose illnesses, plan medical treatment, track patient records, and bill patients. See Figure 1.34. Health maintenance organizations (HMOs) use Web technology to access patients' insurance eligibility and other information stored in databases to cut patient costs.

Professional services firms have information systems to improve the speed and quality of the services they provide to customers. Brodies LLP, one of Scotland's largest law firms, adopted an automated policy management system to ensure that the firm's employees perform their work according to corporate

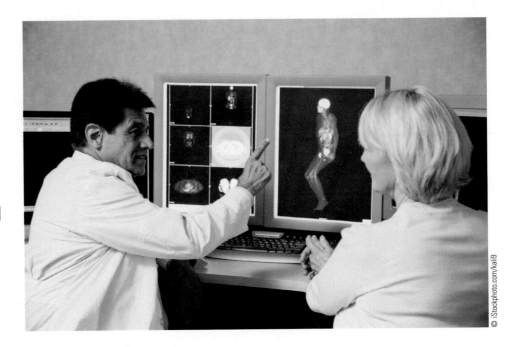

FIGURE 1.34

Information systems in health care

Healthcare organizations use information systems to diagnose illnesses, plan medical treatment, track patient records, and bill patients.

policy. The goal is to increase productivity, reduce operation costs, and ensure that employees follow all applicable laws and guidelines in completing their work.[59]

Banks use information systems to help make sound loans and good investments as well as to provide online services such as check payment and account transfers for account holders.

GLOBAL CHALLENGES IN INFORMATION SYSTEMS

What do Amazon, Coca-Cola, Facebook, Google, Hewlett Packard, IBM, Pepsi Cola, Procter & Gamble, and Unilever along with dozens of other large companies all have in common? They are looking at how and from where they are going to attract their next billion customers. Those billion new customers are not going to come from the Western or developed markets. They will come from emerging markets and will be much different from the first billion in terms of culture, education, income, language, and life style.[60]

In his book *The World Is Flat*, Thomas Friedman describes three eras of globalization, shown in Table 1.3.[61] (According to Friedman, we have progressed from the globalization of countries (Globalization 1.0) to the globalization of multinational corporations (Globalization 2.0) and individuals

TABLE **1-3** Eras of globalization

Era	Dates	Characterized by
Globalization 1.0	Late 1400–1880	Countries with the power to explore and influence the world
Globalization 2.0	1800–2000	Multinational corporations that have plants, warehouses, and offices around the world
Globalization 3.0	2000–today	Individuals from around the world who can compete and influence other people, corporations, and countries by using the Internet and powerful technology tools

(Globalization 3.0). Today, people in remote areas can use the Internet to compete with and contribute to other people, the largest corporations, and entire countries. These workers are empowered by high-speed Internet access, making the world flatter. In the Globalization 3.0 era, designing a new airplane or computer can be separated into smaller subtasks and then completed by a person or small group that can do the best job. These workers can be located in India, China, Russia, Europe, and other areas of the world. The subtasks can then be combined or reassembled into the complete design. This approach can be used to prepare tax returns, diagnose a patient's medical condition, provide computer support, and perform many other tasks.

Success in global markets is imperative today. Global opportunities, however, introduce numerous obstacles and issues, including challenges involving culture and language:

- **Cultural challenges:** Countries and regional areas have their own cultures and customs that can significantly affect individuals and organizations involved in global trade.
- **Language challenges:** Language differences can make it difficult to translate exact meanings from one language to another.
- **Time and distance challenges:** Time and distance issues can be difficult to overcome for individuals and organizations involved with global trade in remote locations. Large time differences make it difficult to talk to people on the other side of the world. With long distance, it can take days to get a product or part from one location to another.
- **Infrastructure challenges:** High-quality electricity and water might not be available in certain parts of the world. Telephone services, Internet connections, and skilled employees might be expensive or not readily available.
- **Currency challenges:** The value of various currencies can vary significantly over time, making international trade more difficult and complex.
- **Product and service challenges:** Traditional products that are physical or tangible, such as an automobile or a bicycle, can be difficult to deliver to the global market. However, electronic products (e-products) and electronic services (e-services) can be delivered to customers electronically over the phone, through networks, through the Internet, or via other electronic means. Software, music, books, manuals, and advice can all be delivered globally and over the Internet.
- **Technology transfer issues:** Most governments don't allow certain military-related equipment and systems to be sold to some countries. Even so, some believe that foreign companies are stealing intellectual property, trade secrets, and copyrighted materials and counterfeiting products and services.
- **State, regional, and national laws:** Each state, region, and country has a set of laws that must be obeyed by citizens and organizations operating in the country. These laws can deal with a variety of issues, including trade secrets, patents, copyrights, protection of personal or financial data, privacy, and much more. Laws restricting how data enters or exits a country are often called transborder data-flow laws. Keeping track of these laws and incorporating them into the procedures and computer systems of multinational and transnational organizations can be very difficult and time consuming, requiring expert legal advice.
- **Trade agreements:** Countries often enter into trade agreements with each other. The North American Free Trade Agreement (NAFTA) and the Central American Free Trade Agreement (CAFTA) are examples.

The European Union (EU) is another example of a group of countries with an international trade agreement. The EU is a collection of mostly European countries that have joined together for peace and prosperity. Additional trade agreements include the Australia–United States Free Trade Agreement (AUSFTA), signed into law in 2005, and the Korean-United States Free Trade Agreement (KORUS-FTA), signed into law in 2007. Free trade agreements have been established between Bolivia and Mexico, Canada and Costa Rica, Canada and Israel, Chile and Korea, Mexico and Japan, the United States and Jordan, Peru and China, and many others.[62]

VF is the world's largest apparel manufacturing company, with $11 billion in annual revenues generated from its over 30 brands, including Wrangler, Lee, North Face, Vans, Timberland, and Eagle Creek. These brands are sold in more than 150 countries through 47,000 retailers, including more than 1,100 retail stores owned and operated by VF itself. Many of its brands are sold directly to consumers over the Internet. It manufactures some 450 million items annually at more than 1,900 facilities, and employs some 57,000 employees working around the world.[63] Because continued global operations and expansion are critical to its future success, VF is working to overcome many global issues including the following challenges:

- **Cultural challenges:** China does not have a strong tradition of outdoor participation, so The North Face brand is trying to build one. Much of the brand's marketing budget for China is invested in events to encourage consumers to get outside and experience the spirit of the brand firsthand. One event was a contest to recruit people for an expedition to climb China's legendary Haba Mountain, a feat accomplished by only 500 people in history.[64]
- **Time and distance challenges:** VF is working to shorten the lead times required to get new products to market by bringing product designers and supply chain experts together to enable face-to-face collaboration in a shared spirit of experimentation and to build new communications tools that make it easier for everyone to work together.[65]
- **State, regional, and national laws:** Uzbekistan, one of the world's largest exporters of cotton, permits forced child labor. VF has pledged to ensure that forced child labor does not find its way into its products.[66]

Competing in such a challenging global environment defines the type of information systems initiatives that VF makes. For example, VF worked to develop new human capital management systems and processes so it could build a global talent pool of internal and external candidates to fill key positions, support business expansion, simplify the recruitment process, and improve the quality of hire.[67] It also implemented information systems to support sales development by determining which customers were shopping in which stores and use this data to make related decisions about product placement. VF has implemented information systems to analyze all its consumer data (such as consumer lifestyle information, demographics, consumer research, Web site registration information, sales rebates, and coupons) and its retail store information (including point-of-sale data and store trade areas) to improve overall profitability and its customer relationships. VF planners and category managers can identify ideal locations for new store locations and determine merchandise stocking levels in new stores.[68] Initiatives such as these are helping VF continue to expand globally and be successful.

Principle:

The value of information is directly linked to how it helps decision makers achieve the organization's goals.

Information systems are used in almost every imaginable career area. Regardless of your college major or chosen career, you will find that information systems are indispensable tools to help you achieve your career goals. Learning about information systems can help you get your first job, earn promotions, and advance your career.

Data consists of raw facts; information is data transformed into a meaningful form. The process of defining relationships among data requires knowledge. Knowledge is an awareness and understanding of a set of information and the way that information can support a specific task. Information has many different attributes. It can be accurate, complete, economical to produce, flexible, reliable, relevant, simple to understand, timely, verifiable, accessible, and secure. Quality information can vary widely in the value of each of these attributes depending on the situation and the kind of decision you are trying to make. The value of information is directly linked to how it helps people achieve their organizations' goals.

Principle:

Computers and information systems help make it possible for organizations to improve the way they conduct business.

A system is a set of elements that interact to accomplish a goal or set of objectives. The components of a system include inputs, processing mechanisms, and outputs. A system uses feedback to monitor and control its operation to make sure that it continues to meet its goals and objectives.

Principle:

Knowing the potential impact of information systems and having the ability to put this knowledge to work can result in a successful personal career and in organizations that reach their goals.

Information systems are sets of interrelated elements that collect (input), manipulate and store (process), and disseminate (output) data and information. Input is the activity of capturing and gathering new data, processing involves converting or transforming data into useful outputs, and output involves producing useful information. Feedback is the output that is used to make adjustments or changes to input or processing activities.

The components of a computer-based information system include hardware, software, databases, telecommunications, people, and procedures. The types of CBISs that organizations use can be classified into four basic groups: (1) e-commerce and m-commerce, (2) transaction processing and enterprise systems, (3) management information and decision support systems, and (4) specialized business information systems.

E-commerce involves any business transaction executed electronically between parties such as companies (business-to-business), companies and consumers (business-to-consumer), business and the public sector, and consumers and the public sector. The major volume of e-commerce and its fastest-growing segment is business-to-business transactions that make purchasing easier for big corporations. E-commerce also offers opportunities for small businesses to market and sell at a low cost worldwide, thus allowing them to enter the global market right from start-up. M-commerce involves anytime, anywhere computing that relies on wireless networks and systems.

The most fundamental system is the transaction processing system. A transaction is any business-related exchange. The TPS handles the large volume of business transactions that occur daily within an organization. An enterprise resource planning system is a set of integrated programs that can manage the vital business operations for an entire multisite, global organization. A management information system uses the information from a TPS to generate information useful for management decision making.

A decision support system is an organized collection of people, procedures, databases, and devices that help make problem-specific decisions. A DSS differs from an MIS in the support given to users, the emphasis on decisions, the development and approach, and the system components, speed, and output.

Specialized business information systems include knowledge management, artificial intelligence, expert systems, multimedia, and virtual reality systems. Knowledge management systems are organized collections of people, procedures, software, databases, and devices used to create, store, share, and use the organization's knowledge and experience. AI includes a wide range of systems in which the computer takes on the characteristics of human intelligence. Robotics is an area of artificial intelligence in which machines perform complex, dangerous, routine, or boring tasks, such as welding car frames or assembling computer systems and components. Vision systems allow robots and other devices to have "sight" and to store and process visual images. Natural language processing involves computers interpreting and acting on verbal or written commands in English, Spanish, or other human languages. Learning systems let computers "learn" from past mistakes or experiences, such as playing games or making business decisions, while neural networks is a branch of artificial intelligence that allows computers to recognize and act on patterns or trends. An expert system is designed to act as an expert consultant to a user who is seeking advice about a specific situation. Virtual reality is an artificial three-dimensional environment created by hardware and software and experienced through our senses and within which an individual can interact to affect what happens in the environment. Augmented reality, a newer form of virtual reality, has the potential to superimpose digital data over real photos or images. Multimedia is a natural extension of virtual reality. It can include photos and images, the manipulation of sound, and special 3D effects.

Principle:

System users, business managers, and information systems professionals must work together to build a successful information system.

Systems development involves creating or modifying existing business systems. The major steps of this process and their goals include investigation (gain a clear understanding of what the problem is), analysis (understand the current system and identify the needs of the end users and the organization), design (determine how the system must work to meet those needs), construction (convert the design into an operational information system), integration and testing (link together all the components of the system to demonstrate that the system meets the user and business requirements), implementation (install the system into a production environment in which it will operate), operation and maintenance (the ongoing running of the system and identifying and making necessary changes), and disposition (those activities at the end of the useful life of the system).

Principle:

Information systems must be applied thoughtfully and carefully so that society, businesses, and industries around the globe can reap their enormous benefits.

Information systems play a fundamental and ever-expanding role in society, business, and industry. But their use can also raise serious security, privacy, and ethical issues. Effective information systems can have a major impact on corporate strategy and organizational success. Businesses around the globe are enjoying better safety and service, greater efficiency and effectiveness, reduced expenses, and improved decision making and control because of information systems. Individuals who can help their businesses realize these benefits will be in demand well into the future.

Computer and information systems literacy are prerequisites for numerous job opportunities, not only for those in the IS field. Computer literacy is knowledge of computer systems, software, and equipment. Information systems literacy is knowledge of how data and information are used by individuals, groups, and organizations. Information literacy is the ability to recognize when there is a need for additional information, and then to be able to find, access, evaluate, and effectively use this information to deal with the issue or problem at hand.

Today, information systems are used in all the functional areas of business, including accounting, finance, sales, marketing, manufacturing, human resource management, and legal. Information systems are also used in every industry, such as agriculture, mining, retail, health care, airlines, investment firms, banks, mining companies, publishing companies, and professional services.

Changes in society as a result of increased international trade and cultural exchange, often called globalization, has always had a significant impact on organizations and their information systems. In his book *The World Is Flat*, Thomas Friedman describes three eras of globalization, spanning the globalization of countries to the globalization of multinational corporations and individuals. Organizations are pursuing their next billion customers and know that they must come from developing companies and that those consumers will be much different than their first billion. These global opportunities, however, introduce numerous obstacles and issues, including challenges involving culture and language.

KEY TERMS

artificial intelligence (AI)

computer literacy

computer-based information system (CBIS)

data

database

decision support system (DSS)

electronic business (e-business)

electronic commerce (e-commerce)

enterprise resource planning (ERP) system

expert system

extranet

feedback

forecasting

hardware

information

information literacy

information system (IS)

information systems literacy

input

Internet

intranet

knowledge

knowledge base
management information system (MIS)
mobile commerce (m-commerce)
network
output
procedures
process
processing

software
system
systems development
technology infrastructure
telecommunications
transaction
transaction processing system (TPS)
virtual reality

CHAPTER 1: SELF-ASSESSMENT TEST

The value of information is directly linked to how it helps decision makers achieve the organization's goals.

1. An information system is a set of interrelated components that collect, manipulate, and disseminate data and information and provide a(n) _____ mechanism to meet an objective.
2. Data, information, and knowledge are all essentially the same thing. True or False?
3. NASA is using a(n) _____ to capture and retain critical knowledge that cannot be lost as workers retire.
   a. expert system
   b. decision support system
   c. management information system
   d. knowledge management system

Computers and information systems help make it possible for organizations to improve the way they conduct business.

4. A recent study in the United Kingdom found that the average organization believes that _____ of its total data is inaccurate.
   a. less than 10 percent
   b. 17 percent
   c. almost 25 percent
   d. nearly one-third
5. Quality information can vary widely in the value of such attributes as accessibility, accuracy, completeness, and timeliness, depending on the situation and the kind of decision you are trying to make. True or False?
6. The _____ of information is directly linked to how it helps decision makers achieve their organization's goals.

Knowing the potential impact of information systems and having the ability to put this knowledge to work can result in a successful personal career and in organizations that reach their goals.

7. _____ means converting or transforming data into useful outputs.

8. The two types of software are _____.
   a. transaction processing and management information systems
   b. mobile and stationary
   c. systems batch processing and online
   d. operating and applications
9. Global laptop shipments are forecast to exceed tablet shipments in 2013. True or False?
10. What is an organized collection of people, procedures, software, databases, and devices used to create, store, share, and use the organization's experience and knowledge?
    a. TPS (transaction processing system)
    b. MIS (management information system)
    c. DSS (decision support system)
    d. KM (knowledge management)
11. _____ is an organized collection of facts and information, typically consisting of two or more files.
12. A(n) _____ is a network based on Web technologies that allows selected outsiders, such as business partners and customers, to access authorized resources of a company's intranet.
13. A set of integrated programs that manage the vital business operations for an entire multisite, global organization is called a(n) _____.

System users, business managers, and information systems professionals must work together to build a successful information system.

14. During the _____ step of the systems development process, it is determined how the system must work, what inputs are required, and what outputs must be produced to meet the defined business needs.
    a. investigation
    b. analysis
    c. design
    d. construction

Information systems must be applied thoughtfully and carefully so that society, businesses, and

industries around the globe can reap their enormous benefits.

15. _____ is the ability to recognize when there is a need for additional information, and then to be able to find, access, evaluate, and effectively use that information to deal with the issue or problem at hand.
   a. Knowledge management
   b. Computer literacy
   c. Information literacy
   d. Information system literacy

CHAPTER 1: SELF-ASSESSMENT TEST ANSWERS

1. Feedback
2. False
3. d
4. b
5. True
6. value
7. Processing
8. d
9. False
10. d
11. database
12. extranet
13. enterprise resource planning system
14. c
15. c

REVIEW QUESTIONS

1. What is an information system? What are its four basic components?
2. How is data different from information? Information from knowledge?
3. Identify and briefly define five attributes that describe the quality of data.
4. What is knowledge management? How might it be used?
5. What is the role of feedback in a system?
6. Identify the five basic components of any computer-based information system.
7. What is meant by an organization's technology infrastructure?
8. Distinguish between a decision support system and an expert system.
9. What is the difference between an intranet and an extranet?
10. What is m-commerce? Give two examples of the use of m-commerce.
11. What are the most common types of computer-based information systems used in business organizations today? Give an example of each.
12. What is the difference between virtual reality and augmented reality?
13. What are computer literacy and information systems literacy? Why are they important?
14. What are some of the benefits organizations seek to achieve through using information systems?
15. Identify the steps in the systems development process and state the goal of each.
16. Identify and briefly discuss several global challenges associated with information systems.

DISCUSSION QUESTIONS

1. Why is the study of information systems important to you? What do you hope to learn from this course that will make it worthwhile for you?
2. Describe how you might use information systems in a career area of interest to you.
3. What are the two basic types of software? Give several examples of software you use at school or home.
4. It is said that the amount of digital data is doubling every two years. Discuss some implications and issues associated with this rapid growth of data.
5. Define the terms "computer literacy," "information systems literacy," and "information literacy." Evaluate yourself in terms of these forms of literacy: Are you below average, average, or above average? Justify your evaluation.
6. Which of your school's information systems is the worst or most difficult for you to deal with? Describe an ideal system that would replace this one. Outline the steps that would be needed to implement this "ideal" system. What role might students play in this effort?
7. Discuss how information systems are linked to the business objectives of an organization.
8. For an industry of your choice, describe how a CBIS could be used to reduce costs or increase profits.

9. Use your imagination and creativity to describe how virtual reality might be used to help students learn in one of your most challenging courses.
10. If you could have an expert system assist you with decision making in some facet of your life, what would it be? Do you think it would be possible to develop such a system? Defend your answer.

PROBLEM-SOLVING EXERCISES

1. Prepare a data disk and a backup disk (using USB flash drives) for the problem-solving exercises and other computer-based assignments you will complete in this class. Create one folder for each chapter in the textbook (you should have 14 folders). As you work through the problem-solving exercises and complete other work using the computer, save your assignments for each chapter in the appropriate folder. Designate one disk as your working copy and the other as your backup.
2. Search through several business magazines (*Bloomberg, Businessweek, Computerworld, PC Week*, etc.) or use an Internet search engine to find recent articles that describe potential social or ethical issues related to the use of an information system. Use word-processing software to write a one-page report summarizing what you discovered.
3. Create a table that lists 10 or more possible career areas, annual salaries, and brief job descriptions, and rate how much you would like the career area on a scale from 1 (don't like) to 10 (like the most). Print the results. Sort the table according to annual salaries from high to low and print the resulting table. Sort the table from the most liked to least liked and print the results.
4. Use a graphics program to create a diagram showing a billing transaction processing system, similar to the payroll transaction processing figure shown in this chapter. Your diagram should show how a company collects sales data and sends out bills to customers. Share your findings with the class.

TEAM ACTIVITIES

1. Before you can do a team activity, you need a team. As a class member, you might create your own team, or your instructor might assign members to groups. After your group has been formed, meet and introduce yourselves to each other. Find out the first name, hometown, major, email address, and phone number of each member. Find out one interesting fact about each member of your team as well. Brainstorm a name for your team. Put the information on each team member into a database and print enough copies for each team member and your instructor.
2. With the other members of your group, use word-processing or group collaboration software to write a summary of the members of your team, the courses each team member has taken, and the expected graduation date of each team member. Send the report to your instructor via email.

WEB EXERCISES

1. Throughout this book, you will see how the Internet provides a vast amount of information to individuals and organizations and examine the important role the Web plays. Most large universities and organizations have an address on the Internet (a Web site or home page). The address of the Web site for this publisher is *www.cengage.com*. You can gain access to the Internet through a browser, such as Internet Explorer or Firefox. Using an Internet browser, go to the Web site for this publisher. What did you find? Try to obtain information on this book. You might be asked to develop a report or send an email message to your instructor about what you found.
2. Do research on the Web to find information on citizen journalism reporting. Find and read several examples of such reporting. Choose one interesting example and perform a critical analysis of the report. What role do you think citizen journalism will play in the future?
3. Do research on the Web to find at least three years of global sales data for tablet computers versus laptop and/or desktop computers. Use a graphics program to illustrate the sales figures. Write a brief summary of your findings.

CAREER EXERCISES

1. In the Career Exercises found at the end of every chapter, you will explore how material in the chapter can help you excel in your college major or chosen career. Identify 10 job characteristics that are important to you in selecting your career (e.g., involves travel to foreign countries, requires working in a project team).

2. Research two or three possible careers that interest you. Describe the job opportunities, job duties, and the possible starting salaries for each career area in a report.

CASE STUDIES

Case One

Campbell Uses Technology to Reach Out to the Younger Generation

Soup. Canned soup. It's been around for ages. What could be said about it that hasn't been said? What could be done to improve soup that hasn't already been done—probably when your grandparents were in school?

Soup companies still find room for improvement. Your grandparents may not have cared about using less salt, but you do. Other opportunities for improvement, however, may not involve the product itself but the business processes used to produce and distribute it. Information systems can do a great deal to improve business processes. The challenge a company faces today is to find those opportunities for improvement. These opportunities are not in the same places that senior managers looked for them a decade or two ago.

Joseph Spagnoletti, senior vice president and CIO of Campbell's Soup, is the person who must figure out how to improve business processes at Campbell's. His challenge is to find opportunities for improvement and take advantage of them. Spagnoletti needs to select the most effective software applications for managing basic business processes, such as maintaining the quality of products, fulfilling orders, and shipping.

"The goal is to get the best outcome, for the lowest cost at the fastest speed, with the least amount of risk," says Spagnoletti. To achieve this goal, Campbell's CIO turned to cloud services that allow companies to spend less on buying and maintaining hardware. In 2013, he cut the amount of money he was spending to maintain the company's back-office hardware and software by 80 percent. Back-office software consists of the applications, such as accounting and inventory management, that do not interface with customers. He invested these funds in consumers and innovation.

One major initiative is to take advantage of crowdsourcing. Crowdsourcing tools use contributions from a large group of people connected together through social media and Web and mobile technologies. For example, Spagnoletti contracted with Field Agent LLC, a company that posts assignments for approximately 240,000 consumers. These assignments include conducting price checks, snapping a photo of product display on a smartphone, answering polling questions, or whatever service a company would usually need field agents to perform. Spagnoletti hopes to use similar efforts to cut costs and improve Campbell's understanding of customers' needs.

Spagnoletti is also investing in fun crowdsourcing marketing initiatives. He has teamed with the marketing department to launch Hack the Kitchen, a contest that invites computer programmers to write code for a Web or mobile tool that helps consumers find good recipes online. The winner receives $25,000 and a $25,000 contract to program for Campbell. By appealing to the online public at large, Campbell hopes to provide innovative online services that boost its image.

Since assuming the role of Campbell's CEO in 2011, Denise Morrison has reversed declining sales and achieved a 9 percent sales growth in the fourth quarter of 2012. Morrison has introduced a new line of soup called Campbell's Go and new varieties of Campbell's Chunky soup. However, she has also charged Spagnoletti not only with maintaining the information systems necessary for basic business processes but also with developing the type of digital technologies that will appeal to the younger generation of consumers. Clearly, Campbell's sees information systems as vital to its future.

Discussion Questions

1. Spagnoletti received his undergraduate degree in computer science and spent his entire career in information systems before being appointed Campbell's CIO in August 2008. Given his current responsibilities, do you think that career path is still appropriate for someone who wants to be a CIO today?

2. How does Campbell's use crowdsourcing? Do you think these initiatives will help the company appeal to younger consumers? Why, or why not?

Critical Thinking Questions

1. Campbell's is a large company. How can cloud tools work for smaller organizations? Consider three types of organizations: a college with about 2,000 students, the police department of a city with a population of about 250,000, and a family-owned chain of five car dealerships in the same region.

2. Spagnoletti has shifted resources from back-office systems to marketing initiatives. Commenting on this choice, he says, "If your strategies are clear, and you understand the risks to your back office versus the opportunities, it's very easy to make those shifts and it's noticeable." What risks is Spagnoletti taking?

SOURCES: Campbell's Web site, "Executive Team: Joseph C. Spagnoletti," 2011, *www.campbellsoupcompany.com/bio_spagnoletti.asp*, accessed November 30, 2011; Boulton, Clint, "Campbell's CIO Uses IT To Soup Up Sales," CIO Journal, *The Wall Street Journal*, January 18, 2013, *http://blogs.wsj.com/cio/2013/01/18/campbells-cio-uses-it-to-soup-up-sales*, accessed July 22, 2013; Field Agent LLC Web site, *www.fieldagent.net*, accessed July 22, 2013.

Case Two

Sketchers USA: Using Loyalty Programs and Customer Data to Grow

Skechers USA, Inc., a billion-dollar company, describes itself as "an award-winning global leader in the lifestyle footwear industry, [and] designs, develops and markets lifestyle footwear that appeals to men, women, and children of all ages…. With more than 3,000 styles, Skechers meets the needs of male and female consumers across every age and demographic."

Any shoe company could say something similar. What separates one from another? Increasingly, it isn't the shoes. It's the *information*.

Information systems are woven into every part of the Skechers's business. Its recent investment in Oracle applications, including cloud computing (introduced in the "Telecommunications and Networks" section of this chapter) demonstrates the company's commitment to information systems. Mark Bravo, Skechers's senior vice president of finance, says, "As we manage growth, we are establishing a business structure that lowers costs and creates more value and flexibility across the business. The … cloud services help us to lighten our IT overhead and enable us to respond more quickly to market opportunities." Therefore, it was natural that Skechers would turn to information systems to help with customer retention.

In a fast-moving consumer product category like shoes, using information to understand, attract, and retain customers is even more important than having the latest technology. Many companies use loyalty programs to help retain customers. A pizza shop might give its customers a card that is punched every time they buy a pizza. When the card has 10 punches, the customer can order a free medium pizza with two toppings. Loyalty programs reduce the chances of a regular customer switching suppliers even if another shop sells pizza for less during a promotion or offers a different advantage.

After Skechers decided to offer a loyalty program, its challenge was this: How to design the program for greatest sales impact? The company had to balance ease of earning rewards, the value of the rewards, and other factors so it gave away as little as possible while retaining as many loyal customers as possible. In the pizza shop, a free pizza after buying five might cost too much revenue; a free pizza after 20 might put the rewards too far out in the future to be attractive. Ten is a good middle ground.

The loyalty program that Skechers designed, planned jointly by its marketing and information systems departments, is called Skechers Elite. Members earn free merchandise ($10 credit for every $150 spent), get free shipping, and enjoy special promotions. In addition, Gold members (who spend at least $750 on Skechers shoes in a calendar year) and Platinum members ($1,000) get higher merchandise credits, sneak peeks at future products, and earn other greater benefits.

Skechers couldn't operate Skechers Elite without information systems. The system that supports this loyalty program records information about members, their purchases, and the rewards they're entitled to, so members can track their participation online. In addition, the system provides Skechers's management with information about the purchase patterns of regular customers, such as shoe designs that appeal to them. The system also lets Skechers send targeted promotional materials to its best customers.

Skechers's CEO Robert Greenberg explains, "2012 was a remarkable year for Skechers. In 2013, the company opened 30 to 35 new retail stores. We grew our existing product divisions, broadened our offering to consumers with several new product lines, established an award-winning performance division, and further grew our heritage business. We have taken a more focused approach to growing our product offering, added features and technologies that consumers desire, and supported these efforts with effective marketing."

Discussion Questions

1. How did Skechers achieve success by looking at what other companies outside its industry were doing with technology?
2. What kind of information does the Skechers Elite program use? Aside from its direct benefit in increasing customer loyalty, what other benefits might the program have? How could Skechers use the information in its planning and sales activities?

Critical Thinking Questions

1. In the five years from 2005 to 2012, Skechers approximately doubled its revenue: from about $1 billion to $2.0 billion. In the next two years, revenue dropped 20 percent to $1.6 billion in 2012. How do you think these changes in revenue growth affected its spending on information systems?
2. Skechers CEO Robert Greenberg explains one reason for his company's success in 2012: "We have taken a more focused approach to growing our product offering, added features and technologies that consumers desire, and supported these efforts with effective marketing." Apart from the loyalty program, how else can Sketcher use information systems to support marketing?

SOURCES: Chu, Peter, "Skechers U.S.A. Has the Best Relative Performance in the Footwear Industry," Financial News Network Online, November 2, 2011, *www.fnno.com/story/fast-lane/331-skechers-usa-has-best-relative-performance-footwear-industry-skx-crox-shoo-icon-nke-fast-lane*, accessed November 6, 2011; Oracle, "Skechers Leverages Oracle Applications, Business Intelligence, and On Demand Offerings to Drive Long-Term Growth," News Release, June 6, 2011, *http://emeapressoffice.oracle.com/Press-Releases/Skechers-Leverages-Oracle-Applications-Business-Intelligence-and-On-Demand-Offerings-to-Drive-Long-Term-Growth-1e2d.aspx*, accessed November 6, 2011; Skechers corporate Web sites, *www.skechers.com* and *www.skx.com*, accessed July 23, 2013.

Questions for Web Case

See the Web site for this book to read about the Altitude Online case for this chapter. The following questions cover this Web case.

Altitude Online: Outgrowing Systems

Discussion Questions

1. Why do you think it's a problem for Altitude Online to use different information systems in its branch locations?
2. What information do you think Jon should collect from the branch offices to plan the new centralized information system?

Critical Thinking Questions

1. With Jon's education and experience, he could design and implement a new information system for Altitude Online himself. What would be the benefits and drawbacks of doing the job himself compared to contracting with an information systems contractor?
2. While Jon is visiting the branch offices, how might he prepare them for the inevitable upheaval caused by the upcoming overhaul to the information system?

NOTES

Sources for the opening vignette: "Building the Technologies for the Mine Sites of the Future," *Viewpoint*, 2008, Issue 4, *https://mining.cat.com/cda/files/2785510/7/Autonomy_Eng.pdf*, accessed July 26, 2013; Hall, Kerry, "Australia's Big Miners Add More Driverless Trucks," Mining.com, March 25, 2013, *www.mining.com/australias-big-miners-add-more-driverless-trucks-88704*, accessed July 26, 2013; Berman, Dennis K., "Daddy, 'What Was a Truck Driver?'" *Wall Street Journal*, July 23, 2013, *http://online.wsj.com/article/SB10001424127887324144304578624221804774116.html*, accessed July 25, 2013; Goodwin, Antuan, "Audi Ready to Test Autonomous Cars on Public Roads," CNET, January 8, 2013, *http://ces.cnet.com/8301-34438_1-57562827/audi-ready-to-test-autonomous-cars-on-public-roads*, accessed July 26, 2013; Cunningham, Wayne, "Volvo Sees Crash-Free Car by 2020," CNET, July 22, 2013, *http://reviews.cnet.com/8301-13746_7-57594979-48/volvo-sees-crash-free-car-by-2020*, accessed July 26, 2013.

1. "Kohl's Careers," *www.kohlscareers.com/corporate/informationsystems/about*, accessed July 1, 2013.
2. "What Is Kaboodle?" *www.kaboodle.com/zd/help/getStarted.html*, accessed July 2, 2013.
3. Thorne, Emma, "Study Reveals Risk Factors for Blood Clots in Pregnant and Post Natal Women," *Bio-Medicine*, April 2, 2013, *www.bio-medicine.org/biology-news-1/Study-reveals-risk-factors-for-blood-clots-in-pregnant-and-postnatal-women-29734-1*.
4. "Expedia CruiseShipCenters Increases Website Inquiries by 65 Percent with Lyris," February 19, 2013, *www.lyris.com/us-en/company/news/2013/expedia-cruiseshipcenters-increases-website-inquiries-by-65-percent-with-lyris-us-en*.
5. "One-Third of Businesses Say Poor Data Quality Leads to Loss of Potential New Customers," *Experian*, February 19, 2013, *http://press.experian.com/United-Kingdom/Press-Release/one-third-of-businesses-say-poor-data-quality-leads-to-the-loss-of-potential-new-customers.aspx*.
6. Neuman, Scott, "Southwest Resumes Flights after Computer Glitch," *NPR*, June 22, 2013, *www.npr.org/blogs/thetwo-way/2013/06/22/194551371/southwest-airlines-computer-outage-causes-delays-cancellations*.

7. Kassab, Chris Rahai, "New Maintenance Operating System Improves Plant Performance," May 21, 2013, *www.at.ford.com/news/cn/Pages/New%20Maintenance%20Operating%20System%20Improves%20Plant%20Performance.aspx*.
8. "Trading at Fidelity," *https://www.fidelity.com/trading/overview*, accessed July 5, 2013.
9. King, Ian and Bass, Dina, "Intel Pushes Haswell Chips at Computex Fighting PC Slump," *Bloomberg*, June 4, 2013, *www.bloomberg.com/news/2013-06-03/intel-pushes-haswell-chips-at-computex-fighting-pc-slump.html*.
10. Clark, Don, "Massive System in China Named World's Fastest Computer," *WSJ Blogs*, June 17, 2013, *http://blogs.wsj.com/digits/2013/06/17/massive-system-in-china-named-worlds-fastest-computer*.
11. Thibodeau, Patrick, "Different and Cheap, New $25 Raspberry Pi Is Selling," *Computerworld*, April 3, 2013, *www.computerworld.com/s/article/9238082/Different_and_cheap_new_25_Raspberry_Pi_is_selling*.
12. Poeter, Damon, "NPD: Tablets to Overtake Laptops in 2013," *PC Magazine*, January 8, 2013, *www.pcmag.com/article2/0,2817,2414022,00.asp*.
13. "Grudi Associates Reports That Powerful New Tablet Computers and Mobile Computing Are Replacing PCs in Businesses," *Streetline*, June 28, 2013, *www.streetinsider.com/Press+Releases/Grudi+Associates+Reports+That+Powerful+New+Tablet+Computers+and+Mobile+Computing+Are+Replacing+PCs+in+Businesses/8457945.html*.
14. Kaneshige, Tom, "How a Big Financial Firm Faced BYOD iPads," *CIO*, January 23, 2013, *www.cio.com/article/727339*.
15. "Number of Available Android Applications," AppBrain, *www.appbrain.com/stats/number-of-android-apps*, accessed July 6, 2013.
16. "Top 20 Best Selling Business & Office Software 2012–2013," *http://topbestprice.com/top-20-best-selling-business-office-software*, accessed July 6, 2013.
17. "Top 10 Small Business Software Products, 2013," W3M4B, *http://wsm4b.com/content/top-10-small-business-software-products-2012*, accessed July 6, 2013.

18. "Meet the Financial Accounting Requirements of Simple or Complex Organizations with Our Software," *www54 .sap.com/solution/lob/finance/software/financial-mana gerial-accounting/index.html*, accessed July 6, 2013.

19. "Carfax Database Surpasses Eleven Billion Records," Market Watch, *The Wall Street Journal*, February 10, 2013, *www.marketwatch.com/story/carfax-database -surpasses-eleven-billion-records-2013-02-10*.

20. Roe, Charles, "The Growth of Unstructured Data: What to Do with All Those Zettabytes?" *Dataversity*, March 15, 2012, *www.dataversity.net/the-growth-of-unstructured -data-what-are-we-going-to-do-with-all-those-zettabytes*.

21. McNamara, Paul, "How Big Is a Zettabyte?" *Tech World*, May 11, 2010, *http://features.techworld.com/storage /3222999/how-big-is-a-zettabyte*.

22. "ESA Telecommunications and Integrated Applications," *http://telecom.esa.int/telecom/www/object/index.cfm? fobjectid=32069*, accessed July 7, 2013.

23. Goldstein, Phil, "Samsung's New '5G' Tech 'Several Hundred Times Faster' Than LTE Advanced," Fierce Wireless, May 13, 2013, *www.fiercewireless.com/story /samsungs-new-5g-tech-several-hundred-times-faster-lte -advanced/2013-05-13*.

24. Ting, Alice, "How Digitization Changed the World," *IDG Connect*, February 27, 2013, *www.idgconnect.com/blog -abstract/754/alice-ting-asia-how-digitization-changed -world*.

25. Becker, Dr. Albercht, et al, "Internet of Things," Atos White Paper, 2013.

26. Reynolds, George W., *Ethics in Information Technology*, 5th edition, Boston: Cengage Learning, 2014.

27. "AWS Case Study: Netflix," *http://aws.amazon.com /solutions/case-studies/netflix/?sc_ichannel=HA&sc_ ipage=homepage&sc_iplace=text_link&sc_icampaigntype= customer_story&sc_icampaign=ha_customer_success_net flix&sc_icountry=US*, accessed July 7, 2013.

28. Knoblich, Trevor, "Can Citizen Reporting Move Beyond Crises Reporting?" PBS, May 13, 2013, *www.pbs.org /idealab/2013/05/can-citizen-journalism-move-beyond -crisis-reporting127*.

29. Wilson, Matt, "The Top 10 Intranets of 2013," *Healthcare Information News*, February 1, 2013, *www.healthcare communication.com/Main/Articles/The_top_10_ intranets_of_2013_10286.aspx#*.

30. Hills, Melanie, "Intranets and Extranets Offer Some Competitive Advantages," *Dallas Business Journal*, April 19, 1998, *www.bizjournals.com/dallas/stories /1998/04/20/smallb4.html?page=all*.

31. Collins, Jim, *Good to Great: Why Some Companies Make the Leap and Others Don't*, New York: Harper Business, 2001.

32. Carroll, Ron, "People Are the Most Important System Component," *The Systems Thinker Blog*, *www.boxtheory gold.com/blog/bid/12164/People-Are-the-Most-Impor tant-System-Component*, accessed July 25, 2013.

33. Whitepaper from COMPOSE, "5 Reasons Every Company Needs Good Standard Operating Procedures," *Virtual Strategy Magazine*, June 27, 2013, *www.virtual -strategy.com/2013/06/27/5-reasons-every-company -needs-good-standard-operating-procedures-newest -whitepaper-compro*.

34. "IRS Implements Changes to ITIN Application," May 1, 2013, *www.irs.gov/uac/IRS-Implements-Changes-to -ITIN-Application-Requirement*.

35. "Internet Retailer 2013 eCommerce Success Stories and Trends," *Commerce Brain*, June 15, 2013, *http://commerce brain.com/2013/06/15/internet-retailer-2013-ecommerce -success-stories-and-trends/#!prettyPhoto*.

36. Rojas, Eileen, "These Retailers' Mobile Commerce Sites Are Shining," *The Motley Fool*, July 7, 2013, *http://beta .fool.com/er529/2013/07/07/these-retailers-are-getting -mobile-commerce-right/39393*.

37. Ibid.

38. "Air21: Achieving Operational Excellence with the SAP ERP," SAP ERP Customer References, *http://download .sap.com/canada*.

39. "Scottish Police Authority Selects Accenture to Implement National Information Management System," July 1, 2013, *http://newsroom.accenture.com/news/scottish -police-authority-chooses-accenture-to-implement -national-information-management-system.htm*.

40. Henschen, Doug, "Big Data Analysis Drives Revolution in Travel," *Information Week*, July 3, 2013, *www .informationweek.com/big-data/news/big-data-analytics /big-data-analysis-drives-revolution-in-travel /240157769*.

41. "APT Test and Learn Restaurants," *www.predictive technologies.com/industries/restaurants.aspx?gclid= COPNrf–sbgCFcOh4AodRwUAZQ*, accessed July 15, 2013.

42. Haque, E., "Gems of KM Success Stories—Story Telling," April 11, 2013, *www.slideshare.net/ehaque2011 /gems-of-km-success-stories*.

43. "Ford Using Robots for Tougher Testing," *Robotics Trends*, June 18, 2013, *www.roboticstrends.com /industry_manufacturing/article/ford_using_robots_ for_tough_testing*.

44. Carroll, James, "Robot Snakes Inspect Nuclear Power Plant," *Vision Systems Design*, July 2013, *www.vision -systems.com/articles/2013/07/robot-snakes-inspect -nuclear-power-plant.html*.

45. Collins, Michael, "Natural Language Processing," Columbia University, *https://www.coursera.org/course /nlangp*, accessed July 13, 2013.

46. "IBM Watson Hard at Work: New Breakthroughs Transform Quality Care for Patients," IBM, February 8, 2013, *www-03.ibm.com/press/us/en/pressrelease/40335 .wss*.

47. Henschen, Doug, "To Avoid Nasty Surprises, Higher Ed Turns to Prediction," *InformationWeek*, January 28, 2013, *www.informationweek.com/education/data-man agement/to-avoid-nasty-surprises-higher-ed-turns /240146949?queryText=neural network*.

48. "Airline Scheduling Case Study, *https://theiqx.com/avia tion/JAL_Scheduling_ES_Case_Study.php*, accessed July 13, 2013.

49. Knowles, Victoria, "Virtual Reality to Improve Freight Design," *Freight International News*, July 6, 2013, *www .freight-int.com/news/virtual-reality-to-improve-freight -design.html*.

50. Wikitude, *www.wikitude.com*, accessed July 13, 2013.

51. "Gartner Executive Program Survey of More Than 2,000 CIOs Shows Digital Technologies Are Top Priorities in

2013," *Gartner Newsroom*, January 16, 2013, *www.gart ner.com/newsroom/id/2304615*.

52. "2013 Information Security Breaches Survey," Department for Business, Innovation & Skills," *https://www.gov.uk /government/uploads/system/uploads/attachment_data /file/191671/bis-13-p184es-2013-information-security -breaches-survey-executive-summary.pdf*, accessed July 14, 2013.

53. Greenwald, Glenn, "NSA Collecting Phone Records of Millions of Verizon Customers Daily," *The Guardian*, June 5, 2013, *www.guardian.co.uk/world/2013/jun/06 /nsa-phone-records-verizon-court-order*.

54. Global Automotive Forecasting Services, J.D. Powers, *http://businesscenter.jdpower.com/?f=/jdpacontent/corp comm/Services/content/forecasting_services.htm*, accessed July 16, 2013.

55. "Kia Motors America Launches 'Kia Service Information System' on the Backbone of Aqueduct Inc.'s 'Partner Relationship Management Solutions,'" *PRNewswire*, April 16, 2013, *www.prnewswire.com/news-releases /kia-motors-america-launches-kia-service-information -system-on-the-backbone-of-aqueduct-incs-partner-rela tionship-management-solutions-70867442.html*.

56. "Farmer Uses Monitor, GPS in the Field," Plandrague, *http://plandrague.com/farmer.html*, accessed July 16, 2013.

57. "About Us, Supply Management," Unilever, *http://www .unilever.com/aboutus/introductiontounilever*, accessed July 16, 2013.

58. Phifer, Maurie, "GIS in Mining," *TechnoMine*, February 2012, *http://technology.infomine.com/reviews/GIS/wel come.asp?view=full*.

59. "Top Legal Firm Adopts Policy Management Software to Improve Information Security," *PRWEB UK*, May 14, 2013, *www.prweb.com/releases/2013/5 /prweb10722370.htm*.

60. Veremis, Marco, "The Next Billion Customers: Emerging Markets Need Services from Brands and Carriers," *Media Post*, May 30, 2013, *www.mediapost.com/publi cations/article/201341/the-next-billion-customers -emerging-markets-need.html#axzz2ZKsqfpxA*.

61. Thomas Friedman, *The World Is Flat*, New York: Farrar, Straus and Giroux, 2005, p. 488.

62. Foreign Trade Information Web site, *www.sice.oas.org*, accessed July 17, 2013.

63. "About VF," *www.vfc.com/about*, accessed July 16, 2013.

64. Ibid.

65. Ibid.

66. Ibid.

67. "VF Unifies Global Talent Management for Strategic Business Results," *www.knowledgeinfusion.com/assets /documents/uploads/KI_VF_CaseStudy.pdf*, accessed July 17, 2013.

68. "VF Corporation Increases Profitability and Stays Ahead of the Competition with Customer Analytics," *www.alteryx .com/resources/vf-corporation*, accessed July 17, 2013.

2 Information Systems in Organizations

Principles	Learning Objectives
• Information systems must be implemented in such a manner that they are accepted and work well within the context of an organization and support its fundamental business goals and strategies.	• Define the term "value chain" and describe the role that information systems play in an organization's supply chain. • Identify and briefly describe four change models that can be used to increase the likelihood of successfully introducing a new information system into an organization.
• Because information systems are so important, businesses need to be sure that improvements or completely new systems help lower costs, increase profits, improve service, or achieve a competitive advantage.	• Define the term "competitive advantage" and identify the factors that lead firms to seek competitive advantage. • Discuss strategic planning for competitive advantage. • Describe three methods for assessing the financial attractiveness of an information system project.
• The information system worker functions at the intersection of business and technology and designs, builds, and implements solutions that allow organizations to effectively leverage information systems.	• Define the types of roles, functions, and careers available in the field of information systems.

At 90 and Counting, Willson Sees Continuous Innovation as Key to Success

© Wilson International, www.willsonintl.com/logistics.aspx

In 1918, William F. Willson opened the first office of Willson International at a ferry landing in Fort Eire in Ontario, Canada, to help broker the import and export of goods coming from Buffalo, New York. Since that year, Willson International has dedicated itself to continuous improvement, constantly seeking ways to improve business processes and adding value to products and services.

"When people talk about length of service—you've been around for about a hundred years, what people are afraid of is that you're not innovating, you're not up-to-date, you're not paying attention to what's going on, and you're slow to react," explains CEO Peter Willson.

The corporation has relied heavily on information technology to put this worry to rest. Willson has kept a careful eye on technology, incorporating personal computers when they first became available in the 1980s. Willson expanded and began offering international freight forwarding services. In 1990, Tim Berners-Lee invented the World Wide Web and Willson unveiled its first electronic processing system of entries and transmissions to customs. In 2005, Willson launched its first customer portal, which today allows customers to upload their shipment information for transmission to the U.S. Customs and Border Protection or the Canadian Border Services Agency.

Then in 2008, Willson acquired a logistics company to add trucking, warehousing, and distribution services. However, with this growth came the need to innovate and reengineer business processes.

"Customs requires all information about a shipment two hours before the truck crosses, but sometimes we may only receive the information from our customer two hours and five minutes before the crossing. That means we have five minutes to process the information and get it to customs," explains Arik Kalinisky, vice president of information technology.

But many customers relying on Willson's new services still used faxes. Willson employed a small army to manually key data from faxes into the database. One paper copy of this shipment paperwork had to be sent to the customer and one had to be stored off-site.

"Each of our 12 branch locations had three or four fax machines spitting out paper around the clock," Kalinisky remembers.

Willson deployed Microsoft Office SharePoint Server, a Web application platform for intranet content management. Willson used the platform to convert incoming faxes to electronic files, improving efficiency by 25 percent. The new system allowed Willson to reduce costs and errors by automating the process and eliminating the need to store millions of paper documents off-site.

The company then developed an intranet solution to connect the information systems from every department. Import analysts, event handlers, and employees from other departments can now collaborate more easily using Willson's online systems. Willson also released an eBilling solution that generates invoices and email confirmations automatically.

Through these ongoing and continuous improvement efforts, Willson has been able to attain its ultimate goal—to improve customer service and to prove that a 90-plus-year-old company can still be innovative.

As you read this chapter, consider the following?

- How has Willson used information systems to achieve continuous improvement?
- What challenges have forced Willson to reengineer its business processes?
- How was Willson constricted by its customers' use of paper-based communication?

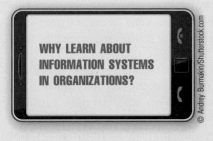

WHY LEARN ABOUT INFORMATION SYSTEMS IN ORGANIZATIONS?

Organizations of all types use information systems to cut costs and increase profits. After graduating, a management major might be hired by a shipping company to help design a computerized system to improve employee productivity. A marketing major might work for a national retailer using a network to analyze customer needs in different areas of the country. An accounting major might work for an accounting or a consulting firm using an information system to audit a client company's financial records. A real estate major might use the Internet and work in a loose organizational structure with clients, builders, and a legal team whose members are located around the world. A biochemist might conduct research for a drug company and use a computer to evaluate the potential of a new cancer treatment. An entrepreneur might use information systems to advertise and sell products and bill customers.

Although your career might be different from those of your classmates, you will almost certainly work with computers and information systems to help you and your company or organization become more efficient, effective, productive, and competitive in its industry. In this chapter, you will see how information systems can help organizations produce higher-quality products and increase their return on investment. We begin by investigating organizations and information systems.

Information systems have changed the way organizations work in recent years. While information systems were once used primarily to automate manual processes, they have transformed the nature of work and the shape of organizations themselves. In this chapter and throughout the book, you will explore the benefits and issues associated with the use of information systems in today's organizations around the globe.

ORGANIZATIONS AND INFORMATION SYSTEMS

organization: A group of people that is structured and managed to meet its mission or set of group goals.

An **organization** is a group of people that is structured and managed to meet its mission or set of group goals. Structured means that there are defined relationships between members of the organization and their various activities, and that processes are defined that assign roles, responsibilities, and authority to complete the various activities. In many cases, the processes are automated using well-defined information systems. Organizations are considered to be open systems, meaning that they affect and are affected by their surrounding environment. See Figure 2.1.

Providing value to a stakeholder—customer, supplier, partner, shareholder, or employee—is the primary goal of any organization. The value chain, first described by Michael Porter in a 1985 *Harvard Business Review* article titled "How Information Gives You Competitive Advantage," reveals how organizations can add value to their products and services. The **value chain** is a series (chain) of activities that an organization performs to transform inputs into outputs in such a way that the value of the input is increased. An organization may have many value chains, and different organizations in different industries will have different value chains. As an example of a simple value chain, the gift wrapping department of an upscale retail store takes packages from customers, covers them with appropriate, decorative wrapping paper, and gives the package back to the customer, thus increasing the customer's perceived value of the gift.

value chain: A series (chain) of activities that an organization performs to transform inputs into outputs in such a way that the value of the input is increased.

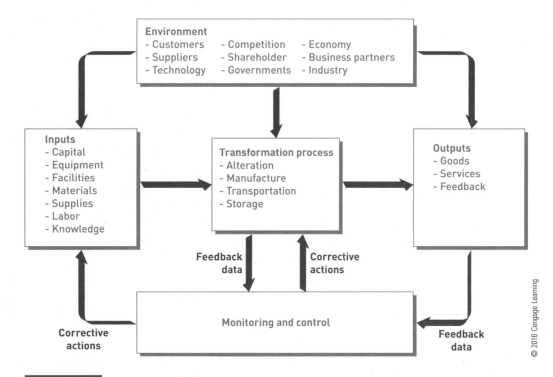

FIGURE **2.1**

General model of an organization

Information systems support and work within the automated portions of an organizational process.

In a manufacturing organization, the supply chain is a key value chain whose primary activities include inbound logistics, operations, outbound logistics, marketing and sales, and service. See Figure 2.2. These primary activities are directly concerned with the creation and/or delivery of the product or service. There are also four main areas of support activities, including technology infrastructure, human resource management, accounting and finance, and procurement. (Technology infrastructure includes not only research and development but information systems hardware, software, and networks.)

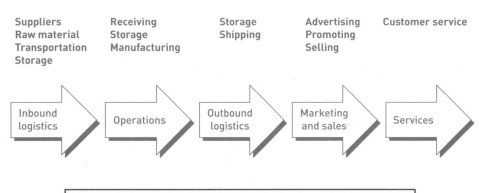

FIGURE **2.2**

Supply chain

The primary and support activities of the manufacturing supply chain are concerned with creating or delivering a product or service.

The concept of value chain is just as important to companies that don't manufacture products, such as tax preparers, restaurants, book publishers, legal firms, and other service providers. By adding a significant amount of value to their products and services, companies ensure their success. See Figure 2.3.

FIGURE **2.3**

Value chain

In a value chain, a company that does not manufacture products, such as a restaurant, adds value to the products and services it provides.

supply chain management (SCM): The management of all the activities required to get the right product into the right consumer's hands in the right quantity at the right time and at the right cost, from acquisition of raw materials through customer delivery.

Supply chain management (SCM) encompasses all the activities required to get the right product into the right consumer's hands in the right quantity at the right time and at the right cost, from acquisition of raw materials through customer delivery. The organizations that compose the supply chain are "linked" together through both physical flows and information flows. Physical flows involve the transformation, movement, and storage of supplies and raw materials. Information flows allow participants in the supply chain to communicate their plans, coordinate their work, and to manage the efficient flow of goods and material up and down the supply chain. See Figure 2.4.

FIGURE **2.4**

Ford Motor Company assembly line

Ford Motor Company's use of information systems is a critical support activity of its supply chain. The company gives suppliers access to its inventory system so that the suppliers can monitor the database and automatically send another shipment of parts and/or raw materials when stocks are low, such as for engine parts, eliminating the need for purchase orders. This procedure speeds delivery and assembly time and lowers Ford's inventory-carrying costs.

Organizations are constantly fine-tuning and adjusting their supply chain. For example, many companies are increasing their use of free shipping to customers in hopes of increasing sales and profits. Amazon, the popular online shopping company, is experimenting with AmazonFresh, a Web site that offers fast, free delivery of groceries and other products in the Los Angeles and Seattle area. Other organizations are outsourcing many of their outbound distribution activities, including the storage and shipping of finished products to customers and the return of items from customers. Amazon, DHL, FedEx, Shipwire, UPS, Webgistics, and other companies are highly skilled and efficient at performing these functions.

What role do information systems play in supply chain management activities and other organizational activities? A traditional view of information systems holds that organizations use them to control and monitor processes and ensure effectiveness and efficiency. In this view, information systems are external to the supply chain management process and serve to monitor or control it.

A more contemporary view, however, holds that information systems are often so intimately involved that they are *part of* the process itself. From this perspective, the information system plays an integral role in the process, whether providing input, aiding product transformation, or producing output. Zara and Coles are two examples of organizations that have incorporated information systems into the supply chain and made them an integral part of this process.

Zara is a Spanish clothing and accessories retailer with headquarters in Arteixo, Spain. Consumer clothing needs change overnight, which creates a highly competitive environment where companies compete not only on price but on their ability to deliver products that are new and stimulating to their customers. To meet this challenge, Zara has developed an extremely responsive supply chain that enables it to go from design stage to sales floor in a maximum of three weeks compared to a six-month industry average. It can then deliver these new products twice a week to some 1,600 stores around the world. Mobile computers and point-of-sales systems are used to capture and review data from stores on an hourly basis to spot new trends as early as possible. This data includes sales and inventory data and anecdotal information gleaned by sales assistants as they chat with customers and as the sales assistants gather unsold items that customers tried on, but left in fitting rooms. All this data is sent to headquarters where it is carefully analyzed by design teams to decide what new designs will be made, prototyped, and produced in small quantities to see what sells. In addition, inventory optimization models help the firm determine the quantities and sizes of existing items that should be delivered to each store. Zara's outstanding supply chain (including information systems as an integral component) has led to improved customer satisfaction, decreased risks of overstocking the wrong items, reduced total costs, and increased sales.[1]

Coles is the second largest supermarket chain in Australia. It employs advanced analytics to improve consumer demand forecasting systems. It uses sophisticated customer loyalty analysis tools to deepen its understanding of customer buying patterns to plan effective marketing programs. Coles has also taken strong measures to improve online data exchange and collaboration with its more than 3,000 suppliers. All these actions have gone a long way toward reducing the number 1 complaint from Coles' customers—item stock-outs. They have also paved the way for improved inventory management and better supplier relationships.[2]

Organizational Structures

organizational structure: Organizational subunits and the way they relate to the overall organization.

Organizational structure refers to organizational subunits and the way they relate to the overall organization. An organization's structure depends on its goals and its approach to management. Organization structure can affect how a company views and uses information systems. The commonly found types of organizational structures include traditional, project, team, and virtual.

Traditional Organizational Structure

A **traditional hierarchical organizational structure**, also called a **functional structure**, is like a managerial pyramid where the hierarchy of decision making and authority flows from the strategic management at the top down to operational management and nonmanagement employees. The military is the classic example of a traditional hierarchical organization structure. The basic functional structure looks like a pyramid, with each level in the hierarchy in charge of the levels below and reports to the level above. See Figure 2.5. Compared to lower levels, the strategic level, including the president of the company and vice presidents, has a higher degree of decision authority, more impact on corporate goals, and more unique problems to solve.

Traditional hierarchical organizational structure (functional structure): An organizational structure in which the hierarchy of decision making and authority flows from the strategic management at the top down to operational management and nonmanagement employees.

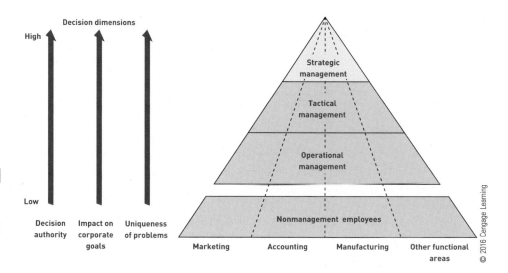

FIGURE 2.5

Levels of management

A simplified model of the organization, showing the managerial pyramid from top-level managers to nonmanagement employees.

The major departments are usually divided according to function and can include accounting, information systems, marketing, production, and human resources. The positions or departments that are directly associated with making, packing, or shipping goods are called line positions. A production supervisor who reports to a vice president of production is an example of a line position. Other positions might not be directly involved with the make, pack, or ship activities, but instead assist these activities. These positions are called staff positions, such as a legal counsel reporting to the president. See Figure 2.6.

In a functional organization, the emphasis is on top-down reporting relationships, with formal reporting relationships clearly defined, where each employee reports to one manager. A weakness of such an organization is that decision making tends to be more autocratic, with little employee involvement. The functional organization also creates vertical and horizontal divisions in the organization that stifles participative management and limits interaction among functions and departments.

In July 2013, following five straight quarters of decline in worldwide PC shipments, Microsoft reacted to this significant market shift. The software giant made a major change by shifting from its organization structure based on eight major product divisions to a four-function structure based on how its products work. See Table 2.1. The goal was to accelerate the pace of innovation at the software giant by dramatically shortening the time required for product releases, customer interactions, and competitive responses.[3] According to CEO Steve Ballmer, the new structure, dubbed "One Microsoft" will focus the entire company on a single strategy, improve Microsoft's capability

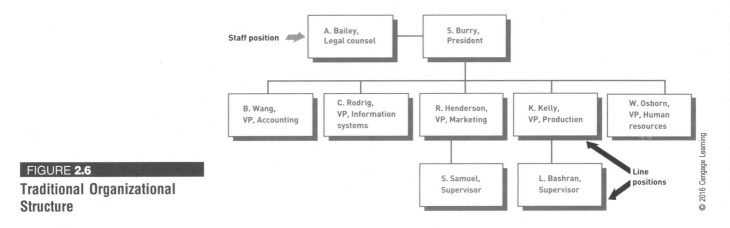

FIGURE 2.6

Traditional Organizational Structure

© 2016 Cengage Learning

TABLE **2.1** Microsoft organizational units before and after reorganization

New Functional Organization Units	Responsibility	Old Divisional Organization Units	Responsibility
Operating systems engineering	All operating systems	Interactive entertainment business	Gaming, music, and video including Xbox, Kinect, PC, and mobile entertainment
Devices and studios engineering	All hardware development	Business solutions	Microsoft Dynamics products and services and Medical Health Solutions
Applications and services engineering	All applications and services used for productivity, communications, and search	Office division	Productivity, collaboration, and entertainment products plus services such as Office, Exchange, SharePoint, Visio
Cloud and enterprise engineering	Development of data centers, database, and technologies for enterprise information systems and development tools	Online services	Search, portal, and personal communications services such as Bing and MSN portals
		Services and tools	Microsoft infrastructure software, developer tools, and cloud platform, including Windows Server, SQL Server, Visual Studio
		Skype	Communications products Skype and Lynch
		Windows and Windows Live	All Windows business, including Windows, Windows Live, and Internet Explorer

Source: "Our Commitment to Our Customers," Company Information, April 18, 2013, *www.microsoft.com/about/companyinformation/ourbusinesses/en/us /business.aspx.*

© 2016 Cengage Learning

in all disciplines and engineering/technology areas and enable employees to work together with more collaboration and agility around common goals.[4]

Today, the trend is to reduce the number of management levels, or layers, in the traditional organizational structure. At the same time, this increases the number of people directly reporting to each manager at every level in the hierarchy. This type of structure, often called a **flat organizational structure**, empowers employees at lower levels to make decisions and solve problems without needing permission from midlevel managers. In theory, by pushing decision making down in the hierarchy, organizations can make decisions quicker to be more responsive to customer needs and changes in the market. See Figure 2.7.

flat organizational structure: An organizational structure with a reduced number of management layers.

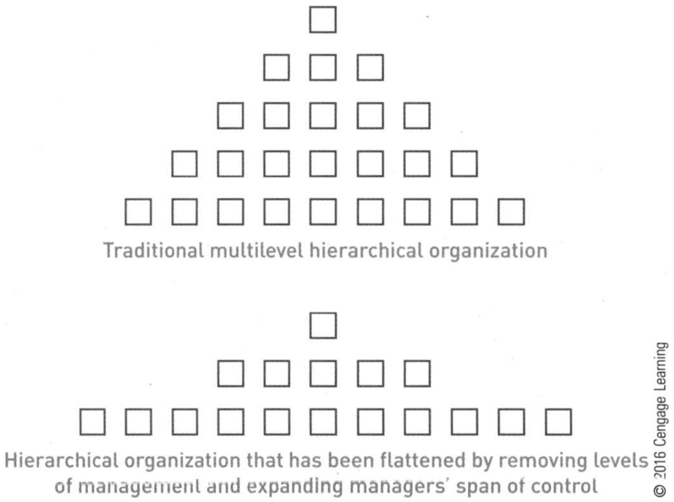

Traditional multilevel hierarchical organization

FIGURE 2.7

Flat organizational structure

A flat organizational structure empowers employees at lower levels to make decisions and solve problems without needing permission from midlevel managers.

Hierarchical organization that has been flattened by removing levels of management and expanding managers' span of control

© 2016 Cengage Learning

empowerment: Giving employees and their managers more responsibility and authority to make decisions, take action, and have more control over their jobs.

Empowerment gives employees and their managers more responsibility and authority to make decisions, take action, and have more control over their jobs. For example, an empowered sales clerk could respond to certain customer requests or problems without needing permission from a supervisor.

Menlo Innovations is small software development firm with about 50 employees organized as a flat organization. The organization structure consists of two layers: two cofounders and a CEO on one layer and everybody else on another layer. Creating a budget, hiring and firing employees, and deciding how best to serve the company's clients are team efforts. Says Rich Sheridan, cofounder and CEO, "If you look at a baseball team in the field, no one would say, hey, who does the pitcher report to, who does the catcher report to? People who really understand baseball would say, well, they have a role to play but their real purpose is to win the game. To be on the field with each other and trust each other to know how to play."[5]

Matrix Organization Structure

matrix organization structure: An organization structure in which an individual has two reporting superiors (managers)—one functional and one operational.

In a **matrix organization structure**, an individual has two reporting superiors (managers)—one functional and one operational. See Figure 2.8. Matrix management is commonly used in multinational organizations that operate in various regions of the world. For example, a financial analyst working in the Tokyo office reports functionally to the vice president of finance and accounting at headquarters in London, but reports operationally to the Asia/Pacific regional manager who works in Hong Kong.

The functional manager oversees how the work is done and distributes works among his or her subordinates. The operational manager decides what is to be done, schedules the work, and coordinates the work of the various subordinates. Working in a matrix organization can result in confusion and conflict because individuals receive (sometimes conflicting) direction from

Functions

Regions	Finance and accounting	Sales	Information systems	Human resources
Asia/Pacific				
Europe/Middle East				
Latin America				
North America				

© 2016 Cengage Learning

FIGURE 2.8

Matrix organization chart

Matrix management is commonly used in multinational organizations that operate in various regions of the world.

two managers. Since the functional manager is responsible for the individual's career (salary, promotion, next assignment), it is the functional manager who usually wins in conflict situations. On the other hand, a matrix form of organization enables the functional managers to focus on hiring, training, developing, and managing in their field of specialty, while operational managers can focus on achieving the goals of their particular area of operation. Employees in a matrix organization have constant contact with members of other functional areas via their participation in operational teams. This provides employees with an opportunity to develop a broader set of skills than they would working in a traditional hierarchical structure.

Project Organizational Structure

project organizational structure: A structure focused on major products or services, with program managers responsible for directing one or more projects.

A **project organizational structure** is focused on major products or services, with program managers responsible for directing one or more projects. Each project is staffed with a project manager who leads a group of people to accomplish the goals of the project. The project team members are carefully selected so that they have the necessary engineering, procurement, human resources, information systems, and whatever other skills are needed to complete the project successfully. See Figure 2.9. Many project teams are temporary so that when the project is complete, the members go on to new teams formed for another project. This form of organization structure is effective for project-driven organizations such as construction companies and companies that work on government contracts.

FIGURE 2.9

Project organizational structure

This form of organization structure is effective for project-driven organizations such as construction companies.

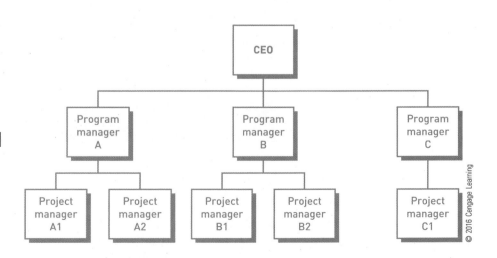

© 2016 Cengage Learning

Virtual Teams and Collaborative Work

virtual team: A group of individuals whose members are distributed geographically, but who work as a coherent unit through the use of information systems technology.

A **virtual team** is a group of individuals whose members are distributed geographically, but who collaborate and complete work through the use of information systems technology. The virtual team may be composed of individuals all from a single organization or may include individuals from multiple organizations (a virtual organization). The strength of a virtual team is that it enlists the best available people to solve important organizational problems. See Figure 2.10.

 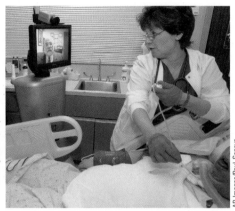

AP Images/Paul Sancya

AP Images/Paul Sancya

FIGURE **2.10**

Virtual teams

Virtual teams let people consult with experts no matter their physical location; they are especially useful in the healthcare industry.

It is difficult for members of a virtual organization to meet at a time that is convenient for all due to the time zone differences in their various geographic locations. Thus, most members of a virtual team seldom meet face to face. However, quick communication exchanges among members are a key to project success.[6] Thus, virtual team members must continually monitor their email, instant messages, and team Web sites and be prepared to participate in an audio or video teleconference on short notice. See Figure 2.11. They must be prepared to do work anywhere, anytime. As a result, members of a virtual team may feel that their work day never ends.

© ACE STOCK LIMITED/Alamy

FIGURE **2.11**

Group videoconference

A virtual organizational structure allows collaborative work in which managers and employees can effectively work in groups, even those composed of members from around the world.

Communications are greatly improved when participants can see one another and pick up facial expressions and body language. Thus, even with sophisticated information system tools, virtual teams still benefit from occasional face-to-face meetings. This is particularly true at the beginning of new projects when the team is just forming and defining goals, roles, and expectations on how its members will work together. Virtual organization members must also be sensitive to the different cultures and practices of the various team members to avoid misunderstandings that can destroy team chemistry. It helps if virtual team members take the time to get to know one another by sharing experiences and personal background information.

According to a recent survey, nearly half of all organizations use virtual teams, while two-thirds of organizations with multinational operations have such teams. Indeed at multinational companies, virtual teams are the norm.[7]

Using virtual teams is a key strategy for operating science and engineering projects funded by the National Science Foundation. For example, an international, multidisciplinary research team studying prehistoric European agricultural villages will form a virtual team with scientists and mentors at laboratories in Hungary, Greece, and the United States. Together they will analyze and interpret the data, present results at international conferences, publish results in peer-reviewed journals, and disseminate findings via Web pages and other media.[8]

A virtual team consisting of the authors and over a dozen others across the United States worked together for over a year to complete this textbook project. We used email to send chapter files and related documents to each other and employed audio-conference sessions to develop the textbook and related materials you are using. Table 2.2 summarizes the strengths and weaknesses of the various organization types.

TABLE 2.2 Strengths and weaknesses of various organizational structures

Organization Type	Strengths	Weaknesses
Traditional hierarchical (functional)	• Formal reporting relationships are clearly defined • Each employee has only one manager	• Stifles participative management • Limits departmental interaction and communications
Matrix	• Enables both functional and operational managers to focus on their strengths • Employees have an opportunity to develop a broader set of skills	• Potential conflicts on work assignments and priorities • Employee morale may be low due to stress and conflicts
Project	• Facilitates team decision making • Good communication among team members	• Limited contact with other teams results in less sharing of learnings across projects • Team may become misaligned with overall organizational goals
Virtual	• Ensures participation of best available people to solve important organizational problems • Opportunity to learn about the cultures and practices of people in foreign countries	• Time zone differences make it inconvenient for all members of the group to meet at the same time • Lack of face-to-face meetings lessens quality of communications

© 2016 Cengage Learning

Innovation

Innovation is the catalyst for the growth and success of any organization. It can build and sustain profits, create new challenges for the competition, and provide added value for customers. Innovation and change are absolutely required in today's highly competitive global environment, or the organization is at risk of losing its competiveness and becoming obsolete.

Nike innovated to create a cutting-edge product, develop new revenue streams, and boost profits. In a breakout move, it diversified from apparel and into technology, with its FuelBand bracelet that measures the user's movements, calories burned, and steps taken throughout the day.[9]

Fab innovated and boldly relaunched itself from a social networking Web site into one of the world's fastest-growing e-commerce Web sites offering thousands of items and with free shipping and free returns. This breakthrough enabled Fab to stake out new markets that attract entirely new customers.[10]

Amazon innovated to improve its supply chain by using robots, investing in modern warehouses, and streamlining order processing to expand its next-day and same-day delivery before rivals Google, eBay, and Walmart expanded. This improved capability has, at least temporarily, provided Amazon with a competitive advantage.[11]

Square innovated to develop a new service to process credit card transactions on mobile devices. This new service enabled Square to win the right to handle payments for all 7,000 U.S. Starbucks, bringing its annual processing volume to more than $10 billion.[12]

Various authors and researchers have identified many ways of classifying innovation. A simple classification developed by Clayton Christensen, a leading researcher in this field, is to think of two types of innovation—sustaining and disruptive.[13]

Sustaining innovation results in enhancements to existing products, services, and ways of operating. Such innovations are important as they enable an organization to continually increase profits, lower costs, and gain market share.

Procter and Gamble has poured hundreds of millions of dollars into making sustaining innovations to its leading laundry detergent, Tide, which was first introduced in 1946. These innovations have made it possible for Tide to get whites whiter and brights brighter, empowered Tide to work in cold as well as hot water, created concentrated Tide, which reduces packaging and distribution costs, and added scented Tide, which makes clothes smell fresher. These innovations have kept Tide as one of the leading detergents with more than $4.5 billion in annual sales.

A *disruptive innovation* is one that initially provides a lower level of performance than the marketplace has grown to accept. Over time, however, the disruptive innovation is improved to provide some new performance characteristics and becomes more attractive to users in a new market. As it continues to improve and begins to provide a higher level of performance, it eventually displaces the former product or way of doing things.

The cell phone is a good example of a disruptive innovation. The first commercial handheld cell phone was invented in 1973. It weighed 2.5 pounds, had a battery life of less than 30 minutes, cost more than $3,000, and had extremely poor sound quality.[14] See Figure 2.12. Compare that with today's ubiquitous cell phones that have one-tenth the weight, one-fifteenth the cost, 25 times longer battery life, and are capable of not only placing calls but serving as a

FIGURE **2.12**

Early mobile phone

The mobile phone is an example of a disruptive innovation.

© iStockphoto.com/Tim Boryer

camera, video recorder, and handheld computer that can run applications and access the Internet.

Reengineering and Continuous Improvement

To stay competitive, organizations must occasionally make fundamental changes in the way they do business. In other words, they must innovate and change the activities, tasks, or processes they use to achieve their goals. **Reengineering**, also called **process redesign** and business process reengineering (BPR), involves the radical redesign of business processes, organizational structures, information systems, and values of the organization to achieve a breakthrough in business results. See Figure 2.13. Reengineering can reduce delivery time, increase product and service quality, enhance customer satisfaction, and increase revenues and profitability.

reengineering (process redesign): The radical redesign of business processes, organizational structures, information systems, and values of the organization to achieve a breakthrough in business results.

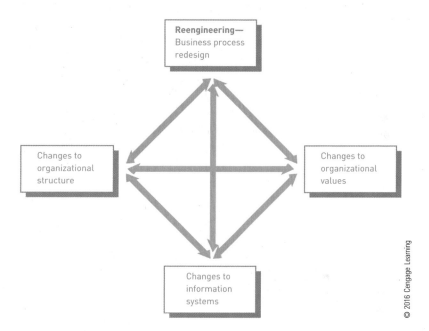

FIGURE 2.13

Reengineering

Reengineering involves the radical redesign of business processes, organizational structure, information systems, and values of the organization to achieve a breakthrough in business results.

© 2016 Cengage Learning

The Food and Drug Administration (FDA) worked with a consulting firm to reengineer its archaic and highly manual business process for submission of drug applications. Today this process is fully automated, with drug applications received electronically, processed, analyzed for conformance to FDA submission guidelines, categorized, and stored on a network. See Figure 2.14. The reengineered process eliminated the need to physically handle and store over 50 million pages of documents annually.[15]

In contrast to reengineering, the idea of **continuous improvement** (often referred to by the Japanese word "Kaizen") is a form of innovation that constantly seeks ways to improve business processes and add value to products and services. This continual change will increase customer satisfaction and loyalty and ensure long-term profitability. Manufacturing companies make continual product changes and improvements. Service organizations regularly find ways to provide faster and more effective assistance to customers. By doing so, these companies increase customer loyalty, minimize the chance of customer dissatisfaction, and diminish the opportunity for competitive inroads.

continuous improvement: Constantly seeking ways to improve business processes and add value to products and services.

Kaiser Permanente employs 180,000 staff members who provide care to 9 million members and patients. The organization has worked hard to instill a strong culture of continuous improvement. As a result, employees know that if they see an opportunity for improvement, they should pursue it. A nurse

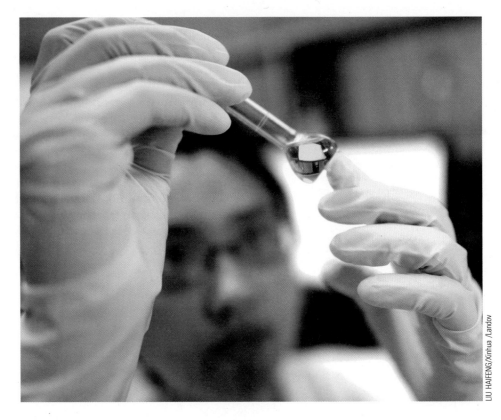

LIU HAIFENG/Xinhua /Landov

FIGURE 2.14

Reengineering to streamline processes

The FDA used reengineering to streamline its business process for submission of drug applications.

came up with an idea for an automated insulin drip calculator. Her idea was tried, and as a result, the old, error-prone method based on manual entries into Excel spreadsheets was eliminated. Through continuous improvement efforts, Kaiser Permanente has achieved the lowest number of pressure ulcers nationwide (less than 1 percent on average compared to a nationwide average of 7 percent of hospital patients).[16]

Table 2.3 compares the two strategies of business process reengineering and continuous improvement.

TABLE 2.3 Comparing business process reengineering to continuous improvement

Business Process Reengineering	Continuous Improvement
Strong action taken to solve serious problem	Routine action taken to make minor improvements
Top-down change driven by senior executives	Bottom-up change driven by workers
Broad in scope; cuts across departments	Narrow in scope; focuses on tasks in a given area
Goal is to achieve a major breakthrough	Goal is continuous, gradual improvements
Often led by outsiders	Usually led by workers close to the business
Information systems are integral to the solution	Information systems provide data to guide the improvement team

culture: A set of major understandings and assumptions shared by a group, such as within an ethnic group or a country.

organizational culture: The major understandings and assumptions for a business, corporation, or other organization.

Organizational Culture and Change

Culture is a set of major understandings and assumptions shared by a group, such as within an ethnic group or a country. **Organizational culture** consists of the major understandings and assumptions for an organization. The understandings, which can include common beliefs, values, and approaches to decision making, are often not stated or documented as goals or formal policies. For example, nonhourly employees might be expected to check their email and instant messages around the clock and be highly responsive to all such messages.

Mark Twain said, "It's not the progress I mind, it's the change I don't like." **Organizational change** deals with how organizations successfully plan for and implement change. Change can be caused by internal factors, such as those initiated by employees at all levels, or by external factors, such as those wrought by competitors, stockholders, federal and state laws, community regulations, natural occurrences (such as hurricanes), and general economic conditions. Organizational change occurs when two or more organizations merge. When organizations merge, integrating their information systems can be critical to future success.

The dynamics of how change is implemented can be viewed in terms of a change model. A **change model** represents change theories by identifying the phases of change and the best way to implement them. Kurt Lewin and Edgar Schein proposed a three-stage approach for change. See Figure 2.15. The first stage, unfreezing, is ceasing old habits and creating a climate that is receptive to change. Moving, the second stage, involves learning new work methods, behaviors, and systems. The final stage, refreezing, involves reinforcing changes to make the new process second nature, accepted, and part of the job.

organizational change: How for-profit and nonprofit organizations plan for, implement, and handle change.

change model: A representation of change theories that identifies the phases of change and the best way to implement them.

Unfreezing Preparing for change	Moving Making the change	Refreezing Institutionalizing
Key Tasks	**Key Tasks**	**Key Tasks**
Communicate what, why, when, who, how	Motivate individuals involved or affected	Monitor progress against success criteria
Draw on others, and seek input, ideas	Coach, train, lead, encourage, manage	Establish processes, systems to institutionalize change
Define objectives, success criteria, resources, schedule, budget	Provide appropriate resources	Establish controls to ensure change is occurring
Finalize work plans	Provide ongoing feedback	Recognize and reward individuals for exhibiting new behavior
Assign leaders and implementation teams		Provide feedback, motivation, additional training to individuals not exhibiting new behavior

FIGURE 2.15

Lewin's change model

Change involves three stages: unfreezing (preparing for change), moving (making the change), and refreezing (institutionalizing the change).

Leavitt's diamond: A theory that proposes that every organizational system is made up of four main components—people, tasks, structure, and technology—with an interaction among the four components so that any change in one of these elements will necessitate a change in the other three elements.

Leavitt's diamond is a second organizational change model that is extremely helpful in successfully implementing change. **Leavitt's diamond** proposes that every organizational system is made up of four main components—people, tasks, structure, and technology—with an interaction among the four components so that any change in one of these elements will necessitate a change in the other three elements. Thus, to successfully implement a new information system, appropriate changes must be made to the people, structure, and tasks affected by the new system. See Figure 2.16.

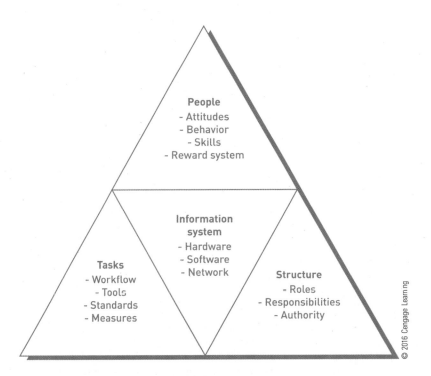

FIGURE 2.16

Leavitt's diamond

Any change in technology, people, task, or structure will necessitate a change in the other three elements.

People are the key to the successful implementation of any change. They must be convinced to take a positive attitude about the change and be willing to exhibit new behaviors consistent with the change. This is likely to require a change in the reward system to recognize those who exhibit the desired new behaviors. Training in any required new skills is also needed.

The organization structure must be modified with appropriate changes in roles, responsibilities, and lines of authority. Along with these changes are required changes in communication patterns, relationships, and coordination among those affected by the change.

The tasks required to complete the work and the flow of work between tasks also need to be changed. For each task, standards on how the work is to be performed need to be set as well as measures for the quality of completion. New tools may be required to perform the tasks.

As a result, the major challenges to successful implementation of an information system are often more behavioral issues than technical. Successful introduction of an information system into an organization requires a mix of both good organizational change skills and technical skills. Strong, effective leadership is required to overcome the behavioral resistance to change and achieve a smooth and successful system introduction.

organizational learning: The adaptations and adjustments based on experience and ideas over time.

Organizational learning is closely related to organizational change. All organizations adapt to new conditions or alter their practices over time— some better than others. Collectively, these adaptations and adjustments based on experience and ideas are called organizational learning. Hourly workers, support staff, managers, and executives learn better ways of fulfilling their role and then incorporate them into their day-to-day activities. In some cases, the adjustments can require a radical redesign of business processes (reengineering). In other cases, adjustments can be more incremental (continuous improvement). Both adjustments reflect an organization's strategy, the long-term plan of action for achieving its goals.

User Satisfaction and Technology Acceptance

technology acceptance model (TAM): A model that specifies the factors that can lead to better attitudes about an information system, along with higher acceptance and usage of it.

Reengineering and continuous improvement efforts (including implementation of new information systems) must be adopted and used to achieve the defined business objectives by targeted users to be effective. The technology acceptance model (TAM) specifies the factors that can lead to better attitudes about the use of a new information system, along with its higher acceptance and usage. See Figure 2.17. In this model, "perceived usefulness" is defined as the degree to which individuals believe that use of the system will improve their performance. The perceived ease of use is the degree to which individuals believe that the system will be easy to learn and use. Both the perceived usefulness and ease of use can be strongly influenced by the expressed opinions of others who have used the system and the degree to which the organization supports use of the system (e.g., incentives, offering training and coaching from key users). Perceived usefulness and ease of use in turn influence an individual's attitude toward the system, which affect their behavioral intention to use the system.[17]

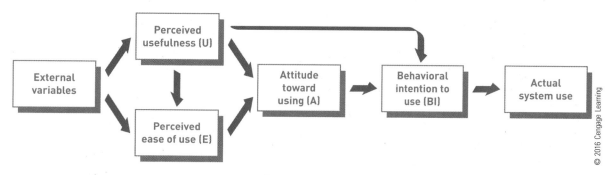

© 2016 Cengage Learning

FIGURE **2.17**

Technology acceptance model

Perceived usefulness (U) and perceived ease of use (E) strongly influence whether someone will use an information system. Management can improve that perception by demonstrating that others have used the system effectively and by providing user training and support.

Today, the world is moving toward the use of electronic medical records (EMRs) that track a patient's entire health and medical history in a digital format.[18] In the United States, the federal government is influencing physicians and hospitals to convert to EMRs by paying physicians up to $18,000 each for using EMRs. To earn this incentive, physicians must reach certain stages of "meaningful use" by 2014. Similar incentives, with different definitions of meaningful use, apply to hospitals and other healthcare organizations.[19] In addition to monetary incentives, those backing the use of EMRs attempt to increase the perceived usefulness of the system by frequently touting benefits, such as a reduction in medication errors, increased patient safety and compliance, around-the-clock access to patient records, and enhanced decision making using EMR data.[20]

Diffusion of Innovation Theory

diffusion of innovation theory: A theory developed by E.M. Rogers to explain how a new idea or product gains acceptance and diffuses (or spreads) through a specific population or subset of an organization.

The diffusion of innovation theory was developed by E.M. Rogers to explain how a new idea or product gains acceptance and diffuses (or spreads) through a specific population or subset of an organization. A key point of this theory is that adoption of any innovation does not happen all at once for all members of the targeted population; rather, it is a drawn-out process, with some people quicker to adopt the innovation than others. See Figure 2.18. Rogers defined five categories of adopters, shown in Table 2.4, each with different attitudes toward innovation. When promoting an innovation to a target population, it is important to understand the characteristics of the target population that will help or hinder adoption of the innovation and then to apply the appropriate strategy. This theory can be useful in planning the rollout of a new information system.

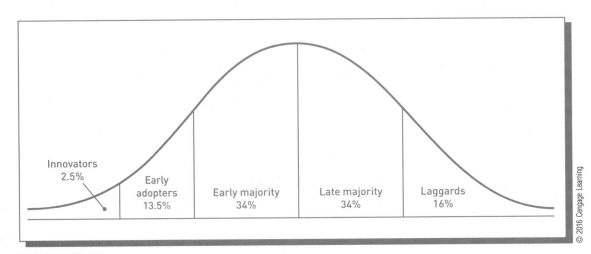

FIGURE 2.18

Innovation diffusion

Adoption of any innovation does not happen all at once for all members of the targeted population; rather, It is a drawn-out process, with some people quicker to adopt the innovation than others.

Source: Everett Rogers, *Diffusion of Innovations*

TABLE 2.4 Five categories of innovation adopters

Adopter Category	Characteristics	Strategy to Use
Innovator	Risk takers, always the first to try new products and ideas	Simply provide them with access to the new system and get out of their way
Early adopter	Opinion leaders whom others listen to and follow, aware of the need for change	Provide them assistance getting started
Early majority	Listen to and follow the opinion leaders	Provide them with evidence of the system's effectiveness and success stories
Late majority	Skeptical of change and new ideas	Provide them data on how many others have tried this and have used it successfully
Laggards	Very conservative and highly skeptical of change	Have their peers demonstrate how this change has helped them and bring pressure to bear from other adopters

Quality

The definition of the term "quality" has evolved over the years. In the early years of quality control, firms were concerned with meeting design specifications, or conforming to standards. If a product performed as designed, it was considered a high-quality product. A product can perform its intended function, however, and still not satisfy customer needs. Today, **quality** means the ability of a product or service to meet or exceed customer expectations.

quality: The ability of a product or service to meet or exceed customer expectations.

United Healthcare operates a myuhc.com portal for its members, which supports the trend toward greater consumer financial responsibility in managing health-related expenses. The service makes it easy for members to see how much they owe each healthcare provider. Members can also check claims for accuracy and resolve discrepancies. United Healthcare recently introduced an online bill payment service that enables its members to pay their bills to healthcare providers by credit card, a first in the industry. United Healthcare is taking strong measures to deliver quality information services that exceed its members' expectations.

Several approaches have been developed to help organizations improve quality and introduce change, including lean enterprise management, total quality management (TQM), and Six Sigma. **Lean enterprise management** is a philosophy that considers using resources for any purpose other than to create value for the customer to be wasteful and therefore a target for elimination. Lean thinking changes the focus of management from optimizing separate technologies, assets, and vertical departments to optimizing the flow of products and services across technologies, assets, and departments to customers.[21] **Total quality management** is a management approach to long-term organizational success through satisfying customer needs. All members of the organization participate in process improvement teams that focus on improving processes, products, and services.[22] **Six Sigma** is a measurement-based strategy to improve processes and reduce variation through completion of Six Sigma projects. The Six Sigma process of define, measure, analyze, improve, and control (DMAIC) is used to improve existing processes that need incremental improvement. The Six Sigma process of define, measure, analyze, design, and verify (DMADV) is used to develop new products at the Six Sigma quality level. A process cannot produce more than 3.4 defects per million opportunities to achieve Six Sigma.[23]

Outsourcing, Offshoring, and Downsizing

A significant portion of an organization's expenses is used to hire, train, and compensate employees. Naturally, organizations try to control costs by determining the number of employees they need to maintain high-quality goods and services. Strategies to contain these personnel costs include outsourcing, offshoring, and downsizing.

Outsourcing is a long-term business arrangement in which a company contracts for services with an outside organization that has expertise in providing a specific function. Organizations often outsource a process so they can focus more closely on their core business—and target their limited resources to meet strategic goals. Typically, the outsourcing firm has expertise and other resources that enable it to perform the service better, faster, and or cheaper.

Many companies now outsource jobs such as call center services, payroll, and security services. The amount of outsourcing activity continues to increase. KPMG, one of the largest professional service firms in the world and one of the big four accounting firms, reports that four out of ten large organizations intend to increase their level of finance and accounting outsourcing. In addition, five out of ten large organizations plan to increase the amount of outsourcing of software application maintenance and development.[24]

Offshore outsourcing (also called **offshoring**) is an outsourcing arrangement where the organization providing the service is located in a country different from the firm obtaining the services. Arizona Chemical is a producer and refiner of pine chemicals used in thousands of everyday products, including personal care items, household cleaners, plastics, and paint. It employs about 1,100 people. The firm offshore outsourced its information systems operations and help desk support to Freudenberg IT, a German global IT services organization with decades of experience and thousands of skilled information systems professionals.[25]

Even small companies employ offshore outsourcing. Mike Scanlin, a software engineer–turned venture capitalist, had an idea to build a new online

lean enterprise management: A philosophy that considers the use of resources for any purpose other than to create value for the customer to be wasteful and therefore a target for elimination.

total quality management: A management approach to long-term organizational success through satisfying customer needs.

Six Sigma: A measurement-based strategy to improve processes and reduce variation through completion of Six Sigma projects.

outsourcing: A long-term business arrangement in which a company contracts for services with an outside organization that has expertise in providing a specific function.

offshore outsourcing (offshoring): An outsourcing arrangement where the organization providing the service is located in a country different than the firm obtaining the services.

ETHICAL& SOCIETAL ISSUES

Outsourcing Background Checks in the United Kingdom

In the United Kingdom as well as in other countries, child abuse is a serious problem. One in five children has experienced sexual abuse, serious physical abuse, or severe physical or emotional neglect. For every victim the government identifies and intervenes to protect, an estimated eight more have suffered mistreatment. In 2011, the British parliament passed the Protection of Freedoms Act. The act regulated surveillance and reduced counterterrorism powers within the United Kingdom, but it also stepped up its protection of vulnerable groups, including children and the elderly.

The act provided for the creation of the Disclosure and Barring Service (DBS) through the merger of the Criminal Records Bureau and the Independent Safeguarding Authority. One of the main purposes of the agency is to provide efficient background checks for organizations and private companies that provide caretaking services. The DBS also bars certain individuals from working in regulated activities, such as childcare.

At the end of 2012, the U.K. Home Office announced that it had awarded Tata Consultancy Services (TCS), the leading IT consultant firm in India, a multimillion pound, multiyear contract to implement electronic background checks, improve decision making within DBS, and reduce processing times.

"Our proposed IT solution supports the U.K. Government's 'Digital by Default' initiative and fully meets the business objectives of DBS to modernize and transform its business," says Shankar Narayanan, head of U.K. and Ireland for TCS.

However, the contract testifies to an increasing willingness on the part of the U.K. government to outsource IT development to TCS and other foreign companies. In 2010, TCS sealed a ten-year deal to provide the IT infrastructure, back-office processing, business applications, and customer-facing systems for the largest universal occupational pension scheme in the United Kingdom, the National Employment and Savings Trust (NEST). Yet, news of this deal was delayed eight months—until after the program was operational.

While the U.K. government is becoming more comfortable with outsourcing IT jobs to India, it is also taking baby steps toward moving its operations—even sensitive operations—into the cloud. In May 2013, Skyscape Cloud Services won a $2.3 million yearly contract with DBS to add cloud connectivity to the solutions TCS builds. Public servants in the United Kingdom have long been wary of the security implications of moving into the cloud. They are, for example, concerned about privacy. Most cloud providers are based in the United States where legal standards give the government and law enforcement easier access to digital data than in Europe.

Skyscape promises that all client data will stay in the United Kingdom. In addition, when the government or a company uses a cloud service provider, it is relying on the cloud service provider to protect its data from physical disruptions and from cyberattacks. If the cloud provider fails to provide adequate data protection, its client is vulnerable. The DBS contract, as well as Skyscape's contract with the British equivalent of the Internal Revenue Service, indicates that the reduced costs and better service delivery made possible by the cloud are overriding these fears.

Discussion Questions

1. The U.K. government is increasingly willing to outsource jobs to India. Is this good stewardship of its citizens' personal data? Are certain activities simply too sensitive to outsource even if it saves money?
2. Do other advantages outweigh these concerns?

Critical Thinking Questions

1. DBS obtains and reveals information about individual's run-ins with law enforcement, arrests, and convictions. Do you think such sensitive information should be supported through cloud services that may not be as secure as traditional IT infrastructure?
2. Why do you think the United Kingdom is embracing the cloud despite its security concerns?

SOURCES: "How Safe Are Our Children?" NSPCC Research April 2013, National Society for the Prevention of Cruelty to Children Web site, *www.nspcc.org.uk/Inform/research/findings/howsafe /how-safe-2013_wda95178.html*, accessed September 30, 2013; Protection of Freedoms Act 2012, *www.legislation.gov.uk/ukpga/2012/9/contents/enacted*, accessed August 13, 2013; "TCS Wins Multi-Million Pound Contract from the United Kingdom's Home Office," Press Release, November 28, 2012, TCS Web site, *www.tcs.com/news_events/press_releases/Pages/TCS_multi-million_pound_con tract_UK_Home_Office.aspx*; Baker, Sophie, "How Tata Helped Build a Nest," *Financial News*, April 15, 2013, *www.efinancialnews.com/story/2013-04-15/tata-consultancy-services-nest?ea9c8a2 de0ee111045601ab04d673622*; Jones, Ben, "How Safe Is Cloud Computing?" Cloud Computing Topics Web site, May 20, 2013, *http://cloudcomputingtopics.com/2013/05/how-safe-is-cloud-comput ing*; Flood, Gary, "British Cloud Firm Wins Background Check Security Contract," *Information Week*, May 20, 2013, *www.informationweek.com/cloud-computing/platform/british-cloud-firm-wins-back ground-check/240155243?queryText=outsourcing*.

investment tool. He investigated using programmers from nearby Silicon Valley, but that would have cost him $600,000 per year. Instead, he offshore outsourced the development effort to programmers in Eastern Europe for just $37,000 per year. The programmers were experienced software developers with master's degrees in computer science. Scanlin feels he did not sacrifice quality for the lower cost.[26]

Companies considering outsourcing need to take into account many factors. A growing number of organizations are finding that outsourcing does not necessarily lead to reduced costs. One of the primary reasons for cost increases is poorly written contracts that allow the service provider to tack on unexpected charges. Other potential drawbacks of outsourcing include loss of control and flexibility, the potential for data breaches of information stored on the service provider's computer hardware, overlooked opportunities to strengthen core competency of the firm's own employees, and low employee morale. In addition, organizations often find that it takes years of ongoing effort and a large up-front investment to develop a good working relationship with an outsourcing firm. Finding a reputable outsourcing partner can be especially difficult for a small or midsized firm that lacks experience in identifying and vetting contractors.

downsizing: Reducing the number of employees to cut costs.

Downsizing is a term frequently associated with outsourcing; it involves reducing the number of employees to cut costs. The term "rightsizing" is also used. Rather than pick a specific business process to downsize, companies usually look to downsize across the entire company. Downsizing clearly reduces total payroll costs, though the quality of products and services and employee morale can suffer.

COMPETITIVE ADVANTAGE

competitive advantage: A significant and ideally long-term benefit to a company over its competition.

A competitive advantage is a significant and ideally long-term benefit to a company over its competition and can result in higher-quality products, better customer service, and lower costs. Many companies consider their IS staff a key competitive weapon against other companies in the marketplace, especially if they have employees with training in the development and use of mobile devices, Internet applications, social networks, and collaborative tools. Firms that gain a competitive advantage often emphasize the alignment of organizational goals and IS goals. In other words, these organizations make sure that their IS departments are totally supportive of the broader goals and strategies of the organization.

To help achieve a competitive advantage, Apple, Inc., requires that companies selling music, books, and other content on Apple's devices, such as iPhones and iPads, give Apple customers the best deals and prices offered. In other words, these companies cannot give customers using other devices better deals and prices than Apple customers can get. Some people, however, believe this policy might violate U.S. antitrust regulations.

In his book *Good to Great*, Jim Collins outlines how technology can be used to accelerate companies to greatness. Table 2.5 shows how a few companies accomplished this. Ultimately, it is not how much a company spends on information systems but how it makes and manages investments in technology. Companies can spend less and get more value.

TABLE **2.5** How some companies used technologies to move from good to great

Company	Business	Competitive Use of Information Systems
Gillette	Shaving products	Developed advanced computerized manufacturing systems to produce high-quality products at low cost
Walgreens	Drug and convenience stores	Developed satellite communication systems to link local stores to centralized computer systems
Wells Fargo	Financial services	Developed 24-hour banking, ATMs, investments, and increased customer service using information systems

Data from Jim Collins, *Good to Great*, New York: Harper Collins Books, 2001, p. 300.

© 2016 Cengage Learning

Factors that Lead Firms to Seek Competitive Advantage

A number of factors can lead to attaining a competitive advantage. Michael Porter, a prominent management theorist, proposed a now widely accepted competitive forces model, also called the five-forces model. The five forces include (1) the rivalry among existing competitors, (2) the threat of new entrants, (3) the threat of substitute products and services, (4) the bargaining power of buyers, and (5) the bargaining power of suppliers. The more these forces combine in any instance, the more likely firms will seek competitive advantage and the more dramatic the results of such an advantage will be.

five-forces model: A widely accepted model that identifies five key factors that can lead to attainment of competitive advantage, including (1) the rivalry among existing competitors, (2) the threat of new entrants, (3) the threat of substitute products and services, (4) the bargaining power of buyers, and (5) the bargaining power of suppliers.

Rivalry among Existing Competitors

Typically, highly competitive industries are characterized by high fixed costs of entering or leaving the industry, low degrees of product differentiation, and many competitors. To gain an advantage over competitors, companies constantly analyze how competitors use their resources and assets. This resource-based view is an approach to acquiring and controlling assets or resources that can help the company achieve a competitive advantage. For example, a transportation company might decide to invest in radio-frequency technology to tag and trace products as they move from one location to another.

Threat of New Entrants

A threat appears when entry and exit costs to an industry are low and the technology needed to start and maintain a business is commonly available. For example, a small restaurant is threatened by new competitors. Owners of small restaurants do not require millions of dollars to start the business, food costs do not decline substantially for large volumes, and food processing and preparation equipment is easily available. See Figure 2.19. When the threat of new market entrants is high, the desire to seek and maintain competitive advantage to dissuade new entrants is also usually high.

FIGURE **2.19**

Restaurant industry

In the restaurant industry, competition is fierce because entry costs are low. Therefore, a small restaurant that enters the market can be a threat to existing restaurants.

Threat of Substitute Products and Services

Companies that offer one type of goods or services are threatened by other companies that offer similar goods or services. The more consumers can obtain similar products and services that satisfy their needs, the more likely firms are to try to establish competitive advantage. For example, consider the photographic industry. When digital cameras became popular, traditional film companies had to respond to try to stay competitive and profitable.

Bargaining Power of Customers and Suppliers

Large customers tend to influence a firm, and this influence can increase significantly if the customers threaten to switch to rival companies. When customers have a lot of bargaining power, companies increase their competitive advantage to retain their customers. Similarly, when the bargaining power of suppliers is strong, companies need to improve their competitive advantage to maintain their bargaining position. Suppliers can also help an organization gain a competitive advantage. Some suppliers enter into strategic alliances with firms and eventually act as a part of the company.

Strategic Planning for Competitive Advantage

To be competitive, a company must be fast, nimble, flexible, innovative, productive, economical, and customer oriented. It must also align its IS strategy with general business strategies and objectives. Given the five market forces previously mentioned, Porter and others have proposed a number of strategies to attain competitive advantage, including cost leadership, differentiation, niche strategy, altering the industry structure, creating new products and services, and improving existing product lines and services:

- **Cost leadership.** Deliver the lowest possible cost for products and services. Walmart, Costco, and other discount retailers have used this strategy for years. See Figure 2.20. Cost leadership is often achieved by reducing the costs of raw materials through aggressive negotiations with suppliers, becoming more efficient with production and manufacturing processes, and reducing warehousing and shipping costs. Some companies use outsourcing to cut costs when making products or completing services.

FIGURE **2.20**

Costco uses cost leadership strategy

Costco and other discount retailers have used a cost leadership strategy to deliver the lowest possible price for products and services.

© iStockphoto.com/slobo

- **Differentiation.** Deliver different products and services. This strategy can involve producing a variety of products, giving customers more choices, or delivering higher-quality products and services. Many car companies make different models that use the same basic parts and components, giving customers more options. Other car companies attempt to increase perceived quality and safety to differentiate their products and appeal to consumers who are willing to pay higher prices for these features. Companies that try to differentiate their products often strive to uncover and eliminate counterfeit products produced and delivered by others.
- **Niche strategy.** Deliver to only a small, niche market. Porsche, for example, doesn't produce inexpensive economy cars, but, rather, it makes high-performance sports cars and sport utility vehicles (SUVs). See Figure 2.21. Rolex makes only high-quality, expensive watches; it doesn't make inexpensive, plastic watches.
- **Altering the industry structure.** Change the industry to become more favorable to the company or organization. The introduction of low-fare airline carriers, such as Southwest Airlines, has forever changed the

FIGURE 2.21

Porsche implements a niche strategy

Porsche is an example of a company with a niche strategy, producing only high-performance sports cars and SUVs.

airline industry, making it difficult for traditional airlines to make high profit margins. See Figure 2.22. Creating strategic alliances can also alter the industry structure. A **strategic alliance**, also called a **strategic partnership**, is an agreement between two or more companies that involves the joint production and distribution of goods and services.

strategic alliance (or strategic partnership): An agreement between two or more companies that involves the joint production and distribution of goods and services.

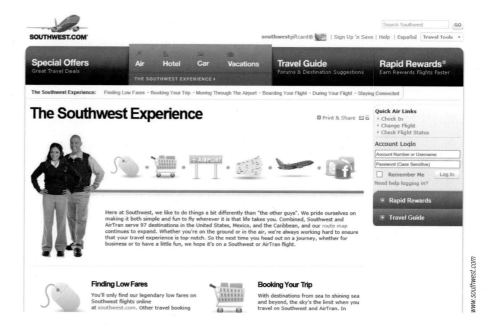

FIGURE 2.22

Southwest Airlines

Low-fare airline carriers such as Southwest Airlines altered the structure of the airline industry.

- **Creating new products and services.** Introduce new products and services periodically or frequently. This strategy always helps a firm gain a competitive advantage, especially in the computer industry and other high-tech businesses. If an organization does not introduce new products and services every few months, the company can quickly stagnate, lose market share, and decline. Companies that stay on top are constantly developing new products and services. Apple Computer, for example, introduced the iPod, iPhone, and iPad as new products.

- **Improving existing product lines and services.** Make real or perceived improvements to existing product lines and services. Manufacturers of household products are always advertising new and improved products. In some cases, the improvements are more perceived than actual refinements; usually, only minor changes are made to the existing product, such as reducing the amount of sugar in a breakfast cereal.

- **Innovation.** Innovation is another competitive strategy. With today's smartphones and tablet computers leapfrogging each other with new innovations, executives are constantly looking for new ways to gain a competitive advantage by developing unique and powerful applications for these newer devices. Innovation led Natural Selection, a San Diego company, to develop a computer program that attempted to analyze past inventions and suggest future ones. Although the original program was not an immediate success, the approach has been used by General Electric, the U.S. Air Force, and others to cut costs and streamline delivery routes of products. According to the common wisdom, "Successful innovations are often built on the back of failed ones."

- **Other strategies.** Some companies seek strong *growth in sales*, hoping they can increase profits in the long run due to increased sales. Being the *first to market* is another competitive strategy. Apple Computer, for instance, was one of the first companies to offer complete and ready-to-use personal computers. Some companies offer *customized* products and services to achieve a competitive advantage. Dell, for example, builds custom PCs for consumers. *Hire the best people* is another example of a competitive strategy. The assumption is that the best people will determine the best products and services to deliver to the market and the best approach to deliver these products and services. Having *agile* information systems that can rapidly change with changing conditions and environments can be a key to information systems success and a competitive advantage.

- Companies can also combine one or more of these strategies. In addition to customization, Dell attempts to offer low-cost computers (cost leadership) and top-notch service (differentiation).

FINANCIAL EVALUATION OF INFORMATION SYSTEM PROJECTS

Most organizations have an entire portfolio of potential information system projects from which to choose. To determine if a specific information system project is even worth pursuing, organizations perform a financial analysis. Three methods for performing a financial analysis will be discussed shortly. First, you should understand the concept of cash flow, which is used in all these methods, and the time value of money, which is used in two of the methods.

cash flow: Takes into account all the increases and decreases in cash flow associated with the project.

The cash flow associated with a specific project takes into account all the increases and decreases in cash flow associated with the project. Some of these are identified in Table 2.6.

time value of money: Takes into account the fact that a dollar today is worth more than a dollar paid in the future.

The time value of money takes into account the fact that a dollar today is worth more than a dollar paid in the future. Why? Because if you have a dollar today, you can invest it and earn a return on that dollar. The rate of return that can be earned on this money is the firm's opportunity cost. Suppose the firm's opportunity cost is 6 percent. If the firm has an additional $1 million today, it could invest it so that in one year it would have $1 million $\times$ (1 + 0.06), or $1.06 million. In two years, it would have $1 million $\times$ (1.06) $\times$ (1.06) or 1.124 million. So the value of future dollars earned must be discounted to determine their value in present-day dollars. One million dollars to be received in three years is worth $1 million$/(1.06)^3$ or $839,619 in today's dollars.

TABLE **2.6** Examples of increases and decreases in cash flow associated with a project

Type	Examples (not exhaustive)
Increases in cash flow	Any new revenue, such as additional sales generated and capture of income earned but not collected under the old methods
	Any cost savings associated with the project, such as savings from reduction in staff, equipment rental fees, and outsourcing fees
	Tax reduction generated from depreciation associated with any capital expenditures
Decreases in cash flow	Any capital investment required to buy equipment, software, or office space
	All ongoing operating costs such as equipment rental, software, office space, additional staff required to operate or support the system, and training of personnel
	All ongoing maintenance costs for equipment and software

Three methods for performing a financial analysis of a potential information systems project involve a payback period, internal rate of return, and net present value method.

Payback Period

payback period: Takes into account all the increases and decreases in cash flow associated with the project.

The **payback period** is the number of years required to recover the initial cost of an investment. The shorter the payback period, the more attractive is the project. A payback period of three years or less is usually considered good.

Assume that an information system project requires an initial investment of $150,000 and it generates net savings of $25,000, $50,000, $75,000, $100,000, and $100,000 over five years of operation. This system has a payback period of three years.

There are two problems with this evaluation method. First, it does not take into account the time value of money. Second, it fails to include cash flows beyond the payback period (years four and five in this example). Consider a project that requires an initial investment of $150,000 and generates net savings of $0, $0, $150,000, $0, $0. It also has a payback period of three years but is not as financially attractive as the first example.

Internal Rate of Return

internal rate of return: The rate of return that makes the net present value of all cash flows (benefits and costs) generated by a project equal to zero.

The **internal rate of return** of an investment is the rate of return that makes the net present value of all cash flows (benefits and costs) generated by a project equal to zero. The higher the internal rate of return, the more attractive the project is from a financial standpoint. Most organizations set a "hurdle rate" for evaluating projects. If the project does not exceed the hurdle rate, it is not acceptable from a financial standpoint.

The equation for determining the internal rate of return is given as follows:

$$\text{Net present value} = \sum_{n=0}^{N} C_n/(1 + r)^n = 0$$

where

N is the total number of periods for which there are cash flow estimates

C_n is the net cash flow for period n

r is the internal rate of return

$C_n/(1+r)^n$ represents the present-day value of net cash flow (C_n) in the nth year.

Online calculators that determine the internal rate of return can be found. Some spreadsheet programs (e.g., Excel's IRR formula in the Financial group on the Formulas tab) calculate the internal rate of return. Also, more expensive calculators have this function.

Net Present Value Method

net present value: A method of evaluating a project is the sum of the present value of the net cash flow for each time period.

The net present value method of evaluating a project is the sum of the present value of the net cash flow for each time period. The higher the net present value, the more financially attractive the project is.

The equation for determining the net present value is given as follows:

$$\text{Net present value} = \sum_{n=0}^{N} C_n/(1+i)^n$$

where

N is the total number of periods for which there are cash flow estimates

C_n is the net cash flow for period n

i is the rate of return associated with an alternative investment; this rate is usually set by a firm's finance or treasury organization. Often, it is the average interest paid by the firm when it must borrow money

$C_n/(1+i)^n$ represents the present-day value of net cash flow (C_n) in the nth year.

A serious problem with both the internal rate of return and net present value methods is that it is difficult to forecast cash flow accurately over a number of years. As Niels Bohr (Danish physicist and winner of the 1922 Nobel Prize in physics) said, "Prediction is very difficult, especially if it is about the future." So while the mathematics involved may make it appear that the results are precise, in actuality, the result is no more accurate than the cash flow estimates, which are often refined guesses. Table 2.7 shows the cash flow model for calculating payback period, internal rate of return, and net present value.

CAREERS IN INFORMATION SYSTEMS

Today, most organizations cannot function or compete effectively without computer-based information systems. Indeed, organizations often attribute their productivity improvement, superior customer service, or competitive advantage in the marketplace to their information systems. The information system worker functions at the intersection of business and technology and designs and builds the solutions that allow organizations to effectively leverage information technology.

Successful information system workers must enjoy working in a fast-paced, dynamic environment where the underlying technology changes all the time. They must be comfortable with meeting deadlines and solving unexpected challenges. They need good communication skills and often serve as translators between business needs and technology-based solutions. They must have solid analytical and decision-making skills and be able to translate ill-defined business problems and opportunities into effective technology-based solutions. They must develop effective team and leadership skills and be adept at implementing organization change. Last, but not least, they need to be prepared to engage in life-long learning in a rapidly changing field.

TABLE 2.7 Cash flow model for calculating payback period, internal rate of return, and net present value

	Years					
	1	2	3	4	5	Total
Initial capital investment	−$2.00					−$2.00
Decreases in cash flow						
Ongoing operating costs		−$0.95	−$0.75	−$0.75	−$0.75	−$3.20
Ongoing maintenance costs		−$0.20	−$0.20	−$0.20	−$0.20	−$0.80
Total costs		−$1.15	−$0.95	−$0.95	−$0.95	−$4.00
Increases in cash flow						$0.00
Additional new revenue		$1.00	$1.25	$1.35	$1.45	$5.05
Savings generated from project		$0.50	$0.75	$0.75	$0.75	$2.75
Total benefits		$1.50	$2.00	$2.10	$2.20	$7.80
Cash flow before taxes	−$2.00	$0.35	$1.05	$1.15	$1.25	$3.80
Accumulated cash flow (to calculate payback period)	−$2.00	−$1.65	−$0.60	−$0.55	$1.80	
Change in income						
Depreciation expense		−$0.45	$0.40	$0.35	$0.30	$1.50
Total costs		−$1.15	−$0.95	−$0.95	−$0.95	−$4.00
Total benefits		$1.25	$1.75	$2.00	$2.25	$7.25
Net change in income		−$0.35	$0.40	$0.70	$1.00	$1.75
Net change in income tax (assume 40% tax rate)		−$0.14	$0.16	$0.28	$0.40	$0.70
Cash flow after taxes	−$2.00	$0.49	$0.89	$0.87	$0.85	$3.10
Discount factor for time value of money (assume 6% cost of money)	1	1.06	$(1.06)^2$	$(1.06)^3$	$(1.06)^4$	
Discounted cash flow (after tax)	−$2.00	$0.46	$0.79	$0.73	$0.67	$0.66
Financial analysis:						
Payback period	4.5 years					
Net present value	$0.54					
Internal rate of return	19%					

Specific technical skills that some experts believe are important for IS workers to possess include the following, all of which are discussed in the chapters throughout this book:

- Mobile applications for smartphones, tablet computers, and other mobile devices
- Program and application development
- Help desk and technical support
- Project management
- Networking
- Business intelligence
- Security
- Web 2.0
- Data center
- Telecommunications

Technology is one of the fastest-growing areas in the U.S. economy, and information systems professionals are in high demand. The Association for Computing Machinery forecasts 150,000 new computing jobs per year from 2012 to 2020. Meanwhile, the unemployment rate among U.S. information system workers is significantly lower than the overall unemployment rate (3.3 percent compared to 7.8 percent overall in the fourth quarter of 2012). One drawback of a career in this field is that as reliance on technology increases, organizations have increasing expectations of their information system workers. According to a Computerworld survey of information systems workers, 68 percent of the respondents said they felt more pressure over the past year to increase productivity and 75 percent felt pressure to take on new tasks. Of those, only 12 percent reported that their salaries had been adjusted to reflect the added workload.[27]

The U.S. Department of Labor's Bureau of Labor Statistics (BLS) (*www.bls.gov*) publishes a list of the fastest-growing occupations. Figure 2.23 identifies the occupations that the BLS predicts to be the fastest-growing IS positions and typical salary in 2013 for people in these positions with one to five years of experience.[28]

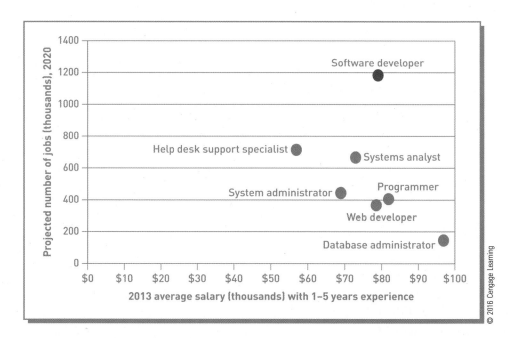

FIGURE 2.23

Occupational outlook for selected information systems positions

This chart shows the typical salary for IS positions in 2013 and the IS positions that BLS predicts will be among the fastest growing in the near future.

Numerous schools have degree programs with titles such as information systems, computer engineering, computer science, and management information systems. Figure 2.24 shows the number of undergraduate degrees awarded in computer science, computer engineering, and information (including information systems, information science, information technology, and informatics) from doctoral-granting computer science departments in the United States and Canada. (Note this is a select subset of schools, not all the schools that award information systems–related degrees.) This number decreased dramatically from a peak of around 21,000 in 2004 to less than 10,000 in 2009. Recently, enrollment in these majors has rebounded at these schools, showing an increase for four straight years, with enrollment among U.S. Computer Science departments increasing just over 16 percent from 2011 to 2012.

Some of the best places to work as an IS professional are listed in Table 2.8. These organizations rate high for a variety of reasons, including career development opportunities, training, benefits, retention, diversity, company facilities including employee gym and swimming pool, and the nature of the work. For example, Quicken Loans is an online mortgage lender that offers its information systems employees over 200 hours of training each year, including 40 hours of external training through industry conferences, guest speakers, and skills development programs directly relating to their area of expertise. Employees also enjoy a casual dress code, spot bonuses, and free trips to amusement parks, concerts, and sporting events such as the Quicken Loans 400 NASCAR race.[29]

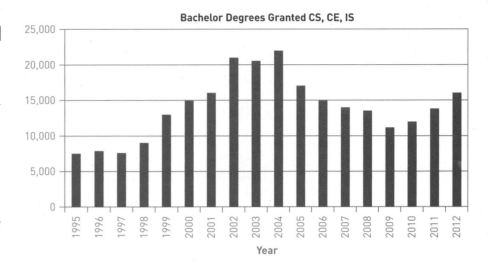

Bachelor Degrees Granted CS, CE, IS

FIGURE 2.24

Undergraduate degrees in IS fields

Number of undergraduate degrees awarded in computer science, computer engineering, and information fields from doctoral-granting computer science departments in the United States and Canada.

Source: © 2016 Cengage Learning. Adapted from "Computing Degree and Enrollment Trends from the 2010-2011 CRA Taulbee Survey" by Stuart Zweben, Computing Research Association.

TABLE 2.8 Best places to work as an IS professional

Rank	According to Computerworld	According to Business Insider
1	Quicken Loans	Facebook
2	USAA	Guidewire
3	Career Builder	Riverbed Technology
4	Commonwealth Financial Network	Riot Games
5	World Wide Technology	Google
6	Sharp Healthcare	SAS Institute
7	Transocean	Workday
8	Qualcomm	Responsys
9	Genentech	Exact Target
10	Pricewatercoopers	Orbitz

Sources: © 2016 Cengage Learning, 100 Best Places to Work in IT," *Computerworld*; "100 Best Places to Work in IT in 2013," *Computerworld*, June 17, 2013, *www.computerworld.com*; "The 25 Best Tech Companies to Work for in 2013," *Business Insider*, July 12, 2013, *www.businessinsider.com*

Opportunities in information systems are also available to people from foreign countries. The U.S. H-1B and L-1 visa programs seek to allow skilled employees from foreign lands into the United States. Opportunities in these programs, however, are limited and are usually in high demand. The L-1 visa program is often used for intracompany transfers for multinational companies. The H-1B program can be used for new employees. The number of H-1B visas offered annually can be political and controversial, with some fearing that the program is being abused to replace high-paid U.S. workers with less expensive foreign workers. Indeed, some believe that companies pretend to seek U.S. workers while actually seeking less expensive foreign workers. Others, however, believe the H-1B program and similar programs are invaluable to the U.S. economy and its competitiveness. Table 2.9 shows the top 10 U.S. employers in H-1B visas in 2012.

The top five countries of birth for H-1B workers in 2011 were India (with 58% of all approved H-1B petitions), China (9%), Canada (4%), the Philippines (3%), and South Korea (3%).[30]

Roles, Functions, and Careers in IS

IS offers many exciting and rewarding careers. Professionals with careers in information systems can work in an IS department or outside a traditional IS department as Web developers, computer programmers, systems analysts, computer operators, and many other positions. There are also opportunities for IS professionals in the public sector. In addition to technical skills, IS professionals

TABLE 2.9 Top H-1B visa employers in 2012

Company	Total H-1B Visas Granted (2012)
Cognizant	9,281
Tata	7,469
Infosys	5,600
Wipro	4,304
Accenture	4,037
HCL America	2,070
Tech Mahindra SATYAM	1,963
IBM & IBM India	1,846
Larsen & Toubro	1,632
Deloitte Touche Tohmatsu	1,668

Source: Ron Hira, "Top 10 Users of H-1B Guest Workers Program Are All Offshore Outsourcing Firms," *Economic Policy Institute* (blog), February 14, 2013, *www.epi.org/blog/top-10-b1b-guestworker-offshore-outsourcing.*

© 2016 Cengage Learning

need skills in written and verbal communication, an understanding of organizations and the way they operate, and the ability to work with people and in groups. At the end of every chapter, you will find career exercises that will help you explore careers in IS and career areas that interest you.

Most medium to large organizations manage information resources through an IS department. In smaller businesses, one or more people might manage information resources, with support from outsourced services. (Recall that outsourcing is also popular with some organizations.) As shown in Figure 2.25, the typical IS organization is divided into three main functions: operations, development, and support.

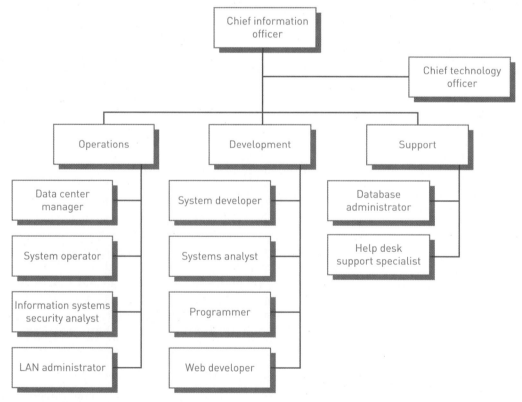

© 2016 Cengage Learning

FIGURE 2.25

Three primary functions of the information systems organization

Each of these functions—operations, development, and support—encompasses several different IS roles.

INFORMATION SYSTEMS @ WORK

Challenges and Responsibilities of a CIO

A CIO, or chief information officer, is the top manager responsible for how an organization uses information systems to advance the purpose of the organization. Aside from supervising programmers and network technicians, what do these people really think about? What's on the mind of a CIO?

Dr. John Halamka is CIO of Beth Israel Deaconess Medical Center (BIDMC) and an emergency room physician. He summarizes his job in a post on his blog of November 1, 2011, as follows: "The modern CIO is no longer a technologist or evangelist for innovation. The modern CIO is a customer relationship manager, a strategic communicator, and a project manager, delicately balancing project portfolios, available resources, and governance."

Dr. Alan Shark is the author of CIO Leadership for Cities and Counties, Emerging Trends and Practices (Washington, DC: Public Technology Institute, 2009). As he puts it, "The new CIO has to be a leader, not a dictator; a technologist, not a technician; a business person, not an accountant; and finally, a diplomat, not a politician." A CIO must lead with "vision, knowledge, and team-building." In that context, BIDMC has been an early adopter of "Electronic health records, patient portals, and clinical decision support tools. [It] began offering subsidized, hosted EHRs to its 300 affiliated doctors more than a year before the American Recovery and Reinvestment Act's HITECH provision provided financial incentives for hospitals to roll out Web-based EHRs to their affiliated physicians in the effort to get more of these doctors wired."

To lead with "vision, knowledge, and team-building," on what should CIOs focus? Gary Beach, publisher emeritus of CIO magazine, surveyed CIOs to learn how they spend their time now and how they want to spend time in the future. He distills their answers as follows:

In the "how they currently spend their time" category, the top three vote-getters are as follows: (1) aligning IT and business goals, (2) implementing new architectures, and (3) managing cost control. For "where they want to spend more time in the future," the list looks like this: (1) developing new go-to-market strategies and technologies, (2) studying market trends for commercial opportunities, and (3) identifying opportunities for competitive differentiation.

Only two of these six items have anything to do with technology. Four and part of a fifth are about business. According to the CIOs surveyed, CIOs are primarily managers.

As managers, CIOs are responsible for developing their staff. BIDMC follows this model. Halamka says, "The only way I am able to succeed is by hiring people smarter than me." He goes on to explain that it's the CIO's job to turn those people into a team.

Halamka also plays an important role outside of the medical center, a role he takes seriously. He speaks at conferences, writes a blog, and gives interviews. He is a forthright advocate for using technology to improve health care and spends about one day a week in Washington, D.C., advising legislators on how to accomplish that goal. A recent InformationWeek article described him as "The hardest-working man in health IT." Not all CIOs are as visible as Halamka, but many are. Because CIOs focus on "aligning IT and business goals," as Gary Beach found, part of the job often involves gathering and communicating business information.

Developing a diverse set of skills that allows a CIO to manage people effectively and keep up with innovations in technology can be challenging. In a recent blog post, Halamka quotes Meg Aranow, the CIO of Boston Medical Center: "The content of our jobs is great, the context is really challenging." Halamka calls that "a profound observation." He goes on to list other challenges of healthcare CIOs, including:

- You don't receive credit for everything that works. Instead, you are held accountable for the 0.01 percent that doesn't work.
- Demand always exceeds supply. Success is finishing half the projects you are asked to complete.
- The pace of change in consumer information systems creates expectations that far exceed the abilities of a thinly staffed IS organization.
- Regulatory burdens will increase exponentially. Compliance is a must-do, though your "customers" do not want their projects or services postponed while you work on compliance.

Why does Halamka keep this job when he could return to the practice of emergency room medicine or move into a different management position? In his blog post of February 24, 2011, he wrote, "The organizations in which I work will last for generations. Their reputations transcend anything I will ever do personally. My role is to champion, support, and publicize a few key innovations every year that will keep the organizations highly visible. That visibility will attract smart people and retain the best employees who want to work for a place on a rising trajectory." These reasons make the work worthwhile.

Discussion Questions

1. What different roles and responsibilities does a CIO take on in a company?
2. Of these roles and responsibilities, which is most challenging? Why?

Critical Thinking Questions

1. Do you think you would enjoy the job of a CIO? Do you think you would be successful as a CIO? Explain why you feel this way.
2. Contact your school's CIO or the CIO of a nearby organization. Find out how the CIO typically allocates time to the following major categories of activity:

   - Meetings with top management and people in other departments
   - Meetings with others in the IS department
   - Meetings with people outside the organization
   - Keeping current: reading, Web research, seminars
   - Individual work: budgeting, writing memos/reports, planning, HR work
   - Other technical tasks (ask for examples)
   - Other nontechnical tasks (ask for examples)

3. Also find out the total hours the CIO works in a week. Combine your results with those of your classmates to assemble a composite picture of the CIO's job.

SOURCES: Beach, Gary, "Time Is Money: What CIOs Should Know about How They Spend Their Time," CIO, *www.cio.com/article/693037/Time_Is_Money_What_CIOs_Should_Know_about_How_they_Spend_Their_Time*, November 2, 2011, accessed November 4, 2011; Halamka, John D., "Life as a Healthcare CIO" (blog) *http://geekdoctor.blogspot.com*, accessed November 1, 2011; McGee, M. K., Mitchell, R. N., and Versel, N., "Healthcare CIO 25: The Leaders behind the Healthcare IT Revolution," *InformationWeek, http://reports.informationweek.com/abstract/105/5954/Healthcare/research-healthcare-cio-25-the-leaders-behind-the-healthcare-it-revolution.html* (free registration required), March 18, 2011, downloaded December 19, 2011; Motorola, "The Evolving Role of the CIO" (interview with Dr. Alan Shark), Enterprise, *http://ezine.motorola.com/enterprise?a=443*, October 2009, accessed November 5, 2011; Opensource.com (under screen name "opensourceway"), "Dr. John Halamka on Openness and Privacy in Medicine" (video), *www.youtube.com/watch?v=4zn_9eiLfcA*, July 6, 2010, accessed December 15, 2011; Versel, Neil, "Halamka to Leave Harvard Med School CIO Post," *InformationWeek, www.informationweek.com/news/healthcare/leadership/231002441*, July 22, 2011, accessed December 18, 2011.

Typical IS Titles and Functions

The organizational chart shown in Figure 2.25 is a simplified model of an IS department in a typical medium-sized or large organization. The following sections provide a brief description of these roles. Smaller firms often combine the roles shown in Figure 2.25 into fewer formal positions.

Chief Information Officer

The role of the CIO is to employ an IS department's equipment and personnel to help the organization attain its goals. CIOs also understand the importance of finance, accounting, and return on investment. They can help companies avoid damaging ethical challenges by monitoring how their firms are complying with a large number of laws and regulations. The high level of the CIO position reflects the fact that information is one of an organization's most important resources. A good CIO is typically a visionary who provides leadership and direction to the IS department to help an organization achieve its goals. CIOs need technical, business, and personal skills.

Senior IS Managers

A large organization may have several people employed in senior IS managerial levels with job titles such as vice president of information systems, manager of information systems, and chief technology officer (CTO). A central role of all these people is to communicate with other areas of the organization to determine changing business needs. Managers outside the IS organization may be part of an advisory or steering committee that helps the CIO and other IS managers make decisions about the use of information systems. Together, they can best decide what information systems will support corporate goals. The CTO, for example, typically works under a CIO and specializes in networks and related equipment and technology.

Operations Roles

The operations group is responsible for the day-to-day running of IS hardware to process the organization's information systems workload. It must also do capacity planning to expand and upgrade equipment to meet changing business needs. It is constantly looking for ways to reduce the overall cost and increase the reliability of the organization's computing. This group is also responsible for protecting the company's IS systems and data from unauthorized access. Professionals in the operations group include those in the following positions:

- **Data center manager**—Data center managers are responsible for the maintenance and operation of the organization's computing facilities that may house a variety of hardware devices—mainframe and or super-computers, large numbers of servers, storage devices, and networking equipment. Data center managers supervise other operations workers to accomplish the day-to-day work needed to support the business operations as well as complete software and hardware upgrades. They also plan for capacity changes and develop business contingency plans in the event of a business disruption due to a fire, power outage, or natural disaster.
- **System operator**—System operators run and maintain IS equipment. They are responsible for efficiently starting, stopping, and correctly operating mainframe systems, networks, tape drives, disk devices, printers, and so on. Other operations include scheduling, maintaining hardware, and preparing input and output.
- **Information systems security analyst**—IS security analysts are responsible for maintaining the security and integrity of their organizations' systems and data. They analyze the security measures of the organization and identify and implement changes to make improvement. They are responsible for developing and delivering training on proper security measures. They also are responsible for creating action plans in the event of a security breach.[31]
- **LAN administrator**—Local area network (LAN) administrators set up and manage the network hardware, software, and security processes. They manage the addition of new users, software, and devices to the network. They also isolate and fix operations problems.

Development Roles

The development group is responsible for implementing the new information systems required to support the organization's existing and future business needs. Importantly, they must also modify existing information systems as the needs of the organization evolve and change. They are constantly on the watch for ways in which to use information systems to improve the competitiveness of the firm. Professionals in the development group include those in the following positions:

- **Software developer**—These individuals are involved in writing the software that customers and employees use. This includes testing and debugging the software as well as maintaining and upgrading software after it is released for operation. Software developers frequently collaborate with management, clients, and others to build a software product from scratch according to a customer's specifications or modify existing software to meet new business needs.[32]
- **Systems analyst**—Systems analysts frequently consult with management and users, as well as convey system requirements to software developers and network architects. They also assist in choosing and configuring hardware and software, matching technology to users' needs, monitoring

and testing the system in operation, and troubleshooting problems after implementation.

- **Programmer**—Programmers convert a program design developed by a systems analyst or software developer into one of many computer languages. To do this, they must write, debug, and test the program to ensure that it will operate in a way that it will meet the users' needs.

- **Web developers**—These professionals design and maintain Web sites, including site layout and function, to meet the client's requirements. The creative side of the job includes creating a user-friendly design, ensuring easy navigation, organizing content, and integrating graphics and audio. The more technical responsibilities include monitoring Web site performance and capacity. See Figure 2.26.

FIGURE 2.26

Web developers

Web developers create and maintain company Web sites.

© iStockphoto.com/warrengoldswain

Support

The support group provides customer service for the employees, customers, and business partners who rely on the firm's information systems and service to accomplish their work. They respond to queries from these constituents and attempt to be proactive in eliminating problems before they occur. They often develop and provide training to users to enable them to better use information systems services and equipment. Professionals in the support group include those in the following positions:

- **Database administrator**—Database administrators (DBAs) design and set up databases to meet an organization's needs. They also ensure that they operate efficiently and perform fine-tuning, upgrading, and testing modifications as needed. They are also responsible for implementing security measures to safeguard the company's most sensitive data.

- **Help desk support specialist**—These skilled specialists respond to telephone calls, electronic mail, and other inquiries from computer users regarding hardware, software, networking, or other IS-related problems or needs. They diagnose the problem through dialogue with the user and research solutions, and implement a plan to resolve the problem or refer the issue to specialized IS staff. Many organizations are setting up "drop in" centers where users can come to meet face-to-face with the help desk specialists to get help. See Figure 2.27.

© racom/Shutterstock.com

FIGURE 2.27

Help desk personnel

Help desk personnel respond to inquiries from computer users regarding hardware, software, networking, or other IS-related problems or needs

certification: A process for testing skills and knowledge, which results in a statement by the certifying authority that confirms an individual is capable of performing particular tasks.

Certification

Often, the people filling IS roles have completed some form of certification. Certification is a process for testing skills and knowledge resulting in an endorsement by the certifying authority that an individual is capable of performing particular tasks or jobs. Certification frequently involves specific, vendor-provided or vendor-endorsed coursework. Popular certification programs include Microsoft Certified Systems Engineer, Certified Information Systems Security Professional (CISSP), Oracle Certified Professional, and Cisco Certified Security Professional (CCSP). Getting certified from a software, database, or network company may open the door to new career possibilities or result in an increase in pay. Not all certifications, however, provide a financial incentive.

Other IS Careers

In addition to working for an IS department in an organization, IS personnel can work for large consulting firms, such as Accenture, IBM, and Hewlett-Packard. Some consulting jobs can entail frequent travel because consultants are assigned to work on various projects wherever the client is. Such jobs require excellent project management and people skills in addition to IS technical skills. Related career opportunities include computer training, computer and computer-equipment sales, and computer repair and maintenance.

Other IS career opportunities include being employed by technology companies, such as Oracle, IBM, HP, Microsoft, Google, and Dell. Such a career enables an individual to work on the cutting edge of technology, which can be challenging and exciting.

As some computer companies cut their services to customers, new companies are being formed to fill the need. With names such as Speak with a Geek and Geek Squad, these companies are helping people and organizations with their computer-related problems that computer vendors are no longer solving.

Some people start their own IS businesses from scratch, such as Craig Newmark, founder of craigslist. In the mid-1990s, Newmark was working for a large financial services firm and wanted to give something back to society by developing an email list for arts and technology events in the San Francisco area. This early email list turned into craigslist. According to Newmark, to run a successful business, you should "Treat people like you want to be treated, including providing good customer service. Listening skills and effective communication are essential."[33] Other people are becoming IS entrepreneurs or freelancers, working from home writing programs, working on IS projects with larger businesses, or developing new applications for the iPhone or similar devices.[34] Some Internet sites, such as *www.freelancer.com*, post projects online and offer information and advice for people working on their own. Many freelancers work for small- to medium-sized enterprises in the U.S. market. If you are thinking of freelance or consulting work, be creative and protect yourself. Aggressively market your talents and make sure you are paid by having some or all of your fees put into an escrow account.

Working in Teams

Most IS careers involve working in project teams that can consist of many of the positions and roles discussed earlier. Thus, it is always good for IS professionals to have good communications skills and the ability to work with other people. Many colleges and universities have courses in information systems and related areas that require students to work in project teams. At the end of every chapter in this book are team activities that require teamwork to complete a project. You may be required to complete one or more of these team-oriented assignments.

Finding a Job in IS

Traditional approaches to finding a job in the information systems area include attending on-campus visits from recruiters and referrals from professors, friends, and family members. Many colleges and universities have excellent programs to help students develop résumés and conduct job interviews. Developing an online résumé can be critical to finding a good job. Many companies accept résumés only online and use software to search for key words and skills used to screen job candidates. Consequently, having the right key words and skills can mean the difference between getting or not getting a job interview. Some corporate recruiters, however, are starting to actively search for employees rather than sifting through thousands of online résumés or posting jobs on their Web sites.[35] Instead, these corporate recruiters do their own Internet searches and check with professional job sites such as *www.linkedin.com* and *www.branchout.com*.[36] Other companies hire college students to help them market products and services to students.[37] In addition to being paid, students can get invaluable career experience. In some cases, it can help them get jobs after graduation. Increasingly, CIOs are becoming actively involved in hiring employees for their IS departments.[38] In the past, many CIOs relied on the company's human resources (HR) department to fill key IS jobs.

Students who use the Internet and other nontraditional sources to find IS jobs have more opportunities to land a job. Many Web sites, such as Monster, Career Builders, Indeed, Simply Hired, Snagged a Job, TheLadders .com, LinkedIn.com, and Computerjobs.com, post job opportunities for Internet careers and more traditional careers. Most large companies list job opportunities on their corporate Web sites. These sites allow prospective job hunters to browse job opportunities, locations, salaries, benefits, and other factors. In addition, some sites allow job hunters to post their résumés. Many people use social networking sites such as Facebook to help get job leads. Corporate recruiters also use the Internet or Web logs (blogs) to gather information on existing job candidates or to locate new job candidates. See Figure 2.28.

In addition, many professional organizations and user groups can be helpful in finding a job, staying current once employed, and seeking new

© iStockphoto.com/skynesher

FIGURE 2.28

Finding an IS job

As with other areas in IS, many top-level administrative jobs, such as Internet systems developers and Internet programmers, are related to the Internet.

career opportunities. These groups include the Association for Computer Machinery (ACM: *www.acm.org*), the Association of Information Technology Professionals (AITP: *www.aitp.org*), Apple User Groups (*www.apple.com /usergroups*), and Linux user groups located around the world.

Over 150 companies use Twitter to advertise job openings in the advertising/ public relations, consulting, consumer products, education, and other industries. Several organizations in the information systems industry, including Google (@googlejobs), Intel (@jobsatIntel), Microsoft (@Microsoft_Jobs), and (YahooEngRecruiter), also use Twitter to advertise job openings.[39]

People who have quit jobs or been laid off often use informal networks of colleagues or business acquaintances from their previous jobs to help find new jobs.

Students need to review and edit what is posted about them on social media sites, as employers often search the Internet to get information about potential employees before they make hiring decisions. A 2012 survey found that 92 percent of respondents either use or plan to use some form of social media—such as Facebook, LinkedIn, or Twitter—in their recruiting.[40] This practice is more common in hiring people for law enforcement positions, such as police officers or 911 dispatchers, so that the interviewer can check for possible gang affiliations or any photos or discussion of illegal or questionable activity.[41]

SUMMARY

Principle:

Information systems must be implemented in such a manner that they are accepted and work well within the context of an organization and support its fundamental business goals and strategies.

Organizations are systems with inputs, transformation processes, outputs, and feedback data used to monitor and control. Organizations affect and are affected by their environment.

Value-added processes increase the relative worth of the combined inputs on their way to becoming final outputs of the organization. The value chain is a series of activities that an organization performs to transform inputs into outputs in such a way that the value of the input is increased.

The supply chain is a key value chain whose primary activities include inbound logistics, operations, outbound logistics, marketing and sales, and service. Supply chain management encompasses all the activities required to get the right product into the right consumer's hands in the right quantity at the right time and at the right cost.

Information systems have transformed the nature of work and the shape of organizations themselves. They are often so intimately involved in the activities of the value chain that they are a part of the process itself.

An organization's structure depends on its goals and its approach to management. Organization structure can affect how an organization views and uses information systems. Four common organizational structures include traditional (functional), matrix, project, and virtual. Each has its strengths and weaknesses.

Innovation is the catalyst for the growth and success of any organization. Innovation may be classified as sustaining or disruptive.

Business process reengineering is a form of innovation that involves the radical redesign of business processes, organizational structures, information systems, and values of the organization to achieve a breakthrough in results. Continuous improvement is a form of innovation that continually improves business processes to add value to products and services.

Organizational change deals with how organizations successfully plan for and implement change. The ability to introduce change effectively is critical to the success of any information system project.

Several change models can be used to increase the likelihood of successfully introducing a new information system into an organization.

Lewin's three-stage organization change model divides the change implementation process into three stages called unfreezing, moving, and refreezing. It also identifies key tasks that need to be performed during each stage.

Leavitt's diamond proposes that to successfully implement a new information system, appropriate changes must be made to the people, structure, and tasks affected by the new system.

The technology acceptance model specifies the factors that can lead to better attitudes about the use of a new information system, along with higher acceptance and use of it.

The diffusion of innovation theory explains how a new idea or product gains acceptance and diffuses through a specific population or subset of an organization. A key point of this theory is that adoption of any innovation does not happen all at once for all people; rather, it is a drawn-out process, with some people quicker to adopt the innovation than others. Indeed, there are five categories of adopters, and a different adoption strategy is recommended for each category.

Organizations use information systems to support their goals.

Organizational culture consists of the major understandings and assumptions for a business, a corporation, or an organization. According to the concept of organizational learning, organizations adapt to new conditions or alter practices over time.

Principle:

Because information systems are so important, businesses need to be sure that improvements or completely new systems help lower costs, increase profits, improve service, or achieve a competitive advantage.

Quality is the ability of a product or service to meet or exceed customer expectations.

Several approaches have been developed to help organizations improve quality and introduce change, including lean enterprise management, total quality management, and Six Sigma.

Outsourcing is a long-term business arrangement in which a company contracts for services with an outside organization that has expertise in providing a specific function. Offshore outsourcing is an outsourcing arrangement where the organization providing the service is located in a country different from the firm obtaining the services. Downsizing involves reducing the number of employees to cut costs. All these staffing alternatives are an attempt to reduce costs or improve services. Each approach is associated with ethical issues and risks.

Competitive advantage is a significant and ideally long-term benefit to a company over its competition and can result in higher-quality products, better customer service, and lower costs. Porter's five-forces model covers factors that lead firms to seek competitive advantage: the rivalry among existing competitors, the threat of new market entrants, the threat of substitute products and services, the bargaining power of buyers, and the bargaining power of suppliers. Strategies to address these factors and to attain competitive advantage include cost leadership, differentiation, niche strategy, altering the industry structure, creating new products and services, and improving existing product lines and services, as well as other strategies.

Financial analysis is performed to determine whether a specific information system project is worth doing. Three commonly used approaches include the payback period, internal rate of return, and net present value.

Principle:

The information system worker functions at the intersection of business and technology and designs, builds, and implements solutions that allow organizations to effectively leverage information systems.

Successful information system workers need to have a variety of personal characteristics and skills, including working well under pressure, good communication skills, solid analytical and decision-making skills, effective team and leaderships, and adeptness at implementing organizational change.

Technology is one of the fastest-growing areas in the U.S. economy, which has a strong demand for information system workers.

Opportunities in information systems are available to people from foreign countries under the H-1B and L-1 visa programs.

The IS organization has three primary functions: operations, development, and support.

Typical operations roles include data center manager, system operators, information system security analyst, and LAN administrator.

Typical development roles include software developer, systems analyst, programmer, and Web developer.

Typical support roles include help desk support specialist and database administrator.

Besides working for an IS department in an organization, IS personnel can work for a large consulting firm or a hardware or software manufacturer. Developing or selling products for a hardware or software vendor is another IS career opportunity.

KEY TERMS

cash flow	downsizing
certification	empowerment
change model	five-forces model
competitive advantage	flat organizational structure
continuous improvement	functional structure
culture	internal rate of return
diffusion of innovation theory	lean enterprise management

Leavitt's diamond

matrix organization structure

net present value

offshore outsourcing (offshoring)

organization

organizational change

organizational culture

organizational learning

organizational structure

outsourcing

payback period

project organizational structure

quality

reengineering (process redesign)

Six Sigma

strategic alliance (strategic partnership)

supply chain management (SCM)

technology acceptance model (TAM)

time value of money

total quality management

traditional hierarchical organizational structure

value chain

virtual team

CHAPTER 2: SELF-ASSESSMENT TEST

Information systems must be implemented in such a manner that they are accepted and work well within the context of an organization and support its fundamental business goals and strategies.

1. A(n) _____ is a series of activities that an organization performs to transform inputs into outputs in such a way that the value of the inputs is increased.

2. _____ is *not* a primary activity of the manufacturing supply chain.
   a. Inbound logistics
   b. Operations
   c. Services
   d. Human resource management

3. _____ encompasses all the activities required to get the right product into the right customer's hands in the right quality at the right time and at the right cost.

4. In the _____ organizational structure, an individual has two reporting superiors.
   a. functional
   b. flat
   c. matrix
   d. team

5. Sustaining innovation results in enhancements to existing products, services, and ways of operating. True or False?

6. An organizational change model that defines three stages of change and the key tasks that must be performed in each stage is _____.
   a. the technology acceptance model
   b. the diffusion of innovation theory
   c. Leavitt's diamond
   d. Lewin's change model

Because information systems are so important, businesses need to be sure that improvements or completely new systems help lower costs, increase profits, improve service, or achieve a competitive advantage.

7. _____ is the ability of a product or service to meet or exceed customer expectations.

8. _____ is a management approach to long-term organizational success through satisfying customer needs.
   a. Agile manufacturing
   b. Lean manufacturing
   c. Six Sigma
   d. Total quality management

9. Offshore outsourcing is a long-term business arrangement in which a company contracts for services with an outside organization that has expertise in providing a specific function. True or False?

10. _____ is *not* one of Porter's five forces that lead firms to seek competitive advantage.
    a. The rivalry among existing competitors
    b. The threat of new market entrants
    c. The threat of government regulation
    d. The threat of substitute products and services

11. The _____ method of financial analysis does not consider the time value of money.
    a. payback
    b. internal rate of return
    c. net present value
    d. all of the above ignore the time value of money

The information system worker functions at the intersection of business and technology and designs, builds, and implements solutions that allow organizations to effectively leverage information systems.

12. _____ frequently collaborate with management, clients, and others to build a software product from scratch according to a customer's

specifications or modify existing software to meet new business needs.

a. Programmers

b. Help desk support specialists

c. Systems developers

d. Chief technical officers

13. The typical information systems organization is typically divided into three functions, including operations, development, and _____.

14. _____ is a process for testing skills and knowledge resulting in an endorsement by the certifying authority that an individual is capable of performing particular tasks or jobs.

CHAPTER 2: SELF-ASSESSMENT TEST ANSWERS

1. value chain
2. d
3. Supply chain management
4. c
5. True
6. d
7. Quality
8. d
9. False
10. c
11. a
12. c
13. support
14. Certification

REVIEW QUESTIONS

1. What is the difference between a value chain and a supply chain?
2. What is supply chain management?
3. What role does an information system play in today's organizations?
4. What is technology diffusion?
5. What are some key differences between reengineering and continuous improvement?
6. What is quality? What is total quality management (TQM)? What is Six Sigma?
7. What is meant by the terms "organizational culture" and "change"?

8. List and define four organizational structures.
9. Sketch and briefly describe the three-stage organizational change model.
10. What is downsizing? How is it different from outsourcing?
11. What are some general strategies employed by organizations to achieve competitive advantage?
12. List and describe popular job-finding Internet sites.
13. Describe the role of a CIO.

DISCUSSION QUESTIONS

1. Identify several personal characteristics needed to be successful in an information system career. Do you feel that you possess any of these characteristics?
2. Your manager has asked for your input on ideas for how to improve the likelihood of successful adoption of a new information system that members of the company's finance department will use. What would you say?
3. What sort of IS career would be most appealing to you: working as a member of an IS organization, consulting, or working for an IT hardware or software vendor? Why?
4. How can a company encourage innovation? Give several examples of companies that have been innovative.
5. You have been asked to assess the success of a recently implemented system that has been deployed across the entire supply chain of a large

organization. How might you go about trying to measure the technology diffusion of this system? How else might you assess the success of this system?

6. You have been asked to participate in preparing your company's strategic plan. Specifically, your task is to analyze the competitive marketplace using Porter's five-forces model. Prepare your analysis using your knowledge of a business you have worked for or have an interest in working for.

7. Based on the analysis you performed in Discussion Question 6, what possible strategies could your organization adopt to address these challenges? What role could information systems play in these strategies? Use Porter's strategies as a guide.

8. Describe the advantages and disadvantages of using the Internet to search for a job.

9. Assume you are the chairperson of a committee responsible for replacing the existing CIO of your organization's IS department. What characteristics would you want in a new CIO? How would you go about identifying qualified candidates?

PROBLEM-SOLVING EXERCISES

1. Identify three companies that make the highest-quality products or services for an industry of your choice. Find the number of employees, total sales, total profits, and earnings growth rate for these three firms. Using a database program, enter this information for the last year. Use the database to generate a report of the three companies with the highest earnings growth rate. Use your word processor to create a document that describes these firms and why you believe they make the highest-quality products and services. What other measures would you use to determine the best company in terms of future profit potential? Does high quality always mean high profits?

2. A new IS project has been proposed that is expected to produce not only cost savings but also an increase in revenue. The initial capital cost to establish the system is estimated to be $500,000. The remaining cash flow data is presented in Table 2.10.

   a. Using a spreadsheet program, calculate the payback period, internal rate of return, and net present value for this project. Assume that the cost of capital is 7 percent and the effective tax rate is 40 percent.

   b. How would the payback, internal rate of return, and net present value change if the capital cost for the project was $750,000 and the cost savings and increased revenue were decreased by 25 percent each year?

3. Using a database program, develop a table listing five popular Internet sites for a job search. The table should include columns on any costs of using the site, any requirements such as salary and job type, important features, advantages, and disadvantages.

TABLE 2.10 Problem solving exercise

	1	2	3	4	5	6
Capital	$500					
Increased revenue		$50	$75	$100	$115	$130
Cost savings		$110	$125	$125	$125	$125
Depreciation expense		$150	$125	$100	$75	$50
Operating and maintenance expense		$75	$50	$50	$50	$50

Note: All amounts are in hundreds of thousands.

© 2016 Cengage Learning

TEAM ACTIVITIES

1. With your team, interview a manager in a successful organization about the organizational culture. Discuss whether any organizational change model is used when introducing a major change.

2. With your team, research a firm that has achieved a competitive advantage. Write a brief report that describes how the company was able to achieve its competitive advantage.

WEB EXERCISES

1. Do research on lean enterprise management and find an example of an organization that uses this process to improve its effectiveness. Outline the steps that the organization followed.

2. Search for information that compares the use of the internal rate of return and net present value method for the financial evaluation of projects. Write a short summary of the strengths and weaknesses of each method. Discuss the use of either method to rank a set of competing projects.

1. Do research on an entrepreneur that you admire. Write a brief description of how the individual was able to start a business. What challenges had to be overcome? Did the individual encounter failure before becoming a success?
2. Go to the U.S. Department of Labor's Bureau of Labor Statistics (*www.bls.gov*) Web site, which publishes a list of the fastest-growing occupations. Write a report identifying the five fastest-growing occupations. What are the growth opportunities of three careers that are most appealing to you?

CASE STUDIES

Case One

Tesco Uses Data and New Information Technologies to Stay Ahead

Tesco has come a long way since it began as a market stall selling surplus groceries in London's East End in 1919. It is now the largest food seller in the United Kingdom, and one of the largest general merchandise retailers in the world. It operates in 14 countries across Europe, Asia, and North America and has over 5,000 stores—about half outside the United Kingdom.

Despite its history of nearly a century, Tesco is up to date with today's information systems. One way it uses these systems is to understand its customers better. As former CEO Sir Terry Leahy puts it, "The hardest thing to know is where you stand relative to your customers, your suppliers and your competitors. Collecting, analyzing, and acting on the insights revealed by customer behavior, at the [cash register] and online, allowed Tesco to find the truth." He added, "Customers [are] the best guide. They have no axe to grind. You have to follow the customers."

To track and analyze customer information, Tesco invested in a data warehousing system from Teradata along with reporting software from Business Objects. A data warehouse is a large collection of historical data to use for analysis and decision making. At Tesco, "large" is no exaggeration: Its data warehouse contains over 100 TB (terabytes) of data. By comparison, a high-end personal computer might have a total storage of 1 TB.

Connecting with customers, though, isn't a one-way process of collecting data about them. Connecting also means reaching out to customers and allowing them to interact in new ways. Tesco is doing that too. Using augmented reality technology from Kishino AR, Tesco lets customers see products online almost as if they were physically in a store. (You can see this in action in the Kishino AR video listed under sources.) Tesco is also putting computers in its U.K. stores that allow customers to check out more products than a store can stock, and view heavy, bulky items from all angles. In Korea, Tesco has opened a complete virtual store: Customers can view over 500 items, scan their bar codes using a special smartphone app, and order products. The products can be delivered later that same day if they order by 1 pm.

Recognizing that many of the customers it wants to connect with are members of social networking sites, Tesco has also developed a Facebook application in which Clubcard holders (or most of its regular customers, 16 million in the United Kingdom alone) can vote on products they want added to its Big Price Drop promotion. Richard Brasher, CEO of Tesco U.K., explains, "We are committed to doing all we can to help our customers, and our new Facebook application will enable them to tell us directly where they most value reduced prices." Aside from the benefits of lower prices, voting on which prices should be lowered gives customers a feeling of being connected with the store and participating in decisions.

Tesco's applications require modern information systems. More importantly, however, they require the ability to see the value of information and conceive of innovative ways to use it.

Discussion Questions

1. How does Tesco's Teradata database add value to the organization?
2. How do Tesco's use of augmented reality and its Facebook application give Tesco a potential competitive advantage?

Critical Thinking Questions

1. Tesco collects and analyzes historical data from customers, such as weekly and monthly spending habits. How might this information help a food seller such as Tesco operate more efficiently, save money, attract customers, and make sure food doesn't go to waste?
2. How do you feel about a company, such as Tesco, collecting data about your spending habits?

SOURCES: Grant, I., "Tesco Uses Customer Data to Stride Ahead of Competition," *ComputerWeekly, www.computerweekly.com/news/1280095684/Tesco-uses-customer-data-to-stride-ahead-of-competition*, April 12, 2011; Kishino AR, "Kishino Augmented Reality for Tesco" (video), *www.youtube.com/watch?v=S5QDRoxuHtk*, November 15, 2011; Sillitoe, B., "Tesco Trials Virtual Store in South Korea," *Retail Gazette, www.retailgazette.co.uk/articles/43224-tesco-trials-virtual-store-in-south-korea*, August 26, 2011; Taylor, G., "Tesco Launches Big Price Drop Facebook App," *Retail Gazette, www.retailgazette.co.uk/articles/41023-tesco-launches-big-price-drop-facebook-app*, October 19, 2011; Tesco PLC, "Interim Results 2011/12," October 5, 2011, downloaded from *www.tescoplc.com/investors/results-and-events*; Whiteaker, J., "Tesco to Trial Augmented Reality In-Store," *Retail Gazette, www.retailgazette.co.uk/articles/44432-tesco-to-trial-augmented-reality-instore*, November 17, 2011.

Case Two

TUI Deutschland Uses Information Systems to Gain a Competitive Advantage

To succeed, a business needs an edge over its competitors: a competitive advantage. A big part of creating a competitive advantage is using information systems effectively, meaning a business can't simply buy computers and expect good results. As Oscar Berg puts it in his blog The Content Economy, "What [creates] competitive advantage is how we use technologies, how we let them affect our practices and behaviors…. If technologies are carefully selected and applied, they can help to create competitive advantage."

This chapter discusses the five forces that define any competitive situation: rivalry among existing firms in an industry, the threats of new competitors and of substitute products/services, and a firm's relationships with suppliers and customers. Firms use these forces to achieve a sustainable competitive advantage, which is one that others cannot copy immediately to eliminate the edge an innovator can have.

TUI Deutschland is Germany's leading tour operator. Targeted pricing is vital in its market, with the travel company that sets prices to accommodate customers' preferences and habits gaining a competitive advantage. For a large tour operator like TUI, setting optimal prices is not easy. Each season, the employee responsible for a particular tour must set around 100,000 prices for each destination region. The factors that affect the final price of hotel rooms, for example, include facilities, types of rooms, arrival dates, and expected demand.

"In the past, decision-making processes were not clear," explains Matthias Wunderlich, head of Business Intelligence at TUI Deutschland GmbH. "There were too many gaps in the system, since the information needed to make pricing decisions was hidden in different places. The result was a pricing process that was complex, laborious, time-consuming, and occasionally inconsistent."

Wunderlich's team developed a new information system to make this process more effective. Used for the first time for the destination of Tenerife, it organizes historical booking data, making relevant information available to pricing specialists. It defines the desired margin for a destination and specifies parameters for results. The system calculates combinations and dependencies until the optimum result is achieved. It forecasts which group of customers will drive demand for particular accommodations at each point of the season, from coastal hotels for families during the school holidays to luxury hotels with first-class amenities for premium customers during the low season.

"We have to ensure that a four-star hotel, for example, is always cheaper on a given date than a five-star hotel in the same customer segment," explains Wunderlich. "With the new solution, this is guaranteed. There is no need for a time-consuming manual procedure to ensure it is done correctly."

Because the new pricing process is based on customer data, it reflects the needs and habits of customers. A pricing specialist can set prices that are attractive to customers while still achieving desired margins.

"Traditional pricing methods are no longer appropriate for today's travel and tourism market," says Wunderlich. "In the past it was practically impossible to set prices in a way that was flexible and customer-focused. This has all changed. The pricing specialist in effect becomes an expert in a particular customer group and knows exactly what a certain customer is prepared to pay for a certain travel service. This increases profits, but not at the expense of our customers."

Discussion Questions

1. Of the five competitive forces discussed in this case, which do you think TUI's system affects?
2. Has TUI's new information system making pricing fairer for its customers? Why or why not?

Critical Thinking Questions

1. What online travel sites have you used? Do you think they make good use of their data? Why or why not?
2. Consider a bookstore that gives customers a card to be punched for each book they buy. With 10 punches, they get a free paperback of their choice. This low-tech system leverages the force of customer power: By promising customers future benefits, it reduces their motivation to switch suppliers even if another store sells books for less. How could a bookstore use technology to make this loyalty program more effective in retaining customers?

SOURCES: Berg, Oscar, "Creating Competitive Advantage with Social Software," The Content Economy (blog), *www.thecontenteconomy.com/2011/06/creating-competitive-advantage-with.html*, June 9, 2011, accessed November 6, 2011; IBM: "Getting the Price Right," IBM Success Stories, *www-01.ibm.com/software/success/cssdb.nsf/CS/STRD-8MQLX4*, October 31, 2011, accessed November 6, 2011; IBM: "Netezza Mediamath—A Nucleus ROI Case Study," IBM Success Stories, *www-01.ibm.com/software/success/cssdb.nsf/CS/JHUN-8N748A*, October 31, 2011, accessed November 6, 2011; Porter, Michael E., "How Competitive Forces Shape Strategy," *Harvard Business Review*, *http://hbr.org/1979/03/how-competitive-forces-shape-strategy/ar/1* (free registration required to read beyond the first page), March/April 1979; accessed November 6, 2011.

NOTES

Sources for the Opening Vignette: "Celebrating 90+ Years," Willson International Web site, *www.willsonintl.com/celebrating-90-years.aspx*, accessed August 11, 2013; Willson International Web site, *www.willsonintl.com*, accessed August 11, 2013; "Willson International, Logistics Firm Gains Competitive Edge with Business-Critical Process Automation," Microsoft Case Study Web site, June 19, 2013, *www.microsoft.com/casestudies/Microsoft-Sharepoint-Designer-2010/Willson-International/Logistics-Firm-Gains-Competitive-Edge-with-Business-Critical-Process-Automation/710000002771*, accessed August 11, 2013.

1. "Zara IT Case," *www.slideshare.net/raulpin101/zara-it-case*, accessed September 3, 2013.
2. Braue, David, "Coles Supply-Chain Revamp Means Stocks Are Down, Down, Down, *ZDNet*, August 15, 2013, *www.zdnet.com/coles-supply-chain-revamp-means-stockouts-are-down-down-down-7000019419*.
3. Molina, Brett and Acohido, Bryon, "Microsoft Reshuffles Company Structure," *USA Today*, July 11, 2013, *www.usatoday.com/story/tech/2013/07/11/microsoft-restructuring/2508175*

4. Ballmer, Steve, "One Microsoft: Company Realigns to Enable Innovation at Greater Speed, Efficiency," *www.microsoft.com/en-us/news/Press/2013/Jul13/07-11One Microsoft.aspx*.

5. Hu, Elise, "Inside the 'Bossless' Office, Where the Team Takes Charge," NPR, August 26, 2013, *www.npr.org/blogs/alltechconsidered/2013/08/27/207039346/What-Works-And-Doesnt-About-Bossless-Offices*.

6. Gratton, Lynda, "Working Together … When Apart," *Wall Street Journal*, June 19, 2012, *http://online.wsj.com/article/SB118165895540732559.html*.

7. Wojciak, Johanna, "The Virtues of Virtual Teams," Finn Partners, July 16, 2013, *www.finnpartners.com/blog/2013/07/16/the-virtues-of-virtual-teams*.

8. "The Körös Regional Archaeological Project: International Research Experiences for Students IRES," *http://fieldmuseum.org/krap_ires*, accessed September 8, 2013.

9. Carr, Austin, "The World's Most Innovative Companies 2013," *Fast Company*, *www.fastcompany.com/section/most-innovative-companies-2013*, accessed September 6, 2013.

10. Ibid.

11. Ibid.

12. Ibid.

13. Christensen, Clayton, "Disruptive Innovation," *www.claytonchristensen.com/key-concepts*, accessed September 19, 2013.

14. Buck, Stephanie, "Cell-ebration! 40 Years of Cellphone History," *Mashable*, April 3, 2013, *http://mashable.com/2013/04/03/anniversary-of-cellphone*.

15. "Process Reengineering at FDA for the Electronic Document Room," *www.zai-inc.com/success-stories/process-reengineering-fda-electronic-document-room*, accessed September 8, 2013.

16. Halvorson, George, "The Culture to Cultivate," Harvard Business Review, July–August 2013, *http://hbr.org/2013/07/the-culture-to-cultivate/ar/*.

17. Davis, F. D., "Perceived Usefulness, Perceived Ease of Use, and User Acceptance of Information Technology," *MIS Quarterly*, volume 13, issue 3, pp. 319–339.

18. Torrey, T., "What Is an EMR Electronic Medical Record or EHR Electronic Health Record?" *About.com*, *http://patients.about.com/od/electronicpatientrecords/a/emr.htm*, accessed September 9, 2013.

19. Fiegl, C., "Early EMR Adopters Get a Break; Tougher Criteria Delayed to 2014," *American Medical News*, *www.ama-assn.org/amednews/2011/12/12/gvl11212.htm*, December 12, 2011, accessed December 19, 2011.

20. iPatientCare, "iPatientCare Helps Brighton Hospital Fulfill Its Passion for Paperless," *www.ipatientcare.com/KnowledgeCenter.aspx*, July 2011.

21. "What Is Lean?" Lean Enterprise Institute, *www.lean.org/whatslean*, accessed September 9, 2013.

22. "Total Quality Management TQM," *http://asq.org/learn-about-quality/total-quality-management/overview/overview.html*, accessed September 9, 2013.

23. "What Is Six Sigma?" *www.isixsigma.com/new-to-six-sigma/getting-started/what-six-sigma*, accessed September 9, 2013.

24. "Enterprises Expand Outsourcing in 2013," *Investors.com*, July 12, 2013, *http://news.investors.com/manage-ment-managing-for-success/071213-663544-enter prises-expand-outsourcing-in-2013.htm*.

25. "Freudenberg IT FIT and Arizona Chemical Partner for Global IT Outsourcing Success," *Yahoo Finance*, August 12, 2013, *http://finance.yahoo.com/news/freudenberg-fit-arizona-chemical-partner-142000975.html*.

26. Pagliery, Jose, "Even Small Companies Are Outsourcing," *CNN Money*, March 28, 2013, *http://money.cnn.com/2013/03/27/smallbusiness/outsourcing/index.html*.

27. Brandel, Mary, "IT Gets Its Grove Back," *Computerworld*, April 8, 2013, *www.computerworld.com/s/article/9237985/IT_gets_its_groove_back?taxonomyId=14&pageNumber=2*.

28. "Computerworld's Smart Salary Tool," *Computerworld*, *www.computerworld.com/s/salary-survey/tool/2013*, accessed September 12, 2013.

29. "100 Best Places to Work in IT in 2013," *Computerworld*, June 17, 2013, *www.computerworld.com/s/article/9238592/100_Best_Places_to_Work_in_IT_2013*, accessed September 30, 2013.

30. U.S. Citizenship and Immigration Services, U.S. Department of Homeland Security, "Characteristics of H-1B Specialty Occupation Workers," March 12, 2012, *www.uscis.gov/USCIS/Resources/Reports20and20Studies/H-1B/h1b-fy-11-characteristics.pdf*.

31. "Security Analyst," Infosec Institute, *www.infosecinstitute.com/jobs/security-analyst.html*, accessed September 22, 2013.

32. "Best Technology Jobs: Software Developer," *U.S. News & World Report*, *http://money.usnews.com/careers/best-jobs/software-developer*, accessed September 22, 2013.

33. Carmichael, Evan, "How Craigslist Was Created without a Business Plan," *Tellus*, June 5, 2012, *http://community.telustalksbusiness.com/blogs/talk_business/2012/06/04/how-craigslist-was-created-without-a-business-plan*.

34. Elance Web site, *www.elance.com*, accessed September 23, 2013.

35. Light, Joe, "Recruiters Rethink Online Playbook," *The Wall Street Journal*, January 18, 2011, p. B7.

36. Berfield, Susan, "Dueling Your Facebook Friends for a New Job," *Bloomberg Businessweek*, March 7, 2011.

37. Rosman, Katherine, "Here, Tweeting Is a Class Requirement," *The Wall Street Journal*, March 9, 2011, p. D1.

38. Lamoreaux, Kristen, "Rethinking the Talent Search," *CIO*, May 1, 2011, p. 30.

39. "Which Employers Post Jobs on Twitter [140 Accounts]," *The Undercover Recruiter*, *http://theundercoverrecruiter.com/list-employers-posting-jobs-twitter*, accessed September 11, 2013.

40. Smith, Darrell, "Job Front: Social Media Expected to Play Bigger Role in Hiring," *Sacramento Bee*, February 4, 2013, *www.sacbee.com/2013/02/04/5162867/job-front-social-media-expected.html*.

41. Valdes, Manuel and McFarland, Shannon, "Job Seekers' Facebook Passwords Asked for During U.S. Interviews," *Huffington Post*, March 20, 2012, *www.huffingtonpost.com/2012/03/20/facebook-passwords-job-seekers_n_1366577.html*.

Information Technology Concepts

CHAPTERS

© Meder Lorant/Shutterstock.com

3 Hardware: Input, Processing, Output, and Storage Devices

Principles	Learning Objectives
• Computer hardware must be carefully selected to meet the evolving needs of the organization and its supporting information systems.	• Describe the role of the central processing unit and primary storage. • State the advantages of multiprocessing, parallel, grid, and cloud-computing systems and provide examples of the types of problems they address. • Describe the access methods, capacity, and portability of various secondary storage devices. • Identify and discuss the speed, functionality, and importance of various input and output devices. • Identify the characteristics of and discuss the usage of various classes of single-user and multiuser computer systems.
• The computer hardware industry is rapidly changing and highly competitive, creating an environment ripe for technological breakthroughs.	• Describe Moore's Law and discuss its implications for future computer hardware developments. • Give an example of recent innovations in computer CPU chips, memory devices, and input/output devices.
• The computer hardware industry and users are implementing green computing designs and products.	• Identify some of the challenges and trade-offs that must be considered in implementing a data center. • Define the term "green computing" and identify the primary goals of this program. • Identify several benefits of green computing initiatives that have been broadly adopted.

Information Systems in the Global Economy
FUJITSU, JAPAN

Supercomputers Are Not Just for Research Anymore

Kyodo/Landov

For decades, only governments and large research institutions used supercomputers, the most powerful computers with the fastest processing speed and highest performance. With the most extensive and rapid computational capabilities, supercomputers supported research in quantum mechanics, molecular modeling, climate, and other scientific fields. Even today, most supercomputers are deployed for scientific research. Fujitsu, for example, is a Japan-based IT and communications multinational corporation and one of the leading manufacturers of supercomputers. In 2013, Fujitsu announced the launch of two supercomputer projects: the ACA Correlator for a Chile-based radio telescope; and Raijin, a supercomputer named after the Japanese god of thunder that will run complex weather and climate modeling. Raijin has the ability to perform the same number of calculations in one hour that it would take 7 billion people, armed with calculators, to perform in 20 years. This same year, other government-sponsored research institutions placed orders for supercomputers.

However, among Fujitsu's 2013 announcements came the notice that Canon, the long-time camera maker and today the leading multinational supplier of laser printers, copying machines, and paper management systems, would be purchasing a Fujitsu supercomputer. The event was unusual enough that several IT analysts picked up the story. What would Canon be doing with a supercomputer?

It turns out that Canon will use the supercomputer as part of its initiative to develop "prototypeless design." A prototype is a physical model of a new product that takes a great deal of time and money to build. Yet building a prototype is necessary so that companies can check whether a product can function in the ways the designers intended without glitches. In the high-tech world, these prototypes have become smaller and increasingly more sophisticated—making the process of building one even more of a challenge. By using Fujitsu's supercomputer to replace physical prototypes with virtual prototyping and analytical simulations, Canon will gain a competitive advantage—a faster, better, cheaper method of developing new products. Canon chose not just any supercomputer, but an updated version of Fujitsu's K computer, which until very recently was the fastest supercomputer in the world and still has relatively low power consumption. Selecting the K computer helps Canon meet its commitment to environment-friendly production.

Canon is not the first corporation to purchase a supercomputer. In fact, in 2004 IBM sold a supercomputer to pharmaceutical company Bristol-Myers Squibb; even though at a billion dollars per K computer, not a lot of corporations could afford them. In 2012, however, sales for supercomputers rocketed by 30 percent as prices dropped as low as half a billion per machine. Companies including PayPal and Procter & Gamble also bought their own supercomputers. Fujitsu's K computer will allow Canon to cut its development costs, and as prices continue to decline, other companies will no doubt find ways to use supercomputers to gain a strategic advantage.

As you read this chapter, consider the following:

- What major competitive advantage does Canon gain from its purchase of the supercomputer?
- Is the way we use hardware, such as supercomputers, changing? If so, how?
- What impact does the decreasing cost of hardware over time have on its use in the corporate world?

WHY LEARN ABOUT HARDWARE?

Organizations invest in computer hardware to improve worker productivity, increase revenue, reduce costs, provide better customer service, speed up time to market, and enable collaboration among employees. Organizations that don't make wise hardware investments are often stuck with outdated equipment that is unreliable and that cannot take advantage of the latest software advances. Such obsolete hardware can place an organization at a competitive disadvantage. Managers, no matter what their career field and educational background, are expected to help define the business needs that the hardware must support. In addition, managers must be able to ask good questions and evaluate options when considering hardware investments for their areas of the business. This need is especially true in small organizations, which might not have information system specialists. Managers in marketing, sales, and human resources often help IS specialists assess opportunities to apply computer hardware and evaluate the options and features specified for the hardware. Managers in finance and accounting especially must keep an eye on the bottom line, guarding against overspending, yet be willing to invest in computer hardware when and where business conditions warrant it.

Today's use of technology is practical—it's intended to yield real business benefits, as demonstrated by the use of a supercomputer at Canon, Bristol-Myers Squibb, PayPal, and Procter & Gamble in the opening vignette. Using the latest information technology and providing additional processing capabilities can increase employee productivity, expand business opportunities, lower costs, reduce time to market, and allow for more flexibility. This chapter concentrates on the hardware component of a computer-based information system (CBIS). Recall that hardware refers to the physical components of a computer that perform the input, processing, output, and storage activities of the computer. When making hardware decisions, the overriding consideration of a business should be how hardware can support the objectives of the information system and the goals of the organization.

COMPUTER SYSTEMS: INTEGRATING THE POWER OF TECHNOLOGY

People involved in selecting their organization's computer hardware must clearly understand current and future business requirements so that they can make informed acquisition decisions. Consider the following examples of applying business knowledge to reach sound decisions on acquiring hardware:

- The city of Bunbury in western Australia decided to upgrade its servers, storage systems, network, and associated software from multiple suppliers to hardware from a single vendor. The goal was to reduce future hardware replacement costs, cut power consumption, and lessen the effort required to manage the multiple devices used to sustain the city's information systems.[1]
- Jason De Vos does video editing for projects such as live streaming Lollaplooza, ACL Fest, and JazzFest music festivals. His work must be of the highest quality and yet still be completed on an extremely tight schedule, often as short as a few hours. Based on these requirements, Jason uses powerful workstations that are dependable and can complete the vast amount of processing required for video editing in the least amount of time.[2]

As these examples demonstrate, choosing the right computer hardware requires understanding the needs of an organization and the demands of the information systems that will run on it.

Hardware Components

Computer system hardware components include devices that perform input, processing, data storage, and output, as shown in Figure 3.1.

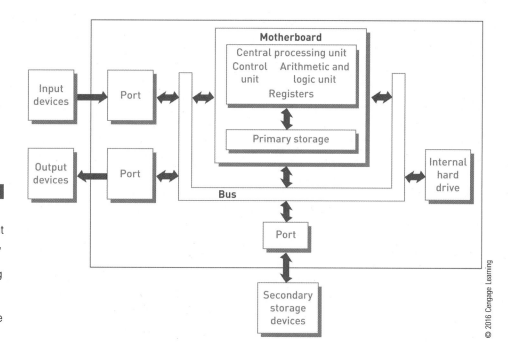

FIGURE **3.1**

Hardware components

These components include the input devices, output devices, ports, bus, primary and secondary storage devices, and the central processing unit (CPU). The control unit, the arithmetic/logic unit (ALU), and the register storage areas constitute the CPU.

primary storage (main memory; memory): The part of the computer that holds program instructions and data.

central processing unit (CPU): The part of the computer that consists of three associated elements: the arithmetic/logic unit, the control unit, and the register areas.

arithmetic/logic unit (ALU): The part of the CPU that performs mathematical calculations and makes logical comparisons.

control unit: The part of the CPU that sequentially accesses program instructions, decodes them, and coordinates the flow of data in and out of the ALU, the registers, the primary storage, and even secondary storage and various output devices.

register: A high-speed storage area in the CPU used to temporarily hold small units of program instructions and data immediately before, during, and after execution by the CPU.

motherboard: The backbone of the computer, connecting all of its components including the CPU and primary storage and providing connectors for peripheral devices such as printers, external hard drives, sound cards, and video cards.

bus: A set of physical connections (cables, printed circuits, etc.) that can be shared by multiple hardware components so they can communicate with one another.

Recall that any system must be able to process (organize and manipulate) data, and a computer system does so through an interplay between one or more central processing units and primary storage. **Primary storage**, also called **main memory** or **memory**, holds program instructions and data immediately before or after the registers. To understand the function of processing and the interplay between the CPU and memory, let's examine the way a typical computer executes a program instruction.

Each **central processing unit (CPU)** consists of three associated elements: the arithmetic/logic unit, the control unit, and the register areas. The **arithmetic/logic unit (ALU)** performs mathematical calculations and makes logical comparisons. The **control unit** sequentially accesses program instructions, decodes them, and coordinates the flow of data in and out of the ALU, the registers, the primary storage, and even secondary storage and various output devices. **Registers** are high-speed storage areas used to temporarily hold small units of program instructions and data immediately before, during, and after execution by the CPU. The **motherboard** is the backbone of the computer, connecting all of its components including the CPU and primary storage and providing connectors for peripheral devices such as printers, external hard drives, sound cards, and video cards. A **bus** is a set of physical connections (e.g., cables and printed circuits) that can be shared by multiple hardware components so they can communicate with one another. A computer can have two fundamental types of bus. An internal bus (also called the *front-side bus*) enables the CPU to communicate with the system's primary storage. The expansion bus (also called the *input/output bus*) allows various motherboard components to communicate with one another and to add new devices using what are called expansion slots connected to the input/output bus.

Hardware Components in Action

Executing any machine-level instruction involves two phases: instruction and execution. During the instruction phase, a computer performs the following steps:

- Step 1: Fetch instruction. The computer reads the next program instruction to be executed and any necessary data into the processor.

- Step 2: Decode instruction. The instruction is decoded and passed to the appropriate processor execution unit. Each execution unit plays a different role. The arithmetic/logic unit performs all arithmetic operations; the floating-point unit deals with noninteger operations; the load/store unit manages the instructions that read or write to memory; the branch processing unit predicts the outcome of a branch instruction in an attempt to reduce disruptions in the flow of instructions and data into the processor; the memory-management unit translates an application's addresses into physical memory addresses; and the vector-processing unit handles vector-based instructions that accelerate graphics operations.

The time it takes to perform the instruction phase (Steps 1 and 2) is called the **instruction time (I-time)**.

The second phase is execution. During the execution phase, a computer performs the following steps:

- Step 3: Execute instruction. The hardware element, now freshly fed with an instruction and data, carries out the instruction. This process could involve making an arithmetic computation, logical comparison, bit shift, or vector operation.
- Step 4: Store results. The results are stored in registers or memory.

The time it takes to complete the execution phase (Steps 3 and 4) is called the **execution time (E-time)**.

After both phases have been completed for one instruction, they are performed again for the second instruction, and so on. Completing the instruction phase followed by the execution phase is called a **machine cycle**, as shown in Figure 3.2. Some processing units can speed processing by using **pipelining**, whereby the processing unit gets one instruction, decodes another, and executes a third at the same time. The Pentium 4 processor, for example, uses two execution unit pipelines. This feature means the processing unit can execute two instructions in a single machine cycle.

instruction time (I-time): The time it takes to perform the fetch instruction and decode instruction steps of the instruction phase.

execution time (E-time): The time it takes to execute an instruction and store the results.

machine cycle: The instruction phase followed by the execution phase.

pipelining: A form of CPU operation in which multiple execution phases are performed in a single machine cycle.

FIGURE 3.2

Execution of an instruction

In the instruction phase, a program's instructions and any necessary data are read into the processor (1). Then the instruction is decoded so that the central processor can understand what to do (2). In the execution phase, the ALU does what it is instructed to do, making either an arithmetic computation or a logical comparison (3). Then the results are stored in the registers or in memory (4). The instruction and execution phases together make up one machine cycle.

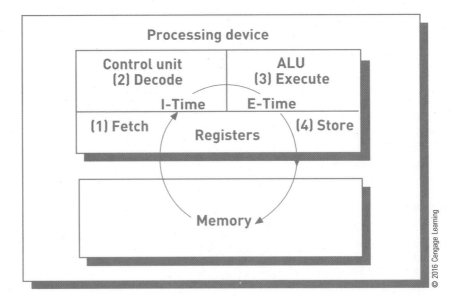

© 2016 Cengage Learning

PROCESSING AND MEMORY DEVICES: POWER, SPEED, AND CAPACITY

The components responsible for processing—the CPU and primary storage—are housed together in the same box or cabinet, called the *system unit*. All other computer system devices, such as the monitor, secondary storage, and keyboard, are linked directly or indirectly into the system unit housing. In this section, we investigate the characteristics of these important devices.

Processing Characteristics and Functions

Because organizations want efficient processing and timely output, they use a variety of measures to gauge processing speed. These measures include the time it takes to complete a machine cycle and clock speed.

Machine Cycle Time

MIPS: Millions of instructions per second, a measure of machine cycle time.

As you've seen, a computer executes an instruction during a machine cycle. The time in which a machine cycle occurs is measured in *nanoseconds* (one-billionth of one second) and *picoseconds* (one-trillionth of one second). Machine cycle time also can be measured by how many instructions are executed in one second. This measure, called MIPS, stands for millions of instructions per second. MIPS is another measure of speed for computer systems of all sizes.

Clock Speed

clock speed: A series of electronic pulses produced at a predetermined rate that affects machine cycle time.

Each CPU produces a series of electronic pulses at a predetermined rate, called the clock speed, which affects machine cycle time. The control unit executes instructions in accordance with the electronic cycle, or pulses of the CPU "clock." Each instruction takes at least the same amount of time as the interval between pulses. The shorter the interval between pulses, the faster each instruction can be executed.

gigahertz (GHz): Billions of cycles per second, a measure of clock speed.

Clock speed is often measured in gigahertz (GHz, billions of cycles per second). Unfortunately, the faster the clock speed of the CPU, the more heat the processor generates. This heat must be dissipated to avoid corrupting the data and instructions the computer is trying to process. Also, CPUs that run at higher temperatures need bigger heat sinks, fans, and other components to eliminate the excess heat. This increases the size and weight of the computing device, whether it is a desktop computer, tablet computer, or smartphone.

Chip designers and manufacturers are exploring various means to avoid heat problems in their new designs. One effective approach is the use of ARM processors. ARM is not a fabricator of computer chips like Advanced Micro Devices (AMD) or Intel. Instead, it creates a design for a family of processors based on Reduced Instruction Set Computing (RISC). RISC processors more quickly execute a small set of simplified instructions compared to complex instruction set computers (CISC), which more slowly execute a larger set of more complex instructions. Its licensees, such as Qualcomm and Nvidia, take those building blocks and design processors with them. Still other companies fabricate the chips under license from ARM. Because RISC processors require fewer transistors to operate, they require less power and generate less heat than standard processors. Thus, ARM processors do not require big heat sinks and fans to remove excess heat, resulting in smaller, lighter, more energy-efficient devices with longer battery life. ARM processors are ideal for use in smartphones and tablet computers.

Manufacturers are also seeking more effective sources of energy as portable devices grow increasingly power hungry. A number of companies are exploring the substitution of fuel cells for lithium ion batteries to provide additional, longer-lasting power. Fuel cells generate electricity by consuming fuel (often methanol), while traditional batteries store electricity and release it through a chemical reaction. A spent fuel cell is replenished in moments by simply refilling its reservoir or by replacing the spent fuel cartridge with a fresh one. Nectar Mobile Power System is developing a portable charger that would be able to fully charge an iPhone every night for two weeks. Its cartridges are filled with butane, which can be taken on airplanes in small amounts.[3] See Figure 3.3.

FIGURE 3.3

Fuel cell

Instead of using lithium ion batteries, companies are exploring the use of fuel cells to provide additional, longer-lasting power in portable devices.

Physical Characteristics of the CPU

Most CPUs are collections of digital circuits imprinted on silicon wafers, or chips, each no bigger than the tip of a pencil eraser. To turn a digital circuit on or off within the CPU, electrical current must flow through a medium from point A to point B. The speed the current travels between points can be increased by either reducing the distance between the points or reducing the resistance of the medium to the electrical current.

Reducing the distance between points has resulted in ever smaller chips, with the circuits packed closer together. Gordon Moore, who would cofound Intel (the largest maker of microprocessor chips) and become its chairman of the board, hypothesized that progress in chip manufacturing ought to make it possible to double the number of transistors (the microscopic on/off switches) on a single chip every two years. The hypothesis became known as **Moore's Law**, and this rule of thumb has become a goal that chip manufacturers have met more or less for more than four decades.

Moore's Law: A hypothesis stating that transistor densities on a single chip will double every two years.

Chip makers have been able to put more transistors on the same size chip while reducing the amount of power required to perform tasks. Furthermore, because the chips are smaller, chip manufacturers can cut more chips from a single silicon wafer and thus reduce the cost per chip. As silicon-based components and computers perform better, they become cheaper to produce and therefore more plentiful, more powerful, and more a part of our everyday lives. This process makes computing devices affordable for an increasing number of people around the world and makes it practical to pack tremendous computing power into the tiniest of devices.

Memory Characteristics and Functions

Primary storage (main memory) is located physically close to the CPU, although not on the CPU chip itself. It provides the CPU with a working storage area for program instructions and data. The chief feature of memory is that it rapidly provides the data and instructions to the CPU.

Storage Capacity

Like the CPU, memory devices contain thousands of circuits imprinted on a silicon chip. Each circuit is either conducting electrical current (on) or not conducting current (off). Data is stored in memory as a combination of on or off circuit states. Usually, 8 bits are used to represent a character, such as the letter *A*. Eight bits together form a **byte (B)**. In most cases, storage capacity is measured in bytes, with 1 byte equivalent to one character of data. The contents of the

byte (B): Eight bits that together represent a single character of data.

Library of Congress, with over 126 million items and 530 miles of bookshelves, would require about 20 petabytes of digital storage. It is estimated that all the words ever spoken by humans represented in text form would equal about 5 exabytes of information.[4] Table 3.1 lists units for measuring computer storage.

TABLE 3.1 Computer storage units

Name	Abbreviation	Number of Bytes
Byte	B	1
Kilobyte	KB	1,000
Megabyte	MB	$1,000^2$
Gigabyte	GB	$1,000^3$
Terabyte	TB	$1,000^4$
Petabyte	PB	$1,000^5$
Exabyte	EB	$1,000^6$
Zettabyte	ZB	$1,000^7$
Yottabyte	YB	$1,000^8$

Types of Memory

random access memory (RAM): A form of memory in which instructions or data can be temporarily stored.

Computer memory can take several forms. Instructions or data can be temporarily stored in and read from random access memory (RAM). As currently designed, RAM chips are volatile storage devices, meaning they lose their contents if the current is turned off or disrupted (as happens in a power surge, brownout, or electrical noise generated by lightning or nearby machines). RAM chips are mounted directly on the computer's main circuit board or in other chips mounted on peripheral cards that plug into the main circuit board. These RAM chips consist of millions of switches that are sensitive to changes in electric current.

RAM comes in many varieties: Static random access memory (SRAM) is byte-addressable storage used for high-speed registers and caches; dynamic random access memory (DRAM) is byte-addressable storage used for the main memory in a computer; and double data rate synchronous dynamic random access memory (DDR SDRAM) is an improved form of DRAM that effectively doubles the rate at which data can be moved in and out of main memory. Other forms of RAM memory include DDR2 SDRAM, DDR3 SDRAM, and DDR4 SDRAM (double data rate fourth-generation synchronous dynamic random access memory).

cache memory: A type of high-speed memory that a processor can access more rapidly than main memory.

Although microprocessor speed has roughly doubled every 24 months over the past decades, memory performance has not kept pace. In effect, memory has become the principal bottleneck to system performance. Cache memory is a type of high-speed memory that a processor can access more rapidly than main memory to help ease this bottleneck. See Figure 3.4. Frequently used data is stored in easily accessible cache memory instead of slower memory such as RAM. Because cache memory holds less data, the CPU can access the desired data and instructions more quickly than when selecting from the larger set in primary storage. Thus, the CPU can execute instructions faster, improving the overall performance of the computer system. Cache memory is available in three forms. The level 1 (L1) cache is on the CPU chip. The level 2 (L2) cache memory can be accessed by the CPU over a high-speed dedicated interface. The latest processors go a step further and place the L2 cache directly on the CPU chip itself and provide high-speed support for a tertiary level 3 (L3) external cache. See Figure 3.5.

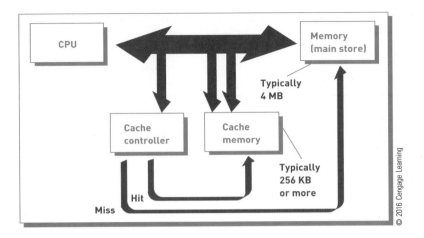

FIGURE 3.4

Cache memory

Processors can access this type of high-speed memory faster than main memory. Located on or near the CPU chip, cache memory works with main memory. A cache controller determines how often the data is used, transfers frequently used data to cache memory, and then deletes the data when it goes out of use.

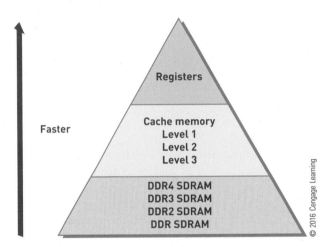

FIGURE 3.5

Relative speed of various types of storage

The closer memory is to the CPU, the faster the CPU can process it.

read-only memory (ROM): A non-volatile form of memory.

Read-only memory (ROM), another type of memory, is nonvolatile, meaning that its contents are not lost if the power is turned off or interrupted. ROM provides permanent storage for data and instructions that do not change, such as programs and data from the computer manufacturer, including the instructions that tell the computer how to start up when power is turned on. ROM memory also comes in many varieties: programmable read-only memory (PROM), which is used to hold data and instructions that can never be changed; erasable programmable read-only memory (EPROM), which is programmable ROM that can be erased and reused; and electrically erasable programmable read-only memory (EEPROM), which is user-modifiable read-only memory that can be erased and reprogrammed repeatedly through the application of higher-than-normal electrical voltage.

Chip manufacturers are competing to develop a nonvolatile memory chip that requires minimal power, offers extremely fast read and write speed, and can store data accurately even after a large number of write-erase cycles. Such a chip could eliminate the need for RAM and simplify and speed up processing. Phase change memory (PCM) is one potential approach to provide such a memory device. PCM employs a specialized glass-like material that can change its physical state, shifting between a low-resistance crystalline state to a high-resistance gaseous state by applying voltage to rearrange the atoms of the material. This technology has been under development for decades and now faces several competing technologies. Micron Technology and Samsung Electronics recently shipped PCM devices for limited applications; however, further improvements are needed to reduce their power consumption and manufacturing costs before they can become broadly used.[5]

Multiprocessing

multiprocessing: The simultaneous execution of two or more instructions at the same time.

Generally, multiprocessing involves the simultaneous execution of two or more instructions at the same time. One form of multiprocessing uses coprocessors. A coprocessor speeds processing by executing specific types of instructions while the CPU works on another processing activity. Coprocessors can be internal or external to the CPU and can have different clock speeds than the CPU. Each type of coprocessor performs a specific function. For example, a math coprocessor chip speeds mathematical calculations, while a graphics coprocessor chip decreases the time it takes to manipulate graphics.

coprocessor: The part of the computer that speeds processing by executing specific types of instructions while the CPU works on another processing activity.

A multicore microprocessor combines two or more independent processors into a single computer so that they share the workload and boost processing speed. In addition, a dual-core processor enables people to perform multiple tasks simultaneously, such as playing a game and burning a CD.

multicore microprocessor: A microprocessor that combines two or more independent processors into a single computer so that they share the workload and improve processing speed.

AMD and Intel are battling for leadership in the multicore processor marketplace, with both companies offering quad-core, six-core, and eight-core CPU chips that can be used to build powerful desktop computers. Apple has redesigned its Mac Pro computer based on one 12-core Intel Xeon E5 CPU chip.[6] A current problem with multicore processors is that as more cores are added, the power consumption increases faster than processing performance. For example, a 16-core processor would drain the life out of a typical smartphone battery in just three hours.[7]

The toughest challenge in designing a processor for a smartphone or tablet is balancing performance and power consumption. Many processor designs rely on a multiple-core configuration ARM calls big.LITTLE that includes high clock speed, powerful cores, and slower, more energy-efficient cores. The powerful cores are used when high performance is needed, such as for gaming. The more energy-efficient cores are used for less taxing tasks such as Web browsing and email. This approach provides sufficient computing power to get the job done, but reduces heating problems and consequentially the drain on the battery to run a cooling fan. Samsung's Galaxy S4 smartphone is powered by eight CPU cores using the big.LITTLE design.[8]

When selecting a CPU, organizations must balance the benefits of processing speed with energy requirements, size, and cost. CPUs with faster clock speeds and shorter machine cycle times require more energy to dissipate the heat generated by the CPU and are bulkier and more expensive than slower ones.

Parallel Computing

parallel computing: The simultaneous execution of the same task on multiple processors to obtain results faster.

Parallel computing is the simultaneous execution of the same task on multiple processors to obtain results faster. Systems with thousands of such processors are known as massively parallel processing systems, a form of multiprocessing that speeds processing by linking hundreds or thousands of processors to operate at the same time, or in parallel, with each processor having its own bus, memory, disks, copy of the operating system, and applications. The processors might communicate with one another to coordinate when executing a computer program, or they might run independently of one another but under the direction of another processor that distributes the work to the various processors and collects their results. The dual-core processors mentioned earlier are a simple form of parallel computing.

massively parallel processing system: A system that speeds processing by linking hundreds or thousands of processors to operate at the same time, or in parallel, with each processor having its own bus, memory, disks, copy of the operating system, and applications.

The most frequent uses for parallel computing include modeling, simulation, and analyzing large amounts of data. For example, parallel computing is used in medicine to develop new imaging systems that complete ultrasound scans in less time with greater accuracy, enabling doctors to provide better, more timely diagnosis to patients. Instead of building physical models of new products, engineers can create virtual models and use parallel computing to test how the products work and then change design elements and materials as needed. The Blue Waters supercomputer is one of the most powerful computers in the world and can perform 1 quadrillion computations per second. Its peak speed is over 3 million times faster than the typical laptop computer. The computer is an example of a massively parallel processing system. It employs over 26,000 processors working together to support scientific and engineering research projects from predicting the behavior of complex biological systems to the simulation of the evolution of the cosmos.[9]

grid computing: The use of a collection of computers, often owned by multiple individuals or organizations, to work in a coordinated manner to solve a common problem.

Grid computing is the use of a collection of computers, often owned by multiple individuals or organizations, to work in a coordinated manner to solve a common problem. Grid computing is a low-cost approach to parallel computing. The grid can include dozens, hundreds, or even thousands of computers that run collectively to solve extremely large processing problems. Key to the success of grid computing is a central server that acts as the grid leader and traffic monitor. This controlling server divides the computing task into subtasks and assigns the work to computers on the grid that have (at least temporarily) surplus processing power. The central server also monitors the processing, and if a member of the grid fails to complete a subtask, the server restarts or reassigns the task. When all the subtasks are completed, the controlling server combines the results and advances to the next task until the whole job is completed.

The World Community Grid is an ongoing project dedicated to building the world's largest public computing grid to tackle projects that benefit humanity. The effort is funded and operated by IBM and includes over 450 organizations and nearly 70,000 registered users. Participants download and install a small program on their computer so that during the computer's idle time, it can request data from the World Community Grid's server, perform computations on this data, and send the results back to the server. Projects running on the World Community Grid include analyzing various aspects of AIDS, cancer, clean water, malaria, and rice crop yields, and identifying compounds that are promising to solar power developers.[10,11]

SECONDARY STORAGE

Storing data safely and effectively is critical to an organization's success. Driven by many factors—such as needing to retain more data longer to meet government regulatory concerns, storing new forms of digital data such as audio and video, and keeping systems running under the onslaught of increasing volumes of email—the world's information is more than doubling every two years. Nearly 6 zettabytes (6×10^{21} bytes) of information was created and stored in 2013 alone.[12] It is mainly unstructured digital content such as video, audio, and image objects that is fueling this growth. For example, the Australian Square Kilometre Array Pathfinder and the Murchison Widefield Array are radio telescope astronomy projects that will probe the depth of the universe. When these projects come online, they will generate 8 petabytes of unstructured data each year.[13]

secondary storage: Devices that store large amounts of data, instructions, and information more permanently than allowed with main memory.

For most organizations, the best overall data storage solution is likely a combination of different secondary storage options that can store large amounts of data, instructions, and information more permanently than allowed with main memory. Compared with memory, secondary storage offers the advantages of nonvolatility, greater capacity, and greater economy. On a cost-per-megabyte basis, secondary storage is considerably less expensive than primary memory. See Table 3.2. The selection of secondary storage media and devices requires understanding their primary characteristics: access method, capacity, and portability.

TABLE **3.2** Cost comparison for various forms of storage

Data Storage Type	Cost Per GB			
	2006	**2009**	**2011**	**2013**
1 TB desktop external hard drive	DNA	$0.12	$0.09	$0.10
25 GB rewritable Blu-ray disc	DNA	$0.44	$0.11	$0.30
500 GB portable hard drive	DNA	$0.23	$0.15	$0.12
72 GB DAT 72 data cartridge	$0.77	$0.21	$0.24	$0.26
50 4.7 GB DVD+R discs	$5.32	$0.09	$0.31	$0.07
8 GB flash drive	$99.99	$2.50	$2.48	$1.25
9.1 GB write-once, read-many optical disk	$10.51	$9.99	$8.12	$7.14
2 GB DDR2 SDRAM computer memory upgrade	$138.46	$25.00	$15.95	$8.00

Source: Office Depot Web site, *www.officedepot.com*, February 5, 2006, December 2009, October 2011, and October 2013.
DNA = data not available.

As with other computer system components, the access methods, storage capacities, and portability required of secondary storage media are determined by the business requirements that must be met. An objective of a credit card company might be to rapidly retrieve stored customer data to approve consumer purchases. In this case, a fast access method is critical. In other cases, such as equipping the Coca-Cola field salesforce with smartphones, portability and ruggedness might be major considerations in selecting and using secondary storage media and devices.

In addition to cost, capacity, portability, and ruggedness, organizations must address security issues to allow only authorized people to access sensitive data and critical programs. Because the data and programs kept on secondary storage devices are so critical to most organizations, all of these issues merit careful consideration.

Access Methods

sequential access: A retrieval method in which data must be accessed in the order in which it is stored.

Data and information access can be either sequential or direct. **Sequential access** means that data must be accessed in the order in which it is stored. For example, inventory data might be stored sequentially by part number, such as 100, 101, and 102. If you want to retrieve information on part number 125, you must read and discard all the data relating to parts 001 through 124.

direct access: A retrieval method in which data can be retrieved without the need to read and discard other data.

Direct access means that data can be retrieved directly without the need to pass by other data in sequence. With direct access, it is possible to go directly to and access the needed data—for example, part number 125—without having to read through parts 001 through 124. For this reason, direct access is usually faster than sequential access. The devices used only to access secondary storage data sequentially are called **sequential access storage devices (SASDs)**; those used for direct access are called **direct access storage devices (DASDs)**.

sequential access storage device (SASD): A device used to sequentially access secondary storage data.

direct access storage device (DASD): A device used for direct access of secondary storage data.

Secondary Storage Devices

Secondary data storage is not directly accessible by the CPU. Instead, computers usually use input/output channels to access secondary storage and transfer the desired data using intermediate areas in primary storage. The most common forms of secondary storage devices are magnetic, optical, and solid state.

Magnetic Secondary Storage Devices

magnetic tape: A type of sequential secondary storage medium, now used primarily for storing backups of critical organizational data in the event of a disaster.

Magnetic storage uses tape or disk devices covered with a thin magnetic coating that enables data to be stored as magnetic particles. **Magnetic tape** is a type of sequential secondary storage medium, which is frequently used for storing backups of critical organizational data in the event of a disaster.

Examples of tape storage devices include cassettes and cartridges measuring a few millimeters in diameter, requiring very little storage space. Magnetic tape has been used as storage media since the time of the earliest computers, such as the 1951 Univac computer.[14] Continuing advancements have kept magnetic tape as a viable storage medium. For example, IBM and FUJIFILM Corporation of Japan have recorded data onto an advanced prototype tape at a density of 29.5 billion bits per square inch, about 39 times denser than current standard magnetic tape products. This breakthrough could lead to tape systems that require much less space and operate at a lower cost.[15]

Over 380 petabytes of magnetic tape storage supports the Blue Waters supercomputer mentioned previously.[16] Other supercomputers use robotic tape backup systems. See Figure 3.6.

Courtesy of Deutsches Klimarechenzentrum GmbH

FIGURE 3.6

Robotic tape backup system

The National Center for Atmospheric Research uses a robotic tape backup system to back up the supercomputer that solves the world's most computationally intensive climate modeling problems.

hard disk drive (HDD): A direct access storage device used to store and retrieve data from rapidly rotating disks coated with magnetic material.

A **hard disk drive (HDD)** is a direct access storage device used to store and retrieve data from rapidly rotating disks coated with magnetic material. A hard disk represents bits of data with small magnetized areas and uses a read/write head to go directly to the desired piece of data. Because direct access allows fast data retrieval, this type of storage is used by organizations that need to respond quickly to customer requests, such as airlines and credit card firms. For example, if a manager needs information on the credit history of a customer or the seat availability on a particular flight, the information can be obtained in seconds if the data is stored on a direct-access hard disk drive. Hard disk drives vary widely in capacity and portability. See Figure 3.7.

FIGURE 3.7

Hard disk drive

A hard disk drive provides direct access to stored data. The read/write head can move directly to the location of a desired piece of data, dramatically reducing access times compared to magnetic tape.

© 29mokara/Shutterstock.com

IBM recently built a huge data repository consisting of 200,000 conventional HDDs working together to provide a storage capacity of 120 petabytes—large enough to hold 60 copies of the 150 billion pages needed to back up the Web. An unnamed client is using the storage device with a supercomputer to perform detailed simulations of real-world events, such as weather forecasts, seismic processing for the petroleum industry, and molecular studies of genomes or proteins.[17]

Putting an organization's data online involves a serious business risk—the loss of critical data can put a corporation out of business. The concern is that the most critical mechanical components inside a HDD storage device—the disk drives, the fans, and read/write heads—can fail. Thus, organizations now require that their data storage devices be fault tolerant, that is, they can continue with little or no loss of performance if one or more key components fail.

redundant array of independent/ inexpensive disks (RAID): A method of storing data that generates extra bits of data from existing data, allowing the system to create a "reconstruction map" so that if a hard drive fails, the system can rebuild lost data.

A redundant array of independent/inexpensive disks (RAID) is a method of storing data that generates extra bits of data from existing data, allowing the system to create a "reconstruction map" so that if a hard drive fails, it can rebuild lost data. With this approach, data can be split and stored on different physical disk drives using a technique called *striping* to evenly distribute the data. RAID technology has been applied to storage systems to improve system performance and reliability.

disk mirroring: A process of storing data that provides an exact copy that protects users fully in the event of data loss.

RAID can be implemented in several ways. RAID 1 subsystems duplicate data on the hard drives. This process, called disk mirroring, provides an exact copy that protects users fully in the event of data loss. However, to keep complete duplicates of current backups, organizations need to double the amount of their storage capacity. Other RAID methods are less expensive because they duplicate only part of the data, allowing storage managers to minimize the amount of extra disk space they must purchase to protect data.

Patients of the Gila Regional Medical Center in Silver City, New Mexico, come to the radiology department for x-rays, ultrasounds, CAT scans, and MRIs. These scans comprised some 600 gigabytes of data stored on 80 double-sided DVDs. However, this data storage approach was fast running out of capacity and would require moving some of the DVDs off-site to make room for additional DVDs. Rather than continue using DVDs, the medical center upgraded to RAID storage devices to provide the radiologists with fast access to the complete set of all medical images. RAID also provided additional backup capabilities to reduce the risk of any lost images.[18]

virtual tape: A storage device for less frequently needed data so that it appears to be stored entirely on tape cartridges, although some parts of it might actually be located on faster hard disks.

Virtual tape is a storage technology for less frequently needed data so that it appears to be stored entirely on tape cartridges, although some parts might actually be located on faster hard disks. The software associated with a virtual tape system is sometimes called a *virtual tape server*. Virtual tape can be used with a sophisticated storage-management system that moves data to slower but less costly forms of storage media as people use the data less often. Virtual tape technology can decrease data access time, lower the total cost of ownership, and reduce the amount of floor space consumed by tape operations.

Optical Secondary Storage Devices

optical storage device: A form of data storage that uses lasers to read and write data.

An optical storage device uses special lasers to read and write data. The lasers record data by physically burning pits in the disk. Data is directly accessed from the disc by an optical disc device, which operates much like a compact disc player. This optical disc device uses a low-power laser that measures the difference in reflected light caused by a pit (or lack thereof) on the disc.

compact disc read-only memory (CD-ROM): A common form of optical disc on which data cannot be modified once it has been recorded.

A common optical storage device is the compact disc read-only memory (CD-ROM) with a storage capacity of 740 MB of data. After data is recorded on a CD-ROM, it cannot be modified—the disc is "read-only." A CD burner, the informal name for a CD recorder, is a device that can record data to a compact disc. *CD-recordable* (*CD-R*) and *CD-rewritable* (*CD-RW*) are the two most common types of drives that can write CDs, either once (in the case of CD-R) or repeatedly (in the case of CD-RW). CD-rewritable (CD-RW) technology allows PC users to back up data on CDs.

A **digital video disc (DVD)** looks like a CD but can store about 135 minutes of digital video or several gigabytes of data. See Figure 3.8. Software, video games, and movies are often stored and distributed on DVDs. At a data transfer rate of 1.352 MB per second, the access speed of a DVD drive is faster than that of the typical CD-ROM drive.

digital video disc (DVD): A secondary storage device that looks similar to a CD ROM but with greater storage capacity and faster data transfer rate.

© Plus69/Shutterstock.com

FIGURE 3.8

Digital video discs and player

DVDs look like CDs but have a greater storage capacity and can transfer data at a faster rate.

DVDs have replaced recordable and rewritable CD discs (CD-R and CD-RW) as the preferred format for sharing movies and photos. Whereas a CD can hold about 740 MB of data, a single-sided DVD can hold 4.7 GB, with double-sided DVDs having a capacity of 9.4 GB. Several types of recorders and discs are currently in use. Recordings can be made on record-once discs (DVD-R and DVD+R) or on rewritable discs (DVD-RW, DVD+RW, and DVD-RAM). Not all types of rewritable DVDs are compatible with other types.

The Blu-ray high-definition video disc format based on blue laser technology stores at least three times as much data as a DVD. The primary use for this new technology is in home entertainment equipment to store high-definition video, though this format can also store computer data. A dual-layer Blu-ray disk can store 50 GB of data in a dual-layer format.[19]

While DVD and Blu-ray discs are commonly used to store data, the discs can become unreliable over time as they are exposed to light, humidity, and chemical changes inside the disk itself. As a result, the data stored on such disks can become unreadable over time. Thus, companies such as Millenniata are developing long-lasting DVD and Blu-ray technology.[20]

The Holographic Versatile Disc (HVD) is an advanced optical disc technology that can store up to 3.9 terabytes, roughly 75–150 times more data than the Blu-ray optical disc system although an HVD is the same size and shape as a regular DVD. One HVD approach records data through the depth of the storage media in three dimensions by splitting a laser beam in two—the signal beam carries the data, and the reference beam positions where the data is written and read. It is believed that HVD can provide safe storage without degradation for 50 years, far exceeding most current storage approaches.[21]

Numerous scientists are experimenting with the use of DNA molecules to store vast amounts of data for long periods of time. DNA molecules consist of four chemicals connected end-to-end, similar to the sequences of ones and zeroes that computers use to represent data. A single gram of DNA is capable of storing 2.2 million gigabytes of data, equivalent to the storage capacity of 468,000 DVDs. DNA is stable for thousands of years, meaning that archival data could be stored safely and reliably. At this time, the cost of synthesizing DNA to store data and the cost of decoding the data stored in DNA are prohibitively expensive unless the data needs to be archived for at least 600 years. It is likely to be a decade or more before the technology evolves to where DNA data storage is practical.[22]

Solid State Secondary Storage Devices

Solid state storage devices (SSDs) store data in memory chips rather than hard disk drives or optical media. These memory chips require less power and provide much faster data access than magnetic data storage devices. In addition, SSDs have no moving parts, so they are less fragile than hard disk drives. All these factors make the SSD a preferred choice over hard disk drives for portable computers.

A universal serial bus (USB) flash drive is one example of a commonly used SSD. See Figure 3.9. USB flash drives are external to the computer and are removable and rewritable. Most weigh less than an ounce and can provide a wide range of storage capacity. Samsung announced solid state storage disks available with capacities from 120 GB to 1,000 GB.[23]

© Zyphyrus/Shutterstock.com

FIGURE 3.9

Flash drive

Flash drives are solid state storage devices.

Infrastructure as a Service (IaaS): A computing model in which an organization outsources the equipment used to support its business operations, including storage, hardware, servers, and networking components, and the service provider owns the equipment and is responsible for housing, running, and maintaining it.

Infrastructure as a Service (IaaS) is a computing model in which an organization outsources the equipment used to support its business operations, including storage, hardware, servers, and networking components. The service provider owns the equipment and is responsible for housing, running, and maintaining it. Cloud Sigma, a European IaaS provider, has announced that its cloud storage will operate completely on solid state drives. One analyst believes that offering an all SSD service provides the firm a competitive advantage because of much improved performance by requiring less CPU and RAM capacity while at the same time speeding up access to data as compared to HDD storage systems.[24]

Enterprise Storage Options

Businesses need to store large amounts of data created throughout an organization. Such large secondary storage is called *enterprise storage* and comes in three forms: attached storage, network-attached storage (NAS), and storage area networks (SANs).

Attached Storage

Attached storage methods include all the options just discussed—tape, hard disk drives including RAID devices, virtual tape, optical devices, and solid state secondary storage devices—which are connected directly to a single computer. Attached storage methods, though simple and cost effective for single users and small groups, do not allow systems to share storage, and they make it difficult to back up data.

Because of the limitations of attached storage, firms are turning to network-attached storage (NAS) and storage area networks (SANs). These alternatives enable an organization to share data storage resources among a much larger number of computers and users, resulting in improved storage efficiency and greater cost effectiveness. In addition, they simplify data backup and reduce the risk of downtime. Nearly one-third of system downtime is a direct result of data storage failures, so eliminating storage problems as a cause of downtime is a major advantage.

Network-Attached Storage

**network-attached storage
(NAS):** A hard disk drive storage
device that is set up with its own network address and provides file-based
storage services to other devices on
the network.

Network-attached storage (NAS) is a hard disk drive storage device that is set up with its own network address and provides file-based storage services to other devices on the network. Figure 3.10 shows a NAS storage device. NAS includes software to manage storage access and file management, relieving the users' computers of those tasks. The result is that both application software and files can be served faster because they are not competing for the same processor resources. Computer users can share and access the same information, even if they are using different types of computers. Common applications for NAS include consolidated storage, Internet and e-commerce applications, and digital media.

Courtesy of Seagate Technology LLC 2016

FIGURE **3.10**

NAS storage device

The Seagate BlackArmor NAS 440 has a capacity of 4 to 12 terabytes at a cost of less than $.27 per GB.

AllPopArt is a company that enables its customers to have photos turned into pop art format. A customer sends in a photo and selects from a variety of art styles. The AllPopArt team of illustrators transforms the photo using the art style requested by the customer. Within a few days, the customer receives a proof and can request as many changes as needed. In another 10 days or so, the customers receive their final artwork. Going from initial photo to final artwork takes a lot of teamwork and sharing of photos and proofs. The AllPopArt team of illustrators, designers, customer service reps, and printing agents needed file-sharing capabilities between Windows and Mac computers and required easy and fast remote access. They chose to implement an on-site NAS solution to meet their business needs.[25]

Storage Area Networks

storage area network (SAN):
A high-speed, special-purpose network
that integrates different types of data
storage devices (e.g., hard disk drives,
magnetic tape, solid state secondary
storage devices) into a single storage
system and connects that to computing
resources across an entire
organization.

A storage area network (SAN) is a high-speed, special-purpose network that integrates different types of data storage devices (e.g., hard disk drives, magnetic tape, solid state secondary storage devices) into a single storage system and connects that to computing resources across an entire organization. See Figure 3.11. SANs can provide important capabilities such as disk mirroring, data backup and restore, data archiving, data migration from one storage device to another, and the sharing of data among computing devices connected to the network.

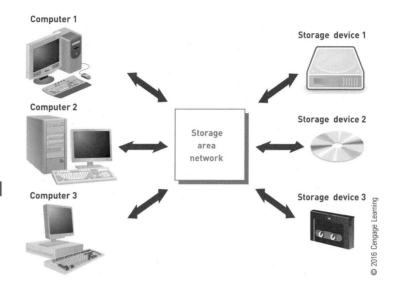

FIGURE 3.11

Storage area network

A SAN provides high-speed connections among data storage devices and computers over a network.

Using a SAN, an organization can centralize the people, policies, procedures, and practices for managing storage, and a data storage manager can apply the data consistently across an enterprise. This centralization eliminates inconsistent treatment of data by different system administrators and users, providing efficient and cost-effective data storage practices.

Revlon is a global manufacturer and seller of beauty products in over 100 countries on six continents. CIO David Giambruno implemented a SAN to meet his organization's data storage needs in a simple, standard manner. The SAN has helped Revlon reduce the time to deliver projects and reduced hardware investment costs by more than $70 million compared to other storage solutions.[26]

A fundamental difference between NAS and SAN is that NAS uses file input/output, which defines data as complete containers of information, while SAN deals with block input/output, which is based on subsets of data smaller than a file. SAN manufacturers include EMC, Hitachi Data Systems Corporation, Xiotech, and IBM.

As organizations set up large-scale SAN systems, they use more computers and network connections than in a NAS environment, and consequently, the network becomes difficult to manage. In response, software tools designed to automate storage using previously defined policies are finding a place in the enterprise. Known as policy-based storage management, the software products from industry leaders such as Veritas Software Corporation, Legato Systems, EMC, and IBM automatically allocate storage space to users, balance the loads on servers and disks, and reroute network traffic when systems go down—all based on policies set up by system administrators.

policy-based storage management: Automation of storage using previously defined policies.

The trend in secondary storage is toward higher capacity, increased portability, and automated storage management. Organizations should select a type of storage based on their needs and resources. In general, storing large amounts of data and information and providing users with quick access make an organization more efficient.

Storage as a Service

storage as a service: Storage as a service is a data storage model where a data storage service provider rents space to individuals and organizations.

Storage as a service is a data storage model in which a data storage service provider rents space to people and organizations. Users access their rented data storage via the Internet. Such a service enables the users to store and back up their data without requiring a major investment to create and maintain their own data storage infrastructure. Businesses can also choose pay-per-use services, where they rent space on massive storage devices housed either at a service provider (such as Hewlett-Packard or IBM) or on the customer's premises, paying only for the amount of storage they use. This approach is sensible for organizations with wildly fluctuating storage needs, such as those involved in the testing of new drugs or in developing software.

Individuals and organizations must be able to access data, documents, databases, presentations, and spreadsheets from anywhere with any sort of Internet-enabled device such as a smartphone, tablet computer, or laptop. In response to this need, numerous cloud-based storage services have emerged, including Amazon's Elastic Compute Cloud, Apple iCloud, Dropbox, Google Drive, Microsoft SkyDrive, and Mozy. These services provide data storage at a rate of $2 or less per gigabyte a year. However, some storage services will not work with the operating systems on some computing devices, so consumers should make sure that their smartphone, tablet, or other device is compatible before subscribing.[27] Amazon's Simple Storage Service allows uploading, storage, and downloading of practically any file or object up to 5 gigabytes (5 GB). The subscriber data is stored on redundant servers across multiple data centers. Subscribers can choose to label their data private or make it publicly accessible. Users can also elect to encrypt data prior to storage.

A Mozy customer who had his laptop stolen was able to provide police with photos of the thief because Mozy continued to back up data after the laptop was stolen, including the thief's photos and documents. The customer accessed the photos from his online storage site, and police captured the thief and returned the laptop.[28]

INPUT AND OUTPUT DEVICES: THE GATEWAY TO COMPUTER SYSTEMS

Your first experience with computers is usually through input and output devices. These devices are the gateways to the computer system—you use them to provide data and instructions to the computer and receive results from it. Input and output devices are part of a computer's user interface, which includes other hardware devices and software that allow you to interact with a computer system.

As with other computer system components, an organization should keep its business goals in mind when selecting input and output devices. For example, many restaurant chains use handheld input devices or computerized terminals that let food servers enter orders and transfer them to the kitchen efficiently and accurately. These systems have also cut costs by helping track inventory and market to customers.

Characteristics and Functionality

In general, businesses want input devices that let them accurately and rapidly enter data into a computer system, and they want output devices that let them produce timely results. Some organizations have very specific needs for input and output, requiring devices that perform specific functions. The more specialized the application, the more specialized the associated system input and output devices.

The Nature of Data

Getting data into the computer—input—often requires transferring human-readable data, such as a sales order, into the computer system. "Human-readable" means data that people can read and understand. The temperature registered on a thermometer is an example of human-readable data. An example of machine-readable data is the universal bar code on many grocery and retail items which indicates the stock keeping identification number for that item. To the human eye, the universal bar code is unintelligible and looks like a series of vertical bars of varying thicknesses. Some data can be read by people and machines, such as magnetic ink on bank checks. Usually, people begin the input process by organizing human-readable data and transforming it into machine-readable data. Every keystroke on a keyboard, for example, turns a letter symbol of a human language into a digital code that the machine can manipulate.

Data Entry and Input

data entry: Converting human-readable data into a machine-readable form.

data input: Transferring machine-readable data into the system.

Getting data into the computer system is a two-stage process. First, the human-readable data is converted into a machine-readable form through data entry. The second stage involves transferring the machine-readable data into the system. This is data input.

Today, many companies are using online data entry and input: They communicate and transfer data to computer devices directly connected to the computer system. Online data entry and input place data into the computer system in a matter of seconds. Organizations in many industries require the instantaneous updating offered by this approach. For example, when ticket agents enter a request for concert tickets, they can use online data entry and input to record the request as soon as it is made. Ticket agents at other terminals can then access this data to make a seating check before they process another request.

Source Data Automation

source data automation: Capturing and editing data where it is initially created and in a form that can be directly entered into a computer, thus ensuring accuracy and timeliness.

Regardless of how data gets into the computer, it should be captured and edited at its source. Source data automation involves capturing and editing data where it is originally created and in a form that can be directly entered into a computer, thus ensuring accuracy and timeliness. For example, using source data automation, salespeople enter sales orders into the computer at the time and place they take the orders. Any errors can be detected and corrected immediately. If an item is temporarily out of stock, the salesperson can discuss options with the customer. Prior to source data automation, orders were written on paper and entered into the computer later (usually by a clerk, not by the person who took the order). Often the handwritten information wasn't legible or, worse yet, got lost. If problems occurred during data entry, the clerk had to contact the salesperson or the customer to "recapture" the data needed for order entry, leading to further delays and customer dissatisfaction.

Input Devices

Data entry and input devices come in many forms. They range from special-purpose devices that capture specific types of data to more general-purpose input devices. Some of the special-purpose data entry and input devices are discussed later in this chapter. First, we focus on devices used to enter and input general types of data, including text, audio, images, and video for personal computers.

Common Personal Computer Input Devices

A keyboard and a computer mouse are the most common devices used for entry and input of data, such as characters, text, and basic commands. Some companies manufacture keyboards that are more comfortable, more easily adjusted, and faster to use than standard keyboards. These ergonomic keyboards, such as the split keyboard, are designed to avoid wrist and hand injuries caused by hours of typing. Other keyboards include touchpads that let you enter sketches on the touchpad while still using keys to enter text. Other innovations are wireless mice and keyboards, which keep a physical desktop free from clutter. See Figure 3.12.

You use a computer mouse to point to and click symbols, icons, menus, and commands on the screen. The computer takes a number of actions in response, such as entering data into the computer system.

FIGURE **3.12**

Drawing pad and integrated keyboard

A drawing pad and integrated keyboard can replace a traditional keyboard and mouse for input.

speech-recognition technology: Input devices that recognize human speech.

Speech-Recognition Technology

Using **speech-recognition technology**, the computer can interpret human speech as an alternative means of providing data or instructions. The most basic systems are designed to support a limited conversation on a fixed topic. For example, your insurance provider may employ a speech-recognition system to support calls to its billing department. The scope of the conversation is very limited, and the caller is guided to make one of a few possible and very distinct responses. For example, a typical prompt is "Do you wish to inquire about your monthly bill or make a payment?" More advanced systems can recognize continuous speech and convert it to text such as in closed-caption live TV broadcasts, sometimes with amusing results when key words are not properly converted to text.

Maxwell Winward, one of the top law firms in the United Kingdom, employs speech-recognition technology to convert its attorneys' dictation directly into text, thus eliminating workflow bottlenecks and freeing up support personnel to undertake a broader range of work.[29]

Motion-Sensing Input Devices

The major video game makers Nintendo, Microsoft, and PlayStation have come out with game controllers based on motion-sensing input devices. These manufacturers hope that their motion-sensing input devices will broaden their user base beyond the typical gamer and increase their market share. However, such input devices may also prove useful in the operation of business information systems.

The Wii Remote is the primary controller for Nintendo's Wii console. It can sense motion in all three dimensions and has an optical sensor that enables it to determine where the Wii Remote is pointing. This allows the user to interact with and manipulate items on the video screen via gestures and pointing.

Kinect is a motion-sensing input device that enables the user to control the Microsoft Xbox as well as computers running the Windows operating system. The sensor is a horizontal bar positioned lengthwise above or below the video display. It includes a Webcam-style device that interprets the user's hand gestures as instructions to quickly swipe through home screens and apps.

PlayStation Move is the motion-sensing game controller from Sony Computer Entertainment. It employs a handheld motion controller wand with sensors that detect its motion and a Webcam to track its position.

Digital Cameras

digital camera: An input device used with a PC to record and store images and video in digital form.

Digital cameras record and store images or video in digital form, so when you take pictures, the images are electronically stored in the camera. You can download the images to a computer either directly or transfer them by using a flash memory card. After you store the images on the computer's hard disk, you can edit and print them, send them to another location, or paste them into another application. This digital format saves time and money by eliminating the need to process film in order to share photos. For example, you can download a photo of your project team captured by a digital camera and then post it on a Web site or paste it into a project status report. Digital cameras have eclipsed film cameras used by professional photographers for photo quality and features such as zoom, flash, exposure controls, special effects, and even video-capture capabilities. With the right software, you can add sound and handwriting to the photo. Many computers, smartphones, and even cell phones come equipped with a digital camera to enable their users to place video calls and take pictures and videos.

Canon, Casio, Nikon, Olympus, Panasonic, Pentax, Sony, and other camera manufacturers offer full-featured, high-resolution digital camera models at prices ranging from $150 to $3,500. Some manufacturers offer pocket-sized camcorders for less than $100.

Scanning Devices

Scanning devices capture image and character data. A page scanner is like a copy machine. You either insert a page into the scanner or place it face down on the glass plate of the scanner and then scan it. With a handheld scanner, you manually move or roll the scanning device over the image you want to scan. Both page and handheld scanners can convert monochrome or color pictures, forms, text, and other images into machine-readable digits. Considering that U.S. enterprises generate an estimated 1 billion pieces of paper daily, many companies are looking to scanning devices to help them manage their documents and reduce the high cost of using and processing paper.

The NeatReceipt filing system is a compact, portable scanner and associated software that enable the user to scan business cards and convert them into digital contacts. NeatReceipt can also scan receipts to convert them into records of vendors and amounts that can be used for tax preparation.[30]

Optical Data Readers

You can also use a special scanning device called an *optical data reader* to scan documents. The two categories of optical data readers are optical mark recognition (OMR) and optical character recognition (OCR). You use OMR readers for grading tests and other purposes such as scanning forms. With this technology, you use pencils to fill in bubbles or check boxes on OMR paper, which is also called a "mark sense form." OMR systems are used in standardized tests, including the SAT and GMAT tests, and to record votes in elections. In contrast, most OCR readers use reflected light to recognize and scan various machine-generated characters. With special software, OCR readers can also convert handwritten or typed documents into digital data. After data is entered, it can be shared, modified, and distributed to the desired recipients.

Traditionally, you had to use a special OCR scanner device to create an image of the characters to be converted and then use expensive OCR software to convert that image into text. It is now possible to complete this process using the camera in an Android smartphone or tablet computer. Once the image is stored on the camera or tablet, you use the Google Drive app for Android to copy the image to Google Drive where Google's software and servers can do the OCR conversion for you at no cost.

Magnetic Ink Character Recognition (MICR) Devices

In the 1950s, the banking industry became swamped with paper checks, loan applications, bank statements, and so on. The result was the development of magnetic ink character recognition (MICR), a system for reading banking data quickly. With MICR, data is placed on the bottom of a check or other form using a special magnetic ink. Using a special character set, data printed with this ink is readable by people and computers. See Figure 3.13.

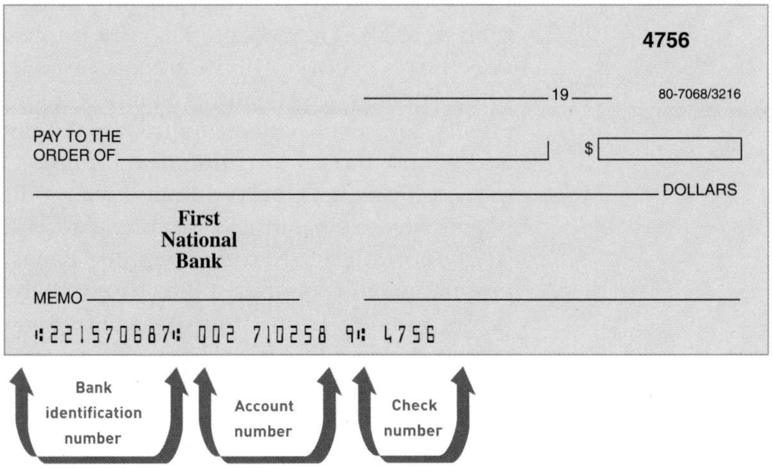

FIGURE 3.13

MICR device

Magnetic ink character recognition technology codes data on the bottom of a check or other form using special magnetic ink, which is readable by people and computers. For an example, look at the bottom of a bank check.

magnetic stripe card: A type of card that stores a limited amount of data by modifying the magnetism of tiny iron-based particles contained in a band on the card.

Magnetic Stripe Cards

A magnetic stripe card stores a limited amount of data by modifying the magnetism of tiny iron-based particles contained in a band on the card. The magnetic stripe is read by physically swiping the card at a terminal. For this reason, such cards are called contact cards. Magnetic stripes are commonly used in credit cards, transportation tickets, and driver's licenses.

Magnetic stripe technology is in wide use in the U.S. credit card industry. The data encoded on the magnetic stripe on the back of the card is read by swiping the card past a magnetic reading head. To protect the consumer, businesses in the United States have invested in extensive computer networks for verifying and processing this data. Software at the point-of-sale (POS) terminal automatically dials a stored telephone number to call an acquirer, an organization that collects credit-authentication requests from merchants and provides the merchants with a payment guarantee. When the acquirer company receives the credit-card authentication request, it checks the transaction for validity by reading the card number, expiration date, and credit card limit recorded on the magnetic stripe. If everything checks out, the authorization is granted. Unfortunately, the magnetic stripe is not really a secure place for sensitive consumer information. The data on the stripe can be read, written, deleted, or changed with easily obtainable hardware and software.

smart cards: Credit cards embedded with computer chips containing key consumer and account data; cardholders must either enter their pin (chip-and-PIN) or sign (chip-and-sign) for each transaction to be approved.

Smart Cards

To better protect the consumer and to avoid setting up and operating expensive computer networks, most European countries use smart card technology. Smart cards are embedded with computer chips containing key consumer and account data. Cardholders must either enter their pin (chip-and-PIN) or sign (chip-and-sign) for each transaction to be approved. The smart cards require different terminals from those used for magnetic stripe cards. All the information needed for authorization is contained in the chip or is captured at the point-of-sale. With smart cards, merchants do not need to send data over networks to obtain authorization.[31]

Although credit card fraud is a problem in the United States, credit card issuers cannot force merchants to invest in the new terminals required for smart cards. As a result, deployment of this technology is lagging in the United States. A few dozen U.S. credit card issuers employ this technology, including select cards from American Express, Bank of America, Chase,

Citibank, and U.S. Bank; however, only a few U.S. merchants are capable of accepting these cards.[32]

Contactless Payment Cards

contactless payment card: A card with an embedded chip that only needs to be held close to a terminal to transfer its data; no PIN number needs to be entered.

Contactless payment cards contain an embedded chip and antenna that enables the consumer to simply hold the card close to a terminal to transfer the data necessary to make a payment. Typically, no signature or PIN entry is required for purchases less than $25, making transactions speedier than payments made by conventional credit or debit card or even cash. Contactless payment cards are ideal in situations where the consumer must make a fast payment, such as when boarding a form of mass transportation. It is estimated that over 32 million people use contactless payment cards in Britain.[33] Some observers are concerned that it is relatively easy to scan details from contactless cards using kits available for less than $75.[34] American Express ExpressPay, ExonMobile SpeedPass, MasterCard PayPass, and Visa PayWave are contactless payment cards used in the United States.

Point-of-Sale Devices

point-of-sale (POS) device: A terminal used to enter data into the computer system.

Point-of-sale (POS) devices are terminals used to capture data. They are frequently used in retail operations to enter sales information into the computer system. The POS device then computes the total charges, including tax. In medical settings, POS devices are often used for remote monitoring in hospitals, clinics, laboratories, doctors' offices, and patients' homes. With network-enabled POS equipment, medical professionals can instantly get an update on the patient's condition from anywhere at any time via a network or the Internet. POS devices use various types of input and output devices, such as keyboards, bar-code readers, scanning devices, printers, and screens. Much of the money that businesses spend on computer technology involves POS devices. Figure 3.14 shows a handheld POS terminal device.

| FIGURE **3.14** |

Handheld POS terminal device

Using a wireless, handheld POS device, restaurant staff can take orders and payments on the floor.

Restaurants, bars, and retail shops are switching from traditional cash registers and costly credit card terminals to simpler devices that plug into smartphones and tablet computers. For example, a device called the Square Stand includes a built-in card reader that connects to an iPad and a hub device that connects to accessories, including a cash drawer, receipt printer, and scanner. With this device, a small retailer can have a cash register that keeps track of inventory and provides instant sales analysis for the cost of an iPad and $450 for the Square Stand, printer, and cash drawer. This is a much less expensive and less bulky solution than a standard cash register system. PayPal and Groupon also offer similar devices.[35]

Automated Teller Machine (ATM) Devices

Another type of special-purpose input/output device, the automated teller machine (ATM) is a terminal that bank customers use to perform transactions with their bank accounts. Companies use various ATM devices, sometimes called *kiosks*, to support their business processes. Some can dispense tickets, such as for airlines, concerts, and soccer games. Some colleges use them to produce transcripts.

Bar-Code Scanners

A bar-code scanner employs a laser scanner to read a bar-coded label and pass the data to a computer. The bar-code reader may be stationary or hand-held to support a wide variety of uses. This form of input is used widely in store checkouts and warehouse inventory control. Bar codes are also used in hospitals, where a nurse scans a patient's wristband and then a bar code on the medication about to be administered to prevent medication errors.

Several companies have created applications that convert your cell phone camera into a bar-code reader. You can scan the code that you find on print ads, packaging, or labels to launch Web sites and buy items with a few clicks.

Radio Frequency Identification

Radio frequency identification (RFID): A technology that employs a microchip with an antenna to broadcast its unique identifier and location to receivers.

Radio frequency identification (RFID) is a technology that employs a microchip with an antenna to broadcast its unique identifier and location to receivers. The purpose of an RFID system is to transmit data by a mobile device, called a tag (see Figure 3.15), which is read by an RFID reader and processed according to the needs of a computer program. One popular application of RFID is to place microchips on retail items and install in-store readers that track the inventory on the shelves to determine when shelves should be restocked. The RFID tag chip includes a special form of EPROM memory that holds data about the item to which the tag is attached. A radio frequency signal can update this memory as the status of the item changes. The data transmitted by the tag might provide identification, location information, or details about the product tagged, such as date of manufacture, retail price, color, or date of purchase.

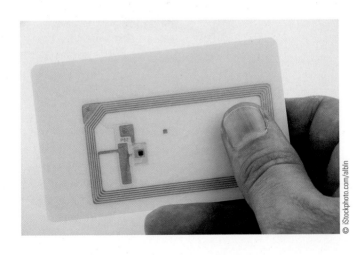

© iStockphoto.com/albin

FIGURE 3.15

RFID tag

An RFID tag is small compared to current bar-code labels used to identify items.

Lone Pine Construction is a general contracting company with annual revenue of $25 million and some 65 employees. The firm has hundreds of pieces of equipment, tools, and a fleet of construction vehicles. Lone Pine lost track of these assets with items disappearing from its warehouses and job sites. To eliminate the problem, the firm assigned a manager for several months to identify all assets, load pertinent data about each asset into a database (including who is responsible for its safe return to the company warehouse), and place RFID tags on key assets. Now a manager can visit the various job sites and quickly count the assets to ensure that none are missing. These measures have saved thousands of dollars, and the firm has decided to increase the number of assets covered by this system.[36]

Pen Input Devices

By touching the screen with a pen input device, you can activate a command or cause the computer to perform a task, enter handwritten notes, and draw objects and figures. See Figure 3.16. Pen input requires special software and hardware. Handwriting recognition software, for example, converts onscreen handwriting into text. Many tablet computers can transform handwriting into typed text and store the "digital ink" just the way a person writes it. People can use a pen to write and send email, add comments to documents, mark up presentations, and even hand draw charts in a document. The data can then be moved, highlighted, searched, and converted into text. If perfected, this interface is likely to become widely used. Pen input is especially attractive if you are uncomfortable using a keyboard. The success of pen input depends on how accurately and at what cost handwriting can be read and translated into digital form.

FIGURE 3.16

Using a pen input device

Using a pen input device directly on a digital pad, graphic designers can precisely edit photos and drawings.

Touch-Sensitive Screens

Advances in screen technology allow display screens to function as input as well as output devices. By touching certain parts of a touch-sensitive screen, you can start a program or trigger other types of action. Touch-sensitive screens can remove the need for a keyboard, which conserves space and increases portability. Touch screens are frequently used at gas stations to allow customers to select grades of gas and request a receipt; on photocopy machines for selecting options; at fast-food restaurants for entering customer choices; at information centers for finding facts about local eating and drinking establishments; and at amusement parks to provide directions to patrons. They also are used in kiosks at airports and department stores. Touch-sensitive screens are also being used for gathering votes in elections.

As touch screens get smaller, the user's fingers begin to block the information on the display. Nanotouch technology is being explored as a means of overcoming this problem. With this technology, users control the touch screen from its backside so that fingers do not block the display. As the user's finger moves on the back of the display, a tiny graphical finger is projected onto the touch screen. Such displays are useful for mobile audio players the size of a coin.

The Thales Group is a French multinational company and a major manufacturer of aircraft cockpits. Its head of cockpit innovation, Denis Bonnet, is a strong advocate of the use of touch screen controls for pilots to replace the current use of buttons, trackballs, and keypads for performing flying tasks. The goals are to reduce complexity by reducing the number of buttons and control panels, make the pilot interaction more intuitive, and enable the pilot to remain focused on flying.[37]

Output Devices

Computer systems provide output to decision makers at all levels of an organization so they can solve a business problem or capitalize on a competitive opportunity. In addition, output from one computer system can provide input into another computer system. The desired form of this output might be visual, audio, or even digital. Whatever the output's content or form, output devices are designed to provide the right information to the right person in the right format at the right time.

Display Screens

The display screen is a device used to show the output from the computer. Today a variety of flat-panel display screens are far lighter and thinner than the traditional cathode-ray tubes (CRTs) associated with early computers. Table 3.3 compares types of flat-panel display screens.

TABLE 3.3 Various types of flat-panel displays

Type	Description	Noteworthy Feature
Liquid crystal display (LCD)	Uses several layers of charged liquid crystals placed between clear plates that are lit from behind by a fluorescent light to create light and images	The viewing angle tends to be worse than that of plasma displays
Light-emitting diode (LED)	An LCD display that uses light-emitting diodes (LEDs) as backlight on the screen rather than a fluorescent lamp	Provides better contrast and lower energy consumption than LCDs
Organic light-emitting diode (OLED)	Functions by exciting organic compounds with electric current to produce bright, sharp images	Does not employ a backlight, which enables improved contrast and lower power consumption than LCD and LED displays
Plasma	Uses electricity to excite gas atoms to light up appropriate phosphors on the screen to emit light and color	Performs well in dark conditions and not as well in well-lit rooms

© 2016 Cengage Learning

With today's wide selection of display screens, price and overall quality can vary tremendously. The quality of a screen image is largely determined by the number of horizontal and vertical pixels used to create it. The images shown on your display device are composed of a million or more pixels. Resolution is the total number of pixels contained in the display; the more pixels, the clearer and sharper the image. A common resolution is 2,040 horizontal pixels × 1,536 vertical pixels. The size of the display monitor also affects the quality of the viewing. The same pixel resolution on a small screen is sharper than on a larger screen, where the same number of pixels is spread out over a larger area.

computer graphics card: A component of a computer that takes binary data from the CPU and translates it into an image you see on your display device.

graphics processing unit (GPU): A powerful processing chip that renders images on the screen display.

The **computer graphics card** takes binary data from the CPU and translates it into an image you see on your display device. It is the computer graphics card that controls the quality of the image and determines how many display devices can be attached to the computer. The computer graphics card holds the **graphics processing unit (GPU)**, a powerful processing chip that renders images on the display screen. The computer graphics card takes binary data from the CPU. The GPU then decides what to do with each pixel on the screen to create the image. As the GPU creates images, it uses RAM on the graphics card (called video RAM or VRAM) to store data about each pixel including its color and location on the screen. One measure of a video card's performance is how many complete images the card can display per second, which is called the frame rate. The human eye can process roughly 25 frames per second; however, many video games require a frame rate of at least 60 frames per second to provide a good user experience.[38]

Because many users leave their computers on for hours at a time, power usage is an important factor when deciding which type of display to purchase. Although power usage varies from model to model, OLED displays are the most energy efficient, with LCD monitors generally consuming between 35 and 50 percent less power than plasma screens. See Figure 3.17.

© iStockphoto.com/Peter Hermus/Beeldbewerking

FIGURE 3.17

Largest LCD screen in Europe
The LCD screen in the Rotterdam Central Station is 40 meters wide, 4.5 meters high, and has more than 5 million LEDs.

Aspect ratio and screen size describe the size of the display screen. *Aspect ratio* is the ratio of the width of the display to its height. The aspect ratio of width to height of 4:3 or 5:4 is good for people who use their computer to view or create Web pages or documents. Widescreen displays typically have an aspect ratio of 16:10 or 16:9 to allow improved viewing of movies and video games.

Companies are competing on the innovation frontier to create thinner, lighter, flexible, and more durable display devices for computers, cell phones, and other mobile devices. Samsung's YOUM display is a flexible OLED made of thin plastic that can bend around surfaces to provide a larger display. Corning has a display device made of bendable glass called Willow Glass that is only as thick as a piece of paper and is extremely light.[39]

Printers and Plotters

One of the most useful and common forms of output is called *hard copy*, which is simply paper output from a printer. The two main types of printers are laser printers and inkjet printers, and they are available with different speeds, features, and capabilities. Some can be set up to accommodate paper forms, such as blank check forms and invoice forms. Newer printers allow businesses to create customized printed output using full color for each customer from standard paper and data input. Ticket-receipt printers such as those used in restaurants, ATMs, and point-of-sale systems are in wide-scale use.

The speed of the printer is typically measured by the number of pages printed per minute (ppm). Like a display screen, the quality, or resolution, of a printer's output depends on the number of dots printed per inch (dpi). A 600-dpi printer prints more clearly than a 300-dpi printer. A recurring cost of using a printer is the inkjet or laser cartridge that must be replaced periodically—every few thousand pages for laser printers and every 500 to 900 pages for inkjet printers.

Inkjet printers that can print 10 to 40 ppm for black and white and 5 to 20 ppm for color are available for less than $175. For color printing, inkjet printers print vivid hues with an initial cost much less than color laser printers and can produce high-quality banners, graphics, greeting cards, letters, text, and photo prints.

Laser printers are generally faster than inkjet printers and can handle a heavier print load volume. A monochrome laser printer can print 25 to 45 ppm and cost anywhere from $200 to $700. Color laser printers can print color pages at a rate of 10 to 35 ppm and are available in a wide range of prices from $300 to more than $3,500 for a high-quality color laser printer.

A number of manufacturers offer multiple-function printers that can copy, print (in color or black and white), fax, and scan. Such multifunctional devices are often used when people need to do a relatively low volume of copying, printing, faxing, and scanning. The typical price of multifunction printers ranges from $100 to $400, depending on features and capabilities. Because these devices take the place of more than one piece of equipment, they are less expensive to acquire and maintain than a stand-alone fax plus a stand-alone printer, copier, and so on. Also, eliminating equipment that was once located on a countertop or desktop clears a workspace for other work-related activities. As a result, such devices are popular in homes and small office settings. Figure 3.18 shows a multifunction inkjet printer.

FIGURE 3.18

Multifunction inkjet printer

The Hewlett-Packard all-in-one 6310 inkjet printer provides printing, scanning, and copying functions.

© iStockphoto.com/Demo

3D printers have created a major breakthrough in how many items will be "manufactured." See Figure 3.19. 3D printing technology takes a three-dimensional model of an object stored on your computer and sends it to a 3D printer to create the object using strands of a plastic filament or synthetic powder. The filament comes in spools of various colors and is fed through a heated extruder that moves in several directions to place layer upon layer on top of each other until the object is created. 3D printers come with a wide range of capabilities as far as how fast they can build objects and how large of an object they can build. 3D Systems sells the highly rated Cubify CubeX and Cubify Cube printers.[40]

FIGURE 3.19

3D printer

3D print technology is making it possible to print objects ranging from everyday objects to houses.

RICH SUGG/MCT/Landov

3D printing is commonly used by aerospace firms, auto manufacturers, and other design-intensive companies. It is especially valuable during the conceptual stage of engineering design when the exact dimensions and material strength of the prototype are not critical. Some architectural design firms are using 3D printers to create full color models of their projects to show clients. eBay has announced a new iPhone app called eBay Exact that allows users to browse and buy customizable print-on-demand merchandise (mainly jewelry and accessories). The items are priced in the $9 to $350 range and can be configured and ordered using the mobile app. eBay's 3D printing partners will then manufacture and ship the products directly to consumers within two weeks.[41] Biomedical engineers are exploring a process called bioprinting that uses 3D printers to build human parts and organs from actual human cells.[42]

Mobile print solutions enable users to wirelessly send documents, email messages and attachments, presentations, and even boarding passes from any smartphone, tablet computer, or laptop to any mobile printer in the world. For example, PrinterOn Enterprise enables any print requests from any mobile or fixed device to be routed to any of over 10,000 printers worldwide configured with the PrinterOn Enterprise service. Mobile users who use the service only need to access a directory of PrinterOn printers and locations and then send an email with attachment to be printed to the email address of the printer. American Airlines Admiral Club, Delta Sky Club, Embassy Suites, and Double-Tree by Hilton have installed PrinterOn printers at many of their locations.[43]

Plotters are a type of hard-copy output device used for general design work. Businesses typically use plotters to generate paper or acetate blueprints, schematics, and drawings of buildings or new products. Standard plot widths are 24 inches and 36 inches, and the length can be whatever meets the need—from a few inches to many feet.

INFORMATION SYSTEMS @ WORK

Printing Livers at Organovo

In San Diego, California, a device the size of an espresso machine shoots a milky paste into six petri dishes filled with opaque goo. With miraculous speed, three little hexagons form in each dish, which soon grow into honeycombs the size of fingernails. The honeycombs are tissue, nearly identical to human liver tissue. The device is a 3D printer, and the company that is planning on using the device to turn human cells into human organs for transplants is Organovo.

Organovo was established in 2007, but its founders began their initial work at universities. In 2003, Dr. Thomas Boland first patented his technique for the inkjet printing of viable cells. Between 2004 and 2005, the National Science Foundation (NSF) granted a team led by Professor Gabor Forgacs $5 million, which the team used to develop and patent the first bioprinting platform. In 2008, Organovo raised $3 million in start-up funds—enough to set up its laboratory in San Diego. Finally, in 2010, Organovo developed its first fully cellular blood vessel, proving that human tissues and eventually human organs can be created using only human cells through 3D printing technology.

Unlike other manufacturing devices, 3D printers have a unique ability to customize a product by tweaking the blueprint that is fed into the printer. As a result, this expensive hardware is making inroads into industries where customization is critical. Nokia, for example, is offering its 3D printer owners a blueprint they can tweak to design their own mobile phone cases. Bespoke Innovations creates specialized coverings that surround an existing prosthetic leg and mimic the shape of the original leg, based on 3D scanning of the remaining leg. To create human tissues and organs, scientists must build highly customized artificial scaffolds to seed the cells temporarily until they are strong enough to stand alone.

Though popular science magazines rave about the potential of this technology for transplants in the future, Organovo already has a much bigger market opportunity in pharmaceutics. Companies spend $1.2 billion and 12 years, on average, to develop and test a new drug. Companies must conduct tests first on cells, then on animals, and finally on humans. Organovo tissues can be used in testing and may generate much more reliable predictions. In fact, in 2012 Organovo partnered with Pfizer and United Therapeutics, two major pharmaceutical companies, to do research into 3D printing of tissues and body parts. Today, Organovo can create liver tissues, but it is working on creating kidney and heart cells as well.

Discussion Questions

1. Why is the use of 3D printers critical to the manufacturing of human organs?
2. What other potential uses does 3D printing technology have in health care and other industries?

Critical Thinking Questions

1. What competitive advantage did technology provide Organovo?
2. Organovo is now a private corporation, but much of the research for the patents it holds was funded by the U.S. government through NSF and the National Institutes of Health. Is it right that Organovo and its investors should be the sole financial beneficiaries of this research? Why or why not?

SOURCES: Organovo Web site, *www.organovo.com/company/history*, accessed August 25, 2012; "Nokia backs 3D printing for mobile phone cases," BBC, January 18, 2013, *www.bbc.co.uk/news/technology -21084430*, accessed August 25, 2013; Bespoke Innovations Web site, *www.bespokeinnovations.com/content/what-fairing*, accessed August 25, 2013; Leckart, Steven, "How 3D Printing Body Parts Will Revolutionize Medicine," *Popular Science*, August 6, 2013, *http://www.popsci.com /science/article/2013-07/how-3-d-printing-body-parts-will-revolutionize -medicine*, accessed August 25, 2013; Stoffel, Brian, "How Big Is Organovo's Market Opportunity?" The Motley Fool, August 23, 2013, *www.fool.com/investing/general/2013/08/23/how-big-is-organovos -market-opportunity.aspx*, accessed August 21, 2013.

Digital Audio Players

digital audio player: A device that can store, organize, and play digital music files.

MP3: A standard format for compressing a sound sequence into a small file.

A digital audio player is a device that can store, organize, and play digital music files. MP3 (MPEG-1 Audio Layer-3) is a popular format for compressing a sound sequence into a very small file while preserving the original level of sound quality when it is played. By compressing the sound file, it requires less time to download the file and less storage space on a hard drive.

You can use many different music devices smaller than a deck of cards to download music from the Internet and other sources. These devices have no moving parts and can store hours of music. Apple expanded into the digital music market with an MP3 player (the iPod) and the iTunes Music Store, which allows you to find music online, preview it, and download it in a way that is safe, legal, and affordable. Other MP3 manufacturers include Dell, Sony, Samsung, Iomega, Creative, and Motorola, whose Rokr product is the first iTunes-compatible phone.

The Apple iPod Touch, with a 3.5-inch widescreen, is a music player that also plays movies and TV shows, displays photos, and connects to the Internet. You can, therefore, use it to view YouTube videos, buy music online, check email, and more. The display automatically adjusts the view when it is rotated from portrait to landscape. An ambient light sensor adjusts brightness to match the current lighting conditions. See Figure 3.20.

BECK DIEFENBACH/Reuters/Landov

FIGURE 3.20

Apple's iPod Touch

The iPod Touch is a music player with a 3.5-inch widescreen for playing movies and TV shows, displaying photos, and connecting to the Internet.

E-book Readers

The digital media equivalent of a conventional printed book is called an e-book (short for electronic book). The Project Gutenberg Online Book Catalog lists over 36,000 free e-books and a total of over 100,000 e-books available. E-books can be downloaded from Project Gutenberg (*www.gutenberg .org*) or many other sites onto personal computers or dedicated hardware devices known as e-book readers. The devices cost anywhere from around $100 to $450, and downloads of the bestselling books and new releases cost around $10. The e-book reader has the capacity to store thousands of books. The most current Amazon.com Kindle, Kobo Aura, and Barnes & Noble Nook are popular e-readers with e-paper displays that look like printed pages or with LCD screens that are bright and shiny but can be difficult to read in bright sunlight.[44] E-books weigh less than three-quarters of a pound, are around one-half inch thick, and come with a display screen ranging from 5 to 8 inches. Thus, these readers are more compact than most paperbacks and can be easily held in one hand. Recent e-book readers display content in 16 million colors and high resolution. See Figure 3.21. On many e-readers, the size of the text can be magnified for readers with poor vision.

FIGURE 3.21

Kindle e-book reader

Kindle uses an e-paper display that looks similar to the printed page.

Amazon.com, Inc.

COMPUTER SYSTEM TYPES

In general, computers can be classified as either special purpose or general purpose. *Special-purpose computers* are used for limited applications, for example, by military, government, and scientific research groups such as the CIA and NASA. Other applications include specialized processors found in appliances, cars, and other products. For example, automobile repair shops connect special-purpose computers to your car's engine to identify specific performance problems. As another example, IBM is developing a new generation of computer chips to develop so-called cognitive computers that are designed to mimic the way the human brain works. Rather than being programmed as today's computers are, cognitive computers will be able to learn through experiences and outcomes and mimic human learning patterns.

General-purpose computers are used for a variety of applications and to execute the business applications discussed in this text. General-purpose computer systems can be divided into two major groups: systems used by one user at a time and systems used by multiple concurrent users. Table 3.4 shows the general ranges of capabilities for various types of computer systems.

Portable Computers

portable computer: A computer small enough to carry easily.

handheld computer: A compact-sized computing device that is small enough to hold comfortably in one hand, and typically includes a display screen with stylus and/or touch screen input along with a compact keyboard or numeric keypad.

Many computer manufacturers offer a variety of **portable computers**, those that are small enough to carry easily. Portable computers include handheld computers, laptop computers, ultrabooks, and tablet computers.

A **handheld computer** is a compact computing device that is small enough to hold comfortably in one hand, and typically includes a display

TABLE **3.4** Types of computer systems

Single-user computer systems can be divided into two groups: portable computers and nonportable computers.

Single-User Computers			
Portable Computers			
Factor	**Handheld**	**Laptop**	**Notebook/Ultrabook**	**Tablet**
Cost	$150–$3,000	$300–$1,200	$300–$800	$350–$700
Weight (pounds)	<0.5	<7	<3	<2
Screen size (inches)	2–4	<17	<13	<13
Typical use	Data collection, organize personal data	Improve worker productivity	Sufficient processing power to run nearly every business application	Capture data at the point of contact, read email, surf the Internet, read e-books, view photos, play games, listen to music, and watch video files

Nonportable Computers			
Factor	**Thin Client**	**Desktop**	**Nettop**	**Workstation**
Cost	$200–$500	$500–$2,500	$150–$350	$1,500–$9,500
Weight (pounds)	<3	20–30	<5	<20–35
Typical use	Enter data and access applications via the Internet	Improve worker productivity	Replace desktop with small, low-cost, low-energy computer	Perform engineering, CAD, and software development

Multiple-user computer systems include servers, mainframes, and supercomputers.

Multiple-User Computers		
Factor	**Server**	**Mainframe**	**Supercomputer**
Cost	>$500	>$75,000	>$250,000
Weight (pounds)	>25	>100	>100
Typical use	Execute network and Internet applications	Execute computing tasks for large organizations and provide massive data storage	Run scientific applications; perform intensive number crunching

© 2016 Cengage Learning

screen with stylus or touch screen input along with a compact keyboard or numeric keypad. Most can communicate with desktop computers over wireless networks. Some even add a built-in GPS receiver with software that can integrate location data into applications run on the device. For example, if you click an entry in an electronic address book, the device displays a map and directions from your current location. Such a computer can also be mounted in your car and serve as a navigation system. One of the shortcomings of handheld computers is that they require a lot of power relative to their size.

Handheld computers frequently serve as point-of-sale devices that can capture credit card data. Rugged versions of handheld computers are designed to meet demanding military standards for drops, vibration, humidity, dust, immersion in water, altitude, and temperature extremes. This version of a handheld computer can be as expensive as $3,000. See Figure 3.22.

FIGURE 3.22

Rugged handheld computer

Rugged handheld computers are used by the military and emergency first responders.

laptop computer: A personal computer designed for use by mobile users, being small and light enough to sit comfortably on a user's lap.

Laptop Computers

A laptop computer is a personal computer designed for use by mobile users, being small and light enough to sit comfortably on a user's lap. Laptop computers use a variety of flat-panel technologies to produce lightweight and thin display screens with good resolution. In terms of computing power, laptop computers can match most desktop computers as they come with powerful CPUs as well as large-capacity primary memory and disk storage. This type of computer is highly popular among students and mobile workers who carry their laptops on trips and to meetings and classes. Many personal computer users now prefer a laptop computer over a desktop because of its portability, lower energy usage, and smaller space requirements.

Ultrabook Computers

Numerous portable computers are smaller than the typical laptop and have various names, including notebook and the even smaller ultrabook. The newest notebook computers come with a natural user interface, including both voice control integration and touch screens; high-quality display screens; always on, always connected capabilities; all-day battery life; and processing power sufficient to run most business applications and games.

tablet computer: A portable, lightweight computer with no keyboard that allows you to roam the office, home, or factory floor carrying the device like a clipboard.

Tablet Computers

Tablet computers are portable, lightweight computers that can come with or without a keyboard and allow you to roam the office, home, or factory floor carrying the device like a clipboard. You can enter text with a writing stylus directly on the screen, thanks to built-in handwriting recognition software. Other input methods include an onscreen keyboard and speech recognition. Tablet computers that support input only via a writing stylus are called *slate computers*. The *convertible tablet PC* comes with a swivel screen and can be used as a traditional notebook or as a pen-based tablet PC. Most new tablets come with a front-facing camera for videoconferencing and a second camera for snapshot photos and video.

Tablet computers are especially popular with students and gamers. They are also frequently used in the healthcare, retail, insurance, and manufacturing industries because of their versatility.

The Apple iPad is a tablet computer capable of running the same software that runs on the older Apple iPhone and iPod Touch devices, giving it a library of over a million applications. It also runs software developed specifically for the iPad. The device has a 9.7-inch screen and an onscreen keypad, weighs 1.5 pounds, and supports Internet access over wireless networks.

A number of computer companies are offering tablet computers to compete with Apple's iPad, including the Playbook from BlackBerry, the Touch-Pad from Hewlett-Packard, the Kindle Fire from Amazon, the Streak by Dell, the Tablet S and Tablet P from Sony, the Thrive by Toshiba, the Galaxy Tab and Galaxy Note from Samsung (see Figure 3.23), the Xoom from Motorola, and the low-cost (less than $75) Aakash and Ubislate from the India-based company Quad.

FIGURE 3.23

Tablet computer

The Samsung Galaxy Note 10.1 Android tablet has a large touch screen and a quad-core processor.

© istockphoto.com/Mixmike

Nonportable Single-User Computers

Nonportable single-user computers include thin client computers, desktop computers, nettop computers, and workstations.

Thin Clients

thin client: A low-cost, centrally managed computer with no internal or external attached drives for data storage.

A **thin client** is a low-cost, centrally managed computer with no internal or external attached drives for data storage. These computers have limited capabilities and perform only essential applications, so they remain "thin" in terms of the client applications they include. As stripped-down computers, they do not have the storage capacity or computing power of typical desktop computers, nor do they need it for the role they play. With no hard disk, they never pick up viruses or suffer a hard disk crash. Unlike personal computers, thin clients download data and software from a network when needed, making support, distribution, and updating of software applications much easier and less expensive. Thin clients work well in a cloud-computing environment to enable users to access the computing and data resources available within the cloud.

Jewelry Television is viewed by over 65 million people in the United States and millions more visit its Web site (*www.jtv.com*). As a result of this exposure, the company has become one of the world's largest jewelry retailers. Its 300 call center representatives handle more than 6 million calls per year using thin client computers to access information to respond to customer queries and to place orders.[45]

Desktop Computers

desktop computer: A nonportable computer that fits on a desktop and provides sufficient computing power, memory, and storage for most business computing tasks.

Desktop computers are single-user computer systems that are highly versatile. Named for their size, desktop computers can provide sufficient computing power, memory, and storage for most business computing tasks.

The Apple iMac is a family of Macintosh desktop computers first introduced in 1998 in which all the components (including the CPU and the disk drives) fit behind the display screen. The Mac Pro is a small and cylindrical shaped computer based on the Intel Xeon E5 chipset with up to 12 cores of processing power and two powerful GPU chips. See Figure 3.24.

FIGURE 3.24

Mac Pro desktop computer

Mac Pro desktop towers are small and cylindrical.

CHRISTOPH DERNBACH/DPA/LANDOV

Nettop Computers

nettop computer: An inexpensive desktop computer designed to be smaller, lighter, and consume much less power than a traditional desktop computer.

A **nettop computer** is an inexpensive desktop computer designed to be smaller and lighter and to consume much less power than a traditional desktop computer. A nettop is designed to perform basic processing tasks such as exchanging email, Internet surfing, and accessing Web-based applications. This computer can also be used for home theater activities such as watching video, viewing pictures, listening to music, and playing games. Unlike netbook computers, nettop computers are not designed to be portable, and they come with or without an attached screen. (Nettops with attached screens are called all-in-ones.) A nettop without an attached screen can be connected to an existing monitor or even a TV screen. It also may include an optical drive (CD/DVD). The CPU is typically a low-power Intel or AMD CPU. A nettop has sufficient processing power to enable you to watch video and do limited processing tasks. Figure 3.25 shows the ASUS EeeBox nettop computer.

Courtesy of ASUS Computers International

FIGURE **3.25**

ASUS EeeBox nettop

The ASUS EeeBox looks like an oversized external hard drive, but includes integrated graphics, wireless networking capabilities, solid state media connections, and an HDMI port so it can play HD video.

Workstations

workstation: A more powerful personal computer used for mathematical computing, computer-assisted design, and other high-end processing but still small enough to fit on a desktop.

Workstations are more powerful than personal computers but still small enough to fit on a desktop. They are used to support engineering and technical users who perform heavy mathematical computing, computer-assisted design (CAD), video editing, and other applications requiring a high-end processor. Such users need very powerful CPUs, large amounts of main memory, and extremely high-resolution graphic displays. Workstations are typically more expensive than the average desktop computer. Some computer manufacturers are now providing laptop versions of their powerful desktop workstations.

Multiple-User Computer Systems

Multiple-user computers are designed to support workgroups from a small department of two or three workers to large organizations with tens of thousands of employees and millions of customers. Multiple-user systems include servers, mainframe computers, and supercomputers.

Servers

server: A computer employed by many users to perform a specific task, such as running network or Internet applications.

A **server** is a computer employed by many users to perform a specific task, such as running network or Internet applications. While almost any computer can run server operating system and server applications, a server computer usually has special features that make it more suitable for operating in a multiuser environment. These features include greater memory and storage capacities, faster and more efficient communications abilities, and reliable backup capabilities. A Web server handles Internet traffic and communications. An enterprise server stores and provides access to programs that meet the needs of an entire organization. A file server stores and coordinates program and data files. Server systems consist of multiuser computers, including supercomputers, mainframes, and other servers. Often, an organization will house a large number of servers in the same room where access to the machines can be controlled and authorized support personnel can more easily manage and maintain the servers. Such a facility is called a *server farm*. Apple, Google, Microsoft, the U.S. government, and many other organizations have built billion-dollar server farms in small rural communities where both land and electricity are cheap.[46]

scalability: The ability to increase the processing capability of a computer system so that it can handle more users, more data, or more transactions in a given period.

Servers offer great **scalability**, the ability to increase the processing capability of a computer system so that it can handle more users, more data, or more transactions in a given period. Scalability is increased by adding more, or more powerful, processors. *Scaling up* adds more powerful processors, and *scaling out* adds many more equal (or even less powerful) processors to increase the total data-processing capacity.

Server manufacturers are competing heavily to reduce the power required to operate their servers and making "performance per watt" a key part of their product differentiation strategy. Low power usage is a critical factor for organizations that run server farms of hundreds or even thousands of servers. Typical servers draw up to 220 watts, while new servers based on Intel's Atom microprocessor draw 8 or fewer watts. The annual power savings from such low-energy usage servers can amount to tens of thousands of dollars for operators of a large server farm. Server farm operators are also looking for low-cost, clean, renewable energy sources. For example, Apple runs a server farm in Maiden, North Carolina, on 167 million kilowatt hours generated from a 100-acre solar energy facility. This is enough power to operate 17,600 homes for a year.

virtual server: A method of logically dividing the resources of a single physical server to create multiple logical servers, each acting as its own dedicated machine.

A **virtual server** is a method of logically dividing the resources of a single physical server to create multiple logical servers, each acting as its own dedicated machine. The server administrator uses software to divide one physical server into multiple isolated virtual environments. For example, a single physical Web server might be divided into two virtual private servers. One of the virtual servers hosts the organization's live Web site, while the other hosts a copy of the Web site. The second private virtual server is used to test and verify updates to software before changes are made to the live Web site. The use of virtual servers is growing rapidly. In a typical data center deployment of several hundred servers, companies using virtualization can build 12 virtual machines for every actual server, with a resulting savings in capital and operating expenses (including energy costs) of millions of dollars per year.

EZZI.net is a Web hosting service provider for many companies, including some of the largest *Fortune* 500 companies. It has data centers located in New York City and Los Angeles that employ virtual servers because they are easy to use, can be supported around the clock, and operate with a 99.7 percent uptime to meet the needs of its many customers.

blade server: A server that houses many individual computer motherboards that include one or more processors, computer memory, computer storage, and computer network connections.

A **blade server** houses many computer motherboards that include one or more processors, computer memory, computer storage, and computer network connections. These all share a common power supply and air-cooling source within a single chassis. By placing many blades into a single chassis, and then mounting multiple chassis in a single rack, the blade server is more powerful but less expensive than traditional systems based on mainframes or server farms of individual computers. In addition, the blade server approach requires much less physical space than traditional server farms. See Figure 3.26.

FIGURE 3.26

Rack-mounted system with blade servers

Blade servers house many motherboards and one or more processors, memory, storage, and network connections.

Bharti Airtel is a telecommunications company with headquarters in New Delhi, India, providing both fixed line and wireless services to some 269 million customers across 20 countries in Asia and Africa. In this highly competitive and rapidly growing market, Bharti Airtel must ensure that growth is achieved with no degradation in service to existing customers. This means reliable and robust performance with services that are always available. To meet these goals, the firm migrated to server-based computing that can be easily scaled to enable it to handle the rapidly increasing customer volume.[47]

Mainframe Computers

mainframe computer: A large, powerful computer often shared by hundreds of concurrent users connected to the machine over a network.

A **mainframe computer** is a large, powerful computer shared by dozens or even hundreds of concurrent users connected to the machine over a network. The mainframe computer must reside in a data center with special HVAC (heating, ventilation, and air conditioning) equipment to control temperature, humidity, and dust levels. In addition, most mainframes are kept in a secure data center with limited access. The construction and maintenance of a controlled-access room with HVAC can add hundreds of thousands of dollars to the cost of owning and operating a mainframe computer.

Mainframe computers have been the workhorses of corporate computing for nearly 50 years. They can support hundreds of users simultaneously and can handle all of the core functions of a corporation. Mainframe computers provide the data-processing power and data storage capacity to enable banks and brokerage firms to deliver new mobile services, credit card companies to detect identity theft, and government agencies to better serve citizens. Indeed, 96 of the world's top 100 banks, 23 of the top 25 retailers, and 9 out of 10 of the world's largest insurance companies run IBM mainframe computers. Mainframe computers process 30 billion business transactions per day, including credit card transactions, billing for telecommunications firms, stock trades, money transfers, and transactions for ERP systems.[48] See Figure 3.27.

F17
301

Courtesy of IBM Corporation

The role of the mainframe is undergoing some remarkable changes as lower-cost, server computers become increasingly powerful. Many computer jobs that used to run on mainframe computers have migrated onto these smaller, less expensive computers. This information-processing migration is called *computer downsizing*.

The new role of the mainframe is as a large information-processing and data storage utility for a corporation—running jobs too large for other computers, storing files and databases too large to be stored elsewhere, and storing backups of files and databases created elsewhere. For example, the mainframe can handle the millions of daily transactions associated with airline, automobile, and hotel/motel reservation systems. It can process the tens of thousands of daily queries necessary to provide data to decision support systems. Its massive storage and input/output capabilities enable it to play the role of a video computer, providing full-motion video to multiple, concurrent users.

Credit Unions System for Brazil (Sicoob) is the largest credit union system in Brazil with over 2.5 million customers. The organization used two mainframe computers to increase its data-processing capacity to handle a 60 percent increase in branch transactions and a 600 percent increase in transactions from mobile users while at the same lowering its annual electricity costs by $1.5 million.[49]

Supercomputers

supercomputer: One of the most powerful computer systems with the fastest processing speed.

Supercomputers are the most powerful computers with the fastest processing speed and highest performance. They are special-purpose machines designed for applications that require extensive and rapid computational capabilities. Originally, supercomputers were used primarily by government agencies to perform the high-speed number crunching needed in weather forecasting, earthquake simulations, climate modeling, nuclear research, study of the origin of matter and the universe, and weapons development and testing. They are now used more broadly for commercial purposes in the life sciences and the manufacture of drugs and new materials. For example, Procter & Gamble uses supercomputers in the research and development of many of its leading commercial brands such as Tide and Pampers to help develop detergent with more soap suds and improve the quality of its diapers. PayPal uses a supercomputer to keep track of its customers and payments.[50]

Most new supercomputers are based on a recent architecture that employs GPU chips in addition to traditional central processing unit chips to perform high-speed processing. The GPU chip is much faster than the typical CPU chip at performing floating point operations and executing algorithms for which processing of large blocks of data is done in parallel. This sort of computing is precisely the type performed by supercomputers.[51] The speed of supercomputers is measured in floating point operations per second (FLOPS). Table 3.5 lists supercomputer processing speeds.

TABLE 3.5 Supercomputer processing speeds

Speed	Meaning
GigaFLOPS	1×10^{9} FLOPS
TeraFLOPS	1×10^{12} FLOPS
PetaFLOPS	1×10^{15} FLOPS
ExaFLOPS	1×10^{18} FLOPS

© 2016 Cengage Learning

The fastest supercomputer as of June 2013 is the Tianhe-2 built by the National University of Defense Technology located in Hunan Province, China. See Figure 3.28. It was built at an estimated cost of about $3 billion and is expected to be used to control traffic lights, predict earthquakes, develop new drugs, design cars, and create movie special effects.[52]

Table 3.6 lists the five most powerful supercomputers in use as of June 2013.

FIGURE 3.28

World's fastest computer

The supercomputer Tianhe-2 can operate as fast as 33.86 petaflops per second, and is currently ranked as the world's fastest computer.

LONG HONGTAO/Xinhua/Landov

TABLE 3.6 Five most powerful operational supercomputers (June 2013)

Rank	Name	Manufacturer	Research Center	Location	Number of Cores	Speed (petaflops)
1	Tianhe-2	NUDT	National University of Defense Technology (NUDT)	China	3.1 million	33.9
2	Titan	Cray	Oak Ridge National Laboratory	United States	0.56 million	17.6
3	Sequoia	IBM	Lawrence Livermore National Laboratory	United States	1.6 million	17.2
4	K	Fujitsu	Riken Advanced Institute for Computational Science	Japan	0.8 million	10.5
5	Mira	IBM	Argonne National Laboratory	United States	0.8 million	8.6

Source: Slides from the Top 500 Session at Isc13 in Leipzig, *Top 500 Computer Sites*, June 18, 2013, *www.top500.org/blog/slides-from-the-top500-session-at-isc13-in-leipzig/*.

Figure 3.29 shows the rate of increased processing speed for the world's fastest supercomputers. If computer scientists can maintain this rate of improvement, by 2018 the world's fastest computer will exceed 1.0 exaflop (five times faster than the *combined* speed of world's 500 fastest supercomputers in June 2013). Such processing speed will be needed for future projects such as the

FIGURE **3.29**

Increasing processing speed of the world's fastest computer

If computer scientists maintain this rate of improvement, by 2018 the world's fastest computer will exceed 1.0 exaflop.

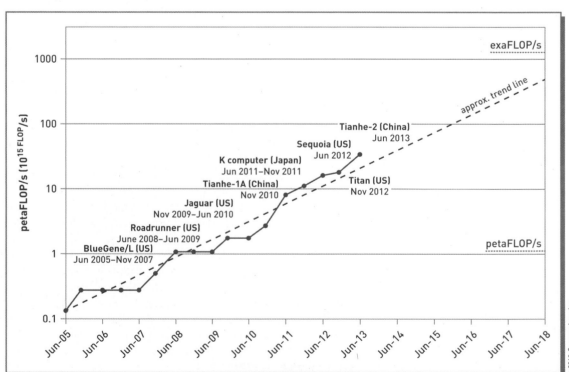

Source: Dorrier, Jason, "China's Tianhe-2 Doubles World's Top Supercomputing Speed Two Years Ahead of Schedule," Singularity Hub, July 1, 2013. Adapted from Top500 Supercomputer Sites.

Human Brain Project (requires exascale computing to build a complete digital model of the human brain) and the Square Kilometer Array radio telescope (requires exascale processing to operate a new telescope 50 times as sensitive and 10,000 times faster than any telescope in existence today).

DATA CENTERS

data center: A climate-and-access-controlled building or a set of buildings that houses the computer hardware that delivers an organization's data and information services.

A data center is a climate-and-access-controlled building or a set of buildings that houses the computer hardware that delivers an organization's data and information services.

The rapid growth in the demand of additional computing capacity is causing an explosion in the growth of new and existing data centers. Rackspace is a major cloud-computing service provider that is adding new servers to its data centers at the rate of over 1,500 per month.[53] Apple, Facebook, AT&T, Rackspace, and IT services company Wipro are among firms that have spent hundreds of millions in a single year on new data centers. Indeed, Google spends on the order of $4 billion a year on building data centers in an attempt to keep up with the burgeoning demand of its existing and new customers.

The need for additional data storage capacity is another factor driving the growth in data centers. According to one study, somewhere between one-third and one-half of all data centers will run out of space in the next several years. Of those organizations needing more database capacity, about 40 percent indicated that they would build new data centers, about 30 percent said they would lease additional space, and the rest indicated that they would investigate other options, including the use of cloud computing.

A further driving force behind the increased spending on new data centers is that organizations are consolidating their data centers from many locations to a few locations. The goal of consolidation is to lower ongoing operating costs—less spending on utilities, property taxes, and labor. General Motors recently consolidated from 23 data center locations to just two. This has reduced both its operating costs and energy usage.[54] Overall, research group Gartner estimates that spending on data centers will reach a whopping $143 billion in 2013.[55]

Traditional data centers consist of warehouse-size buildings filled with row upon row of server racks and powerful air conditioning systems to remove dust and humidity from the air and to offset the heat generated by the processors. Such data centers can use as much energy as a small city and run up a power bill of millions of dollars per year. Indeed, energy costs can be 25 percent of the total cost of operating a data center, with hardware expenses and labor costs the other 75 percent.

Businesses and technology vendors are working to develop data centers that run more efficiently and require less energy for processing and cooling. For example, Microsoft is investing nearly $1 billion in a modular data center campus in Boydton, Virginia. This state-of-the-art data center employs prefabricated, container-like data center modules called IT-PACS, each with the capacity to hold thousands of servers. Individual modules sit on slabs completely exposed to the elements and provide weather-tight protection for the servers, data storage devices, and other equipment inside. The servers inside the module are cooled efficiently by water and fan-driven cooling systems that require much less energy than air conditioning units. This data center design approach enables Microsoft to deploy additional computing capacity quicker and at a lower initial cost and a lower ongoing operating cost.[56] Google, Dell, Hewlett-Packard, and others have adopted similar modular data center approaches.[57] See Figure 3.30.

About half the energy usage of a traditional data center goes to operate its computers. The other half goes to cooling the computers and removing dust

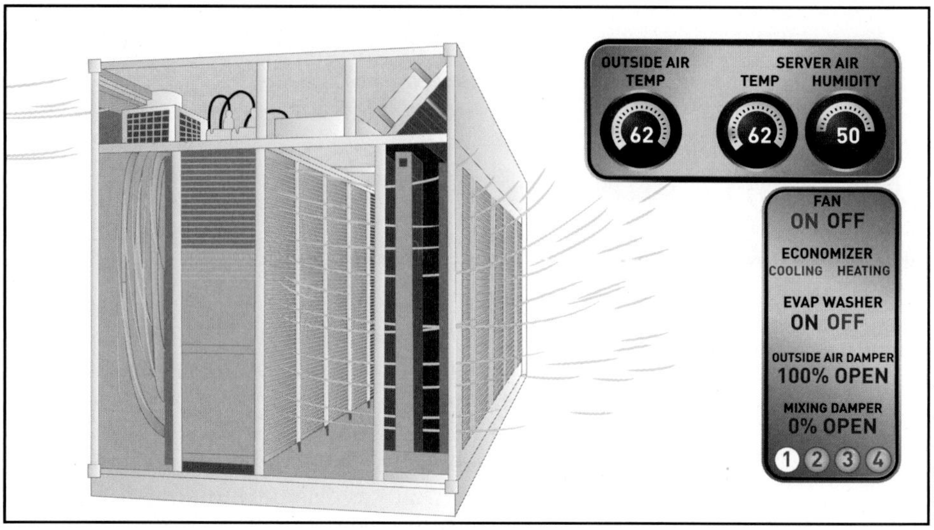

FIGURE 3.30

Modular data center

Each module in a modular data center has a server that is cooled efficiently by water and by fans that require much less energy than air conditioning units.

and humidity from the air, lighting, and other systems that sustain the data center. Such a data center has a power usage effectiveness (PUE) of 2.0. (PUE = total power consumed/power required to run the computers). The ideal goal is a PUE of 1.0, which means that all the power goes to running the computers. Google has been able to build data centers that operate with a PUE of 1.14.[58]

In a further attempt to lower ongoing operating costs, organizations are locating their data centers in areas with milder climates and lower energy rates and land costs. For organizations in the United States, this translates to rural locations in the south and the northwest. Apple's $1 billion data center, Google's $600 million data center, and Facebook's $450 million data center are all located in rural North Carolina.[59]

The ability to absorb the impact of a disaster (e.g., hurricane, earthquake, terrorism attack, or war) and quickly restore services is a critical concern when it comes to the planning for new data centers. As a result, data centers of large information systems service organizations are often distributed among multiple locations in different areas of the country or even different countries to ensure continuous operations in the event of a disaster. If a data center is affected by a disaster, it is possible to redirect that center's work load to one or more of the distributed data centers not affected. IBM is an extreme example of distributed data centers. Since 2009, IBM has opened nine data centers in Brazil, Mexico, Costa Rica, Chile, Colombia, Peru, and Uruguay to ensure around-the-clock services to its Latin American customers. Globally, IBM has more than 400 widely distributed data centers to meet the needs of its customers.[60] In addition to the distribution strategy, most data centers have implemented some form of backup generator or uninterruptible power supply in the event that the local power provider fails.

GREEN COMPUTING

Electronic devices such as computer hardware and cell phones contain hundreds or even thousands of components. The components, in turn, are composed of many different materials, including some that are known to be potentially harmful to humans and the environment, such as beryllium, cadmium, lead, mercury, brominated flame retardants (BFRs), selenium, and polyvinyl chloride.[61] Electronics manufacturing employees and suppliers at all steps along the supply chain and manufacturing process are at risk of unhealthy exposure to these raw materials. Users of these products can also be exposed to these materials when using poorly designed or improperly manufactured devices. Care must also be taken when recycling or destroying these devices to avoid contaminating the environment.

green computing: A program concerned with the efficient and environmentally responsible design, manufacture, operation, and disposal of IS-related products.

Green computing is concerned with the efficient and environmentally responsible design, manufacture, operation, and disposal of IS-related products, including all types of computers, printers, and printer materials such as cartridges and toner. Business organizations recognize that going green is in their best interests in terms of public relations, safety of employees, and the community at large. They also recognize that green computing presents an opportunity to substantially reduce total costs over the life cycle of their IS equipment. Green computing has three goals: reduce the use of hazardous material, allow companies to lower their power-related costs (including potential cap and trade fees), and enable the safe disposal or recycling of computers and computer-related equipment.

It is estimated that 51.9 million computers, 35.8 million monitors, and 33.6 million hard copy devices (printers, faxes, etc.)—representing a total of 1.3 million tons of waste—were disposed of in the United States in 2010.[62] Because it is impossible to ensure safe recycling or disposal, the best practice is to eliminate the use of toxic substances, particularly since recycling of used computers, monitors, and printers has raised concerns about toxicity and carcinogenicity of some of the substances. Safe disposal and reclamation operations must be carried out carefully to avoid exposure in recycling operations and leaching of materials such as heavy metals from landfills and incinerator ashes. In many cases, recycling companies export large quantities of used electronics to companies in undeveloped countries. Unfortunately, many of these countries do not have strong environmental laws, and they sometimes fail to recognize the potential dangers of dealing with hazardous materials. In their defense, these countries point out that the United States and other first-world countries were allowed to develop robust economies and rise up out of poverty without the restrictions of strict environmental policies.

Electronic Product Environmental Assessment Tool (EPEAT): A system that enables purchasers to evaluate, compare, and select electronic products based on a total of 51 environmental criteria.

Electronic Product Environmental Assessment Tool (EPEAT) is a system that enables purchasers to evaluate, compare, and select electronic products based on a total of 51 environmental criteria. Products are ranked in EPEAT according to three tiers of environmental performance: bronze, silver, and gold. See Table 3.7.[63] Individual purchasers as well as corporate purchasers of computers, printers, scanners, and multifunction devices can use the EPEAT Web site (*www.epeat.net*) to screen manufacturers and models based on environmental attributes.[64]

TABLE **3.7** EPEAT product tiers

Tier	Number of Required Criteria That Must Be Met	Number of Optional Criteria That Must Be Met
Bronze	All 23	None
Silver	All 23	At least 50%
Gold	All 23	At least 75%

© 2016 Cengage Learning

European Union's Restriction of Hazardous Substances Directive: A directive that restricts the use of many hazardous materials in computer manufacturing and requires manufacturers to use at least 65 percent reusable or recyclable components, implement a plan to manage products at the end of their life cycle in an environmentally safe manner, and reduce or eliminate toxic material in their packaging.

The European Union's Restriction of Hazardous Substances Directive, which took effect in 2006, restricts the use of many hazardous materials in computer manufacturing. The directive also requires manufacturers to use at least 65 percent reusable or recyclable components, implement a plan to manage products at the end of their life cycle in an environmentally safe manner,

ETHICAL& SOCIETAL ISSUES

Challenges to E-Waste Recycling

Every day, Americans throw approximately 150,000 computers in the trash—along with approximately 100,000 monitors and 225,000 keyboards and mice. And that's nothing compared to the rush to get rid of mobile devices. Americans throw out over 400,000 cell phones and other mobile equipment every year. In fact, e-waste (electronic waste) is the fastest-growing source of municipal waste. Moreover, electronics contain both precious metals, such as gold, silver, and copper, and hazardous materials, so dumping electronics is both wasteful and harmful to the environment. The obvious solution is to encourage Americans to recycle, but this simple solution is a lot more complicated than it seems.

About 20 percent of Americans are dutifully bringing their old electronics to e-waste recyclers—where it may, or may not, be recycled, reused, or disposed of safely. E-waste recyclers have found it more profitable to ship the material overseas to Africa or Asia, where wages are so low that removing the metals from electronic devices is economically viable. Guiyu, China, is known as one of the e-waste capitols of the world. There, peasants bash open cathode-ray tubes, releasing the toxic phosphor dust. They cook circuit boards in woks to retrieve the lead, breathing in the fumes in the process. They burn plastic parts, sending poisonous dioxins and furans into the air they breathe—and the environment.

Still, many e-waste recyclers were doing their best to accommodate the massive tonnage of e-waste sent their way, and they were making a profit. In the first decade of the twenty-first century, for example, recyclers earned more than $200 per ton of glass from computer and television monitors, which was then melted and reused in cathode-ray tubes at one of the 12 U.S. or 13 global plants. In 2009, on orders from the U.S. government, television stations stopped broadcasting their analog signals and consumers rushed to buy the new flat-screen monitors that do not use cathode-ray tubes. By 2013, all but two of the cathode tube recycling plants had shut their doors and e-waste recyclers had to pay to get rid of the glass. Some e-waste recyclers are illegally storing their waste in large warehouses where it begins to break down and harm the environment. In California, one owner of a recycling company simply disappeared, leaving the state to pick up the mess. Small e-waste companies simply can't cope with the demands of changing technology.

Instead, governments are demanding that manufacturers take back their old products and safely dispose of them, and many are doing so. In fact, Acer launched an e-waste reward program whereby Australians who turned in their old computers received $120 in vouchers to be used at the company's online store. Clearly, e-waste is a problem that will require the cooperation of recyclers, manufacturers, and governments around the world.

Discussion Questions

1. Why was e-waste recycling initially profitable, and what happened to make it less profitable or even costly?
2. What challenges will e-waste recycling face in the future?

Critical Thinking Questions

1. What role should manufacturers and governments play in solving the e-waste problem?
2. What steps can you take to help solve the problem?

SOURCES: "Facts and Figures on E-Waste and Recycling," Electronics Take Back Coalition Web site, June 25, 2013, *www.electronicstakeback.com/wp-content/uploads/Facts_and_Figures_on_EWaste_and_Recycling.pdf*, accessed August 21, 2013; "E-Waste Facts," E-Waste Collection Center, University of San Diego, *www.sandiego.edu/ewaste/facts.php*, accessed August 21, 2013; "Global E-Waste Dumping," Electronics Take Back Coalition Web site, *www.electronicstakeback.com/global-e-waste-dumping*, accessed August 21, 2013; Urbina, Ian, "Unwanted Electronic Gear Rising in Toxic Piles,"*The New York Times*, March 18, 2013, *www.nytimes.com/2013/03/19/us/disposal-of-older-monitors-leaves-a-hazardous-trail.html?pagewanted=all&_r=0*, accessed August 21, 2013; Spandas, Lui, "Acer Launches E-Waste Rewards Program,"*ZDNet*, January 21, 2013, *www.zdnet.com/au/acer-launches-e-waste-rewards-program-7000010047*, accessed August 21, 2013.

and reduce or eliminate toxic material in their packaging. The state of California has passed a similar law, called the Electronic Waste Recycling Act. Because of these two acts, manufacturers had a strong motivation to remove brominated flame retardants from their PC casings.[65]

Some electronics manufacturers have developed programs to assist their customers in disposing of old equipment. For example, Dell offers a free worldwide recycling program for consumers. It also provides no-charge recycling of any brand of used computer or printer with the purchase of a new Dell computer or printer. This equipment is recycled in an environmentally responsible manner, using Dell's stringent and global recycling guidelines.[66] HP and other manufacturers offer similar programs. The HP Planet Partners program enables customers to recycle used HP cartridges in 56 countries and territories in collaboration with some 9,000 retailer outlets worldwide (e.g., Office Depot, Office Max, Staples, and Walmart). HP customers have recycled more than half a billion HP ink and LaserJet toner cartridges to date and expect to recycle 3.5 billion pounds of electronic products and supplies by the end of 2015. This recycling effort has kept 280 million cartridges out of landfills.[67]

Computer manufacturers such as Apple, Dell, and Hewlett-Packard have long competed on the basis of price and performance. As the difference among the manufacturers in these two arenas narrows, support for green computing is emerging as a new business strategy for these companies to distinguish themselves from the competition. Apple claims to have the "greenest lineup of notebooks," and is making progress at removing toxic chemicals. Dell's new mantra is to become "the greenest technology company on Earth." Hewlett-Packard highlights its long tradition of environmentalism and is improving its packaging to reduce the use of materials. It is also urging computer users around the world to shut down their computers at the end of the day to save energy and reduce carbon emissions.

SUMMARY

Principle:

Computer hardware must be carefully selected to meet the evolving needs of the organization and its supporting information systems.

Computer hardware should be selected to meet specific user and business requirements. These requirements can evolve and change over time.

The central processing unit (CPU) and primary storage cooperate to execute data processing. The CPU has three main components: the arithmetic/logic unit (ALU), the control unit, and the register areas. Instructions are executed in a two-phase process called a machine cycle, which includes the instruction phase and the execution phase.

Computer system processing speed is affected by clock speed, which is measured in gigahertz (GHz). As the clock speed of the CPU increases, heat is generated, which can corrupt the data and instructions the computer is trying to process. Bigger heat sinks, fans, and other components are required to eliminate the excess heat. Chip designers and manufacturers are exploring various means to avoid heat problems in their new designs.

Primary storage, or memory, provides working storage for program instructions and data to be processed and provides them to the CPU. Storage capacity is measured in bytes.

A common form of memory is random access memory (RAM). RAM is volatile; loss of power to the computer erases its contents. RAM comes in many different varieties including dynamic RAM (DRAM), synchronous DRAM (SDRAM), Double Data Rate SDRAM, and DDR2 SDRAM.

Read-only memory (ROM) is nonvolatile and contains permanent program instructions for execution by the CPU. Other nonvolatile memory types include programmable read-only memory (PROM), erasable programmable read-only memory (EPROM), electrically erasable PROM (EEPROM), and phase change memory.

Cache memory is a type of high-speed memory that CPUs can access more rapidly than RAM.

A multicore microprocessor is one that combines two or more independent processors into a single computer so that the independent processors can share the workload. Intel has introduced 12-core processors that are effective in working on problems involving large databases and multimedia. ARM designs chips based on the big.LITTLE architecture, which employs high clock speed, powerful processors, and slower, more energy-efficient cores.

Parallel computing is the simultaneous execution of the same task on multiple processors to obtain results faster. Massively parallel processing involves linking many processors to work together to solve complex problems.

Grid computing is the use of a collection of computers, often owned by multiple individuals or organizations, to work in a coordinated manner to solve a common problem.

Computer systems can store larger amounts of data and instructions in secondary storage, which is less volatile and has greater capacity than memory. The primary characteristics of secondary storage media and devices include access method, capacity, portability, and cost. Storage media can implement either sequential access or direct access. Common forms of secondary storage include magnetic storage devices such as tape, hard disk drive, virtual tape; optical storage devices such as optical disc, digital video disc (DVD), and Holographic Versatile Disc (HVD); and solid state storage devices such as flash drives.

Infrastructure as a Service is a computing model in which an organization outsources the equipment to support its business operations, including storage, hardware, servers, and networking components.

Redundant array of independent/inexpensive disks (RAID) is a method of storing data that generates extra bits of data from existing data, allowing the system to more easily recover data in the event of a hardware failure.

Network-attached storage (NAS) and storage area networks (SAN) are alternative forms of data storage that enable an organization to share data storage resources among a much larger number of computers and users for improved storage efficiency and greater cost effectiveness.

Storage as a service is a data storage model in which a data storage service provider rents space to people and organizations.

Input and output devices allow users to provide data and instructions to the computer for processing and allow subsequent storage and output. These devices are part of a user interface through which human beings interact with computer systems.

Data is placed in a computer system in a two-stage process: Data entry converts human-readable data into machine-readable form; data input then transfers it to the computer. Common input devices include a keyboard, a mouse, speech recognition, motion-sensing input devices, digital cameras, scanning devices, optical data readers, magnetic ink character recognition devices, magnetic stripe cards, smart cards, contactless cards, point-of-sale devices, automated teller machines, pen input devices, touch-sensitive screens, bar-code scanners, and radio frequency identification (RFID) tags.

There are numerous flat-panel display screens, including liquid crystal display, light-emitting diode, organic light-emitting diode, and plasma devices. Display screen quality is determined by aspect ratio, size, color, and resolution. Other output devices include printers, plotters, surface touch tables, digital audio players, and e-book readers. Computer systems are generally divided into two categories: single user and multiple users. Single-user systems include portable computers, such as handheld, laptop, notebook, and tablet computers. Nonportable single-user systems include thin client, desktop, nettop, and workstation computers.

Multiuser systems include servers, blade servers, mainframes, and supercomputers.

Principle:

The computer hardware industry is rapidly changing and highly competitive, creating an environment ripe for technological breakthroughs.

CPU processing speed is limited by physical constraints such as the distance between circuitry points and circuitry materials. Moore's Law is a hypothesis stating that the number of transistors on a single chip doubles every two years. This hypothesis has been accurate since it was introduced in 1970.

Manufacturers are competing to develop a nonvolatile memory chip that requires minimal power, offers extremely fast write speed, and can store data accurately even after it has been stored and written over many times. Such a chip could eliminate the need for RAM forms of memory.

3D printing has created a major breakthrough in how many items will be manufactured.

The rapid growth in data centers is stimulated by the increased demand for additional computing and data storage capacity plus the consolidation from many to a few data centers.

Organizations are trying a number of strategies to lower the ongoing cost of data center operations.

Principle:

The computer hardware industry and users are implementing green computing designs and products.

Green computing is concerned with the efficient and environmentally responsible design, manufacture, operation, and disposal of IT-related products.

Business organizations recognize that going green can reduce costs and is in their best interests in terms of public relations, safety of employees, and the community at large.

Three specific goals of green computing are to reduce the use of hazardous material, lower power-related costs, and enable the safe disposal and/or recycling of IT products.

Two key green computing initiatives are the European Union Directive 2002/95/EC to reduce the use of hazardous materials, and the use of the Electronic Product Environmental Assessment Tool (EPEAT) to evaluate and purchase green computing systems.

KEY TERMS

arithmetic/logic unit (ALU)

blade server

bus

byte (B)

cache memory

central processing unit (CPU)

clock speed

compact disc read-only memory (CD-ROM)

computer graphics card

contactless payment card

control unit

coprocessor

data center

data entry

data input

desktop computer

digital audio player

digital camera

digital video disc (DVD)

direct access

direct access storage device (DASD)

disk mirroring

Electronic Product Environmental Assessment Tool (EPEAT)

European Union's Restriction of Hazardous Substances Directive

execution time (E-time)

gigahertz (GHz)

graphics processing unit (GPU)

green computing

grid computing

handheld computer

hard disk drive (HDD)

Infrastructure as a Service (IaaS)

instruction time (I-time)

laptop computer

machine cycle

magnetic stripe card

magnetic tape

mainframe computer

massively parallel processing system

MIPS

Moore's Law

motherboard

MP3

multicore microprocessor

multiprocessing

nettop computer

network-attached storage (NAS)

optical storage device

parallel computing

pipelining

point-of-sale (POS) device

policy-based storage management

portable computer

primary storage (main memory; memaroy)

Radio frequency identification (RFID)

random access memory (RAM)

read-only memory (ROM)

redundant array of independent/inexpensive disks (RAID)

register

scalability

secondary storage

sequential access

sequential access storage device (SASD)

server

smart cards

source data automation

speech-recognition technology

storage area network (SAN)

storage as a service

supercomputer

tablet computer

thin client

virtual server

virtual tape

workstation

CHAPTER 3: SELF-ASSESSMENT TEST

Computer hardware must be carefully selected to meet the evolving needs of the organization and its supporting information systems.

1. The _____ is a set of physical connections that can be shared by multiple computer hardware components to communicate with one another.
   a. motherboard
   b. register
   c. bus
   d. control unit

2. A high-speed storage area in the CPU used to temporarily hold small units of program instructions and data immediately before, during, and after execution by the CPU is called the _____.

3. The time it takes to perform the fetch instruction and decode instruction steps is called the execution time. True or false?

4. Each CPU produces a series of electronic pulses at a predetermined rate called the _____, which affects machine cycle time.

5. An advantage of ARM processors over traditional complex instruction set processors is that _____.
   a. they do not require large heat sinks and fans to remove excess heat
   b. they weigh less
   c. they are more energy efficient
   d. all of the above

6. The _____ is the largest amount of storage.
   a. petabyte
   b. exabyte
   c. terabyte
   d. zettabyte

7. DDR SDRAM is faster than SRAM memory. True or false?

8. The toughest challenge in designing a processor for a smartphone or tablet is balancing power consumption with _____.

9. The optical storage device capable of storing the most data is the _____.
   a. CD-ROM
   b. DVD
   c. HVD
   d. Blu-ray

The computer hardware industry is rapidly changing and highly competitive, creating an environment ripe for technological breakthroughs.

10. Many computer jobs that used to run on mainframe computers have migrated onto smaller, less expensive computers. This information-processing migration is called _____.

11. Moore's Law is an indisputable law of physics. True or false?

12. _____ is a measure of the total power consumed by a data center divided by the power required to operate just its computers.

The computer hardware industry and users are implementing green computing designs and products.

13. Green computing is about saving the environment; there are no real business benefits associated with this program. True or false?

14. The disposal and reclamation operations for IT equipment must be careful to avoid unsafe exposure to _____.

CHAPTER 3: SELF-ASSESSMENT TEST ANSWERS

1. c
2. register
3. False
4. clock rate
5. d
6. d
7. True
8. performance
9. c
10. computer downsizing
11. False
12. Power usage effectiveness (PUE)
13. False
14. hazardous materials

REVIEW QUESTIONS

1. Identify the three elements of a CPU and describe the role of each.
2. What is the computer motherboard?
3. How does the role of primary storage differ from secondary storage?
4. Identify and briefly discuss the fundamental characteristic that distinguishes RAM from ROM memory.
5. What is RFID technology? Identify three practical uses for this technology.
6. What is a fuel cell? What advantages do fuel cells offer over batteries for use in portable electronic devices? Do they have any disadvantages?
7. What is RAID storage technology? Why is it used?
8. When speaking of computers, what is meant by scalability? What are the two types of scalability?

9. What is a massively parallel processing computer system? How is grid computing different from such a system? How is it similar?
10. How is a blade server different from a regular server?
11. Identify and briefly describe the various classes of single-user, portable computers.
12. What is a solid state storage device?
13. Identify three reasons for increased spending in data centers.
14. Define the term "green computing" and state its primary goals.
15. What is the EPEAT? How is it used?

DISCUSSION QUESTIONS

1. Discuss the role of the business manager in helping determine the computer hardware to be used by the organization.
2. Compare and contrast the role of the CPU and GPU.
3. Briefly describe the concept of multiprocessing. How does parallel processing differ from multiprocessing?
4. What is 3D printing? Identify three objects that you think would be practical to create using 3D printing.
5. Briefly discuss the advantages and disadvantages of installing thin clients for use in a university computer lab versus desktop computers.
6. What is a 12-core processor? What advantages does it offer users over a single-core processor? Are there any potential disadvantages?
7. Outline the Electronic Product Environment Assessment Tool (EPEAT) for rating computer products.

8. Briefly describe Moore's Law. What are the implications of this law? Are there any practical limitations to Moore's Law?
9. Identify and briefly discuss the advantages and disadvantages of solid state secondary storage devices compared to magnetic secondary storage devices.
10. Briefly discuss the advantages and disadvantages of attached storage, network-attached storage, and storage area networks in meeting enterprise data storage challenges.
11. If cost were not an issue, describe the characteristics of your ideal computer. What would you use it for? Would you choose a handheld, portable, desktop, or workstation computer? Why?
12. Briefly explain the differences between the magnetic stripe card and the smart card.
13. Fully discuss why some organizations are consolidating many data centers into a few.
14. Discuss potential issues that can arise if an organization is not careful in selecting a reputable service organization to recycle or dispose of its IS equipment.

PROBLEM-SOLVING EXERCISES

1. Do research to find the total worldwide sales in units for smartphones, tablet computers, laptop computers, and desktop computers for the last five or six years. Use graphing software to draw a chart showing these sales figures. Write a paragraph summarizing your findings.
2. Use word-processing software to document what your needs are as a computer user and your justification for selecting either a desktop or a portable computer. Find a Web site that allows you to order and customize a computer and select

those options that best meet your needs in a cost-effective manner. Assume that you have a budget of $650. Enter the computer specifications you selected and associated costs from the Web site into an Excel spreadsheet that you cut and paste into the document defining your needs. Email the document to your instructor.
3. Develop a spreadsheet that compares the features, initial purchase price, and a two-year estimate of operating costs (paper, cartridges, and toner) for three color laser printers. Assume that

you will print 25 color pages and 100 black-and-white pages each month. Now do the same for three inkjet printers. Write a brief memo on which printer you would choose and why. Cut and paste the spreadsheet into a document. Repeat your analysis, but this time assume 150 color pages and 1,000 black and white pages per month.

TEAM ACTIVITIES

1. With one or two of your classmates, visit a data center or server farm. As you tour the facility, draw a simple diagram showing the locations of various pieces of hardware equipment. Label each piece of equipment. Discuss the need for power backup, surge protection, and HVAC. Be sure to obtain permission from the appropriate company resources prior to your visit.
2. With one or two of your classmates, visit three different retail stores in search of your ideal e-book reader. Document the costs, features, advantages, and disadvantages of three different readers using a spreadsheet program. Be sure to consider the cost and ease with which e-books can be purchased and downloaded for each reader. Analyze your data and write a recommendation on which one you would buy. Be sure to clearly explain your decision.

WEB EXERCISES

1. Do research on the Web to learn more about why Apple decided to cease registering its products in EPEAT and then later reversed that decision. Write a one-page report summarizing your findings.
2. There is great competition among countries and manufacturers to develop the fastest supercomputer. Do research on the Web to identify the current three fastest supercomputers and how they are being used. Develop a spreadsheet that documents your findings.

CAREER EXERCISES

1. Examine the possibility of a career in computer hardware sales. Which area of sales do you believe holds the brightest prospects for young college graduates—mainframe computers, supercomputers, or high-volume storage devices? Why? What would be some of the advantages and disadvantages of a career in computer hardware sales?
2. Your organization earns $50 million in annual sales, has 500 employees, and plans to acquire 100 new portable computers. The chief financial officer has asked you to lead a project team to define users' computer hardware needs and recommend the most cost-effective solution for meeting those needs. Who else (role, department) and how many people would you select to be a member of the team? How would you go about defining users' needs? Do you think that only one kind of portable computer will meet everyone's needs? Should you define multiple portable computers based on the needs of various classes of end user? What business rationale can you define to justify this expenditure of roughly $50,000?

CASE STUDIES

Case One

Sending Computers into the Cloud

Since the modern electronic computer was invented in the 1940s, the trend has been toward reducing the size of the computer while increasing its capability. The logical end of this trend is to remove the physical computer altogether. While that isn't likely to happen in business, companies have found ways to make their central computers disappear.

Central computers still exist, of course, but if you look around business offices, follow the cables from a desktop or wireless router through walls and down halls, you may not find a central computer. What you'll find instead in more and more organizations are signals going "into the cloud." That saying refers to cloud computing, which provides computing services and database access over the Internet that are accessible from anywhere in the world rather than from a specific computer in a specific location.

Deutsche Bank (DB), the German financial services firm, made a decision to send its computers into the cloud. As Alistair McLaurin of its Global Technology Engineering group put it, the bank "wanted to create something radically different," to "challenge assumptions around what centrally provided IT services could be and how much they must cost." DB created a system in which computing is done by virtual machines (VMs): software-managed "slices" of real computers that behave in every respect like a full computer but that share the hardware of one real computer with many other VMs. A virtual machine is an extension of the familiar concept of running more than one program at a time. In a VM, you run more than one operating system at a time, with each completely isolated from the others. The result is substantial savings in hardware cost and everything that goes with it, such as space and electricity. By putting the computers that host its virtual machines in the cloud, DB freed itself from the constraints of being at a particular physical location. DB can thus optimize the use of these virtual computers across the entire company.

Another advantage of the virtual approach is that someone who needs a new computer doesn't have to purchase one. Instead, they can use a virtual computer inside a real computer that the company already has; such a VM is easier to set up than a new system. In fact, "a user who is a permanent employee, who wants a new Virtual Machine for their own use only, can do it by visiting one Web site, selecting an operating system [Windows, Solaris, or Linux] and clicking three buttons. The new VM will be ready and available for them within an hour."

The Open Data Center Alliance recently chose DB as the grand prize winner of its Conquering the Cloud Challenge. The specific basis for the award was the way DB's cloud-based system manages user identities. When a user requests a virtual machine, the system already knows who has to approve the request (if anyone), where its cost should be billed, and who should be allowed to administer the machine. The cloud-based system means users don't have to worry about how virtual machines are created, making it more practical to use them. Because a virtual machine is less expensive than a new desktop computer, DB management wanted to encourage employees to use the virtual machines. Removing barriers to their adoption was important, which is why DB designed the cloud-based system to manage user identities.

Currently, programmers and other systems developers use DB's cloud system for application development and testing. If a developer is working with a computer that runs Solaris and wants to test an application under Windows 7 or Windows Vista, he or she can do so using a virtual machine quickly and efficiently. The cloud system will be used next for DB production applications, except for those that need 100 percent uptime (such as the one that operates a network of ATMs). After that? Who knows?

Discussion Questions

1. What was innovative about the manner in which the Deutsche Bank manages identities?
2. What other types of companies could use this innovation to cut IT costs?

Critical Thinking Questions

1. Would cloud computing be useful to your school? To a specific small business you can think of?
2. How does the location independence of cloud computing help Deutsche Bank or any other organization?

SOURCES: King, L., "Deutsche Bank Completes Cloud Computing Overhaul," *Computerworld UK, www.itworld.com/it-management strategy/229793/deutschebank-completes-cloud-computing-overhaul*, December 2, 2011; McLaurin, A., "Identity Management in the New Hybrid Cloud World," Deutsche Bank's Entry in the Open Data Center Alliance 2011 Conquering the Cloud Challenge, downloaded December 19, 2011, from *www.opendatacenteralliance.org/contest*; Morgan, G., "Deutsche Bank Lifts the Hood on Cloud Transition," *Computing, www.computing.co.uk/ctg/news/2128892/deutsche-bank-liftshood-cloud-transition*, November 30, 2011.

Case Two

AT&T and the Dallas Cowboys Leverage Technology in the Stadium

When you visit the Web site of the Dallas Cowboys professional football team, you have a good chance of seeing a banner ad for the team's stadium with the headline, "It's a data center with 80,000 seats." Calling a stadium a data center may be an exaggeration, but today's professional sports arenas aren't just seats around a grass field. For at least a few hours a week, they are in effect good-sized cities. It would be impossible to manage such stadiums without technology.

Professional sports teams are also businesses. Making a profit is close to the top of their agendas. Costs must be controlled, expenditures minimized. These needs apply to computer hardware as much as it does anywhere else in the Cowboys organization.

The team's first major step toward reducing costs through IT came when it designed its new stadium for the 2009–10 NFL season. The new technology infrastructure had to handle stadium operations as well as the customer experience (such as ticketing, running the huge screens along the sidelines and in the end zone, and operating 2,900 other screens in the stadium) for the next 15 to 20 years. "At our previous home, 30-year-old Texas Stadium, all you really did was turn on the lights and bring out the football," says Bill Haggard, director of enterprise infrastructure for the Cowboys. "This is different."

"If we had gone all physical with the servers, we would have in the neighborhood of 500 physical servers," Haggard observes. Aside from the cost of the servers and the space they'd occupy, they would have cost about $2.2 million per year just in power and cooling. That expense was too high for the organization. By using two technologies, blade servers and virtualization, the Cowboys reduced these numbers: from 500 to 130 servers and from $2.2 million to $365,000 for power and cooling.

Then in 2013, the Cowboys struck a deal with the telecommunications giant AT&T. The two organizations worked together to double the capacity of the fastest and most reliable mobile network in the United States, which is now available within the stadium, in the plazas, and even in the parking lots. The stadium also doubled the capacity of its Wi-Fi network while providing new mobile apps with maps and navigation tools to help Cowboys fans on game days. To acknowledge AT&T's contribution and this move toward high-tech football, the stadium changed its name from Cowboys Stadium to AT&T Stadium.

Discussion Questions

1. One clear benefit of the combination of virtualization and blade servers to the Dallas Cowboys is the financial savings. What other benefits did the Cowboys obtain by using these technologies?
2. What advantage does AT&T gain by providing the stadium with a 4G LTE mobile network?

Critical Thinking Questions

1. The Cowboys estimate that the team will save a total of $8.2 million over five years by using the approaches outlined in this case rather than by using separate servers. What do you think will happen at the end of this period?
2. What strategic advantages have the Cowboys gained from the technological transformations of its stadium?

SOURCES: Home of the Dallas Cowboys Is Now AT&T Stadium, New Release Archives, AT&T Web site, July 25, 2013, *www.att.com/gen/press -room?pid=24565&cdvn=news&newsarticleid=36769*, accessed August 23, 2013; Dallas Cowboys Web site, *www.dallascowboys.com*, accessed January 2, 2012; Dallas Cowboys stadium fact sheet (no date), down loaded January 2, 2012, from *http://stadium.dallascowboys.com /assets/pdf/mediaArchitectureFactSheet.pdf*; Hewlett-Packard, "Dallas

Cowboys Generate 30% More Revenue with New Stadium and HP Solutions," *www.convergedinfrastructure.com/document /1319477924_337* (free registration required), October 27, 2011.

Questions for Web Case

See the Web site for this book to read about the Altitude Online Consulting case for this chapter. Following are questions concerning this Web case.

Altitude Online Consulting: Choosing Hardware

Discussion Questions

1. How might Altitude Online Consulting determine what new hardware devices it requires to support the service that its employees use?
2. How will Altitude Online Consulting determine the computing power and storage requirements of the new system?

Critical Thinking Questions

1. What should Altitude Online Consulting do with its old computer hardware as it is replaced with new hardware?
2. Why do you think Altitude Online Consulting decided to phase in new desktop computers, but replace mobile devices all at once?

NOTES

Sources for the opening vignette: "Fujitsu and NAOJ Begin Operation of Supercomputer for ALMA," Press Release, Fujitsu Web site, March 14, 2013, *www.fujitsu.com/global /news/pr/archives/month/2013/20130314-01.html*, accessed August 23, 2013; "Fujitsu PRIMERGY Computational Power at Australian National University Takes High Capability Australian Research to the World Stage," Press Release, Fujitsu Web site, July 31, 2013, *www.fujitsu.com/au/news/pr /archives/2013/20130731-01.html*, accessed August 23, 2013; Fujitsu Press Release Archives, *www.fujitsu.com /global/news/pr/archives*, accessed August 22, 2013; "Fujitsu Receives Order for New Supercomputer System from Canon," Press Release, Fujitsu Web site, August 6, 2013, *www.fujitsu .com/global/news/pr/archives/month/2013/20130806-01 .html*, accessed August 23, 2013; "IBM sells Opteron Supercomputer to Drug Company," Geek.com, January 15, 2004, *www.geek.com/chips/ibm-sells-opteron-supercomputer -to-drug-company-555169*, accessed August 23, 2013; Gohring, Nancy, "Own Your Own Cray Supercomputer for a Mere $500,000," CNNMoneyTech, May 7, 2013, *http://money .cnn.com/2013/05/07/technology/enterprise/cray -supercomputer/index.html*, accessed August 23, 2013.

1. "City of Bunbury Selects IBM PureSystems to Take the Lead with Government Cloud," *IBM News Room*, April 2, 2013, *www-03.ibm.com/press/us/en/pressrelease /40730.wss*.
2. De Vos, Jason, "Video Editors Choose Dell for Performance over Apple Mac Pro," *Studio Daily*, January 1, 2013, *www.studiodaily.com/2013/01/video-editors-choose-dell -for-performance-over-apple-mac-pro*.
3. Shrout, Ryan, "CES 2013: Lilliputian Nectar Mobile Power System Brings Fuel Cells to Consumers," *General Tech*, January 6, 2013, *www.pcper.com/news/General -Tech/CES-2013-Lilliputian-Nectar-Mobile-Power -System-brings-Fuel-Cells-Consumers*.
4. Seubert, Curtis, "How Many Bytes Is an Exabyte," *www .ehow.com/about_6370860_many-bytes-exabyte_.html*, accessed August 8, 2013.
5. "Manufacturing Bits," Semiconductor Manufacturing and Design, March 19, 2013, *http://semimd.com/blog /tag/phase-change-memory*.
6. Cooper, Daniel, "Apple Announces New Mac Pro with Cylindrical Design, 12-Core Intel Xeon E5 CPU, Flash Storage, Thunderbolt 2.0 and Support for up to Three 4K Displays," *engadget*, June 10, 2013, *www.engadget .com/2013/06/10/apple-mac-pro-2013-redesign*.
7. Heath, Nick, "Cracking the 1,000-Core Processor Power Challenge," *ZDNet*, May 21, 2013, *www.zdnet.com /cracking-the-1000-core-processor-power-challenge -7000015554*.
8. Cunningham, Andrew, "Samsung Galaxy S4 Processor: How the Eight Core CPU Works," *Wired.CO.UK*, March 19, 2013, *www.wired.co.uk/news/archive/2013-03/19 /exynos-5-octa*.
9. "About Blue Waters," Blue Waters Sustained Petascale Computing, *https://bluewaters.ncsa.illinois.edu /blue-waters*, accessed August 10, 2013.

10. Mearian, Lucas, "Harvard Global Grid Computing Project Will Help Create Printable Solar Cells," *Computerworld*, April 16, 2013, *www.computerworld.com/s/article /9238429/Harvard_global_grid_computing_project_ will_help_create_printable_solar_cells*.

11. "Statistics by Project," World Community Grid, *www .worldcommunitygrid.org/stat/viewProjects.do*, accessed August 9, 2013.

12. Malle, Jean-Pierre, "Big Data: Farewell to Cartesian Thinking?" *Paris Tech Review*, March 15, 2013, *www .paristechreview.com/2013/03/15/big-data-cartesian -thinking*.

13. "SGI to Provide Massive Data Storage Capability for the Australian Square Kilometer Array Pathfinder," SGI Press Release, April 29, 2013, *www.sgi.com /company_info/newsroom/press_releases/2013/april /askap.html*.

14. Mims, Christopher, "And the Longest Running Digital Storage Medium is …," *MIT Technology Review*, July 13, 2011, *www.technologyreview.com/view/424669/and -the-longest-running-digital-storage-medium-is*.

15. "Made in IBM Labs: IBM Research Sets New Record in Magnetic Tape Density," *PR Newswire*, January 22, 2013, *www.prnewswire.com/news-releases/made-in-ibm-labs -ibm-research-sets-new-record-in-magnetic-tape-data -density-82330257.html*.

16. "Tape Systems Are Down but Not Out," Emerging Tech blog, *GCN*, January 28, 2013, *http://gcn.com/blogs /emerging-tech/2013/01/tape-storage-systems-are-down -but-not-out.aspx*.

17. Simonite, Tom, "IBM Builds Biggest Data Drive Ever," *MIT Technology Review*, August 25, 2011, *www.technology review.com/news/425237/ibm-builds-biggest-data-drive -ever*.

18. "Out with the Old, in with the New: Gila Regional Medical Center Moves Radiology Departments Imaging Library to ATA boy2 RAID Array," *www.rad-direct.com /Success_Story_GRMC.htm*, accessed August 10, 2013.

19. Inglis, Blair, "Sony Working on Blue-Ray Successor— Are PS4 Discs Soon to be Outdated?" *The Six Axis*, July 30, 2013, *www.thesixthaxis.com/2013/07/30/sony -working-on-blu-ray-successor-are-ps4-discs-soon-to-be -out-dated*.

20. Williams, Martyn, "New Blu-ray Disc Offers 'Lifetime of Storage,'" *Computerworld*, January 6, 2013, *www .computerworld.com/s/article/9235318/New_Blu_ray _Disc_offers_39_lifetime_of_storage_39_*.

21. "Holographic Versatile Disc," *TechTwick*, April 14, 2013, *www.techtwick.com/holographic-versatile-disc-hvd /#chitika_close_button*.

22. Keith, Jonathan, "DNA Data Storage: 100 Million Hours of HD Video in Every Cup," Phys Org, January 25, 2013, *http://phys.org/news/2013-01-dna-storage-million-hours -hd.html*

23. "Samsung Unveils New Solid State Drives at Its Annual SSD Global Summit," *Samsung Press Release*, July 18, 2013, *www.samsung.com/global/business/semiconductor /news-events/press-releases/detail?newsId=12961*.

24. Butler, Brandon, "Cloud Sigma Goes All SSD in Its Cloud," *Network World*, April 2, 2013, *www.networkw orld.com/news/2013/040213-cloudsigma-ssd-268301 .html*.

25. Synology Web site, "All Pop Art Replaces Their SBS Server with Network Attached Storage and Doesn't Look Back," *www.vst.co.nz/storage%20solution /synology/synology_for_industry/synology%20case %20study/Creative%20Concepts%20Engineering %20Finds%20Value,%20Peace%20of%20Mind,%20With %20Synology%20DiskStation/Creative%20Concepts %20Engineering.pdf, accessed September 13, 2013*.

26. "IT Simplicity Drives Business Agility at Revlon," NetApp Web site, *www.netapp.com/us/media/ds-3411 -0213.pdf*, access September 13, 2013.

27. Vaughan-Nichols, Stephen J., "The Top 10 Personal Cloud-Storage Services," *ZD Net*, February 25, 2013, *www.zdnet.com/the-top-10-personal-cloud-storage -services-7000011729/*.

28. "I Found My Stolen Laptop", *http://mozy.ie/home /reviews*, accessed August 14, 2013.

29. Big Hand Web site, "Maxwell Winward Deploys BigHand Speech Recognition to Improve Fee-Earners' Self-Sufficiency and Broaden the Scope of Secretarial Support", May 30, 2012, *www.bighand.com/digital dictation/BHforBlackBerry10_658.html*.

30. France, Jasmine, "NeatReceipts," *PC World*, April 30, 2013, *www.pcworld.com/article/2035998/neatreceipts -scanner-makes-filing-a-snap.html*.

31. "US Credit Cards with Smart Chip Technology, The Points Guy, May 30, 2013, *http://thepointsguy.com /2013/05/us-credit-cards-with-smart-chips*.

32. Ibid.

33. Britten, Nick, "Your Contactless Card Could Be Hacked by Mobile Phone," *Telegraph*, June 3, 2013, *www.tele graph.co.uk/finance/personalfinance/borrowing /creditcards/10095303/Your-contactless-card-could-be -hacked-by-mobile-phone.html*.

34. "Contactless Debit and Credit Cards: What Are the Risks?" *The Week*, May 30, 2013, *www.theweek.co.uk /prosper/53317/contactless-cards-what-are-risks*.

35. Flores, Adolfo, "Technology Taking Swipe at Old Point- of-Sale Devices," *The Spokesman Review*, June 20, 2013, *www.spokesman.com/stories/2013/jun/20/technology -taking-swipe-at-old-point-of-sale*.

36. Five, Dave, "RFID Solution for Asset Tracking—Lone Pine Construction," *Silent Partner Tech*, June 28, 2013, *www.silentpartnertech.com/news-and-articles/success- stories/lone-pine-construction*.

37. Clark, Nicola, "Touch Screens Are Tested for Piloting Passenger Jets," *New York Times*, July 5, 2013, *www .nytimes.com/2013/07/06/technology/passenger-jets -testing-touch-screen-technology.html?_r=0*.

38. Tyson, Jeff and Wilson, Terry V., "How Graphics Cards Work, How Stuff Works," *http://computer.howstuff works.com/graphics-card.html*, accessed August 18, 2013.

39. Blecher, Joni, "CES 2013: Bending the Future of Mobile Phones," *RealPlayer*, January 17, 2013, *www.real.com /resources/ces-future-mobile-phones*.

40. "2013 Best 3D Printer Reviews and Comparisons," *http://3d-printers.toptenreviews.com*, accessed August 19, 2013.

41. Perez, Sarah, "eBay Is Latest to Join 3D Printing Craze with New App for Customizable Goods, eBay Exact," *Tech Crunch*, July 12, 2013, *http://techcrunch.com /2013/07/12/ebay-is-latest-to-join-3d-printing-craze -with-new-app-for-customizable-goods-ebay-exact.*

42. Leckart, Steven, "How 3D Printing Body Parts Will Revolutionize Medicine," *Popular Science*, August 6, 2013, *www.popsci.com/science/article/2013-07/how-3 -d-printing-body-parts-will-revolutionize-medicine.*

43. PrinterOn Web site, *www.printeron.com/images/docs /PrinterOnAirportPrintingSolutions.pdf*, accessed August 19, 2013.

44. "Ebook Readers," *PC Magazine, www.pcmag.com /reviews/ebook-readers*, accessed August 19, 2013.

45. "Wyse TV Jewelry Case Study," *www.wyse.com /solutions/industries/retail*, accessed August 27, 2013.

46. Miller, Rich, "The Billion Dollar Data Centers," *Data Center Knowledge*, April 29, 2013, *www.datacenter knowledge.com/archives/2013/04/29/the-billion-dollar -data-centers.*

47. "Network and Services Availability Secures Bharti Airtel Drive for New Highs," HP Case Studies, August 16, 2013, *http://h20195.www2.hp.com/V2/GetDocument .aspx?docname=4AA4-7964EEW&doctype=success story&doclang=EN_GB&searchquery=All sizes|All Industries|virtual servers&cc=us&lc=en.*

48. Barker, Colin, "With the World Embracing Cloud Computing, Who Needs Mainframes?" *ZDNet*, July 4, 2013, *www.zdnet.com/with-the-world-embracing-cloud -computing-who-needs-mainframes-7000017087.*

49. "Sicoob Avoids USD 1.5 Million in Annual Costs with IBM," July 18, 2013, *https://www-01.ibm.com/software /success/cssdb.nsf/CS/STRD-99GKQN?OpenDocument& Site=default&cty=en_us.*

50. Gohring, Nancy, "Own Your Own Cray Supercomputer for a Mere $500,000," *CNN Money Tech*, May 7, 2013, *http://money.cnn.com/2013/05/07/technology/enterprise /cray-supercomputer/index.html.*

51. "Introducing Titan, Advancing the Era of Accelerated Computing," *www.olcf.ornl.gov/titan*, accessed August 22, 2013.

52. Chen, Stephen, "World's Fastest Supercomputer, Tianhe-2, Might Get Very Little Use," *South China Morning Post*, August 22, 2013, *www.scmp.com/news /china/article/1264529/worlds-fastest-computer-tianhe -2-might-get-very-little-use.*

53. Miller, Rich, "Rackspace Adding 50 Servers per Day," *Data Center Knowledge*, August 12, 2013, *http://www .datacenterknowledge.com/archives/2013/08/12 /rackspace-adding-servers-per-day/.*

54. "GM's Latest Michigan Data Center Gets LEED Gold," *Data Center Dynamics*, September 13, 2013, *www .datacenterdynamics.com/focus/archive/2013/09 /gms-latest-michigan-data-center-gets-leed-gold.*

55. Arthur Charles, "Technology Firms to Spend $150 Billion on Building New Data Centres," *The Guardian*, August 23, 2013, *www.theguardian.com/business/2013/aug/23 /spending-on-data-centres-reaches-150-billion-dollars.*

56. Miller, Rich, Microsoft's $1 billion Data Center," *Data Center Knowledge*, January 21, 2013, *www.datacenter knowledge.com/archives/2013/01/31/microsofts-1 -billion-roofless-data-center/.*

57. Morthen, Ben, "Data Centers Boom," *Wall Street Journal*, April 11, 2011, p. B6.

58. Babcock, Charles, "5 Data Center Trends for 2013," *InformationWeek*, January 2, 2013, *www.information week.com/hardware/data-centers/5-data-center-trends -for-2013/240145349?printer_friendly=this-page.*

59. Thibodeau, P., "Rural N.C. Becomes Popular IT Location," *Computerworld*, June 20, 2011, p. 2.

60. "IBM Opens New Cloud Data Center in Peru to Meet Demand for Big Data Analytics," IBM News room, August 22, 2013, *www-03.ibm.com/press/us/en /pressrelease/41809.wss.*

61. Wells, Brad, "What Truly Makes a Computer 'Green'?" *OnEarth* (blog), September 8, 2008, *www.onearth.org /node/658.*

62. "Facts and Figures on E-Waste and Recycling," Electronics TakeBack Coalition, June 25, 2013, *www .electronicstakeback.com/wp-content/uploads/Facts _and_Figures_on_EWaste_and_Recycling.pdf.*

63. "EPEAT Environmental Criteria," *www.epeat.net /resources/criteria/*, accessed August 19, 2013.

64. "EPEAT Recognizing Environmental Performance," Ricoh Web site, *www.ricoh-usa.com/about/epeat*, accessed June 20, 2013.

65. "Restriction of Hazardous Substances Directive," Compliance Web Site, *http://leadfree.ipc.org/RoHS _4-1-2.asp*, accessed August 19, 2013.

66. "Dell's Worldwide Technology Recycling Options," *www.dell.com/learn/us/en/uscorp1/corp-comm/global recycling*, accessed July 12, 2013.

67. "HP Expands Recycling Program, Adds Certified Paper Portfolio," *Environmental Leader*, April 17, 2013, *www .environmentalleader.com/2013/04/17/hp-expands -recycling-program-adds-certified-paper-portfolio.*

4 Software: Systems and Application Software

Principles	Learning Objectives
• Systems and application software are critical in helping individuals and organizations achieve their goals.	• Identify and briefly describe the functions of two basic kinds of software. • Outline the role of the operating system and identify the features of several popular operating systems.
• Organizations use off-the-shelf application software for common business needs and proprietary application software to meet unique business needs and provide a competitive advantage.	• Discuss how application software can support personal, workgroup, and enterprise business objectives. • Identify three basic approaches to developing application software and discuss the pros and cons of each.
• Organizations should choose programming languages with functional characteristics that are appropriate for the task at hand and well suited to the skills and experience of the programming staff.	• Outline the overall evolution and importance of programming languages and clearly differentiate among the generations of programming languages.
• The software industry continues to undergo constant change; users need to be aware of recent trends and issues to be effective in their business and personal life.	• Identify several key software issues and trends that have an impact on organizations and individuals.

Information Systems in the Global Economy
CREATIVESYSTEMS, PORTUGAL

Developing Software to Leverage RFID Innovation

© havesen/Shutterstock.com, © Tang Yan Song/Shutterstock.com

Operating out of its headquarters in Portugal and Span, Creativesystems develops radio frequency identification (RFID) software. RFID is a technology that employs a microchip with an antenna to broadcast its unique identifier and location to receivers. The purpose of an RFID system is to transmit data by a mobile device, called a tag, which is read by an RFID reader and processed according to the needs of a computer program. Creativesystems develops computer programs that not only process the tag information but make decisions based on this input. This software is improving the efficiency of supply chains across the world.

In 2013, for example, the Dutch clothing store C&A decided to implement Creativesystems's RFID solutions. C&A manufactures clothing and footwear for men, women, and children made out of organic cotton and other sustainable materials. C&A also operates 1,600 stores in 20 countries; it manufactures garments and footwear based on the orders sent in by each store. Because the process is logistically challenging, C&A began to use RFID technology and Creativesystems software to track orders. Now when the manufacturers receive an order, they attach and scan an RFID tag to each unit ordered and then ship it. The Creativesystems software immediately sends an advance shipping notice to the store. When the store receives the units, employees scan the tags to update the store's inventory system and to indicate that the items have been placed on the sales floor. As customers purchase items, the inventory system is updated and notifies the managers when it is necessary to reorder. Since implementing Creativesystems software, C&A has achieved a lower out-of-stock rate and improved the number of items that are on the shelf and ready to purchase.

Creativesystems not only develops RFID software solutions for supply chain and manufacturing challenges but also actively works with industrial partners and research institutions to find new solutions in areas such as embedding intelligence and near field communication. Because RFIDs can be read only by mobile devices within a limited physical range, Creativesystems is cooperating with Universidade do Minho, We Adapt, and other organizations to extend the distance at which RFID tags can be read.

In addition to its commercial success, Creativesystems has received numerous awards, including Motorola Solutions's Best Mobile Application Solutions Award. It is also recognized by global media company Red Herring as one of Europe's top 100 technology companies. Creativesystems recently received its first U.S. patent for its RFID software innovations, signaling its move into the North American market.

As you read this chapter, consider the following:

- How is software development tied to or limited by advances in hardware?
- What type of solutions can Creativesystems and other software developers provide to industry?
- Can the use of RFID tags reduce human input errors?

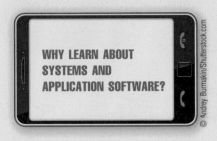

WHY LEARN ABOUT SYSTEMS AND APPLICATION SOFTWARE?

Software is indispensable for any computer system and the people using it. In this chapter, you will learn about systems and application software. Without systems software, computers would not be able to accept data input from a keyboard, process data, or display results. The ability to use application software effectively is one of the keys to helping you achieve your career goals. Sales representatives use software on their smartphones and tablet computers to enter sales orders and help their customers get what they want. Stock and bond traders use software to make split-second decisions involving millions of dollars. Scientists use software to analyze the threat of climate change. Regardless of your job, you most likely will use software to help you advance in your career and earn higher wages. You can also use software to help you prepare your personal income taxes, keep a budget, and stay in contact with friends and family online. Software can truly advance your career and enrich your life. We begin with an overview of software.

The effective use of software has a profound impact on individuals and organizations. It can make the difference between profits and losses and between financial health and bankruptcy. As Figure 4.1 shows, companies recognize this impact, spending more on software than on computer hardware or other areas of information systems. This is far different from when computers first were available; software was given away and customers paid only for the hardware. Today, spending on software actually exceeds spending on hardware.[1]

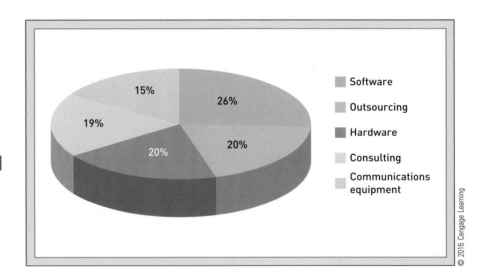

FIGURE 4.1

Software expenditures exceed spending on hardware

Since the 1950s, businesses have greatly increased their expenditures on software compared with hardware.

AN OVERVIEW OF SOFTWARE

computer program: A sequence of instructions for the computer.

documentation: Text that describes a program's functions to help the user operate the computer system.

Software consists of computer programs that control the workings of computer hardware. Computer programs are sequences of instructions for the computer. Documentation describes how the program works to help the user operate the computer system. Some documentation is given onscreen or online, while other forms appear in external resources, such as printed manuals.

Worldwide spending on software has been affected by the slowdown in the economy. Software spending over the five-year period from 2012 to 2017 in the emerging economies of Asia/Pacific (excluding Japan), Latin America, Central, Eastern, Middle East (CEMA), and Africa is expected to grow at an average compound rate of 8.8 percent compared to 5.0 percent for the mature regions of North America, Western Europe, and Japan.[2]

Systems Software

Systems software is the set of programs that coordinates the activities and functions of the hardware and other programs throughout the computer system. Each type of systems software is designed for a specific CPU and class of hardware. The combination of a hardware configuration and systems software is known as a computer system platform.

Application Software

Application software consists of programs that help users solve particular computing problems. See Figure 4.2. American Modern Insurance Group is a specialty insurer that covers items such as rental property, seasonal homes, mobile homes, motorcycles, and collector cars.[3] The firm recently implemented application software called InsuranceSuite to support its underwriting and policy administration, as well as its claims, billing, payment, and commission management processes. The software enables it to provide full-policy lifecycle servicing, faster quoting, and standardized underwriting.[4] The Brain Academy software application provides a fun way to exercise your brain and make it stronger. The software features a dozen fun and mentally stimulating games to help players of all ages have a fit and healthy brain.[5]

FIGURE 4.2

Application software

Application software has the greatest potential to affect processes that add value to a business because it is designed for specific organizational activities and functions.

© iStockphoto.com/Avatar_023

You can find millions of software applications, with over 1.6 million apps alone designed to run on Android and iPhone smartphones.[6] Following are some of the dozens of categories of applications.

Business	Genealogy	Personal information manager
Communications	Language	Photography
Computer-aided design	Legal	Science
Desktop publishing	Library	Simulation
Educational	Multimedia	Video games
Entertainment	Music	Video

In most cases, application software resides on the computer's hard disk before it is brought into the computer's memory and run. Application software can also be stored on CDs, DVDs, and even USB flash drives. An increasing amount of application software is available on the Web. Sometimes referred to as a *rich Internet application (RIA)*, a Web-delivered application combines hardware resources of the Web server and the PC to deliver valuable software services through a Web browser interface. Before a person, a group, or an enterprise decides on the best approach for acquiring application software, they carefully analyze computing goals, business needs, and budget.

Supporting Individual, Group, and Organizational Goals

Every organization relies on the contributions of people, groups, and the entire enterprise to achieve its business objectives. One useful way of classifying the many potential uses of information systems is to identify the scope of the problems and opportunities that the system is intended to address. This scope is called the *sphere of influence*. For most companies, the spheres of influence are personal, workgroup, and enterprise. Table 4.1 shows how various kinds of software support these three spheres.

TABLE **4.1** Software supporting individuals, workgroups, and enterprises

Software	Personal	Workgroup	Enterprise
Systems software	Smartphone, tablet computer, personal computer, and workstation operating systems	Network operating systems	Server and mainframe operating systems
Application software	Word processing, spreadsheet, database, and graphics	Electronic mail, group scheduling, shared work, and collaboration	General ledger, order entry, payroll, and human resources

© 2016 Cengage Learning

personal sphere of influence: The sphere of influence that serves the needs of an individual user.

personal productivity software: The software that enables users to improve their personal effectiveness, increasing the amount of work and quality of work they can do.

workgroup: Two or more people who work together to achieve a common goal.

workgroup sphere of influence: The sphere of influence that helps workgroup members attain their common goals.

enterprise sphere of influence: The sphere of influence that serves the needs of the firm in its interaction with its environment.

Information systems that operate within the **personal sphere of influence** serve the needs of individual users. These information systems help users improve their personal effectiveness, increasing the amount and quality of work they can do. Such software is often called **personal productivity software**. For example, Clear is a user-friendly "to-do" list app for the iPhone and Mac,[7] while Bump lets you swap contacts and other content with nearby mobile devices over a Wi-Fi network.[8]

When two or more people work together to achieve a common goal, they form a **workgroup**. A workgroup might be a large formal, permanent organizational entity, such as a section or department, or a temporary group formed to complete a specific project. An information system in the **workgroup sphere of influence** helps workgroup members attain their common goals. Often, software designed for the personal sphere of influence can extend into the workgroup sphere. See Figure 4.3. For example, SignNow is a free app that speeds up the approval process for important documents by letting you print documents, and then sign, scan, format, and send them to the next person on the approval chain.[9] Cooper is a project management application that lets you create a project plan, add people resources to the project, and then have them sign in and update the status of their tasks.[10]

Information systems that operate within the **enterprise sphere of influence** support the firm in its interaction with its environment, which includes customers, suppliers, shareholders, competitors, special-interest groups, the financial community, and government agencies. This means the enterprise sphere of influence includes business partners, such as suppliers that provide raw materials; retail companies that store and sell a company's products; and shipping companies that transport raw materials to the plant and finished goods to retail outlets. For example, many enterprises use IBM Cognos

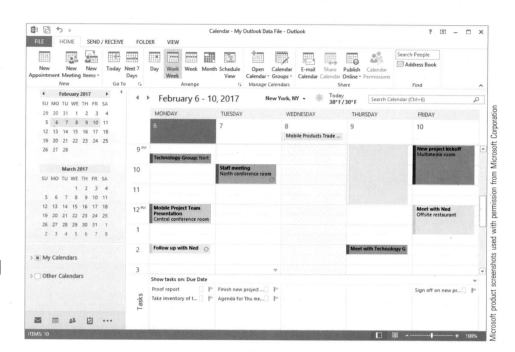

FIGURE 4.3

Microsoft Outlook

Outlook is an application that workgroups can use to schedule meetings and coordinate activities.

software as a centralized Web-based system where employees, partners, and stakeholders can report and analyze corporate financial data.

SYSTEMS SOFTWARE

The primary role of systems software is to control the operations of computer hardware. Systems software also supports the application programs' problem-solving capabilities. There are three types of systems software: operating systems, utility programs, and middleware.

Operating Systems

operating system (OS): A set of computer programs that controls the computer hardware and acts as an interface with applications.

An **operating system (OS)** is a set of programs that controls the computer hardware and acts as an interface with applications. See Figure 4.4. Operating systems can control one or more computers, or they can allow multiple users to interact with one computer. The various combinations of OSs, computers, and users include the following:

- **Single computer with a single user.** This system is commonly used in a personal computer, a tablet computer, or a smartphone that supports one user at a time. Examples of OSs for this setup include Microsoft Windows, Mac OS X, and Google Android.
- **Single computer with multiple simultaneous users.** This system is typical of larger server or mainframe computers that can support hundreds or thousands of people, all using the computer at the same time. Examples of OSs that support this kind of system include UNIX, z/OS, and HP-UX.
- **Multiple computers with multiple users.** This type of system is typical of a network of computers, such as a home network with several computers attached or a large computer network with hundreds of computers attached supporting many users, sometimes located around the world. Network server OSs include Red Hat Enterprise Linux Server, Windows Server, and Mac OS X Server.
- **Special-purpose computers.** This type of system is typical of a number of computers with specialized functions, such as those that control sophisticated military aircraft, space shuttles, digital cameras, or home

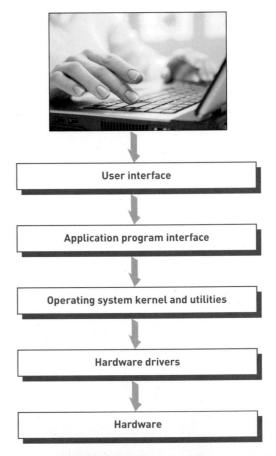

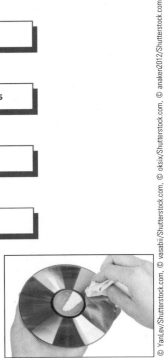

FIGURE 4.4

Role of operating systems

The role of the operating system is to act as an interface between application software and hardware.

kernel: The heart of the operating system and controls its most critical processes.

appliances. Examples of OSs for these purposes include Windows Embedded, Symbian, and some distributions of Linux.

The OS, which plays a central role in the functioning of the complete computer system, is usually stored on disk on general-purpose computers and in solid state memory on mobile computers such as tablets and smartphones. After you start, or boot up, a computer system, the kernel of the OS is loaded into primary storage and remains there for as long as the computer is powered on. The kernel, as its name suggests, is the heart of the OS and controls its most critical processes. The kernel ties all of the OS components together and regulates other programs.

Other portions of the OS are transferred to memory as the system needs them. OS developers are continuously working to shorten the time required to boot devices from being shut down and wake devices from sleep mode.

You can also boot a computer from a CD, a DVD, or even a USB flash drive. A storage device that contains some or all of the OS is often called a *rescue disk* because you can use it to start the computer if you have problems with the primary hard disk.

The set of programs that makes up the OS performs a variety of activities, including the following:

- Controlling common computer hardware functions
- Providing a user interface and input/output management
- Providing a degree of hardware independence
- Managing system memory
- Managing processing tasks
- Providing networking capability
- Controlling access to system resources
- Managing files

Common Hardware Functions

All applications must perform certain hardware-related tasks, such as the following:

- Get input from the keyboard or another input device
- Retrieve data from disks
- Store data on disks
- Display information on a monitor or printer

Each of these tasks requires a detailed set of instructions. The OS converts a basic request into instructions that the hardware requires. In effect, the OS acts as an intermediary between the application and the hardware. The OS uses special software provided by device manufacturers, called hardware drivers, to communicate with and control a device. Hardware drivers are typically downloaded from the device manufacturer's Web site or read from an installation DVD and installed when the hardware is first connected to the computer system.

User Interface and Input/Output Management

user interface: The element of the operating system that allows people to access and interact with the computer system.

One of the most important functions of any OS is providing a user interface, which allows people to access and interact with the computer system. The first user interfaces for mainframe and personal computer systems were command based. A command-based user interface requires you to give text commands to the computer to perform basic activities. For example, the command ERASE 00TAXRTN would cause the computer to erase a file named 00TAXRTN. RENAME and COPY are other examples of commands used to rename files and copy files from one location to another. Today's systems engineers and administrators often use a command-based user interface to control the low-level functioning of computer systems. Most modern OSs (including popular graphical user interfaces such as Windows) provide a way to interact with the system through a command line. See Figure 4.5.

command-based user interface: A user interface that requires you to give text commands to the computer to perform basic activities.

graphical user interface (GUI): An interface that displays pictures (icons) and menus that people use to send commands to the computer system.

A graphical user interface (GUI) displays pictures (called *icons*) and menus that people use to send commands to the computer system. GUIs are more intuitive to use because they anticipate the user's needs and provide easy-to-recognize options. Microsoft Windows is a popular GUI. As the name suggests, Windows is based on the use of a window, or a portion of the display screen dedicated to a specific application. The screen can display several windows at once.

While GUIs have traditionally been accessed using a keyboard and mouse, more recent technologies allow people to use touch screens and spoken commands. Today's mobile devices and some PCs, for example, use a touch user interface also called a *natural user interface* (*NUI*) or multitouch interface by some.

Speech recognition is also available with some operating systems. Microsoft and other operating system manufacturers have developed voice command computer control software. Microsoft employs a special programming language

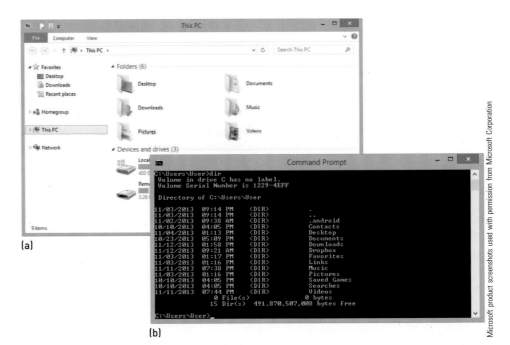

(a)

(b)

FIGURE **4.5**

Command-based and graphical user interfaces

A Windows file system viewed with a GUI (a) and from the command prompt (b).

called Speech Application Program Interface (SAPI) to associate your voice commands with specific actions performed by the computer. OpenEars makes it simple for you to add speech recognition to your iPhone, iPad, or iPod. Adacel develops advanced simulation and control systems for aviation and defense. It is working on a voice-activated control system to operate the display system on aircrafts. See Figure 4.6. Siri, the personal assistant that acts as an app on the Apple iOS operating system, uses a natural language user interface to answer questions.

FIGURE **4.6**

Voice recognition

Software developers are working on voice control systems to operate aircraft.

Sight interfaces use a camera on the computer to determine where a person is looking on the screen and performs the appropriate command or operation. Some companies are also experimenting with sensors attached to the human brain (brain interfaces) that can detect brain waves and control a computer as a result. Sight and brain interfaces can be very helpful to disabled individuals.

Operating system developers must be extremely careful in making changes to their user interface. The Windows 8 touch interface represented a major change from its traditional mouse-driven point-and-click user interface. Initial user reaction has been lukewarm at best with users complaining about the loss of the Start button to display a pop-up menu of programs, folders, and icons.

Hardware Independence

application programming interface (API): A set of programming instructions and standards for one software program to access and use the services of another software program.

An **application programming interface (API)** is a set of programming instructions and standards for one software program to access and use the services of another software program. It provides a software-to-software interface, not a user interface. The API also provides software developers with tools they can use to build application software without needing to understand the inner workings of the OS and hardware. Software applications are designed to run on a particular OS by using the operating system's application program interface.

Being able to develop software without concern for the specific underlying hardware is referred to as *hardware independence*. When new hardware technologies are introduced, the operating system, not the application software, is required to adjust to enable use of those changes.

A software manufacturing company or service provider will often release its API to the public so that other software developers can design products that employ its service. For example, Amazon.com released its API to enable other Web site developers to use defined programming instructions and standards to access Amazon's product information so that third-party Web sites can post direct links to Amazon products with updated prices and an option to "buy now."[11]

Memory Management

The OS also controls how memory is accessed, maximizing the use of available memory and storage to provide optimum efficiency. The memory-management feature of many OSs allows the computer to execute program instructions effectively and to speed processing. One way to increase the performance of an old computer is to upgrade to a newer OS and increase the amount of memory.

Most OSs support *virtual memory*, which allocates space on the hard disk to supplement the immediate, functional memory capacity of RAM. Virtual memory works by swapping programs or parts of programs between memory and one or more disk devices—a concept called paging. This procedure reduces CPU idle time and increases the number of jobs that can run in a given time span.

Processing Tasks

Operating systems use the following five basic task management techniques to increase the amount of processing that can be accomplished in a given amount of time.

- **Multiuser:** Allows two or more users to run programs at the same time on the same computer. Some operating systems permit hundreds or even thousands of concurrent users. The ability of the computer to handle an increasing number of concurrent users smoothly is called scalability.
- **Multiprocessing:** Supports running a program on more than one CPU.
- **Multitasking:** Allows more than one program to run concurrently.
- **Multithreading:** Allows different threads of a single program to run concurrently. A thread is a set of instructions within an application that is independent of other threads. For example, in a spreadsheet program, the thread to open the workbook is separate from the thread to sum a column of figures.
- **Real time:** Responds to input instantly. To do this, the operating system task scheduler can stop any task at any point in its execution if it determines that another higher priority task needs to run immediately. Such systems are used to control the operation of jet engines, deployment of air bags, the operation of anti-lock braking systems, and other real-time operations.

Not all operating systems employ all these techniques. For example, the general-purpose operating systems with which we are most familiar (e.g., Windows, Mac OS, and Linux) cannot support real-time processing.

Networking Capability

Most operating systems include networking capabilities so that computers can join together in a network to send and receive data and share computing resources. Operating systems for larger server computers are designed specifically for computer networking environments.

Access to System Resources and Security

Because computers often handle sensitive data that can be accessed over networks, the OS needs to provide a high level of security against unauthorized access to the users' data and programs. Typically, the OS establishes a logon procedure that requires users to enter an identification code, such as a user name, and a matching password. Operating systems may also control what system resources a user may access. When a user successfully logs on to the system, the OS allows access to only portions of the system for which the user has been cleared. The OS records who is using the system and for how long and reports any attempted breaches of security.

File Management

The OS manages files to ensure that files in secondary storage are available when needed and that they are protected from access by unauthorized users. Many computers support multiple users who store files on centrally located disks or tape drives. The OS keeps track of where each file is stored and who can access them.

Current Operating Systems

Today's operating systems incorporate sophisticated features and impressive graphic effects. Table 4.2 classifies a few current computer OSs by sphere of influence.

TABLE 4.2 Operating systems serving three spheres of influence

Personal	Workgroup	Enterprise
Microsoft Windows	Microsoft Windows Server	Microsoft Windows Server
Mac OS X, iOS	Mac OS X Server	
Linux	Linux	Linux
Google Android, Chrome OS		
HP webOS		
	UNIX	UNIX
	IBM i and z/OS	IBM i and z/OS
	HP-UX	HP-UX

Microsoft PC Operating Systems

IBM met with Bill Gates in 1980 about creating an operating system for its new personal computer. The Microsoft Disk Operating System (MS-DOS) was based on Microsoft's purchase of the Quick and Dirty Operating System (QDOS) written by Tim Paterson of Seattle Computer Products. Microsoft bought the rights to QDOS for $50,000. QDOS, in turn, was based on Gary Kildall's Control Program for Microcomputers (CP/M). Bill Gates then convinced IBM into letting Microsoft retain the rights to MS-DOS and to market

MS-DOS separate from the IBM personal computer. The rest is history, with Gates and Microsoft earning a fortune from the licensing of MS-DOS and its descendants.[12]

MS-DOS had command-driven interfaces that were difficult to learn and use. MS-DOS gave way to Windows, which opened the PC market to everyday users. Windows evolved through several versions, including Windows 1.01, 2.03, 3.0, and 3.1, Windows 95, 98, and Me, Windows NT, Windows 2000, Windows XP, Windows Vista, Windows 7, and Windows 8.

Windows 7 has strong support for touch displays and netbooks, ushering in a new era of mobile computing devices. Windows 7 is available in configurations designed for 32-bit or 64-bit processors. Users running newer computers are advised to install the 64-bit version, if their computers can support it, to experience faster processor performance. One of the greatest advantages of using a 64-bit version computer is the ability to access physical memory (RAM) above the 4-gigabyte (GB) range, which is not addressable by 32-bit computers. The 4-GB limit can be a severe problem for servers and computers accessing large databases.

Microsoft Windows 8 includes a touch interface and many new features for the consumer market. The Start screen displays colorful application "tiles" instead of icons. Windows 8 is available for a number of platforms, including smartphones, tablet computers, PCs, and servers. Many smartphone and mobile device makers plan to use Windows in their devices. See Figure 4.7.

FIGURE 4.7

Microsoft Windows 8

Windows 8 uses a Start screen rather than a Start menu.

Microsoft product screenshots used with permission from Microsoft Corporation

Windows 9 is expected to be released in 2014 and will be capable of running on smartphones, tablets, and desktop computers.[13]

Apple Computer Operating Systems

In July 2001, Mac OS X was released as an entirely new OS for the Mac based on the UNIX operating system. It included a new user interface, which provided a new visual appearance for users—including luminous and semitransparent elements, such as buttons, scroll bars, windows, and fluid animation to enhance the user's experience.

Since its first release, Apple has upgraded OS X several times. OS X 10.9 Mavericks is Apple's latest operating system. See Figure 4.8. It offers the ability to launch the iBooks app, and books you've already downloaded to your iPad, iPhone, or iPod Touch will appear in your library. Directions, bookmarks, and recent searches are automatically passed on to all your iOS devices. You can

© Apple, Inc.

MacBook Pro

FIGURE 4.8

Mac OS X Mavericks

Mavericks incorporates many features of Apple's mobile devices into its desktop operating system.

open multiple displays on multiple screens, and use power-saving technology that enables you to browse up to an hour longer without running out of power.

Because Mac OS X runs on Intel processors, Mac users can set up their computer to run both Windows and Mac OS X and select the platform they want to work with when they boot their computer. Such an arrangement is called *dual booting*. While Macs can dual boot into Windows, the opposite is not true. Apple does not allow OS X to be run on any machine other than an Apple. However, Windows PCs can dual boot with Linux and other OSs.

Linux

Linux is an OS developed by Linus Torvalds in 1991 as a student in Finland. The OS is distributed under the *GNU General Public License*, and its source code is freely available to everyone. It is, therefore, called an *open-source* operating system.

Individuals and organizations can use the open-source Linux code to create their own distribution (flavor) of Linux. Such a distribution consists of the Linux kernel (core of the operating system) that controls the hardware, manages files, separates processes, and performs other basic functions along with other software. This other software defines the terminal interface and the commands you use, produces the graphical user interface that you see, and provides other useful utility programs. The Linux distributor takes all the code for these programs and combines it into a single operating system that can be installed on a computer. The distributor may also add finishing touches, such as what the desktop looks like, what color schemes and character sets are displayed, and what browser and other optional software is included with the operating system. Typically, the distribution is "optimized" to perform in a particular environment such as for a desktop computer, server, or TV cable box controller.

Well in excess of 100 distributions of Linux have been created.[14] Many distributions are available as free downloads. Three of the most widely used distributions come from software companies RedHat, SUSE, and Canonical. Although the Linux kernel is free software, both Red Hat and SUSE produce retail versions of the operating system that earned them revenues of hundreds of millions in 2012 by distributing and servicing the software.[15] OpenSUSE is the distribution sponsored by SUSE. See Figure 4.9.

Ubuntu is a Linux-based operating system used on desktop and laptop computers and on servers. The development of Ubuntu is led by Canonical Ltd. Emphony Technologies is a software firm that builds and hosts project management software for the engineering, construction, petrochemical, and pharmaceutical industries. The firm required a cost-effective IT infrastructure

FIGURE 4.9

OpenSUSE operating system

OpenSUSE is a distribution of Linux available as a free download.

that was always available to support its customer project management applications around the clock. It also needed a computing environment on which traditional file, print, and email applications could run. The company chose to implement the Ubuntu Server Edition operating system on six servers residing at customer sites running its project management applications. The Ubuntu operating system is also installed on four additional servers in the company's data center that run customer applications, handle backups, support the company's email system, and host the Emphony Web site. Ubuntu has provided the high availability needed—neither Emphony nor its customers have experienced any downtime since the implementation took place over a year ago.[16]

Google

Over the years, Google has extended its reach from providing a popular search engine (Google) to application software (Google Docs), email (Gmail), mobile operating system (Android), Web browser (Chrome), and, more recently, PC operating system (Chrome OS). The various releases of the Android operating system have been given tasty names such as Gingerbread, Jelly Bean, and Ice Cream Sandwich. Android is estimated to surpass 1 billion users across all devices in 2014.[17]

Chrome OS is a Linux-based operating system for netbooks and nettops, which are notebooks and desktop PCs primarily used to access Web-based information and services such as email, Web browsing, social networks, and Google online applications. The OS is designed to run on inexpensive low-power computers. Chrome OS for personal computers is designed to start fast and provide quick access to applications through the Internet. An open-source version of Chrome OS, named Chromium OS, was made available at the end of 2009. Because it is open-source software, developers can customize the source code to run on different platforms, incorporating unique features.

Workgroup Operating Systems

To keep pace with user demands, the technology of the future must support a world in which network usage, data storage requirements, and data-processing speeds increase at a dramatic rate. Powerful and sophisticated OSs are needed to run the servers that meet these business needs for workgroups.

Windows Server

Microsoft designed *Windows Server* to perform a host of tasks that are vital for Web sites and corporate Web applications. For example, Microsoft

INFORMATION SYSTEMS @ WORK

The Linux Business Advantage

If you use a computer as a university business student, odds are that it runs either Microsoft Windows or Apple Mac OS. Few students outside computer science, and even fewer business school computer labs, use any other platform.

That's not the case in business. In May 2013, about 53 percent of 673 million Web servers surveyed use the Linux operating system, described in this chapter, to run a Web server application called Apache. Apache's market share fluctuates but has been above 40 percent since 1997. Linux is popular among businesses in other application areas as well.

Why do businesses use Linux? Their reasons for choosing it vary. For PrintedArt, an online shop that sells limited editions of fine art photography, the reasons involved the availability of open-source applications developed for Linux. President and CEO of PrintedArt, Klaus Sonnenleiter, explains the company's choice of the open-source package Drupal for managing Web content. "Before settling on Drupal, we went through a major evaluation shoot-out between the different CMS [Content Management System] options. After looking at a fairly large number of options, Joomla, Drupal, Alfresco, and Typo3 became the finalists. Drupal came out on top because of its layered API [Application Program Interface] that lets PrintedArt … create their own integrations and modules."

Ubercart, the free open-source e-commerce shopping cart module, is also a core part of the PrintedArt system. "In addition, we use Capsule running as a Google App as our CRM," Sonnenleiter adds. "We also use MailChimp, and we are evaluating Producteev as our project and to do-list manager."

Gompute of Göteborg, Sweden, is larger than the six-person PrintedArt. Gompute operates a cluster of 336 IBM servers to provide high-performance computing on-demand for technical and scientific users. Those people use Gompute's computers in fields such as fluid dynamics, stress analysis, and computational chemistry. Linux gives them the ability to run the variety of applications that the company's customers require. These include proprietary applications such as ANSYS for computer-aided engineering and PERMAS for structural analysis for which users must purchase a license and open-source programs such as

OpenFOAM for advanced computation, which are free for anyone to use. If none of these applications meet users' needs, users can write their own programs and then run them on Gompute's advanced hardware.

The Linux groundswell in business is so strong that not even Microsoft is immune. In 2012, Microsoft announced that its Azure cloud-computing service will let customers run Linux as well as Windows. Linux provides important features in this environment, such as the ability to retain data even after a virtual machine is rebooted. By offering Linux, Microsoft can pursue customers that need data retention and other Linux capabilities.

Discussion Questions

1. When you bought your computer, had you heard of Linux? If so, where had you heard about it?
2. As the case mentions, more than half of all Web servers run Linux but only about 1 percent of personal computers do. What factors do you think account for this difference?

Critical Thinking Questions

1. Basic applications are available for all operating systems. Beyond those applications, some users depend on packages while others tend to write their own applications. How does application availability affect their choice of an operating system?
2. Why is Microsoft offering support for Linux in its Azure cloud-computing service? Is this a good business decision? Why or why not?

SOURCES: Endsley, R., "How Small Business PrintedArt Uses Linux and Open Source," *www.linux.com/learn/tutorials/539523-case-study-how-small-business-printedart-uses-linux-and-open-source*, January 25, 2012; Staff, "Gompute Harnesses Sophisticated IBM High Performance Computing," IBM, *www-01.ibm.com/software/success/cssdb.nsf/CS/STRD-8SYJ2K*, April 3, 2012; Metz, C., "Microsoft Preps for Public Embrace of Linux," Wired, *www.wired.com/wiredenterprise/2012/05/microsoft-linux*, May 30, 2012; Meyer, D., "Microsoft Azure Starts Embracing Linux and Python," ZDNet UK, *www.zdnet.com/microsoft-azure-starts-embracing-linux-and-python-3040155346*, June 7, 2012; Staff, May 2013; Web Server Survey, Netcraft, *http://news.netcraft.com/archives/2013/05/03/may-2013-web-server-survey.html*, August 28, 2013; PrintedArt Web site, *www.printedart.com*, accessed May 31, 2012.

Windows Server can be used to coordinate the many servers in large data centers. It delivers benefits such as a powerful Web server management system, virtualization tools that allow various operating systems to run on a single server, advanced security features, and robust administrative support. Windows Home Server allows individuals to connect multiple PCs, storage devices, printers, and other devices into a home network. It provides a convenient way to store and manage photos, video, music, and other digital content. It also provides backup and data recovery functions.

UNIX

UNIX is a powerful OS originally developed by AT&T for minicomputers—the predecessors of servers that are larger than PCs and smaller than mainframes. UNIX can be used on many computer system types and platforms, including workstations, servers, and mainframe computers. UNIX also makes it much easier to move programs and data among computers or to connect mainframes and workstations to share resources. There are many variants of UNIX, including HP-UX from Hewlett-Packard, AIX from IBM, and Solaris from Oracle. The UNIX platform (computer capable of running the UNIX operating system plus the operating system itself) is considered a high-cost platform compared to Linux and Windows Server.

Oracle, known primarily as a database management software firm, acquired Sun in 2010. Sun products included server hardware, the Solaris operating system, and the Java programming language. Oracle now offers so-called general-purpose engineered systems that include a combination of Oracle and the Sun software running on Sun servers under the Solaris operating system.[18] KASIKORNBANK is a Thai financial institution that provides a variety of financial services. It operates 897 branches and sub-offices across the country and has 10 overseas offices. The bank consolidated its disparate security systems onto Sun servers running under the Solaris operating system.[19]

Red Hat Linux

Red Hat Software offers Red Hat Enterprise Linux Server, an operating system that is very efficient at serving Web pages and can manage a cluster of several servers. Distributions such as SUSE and Red Hat have proven Linux to be a very stable and efficient OS. Red Hat Enterprise Virtualization (RHEV) software provides virtualization capabilities for servers and desktop computers to enable the hardware to run more than one operating system. See Figure 4.10.

Mac OS X Server

The *Mac OS X Server* is the first modern server OS from Apple Computer and is based on the UNIX OS. The most recent version is OS X Mavericks Server. It includes support for 64-bit processing, along with several server functions and features that allow the easy management of network and Internet services such as email, Web site hosting, calendar management and sharing, wikis, and podcasting.

HP-UX

The HP-UX is a robust UNIX-based OS from Hewlett-Packard designed to handle a variety of business tasks, including online transaction processing and Web applications. It supports Hewlett-Packard's largest and most powerful computers and those designed to run Intel's Itanium processors.

Kenya Woman Finance Trust (KWFT) serves women only in Africa and is the leading deposit-taking microfinance institution in Kenya. It targets low-income women as an entry and contact point to their families with the objective of alleviating poverty by offering innovative savings and credit products. Initially, KWFT was limited to providing loans, but as it grew, KWFT took actions to become licensed as a Deposit Taking Microfinance (DTM) to offer financial

FIGURE **4.10**

Red Hat Linux

Red Hat Enterprise Virtualization (RHEV) software provides virtualization capabilities for servers and desktop computers.

services related to savings. One key step was to make a significant upgrade to its information system infrastructure. KWFT acquired Temenos T24 core banking software and an HP Integrity Superdome 2 server designed to run an organization's mission-critical applications. The server runs using the HP-UX operating system and provides KWFT with the processing power and reliability necessary to handle more than 30,000 small transactions each day.[20]

Enterprise Operating Systems

Mainframe computers, often referred to as "Big Iron," provide the computing and storage capacity to meet massive data-processing requirements and offer many users high performance and excellent system availability, strong security, and scalability. In addition, a wide range of application software has been developed to run in the mainframe environment, making it possible to purchase software to address almost any business problem. Examples of mainframe OSs include z/OS from IBM, HP-UX from Hewlett-Packard, and Linux. The *z/OS* is IBM's first 64-bit enterprise OS and is capable of handling very heavy workloads, including serving thousands of concurrent users and running an organization's critical applications. (The z stands for zero downtime.)

Mobile Operating Systems

Smartphones now employ full-fledged personal computer operating systems such as the Google Android, Apple iOS, and Microsoft Windows Phone that determine the functionality of your phone and the applications that you can run. These operating systems have software development kits that allow developers to design thousands of apps providing a myriad of mobile services.

Table 4.3 lists the top four mobile operating systems for smartphones and tablets based on worldwide market share of sales as of the second quarter (2Q) of 2013. Table 4.4 lists the top four tablet operating systems based on sales in 1Q 2013.

TABLE **4.3** Comparison of smartphone operating systems

Smartphone Operating System	Worldwide Market Share of Sales during 2Q 2013	Estimated Total Number of Applications Mid-2013	Estimated Rate of Increase in Number of New Applications
Google Android	56.5%	>1,000,000	800/day
Apple iPhone OS	39.6%	900,000	600/day
Microsoft Windows Mobile	3.3%	145,000	130/day
Blackberry Limited, Blackberry	2.9%	120,000	NA

Sources: Etherington, Darrell, "Android Nears 80% Market Share in Global Smartphone Shipments, As iOS And BlackBerry Share Slides, per IDC," Tech Crunch, August 7, 2013, *http://techcrunch.com/2013/08/07/android-nears-80-market-share-in-global-smartphone-shipments-as-ios-and-blackberry-share-slides-per-idc*; Cunningham, Andrew, "One Developer Makes over 47,000 of BlackBerry 10's 120,000 Apps," Ars Technica, August 21, 2013, *http://arstechnica.com/gadgets/2013 /08/one-developer-makes-over-47000-of-blackberry-10s-120000-apps*; Rowinski, Dan, ReadWrite, January 08, 2013, Google Play Will Beat Apple App Store to 1,000,000 Apps, *http://readwrite.com/2013/01/08/google-play-to-hit-1-million-apps-before-apple-app-store#awesm=~okUaRI5V5A0WOR*.

TABLE **4.4** Worldwide market share of tablet computer operating systems—1Q 2013 shipments

Table Computer Operating System	Worldwide Market Share
Android	27.8%
iOS	19.5%
Windows	1.6%
Others	0.3%

Source: Kovach, Steve, "Android Now Ahead of Apple's iOS in Tablet Market Share," *www.businessinsider .com/android-ahead-of-ios-tablet-market-share-2013-5#ixzz2kfajQMiW*, May 1, 2013.

Embedded Operating Systems

An embedded system is a computer system (including some sort of processor) that is implanted in and dedicated to the control of another device. Embedded systems control many devices in common use today, including TV cable boxes, cell phones, digital watches, digital cameras, MP3 players, calculators, microwave ovens, washing machines, and traffic lights. The typical auto contains many embedded systems to control anti-lock brakes, air bag deployment, fuel injection, active suspension devices, transmission control, and cruise control. A global positioning system (GPS) device uses an embedded system to help people find their way around town or more remote areas. See Figure 4.11.

Some embedded systems include specialized operating systems. For example, Hewlett-Packard purchased Palm, an early smartphone manufacturer, and its respected Palm webOS operating system used to run its Pre and Pixi smartphones in 2010. The smartphones were a market failure, and in early 2013, LG bought all the assets associated with webOS from HP. It plans to use the software in its smart TVs to enable users to watch streaming movies and TV and YouTube videos, connect to social networks, play games, get news, and download apps.[21]

Some of the more popular OSs for embedded systems are described in the following section.

FIGURE 4.11

GPS devices use embedded operating systems

A GPS device uses an embedded system to acquire information from satellites, display your current location on a map, and direct you to your destination.

Windows Embedded

Windows Embedded is a family of Microsoft OSs included with or embedded into small computer devices. Windows Embedded Compact includes several versions that provide computing power for TV set top boxes, automated industrial machines, media players, medical devices, digital cameras, PDAs, GPS receivers, ATMs, gaming devices, and business devices such as cash registers. Microsoft Windows Embedded Automotive helps manufacturers provide drivers with everything they need to stay in touch with others, be entertained, and be informed. Drivers can also monitor vehicle performance, screen for maintenance issues, and allow remote tracking of the car's location. Speech recognition, touch interface, and hands-free technologies enable drivers to stay focused on the road and in control of their surroundings. The Ford Sync system uses an in-dashboard display and wireless networking technologies to link automotive systems with cell phones and portable media players. See Figure 4.12.

FIGURE 4.12

Microsoft Auto and Ford Sync

The Ford Sync system, developed on the Microsoft Auto operating system, allows drivers to wirelessly connect cell phones and media devices to automotive systems.

Proprietary Linux-Based Systems

Because embedded systems are usually designed for a specific purpose in a specific device, they are usually proprietary or custom-created and owned by the manufacturer. Sony's Wii, for example, uses a custom-designed OS based on the Linux kernel. Linux is a popular choice for embedded systems because it is free and highly configurable. It has been used in many embedded systems, including e-book readers, ATMs, cell phones, networking devices, and media players.

Utility Programs

utility program: Program that helps to perform maintenance or correct problems with a computer system.

Utility programs help perform a variety of tasks. For example, some utility programs merge and sort sets of data, keep track of computer jobs being run, compress files of data before they are stored or transmitted over a network (thus saving space and time), and perform other important tasks.

Just as your car engine runs best if you have regular tune-ups, computers also need regular maintenance to ensure optimal performance. Over time your computer's performance can start to diminish as system errors occur, files clutter your hard drive, and security vulnerabilities materialize. The Sysinternals Suite is a popular personal computer utility for maintaining the performance of your Windows system by repairing errors in the registry and on your hard drive, protecting your system and privacy, and optimizing sluggish system processes.[22] The Sysinternals window shown in Figure 4.13 summarizes the tasks the troubleshooting utility can perform on a PC. The Sysinternals Suite includes utilities for files, disks, networking, security, and system information.

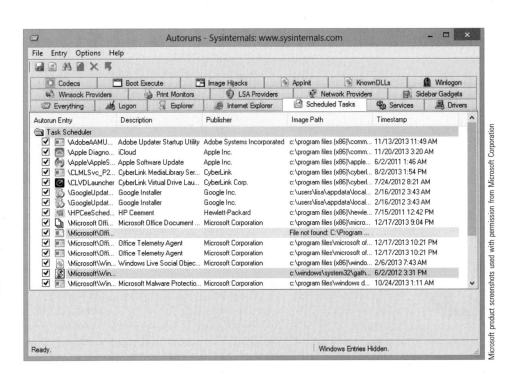

FIGURE **4.13**

Sysinternals Suite

The Sysinternals Suite is a collection utilities for troubleshooting and maintaining a Windows system.

Although many PC utility programs come installed on computers, you can also purchase utility programs separately. The following sections examine some common types of utilities.

Hardware Utilities

Some hardware utilities are available from companies such as Symantec, which produces Norton Utilities. Hardware utilities can check the status of all parts of the PC, including hard disks, memory, modems, speakers, and printers. Disk utilities check the hard disk's boot sector, file allocation tables, and directories and analyze them to ensure that the hard disk is not damaged. Disk utilities can also optimize the placement of files on a crowded disk.

Security Utilities

Computer viruses and spyware from the Internet and other sources can be a nuisance—and sometimes can completely disable a computer. Antivirus and antispyware software can be installed to constantly monitor and protect the computer. If a virus or spyware is found, it can often be removed. It is also a good idea to protect computer systems with firewall software. Firewall software filters incoming and outgoing packets, making sure that neither hackers nor their tools are attacking the system. Symantec, McAfee, and Microsoft are the most popular providers of security software.

File-Compression Utilities

File-compression programs can reduce the amount of disk space required to store a file or reduce the time it takes to transfer a file over the Internet. Both Windows and Mac operating systems let you compress or decompress files and folders. A zip file has a .zip extension, and its contents can be easily unzipped to the original size. *MP3 (Motion Pictures Experts Group-Layer 3)* is a popular file-compression format used to store, transfer, and play music and audio files, such as podcasts—audio programs that can be downloaded from the Internet.

Spam-Filtering Utilities

Receiving unwanted email (spam) can be a frustrating waste of time. Email software and services include spam-filtering utilities to assist users with these annoyances. Email filters identify spam by learning what the user considers spam and routing it to a junk mail folder. However, this method is insufficient for protecting enterprise-level email systems where spam containing viruses is a serious threat. Businesses often use additional spam-filtering software from companies including Cisco, Barracuda Networks, and Google at the enterprise level to intercept dangerous spam as it enters the corporate email system.

The use of iOS and Android smartphones and tablets has been increasing rapidly in grades K–12. The EdgeWave iPrism Web filter utility is designed to protect students from inappropriate Web content.[23] The Palm Springs California Unified school district implemented this software to safeguard 118 servers and 5,850 computers spread across 24 schools to ensure that it was in compliance with federal requirements to continue to receive funds from the E-Rate program.[24]

Network and Internet Utilities

A broad range of network- and systems-management utility software is available to monitor hardware and network performance and trigger an alert when a server is crashing or a network problem occurs. IBM's Tivoli Netcool, Hewlett-Packard's Automated Network Management Suite, and Paessler's PRTG Network Monitor can be used to solve computer-network problems and help save money. As shown in Figure 4.14, PRTG Network Monitor creates a sensor for each network device and then monitors the device to make sure it is connected and working properly. If a device encounters a problem, the software can alert you via email or text message, for example.

Česká pojišt'ovna in Prague, Czech Republic, provides life insurance and other insurance products for individuals and businesses. It employs some 4,900 people and works with 65,000 agents across its 70 branches. The firm needed a complete IT service monitoring and management solution to avoid system downtime and eliminate service disruptions. It implemented Tivoli Netcool to gain insight into its IT resource performance and usage. The network utility enables Ceská pojišt'ovna to predict fluctuations in resource

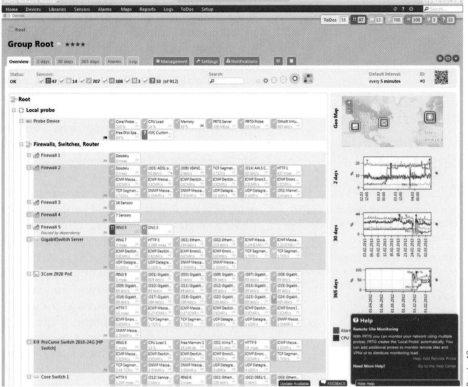

FIGURE 4.14

PRTG Network Monitor

PRTG Network Monitor and other network utility software can help you to keep track of network components, traffic flows, and network performance.

requirements that enable more accurate capacity planning and avoid costly system failures.[25]

Server and Mainframe Utilities

Some utilities enhance the performance of servers and mainframe computers. Blue Cross and Blue Shield of Kansas provides medical, dental, and life insurance coverage to 800,000 customers. As part of its service, it offers online access to health information stored in an IBM DB2 database running on an IBM z/OS mainframe. It employs IBM mainframe utility programs to manage this operation effectively. The IBM z/OS Data Facility System Managed Storage utility applies the appropriate retention policies to data stored on direct access storage devices. The IBM Tivoli Workload Scheduler is used to perform automated job scheduling to ensure critical jobs are completed on time.[26]

IBM and other companies have created systems-management software that allows a support person to monitor the growing number of desktop computers attached to a server or mainframe computer. Similar to the virtual machine software discussed earlier, *server virtualization software* allows a server to run more than one operating system at the same time. For example, you could run four different virtual servers simultaneously on one physical server.

Other Utilities

Utility programs are available for almost every conceivable task or function. Managing the vast array of operating systems for smartphones and mobile devices, for example, has been difficult for many companies. Many organizations unwisely allow employees to connect to corporate databases using smartphones and mobile devices with little or no guidance. Utility programs called *mobile device management* (*MDM*) software can help a company manage security, enforce corporate strategies, and control downloads and content streaming from corporate databases into smartphones and mobile devices. The Naval Supply Systems Command employs an MDM approach to manage over 600 handheld mobile devices across the Unites States and Japan to immediately process thousands of daily warehouse and inventory management business transactions from anywhere in the world.[27]

In addition, a number of companies, such as CNET, offer utilities that can be downloaded for most popular operating systems. CNET offers hundreds of utilities for Windows operating systems, including defraggers (fixes the problem of fragmentation, which occurs when data is broken up into discontinuous pieces that waste space on your hard drive), system cleaners (cleans tracks on your hard drive, deletes temporary files, and cleans your registry), uninstallers (safely removes unwanted software), and replacements for Notepad and Task Manager.

Middleware

middleware: Software that allows various systems to communicate and exchange data.

enterprise application integration (EAI): The systematic tying together of disparate applications so that they can communicate.

Middleware is software that provides messaging services so that different applications can communicate. This systematic tying together of disparate applications, often through the use of middleware, is known as **enterprise application integration (EAI)**. It is often developed to address situations where a company acquires different types of information systems through mergers, acquisitions, or expansion and wants the systems to share data and interact. Middleware can also serve as an interface between the Internet and private corporate systems. For example, it can be used to transfer a request for information from a corporate customer on the corporate Web site to a traditional database on a mainframe computer and return the results to the customer on the Internet.

service-oriented architecture (SOA): A software design approach based on the use of discrete pieces of software (modules) to provide specific functions as services to other applications.

The use of middleware to connect disparate systems has evolved into an approach for developing software and systems called SOA. **Service-oriented architecture (SOA)** is a software design approach based on the use of discrete pieces of software (modules) to provide specific functions (such as displaying a customer's bill statement) as services to other applications. Each module is built in such a way that ensures that the service it provides can exchange information with any other service without human interaction and without the need to make changes to the underlying program itself. In this manner, many modules can be combined to provide the complete functionality of a large, complex software application. Systems developed with SOA are highly flexible as they allow for the addition of new modules that provide new services required to meet the needs of the business as they evolve and change over time.

Florida State College at Jacksonville is one of the largest baccalaureate colleges in the United States, serving over 80,000 students per year. It is experiencing a rapid growth in enrollment that is increasing the workload on its enrollment systems and student advisory services. The college implemented a new Web-based student portal built on SOA to enable students to self-enroll and select courses online. The portal provides access to six self-service modules, including a student's college email account, My Records to see grades, My Classes to find available classes and register, and My Advisor to review graduation requirements and obtain guidance on which courses to take. Now students can save time and costs with constant access to these services.[28]

APPLICATION SOFTWARE

The primary function of application software is to apply the power of the computer to enable people, workgroups, and the entire enterprise to solve problems and perform specific tasks.

In almost any category of software, you will find many options from which to choose. For example, Internet Explorer, Mozilla Firefox, Google

Chrome, Apple Safari, and Opera are all popular Web browsers that enable you to surf the Web. The availability of many software options enables users to select the software that best meets the needs of the individual, workgroup, or enterprise. For example, a large, multinational organization such as Procter & Gamble chose the SAP Enterprise Resource Planning software with its vast array of options, features, and functionality to meet its complex global accounting needs. Meanwhile, the tiny, neighborhood Just Right Bakery found that Intuit's Quicken worked well to meet its simple accounting needs.

Take care when adopting new applications because software is sometimes initially released with inherent problems. For example, the Web-based application introduced by the federal government to enable people to apply for the new healthcare options made available by the Affordable Care Act was poorly designed and was unable to handle the large number of initial applicants, causing many users to abandon the site in frustration.

Overview of Application Software

Proprietary software and off-the-shelf software are important types of application software. Proprietary software is one-of-a-kind software designed for a specific application and owned by the company, organization, or person that uses it. Proprietary software can give a company a competitive advantage by providing services or solving problems in a unique manner, better than methods used by a competitor. Off-the-shelf software is mass-produced by software vendors to address needs that are common across businesses, organizations, or individuals. For example, Amazon.com uses the same off-the-shelf payroll software as many businesses, but the company uses custom-designed proprietary software on its Web site that allows visitors to more easily find items to purchase. The relative advantages and disadvantages of proprietary software and off-the-shelf software are summarized in Table 4.5.

proprietary software: One-of-a-kind software designed for a specific application and owned by the company, organization, or person that uses it.

off-the-shelf software: Software mass-produced by software vendors to address needs that are common across businesses, organizations, or individuals.

TABLE **4.5** Comparison of proprietary and off-the-shelf software

Proprietary Software		Off-the-Shelf Software	
Advantages	Disadvantages	Advantages	Disadvantages
You can get exactly what you need in terms of features, reports, and so on.	It can take a long time and significant resources to develop required features.	The initial cost is lower because the software firm can spread the development costs over many customers.	An organization might have to pay for features that are not required and never used.
Being involved in the development offers control over the results.	In-house system development staff may be hard pressed to provide the required level of ongoing support and maintenance because of pressure to move on to other new projects.	The software is likely to meet the basic business needs—you can analyze existing features and the performance of the package before purchasing.	The software might lack important features, thus requiring future modification or customization. This lack can be very expensive because users must adopt future releases of the software as well.
You can modify features that you might need to counteract an initiative by competitors or to meet new supplier or customer demands.	The features and performance of software that has yet to be developed presents more potential risk.	The package is likely to be of high quality because many customer firms have tested the software and helped identify its bugs.	The software might not match current work processes and data standards.

Many companies use off-the-shelf software to support business processes. Key questions for selecting off-the-shelf software include the following:

- Will the software run on the OS and hardware you have selected?
- Does the software meet the essential business requirements that have been defined?
- Is the software manufacturer financially solvent and reliable?
- Does the total cost of purchasing, installing, and maintaining the software compare favorably to the expected business benefits?

The Rhode Island Division of Taxation chose an off-the-shelf Integrated Tax System to provide a wide range of processing and administration functionality for the 56 taxes and fees currently administered by the state. The software is flexible enough that it can be modified to handle new tax programs that may be ratified in the future. Rhode Island Tax Administrator David M. Sullivan expects that the system will enable the Division of Taxation to operate more effectively and efficiently, generate additional revenue for the state, and create useful new online tools for tax practitioners, taxpayers, and other stakeholders.[29]

application service provider (ASP): A company that provides the software, support, and computer hardware on which to run the software from the user's facilities over a network.

Another approach to obtaining a customized software package is to use an application service provider. An **application service provider (ASP)** is a company that can provide the software, support, and computer hardware on which to run the software from the user's facilities over a network. Some vendors refer to the service as *on-demand software*. Table 4.6 lists a few ASPs.

TABLE 4.6 Short list of application service providers

Application Service Provider	Description
5 PointAG	Provides project management, ERP, time recording, billing, and online documentation management software.
ACS	Provides diversified business process outsourcing and information technology services and solutions.
Alliance Systems	Delivers comprehensive set of design and manufacturing services to OEMs to enhance profit and reduce time to market.
Click Commerce	Provides collaborative commerce and channel management software to help companies optimize processes, lower costs to serve business partners and customers, accelerate revenue, and improve customer service.
Epicor Software	Delivers ERP and other software solutions.
InfoStreet	Develops and hosts software that facilitates group interaction.
Ryder	Provides transportation, logistics, and supply chain management solutions worldwide.
WordSecure	Provides Web-based SaaS alternative to secure email to ensure HIPAA compliance.

© 2016 Cengage Learning

As mentioned in Chapter 1, workers in many organizations operate in a cloud-computing environment in which software, data storage, and other services are provided by the Internet ("the cloud"); the services are run on another organization's computer hardware and both software and data are easily accessed. Examples of public cloud service providers, which make their services available to the general public, include Amazon Elastic Compute Cloud (EC2), IBM's Blue Cloud, Sun Cloud, Google AppEngine, and Windows Azure Services Platform. Public cloud users can realize a considerable cost savings because the very high initial hardware, application, and bandwidth costs are paid for by the service provider and passed along to users as a relatively small monthly fee or per-use fee. Furthermore, the amount of services used can be easily scaled up or down depending on user demand for services.

The cloud services are given popular acronyms such as SaaS (Software as a Service), PaaS (Platform as a Service), IaaS (Infrastructure as a Service), and

Software as a Service (SaaS):
A service that allows businesses to subscribe to Web-delivered application software.

HaaS (Hardware as a Service). **Software as a Service (SaaS)** allows organizations to subscribe to Web-delivered application software. In most cases, the company pays a monthly service charge or a per-use fee. Many business activities are supported by SaaS. SaaS vendors include Oracle, SAP, Net Suite, Salesforce, and Google. General Electric Aviation uses the SaaS software Salesforce to communicate with commercial customers and manage sales opportunities. Initially it used Salesforce to provide everyone with access to customer data, but eventually it enabled a level of collaboration among sales and marketing people that changed the way it ran its day-to-day business.[30]

Amazon is considered one of the leading public cloud service providers because of the variety of services that it provides. It is also rapidly adding new services such as tools for software developers and services to support version control and collaboration. A negative of the Amazon Web Services (AWS) is that organizations storing and serving their data with Amazon never know exactly where Amazon keeps this data, and Amazon does not run dedicated servers that ensure company data is separate from data belonging to other companies.[31]

Coursera is an educational company that collaborates with Stanford, Duke, Princeton, the London School of Economics, and other institutions to offer some 300 free online classes. Coursera uses AWS to track student data, store and deliver videos, and enable students and teachers to interact with each other.[32]

Google launched a family of new personal computers built by Samsung and Acer called Chromebooks that include only an Internet browser with all of the software applications accessed through an Internet connection. Rather than installing, storing, and running software on your own computer, you use the Web browser to access software stored and delivered from a Web server. Typically the data generated by the software is also stored on the Web server. For example, Tableau software allows users to import databases or spreadsheet data to create powerful visualizations that provide useful information. Figure 4.15 shows a Tableau visualization that tracks the unemployment rate across the country over time. Orange indicates an unemployment rate exceeding the national average, while blue indicates rates below the national average. Cloud computing also provides the benefit of being able to easily collaborate with others by sharing documents on the Internet.

FIGURE 4.15
Tableau software
Tableau is available in desktop and cloud versions, and helps you visualize data, such as how the unemployment rate changes over a 20-year period.

Dillon Supply Company is an industrial distributor serving contractors, steel fabricators, and other customers. It employs 280 workers and had recent revenues of $100 million. The firm employed an ASP to help it implement its strategic pricing strategy. This strategy is based on finding the optimal price for each product/customer sales combination. The optimal price is the highest price that the distributor can charge and still retain the customer's business. Successful implementation of this strategy has increased the firm's profit margin by two percentage points, resulting in millions of additional profits.[33]

ASP, SaaS, and cloud computing, however, involve some risks. For example, sensitive information could be compromised in a number of ways, including unauthorized access by employees or computer hackers; the host might not be able to keep its computers and network up and running as consistently as necessary; or a disaster could disable the host's data center, temporarily putting an organization out of business. It can also be difficult to integrate the SaaS approach with existing software.

Personal Application Software

Hundreds of computer applications can help people at school, home, and work. New computer software under development and existing GPS technology, for example, will enable people to see 3D views of where they are, along with directions and 3D maps to where they would like to go. Absolute software, which uses GPS technology, helps people and organizations retrieve stolen computers. The company has recovered almost 30,000 devices in over 100 countries.[34]

The features of some popular types of personal application software are summarized in Table 4.7. In addition to these general-purpose programs,

TABLE **4.7** Examples of personal application software

Type of Software	Explanation	Example
Word processing	Create, edit, and print text documents	Microsoft Word Google Docs Apple Pages OpenOffice Writer
Spreadsheet	Provide a wide range of built-in functions for statistical, financial, logical, database, graphics, and date and time calculations	Microsoft Excel IBM Lotus 1-2-3 Google Spreadsheet Apple Numbers OpenOffice Calc
Database	Store, manipulate, and retrieve data	Microsoft Access IBM Lotus Approach Borland dBASE Google Base OpenOffice Base
Graphics	Develop graphs, illustrations, and drawings	Adobe Illustrator Adobe FreeHand Microsoft PowerPoint OpenOffice Impress
Project management	Plan, schedule, allocate, and control people and resources (money, time, and technology) needed to complete a project according to schedule	Microsoft Project Symantec On Target Scitor Project Scheduler Symantec Time Line
Financial management	Provide income and expense tracking and reporting to monitor and plan budgets (some programs have investment portfolio management features)	Intuit Quicken
Desktop publishing (DTP)	Use with personal computers and high-resolution printers to create high-quality printed output, including text and graphics; various styles of pages can be laid out; art and text files from other programs can also be integrated into published pages	QuarkXpress Microsoft Publisher Adobe InDesign Corel Ventura Publisher Apple Pages

thousands of other personal computer applications perform specialized tasks that help you do your taxes, get in shape, lose weight, get medical advice, write wills and other legal documents, repair your computer, fix your car, write music, and edit your pictures and videos. This type of software, often called *user software* or *personal productivity software*, includes the general-purpose tools and programs that support individual needs.

Word Processing

Word-processing applications are installed on most PCs today. These applications come with a vast array of features, including those for checking spelling, creating tables, inserting formulas, and creating graphics. See Figure 4.16. Much of the work required to create this book used the popular word-processing software, Microsoft Word.

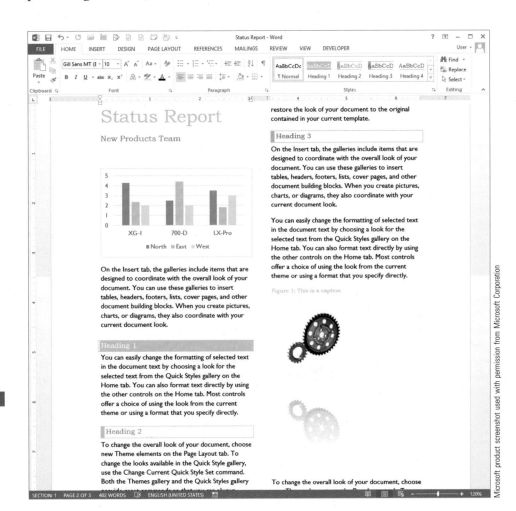

FIGURE 4.16

Word-processing program

Word-processing applications, such as Microsoft Word, can be used to write letters, professional documents, work reports, and term papers.

A team of people can use a word-processing program to collaborate on a project. The authors and editors who developed this book, for example, used the Track Changes and Reviewing features of Microsoft Word to track and make changes to chapter files. With these features, you can add comments or make revisions to a document that a coworker can review and either accept or reject.

Spreadsheet Analysis

Spreadsheets are powerful tools for manipulating and analyzing numbers and alphanumeric data. Individuals and organizations use spreadsheets. Features of spreadsheets include formulas, statistical analysis, built-in business functions, graphics, and limited database capabilities. See Figure 4.17. The business

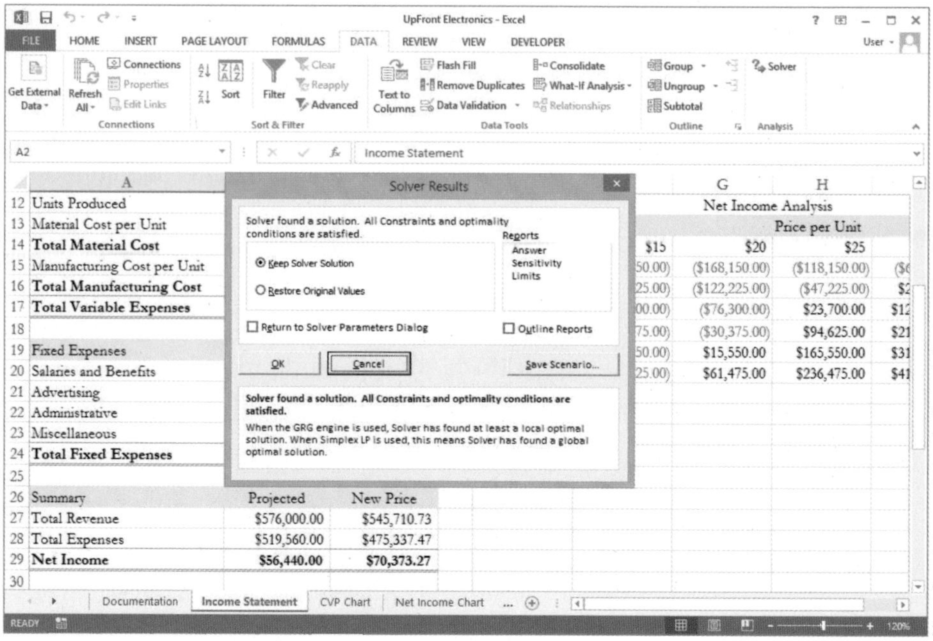

FIGURE 4.17

Spreadsheet program

Consider spreadsheet programs, such as Microsoft Excel, when calculations are required.

functions include calculation of depreciation, present value, internal rate of return, and the monthly payment on a loan. Optimization is another powerful feature of many spreadsheet programs. *Optimization* allows the spreadsheet to maximize or minimize a quantity subject to certain constraints. For example, a small furniture manufacturer that produces chairs and tables might want to maximize its profits. The constraints could be a limited supply of lumber, a limited number of workers who can assemble the chairs and tables, or a limited amount of various hardware fasteners that might be required. Using an optimization feature, such as Solver in Microsoft Excel, the spreadsheet can determine what number of chairs and tables to produce with labor and material constraints to maximize profits.

Carmen Reinhart and Kenneth Rogoff's famous 2010 study "Growth in a Time of Debt," concluded that a country's economic growth is reduced when its public debt level reaches 90 percent of GDP. This finding has been used as justification in recent years for countries to reduce their deficits. However, a new study by Thomas Herndon, Michael Ash, and Robert Pollin has uncovered that the original study has three major flaws. First, it excluded three occurrences of high-debt, high-growth nations. Second, it made some questionable assumptions about weighting different historical episodes. Third, it had an error in an Excel spreadsheet formulas that excluded Belgium from their analysis. Correcting for these problem leads to an entirely different conclusion—"The average real GDP growth rate for countries carrying a public debt-to-GDP ratio of over 90 percent is actually 2.2 percent, not –0.1 percent as published in Reinhart and Rogoff."[35]

Database Applications

Database applications are ideal for storing, organizing, and retrieving data. These applications are particularly useful when you need to manipulate a large amount of data and produce reports and documents. Database manipulations include merging, editing, and sorting data. The uses of a database application are varied. You can keep track of a CD collection, the items in your apartment, tax records, and expenses. A student club can use a database to store names, addresses, phone numbers, and dues paid. In business, a database application can help process sales orders, control inventory, order new supplies, send letters to customers, and pay employees. Database management systems can be used to track orders, products, and customers; analyze weather data to make forecasts for the next several days; and summarize medical research results. A database can also be a front end to another application. For example, you can use a database application to enter and store income tax information and then export the stored results to other applications, such as a spreadsheet or tax-preparation application.

Presentation Graphics Program

It is often said that a picture is worth a thousand words. With today's graphics programs, it is easy to develop attractive graphs, illustrations, and drawings that assist in communicating important information. See Figure 4.18. Presentation graphics programs can be used to develop advertising brochures, announcements, and full-color presentations and to organize and edit photographic images. If you need to make a presentation at school or work, you can use a special type of graphics program called a presentation application to develop slides and then display them while you are speaking. Because of their popularity, many colleges and departments require students to become proficient at using presentation graphics programs.

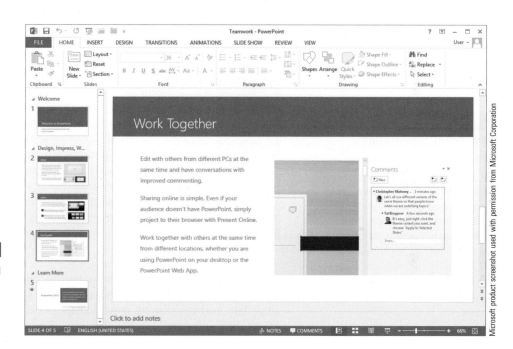

FIGURE 4.18

Presentation graphics program

Presentation graphics programs, such as Microsoft PowerPoint, can help you make a presentation at school or work.

Microsoft product screenshot used with permission from Microsoft Corporation

Many graphics programs, including Microsoft PowerPoint, consist of a series of slides. Each slide can be displayed on a computer screen, printed as a handout, or (more commonly) projected onto a large viewing screen for audiences. Powerful built-in features allow you to develop attractive slides and complete presentations. You can select a template for a type of presentation, such as recommending a strategy for managers, communicating news to a salesforce, giving a training presentation, or facilitating a brainstorming session. The presentation graphics program lets you create a presentation step-by-step, including applying color and attractive formatting. You can also design a custom presentation using the many types of charts, drawings, and formatting available. Most presentation graphics programs come with many pieces of *clip art*, such as drawings and photos of people meeting, medical equipment, telecommunications equipment, entertainment, and much more.

Personal Information Managers

Personal information management (PIM) software helps people, groups, and organizations store useful information, such as a list of tasks to complete or a set of names and addresses. PIM software usually provides an appointment calendar, an address book or contacts list, and a place to take notes. In addition, information in a PIM can be linked. For example, you can link an appointment with a sales manager in the calendar to information on the sales manager in the address book. When you click the appointment in the calendar, a window opens displaying information on the sales manager from the address book. Microsoft Outlook is an example of very popular PIM software. Increasingly, PIM software is moving online where it can be accessed from any Internet-connected device. See Figure 4.19.

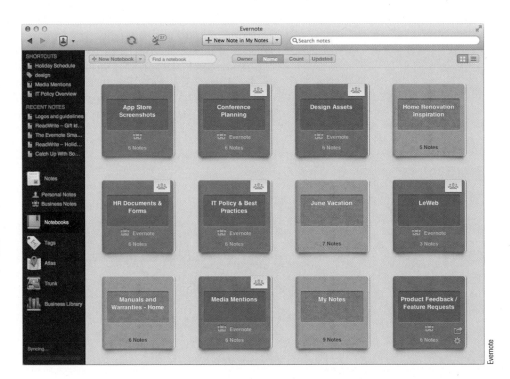

FIGURE **4.19**

Personal information management software

Evernote lets you take notes, sync files across devices, save Web pages, and share your ideas with friends and colleagues. It runs on computers and smartphones.

Some PIMs allow you to schedule and coordinate group meetings. If a computer or handheld device is connected to a network, you can upload the PIM data and coordinate it with the calendar and schedule of others using the same PIM software on the network. You can also use some PIMs to coordinate emails inviting others to meetings. As users receive their invitations, they click a link or button to be automatically added to the guest list.

Software Suites and Integrated Software Packages

software suite: A collection of programs packaged together in a bundle.

A software suite is a collection of programs packaged together in a bundle. Software suites can include a word processor, spreadsheet program, database management system, graphics program, communications tools, and organizers. Some suites support the development of Web pages, note taking, and speech recognition so that applications in the suite can accept voice commands and record dictation. Software suites offer many advantages. The software programs have been designed to work similarly so that, after you learn the basics for one application, the other applications are easy to learn and use. Buying software in a bundled suite is cost effective; the programs usually sell for a fraction of what they would cost individually.

Table 4.8 lists the most popular general-purpose software suites for personal computer users. Microsoft Office has the largest market share. Most of these software suites include a spreadsheet program, word processor,

TABLE **4.8** Major components of leading software suites

Personal Productivity Function	Microsoft Office	IBM Lotus Symphony	Corel WordPerfect Office	Apache OpenOffice	Apple iWork	Google Apps
Word processing	Word	Documents	WordPerfect	Writer	Pages	Docs
Spreadsheet	Excel	Spreadsheets	Quattro Pro	Calc	Numbers	Sheets
Presentation graphics	PowerPoint	Presentations	Presentations	Impress and Draw	Keynote	Slides
Database	Access	Approach		Base		

© 2016 Cengage Learning

database program, and graphics presentation software. All can exchange documents, data, and diagrams. In other words, you can create a spreadsheet and then cut and paste that spreadsheet into a document created using the word-processing application.

Some companies offer Web-based productivity software suites that require the installation of no hardware on your device—only a Web browser. Google, Zoho, and Thinkfree offer free online word processors, spreadsheets, presentations, and other software that require no installation on the PC.

After observing this trend, Microsoft responded with an online version of some of its popular Office applications. Microsoft Office 365 offers basic software suite features over the Internet using cloud computing. See Figure 4.20. Microsoft Word, Outlook, Excel, Exchange for messaging, SharePoint for collaboration, and Lync for conferencing can be accessed. These cloud-based applications cost on the order of $10 per user per month depending on the features used. Microsoft offers plans for professionals and small businesses, enterprises, and education. For example, any institution worldwide that licenses Office 365 ProPlus or Office Professional Plus for staff and faculty can provide access to Office 365 ProPlus for students at no additional cost. The online versions of Word, Excel, PowerPoint, and OneNote are tightly integrated with Microsoft's desktop Office suite for easy sharing of documents among computers and collaborators.

FIGURE **4.20**

Web suite

Microsoft Office 365 is a Web suite that offers basic software suite features over the Internet using cloud computing.

What's included

Get the latest Office, business-class email, document sharing, and web meetings—rich productivity services for modern users with the IT flexibility and control you need.

Office applications

Compliance and BI
Control access, prevent data loss, and gain insight fast with advanced tools

IT flexibility and control
Deploy on your terms and monitor your system's health in real time

Microsoft screenshot used with permission from Microsoft Corporation

FHI 360 is a nonprofit global health and development organization working on family planning, reproductive health, and HIV/AIDS. It has 60 offices in the United States and around the world and employs 4,400 professional staff, including experts in health, nutrition, education, economic development, civil society, environment, and research.[36] FHI 360 selected Microsoft Office 365 for its productivity software solution because the service supports a hybrid model in which Active Directory (a key security application that authenticates and authorizes all users and computers) and a number of applications are hosted locally by the nonprofit, while other documents and resources are stored off-site by Microsoft. This model enables FHI 360 to store sensitive patient data subject to HIPAA compliance on its own hardware rather than in the cloud. Office 365 also enables FHI 360 to do email, instant messaging, Web conferencing, document sharing, and collaboration. In addition, Office 365's videoconferencing and instant messaging capabilities will save FHI 360 approximately $20,000 annually.[37]

Other Personal Application Software

In addition to the software already discussed, people can use many other interesting and powerful application software tools. In some cases, the features and capabilities of these applications can more than justify the cost of an entire computer system. TurboTax, for example, is a popular tax-preparation program, which annually saves many people lots of hours and even dollars in preparing their taxes. You can find software for creating Web pages and sites, composing music, and editing photos and videos. Many people use educational and reference software and entertainment, games, and leisure software. Game-playing software is popular and can be very profitable for companies that develop games and various game accessories, including virtual avatars such as colorful animals, fish, and people. Recent studies proved that middle-school students who played enough active video games (e.g., Wii Boxing and Dance, Dance Revolution) get enough exercise to meet recommendations for physical exercise. Retirement communities use video games to keep seniors physically active.[38] Engineers, architects, and designers often use computer-assisted design (CAD) software to design and develop buildings, electrical systems, plumbing systems, and more. Autosketch, CorelCAD, and AutoCad are examples of CAD software. Other programs perform a wide array of statistical tests. Colleges and universities often have a number of courses in statistics that use this type of application software. Two popular applications in the social sciences are SPSS and SAS.

Mobile Application Software

The number of applications (apps) for smartphones and other mobile devices has exploded in recent years. Besides the valuable mobile applications that come with these devices, hundreds of thousands of applications have been developed by third parties. For example, iPhone users can download and install thousands of applications using the Apple App Store. Many iPhone apps are free, while others range in price from 99 cents to hundreds of dollars. Over 1 million mobile apps are available at the Google Play site for users of Android handsets. Microsoft and other software companies are also investing in mobile applications for devices that run on their software. SceneTap, an application for iPhones and Android devices, can determine the number of people at participating bars, pubs, or similar establishments and the ratio of males to females. The application uses video cameras and facial-recognition software to identify males and females. SocialCamera, an application for Android phones, allows people to take a picture of someone and then search their Facebook friends for a match. Many people consider facial-recognition software, however, a potential invasion to privacy. Table 4.9 lists a few mobile application categories.

TABLE 4.9 Categories of mobile applications

Category	Description
Books and reference	Access e-books, subscribe to journals, or look up information in Webster's or Wikipedia
Business and finance	Track expenses, trade stocks, and access corporate information systems
Entertainment	Access all forms of entertainment, including movies, television programs, music videos, and local night life
Games	Play a variety of games, from 2D games such as Pacman and Tetris to 3D games such as Need for Speed, Rock Band, and The Sims
Health and fitness	Track workout and fitness progress, calculate calories, and even monitor your speed and progress from your wirelessly connected Nike shoes
Lifestyle	Find good restaurants, select wine for a meal, and more
Music	Find, listen to, and create music
News and weather	Access major news and weather providers including Reuters, AP, the *New York Times*, and the Weather Channel
Photography	Organize, edit, view, and share photos taken on your camera phone
Productivity and utilities	Create grocery lists, practice PowerPoint presentations, work on spreadsheets, synchronize with PC files, and more
Social networking	Connect with others via major social networks including Facebook, Twitter, and MySpace
Sports	Keep up with your favorite team or track your own golf scores
Travel and navigation	Use the GPS in your smartphone to get turn-by-turn directions, find interesting places to visit, access travel itineraries, and more

Workgroup Application Software

workgroup application software: Software that supports teamwork, whether team members are in the same location or dispersed around the world.

Workgroup application software is designed to support teamwork, whether team members are in the same location or dispersed around the world. This support can be accomplished with software known as *groupware* that helps groups of people work together effectively. Microsoft Exchange Server, for example, has groupware and email features. Also called *collaborative software*, this approach allows a team of managers to work on the same production problem, letting them share their ideas and work via connected computer systems.

Examples of workgroup software include group-scheduling software, electronic mail, and other software that enables people to share ideas. Notes and Domino are examples of workgroup software from IBM. See Figure 4.21. Web-based software is ideal for group use. Because documents are stored on an Internet server, anyone with an Internet connection can access them easily. Google provides options in its online applications that allow users to share documents, spreadsheets, presentations, calendars, and notes with other specified users or everyone on the Web. This sharing makes it convenient for several people to contribute to a document without concern for software compatibility or storage. Google also provides a tool for creating Web-based forms and surveys. When invited parties fill out the form, the data is stored in a Google spreadsheet.

Clark Construction Group is a large general contractor with 11 regional offices and 4,000 employees. Clark needed a new IT solution to support document sharing, instant messaging, and the archiving of documents for legal discovery. Because its current system did not support users with mobile devices, software updates were delayed until they could be scheduled and pushed out to PCs scattered around job sites across the country. Clark selected Google Apps for Business and Postini Archiving & Discovery as its new solution. Cloud-based Google Apps would enable employees and business partners to collaborate easily. It also gave immediate access to software upgrades and enabled users to add new Apps via the Google Apps Marketplace.[39]

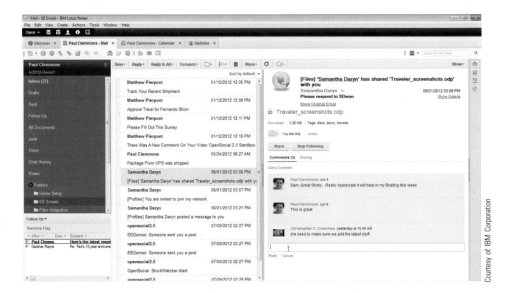

FIGURE **4.21**

IBM Notes Social Edition

IBM Notes Social Edition is work-group software.

Enterprise Application Software

Software that benefits an entire organization—enterprise application software—can also be developed specifically for the business or purchased off the shelf. Taylor Wimpey is one of the largest home builders in the United Kingdom, with offices in England, Scotland, and Wales. The firm implemented a cloud-based software solution that enabled the entire enterprise to reengineer its formerly labor-intensive annual budget forecasting process and meet its long-range financial planning requirements. Users access the system to perform analysis, modeling, forecasting, and generate key reports. The new forecasting process yields far more accurate results and enables separate business units to collaborate in real time.[40]

Enterprise software also helps managers and workers stay connected. At one time, traditional email kept managers and workers in touch with each other, but that may no longer be the best approach. Many workers spend much of their time sifting through email messages. One study claims that U.K. workers spend over 10 percent of their time reading and responding to messages. Furthermore, many workers compulsively check their email, becoming distracted and losing concentration on other work. Some believe that business collaboration tools such as Asana, Blue Kiwi, and Jive will eventually replace traditional email. Multinational IT consulting firm Atos is moving from email to a social collaboration service for communications.[41]

Following are categories of enterprise software:

Accounts payable	Credit and charge card administration
Invoicing	Retail operations
Accounts receivable	Distribution control
Manufacturing control	Sales ordering
Airline industry operations	Fixed asset accounting
Order entry	Savings and time deposits
Automatic teller systems	General ledger
Payroll	Shipping
Cash-flow analysis	Human resource management
Receiving	Stock and bond management
Check processing	Inventory control
Restaurant management	Tax planning and preparation

The total cost, ease of installation, ease of management, and the ability to integrate the software with other enterprise software are the major considerations in selecting enterprise software. Extending enterprise applications so that they can run on smartphones and other mobile devices is increasingly becoming a priority for organizations. In one survey, over 80 percent of respondents believe that having enterprise application software that can be used on smartphones and mobile devices was an important factor in selecting enterprise software.[42]

Most software spending goes to application software, as shown in Figure 4.22.[43]

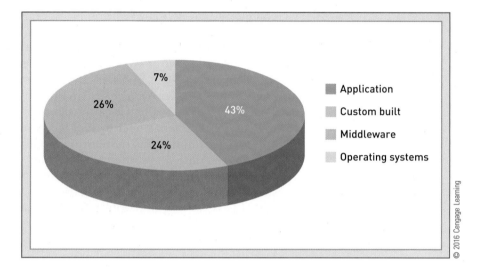

FIGURE 4.22

Spending by type of software

Of all software types, businesses spend the most on application software.

Application Software for Information, Decision Support, and Competitive Advantage

Specialized application software for information, decision support, and competitive advantage is available in every industry. For example, many schools and colleges use Blackboard or other learning management software to organize class materials and grades. Genetic researchers, as another example, are using software to visualize and analyze the human genome. Music executives use decision support software to help pick the next hit song.

Playa lakes appear only after spring rainstorms cause freshwater to collect in the round depressions of the otherwise flat landscape of parts of West Texas, Oklahoma, New Mexico, Nebraska, Colorado, and Kansas. Playas are an important habitat for migratory birds and waterfowl. The Playa DSS is used by natural resource professionals, land managers, and developers to enable them to make better decisions regarding how their collective actions may impact the playas and their associated wildlife.[44]

But how are all these systems actually developed and built? The answer is through the use of programming languages, discussed next.

PROGRAMMING LANGUAGES

programming languages: Sets of keywords, commands, symbols, and rules for constructing statements by which humans can communicate instructions to a computer.

Both system and application software are written in coding schemes called *programming languages.* The primary function of a programming language is to provide instructions to the computer system so that it can perform a processing activity. Information systems professionals work with **programming languages**, which are sets of keywords, symbols, and rules for constructing statements that people can use to communicate instructions to a computer. Programming involves translating what a user wants to accomplish into

Digital Software Systems May Improve Nuclear Power Plant Safety

The safety of nuclear power plants has always been an important consideration in their design. In the wake of the Fukushima plant failure after a record tsunami in March 2011, safety has an even higher priority. Using software to control power plants offers the potential of increased safety compared to earlier methods.

Duke Energy's Oconee nuclear power plant on the eastern shore of Lake Keowee near Seneca, South Carolina, was commissioned in 1973. As it entered the twenty-first century, its older analog control systems were showing their age. The plant suffered minor control failures during the 1990s, though no people were injured and no radiation leaked out as a result. Digital controls were added to some parts of the system in the late 1990s and early 2000s to deal with the most acute problems, but it was clear that Oconee's entire control structure needed to be replaced.

The purpose of a reactor protection system (RPS) is to protect the integrity of the plant's nuclear fuel by monitoring inputs from the reactor core. To accomplish this monitoring, application software must check sensors located throughout the reactor. If any safe operating values are exceeded, the software takes action, such as injecting cooling water or shutting the reactor down by inserting control rods.

After reviewing RPS applications, Duke Energy chose the Teleperm XS (TXS) system from Areva of France because TXS is designed to modernize existing analog instrumentation and control systems, and because its design includes features to ensure reliability. TXS is licensed in 11 countries and was already in use in other nuclear reactors outside the United States, thus assuring Duke that Oconee would not be a test site. TXS encompasses three functional systems:

- **Protection:** Monitoring safety parameters, enabling automatic protection and safeguard actions when an initiating event occurs
- **Surveillance:** Monitoring the core, rod control, and reactor coolant system and performing actions to protect reactor thresholds from being breached
- **Priority and actuator control system:** Managing the control and monitoring of operational and safety system actuators

Reactor Unit 1 of the Oconee facility became the first U.S. nuclear power plant to convert to fully digital control in 2011, Unit 3 in 2012, and Unit 2 in 2013. The conversions took place during the respective reactors' scheduled refueling shutdowns.

The nuclear power industry has recognized the importance of this instrumentation and control system upgrade. In 2012, the Nuclear Energy Institute awarded Duke Energy its "Best of the Best" Top Industry Practice award. Speaking at the award ceremony, Preston Gillespie, vice president at the Oconee site, said, "When I look back over the decision of leaders that I worked for ten years ago, who had the vision of what it would take to install a safety-related digital system, I stand very much in respect of what those leaders did. They knew it would be hard; they knew the cost would be great; they knew they had to find the right partner; they knew they had to get it through the licensing process. All of this, they knew, would result in reliable and safe operation of the plant. Because of that vision, the trail is now blazed for the rest of the industry to take advantage of the fruits of their labor."

"If the conversion improves safety and reliability over time, other nuclear power plants will likely follow Oconee's lead as soon as they can afford it," said David Lochbaum, director of the Nuclear Safety Project for the Union of Concerned Scientists: "There are a lot of eyes on that. If it goes well, you'll probably see many people in the queue making it happen. If it doesn't go well, they are going to wait for Duke Energy to iron out the kinks."

Discussion Questions

1. What functions does Duke's new reactor protection system (RPS) software perform?
2. Duke Energy selected off-the-shelf software for Oconee rather than writing custom software (or having a software development firm write it for them). Discuss the pros and cons of these two approaches in this situation. Do you think Duke Energy made the correct choice? Why or why not?

Critical Thinking Questions

1. What advantages does transforming from analog to digital systems convey? What advantages is the digital upgrade of the RPS expected to afford to Duke?
2. Computers are increasingly used to control systems that affect human lives. Besides nuclear power plants, examples include passenger aircraft, elevators, and medical equipment. Should the programmers who write software for those systems be licensed, be certified, or be required to pass standardized official examinations?

SOURCES: Areva Web site, *www.areva.com*, accessed May 31, 2012; Collins, J., "S.C. Nuke Plant First in U.S. to Go Digital," Desert News, *www.deseretnews.com/article/700139845/SC-nuclear-plant -becoming-1st-in-US-to-go-digital.html*, May 29, 2011; Staff, "Oconee Nuclear Station Projects Honored with Three Awards by the Nuclear Energy Institute," Duke Energy, *www.duke-energy.com /news/releases/2012052301.asp*, May 23, 2012; Hashemian, H., "USA's First Fully Digital Station," Nuclear Engineering International, *www.neimagazine.com/features/featureusa-s-first-fully-digital -station/*, January 21, 2011; Staff, "Duke Energy Employees Win Top Nuclear Industry Award for Improving Safety with Digital Milestone," Nuclear Energy Institute, *www.nei.org/newsandevents /newsreleases/duke-energy-employees-win-top-nuclear-industry-award-for-improving-safety-with -digital-milestone*, May 23, 2012.

a code that the computer can understand and execute. *Program code* is the set of instructions that signal the CPU to perform circuit-switching operations. In the simplest coding schemes, a line of code typically contains a single instruction such as, "Retrieve the data in memory address X." The instruction is then decoded during the instruction phase of the machine cycle.

Like writing a report or a paper in English, writing a computer program in a programming language requires the programmer to follow a set of rules. Each programming language uses symbols, keywords, and commands that have special meanings and usage. Each language also has its own set of rules, called the **syntax** of the language. The language syntax dictates how the symbols, keywords, and commands should be combined into statements capable of conveying meaningful instructions to the CPU. Rules such as "statements must terminate with a semicolon," and "variable names must begin with a letter," are examples of a language's syntax. A variable is a quantity that can take on different values. Program variable names such as SALES, PAYRATE, and TOTAL follow the syntax because they start with a letter, whereas variables such as %INTEREST, $TOTAL, and #POUNDS do not.

syntax: A set of rules associated with a programming language.

The Evolution of Programming Languages

The desire for faster, more efficient, more powerful information processing has pushed the development of new programming languages. The evolution of programming languages is typically discussed in terms of generations of languages. See Table 4.10.

TABLE **4.10** Evolution of programming languages

Generation	Language	Approximate Development Date	Sample Statement or Action
First	Machine language	1940s	00010101
Second	Assembly language	1950s	MVC
Third	High-level language	1960s	READ SALES
Fourth	Query and database languages	1970s	PRINT EMPLOYEE NUMBER IF GROSS PAY > 1000
Beyond Fourth	Natural and intelligent languages	1980s	IF hours worked is greater than 40, THEN pay the employee overtime pay

© 2016 Cengage Learning

Visual, Object-Oriented, and Artificial Intelligence Languages

Today, programmers often use visual and object-oriented languages. In the future, they may be using artificial intelligence languages to a greater extent. In general, these languages are easier for nonprogrammers to use, compared with older generation languages.

Visual programming uses a graphical or "visual" interface combined with text-based commands. Prior to visual programming, programmers were required to describe the windows, buttons, text boxes, and menus that they were creating for an application by using only text-based programming language commands. With visual programming, the software engineer drags and drops graphical objects such as buttons and menus onto the application form. Then, using a programming language, the programmer defines the capabilities of those objects in a separate code window. Visual Basic was one of the first visual programming interfaces. Today, software engineers use Visual Basic.NET, Visual C++, Visual C# (# is pronounced "sharp" as in music), and other visual programming tools.

Many people refer to visual programming interfaces such as Visual C# as "visual programming languages." This custom is fine for casual references, but a lesser-known category of programming language is more truly visual. With a true visual programming language, programmers create software by manipulating programming elements only graphically, without the use of any text-based programming language commands. Examples include Alice, Mindscript, and Microsoft Visual Programming Language (VPL). Visual programming languages are ideal for teaching novices the basics about programming without requiring them to memorize programming language syntax.

Some programming languages separate data elements from the procedures or actions that will be performed on them, but another type of programming language ties them together into units called *objects*. An object consists of data and the actions that can be performed on the data. For example, an object could be data about an employee and all the operations (such as payroll calculations) that might be performed on the data. Programming languages that are based on objects are called *object-oriented programming languages*. C++ and Java are popular general-purpose object-oriented programming languages. Languages used for Web development, such as Javascript and PHP, are also object oriented. In fact, most popular languages in use today take the object-oriented approach—and for good reason.

Using object-oriented programming languages is like constructing a building using prefabricated modules or parts. The object containing the data, instructions, and procedures is a programming building block. The same objects (modules or parts) can be used repeatedly. One of the primary advantages of an object is that it contains reusable code. In other words, the instruction code within that object can be reused in different programs for a variety of applications, just as the same basic prefabricated door can be used in two different houses. An object can relate to data on a product, an input routine, or an order-processing routine. An object can even direct a computer to execute other programs or to retrieve and manipulate data. So, a sorting routine developed for a payroll application could be used in both a billing program and an inventory control program. By reusing program code, programmers can write programs for specific application problems more quickly. See Figure 4.23. By combining existing program objects with new ones, programmers can easily and efficiently develop new object-oriented programs to accomplish organizational goals.

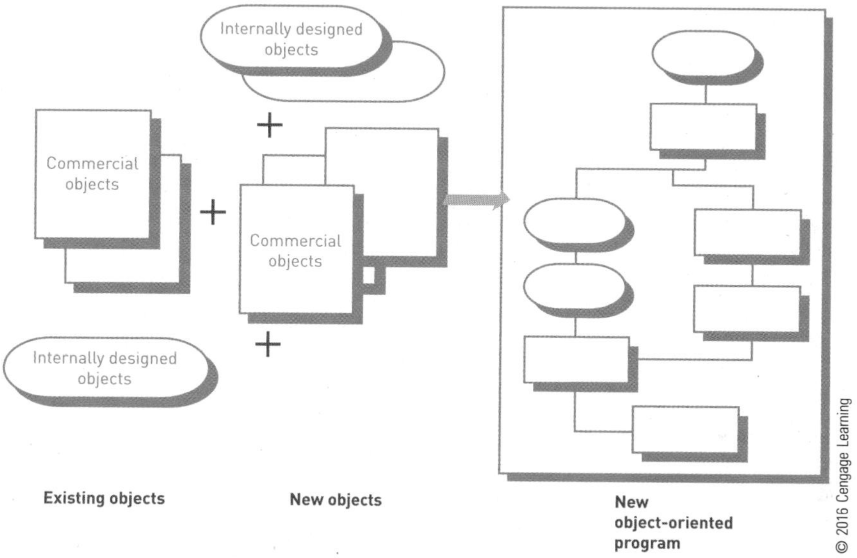

FIGURE **4.23**

Reusable code in object-oriented programming

By combining existing program objects with new ones, programmers can easily and efficiently develop new object-oriented programs to accomplish organizational goals. Note that these objects can be either commercially available or designed internally.

© 2016 Cengage Learning

Programming languages used to create artificial intelligence or expert systems applications are often called *fifth-generation languages (5GLs)*. Fifth-generation languages are sometimes called *natural languages* because they use even more English-like syntax than 4GLs. They allow programmers to communicate with the computer by using normal sentences. For example, computers programmed in fifth-generation languages can understand queries such as "How many athletic shoes did our company sell last month?"

With third-generation and higher-level programming languages, each statement in the language translates into several instructions in machine language. A special software program called a compiler converts the programmer's source code into the machine-language instructions, which consist of binary digits, as shown in Figure 4.24. A compiler creates a two-stage process for program execution. First, the compiler translates the program into a machine language; second, the CPU executes that program. Another approach is to use an *interpreter*, which is a language translator that carries out the operations called for by the source code. An interpreter does not produce a complete machine-language program. After the statement executes, the machine-language statement is discarded, the process continues for the next statement, and so on.

The majority of software used today is created using an integrated development environment. An *integrated development environment (IDE)* combines all

compiler: A special software program that converts the programmer's source code into the machine-language instructions, which consist of binary digits.

Stage 1: Convert program

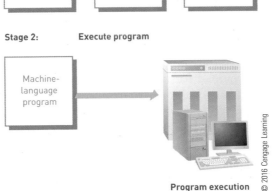

Stage 2: Execute program

FIGURE 4.24

How a compiler works

A compiler translates a complete program into a complete set of binary instructions (Stage 1). After this is done, the CPU can execute the converted program in its entirety (Stage 2).

Program execution

© 2016 Cengage Learning

the tools required for software engineering into one package. For example, the popular IDE Microsoft Visual Studio includes an editor that supports several visual programming interfaces and languages, a compiler and an interpreter, programming automation tools, a debugger (a tool for finding errors in the code), and other tools that provide convenience to the developer.

Software development kits (SDKs) often serve the purpose of an IDE for a particular platform. For example, software developers for Google's Android smartphone platform use Java (an object-oriented programming language) along with the Eclipse SDK with built-in Android Developer Tools to stream-line their Android app development. They can also use special code libraries provided by Google for Android functionality, and they test out their applications in an Android Emulator.[45] See Figure 4.25.

FIGURE 4.25

Emulator for Android smartphones

To develop for the Android, you use an SDK with a mobile device emu-lator so you can prototype, develop, and test Android applications with-out transferring them to a physical device.

Courtesy of Google

IDEs and SDKs have made software development easier than ever. Many novice coders and some who might have never considered developing software are publishing applications for popular platforms such as Facebook and the iPhone.

SOFTWARE ISSUES AND TRENDS

Because software is such an important part of today's computer systems, issues such as software bugs, licensing, upgrades, global software support, and even software taxation have received increased attention. For example, Massachusetts Governor Patrick signed the repeal of the computer software and services tax in September 2013 just two months after the tax took effect. From the outset, the tax was widely denounced by critics, saying the tax was too broad and confusing and would apply to virtually any business that upgraded software.[46]

Software Bugs

A software bug is a defect in a computer program that keeps it from performing as its users expect it to perform. Some software bugs are obvious and cause the program to terminate unexpectedly. Other bugs are subtler and allow errors to creep into your work.

Knight Capital Americas LLC experienced a significant software error in the operation of its automated routing system for equity orders. Over a 45-minute period, the system erroneously routed some 4 million executions in 154 stocks for more than 397 million shares. By the time that Knight stopped sending the orders, the firm had built a net long position in 80 stocks of approximately $3.5 billion and a net short position in 74 stocks of approximately $3.15 billion. When everything was sorted out, Knight lost more $460 million from these unwanted positions.[47] Following this disastrous trading error, the firm agreed to be acquired by Getco LLC to form KCG Holdings.[48]

Computer and software vendors say that as long as people design and program hardware and software, bugs are inevitable. The following list summarizes tips for reducing the impact of software bugs:

- Register all software so that you receive bug alerts, fixes, and patches.
- Check the manual or read-me files for solutions to known problems.
- Access the support area of the manufacturer's Web site for patches.
- Install the latest software updates.
- Before reporting a bug, make sure that you can recreate the circumstances under which it occurs.
- After you can recreate the bug, call the manufacturer's tech support line.
- Consider waiting before buying the latest release of software to give the vendor a chance to discover and remove bugs. Many schools and businesses don't purchase software until the first major revision with patches is released.

Copyrights and Licenses

Most companies aggressively guard and protect the source code of their software from competitors, lawsuits, and other predators. As a result, most software products are protected by law using copyright or licensing provisions. Those provisions can vary, however. In some cases, you are given unlimited use of software on one or two computers. This stipulation is typical with many applications developed for personal computers. In other cases, you pay for your usage: If you use the software more, you pay more. This approach is becoming popular, with software placed on networks or larger computers. Most of these protections prevent you from copying software and giving it to others. Some software now requires that you *register* or *activate* it before it can be fully used. This requirement is another way software companies prevent illegal distribution of their products.

When people purchase software, they don't actually own the software, but rather they are licensed to use the software on a computer. This is called a **single-user license**. A single-user license permits you to install the software on one or more computers, used by one person. A single-user license does not allow you to copy and share the software with others. Table 4.11 describes different types of software licenses.[49] Licenses that accommodate multiple users are usually provided at a discounted price.

single-user license: A software license that permits you to install the software on one or more computers, used by one person.

TABLE **4.11** Software licenses

License	Subtype	Description
Single-user license	General	This license type allows the program to be installed and used on one CPU which is not accessed by other users over a network. The software will be used only on a single computer, and other users will not be able to access or run the software while connected to your computer.
	Perpetual license	Allows the customer to install and use the software indefinitely. Technical support is included for a limited term, usually 90 days.
	Subscription license	Allows the user to use the software for a specified time period. This license usually includes technical support and access to upgrades and patches released during the term of the subscription. At the end of the term, the user has several options: (1) renew the subscription; (2) purchase a perpetual license at a discounted cost; or (3) remove the software from the computer.
	Freeware license	This license type is offered as freeware by the author and does not require paying any fee for use.
	Shareware license	This is a license to use software for a trial period and then, if you continue to use the software, you must pay a shareware fee or cease using the software.
Individual/multiuser licensing	Volume licenses	Allows the licensee to install the software on a certain number of computers. The licensee usually has to satisfy a minimum purchase requirement and obtains reduced prices in exchange. When purchasing the licenses, the licensee usually receives one copy of the media and documentation with the option of purchasing more.
	Site/enterprise	This license provides access to software at a single location. Typically, these licenses are individually negotiated with the publisher and vary widely in their provisions
Network/multiuser licenses	Server (network)	Licensed per server—this license type requires that you have a single copy of the software residing on the file server. With Per Server licensing, a specified number of CALs are associated with a particular server. The number of devices that can legally access that server simultaneously is limited in Per Server licensing to the number of CALs purchased for that particular server.
	Per Seat (machine)	Licensed per machine/seat—this license requires that you purchase a license for each client computer and/or device where access to services is needed. This license is typically used in conjunction with a network license.
	Per Processor	Under the Per Processor model, you acquire a Processor License for each processor in the server on which the software is running. A Processor License usually includes access for an unlimited number of users to connect. You do not need to purchase additional server licenses, CALs, or Internet Connector Licenses.

Source: Olshan, Jeremy, "88% of Spreadsheets Have Errors," MarketWatch, April 20, 2013, *www.marketwatch.com/story/88-of-spreadsheets-have-errors-2013-04-17.*

Freeware and Open-Source Software

Some software developers are not as interested in profiting from their intellectual property as others and have developed alternative copyrights and licensing agreements. *Freeware* is software that is made available to the public for free. Software developers might give away their product for several reasons. Some want to build customer interest and name recognition. Others simply don't need the money and want to make a valuable donation to society. Still others, such as those associated with the Free Software Foundation (*www.fsf .org*), believe that all software should be free. Some freeware is placed in the public domain where anyone can use the software free of charge. (Creative works that reach the end of their term of copyright revert to the public domain.) Table 4.12 shows some examples of freeware.

TABLE 4.12 Examples of freeware

Software	Description
Adobe Reader	Software for viewing Adobe PDF documents
AVG Anti-Virus	Antivirus security software
IrfanView	Photo-editing software
Pidgin	Instant messaging software
Thunderbird	Email and newsgroup software
WinPatrol	Antispyware software

© 2016 Cengage Learning

Freeware differs slightly from free software. Freeware simply implies that the software is distributed for free. The term "free software" was coined by Richard Stallman and the Free Software Foundation and implies that the software is not only freeware, but it is also open source. Open-source software is distributed, typically for free, with the source code also available so that it can be studied, changed, and improved by its users. Open-source software evolves from the combined contribution of its users. The Code For America (CFA) organization, for example, used open-source software in Boston and other American cities to help cities and municipalities solve some of their traffic problems, such as locating fire hydrants that might be completely covered with snow in the winter. CFA made its efforts free to other cities and municipalities. Table 4.13 provides examples of popular open-source software applications.

open-source software: Software that is distributed, typically for free, with the source code also available so that it can be studied, changed, and improved by its users.

TABLE 4.13 Examples of open-source software

Software	Category
Drupal	Web publishing system
Gimp	Photo editing
Grisbi	Personal accounting
Linux	Operating system
Mozilla Firefox	Internet browser
MySQL	Database software
Open Office	Application software
OpenProj	Project management

© 2016 Cengage Learning

Open-source software is not completely devoid of restrictions. Much of the popular free software in use today is protected by the GNU General Public License (GPL). The GPL grants you the right to do the following:

- Run the program for any purpose
- Study how the program works and adapt it to your needs
- Redistribute copies so you can help others
- Improve the program and release improvements to the public

Software under the GPL is typically protected by a "copyleft" (a play on the word "copyright"), which requires that any copies of the work retain the same license. A copyleft work cannot be owned by any one person, and no one is allowed to profit from its distribution. The Free Software Directory (*http://directory.fsf.org*) lists over 5,000 software titles in 22 categories licensed under the GPL.

Why would an organization run its business using software that's free? Can something that's given away over the Internet be stable, reliable, or sufficiently supported to place at the core of a company's day-to-day operations? The answer is surprising—many believe that open-source software is often *more* reliable and secure than commercial software. How can this be? First, because a program's source code is readily available, users can fix any problems they discover. A fix is often available within hours of the problem's discovery. Second, because the source code for a program is accessible to thousands of people, the chances of a bug being discovered and fixed before it does any damage are much greater than with traditional software packages.

However, using open-source software does have some disadvantages. Although open-source systems can be obtained for next to nothing, the upfront costs are only a small piece of the total cost of ownership that accrues over the years that the system is in place. Some claim that open-source systems contain many hidden costs, particularly for user support or solving problems with the software. Licensed software comes with guarantees and support services, while open-source software does not. Still, many businesses appreciate the additional freedom that open-source software provides. The question of software support is the biggest stumbling block to the acceptance of open-source software at the corporate level. Getting support for traditional software packages is easy—you call a company's toll-free support number or access its Web site. But how do you get help if an open-source package doesn't work as expected? Because the open-source community lives on the Internet, you look there for help. Through use of Internet discussion areas, you can communicate with others who use the same software, and you might even reach someone who helped develop it. Users of popular open-source packages can get correct answers to their technical questions within a few hours of asking for help on the appropriate Internet forum. Another approach is to contact one of the many companies emerging to support and service such software—for example, Red Hat for Linux and Sendmail, Inc., for Sendmail. These companies offer high-quality, for-pay technical assistance.

Software Upgrades

Software companies revise their programs periodically. Software upgrades vary widely in the benefits that they provide, and what some people call a benefit others might call a drawback. Deciding whether to upgrade to a new version of software can be a challenge for corporations and people with a large investment in software. Should the newest version be purchased when it is released? Some users do not always get the most current software upgrades or versions unless it includes significant improvements or capabilities. Developing an upgrading strategy is important for many businesses. American Express, for example, has standardized its software upgrade process around the world to make installing updated software faster and more efficient. The standardized process also helps the company make sure that updated software is more stable with fewer errors and problems.

Global Software Support

Large global companies have little trouble persuading vendors to sell them software licenses for even the most far-flung outposts of their company. But can those same vendors provide adequate support for their software customers in all locations? Supporting local operations is one of the biggest challenges IS teams face when putting together standardized companywide systems. Slower technology growth markets, such as Eastern Europe and Latin America, might not have any official vendor presence. Instead, large vendors such as Sybase, IBM, and Hewlett-Packard typically contract with local providers to support their software.

One approach that has been gaining acceptance in North America is to outsource global support to one or more third-party distributors. The user company can still negotiate its license with the software vendor directly, but it then hands the global support contract to a third-party supplier. The supplier acts as a middleman between software vendor and user, often providing distribution, support, and invoicing.

In today's computer systems, software is an increasingly critical component. Whatever approach people and organizations take to acquire software, everyone must be aware of the current trends in the industry. Informed users are wise consumers.

SUMMARY

Principle:

Systems and application software are critical in helping individuals and organizations achieve their goals.

Software consists of programs that control the workings of the computer hardware. Two main categories of software are systems software and application software. Systems software is a collection of programs that interacts between hardware and application software and includes operating systems, utility programs, and middleware. Application software can be proprietary or off the shelf and enables people to solve problems and perform specific tasks.

An operating system (OS) is a set of computer programs that controls the computer hardware and acts as an interface with applications. An OS converts an instruction from an application into a set of instructions needed by the hardware. This intermediary role allows hardware independence. An OS also manages memory, which involves controlling storage access and use by converting logical requests into physical locations and by placing data in the best storage space, including virtual memory.

Operating systems use multitasking, multiprocessing, and multithreading to increase the amount of processing that can be accomplished in a given amount of time. With multitasking, users can run more than one application at a time. Multiprocessing supports running a program on more than one CPU. Multitasking allows more than one program to run concurrently. Multithreading allows different threads of a single program to run concurrently.

The ability of a computer to handle an increasing number of concurrent users smoothly is called *scalability*, a feature critical for systems expected to handle a large number of users.

An OS also provides a user interface, which allows users to access and command the computer. A command-based user interface requires text commands to send instructions. A graphical user interface (GUI), such as

Windows, uses icons and menus. Other user interfaces include touch, speech, and motion.

Software applications use the OS by requesting services through a defined application program interface (API). Programmers can use APIs to create application software without having to understand the inner workings of the OS. APIs also provide a degree of hardware independence so that the underlying hardware can change without necessarily requiring a rewrite of the software applications.

Over the years, many popular OSs have been developed, including Microsoft Windows, the Mac OS X, and Linux. There are several options for OSs in the enterprise as well, depending on the type server. UNIX is a powerful OS that can be used on many computer system types and platforms, from workstations to mainframe systems. Linux is the kernel of an OS whose source code is freely available to everyone. Some OSs, such as Mac iOS, Windows Embedded, Symbian, Android, webOS, and variations of Linux, have been developed to support mobile communications and consumer appliances. When an OS is stored in a computer system, including a processor, and then implanted in another device to control it, it is referred to as an embedded operating system or an embedded system for short.

Utility programs can perform many useful tasks and often come installed on computers along with the OS. This software is used to merge and sort sets of data, keep track of computer jobs being run, compress files of data, protect against harmful computer viruses, monitor hardware and network performance, and perform dozens of other important tasks. Virtualization software simulates a computer's hardware architecture in software so that computer systems can run operating systems and software designed for other architectures or run several operating systems simultaneously on one system. Middleware is software that allows different systems to communicate and transfer data back and forth.

Principle:

Organizations use off-the-shelf application software for common business needs and proprietary application software to meet unique business needs and provide a competitive advantage.

Application software applies the power of the computer to solve problems and perform specific tasks. One useful way of classifying the many potential uses of information systems is to identify the scope of problems and opportunities addressed by a particular organization or its sphere of influence. For most companies, the spheres of influence are personal, workgroup, and enterprise.

User software, or personal productivity software, includes general-purpose programs that enable users to improve their personal effectiveness, increasing the quality and amount of work that can be done. Software that helps groups work together is often called workgroup application software. It includes group-scheduling software, electronic mail, and other software that enables people to share ideas. Enterprise software that benefits the entire organization, called enterprise resource planning software, is a set of integrated programs that help manage a company's vital business operations for an entire multisite, global organization.

Three approaches to acquiring application software are to build proprietary application software, buy existing programs off the shelf, or use a combination of customized and off-the-shelf application software. Building proprietary software (in-house or on contract) has the following advantages. The organization gets software that more closely matches its needs. Further, by being involved with the development, the organization has further control over the results. Finally, the organization has greater control in making changes. The disadvantages include the following. It is likely to take longer and cost more to develop. Additionally, the in-house staff will be hard pressed to provide ongoing support and maintenance. Lastly, there is a greater risk that the software features will not work as expected or that other performance problems will occur.

Some organizations have taken a third approach—customizing software packages. This approach usually involves a mixture of the preceding advantages and disadvantages and must be carefully managed.

An application service provider (ASP) is a company that provides the software, support, and computer hardware on which to run the software from the user's facilities over a network. ASPs customize off-the-shelf software on contract and speed deployment of new applications while helping IS managers avoid implementation headaches. ASPs reduce the need for many skilled IS staff members and also lower a project's start-up expenses. Software as a Service (SaaS) allows businesses to subscribe to Web-delivered business application software by paying a monthly service charge or a per-use fee.

SaaS and recent Web development technologies have led to a new paradigm in computing called cloud computing. "Cloud computing" refers to the use of computing resources, including software and data storage, on the Internet (the cloud), not on local computers. Rather than installing, storing, and running software on your own computer, with cloud computing, you access software stored on and delivered from a Web server.

Although hundreds of computer applications can help people at school, home, and work, the most popular applications are word processing, spreadsheet analysis, database, graphics, and personal information management. A software suite, such as Office, Symphony, WordPerfect, Lotus Symphony, OpenOffice, Apple iWorks, or Google Apps, offers a collection of these powerful programs sold as a bundle.

Many thousands of applications are designed for businesses and workgroups. Business software generally falls under the heading of information systems that support common business activities, such as accounts receivable, accounts payable, inventory control, and other management activities.

Principle:

Organizations should choose programming languages with functional characteristics that are appropriate for the task at hand and well suited to the skills and experience of the programming staff.

All software programs are written in coding schemes called *programming languages*, which provide instructions to a computer to perform some processing activity. The several classes of programming languages include machine, assembly, high-level, query and database, object-oriented, and visual programming.

Programming languages have changed since their initial development in the early 1950s. In the first generation, computers were programmed in machine language, and in the second, assembly languages were used. The third generation consists of many high-level programming languages that use English-like statements and commands. They must be converted to machine language by special software called a compiler and include BASIC, COBOL, and FORTRAN. Fourth-generation languages include database and query languages such as SQL.

Fifth-generation programming languages combine rule-based code generation, component management, visual programming techniques, reuse management, and other advances. Object-oriented programming languages use groups of related data, instructions, and procedures called *objects*, which serve as reusable modules in various programs. These languages can reduce program development and testing time. Java can be used to develop applications on the Internet. Visual programming environments, integrated development environments (IDEs), and software development kits (SDKs) have simplified and streamlined the coding process and have made it easier for more people to develop software.

Principle:

The software industry continues to undergo constant change; users need to be aware of recent trends and issues to be effective in their business and personal life.

Software bugs, software copyrights and licensing, freeware and open-source software, software upgrades, and global software support are all important software issues and trends.

A software bug is a defect in a computer program that keeps it from performing in the manner intended. Software bugs are common, even in key pieces of business software.

Freeware is software that is made available to the public for free. Open-source software is freeware that also has its source code available so that others may modify it. Open-source software development and maintenance is a collaborative process, with developers around the world using the Internet to download the software, communicate about it, and submit new versions of it.

Software upgrades are an important source of increased revenue for software manufacturers and can provide useful new functionality and improved quality for software users.

Global software support is an important consideration for large global companies putting together standardized companywide systems. A common solution is outsourcing global support to one or more third-party software distributors.

KEY TERMS

application programming interface (API)

application service provider (ASP)

command-based user interface

compiler

computer program

documentation

enterprise application integration (EAI)

enterprise sphere of influence

graphical user interface (GUI)

kernel

middleware

off-the-shelf software

open-source software

operating system (OS)

personal productivity software

personal sphere of influence

programming languages

proprietary software

service-oriented architecture (SOA)

single-user license

Software as a Service (SaaS)

software suite

syntax

user interface

utility program

workgroup

workgroup application software

workgroup sphere of influence

CHAPTER 4: SELF-ASSESSMENT TEST

Systems and application software are critical in helping individuals and organizations achieve their goals.

1. Which of the following is an example of a command-driven operating system?

a. XP

b. Mavericks

c. MS DOS

d. Windows 7

2. It will be years before computers are smart enough to use speech or motion user interface. True or False?

3. _____ is an open-source OS that is used on all computer platforms: PC, server, embedded, smartphones, and other.

4. Internet filtering designed to protect students from inappropriate Web sites is a function of the operating system. True or False?

5. Some companies use _____ to run multiple operating systems on a single computer.
   a. multitasking
   b. middleware
   c. service-oriented architecture
   d. virtualization

Organizations use off-the-shelf application software for common business needs and proprietary application software to meet unique business needs and provide a competitive advantage.

6. Application software that enables users to develop a spreadsheet for tracking their exercise and eating habits is software for the personal sphere of influence. True or False?

7. Software that enables users to improve their personal effectiveness, increasing the amount of work they can do and its quality, is called _____.
   a. personal productivity software
   b. operating system software
   c. utility software
   d. graphics software

8. The capability to do forecasting can be found in which type of application software?
   a. word-processing programs
   b. spreadsheets
   c. personal information management programs
   d. presentation graphics programs

9. _____ software is one-of-a-kind software designed for a specific application and owned by the company, organization, or person that uses it.

10. _____ allows businesses to subscribe to Web-delivered business application software by paying a monthly service charge or a per-use fee.
    a. Software as a Service (SaaS)
    b. An application service provider (ASP)
    c. Proprietary software
    d. Off-the-shelf software

Organizations should choose programming languages with functional characteristics that are appropriate for the task at hand and well suited to the skills and experience of the programming staff.

11. Most software purchased to run on a server uses a single-user license. True or False?

12. One of the primary advantages of _____ programming is the use of reusable code modules that save developers from having to start coding from scratch.

13. Each programming language has its own set of rules, called the _____ of the language.

14. A(n) _____ converts a programmer's source code into the machine-language instructions consisting of binary digits.

The software industry continues to undergo constant change; users need to be aware of recent trends and issues to be effective in their business and personal life.

15. _____ allows users to tweak the software to their own needs.
    a. Freeware
    b. Off-the-shelf software
    c. Open-source software
    d. Software in the public domain

16. An enterprise is likely to purchase a(n) _____ license for software that it intends all of its employees to use while on site.

CHAPTER 4: SELF-ASSESSMENT TEST ANSWERS

1. c
2. False
3. Linux
4. False
5. d
6. True
7. a
8. b
9. Proprietary
10. a
11. False
12. object-oriented
13. syntax
14. compiler
15. c
16. site

REVIEW QUESTIONS

1. What trends are expected in software spending for the time period 2012–2017?
2. What is a computer platform?
3. Identify and briefly describe the three spheres of influence.
4. What is the kernel of the operating system?
5. Identify and briefly discuss five types of operating system user interfaces.
6. What is an application programming interface?
7. Identify and briefly describe five basic task management techniques employed in operating systems.
8. What role does a Linux distributor play?
9. What is the greatest advantage of using a 64-bit computer?
10. What is an embedded system? Give three examples of such a system.
11. Distinguish between proprietary software and off-the-shelf software.
12. What is middleware?
13. What is Software as a Service (SaaS)?
14. What is an application server provider (ASP)?
15. What is cloud computing? What are some pros and cons of cloud computing?
16. What is open-source software? What are the benefits and drawbacks for a business that uses open-source software?
17. Briefly discuss the advantages and disadvantages of frequent software upgrades.
18. What is the difference between freeware and open-source software?

DISCUSSION QUESTIONS

1. Assume that you must take a computer-programming language course next semester. How would you decide which language would be best for you to study? Do you think that a professional programmer needs to know more than one programming language? Why or why not?
2. You are going to buy a personal computer. What operating system features are important to you? What operating system would you select and why?
3. You have been asked to develop a user interface for someone with limited sight—someone without the ability to recognize shapes on a computer screen. Describe the user interface you would recommend.
4. You are using a new release of an application software package. You think that you have discovered a bug. Outline the approach that you would take to confirm that it is indeed a bug. What actions would you take if it truly were a bug?
5. For a company of your choice, describe the three most important application software packages you would recommend for the company's profitability and success.
6. What are some of the advantages and disadvantages of employing Software as a Service (SaaS)? What precautions might you take to minimize the risk of using one?
7. Describe three personal productivity software packages you are likely to use the most. What personal productivity software packages would you select for your use?
8. Describe the most important features of an operating system for a smartphone.
9. If you were the IS manager for a large manufacturing company, what issues might you have with the use of open-source software? What advantages might there be for use of such software?
10. Identify four types of software licenses frequently used. Which approach does the best job of ensuring a steady, predictable stream of revenue from customers? Which approach is most fair for the small company that makes infrequent use of the software?
11. How have software development kits (SDKs) influenced software development?
12. How can virtualization save a company a lot of money?

PROBLEM-SOLVING EXERCISES

1. "Spreadsheets, even after careful development, contain errors in 1% or more of all formula cells," according to Ray Panko, a professor of IT management at the University of Hawaii and an

authority on bad spreadsheet practices. This means that in large spreadsheets there could be dozens of undetected errors.[50] Outline several measures that could be taken to ensure the accuracy of a large spreadsheet that is used to make key business decisions.

2. Use a database program to enter four candidates for your next computer. List the make, model, cost, and key features in the columns of a database table. Use a word processor to write a paragraph summarizing the pros and cons for each choice. Copy the database table into the word-processing program.

3. Use a spreadsheet package to prepare a monthly budget that itemizes your various income sources and at least six expense items (make up numbers rather than using actual ones). Forecast your cash flow—total income minus total expenses—for the next six months. Now use a graph to plot your cash flow over this period of time. Use word-processing software to prepare a paragraph that documents your financial situation over the next six months. Cut and paste the graph of your cash flow into this document.

TEAM ACTIVITIES

1. Form a group of three or four classmates. Find articles from business periodicals, search the Internet, and interview people on the topic of modifying off-the-shelf software packages. Identify the three greatest pros and cons of this strategy. Compile your results for an in-class presentation or a written report.

2. Form a group of three or four classmates. Identify and contact an employee of any local business or organization. Interview the individual and describe the application software the company uses and discuss the importance of the software to the organization. Write a brief report summarizing your findings.

3. Team members should learn how to use a computer operating system with which they are unfamiliar. Explore how to launch applications, minimize and maximize windows, close applications, save and view files on the system, and change system settings such as the wallpaper. Assess ease of learning and ease of use. Team members should collaborate on a report, using the track changes features of Word or collaborative features of Google Docs to summarize findings and opinions on at least three PC OSs.

WEB EXERCISES

1. Use the Internet to identify the three most popular smartphone operating systems. Write a report that describes the key features and the pros and cons of these three operating systems.

2. Use the Web to find multiple reviews and reports on four different personal productivity software suites from various vendors. Create a table in a word-processing document to show what applications are provided by the competing suites. For each suite, write a paragraph summarizing its strengths and weaknesses. Write a final

paragraph stating which suite you would choose and why.

3. Use the Internet to search for information on real-time operating systems. Identify the key difference between real time and non-real–time operating systems. Identify three examples where real-time operating systems are needed.

4. Do research on the Web about application software that is used in an industry and is of interest to you. Write a brief report describing how the application software can be used to increase profits or reduce costs.

CAREER EXERCISES

1. Identify three specific smartphone applications that would greatly help you in your current or next job. (The applications may already exist or you may identify ones you wish did exist.) Describe specific features of each application and how you would use them.

2. Think of your ideal job. Identify two application software packages for each sphere of influence that you would likely use in this career.

CASE STUDIES

Case One

Kaiser Permanente Implements Electronic Health Record (EHR) System

Kaiser Permanente is an integrated healthcare organization founded in 1945. The company operates one of the largest not-for-profit health plans in the United States, with over 9 million health plan subscribers. Kaiser Permanente also includes Kaiser Foundation Hospitals (encompassing 37 hospitals) and The Permanente Medical Groups, with 611 medical offices. The company employs nearly 176,000 people, including 17,157 physicians. Its 2012 operating revenue was almost $51 billion.

HealthConnect is the name of Kaiser's comprehensive health information system. Over the past decade, HealthConnect has been a leader in the implementation of electronic health records (EHR), computer-readable records of health-related information on individuals. In 2003, Kaiser had announced its intention to work with Epic Systems Corporation over a three-year period to build an integrated set of systems to support EHRs, computerized physician order entry, scheduling and billing, and clinical decision support at an estimated cost of $1.8 billion. This decision came after Kaiser had already made several unsuccessful attempts at clinical automation projects. The project eventually ballooned into a seven-year, $4.2 billion effort as the scope of the project was expanded time and again. Training and productivity losses made up more than 50 percent of the cost of the project, as Kaiser had to cut physicians' hours at clinics during training and was forced to hire physicians temporarily to handle the workload.

However, in 2010, Kaiser announced that it had fully implemented EHR applications at all of its hospitals and clinics. Finally, it could begin reaping the benefits from its efforts.

The HealthConnect system connects Kaiser plan subscribers to their healthcare providers and to their personal healthcare information. The system uses EHRs to coordinate patient care among physicians' offices, hospitals, testing labs, and pharmacies. The EHR is designed to ensure that patients and their healthcare providers all have access to current, accurate, and complete patient data. The system and its data are now accessible via smartphone as well as personal computer. During 2012, there were over 88 million subscriber sign-ons to the system.

Physicians and nurses in hospitals, clinics, and private offices document treatment in the EHR system. After physicians enter a diagnosis into the system, they may receive a system message indicating that there is a "best practice order set" available for treating the condition. When they enter a medication order, physicians receive alerts about potential allergic reactions or adverse drug reactions based on other medications a patient is already taking. Physicians also receive automatic notifications about how lab test results should affect medication orders.

HealthConnect also provides capabilities to support bar coding for the safe administration of medicine. Under this system of administering medication, the nurse first scans the patient's barcoded identification wristband. The nurse next scans a bar code on the medication container that identifies the specific medicine and dosage. The system verifies that this medicine and dosage have been ordered for this patient. If these do not match, the nurse receives an audible warning signal.

Kaiser has found that use of a comprehensive EHR improves health plan subscribers' satisfaction with the healthcare delivery system. In addition, HealthConnect empowers healthcare plan subscribers to take more responsibility for managing their own health care. Kaiser subscribers can access HealthConnect via a Web portal at kp.org. Here they are able to view most of their personal health records online, including their lab results, medication history, and treatment summaries. Patients can enter their own readings from blood pressure and glucose meters.

They can also securely email their healthcare providers, which cuts down on the amount of time patients spend on hold waiting to speak to a doctor and on the number of office visits (the number of outpatient visits has dropped an average of 8 percent in the one and one-half years following EHR implementation at each hospital). Each month patients send over 1 million emails to their doctors and healthcare teams through this component of the system. Over 29 million lab test results were viewed online in 2011. In addition, approximately 827,000 prescriptions are being refilled online monthly, and 230,000 appointments are scheduled monthly.

HealthConnect enables physicians to benchmark their performance against colleagues on a number of fronts— efficiency, quality, safety, and service. Hospitals can also benchmark each other on measures such as adverse events and complications. "Best in class" practices can be identified, and physicians and hospitals can borrow these best practices from one another to further improve the overall quality of care.

As the EHR system is further enhanced, Kaiser will likely find new ways to reap benefits from its system to improve efficiency and the quality of health care.

Kaiser began working on implementing an EHR system in 2003 and finally completed the implementation in 2010. Along the way, the company tried several different approaches, ran into numerous problems, and spent millions of dollars. It is just now beginning to reap the benefits from this effort. It likely will take time, further system enhancements, and additional expenditures for many other organizations to see similar benefits.

Discussion Questions

1. What troubles did Kaiser run into when it first tried to implement the EHR system? Is Kaiser's experience typical of leading-edge companies? If so, how?
2. Researchers associated with Kaiser Permanente have used the patient record database to make numerous worthwhile discoveries in the areas of preventing whooping cough, determining the correlation between HPV vaccination and sexual activity in young girls, improving methods of cancer detection, avoiding blood clots in women using birth control pills, and lowering cholesterol. Do you think that access to this

valuable data should be granted to researchers not associated with Kaiser Permanente? Should researchers be charged a fee to access this data to help offset the ongoing cost of upgrading the system?

Critical Thinking Questions

1. What strategic advantage does Kaiser gain from its EHR system?
2. What do you think are the greatest benefits of the HealthConnect system for Kaiser Permanente subscribers? Can you identify any potential risks or ethical issues associated with the use of this system for Kaiser healthcare plan subscribers? How would you answer these questions from the perspective of a physician or nurse?

SOURCES: Kaiser Permanente, "About Kaiser Permanente," *http://xnet .kp.org/newscenter/aboutkp/fastfacts.html*, accessed August 27, 2013; Versel, Neil, "As EHR Installation Nears Completion, Kaiser Recommends 'Big Bang,' " FierceEMR, July 30, 2009, *www.fierceemr.com/story/ehr -installation-nears-completionkaiser-recommends-big-bang/2009-07 -30*; Anderson, Howard, J., "Kaiser's Long and Winding Road," Health Data Management, August 1, 2009, *www.healthdatamanagement.com /issues/2009_69/-38718-1.html*; McPartland, Ginny, "Decades of Health Records Fuel Kaiser Permanente Research", March 6, 2013, *http:// kaiserpermanentehistory.org/tag/kaiser-permanente-healthconnect/*; Kaiser Permanente "Kaiser Permanente HealthConnect® Electronic Health Record," *http://xnet.kp.org/newscenter/aboutkp/healthconnect /index.html*, accessed April 13, 2013; Sarasohn-Kahn, Jane, "The Story of Kaiser Permanente's EHR," Health Populi, September 15, 2010, *http://healthpopuli.com/2010/09/15/the-story-of-kaiser-permanentes-ehr*.

Case Two

Your Next Car on iPad, iPhone, or Android

Like most companies today, automotive information publisher Edmunds collects and analyzes statistical data about visitors to its Web site. When chief operating officer Seth Berkowitz saw a spike in the percentage of mobile page views that came from iPads in the summer of 2010, he knew something was up.

In 2011, Edmunds launched an iPhone app (application program) for its Inside Line car fan site, followed by an iPad and Android version in 2012.

However, for a business, the decision is never as simple as "Let's develop an iPhone app." It's not enough to know that visitors to its Web site use certain mobile devices. A business must also know why. To develop an app without that knowledge is to risk developing the wrong app. That would be worse than not having one at all. However, that information, the why, cannot be obtained from statistical analysis of Web-visit data. Coming up with an app that would earn a five-star rating on the iTunes store requires more than programming skills. It calls for a deep understanding of why mobile users access a site and how their needs differ from those of people who use other devices. For example, knowing that users of smartphones have small screens but may still need to see details, Edmunds included high-quality car photos that users can zoom to enlarge.

To Edmunds users, the Inside Line iPhone app can be the most convenient way to access the Edmunds site. Not all car buyers prefer or even use tablets (any more than people in any other group), but some do. In a competitive market,

being accessible to all potential customers, not just some, can help companies gain an advantage over competitors. As one blogger put it, "I'll be in the market for another car soon. Used, of course. Which is where the value of the Edmunds site really comes into play, since owners are free to review these cars and post them on the site."

But to Edmunds, tablets such as the iPad offer more than a way to connect with its customers. They also support valuable business analysis tools. Using an app that Edmunds.com developed with tools from software company MicroStrategy, Edmunds management can sort and analyze huge volumes of data about auto sales. President Avi Steinlauf refers to this app when he says that "As a result of having more data at his fingertips [a manager] can ask more specific questions of his staff and make quicker decisions."

The analytics software indicates such tendencies as the propensity of a consumer to consider other models when researching a particular vehicle. Automakers can review and interact with the data on their iPads to help them with marketing and advertising decisions. Solomon Kang, director of client analytic services at Edmunds.com, explains: "Our new iPad app is particularly critical for executives who are always on the go and need to be able to react quickly."

Discussion Questions

1. Why did Edmunds develop the Inside Line iPhone app? It's nice to provide Inside Line as a free news service and discussion forum for car fans, but companies that provide free services for no reason don't stay in business. How does Edmunds expect to earn enough money with this app to justify its development and support costs?
2. What piece of data inspired Edmunds to create a mobile app? What types of data in general should IT managers watch when considering innovative software development?

Critical Thinking Questions

1. This case study says that Edmunds's Inside Line app includes full-resolution photos that users can zoom. The other possible decision would have been to include low-resolution photos that load faster and use fewer megabytes of a smartphone's data cap but do not offer the zoom option. For what market or application might that software design decision have been the better choice? What differences between the two make you think so?
2. What different types of users does Edmunds appeal to? How does Edmunds and other companies develop their applications to appeal to different types of users?

SOURCES: Campbell, J., "Edmunds Has Their Own App (Finally!)," Apple Thoughts, *forums.thoughtsmedia.com/f387/edmunds-has-their -own-app-finally-124564.html*, December 5, 2011; Taylor, P., "iPad Case Study: Edmunds.com," *Financial Times, www.ft.com/intl/cms/s/0 /d8e5eda6-613c-11e0-ab25-00144feab49a.html#axzz1b6VLxELL* (free registration required), April 8, 2011; Edmunds, "Inside Line App Comes to iPad," Inside Line, *www.insideline.com/car-news/inside-line-app -comes-to-ipad.html*, June 3, 2011; Staff, "Inside Line Launches iPhone App," Edmunds, Inside Line, *www.insideline.com/car-news/inside-line*

-launches-iphone-app.html, April 14, 2011; Staff, "Edmunds' InsideLine iPhone and iPad Apps Earn Five-Star Ratings in iTunes Store," Edmunds, Business Wire, *www.businesswire.com/news/home/20110826005691 /en/Edmunds'-InsideLine-iPhone-iPad-Apps-Earn-Five-Star*, August 26, 2011; Konrad, A., "Tablets Storm the Corner Office," Fortune, *tech.fortune.cnn.com/2011/10/13/ipad-executives-managing*, October 17, 2011; Moore, C. W., "Edmunds InsideLine iPhone and iPad Automotive Enthusiast App," PowerBook Central, *www.pbcentral.com /blog/2011/08/29/edmunds-insideline-iphone-and-ipad-automotive -enthusiast-app*, August 29, 2011.

Questions for Web Case

See the Web site for this book to read about the Altitude Online case for this chapter. Following are questions concerning this Web case.

Altitude Online: Systems and Application Software

Discussion Questions

1. Why do you think Altitude Online uses two PC platforms—Windows and Mac—rather than

standardizing on one? What are the benefits and drawbacks of this decision?

2. Why do you think a business is required to keep copies of all of its software licenses?

Critical Thinking Questions

1. How much freedom should a company like Altitude Online allow for its employees to choose their own personal application software? Why might a company prefer to standardize around specific software packages?

2. What benefits might be provided to an advertising media company like Altitude Online by upgrading to the latest media development and production software? How might upgrading provide the company with a competitive advantage?

NOTES

Sources for the opening vignette: Swedberg, Claire, "C&A Expands RFID Usage to Track Inventory," RFID Journal, May 29, 2013, *www.rfidjournal.com/articles/view?10556*, accessed August 26, 2013; Creativesystems Web site, *www.creativesystems.eu*, accessed August 26, 2013; "Creativesystems Wins Motorola Solutions' Best Mobile Applications Solutions Award," Creativesystems News Release, April 2, 2013, *www.creativesystems.eu/en/press /news/568/creativesystems-wins-motorola-solutions-best -mobile-applications-solutions-award.html*, accessed August 28, 2013; Red Herring Web site, *www.redherring.com/events /red-herring-europe/2013-red-herring-europe-top-100-2/*, accessed August 28, 2013.

1. Devery, Quinn, "2012 Breakdown of Global IT Services, Software, and Hardware," posted August 8, 2013, *www .paranet.com/blog/bid/151090/2012-Breakdown-of -Global-IT-Services-Software-and-Hardware-Spending*.

2. "Worldwide Software Market Forecast to Continue on Modest Growth Trajectory through 2017, According to IDC," IDC Press Release, May 23, 2013, *www.idc.com /getdoc.jsp?containerId=prUS24127113*.

3. "About Us, American Modern Insurance Company Web site, *www.amig.com/aboutus.html*, accessed October 11, 2013.

4. Patel, Zarna, "American Modern Ready to Roll with Guidewire Suite," Insurance & Technology, August 13, 2013, *www.insurancetech.com/policy-administration /american-modern-ready-to-roll-with-guide/240159914*.

5. "Brain Academy by Manthan Studios," Intel Web site, *http://software.intel.com/en-us/articles/brain-academy -by-manthan-studios*, accessed October 12, 2013.

6. McCracken, Harry, "Who's Winning, iOS or Android? All the Numbers, All in One Place," April 16, 2013, *http://techland.time.com/2013/04/16/ios-vs-android/*.

7. "7 Productivity Apps to Help You Get It All Done— Fast," *Huffington Post*, July 11, 2013, *www.huffington post.com/2013/07/11/productivity-apps-10-ipho_n _3560671.html*.

8. "The 18 Best Productivity Apps in the World," Business Insider, September 8, 2012, *www.businessinsider.com /best-productivity-apps-2012-9#bump-for-sharing-stuff -between-phones-3*.

9. "8 Apps for Improving Work Productivity," January 13, 2013, *Mac Life*, *www.maclife.com/article/gallery/8 _apps_boosting_work_productivity*.

10. "Cooper Project Management Software," *www.copper project.com/?gclid=CJn00ZCLlroCFRCg4AodnF4AFQ*, accessed October 14, 2013.

11. Roos, Dave, "How to Leverage an API for Conferencing," How Stuff Works, *http://money.howstuffworks .com/business-communications/how-to-leverage-an-api -for-conferencing1.htm*, accessed September 27, 2013.

12. Bellis, Mary, "Putting Microsoft on the Map," *http://inventors.about.com/od/computersoftware/a /Putting-Microsoft-On-The-Map.htm*, accessed September 30, 2013.

13. Anthony, Sebastian, "Windows 9 Will Unify the Smartphone, Tablet, Desktop, and Console, but Is It Too Little, Too Late?" ExtremeTech, October 8, 2013, *www.extremetech.com/computing/168168-windows-9 -will-unify-the-smartphone-tablet-desktop-and -console-but-is-it-too-little-too-late*.

14. Linux Definition, *linfo.org/linuxdef.html*, accessed October 21, 2013.

15. "Linux Profitability (Red Hat, SUSE, and Canonical)," *http://zoumpis.wordpress.com/2013/06/06/linux-profit ability-red-hat-suse-canonical/*, accessed October 14, 2013.

16. "Emphony Technologies Achieves 100 Per Cent Uptime with Ubuntu," *canonical.com/about-canonical /resources/case-studies/emphony-technologies-achieves -100-cent-uptime-ubuntu*, accessed October 19, 2013.

17. "Gartner Says Worldwide Traditional PC, Tablet, Ultra-mobile and Mobile Phone Shipments On Pace to Grow 7.6 percent in 2014", Gartner Newsroom, January 7, 2014, *www.gartner.com/newsroom/id/2645115*.

18. Furrier, John and Vellente, Dave, "Analysis: Is Sun Better Off after Acquiring Sun?" *Forbes*, July 9, 2013, *www.forbes.com/sites/siliconangle/2013/07/09/analysis-is-oracle-better-off-after-sun-acquisition/*.

19. "KASIKORNBANK—Secure on Solaris 10 and Sun Fire V20z Servers," Oracle, *www.oracle.com*, accessed October 15, 2013.

20. "HP Case Study: KWFT Empowers Kenyan Women with HP Superdome 2," *http://h20195.www2.hp.com/v2/GetDocument.aspx?docname=4AA4-7130ENW&cc=us&lc=en*, accessed October 17, 2013.

21. Pepitone, Julianne, "HP Sells Off the Last Scraps of Palm: WebOS," CNN Money, February 25, 2013, *http://money.cnn.com/2013/02/25/technology/hp-sells-webos-lg/*.

22. "Windows Sysinternals," *http://technet.microsoft.com/en-us/sysinternals/bb545021.aspx*, accessed March 27, 2014.

23. "EdgeWave Secures Smartphones and Tablets for Corporations and Schools," EdgeWave Press Release, March 19, 2013, *www.edgewave.com/press_releases/2013/EdgeWave_Secure_Browser.pdf*.

24. "iPrism Case Study: Palm Springs Unified School District," *www.edgewave.com/docs/casestudy/EdgeWave_iPrism_PalmSpringsUnified.pdf*, accessed October 31, 2013.

25. "IBM Case Study: Česká Pojištovna," August 15, 2013, *www-01.ibm.com/software/success/cssdb.nsf/cs/KJON-8RL3LX?OpenDocument&Site=corp&ref=crdb*.

26. "BCBSKS Cuts Mainframe Software Costs with IBM," IBM Case Studies, May 31, 2013, *www-01.ibm.com/software/success/cssdb.nsf/CS/STRD-988E7F*.

27. "CACI Fills Government's Need to Securely Manage Mobile Devices and Apps," *www.caci.com/special/Mobility.shtml*, accessed October 31, 2013.

28. "College Makes Smart Move Using SOA to Launch Self-Service Student Portal," *www.softwareag.com/us/images/200912_SAG_ETS_FSCJ_Con_tcm89-58321.pdf*, accessed October 17, 2013.

29. "Revenue Solutions, Inc. and the State of Rhode Island Division of Taxation Partner to Implement a Commercial-off-the-Shelf (COTS) Integrated Tax System (ITS)," Revenue Solutions, Inc., July 18, 2013, *www.revenuesolutionsinc.com/news/2013/07-18-13.html*.

30. "Collaboration Helps GE Aviation Bring Its Best Inventions to Life," *www.salesforce.com/customers/stories/ge.jsp*, accessed October 26, 2013.

31. Marshall, Matt, "The Top 10 'Arms Merchants' of the Cloud," Cloud, August 23, 2013, *http://venturebeat.com/2013/08/23/the-top-10-arms-merchants-of-the-cloud/#W5ToYJRwdw7iQQjP.99Google*.

32. "AWS Case Study: Coursera," *https://aws.amazon.com/solutions/case-studies/coursera/?sc_ichannel=HA&sc_ipage=homepage&sc_iplace=editorial_r3_left_subheader&sc_icampaigntype=customer_story&sc_icampaign=ha_customer_success_cours era&sc_icountry=US&playIt=now#courseraVid*, accessed October 18, 2013.

33. "Epicor Success Story: Dillon Supply Company," *www.epicor.com/MRCPR/Epicor-Dillon20Supply-A4-CS-ENS.pdf*, accessed November 1, 2013.

34. "Absolute Software Expands LoJack for Mobile Devices Theft Recovery Solution to the Samsung GALAXY Note 3 and Samsung GALAXY Note 10.1 (2014 Edition)," Absolute Software, October 23, 2013, *www.absolute.com/en/about/pressroom/press-releases/2013/10/23/absolute-software-expands-loJack-for-mobile-devices-theft-recovery-solution-to-the-samsung*.

35. Plumer, Brad, "Is the Evidence for Austerity Based on an Excel Spreadsheet Error?" *Washington Post*, April 16, 2013, *www.washingtonpost.com/blogs/wonkblog/wp/2013/04/16/is-the-best-evidence-for-austerity-based-on-an-excel-spreadsheet-error/*.

36. FHI 360, *www.who.int/workforcealliance/members_partners/member_list/fhi/en/*, accessed November 2, 2013.

37. Endler, Michael, "Microsoft Office 365 Steps on Google Enterprise Ambitions," InformationWeek, May 14, 2013, *www.informationweek.com/software/productivity-applications/microsoft-office-365-steps-on-google-ent/240154836*.

38. "Games: Improving Health," Entertainment Software Association, *www.theesa.com/games-improving-what-matters/health.asp*, accessed October 25, 2013.

39. "Clark Construction Group 'Goes Google' to Communicate on Projects from Anywhere," *www.ditoweb.com/clark-construction-group-and-google-apps*, accessed November 2, 2013.

40. Bateman, Kayleigh, "Computer Weekly European User Awards for Enterprise Software: Winners," ComputerWeekly, June 26, 2013, *www.computerweekly.com/news/2240186855/Computer-Weekly-European-User-Awards-for-Enterprise-Software-Winners*.

41. Goldberg, Margaret, "Atos: From Zero Email to Social Collaboration Services," Ovum, April 13, 2013, *http://ovum.com/research/atos-from-zero-email-to-social-collaboration-services/*.

42. "81 percent Find Mobile ERP Software Interface Important," *Business Wire*, July 12, 2011.

43. Lunden, Ingrid, "Forrester: $2.1 Trillion Will Go into IT Spend in 2013; Apps and the U.S. Lead the Charge," TechCrunch, July 15, 2013, *http://techcrunch.com/2013/07/15/forrester-2-1-trillion-will-go-into-it-spend-in-2013-apps-and-the-u-s-lead-the-charge/*.

44. "Playa Lakes Decision Support System," Environmental Protection Agency, *water.epa.gov/type/wetlands/playa.cfm*, accessed November 2, 2013.

45. "Get the Android SDK," *http://developer.android.com/sdk/index.html*, accessed October 28, 2013.

46. Cole, Gail, "Massachusetts Computer Software and Services Tax Repealed," TaxRates.com, September 30, 2013, *www.taxrates.com/blog/2013/09/30/massachusetts-computer-software-and-services-tax-repealed/*.

47. Gibbs, Mark, "Knight Capital Fined a Measly $12M for a Software Bug That Cost $460M," Network World, October 23, 2013, *www.networkworld.com/community/blog/knight-capital-fined-measly-12m-software-bug-cost-460m*.

48. Ecker, Elizabeth, "Knight Capital Group Completes Merger with Getco," Reverse Mortgage, July 1, 2013, *http://reversemortgagedaily.com/2013/07/01/knight-capital-group-completes-merger-with-getco/*.

49. "Software Licenses Types," Tulane University, Technology Services, *http://tulane.edu/tsweb/software/software-license-types.cfm*, accessed November 3, 2013.

50. Olshan, Jeremy, "88\char"0025 of Spreadsheets Have Errors," MarketWatch, April 20, 2013, *www.marketwatch.com/story/88-of-spreadsheets-have-errors-2013-04-17*.

5 Database Systems and Applications

Principles	Learning Objectives
• Data management and modeling are key aspects of organizing data and information.	• Define general data management concepts and terms, highlighting the advantages of the database approach to data management. • Describe logical and physical database design considerations and the relational database model.
• A well-designed and well-managed database is an extremely valuable tool in supporting decision making.	• Identify the common functions performed by all database management systems, and identify popular database management systems.
• The number and types of database applications will continue to evolve and yield real business benefits.	• Identify and briefly discuss business intelligence, data mining, and other database applications.

Information Systems in the Global Economy
VELUX, DENMARK

Implementing the Next Generation of Business Intelligence

Adam Mork

The VELUX Group is one of the largest international building materials manufacturers in the world. Headquartered in Denmark, the VELUX group employs about 10,000 people who work in manufacturing plants in 11 countries and sales offices in just under 40 countries spread across Europe, the Americas, Asia, and Australia. It is so successful that in many countries, in fact, a flat roof window is simply called a velux.

Not surprising, then, is the VELUX Group's early adoption of information systems technology to support business intelligence. Business intelligence (BI) involves gathering and analyzing data in a timely manner to support the development of effective business strategies, tactics, and operations. In 2000, the VELUX Group turned to the IT department to initiate the introduction of a BI system. The IT group successfully generated financial reports, but few people used the system.

The VELUX Group's experience was not atypical. At that time, BI systems development was often left to IT departments that did not supply the type of reports that managers, the users of the system, needed. By 2005, VELUX top executives became involved in shaping the BI system, deciding what data and analyses the BI system should provide. The number of users increased to 800 company-wide. Yet, many lower-level managers were still not relying on the BI reports.

As a result, in 2011, the VELUX Group conducted a thorough investigation to find out why more managers were not using the reports. It created a team to explore the needs of its end users prior to developing and adopting new SAP BI technology. It discovered that many potential users did not understand the existing data and those that did often had little use for standard reports, but rather needed customized analyses. As a result, some business units and subsidiaries had invested in their own systems, incurring additional costs. The company realized that it would have to develop a user-friendly interface to enable these users to use one centralized, cheaper, faster system. The system had to access a rapidly growing bank of internal and external data in a timely manner.

In 2013, the VELUX Group launched its new SAP BI system. The pool of BI users is now expanding from 800 users to 4,000. The SAP team is also working with users to make sure they have the analytical skills that they need to make use of the new tools at their disposal. Rather than simply generating budgets and financial targets, the new systems use simulation models to allow managers to plan the number of units and prices to be manufactured at a granular level.

The VELUX Group's endeavors represent the next generation of BI development, in which companies are learning how to tailor their systems to the needs of a wider body of users operating at lower levels of the decision-making process. The hope is to extend the advantages of BI while reducing the costs.

As you read this chapter, consider the following:

- Why is it important for all business units to be involved in the development and adoption of data management, data modeling, and business information systems?
- How can businesses use the information in their databases to be more effective?

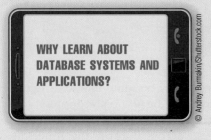

WHY LEARN ABOUT DATABASE SYSTEMS AND APPLICATIONS?

A huge amount of data is captured for processing by computers every day. Where does all this data go, and how is it used? How can it help you on the job? In this chapter, you will learn about database systems and applications that can help you make the most effective use of information. If you become a marketing manager, you can access a vast store of data on existing and potential customers from surveys, their Web habits, and their past purchases. This information can help you sell products and services. If you become a corporate lawyer, you will have access to past cases and legal opinions from sophisticated legal databases. This information can help you win cases and protect your organization legally. If you become a human resource (HR) manager, you will be able to use databases and applications to analyze the impact of raises, employee insurance benefits, and retirement contributions on long-term costs to your company. Regardless of your field of study in school, using database systems and applications will likely be a critical part of your job. As you read this chapter, you will see how you can use databases and applications to extract and analyze valuable information to help you succeed. This chapter starts by introducing basic concepts of database management systems.

A database is a well-designed, organized, and carefully managed collection of data. Like other components of an information system, a database should help an organization achieve its goals. A database can contribute to organizational success by providing managers and decision makers with timely, accurate, and relevant information built on data. Databases also help companies analyze information to reduce costs, increase profits, add new customers, track past business activities, and open new market opportunities.

A **database management system (DBMS)** consists of a group of programs that manipulate the database and provide an interface between the database and its users and other application programs. Usually purchased from a database company, a DBMS provides a single point of management and control over data resources, which can be critical to maintaining the integrity and security of the data. Oracle's DBMS, for example, now includes a firewall to help secure the databases of its customers.[1] A database, a DBMS, and the application programs that use the data make up a database environment.

Databases and database management systems are becoming even more important to organizations as they deal with rapidly increasing amounts of information. Indeed, although many organizations today have dozens of databases, without good data management, it is nearly impossible for anyone to find the right and related information for accurate and business-critical decision making.[2]

database management system (DBMS): A group of programs that manipulate the database and provide an interface between the database and the user of the database and other application programs.

DATA MANAGEMENT

Without data and the ability to process it, an organization cannot successfully complete most business activities. It cannot pay employees, send out bills, order new inventory, or produce information to assist managers in decision making. As you recall, data consists of raw facts, such as employee numbers and sales figures. For data to be transformed into useful information, it must first be organized in a meaningful way.

Hierarchy of Data

Data is generally organized in a hierarchy that begins with the smallest piece of data used by computers (a bit) and progresses through the hierarchy to a database. A bit (a binary digit) represents a circuit that is either on or off. Bits can be organized into units called *bytes*. A byte is typically eight bits. Each byte represents a **character**, which is the basic building block of most information. A character can be an uppercase letter (A, B, C, ..., Z), a lowercase letter (a, b, c, ..., z), a numeric digit (0, 1, 2, ..., 9), or a special symbol (., !, +, −, /, etc.).

character: A basic building block of most information, consisting of uppercase letters, lowercase letters, numeric digits, or special symbols.

field: Typically a name, number, or combination of characters that describes an aspect of a business object or activity.

record: A collection of data fields all related to one object, activity, or individual.

file: A collection of related records.

hierarchy of data: Bits, characters, fields, records, files, and databases.

Characters are put together to form a field. A **field** is typically a name, number, or combination of characters that describes an aspect of a business object (such as an employee, a location, or a truck) or activity (such as a sale). In addition to being entered into a database, fields can be computed from other fields. *Computed fields* include the total, average, maximum, and minimum value. A collection of data fields all related to one object, activity, or individual is called a **record**. By combining descriptions of the characteristics of an object, activity, or individual, a record can provide a complete description of it. For instance, an employee record is a collection of fields about one employee. One field includes the employee's name, another field contains the address, and still others the phone number, pay rate, earnings made to date, and so forth. A collection of related records is a **file**—for example, an employee file is a collection of all company employee records. Likewise, an inventory file is a collection of all inventory records for a particular company or organization.

At the highest level of the data hierarchy is a *database*, a collection of integrated and related files. Together, bits, characters, fields, records, files, and databases form the **hierarchy of data**. See Figure 5.1. Characters are combined to make a field, fields are combined to make a record, records are combined to make a file, and files are combined to make a database. A database houses not only all these levels of data but also the relationships among them.

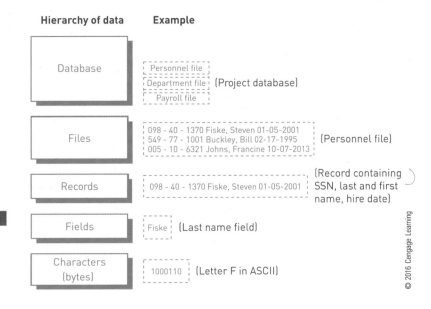

FIGURE 5.1

Hierarchy of data

Together, bits, characters, fields, records, files, and databases form the hierarchy of data.

Data Entities, Attributes, and Keys

entity: A person, place, or thing for which data is collected, stored, and maintained.

attribute: A characteristic of an entity.

data item: The specific value of an attribute.

Entities, attributes, and keys are important database concepts. An **entity** is a person, place, or thing (object) for which data is collected, stored, and maintained. Examples of entities include employees, products, and plants. Most organizations organize and store data as entities.

An **attribute** is a characteristic of an entity. For example, employee number, last name, first name, hire date, and department number are attributes for an employee. See Figure 5.2. The inventory number, description, number of units on hand, and location of the inventory item in the warehouse are attributes for items in inventory. Customer number, name, address, phone number, credit rating, and contact person are attributes for customers. Attributes are usually selected to reflect the relevant characteristics of entities such as employees or customers. The specific value of an attribute, called a **data item**, can be found in the fields of the record describing an entity.

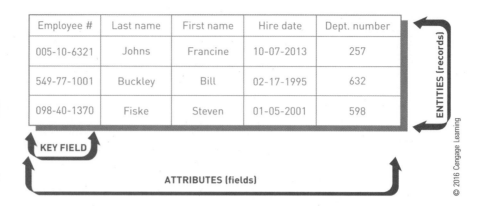

FIGURE 5.2

Keys and attributes

The key field is the employee number. The attributes include last name, first name, hire date, and department number.

Many organizations create databases of attributes and enter data items to store data needed to run their day-to-day operations, as in the following examples.

- The German government implemented a Visa Alert database to be used by immigration officials worldwide to review Visa applications. Immigration authorities, police, and public prosecutor offices upload information on visa overstays, visa fraud, unlawful employment, and criminal offenses to the database. Local police and immigration offices can request access to the database to verify information for local immigration procedures, such as visa extensions and deportation proceedings.[3]
- Wireless network providers are implementing a database using unique smartphone identifying numbers to prevent stolen smartphones from being activated or provided service on their networks.[4]
- dunnhumby, a U.K.-based customer analytics company, is building databases that combine consumers' TV viewing data with their supermarket purchasing data. The firm can then work with brand marketers responsible for media buying to make their TV advertising purchase decisions based on actual consumer purchase data.[5]
- Zoomlion is a leading Chinese manufacturer of construction equipment and industrial machinery with operations in 80 countries across six continents. A Zoomlion database enables the firm to rank the performance of its after-sales subcontractors and identify where it needs to improve service to avoid losing customers.[6]

As discussed earlier, a collection of fields about a specific object is a record. A **primary key** is a field or set of fields that uniquely identifies the record. No other record can have the same primary key. For an employee record, such as the one shown in Figure 5.2, the employee number is an example of a primary key. The primary key is used to distinguish records so that they can be accessed, organized, and manipulated. Primary keys ensure that each record in a file is unique. For example, eBay assigns an "Item number" as its primary key for items to make sure that bids are associated with the correct item. See Figure 5.3.

Locating a particular record that meets a specific set of criteria might be easier and faster using a combination of secondary keys. For example, a customer might call a mail-order company to place an order for clothes. The order clerk can easily access the customer's mailing and billing information by entering the primary key—usually a customer number—but if the customer does not know the correct primary key, a secondary key such as last name can be used. In this case, the order clerk enters the last name, such as Adams. If several customers have a last name of Adams, the clerk can check other fields, such as address and first name, to find the correct customer record. After locating the correct record, the order can be completed and the clothing items shipped to the customer.

primary key: A field or set of fields that uniquely identifies the record.

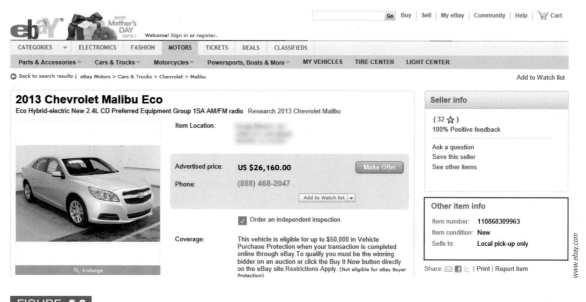

FIGURE 5.3

Primary key

eBay assigns an Item number as a primary key to keep track of each item in its database.

The Database Approach

At one time, information systems referenced specific files containing relevant data. For example, a payroll system would use a payroll file. Each distinct operational system used data files dedicated to that system. This approach to data management is called the traditional approach to data management.

Today, most organizations use the database approach to data management, where multiple information systems share a pool of related data. A database offers the ability to share data and information resources. Federal databases, for example, often include the results of DNA tests as an attribute for convicted criminals. The information can be shared with law enforcement officials around the country. Often, distinct yet related databases are linked to provide enterprise-wide databases. For example, many Walgreens stores include in-store medical clinics for customers. Walgreens uses an electronic health records database that stores the information of all patients across all stores. The database provides information about customers' interactions with the clinics and pharmacies.

To use the database approach to data management, additional software—a database management system (DBMS)—is required. As previously discussed, a DBMS consists of a group of programs that can be used as an interface between a database and the user of the database. Typically, this software acts as a buffer between the application programs and the database itself. Figure 5.4 illustrates the database approach.

traditional approach to data management: An approach to data management whereby each distinct operational system uses data files dedicated to that system.

database approach to data management: An approach to data management where multiple information systems share a pool of related data.

DATA MODELING AND DATABASE CHARACTERISTICS

Because today's businesses must keep track of and analyze so much data, they must keep the data well organized so that it can be used effectively. A database should be designed to store all data relevant to the business and provide quick access and easy modification. Moreover, it must reflect the business processes of the organization. When building a database, an organization must carefully consider these questions:

- **Content.** What data should be collected and at what cost?
- **Access.** What data should be provided to which users and when?

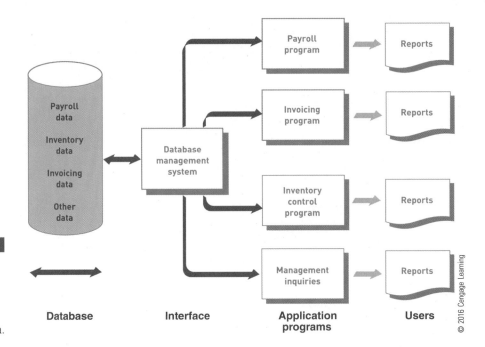

| Database | Interface | Application programs | Users |

Database approach to data management

In a database approach to data management, multiple information systems share a pool of related data.

- **Logical structure.** How should data be arranged so that it makes sense to a given user?
- **Physical organization.** Where should data be physically located?

Data Modeling

When organizing a database, key considerations include determining what data to collect, what will be the source of the data, who will have access to it, how one might want to use it, and how to monitor database performance. For example, Harrison College serves a student population of 5,000, with 12 campuses throughout Indiana and Ohio, and online at Harrison.edu. The college uses networking and storage devices from HP, Dell, F5 Networks, and Cisco. The college implemented a database-monitoring tool to gain insight into the status of its database applications and the hardware on which those applications run. During a datacenter power outage, the monitoring tool helped the IT support staff to determine quickly which servers had come back online and take prompt action to restart them without a major loss of services.[7]

One of the tools database designers use to show the logical relationships among data is a data model. A data model is a diagram of entities and their relationships. Data modeling usually involves understanding a specific business problem and analyzing the data and information needed to deliver a solution. When done at the level of the entire organization, this procedure is called enterprise data modeling. Enterprise data modeling is an approach that starts by investigating the general data and information needs of the organization at the strategic level and then examines more specific data and information needs for the functional areas and departments within the organization. Various models have been developed to help managers and database designers analyze data and information needs. An entity-relationship diagram is an example of such a data model.

Entity-relationship (ER) diagrams use basic graphical symbols to show the organization of and relationships between data. In other words, ER diagrams show data items in tables (entities) and the ways they are related.

ER diagrams help ensure that the relationships among the data entities in a database are correctly structured so that any application programs developed are consistent with business operations and user needs. In addition, ER

data model: A diagram of data entities and their relationships.

enterprise data modeling: Data modeling done at the level of the entire enterprise.

entity-relationship (ER) diagrams: Data models that use basic graphical symbols to show the organization and relationships between data.

diagrams can serve as reference documents after a database is in use. If changes are made to the database, ER diagrams help design them. Figure 5.5 shows an ER diagram for an order database. In this database design, one salesperson serves many customers. This is an example of a one-to-many relationship, as indicated by the one-to-many symbol (the "crow's-foot") shown in Figure 5.5. The ER diagram also shows that each customer can place one-to-many orders, that each order includes one-to-many line items, and that many line items can specify the same product (a many-to-one relationship). This database can also have one-to-one relationships. For example, one order generates one invoice.

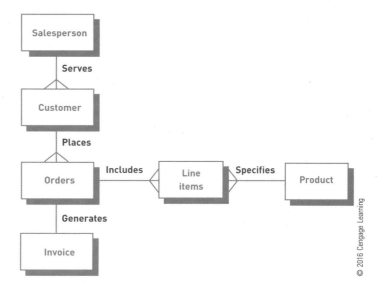

FIGURE 5.5

Entity-relationship (ER) diagram for a customer order database

Development of ER diagrams helps ensure that the logical structure of application programs is consistent with the data relationships in the database.

Relational Database Model

The relational database model has been an outstanding success and is dominant in the commercial world today, although many organizations are beginning to use new nonrelational models to meet some of their business needs. The **relational model** is a simple but highly useful way to organize data into collections of two-dimensional tables called relations. Each row in the table represents an entity, and each column represents an attribute of that entity. See Figure 5.6.

relational model: A simple but highly useful way to organize data into collections of two-dimensional tables called relations.

Databases based on the relational model include Oracle, IBM DB2, Microsoft SQL Server, Microsoft Access, MySQL, and Sybase. Oracle holds 48 percent of the 2012 worldwide relational database management systems market share according to market research firm Gartner. This is a larger market share than its four closest competitors combined (IBM, Microsoft, SAP, and Teradata).[8]

Each attribute can be constrained to a range of allowable values called its **domain**. The domain for a particular attribute indicates what values can be placed in each column of the relational table. For instance, the domain for an attribute such as gender could be limited to the two characters M (male) or F (female). If someone tried to enter a "1" in the gender field, the data would not be accepted. The domain for pay rate would not include negative numbers. In this way, defining a domain can increase data accuracy.

domain: The range of allowable values for a data attribute.

Manipulating Data

After entering data into a relational database, users can make inquiries and analyze the data. Basic data manipulations include selecting, projecting, and joining. **Selecting** involves eliminating rows according to certain criteria. Suppose an HR manager wants to use an employee table that contains the project

selecting: Manipulating data to eliminate rows according to certain criteria.

Data Table 1: Project Table

Project	Description	Dept. number
155	Payroll	257
498	Widgets	632
226	Sales manual	598

Data Table 2: Department Table

Dept.	Dept. name	Manager SSN
257	Accounting	005-10-6321
632	Manufacturing	549-77-1001
598	Marketing	098-40-1370

Data Table 3: Manager Table

SSN	Last name	First name	Hire date	Dept. number
005-10-6321	Johns	Francine	10-07-2013	257
549-77-1001	Buckley	Bill	02-17-1995	632
098-40-1370	Fiske	Steven	01-05-2001	598

© 2016 Cengage Learning

FIGURE 5.6

Relational database model

In the relational model, data is placed in two-dimensional tables, or relations. As long as they share at least one common element, these relations can be linked to provide output useful information.

projecting: Manipulating data to eliminate columns in a table.

joining: Manipulating data to combine two or more tables.

linking: The ability to combine two or more tables through common data attributes to form a new table with only the unique data attributes.

number, description, and department number for all projects a company is performing. The manager might want to find the department number for Project 226, a sales manual project. Using selection, the manager can eliminate all rows but the one for Project 226 and see that the department number for the department completing the sales manual project is 598.

Projecting involves eliminating columns in a table. For example, a department table might contain the department number, department name, and Social Security number (SSN) of the manager in charge of the project. A sales manager might want to create a new table with only the department number and the Social Security number of the manager in charge of the sales manual project. The sales manager can use projection to eliminate the department name column and create a new table containing only the department number and SSN.

Joining involves combining two or more tables. For example, you can combine the project table and the department table to create a new table with the project number, project description, department number, department name, and Social Security number for the manager in charge of the project.

As long as the tables share at least one common data attribute, the tables in a relational database can be linked to provide useful information and reports. **Linking**, the ability to combine two or more tables through common data attributes to form a new table with only the unique data attributes, is one of the keys to the flexibility and power of relational databases. Suppose the president of a company wants to find out the name of the manager of the sales manual project and the length of time the manager has been with the company. Assume that the company has the manager, department, and project tables shown in Figure 5.6. A simplified ER diagram showing the relationship between these tables is shown in Figure 5.7.

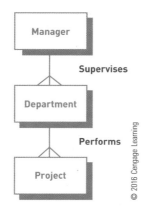

FIGURE **5.7**

Simplified ER diagram

This diagram shows the relationship among the Manager, Department, and Project tables.

Note the crow's-foot by the Project table. This symbol indicates that a department can have many projects. The president would make the inquiry to the database, perhaps via a personal computer. The DBMS would start with the project description and search the Project table to find out the project's department number. It would then use the department number to search the Department table for the manager's Social Security number. The department number is also in the Department table and is the common element that links the Project table to the Department table. The DBMS uses the manager's Social Security number to search the Manager table for the manager's hire date. The manager's Social Security number is the common element between the Department table and the Manager table. The final result is that the manager's name and hire date are presented to the president as a response to the inquiry. See Figure 5.8.

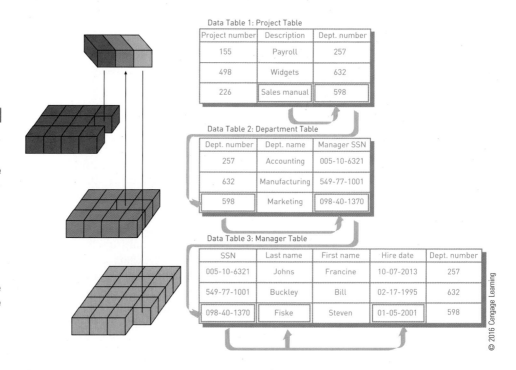

FIGURE **5.8**

Linking data tables to answer an inquiry

To find the name and hire date of the manager working on the sales manual project, the president needs three tables: Project, Department, and Manager. The project description (Sales manual) leads to the department number (598) in the Project table, which leads to the manager's SSN (098-40-1370) in the Department table, which leads to the manager's name (Fiske) and hire date (01-05-2001) in the Manager table.

Data Table 1: Project Table

Project number	Description	Dept. number
155	Payroll	257
498	Widgets	632
226	Sales manual	598

Data Table 2: Department Table

Dept. number	Dept. name	Manager SSN
257	Accounting	005-10-6321
632	Manufacturing	549-77-1001
598	Marketing	098-40-1370

Data Table 3: Manager Table

SSN	Last name	First name	Hire date	Dept. number
005-10-6321	Johns	Francine	10-07-2013	257
549-77-1001	Buckley	Bill	02-17-1995	632
098-40-1370	Fiske	Steven	01-05-2001	598

One of the primary advantages of a relational database is that it allows tables to be linked, as shown in Figure 5.8. This linkage reduces data redundancy and allows data to be organized more logically. The ability to link to the manager's SSN stored once in the Manager table eliminates the need to store it multiple times in the Project table.

The relational database model is currently the most widely used. It is easier to control, more flexible, and more intuitive than other approaches because it organizes data in tables. As shown in Figure 5.9, a relational database management system, such as Microsoft Access, can be used to store data in rows and columns. In this figure, hyperlinks at the top of the Access database can be used to create, edit, and manipulate the database. The ability to link relational tables also allows users to relate data in new ways without having to redefine complex relationships. Because of the advantages of the relational model, many companies use it for large corporate databases, such as those for marketing and accounting.

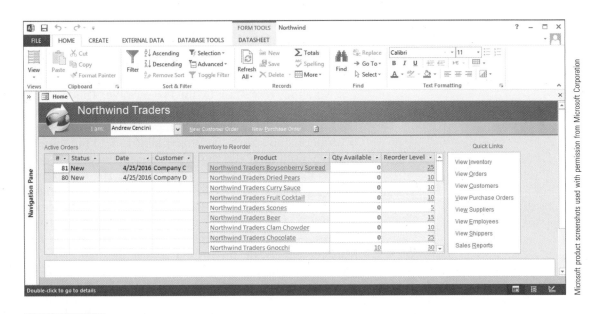

FIGURE 5.9

Building and modifying a relational database

Relational databases provide many tools, tips, and shortcuts to simplify the process of creating and modifying a database.

Data Cleansing

Data cleansing (data cleaning or data scrubbing): The process of detecting and then correcting or deleting incomplete, incorrect, inaccurate, irrelevant records that reside in a database.

Data used in decision making must be accurate, complete, economical, flexible, reliable, relevant, simple, timely, verifiable, accessible, and secure. **Data cleansing (data cleaning or data scrubbing)** is the process of detecting and then correcting or deleting incomplete, incorrect, inaccurate, irrelevant records that reside in a database. The goal is to improve the quality of the data used in decision making. The "bad data" may have been caused by user data-entry errors or by data corruption during data transmission or storage. Data cleansing is different from data validation, which involves the identification of "bad data" and its rejection at the time of data entry.

One data cleansing solution is to identify and correct the data by cross-checking it against a validated data set. For example, street number, street name, city, state, and zip code entries in an organization's database may be cross-checked against the United States Postal Zip Code database. Data cleansing may also involve standardization of data, such as the conversion of various possible abbreviations (St., St, st., st) to one standard name (Street).

Data enhancement augments the data in a database by adding related information such as using the zip code information for a given record to append the county code or census tract code.

The cost of performing data cleansing can be quite high. It is prohibitively expensive to eliminate all "bad data" to achieve 100 percent database accuracy, as shown in Figure 5.10.

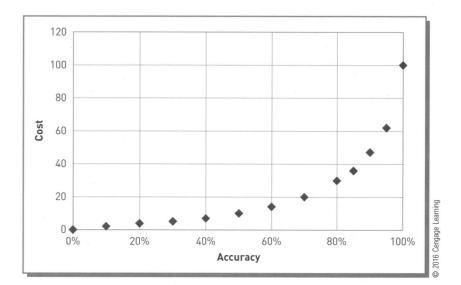

FIGURE 5.10

Tradeoff of cost versus accuracy

The cost of performing data cleansing to achieve 100 percent database accuracy can be prohibitively expensive.

DATABASE MANAGEMENT SYSTEMS

Creating and implementing the right database system ensures that the database will support both business activities and goals. But how do we actually create, implement, use, and update a database? The answer is found in the database management system. As discussed earlier, a DBMS is a group of programs used as an interface between a database and application programs or a database and the user. There is a wide range of capabilities and types of database systems.

Overview of Database Types

Database management systems can range from small inexpensive software packages to sophisticated systems costing hundreds of thousands of dollars. The following sections discuss a few popular alternatives. See Figure 5.11 for one example.

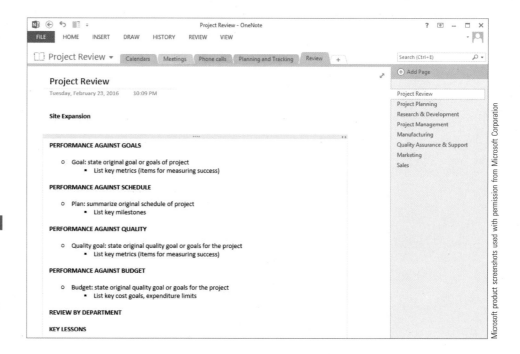

FIGURE 5.11

Microsoft OneNote

Microsoft OneNote lets you gather any type of information and then retrieve, copy, and paste the information into other applications, such as word-processing and spreadsheet programs.

Single-User DBMS

A database installed on a personal computer is typically meant for a single user. This means that when user A is accessing the database, user B must wait until user A is finished. Microsoft Access and InfoPath, Lotus Approach, Personal Oracle, and DB Everyplace are designed to support single-user implementations.

Multiple-User DBMS

Small, midsize, and large businesses need multiuser DBMSs to share information throughout the organization over a network. These more powerful, expensive systems allow dozens or hundreds of people to access the same database system at the same time. Popular vendors for multiuser database systems include Oracle, Microsoft, Sybase, and IBM. Many single-user databases, such as Microsoft Access, can be implemented for multiuser support over a network, though they often are limited in the number of users they can support.

Flat Files

A flat file is a simple database program whose records have no relationship to one another. Flat file databases are often used to store and manipulate a single table or file. Many spreadsheet and word-processing programs have flat file capabilities. These software packages can sort records and make simple calculations and comparisons. Microsoft OneNote is designed to let people put ideas, thoughts, and notes into a flat file. Similar to OneNote, Evernote is a free online database service that can store notes and other pieces of information, including photos, voice memos, or handwritten notes. Evernote can be used on computers, smartphones, tablet computers, and other mobile devices.

Intuit, Inc., provides financial management software for small- and mid-sized organizations. It has over 4 million active users, with the popular QuickBooks one of its leading products. Intuit is continually meeting with its customers to better understand their needs. These discussions led to the discovery of a need to provide increased functionality, improved performance, and better reporting capabilities. The solution that the Intuit engineering team came up with was to convert from the existing flat file data management system to a relational database management system. "We realized that by moving to a true relational database we could enhance the capabilities and the value of QuickBooks for our customers" says Siddharth Ram, Intuit group architect.[9]

SQL Databases

SQL is a special-purpose programming language for accessing and manipulating data stored in a relational database. It was originally defined by Donald D. Chamberlin and Raymond Boyce of the IBM Research Center and described in their paper "SEQUEL: A Structured English Query Language," *Proceedings of the ACM SIGFIDET Conference, May 1974.* Their work was based on the relational database model described by Edgar F. Codd in his groundbreaking paper from 1970, "A Relational Model of Data for Large Shared Data Banks."

SQL databases conform to ACID properties (Atomicity, Consistency, Isolation, Durability), defined by Jim Gray soon after Codd's work. These properties guarantee database transactions are processed reliably and ensure the integrity of data in the database. Basically, these principles mean that data is broken down to atomic values (employee_ID, last_name, first_name, address_line_1, address_line_2, city, and so on) while remaining consistent across the database, isolated from other transactions until the current transaction is finished, and durable in the sense that the data should never be lost.[10]

SQL databases rely upon concurrency control by locking database records to ensure that other transactions do not modify the database until the first transaction succeeds or fails. As a result, 100 percent ACID-compliant SQL databases can suffer from slow performance.

In 1986, the American National Standards Institute (ANSI) adopted SQL as the standard query language for relational databases. Since ANSI's acceptance of SQL, interest in making SQL an integral part of relational databases on both mainframe and personal computers has increased. SQL has many built-in functions, such as average (AVG), the largest value (MAX), and the smallest value (MIN). Table 5.1 contains examples of SQL commands.

TABLE 5.1 Examples of SQL commands

SQL Command	Description
SELECT ClientName, Debt FROM Client WHERE Debt > 1000	This query displays all clients (ClientName) and the amount they owe the company (Debt) from a database table called Client for clients who owe the company more than $1,000 (WHERE Debt > 1000).
SELECT ClientName, ClientNum, OrderNum FROM Client, Order WHERE Client.ClientNum=Order.ClientNum	This command is an example of a join command that combines data from two tables: the Client table and the Order table (FROM Client, Order). The command creates a new table with the client name, client number, and order number (SELECT ClientName, ClientNum, OrderNum). Both tables include the client number, which allows them to be joined. This ability is indicated in the WHERE clause, which states that the client number in the Client table is the same as (equal to) the client number in the Order table (WHERE Client.ClientNum=Order.ClientNum).
GRANT INSERT ON Client to Guthrie	This command is an example of a security command. It allows Bob Guthrie to insert new values or rows into the Client table.

SQL lets programmers learn one powerful query language and use it on systems ranging from PCs to the largest mainframe computers. See Figure 5.12. Programmers and database users also find SQL valuable because SQL statements can be embedded into many programming languages, such as the widely used C++ and Java. Because SQL uses standardized and simplified procedures for retrieving, storing, and manipulating data, the popular database query language can be easy to understand and use.

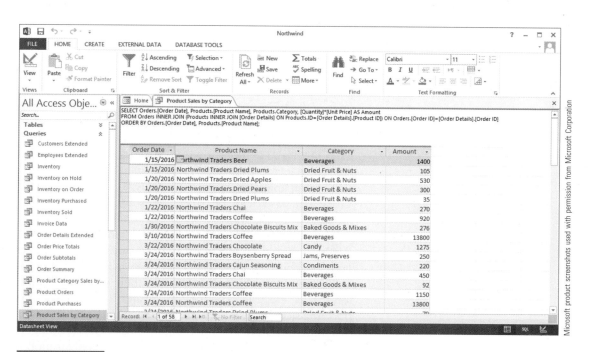

FIGURE 5.12

Structured Query Language

Structured Query Language (SQL) has become an integral part of most relational databases, as shown by this example from Microsoft Access 2013.

NoSQL Databases

A NoSQL database is designed to store and retrieve data in a manner that does not rigidly enforce the atomic conditions associated with the relational database model. The goal of a NoSQL database is to provide faster performance and greater scalability. NoSQL databases lack strong data consistency—the ability to ensure that an update to data in one part of the database is *immediately* propagated to all other parts of the database. NoSQL databases are finding significant and growing industry use in dealing with extremely large database and real-time Web applications.

A NoSQL database stores data as highly optimized key-value stores wherein the data is stored in a simple two-column table, with one column reserved for the primary key and the other for the value. A NoSQL database is highly scalable, meaning that a large database may be distributed across hundreds, thousands, or even tens of thousands of servers running the same NoSQL database management system. This distribution of the database improves system uptime as the database can still process almost all transactions even if a server or two someplace is down. (Scaling a traditional SQL database is much more complicated.) Facebook employs thousands of servers running the NoSQL database Cassandra to handle millions of queries per second and ensure around-the-clock processing.

Amazon uses the DynamoDB NoSQL database to track millions of daily sales transactions. The database employs an *eventually consistent* approach to processing transactions to gain speed and increase system uptime.[11]

Hadoop is an open-source software framework including several software modules that provide a means for storing and processing extremely large data sets. For years, Yahoo! used Hadoop to better personalize the ads and articles that its visitors see. Now Hadoop is used by many popular Web sites and services (such as eBay, Etsy, Twitter, and Yelp).[12] Hadoop divides the data into subsets and distributes the subsets onto different servers for processing. The Hadoop MapReduce software module is a programming model designed for processing large volumes of data in parallel by dividing the work into a set of independent tasks. This approach creates a very robust computing environment that allows the application to keep running even if individual servers fail.

Visual, Audio, and Other Database Systems

In addition to raw data, organizations are finding a need to store large amounts of visual and audio signals in an organized fashion. Credit card companies, for example, enter pictures of charge slips into an image database using a scanner. The images can be stored in the database and later sorted by customer name, printed, and sent to customers along with their monthly statements. Image databases are also used by physicians to store X-rays and transmit them to clinics away from the main hospital. Financial services, insurance companies, and government branches are using image databases to store vital records and replace paper documents. Drug companies often need to analyze many visual images from laboratories. Visual databases can be stored in some object-relational databases or special-purpose database systems. Many relational databases can also store images.

In addition to visual, audio, and virtual databases, other special-purpose database systems meet particular business needs. For example, *spatial databases* provide location-based services, where business and public sector Web sites embed location and maps into their Web applications and operational systems. Gas, electric, pipeline, and water agencies use spatial databases to support mission-critical applications such as mobile asset maintenance, outage management, network maintenance, and crisis management. See Figure 5.13. Retailers use spatial analytics and map visualization techniques to decide where to locate new stores and where to deploy sales personnel based on customer demographic analysis. Highway agencies, railways, public transport, and delivery services use spatial technology to track and maintain assets, develop delivery and transportation schedules, and optimize routes to reduce transit time and costs. Government agencies such as police and fire departments, land management, homeland security, public works, and urban planning use spatial databases to improve planning and operations.[13]

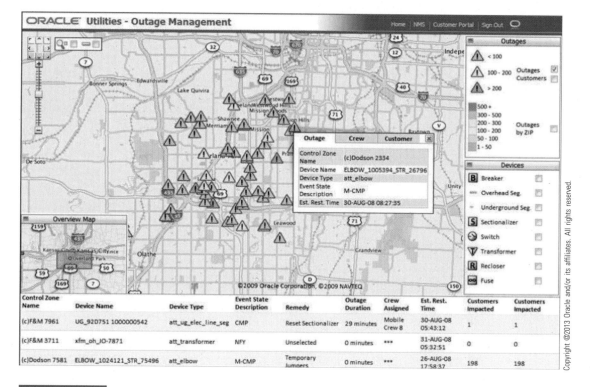

FIGURE 5.13

Spatial data technology

Oracle Spatial Network Data Model is used by gas, electric, pipeline, and water agencies for live, mission-critical network applications such as mobile asset maintenance, outage management, network maintenance, and crisis management.

Database Activities

You use a database to provide a user view of the database, to add and modify data, to store and retrieve data, and to manipulate the data and generate reports. Each of these activities is discussed in greater detail in the following sections.

Providing a User View

schema: A description of the entire database.

Because the DBMS is responsible for access to a database, one of the first steps in installing and using a large database involves "telling" the DBMS the logical and physical structure of the data and the relationships among the data for each user. This description is called a schema (as in a schematic diagram). Large database systems, such as Oracle, typically use schemas to define the tables and other database features associated with a person or user. A schema can be part of the database or a separate schema file. The DBMS can reference a schema to find where to access the requested data in relation to another piece of data.

Creating and Modifying the Database

data definition language (DDL): A collection of instructions and commands used to define and describe data and relationships in a specific database.

Schemas are entered into the DBMS (usually by database personnel) via a data definition language. A data definition language (DDL) is a collection of instructions and commands used to define and describe data and relationships in a specific database. A DDL allows the database's creator to describe the data and relationships that are to be contained in the schema. In general, a DDL describes logical access paths and logical records in the database. Figure 5.14 shows a simplified example of a DDL used to develop a general schema. The use of the letter *X* in Figure 5.14 reveals where specific information concerning the database should be entered. File description, area description, record description, and set description are terms the DDL defines and uses in this example. Other terms and commands can be used, depending on the DBMS employed.

```
SCHEMA DESCRIPTION
SCHEMA NAME IS XXXX
AUTHOR        XXXX
DATE          XXXX
FILE DESCRIPTION
      FILE NAME IS XXXX
        ASSIGN XXXX
      FILE NAME IS XXXX
        ASSIGN XXXX
AREA DESCRIPTION
      AREA NAME IS XXXX
RECORD DESCRIPTION
      RECORD NAME IS XXXX
      RECORD ID IS XXXX
      LOCATION MODE IS XXXX
      WITHIN XXXX AREA FROM XXXX THRU XXXX
SET DESCRIPTION
      SET NAME IS XXXX
      ORDER IS XXXX
      MODE IS XXXX
      MEMBER IS XXXX
```

FIGURE 5.14

Data definition language

You use a data definition language to define a schema.

data dictionary: A detailed description of all the data used in the database.

Another important step in creating a database is to establish a **data dictionary**, a detailed description of all data used in the database. The data dictionary contains the following information:

- Name of the data item
- Aliases or other names that may be used to describe the item
- Range of values that can be used
- Type of data (such as alphanumeric or numeric)
- Amount of storage needed for the item
- Notation of the person responsible for updating it and the various users who can access it
- List of reports that use the data item

A data dictionary can also include a description of data flows, the way records are organized, and the data-processing requirements. Figure 5.15 shows a typical data dictionary entry.

For example, the information in a data dictionary for the part number of an inventory item can include the following information:

- Name of the person who made the data dictionary entry (D. Bordwell)
- Date the entry was made (August 4, 2016)
- Name of the person who approved the entry (J. Edwards)
- Approval date (October 13, 2016)
- Version number (3.1)

NORTHWESTERN MANUFACTURING

PREPARED BY: D. BORDWELL
DATE: 04 AUGUST 2016
APPROVED BY: J. EDWARDS
DATE: 13 OCTOBER 2016
VERSION: 3.1
PAGE: 1 OF 1

DATA ELEMENT NAME: PARTNO
DESCRIPTION: INVENTORY PART NUMBER
OTHER NAMES: PTNO
VALUE RANGE: 100 TO 5000
DATA TYPE: NUMERIC
POSITIONS: 4 POSITIONS OR COLUMNS

© 2016 Cengage Learning

FIGURE 5.15

Data dictionary entry

A data dictionary provides a detailed description of all data used in the database.

- Number of pages used for the entry (1)
- Part name (PARTNO)
- Other part names that might be used (PTNO)
- Range of values (part numbers can range from 100 to 5000)
- Type of data (numeric)
- Storage required (four positions are required for the part number)

A data dictionary is valuable in maintaining an efficient database that stores reliable information with no redundancy, and it makes it easy to modify the database when necessary. Data dictionaries also help computer and system programmers who require a detailed description of data elements stored in a database to create the code to access the data.

Adherence to the standards defined in the data dictionary also makes it easy to share data among various organizations. For example, the U.S. Department of Energy (DOE) developed a data dictionary of terms to provide a standardized approach for the evaluation of energy data. The Building Energy Data Exchange Specification (BEDES) provides a common language of key data elements, including data formats, valid ranges, and definitions that will improve communications between contractors, software vendors, finance companies, utilities, and Public Utility Commissions. Adherence to these data standards will allow information to be easily shared and aggregated without the need for extensive data scrubbing and translation. All stakeholders can use this standard set of data to answer key questions related to the energy savings and financial performance of commercial and residential buildings.[14]

Storing and Retrieving Data

One function of a DBMS is to be an interface between an application program and the database. When an application program needs data, it requests the data through the DBMS. Suppose that to calculate the total price of a new car, a pricing program needs price data on the engine option—six cylinders instead of the standard four cylinders. The application program requests this data from the DBMS. In doing so, the application program follows a logical access path. Next, the DBMS, working with various system programs, accesses a storage device, such as disk drives and solid state storage devices (SSDs), where the data is stored. When the DBMS goes to this storage device to retrieve the data, it follows a path to the physical location (physical access path) where the price of this option is stored. In the pricing example, the DBMS might go to a disk drive to retrieve the price data for six-cylinder engines. This relationship is shown in Figure 5.16.

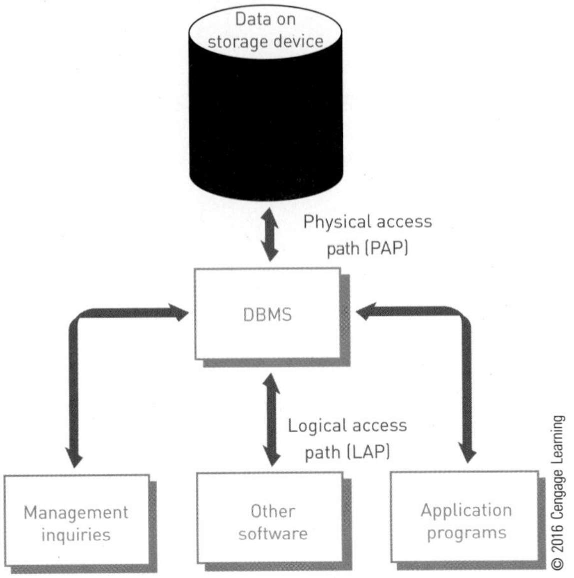

© 2016 Cengage Learning

FIGURE 5.16

Logical and physical access paths

When an application requests data from the DBMS, it follows a logical access path to the data. When the DBMS retrieves the data, it follows a path to the physical access path to the data.

This same process is used if a user wants to get information from the database. First, the user requests the data from the DBMS. For example, a user might give a command, such as LIST ALL OPTIONS FOR WHICH PRICE IS GREATER THAN $200. This is the logical access path (LAP). Then, the DBMS might go to the options price section of a disk to get the information for the user. This is the physical access path (PAP).

Two or more people or programs attempting to access the same record at the same time can cause a problem. For example, an inventory control program might attempt to reduce the inventory level for a product by 10 units because 10 units were just shipped to a customer. At the same time, a purchasing program might attempt to increase the inventory level for the same product by 200 units because inventory was just received. Without proper database control, one of the inventory updates might be incorrect, resulting in an inaccurate inventory level for the product. Concurrency control can be used to avoid this potential problem. One approach is to lock out all other application programs from access to a record if the record is being updated or used by another program.

concurrency control: A method of dealing with a situation in which two or more users or applications need to access the same record at the same time.

Manipulating Data and Generating Reports

After a DBMS has been installed, employees, managers, and other authorized users can use it to review reports and obtain important information. Using a DBMS, a company can manage this requirement. Some databases use *Query by Example (QBE)*, which is a visual approach to developing database queries or requests. Like Windows and other GUI (graphical user interface) operating systems, you can perform queries and other database tasks by opening windows and clicking the data or features you want. See Figure 5.17.

In other cases, database commands can be used in a programming language. For example, C++ commands can be used in simple programs that will access or manipulate certain pieces of data in the database. Here's another example of a DBMS query: SELECT * FROM EMPLOYEE WHERE JOB_CLASSIFICATION="C2." The asterisk (*) tells the program to include all columns from the EMPLOYEE table. In general, the commands that are used to manipulate the database are part of the data manipulation language (DML). This specific language, provided with the DBMS, allows managers and other database users to access and modify the data, to make queries, and to generate reports. Again, the application programs go through schemas and the DBMS before getting to the data stored on a device such as a disk.

data manipulation language (DML): A specific language, provided with a DBMS, which allows users to access and modify the data, to make queries, and to generate reports.

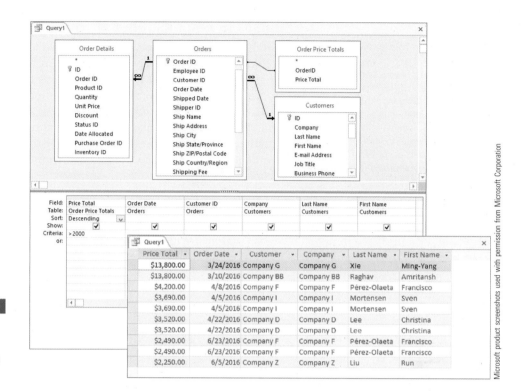

FIGURE 5.17

Query by Example

Some databases use Query by Example (QBE) to generate reports and information.

After a database has been set up and loaded with data, it can produce desired reports, documents, and other outputs. See Figure 5.18. These outputs usually appear in screen displays or hard copy printouts. The output-control features of a database program allow you to select the records and fields you want to appear in reports. You can also make calculations specifically for the report by manipulating database fields. Formatting controls and organization options (such as report headings) help you to customize reports and create flexible, convenient, and powerful information-handling tools.

Top Ten Biggest Orders

Top 10 Biggest Orders

#	Invoice #	Order Date	Company	Sales Amount
1	38	3/10/2016	Company BB	$13,800.00
2	41	3/24/2016	Company G	$13,800.00
3	47	4/8/2016	Company F	$4,200.00
4	46	4/5/2016	Company I	$3,690.00
5	58	4/22/2016	Company D	$3,520.00
6	79	6/23/2016	Company F	$2,490.00
7	77	6/5/2016	Company Z	$2,250.00
8	36	2/23/2016	Company C	$1,930.00
9	44	3/24/2016	Company A	$1,674.75
10	78	6/5/2016	Company CC	$1,560.00

FIGURE 5.18

Database output

A database application offers sophisticated formatting and organization options to produce the right information in the right format.

A DBMS can produce a wide variety of documents, reports, and other output that can help organizations achieve their goals. The most common reports select and organize data to present summary information about some aspect of company operations. For example, accounting reports often summarize financial data such as current and past due accounts. Many companies base their routine operating decisions on regular status reports that show the progress of specific orders toward completion and delivery.

Database Administration

database administrators (DBAs): Skilled and trained IS professionals who hold discussions with users to define their data needs; apply database programming languages to craft a set of databases to meet those needs; test and evaluate databases; implement changes to improve their performance; and assure that data is secure from unauthorized access.

Database administrators (DBA) are skilled and trained IS professionals who hold discussions with users to define their data needs; apply database programming languages to craft a set of databases to meet those needs; test and evaluate databases; implement changes to improve their performance; and assure that data are secure from unauthorized access. Database systems require a skilled database administrator (DBA), who is expected to have a clear understanding of the fundamental business of the organization, be proficient in the use of selected database management systems, and stay abreast of emerging technologies and new design approaches. The role of the DBA is to plan, design, create, operate, secure, monitor, and maintain databases. Typically, a DBA has a degree in computer science or management information systems and some on-the-job training with a particular database product or more extensive experience with a range of database products. See Figure 5.19.

FIGURE 5.19

Database administrator

The role of the database administrator (DBA) is to plan, design, create, operate, secure, monitor, and maintain databases.

© iStockphoto.com/OJO_Images

The DBA works with users to decide the content of the database—to determine exactly what entities are of interest and what attributes are to be recorded about those entities. Thus, personnel outside of IS must have some idea of what the DBA does and why this function is important. The DBA can play a crucial role in the development of effective information systems to benefit the organization, employees, and managers.

The DBA also works with programmers as they build applications to ensure that their programs comply with database management system standards and conventions. After the database is built and operating, the DBA monitors operations logs for security violations. Database performance is also monitored to ensure that the system's response time meets users' needs and that it operates efficiently. If there is a problem, the DBA attempts to correct it before it becomes serious.

A large responsibility of a DBA is to protect the database from attack or other forms of failure. DBAs use security software, preventive measures, and redundant systems to keep data safe and accessible. In spite of the DBA's best efforts, database security breaches are all too common. An individual was accused of hacking into numerous U.S. government databases in a year-long series of attacks. Large amounts of military data and personal identification information was stolen from databases belonging to the army, the U.S. Missile Defense Agency, NASA, the Environmental Protection Agency, and others. The hacker's motivation was to disrupt the operations and infrastructure of the U.S. government.[15]

Some organizations have also created a position called the **data administrator**, a nontechnical, but important position responsible for defining and implementing consistent principles for a variety of data issues, including setting data standards and data definitions that apply across all the databases in an organization. For example, the data administrator would ensure that a term such as "customer" is defined and treated consistently in all corporate databases. This person also works with business managers to identify who should have read or update access to certain databases and to selected attributes within those databases. This information is then communicated to the database administrator for implementation. The data administrator can be a high-level position reporting to top-level managers.

Popular Database Management Systems

Many popular database management systems address a wide range of individual, workgroup, and enterprise needs as shown in Table 5.2. The complete DBMS market encompasses software used by people ranging from nontechnical individuals to highly trained, professional programmers and runs on all types of computers from tablets to supercomputers. The entire market generates billions of dollars per year in revenue for companies such as IBM, Oracle, and Microsoft.

TABLE 5.2 Popular database management systems

Open-Source Relational DBMS	Relational DBMS for Individuals and Workgroups	Relational DBMS for Workgroups and Enterprise	NoSQL DBMS
MySQL	Microsoft Access	Oracle	Mongo DB
PostgreSQL	IBM Lotus Approach	IBM DB2	Cassandra
MariaDB	Google Base	Sybase	Redis
SQL Lite	OpenOffice Base	Teradata	CouchDB
		Microsoft SQL Server	
		Progress OpenEdge	

© 2016 Cengage Learning

Like other software products, numerous open-source database systems are also available. CouchDB by Couchbase is an open-source database system used by Zynga, the developer of the popular Internet game FarmVille, to process 250 million visitors a month.

Database as a Service (DaaS or Database 2.0) is similar to Software as a Service (SaaS). With DaaS, the database is stored on a service provider's servers and accessed by the client over a network, typically the Internet, with the database administration handled by the service provider. More than a dozen companies are moving in the DaaS direction, including Amazon, Database.com, Google, Heroku, IBM, Intuit, Microsoft, MyOwnDB, Oracle, and Trackvia.

Amazon Relational Database Service (Amazon RDS) is a Database as a Service that enables organizations to set up and operate their choice of a MySQL, Microsoft SQL, Oracle, or PostgreSQL relational database in the cloud. The service automatically backs up the database and stores those backups based on a user-defined retention period. Fairfax Media is a major media company in Australia and New Zealand that publishes some of the region's biggest newspapers and magazines. The firm employs Amazon RDS to avoid the cost of acquiring and maintaining its own database software and computing hardware. Management also believes that the DaaS environment enables it to bring new products to market more quickly and to better respond to changing customer preferences.[16]

Using Databases with Other Software

Database management systems are often used with other software and with the Internet. A DBMS can act as a front-end application or a back-end application. A *front-end application* is one that people interact with directly. Marketing researchers often use a database as a front end to a statistical analysis program. The researchers enter the results of market questionnaires or surveys into a database. The data is then transferred to a statistical analysis program to perform analysis such as to determine the potential for a new product or the effectiveness of an advertising campaign. A *back-end application* interacts with other programs or applications; it only indirectly interacts with people or users. When people request information from a Web site, the site can interact with a database (the back end) that supplies the desired information. For example, you can connect to a university Web site to find out whether the university's library has a book you want to read. The site then interacts with a database that contains a catalog of library books and articles to determine whether the book you want is available. See Figure 5.20.

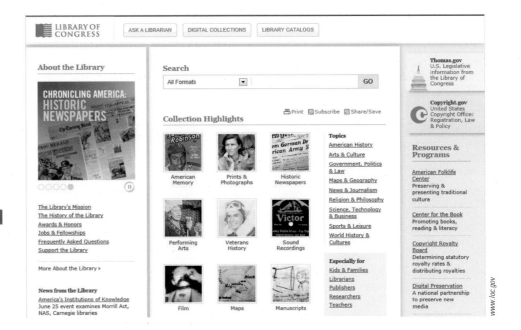

FIGURE 5.20

Library of Congress Web site

The Library of Congress (LOC) provides Web access to its databases, which include references to books and digital media in the LOC collection.

DATABASE APPLICATIONS

Databases have proven to be an extremely valuable asset for organizations. The existence of databases has spun off numerous database applications, including big data, data warehouses and data marts, and business intelligence. These topics will now be covered.

Big Data

big data: The term used to describe data collections that are so large and complex that traditional data management software, hardware, and analysis processes are incapable of dealing with them.

Big data is the term used to describe data collections that are so enormous (terabytes or more) and complex (from sensor data to social media data) that traditional data management software, hardware, and analysis processes are incapable of dealing with them. Computer technology analyst Doug Laney associated the three characteristics of volume, velocity, and variety with big data:[17]

- **Volume.** In 2012, IBM estimated that the volume of data that exists in the digital universe was 2.7 zetabytes.[18]
- **Velocity.** The velocity at which data is currently coming at us exceeds 5 trillion bits per second.[19] This rate will accelerate so that the volume of digital data is expected to double every two years between now and 2020.[20] Table 5.3 lists just a few of the generators of large amounts of data.
- **Variety.** Data today comes in a variety of formats. Some of the data is what computer scientists call structured data whose format is known in advance

TABLE **5.3** Big data generators

Source	Magnitude of Data Generated
Large Hadron particle accelerator at CERN	40 terabytes of data per second
Commercial aircraft engines	More than 1 petabyte per day of sensor data
Cell phones	More than 5 billion people worldwide are making cell phone calls, exchanging text messages, and accessing Web sites
YouTube	48 hours of video uploaded per minute
Facebook	100 terabytes uploaded per day
Twitter	500 million tweets per day
RFID tags	1,000 times the volume of data generated by bar codes

and fits nicely into traditional databases. An example of structured data is the well-defined business transactions that are used to update corporate databases containing customer, product, inventory, financial, and employee data. However, most of the data that an organization must deal with is unstructured data, meaning that it is not organized in any predefined manner.[21] Unstructured data comes from sources such as word-processing documents, social media, email, surveillance video, phone messages, and scientific research. For example, Figure 5.21 shows the Large Hadron Collider (LHC) tunnel at CERN (European Organization For Nuclear Research). The LHC generates 40 TB of data per second for scientific analysis.[22]

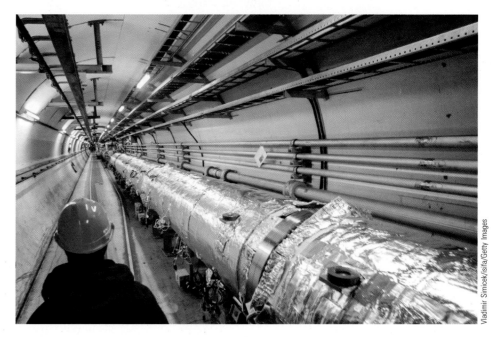

FIGURE 5.21

Large Hadron Collider (LHC)

The LHC at CERN generates 40 TB of data per second, amounting to tens of petabytes per year. The data is analyzed by a grid network that connects 140 computing centers in 35 countries and is provided to scientists seeking to answer complex questions in physics.

Challenges of Big Data

Individuals, organizations, and indeed society itself must find a way to deal with this ever-growing data tsunami or they will be paralyzed by information overload. The challenge is manifold—how to choose what subset of this data to store, where and how to store this data, how to find those nuggets of data that are relevant to the decision making at hand, and how to derive value from the relevant data. Optimists believe that we can conquer these challenges and that more data will lead to more accurate analyses and better decision making, which in turn will result in deliberate actions that improve matters. Some organizations are obtaining good results from a combination of big data and high-powered analytics, as shown in Table 5.4.

TABLE 5.4 Big data and analytics applications

Organization	How It Uses Big Data and Analytics
Apple	To gain a better understanding of its customers across its product groups
Continental Airlines	To determine each flyer's lifetime value and make decisions that affect individual customers
Disney	To understand its customers better so it can enhance their park experience and enable its employees to interact with visitors in a more personalized manner
Google Trends	To analyze a portion of the Google Web searches to help marketers to identify search trends and advertize or market accordingly
Harrah's	To know how much individual gamblers can afford to lose in a day before they won't come back the next day
Polkomtel (Polish wireless communications provider)	To reduce its credit-scoring expenses, speed the approval process for new customers, and fine-tune its collections operations
Walmart	To enable its suppliers to optimize the shelf space they are allocated in its stores

Not everyone, however, is happy with big data applications. Some people have privacy concerns that corporations are harvesting huge amounts of personal data that can be shared with other organizations. With all this data, organizations can develop extensive profiles of people without their knowledge or consent. Big data also introduces security concerns. Can an organization keep big data secure from competitors and malicious hackers? Some experts believe companies that collect and store big data could be open to liability suits from individuals and organizations. Even with these potential disadvantages, many companies are rushing into big data with its potential treasure trove of information and new applications.

In-Memory Databases

in-memory database A database management system that stores the entire database in random access memory (RAM).

An **in-memory database (IMDB)** is a database management system that stores the entire database in random access memory (RAM). This approach provides access to data at rates of up to 100,000 times faster than storing data on some form of secondary storage (e.g., a hard drive or flash drive) as is done with traditional database management systems. IMDB is an enabler for the analysis of big data and other challenging data-processing applications. IMDBs have become feasible because of the increase in RAM capacities and a corresponding decrease in RAM costs. In addition, in-memory databases perform best on multiple multicore CPUs that can process parallel requests to the data, further speeding access to and processing of large amounts of data.[23] Furthermore, the advent of 64-bit processors enabled the direct addressing of larger amounts of main memory. Some of the leading providers of IMDBs are shown in Table 5.5.

TABLE 5.5 IMDB providers

Database Software Manufacturer	Product Name	Major Customers
Altibase	HDB	E*Trade, China Telecom
Oracle	Times Ten	Lockheed Martin, Verizon Wireless
SAP	High Performance Analytic Appliance (HANA)	eBay, Colgate
Software AG	Terracotta Big Memory	AdJuggler

Critical Thinking Questions

1. What analyses does the NSA perform using the data it is collecting?
2. Should the NSA be allowed to perform these types of analyses? Why or why not?

SOURCES: Greenwald, Glenn, "NSA Collecting Phone Records of Millions of Verizon Customers Daily," *The Guardian*, June 5, 2013; Gellman, Barton and Poitras, Laura, "U.S., British Intelligence Mining Data from Nine U.S. Internet Companies in Broad Secret Program," *The Washington Post*, June 6, 2013; Harris, Derrick, "Under the Covers of the NSA's Big Data Effort," Gigaom, June 7, 2013, *http://gigaom.com/2013/06/07/under-the-covers-of-the-nsas-big-data-effort/*; Harris, Derrick, "Here's How the NSA Analyzes All That Call Data," Gigaom, June 6, 2013, *http://gigaom.com/2013 /06/06/heres-how-the-nsa-analyzes-all-that-call-data/*.

Data warehouses are used for decision making, so the quality of their data is vital to avoid wrong conclusions. For instance, duplicated or missing information will produce incorrect or misleading statistics ("garbage in, garbage out"). Due to the wide range of possible data inconsistencies and the sheer data volume, data quality is considered one of the biggest issues in data warehousing.

Data warehouses are continuously refreshed with huge amounts of data from a variety of sources so the probability that some of the sources contain "dirty data" is high. The ETL (extract, transform, load) process takes data from a variety of sources, edits and transforms it into the form to be used in the data warehouse, and then loads this data into the warehouse. This process is essential in ensuring the quality of the data in the data warehouse.

- **Extract.** Source data for the data warehouse comes from many sources and systems. The data may be represented in a variety of forms, such as relational databases and flat files. The goal of this process is to extract the source data from all the various sources and convert it into a single format suitable for processing. During the extract step, data that fails to meet expected patterns or values may be rejected from further processing (e.g., blank or nonnumeric data in net sales field, a product code outside the defined range of valid codes).
- **Transform.** During this stage of the ETL process, a series of rules or algorithms are applied to the extracted data to derive the data that will be stored in the data warehouse. A common transformation that may be made is to convert the customer's street address, city, state, and zip code to an organization-assigned sales district or government census tract. Also, data is often aggregated to reduce the processing time required to create anticipated reports. For example, total sales may be accumulated by store or sales district.
- **Load.** During this stage of the ETL process, the extracted and transformed data is loaded into the data warehouse. As the data is being loaded into the data warehouse, new indices are created and the data is checked against the constraints defined in the database schema to ensure its quality. As a result, the data load stage for a large data warehouse can take days.

A large number of software tools are available to support these ETL tasks, including Ab Initio, IBM InfoSphere Datastage, Oracle Data Integrator, and the SAP Data Integrator. See Figure 5.23. Several open-source ETL tools are also available, including Apatar, Clover ETL, Pentaho, and Talend. Unfortunately, much of the ETL work must be done by low-level proprietary programs that are difficult to write and maintain.

© iStockphoto.com/nullplus

FIGURE **5.23**

Data warehouse tools

Data warehouses can use tools such as Oracle's Warehouse Management software to acquire data from unique sources such as scans of RFID tags.

data mart: A subset of a data warehouse that is used by small- and medium-sized businesses and departments within large companies to support decision making.

business intelligence (BI): A broad range of technologies and applications that enable an organization to transform mostly structured data obtained from information systems to perform analysis, generate information, and improve the decision making of the organization.

data mining: An information-analysis tool that involves the automated discovery of patterns and relationships in a data warehouse.

online analytical processing (OLAP): A form of analysis that allows users to explore data from a number of perspectives, enabling a style of analysis known as "slicing and dicing."

Data Marts

A **data mart** is a subset of a data warehouse. Data marts bring the data warehouse concept—online analysis of sales, inventory, and other vital business data that have been gathered from transaction processing systems—to small- and medium-sized businesses and to departments within larger companies. Rather than store all enterprise data in one monolithic database, data marts contain a subset of the data for a single aspect of a company's business—for example, finance, inventory, or personnel. In fact, a specific area in the data mart might contain greater detailed data than the data warehouse.

Business Intelligence

Business intelligence (BI) is a broad range of technologies and applications that enable an organization to transform mostly structured data obtained from information systems to perform analysis, generate information, and improve the decision making of the organization.[26] BI technologies include data mining, online analytical processing, predictive analytics, data visualization, and competitive intelligence. Some key BI vendors are IBM Cognos, Information Builders, Microsoft, Micro Strategy, Oracle, SAP, and SAS.

Data Mining

Data mining is an information-analysis process that involves the automated discovery of patterns and relationships in a data warehouse. Like gold mining, data mining sifts through mountains of data to find a few nuggets of valuable information. For example, a midwest grocery chain used data mining to analyze its customers' buying patterns. Data mining revealed that when men bought diapers on Thursdays, they also tended to buy beer. The grocery chain used this newly discovered information to increase revenue by moving the beer display closer to the diaper display or by ensuring that beer and diapers were sold at full price on Thursdays.[27]

Sprouts Farmers Market employs data mining to view retail data from multiple sources to gain insights into business performance. People across the entire organization can drill down or drill across the data using various devices, including smartphones and tablet computers.[28] Janssen Pharmaceutical mined discussions and patient reviews in social media regarding Xanax, a drug used to treat anxiety and panic disorder, to segment customer insights, to improve advertising and branding, and to discover new patient concerns.[29] Samsung's newest TVs track what viewers watch on cable, satellite, and premium view-on-demand services over the past six months and then apply data-mining techniques to offer them personalized viewing recommendations.[30]

Online Analytical Processing (OLAP)

Online analytical processing (OLAP) allows users to explore data from a number of perspectives, enabling a style of analysis known as "slicing and dicing." OLAP databases support business intelligence discussed earlier and have been optimized to provide useful reports and analysis. The leading OLAP database vendors include Microsoft, IBM Cognos, SAP, Business Objects, MicroStrategy, Applix, Infor, and Oracle.

Unlike data mining that provides bottom-up, discovery-driven analysis, OLAP provides top-down, query-driven data analysis. Whereas data mining requires no assumptions and instead identifies facts and conclusions based on patterns discovered, OLAP requires repetitive testing of user-originated theories. OLAP, or multidimensional analysis, requires a great deal of human ingenuity and interaction with the database to find information in the database. A user of a data-mining tool does not need to figure out what questions to ask; instead, the approach is, "Here's the data, tell me what interesting patterns emerge." For example, a data-mining tool in a credit card company's customer database can construct a profile of fraudulent activity from historical information. Then, this profile can be applied to all incoming transaction data to identify and stop fraudulent behavior, which might otherwise go undetected. Verafin develops data-mining software for financial institutions that analyzes transactions and detects financial crimes. See Figure 5.24.

Table 5.6 compares OLAP and data mining.

Predictive Analysis

Predictive analysis is a form of data mining that combines historical data with assumptions about future conditions to predict outcomes of events, such as future product sales or the probability that a customer will default on a

predictive analysis (also called predictive analytics): A form of data mining that combines historical data with assumptions about future conditions to predict outcomes of events, such as future product sales or the probability that a customer will default on a loan.

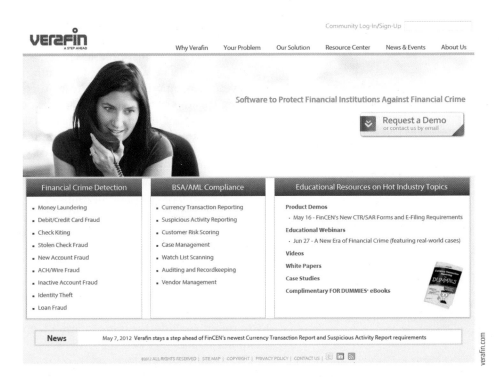

FIGURE 5.24

Data-mining software

To meet its mission of helping financial institutions fight fraud, Verafin develops data-mining software to analyze transactions and detect financial crimes.

TABLE 5.6 Comparison of OLAP and data mining

Characteristic	OLAP	Data Mining
Purpose	Supports data analysis and decision making	Supports data analysis and decision making
Type of analysis supported	Top-down, query-driven data analysis	Bottom-up, discovery-driven data analysis
Skills required of user	Must be very knowledgeable of the data and its business context	Must trust in data-mining tools to uncover valid and worthwhile hypotheses

loan. The key element in predictive analytics is the *predictor*, one or more variables that can be measured for an individual to predict future behavior. For example, a life insurance company is likely to take into account potential life expectancy predictors such as age, gender, and health record when issuing life insurance policies.

The FICO score is a widely used credit score model based on predictive analysis. Credit reporting bureaus such as Experian, Equifax, and TransUnion calculate consumers' FICO scores based on their credit histories. The score provides a prediction of the likelihood of the consumer to repay a loan and is used by banks and other financial institutions to make lending decisions. Consumers with higher FICO scores might be offered better interest rates on mortgages or automobile loans as well as higher credit limit amounts. Predictive analysis is also being used to better understand the behavior patterns of large groups of employees, such as in a call center, to predict the number of workers likely to leave in a month.[31] Condé Nast attracts more than 164 million consumers across its 20 print and digital media brands, including *Vogue, Vanity Fair, The New Yorker, Architectural Digest, Bon Appétit, Wired, Golf Digest*, and *Ars Technica*.[32] Its in-house marketing analytic team used predictive analysis methods and software to perform market segmentation and develop more effective subscription marketing programs.[33]

Data Visualization

One of the best ways to gain insights into data is through data visualization techniques that can help quickly draw conclusions and see relationships among the data. The analysis of big data brings additional challenges of trying to make sense out of the data. Excel, SAS Visual Analytics, and other software are available to prepare charts and graphs to make it easier to see trends and patterns and to identify opportunities for further analysis. Line charts, bar charts, scatter diagrams, bubble charts, and pie charts are frequently used.

social graph analysis: A data visualization technique in which data is represented as networks where the vertices are the individual data points (social network users) and the edges are the connections among them.

Social media networks are generating enormous amounts of data that progressive organizations are using to gain competitive advantage by better understanding customer needs and brand experience. Social graph analysis is a data visualization technique in which data is represented as networks where the vertices are the individual data points (social network users) and the edges are the connections among them.[34] Facebook is performing social graph analysis with billions of nodes and trillions of edges. Social graph analysis is also being used in fraud detection, influence analysis, sentiment monitoring, market segmentation, engagement optimization, experience optimization, and other applications where complex behavioral patterns must be rapidly identified. Figure 5.25 represents millions of pieces of social media data indicating connections among millions of people.

key performance indicators (KPIs): Quantifiable measurements that assess progress toward organizational goals and reflect the critical success factors of an organization.

Key performance indicators (KPIs) are quantifiable measurements that assess progress toward organizational goals and reflect the critical success factors of an organization. They differ from one organization to another and from department to department within a given organization. Manufacturing KPIs might include the percentage of on-time deliveries and the number of customer complaints per 100 orders.

dashboard: A data visualization tool that displays the current status of the key performance indicators (KPIs) for an organization.

A business intelligence dashboard is a data visualization tool that displays the current status of the KPIs for an organization. The dashboard may be tailored to display metrics targeted for a single point or department. Figure 5.26 shows an example of a dashboard highlighting the KPIs for a supply chain.

Competitive Intelligence

competitive intelligence: One aspect of business intelligence and encompasses information about competitors and the ways that knowledge affects strategy, tactics, and operations.

Competitive intelligence is one aspect of business intelligence and encompasses information about competitors and the ways that knowledge affects strategy, tactics, and operations. Competitive intelligence is a critical part of a company's ability to see and respond quickly and appropriately to the changing marketplace. Competitive intelligence is not espionage—the use of illegal

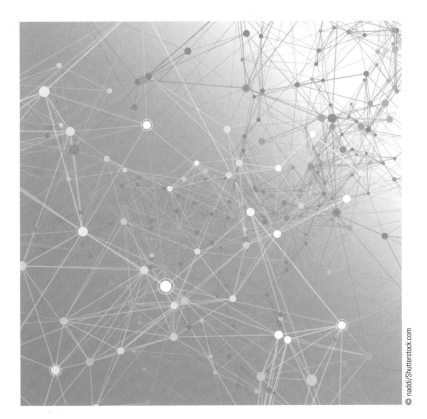

Microsoft product screenshots used with permission from Microsoft Corporation

FIGURE **5.25**

Social graph analysis

Data is represented as networks where the vertices are the individual data points (social network users) and the edges are the connections among them.

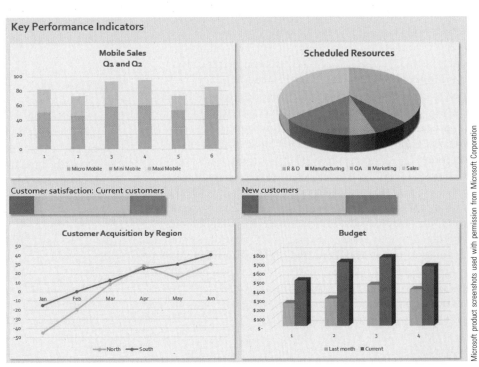

FIGURE **5.26**

KPI dashboard

This dashboard highlights the current status of the key performance indicators (KPIs) for sales, resources, customers, and budget.

means to gather information. In fact, almost all the information a competitive-intelligence professional needs can be collected by examining published information sources, conducting interviews, and using other legal and ethical methods. Using a variety of analytical tools, a skilled competitive-intelligence professional can by deduction fill the gaps in information already gathered. For example, Omgili is a search engine that focuses on only Internet message boards and allows its users to find topics on discussion boards that are relevant to their interests.

INFORMATION SYSTEMS @ WORK

Brandwatch: Applying Business Intelligence to Social Media Data to Make Advertising Decisions

Social networks are big in professional sports. About 5.3 million people follow the National Football League (NFL) on Twitter, and about 8.5 million "like" its Facebook page. The 2012 NFL championship game, Super Bowl 46 between the New York Giants and the New England Patriots, was watched by about 100 million television viewers. During the game, people posted 7,366,400 tweets about it. Of those, 324,221 mentioned one or more advertisers. With social media attention on such a large scale, it's no wonder that advertisers analyze social media as one indicator of whether their money was well spent.

Aside from sheer volume, the data from social media is unstructured. That puts this social media activity squarely into the "big data" category. What can advertisers learn from it?

If you measure advertising effectiveness by cost per tweet, Swedish high-fashion clothing chain H&M did best. According to Brandwatch, a firm that analyzes big data on the Web, H&M's 30-second commercial was mentioned in 17,190 tweets and cost $3.5 million, or $204 per tweet. Pepsi, which had the second-highest number of tweets with 28,996, ran two such commercials for a second-lowest $253 per tweet. Budweiser, the highest-spending brand in the 10 most-tweeted about commercials (for an estimated total of $35 million), had only 13,910 tweets for a cost of $2,265 each.

Do these findings mean that Budweiser wasted its money? Not necessarily. Perhaps beer drinkers tweet less than high-fashion customers or cola drinkers. It's more useful to compare within a category. Coca-Cola spent half again as much as Pepsi but had slightly more than half as many tweets (17,334). Similarly, Volkswagen had 20,818 tweets for $7 million worth of air time, or $336 per tweet. Hyundai, with 4,325 tweets for the same cost, was far less effective in generating Twitter buzz.

You can also look for the sentiment of tweets. The way words are used can affect their meaning, but when taken over a large number of messages and compared across advertisers, the results of sentiment analysis are informative. Most tweets are neutral, and most advertisers show a small excess of positive over negative tweets. For example, Pepsi had 7 percent positive tweets, 2 percent negative, with the rest neutral. More negative Twitter sentiment suggests a problem. Skechers had 11 percent negative tweets and only 4 percent positive. The data don't say why,

but it suggests that Skechers ought to look into the reason. (It may have been due to a protest based on its commercial having been filmed at a location where dogs were allegedly mistreated. If that's the reason, it's unlikely to affect shoe sales.)

The Brandwatch process begins by gathering data. Brandwatch monitors blogs, microblogs such as Twitter, social sites such as Facebook, image sites such as Flickr, video sites such as YouTube and Vimeo, discussion forums, and news sites. Clients can choose the site they want to monitor.

Brandwatch then cleans the data. It removes duplicates, eliminates navigation text and ads, separates actual mentions of a brand from uses of the same word (an apple isn't necessarily an Apple), and analyzes the site to determine its date so that trends can be tracked.

The third step is data analysis, including sentiment analysis. Combined with date information, data analysis gives sentiment trends over time.

Finally, Brandwatch presents the data in several ways, including a digital dashboard. The net result is insight into the success of an ad campaign that could probably not be obtained any other way.

Discussion Questions

1. Brandwatch can create a graph of Twitter activity over time. The time at which a commercial airs can be indicated on that graph. What could an advertiser do with this information?
2. Is Brandwatch as helpful for small companies as it is for large companies? Why or why not?

Critical Thinking Questions

1. Draw an entity-relationship diagram for the tables that a database would need to store information about tweets related to Super Bowl ads after data cleaning is complete. List the attributes that the database must store for each entity.
2. How accurate do you think sentiment analysis is? How do you think it is carried out?

SOURCES: Brandwatch Web site, *www.brandwatch.com*, accessed May 16, 2012; Staff, "Visualizing Big Social Media Data," Brandwatch, *www.brandwatch.com/wp-content/uploads/brandwatch/The-Brandwatch-Super-Bowl-2012.pdf*, March 14, 2012; Staff, "Brandwatch Superbowl 2012," Brandwatch, *labs.brandwatch.com/superbowl*, accessed May 16, 2012; Horovitz, B., "Even without Kardashian, Skechers Ad Stirs Controversy," *USA Today, www.usatoday.com/money/advertising/story/2012–01-11/kim-kardashian-skechers-super-bowl-ad/52506236/1*, January 12, 2012; Tofel, K., "Super Bowl 46 Mobility by the Numbers," *gigaom.com/mobile/super-bowl-46-mobility-by-the-numbers*, February 5, 2012.

Fuld & Company is a research and consulting firm in the field of competitive intelligence. A leading U.K. bank hired Fuld to examine new entrants and nontraditional business models that could threaten its market position. Based on results of this study, the client moved quickly to change its direction and to educate its executives on critical strategic threats.[35]

The term **counterintelligence** describes the steps an organization takes to protect information sought by "hostile" intelligence gatherers. One of the most effective counterintelligence measures is to define "trade secret" information relevant to the company and control its dissemination.

counterintelligence: The steps an organization takes to protect information sought by "hostile" intelligence gatherers.

SUMMARY

Principle:

Data management and modeling are key aspects of organizing data and information.

Data is one of the most valuable resources that a firm possesses. It is organized into a hierarchy that builds from the smallest element to the largest. The smallest element is the bit, a binary digit. A byte (a character such as a letter or numeric digit) is made up of eight bits. A group of characters, such as a name or number, is called a field (an object). A collection of related fields is a record; a collection of related records is called a file. The database, at the top of the hierarchy, is an integrated collection of records and files.

An entity is a generalized class of objects for which data is collected, stored, and maintained. An attribute is a characteristic of an entity. Specific values of attributes—called data items—can be found in the fields of the record describing an entity. A primary key uniquely identifies a record, while a secondary key is a field in a record that does not uniquely identify the record.

When building a database, an organization must consider content, access, logical structure, and physical organization of the database. One of the tools that database designers use to show the logical structure and relationships among data is a data model. A data model is a map or diagram of entities and their relationships. Enterprise data modeling involves analyzing the data and information needs of an entire organization. Entity-relationship (ER) diagrams can be used to show the relationships among entities in the organization.

The relational model places data in two-dimensional tables. Tables can be linked by common data elements, which are used to access data when the database is queried. Each row represents a record, and each column represents an attribute (or field). Allowable values for these attributes are called the domain. Basic data manipulations include selecting, projecting, and joining. The relational model is easier to control, more flexible, and more intuitive than the other models because it organizes data in tables.

Data cleansing is the process of detecting and then correcting or deleting incomplete, incorrect, inaccurate, or irrelevant records that reside in the database. The goal is to improve the quality of the data used in decision making.

Principle:

A well-designed and well-managed database is an extremely valuable tool in supporting decision making.

A DBMS is a group of programs used as an interface between a database and its users and other application programs. When an application program requests data from the database, it follows a logical access path. The actual retrieval of the data follows a physical access path. Records can be considered in the same way: A logical record is what the record contains; a physical record is where the record is stored on storage devices. Schemas are used to describe the entire database, its record types, and its relationships to the DBMS.

There are both single-user and multiple-user DBMS systems, and flat files, SQL databases, NoSQL databases, and visual, audio, and other database systems.

A DBMS provides four basic functions: offering user views, creating and modifying the database, storing and retrieving data, and manipulating data and generating reports. Schemas are entered into the computer via a data definition language, which describes the data and relationships in a specific database. Another tool used in database management is the data dictionary, which contains detailed descriptions of all data in the database.

After a DBMS has been installed, the database can be accessed, modified, and queried via a data manipulation language. A more specialized data manipulation language is the query language, the most common being Structured Query Language (SQL). SQL is used in several popular database packages today and can be installed in PCs and mainframes.

A database administrator (DBA) plans, designs, creates, operates, secures, monitors, and maintains databases. A data administrator is a nontechnical position responsible for defining and implementing consistent principles for a variety of data issues, including setting data standards and data definitions that apply across all the databases in an organization. Selecting a DBMS begins by analyzing the information needs of the organization. Important characteristics of databases include the size of the database, the number of concurrent users, performance of the database, the ability of the DBMS to be integrated with other systems, the features of the DBMS, the vendor considerations, and the cost of the database management system.

Many popular database management systems are available to address a wide range of individual, workgroup, and enterprise needs.

Database as a Service (DaaS) is a new form of database service in which clients lease use of a database on a service provider's site. In DaaS, the database is stored on a service provider's servers and accessed by the client over a network, typically the Internet. In DaaS, database administration is provided by the service provider.

Principle:

The number and types of database applications will continue to evolve and yield real business benefits.

"Big data" is the term used to describe data collections that are so enormous and complex that traditional data management software, hardware, and analysis processes are incapable of dealing with them.

An in-memory database is a database management system that stores the entire database in random access memory to improve storage and retrieval speed.

Traditional online transaction processing (OLTP) systems put data into databases very quickly, reliably, and efficiently, but they do not support the types of data analysis that today's businesses and organizations require. To address this need, organizations are building data warehouses specifically designed to support management decision making.

An extract, transform, load process takes data from a variety of sources, edits and transforms it into the form to be used in the data warehouse, and then loads the data into the warehouse.

Data marts are subdivisions of data warehouses and are commonly devoted to specific purposes or functional business areas.

Business intelligence is a broad range of technologies and applications that enable an organization to transform mostly structured data obtained from information systems to perform analysis, generate information, and improve the decision making of the organization.

Data mining, which is the automated discovery of patterns and relationships in a data warehouse, is a practical approach to generating hypotheses about the data that can be used to predict future behavior.

Online analytical processing (OLAP) allows users to explore data from a number of perspectives, enabling a style of analysis known as "slicing and dicing."

Predictive analysis is a form of data mining that combines historical data with assumptions about future conditions to forecast outcomes of events.

Data visualization employs a variety of techniques such as social graph analysis and dashboards to help quickly draw conclusions and see relationships among the data.

Competitive intelligence is one aspect of business intelligence limited to information about competitors and the ways that information affects strategy, tactics, and operations. Competitive intelligence is not espionage—the use of illegal means to gather information. Counterintelligence describes the steps an organization takes to protect information sought by "hostile" intelligence gatherers.

KEY TERMS

attribute

big data

business intelligence (BI)

character

competitive intelligence

concurrency control

counterintelligence

dashboard

data administrator

database administrators (DBAs)

database approach to data management

database management system (DBMS)

data cleansing (data cleaning or data scrubbing)

data definition language (DDL)

data dictionary

data item

data manipulation language (DML)

data mart

data mining

data model

data warehouse

domain

enterprise data modeling

entity

entity-relationship (ER) diagrams

field

file

hierarchy of data

in-memory database

joining

key performance indicators (KPIs)

linking

NoSQL database

online analytical processing (OLAP)

predictive analysis (also called predictive analytics)

primary key

projecting

record

relational model

schema

selecting

social graph analysis

traditional approach to data management

CHAPTER 5: SELF-ASSESSMENT TEST

Data management and modeling are key aspects of organizing data and information.

1. _____ is a skilled and trained IS professional who holds discussions with users to define their data needs; applies database programming languages to craft a set of databases to meet those needs; tests and evaluates databases; implements changes to improve their performance; and assures that data is secure from unauthorized access.

2. A collection of data fields all related to one object, activity, or individual is called a(n) _____.
   a. attribute
   b. byte

   c. record
   d. column

3. Multiple records can have the same primary key. True or False?

4. A(n) _____ is a field or set of fields that uniquely identifies a database record.
   a. attribute
   b. data item
   c. key
   d. primary key

5. A(n) _____ is a diagram of entities and their relationships.
   a. database
   b. data model

   c. data entity
   d. database management system
6. The _____ is a simple but highly useful way to organize data into collections of two-dimensional tables called relations.

A well-designed and well-managed database is an extremely valuable tool in supporting decision making.

7. _____ involves eliminating columns in a table.
   a. Projecting
   b. Joining
   c. Selecting
   d. Linking
8. Because the DBMS is responsible for providing access to a database, one of the first steps in installing and using a database involves telling the DBMS the logical and physical structure of the data and relationships among the data in the database. This description of an entire database is called a(n) _____.
9. _____ is a special-purpose programming language for accessing and manipulating data stored in a relational database.
10. SQL databases conform to ACID properties that guarantee database transactions are processed reliably and ensure the integrity of data in the database. True or False?
11. A(n) _____is a collection of instructions and commands used to define and describe data and relationships in a specific database.
   a. data manipulation language
   b. schema
   c. data model
   d. data definition language
12. The _____ is a nontechnical, but important position responsible for defining and implementing consistent principles for a variety of data issues, including setting data standards and data definitions that apply across all the databases in an organization.
   a. database administrator
   b. systems analyst
   c. programmer
   d. data administrator

13. A trend in database management, known as Database as a Service, places the responsibility of storing and managing a database on a service provider. True or False?

The number and types of database applications will continue to evolve and yield real business benefits.

14. _____ is a term used to describe data collections that are so large and complex that traditional data management software, hardware, and analysis processes are incapable of dealing with them.
15. An in-memory database (IMDB) is a database management system that stores the entire database in _____.
   a. random access memory
   b. read-only memory
   c. distributed servers
   d. virtual memory
16. A(n) _____ is a database that holds business information from many sources in the enterprise covering all aspects of the company's processes, products, and customers.
17. An information-analysis process that involves the automated discovery of patterns and relationships in a data warehouse is called _____.
   a. a data mart
   b. data mining
   c. predictive analysis
   d. business intelligence
18. _____ allows users to explore data from a number of perspectives, enabling a style of analysis known as "slicing and dicing."
   a. Data mining
   b. Online analytical processing (OLAP)
   c. Predictive analysis
   d. None of the above
19. _____is a form of data mining that combines historical data with assumptions about future conditions to predict outcomes of events.
20. _____ is a data visualization technique in which data is represented as networks where the vertices are the individual data points (social network users) and the edges are the connections among them.

CHAPTER 5: SELF-ASSESSMENT TEST ANSWERS

1. Database administrator
2. c
3. False
4. d
5. b
6. relational model
7. Projecting
8. schema
9. SQL
10. True

11. d
12. d
13. True
14. Big data
15. a
16. data warehouse
17. b
18. b
19. Predictive analysis
20. Social graph analysis

REVIEW QUESTIONS

1. Identify all the components in the data hierarchy from the bit to the database.
2. What is the difference between a data attribute and a data item?
3. What is the purpose of a primary key? What field or fields might be the primary key in an airline reservation system used to identify a specific seat on a specific flight for a specific airline on a specific day?
4. What is enterprise data modeling?
5. What is an entity-relationship model and what is its purpose?
6. What is data cleansing?
7. What is SQL and how is it used?
8. What are the essential differences between an SQL database and a NoSQL database?
9. What is Database as a Service (DaaS)? What are the advantages and disadvantages of using the DaaS approach?
10. What is Hadoop?
11. What is a schema and how is it used?
12. What is concurrency control? Why is it important?
13. What is in-memory database processing and what advantages does it provide?
14. What is the difference between projecting and joining?
15. What is big data? Identify three characteristics associated with big data.
16. What is a data warehouse, and how is it different from a traditional database used to support OLTP?
17. What is meant by the "front end" and the "back end" of a DBMS?
18. What is the relationship between the Internet and databases?
19. What is data mining? What is OLAP? How are they different?
20. What is business intelligence? Identify five specific business intelligence technologies.
21. What is predictive analysis? Give an example where this could be used.

DISCUSSION QUESTIONS

1. When building a database, an organization must carefully consider these topics: content, access, logical structure, and physical organization. Elaborate on these points.
2. Outline some specific steps an organization might take to perform data cleansing to ensure the accuracy and completeness of its customer database before adding this data to a data warehouse. How would you decide when the data is accurate enough?
3. Briefly describe the ACID properties to which an SQL database must conform. Identify one advantage and one disadvantage associated with ACID conformance.
4. Briefly describe how a NoSQL database operates.
5. Identify and briefly describe some of the challenges and issues associated with big data.
6. Identify and briefly describe the steps in the ETL process. What is the goal of the ETL process?
7. You are the vice president of information technology for a large multinational consumer packaged goods company (such as Procter & Gamble or Unilever). You must make a presentation to persuade the board of directors to invest $25 million to establish a state-of-the-art competitive-intelligence organization—including people, data-gathering services, and software tools. What key points do you need to make in favor of this investment? What arguments can you anticipate that the board might make?
8. What counterintelligence strategy might a large multinational consumer packaged goods company employ? Identify at least three specific actions that might be taken.
9. Your luxury car dealership wants to identify likely future customers in your local geographic area. What key pieces of data might be useful in making this determination? What are some possible sources for this data? How could data mining be used to accomplish this objective?
10. Make a list of the databases in which data about you exists. How is the data in each database captured? Who updates each database and how often? Is it possible for you to request a printout of the contents of your data record from each database? What data privacy concerns do you have?
11. If you were the database administrator for the iTunes store, how might you use predictive analysis to determine which artists and movies will sell the most next year?
12. Identity theft, where people steal personal information, which continues to be a problem for consumers and businesses. Assume that you are the database administrator for a corporation with a large database that is accessible from the Web. What steps would you implement to prevent people from stealing personal information from the corporate database?
13. You have been hired to set up a database for a company similar to Netflix that rents movies over the Internet. Describe what type of database management system you would recommend for this application.

PROBLEM-SOLVING EXERCISES

1. Develop a simple data model for the music you have on your digital music player or in your CD collection. The data model includes three tables: songs, artists, and awards earned by the song. For each table, what attributes should you capture? What will be the primary key and foreign keys for the tables in your database? Use a relational database management system to create this database for a dozen or so songs and artists.

2. An online video movie rental store is using a relational database to store information on movies to answer customer questions. Each entry in the database contains the following items: Movie Number (the primary key), Movie Title, Year Made, Movie Type, MPAA Rating, Starring actor #1, Starring actor #2. Movie Types are comedy, family, drama, horror, science fiction, and western. MPAA ratings are G, PG, PG-13, R, NC-17, and NR (not rated). Use a single-user database management system to build a data-entry screen to enter this data. Build a small database with at least 10 entries.

3. To improve service to their customers, the workers at the online video rental store have proposed a list of changes being considered for the database in the previous exercise. From this list, choose two database modifications and modify the data-entry screen to capture and store this new information.
   Proposed changes are as follows:

   a. To help customers locate the newest releases, add the date that the movie was first available.
   b. Add the director's name.
   c. Add a customer rating of one, two, three, or four stars based on number of rentals.
   d. Add the number of Academy Award nominations.

4. Using a graphics program, develop an entity-relationship diagram for a database application for an Internet bookstore where students buy textbooks from a salesperson and receive invoices for their purchases. Use Figure 5.5 as a guide.

TEAM ACTIVITIES

1. You and your team have been selected to represent the student body in defining the user requirements for a new student database for your school. What actions would you take to ensure that the student reporting needs and data privacy concerns of the students are fully identified? What other resources might you enlist to help you in defining these requirements?

2. As a team of three or four classmates, interview managers from three different organizations that have implemented a customer database. What data entities and data attributes are contained in each database? What database management system did each company select to implement its database and why? How does each access the database to perform analysis? Have the companies received training in any query or reporting tools? What do they like about their databases, and what could be improved? Do any of them use data-mining or OLAP techniques? Weighing the information obtained, identify which company has implemented the best customer database.

3. Imagine that you and your classmates are a research team developing a system based on predictive analysis to identify "at risk" students who are likely to withdraw from school because of poor academic performance rather than complete their course of studies. Prepare a brief report for your instructor addressing these questions:

   a. What data do you need for each student?
   b. Where might you get this data?
   c. Take a first cut at designing a database for this application. Using the material in this chapter on designing a database, draw the logical structure of the relational tables for this proposed database. In your design, include the data attributes you believe are necessary for this database and show the primary keys in your tables. Keep the size of the fields and tables as small as possible to minimize required disk drive storage space. Fill in the database tables with the sample data for demonstration purposes (10 records). After your design is complete, implement it using a relational DBMS.

WEB EXERCISES

1. Use a Web search engine to find information on social graph analysis. Identify at least three organizations that are using this technique to analyze big data and discuss their findings.

2. Do research to find three different estimates of the rate at which the amount of data is growing. Discuss why there are differences in these estimates.

CAREER EXERCISES

1. Do research to find what career opportunities are available in the field of competitive intelligence. Identify colleges or universities that offer courses in competitive intelligence and what certifications are available. What is the expected growth in the number of such positions and what are typical salaries?

2. How could you use business intelligence (BI) to do a better job at work? Give some specific examples of how BI can give you a competitive advantage.

CASE STUDIES

Case One

Medihelp: Transforming Traditional Databases into Business Intelligence

Medihelp is South Africa's third-largest health insurance company. It covers about 220,000 people, with plans ranging from R828 to R2,700 (about U.S. $80 to $260) per month per person. Medihelp needed a better way to access and analyze data on customers, claims, and third-party providers to monitor the effectiveness of its insurance products and to fine-tune and create new products as needed.

Medihelp's problem was that its data was stored in a traditional database. As discussed in this chapter, traditional databases are not designed to support decision making. They're not efficient at the types of information retrieval that decision making uses. With Medihelp's existing database, reports took unacceptably long times to run. Reports based on the content of the full database couldn't be run at all. This inefficiency detracted from Medihelp's ability to make informed business decisions.

For example, Medihelp's claim file had about 55 million rows. Each row contained about 35 data values describing medical conditions, treatments, and payments. Each row was associated with one of 15 million rows of historical member data, which held another 15 or so data values describing the member and his or her coverage. For claim processing, accessing the data for a single claim was fast and efficient. Combining data from thousands of rows, as decision support calls for, was not.

"Logging into our [traditional] database ... was not providing us the information we needed to make the best business decisions," explains Jan Steyl, senior manager of business intelligence at Medihelp. "We needed a dedicated, high-performance data warehouse."

After looking at several options, Medihelp made a preliminary selection of Sybase IQ as the basis for its data warehouse. Working with B.I. Practice, a Sybase subsidiary in South Africa, Medihelp carried out a proof of concept to confirm that Sybase IQ could deliver the needed performance at an acceptable cost. This procedure involved loading a subset of the tables from the operational database into Sybase IQ, executing queries that used only that subset of the data, and evaluating the results.

Because these queries now used a database designed for queries, performance improved dramatically. Response time was reduced by an average of 71.5 percent. Response time for ad hoc queries, those which were not programmed into the database system ahead of time, was reduced by an average of 74.1 percent. One query's response time dropped by 92.8 percent.

Theo Els, Medihelp's senior manager of client relations, likes the new system. "Health insurers supply data to employer groups. These demographic and claims profiles are essential for employer groups seeking to understand their employees' health risks ... and the consequent impact that risk can have on business productivity. Brokers and healthcare consultants also use this information in their annual client reviews to ensure that employees receive the most suitable coverage. It is imperative that the ... data warehouse provide accurate information in a format that is easily understood."

The biggest beneficiary of Medihelp's data warehouse is its product development team. The team uses data from the data warehouse to understand trends in claims by benefit code, condition, area, age group, and other factors. Medihelp also uses its data warehouse to determine what financial effects changes to a benefit in a specific product will have. This provides the salesforce with the right offering at the right price for specific target markets in South Africa.

Discussion Questions

1. How did Medihelp's use of a traditional database limit what it could do with its data?
2. How does Medihelp's salesforce now use the information in the company's data warehouse?

Critical Thinking Questions

1. How did B.I. Practice improve the efficiency of queries run by Medihelp employees?
2. How does the new query system help Medihelp make better decisions for the company? Does Medihelp also use the system to help its clients make better decisions? If so, how?

SOURCES: "Medihelp Recognized by Computerworld as 2011 Honors Laureate," *www.bipractice.co.za/index.php?option=com_content&view= article&id=65:medihelp-recognised-by-computerworld-as-a-2011-honors -laureate&catid=2:bi-news&Itemid=8*, accessed November 18, 2013; "Medihelp Customer Case Study," Success Stories, Sybase Web site, *www.sybase.com/detail?id=1095243*, accessed November 18, 2013.

Case Two

HanaTour: Gaining Customer Trust through Increased Security

HanaTour International Service is South Korea's largest provider of overseas travel services and air tickets. HanaTour employs nearly 2,500 people in Korea and travel agents outside Korea to provide clients with travel information for about 26 regions worldwide.

HanaTour customers who book travel provide the company with personal details, including their addresses, contact phone numbers, dates of birth, passport numbers, and payment information. These details, along with their airline and tour bookings and travel itineraries, are stored in HanaTour's database. The confidential nature of this information means HanaTour must have security measures in place to protect the database from unauthorized access.

In addition to these marketplace requirements, HanaTour must comply with South Korea's Electronic Communication Privacy Act. This act requires industries to take measures to protect the privacy of personal information. Thus, protecting customer data is not only good business, but also a legal requirement.

To improve database security, HanaTour added data encryption, both in the database and during transmission. The company also implemented access control based on individual authorizations and assigned tasks. To discourage hacker attacks, HanaTour blocked database access even if a hacker obtained top-level administrator privileges for the system. It created an audit trail of database access to spot suspicious activities so that action could be taken immediately. It also published reports to show compliance with security requirements and used audit information to develop further security plans.

Like most small- and medium-sized firms, HanaTour does not need the skills that this security upgrade called for on a permanent full-time basis. Rather than hiring and training staff members to address short-term needs and then releasing or finding other work for these employees, HanaTour engaged specialists. The company worked with Korean database consulting firm Wizbase. HanaTour had worked with Wizbase previously, so it didn't have to spend time explaining basic information about how HanaTour's business works.

The net result of these actions was to make it much more difficult for unauthorized people to see any of the personal information that HanaTour customers supplied. Did this help HanaTour? According to Kim Jin-hwan, director of the HanaTour's IT department, "Our business is based on service. We do not want anything to go wrong on a customer's holiday that will inconvenience them. Lost data or any disruptions to our system would affect our ability to provide optimum service. We upgraded our database to improve performance and take advantage of new security features, which would minimize the risk of losing confidential customer data and strengthen our database and systems from unlawful access."

Discussion Questions

1. From the user side, Mr. Kim said that HanaTour upgraded to a new release of its database management software due to its improved security features. What are the business advantages of improved security?
2. How does HanaTour use the data it collects from the audit to increase the security of its data?

Critical Thinking Questions

1. HanaTour chose Wizbase as its implementation partner in part because of prior experience with that firm. Many small-to-medium companies need to outsource security tasks because they lack the expertise. Does this present an added security risk? Why or why not?
2. Think of the data that your university's database has about students as a large table, with a row for each student and a column for each data element. Group the data into major categories such as contact data, medical data, financial data, and academic data. Which groups of people, by job, should have access to each category? Within a group, who should have access to only one row, who should have access to more than one row but not all rows, and who should have access to all rows of the table? Should anyone be allowed to see data but not change it?

SOURCES: Forrester Research, "Formulate a Database Security Strategy to Ensure Investments Will Actually Prevent Data Breaches and Satisfy Regulatory Requirements," *www.oracle.com/us/corporate/analystreports /infrastructure/forrester-thlp-db-security-1445564.pdf*, July 13, 2011; HanaTour Web site, *www.hanatour.com*, accessed May 8, 2012; Staff, "HanaTour International Service Tightens Customer Data Security by Introducing Data Encryption, Access Control, and Audit Solutions," Oracle, *www.oracle.com/us/corporate/customers/customersearch/hanatour -intl-1-database-cs-1521219.html*, accessed February 13, 2012.

Questions for Web Case

See the Web site for this book to read about the Altitude Online case for this chapter. Following are questions concerning this Web case.

Altitude Online: Database Systems, Data Centers, and Business Intelligence

Discussion Questions

1. What work is involved in merging multiple databases into one central database, as Altitude Online is doing?
2. Why do you think Altitude Online found it necessary to hire a database administrator? How will the ERP affect the responsibilities of IS personnel across the organization?

Critical Thinking Questions

1. In a major move such as this, what opportunities can Altitude Online take advantage of as it totally revamps its database system that it perhaps wouldn't have considered before?
2. Why do you think Altitude Online is beginning work on its database prior to selecting an ERP vendor?

NOTES

Sources for the opening vignette: Reinhardt, Anders, "SAP: VELUX 100% BI Strategy—100% Technology—100% Business Value," presentation by Anders Reinhardt, head of global business intelligence for VELUS, in Oslo, Norway, June 11, 2013; Elliott, Timo, "VELUX: A New Business Intelligence Strategy to Meet New Needs," Business Analytics, June 18, 2013. The VELUX Group Web site.

1. "Oracle Audit Vault and Database Firewall," Oracle, *www.oracle.com/us/products/database/security/audit*

-vault-database-firewall/overview/index.html accessed November 7, 2013.

2. Auditore, Peter and Everitt, George, "The Anatomy of Big Data," Sand Hill, September 11, 2012, *http://sandhill .com/article/the-anatomy-of-big-data*.

3. "New Government Database Tracks Immigration Violations," June 21, 2013, *www.fragomen.com/germany-06-21-2013*.

4. "Letter from Kris Monteith, Acting Bureau Chief Consumer and Governmental Affairs Bureau," July 1, 2013, *http://files.ctia.org/pdf/130701_-_FILED_CTIA_July_ 1st_Stolen_Phones_Status_Report.pdf*.

5. Neff, Jack, "Dunnhumby: Time to Ditch the Demographic," *Advertising Age*, February 11, 2013, *http://adage.com/article/news/dunnhumby-time-ditch -demographic/239689*.

6. "Zoomlion Combines Quality, Efficiency and Global Value with SAP and IBM," IBM Alliance Solutions, November 24, 2013, *www-01.ibm.com/software /success/cssdb.nsf/CS/STRD-9CRFMA?OpenDocument& Site=default&cty=en_us*.

7. "Harrison College Replaces WhatsUp Gold with Server & Application Monitor for More Robust Application Monitoring," *http://web.swcdn.net/creative/pdf /casestudies/1211_sam_harrison_college_cs.pdf*, accessed November 10, 2013.

8. "Oracle Is #1 in the RDBMS Market Share Worldwide for 2012," *www.oracle.com/us/corporate/features /number-one-database/index.html*, accessed November 10, 2013.

9. "Intuit, Inc.," *www.sybase.com/detail?id=1061721*, accessed November 11, 2013.

10. Proffitt, Brian, "FoundationDB's NoSQL Breakthrough Challenges Relational Database Dominance," Read Write, March 8, 2013, *http://readwrite.com/2013/03/08 /foundationdbs-nosql-breakthrough-challenges-relational -database-dominance#awesm=~oncfIkqw3jiMOJ*.

11. Ibid.

12. Harris, Derrick, "The History of Hadoop from 4 Nodes to the Future of Data," Gigaom, March 4, 2013, *http:// gigaom.com/2013/03/04/the-history-of-hadoop-from-4 -nodes-to-the-future-of-data/2/*.

13. Palmer, Carol, Steinger, Jim, Lopez, Xavier, Ihm, Jean, "Oracle Database 12c: An Introduction to Oracle's Loca- tion Technologies, Oracle Corporation, June 2013, *http:// download.oracle.com/otndocs/products/spatial /pdf/12c/oraspatialandgraph_12c_wp_intro_to_ location_technologies.pdf*.

14. Golden, Matt, "New DOE Effort to Standardize the Energy Efficiency Data Dictionary," EDF Blogs, August 8, 2013, *http://blogs.edf.org/energyexchange/2013/08/08 /new-doe-effort-to-standardize-the-energy-efficiency -data-dictionary*.

15. Goodin, Dan, "Database Hacking Spree on US Army, NASA, and Others Costs Gov't Millions," *ars technica*, October 28, 2013, *http://arstechnica.com/security/2013 /10/database-hacking-spree-on-us-army-nasa-and -others-cost-gov-millions*.

16. "AWS Case Study: Fairfax Media," *http://aws.amazon .com/solutions/case-studies/fairfax-media*, accessed November 20, 2013.

17. Laney, Doug, "3D Data Management: Controlling Data Volume, Velocity, and Variety," META Group, February 6, 2001, *http://blogs.gartner.com/doug-laney/files/2012 /01/ad949-3D-Data-Management-Controlling-Data -Volume-Velocity-and-Variety.pdf*.

18. Karr, Douglas, "Infographic: Big Data Brings Marketing Big Numbers," Marketing Tech Blog, May 9, 2012, *www .marketingtechblog.com/ibm-big-data-marketing*.

19. "Seminars about Long Term Thinking," *http://longnow .org/seminars/02013/mar/19/no-time-there-digital -universe-and-why-things-appear-be-speeding*, accessed November 8, 2013.

20. Rosenbaum, Steven, "Is It Possible to Analyze Digital Data If It's Growing Exponentially?" Fast Company, January 13, 2013, *www.fastcompany.com/3005128/it-possible -analyze-digital-data-if-its-growing-exponentially*.

21. Ibid.

22. "The Large Hadron Collider," *http://home.web.cern .ch/topics/large-hadron-collider*, accessed April 7, 2014.

23. Brocke, Jan vom, "In-Memory Database Business Value," Business Innovation, July 25, 2013.

24. "About the United States Postal Service," *http://about .usps.com/who-we-are/postal-facts/welcome.htm#H1*, accessed November 9, 2013.

25. Moore, John, "In-Memory Technology Speeds Up Data Analytics," CIO, June 26, 2013, *www.cio.com/article /735379/In_Memory_Technology_Speeds_Up_Data _Analytics*.

26. De La Hera, Maria, "Business Intelligence, The Key to Company Success," EzineArticles, November 16, 2013, *http://ezinearticles.com/?Business-Intelligence,-The-Key -To-Company-Success&id=8125069*.

27. Palace, Bill, "Data Mining—What Is Data Mining?" *www.anderson.ucla.edu/faculty/jason.frand/teacher /technologies/palace/datamining.htm*, accessed November 21, 2013.

28. Berthiaume, Dan, "Sprouts Rolls Out Manthan BI Solution," Chain Store Age, *www.chainstoreage.com /article/sprouts-rolls-out-manthan-bi-solution*, accessed November 21, 2013.

29. "Chatmine Success Stories Jansen Pharmaceuticals", *www.chatmine.com/success-stories*, accessed November 21, 2013.

30. Ungerleider, Neal, "Samsung's New TVs Data-Mine Viewing Habits," Fast Company, March 30, 2013, *www .fastcompany.com/3007270/most-innovative-companies -2013/samsungs-new-tvs-data-mine-viewing-habits*.

31. Booker, Ellis, "Human Resources Tentatively Tries Predictive Analytics," *Information Week*, November 20, 2013, *www.informationweek.com/strategic-cio/team -building-and-staffing/human-resources-tentatively -tries-predictive-analytics/d/d-id/1112697*.

32. Condé Nast About Us, *www.condenast.com/about-us*, accessed November 21, 2013.

33. "Condé Nast: Marketing Analytics," *www.angoss.com /wp-content/uploads/2011/06/Conde_Nast_Segmentation _Response_Modeling.pdf*, accessed November 21, 2013.

34. Auditore, Peter and Everitt, George, "The Anatomy of Big Data," Sand Hill, September 11, 2012, *http:// sandhill.com/article/the-anatomy-of-big-data*.

35. Financial Services Practice Client Success Stories, *www .fuld.com/services/case-studies*, accessed November 22, 2013.

6 Telecommunications and Networks

© Iiolab/Shutterstock.com

Principles	Learning Objectives
A telecommunications system consists of several fundamental components.	• Identify and describe the fundamental components of a telecommunications system. • Discuss two broad categories of telecommunications media and their associated characteristics. • Briefly describe several options for short-range, medium-range, and long-range communications.
Networks are an essential component of an organization's information technology infrastructure.	• Identify the benefits of using a network. • Describe three distributed processing alternatives and discuss their basic features. • Identify several telecommunications hardware devices and discuss their functions.
Network applications are essential to organizational success.	• List and describe several network applications that organizations benefit from today.

Information Systems in the Global Economy
WESTERMO, SWEDEN

Working to Reduce Railway Accidents

© iStockphoto.com/JPecha

In the early morning hours of Sunday, December 1, 2013, train engineer William Rockefeller succumbed to what his lawyer called "highway hypnosis." Dozing off for a minute or so, Rockefeller didn't slow the Hudson line train as it came around a sharp bend at the intersection of the Harlem and Hudson rivers. The speed limit at the bend was 30 miles an hour. The train derailed from the track at 82 miles per hour, killing four and injuring dozens of others. The city and the nation were in shock, and some began asking why an alarm did not sound when the train exceeded the speed limit to alert a control room or wake the engineer.

Around the world—in Egypt, Chile, South Africa, Japan, and many other countries—hundreds of people die or are injured in railway accidents. To reduce derailments and collisions, the railway industry has been looking for affordable strategies. Some companies are increasingly turning to new Ethernet technologies, a family of computer network technologies that specify the communications media and signaling to be used on a local area network.

Westermo, a global industrial data communications company based in Sweden, is at the forefront of developing these technologies. Electronic devices located along the track and within the train car send input about a train's speed, position, status, track shifters, and gates to a control room, located in the station. This station is often located far from these devices, and the control room must receive and analyze a large amount of data simultaneously. The data must be sent through a speedy and reliable system.

Previously, this communication was carried out through analog devices. Unlike digital devices, analog devices communicate through signals that represent physical quantities that change continuously and degrade as they are transmitted over long distances. Westermo's Ethernet solutions, however, provide for a massive 100 Mbits data flow of digital signals along the cables. Its Ethernet switches are built tough, with metal housing that allows the switches to withstand extreme temperatures and temporary power glitches. The company uses Fast Reconfiguration of Networks Topology (FRNT) to overcome failures in network links and switches.

Ferrovie Nord Milano, the second-largest railway company in Italy, recently installed Westermo's Ethernet solutions in 32 stations along fiber-optic cables, which support faster communications, but are more expensive than telephone wires. However, Westermo technology can also be used to run Ethernet networks over old copper wires. The Massachusetts Bay Commuter Railroad, servicing a 500-mile area within and around the city of Boston, used Westermo Ethernet extenders, devices that can physically extend an Ethernet or a network beyond its standard 330-foot limitation, to run a network on copper wires that had been installed in the Worcester area 35 years ago. The networks run over long distances, with data rates as high as 15.3 Mbits.

Ethernet networks are key to helping major railroad companies gather and interpret data so that they can increase efficiency, reduce costs, and increase safety. Although the railway system in New York did not have a system in place to prevent the tragic derailment in December 2013, companies such as Westermo are developing solutions that railway companies around the world will be able to leverage to prevent accidents like this in the future.

As you read this chapter, consider the following:

- How are telecommunications and network technologies supporting economic progress and improving safety?
- What qualities do these technologies have that make them so useful?

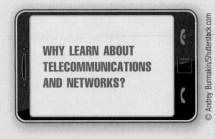

WHY LEARN ABOUT TELECOMMUNICATIONS AND NETWORKS?

Effective communication is essential to the success of every major human undertaking, from building great cities to waging war to running a modern organization. Today, we use electronic messaging and networking to enable people everywhere to communicate and interact effectively without requiring face-to-face meetings. Regardless of your chosen major or career field, you will need the communications capabilities provided by telecommunications and networks, especially if your work involves the supply chain. Among all business functions, supply chain management probably uses telecommunications and networks the most because it requires cooperation and communications among workers in inbound logistics, warehouse and storage, production, finished product storage, outbound logistics, and, most important, with customers, suppliers, and shippers. All members of the supply chain must work together effectively to increase the value perceived by the customer, so partners must communicate well. Other employees in human resources, finance, research and development, marketing, and sales positions must also use communications technology to communicate with people inside and outside the organization. To be a successful member of any organization, you must be able to take advantage of the capabilities that these technologies offer you. This chapter begins by discussing the importance of effective communications.

In today's high-speed global business world, organizations need always-on, always-connected computing for traveling employees and for network connections to their key business partners and customers. Forward-thinking organizations strive to increase revenue, reduce time to market, and enable collaboration with their suppliers, customers, and business partners by using telecommunications systems. Here are just a few examples of organizations using telecommunications and networks to move ahead:

- Wasko S.A., a leading Polish information systems organization, designed and implemented a major computing center to serve the BIO-PHARMA consortium consisting of the Silesian University of Technology, the Maria Sklodowska-Curie Memorial Cancer Center, the Medical University of Silesia, and the University of Silesia. The cluster consists of 105 blade servers and a large data storage system interconnected via a telecommunications backbone capable of transporting data at 10 Gb/sec. The system is used to support scientists in their search for an effective cure for cancer. The computing center is designed to perform extremely fast calculations and provide security and backup to prevent data loss.[1]
- Telecommunications and networks make it possible for you to access a wealth of educational material and earn certifications or an online degree. A wide range of courses are available online from such leading educational institutions as Cornell, Carnegie Mellon, Harvard, MIT, UCLA, and Yale. Many education organizations such as Coursesa, ed2Go, and Kahn Academy offer continuing education, certification programs, and professional development courses. Schools such as the University of Phoenix and Strayer University enable students to earn online degrees.
- US Storage Centers is a self-storage operator with over 70 facilities in 12 states. It is the first firm in the storage industry to offer an electronic cash-transaction service to its tenants. The service runs on the PayNearMe network and enables tenants to pay their rent at any of 10,000 retail

locations nationwide. Tenants submit a barcoded PayNearMe PaySlip along with their payment to the cashier, and their accounts are immediately credited.[2]

- The New Orleans Ernest N. Morial Convention Center with 1.1 million square feet of exhibit space is the sixth-largest convention center in the nation and a consistent Top 10 host of the largest number of conventions and tradeshows annually. The convention center implemented a wireless network to provide a high-density, portable Wi-Fi connectivity solution, supporting voice, video, and data access across a large area to serve thousands of users simultaneously.[3]

AN OVERVIEW OF TELECOMMUNICATIONS

Telecommunications refers to the electronic transmission of signals for communications by means such as telephone, radio, and television. Telecommunications is creating profound changes in business because it lessens the barriers of time and distance. Advances in telecommunications technology allow us to communicate rapidly with business partners, clients, and coworkers almost anywhere in the world. Telecommunications also reduces the amount of time needed to transmit information that can drive and conclude business actions. It is changing not only the way organizations operate but the nature of commerce itself. As networks connect to one another and transmit information more freely, a competitive marketplace demands excellent quality and service from all organizations.

Figure 6.1 shows a general model of telecommunications. The model starts with a sending unit (1) such as a person, a computer system, a terminal, or another device that originates the message. The sending unit transmits a signal (2) to a telecommunications device (3). The telecommunications device—a hardware component that facilitates electronic communication—performs many tasks, which can include converting the signal into a different form or from one type to another. The telecommunications device then sends the signal through a medium (4). A **telecommunications medium** is any material substance that carries an electronic signal to support communications between a sending and a receiving device. Another telecommunications device (5) connected to the receiving device (6) receives the signal. The process can be reversed, and the receiving unit (6) can send a message to the original sending unit (1). An important characteristic of telecommunications is the speed at which information is transmitted, which is measured in bits per second (bps). Common speeds are in the range of thousands of bits per second (Kbps) to millions of bits per second (Mbps) and even billions of bits per second (Gbps).

telecommunications medium: Any material substance that carries an electronic signal to support communications between a sending and a receiving device.

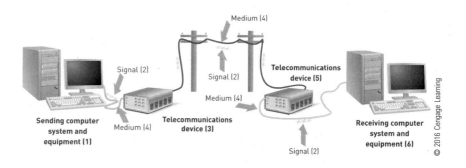

FIGURE 6.1

Elements of a telecommunications system

Telecommunications devices relay signals between computer systems and transmission media.

networking protocol: A set of rules, algorithms, messages, and other mechanisms that enable software and hardware in networked devices to communicate effectively.

A **networking protocol** is a set of rules, algorithms, messages, and other mechanisms that enable software and hardware in networked devices to communicate effectively. The goal is to ensure fast, efficient, error-free communications and to enable hardware, software, and equipment manufacturers and service providers to build products that interoperate effectively. The Institute of Electrical and Electronics Engineers (IEEE) is a leading standards-setting organization whose IEEE network standards are the basis for many telecommunications devices and services. The International Telecommunication Union (ITU) is a specialized agency of the United Nations, with headquarters in Geneva, Switzerland. The international standards produced by the ITU are known as Recommendations and carry a high degree of formal international recognition.

Communications between two people can occur synchronously or asynchronously. With synchronous communications, the receiver gets the message as soon as it is sent. Voice and phone communications are examples of synchronous communications. With asynchronous communications, the receiver gets the message after some delay—a few seconds to minutes or hours or even days after the message is sent. Sending a letter through the post office or an email over the Internet are examples of asynchronous communications. Both types of communications are important in business. See Figure 6.2.

FIGURE **6.2**

Telecommunications increases collaboration

Telecommunications technology enables businesspeople to communicate with coworkers and clients from remote locations.

Most colleges and universities today offer distance learning courses using telecommunications hardware and software that enables instructors to connect to students anywhere in the world. Students can elect to attend a synchronous class where they attend the online course with the instructor at the same time and where they can see and hear the instructor in real time and interact by asking questions. Other students can attend asynchronous classes in which they participate at any time that is convenient to them. They see a slide presentation, and if they have questions, they can correspond with the instructor via email. Harvard University Extension School offers hundreds of distance learning courses each term. The courses employ either online video of faculty lecturing on campus or Web conferencing where students communicate in a live session with the instructor by chat or voice technology.[4]

Basic Telecommunications Channel Characteristics

The transmission medium carries messages from the source of the message to its receivers. A transmission medium can be divided into one or more telecommunications channels, each capable of carrying a message. Telecommunications channels can be classified as simplex, half-duplex, or full-duplex.

simplex channel: A communications channel that can transmit data in only one direction and is seldom used for business telecommunications.

half-duplex channel: A communications channel that can transmit data in either direction but not simultaneously.

full-duplex channel: A communications channel that permits data transmission in both directions at the same time; a full-duplex channel is like two simplex channels.

channel bandwidth: The rate at which data is exchanged, usually measured in bps.

broadband communications: A relative term but it generally means a telecommunications system that can transmit data very quickly.

circuit-switching network: A network that sets up a circuit between the sender and receiver before any communications can occur; this circuit is maintained for the duration of the communication and cannot be used to support any other communications until the circuit is released and a new connection is set up.

packet-switching network: A network in which no fixed path is created between the communicating devices, and the data is broken into packets, with each packet transmitted individually and capable of taking various paths from sender to recipient.

A simplex channel can transmit data in only one direction and is seldom used for business telecommunications. Doorbells and the radio operate using a simplex channel. A half-duplex channel can transmit data in either direction but not simultaneously. For example, A can begin transmitting to B over a half-duplex line, but B must wait until A is finished to transmit back to A. Personal computers are usually connected to a remote computer over a half-duplex channel. A full-duplex channel permits data transmission in both directions at the same time, so a full-duplex channel is like two simplex channels. Private leased lines or two standard phone lines are required for full-duplex transmission.

Channel Bandwidth

In addition to the direction of data flow supported by a telecommunications channel, you must consider the speed at which data can be transmitted. Telecommunications channel bandwidth refers to the rate at which data is exchanged, usually measured in bps—the broader the bandwidth, the more information can be exchanged at one time. Broadband communications is a relative term, but it generally means a telecommunications system that can transmit data very quickly. For example, for wireless networks, broadband lets you send and receive data at a rate greater than 1.5 Mbps.

Telecommunications professionals consider the capacity of the channel when they recommend transmission media for a business. In general, today's organizations need more bandwidth than they did even a few years ago for increased transmission speed to carry out their daily functions.

Circuit Switching and Packet Switching

Circuit switching and packet switching are two different means for routing data from the communications sender to the receiver. In a circuit-switching network, a dedicated path is first established to create a permanent circuit that connects the communicating devices. This path is committed and then used for the duration of the communication. Because it is dedicated, the circuit cannot be used to support communications from other users or sending devices until the circuit is released and a new connection is set up. The traditional telephone network is a circuit-switching network.

In a packet-switching network, no fixed path is created between the communicating devices, and the data is broken into packets for sending over the network. Each packet is transmitted individually and is capable of taking various paths from sender to receiver. Because the communication paths are not dedicated, packets from multiple users and communicating devices can travel over the same communication path. Once all the packets forming a message arrive at the destination, they are compiled into the original message. The Internet is an example of a packet-switching network that employs the packet-switching protocol called TCP/IP.

The advantage of a circuit-switching network is that it provides for the nonstop transfer of data without the overhead of assembling and disassembling data into packets and determining which routes packets should follow. Circuit-switching networks are best when data must arrive in exactly the same order in which it is sent. This is the case with most real-time data such as live audio and video.

Packet-switching networks are more efficient at using the channel bandwidth because packets from multiple conversations can share the same communications links. However, there can be delays in the delivery of messages due to network congestion and the loss of packets or the delivery of packets out of order. Thus, packet-switching networks are used to communicate data that can withstand some delays in transmission, such as email messages and the sending of large data files. Another key consideration in setting up a network is choosing the type of telecommunications media to use.

Telecommunications Media

Each telecommunications media type can be evaluated according to characteristics such as cost, capacity, and speed. In designing a telecommunications system, the transmission media selected depends on the amount of information to be exchanged, on the speed at which data must be exchanged, on the level of concern for data privacy, on whether the users are stationary or mobile, and on many other business requirements. The transmission media are selected to support the communications goals of the organization systems that are at the lowest cost but that still allow for possible modifications should business requirements change. Transmission media can be divided into two broad categories: *wired* (sometimes called *guided*) *transmission media*, in which telecommunications signals are guided along a solid medium, and *wireless*, in which the telecommunications signal is broadcast over airwaves as a form of electromagnetic radiation.

Guided Transmission Media Types

There are many types of wired transmission media. Table 6.1 summarizes three common wired media types by physical media type. These wired transmission media types are discussed in the following sections.

TABLE **6.1** Guided transmission media types

Media Type	Description	Advantages	Disadvantages
Twisted-pair wire	Twisted pairs of copper wire, shielded or unshielded	Used for telephone service; widely available	Transmission speed and distance limitations
Coaxial cable	Inner conductor wire surrounded by insulation	Cleaner and faster data transmission than twisted-pair wire	More expensive than twisted-pair wire
Fiber-optic cable	Many extremely thin strands of glass bound together in a sheathing; uses light beams to transmit signals	Diameter of cable is much smaller than coaxial cable; less distortion of signal; capable of high transmission rates	Expensive to purchase and install

© 2016 Cengage Learning

Twisted-Pair Wire

Twisted-pair wire contains two or more twisted pairs of wires, usually copper, as shown in Figure 6.3 (left). Proper twisting of the wire keeps the signal from "bleeding" into the next pair and creating electrical interference. Because the twisted-pair wires are insulated, they can be placed close together and packaged in one group, with hundreds of wire pairs being grouped into one large wire cable. Twisted-pair wires are classified by category (Category 2, 3, 5, 5E, and 6—there is no Category 1, and Category 4 is no longer used). The lower categories are used primarily in homes. Higher categories are used in networks and can carry data at higher speeds. For example, 10-Gigabit Ethernet is a standard for transmitting data in full-duplex mode at the speed of 10 billion bps for limited distances over Category 5 or 6 twisted-pair wire. The 10-Gigabit Ethernet cable can be used for the high-speed links that connect groups of computers or to move data stored in large databases on large computers to stand-alone storage devices.

Chi-X Japan provides investors with an alternative venue for trading in Tokyo-listed stocks. Its goal is to attract new international investors, in turn increasing overall Japanese market volumes, reducing transaction costs, and improving investment performance.[5] The firm implemented 10 Gbps Ethernet network adapters to upgrade its network and provide customers minimal transaction processing delays. "We are excited about our upgrade to 10GbE, as it will introduce greater trading efficiencies and enhancements for all participants from day one," said Samson Yuen, CTO, Chi-X Japan. "As we look ahead, Chi-X Japan is committed to technology investments that reduce trading costs and introduce greater trading efficiencies to our customers."[6]

Coaxial Cable

Figure 6.3 (middle) shows a typical coaxial cable, similar to that used in cable television installations. When used for data transmission, coaxial cable falls in the middle of the guided transmission media in terms of cost and performance. The cable itself is more expensive than twisted-pair wire but less than fiber-optic cable (discussed next). However, the cost of installation and other necessary communications equipment makes it difficult to compare the total costs of each medium. Coaxial cable offers cleaner and crisper data transmission (less noise) than twisted-pair wire and also a higher data transmission rate.

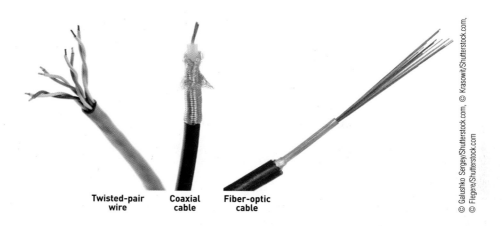

FIGURE 6.3

Types of guided transmission media

Common guided transmission media include twisted-pair wire, coaxial cable, and fiber-optic cable.

Twisted-pair wire   Coaxial cable   Fiber-optic cable

© Galushko Sergey/Shutterstock.com, © Krasowit/Shutterstock.com, © Flegere/Shutterstock.com

Many cable companies, including Time Warner, Cox Communications, Cablevision, and Comcast, aggressively court customers for telephone service. They entice people away from phone companies by offering highly discounted rates for bundled high-speed Internet and phone services along with services phone companies do not offer, such as TV and new movies on-demand the same day as the DVD is released.

Fiber-Optic Cable

Fiber-optic cable, consisting of many extremely thin strands of glass or plastic bound together in a sheathing (also known as a jacket), transmits signals with light beams. See Figure 6.3 (right). These high-intensity light beams are generated by lasers and are conducted along the transparent fibers. These fibers have a thin coating, called *cladding*, which works like a mirror, preventing the light from leaking out of the fiber. The much smaller diameter of fiber-optic cable makes it ideal when there is no room for bulky copper wires—for example, in crowded conduits, which can be pipes or spaces carrying both electrical and communications wires. Fiber-optic cable and associated telecommunications devices are more expensive to purchase and install than their twisted-pair wire counterparts, although the cost is decreasing.

FiOS is a bundled set of communications services, including Internet, telephone, and high-definition TV, that operates over a total fiber-optic communications network. With this service, fiber-optic cable is run from the carrier's local exchange all the way to the customer's premises. (Cable networks often use fiber optic in their network backbone that connects their local exchanges, but they do not run fiber optic to the customer's premises). FiOS is offered from Verizon in selected portions of the United States with Internet speeds of 15 to 150 Mbps. At top speed, it takes just four minutes to download a two-hour movie (500 MB).[7] A shortcoming of this service is that a power outage at the premises means no FiOS service. A battery backup unit is advisable to avoid this potential problem.

Wireless Communications Options

Wireless communications coupled with the Internet are revolutionizing how and where we gather and share information, collaborate in teams, listen to music or watch videos, and stay in touch with our families, friends, and co-workers while on the road. With wireless capability, a coffee shop can become our living room, and the bleachers at a ball park can become our office. The many advantages and freedom provided by wireless communications are causing many organizations to consider moving to an all-wireless environment.

Wireless transmission involves the broadcast of communications in one of three frequency ranges: radio, microwave, or infrared, as shown in Table 6.2. In some cases, the use of wireless communications is regulated, and the signal must be broadcast within a specific frequency range to avoid interference with other wireless transmissions. For example, radio and TV stations must gain Federal Communications Commission (FCC) approval to use a certain frequency to broadcast their signals. Where wireless communications are not regulated, there is a high potential for interference between signals.

TABLE 6.2 Frequency ranges used for wireless communications

Technology	Description	Advantages	Disadvantages
Radio frequency range	Operates in the 3 kHz–300 MHz range	Supports mobile users; costs are dropping	Signal highly susceptible to interception
Microwave—terrestrial and satellite frequency range	High-frequency radio signal (300 MHz–300 GHz) sent through atmosphere and space (often involves communications satellites)	Avoids cost and effort to lay cable or wires; capable of high-speed transmission	Must have unobstructed line of sight between sender and receiver; signal highly susceptible to interception
Infrared frequency range	Signals in the 300 GHz–400 THz frequency range sent through air as light waves	Allows you to move, remove, and install devices without expensive wiring	Must have unobstructed line of sight between sender and receiver; transmission effective only for short distances

© 2016 Cengage Learning

With the spread of wireless network technology to support devices such as smartphones, mobile computers, and cell phones, the telecommunications industry needed new protocols to define how these hardware devices and their associated software would interoperate on the networks provided by telecommunications carriers. More than 70 active groups are setting standards at the regional, national, and global levels, resulting in a dizzying array of communications standards and options. Some of the more widely used wireless communications options are discussed next.

Short-Range Wireless Options

Many wireless solutions provide communications over very short distances, including Near Field Communications, Bluetooth, ultra wideband, infrared transmission, and ZigBee.

Near Field Communication (NFC)

Near Field Communication (NFC): A very short-range wireless connectivity technology designed for consumer electronics, cell phones, and credit cards.

Near Field Communication (NFC) is a very short-range wireless connectivity technology designed for consumer electronics, cell phones, and credit cards. Once two NFC-enabled devices are in proximity (touching or a few centimeters apart), they exchange the necessary communications parameters and passwords to enable Bluetooth, Wi-Fi, or other wireless communications between the devices. Because only two devices participate in the communications, NFC establishes a peer-to-peer network.

France-based Store Electronic Systems is deploying millions of NFC tags in electronic retail chains throughout France. Shoppers can tap their NFC phones to view product information, including allergens and nutritional data as well as information on the product's origins and manufacturing chain. See Figure 6.4. Shoppers can also gain access to loyalty programs to earn points, view marketing information, and share content and interact with brands via social media.[8]

FIGURE **6.4**

NFC-enabled shelf tags

Shoppers can tap their NFC phones to view product information, including price, allergens, and nutritional data.

Bluetooth: A wireless communications specification that describes how cell phones, computers, faxes, personal digital assistants, printers, and other electronic devices can be interconnected over distances of 10 to 30 feet at a rate of about 2 Mbps.

Bluetooth is a wireless communications specification that describes how cell phones, computers, printers, and other electronic devices can be interconnected over distances of 10 to 30 feet at a rate of about 2 Mbps and allows users of multifunctional devices to synchronize with information in a desktop computer, send or receive faxes, print, and, in general, coordinate all mobile and fixed computer devices. The Bluetooth technology is named after the tenth-century Danish King Harald Blatand, or Harold Bluetooth in English. He had been instrumental in uniting warring factions in parts of what is now Norway, Sweden, and Denmark, just as the technology named after him is designed to allow collaboration among differing devices such as computers, phones, and other electronic devices.

As more states are banning the use of handheld cell phones in cars, one of the most important accessories for smartphone users is their hands-free Bluetooth headset. Drivers can also use the hands-free system in their cars to have their email messages, notes, calendar entries, and text messages read aloud over the car's speakers.

The Bluetooth G-Shock watch enables you to make a connection between your watch and phone. For example, you can control the phone's music player from the watch and watch's timekeeping functions from the phone.

Ultra Wideband

ultra wideband (UWB): A form of short-range communications that employs extremely short electromagnetic pulses lasting just 50 to 1,000 picoseconds that are transmitted across a broad range of radio frequencies of several gigahertz.

Ultra wideband (UWB) communications involves the transmission of extremely short electromagnetic pulses lasting just 50 to 1,000 picoseconds. (One picosecond is one trillionth or one-millionth of one-millionth of a second.) The pulses are capable of supporting data transmission rates of 480 to 1,320 Mbps over a relatively short range of 10 to 50 meters.[9] UWB provides several advantages over other communications methods, including a high throughput rate, the ability to transmit virtually undetected and impervious to interception or jamming, and a lack of interference with current communications services.

Potential UWB applications include wirelessly connecting printers and other devices to desktop computers or enabling completely wireless home multimedia networks. Manufacturers of medical instruments are using UWB for video endoscopes, laryngoscopes, and ultrasound transducers.[10]

Infrared Transmission

infrared transmission: A form of communications that sends signals at a frequency of 300 GHz and above—higher than those of microwaves but lower than those of visible light.

Infrared transmission sends signals at a frequency of 300 GHz and above—higher than those of microwaves but lower than those of visible light. It is frequently used in wireless networks, intrusion detectors, home entertainment remote control, and fire sensors. Infrared transmission requires line-of-sight transmission and short distances—such as a few yards. It allows handheld computers to transmit data and information to larger computers within the same room and to connect a display screen, printer, and mouse to a computer.

Temperature and humidity monitoring sensors are frequently used in computer data centers, hospitals, laboratories, museums, warehouses, wine production, and storage facilities.

ZigBee

ZigBee: A developing network wireless communications standard designed to carry small amounts of data at fairly low bandwidth of 20 Kbps to 250 Kbps over midrange distances or 100 meters or so using very little power.

ZigBee is a developing network wireless communications standard designed to carry small amounts of data at a fairly low bandwidth of 20 Kbps to 250 Kbps over midrange distances (100 meters or so) using very little power. It is frequently used in security systems and for sensing and controlling energy-consuming devices, such as lighting and heating, ventilation, and air conditioning (HVAC) in both residential homes and commercial buildings.

A smart home employs a network to connect sensors that control devices within the home to the Internet. Users control the devices by accessing a Web site or using mobile devices such as a smartphone or tablet computer. The sensors communicate over a wireless network to a central controller that has access to the Internet. The home owner can remotely adjust the lights, control the climate, arm the security system, lock and unlock doors, and measure carbon monoxide and smoke levels. A number of organizations such as Lowe's, AT&T, Verizon, and Home Depot sell or install such systems for the home. ZigBee is often used as the wireless network to connect all the sensors within the home.

Medium-Range Wireless Options

Wi-Fi: A medium-range wireless telecommunications technology brand owned by the Wi-Fi Alliance.

Wi-Fi is a wireless telecommunications technology brand owned by the Wi-Fi Alliance, which consists of about 300 technology companies, including AT&T, Dell, Microsoft, Nokia, and Qualcomm. The alliance exists to improve the interoperability of wireless local area network products based on the IEEE 802.11 series of telecommunications standards. IEEE is a nonprofit organization and one of the leading standards-setting organizations. Table 6.3 summarizes several variations of this standard.

With a Wi-Fi wireless network, the user's computer, smartphone, or cell phone has a wireless adapter that translates data into a radio signal and transmits it using an antenna. The antennas transmit at frequencies of 2.4 GHz or 5.0 GHz. A wireless access point, which consists of a transmitter with an antenna, receives the signal and decodes it. The access point then sends the information to the Internet over a wired connection, as shown in Figure 6.5. When receiving data, the wireless access point takes the information from the Internet, translates it into a radio signal, and sends it to the device's wireless adapter. These devices typically come with built-in wireless transmitters and software that enable them to alert the user to the existence of a Wi-Fi network. The area covered by one or more interconnected wireless access points is called

TABLE **6.3** IEEE 802.11 wireless local area networking standards

Wireless Networking Protocol	Maximum Data Rate per Data Stream	Comments
IEEE 802.11a	54 Mbps	Transmits at 5 GHz so that it is incompatible with 802.11b and 802.11g
IEEE 802.11b	11 Mbps	First widely accepted wireless network standard and transmits at 2.4 GHz; equipment using this protocol may occasionally suffer from interference from microwave ovens, cordless telephones, and Bluetooth devices
IEEE 802.11g	54 Mbps	Equipment using this protocol transmits at 2.4 GHz and may occasionally suffer from interference from microwave ovens, cordless telephones, and Bluetooth devices
IEEE 802.11n	300 Mbps	Employs multiple input, multiple output (MIMO) technology that allows multiple data streams to be transmitted over the same channel using the same bandwidth used for only a single data stream in 802.11a/b/g
IEEE 802.11ac	400 Mbps–1.3 Gbps	An emerging 802.11 standard that provides higher data transmission speeds and more stable connections. It can transmit at either 2.4 GHz or 5 GHz

© 2016 Cengage Learning

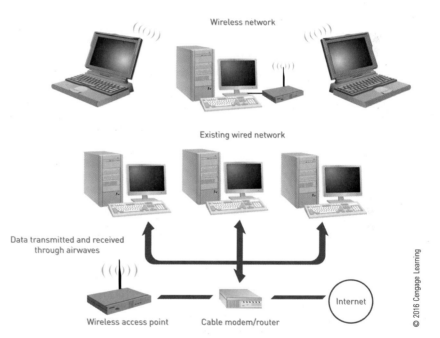

FIGURE 6.5

Wi-Fi network

In a Wi-Fi network, the user's computer, smartphone, or cell phone has a wireless adapter that translates data into a radio signal and transmits it using an antenna.

© 2016 Cengage Learning

a "hot spot." Current Wi-Fi access points have a maximum range of about 300 to 900 feet outdoors and 100 to 300 feet within a dry-walled building. Wi-Fi has proven so popular that hot spots are established in many public places such as airports, coffee shops, college campuses, libraries, and restaurants.

The availability of free Wi-Fi within a hotel's premises has become very popular with business travelers. Many hotels offer free Wi-Fi, including Best Western, Carlson Rezidor, Choice Hotels, Hilton, Hyatt, Holiday Inn, Starwood, The Four Seasons Hotels and Resorts, and Wyndham hotels.[11]

Many cities around the world have implemented Wi-Fi networks for use by meter readers and other municipal workers and to partially subsidize Internet access to their citizens and visitors. Santa Clara, California, was the first city in the United States to provide free citywide Internet access by adding a public Wi-Fi channel on its wireless network used to carry utility meter data.[12] Singapore provides free Wi-Fi access at the Gardens by the Bay, a 101 hectare (one hectare equals 10,000 square meters or 2.47 acres) park of beautiful waterfalls, arboretums, and flower gardens.[13] Supporters of the networks believe that the presence of such networks stimulates economic development by attracting new businesses. Critics doubt the long-term viability of municipal Wi-Fi networks because the technology cannot easily handle rapidly increasing numbers of users. Also, because municipal Wi-Fi networks use an unlicensed bandwidth available to any user and they operate at up to 30 times the power of existing home and business Wi-Fi networks, critics claim interference is inevitable with these networks. As a result, cities are considering other options including WiMAX and fiber-optic networks, slowing the growth of municipal Wi-Fi networks.

Wide Area Wireless Network Types

Wide area network options include satellite and terrestrial microwave transmission, wireless mesh, 3G, 4G, and WiMAX.

Microwave Transmission

Microwave is a high-frequency (300 MHz–300 GHz) signal sent through the air, as shown in Figure 6.6. Terrestrial (Earthbound) microwaves are transmitted by line-of-sight devices, so the line of sight between the transmitter and receiver must be unobstructed. Typically, microwave stations are placed in a series—one station receives a signal, amplifies it, and retransmits it to the next microwave transmission tower. Such stations can be located roughly 30 miles apart before the curvature of the Earth makes it impossible for the towers to "see" one another. Microwave signals can carry thousands of channels at the same time.

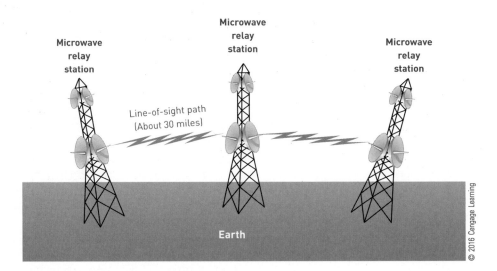

FIGURE 6.6

Microwave communications

Because they are line-of-sight transmission devices, microwave dishes are frequently placed in relatively high locations, such as mountains, towers, or tall buildings.

A communications satellite also operates in the microwave frequency range. See Figure 6.7. The satellite receives the signal from the Earth station, amplifies the relatively weak signal, and then rebroadcasts it at a different frequency. The advantage of satellite communications is that satellites can receive and broadcast over large geographic regions. Such problems as the curvature of the Earth, mountains, and other structures that block the line-of-sight microwave transmission make satellites an attractive alternative. Geostationary, low earth orbit, and small mobile satellite stations are the most common forms of satellite communications.

A *geostationary satellite* orbits the Earth directly over the equator, approximately 22,300 miles above the Earth so that it appears stationary. The U.S. National Weather Service relies on the Geostationary Operational

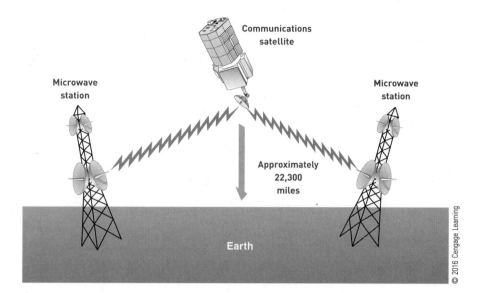

© 2016 Cengage Learning

FIGURE 6.7

Satellite transmission

Communications satellites are relay stations that receive signals from one Earth station and rebroadcast them to another.

Environmental Satellite program for weather imagery and quantitative data to support weather forecasting, severe storm tracking, and meteorological research.

A *low earth orbit (LEO) satellite* system employs many satellites, each in an orbit at an altitude of less than 1,000 miles. The satellites are spaced so that, from any point on the Earth at any time, at least one satellite is on a line of sight. Iridium Communications, Inc., provides a global communications network that spans the entire Earth using 66 satellites in a near polar orbit at an altitude of 485 miles. Calls are routed among the satellites to create a reliable connection between call participants that cannot be disrupted by natural disasters such as earthquakes, tsunamis, or hurricanes that knock out ground-based wireless towers and wire- or cable-based networks.[14] Sarah Outen, while attempting to become the first woman to row solo across the dangerous north Pacific Ocean, was hit by a tropical storm with winds of 65 knots and waves of 15 feet. After two days, her boat was so damaged that she had no choice but to call for an emergency pickup using her satellite phone to keep in contact with the rescue team as it took 30 hours to reach her.[15]

A *very small aperture terminal (VSAT)* is a satellite ground station with a dish antenna smaller than 3 meters in diameter. Carnival Corporation uses VSAT to provide communications for crew and passengers onboard its 100 cruise chips. Richard Ames, senior vice president of business services, says: "At Carnival, our most important goal is to give our guests a great experience. For many guests, this means staying connected by phone and Internet, even when they're on our ships in the middle of the sea."[16]

4G Wireless Communications

Wireless communications has evolved through four generations of technology and services. The 1G (first generation) of wireless communications standards originated in the 1980s and was based on analog communications. The 2G (second generation) employed fully digital networks that superseded 1G networks in the early 1990s. Phone conversations were encrypted, mobile phone usage was expanded, and short message services (SMS), or texting, was introduced. 3G wireless communications supports wireless voice and broadband speed data communications in a mobile environment at speeds of 2 to 4 Mbps. Additional capabilities include mobile video, mobile e-commerce, location-based services, mobile gaming, and the downloading and playing of songs.

Long Term Evolution (LTE):
A standard for wireless communications for mobile phones based on packet switching.

Worldwide Interoperability for Microwave Access (WiMAX): A 4G alternative based on a set of IEEE 802.16 metropolitan area network standards that support various types of communications access.

4G broadband mobile wireless is expected to deliver more advanced versions of enhanced multimedia, smooth streaming video, universal access, portability across all types of devices, and, eventually, worldwide roaming. 4G will also deliver 3 to 20 times the speed of 3G networks for mobile devices such as smartphones, tablets, laptops, and wireless hotspots.[17]

Each of the four major U.S. wireless network operators (AT&T, Verizon, Sprint, and T-Mobile) is rapidly expanding its 4G networks based on the Long Term Evolution (LTE) standard. **Long Term Evolution (LTE)** is a standard for wireless communications for mobile phones based on packet switching, which is an entirely different approach from the circuit-switching approach employed in 3G telecommunications networks. Carriers must reengineer their voice call networks to convert to the LTE standard.

The biggest benefit of LTE is how quickly a mobile device can connect to the Internet and how much data it can download or upload in a given amount of time. LTE makes it reasonable to stream video to your phone, using services such as Hulu Plus, Netflix, or YouTube. It also speeds up Web browsing, with most pages loading in seconds. LTE enables video calling using services such as Skype or Google+ Hangouts. LTE's faster speed also makes sharing photos and videos from your phone quick and easy.

Worldwide Interoperability for Microwave Access (WiMAX) is a 4G alternative based on a set of IEEE 802.16 wireless metropolitan area network standards that support various types of communications access. In many respects, WiMAX operates like Wi-Fi, only over greater distances and at faster transmission speeds. Fewer WiMAX base stations (towers) are required to cover the same geographical area than when Wi-Fi technology is used. While Wi-Fi's range is limited to hundreds of feet, WiMAX has a range of 30 miles due to the frequencies used (2 to 11 GHz and 10 to 66 GHz).

Most telecommunications experts agree that WiMAX is an attractive option for developing countries with little or no wireless telephone infrastructure. However, as mentioned earlier, the major U.S. carriers have selected 4G LTE.

5G Wireless Communications

A new mobile telecommunications generation has come on the scene about every ten years since the first 1G system. 5G is a term used to identify the next major phase of mobile telecommunications standards beyond 4G. No 5G mobile standard has been formally defined yet, but some industry observers predict the new 5G standards may be introduced in the early 2020s. 5G may bring with it higher data transmission rates, lower power consumption, higher connect reliability with fewer dropped calls, increased geographic coverage, and lower infrastructure costs.[18]

Growth in Wireless Data Traffic

Over the next several years, the growth in the amount of wireless data traffic will create many opportunities for innovators to solve network capacity problems and avoid user service issues. The volume of mobile data traffic reached 8.1 exabytes worldwide in 2012, and some predict a compound average growth rate of roughly 44 percent over the next five years. (One exabyte is $1,000^6$ bytes or sufficient storage to hold 50,000 years of DVD-quality video.)[19] Cisco estimates that worldwide wireless data traffic will grow at a higher average rate of 66 percent per year from 2013 to 2017 when smartphones are expected to represent 27 percent of the connected devices consuming 68 percent of the data. Video is expected to make up as much as two-thirds of the data volume.[20] Although 4G LTE networks have 20 times the data-carrying capacity of 3G networks, even 4G networks may not be able to keep pace with such rapid growth rates.

NETWORKS AND DISTRIBUTED PROCESSING

computer network: The communications media, devices, and software needed to connect two or more computer systems or devices.

A **computer network** consists of communications media, devices, and software needed to connect two or more computer systems or devices. The computers and devices on the networks are also called *network nodes*. After they are connected, the nodes can share hardware and software and data, information, and processing jobs. Increasingly, businesses are linking computers in networks to streamline work processes and enable employees to collaborate on projects. If a company uses networks effectively, it can grow into an agile, powerful, and creative organization, giving it a long-term competitive advantage. Organizations can use networks to share hardware, programs, and databases. Networks can transmit and receive information to improve organizational effectiveness and efficiency, and they enable geographically separated workgroups to share documents and opinions, which fosters teamwork, innovative ideas, and new business strategies.

Network Topology

network topology: A diagram that indicates how the communications links and hardware devices of the network are arranged.

Network topology indicates how the communications links and hardware devices of the network are arranged. The topology is the shape or structure of the network so that the transmission rates, distances between devices, signal types, and physical interconnection may differ between networks, but they may all have the same topology. The three most common network topologies in use today are the star, bus, and mesh.

star network: A network in which all network devices connect to one another through a single central device called the hub node.

In a **star network**, all network devices connect to one another through a single central device called the hub node. See Figure 6.8. Many home networks employ the star topology. A failure in any link of the star network will isolate only the device connected to that link. However, should the hub fail, all devices on the entire network are unable to communicate.

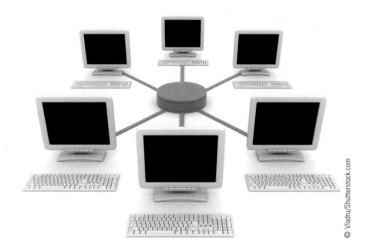

FIGURE 6.8

Star network

In a star network, all network devices connect to one another through a single central hub node.

bus network: A network in which all network devices are connected to a common backbone that serves as a shared communications medium.

In a **bus network**, all network devices are connected to a common backbone that serves as a shared communications medium. See Figure 6.9. To communicate with any other device on the network, a device sends a broadcast message onto the communications medium. All devices on the network can "see" the message, but only the intended recipient actually accepts and processes the message.

mesh network: A network that uses multiple access points to link a series of devices that speak to each other to form a network connection across a large area.

Mesh networks use multiple access points to link a series of devices that speak to each other to form a network connection across a large area. See Figure 6.10. Communications are routed among network nodes by allowing

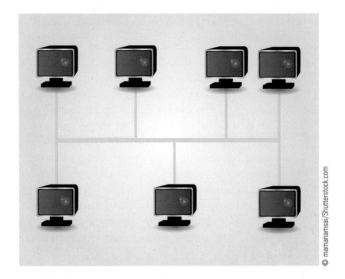

FIGURE **6.9**

Bus network

In a bus network, all network devices are connected to a common backbone that serves as a shared communications medium.

FIGURE **6.10**

Mesh network

Mesh networks use multiple access points to link a series of devices that speak to each other to form a network connection across a large area.

for continuous connections and bypassing blocked paths by "hopping" from node to node until a connection can be established. Mesh networks are very robust: If one node fails, all the other nodes can still communicate with each other, directly or through one or more intermediate nodes.

The Piedmont City School District, located in rural Alabama, implemented a citywide wireless mesh network to enable its 1,200 students to access computer services. Many of the families could not afford Internet access from their homes. The network enables all students to access Odyssey, a Web-based learning system for reading, language, and math. They can also participate in distance learning and advanced placement classes.[21]

Network Types

Depending on the physical distance between nodes on a network and the communications and services it provides, networks can be classified as personal area, local area, metropolitan area, or wide area.

Personal Area Networks

A **personal area network (PAN)** is a wireless network that connects information technology devices close to one person. With a PAN, you can connect a laptop, digital camera, and portable printer without cables. You can download digital image data from the camera to the laptop and then print it on a high-quality printer—all wirelessly. Additionally, a PAN enables data captured by sensors placed on your body to be transmitted to your smartphone as input to applications that can serve as calorie trackers, heart monitors, glucose monitors, and pedometers.

personal area network (PAN): A network that supports the interconnection of information technology close to one person.

Local Area Networks

A network that connects computer systems and devices within a small area, such as an office, home, or several floors in a building, is a **local area network (LAN)**. Typically, LANs are wired into office buildings and factories, as shown in Figure 6.11. Although LANs often use unshielded twisted-pair wire, other media—including fiber-optic cable—are also popular. Increasingly, LANs are using some form of wireless communications. You can build LANs to connect personal computers, laptop computers, or powerful mainframe computers.

local area network (LAN): A network that connects computer systems and devices within a small area, such as an office, home, or several floors in a building.

FIGURE 6.11

Typical LAN

All network users within an office building can connect to each other's devices for rapid communication. For instance, a user in research and development could send a document from her computer to be printed at a printer located in the desktop publishing center. Most computer labs employ a LAN to enable the users to share the use of high-speed and/or color printers and plotters as well as to download software applications and save files.

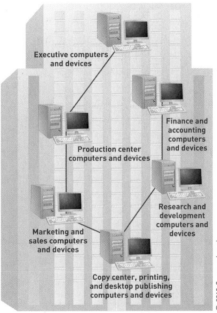

© 2016 Cengage Learning

A basic type of LAN is a simple peer-to-peer network that a small business might use to share files and hardware devices such as printers. In a peer-to-peer network, you set up each computer as an independent computer, but you let other computers access specific files on its hard drive or share its printer. These types of networks have no server. Instead, each computer is connected to the next machine. Examples of peer-to-peer networks include Windows for Workgroups, Windows NT, Windows 2000, AppleShare, and Windows 7 Homegroup. Performance of the computers on a peer-to-peer network is usually slower because one computer is actually sharing the resources of another computer.

With more people working at home, connecting home computing devices and equipment into a unified network is on the rise. Small businesses are also connecting their systems and equipment. A home or small business can connect network resources, computers, printers, scanners, and other devices. A person working on one computer, for example, can use data and programs stored on another computer. In addition, several computers on the network can share a single printer. To make home and small business networking a reality, many companies are offering networking standards, devices, and procedures.

Metropolitan Area Networks

metropolitan area network (MAN): A telecommunications network that connects users and their computers in a geographical area that spans a campus or city.

A **metropolitan area network (MAN)** is a telecommunications network that connects users and their computers in a geographical area that spans a campus or city. A MAN might redefine the many networks within a city into a single larger network or connect several LANs into a single campus LAN. Often the MAN is owned either by a consortium of users or by a single network provider who sells the service to users.

PIONIER is a Polish national research and education network created to provide high-speed Internet access and to conduct network-based research. The network connects 21 MANs and 5 high-performance computing centers using fiber-optic transmission media for a distance of 6,467 km.[22]

Wide Area Networks

wide area network (WAN): A telecommunications network that connects large geographic regions.

A **wide area network (WAN)** is a telecommunications network that connects large geographic regions. A WAN might be privately owned or rented and includes public (shared-users) networks. When you make a long-distance phone call or access the Internet, you are using a WAN. WANs usually consist of computer equipment owned by the user, together with data communications equipment and telecommunications links provided by various carriers and service providers. See Figure 6.12. The Schools 100 Mbit/s High-Speed Programme is an Irish government project to connect all 730 post-primary schools across the country to a high-speed WAN and enable students to learn and collaborate online.[23]

North America

© 2016 Cengage Learning

FIGURE 6.12

Wide area network

WANs are the basic long-distance networks used around the world. The actual connections between sites, or nodes (shown by dashed lines), might be any combination of guided and wireless media. When you make a long-distance telephone call or access the Internet, you are using a WAN.

WANs often provide communications across national borders, which involves national and international laws regulating the electronic flow of data across international boundaries or *transborder data flow*. Many countries, including those in the European Union, have strict laws placing limits on the transmission of personal data about customers and employees across national borders.

Basic Processing Alternatives

centralized processing: An approach to processing wherein all processing occurs in a single location or facility.

When an organization needs to use two or more computer systems, it can implement one of three basic processing alternatives: centralized, decentralized, or distributed. With **centralized processing**, all processing occurs in a single location or facility. This approach offers the highest degree of control because a single centrally managed computer performs all data processing. The Ticketmaster reservation service is an example of a centralized system. One central computer with a database stores information about all events and records the purchases of seats. Ticket clerks at various ticket selling locations can enter order data and print the results, or customers can place orders directly over the Internet.

decentralized processing: An approach to processing wherein processing devices are placed at various remote locations.

With **decentralized processing**, processing devices are placed at various remote locations. Each processing device is isolated and does not communicate with any other processing device. Decentralized systems are suitable for companies that have independent operating units, such as 7-Eleven, where each of its 8,700 stores in the United States and Canada is managed to meet local retail conditions.[24] Each store has a computer that runs more than 50 business applications, such as cash register operations, gasoline pump monitoring, and merchandising.

distributed processing: An approach to processing wherein processing devices are placed at remote locations but are connected to each other via a network.

With **distributed processing**, processing devices are placed at remote locations but are connected to each other via a network. One benefit of distributed processing is that managers can allocate data to the locations that can process it most efficiently. Kroger operates over 2,424 supermarkets and multi-department stores, each with its own computer to support store operations such as customer checkout and inventory management. These computers are connected to a network so that sales data gathered by each store's computer can be sent to a huge data repository on a mainframe computer for efficient analysis by marketing analysts and product supply chain managers.

Ongoing terrorist attacks around the world and the heightened sensitivity to natural disasters (such as a major earthquake in China; major flooding in Argentina, China, Colorado, and the Philippines; a cyclone in Bangladesh; major forest fires in California, Colorado, and Idaho; and tornados in Oklahoma, all happening in 2013) have motivated many companies to distribute their workers, operations, and systems much more widely, a reversal of the previous trend toward centralization. The goal is to minimize the consequences of a catastrophic event at one location while ensuring uninterrupted systems availability.

File Server Systems

Users can share data through file server computing, which allows authorized users to download entire files from certain computers designated as file servers. After downloading data to a local computer, a user can analyze, manipulate, format, and display data from the file, as shown in Figure 6.13.

FIGURE 6.13

File server connection

The file server sends the user the entire file that contains the data requested. The user can then analyze, manipulate, format, and display the downloaded data with a program that runs on the user's personal computer.

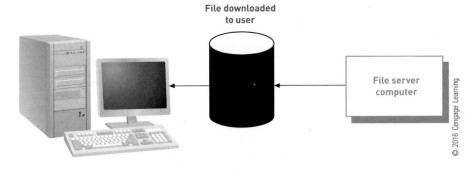

File downloaded to user

File server computer

© 2016 Cengage Learning

Client/Server Systems

client/server architecture: An approach to computing wherein multiple computer platforms are dedicated to special functions, such as database management, printing, communications, and program execution.

In **client/server architecture**, multiple computer platforms are dedicated to special functions, such as database management, printing, communications, and program execution. These platforms are called *servers*. Each server is accessible by all computers on the network. Servers can be computers of all sizes; they store both application programs and data files and are equipped with operating system software to manage the activities of the network. The server distributes programs and data to the other computers (clients) on the network as they request them. An application server holds the programs and data files for a particular application, such as an inventory database. The client or the server can do the processing.

A client is any computer (often a user's personal computer) that sends messages requesting services from the servers on the network. A client can converse with many servers concurrently. For example, a user at a personal computer initiates a request to extract data that resides in a database somewhere on the network. A data request server intercepts the request and determines on which database server the data resides. The server then formats the user's request into a message that the database server will understand. When it receives the message, the database server extracts and formats the requested data and sends the results to the client. The database server sends only the data that satisfies a specific query—not the entire file. See Figure 6.14. As with the file server approach, when the downloaded data is on the user's machine, it can then be analyzed, manipulated, formatted, and displayed by a program that runs on the user's personal computer.

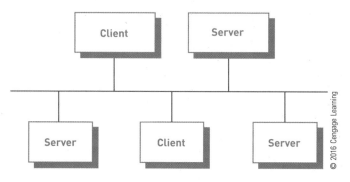

FIGURE 6.14

Client/server connection

Multiple computer platforms, called *servers*, are dedicated to special functions. Each server is accessible by all computers on the network. The client requests services from the servers, provides a user interface, and presents results to the user.

Table 6.4 lists the advantages and disadvantages of client/server architecture.

TABLE 6.4 Advantages and disadvantages of client/server architecture

Advantages	Disadvantages
Moving applications from mainframe computers and terminal-to-host architecture to client/server architecture can yield significant savings in hardware and software support costs	Moving to client/server architecture is a major two- to five-year conversion process
Minimizes traffic on the network because only the data needed to satisfy a user query is moved from the database to the client device	Controlling the client/server environment to prevent unauthorized use, invasion of privacy, and viruses is difficult
Security mechanisms can be implemented directly on the database server through the use of stored procedures	Using client/server architecture leads to a multivendor environment with problems that are difficult to identify and isolate to the appropriate vendor

An electronic health record (EHR) is a summary of health information generated by each patient encounter in any healthcare delivery setting. It includes patient demographics, medical history, immunization records, lab data, medications, and vital signs. The federal government earmarked $33 billion in incentives for healthcare providers that can demonstrate they are "meaningful users" of EHR technology. To earn this incentive, which can amount to millions of dollars, a hospital must show that it is achieving key desired policy outcomes in efficiency, patient safety, and care coordination. Mecosta County Medical Center is a 74-bed acute-care hospital in Michigan that implemented a client/server hospital information system to capture and display meaningful use data to ensure that the hospital is on track to earn its incentive.[25]

Safaricom's Moves against Hate Speech

On December 30, 2007, Kenya held its breath as it awaited the results of its presidential election. Many were sure that Raila Odinga, the challenger, had ousted incumbent Mwai Kibaki. The election was too close to call, and three days later, when officials announced Kibaki's victory, the nation descended into violent clashes between the party and tribal supporters of each of the two candidates. The clashes claimed 1,200 lives and displaced over half a million people. In the inquiries that followed, officials found that hate speech posted to blogs and delivered over SMS was rampant prior to the election and during the violence.

Unlike many developed European and North American countries, mobile telephony dominates the Internet and communications technology sector in Africa. Prepaid and pay-as-you-go plans make up about 99 percent of all mobile plans, and mobile phones provide Internet access to those who cannot afford laptops and Internet services. As Kenya headed into its March 2013 national election, many worried about the possibility of another outbreak of violence. Safaricom, a leading telecommunications company in East Africa and the leading mobile network provider, took a radical step to eliminate hate speech transmitted over its network. It issued guidelines to its clients that transmitted bulk SMS from political candidates and parties, vetted the SMS content, and retained the right to refuse to transfer messages with content that attacked members of a particular party or tribe.

The guidelines specified that senders, the political party representatives or political candidates, had to identify themselves and provide registration documents or ID numbers. The message could only be sent in one of the two official languages in Kenya, Swahili or English. The content could not use abusive or profane language, incite people to violence, ridicule members of a particular group, or attack individuals, their families, or their tribes. In creating these guidelines, Safaricom had to traverse carefully between the hate speech provisions in the new Kenyan constitution, privacy rights, and customer expectations. Since Safaricom was only intercepting bulk SMS rather than peer-to-peer SMS, privacy rights were not a concern. For-profit companies, political parties, and other organizations pay to send bulk SMS messages. Because these messages are not considered personal communications, they are not subject to privacy laws. However, Safaricom later noticed an increase in SMS sent from outside of Kenya and, in the final days of the election, blocked messages sent to over 100 recipients.

In all, Safaricom refused 18 requests and 13 of these were modified, resubmitted, and approved. Only one request was blocked due to its content. Initial reports have pointed out that Safaricom was able to eliminate only one of the many options available: Many people still received messages containing hate speech through peer-to-peer SMS and others posted hate speech on social media sites such as Facebook.

Still, the March 2013 Kenyan election passed with only one attack, which killed six police officers. By comparison to 2007, the election was a great success for democracy and those who support peaceful change, and some of the credit is due to Safaricom and other groups that worked to stop the spread of hate speech and incitement.

Discussion Questions

1. What steps did Safaricom take to prevent hate speech during the 2013 elections? Did Safaricom act ethically? Why or why not?
2. Were these steps effective? Why or why not?

Critical Thinking Questions

1. Violence broke out a few months prior to the elections. Should Safaricom and other organizations do more to stop hate speech? If so, what measures should they take?
2. Should Safaricom be allowed to intercept and vet peer-to-peer messages? Or should the right to privacy trump the need to stop hate crime?

SOURCES: "Kenya Election Violence: ICC Names Suspects," BBC, December 15, 2010; Purdon, Lucy, "Corporate Responses to Hate Speech in the 2013 Kenyan Presidential Elections," Case Study Number 1: November 2013, Institution for Human Rights and Business; Okutoyi, Elly, "Safaricom Spearheads Fight Against Campaign Hate Speech with Tough New Rules," humanipo, Home to African Tech, June 18, 2012.

Telecommunications Hardware

Networks require various telecommunications hardware devices to operate, including modems, multiplexers, private branch exchanges, switches, bridges, routers, and gateways.

Modems

modem: A telecommunications hardware device that converts (modulates and demodulates) communications signals so they can be transmitted over the communication media.

At each stage of the communications process, transmission media of differing types and capacities may be used. If you use an analog telephone line to transfer data, it can accommodate only an analog signal. Because a computer generates a digital signal represented by bits, you need a special device to convert the digital signal to an analog signal and vice versa. See Figure 6.15. Translating data from digital to analog is called *modulation*, and translating data from analog to digital is called *demodulation*. Thus, these devices are modulation/demodulation devices, or modems. Penril/Bay Networks, Hayes, Microcom, Motorola, and U.S. Robotics are modem manufacturers.

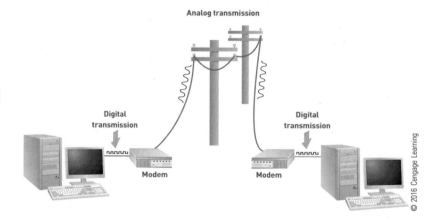

FIGURE 6.15

How a modem works

Digital signals are modulated into analog signals, which can be carried over existing phone lines. The analog signals are then demodulated back into digital signals by the receiving modem.

Modems can dial telephone numbers, originate message sending, and answer incoming calls and messages. Modems can also perform tests and checks on how well they are operating. Some modems can vary their transmission rates based on detected error rates and other conditions. Wireless modems in laptop personal computers allow people on the go to connect to wireless networks and communicate with other users and computers. These modems are also called network adapters.

Cable company network subscribers use a cable modem to connect to the Internet and pay their ISP around $7 per month for the device. See Figure 6.16. You can save money by buying your own cable modem for less than $70. Digital subscriber line (DSL) refers to a family of services that provides Internet connection over the wires as a regular telephone connection.

This service is slower than cable connection. Subscribers use a DSL modem to connect their computers to this service.

FIGURE 6.16

Cable modem

A cable modem can deliver network and Internet access up to 500 times faster than a standard modem and phone line.

router: A telecommunications device that forwards data packets between computer networks.

Routers, Switches, and Other Devices

Telecommunications hardware routes messages and data from one network to another at high speeds.

A **router** is a device that forwards data packets between computer networks. A network may have multiple routers, with each router connected to two or more data lines from different networks. When a data packet arrives on one of the lines, the router reads the address information in the packet to determine its intended destination. The router then uses information in its routing table to direct the packet to the next router on its journey to the intended destination. In this manner, a data packet is forwarded from one router to another through the network until it reaches its final destination. A router for a home network is designed to join the home LAN to the Internet WAN for the purpose of Internet connection sharing.

switch: A telecommunications device that contains ports to which all the devices on the network can connect and uses the physical device address in each incoming message to determine to which output port it should forward the message to reach its intended destination.

A **switch** is a telecommunications device that contains ports to which all the devices on the network can connect and uses the physical device address in each incoming message to determine to which output port it should forward the message to reach its intended destination. A switch is not capable of joining multiple networks or sharing an Internet connection.

gateway: A telecommunications device that serves as an entrance to another network.

A **gateway** is a network device that serves as an entrance to another network. A network with only switches must designate one computer in the network to serve as the gateway to the Internet, and that device must possess two network adapters for sharing, one for the home LAN and one for the Internet WAN. With a router, all home computers connect to the router as peers, and the router performs all gateway functions.

wireless access point: A device that enables wireless devices to connect to a wired network using Wi-Fi, or other wireless network standards.

A **wireless access point** is a device that enables wireless devices to connect to a wired network using Wi-Fi, or other wireless network standards. The access point may connect to a router (via a wired network) as a standalone device, or it can also be an integral component of the router itself.

Private Branch Exchange (PBX)

private branch exchange (PBX): A telephone switching exchange that serves a single organization.

A **private branch exchange (PBX)** is a telephone switching exchange that serves a single organization. It enables users to share a certain number of outside lines (trunk lines) to make telephone calls to people outside the organization. This sharing reduces the number of trunk lines required, which in turn reduces the organization's telephone expense. A PBX also enables the routing of calls from department to department or individual to individual with the organization. The PBX can also provide many other functions, such as voice mail, voice paging, three-way calling, call transfer, and call waiting.

A VoIP-PBX can accept Voice over IP (VoIP) calls as well as traditional analog phone calls. With Voice over IP calls, the callers' voice communications are converted into packets of data for routing over the Internet.

The Township of North Glengarry, Ontario, implemented a hosted PBX service to connect its municipal offices, fire stations, recreation centers, and service centers that provide services to over 10,000 residents. With a hosted PBX, small- and medium-sized businesses can use an advanced telephone system without needing to purchase expensive telephone equipment. The hosted PBX is owned, operated, and maintained by a PBX service provider. Prior to this change, all the township's locations paid individually for phone, fax, and Internet services, and workers had to place external calls to reach one another. The hosted PBX solution treats the township's multiple locations as if they were one single campus. Phone-related expenses were reduced nearly 80 percent, and workers using mobile phones can now easily answer and make calls even from remote locations.[26]

Telecommunications Software

network operating system (NOS): Systems software that controls the computer systems and devices on a network and allows them to communicate with each other.

A network operating system (NOS) is systems software that controls the computer systems and devices on a network and allows them to communicate with each other. The NOS performs similar functions for the network as operating system software does for a computer, such as memory and task management and coordination of hardware. When network equipment (such as printers, plotters, and disk drives) is required, the NOS makes sure that these resources are used correctly. Novell NetWare, Windows 2000, Windows 2003, and Windows 2008 are common network operating systems.

Standard Chartered Bank operates with 89,000 employees in over 1,700 branches and outlets in 68 countries around the world. It derives 90 percent of its income and profits from operations in Asia, Africa, and the Middle East.[27] For any bank, processing and telecommunications system availability is essential. Standard Chartered implemented a telecommunications infrastructure consisting of switches and gateways running under the Junos network operating system to lower the cost and complexity of managing its networks and to provide full redundancy.[28]

Because companies use networks to communicate with customers, business partners, and employees, network outages or slow performance can mean a loss of business. Network management includes a wide range of technologies and processes that monitor the network and help identify and address problems before they can create a serious impact.

network-management software: Software that enables a manager on a networked desktop to monitor the use of individual computers and shared hardware (such as printers), scan for viruses, and ensure compliance with software licenses.

Software tools and utilities are available for managing networks. With network-management software, a manager on a networked personal computer can monitor the use of individual computers and shared hardware (such as printers), scan for viruses, and ensure compliance with software licenses. Network-management software also simplifies the process of updating files and programs on computers on the network—a manager can make changes through a communications server instead of having to visit each individual computer. In addition, network-management software protects software from being copied, modified, or downloaded illegally. It can also locate telecommunications errors and potential network problems. Some of the many benefits of network-management software include fewer hours spent on routine tasks (such as installing new software), faster response to problems, and greater overall network control.

Banks use a special form of network-management software to monitor the performance of their automated teller machines (ATMs). Status messages can be sent over the network to a central monitoring location to inform support people about situations such as low cash or receipt paper levels, card reader problems, and printer paper jams. Once a status message is received, a service provider or branch location employee can be dispatched to fix the ATM problem.

Today, most IS organizations use network-management software to ensure that their network remains up and running and that every network component and application is performing acceptably. The software enables IS staff to identify and resolve fault and performance issues before they affect customers and service. The latest network-management technology even incorporates automatic fixes: The network-management system identifies a problem, notifies the IS manager, and automatically corrects the problem before anyone outside the IS department notices it.

The Covell Group is a small IT consulting group in San Diego that provides server and Web site monitoring for primarily small- and medium-sized companies. The firm uses network-monitoring software to watch sensors and remote probes that track CPU, disk space, and Windows services. Constant monitoring enables the firm to detect if a communications line is down or if there is a power failure overnight so that everything is up and ready by the start of the next work day. Covell even monitors a freezer probe for one of its customers that stores human tissue and expensive, temperature-sensitive chemicals. Should the temperature rise above freezing, appropriate individuals are immediately paged.[29]

Software Defined Networking (SDN)

software defined networking: An emerging approach to networking that allows network administrators to have programmable central control of the network via a controller without requiring physical access to all the network devices.

In today's current network environment, each network device must be configured individually, usually via manual keyboard input. For a network of any size, this becomes a labor-intensive and error-prone effort, making it difficult to change the network so it can meet the needs of the organization. Software Defined Networking (SDN) is an emerging approach to networking that allows network administrators to manage a network via a controller that does not require physical access to all the network devices. This approach automates tasks such as configuration and policy management and enables the network to dynamically respond to application requirements. As a pioneer in the use of SDN, Google is so pleased with its benefits that the company plans to extend its current international SDN-based inter-data center network and build other new networks using the same capabilities.[30] Benefits of SDN for Google include the following:

- Makes it possible to better leverage Google's massive computing power
- Enables faster response to changes in business needs
- Reduces the manual effort and personnel costs of running and maintaining the network
- Enables applications to be more quickly deployed
- Reduces network disruption due to network changes

Securing Data Transmission

The interception of confidential information by unauthorized individuals can compromise private information about employees or customers, reveal marketing or new product development plans, or cause organizational embarrassment. Organizations with widespread operations need a way to maintain the security of communications with employees and business partners, wherever their facilities are located.

Guided media networks have an inherently secure feature: Only devices physically attached to the network can access the data. Wireless networks, on the other hand, are surprisingly often configured by default to allow access to any device that attempts to "listen to" broadcast communications. Action must be taken to override the defaults.

encryption: The process of converting an original message into a form that can be understood only by the intended receiver.

encryption key: A variable value that is applied (using an algorithm) to a set of unencrypted text to produce encrypted text (ciphertext) or to decrypt encrypted text.

Encryption of data is one approach taken to protect the security of communications over both wired and wireless networks. Encryption is the process of converting an original message into a form that can be understood only by the intended receiver. An encryption key is a variable value that is applied (using an algorithm) to a set of unencrypted text to produce encrypted text (also called ciphertext) or to decrypt encrypted text. See Figure 6.17.

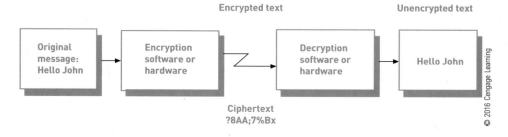

FIGURE **6.17**

Encryption process

Encryption converts an original message into a form that can be understood only by the intended receiver.

Encryption algorithms typically employ two types of data manipulation—substitution with each element of plaintext mapped into another element (e.g., "A" becomes "U") and permutation with elements in the plaintext rearranged (e.g., "the" becomes "het"). There are two types of encryption algorithms: symmetric and asymmetric. Symmetric algorithms use the same key for both encryption and decryption. Asymmetric algorithms use one key for encryption and a different key for decryption.

The ability to keep encrypted data secret is not based on the encryption algorithm, which is widely known, but on the encryption key. The encryption key is chosen from one of a large number of possible encryption keys. In general, the longer the key, the stronger the encryption. Thus, an encryption protocol based on a 56-bit key is not as strong as one based on a 128-bit key. Of course, it is essential that the key be kept secret from possible interceptors. A hacker who obtains the key by whatever means can recover the original message from the encrypted data.

Wi-Fi communications are broadcast over a wireless radio network. Communications over such a network can easily be intercepted by anyone within the range of the Wi-Fi hot spot. Therefore, Wi-Fi communications need to be encrypted to be secure. Wireless Protected Access 2 (WPA2) is the most commonly used security protocol for Wi-Fi networks today. WPA2 represents an improvement over the older WPA protocol in that it does not allow the use of a security algorithm called TKIP, which has known vulnerabilities that can be exploited by hackers. WPA2 employs the more powerful Advanced Encryption Standard (AES) encryption algorithm and Counter Cipher Mode with Block Chaining Message Authentication Code protocol (CCMP) based on the IEEE 802.11i standard for data encryption. *War driving* involves hackers driving around with a laptop and antenna trying to detect insecure wireless access points. Once connected to such a network, the hacker can gather enough traffic to analyze and crack the encryption.

Hotspot 2.0 is a specification developed by the Wi-Fi Alliance to simplify the process of securely connecting to one Wi-Fi network and then roaming among different Wi-Fi networks. This allows Hotspot 2.0–capable mobile devices to discover Hotspot 2.0 access points connected to wireless LANS whose owners have roaming arrangements with the user's home network. Hotspot 2.0 automates the connection process and provides secure transmission based on the AES encryption algorithm. This creates an opportunity to build major roaming consortiums with potentially thousands of partners and millions of access points. AT&T is one of the first organizations to establish such a consortium with an international roaming program.[31]

Encryption methods rely on the limitations of computing power for their security. If breaking a code requires too much computing power, even the most determined hacker cannot be successful.

In late 2013, former U.S. National Security Agency (NSA) contractor and whistle-blower Edward Snowden provided a number of revelations about the efforts of the NSA and its British counterpart, Government Communications Headquarters (GCHQ), to defeat encryption. These revelations include the following: The NSA has worked for over a decade to collect and decrypt vast amounts of data; NSA spends $250 million per year working with technology

INFORMATION SYSTEMS @ WORK

Is a "Zero-Email" Policy Achievable, or Even Desirable?

It's hard to imagine business without email, which is as common as the water cooler—and probably more useful. Is it, however, time to move on?

That's what IT services firm Atos, based in Bezons just outside Paris, France, thinks. In 2011, the company made a big splash in international IT news by announcing its aim to become a "zero-email company" by 2011 to help tackle what it calls "information pollution," which Atos sees as bogging down company progress because employees overuse email rather than turning to more effective forms of interaction.

As one example of information pollution, consider a six-person project group. One member sends the others an email message with a suggestion. The other five respond, with copies to all group members (as is standard business email practice). Three of the members reply to the other comments. Soon each project member receives two or three dozen email messages. Most of those messages repeat the same content with a new sentence or two at the top.

The time spent sifting through email adds up, says Atos. In 2010, corporate employees received approximately 200 email messages a day, almost one-fifth of which was spam. Middle managers, Atos reported, spent one-fourth of their day searching for information.

Atos chairman and CEO Thierry Breton, speaking at a conference in February 2011, announced his plans to end all internal emails among Atos employees. "We are producing data on a massive scale that is fast polluting our working environments and also encroaching into our personal lives," he said. "We are taking action now to reverse this trend, just as organizations took measures to reduce environmental pollution after the industrial revolution."

Though its name may not be a household word in the United States, Atos is not a small firm. It is a major information technology service provider, with 77,000 employees in 47 countries and annual revenues in excess of U.S. $12 billion. If it can eliminate email, size should not prevent other companies from doing the same.

As in most companies, Atos employees regularly used email to communicate with one another and to share documents and other files. What were they to use instead? Collaboration and social media tools. A collaboration tool lets employees use an online discussion group instead of sending emails to each other. (An online discussion group would have helped the six-person project team in the earlier example.) Rather than bandy documents about on email, Atos employees use SharePoint.

Social media tools include using familiar sites such as Facebook to keep others informed about their business activities. Groups can also use wikis to create shared repositories of information on topics of interest. Atos has found that making such tools available reduces email volume by 10 to 20 percent immediately.

Not everyone thinks that eliminating internal email is practical. Industry analyst Brian Prentice of Gartner Group faults the bureaucracy that leads to overuse of email, not the medium itself. In his view, "The only solution is to tackle the ballooning administration and bureaucracy overhead in organizations that is fuelling the number of e-mails being generated. Specifically, our criticism of e-mail as a collaboration tool needs to shift towards the unchecked growth of bureaucracy it enables." In other words, e-mail is a symptom, not the problem.

Not surprisingly, Hubert Tardieu, an advisor to Atos CEO Breton, disagrees. He believes that email does not lend itself to creating communities of shared interests within an organization but that other forms of electronic communication do. "Zero mail is not an objective in itself," he writes, "but the recognition that companies are suffering from e-mail overload."

By the end of 2013, while Atos still had its "zero-email" goal, the company was changing its tune. In a September 2013 interview, after the U.K. office reported a 65 percent drop in email usage (rather than the targeted 100 percent drop), Lee Timmons, senior vice president, explained that "e-mails still have a place with our delivery consultants but it sits alongside instant messaging, it sits alongside an enterprise social networking tool, and it sits alongside SharePoint. Our role has been to help people understand for which tasks and under which circumstances e-mail is the right tool for the job or whether one of the others is better."

Atos failed to achieve its zero-email goal, but in the process, the company has called attention to the great need to increase company efficiency through the use of the most appropriate new communication tools.

Discussion Questions

1. What purpose did Atos's zero-email policy achieve for Atos and for others?
2. What purposes do you use email for? What communication tools might be more effective or efficient at accomplishing those purposes?

Critical Thinking Questions

1. Think about your use of social media. If you could count on all your friends to see updates to your Facebook page and if they knew that was the only way they would hear from you, what fraction of your emails do you think you could avoid sending? Would it be more or less work to update your Facebook page than to send email messages?

2. Atos is a large firm and can afford to set up several social media and collaboration sites, each of which eliminates some need for email. Suppose you work for a small firm with fewer technology resources and people to support them. Can you use this approach? If not all of it, then can you use any of it? Should you?

SOURCES: Scott, Wayne, "Can a Zero E-Mail Policy in Organisations Improve Efficiency?" ITProPortal, September 2, 2013; Savvas, A., "Atos Origin Abandoning E-mail," *Computerworld UK*, February 9, 2011; Savvas, A., "Defiant Atos Sticks with Company-Wide E-Mail Ban," *Computerworld UK*, December 7, 2011; Prentice, B., "Why Will 'Zero E-Mail' Policies Fail? Bureaucracy!" Gartner blog, December 11, 2011; Tardieu, H., "Achieving a Zero E-Mail Culture: Is Bureaucracy a Showstopper?" Atos blog, December 21, 2011; Atos S.A. Web site, *www.atos.net*, accessed December 15, 2013.

companies to "covertly influence" the design of their products to enable collection and decryption of data; and the GCHQ has been working to develop the means to collect and decrypt encrypted data traffic on Hotmail, Google, Yahoo!, and Facebook.[32] Privacy groups consider these efforts an invasion of privacy and a violation of the Fourth Amendment of the U.S. Constitution, which guarantees the right of the people to be secure in their persons, houses, papers, and effects, against unreasonable searches and seizures. Others believe that the NSA must do everything within its power to fight terrorists, cybercriminals, and others who encrypt their messages to hide their activities.

Virtual Private Network (VPN)

virtual private network (VPN):
A private network that uses a public network (usually the Internet) to connect multiple remote locations.

The use of a virtual private network is another means used to secure the transmission of communications. A virtual private network (VPN) is a private network that uses a public network (usually the Internet) to connect multiple remote locations. A VPN provides network connectivity over a potentially long physical distance and thus can be considered a form of wide area network. VPNs support secure, encrypted connections between a company's employees and remote users through a third-party service provider. Telecommuters, salespeople, and frequent travelers find the use of a VPN to be a safe, reliable, low-cost way to connect to their corporate intranets. Often, users are provided with a security token that displays a constantly changing password to log onto the VPN. See Figure 6.18. This solution avoids the problem of users forgetting their password while providing added security through use of a password constantly changing every 30 to 60 seconds.

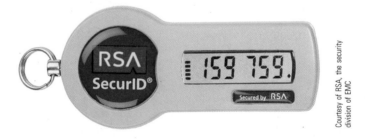

Courtesy of RSA, the security division of EMC

FIGURE 6.18

RSA SecurID security token

The six digits displayed on the token are used as an access code to gain access to a VPN network. The digits change every 60 seconds.

Yahoo! employs VPN to enable remote workers to securely log into the Yahoo! network and do their work from any location, often from home. When CEO Melissa Mayer noticed how empty Yahoo! parking lots were, she examined the firm's VPN logs to see if absent employees were logging onto the network to do work. They were not. Mayer then put out the word that employees were banned from doing work at home.[33]

All major car manufacturers such as BMW, Chrysler, Ford, GM, Mercedes, Toyota, and Volkswagen have announced their intentions to provide Internet access in their vehicles. BMW, in fact, has demonstrated a sedan equipped with an LTE router for up to eight devices. IST-G5 is a new Wi-Fi standard specifically developed for use in vehicles. This evolving technology can provide vehicle passengers with a secure VPN connection to their company's network and enable them to download sensitive information stored on its servers.[34]

TELECOMMUNICATIONS SERVICES AND NETWORK APPLICATIONS

Telecommunications and networks are vital parts of today's information systems. In fact, it is hard to imagine how organizations could function without them. For example, when a business needs to develop an accurate monthly production forecast, a manager simply downloads sales forecast data gathered directly from customer databases. Telecommunications provides the network link, allowing the manager to access the data quickly and generate the production report, which supports the company's objective of better financial planning. This section looks at some of the more significant telecommunications services and network applications.

Cellular Phone Services

The cell phone has become ubiquitous and is an essential part of life in the twenty-first century. Out of the world's estimated 7 billion people, 6 billion have access to mobile phones. Far fewer—only 4.5 billion people—have access to working toilets. Although many of the people who live in these countries do not have ready access to clean drinking water, electricity, or the Internet, more than half of these individuals are expected to have mobile phones by 2012.

Cellular phones operate using radio waves to provide two-way communications. With cellular transmission, a local area such as a city is divided into cells. As a person with a cellular device such as a mobile phone moves from one cell to another, the cellular system passes the phone connection from one cell to another (see Figure 6.19). The signals from the cells are transmitted to a receiver and integrated into the regular phone system. Cellular phone users can thus connect to anyone who has access to either a cell phone or a regular phone service, from a child at home to your friend on the road to a business associate in another country. Because cellular transmission uses

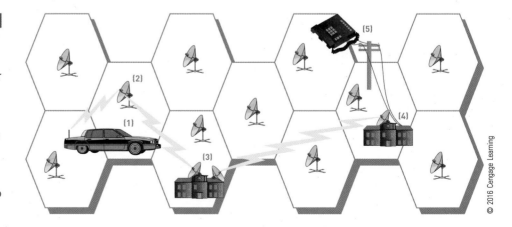

FIGURE 6.19

Typical cellular transmission scenario

Using a cellular car phone, the caller dials the number (1). The signal is sent from the car's antenna to the low-powered cellular antenna located in that cell (2). The signal is sent to the regional cellular phone switching office, also called the *mobile telephone subscriber office* (MTSO) (3). The signal is switched to the local telephone company switching station located nearest to the call destination (4). Now integrated into the regular phone system, the call is switched to the number originally dialed (5), all without the need for operator assistance.

small cell: A miniature cellular base station designed to provide improved cellular coverage and capacity for homes and organizations and even metropolitan and rural public spaces.

radio waves, people with special receivers can listen to cellular phone conversations, so such conversations are not secure.

Increasingly, workers rely on their mobile phones as their primary business phones. However, they frequently encounter problems with poor coverage and can find it difficult to place calls or conduct an extended conversation. A small cell is a miniature cellular base station designed to provide improved cellular coverage and capacity for homes and organizations and even metropolitan and rural public spaces. Various types of small cells ranging in order of increasing coverage include femtocells, picocells, metrocells, and microcells.

Many communications companies now offer small cell solutions to boost cell phone signals or enable the cell phone to operate over other wireless networks, thus guaranteeing a strong, reliable cell signal. Cell phones may also be linked to a cordless phone via a Bluetooth connection so that if someone calls you on your cell phone, you can answer the call on the cordless phone. This improves the range of cell phone coverage and eliminates dropped calls, especially for those times you cannot find your cell phone in time.

Some observers are concerned that these small cell devices can be hacked and intruders can intercept and decode voice and text messages.

Digital Subscriber Line (DSL) Service

digital subscriber line (DSL): A telecommunications service that delivers high-speed Internet access to homes and small businesses over the existing phone lines of the local telephone network.

A digital subscriber line (DSL) is a telecommunications service that delivers high-speed Internet access to homes and small businesses over the existing phone lines of the local telephone network. See Figure 6.20. Most home and small business users are connected to an *asymmetric DSL (ADSL)* line designed to provide a connection speed from the Internet to the user (download speed) that is three to four times faster than the connection from the user back to the Internet (upload speed). ADSL does not require an additional phone line and yet provides "always-on" Internet access. A drawback of ADSL is that the farther the subscriber is from the local telephone office, the poorer the signal quality and the slower the transmission speed. ADSL provides a dedicated connection from each user to the phone company's local office, so the performance does not decrease as new users are added. Cable modem users generally share a network loop that runs through a neighborhood so that adding users means lowering the transmission speeds. *Symmetric DSL (SDSL)* is used mainly by small businesses; it does not allow you to use the phone at the same time, but the speed of receiving and sending data is the same.

FIGURE 6.20

Digital subscriber line (DSL)

At the local telephone company's central office, a DSL Access Multiplexer (DSLAM) takes connections from many customers and multiplexes them onto a single, high-capacity connection to the Internet. Subscriber phone calls can be routed through a switch at the local telephone central office to the public telephone network.

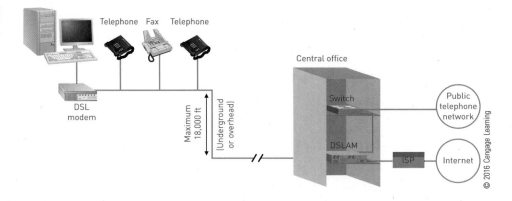

Linking Personal Computers to Mainframes and Networks

One of the most basic ways that telecommunications connect users to information systems is by connecting personal computers to mainframe computers so that data can be downloaded or uploaded. For example, a user can download a data file or document file from a database to a personal computer.

Some telecommunications software programs instruct the computer to connect to another computer on the network, download or send information, and then disconnect from the telecommunications line. These programs are called *unattended systems* because they perform the functions automatically without user intervention.

Voice Mail

voice mail: Technology that enables users to send, receive, and store verbal messages to and from other people around the world.

With voice mail, users can send, receive, and store verbal messages to and from other people around the world. Some voice mail systems assign a code to a group of people. Suppose the code 100 stands for all the sales representatives in a company. If anyone calls the voice mail system, enters the number 100, and leaves a message, all the sales representatives receive the same message. Call management systems can be linked to corporate email and instant messaging systems. Calls to employees can be generated from instant messages or converted into email messages to ensure quicker access and response.

Voice Mail-to-Text Services

voice mail-to-text service: A service that captures voice mail messages, converts them to text, and sends them to an email account.

Voice mail is more difficult to manage than email because you must deal with messages one by one without knowing who has called you and without being able to prioritize the messages. In recognition of these shortcomings of voice mail, several services (e.g., Jott, SpinVox, GotVoice, and SimulScribe) are now available to convert speech to text so that you can manage voice mails more effectively. If you subscribe to a voice mail-to-text service, your voice mail no longer reaches your phone service provider's voice mail service. Instead, it is rerouted to the voice-to-text service, translated into text, and then sent to your regular email account or a special account for converted email messages. You can also temporarily disable the voice-to-text service and receive voice messages.

Reverse 911 Service

reverse 911 service: A communications solution that delivers emergency notifications to users in a selected geographical area.

Reverse 911 service is a communications solution that delivers recorded emergency notifications to users in a selected geographical area. The technology employs databases of phone numbers and contact information. Some systems can send more than 250,000 voice or text messages per hour via phone, pager, cell phone, and email.

Bladen County in North Carolina purchased a reverse 911 service integrated with a geographic information system to target areas simply by choosing a street or drawing a circle around a portion of a county map. Initially, the database was filled only with the landline numbers of residents. Residents can also enter unlisted phone numbers, cell phone numbers, and secondary numbers into the system for future contact.

Police in Virginia Beach defended the use of a reverse 911 call system to wake over 17,000 residents at 3:20 am. The police used the system to send an automated message to alert people that they were searching for a missing 12-year-old-girl. The police decided to take this measure only after they had searched unsuccessfully for three hours using K-9s, helicopters, and foot patrols, and were unable to find the girl with her friends or through social media or her cell phone.[35]

Home and Small Business Networks

Some small businesses and many families own more than one computer and want to set up a simple network to share printers or an Internet connection; access shared files, such as photos, MP3 audio files, spreadsheets, and documents, on different machines; play games that support multiple concurrent players; and send the output of network-connected devices, such as a security camera or DVD player, to a computer.

One simple solution is to establish a wireless network that covers your home or small business. To do so, you can buy an 802.11n access point, connect it to your cable modem or DSL modem, and then use it to communicate with all your devices. For less than $100, you can purchase a combined router, firewall, Ethernet hub, and wireless hub in one small device. Computers in your network connect to this box with a wireless card, which is connected by cable or DSL modem to the Internet. This box enables each computer in the network to access the Internet. The firewall filters the information coming from the Internet into your network. You can configure it to reject information from offensive Web sites or potential hackers. The router can also encrypt all wireless communications to keep your network secure.

In addition, you can configure your computers to share printers and files. Recent versions of Windows include a Network and Sharing Center that helps with network configuration. Some of the basic configuration steps include assigning each computer to a workgroup and giving it a name, identifying the files you want to share (placing an optional password on some files), and identifying the printers you want to share.

Electronic Document Distribution

electronic document distribution: A process that enables the sending and receiving of documents in a digital form without being printed (although printing is possible).

Electronic document distribution lets you send and receive documents in a digital form without printing them (although printing is possible). It is much faster to distribute electronic documents via networks than to mail printed forms. While creating the new edition of this textbook, the authors distributed drafts of the chapters to a developmental editor, copyeditor, proofreader, and reviewers to obtain quick feedback and suggestions for improvements to be incorporated into a second and then final draft. Viewing documents on screen instead of printing them also saves paper and document storage space. Accessing and retrieving electronic documents is also much faster.

The YMCA of metropolitan Los Angeles serves over 200,000 members in 25 branch locations across the city. It linked its procurement system with an electronic document distribution system to produce documents that can be delivered quickly and cost effectively to its suppliers via print, fax, email, or the Web. The documents provide a full audit trail of all purchasing transactions.

Call Centers

A call center is a location where an organization handles customer and other telephone calls, usually with some amount of computer automation. See Figure 6.21. Call centers are used by customer service organizations, telemarketing companies, computer product help desks, charitable and political campaign organizations, and any organization that uses the telephone to sell or support its products and services. An automatic call distributor (ACD) is a telephone facility that manages incoming calls, handling them based on the

FIGURE **6.21**

Call center

Offshore call centers provide technical support services for many technology vendors and their customers.

STR/AFP/Getty Images

number called and an associated database of instructions. Call centers frequently employ an ACD to validate callers, place outgoing calls, forward calls to the right party, allow callers to record messages, gather usage statistics, balance the workload of support personnel, and provide other services.

The Philippines is now considered the call center capital of the world. U.S. companies prefer Filipinos because their customers can more easily understand them than they can Indian agents. Another factor is that the Philippines has excellent training facilities. In addition, the Philippines has a more reliable power grid, and its cities have better public transportation so employees can get to work safely and on time. Although the country is first in the voice sector, the top provider of technical support is still India because of its cheaper labor.[36]

Some U.S. companies are moving their call centers back to the United States. As a result, contact center deployment in the United States has been rising since 2010, including a 1.6 percent rise in 2013 resulting in a gain of 10,000 jobs in the sector per quarter. Service complaints from consumers frustrated with oversees call centers is the primary reason for the change. In addition, U.S. call centers increasingly are using integrated telephony solutions to improve customer support, while mining data to observe trends, such as account cancelation.[37]

The National Do Not Call Registry was set up in 2003 by the U.S. Federal Trade Commission (FTC). Telemarketers who call numbers on the list face penalties of up to $11,000 per call, as well as possible consumer lawsuits. More than 221 million active registrants have been created by individuals logging on to *www.donotcall.gov* or calling 888–382-1222. The Do Not Call Rules require that, at least every 31 days, sellers and telemarketers remove from their call lists the numbers found in the registry. The number of registrants is increasing dramatically, over 60 percent from 2011 to 2012. The FTC now receives an average of 308,000 complaints a month.[38]

Even if you have registered, you can still receive calls from political organizations, charities, educational organizations, and telephone surveyors. You can also receive calls from companies with which you have an existing business relationship, such as your bank or credit card companies. Although the registry has greatly reduced the number of unwanted calls to consumers, it has created several compliance-related issues for direct marketing companies.

Telecommuting and Virtual Workers and Workgroups

telecommuting: The use of computing devices and networks so that employees can work effectively away from the office.

Employees are performing more and more work away from the traditional office setting. Many enterprises have adopted policies for telecommuting so that employees can work away from the office using computing devices and networks. This practice means workers can be more effective and companies can save money on office and parking space and office equipment. According to a recent study by Forrester Research, 17 percent of North American enterprises and 14 percent of European enterprises report having employees who spend at least 20 percent of their time away from their normal work desk or who work from home.

Telecommuting is popular among workers for several reasons. Parents find that eliminating the daily commute helps balance family and work responsibilities. Qualified workers who otherwise might be unable to participate in the normal workforce (e.g., those who are physically challenged or who live in rural areas too far from the city office to commute regularly) can use telecommuting to become productive workers. When gas prices soar, telecommuting can help workers reduce significant expenses. Extensive use of telecommuting can lead to decreased need for office space, potentially saving a large company millions of dollars. Corporations are also being encouraged by public policy to try telecommuting as a means of reducing their carbon footprint and traffic congestion. Large companies also view telecommuting as a means to distribute their workforce and reduce the impact of a disaster at a central facility.

Some types of jobs are well suited to telecommuting, including jobs held by salespeople, secretaries, real estate agents, computer programmers, and legal assistants, to name a few. Telecommuting also requires a certain personality type to be effective. Telecommuters need to be strongly self-motivated, be organized, be focused on their tasks with minimal supervision, and have a low need for social interaction. Jobs unsuitable for telecommuting include those that require frequent face-to-face interaction, need much supervision, and have many short-term deadlines. Employees who choose to work at home must be able to work independently, manage their time well, and balance work and home life.

Electronic Meetings

videoconferencing: A set of interactive telecommunications technologies that enable people at multiple locations to communicate using simultaneous two-way video and audio transmissions.

Videoconferencing comprises a set of interactive telecommunications technologies that enable people at multiple locations to communicate using simultaneous two-way video and audio transmissions. Videoconferencing can reduce travel expenses and time, and it can increase managerial effectiveness through faster response to problems, access to more people, and less duplication of effort by geographically dispersed sites. Almost all videoconferencing systems combine video and phone call capabilities with data or document conferencing, as shown in Figure 6.22. You can see the other person's face, view the same documents, and swap notes and drawings. With some systems, callers can change live documents in real time. Many businesses find that the document- and application-sharing feature of the videoconference enhances group productivity and efficiency. It also fosters teamwork and can save corporate travel time and expense.

FIGURE **6.22**

Videoconferencing

Videoconferencing allows participants to conduct long-distance meetings face-to-face while eliminating the need for costly travel.

© Andrey_Popov/Shutterstock.com

Group videoconferencing is used daily in a variety of businesses as an easy way to connect work teams. Members of a team meet in a specially prepared videoconference room equipped with sound-sensitive cameras that automatically focus on the person speaking, large TV-like monitors for viewing the participants at the remote location, and high-quality speakers and microphones. Videoconferencing costs have declined steadily, while video quality and synchronization of audio to video—once weak points of the technology—have improved.

Facebook has rapidly expanded to hundreds of millions of active users around the globe. It is a challenge to get members of a global operation to collaborate effectively and perform at a high level, especially when the members are separated by thousands of miles and multiple time zones as well as vast differences in culture and experiences. Videoconferencing has been a key strategy at Facebook to meet these challenges. Early on the firm implemented large room videoconferencing at its headquarters and larger office locations. More recently it has set up the Blue Jeans Network, a cloud-based videoconferencing service, to enable videoconferencing for employees who do not have easy access to these sites but can use desktop and mobile devices.

Electronic Data Interchange

Electronic data interchange (EDI) is a way to communicate data from one company to another and from one application to another in a standard format, permitting the recipient to perform a standard business transaction, such as processing purchase orders. Connecting corporate computers among organizations is the idea behind EDI, which uses network systems and follows standards and procedures that can process output from one system directly as input to other systems—without human intervention. EDI can link the computers of customers, manufacturers, and suppliers, as shown in Figure 6.23. This technology eliminates the need for paper documents and substantially cuts down on costly errors. Customer orders and inquiries are transmitted from the customer's computer to the manufacturer's computer. The manufacturer's computer determines when new supplies are needed and can place orders by connecting with the supplier's computer.

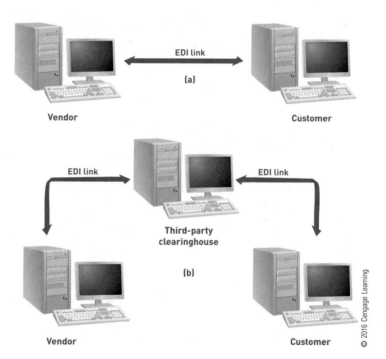

FIGURE 6.23

Two approaches to electronic data interchange

Many organizations now insist that their suppliers use EDI systems. Often, the vendor and customer (a) have a direct EDI connection or (b) the link is provided by a third-party clearinghouse that converts data and performs other services for the participants.

© 2016 Cengage Learning

Audubon Metals recovers metal from automobile scrap, including brass, copper, magnesium, and zinc. The company produces on the order of 120 million pounds of aluminum alloy per year. One of the purchasers of its recycled metal, Nissan, demands accurate and time EDI processing from all of its suppliers so that it can streamline the processing of purchase orders, invoices, and other documents.

Electronic Funds Transfer

Electronic funds transfer (EFT) is a system of transferring money from one bank account directly to another without any paper money changing hands. It is used both for credit transfers, such as payroll payments, and for debit transfers, such as mortgage payments. The benefits of EFT include reduced administrative costs, increased efficiency, simplified bookkeeping, and greater security. One of the most widely used EFT programs is direct deposit, which deposits employee payroll checks directly into the designated bank accounts. The two primary components of EFT, wire transfer and automated clearing house, are summarized in Table 6.5.

TABLE **6.5** Comparison of ACH payments and wire transfers

	ACH Payments	Wire Transfers
When does payment clear?	Overnight	Immediately
Can payment be canceled?	Yes	No
Are sufficient funds guaranteed?	No	Yes
What is the approximate cost per transaction?	$0.25	$10–$40

© 2016 Cengage Learning

The STAR Network is part of the payment services offered by First Data Corporation and provides EFT services to some 2 million retailers, their financial institutions, and customers nationwide.

Unified Communications

Unified communications provides a simple and consistent user experience across all types of communications, such as instant messaging, fixed and mobile phone, email, voice mail, and Web conferencing. The concept of *presence* (knowing where one's desired communication participants are and if they are available at this instant) is a key component of unified communications. The goal is to reduce the time required to make decisions and communicate results, thus greatly improving productivity.

All of the ways that unified communications can be implemented rely on fast, reliable communications networks. Typically, users have a device capable of supporting the various forms of communications (e.g., laptop with microphone and video camera or a smartphone) that is loaded with software supporting unified communications. The users' devices also connect to a server that keeps track of the presence of each user.

Quick Response Codes

Quick Response (QR) codes are a type of two-dimensional bar code that can be scanned by users with a smartphone camera. The camera must be equipped with the appropriate software to display text or connect to a wireless network and open a Web page in the smartphone's browser. The code consists of black modules arranged in a square pattern on a white background. See Figure 6.24. Air New Zealand was one of the first airlines to use QR codes to read boarding passes. Sign posts with QR codes can be found in some parks and nature areas. When you scan the code, you are provided with

FIGURE 6.24

Quick Response code

QR codes are a type of two-dimensional bar code that can be scanned by users with a smartphone camera.

© iStockphoto.com/Oehoeboeroe

information about the trail, flora and fauna of the location, and interesting spots along the trail. At Findlay Market in Cincinnati, shoppers can use their smartphones to scan a QR code on a sign for squash at Daisy Mae's Market, and then display a short YouTube video on "How to Make Spaghetti Squash." In addition, the Cincinnati zoo uses the QR codes on exhibits, zoo maps, and membership booklets.

Global Positioning System Applications

The global positioning system (GPS) is a global navigation satellite system that uses two dozen satellites orbiting roughly 11,000 miles above the Earth. See Figure 6.25. These satellites are used as reference points to calculate positions on Earth to an accuracy of a few yards or even less. GPS receivers have become as small as a cell phone and relatively inexpensive, making the technology readily accessible. The technology, originally developed for national defense and military applications, has migrated to consumer devices and is used in navigational and location tracking devices. GPS receivers are commonly found in automobiles, boats, planes, laptop computers, and cell phones.

FIGURE 6.25

Global positioning system

A global positioning system (GPS) can guide you along a route whether you are mobile or on foot.

© iStockphoto.com/DOUGBERRY

To determine its position, a GPS receiver receives the signals from four GPS satellites and determines its exact distance from each satellite. (While the position of the receiver could be determined with just three measurements, a fourth distance measurement helps to adjust for any impreciseness in the other three.) This determination is done by very accurately measuring the time it takes for a signal to travel at the speed of light from the satellite to the receiver (distance = time $\times$ 186,000 miles/second). The GPS receiver then uses these distances to triangulate its precise location in terms of latitude, longitude, and altitude.

GPS tracking technology has become the standard by which fleet managers monitor the movement of their cars, trucks, and vehicles. GPS tracking quickly exposes inefficient routing practices, wasted time on the job, and speeding. Even small fleet operators can achieve significant benefits from the use of GPS tracking.

Computer-based navigation systems are also based on GPS technology. These systems come in all shapes and sizes and with varying capabilities—from PC-based systems installed in automobiles for guiding you across the country to handheld units you carry while hiking. All systems need a GPS antenna to receive satellite signals to pinpoint your location. On most of these systems, your location is superimposed on a map stored on CDs or a DVD. Portable systems can be moved from one car to another or carried in your backpack. Some systems come with dynamic rerouting capability, where the path recommended depends on weather and road conditions, which are continually transmitted to your car via a receiver connected to a satellite radio system.

All of the major U.S. wireless carriers offer cell phones that include an additional GPS antenna and internal GPS chip that can pinpoint a given location within a hundred yards or so. (The accuracy really depends on the accuracy of the timing mechanism of the cell phone. A tiny timing error can result in an error of 1,000 feet.) Verizon customers can use Verizon VZ Navigator software, while AT&T, Sprint, T-Mobile, and Verizon Wireless customers can use TeleNav's GPS Navigator software.

Some employers use GPS-enabled phones to track their employees' locations. The locator phone provides GPS-enabled tracking devices that can provide its wearer's coordinates and dial emergency phone numbers. In addition to employers, parents and caregivers can track the phone's location by phone or online and can receive notification if it leaves a designated safe area. Many people suffering from dementia have wandered off but were quickly found because they were wearing such a device.

Google Maps, Navigon USA, Network in Motion's Gokivo, and MapQuest are among the more popular navigation apps for GPS-enabled devices. With these apps, users can find their way around and receive voice directions on how to get from one place to another. SpotCrime is an innovative GPS app that uses GPS technology to determine exactly where you are and then provides a criminal history of that area providing details of various crimes committed such as arson, assault, burglary, and vandalism.

SUMMARY

Principle:

A telecommunications system consists of several fundamental components.

In a telecommunications system, the sending unit transmits a signal to a telecommunications device, which performs a number of functions such as converting the signal into a different form or from one type to another. The telecommunications device then sends the signal through a medium that carries the electronic signal. The signal is received by another telecommunications device that is connected to the receiving computer.

A networking protocol defines the set of rules that governs the exchange of information over a telecommunications channel to ensure fast, efficient, error-free communications and to enable hardware, software, and equipment manufacturers and service providers to build products that interoperate effectively. There is a myriad of telecommunications protocols, including international, national, and regional standards.

Communications among people can occur synchronously or asynchronously. With synchronous communications, the receiver gets the message as soon as it is sent. With asynchronous communications, the receiver gets the message after some delay—a few seconds to minutes or hours or even days after the message is sent.

A transmission medium can be divided into one or more communications channels, each capable of carrying a message. Telecommunications channels can be classified as simplex, half-duplex, or full-duplex.

Channel bandwidth refers to the rate at which data is exchanged, usually expressed in bits per second.

A circuit-switching network uses a dedicated path for the duration of the communications. A packet-switching network does not employ a dedicated path for communications and breaks data into packets for transmission over the network.

The telecommunications media that physically connect data communications devices can be divided into two broad categories: guided transmission media and wireless media. Guided transmission media include twisted-pair wire, coaxial cable, and fiber-optic cable. Wireless transmission involves the broadcast of communications in one of three frequency ranges: radio, microwave, or infrared.

Wireless communications solutions for very short distances include Near Field Communications, Bluetooth, ultra wideband, infrared transmission, and ZigBee. Wi-Fi is a popular wireless communications solution for medium-range distances. Wireless communications solutions for long distances include satellite and terrestrial microwave transmission, wireless mesh, 3G and 4G cellular communications service, and WiMAX.

Principle:

Networks are an essential component of an organization's information technology infrastructure.

Network topology indicates how the communications links and hardware devices of the network are arranged. The three most common network topologies in use today are the star, bus, and mesh.

The geographic area covered by a network determines whether it is called a personal area network, local area network, metropolitan area network, or wide area network.

The electronic flow of data across international and global boundaries is often called transborder data flow.

When an organization needs to use two or more computer systems, it can follow one of three basic data-processing strategies: centralized (all processing at a single location, high degree of control), decentralized (multiple processors that do not communicate with one another), or distributed (multiple processors that communicate with each other). Distributed processing minimizes the consequences of a catastrophic event at one location while ensuring uninterrupted systems availability.

A client/server system is a network that connects a user's computer (a client) to one or more host computers (servers). A client is often a PC that requests services from the server, shares processing tasks with the server, and displays the results.

Numerous popular telecommunications devices include smartphones, modems, multiplexers, PBX systems, switches, bridges, routers, and gateways.

Telecommunications software performs important functions, such as error checking and message formatting. A network operating system controls the computer systems and devices on a network, allowing them to communicate with one another. Network-management software enables a manager to monitor the use of individual computers and shared hardware, scan for viruses, and ensure compliance with software licenses.

The interception of confidential information by unauthorized parties is a major concern for organizations. Encryption of data and the use of virtual private networks are two common solutions to this problem. Special measures must be taken to secure wireless networks.

Principle:

Network applications are essential to organizational success.

Telecommunications and networks are creating profound changes in business because they remove the barriers of time and distance.

The effective use of networks can turn a company into an agile, powerful, and creative organization, giving it a long-term competitive advantage. Networks let users share hardware, programs, and databases across the organization. They can transmit and receive information to improve organizational effectiveness and efficiency. They enable geographically separated workgroups to share documents and opinions, thus fostering teamwork, innovative ideas, and new business strategies.

The wide range of telecommunications and network applications includes cellular phone services, digital subscriber line, linking personal computer to mainframes, voice mail, voice-to-text services, reverse 911 service, home and small business networks, electronic document distribution, call centers, telecommuting, videoconferencing, electronic data interchange, electronic funds transfer, unified communications, Quick Response codes, and global positioning system applications.

KEY TERMS

Bluetooth	network topology
broadband communications	networking protocol
bus network	network-management software
centralized processing	packet-switching network
channel bandwidth	personal area network (PAN)
circuit-switching network	private branch exchange (PBX)
client/server architecture	reverse 911 service
computer network	router
decentralized processing	simplex channel
digital subscriber line (DSL)	small cell
distributed processing	software defined networking
electronic document distribution	star network
encryption	switch
encryption key	telecommunications medium
full-duplex channel	telecommuting
gateway	ultra wideband (UWB)
half-duplex channel	videoconferencing
infrared transmission	virtual private network (VPN)
local area network (LAN)	voice mail
Long Term Evolution (LTE)	voice mail-to-text service
mesh network	wide area network (WAN)
metropolitan area network (MAN)	Wi-Fi
modem	wireless access point
Near Field Communication (NFC)	Worldwide Interoperability for Microwave Access (WiMAX)
network operating system (NOS)	ZigBee

CHAPTER 6: SELF-ASSESSMENT TEST

A telecommunications system consists of several fundamental components.

1. With asynchronous communications, the receiver gets the message as soon as it is sent. True or False?
2. Telecommunications channel _____ refers to the rate at which data is exchanged.
3. A _____ defines a set of rules, algorithms, messages, and other mechanisms that enable software and hardware in networked devices to communicate effectively.
   a. network channel
   b. network bandwidth
   c. network protocol
   d. circuit switching
4. A _____ permits data transmission in both directions at the same time.
   a. circuit-switching network
   b. packet-switching network
   c. simple channel
   d. full-duplex channel
5. _____ involves the transmission of extremely short electromagnetic pulses lasting just 50 to 1,000 picoseconds.

Networks are an essential component of an organization's information technology infrastructure.

6. A(n) _____ network uses multiple access points to link a series of nodes that speak to each other to form a network connection across a large area.

7. The Ticketmaster reservation service is an example of an organization that uses decentralized processing to store information about events and record the purchases of seats. True or False?

8. A _____ is a network device that serves as an entrance to another network.
   a. modem
   b. gateway
   c. bridge
   d. PBX

Network applications are essential to organizational success.

9. A(n) _____ private network uses a public network (usually the Internet) to connect multiple remote locations.
   a. circuit-switching network

   b. packet-switching network
   c. virtual private network
   d. encrypted network

10. _____ enables a manager on a networked personal computer to monitor the use of individual computers and shared hardware, scan for viruses, and ensure compliance with software licenses.

11. _____ is the process of converting an original message into a form that can be understood only by the intended receiver.

12. Reverse 911 is a communications solution that delivers recorded emergency notifications to users in a selected geographical area. True or False?

13. _____ is a way to communicate data from one company to another and from one application to another in a standard format, permitting recipients to perform a standard business transaction.

CHAPTER 6: SELF-ASSESSMENT TEST ANSWERS

1. False
2. bandwidth
3. c
4. d
5. Ultra wideband
6. mesh
7. False

8. b
9. c
10. Network-management software
11. Encryption
12. True
13. Electronic data interchange or EDI

REVIEW QUESTIONS

1. Define the term telecommunications medium. Name three media types.
2. What is meant by network topology? Identify and briefly describe different network topologies.
3. What is a telecommunications protocol? Give the names of two specific telecommunications protocols.
4. What are the names of the three primary frequency ranges used in wireless communications?
5. Briefly describe the differences between a circuit-switching and a packet-switching network.
6. Identify two organizations that lead in the setting of communications standards.
7. Identify and briefly describe three types of telecommunications channels.
8. What is Bluetooth? How is it used?
9. What is a wireless mesh network? What is one of the key advantages of such a network?

10. Briefly explain how a Wi-Fi network operates.
11. What are some of the advantages of videoconferencing? Describe a recent meeting you attended that could have been conducted using videoconferencing.
12. What is the difference between a network operating system and a network-management software?
13. Distinguish between a router and a switch.
14. Identify two approaches to securing the transmission of confidential data.
15. What is a reverse 911 service? Give two examples of how such a system might be used.
16. What is electronic data interchange? List three types of data that a manufacturer and supplier might exchange electronically.

DISCUSSION QUESTIONS

1. What are the risks of transmitting data over an unsecured Wi-Fi network? What steps are necessary to secure a Wi-Fi Protected Access network?
2. Briefly discuss the differences between centralized and decentralized processing.

3. Distinguish between client/server and file server architecture.
4. What is the issue associated with transborder data flow? How might this issue limit the use of an organization's WAN?

5. Distinguish between centralized and distributed data processing.
6. Briefly describe how a cellular phone service works.
7. Briefly explain how the GPS system determines the position of a transmitter.
8. Briefly discuss some of the changes that are affecting the operations of a telephone call center.
9. Imagine that you are responsible for signage on your campus to help visitors learn about your school and more easily find their way around.

Discuss how you might employ Quick Response code technology in this effort.
10. Identify some of the features and capabilities that 5G networks might provide.
11. Is telecommuting aimed solely at enabling employees to work from home? Explain your answer.
12. Discuss the role of the PBX and identify some of the features that it can provide.

PROBLEM-SOLVING EXERCISES

1. You have been hired as a telecommunications consultant to help a software firm identify new ideas for GPS applications. Use PowerPoint or similar software to produce a presentation of your top three ideas.
2. As a member of the information systems organization of a mid-sized firm, you are convinced that telecommuting represents an excellent

opportunity for the firm to both reduce expenses and improve employee morale. Use PowerPoint or similar software to make a convincing presentation to management for adopting such a program. Your presentation must identify benefits and potential issues that must be overcome to make such a program a success.

TEAM ACTIVITIES

1. Form a team to interview a manager employed in a telecommunications service provider. Identify the greatest challenges and opportunities that the company faces in the next two to three years.
2. Form a team to identify the public locations (such as an airport, public library, or café) in your area

where wireless LAN connections are available. Visit two locations and write a brief paragraph discussing your experience at each location trying to connect to the Internet.

WEB EXERCISES

1. Do research on the Web to identify the latest revelations about the NSA from Edward Snowden. In your opinion, should he be considered a patriot or a traitor? Defend your position.
2. Go online to find out more about the rapid growth of wireless data traffic. Document the

current growth trend. Identify actions taken by two different wireless carriers to meet this increase in demand. Briefly summarize your findings in a written report.

CAREER EXERCISES

1. Identify three telecommunications organizations that appear to have excellent growth opportunities. Do research to identify current job openings and the qualifications needed to fill these positions. Do any of these positions appeal to you? Why or why not?
2. Do research to assess potential career opportunities in the telecommunications or networking industry. Consider resources such as the Bureau of Labor

Statistics list of fastest-growing positions, *Network World*, and *Computerworld*. Are there particular positions within these industries that offer good opportunities? What sort of background and education is required for candidates for these positions? You might be asked to summarize your findings for your class in a written or an oral report.

CASE STUDIES

Case One

NetHope Worldwide Disaster Relief

When disaster strikes, it has both an economic and a human impact. People who are not affected by the disaster often feel

a moral obligation to come to the aid of the disaster's victims. People feel this obligation even more strongly if they have specific skills that can help alleviate the effects of the disaster.

One skill needed in many natural disasters is the ability to set up networks so the people affected, their governments, and organizations that want to help can communicate with each other. That need for long-distance communication places a particular responsibility on the technology community. Many high-tech companies fulfill this responsibility under the auspices of NetHope, a group of large humanitarian relief organizations.

Consider, for example, the 2013 typhoon that hit the Philippines. With tens of thousands of people missing and over 6,000 people confirmed dead, humanitarian organizations were in a race against time. If relief is not provided quickly in such situations, the effects of a disaster can worsen and spread. Yet where and how to provide relief in the chaotic situation was not clear. So, NetHope sent a civil drone to scout out the situation on the ground. The drone helped NGO rescue teams identify the best locations to set up base camps. Then the drone provided detailed visual information needed to clear roads blocked by debris and to repair the Carigara Hospital. Later the drone conducted search-and-rescue operations in the Bay of Tacloban.

NetHope and its partners have been on site in all recent natural disasters. In the first two months after the Haiti earthquake of 2010, NetHope and its partner Microsoft helped launch a Web site for interagency collaboration, set up cloud-computing solutions for Haiti's government and for organizations working in the country, and had Bing and MSN each set up Web pages where people could donate to Haiti. Communication between Haitians and aid workers was hampered because few workers spoke Haitian Creole. To solve this problem, Microsoft added Haitian Creole to Microsoft Translator, a free automatic translation tool, and provided the tool to aid workers.

In the 2011 tsunami in Japan, NetHope partners provided a cloud-based community communication portal for Second Harvest Japan. The organization uses the portal to coordinate food donors, transportation providers, and distributors in the Japanese relief effort. Cloud services avoid problems such as damaged infrastructure and equipment, power shortages, and telecommunications service interruptions.

One of NetHope's five major missions is connectivity. According to the NetHope Web site, the connectivity objective is to "improve communications between organizations and field offices in remote parts of the world, where infrastructure is limited or absent." Until recently, NetHope tried to meet this objective by placing very small aperture terminals (VSATs) in remote areas with little to no terrestrial infrastructure. VSAT systems include an Earth station (usually less than 3 meters, or 10 feet, wide) placed outdoors in line of sight to the sky to link to a satellite in geosynchronous orbit. The satellite can relay messages to anywhere else on Earth, permitting communication with isolated areas.

However, as Gisli Olafsson, emergency response director of NetHope (and a former Microsoft employee) learned, "Using VSAT as the preferred way to connect is not always the most effective and economical method." Olafsson continues: "With most countries moving toward a 3G wireless broadband mobile network … we have seen that mobile networks are becoming more resilient to large-scale disasters, with core services generally being available within two weeks of a major incident…. It is more economical and easier to stockpile and transfer 3G modems than VSAT kits."

Technology, of course, is never the entire answer. People are an important part of any system. After the 2010 Haiti earthquake, NetHope launched NetHope Academy to provide IT skills training and on-the-job work experience to unemployed Haitians so they could build in-country technical expertise. The first group of NetHope Academy interns spent three weeks in intensive boot camp–style classroom training. They were then placed with teams rebuilding devastated areas of Haiti, using their new skills to help team members keep in touch with people outside their immediate area.

In addition to Microsoft, NetHope partners include such well-known technology firms as Accenture, Cisco, Hewlett-Packard, and Intel. The technology community can be proud of its commitment to humanitarian aid and economic recovery.

Discussion Questions

1. How does the destruction of technology during natural disasters stifle relief efforts?
2. How does NetHope partner with other organizations to assist disaster relief efforts?

Critical Thinking Questions

1. Which of the telecommunications and networking technologies would be useful in natural disasters?
2. Major natural disasters, while not as rare as one might wish, are not common enough that companies develop network and communications products for that use alone. The technologies that NetHope partners use were originally developed for other reasons. What additional uses could these technologies have?

SOURCES: Dearing, Paige, "Civil Drone Helps NetHope Haitian Relief Efforts in the Philippines," NetHub, Our Blog, NetHope Web Site, December 17, 2013; Microsoft case study, "Microsoft Disaster Response," Computerworld Honors Awards, 2011, *www.eiseverywhere.com/file_up loads/1731e3ed9282e5b4b81db8572c9d5e4f_Microsoft_Corporation _Microsoft_Disaster_Response.pdf*, accessed January 28, 2012; Microsoft Web site, "Microsoft Supports Relief Efforts in Haiti" (video), *www .microsoft.com/en-us/showcase/details.aspx?uuid=ed1d948f-5dfb-45f1 –9c39–20050b7d752c*, August 19, 2010; Microsoft Citizenship Team, "How Technology Is Helping Distribute Food in Japan," Microsoft Citizenship (blog), *blogs.technet.com/b/microsoftupblog/archive/2011 /03/18/how-technology-is-helping-distribute-food-in-japan.aspx*, March 18, 2011; Microsoft Web site, "Serving Communities: Disaster and Humanitarian Response," *www.microsoft.com/about/corporatecitizen ship/en-us/serving-communities/disaster-and-humanitarian-response*, accessed January 30, 2012; NetHope Web site, *www.nethope.org*, accessed January 31, 2012; Olafsson, G., "Information and Communication Technology Usage in the 2010 Pakistan Floods," NetHope (blog), *blog.disasterexpert.org/2011/09/pakistan-floods-use-of-information -and.html*, September 9, 2011.

Case Two

Rural Africa Reaches to the Sky for Internet Access

In Africa, only about 16 percent of the population has access to the Internet. By comparison, about 63 percent of the population in Europe has Internet access. Furthermore, Internet connectivity is plagued by the low bandwidth, unreliability, and high cost. Overcoming this digital divide is not an easy task, as the content lacks terrestrial connectivity between the submarine cables, the Internet exchange points—the infrastructure Internet service providers (ISP) need to exchange traffic between their different networks—and "last mile" delivery systems. As a result, individuals, organizations, and businesses rely heavily on mobile telephony and satellite technology.

SkyVision has stepped into the African market and other emerging markets with customized satellite-based virtual private networks that are supporting economic development. The VPN allows companies to connect their WAN sites to share data and support significantly more efficient collaboration. Through its satellite systems, SkyVision is able to offer reliable broadband and high-speed data services to the most remote locations.

For example, only 12 percent of the rural population in Zimbabwe has access to banking services. Banks simply cannot provide connectivity to rural areas where 65 percent of the population lives. SkyVision VPN connected the Harare headquarters to the rural branches so that they could offer the wide range of banking services that rely on core banking systems, email, Internet, and point-of-sale (POS) services. SkyVision satellite and fiber-optic VPN technology allowed one Nigerian bank to install and connect 90 ATM sites to never-before–served rural locations. Within the developing oil and gas industries, SkyVision has also established reliable connectivity between companies' headquarters and remote depots—as well as between onshore and offshore operations.

SkyVision technology has also promoted the development of economic ties between Europe and Africa. The Agro-Industrial Group, for example, needs to connect several private African agro-industrial companies to each other and to their European headquarters. SkyVision established reliable and secure data sharing system.

Despite these advances, analysts point out that the prices of more reliable connectivity solutions are prohibitive for many companies, organizations, and businesses. So, many organizations and corporations are continuing to take initiatives. In late 2013, Google announced Project Link, a plan to build fiber-optic networks that would allow for high-speed Internet connectivity. The project is headquartered in Kampala, the capital of Uganda, a dense urban center that lacks broadband access. Google is hoping to fund the project by charging the mobile telephony providers who will link into the network.

These efforts, however, will focus on major cities and support development in urban Africa. Yet a number of barriers exist to high-speed terrestrial networks. African governments sometimes charge high licensing fees and tax technology equipment heavily. Policy-makers also need to cooperate to facilitate cross-border terrestrial connectivity and encourage private investment. Until governments take these steps, it will be left to initiatives, like those of SkyVision, to reach out to those remote rural areas.

Discussion Questions

1. Where does Africa stand in relation to Europe and other developed nations with regard to Internet connectivity and use?
2. What technological barriers do companies face when trying to link networks that are located in different locations and how do companies like SkyVision help these companies?

Critical Thinking Questions

1. Do you think that innovators like SkyVision or Google will have more success?
2. What role do you think governments and international organizations should take in overcoming the digital divide in urban and rural Africa?

SOURCES: Donnelly, Caroline, "Google to Improve Internet Access in Africa via Project Link," ITPRO, November 21, 2013; "Lifting Barriers to Internet Connectivity in Africa," Analysis Mason, October 2013; Internet Work Statistics, *www.internetworldstats.com/*, accessed December 26, 2013; SkyVision Case Studies: Agro-Industrial Group; Banking & Finance Solution, Nigeria; Bank in Zimbabwe; Oil & Gas Corporation.

Questions for Web Case

See the Web site for this book to read about the Altitude Online case for this chapter. The following are questions concerning this Web case.

Altitude Online: Telecommunications and Networks

Discussion Questions

1. What telecommunications equipment is needed to fulfill Altitude Online's vision?
2. Why is it necessary to lease a line from a telecommunications company?

Critical Thinking Questions

1. What types of services will be provided over Altitude Online's network?
2. What considerations should Jon and his team take into account as they select telecommunications equipment?

NOTES

Sources for the opening vignette: "Westermo's Ethernet Switches Reduce the Cost of Traffic Data Collection in Milan," Eternity Sales Web site, *www.eternity-sales.com*, accessed December 15, 2013; "Robust Network Solution Using Pre-existing Cables," Success Stories, Westermo Web site, *www.westermo.com/web/web_en_idc_com.nsf/alldocuments/DF212ABC5B1E2364C1257C0B003D2D7A*, accessed December 15, 2013; Sanchez, Ray and Patterson, Thom, "Man vs. Machine: Who Should Be at the Wheel?" CNN, December 8, 2013, accessed December 15, 2013; Xiang Liu, Xiang, Saat, M. Rapik, and Barkan, Christopher P. L., "Analysis of Causes of Major Train Derailment and Their Effect on Accident Rates," Transportation Research Record, 2012, Illinois Center for Transportation Web site, *http://ict.illinois.edu/railroad/CEE/pdf/Journal%20Papers/2012/Liu%20et%20al%202012.pdf*, accessed December 15, 2013.

1. Hitachi Success Story: Silesian University of Technology: BIO-FARMA Project, *www.hds.com/assets/pdf/hitachi-success-story-silesian-university-of-technology.pdf*, accessed December 5, 2013.
2. "Self-Storage Operator US Storage Centers Implements National PayNearMe Cash-Transaction Network," October 21, 2013, *www.insideselfstorage.com/news/2013/10/self-storage-operator-us-storage-centers-implements-national-paynearme-cash-transaction-network.aspx*.
3. "High-Density Wireless Networks Implemented at New Orleans Ernest N. Morial Convention Center," December 2, 2013, *www.mccno.com/high-density-wireless-networks-implemented-at-new-orleans-ernest-n-morial-convention-center/#sthash.feWe7mBq.dpuf*.
4. "How Distance Education Works," Harvard Extension School, *http://www.extension.harvard.edu/distance*

-education/how-distance-education-works, accessed December 7, 2013.

5. "About Chi-X," *www.chi-x.jp/ABOUTUS.aspx*, accessed January 5, 2013.

6. "Chi-X Japan Goes Live with Solarflares 10 Gigabit Ethernet to Accelerate Low Latency Network Performance," *www.solarflare.com/12-03-13-Chi-X -Japan-Goes-Live-with-Solarflares-10-Gigabit-Ethernet -to-Accelerate-Low-Latency-Network-Performance*, accessed January 5, 2014.

7. McCormick, Melissa, "How Fast Is FIOS Business Class?" *www.ehow.com/facts_7766577_fast-fios-business-class .html*, accessed December 9, 2013.

8. "Retail Chains in France, Other Countries Plan Rollout of NFC-Enabled Shelf Labels," *NFC Times*, June 7, 2013, *http://nfctimes.com/news/retail-chains-plan-major-roll out-nfc-enabled-shelf-labels*.

9. Gelke, Hans, "Harnessing Ultra-Wideband for Medical Applications," *Medical Electronic Design*, *www.medical electronicsdesign.com/article/harnessing-ultra-wideband -medical-applications*, accessed November 14, 2011.

10. Ibid.

11. "Hotel Chatter Annual WiFi Report 2013: Free Hotel WiFi," *www.hotelchatter.com/special/free-WiFi-Hotels -2013*, accessed December 12, 2013.

12. Vos, Esme, "Santa Clara Free Wi-Fi Service More Popular Than Expected," MuniWireless, November 14, 2013, *www.muniwireless.com/2013/11/14/people-use -santa-claras-free-wi-fi-expected/*.

13. Vos, Esme, "Singapore Rolls Out Free Wi-Fi at Gardens by the Bay," MuniWireless, November 6, 2013, *www .muniwireless.com/2013/11/06/singapore-rolls-free-wifi -gardens-bay/*.

14. "About Iridium Global Network," *http://iridium.com /About/IridiumGlobalNetwork.aspx*, accessed December 12, 2013.

15. "Capsized at Sea: The Sarah Outen Story," *http://iridium .com/IridiumConnected/ViewAllStories/CapsizedAtSea .aspx*, accessed December 12, 2013.

16. "Harris CapRock to Provide Communications Services for Carnival Corporation's Global Cruise Line Fleet," *www.harriscaprock.com/press_releases/2013-10-15 _Harris_CapRock_to_Provide_Communications _Services_for_Carnival.php*, accessed December 12, 2013.

17. "4G LTE," Webopedia, *www.webopedia.com/TERM /4/4G_LTE.html*, accessed December 12, 2013.

18. Lawson, Stephen, "5G Will Have to Do More Than Just Speed Up Your Phone, Ericsson Says," *PC World*, October 17, 2013, *www.pcworld.com/article/2055880 /5g-will-have-to-do-more-than-send-speed-up-your -phone-ericsson-says.html*.

19. Wood, Rupert, "Analysys Mason: Mobile Data Growth Will Be Strongest Outside Europe and North America, Fierce Wireless Europe," October 18, 2013, *www.fiercewireless. com/europe/story/analysys-mason-mobile-data-growth -will-be-strongest-outside-europe-and-nort/2013-10-18*.

20. Kelleher, Kevin, "Mobile Growth Is about to be Staggering," Fortune, February 20, 2013, *http://tech.fortune.cnn.com/ 2013/02/20/mobile-will-growth-is-about-to-be-staggering/*.

21. Schaffhauser, Dian, "Alabama District Taps Wireless Mesh, Differentiate Instruction as Part of 1-to-1 Initiative," *The Journal*, October 24, 2013, *www.tropos.com /onladv/adwords/mesh-networks/adgroup1/landing-a .php?gclid=CMmp8MO3q7sCFRBnOgodNCYAHg*.

22. "PIONIER—Polish Optical Internet," *http://blog.pionier .net.pl/sc2013/pionier/*, accessed January 6, 2014.

23. "Schools 100Mbps Project," *www.heanet.ie/schools /100Mb_project*, accessed December 13, 2013.

24. "About Us," 7-eleven, *http://corp.7-eleven.com/AboutUs /tabid/73/Default.aspx*, accessed December 13, 2013.

25. "Mecosta County Medical Center Automates Health Data Delivery to State Agencies Using Iatric Systems Public Health Interfaces," *www.iatric.com/images/Public /Documents/IatricPublicHealthInterfacesSuccess _Mecosta.pdf*, accessed December 13, 2013.

26. Simpson, Adam, "New Customer Success Story— Municipality of over 10,000 Residents Chooses Easy Office Phone's Hosted PBX," January 24, 2013, *http:// blog.easyofficephone.com/2013/new-customer-success -story-municipality-of-over-10000-residents-chooses -easy-office-phones-hosted-pbx/*.

27. Standard Chartered Web site, "Who We Are," *www.sc .com/en/about-us/who-we-are/index.html*, accessed December 14, 2013.

28. Marketwire Web site, "Standard Chartered Bank Adopts Juniper Networks Infrastructure," October 19, 2011, *http://newsroom.juniper.net/press-releases/standard -chartered-bank-adopts-juniper-networks-in-nyse-jnpr -0811554*.

29. "PRTG Network Monitor Helps Small, Family-Owned IT Consulting Business Provide World-Class Reliability," *www.paessler.com/company/casestudies/covell_group _uses_prtg*, accessed December 14, 2013.

30. Le Maistre, Ray, "SDN Works for Us," Light Reading, October 23, 2012, *www.lightreading.com/carrier-sdn /sdn-architectures/google-sdn-works-for-us/d/d-id /699197*.

31. Vos, Esme, "Guest Post: Cashing in on Hotspot 2.0," MuniWireless, December 2, 2013, *www.muniwireless .com/2013/12/02/cashing-in-on-hotspot-2-0/*.

32. Ball, James, "NSA Decryption Revelations 'Provide Roadmap' to Adversaries, US Warns," *The Guardian*, September 6, 2013.

33. Carlson, Nicholas, "How Marissa Mayer Figured Out Work-at-Home Yahoos Were Slacking Off," Business Insider, March 2, 2013, *www.businessinsider.com/how -marissa-mayer-figured-out-work-at-home-yahoos-were -slacking-off-2013-3#ixzz2njx6L5fr*.

34. "Vehicle VPNs, Part Two: Business World Implications," VPN Haus, November 4, 2013, *http://vpnhaus.ncp-e.com /2013/11/04/vehicle-vpns-part-two-business-world -implications/*.

35. Cleavelin, Mary Beth, "Va. Beach Police Defend Late Night Reverse 911 Call," The Virginian Pilot Online, July 26, 2013, *http://hamptonroads.com/2013/07 /va-beach-police-defend-latenight-reverse-911-call*.

36. Periabras, Rosalie C., "Philippines: The New Call Center Capital of the World," *The Manila Times*, October 23, 2013, *http://manilatimes.net/philippines-the-new-call -center-capital-of-the-world/47984/*.

37. "Companies Moving Contact Centers Back to U.S.," Sangoma, *www.sangoma.com/companies-moving-con tact-centers-back-to-u-s/*, accessed December 19, 2013.

38. Kowalski, Megan and Hoyer, Meghan, "Robocallers Doing a Number on the Do Not Call List," *USA Today*, August 26, 2013, *www.usatoday.com/story/news /nation/2013/08/26/do-not-call-list/2609855/*.

7 The Internet, Web, Intranets, and Extranets

Principles	Learning Objectives
• The Internet provides a critical infrastructure for delivering and accessing information and services.	• Briefly describe how the Internet works, including methods for connecting to it and the role of Internet service providers.
• Originally developed as a document-management system, the World Wide Web has grown to become a primary source of news and information, an indispensable conduit for commerce, and a popular hub for social interaction, entertainment, and communication.	• Describe the World Wide Web and how it works. • Explain the use of markup languages, Web browsers, and Web servers. • Identify and briefly describe the process of creating software applications for the Web.
• The Internet and Web provide numerous resources for finding information, communicating and collaborating, socializing, conducting business and shopping, and being entertained.	• List and describe several sources of information on the Web. • Describe methods of finding information on the Web. • List and describe several forms of online communication, along with the benefits and drawbacks of each, in terms of convenience and effectiveness. • Explain Web 2.0 and provide examples of Web 2.0 sites.
• Popular Internet and Web technologies have been applied to business networks in the form of intranets and extranets.	• Explain how intranets and extranets use Internet and Web technologies and describe how the two differ.

Google? In China, People Baidu It

Courtesy of Baidu

You're studying Chinese in Beijing for a semester. One evening, you're out with friends searching for a good restaurant. Do you Google it on your mobile device? You might be better off if you Baidu it.

Founded in 2000, Baidu is the most popular search engine in China, capturing a whopping 80 percent of the market. Baidu employs almost 21,000 people and earns approximately $3.5 billion in sales annually. In 2007, Baidu became the first Chinese company to join the Nasdaq 100. It publishes its quarterly reports and SEC filings publically on its Web site and has long set its sights not only on capturing the Chinese market, but on moving into the global market.

Like Google, most of its revenue is generated from Internet search advertising, though it provides many other services. The company began with both a Yahoo-like Web directory and a search engine for Web sites. It soon expanded its search tools to include images, music, videos, and news. Next, it released its map tool. It partnered with Qualcomm to move into the cloud and has vigorously pursued the mobile market since 2011. By 2014, Baidu's pool of mobile search tool users was climbing toward the 150 million mark. Like Google, Baidu has plunged into social media and marketing solutions—enabling throngs of businesses in rural China to access and leverage the Internet.

Unlike Google, however, Baidu has carefully complied with Chinese censorship laws. In fact, in 2011, when Google announced that it was no longer willing to censor search engine results, Baidu captured most of the 7 percent Chinese market share that Google lost. Moreover, Baidu so impressed Chinese authorities that the company was granted a license to establish its own news department, with its own staff, rather than simply act as a portal for other licensed channels. In addition, Baidu has built knowledge communities and launched its own online encyclopedia for the Chinese public. China has, in the past, blocked access to Wikipedia. As an alternative, Baidu's knowledge communities allow people to exchange information.

In 2011, pro-democracy writers and videographers in New York filed suits against Baidu and the People's Republic of China after they discovered that Baidu had blocked access to their online content. Demonstrating that their political speech was accessible through Google, Bing, and Yahoo, they charged the company with violating their human rights by impinging on their freedom of speech. In 2014, the case was still waiting to be heard in U.S. District Court.

Google has fallen to fourth place in the Chinese search engine market behind Baidu, Qihoo, and Sogou. Meanwhile, Baidu has launched Web sites in the Thai and Egyptian markets. This expansion, Baidu hopes, is the first of many as Baidu makes a bid to oust Google from its first-place position in the global market. It's unclear, however, how Baidu will fare in a democratic Europe and North America.

As you read this chapter, consider the following:

- What tools do search engines, social networks, and other Internet services provide to make organizations successful?
- How do Internet companies leverage new technologies to improve their market position?

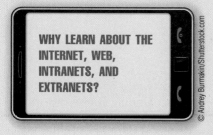

WHY LEARN ABOUT THE INTERNET, WEB, INTRANETS, AND EXTRANETS?

To say that the Internet has had a big impact on organizations of all types and sizes would be an understatement. Since the early 1990s, when the Internet was first used for commercial purposes, it has affected all aspects of business. Businesses use the Internet to sell and advertise their products and services, reaching out to new and existing customers. If you are undecided about a career, you can use the Internet to investigate career opportunities and salaries using sites such as *www.monster.com* and *www.linkedin.com*. Most companies have Web sites that list job opportunities, descriptions, qualifications, salaries, and benefits. If you have a job, you probably use the Internet daily to communicate with coworkers and your boss. People working in every field and at every level use the Internet in their work. Purchasing agents use the Internet to save millions of dollars in supplies every year. Travel and events-management agents use the Internet to find the best deals on travel and accommodations. Automotive engineers use the Internet to work with other engineers around the world developing designs and specifications for new automobiles and trucks. Property managers use the Internet to find the best prices and opportunities for commercial and residential real estate. Whatever your career, you will probably use the Internet daily. This chapter starts by exploring how the Internet works and then investigates the many exciting opportunities for using the Internet to help you achieve your goals.

The Internet is the world's largest computer network. The Internet is actually a collection of interconnected networks, all freely exchanging information using a common set of protocols. More than 1 billion computers, or hosts, make up today's Internet, supporting nearly 2.7 billion users. China, United States, India, and Japan are the countries with the most Internet users today.[1] The number of worldwide users is expected to continue growing with an additional 1 billion users by 2017. Some 61 percent of these new users will come from the Asia-Pacific region, primarily China, India, and Indonesia.[2] Figure 7.1 shows the staggering growth of the Internet, as measured by the number of Internet host sites, or domain names. Domain names are discussed later in the chapter.

FIGURE 7.1

Internet growth: Number of Internet hosts

The number of worldwide Internet hosts is expected to continue growing.

Source: Data from "2012 The Internet Domain Survey," *www.isc.org /services/survey/references/*

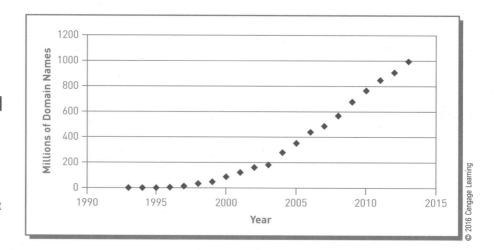

USE AND FUNCTIONING OF THE INTERNET

The Internet is truly international in scope, with users on every continent—including Antarctica. See Figure 7.2. Although the United States has high Internet penetration among its population, it does not constitute the majority

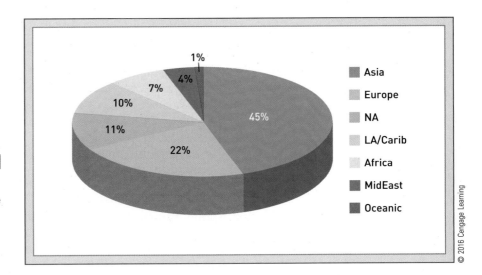

FIGURE 7.2

Distribution of Internet users

Most of the world's Internet users are in Asia.

Source: Data from "Internet World Stats," *www.internetworldstats.com /stats.htm*

© 2016 Cengage Learning

of people online. Of all the people using the Internet, citizens of Asian countries make up about 45 percent, Europeans about 22 percent, and North Americans about 11 percent. China has by far the most Internet users with 538 million, which is more users than the next three countries combined (United States, 245 million; India, 137 million; and Japan, 101 million).[3] Being connected to the Internet provides global economic opportunity to individuals, businesses, and countries.

The Internet and social media Web sites have emerged as important new channels for learning about world events, protesting the actions of organizations and governments, and urging others to support one's favorite causes or candidates. For example, some believe that Barrack Obama's effective use of the Internet and social media provided him with a distinct advantage over his opponents in the presidential elections of 2008 and 2012.[4] In another example, Syrian rebels used the Internet to communicate about events within the country and to provide a useful link to others around the world.[5]

Internet censorship: The control or suppression of the publishing or accessing of information on the Internet.

On the other hand, Internet censorship, the control or suppression of the publishing or accessing of information on the Internet, is a growing issue. For example, riot police in Istanbul used water cannons to disperse protesters who objected to a draft law that would grant the government sweeping new powers over Turkish Internet service providers.[6]

ARPANET: A project started by the U.S. Department of Defense (DoD) in 1969 as both an experiment in reliable networking and a means to link the DoD and military research contractors, including many universities doing military-funded research.

The ancestor of the Internet was the ARPANET, a project started by the U.S. Department of Defense (DoD) in 1969. The ARPANET was both an experiment in reliable networking and a means to link the DoD and military research contractors, including many universities doing military-funded research. (*ARPA* stands for the Advanced Research Projects Agency, the branch of the DoD in charge of awarding grant money. The agency is now known as DARPA—the added "D" is for *Defense.*) The ARPANET was eventually broken into two networks: MILNET, which included all military sites, and a new, smaller ARPANET, which included all the nonmilitary sites. The two networks remained connected, however, through the use of the Internet Protocol (IP), which enables computers to route communications traffic from one network to another as needed. All the networks connected to the Internet use IP so that they can communicate.

Internet Protocol (IP): A communication standard that enables computers to route communications traffic from one network to another as needed.

To speed Internet access, a group of corporations and universities called the University Corporation for Advanced Internet Development (UCAID) is working on a faster alternative Internet called Internet2 (I2). The Internet2 offers the potential of faster Internet speeds—up to 10 Gbps or more. The goal is to enable collaboration with anyone, anywhere without constraints.[7] The National LambdaRail (NLR) is a cross-country, high-speed (10 Gbps) fiber-optic network dedicated to research in high-speed networking applications.[8] The NLR provides a "unique national networking infrastructure" to advance networking research and next-generation network-based applications in science, engineering, and medicine. This new high-speed fiber-optic network will support the ever-increasing need of scientists to gather, transfer, and analyze massive amounts of scientific data.

How the Internet Works

In the early days of the Internet, the major telecommunications (telecom) companies around the world agreed to connect its networks so that users on all the networks could share information over the Internet. These large telecom companies are called *network service providers* (*NSPs*). Examples include Verizon, Sprint, British Telecom, and AT&T. The cables, routers, switching stations, communication towers, and satellites that make up these networks are the hardware over which Internet traffic flows. The combined hardware of these and other NSPs—the fiber-optic cables that span the globe over land and under sea—make up the Internet backbone.

backbone: One of the Internet's high-speed, long-distance communications links.

The Internet transmits data from one computer, called a *host*, to another. See Figure 7.3. If the receiving computer is on a network to which the first computer is directly connected, it can send the message directly. If the receiving and sending computers are not directly connected to the same network, the sending computer relays the message to another computer that can forward it. The message is typically sent through one or more routers to reach its destination. It is not unusual for a message to pass through a dozen or more routers on its way from one part of the Internet to another. Thus, the Internet routes data packets over the network backbone from router to router to reach their destinations.

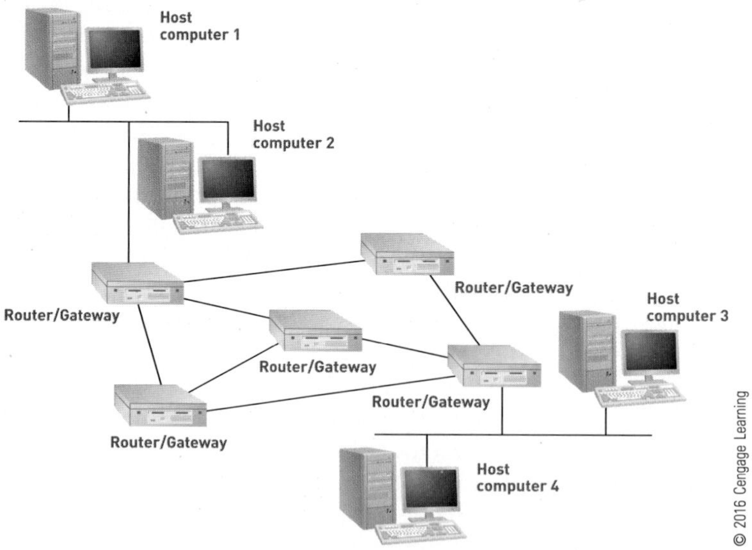

FIGURE 7.3

Routing messages over the Internet

Data is transmitted from one host computer to another on the Internet.

Transmission Control Protocol (TCP): The widely used transport layer protocol that most Internet applications use with IP.

The various telecommunications networks that are linked to form the Internet work much the same way—they pass data around in chunks called *packets*, each of which carries the addresses of its sender and its receiver along with other technical information. The set of conventions used to pass packets from one host to another is the IP. Many other protocols are used in connection with IP. The best known is the Transmission Control Protocol (TCP). Many people use "TCP/IP" as an abbreviation for the combination of TCP and IP used by most Internet applications. After a network following these standards links to the Internet's backbone, it becomes part of the worldwide Internet community.

IP address: A 64-bit number that identifies a computer on the Internet.

Each computer on the Internet has an assigned address, called its IP address, that identifies it on the Internet. An IP address is a 64-bit number that identifies a computer on the Internet. The 64-bit number is typically divided into four bytes and translated to decimal; for example, 69.32.133.11. The Internet is migrating to Internet Protocol version 6 (IPv6), which uses 128-bit addresses to provide for many more devices, however, this change is expected to take years. As of mid-2013, the volume of Internet traffic using IPv6 is small, but growing, with Google reporting that just 1.37 percent of its traffic comes in over IPv6.[9]

Because people prefer to work with words rather than numbers, a system called the Domain Name System (DNS) was created. Domain names such as *www.cengage.com* are mapped to IP addresses such as 69.32.133.11 using the DNS. If you type either *www.cengage.com* or 69.32.133.11 into your Web browser, you will access the same Web site. To make room for more Web addresses, efforts are underway to increase the number of available domain names.

Uniform Resource Locator (URL): A Web address that specifies the exact location of a Web page using letters and words that map to an IP address and a location on the host.

A Uniform Resource Locator (URL) is a Web address that specifies the exact location of a Web page using letters and words that map to an IP address and a location on the host. The URL gives those who provide information over the Internet a standard way to designate where Internet resources such as servers and documents are located. Consider the URL for Course Technology, *http://www.cengage.com/coursetechnology*.

The "http" specifies the access method and tells your software to access a file using the Hypertext Transfer Protocol. This is the primary method for interacting with the Internet. In many cases, you don't need to include http:// in a URL because it is the default protocol. The "www" part of the address signifies that the address is associated with the World Wide Web service. The URL *www.cengage.com* is the domain name that identifies the Internet host site. The part of the address following the domain name—/coursetechnology—specifies an exact location on the host site.

Domain names must adhere to strict rules. They always have at least two parts, with each part separated by a dot (period). For some Internet addresses, the far right part of the domain name is the country code, such as au for Australia, ca for Canada, dk for Denmark, fr for France, de (Deutschland) for Germany, and jp for Japan. Many Internet addresses have a code denoting affiliation categories, such as com for business sites and edu for education sites. Table 7.1 contains a few popular categories. The far left part of the domain name identifies the host network or host provider, which might be the name of a university or business. Countries outside the United States use different top-level domain affiliations from the ones described in the table.

TABLE 7.1 U.S. top-level domain affiliations

Affiliation ID	Affiliation	Number of Hosts
com	Business sites	112,259,193
edu	Post-secondary educational sites	7,500
gov	Government sites	2,174
net	Networking sites	15,221,763
org	Nonprofit organization sites	10,395,604

Source: Whois Source Domain Counts & Internet Statistics (January 7, 2014), *www.whois.sc/internet-statistics*

The Internet Corporation for Assigned Names and Numbers (ICANN) is responsible for managing IP addresses and Internet domain names. One of its primary concerns is to make sure that each domain name represents only one individual or entity—the one that legally registers it. For example, if your teacher wanted to use *www.cengage.com* for a course Web site, he or she would discover that domain name has already been registered by Cengage Learning and is not available. ICANN uses companies called *accredited domain name registrars* to handle the business of registering domain names. For example, you can visit *www.namecheap.com*, an accredited registrar, to find out if a particular name has already been registered. If not, you can register the name for around $9 per year. Once you do so, ICANN will not allow anyone else to use that domain name as long as you pay the yearly fee.

Accessing the Internet

Although you can connect to the Internet in numerous ways, Internet access is not distributed evenly throughout the world or even throughout a city. Which access method you choose is determined by the size and capability of your organization or system, your budget, and the services available to you. See Figure 7.4.

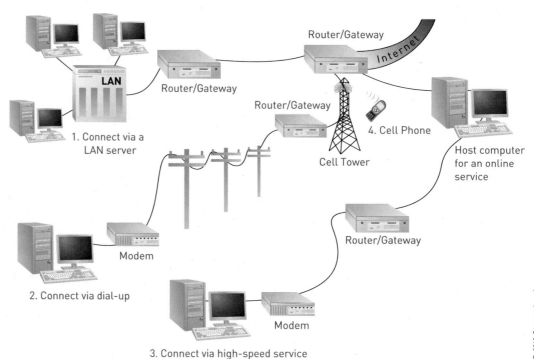

© 2016 Cengage Learning

FIGURE 7.4

Several ways to access the Internet

Users can access the Internet in several ways, including using a LAN server, telephone lines, a high-speed service, or a wireless network.

Connecting via LAN Server

Businesses and organizations that manage a local area network (LAN) connect to the Internet via server. By connecting a server on the LAN to the Internet using a router, all users on the LAN are provided access to the Internet. Business LAN servers are typically connected to the Internet at very fast data rates, sometimes in the hundreds of Mbps. In addition, you can share the higher cost of this service among several dozen LAN users to allow a reasonable cost per user.

Connecting via Internet Service Providers

Companies and residences unable to connect directly to the Internet through a LAN server must access the Internet through an Internet service provider.

Internet service provider (ISP):
Any organization that provides Internet access to people.

An **Internet service provider (ISP)** is any organization that provides Internet access to people. Thousands of organizations serve as ISPs, ranging from universities that make the Internet available to students and faculty to small Internet businesses to major telecommunications giants such as AT&T and Comcast. To connect to the Internet through an ISP, you must have an account with the service provider (for which you usually pay) along with software (such as a browser) and devices (such as a computer or smartphone) that support a connection via TCP/IP.

Perhaps the least expensive but slowest connection provided by ISPs is a dial-up connection. A *dial-up Internet connection* uses a modem and standard phone line to "dial-up" and connect to the ISP server.

Several high-speed Internet services are available for home and business. They include cable modem connections from cable television companies, DSL connections from phone companies, and satellite connections from satellite television companies. These technologies were discussed in Chapter 6. High-speed services provide data transfer rates between 1 and 15 Mbps. Some businesses and universities use the very fast T1 or T3 lines to connect to the Internet.

In addition to connecting to the Internet through wired systems such as phone lines and television cables, wireless Internet over cellular and Wi-Fi networks has become common. See Figure 7.5. Thousands of public Wi-Fi services are available in coffee shops, airports, hotels, and elsewhere, where Internet access is provided free, for an hourly rate, or for a monthly subscription fee.

FIGURE 7.5

Connecting wirelessly

The iPad connects to the Internet over cellular or Wi-Fi networks.

Cell phone carriers also provide Internet access for handsets, notebooks, and tablets. New 4G mobile phone services rival wired high-speed connections enjoyed at home and work. Sprint, Verizon, AT&T, and other popular carriers are working to bring 4G service to subscribers, beginning in large metropolitan areas.

When Apple introduced the iPhone, one of its slogans was the "Internet in your pocket." The iPhone proves the popularity of and the potential for Internet services over a handset. Many other smartphones followed the iPhone, offering similar services on all of the cellular networks. More recently, the iPhone brought video calling into vogue, while the iPad and other tablet computers provide anywhere, anytime access to all types of Internet services on a larger display.

ETHICAL& SOCIETAL ISSUES

Bringing High-Speed Internet to Poland

Full business or personal participation in today's society is impossible without good Internet access. A country that wants to progress economically and provide opportunities for its citizens must ensure that Internet access is widely available.

The government of Poland understands this principle. The government has taken several steps to make high-speed Internet connections widely available.

In 2009, Poland passed legislation to support and encourage the development of telecommunications networks, reducing regulatory barriers to new infrastructure and increasing competition. Many new projects were initiated after this legislation was adopted. For example, on January 14, 2011, the Łódźkie voivodship (province) in central Poland opened the bidding for operating a network to give all of its nearly 3 million residents Internet access at their homes.

Consistent with this philosophy, in October 2009, the Polish government reached an agreement with the largest telecommunications carrier, Telekomunikacja Polska (TP), to deploy at least 1.2 million broadband lines by the end of 2012. By the end of 2010, TP had built more than 454,000 such lines, including more than 420,000 over 6 Mbps. They also increased the percentage that will go into unprofitable rural areas from the initially planned 23 percent to 30 percent. In April 2011, TP started regulatory discussions about deploying 3 million Fiber to the Home (FTTH) lines, beginning in 2012.

Other legislation supports this aim. For example, new apartment buildings must have high-speed data connections from the building access point to each unit. Knowing that the most expensive part of broadband installation is already done for them, telecommunications companies are more likely to bring high-speed Internet connections to the building itself and to compete in offering that service to the building's residents.

The European Union (EU) is also contributing to Poland's Internet infrastructure. The EU gets a portion of each member country's Value-Added Tax (VAT revenue) collections and allocates those funds to development projects throughout the EU. The Broadband Network of Eastern Poland will provide broadband Internet access to most residents of five low-income voivodships in that part of the country. This is the largest EU-funded information technology project anywhere, with a total budget of PLN 1.4 billion (about U.S. $400 million) through 2015. The EU will supply about 85 percent of that budget, with Poland providing the remaining 15 percent directly.

As of the end of 2011, 62 percent of Poland's residents had high-speed Internet access. This is above the worldwide average of 32.7 percent, but below the EU average of 71.5 percent. Actions such as those described here should bring Poland up to the European average—which is, of course, a moving target as all EU countries are also moving forward. The International Telecommunications Union estimates that 90 percent of all Poles will have broadband Internet access at a fixed location by the end of 2015. Since many of the remaining 10 percent will have mobile access, and many of those who have no personal access will have convenient Internet access through their public libraries, high-speed Internet access in some form will be nearly universal. This will be a key factor in Poland's future economic success.

Discussion Questions

1. The case states that "A country that wants to progress economically and provide opportunities for its citizens must ensure that Internet access is widely available." Do you agree? Why or why not?

2. The case states that the EU takes a fraction of each member's VAT revenue and returns that money to member countries for economic development projects. Less prosperous countries get back more than they put in; more prosperous ones get back less. The intent of this European Funds program is to reduce developmental differences among regions. Poland gets back considerably more than it contributes to this fund. About 30 percent of the funds Poland gets go into telecommunications infrastructure, with most of the rest going to transportation infrastructure. Do you think this is an appropriate split? How would you divide these funds? Consider other uses besides these two as well.

Critical Thinking Questions

1. As a university student, you almost certainly have high-speed Internet access on campus and most likely where you live as well. What difficulties would not having it create for you? How hard would it be to do the job you hope to have after graduation without good Internet access?
2. As of September 2013, 14 million Poles out of a population of 38.5 million were Facebook members—about 36 percent. The corresponding fraction for the United States was just over 50 percent. How much of the difference do you think is due to lack of high-speed Internet access, and how much to other factors? What do you think will be the effect of better high-speed Internet availability on Facebook membership in Poland?

SOURCES: International Telecommunications Union, "Poland—Impact of the regulations on the stimulation of the infrastructural investments and actions concerning development of the information society," *www.itu.int/ITU-D/eur/NLP-BBI/CaseStudy/CaseStudy_POL_Impact_of_Regulation.html*, June 29, 2011; Point-Topic, "Poland Broadband Overview," *http://point-topic.com/content/operator Source/profiles2/poland-broadband-overview.htm*, August 26, 2011; Polish Information and Foreign Investment Agency, "Broadband Network in Eastern Poland," *www.paiz.gov.pl/20111114 /broadband_network_in_eastern_poland*, November 14, 2011; Internet World Stats, "Internet Usage in Europe," *www.internetworldstats.com/stats4.htm*, June 30, 2012.

Cloud Computing

cloud computing: A computing environment where software and storage are provided as an Internet service and are accessed with a Web browser.

Cloud computing refers to a computing environment where software and storage are provided as an Internet service and accessed with a Web browser. See Figure 7.6. Google and Yahoo!, for example, store the email of many users, along with calendars, contacts, and to-do lists. Apple Computer has

FIGURE **7.6**

Cloud computing

Cloud computing uses applications and resources delivered via the Web.

© Helder Almeida/Shutterstock.com

developed a service called iCloud to allow people to store their documents, music, photos, apps, and other content on its server.[10] Facebook provides social interaction and can store personal photos, as can Flickr and a dozen other photo sites. Pandora delivers music, and Hulu and YouTube deliver movies. Google Docs, Zoho, 37signals, Flypaper, Adobe Buzzword, and others provide Web-delivered productivity and information management software. With its Office 365 software product, Microsoft is emphasizing cloud computing to a greater extent. Office 365 competes with other online software suites such as Apache Open Office, Google Apps, and NeoOffice.[11] Communications, contacts, photos, documents, music, and media are available to you from any Internet-connected device with cloud computing.

Cloud computing offers many advantages to businesses. By outsourcing business information systems to the cloud, a business saves on system design, installation, and maintenance. The New York Stock Exchange (NYSE), for example, is starting to offer cloud-computing applications that let customers pay for the services and data they use on Euronext—a European market for stocks, bonds, and other investments.

Cloud computing can have several methods of deployment. Those that have been discussed thus far are considered public cloud services. *Public cloud* refers to service providers that offer their cloud-based services to the general public, whether that is an individual using Google Calendar or a corporation using the Salesforce.com application. In a *private cloud* deployment, cloud technology is used within the confines of a private network.

Since 1992, The College Network and its partner universities have provided accessible educational programs for individuals seeking degrees or professional certificates, entirely through distance learning. Its small information systems team supported 50 servers located in Las Vegas and another 65 in Indianapolis. These servers enabled students to register and take a large variety of online courses. The team was stretched to its limits and tried to do everything themselves, including managing the physical servers and troubleshooting problems. This left little time for them to focus on solving business challenges such as developing a disaster recovery plan to avoid system outages they had experienced. The College Network realized that it had to change the way it ran its business, and began an evaluation of private cloud providers. EarthLink was eventually chosen to provide a customized private cloud with dedicated servers. Conversion to the private network reduced the capital required for computer hardware and software. It has also increased systems availability and avoided outages by providing backup servers with multilink connectivity between Indianapolis and the EarthLink data center. The College Network has been able to reallocate its valuable IT resources to address issues that bring greater value to the business while EarthLink resources troubleshoot any systems issues.[12]

Businesses may also elect to combine public cloud and private cloud services to create a *hybrid cloud*. In another version of cloud computing known as a *community cloud*, several businesses share cloud-computing resources. The New York Stock Exchange Technologies Capital Markets Community Platform is a financial services cloud that provides platform services to the capital markets community. This platform provides the secure and high-performance technology that clients require to handle their trading.

THE WORLD WIDE WEB

The World Wide Web was developed by Tim Berners-Lee at CERN, the European Organization for Nuclear Research in Geneva, Switzerland. He originally conceived of it as an internal document-management system. From this modest beginning, the Web has grown to become a primary source of news and information, an indispensable conduit for commerce, and a popular hub for social interaction, entertainment, and communication.

How the Web Works

While the terms Internet and Web are often used interchangeably, technically, the two are different technologies. The Internet is the infrastructure on which the Web exists. The Internet is made up of computers, network hardware such as routers and fiber optic cables, software, and the TCP/IP protocols. The Web, on the other hand, consists of server and client software, the Hypertext Transfer Protocol (HTTP), standards, and markup languages that combine to deliver information and services over the Internet.

The Web was designed to make information easy to find and organize. It connects billions of documents, which are now called Web pages, stored on hundreds of millions of servers around the world. These are connected to each other using hyperlinks, specially denoted text or graphics on a Web page that, when clicked, open a new Web page containing related content. Using hyperlinks, users can jump between Web pages stored on various Web servers, creating the illusion of interacting with one big computer. Because of the vast amount of information available on the Web and the wide variety of media, the Web has become the most popular means of information access in the world today.

In short, the Web is a hyperlink-based system that uses the client/server model. It organizes Internet resources throughout the world into a series of linked files, called pages, accessed and viewed using Web client software called a Web browser. Google Chrome, Mozilla Firefox, Internet Explorer, Apple Safari, and Opera Software's Opera are popular Web browsers. See Figure 7.7. A collection of pages on one particular topic, accessed under one Web domain, is called a Web site. The Web was originally designed to support formatted text and pictures on a page. It has evolved to support many more types of information and communication, including user interactivity, animation, and video. Web *plug-ins* help provide additional features to standard Web sites. Adobe Flash and Real Player are examples of Web plug-ins.

Web: Server and client software, the Hypertext Transfer Protocol (HTTP), standards, and markup languages that combine to deliver information and services over the Internet.

hyperlink: Highlighted text or graphics in a Web document that, when clicked, opens a new Web page containing related content.

Web browser: Web client software, such as Chrome, Firefox, Internet Explorer, Safari, and Opera, are used to view Web pages.

FIGURE 7.7

Google Chrome

Web browsers such as Google Chrome let you access Internet resources such as email and other online applications.

Hypertext Markup Language (HTML): The standard page description language for Web pages.

Hypertext Markup Language (HTML) is the standard page description language for Web pages. HTML is defined by the World Wide Web Consortium (referred to as "W3C") and has developed through numerous revisions. It is currently in its fifth revision—HTML5. HTML tells the browser how to display font characteristics, paragraph formatting, page layout, image

tag: Code that tells the Web browser how to format text—as a heading, as a list, or as body text—and whether images, sound, and other elements should be inserted.

placement, hyperlinks, and the content of a Web page. HTML uses tags, which are codes that tell the browser how to format the text or graphics, as a heading, list, or body text, for example. Web site creators mark up a page by placing HTML tags before and after one or more words. For example, to have the browser display a sentence as a heading, you place the <h1> tag at the start of the sentence and an </h1> tag at the end of the sentence. When you view this page in your browser, the sentence is displayed as a heading.

HTML also provides tags to import objects stored in files, such as photos, pictures, audio, and movies, into a Web page. In short, a Web page is made up of three components: text, tags, and references to files. The text is your Web page content, the tags are codes that mark the way words will be displayed, and the references to files insert photos and media into the Web page at specific locations. All HTML tags are enclosed in a set of angle brackets (< and >), such as <h2>. The closing tag has a forward slash in it, such as </b> for closing bold. Consider the following text and tags:

```
<html>
<head>
<title>Table of Contents</title>
<link href="style.css" rel="stylesheet" type="text/css" />
</head>
<body style="background-color:#333333">
<div id="container">
<p><img src="header.png" width="602" height="78" /></p>
<h1 align=center>Principles of Information Systems</h1>
<ol>
<li>An Overview</li>
<li>Information Technology Concepts</li>
<li>Business Information Systems</li>
<li>Systems Development</li>
<li>Information Systems in Business and Society</li>
</ol>
</div>
</body>
</html>
```

The <html> tag identifies this as an HTML document. HTML documents are divided into two parts: the <head> and the <body>. The <body> contains everything that is viewable in the Web browser window, and the <head> contains related information such as a <title>to place on the browser's title bar. The background color of the page is specified in the <body> tag using a hexadecimal code. The heading "Principles of Information Systems" is identified as the largest level 1 heading with the <h1> tag, typically a 16–18 point font, centered on the page. The <ol> tag indicates an ordered list, and the <li> tags indicate list items. The resulting Web page is shown in Figure 7.8.

HTML works hand in hand with another markup language called CSS. CSS, which stands for Cascading Style Sheets, has become a popular tool for designing groups of Web pages. CSS uses special HTML tags to globally define font characteristics for a variety of page elements as well as how those elements are laid out on the Web page. Rather than having to specify a font for each occurrence of an element throughout a document, formatting can be specified once and applied to all occurrences. CSS styles are often defined in a separate file and then can be applied to many pages on a Web site. In the

Cascading Style Sheets (CSS): A markup language for defining the visual design of a Web page or group of pages.

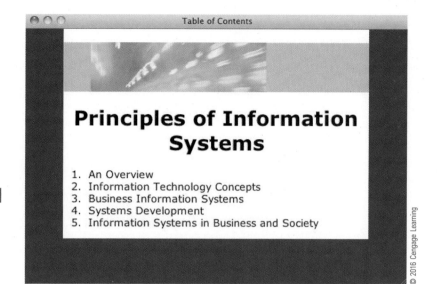

© 2016 Cengage Learning

FIGURE 7.8

HTML code interpreted by a browser

The example HTML code as interpreted by the Firefox Web browser on a Mac.

Extensible Markup Language (XML): The markup language designed to transport and store data on the Web.

previous example code, you may have noticed the <link> tag that refers to an external style sheet file, style.css.

Extensible Markup Language (XML) is a markup language designed to transport and store data on the Web. Rather than using predefined tags like HTML, XML allows the coder to create custom tags that define data. For example, the following XML code identifies the components of a book:

```
<book>
<chapter>Hardware</chapter>
<topic>Input Devices</topic>
<topic>Processing and Storage Devices</topic>
<topic>Output Devices</topic>
</book>
```

XML is extremely useful for organizing Web content and making data easy to find. Many Web sites use CSS to define the design and layout of Web pages, XML to define the content, and HTML to join the content (XML) with the design (CSS). See Figure 7.9. This modular approach to Web design allows you to change the visual design without affecting the content and to change the content without affecting the visual design.

Web Programming Languages

Many of the services offered on the Web are delivered through the use of programs and scripts. A Web program may be something as simple as a menu that expands when you click it or as complicated as a full-blown spreadsheet application. Web applications may run on the Web server, delivering the results of the processing to the user, or they may run directly on the client, the user's PC. These two categories are commonly referred to as server-side and client-side software.

Java: An object-oriented programming language from Sun Microsystems based on the C++ programming language, which allows applets to be embedded within an HTML document.

JavaScript is a popular programming language for client-side applications. Using JavaScript, you can create interactive Web pages that respond to user actions. JavaScript can be used to validate data entry in a Web form, to display photos in a slideshow style, to embed simple computer games in a Web page, and to provide a currency conversion calculator. **Java** is an object-oriented programming language from Sun Microsystems based on the C++ programming language, which allows small programs, called *applets*, to be embedded within an HTML document. When the user clicks the appropriate

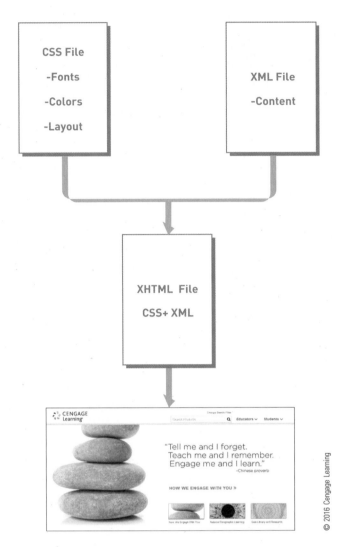

FIGURE 7.9

XML, CSS, and HTML

Today's Web sites are created using XML to define content, CSS to define the visual style, and HTML to put it all together.

part of an HTML page to retrieve an applet from a Web server, the applet is downloaded onto the client workstation where it begins executing. Unlike other programs, Java software can run on any type of computer. It can be used to develop client-side or server-side applications. Programmers use Java to make Web pages come alive, adding splashy graphics, animation, and real-time updates.

Hypertext Preprocessor, or *PHP*, is an open-source programming language that is popular for server-side application development. Unlike some other Web programming languages, PHP is easy to use because its code, or instructions, can be embedded directly into HTML code. PHP can be used with a variety of database management systems, such as MySQL, DB2, Oracle, Informix, and many others. PHP's flexibility, power, and ease of use make it popular with many Web developers. Perl is another popular server-side programming language.

Adobe Flash and *Microsoft Silverlight* provide development environments for creating rich Web animation and interactive media. Both Flash and Silverlight require the user to install a browser plug-in to run. Flash became so common that popular browsers included it as a standard feature. The introduction of HTML5 provided Web developers the ability to create interactive Web content and media natively in HTML without the need for Flash or Silverlight. A number of technology companies, led by Apple, are moving away from Flash to HTML5. See Figure 7.10.

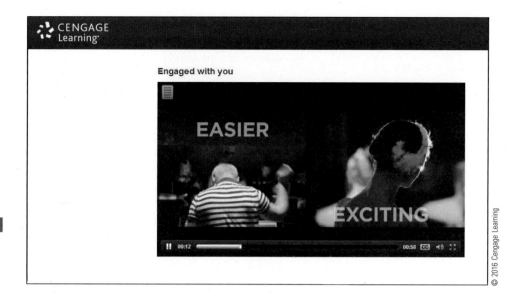

FIGURE 7.10

HTML5 video

HTML5 supports interactive media, including video and audio.

Web Services

Web services consist of standards and tools that streamline and simplify communication among Web sites and that promise to revolutionize the way we develop and use the Web for business and personal purposes. Internet companies, including Amazon, eBay, and Google, use Web services.

Amazon, for example, has developed Amazon Web Services (AWS) to make the contents of its huge online catalog available to other Web sites or software applications. Airbnb is a community marketplace that enables property owners and travelers to interact for the purpose of renting distinctive vacation spots in nearly 25,000 cities in 192 countries. These interactions are conducted on the company's Web site via clients using Airbnb iPhone and Android applications. Shortly after Airbnb began operations, it migrated its cloud computing functions to AWS because of issues with its original provider. The company now uses some 200 AWS instances for its application, memory storage, and search servers to support its Web site. Incoming traffic is automatically distributed across these multiple instances to ensure high availability and fast response time. AWS allows Airbnb to store backups and static files, including 10 TB of user pictures. Airbnb is also able to monitor all of its server resources. As a result of these AWS services, Airbnb has saved the expense of at least one operations position and gained increased flexibility to meet the demand for future growth.[13]

The key to Web services is XML. Just as HTML was developed as a standard for formatting Web content into Web pages, XML is used within a Web page to describe and transfer data between Web service applications. It is easy to read and has wide industry support. In addition to XML, three other components are used in Web service applications:

1. SOAP (Simple Object Access Protocol) is a specification that defines the XML format for messages. It allows businesses, their suppliers, and their customers to communicate with each other. It provides a set of rules that makes information and data easier to move over the Internet.
2. WSDL (Web Services Description Language) provides a way for a Web service application to describe its interfaces in enough detail to allow a user to build a client application to talk to it. In other words, WSDL allows one software component to connect to and work with another software component on the Internet.
3. UDDI (Universal Discovery Description and Integration) is used to register Web service applications with an Internet directory so that potential users can easily find them and carry out transactions over the Web.

Developing Web Content and Applications

If you need to create a Web site, you have lots of options. You can hire someone to design and build it, or you can do it yourself. If you do it yourself, you can use an online service to create the Web pages, use a Web page creation software tool, or use a plain text editor to create the site. Today's Web development applications allow developers to create Web sites using software that resembles a word processor. The software includes features that allow the developer to work directly with the HTML code or to use auto-generated code. Web development software also helps the designer keep track of all files in a Web site and the hyperlinks that connect them. See Figure 7.11.

FIGURE 7.11

Creating Web pages

Microsoft Expression Web makes Web design nearly as easy as using a word processor.

Adobe Dreamweaver CC is a highly popular software tool for Web page creation. It has evolved over time from being a creator of HTML pages with a WYSIWYG (what you see is what you get) interface to being able to handle programming pages in PHP, ColdFusion, and JavaScript. Its allows you to preview how Web pages look using different browsers and screen sizes—from smartphones to large screen personal computers. Muse is an alternate choice from Adobe that comes with templates and generates a site view map that lets you see how your site will look.

Those using a Mac to develop their Web sites can use RapidWeaver 5, also a WYSIWYG Web page editor that includes many built-in templates to help you get started. On a Windows computer, Web developers have a plethora of choices. Xara Web Designer 9 is for Windows-based Web development. It also provides templates so designers do not need to know HTML or JavaScript to create a Web site.

The task of designing a Web site has become much more complicated as the range of mobile devices we use to access the Web has expanded. Soon, if not already, more people will access the Web using some type of mobile device rather than a desktop computer. The challenge for Web site designers is to figure out how to provide a pleasing Web browsing experience on various devices. One approach is the use of responsive Web design—a means of providing custom layouts to devices based on the size of the browser window.[14]

Most browsers that run on small screen devices such as smartphones and tablets shrink a Web page down to fit the screen and provide ways for zooming and moving around the page. Although this approach works, it does not

responsive Web design: A means of providing custom layouts to devices based on the size of the browser window.

CHAPTER 7 • The Internet, Web, Intranets, and Extranets **323**

provide a pleasing browsing experience. The text is too small to read, the links too small to tap, and too much zooming and panning is tedious. An alternative approach is to use responsive Web design to serve a single HTML document to all devices by applying different style sheets based on the screen size to provide an optimal layout for that device. For example, when the page is viewed on a desktop computer with a large screen, the content can be placed into multiple columns with normal navigation elements. But when that same page is viewed on a small smartphone screen, it appears in one column with large links for easy tapping.

A **Web design framework** is a collection of files and folders of standardized code (HTML, CSS, and JavaScript documents) that can be used to support the development of Web sites.[15] Responsive Web design is made easier through the use of frameworks that enable you to create standard-compliant Web sites with minimum effort while at the same time keeping everything simple and consistent. The advantage of using frameworks is that they speed up and simplify the design of the Web site and provide consistency across different devices.[16] Bootstrap, Kickstrap, Foundation, Groundwork CSS, Skelton, Gumby, and IVORY are a few of the dozens of Web design frameworks.[17]

Web application frameworks that support full enterprise-level needs are referred to as online content management systems. Most content management systems use a database to store and deliver Web content. ExpressionEngine, ezPublish, Vivvo CMS, and SquareSpace are examples of content management systems. The federal government used the Drupal framework to develop the *www.whitehouse.gov* Web site. See Figure 7.12.

Web design framework: A collection of files and folders of standardized code (HTML, CSS, and Javascript documents), which can be used to support the development of Web sites.

FIGURE **7.12**

Web application framework

Whitehouse.gov was created with the Drupal Web content management system.

Web sites are typically developed on personal computers and then uploaded to a Web server. Although a business may manage its own Web server, the job is often outsourced to a Web-hosting company. Web hosts maintain Web servers, storage systems, and backup systems, and they provide Web development software and frameworks, Web analytics tools, and e-commerce software when required. A Web host can charge $15 or more per month, depending on the services delivered. Some Web-hosting sites also include domain name registration and Web site design services.

Many products make it easy to develop Web content and interconnect Web services, as discussed in the next section. Microsoft, for example, provides a development and Web services platform called .NET, which allows developers to use various programming languages to create and run programs, including those for the Web. The .NET platform also includes a rich library of programming code to help build XML Web applications. Other popular Web development platforms include JavaServer Pages, Microsoft ASP, and Adobe ColdFusion.

INTERNET AND WEB APPLICATIONS

The types of Internet and Web applications available are vast and ever expanding. Individuals and organizations around the world rely on Internet and Web applications. Using the Internet, entrepreneurs can start online companies and thrive. Joshua Opperman and Nell Garcia were voted Entrepreneur of 2013 award winners by *Entrepreneur* magazine. Opperman developed an online market for discarded wedding rings from the lovelorn; Garcia for taking her successful cake-baking skills to the masses via Internet workshops.[18] Meanwhile, four-year-old Altitude Digital, which matches online content publishers with advertisers using an eBay-like bidding platform, is on target to generate $20 million in revenue this year.[19] Internet companies such as *www .elance.com* or *www.guru.com* can help entrepreneurs prosper on the Internet.

For businesses of all sizes, lackluster Web sites mean fewer people visiting the sites, which usually translates into lower sales and profits. Today, many organizations are concerned about the profitability of their Internet business model. In the early days of the Internet, many media companies placed free content on their Web sites. Now, media companies and others are investigating ways to generate revenues from their Web sites or removing content from their Web sites that could compete with traditional newspapers, magazines, or TV content and hurt profitability in their traditional businesses.

The newspaper industry has had to deal with competition from Internet media, climbing newsprint prices, the loss of much classified advertising, and rapid declines in circulation. In an attempt to deal with these challenges, over one-third of the 1,380 daily newspapers in the United States and many newspapers in Canada and the United Kingdom have adopted digital pay plans. Under this strategy, frequent users of a newspaper's Web site eventually are requested to pay $10 to $20 per month for a digital subscription or lose access to the site. Less frequent users are allowed free access to a limited number of articles each month and articles found through search, links, and social media references. Digital access is typically offered at a greatly reduced rate to print subscribers. For example, for *The Los Angeles Times* and some other papers, the cost of a subscription for digital access and the Sunday paper is cheaper than digital alone.[20]

Internet advertising has been an important revenue source for many organizations. Internet companies, however, have to be careful about how they conduct their advertising. For example, Google, LinkedIn, and Yahoo have been accused in lawsuits of intercepting emails sent to users of their mail service and using those communications to tailor advertisements to them to increase their revenue.[21]

Social media Web sites, such as Facebook, represent a large percentage of all Internet advertising. Indeed, some 93 percent of marketers use social media for business.[22] Without question, social media Web sites like Facebook and newer Web approaches have exploded in popularity and importance.

Web 2.0 and the Social Web

Over the years, the Web has evolved from a one-directional resource where users only obtain information to a two-directional resource where users obtain and contribute information. Consider Web sites such as Facebook, YouTube,

Wikipedia, WordPress, Pinterest, Tumblr, Craigslist, IMDB, Yelp, and Flickr as examples. The Web has also grown in power to support full-blown software applications such as Google Docs and is becoming a computing platform itself. These two major trends in how the Web is used and perceived have created dramatic changes in how people, businesses, and organizations use the Web, creating a paradigm shift to Web 2.0.

Web 2.0: The Web as a computing platform that supports software applications and the sharing of information among users.

The Social Web

The original Web—Web 1.0—provided a platform for technology-savvy developers and the businesses and organizations that hired them to publish information for the general public to view. Web sites such as YouTube and Flickr allow users to share video and photos with other people, groups, and the world. Microblogging sites such as Twitter allow people to post thoughts and ideas throughout the day for friends to read. See Figure 7.13.

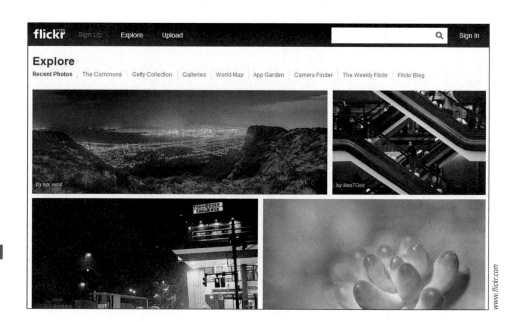

FIGURE **7.13**

Flickr

Flickr allows users to share photos with other people around the world.

Social networking Web sites provide Web-based tools for users to share information about themselves with people on the Web and to find, meet, and converse with other members. Some of these characteristics can be seen in *The Social Network*, a popular movie about the start and growth of Facebook. Google began Google+, a social networking site, in 2011 and today it is the second largest social network in the world with over 230 million active users.[23] LinkedIn is designed for professional use to assist its members with creating and maintaining valuable professional connections. Ning provides tools for Web users to create their own social networks dedicated to a topic or interest. Table 7.2 lists the top social network sites based on estimated unique monthly visitors.[24]

Social networking sites provide members with a personal Web page and allow them to post photos and information about themselves. Special interest groups can be created and joined as well. Social networking Web sites have also been used to help encourage medical research on unusual diseases, help people find important health information, and even sign up to be an organ donor or locate organ donors.

Social networks have become very popular for finding old friends, staying in touch with current friends, and making new friends. Besides their personal value, these networks provide a wealth of consumer information and opportunity to businesses as well. Some businesses are including social networking

TABLE **7.2** Most popular social network sites

Web Site	Estimated Unique Monthly Visitors (Millions)
Facebook	800
Twitter	250
LinkedIn	200
Google+	150
Pinterest	140
Flickr	67
VK	65
Instagram	50
MySpace	26

features in their workplaces. The use of social media in business is called Enterprise 2.0. Enterprise 2.0 applications, such as Salesforce's Chatter, Jive Software's Engage, and Yammer enable employees to create business wikis, support social networking, perform blogging, and create social bookmarks to quickly find information.

Tyco is a dedicated fire protection and security company. The company recently went through a major restructuring, changing from a conglomerate of holding companies to a united global enterprise with more than 69,000 employees in 50 countries. Tyco relied on Yammer rather than email to educate its workforce on the difference between the old Tyco and the new Tyco and to increase employee engagement across the company.[25]

Not everyone is happy with social networking sites, however. Employers might use social networking sites to find personal information about you. Some people worry that their privacy will be invaded or their personal information used without their knowledge or consent.

Rich Internet Applications

The introduction of powerful Web-delivered applications, such as Google Docs, Adobe Photoshop Express, Xcerion Web-based OS, and Microsoft Office Web Apps, has enabled the Web to serve as a platform for computing. Many of the computer activities traditionally provided through software installed on a PC can now be carried out using rich Internet applications (RIAs) in a Web browser without installing any software. A rich Internet application is software that has the functionality and complexity of traditional application software but that runs in a Web browser and does not require local installation. See Figure 7.14. RIAs are the result of continuously improving programming languages and platforms designed for the Web.

Most RIAs take advantage of being online by emphasizing their collaborative benefits. Microsoft and Google support both online document sharing and collaborative editing. A site called 37signals provides online project management, contact management, calendar, and group chat applications. Microsoft SharePoint provides businesses with collaborative workspaces and social computing tools to allow people at different locations to work on projects together.

rich Internet application (RIA): Software that has the functionality and complexity of traditional application software but that does not require local installation and runs in a Web browser.

Online Information Sources

The Web has become the most popular source for daily news, surpassing newspapers and television. It has become the first place people look when they want news or are faced with a challenge or question.

FIGURE 7.14

Rich Internet application

Adobe Photoshop Creative Cloud (CC) is a rich Internet application for graphic designers and other media professionals.

News

The Web is a powerful tool for keeping informed about local, state, national, and global news. It has an abundance of special-interest coverage and provides the capacity to deliver deeper analysis of the subject matter. Text and photos are supported by the HTML standard. Video (sometimes called a Webcast) and audio are provided in the browser through plug-in technology and in podcasts. See Figure 7.15.

FIGURE 7.15

Online news

Online news is available in text, audio, and video formats providing the ability to drill down into stories.

As traditional news sources migrate to the Web, new sources are emerging from online companies. News Web sites from Google, Yahoo!, Digg, and Newsvine provide popular or interesting stories from a variety of news sources. In a trend some call social journalism or citizen journalism, ordinary citizens are more involved in reporting the news than ever before. The online community is taking journalism into its hands and reporting the news from each person's perspective using an abundance of online tools. Although social journalism provides important news not available elsewhere, its sources may not be as reliable as mainstream media sources. It is sometimes difficult to discern news from opinion.

Education and Training

As a tool for sharing information and a primary repository of information on all subjects, the Web is ideally suited for education and training. Advances in interactive Web technologies further support important educational relationships between teacher and student and among students. See Figure 7.16.

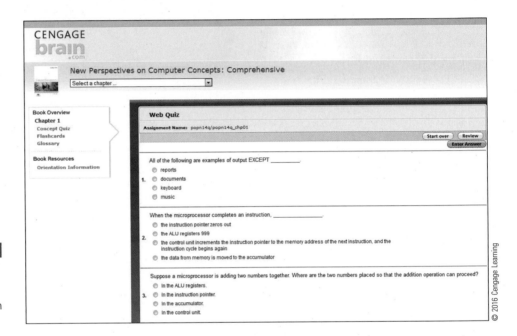

FIGURE 7.16

Cengage Brain instruction resources

The Internet supports education from pre-K to lifelong learning.

Today, schools at all levels provide online education and training. Khan Academy, for example, provides free online training and learning in economics, math, banking and money, biology, chemistry, history, and many other subjects.[26] NPower helps nonprofit organizations, schools, and individuals to develop information system skills. The nonprofit organization gives training and hope to hundreds of disadvantaged young adults through a 22-week training program that can result in certification from companies such as Microsoft and Cisco.[27] Online training programs can be accessed via PCs, tablet computers, and smartphones. High school and college students are also starting to use these devices to read electronic textbooks instead of carrying heavy printed textbooks to class.

Educational support products, such as Blackboard, provide an integrated Web environment that includes virtual chat for class members; a discussion group for posting questions and comments; access to the class syllabus and agenda, student grades, and class announcements; and links to class-related material. Conducting classes over the Web with no physical class meetings is called *distance education*.

In a program it calls Open Courseware, the Massachusetts Institute of Technology (MIT) offers the course material from virtually all of its 2,150 courses free online.[28] See Figure 7.17. Organizations such as the Open Courseware Consortium and the Center for Open Sustainable Learning have been established to support open education around the world.

Beyond traditional education, corporations such as Skillsoft offer professional job skills training through some 6,000 courses accessible over the Web.

MIT's Open Courseware

The Massachusetts Institute of Technology offers course material from nearly all of its courses free online.

Job seekers often use these services to acquire specialized business or technical training.[29] Museums, libraries, private businesses, government agencies, and many other types of organizations and individuals offer educational materials online for free or a fee. Consider eHow, the Web site that claims to teach you "How to do just about everything!"[30] Certiport offers training and testing for technology certification, including application software from Adobe, Autodesk, Intuit, and Microsoft.[31]

Business and Job Information

Providing news and information about a business and its products through the company's Web site and online social media can assist in increasing a company's exposure to the general public and improving its reputation. Providing answers to common product questions and customer support online can help keep customers coming back for more. For example, natural food company Kashi used its Web site to promote healthy living, with a blog about leading a natural lifestyle, recipes, and personal stories from Kashi employees. The Web site helps build a community around the Kashi brand and promotes awareness of Kashi's philosophy and products.[32]

The Web is also an excellent source of job-related information. People looking for their first jobs or seeking information about new job opportunities can find a wealth of information on the Web. Search engines, such as Google or Bing (discussed next), can be a good starting point for searching for specific companies or industries. You can use a directory on Yahoo's home page, for example, to explore industries and careers. Most medium and large companies have Web sites that list open positions, salaries, benefits, and people to contact for further information. The IBM Web site at *www.ibm.com /employment* provides information about jobs available at the firm. When you visit the site, you can find information on jobs with IBM around the world. In addition, several Internet sites specialize in helping you find job information and even apply for jobs online, including *www.linkedin.com* (see Figure 7.18), *www.monster.com*, *www.hotjobs.com*, and *www.careerbuilder.com*.

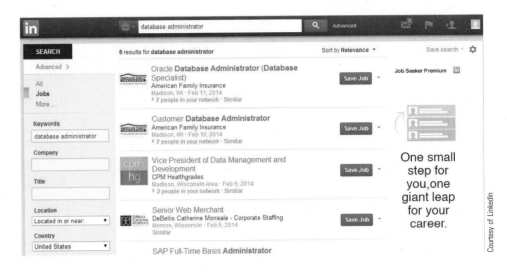

FIGURE **7.18**

LinkedIn jobs listing

LinkedIn and several other Web sites specialize in helping people get job information and even apply for jobs online.

---

search engine: A valuable tool that enables you to find information on the Web by specifying words that are key to a topic of interest, known as keywords.

Search Engines and Web Research

A search engine is a valuable tool that enables you to find information on the Web by specifying words or phrases known as keywords, which are related to a topic of interest. You can also use operators such as OR and NOT for more precise search results. Table 7.3 provides examples of the use of operators in Google searches as listed on Google's help page (*https://support.google.com /websearch/answer/136861*).

TABLE 7.3 Using operators in Google Web searches

Keywords and Operator Entered	Search Engine Interpretation
vacation Hawaii	The words "vacation" and "Hawaii"
Maui OR Hawaii	Either the word "Maui" or the word "Hawaii"
"To each his own"	The exact phrase "To each his own"
virus -computer	The word virus, but not the word computer
Star Wars Episode +I	The movie title "Star Wars Episode," including the Roman numeral I
~auto loan	Loan information for both the word "auto" and its synonyms, such as "truck" and "car"
define:computer	Definitions of the word "computer" from around the Web
red * blue	The words "red" and "blue" separated by one or more words

The search engine market is dominated by Google. Other popular search engines include Yahoo!, Bing, Ask, Dogpile, and China's Baidu. Google has taken advantage of its market dominance to expand into other Web-based services, most notably email, scheduling, maps, social networking, Web-based applications, and mobile device software. Search engines like Google often have to modify how they display search results, depending on pending litigation from other Internet companies and government scrutiny, such as antitrust investigations.

To help users get the information they want from the Web, most search engines use an automated approach that scours the Web with automated programs called spiders. These spiders follow all Web links in an attempt to catalog every Web page by topic; each Web page is analyzed and ranked using unique algorithms, and the resulting information is stored in a database.

INFORMATION SYSTEMS @ WORK

Improved Insight via Clickstream Analysis

When you visit a site, your clickstream is the sequence of pages you click as you spend time on the site. Clickstream analysis is the process of analyzing many clickstreams to understand visitors' collective behavior. The goal of clickstream analysis usually is to optimize a site for its users.

For example, clickstream analysis may find that many users want to see a list of a company's sales offices. Rather than making them reach that page by clicking "About Our Company," then "International Regions," then their local region, and finally, a list of its locations, the company might put a "Sales Offices" link on its home page. That would take the user directly to a page with a list of regions. Click a region, and it expands to show a list of its sales offices on the same page. Besides improving visitor satisfaction with the site, such a change to the site design also reduces the page-serving load on the site owner's Web servers. That, in turn, improves performance and may defer the need for an expensive upgrade.

Clickstream analysis is vital to organizations that depend on the Web for their existence. Greg Linden explains that "Google [search] and Microsoft [Bing] learn from people using Web search. When people find what they want, Google notices. When other people do that same search later, Google has learned from earlier searchers, and makes it easier for the new searchers to get where they want to go."

Learning from clickstreams could be useful in online education. Discussing algebra, Linden notes, "As millions of students try different exercises, we [that is, our computer] forget the paths that consistently led to continued struggles, remember the ones that lead to rapid mastery, and, as new students come in, we put them on the successful paths we have seen before." Therefore, students learn algebra more quickly and more easily. The improved experience may affect their overall attitude toward learning mathematics.

The benefits of clickstream analysis aren't just for online companies. In an interview with MIT's *Sloan Management Review*, David Kreutter, Pfizer's vice-president of U.S. commercial operations, described its value to Pfizer: "When physicians visit our Web site, we know what they're clicking on, we know what they're clicking through to…. We've got more data from which

to try to discern patterns, which we can use in a predictive way. That's really what we're trying to focus on now: can we detect patterns early on, or at least much earlier than prescription writing, that will allow us to adapt more quickly to our customers' needs as well as to the competitive environment?"

Clickstream analysis helps Pfizer monitor what happens when its representatives visit physicians. Kreutter continues, "If our strategy is to deliver certain messages in a certain order, we can see if the message was delivered that way. For example, if we know that a certain segment of doctors in South Florida have a heavy proportion of elderly patients, they will often want to hear about drug-drug interactions first (because their patients are on many medications). We can track if we executed against that strategy, and we can track if that strategy had the impact, the literal prescribing behavior, that we anticipated. It … helps us to figure out, if we don't have the impact we hoped for, if our strategy was right but the execution was flawed, or if the strategy fundamentally needs to be rethought."

Discussion Questions

1. Consider Greg Linden's example of search engines learning from watching which search results users chose to click. What are the benefits to the search engine company (e.g., Google or Microsoft in Linden's examples) of having this information?
2. How could other companies benefit from clickstream analysis?

Critical Thinking Questions

1. Some people fear that clickstream analysis constitutes an invasion of privacy. Do you agree? Why or why not?
2. How does clickstream analysis benefit you as a user? Does clickstream analysis offer more advantages than disadvantages to individuals?

SOURCES: Kiron, D. and Shockley, R., "How Pfizer Uses Tablet PCs and Click-Stream Data to Track Its Strategy," *Sloan Management Review*, sloanreview.mit.edu/the-magazine/2011-fall/53118/how-pfizer-uses -tablet-pcs-and-click-stream-data-to-track-its-strategy, August 25, 2011; Linden, G., "Massive-Scale Data Mining for Education," *Communications of the ACM*, vol. 54, no. 11, November 2011, p. 13; Pfizer Web site, *www.pfizer.com*, accessed June 8, 2012.

A keyword search at Yahoo!, Bing, or Google isn't a search of the Web but rather a search of a database that stores information about Web pages. The database is continuously checked and refreshed so that it is an accurate reflection of the current status of the Web.

Some search companies have experimented with human-powered and human-assisted search, such as Mahalo.[33] Human-powered search provides search results created by human researchers. Because the system is human powered, the search results are typically more accurate, definitive, and complete. The Web site *www.liveperson.com* takes human power one step further and allows visitors to chat and seek advice from human experts. The Web service contracts thousands of experts in a wide variety of fields to answer questions from users for a fee.[34]

The Bing search engine has attempted to innovate with its design. Bing refers to itself as a decision engine because it attempts to minimize the amount of information that it returns in its searches that is not useful or pertinent.[35] Bing also includes media—music, videos, and games—in its search results. See Figure 7.19.

A meta search engine allows you to run keyword searches on several search engines at once. For example, a search run from *www.dogpile.com* returns results from Google, Yahoo!, MSN, Ask, and other search engines.

Savvy business owners know that the results gained from search engines are tools that draw visitors to the certain Web sites. Many businesses invest in search engine optimization (SEO)—a process for driving traffic to a Web site by using techniques that improve the site's ranking in search results. Normally, when a user gets a list of results from a Web search, the links listed highest on the first page of search results have a far greater chance of being clicked. SEO professionals, therefore, try to get the Web sites of their businesses to be listed with as many appropriate keywords as possible. They study the algorithms that search engines use, and then they alter the contents of their Web pages to improve the page's chance of being ranked number one. SEO professionals use *Web analytics software* to study detailed statistics about visitors to their sites. Top-rated search engine optimization companies include Netmark, Customer Magnetism, SEOP, Higher Visibility, and 180Fusion. These companies help organizations like Hallmark, SelectQuote, Experian, SallieMae, Siemens, Mercedes, Toyota, and *Women's Running* magazine.[36]

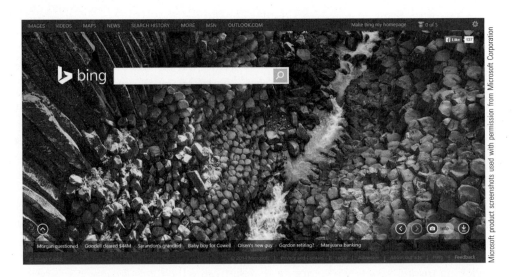

FIGURE 7.19

Microsoft Bing decision engine

Microsoft calls its search engine a decision engine to distinguish it from other search software.

In addition to search engines, you can use other Web sites to research information. Wikipedia, an online encyclopedia with over 3 million English-language entries created and edited by millions of users, is another example of a Web site that can be used to research information. See Figure 7.20. In Hawaiian, *wiki* means quick, so a "wikipedia" provides quick access to information. The Web site is both open source and open editing, which means that people can add or edit entries in the encyclopedia at any time. More than 77,000 active contributors are working on more than 30 million articles written in some 285 languages. Besides being self-regulating, Wikipedia articles are vetted by around 1,400 administrators.[37] However, even with so many administrators, it is possible that some entries are inaccurate and biased.

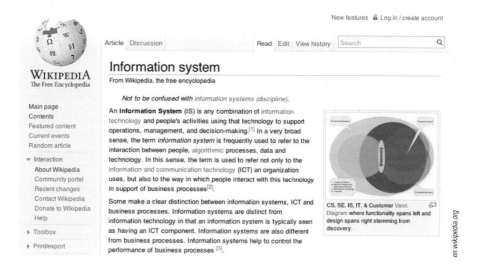

FIGURE 7.20

Wikipedia

Wikipedia captures the knowledge of tens of thousands of experts.

The wiki approach to content development is referred to as *crowd sourcing*, which uses the combined effort of many individuals to accomplish some task. Another example of crowd sourcing is the OpenStreetMap.org project. OpenStreetMap uses a wiki and the power of the crowd to develop a detailed map of the world.

Besides online catalogs, libraries typically provide links to public and sometimes private research databases on the Web. Online research databases allow visitors to search for information in thousands of journal, magazine, and newspaper articles. Information database services are valuable because they offer the best in quality and convenience. They conveniently provide full-text articles from reputable sources over the Web. College and public libraries typically subscribe to many databases to support research. One of the most popular private databases is LexisNexis Academic Universe. See Figure 7.21.

Web Portals

Web portal: A Web page that combines useful information and links and acts as an entry point to the Web; portals typically include a search engine, a subject directory, daily headlines, and other items of interest. Many people choose a Web portal as their browser's home page (the first page you open when you begin browsing the Web).

A **Web portal** is a Web page that combines useful information and links and acts as an entry point to the Web; portals typically include a search engine, a subject directory, daily headlines, and other items of interest. Because many people choose a Web portal as their browser's home page (the first page you open when you begin browsing the Web), the two terms are used interchangeably.

Many Web pages have been designed to serve as Web portals. Yahoo!, AOL, and MSN are examples of horizontal portals; "horizontal" refers to the fact that these portals cover a wide range of topics. MyYahoo! allows users to custom design their pages, selecting from hundreds of widgets—small applications that deliver information and services. Yahoo! also integrates with Facebook so that Facebook users can access their friends and news streams from the MyYahoo portal. See Figure 7.22.

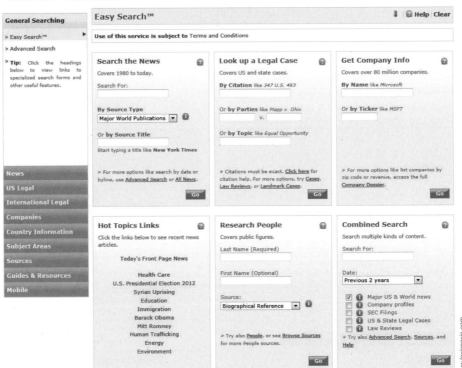

FIGURE 7.21

LexisNexis

At LexisNexis Academic Universe, you can search the news, legal cases, company information, people, or a combination of categories.

FIGURE 7.22

MyYahoo! personalized portal

MyYahoo! and other personalized portals can contain custom designs and widgets.

Vertical portals are pages that provide information and links for special-interest groups. For example, the portal at *www.iVillage.com* focuses on items of interest to women, and *www.AskMen.com* is a vertical portal for men. Many businesses set up corporate portals for their employees to provide access to work-related resources, such as corporate news and information, along with access to business tools, databases, and communication tools to support collaboration.

Email

Email is a useful form of Internet communication that supports text communication, HTML content, and sharing documents as email attachments. Email is accessed through Web-based systems or through dedicated email applications, such as Microsoft Outlook and Mozilla Thunderbird. Email can also be distributed through enterprise systems to desktop computers, notebook computers, and smartphones. Email services must be reliable and impervious to hacking attacks. British Telecom pulled its 6 million users off Yahoo allegedly because its users complained about spam and hacking attacks.[38]

Many people use online email services, such as Outlook.com, Yahoo, and Gmail. See Figure 7.23. Online email services store messages on the server, not the user's computer, so that users need to be connected to the Internet to view, send, and manage email. Other people prefer to use software such as Microsoft Outlook, Apple Mail, or Thunderbird, which retrieve email from the server and deliver it to the user's PC.

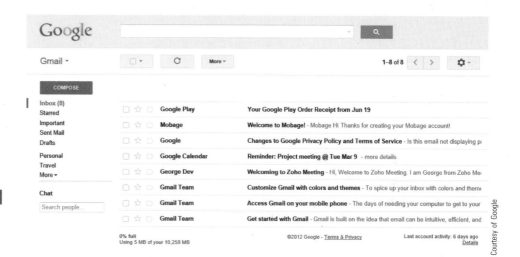

FIGURE 7.23

Gmail

Gmail is one of several free online email services.

Business users who access email from smartphones, such as the BlackBerry, take advantage of a technology called push email. Push email uses corporate server software that transfers, or pushes, email to the handset as soon as it arrives at the corporate email server. To the BlackBerry user, it appears as though email is delivered directly to the handset. See Figure 7.24.

FIGURE 7.24

Blackberry email

BlackBerry users have instant access to email sent to their business accounts.

Push email allows the user to view email from any mobile or desktop device connected to the corporate server. This arrangement allows users flexibility in where, when, and how they access and manage email.

Some email services scan for possible junk or bulk mail, called *spam*, and the service deletes it or places it in a separate folder. A study by the IT Security firm Kaspersky found that 70 percent of email sent in April, May, and June of 2013 was spam.[39] While spam-filtering software can prevent or discard unwanted messages, other software products can help users sort and answer large amounts of legitimate email. For example, software from Clear-Context, Seriosity, and Xobni rank and sort messages based on sender, content, and context, allowing individuals to focus on the most urgent and important messages first.

Instant Messaging

instant messaging: A method that allows two or more people to communicate online in real time using the Internet.

Instant messaging is online, real-time communication between two or more people who are connected to the Internet. See Figure 7.25. With instant messaging, participants build buddy lists, or contact lists, that let them see which contacts are currently logged on to the Internet and available to chat. If you send messages to one of your online buddies, a small dialog box opens on your buddy's computer and allows the two of you to chat via the keyboard. Although chat typically involves exchanging text messages with one other person, more advanced forms of chat exist. Today's instant messaging software supports not only text messages but also the sharing of images, sounds, files, and voice communications. These apps allow users to send messages from their mobile devices to other mobile devices without paying for wireless

FIGURE 7.25

Instant messaging

Instant messaging lets you converse with another Internet user by exchanging messages instantaneously.

service. As a result, it is estimated that mobile operators lost $23 billion in revenue in just 2012.[40] Table 7.4 lists the most popular instant messaging applications as of November 2013 based on number of registered users worldwide.[41]

TABLE **7.4** Most popular instant messaging applications

Application	Number of Registered Users	Originates From
WeChat	600 million	China
WhatsApp	590 million	United States
Facebook Messenger	550 million	United States
Line	300 million	Japan
Viber	200 million	Israel
Snapchat	100 million	United States
Talk	100 million	South Korea

© 2016 Cengage Learning

Microblogging, Status Updates, and News Feeds

Twitter is a Web application that allows members to report on what they are doing throughout the day. Referred to as a microblogging service, Twitter allows users to send short text updates (up to 140 characters) from a smartphone or a Web account to their Twitter followers. While Twitter has been hugely successful for personal use, businesses are finding value in the service as well. Business people use Twitter to stay in close touch with associates by sharing their location and activities throughout the day. Businesses also find Twitter to be a rich source of consumer sentiment that can be tapped to improve marketing, customer relations, and product development. Many businesses have a presence on Twitter, dedicating personnel to communicate with customers by posting announcements and reaching out to individual users. Village Books, an independent bookstore, uses Twitter to build relationships with its customers and to make them feel part of their community.

The popularity of Twitter has caused social networks, such as Facebook, LinkedIn, and MySpace, to include Twitter-like news feeds. Previously referred to as Status Updates, Facebook users share their thoughts and activities with their friends by posting messages to Facebook's News Feed.

Conferencing

Some Internet technologies support real-time online conferencing. Participants dial into a common phone number to share a multiparty phone conversation. The Internet has made it possible for those involved in teleconferences to share computer desktops. Using services such as WebEx or GoToMeeting, conference participants log on to common software that allows them to broadcast their computer display to the group. This ability is quite useful for sharing PowerPoint presentations, demonstrating software, training, or collaborating on documents. Participants verbally communicate by phone or PC microphone. Some conferencing software uses Webcams to broadcast video of the presenter and group participants. The Addison Fire Protection District provides professional fire protection and paramedic services to the 35,000 residents of Addison, Illinois. The district uses GoToMeeting to enable its employees to attend training and to support chief-to-chief meetings without requiring personnel to leave their assigned stations.[42]

Telepresence takes video conferencing to the ultimate level. Telepresence systems such as those from Cisco and Polycom use high-resolution video and audio with high-definition displays to make it appear that conference participants are actually sitting around a table. See Figure 7.26. You can see eyes

Courtesy of Polycom

FIGURE 7.26

Halo Collaboration Meeting Room

The Halo telepresence system allows people at various locations to meet as though they were gathered around a table.

blinking and people breathing. Participants enter a telepresence studio where they sit at a table facing display screens that show other participants in other locations. Cameras and microphones collect high-quality video and audio at all locations and transmit them over high-speed network connections to provide an environment that replicates actual physical presence. Document cameras and computer software are used to share views of computer screens and documents with all participants.

You don't need to be a big business to enjoy the benefits of video conversations. Free software is available to make video chat easy to use for anyone with a computer, a Webcam, and a high-speed Internet connection. Online applications such as Google Chat support video connections between Web users. For spontaneous, random video chat with strangers, you can use *www.chatroulette.com* and Internet Conga Line. Software, such as Apple Messages and Skype, provide computer-to-computer video chat so users can speak to each other face to face. In addition to offering text, audio, and video chat on computers, Skype offers its video phone service over Internet-connected TVs. Recent Internet-connected sets from Panasonic and Samsung ship with the Skype software preloaded. You attach a Webcam to your TV to have a video chat from your sofa.

Blogging and Podcasting

Web log (blog): A Web site that people can create and use to write about their observations, experiences, and opinions on a wide range of topics.

A Web log, typically called a blog, is a Web site that people can create and use to write about their observations, experiences, and opinions on a wide range of topics. The community of blogs and bloggers is often called the *blogosphere*. A *blogger* is a person who creates a blog, whereas *blogging* refers to the process of placing entries on a blog site. A blog is like a journal. When people post information to a blog, it is placed at the top of the blog page. Blogs can include links to external information and an area for comments submitted by visitors. Video content can also be placed on the Internet using the same approach as a blog. This is often called a *video log* or *vlog*.

Internet users may subscribe to blogs using a technology called Really Simple Syndication (RSS). RSS is a collection of Web technologies that allows users to subscribe to Web content that is frequently updated, such as news sites and blogs. With RSS, you can receive a blog update and the latest headlines without actually visiting the blog or news Web site. Software used to subscribe to RSS feeds is called *aggregator software*. Feedly is a popular aggregator for subscribing to blogs, and is available as an iOS, Android, or Web app.

To set up a blog, you can go to the Web site of a blog service provider, such as *www.blogger.com* or *www.wordpress.com*, create a user name and password, select a theme, choose a URL, follow any other instructions, and start making your first entry. You can also use software such as Blogger, WordPress, and Tumblr to create your blogs. People who want to find a blog on a certain topic can use blog search engines, such as Technorati, Feedster, and Blogdigger. You can also use Google to locate a blog.

A *podcast* is an audio broadcast over the Internet. The name "podcast" originated from the Apple *iPod* combined with the word *broadcast*. A podcast is like an audio blog. Using PCs, recording software, and microphones, you can record podcast programs and place them on the Internet. Apple iTunes provides free access to tens of thousands of podcasts, which are sorted by topic and searchable by key word. See Figure 7.27. After you find a podcast, you can download it to your PC (Windows or Mac), to an MP3 player such as the iPod, or to any smartphone or tablet. You can also subscribe to podcasts using RSS software included in iTunes and other digital audio software.

1. **NPR: Science Friday Podcast**
by Ira Flatow

Science Friday, as heard on NPR, is a weekly discussion of the latest news in science, technology, health, and the environment hosted by Ira Flatow.

▶ PLAY

2. **TEDTalks Podcast**
by Anthony Robbins

Each year, TED hosts some of the world's most fascinating people: Trusted voices and convention-breaking mavericks, icons and geniuses.

▶ PLAY

3. **Entrepreneurial Thought Leaders Podcast**
by Forrest Glick

The DFJ Entrepreneurial Thought Leaders Seminar (ETL) is a weekly seminar series on entrepreneurship, co-sponsored by BASES (a student entrepreneurship group), Stanford Technology Ventures Program, and the Department of Management Science and Engineering.

▶ PLAY

4. **Mixergy Video Podcast**
by Andrew Warner

 Interviews with a mix of successful online businesspeople. Andrew Warner asks them to teach ambitious startups how to build companies that leave a legacy...

▶ PLAY

5. **Ruby on Rails Podcast**
by Scott Barron

The Rails podcast is a super-agile way for you to get the inside scoop on the Rails community.

www.learnoutloud.com

content streaming: A method for transferring large media files over the Internet so that the data stream of voice and pictures plays more or less continuously as the file is being downloaded.

Online Media and Entertainment

Like news and information, all forms of media and entertainment have followed their audiences online. Music, movies, television program episodes, user-generated videos, e-books, and audio books are all available online to download and purchase or stream.

Content streaming is a method of transferring large media files over the Internet so that the data stream of voice and pictures plays more or less continuously as the file is being downloaded. For example, rather than wait for an entire 5 MB video clip to download before they can play it, users can begin viewing a streamed video as it is being received. Content streaming works best when the transmission of a file can keep up with the playback of the file.

Music

The Internet and the Web have made music more accessible than ever, with artists distributing their songs through online radio, subscription services, and download services. Spotify, Pandora, Napster, and Grooveshark are just a few examples of free Internet music sites. Other Internet music sites charge a fee for music. Rhapsody has about 800,000 paid listeners and Slacker Radio has about 300,000 paid listeners. See Figure 7.28. Internet music has even helped sales of classical music by Mozart, Beethoven, and others. Internet companies, including Facebook, are starting to make music, movies, and other digital content available on their Web sites. Facebook, for example, allows online music companies, such as Spotify and Rdio, to post music activity on its Web site.

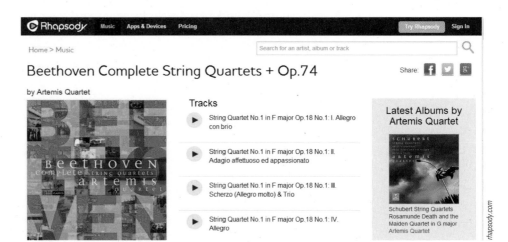

FIGURE 7.28

Rhapsody

Rhapsody provides streaming music by subscription.

Apple iTunes was one of the first online music services to find success. Microsoft, Amazon, Walmart, and other retailers also sell music online. The going rate for music downloads is $0.89 to $0.99 per song. Downloaded music may include digital rights management (DRM) technology that prevents or limits the user's ability to make copies or to play the music on multiple players.

Podcasts are yet another way to access music on the Web. Many independent artists provide samples of their music through podcasts. Podcast Alley includes podcasts from unsigned artists.

Movies, Video, and Television

Television and movies are expanding to the Web in leaps and bounds. Web sites such as Hulu and Internet-based television platforms such as Netflix and Joost provide television programming from hundreds of providers, including most mainstream television networks. See Figure 7.29. Walmart's acquisition of Vudu has allowed the big discount retailer to successfully get into the Internet movie business. Increasingly, TV networks have iPad and other mobile applications (apps) that stream TV content to tablet computers and other mobile devices. Other TV networks are starting to charge viewers to watch their episodes on the Internet. The Roku LT Streaming Media Box connects wirelessly to your TV and streams TV shows and movies from online sources such as Amazon Instant, Crackle, Disney, Hulu, Netflix, Pandora, and Xfinity TV.

No discussion of Internet video would be complete without mentioning YouTube. YouTube supports the online sharing of user-created videos. YouTube videos are relatively short and cover a wide range of categories from the nonsensical to college lectures. See Figure 7.30. It is estimated that 100 hours of video are uploaded to YouTube every minute and that over 6 billion hours of video are watched each month on YouTube. YouTube reaches more United States adults in the 18–34 age category than any cable network.[43] Other video-streaming sites include Google Video, Yahoo! Video, Metacafe, and AOL Video.

© Twin Design/Shutterstock.com

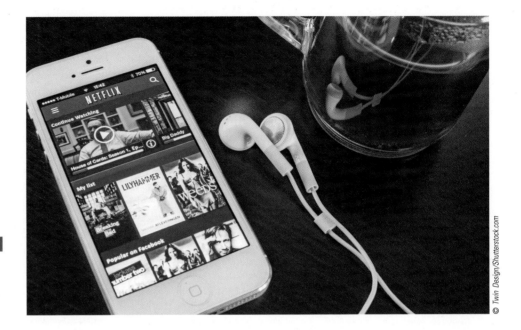

FIGURE 7.29
Netflix

Netflix provides online access to thousands of movies and television shows.

youtube.com/edu

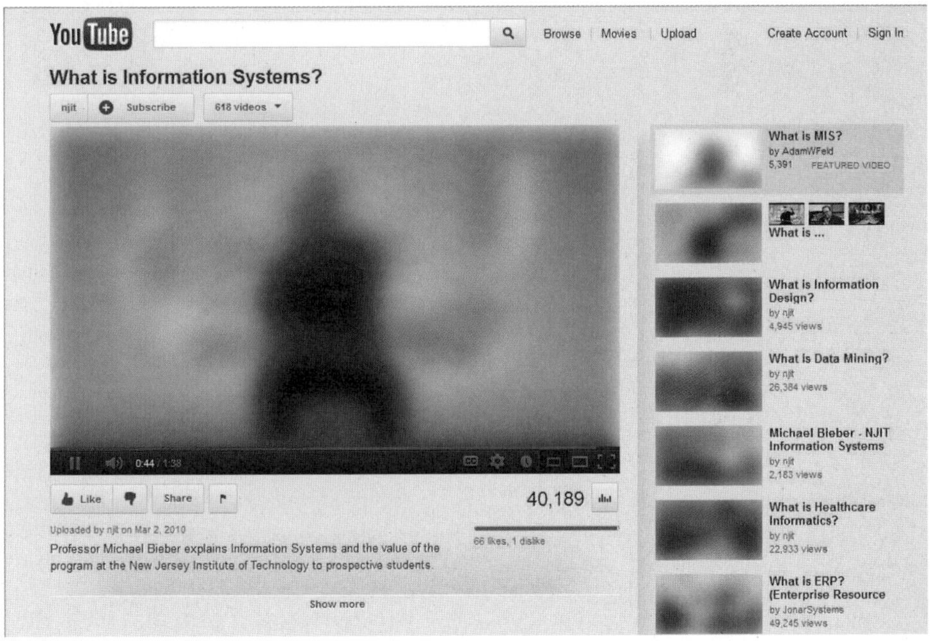

FIGURE 7.30
YouTube EDU

YouTube EDU provides thousands of educational videos from hundreds of universities.

As more companies create and post videos to Web sites like YouTube, some IS departments are creating a new position—video content manager.

E-Books and Audio Books

An e-book is a book stored digitally rather than on paper and read on a display using e-book reader software. E-books have been available for quite a while, nearly as long as computers. However, it wasn't until the introduction of Amazon's e-book reading device, the Kindle, in 2007 that they became more widely accepted. Several features of the Kindle appeal to the general public. First, it features ePaper, a display that does not include backlighting like traditional displays. Some feel that ePaper is less harsh on your eyes than using a backlit display. Second, the Kindle is light and compact, similar in size and weight to a paperback book, although thinner than most books. Finally, Amazon created a vast library of e-books that could be purchased and downloaded to the Kindle over whispernet—a wireless network provided free of charge by Sprint. Today, dozens of electronics manufacturers are offering e-book readers.

The Apple iPad changed the e-book industry by providing a form factor that is similar to but larger than the Kindle. The iPad also includes a color backlit display. As an e-book reader, the iPad functions much like the Kindle; however, the iPad provides thousands of applications in addition to e-books. Besides using the Kindle, iPad, and other slate devices, you can access e-books on the Web, download them as PDF files to view on your computer, or you can read them on your smartphone. While e-books are convenient, some have accused e-book publishers and distributors with conspiring to raise e-book prices.

There are dozens of e-book formats. Some are proprietary, such as Kindle's .azw format, which can be viewed only on a Kindle. Others formats are open, such as Open e-book's .opf format and the .epub format, both of which can be read on many different devices and software packages, including Samsung tablets and the iPad. See Figure 7.31.

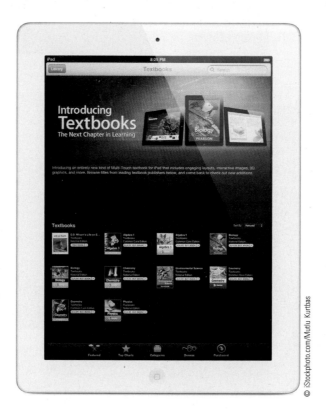

FIGURE 7.31

iPad publishing

The iPad provides an interactive platform for magazines and books.

Audio books have become more popular due to the popularity of the iPod, the iPhone, and other mobile devices along with services such as Audible that allow you to download audio books. Audio books are read by a narrator without much inflection or varying voices or they can be performed by actors who add dramatic interpretations of the book to the reading. Audio books may be abridged (consolidated and edited for audio format) or unabridged (read word for word from the book). Audio book services may allow you to purchase books individually or sign up for a membership and receive a new book each month.

Online Games and Entertainment

Video games have become a huge industry with worldwide annual revenue projected to exceed $100 billion by 2017.[44] Zynga, a fast-growing Internet company, sells virtual animals and other virtual items for games, such as FarmVille. The company, for example, sells a clown pony with colorful clothes for about $5. Zynga has a VIP club for people that spend a lot on virtual items it offers for sale. Some Internet companies also sell food for virtual animals. People can feed and breed virtual animals and sell their offspring. With all the money being made with virtual animals and their pet food, lawsuits are likely. The market for Internet gaming is very competitive and constantly changing. After Google included online games on its Web site, Facebook updated its online gaming offerings. Many video games are available online. They include single-user, multiuser, and massively multiuser games. The Web offers a multitude of games for all ages.

Game consoles such as the Wii, Xbox, and PlayStation provide multiplayer options for online gaming over the Internet. Subscribers can play with or against other subscribers in 3D virtual environments. They can even talk to each other using a microphone headset. The Microsoft Xbox One integrates with live TV and can control your cable or satellite cable box, TV, and receiver.

Shopping Online

Shopping on the Web can be convenient, easy, and cost effective. You can buy almost anything via the Web, from books and clothing to cars and sports equipment. Groupon, for example, offers discounts at restaurants, spas, auto repair shops, music performances, and almost any other product or service offered in your area or city. See Figure 7.32. Revenues for Groupon were expected to exceed $2 billion in 2013.[45]

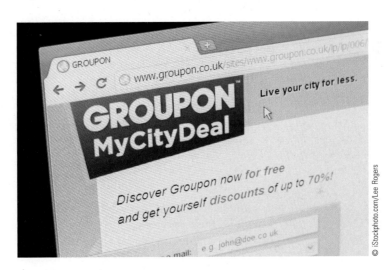

FIGURE 7.32

Groupon

Groupon offers discounts at restaurants, spas, auto repair shops, music performances, and almost any other product or service offered in your area or city.

Other online companies offer different services. Dell.com and many other computer retailers provide tools that allow shoppers to specify every aspect and component of a computer system to purchase. ResumePlanet.com would be happy to create your professional résumé. Peapod or Amazon Grocery would be happy to deliver groceries to your doorstep. Products and services abound online.

Many online shopping options are available to Web users. E-tail stores—online versions of retail stores—provide access to many products that may be unavailable in local stores. JCPenney, Target, Walmart, and many others carry only a percentage of their inventory in their retail stores; the other inventory is available online. To add to their other conveniences, many Web sites offer free shipping and pickup for returned items that don't fit or otherwise meet a customer's needs.

Like your local shopping mall, cybermalls provide access to a collection of stores that aim to meet your every need. Cybermalls are typically aligned with popular Web portals such as Yahoo!, AOL, and MSN.

Web sites such as *www.mySimon.com*, *www.DealTime.com*, *www.Price SCAN.com*, *www.PriceGrabber.com*, and *www.NexTag.com* provide product price quotations from numerous e-tailers to help you to find the best deal. An application for Android smartphones and tablets called Compare Everywhere allows users to compare the price of an item offered by many retailers. Even if the best price is offered at your local warehouse store, shopping online provides the assurance that you are getting the best deal.

Online clearinghouses, Web auctions, and marketplaces offer a platform for businesses and individuals to sell their products and belongings. Online clearinghouses, such as *www.uBid.com*, provide a method for manufacturers to liquidate stock and for consumers to find a good deal. Outdated or overstocked items are put on the virtual auction block and users bid on the items. The highest bidder when the auction closes gets the merchandise—often for less than 50 percent of the advertised retail price. Credit card numbers are collected at the time that bids are placed. A good rule to keep in mind is not to place a bid on an item unless you are prepared to buy it at that price.

The most popular online auction or marketplace is *www.eBay.com*. See Figure 7.33. eBay provides a public platform for global trading where anyone can buy, sell, or trade practically anything. It offers a wide variety of features and services that enable members to buy and sell on the site quickly and conveniently. Buyers have the option to purchase items at a fixed price or in auction-style format, where the highest bid wins the product.

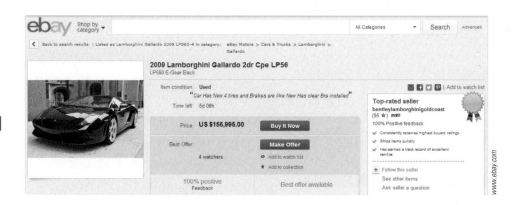

FIGURE 7.33

eBay

eBay provides an online marketplace where anyone can buy, sell, or trade practically anything.

Internet auction sites have even been used by attorneys to market and advertise their services. One Internet auction site, for example, allows lawyers to bid for clients and legal cases online.

Auction houses such as eBay accept limited liability for problems that buyers or sellers may experience in their transactions. Transactions that make use of eBay's PayPal service are protected. Others, however, may be risky. Participants should be aware that auction fraud is the most prevalent type of fraud on the Internet.

Craigslist is a network of online communities that provides free online classified advertisements. It is a popular online marketplace for purchasing items from local individuals. Many shoppers turn to Craigslist rather than going to the classifieds in the local paper.

Businesses benefit from shopping online as well. *Global supply management (GSM)* online services provide methods for businesses to find the best deals on the global market for raw materials and supplies needed to manufacture their products. *Electronic exchanges* provide an industry-specific Web resource created to deliver a convenient centralized platform for B2B e-commerce among manufacturers, suppliers, and customers. You can read more about this topic in Chapter 8.

Travel, Geolocation, and Navigation

The Web has had a profound effect on the travel industry and the way people plan and prepare for trips. From getting assistance with short trips across town to planning long holidays abroad, travelers are turning to the Web to save time and money and overcome much of the risk involved in visiting unknown places.

Travel Web sites, such as *www.travelocity.com*, *www.expedia.com*, *www.kayak.com*, and *www.priceline.com*, help travelers find the best deals on flights, hotels, car rentals, vacation packages, and cruises. Priceline offers a slightly different approach from the other Web sites. In addition to searching for travel deals, Priceline allows shoppers to name a price they're willing to pay for a ticket and then works to find an airline that can meet that price. In addition to reserving flights, travelers can use these Web sites to book hotels and rental cars, often at discounted prices.

Mapping and geolocation tools are among the most popular and successful Web applications. MapQuest, Google Maps, and Bing Maps are examples. See Figure 7.34. By offering free street maps for cities around the world, these tools help travelers find their way. Provide your departure location and destination, and these online applications produce a map that displays the fastest route. Now with GPS technologies, these tools can detect your current location and provide directions from where you are.

FIGURE 7.34

Google Maps

Mapping software, such as Google Maps, provide streetside views of Times Square.

Google Maps also provides extensive location-specific business information, satellite imagery, up-to-the-minute traffic reports, and Street View. The latter is the result of Google employees driving the streets of the world's cities in vehicles with high-tech camera gear, taking 360-degree images. These images are integrated into Google Maps to allow users to get a "street view" of an area that can be manipulated as if they were actually walking down the street looking around. Bing Maps takes it a step further with high-resolution aerial photos and street-level 3D photographs.

Map applications like Google Maps provide tool kits that allow them to be combined with other Web applications. For example, Google Maps can be used with Twitter to display the location where various tweets were posted. Likewise, Google Maps combined with Flickr can overlay photos of specific geographic locations. Combined Web applications are commonly referred to as a *mashup*.

Geographic information systems (GIS) provide geographic information layered over a map. For example, Google Earth provides options for viewing traffic, weather, local photos and videos, underwater features such as shipwrecks and marine life, local attractions, businesses, and places of interest. Software such as Google+ Location and Loopt allow you to find your friends on a map—with their permission—and will automatically notify you if a friend is near.

Geo-tagging is technology that allows for tagging information with an associated location. For example, Flickr and other photo software and services allow photos to be tagged with the location they were taken. Once tagged, it becomes easy to search for photos taken, for example, in Arizona. Geo-tagging also makes it easy to overlay photos on a map, as Google Maps and Bing Maps have done. Twitter, Facebook, and other social networks have made it possible for users to geo-tag photos, comments, tweets, and posts.

Geolocation information does pose a risk to privacy and security. Many people prefer that their location remain unknown, at least to strangers and often to acquaintances and even friends. Recently, criminals have made use of location information to determine when people are away from their residences so that they can burglarize without fear of interruption.

Internet Utilities

Just as the Web is an application that runs on the Internet to provide a framework for delivering information and services, other applications have been designed to run on the Internet for other purposes. Many of these applications serve as utilities for accessing and maintaining resources on the Internet. A few such utilities that predate the Web and http, and still remain useful, are telnet, SSH, and FTP.

Telnet is a network protocol that enables users to log on to networks remotely over the Internet. Telnet software uses a command-line interface that allows the user to work on a remote server directly. Because Telnet is not secured with encryption, most users are switching to *secure shell* (*SSH*), which provides Telnet functionality through a more secure connection.

File Transfer Protocol (FTP): A protocol that provides a file transfer process between a host and a remote computer and allows users to copy files from one computer to another.

File Transfer Protocol (FTP) is a protocol that supports file transfers between a host and a remote computer. See Figure 7.35. Using FTP, users can copy files from one computer to another. For example, the authors and editors of this book used an FTP site provided by the publisher, Cengage Learning, to share and transfer important files during the publication process. Chapter files and artwork, for example, were uploaded to a Cengage Learning FTP site and downloaded by authors and editors to review. Like Telnet, FTP connections are not encrypted, and are, therefore, not secure. Many users are switching to secure FTP (SFTP) for more protected file transfers.

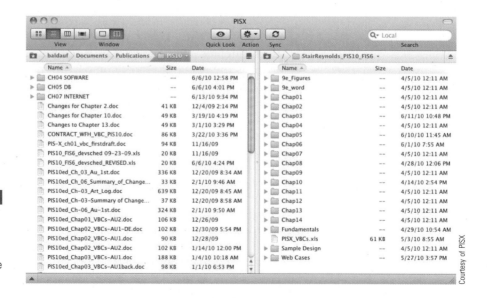

FIGURE 7.35

FTP applications

FTP applications allow you to transfer files between computers by clicking and dragging them from one window to another.

INTRANETS AND EXTRANETS

An intranet is an internal corporate network built using Internet and World Wide Web standards and technologies. Employees of an organization use it to gain access to corporate information. After getting their feet wet with public Web sites that promote company products and services, corporations are seizing the Web as a swift way to streamline—even transform—their organizations. These private networks use the infrastructure and standards of the Internet and the Web. Using an intranet offers one considerable advantage: Many people are already familiar with Internet technology so that they need little training to make effective use of their corporate intranet.

An intranet is an inexpensive yet powerful alternative to other forms of internal communication, including conventional computer networks. One of an intranet's most obvious virtues is its ability to reduce the need for paper. Because Web browsers run on any type of computer, the same electronic information can be viewed by any employee. That means that all sorts of documents (such as internal phone books, procedure manuals, training manuals, and requisition forms) can be inexpensively converted to electronic form on the Web, easily distributed, and constantly updated. An intranet provides employees with an easy and intuitive approach to accessing information that was previously difficult to obtain. For example, it is an ideal solution for providing information to a mobile sales force that needs access to rapidly changing information.

A growing number of companies offer limited access to their private corporate network for selected customers and suppliers. Such networks are referred to as extranets; they connect people who are external to the company. An **extranet** is a network that links selected resources of the intranet of a company with its customers, suppliers, or other business partners. Like intranets, an extranet is built around Web technologies.

extranet: A network based on Web technologies that links selected resources of a company's intranet with its customers, suppliers, or other business partners.

Security and performance concerns are different for an extranet than for a Web site or network-based intranet. User authentication and privacy are critical on an extranet so that information is protected. Obviously, the network must perform well to provide quick response to customers and suppliers. Table 7.5 summarizes the differences between users of the Internet, intranets, and extranets.

TABLE **7.5** Summary of Internet, intranet, and extranet users

Type	Users	Need User ID and Password?
Internet	Anyone	No
Intranet	Employees and managers	Yes
Extranet	Business partners	Yes

© 2016 Cengage Learning

Secure intranet and extranet access applications usually require the use of a *virtual private network (VPN)*, a secure connection between two points on the Internet. VPNs transfer information by encapsulating traffic in IP packets and sending the packets over the Internet, a practice called **tunneling**. Most VPNs are built and run by ISPs. Companies that use a VPN from an ISP have essentially outsourced their networks to save money on wide area network equipment and personnel.

tunneling: The process by which VPNs transfer information by encapsulating traffic in IP packets over the Internet.

INTERNET ISSUES

The Internet has greatly benefited individuals and organizations, but some Internet issues can have negative consequences. Privacy invasion can be a potential problem with Internet and social networking sites. A number of Web sites, for example, collect personal and financial information about people who visit their sites without the user's knowledge or consent. Some Internet

The Problem with Prosecuting Cyberbullies

On January 2, 2014, 14-year-old Viviana Aguirre logged onto Facebook and posted a message: "Before I do this, thank you to all who tried to keep me up. But hey, it didn't work. Bye." She then hung herself in her El Paso, Texas home. Devastated, her family and friends pointed to four teenage girls who had constantly taunted her online.

"They used to just call her names, but recently, they actually started telling her how she should kill herself," Viviana's cousin Albert Fernandez told reporters. "They would send her messages and they were some of the meanest messages I've ever read. They told her a few ways how they'd like her to kill herself. They made fun of her, telling her to go cry to her therapist, calling her 'emo' and worthless and that nobody would miss her."

On January 3, 2014, about 100 people gathered at Capistrano Park for a candlelight vigil in memory of Viviana.

"I hope they learn, and I hope they're guilty for what they did and not in denial," Albert Fernandez said at the vigil.

Many teens who engage in cyberbullying, however, are in denial and explain that they were just having fun. Katelyn Roman, a 13-year-old Florida teen, and her 14-year-old girlfriend were both arrested for the aggravated stalking of 12-year-old Rebecca Sedwick who took her own life on September 9, 2013. The 14-year-old girlfriend had allegedly posted a Facebook message admitting, "Yes ik [I know] I bullied Rebecca nd she killed herself but IDGAF [I don't give a f---]." The day after the charges were dropped, Katelyn appeared on the Today Show with her parents and lawyer and told her interviewer, "No, I do not feel I did anything wrong."

A recent survey by the Centers for Disease Control reveals that 16.2 percent of high school students report being bullied within the last year through social media portals, email, chat rooms, instant messaging, texting, online games, and Web sites. Teens who are bullied have a higher risk of drug and alcohol use, low self esteem, poor grades, truancy, and health problems.

What makes cyberbullying different from in-person bullying is that it is pervasive. Cyberbullying can be carried out 24 hours a day, 7 days a week, and a teen can't avoid it simply by skipping school.

Only about 20 to 30 percent of children who are bullied notify an adult. Viviana's mother told reporters the Viviana did mention the bullying, "She would tell me sometimes, and I would tell her to cut off that friend. I think she got to the point where she wouldn't tell me anymore."

Texas has no law against cyberbullying. El Paso's state representative says the Texas legislature has had trouble agreeing on exactly how to define "cyberbullying." Many other states have passed cyberbullying laws. However, states often have trouble implementing them.

In the Rebecca Sedwick's case, the Florida state attorney's office opted to drop the charges against Katelyn Roman and her 14-year-old friend. The following day, Katelyn's lawyer announced that he planned to pursue legal action against Polk County Sheriff Grady Judd who made the arrests: "He should get a lawyer and a darn good one, because he's going to need it."

Discussion Questions

1. How culpable are cyberbullies for the suicides of Rebecca Sedwick and Viviana Aguirre? Do you think they should have been arrested and charged?
2. Why do you think it might be hard to define cyberbullying in legal terms? What complications can arise?

Critical Thinking Questions

1. What are the differences between cyberbullying and in-person bullying?
2. What actions should families, schools, police, and government take to stop cyberbullying?

SOURCES: Welsh, Stacey, "El Paso teen's family says cyberbullying forced her to kill herself," *KFox14 News*, January 4, 2014, *www.kfoxtv.com/news/features/top-stories/stories/el-paso-teens-fam ily-says-cyberbullying-forced-her-kill-herself-3010.shtml*; Martinez, Aaron, "Cyberbullying: El Paso girl's suicide puts spotlight on social media dangers," *El Paso Times*, January 12, 2014, *www .elpasotimes.com/news/ci_24895008/activist-lawmakers-battle-increasing-threat-cyber-bullying*; "Cyberbullying" and "Facts About Bullying," *www.stopbullying.gov/cyberbullying/index.html*; "Youth Risk Behavior Surveillance — United States, 2011" *Morbidity and Mortality Weekly Report*, Surveillance Summaries/Vol.61/No. 4, June 8, 2012, *www.cdc.gov/mmwr/pdf/ss/ss6104.pdf*; NG, Christina and Gutman, Matt, "Charges Dropped Against 'Cyberbullies' in Rebecca Sedwick Suicide," *ABC News*, November 20, 2013, *http://abcnews.go.com/US/charges-dropped-cyberbullies-rebecca -sedwick-suicide/story?id=20954020*; Stump, Scott, "Fla. teen cleared of cyberbullying: I didn't do 'anything wrong'" *Today News*, November 21, 2013, *www.today.com/news/fla-teen-cleared -cyberbullying-case-i-didnt-do-anything-wrong-2D11632710*.

companies, however, are now starting to allow people to select a "do-not-track" feature that informs Web sites that they do not want their personal and financial information gathered and stored. Some people fear that new facial recognition software used by some Internet companies could also be an invasion of privacy. Facial recognition software, for example, is used to identify people in photos on social networking sites and other Internet sites. Additionally, some workers have been fired by their employers when they criticized them or their companies using Facebook, Twitter, and other social networking sites. Some fired employees are fighting back by suing their employers. Frequently, individuals attack others in a form of online cyberbullying.

Many states and local governments are trying to collect sales tax on Internet sales. Lost sales tax from United States Internet businesses is estimated at more than 11 billion.[46]

The scope and frequency of Internet attacks and hacks are also important Internet issues. Kaspersky Lab products detected and neutralized a total of 979 million threats in just the third quarter of 2013.[47] Increasingly, countries are charging and arresting people involved in Internet attacks by individuals as well as groups like Anonymous.

SUMMARY

Principle:

The Internet provides a critical infrastructure for delivering and accessing information and services.

The Internet is truly international in scope, with users on every continent. It started with ARPANET, a project sponsored by the U.S. Department of Defense (DoD). Today, the Internet is the world's largest computer network. Actually, it is a collection of interconnected networks, all freely exchanging information. The Internet transmits data from one computer (called a host) to another. The set of conventions used to pass packets from one host to another is known as the Internet Protocol (IP). Many other protocols are used with IP. The best known is the Transmission Control Protocol (TCP). TCP is so widely used that many people refer to the Internet protocol as TCP/IP, the combination of TCP and IP used by most Internet applications. Each computer on the Internet has an assigned IP address for easy identification. A Uniform Resource Locator (URL) is a Web address that specifies the exact location of a Web page (using letters and words that map to an IP address) and the location on the host.

Cloud computing refers to a computing environment where software and storage are provided as an Internet service and accessed with a Web browser rather than installed and stored on PCs. As Internet connection speeds improve and wireless Internet access becomes pervasive, computing activities are increasing. Cloud computing offers many advantages. By outsourcing business information systems to the cloud, a business saves on system design, installation, and maintenance. Employees can also access corporate systems from any Internet-connected computer using a standard Web browser.

People can connect to the Internet backbone in several ways: via a LAN, whose server is an Internet host; a dial-up connection; high-speed service; or wireless service. An Internet service provider (ISP) is any organization that provides access to the Internet. To use this type of connection, you must have an account with the service provider and software that allows a direct link via TCP/IP.

Principle:

Originally developed as a document-management system, the World Wide Web has grown to become a primary source of news and information, an indispensable conduit for commerce, and a popular hub for social interaction, entertainment, and communication.

The Web is a collection of hundreds of millions of servers providing information via hyperlink technology to billions of users worldwide. Thanks to the high-speed Internet circuits connecting them and to hyperlink technology, users can jump between Web pages and servers effortlessly, creating the illusion of using one big computer. Because of its ability to handle multimedia objects and hypertext links between distributed objects, the Web is emerging as the most popular means of information access on the Internet today.

As a hyperlink-based system that uses the client/server model, the Web organizes Internet resources throughout the world into a series of linked files, called pages, accessed and viewed using Web client software, called a Web browser. Chrome, Firefox, Internet Explorer, Opera, and Safari are popular Web browsers. A collection of pages on one particular topic, accessed under one Web domain, is called a Web site.

Hypertext Markup Language (HTML) is the standard page description language for Web pages. The HTML tags tell the browser how to format the text: as a heading, as a list, or as body text, for example. HTML also indicates where images, sound, and other elements should be inserted. Some other Web standards include Extensible Markup Language (XML) and Cascading Style Sheets (CSS).

Web 2.0 refers to the Web as a computing platform that supports software applications and the sharing of information among users with Web sites such as Facebook and Twitter. Over the past few years, the Web has been changing from a one-directional resource where users find information to a two-directional resource where users find and share information. The Web has also grown in power to support complete software applications and is becoming a computing platform itself. A rich Internet application (RIA) is software that has the functionality and complexity of traditional application software, but that runs in a Web browser and does not require local installation. Java, PHP, AJAX, MySQL, .NET, and Web application frameworks are all used to create interactive Web pages.

Principle:

The Internet and Web provide numerous resources for finding information, communicating and collaborating, socializing, conducting business and shopping, and being entertained.

The Web has become the most popular medium for distributing and accessing information. It is a powerful tool for keeping informed about local, state, national, and global news. As a tool for sharing information and a primary repository of information on all subjects, the Web is ideally suited for education and training. Museums, libraries, private businesses, government agencies, and many other types of organizations and individuals offer educational materials online. Many businesses use the Web browser as an interface to corporate information systems. Web sites have sprung up to support every subject and activity of importance.

A search engine is a valuable tool that enables you to find information on the Web by specifying words that are key to a topic of interest—known as keywords. Some search companies have experimented with human-powered and human-assisted searches. In addition to search engines, you can use other Internet sites to research information. *Wikipedia*, an online encyclopedia created and edited by millions of users, is an example of a Web site that can be used to research information. While *Wikipedia* is the best-known, general-purpose wiki, other wikis are designed for special purposes. Online research is also greatly assisted by traditional resources that have migrated from libraries to Web sites such as online databases.

A Web portal is a Web page that combines useful information and links onto one page and that often acts as an entry point to the Web—the first page you open when you begin browsing the Web. A Web portal typically includes a search engine, a subject directory, daily headlines, and other items of interest. It can be general or specific in nature.

The Internet and Web provide many applications for communication and collaboration. Email is an incredibly useful form of Internet communication that not only supports text communication but also supports HTML content and file sharing as email attachments. Instant messaging is online, real-time communication between two or more people who are connected to the Internet. Referred to as a microblogging service, Twitter allows users to send short text updates (up to 140 characters long) from smartphone or Web to their Twitter followers. A number of Internet technologies support real-time online conferencing. The Internet has made it possible for those involved in teleconferences to share computer desktops. Using services such as WebEx or GoToMeeting, conference participants log on to common software that allows them to broadcast their computer displays to the group. Telepresence systems such as those from Cisco and HP use high-resolution video and audio with high-definition displays to make it appear that conference participants are actually sitting around a table.

Web sites such as YouTube and Flickr allow users to share video and photos with other people, groups, and the world. Microblogging sites such as Twitter allow people to post thoughts and ideas throughout the day for friends to read. Social networking Web sites provide Web-based tools for users to share information about themselves with people on the Web and to find, meet, and converse with other members.

A Web log, typically called a blog, is a Web site that people can create and use to write about their observations, experiences, and opinions on a wide range of topics. Internet users may subscribe to blogs using a technology called Really Simple Syndication (RSS). RSS is a collection of Web technologies that allows users to subscribe to Web content that is frequently updated. A podcast is an audio broadcast over the Internet.

Like news and information, all forms of media and entertainment have followed their audiences online. The Internet and the Web have made music more accessible than ever, with artists distributing their songs through online radio, subscription services, and download services. With increasing amounts of Internet bandwidth available, streaming video and television are becoming commonplace. E-books have been available for quite a while, nearly as long as computers. However, it wasn't until the birth of Amazon's e-book reading device, the Kindle, in 2007 that they became more widely accepted. Online games include the many different types of single-user, multiuser, and massively multiuser games played on the Internet and the Web.

The Web has had a profound effect on the travel industry and the way people plan and prepare for trips. From getting assistance with short trips across town to planning long holidays abroad, travelers are turning to the Web to save time and money and overcome much of the risk involved in visiting unknown places. Mapping and geolocation tools are among the most popular and successful Web applications. MapQuest, Google Maps, and Bing Maps are examples. Geo-tagging is technology that allows for tagging information with an associated location.

Just as the Web is an application that runs on the Internet to provide a framework for delivering information and services, other applications have been designed to run on the Internet for other purposes. Telnet is a network protocol that enables users to log on to networks remotely over the Internet. File Transfer Protocol (FTP) is a protocol that supports file transfers between a host and a remote computer. Like Telnet, FTP connections are not encrypted and are, therefore, not secure. Many users are switching to secure FTP (SFTP) for more secure file transfers.

Principle:

Popular Internet and Web technologies have been applied to business networks in the form of intranets and extranets.

An intranet is an internal corporate network built using Internet and World Wide Web standards and products. Because Web browsers run on any type of computer, the same electronic information can be viewed by any employee. That means that all sorts of documents can be converted to electronic form on the Web and constantly be updated.

An extranet is a network that links selected resources of the intranet of a company with its customers, suppliers, or other business partners. It is also built around Web technologies. Security and performance concerns are different for an extranet than for a Web site or network-based intranet. User authentication and privacy are critical on an extranet. Obviously, the network must perform well to provide quick response to customers and suppliers.

KEY TERMS

ARPANET	Java
backbone	responsive Web design
Cascading Style Sheets (CSS)	rich Internet application (RIA)
cloud computing	search engine
content streaming	tag
Extensible Markup Language (XML)	Transmission Control Protocol (TCP)
extranet	tunneling
File Transfer Protocol (FTP)	Uniform Resource Locator (URL)
hyperlink	Web
Hypertext Markup Language (HTML)	Web 2.0
instant messaging	Web browser
Internet censorship	Web design framework
Internet Protocol (IP)	Web log (blog)
Internet service provider (ISP)	Web portal
IP address	

CHAPTER 7: SELF-ASSESSMENT TEST

The Internet provides a critical infrastructure for delivering and accessing information and services.

1. The country with the most Internet users today is
   _____.
   a. United States
   b. Japan
   c. China
   d. India
2. An IP address is a number that identifies a computer on the Internet. True or False?
3. The _____ enables computers to route communications traffic from one network to another as needed.
   a. LAN server
   b. ARPANET
   c. Uniform Resource Locator
   d. Internet Protocol
4. More than 1 billion computers, or hosts, make up today's Internet, supporting nearly 2.7 billion users. True or False?
5. _____ is a computing environment where software and storage are provided as an Internet service and accessed with a Web browser.
   a. Cloud computing
   b. Internet Society (ISOC)
   c. The Web
   d. America Online (AOL)
6. A(n) _____ is an organization that provides people with access to the Internet.

Originally developed as a document-management system, the World Wide Web has grown to become a primary source of news and information, an indispensable conduit for commerce, and a popular hub for social interaction, entertainment, and communication.

7. While the terms Internet and Web are often used interchangeably, technically, the two are different technologies. True or False?
8. Which technology was developed to assist in more easily specifying the visual appearance of Web pages in a Web site?
   a. HTML
   b. XHTML
   c. XML
   d. CSS
9. HTML uses _____, which are codes that tell the browser how to format the text or graphics, as a heading, list, or body text.
10. What is the standard page description language for Web pages?
    a. Home Page Language (HPL)
    b. Hypermedia Language (HML)
    c. Java
    d. Hypertext Markup Language (HTML)
11. Web development software that provides the foundational code—or framework—for a professional interactive Web site, allowing developers to customize the code to specific needs, is called a(n) _____.

The Internet and Web provide numerous resources for finding information, communicating and collaborating, socializing, conducting business and shopping, and being entertained.

12. Web sites such as Facebook and LinkedIn are examples of _____ Web sites.
    a. media sharing
    b. social network
    c. social bookmarking
    d. content streaming
13. _____ is a collection of Web technologies that allows users to subscribe to Web content that is frequently updated, such as news sites and blogs.
14. _____ uses high-resolution video and audio with high-definition displays to make it appear that conference participants are actually sitting around a table.

Popular Internet and Web technologies have been applied to business networks in the form of intranets and extranets.

15. A(n) _____ is a network based on Web technology that links customers, suppliers, and others to the company.
16. An intranet is an internal corporate network built using Internet and World Wide Web standards and products. True or False?

CHAPTER 7: SELF-ASSESSMENT TEST ANSWERS

1. c
2. True
3. d
4. True
5. a
6. Internet service provider (ISP)
7. True
8. d
9. tags
10. d
11. Web application framework
12. b
13. Really Simple Syndication (RSS)
14. Telepresence
15. extranet
16. True

REVIEW QUESTIONS

1. What is the Web? Is it another network like the Internet or a service that runs on the Internet?
2. What is MILNET?
3. What is HTML? How does it work?
4. Explain the naming conventions used to identify Internet host computers.
5. What is a Web browser? Identify four popular Web browsers.
6. What is cloud computing? How is it used?
7. Briefly describe three ways to connect to the Internet. What are the advantages and disadvantages of each approach?
8. What is Internet censorship?
9. How do Web design frameworks assist Web developers?
10. What is clickstream data analysis? How is it used?
11. What is a podcast?
12. How do human-powered search engines work?
13. For what are Telnet and FTP used?
14. What is content streaming?
15. What is ICANN and what role does it play?
16. What is a URL, and how is it used?
17. What are the advantages and disadvantages of streaming movies and TV programs over the Internet?
18. What is an intranet? Provide three examples of the use of an intranet.
19. What is an extranet? How is it different from an intranet?

DISCUSSION QUESTIONS

1. Briefly explain how the Internet works and mention the primary protocols and naming conventions used.
2. Social networks are widely used. Describe how this technology could be used in a business setting. Are there any drawbacks or limitations to using social networks in a business setting?
3. Your company is about to develop a new Web site. Identify three different options for how the Web site could be built and operated. What are the pros and cons of each approach?
4. Why is it important to have an organization that manages IP addresses and domain names?
5. What are the benefits and risks involved in using cloud computing?
6. You are the owner of a small business with five employees. Describe what approach you would use to enable your employees to connect to the Internet.
7. Describe how a company could use a blog and podcasting.
8. Why is XML an important technology?
9. Discuss how a virtual private network operates.
10. Briefly describe the importance of Web services. What is involved?
11. What are the defining characteristics of a Web 2.0 site?
12. What is cyberbullying? In your opinion, how significant of an issue is it?
13. What social concerns surround geolocation technologies?
14. One of the key issues associated with the development of a Web site is getting people to visit it. If you were developing a Web site, how would you attract others to your site?
15. Downloading music, radio, and video programs from the Internet is easier and more regulated than in the past, but some companies are still worried that people will illegally obtain copies of this programming without paying the artists and producers royalties. If you were an artist or producer, what would you do?
16. Keep track of the amount of time you spend on social networking sites for one week. Do you think that this is time well spent? Why or why not?
17. Briefly summarize the differences in how the Internet, a company intranet, and an extranet are accessed and used.

PROBLEM-SOLVING EXERCISES

1. Do research on the Web to identify the three most frequently visited non-U.S.-based social networking sites. Use a word processor to write a report that identifies and then compares and contrasts their services. Also discuss the advantages and potential problems of sharing personal information online. What information collected by social networking sites do you think should be kept private from the general public?

2. Think of a business that you might like to establish. Use a word processor to define the business in terms of what product(s) or service(s) it provides, where it is located, and its name. Go to *www.godaddy.com* and find an appropriate domain name for your business that is not yet taken. Shop around online for the best deal on Web site hosting. Write a paragraph about your experience finding a name, why you chose the name that you did, and how much it will cost you to register the name and host a site.

3. Develop a brief proposal for creating a business Web site. Generate a list of those tasks you need to complete to create and begin to operate the Web site. Use a spreadsheet program to capture your estimate of the time and costs required to complete each step. How soon and at what cost could you launch your Web site?

4. You have been hired to develop a business model for a Web site for a small local bakery. Develop a spreadsheet that shows the revenues from operating the Web site and the costs involved in setting it up and running the Web site.

5. Develop a slide show using a graphics program, such as PowerPoint, to show how a new Web site to sell used bicycles on campus can be started and profitably run.

TEAM ACTIVITIES

1. Plan, set up, and execute a meeting with another team wherein you do not meet physically but via use of a Web service such as GoToMeeting or WebEx. What are some of the problems you encounter in setting up and executing the meeting? How would you evaluate the effectiveness of the meeting? What could have been done to make the meeting even more effective?

2. Try using the search engine Baidu to find information on several topics. Write a brief summary of your experience.

3. Have your team describe a new and exciting Internet game. The game should include students, professors, and university administrators as players in the game. Write a report using Google Docs or a similar word-processing program describing how your game will work.

4. Each team member should use a different search engine to find information about podcasting. Meet as a team and decide which search engine was the best for this task. Write a brief report to your instructor summarizing your findings.

WEB EXERCISES

1. Do research to identify the top three Internet issues of today. Write a paragraph on each issue and why it is considered significant.

2. Using the Internet, identify three organizations that make extensive use of extranets to collaborate with their business partners. Write a report summarizing the advantages and disadvantages of using extranets.

3. Identify half a dozen blogs of interest to you. Use Really Simple Syndication to receive a blog update from each site. Write a brief report on your experience of setting up and using RSS.

CAREER EXERCISES

1. Explore LinkedIn, a social media network for professional networking. Use some of its features to find former students of your school or coworkers at your place of employment. What are some of the advantages of using such a Web site? What are some of the potential problems?

2. Consider how the Internet and Web can be useful to businesses in fields that interest you. Select two such businesses and research how they use the Web. Write a summary of the results of your research, including the benefits of the Web to these businesses and recommendations for how they might extend their use of the Web to increase profits.

CASE STUDIES

Case One

Social Networking Inside a Business

PepsiCo Russia, an organizational element of PepsiCo Europe, is the largest food and beverage business in Russia and the countries of the former Soviet Union. Much of PepsiCo Russia's growth has been through acquisitions as PepsiCo management recognizes the business potential of Russia and neighboring countries. For example, its $3.8 billion acquisition of 18,000-employee Wimm-Bill-Dann is the largest foreign investment to date in the Russian food industry. PepsiCo had previously acquired a majority stake in JSC Lebedyanski, Russia's leading juice producer and a major baby food company, for $1.4 billion. Because of these and other acquisitions, PepsiCo Russia now consists of dozens of employee groups that have no shared history. Making them work as a unit creates a management challenge.

To deal with this challenge, PepsiCo Russia decided to create an employee intranet portal with a social focus. To learn what users expect of social sites, the project team looked at Facebook, VK (previously VKontakte, a Russian social site comparable to Facebook), LinkedIn, and Google+. "We studied the [user] experience of the world's best social networking sites, and combined it with the concepts of enterprise portals," says project leader Eugene Karpov.

PepsiCo Russia used Microsoft SharePoint collaboration software to integrate social networking concepts with its portal. The current SharePoint release has social networking features: users can find information from others with matching interests; they can bookmark, tag, and rate content, making it accessible to those on a team; and they get consolidated views of what other users are tracking or have written. Wikis also made their debut in SharePoint.

The intranet uses a Quick Poll feature to gauge employee sentiment on topics of interest and to provide feedback on the portal itself.

Because PepsiCo Russia's programmers had little experience with SharePoint, the company partnered with an experienced SharePoint developer to build its intranet site. This firm, WSS Consulting, carried out the project. WSS Consulting had already developed a general-purpose portal for SharePoint called WSS Portal. WSS Portal provided a ready-made basis for PepsiCo Russia's portal, reducing the cost and time required to complete the project and ensuring good performance with the server typically returning pages in less than 0.2 seconds.

Features of the new portal include social profiles, community membership, quick polls, document management, and location-specific information such as weather. Since 2012, thousands of office employees and factory-floor workers have had portal access. Employee reception of the portal has been positive, which is vital to PepsiCo Russia's overall business strategy. The company has a highly innovative business plan, testing out new products, such as caviar and crab-flavored Lays potato chips, to see how they fare in Russia so that they can expand in the former-Soviet Union market with its burgeoning middle class. With equipment used to make Cheetos, PepsiCo Russia developed a new product similar to a traditional homemade Russian bread-crumb snack. Implementation of

PepsiCo's ambitious goal requires efficient and effective communication between the different employee groups. PepsiCo hopes that its new enterprise portal with its document management system and social media utilities will help it achieve success.

Discussion Questions

1. Why did PepsiCo Russia invest in a new portal with social network capabilities?
2. How can intranets help companies achieve their business objectives?

Critical Thinking Questions

1. How do document sharing platforms support product development?
2. In providing document sharing and social media capabilities through an intranet, what concerns should a company like PepsiCo Russia keep in mind?

SOURCES: Standford, Duane, PepsiCo's East European Snack Attack, *Bloomberg Businessweek*, February 28, 2013, *www.businessweek.com /articles/2013-02-28/pepsicos-east-european-snack-attack*; Microsoft SharePoint Web site, *sharepoint.microsoft.com*, accessed June 6, 2012; PepsiCo Europe Web page, *www.pepsico.com/Company/The-Pepsico -Family/PepsiCo-Europe.html*, accessed June 6, 2012; Staff, "PepsiCo Announces Completion of Wimm-Bill-Dann Acquisition," PepsiCo, *www.pepsico.com/PressRelease/PepsiCo-Announces-Completion-of -Wimm-Bill-Dann-Acquisition09092011.html*, September 9, 2011; Schwartz, J., "What To Expect in SharePoint 15," *Redmond, redmondmag.com/articles/2012/04/01/whats-next-for-sharepoint.aspx*, April 4, 2012; Ward, T., "Social Intranet Case Study: PepsiCo Russia," *www.intranetblog.com/social-intranet-case-study-pepsico-russia/2012 /03/28*, March 28, 2012; Weis, R. T., "How Pepsi Won the Cola Wars in Russia," *www.frumforum.com/how-pepsi-won-the-cola-wars-in-russia*, October 28, 2011; WSS Consulting Web site (in Russian/по-русски), *www.wss-consulting.ru*, accessed June 7, 2012.

Case Two

War Games: Now More Real Than Ever

Earth is under invasion. Our only hope lies with the team of soldiers who are being trained on massive multiplayer virtual simulators. Sound familiar? It's the plot line of the wildly popular futuristic novel entitled "Ender's Game."

But just how futuristic is the scenario? True, we have yet to be invaded by an alien race. But the U.S. military is already developing massive multiplayer virtual online gaming systems for training purposes. Since 2009, the United States Army Simulation and Training Technology Center (STTC) has been working with the DOD, the Department of Homeland Security (DHS), and private contractors to create a virtual online gaming platform to train soldiers to master strategic skills needed under fire.

Currently, the U.S. army uses numerous simulation tools and online apps. For example, soldiers about to be deployed to Afghanistan might watch detailed videos of a recent skirmish to learn techniques they will require to clear a building where enemy forces are hiding.

But in 2014, the army tested its first avatar-based multiplayer online training game that simulates conditions on the ground in Afghanistan. The project called MOSES, military open simulator enterprise strategy, simulates a 25-by-25 kilometer Afghan terrain into which 700 trainees can project their avatars. Soldiers will interact with each other as well as with simulated Afghan civilians and enemy combatants. They will have to cooperate as they carry out maneuvers and make good choices, such as which village elders to trust as they collect information they need to carry out a maneuver.

Unlike other gaming environments in which bullets fly in a straight line, ignoring the physics that would determine the course of a real-life bullet, MOSES and its predecessor EDGE (Enhanced Dynamic Geosocial Environment) have created a life-like simulation in which objects and people behave as they would in the real world. STTC Director Douglas Maxwell and his team of government and private engineers have developed a flexible virtual environment using artificial intelligence and advanced computational steering of objects. For example, as soldiers' avatars work to disarm improvised explosive devices (IEDs), MOSES's flexible environment even captures real-time terrain warping in response to an exploding IED.

As teams are working to develop MOSES, EDGE technology has already been adapted to develop another project that will service federal, state, and local emergency agencies and private sector partners across the nation in the event of a terrorist threat. The project, called Virtual Training Active Shooter Response, is an online gaming system that trains first responders for active shooter incidents.

Sacramento police and fire departments were the first to pilot the program in 2013. Trainees were placed in a scenario in which a bomb planted in a hotel sets off a fire. Terrorists are in position picking off people as they try to make it to safety. The game featured a realistic replica of a popular Sacramento hotel with a lobby, restaurant and bar, ballrooms, 27 guest room floors, a basement, and two main entrances. Teams from the different Sacramento city departments, police, fire, and emergency medical services, had to work together to neutralize the threat. Unlike simulations in which individuals work through a computer-generated simulation, this product improves collaboration between different groups of first responders—a valuable skill that is difficult to develop without actually being in the field.

Researchers have found that massive multiplayer online fantasy games tend to encourage addiction and lead to depression, allowing individuals to avoid solving real-world problems. EDGE indicates, however, that developers might be able to produce games that allow people to develop skills necessary to succeed in the real world.

Discussion Questions

1. What purposes do massive multiplayer games serve today? What purposes could they serve in the future?

2. What advantage do projects developed with EDGE have over other training software?

Critical Thinking Questions

1. Do massive multiplayer games serve a useful function in today's society? Why or why not?
2. What types of technologies are used by massive multiplayer games that could be used in other ways?

SOURCES: Hugh, Lessig, "The New Army: A Newport News tech center uses gaming and apps to train soldiers," *Daily Press*, January 28, 2012, *http://articles.dailypress.com/2012-01-28/news/dp-nws-high-tech-training-20120128_1_training-exercises-army-s-training-latest-training-tool*; Korolov, Maria, "Army takes a flier on OpenSim," *Network World*, March 25, 2013, *www.networkworld.com/news/2013/032513-army-opensim-267405.html?page=3*; Montalbano, Elizabeth, "DOD Explores Virtual Worlds For Military Training," *InformationWeek*, May 12, 2011, *www.informationweek.com/security/risk-management/dod-explores-virtual-worlds-for-military-training/d/d-id/1097729?*; Pellerin, Cheryl, "Fighting Bombs in Cyberspace Gives Army an 'EDGE,'" American Forces Press Service, U.S. Department of Defense, May 12, 2011, *www.defense.gov/News/NewsArticle.aspx?ID=63924*; Barrie, Allison, Army, "DHS join forces for virtual traiing tech for first responders," *Fox News*, November 21, 2013, *www.foxnews.com/tech/2013/11/21/army-dhs-join-forces-for-virtual-training-tech-for-first-responders/*; "DHS is training first responders to respond to an active shooter," *Government Security News*, November 20, 2013, *www.gsnmagazine.com/node/39069*.

Questions for Web Case

See the Web site for this book to read about the Altitude Online case for this chapter. Following are questions concerning this Web case.

Altitude Online: The Internet, Web, Intranets, and Extranets

Discussion Questions

1. What impact will the new ERP system have on Altitude Online's public-facing Web site? How will it affect its intranet?
2. What types of applications will be available from the employee dashboard?

Critical Thinking Questions

1. Altitude Online employees have various needs, depending on their position within the enterprise. How might the dashboard and intranet provide custom support for individual employee needs?
2. What Web 2.0 applications should Altitude Online consider for its dashboard? Remember that the applications must be available only on the secure intranet.

NOTES

Sources for the opening vignette: Robertson, Jordan, "A Tale of Two Search Engines: Why Google Is Winning, Baidu Isn't," Bloomberg Technology, April 30, 2013, *www.bloomberg.com/news/2013-04-30/a-tale-of-two-search*

-engines-why-google-s-winning-and-baidu-isn-t.html; "Baidu Launched News Search Engine and Pictures Search Engine," SinoCast via COMTEX, Highbeam Business, July 31, 2003, *http://business.highbeam.com/436093/article-1G1-1056*

19810/baidu-launched-news-search-engine-and-pictures-search; Chmielewski, Dawn C., "Search site moves at the speed of China," Los Angeles Times, December 10, 2007, http://articles.latimes.com/2007/dec/10/business/fi-baidu10; Betters, Elyse, "Did Google really lose 7 percent of its search market share last month, mostly to Baidu?" 9To5Google, March 1, 2012, http://9to5google.com/2012/03/01/did-google-really-lose-7-percent-of-its-search-market-share-last-month-mostly-to-baidu/; "Sina and Baidu team up in China to focus on mobile," BBC, July 31, 2012, www.bbc.co.uk/news/technology-19061997; Stempel, Jonathan, "Censorship lawsuit against Baidu and China gets new life in U.S.," Reuters, June 10, 2012, www.reuters.com/article/2013/06/10/us-baidu-china-lawsuit-idUSBRE9590R620130610; Taylor, Sophie, and Chen, George, "China's Baidu receives license to provide news," Washington Post, January 23, 2007, www.washingtonpost.com/wp-dyn/content/article/2007/01/23/AR2007012300201.html.

1. "India is Now the World's Third Largest Internet User After China, U.S.," The Hindu, August 24, 2013, www.thehindu.com/sci-tech/technology/internet/india-is-now-worlds-third-largest-internet-user-after-us-china/article5053115.ece.

2. Casti, Taylor, "Who Will the Next Billion Internet Users Be?" Mashable, August 30, 2013, http://mashable.com/2013/08/30/next-billion-internet-users.

3. "Internet World Stats," www.internetworldstats.com/stats3.htm, accessed January 7, 2014.

4. Alexandrova, Katerina, "Using New Media Effectively: An Analysis of Barack Obama's Election Campaign Aimed at Young Americans," Thesis, New York 2010, www.academia.edu/1526998/Using_New_Media_Effectively_an_Analysis_of_Barack_Obamas_Election_Campaign_Aimed_at_Young_Americans.

5. "Electronic Weapons Syria Shows the Way," Strategy-Page, January 13, 2014, www.strategypage.com/htmw/htecm/articles/20140113.aspx.

6. "Clashes in Turkey as Internet Censorship Protests Turn Violent," Euronews, January 18, 2014, www.euronews.com/2014/01/18/clashes-in-turkey-as-internet-censorship-protests-turn-violent/.

7. "About Internet2: Accelerating Research and Education Through Community Developed Technology," March 2013, www.internet2.edu/media/medialibrary/2013/09/16/about-internet2-2013.pdf.

8. "Company Overview of National LamdaRail, Inc.," Bloomberg BusinessWeek, http://investing.businessweek.com/research/stocks/private/snapshot.asp?privcapId=7804267, accessed January 7, 2014.

9. Kerner, Michael Sean, "IPv6 in 2013: Where Are We Now?" Internet New.com, June 7, 2013, www.internetnews.com/infra/ipv6-in-2013-where-are-we-now.html.

10. "iCloud," www.apple.com/icloud/, accessed January 8, 2014.

11. Gregg, Cindy, "List of Cloud or Web-Based Office Software & Apps," http://office.about.com/od/WebApps/tp/List-Of-Cloud-Office-Software-Suites-And-Apps.htm, accessed January 8, 2014.

12. "The College Network," www.slideshare.net/EarthLinkBusiness/private-cloud-case-study-the-college-network-earth-link-business, accessed January 9, 2014.

13. "AWS Case Study: Airbnb," http://aws.amazon.com/solutions/case-studies/airbnb/, accessed January 10, 2014.

14. Awwwards Team, "What are Frameworks? 22 Best Responsive CSS Frameworks for Web Design," Web Design, February 20, 2013, www.awwwards.com/what-are-frameworks-22-best-responsive-css-frameworks-for-web-design.html.

15. Ibid.

16. Gerchev, Ivaylo, "Top 10 Front-End Development Frameworks," June 16, 2013, www.sitepoint.com/top-10-front-end-development-frameworks/.

17. Griffith, Eric, "How to Build a Website," PC Magazine, September 4, 2013.

18. Schnuer, Jenna, "Meet the Innovative Entrepreneurs Who Won Our Top Awards for 2013," Entrepreneur, December 24, 2013, www.entrepreneur.com/article/230243#ixzz2q6bQD3Vo.

19. Port, David, "How to Start a Business in 10 Days," Entrepreneur, October 15, 2013, www.entrepreneur.com/article/228659.

20. Edmonds, Rick, Guskin, Emily, Mitchell, Amy, and Jurkowitz, Mark, "The State of News Media 2013," Pew Research Center, July 18, 2013, http://stateofthemedia.org/2013/newspapers-stabilizing-but-still-threatened/.

21. Sandler, Linda, "Yahoo Sued Over E-mail Scans that Beget Ads," Boston Globe, November 18, 2013, www.bostonglobe.com/business/2013/11/18/yahoo-sued-and-accused-analyzing-mails-target-advertising/7ZN56rFH5ec4zmu7FPb8MI/story.html.

22. Cooper, Belle Beth, "10 Surprising Social Media Statistics That Might Make You Rethink Your Social Strategy," Buffer, July 16, 2013, http://blog.bufferapp.com/10-surprising-social-media-statistics-that-will-make-you-rethink-your-strategy.

23. Lytle, Ryan, "The Beginner's Guide to Google+," Mashable, October 27, 2013, http://mashable.com/2013/10/27/google-plus-beginners-guide/.

24. "Top 14 Most Popular Social Networking Websites: January 2014," eBiz/MBA, www.ebizmba.com/articles/social-networking-websites, accessed January 13, 2014.

25. "Transforming Tyco with Yammer," https://about.yammer.com/customers/tyco/, accessed January 13, 2014.

26. "About Khan Academy," www.khanacademy.org/about, accessed January 16, 2014.

27. "NPower," www.npower.org/Our-Purpose/Our-Purpose.aspx, accessed January 16, 2014.

28. "About OCW," http://ocw.mit.edu/about/, accessed January 16, 2014.

29. "About Skillsoft," http://learn.skillsoft.com/PaidMedia-PPC-MaximizeBusiness_RegistrationPage.html?gclid=CLnksvS_g7wCFSHNOgod0EoAzw, accessed January 16, 2014.

30. "About eHow," www.ehow.com/about-us.html, accessed January 16, 2014.

31. "Certiport Products," www.certiport.com/PORTAL/desktopdefault.aspx?tabid=663&roleid=101, accessed January 16, 2014.

32. "Kashi," kashi.com, accessed January 16, 2014.

33. "Mahalo," CrunchBase, www.crunchbase.com/company/mahalo, accessed January 16, 2014.

34. "Live Persons," *www.liveperson.com/services*, accessed January 16, 2014.

35. Briggs, Josh, "How Microsoft Bing Works," How Stuff Works, *http://computer.howstuffworks.com/internet /basics/microsoft-bing1.htm*, accessed January 16, 2014.

36. Top 100 Search Engine Optimization Companies, January 2014, *www.topseos.com/rt/rankings-of-best-seo -companies*.

37. "About Wikipedia," *http://en.wikipedia.org/wiki /Wikipedia:About*, accessed January 21, 2014.

38. Wasserman, Todd, "BT Pulls 6 Million Customers Off Yahoo," Mashable, May 31, 2013, *http://mashable.com /2013/05/31/bt-6-million-yahoo-mail*.

39. Wagner, Kurt, "More Than 70% of Email is Spam," Mashable, August 9, 2013, *http://mashable.com/2013 /08/09/70-percent-email-is-spam/*.

40. Clifford, Catherine, "Top 10 Apps for Instant Messaging," Entrepreneur, *www.entrepreneur .com/article/230335*, accessed January 21, 2014.

41. Ibid.

42. "Addison Fire Saves $5k Yearly Using GoToMeeting with HD Faces Videoconferencing," *http://news.citrix online.com/wp-content/uploads/2013/07/Addision-Fire -District_G2M_ss.pdf*, accessed January 30, 2014.

43. "YouTube Statistics," *www.youtube.com/yt/press/statis tics.html*, accessed January 21, 2014.

44. Takahashi, Dean, "Mobile Gaming Could Drive Entire Video Game Industry to $100 Billion in Revenue by 2017," Gamesbeat, January 14, 2014, *http://venturebeat .com/2014/01/14/mobile-gaming-could-drive-entire -game-industry-to-100b-in-revenue-by-2017/*.

45. Yarrow, Jay and Edwards, Jim, "Groupon Whiffs on Earnings, Stock Crashes ....Then Stages an Amazing Comeback," Business Insider, November 7, 2013, *www .businessinsider.com/groupon-q3-earnings-2013-10*.

46. Maguire, Stephen, "State Taxation of Internet Transactions," Congressional Research Service, May 7, 2013, *www.fas.org/sgp/crs/misc/R41853.pdf*.

47. "IT Threat Evaluation: 3Q 2013," SecureList *www .securelist.com/en/analysis/204792312/IT_Threat_ Evolution_Q3_2013*, accessed January 29, 2014.

Business Information Systems

8 Electronic and Mobile Commerce

Principles	Learning Objectives
• Electronic and mobile commerce are evolving, providing new ways of conducting business that present both potential benefits and problems.	• Describe the current status of various forms of e-commerce, including B2B, B2C, C2C, and e-Government. • Outline a multistage purchasing model that describes how e-commerce works. • Define m-commerce and identify some of its unique challenges.
• E-commerce and m-commerce can be used in many innovative ways to improve the operations of an organization.	• Identify several e-commerce and m-commerce applications. • Identify several advantages associated with the use of e-commerce and m-commerce.
• E-commerce and m-commerce offer many advantages yet raise many challenges.	• Identify the many benefits and challenges associated with the continued growth of e-commerce and m-commerce.
• Organizations must define and execute a strategy to be successful in e-commerce and m-commerce.	• Outline the key components of a successful e-commerce and m-commerce strategy.
• E-commerce and m-commerce require the careful planning and integration of a number of technology infrastructure components.	• Identify the key components of technology infrastructure that must be in place for e-commerce and m-commerce to work. • Discuss the key features of the electronic payment systems needed to support e-commerce and m-commerce.

Information Systems in the Global Economy
BHARTI AIRTEL, INDIA

Airtel Money Boosts M-Commerce in Asia and Africa

Source: Bharti Enterprises

Feeling peckish in Mumbai at about 8 pm local time, but too tired to cook or go out to eat? Pick up your cell phone and order Domino's pizza. It's no problem. You don't even need cash. You don't need a credit or debit card. You just need your mobile phone and an Airtel Money account.

Bharti Airtel (Airtel) is one of the top four mobile service providers globally. Based in New Delhi, India, the company services over 370 million subscribers in 20 countries across Africa, Asia, and the Channel Islands (in the English Channel, off the French coast of Normandy). It offers 2G and 3G wireless service, m-commerce, and Airtel Money. Within India, the company also provides fixed-line services, Internet access and satellite television, high-speed DSL broadband connections, and enterprise services linking Africa and South Asia to international long-distance carriers.

Recently, however, Airtel has experienced intense growth in the mobile industry. Its consumers, especially in India, are flocking toward m-commerce—for some very good reasons. First, mobile devices, such as cell phones and tablets, are significantly cheaper than computers. As m-commerce develops, consumers don't even need expensive smartphones to navigate these sites, compare prices, and make purchases. So, access to m-commerce has become affordable to a growing consumer base with lower incomes. In fact, because these devices are cheaper, the Indian government has invested in and distributed cell phones and tablets as part of its programs to overcome the digital divide between urban and rural areas. Other developing countries may follow this lead. Moreover, Bharti Airtel pioneered the strategy of lowering its mobile rates to increase affordability and traffic.

Unlike personal computers and laptops, mobile phones are always connected. So, you don't have to be at home, at work, or at an Internet café to make your purchases. Furthermore, mobile devices are relatively secure because they are not yet subject to the onslaught of virus and pernicious attacks that PC users must constantly fend off. Moreover, owners keep their mobile devices on-hand, decreasing the risk that others will access their personal electronic information.

Finally, the increasing prevalence of Airtel Money is fueling the growth in the mobile industry. In 2011, Airtel launched its mobile money service, allowing customers to make cash payments at service centers or transfer money directly from their banks or credit card companies. Customers can shop online, pay utility bills, book train or movie tickets, and transfer money from wherever they happen to be. Airtel also has deals with online vendors to offer special Airtel Money discounts. The good news is that even if you do lose your phone or laptop, your Airtel Money is protected by a PIN number, so at least that personal information is secure.

As you read this chapter, consider the following:

- What are the advantages of e-commerce and m-commerce?
- How do innovations in technology and infrastructure affect regions across the globe?

WHY LEARN ABOUT ELECTRONIC AND MOBILE COMMERCE?

Electronic and mobile commerce have transformed many areas of our lives and careers. One fundamental change has been the manner in which companies interact with their suppliers, customers, government agencies, and other business partners. As a result, most organizations today have set up business on the Internet or are considering doing so. To be successful, all members of the organization need to plan and participate in that effort. As a sales or marketing manager, you will be expected to help define your firm's e-commerce business model. As a customer service employee, you can expect to participate in the development and operation of your firm's Web site. As a human resource or public relations manager, you will likely be asked to provide Web site content for use by potential employees and shareholders. As an analyst in finance, you will need to know how to measure the business impact of your firm's Web operations and how to compare that to competitors' efforts. Clearly, as an employee in today's organization, you must understand what the potential role of e-commerce is, how to capitalize on its many opportunities, and how to avoid its pitfalls. The emergence of m-commerce adds an exciting new dimension to these opportunities and challenges. Future customers, potential employees, and shareholders will be accessing your firm's Web site via smartphones and tablet computers from places other than their homes or places of business. This chapter begins by providing a brief overview of the dynamic world of e-commerce.

AN INTRODUCTION TO ELECTRONIC COMMERCE

electronic commerce (e-commerce): Conducting business activities (e.g., distribution, buying, selling, marketing, and servicing of products or services) electronically over computer networks.

Electronic commerce (e-commerce) is the conducting of business activities (e.g., distribution, buying, selling, marketing, and servicing of products or services) electronically over computer networks. It includes any business transaction executed electronically between companies (business-to-business), companies and consumers (business-to-consumer), consumers and other consumers (consumer-to-consumer), public sector and business (government-to-business), the public sector to citizens (government-to-citizen), and public sector to public sector (government-to-government). Business activities that are strong candidates for conversion to e-commerce are ones that are paper based, time consuming, and inconvenient for customers.

Business-to-Business E-Commerce

business-to-business (B2B) e-commerce: A subset of e-commerce in which all the participants are organizations.

Business-to-business (B2B) e-commerce is a subset of e-commerce in which all the participants are organizations. B2B e-commerce is a useful tool for connecting business partners in a virtual supply chain to cut resupply times and reduce costs. Although the business-to-consumer market grabs more of the news headlines, the B2B market is considerably larger and is growing more rapidly. B2B sales within the United States (excluding EDI transactions) was estimated to be $559 billion in 2013, twice the size of B2C commerce.[1]

Popular B2C Web sites have helped raise expectations as to how an e-commerce site must operate. In addition, a recent survey by Forrester Research Inc. and Internet Retailer revealed that 46 percent of responding e-commerce executives expect that more than half their customers will be buying online by 2016. As a result, nearly half of B2B organizations plan to upgrade the e-commerce platform they use to conduct their B2B transactions by the end of 2015. Other top IS priorities related to e-commerce include integration of the B2B platform with accounting and order management systems and establishing mobile sites and apps.[2]

Moving more customers online is key to B2B commerce success. Indeed, in a recent survey by Oracle, 57 percent of respondents said customer acquisition is a top metric used to measure e-commerce success and 42 percent said customer retention.[3]

An organization will use both *buy-side e-commerce* to purchase goods and services from its suppliers and *sell-side e-commerce* to sell products to its customers. Buy-side e-commerce activities may include identifying and comparing competitive suppliers and products, negotiating and establishing prices and terms, ordering and tracking shipments, and steering organizational buyers to preferred suppliers and products. Sell-side e-commerce activities may include enabling the purchase of products online, providing information for customers to evaluate the organization's goods and services, encouraging sales and generating leads from potential customers, providing a portal of information of interest to the customer, and enabling interactions among a community of consumers. Thus, buy-side and sell-side e-commerce activities support the organization's value chain and help the organization provide lower prices, better service, higher quality, or uniqueness of product and service, as first mentioned in Chapter 2.

Grainger is a B2B distributor of products for facilities maintenance, repair, and operations (a category called MRO) with more than 1.2 million different items offered online. See Figure 8.1. The company exceeded $3 billion in online sales in 2013, which represented one-third of total sales.[4] The firm provides a suite of mobile apps that makes it possible to access products online and quickly find and order products via your smartphone or mobile device.[5]

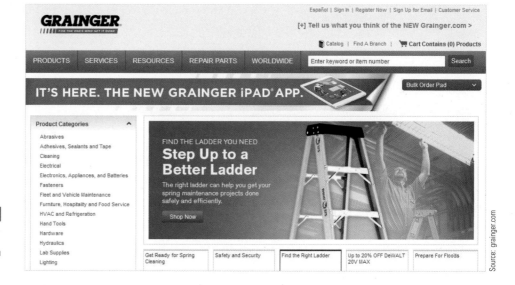

FIGURE 8.1

Grainger e-commerce

Grainger offers more than 1.2 million items online.

Business-to-Consumer E-Commerce

business-to-consumer (B2C) e-commerce: A form of e-commerce in which customers deal directly with an organization and avoid intermediaries.

Business-to-consumer (B2C) e-commerce is a form of e-commerce in which customers deal directly with an organization and avoid intermediaries. Early B2C pioneers competed with the traditional "brick-and-mortar" retailers in an industry, selling their products directly to consumers. For example, in 1995, upstart Amazon.com challenged well-established booksellers Waldenbooks and Barnes & Noble. Amazon did not become profitable until 2003; the firm has grown from selling only books on a United States-based Web site to selling a wide variety of products through international Web sites in Canada, China, France, Germany, Japan, and the United Kingdom. A recent Forrester Research Inc. and Internet Retailer survey found that the average order value was $491 for B2B versus $147 for B2C.[6]

The Asia-Pacific region has overtaken North America as the region with the largest B2C sales and now accounts for over one-third of total worldwide B2C sales. China is projected to have 2.5 times the number of B2C shoppers as the United States by 2016. Brazil, Russia, India, and Mexico are expected to see rapid growth in B2C as well.[7]

Table 8.1 shows the estimated B2C e-commerce sales by world region in 2016. Roughly 5 percent of total retail sales is spent by online shoppers.[8]

TABLE **8.1** Forecasted global B2C e-commerce spending (USD billions)

Region/Selected Countries	2014	2016	Increase
North America	$469	$580	24%
United States	$442	$546	24%
Canada	$28	$34	21%
Asia/Pacific	$502	$708	41%
China	$275	$440	60%
Australia	$28	$31	11%
India	$21	$30	43%
Western Europe	$326	$388	19%
UK	$111	$133	20%
Germany	$58	$66	12%
Spain	$25	$30	25%
Central and Eastern Europe	$58	$69	19%
Russia	$21	$25	19%
Latin America	$56	$70	25%
Brazil	$24	$27	12%
Mexico	$10	$13	30%
Middle East and Africa	$34	$45	32%
Worldwide	$1,445	$1,860	29%

Source: Indvik, Lauren, "Study: Global E-Commerce to Hit $1.2 Trillion Led by Asia," *Mashable*, June 27, 2013, *http://mashable.com/2013/06/27/ecommerce-study-china-asia/*.

One reason for the steady growth in B2C e-commerce is shoppers find that many goods and services are cheaper when purchased via the Web, including stocks, books, newspapers, airline tickets, and hotel rooms.

Another reason for the growth in B2C e-commerce is that online B2C shoppers have the ability to design a personalized product. Brooks Brothers provides an example of this personalization. Suits have what is called a "drop," which is the difference between the number given in the suit size and your pant size. American suits typically have a six-inch drop; an American suit in size 38R would have pants in size 32. On their newly designed Web site, Brooks Brothers allows men to pair any size pant with any size jacket, an offer especially attractive to men who do not fit into the traditional jacket and pants size combinations. In addition, fabric choices and linings can also be customized. Brooks Brothers also offers custom shirts. Ken Seiff, executive vice president of digital and omnichannel for the retailer states: "Our goal is to make suits and shirts that are personalized. This will give our customer a chance to build product in a way that suits their personal taste and character."[9]

Yet a third reason for the continued growth of B2C e-commerce is the use of social media networks to promote products and reach consumers. Vera Bradley is a luggage design company that produces a variety of products, including quilted cotton luggage, handbags, and accessories. The firm has more than 1 million Facebook followers and is one of the most followed Internet retailers on Pinterest. Indeed, Vera Bradley has been extremely conscientious in cross-posting items from Facebook, Flickr, and YouTube to Pinterest. When you visit the Vera Bradley Web site, Pinterest and other social buttons appear on the product pages so that shoppers can share their likes with friends. Vera Bradley is an example of a B2C retailer that makes social media channels work together effectively to reach more potential customers.[10]

By using B2C e-commerce to sell directly to consumers, producers or providers of consumer products can eliminate the middlemen, or intermediaries, between them and the consumer. In many cases, this squeezes costs and inefficiencies out of the supply chain and can lead to higher profits for businesses and lower prices for consumers. The elimination of intermediate organizations between the producer and the consumer is called *disintermediation*.

More than just a tool for placing orders, the Internet enables shoppers to compare prices, features, and value, and to check other customers' opinions. Consumers can, for example, easily and quickly compare information about automobiles, cruises, loans, insurance, and home prices to find better values. Internet shoppers can, for example, unleash shopping bots or access sites such as eBay Shopping.com, Google Shopping, Shopzilla, PriceGrabber, Yahoo! Shopping, or Excite to browse the Internet and obtain lists of items, prices, and merchants. Many B2C merchants have added what is called "social commerce" to their Web sites by creating a section where shoppers can go to see only those products that have been reviewed and listed by other shoppers. Walmart implemented its Shopycat application that refers to information from a shopper's friends on Facebook to make gift recommendations for the shopper. He or she can then purchase these items from Walmart or other stores online or via a personal visit.[11]

One growing trend is consumers researching products online but then purchasing those products at their local brick-and-mortar stores. Sales in local stores that are stimulated through online marketing and research are called Web-influenced sales. Such sales are estimated to already exceed $1.3 trillion (roughly 25 percent of total retail sales) and are growing at the rate of over 100 billion dollars per year in the United States.[12] Table 8.2 lists the five largest B2C retailers in the United States.

TABLE 8.2 Largest business-to-consumer retailers in the United States 2013

Rank	Company	Total Web Sales (Billions of Dollars)	2011 Growth
1	Amazon	$48.1	+40.6%
2	Staples	$10.6	+3.9%
3	Apple	$6.7	+27.4%
4	Walmart	$4.9	+19.7%
5	Dell	$4.6	−4.0%

Source: "Top 5 Online Retailers—Who Are These Companies and How did They Make It to the Top?" *Netonomy.Net*, January 30, 2013, *http://netonomy.net/2013/01/30/top-5-largest-online-retailers-who-companies -how-did-they-make-it/*.

© 2016 Cengage Learning

As a result of a 1992 Supreme Court ruling that says online retailers don't have to collect sales taxes in states where they lack a physical presence, millions of online shoppers do not pay state or local tax on their online purchases. Consumers who live in states with sales tax are supposed to keep track of their out-of-state purchases and report those "use taxes" on their state income tax returns. However, few tax filers report such purchases. Thus, despite having a legal basis to do so, the states find it very difficult to collect sales taxes on Internet purchases. This avoidance of sales tax creates a price advantage for online retailers over brick-and-mortar stores where sales taxes

INFORMATION SYSTEMS @ WORK

eBay Latin American Style

E-commerce is taking off in Latin America and the most powerful corporation behind this movement into online shopping is MercadoLibre.com. MercadoLibre .com was established in 1999 when only about 2 percent of the region's population had Internet access and only about 10 percent of online users shopped online. Yet, within one year, by 2000, MercadoLibre.com was up and running in six Latin American countries.

Finishing his MBA at Stanford University in 1999, the company's founder and current CEO Marcos Galperin noted that across the continent, only large cities had good retail alternatives. His plan was to open up e-commerce to people living in the smaller cities and towns. Often called the "eBay of Latin America," MercadoLibre.com originally offered an auction marketplace, but quickly developed the preferred "fixed-price" model, in which sellers offer their goods for a fixed price.

Galperin explains, "The goal was to capture an increasingly larger share of all e-commerce activity occurring in the region. This meant improving MercadoLibre, our online marketplace, as well as the MercadoPago payments business unit, MercadoClics advertising group, and MercadoShops e-building solutions, respectively."

Galperin's plan worked. Headquartered in Argentina, today the company services 11 other countries in Latin America—Brazil, Chile, Colombia, Costa Rica, Dominican Republic, Ecuador, Mexico, Panama, Peru, Uruguay, Venezuela—and recently launched operations in Portugal. Within the first nine months of 2013, over 60 million transactions took place on MercadoLibre.com. This represents a growth of over 25 percent from the previous year.

Yet the rapid growth of e-commerce does have its dangers to shaky South American economies. Between 2012 and 2013, the number of Argentinians engaged in cross-border online shopping doubled to 1.5 million citizens. Argentina, however, has been using its foreign currency reserves to pay back its foreign debt since its 2000–2001 economic crisis. As e-commerce has risen, the country has watched its foreign currency reserves seep across the border. Argentina's foreign currency reserves dropped by 30 percent in 2013. Worried about its already shaky financial position, the government placed tight restrictions on cross-border e-commerce in 2014. Individuals can buy $25 worth of cross-border merchandise each year with no tax. Once they exceed the $25 limit, they pay a tax of 50 percent. Moreover, overseas goods can no longer be shipped directly to the consumers' homes. Instead, the shopper must travel to a customs office, wait in line, and fill out the necessary paperwork before the purchase is handed over.

Obviously, this new policy will put a dent on MercadoLibre.com's sales. However, it is likely to hit U.S. and European-based e-commerce giants, such as Amazon and eBay, much harder. Still, the company's name, Mercado Libre, means "free trade" and many consumers and sellers will no doubt see these new restrictions as an encroachment of this principle.

Discussion Questions

1. What were the market conditions prior to MercadoLibre.com's launch? Were these ideal conditions for the company? Why or why not?
2. What technological tools did MercadoLibre.com need to develop to make its e-commerce platform viable?

Critical Thinking Questions

1. Why did the "fixed-price" option work best in Latin America?
2. Is Argentina justified in restricting cross-border e-commerce? Why or why not?

SOURCES: "MercadoLibre, Inc. to Report Fourth Quarter and Full Year 2013 Financial Results," *iStockAnalyst*, February 20, 2014, *www .istockanalyst.com/business/news/6747567/mercadolibre-inc-to-report -fourth-quarter-and-full-year-2013-financial-results*; "Endeavor Entrepreneur Marcos Galperin on MercadoLibre," *Endeavor*, May 25, 2011, *www.endeavor.org/blog/mercadolibre-wef-report*; MercadoLibre Investor Web site, *http://investor.mercadolibre.com/releases.cfm*; "El Promisorio Negocio De Vender A Través De Internet," *EntornoInteligente.com*, February 17, 2014, *http://www.entornointeli gente.com/articulo/2057834/El-promisorio-negocio-de-vender-a-traves -de-internet-17022014*; "Argentina Restricts Online Shopping as Foreign Reserves Drop," *BBC News*, January 22, 2014, *www.bbc.co.uk/news /world-latin-america-25836208*; "Argentina Imposes Tight Restrictions on Cross-Border E-Commerce," *Post and Parcel*, January 22, 2014, *http:// postandparcel.info/59698/news/regulation/argentina-imposes-tight -restrictions-on-cross-border-e-commerce/*.

must be collected. It also results in the loss of about $23 billion in tax revenue that could go to state and local governments to provide services for their citizens. In 2013, the United States Supreme Court declined to get involved in state efforts to force Web retailers such as Overstock and eBay to collect sales tax from customers. The court's failure to act puts pressure on Congress to devise a national solution, as both online and traditional retailers complain about a patchwork of state laws and conflicting lower-court decisions.[13]

Consumer-to-Consumer E-Commerce

consumer-to-consumer (C2C) e-commerce: A subset of e-commerce that involves electronic transactions between consumers using a third party to facilitate the process.

Consumer-to-consumer (C2C) e-commerce is a subset of e-commerce that involves electronic transactions between consumers using a third party to facilitate the process. eBay is an example of a C2C e-commerce site; customers buy and sell items to each other through the site. Founded in 1995, eBay has become one of the most popular Web sites in the world.

Other popular C2C sites include Bidz.com, Craigslist, eBid, ePier, Ibidfree, Kijiji, Ubid, and Tradus. The growth of C2C is responsible for reducing the use of the classified pages of newspapers to advertise and sell personal items, so it has a negative impact on that industry. On the other hand, C2C has created an opportunity for many people to make a living out of selling items on auction Web sites.

Companies and individuals engaging in e-commerce must be careful that their sales do not violate the rules of various county, state, or country legal jurisdictions. More than 4,000 Web sites offer guns for sale and over 20,000 gun ads are posted each week on the Web site Armslist alone. Extending background checks to the flourishing world of online gun sales has become a highly controversial issue in the United States. Under current law, the question of when a background check must occur depends on who is selling the gun. Federal regulations require licensed dealers to perform checks, but the legal definition of who must be licensed is unclear. With no requirements for background checks on most private transactions, the anonymity of the Internet enables unlicensed sellers to advertise weapons and people legally barred from gun ownership (convicted felons) to buy them.[14]

Table 8.3 summarizes the key factors that differentiate among B2B, B2C, and C2C e-commerce.

TABLE 8.3 Differences among B2B, B2C, and C2C

Factors	B2B	B2C	C2C
Value of sale	Thousands or millions of dollars	Tens or hundreds of dollars	Tens of dollars
Length of sales process	Days to months	Days to weeks	Hours to days
Number of decision makers involved	Several people to a dozen or more	One or two	One or two
Uniformity of offer	Typically a uniform product offering	More customized product offering	Single product offering, one of a kind
Complexity of buying process	Extremely complex; much room for negotiation on price, payment and delivery options, quantity, quality, and options and features	Relatively simple; limited discussion over price and payment and delivery options	Relatively simple; limited discussion over payment and delivery options; negotiation over price
Motivation for sale	Driven by a business decision or need	Driven by an individual consumer's need or emotion	Driven by an individual consumer's need or emotion

© 2016 Cengage Learning

E-Government

E-government is the use of information and communications technology to simplify the sharing of information, speed formerly paper-based processes, and improve the relationship between citizens and government. Government-to-citizen (G2C), government-to-business (G2B), and government-to-government (G2G) are all forms of e-government, each with different applications.

Citizens can use G2C applications to submit their state and federal tax returns online, renew auto licenses, purchase postage, apply for student loans, and make campaign contributions. Citizens can purchase items from the U.S. government through its GSA Auctions Web site, which offers the general public the opportunity to bid electronically on a wide range of government assets. Healthcare.gov is a healthcare exchange website created by and operated under the United States federal government as specified in the Patient Protection and Affordable Care Act. It is designed for use by residents in the 36 U.S. states that opted not to create their own state exchanges. By accessing this Web site, users can view healthcare options and determine if they are eligible for healthcare subsidiaries.[15]

G2B applications support the purchase of materials and services from private industry by government procurement offices, enable firms to bid on government contracts, and help businesses identify government contracts on which they may bid. Business.gov allows businesses to access information about laws and regulations and to download relevant forms needed to comply with federal requirements for their businesses. The Buyers.gov Web site is a business and auction exchange that helps federal government agencies purchase information system products by using reverse auctions and by aggregating demand for commonly purchased products. FedBizOpps is a Web site where government agencies post procurement notices to provide an easy point of contact for businesses that want to bid on government contracts.

G2G applications support transactions between governments such as between the federal government and state or local governments. Government to Government Services online is a suite of Web applications that enables government organizations to report information, such as birth and death data, arrest warrant information, and information about the amount of state aid being received, to the Social Security Administration. This information can affect the payment of benefits to individuals. Oregon e-Government provides e-commerce services to various state agencies. For example, the Oregon transaction payment engine option enables agencies to use an efficient Internet payment solution while adhering to statewide policies and procedures.[16]

INTRODUCTION TO MOBILE COMMERCE

As discussed briefly in Chapter 1, mobile commerce (m-commerce) relies on the use of mobile wireless devices, such as cell phones and smartphones, to place orders and conduct business. Handset manufacturers such as Apple, Ericsson, Samsung, Nokia, and Qualcomm are working with communications carriers such as AT&T, Cingular, Sprint/Nextel, and Verizon to develop wireless devices, related technology, and services to support m-commerce. The Internet Corporation for Assigned Names and Numbers (ICANN) created a .mobi domain to help attract mobile users to the Web. mTLD Top Level Domain Ltd of Dublin, Ireland, administers this domain and helps to ensure that the .mobi destinations work quickly, efficiently, and effectively with user handsets.

Mobile Commerce in Perspective

The market for m-commerce in North America is maturing much later than in Western Europe and Japan for several reasons. In North America, responsibility for network infrastructure is fragmented among many providers, consumer payments are usually made by credit card, and many Americans are unfamiliar with mobile data services. In most Western European countries, communicating via wireless devices is common, and consumers are much more willing to use m-commerce. Japanese consumers are generally enthusiastic about new technology and are therefore much more likely to use mobile technologies for making purchases.

Worldwide m-commerce is expected to grow to more than one-half billion customers shopping by mobile devices by 2016.[17] In the United States, it is estimated that m-commerce generated about $42 billion in revenue for 2013—an increase of 68 percent from 2012. By 2017 m-commerce sales are estimated to reach over $113 billion—representing a compound annual growth rate (CAGR) of 28 percent.[18] Clearly mobile commerce is a rapidly growing segment of e-commerce

The number of mobile Web sites worldwide is expected to grow rapidly because of advances in wireless broadband technologies, the development of new and useful applications, and the availability of less costly but more powerful handsets. Experts point out that the relative clumsiness of mobile browsers and security concerns must be overcome to ensure rapid m-commerce growth.

M-Commerce Web Sites

A number of retailers have established special Web sites for users of mobile devices. Table 8.4 provides a list of some of the best mobile Web sites as of 2013 based on depth of content, personalization, social media integration, mobile coupons, and use of video.

TABLE **8.4** Highly rated m-commerce retail Web sites

Rank	Company
1	Toys "R" Us
2	American Eagle Outfitters
3	Crate & Barrel
4	Nordstrom
5	Sephora USA
6	Foot Locker

Source: Siwicki, Bill, "Which Six Retailers Offer the Best M-Commerce Sites?" *Internet Retail*, October 6, 2013, *www.internetretailer.com/2013/10/09/which-six-retailers-offer-best-mobile-commerce-web-sites*.

© 2016 Cengage Learning

An interesting service can be accessed from Twitter by sending a shopping-related question to @IMshopping. Your question is routed to an appropriate expert who can provide unbiased opinions and links to products within about 15 minutes. (Experts are rated over time based on their answers.) The expert's response is a URL link to a page at IMshopping.com that will provide a longer answer than the 140-character limit imposed by Twitter.

Advantages of Electronic and Mobile Commerce

Conversion to an e-commerce or m-commerce system enables organizations to reach new customers, reduce the cost of doing business, speed the flow of goods and information, increase the accuracy of order-processing and order fulfillment, and improve the level of customer service.

Reach New Customers

The establishment of an e-commerce Web site enables a firm to reach new customers in new markets. Indeed, this is one of the primary reasons organizations give for establishing a Web site.

Harry Corry is a northern Irish home décor store with 50 stores in Ireland and Scotland. The stores primarily sell curtains, bedding, curtain poles, lamps, and towels. The firm started a new e-commerce Web site to help the brand reach new markets. Marketing manager Mark Corry said: "We recognised the need for an online shopping option after conducting research to understand the changing buying patterns of Irish consumers, where we found a growing demand for an online home interiors offering. Functionality and ease of use are two key elements we've developed with the new site."[19]

Reduce Costs

By eliminating or reducing time-consuming and labor-intensive steps throughout the order and delivery process, more sales can be completed in the same period and with increased accuracy. With increased speed and accuracy of customer order information, companies can reduce the need for inventory—from raw materials to safety stocks and finished goods—at all the intermediate manufacturing, storage, and transportation points.

EquaShip is an e-commerce company that consolidates the goods from many small shippers into the same trailers so that the latter can earn the same high-volume shipping discounts that large companies like Amazon.com do. The downside is that the delivery time is a little longer. However, the cost savings enables small companies to offer free shipping at essentially the same cost to themselves as large companies. Shippers communicate their pick-up and delivery needs as well as print labels using online software provided by EquaShip.[20]

Speed the Flow of Goods and Information

When organizations are connected via e-commerce, the flow of information is accelerated because electronic connections and communications are already established. As a result, information can flow from buyer to seller easily, directly, and rapidly.

Bypass Lane, SnagMobile, and Yorder are mobile apps that enable sports fans to order merchandise using their smartphones. The items can be delivered to their seat or picked up at a special window at the concession stand. These mobile apps not only increase the convenience of ordering food and enjoyment of the sporting event, they also increase concession stand sales by 30 to 40 percent.[21]

Increase Accuracy

By enabling buyers to enter their own product specifications and order information directly, human data-entry error on the part of the supplier is eliminated. R.O. Writer is shop management software used by thousands of auto repair, quick lube, and tire repair shops across the United States. It integrates with the electronic parts catalogs of various parts distributors to allow repair people to correctly order the specific parts needed for each repair job. The data is then transferred onto customer repair orders to produce timely and accurate customer invoices.[22]

Improve Customer Service

Increased and more detailed information about delivery dates and current status can increase customer loyalty. In addition, the ability to consistently meet customers' desired delivery dates with high-quality goods and services eliminates any incentive for customers to seek other sources of supply.

Mobile Money from T-Mobile is a money management application for smartphones used with a reloadable T-Mobile Visa Prepaid Card. The service provides improved customer service by enabling users to make direct deposits of their paychecks and to deposit checks using their smartphone camera—without fees. The service is a strong competitor to many bank services that come with high fees for checking services. "Millions of Americans pay outrageous fees to check cashers, payday lenders, and other predatory businesses—just for the right to use their own money," said John Legere, president and chief executive officer of T-Mobile.[23]

ETHICAL& SOCIETAL ISSUES

AbilityOne: E-Commerce Not Just for the Sighted

In the United States, 7 out of 10 working-age people with visual impairments are not employed. National Industries for the Blind (NIB) aims to reduce that number. Their mission is "to enhance the opportunities for economic and personal independence of persons who are blind, primarily through creating, sustaining, and improving employment."

In the United States, the Javits-Wagner-O'Day Act of 1971 has a similar goal. It requires the federal government to purchase certain supplies and services from nonprofit organizations that employ people with visual impairments or other significant disabilities. This law is administered by the U.S. AbilityOne Commission, a government agency that operates in conjunction with NIB and National Industries for the Severely Handicapped (NISH). These two organizations, in turn, are authorized to provide supplies and services under this act. They coordinate offerings from many small nonprofits that produce items or provide services that the government needs and sell them through AbilityOne.

Today, people expect to be able to obtain goods and services via e-commerce. AbilityOne, therefore, needed an e-commerce Web site that would let government agencies order from them. The commission's challenges in developing its site were to make it accessible to the visually impaired while basing it on standard software to reduce development effort and keeping it easily usable by people with full vision. (Most external site users, those who purchase goods and services for government agencies, have full vision, but accessibility was still required for two reasons: Many internal users at NIB are vision-impaired, and accessibility is part of NIB's mission.)

To address these challenges, AbilityOne decided to work with NIB to develop its site. The agencies began with a commitment to meet all the requirements of Section 508c of the Rehabilitation Act of 1998. That act specifies accommodations to make information systems accessible to people with disabilities, such as ensuring that all graphics on a site have text descriptions that can be read aloud by a screen reader. Section 508c compliance was a requirement throughout the vendor selection process for the new site. Ultimately, NIB decided to base its site on Oracle's E-Business Suite and its iStore e-commerce application. NIB found that iStore offered sufficient user interface flexibility to meet the accessibility requirements. For example, iStore allows each user to customize the site's colors to black and white, high contrast, or a mix of settings that optimizes the site for his or her vision. NIB also chose BizTech, an IT services firm and Oracle developer, to lead the implementation project.

After confirming that the AbilityOne site met Section 508c requirements, NIB tested the site further against the Web Content Accessibility Guidelines of the World Wide Web Consortium (W3C) and against NIB's own internal usability guidelines. Only after passing all these tests was the site made available to AbilityOne's customers.

The result was a site that is fully usable by sighted and visually impaired people, that is visually attractive to sighted people, that allows government agencies to obtain any of the 8,000 products that are available through AbilityOne, and that facilitates the employment of visually impaired people as AbilityOne customer representatives. Commercial e-commerce sites can lose nothing, but can only gain, by making their sites equally accessible.

Discussion Questions

1. How can a company with a general e-commerce site benefit from conforming to accessibility guidelines such as those mentioned above?
2. Visit the *www.abilityone.gov* Web site. Identify some of its unique features used to accommodate the disabled.

Critical Thinking Questions

1. U.S. federal government agencies are required by law to purchase certain supplies and services through AbilityOne, thus ensuring that visually impaired and other severely handicapped people have a major role in producing or providing them. Do you agree with this law? Why or why not?
2. With some exceptions, complying with accessibility standards is voluntary on the part of companies that sell software. However, it costs money in added development effort. How should these costs be offset?

SOURCES: AbilityOne Web site, *www.abilityone.com*, accessed February 29, 2012; National Industries for the Blind, "AbilityOne eCommerce Site," *Computerworld* case study, *www.eisevery where.com/file_uploads/13271db4a95e3264477277f0829035c6_National_Industries_for_the_ Blind_-_AbilityOne_eCommerce_Site.pdf*, accessed February 29, 2012; National Industries for the Blind Web site, *www.nib.org*, accessed February 29, 2012; U.S. Government, "Resources for Understanding and Implementing Section 508," *www.section508.gov*, accessed February 29, 2012; "Javits–Wagner–O'Day Act," "Javits-Wagner-O'Day Act *www.abilityone.gov/laws_and_regulations /jwod.html*, accessed February 29, 2012; "Web Content Accessibility Guidelines (WCAG) 2.0," World Wide Web Consortium, *www.w3.org/TR/WCAG20*, December 11, 2008.

Multistage Model for E-Commerce

A successful e-commerce system must address the many stages that consumers experience in the sales life cycle. At the heart of any e-commerce system is the user's ability to search for and identify items for sale; select those items and negotiate prices, terms of payment, and delivery date; send an order to the vendor to purchase the items; pay for the product or service; obtain product delivery; and receive after-sales support. Figure 8.2 shows how e-commerce can support each of these stages. Product delivery can involve tangible goods delivered in a traditional form (e.g., clothing delivered via a package service) or goods and services delivered electronically (e.g., software downloaded over the Internet).

Search and Identification

An employee ordering parts for a storeroom at a manufacturing plant would follow the steps shown in Figure 8.2. Such a storeroom stocks a wide range of office supplies, spare parts, and maintenance supplies. The employee prepares a list of needed items—for example, fasteners, piping, and plastic tubing. Typically, for each item carried in the storeroom, a corporate buyer has already identified a preferred supplier based on the vendor's price competitiveness, level of service, quality of products, and speed of delivery. The employee then logs on to the Internet and goes to the Web site of the preferred supplier.

From the supplier's home page, the employee can access a product catalog and browse until he or she finds the items that meet the storeroom's specifications. The employee fills out a request-for-quotation form by entering the item codes and quantities needed. When the employee completes the quotation form, the supplier's Web application calculates the total charge of the

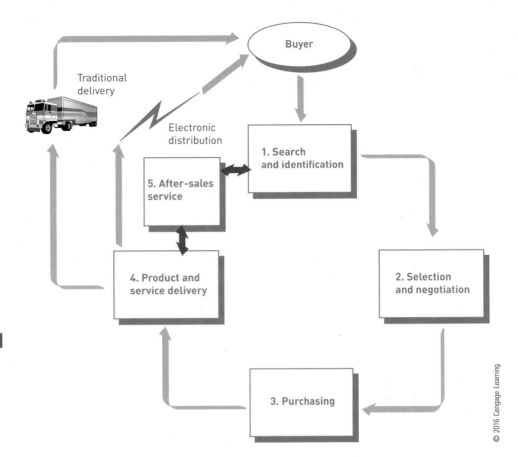

FIGURE 8.2

Multistage model for e-commerce (B2B and B2C)

A successful e-commerce system addresses the stages that consumers experience in the sales life cycle.

order with the most current prices and shows the additional cost for various forms of delivery—overnight, within two working days, or the next week. The employee might elect to visit other suppliers' Web home pages and repeat this process to search for additional items or obtain competing prices for the same items.

Select and Negotiate

After the price quotations have been received from each supplier, the employee examines them and indicates by clicking the request-for-quotation form which items to order from a given supplier. The employee also specifies the desired delivery date. This data is used as input into the supplier's order-processing system. In addition to price, an item's quality and the supplier's service and speed of delivery can be important in the selection and negotiation process.

B2B e-commerce systems need to support negotiation between a buyer and the selected seller over the final price, delivery date, delivery costs, and any extra charges. However, these features are not fundamental requirements of most B2C systems, which offer their products for sale on a "take-it-or-leave-it" basis.

Purchase Products and Services Electronically

The employee completes the purchase order specifying the final agreed-to terms and prices by sending a completed electronic form to the supplier. Complications can arise in paying for the products. Typically, a corporate buyer who makes several purchases from the supplier each year has established credit with the supplier in advance, and all purchases are billed to a corporate account. But when individual consumers make their first, and perhaps only, purchase from the supplier, additional safeguards and measures are required. Part of the purchase transaction can involve the customer providing a credit card number. Another approach to paying for goods and services purchased over the Internet is using electronic money, which can be exchanged for hard cash, as discussed later in the chapter.

Deliver Product and Service

Electronic distribution can be used to download software, music, pictures, videos, and written material through the Internet faster and for less expense than shipping the items via a package delivery service. Most products cannot be delivered over the Internet, so they are delivered in a variety of other ways: overnight carrier, regular mail service, truck, or rail. In some cases, the customer might elect to drive to the supplier and pick up the product.

Many manufacturers and retailers have outsourced the physical logistics of delivering merchandise to cybershoppers—those who take care of the storing, packing, shipping, and tracking of products. To provide this service, DHL, Federal Express, United Parcel Service, and other delivery firms have developed software tools and interfaces that directly link customer ordering, manufacturing, and inventory systems with their own system of highly automated warehouses, call centers, and worldwide shipping networks. The goal is to make the transfer of all information and inventory, from the manufacturer to the delivery firm to the consumer, fast and simple.

For example, when a customer orders a printer at the Hewlett-Packard (HP) Web site, that order actually goes to FedEx, which stocks all the products that HP sells online at a dedicated e-distribution facility in Memphis, Tennessee, a major FedEx shipping hub. FedEx ships the order, which triggers an email notification to the customer that the printer is on its way and an inventory notice is sent to HP that the FedEx warehouse now has one fewer printers in stock. See Figure 8.3.

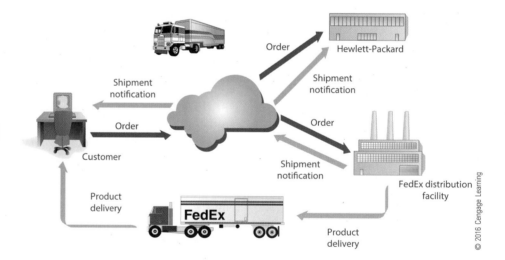

FIGURE 8.3

Product and information flow

When a customer orders an HP printer over the Web, the order goes first to FedEx, which ships the order, triggering an email notification to the customer and an inventory notice to HP.

For product returns, HP enters return information into its own system, which is linked to FedEx. This information signals a FedEx courier to pick up the unwanted item at the customer's house or business. Customers don't need to fill out shipping labels or package the item. Instead, the FedEx courier uses information transmitted over the Internet to a computer in his truck to print a label from a portable printer attached to his belt. FedEx has control of the return, and HP can monitor its progress from start to finish.

After-Sales Service

In addition to the information to complete the order, comprehensive customer information is also captured from the order and stored in the supplier's customer database. This information can include the customer name, address, telephone numbers, contact person, credit history, and other details. For example, if the customer later contacts the supplier to complain that not all items were received, that some arrived damaged, or even that the product provides unclear instructions, any customer service representative can retrieve the order information from the database via a computing/communications device. Companies are adding to their Web sites the capability to answer many after-sales questions, such as how to maintain a piece of equipment, how to effectively use the product, and how to receive repairs under warranty.

E-Commerce Challenges

A company must overcome many challenges to convert its business processes from the traditional form to e-commerce processes, especially for B2C e-commerce. As a result, not all e-commerce ventures are successful. For example, Borders began an online Web site in the late 1990s, but after three years of operating in the red, the bookseller outsourced its e-commerce operations to Amazon in 2001. In 2006, Borders reversed course and decided to relaunch its own Borders.com Web site in May 2008. Since then, Borders generated disappointing sales figures. As a result of the substandard results, many decision makers were replaced, including the CIO and senior vice president of sales. Finally in early 2011, Borders applied for bankruptcy protection and began closing its stores.[24]

Dealing with Consumer Privacy Concerns

The following are three key challenges to e-commerce: (1) dealing with consumer privacy concerns, (2) overcoming consumers' lack of trust, and (3) overcoming global issues. While two-thirds of U.S. Internet users have purchased an item online and most Internet users say online shopping saves them time, about one-third of all adult Internet users will not buy anything online primarily because they have privacy concerns or lack trust in online merchants. In addition to having an effective e-commerce model and strategy, companies must carefully address consumer privacy concerns and overcome consumers' lack of trust.

Following are a few examples of recent security beaches in which personal data was compromised:

- Target reported that cyber thieves compromised the credit card data and personal information of as many as 110 million customers. That data includes phone numbers, email and home addresses, credit and debit card numbers, PINs, expiration dates and magnetic strip information.[25]
- A security vulnerability exposed the email addresses and telephone numbers of an estimated 6 million Facebook users.[26]
- The credit card data of more than 2 million customers of Schnucks Markets, a St. Louis area grocery store chain, was stolen by cybercriminals.[27]
- Luxury retailer Neiman Marcus revealed that hackers invaded its systems for several months in a breach that involved 1.1 million credit and debit cards.[28]

identify theft: Someone uses your personal identification information without your permission often to commit fraud or other crimes.

In some cases, the compromise of personal data can lead to identity theft. According to the Federal Trade Commission (FTC), "Identity theft occurs when someone steals your personal information and uses it without your permission."[29] Often stolen personal identification information (PII), such as your name, Social Security number, or credit card number, is used to commit fraud or other crimes. Thieves may use a consumer's credit card numbers to charge items to that person's accounts, use identification information to apply for a new credit card or a loan in a consumer's name, or use a consumer's name and Social Security number to receive government benefits.

Companies must be prepared to make a substantial investment to safeguard their customers' privacy or run the risk of losing customers and generating potential class action law suits should the data be compromised. It is not uncommon for customers to initiate a class action lawsuit for millions of dollars in damages for emotional distress and loss of privacy. In addition to potential damages, companies must frequently pay for customer credit monitoring and identity theft insurance to ensure that their customers' data is secure.

Within two days after the Target data breach was announced, the first lawsuit was filed. The California class action lawsuit claims that Target was negligent in its failure to implement and maintain reasonable security procedures and practices. A second lawsuit claims that Target broke Minnesota law by not alerting customers quickly enough after learning of the security issue. A third lawsuit was filed in California alleging both negligence and invasion of privacy.[30]

Most Web sites invest in the latest security technology and employ highly trained security experts to protect their consumers' data. The presence of the McAfee Secure security icon on the pages of an e-commerce Web site indicates that the site meets all guidelines set by the payment card industry. It also signifies that the site is secure from hackers and malicious software that could access customer identity information, passwords, or account numbers.

Longmont United Hospital employs more than 280 staff members in their location of Longmont, Colorado. The Health Insurance Portability and Accountability Act of 1996 (HIPAA) was passed by Congress to improve the efficiency and effectiveness of the healthcare system, and reduce the incidence of fraud. This policy requires increasing the secure automation of patient records and electronic healthcare information transfers. Longmont employs McAfee Secure Computing solutions to meet these requirements by providing identity and access control, detailed auditing of action on data, strong authentication of users, and role-based authorization to data.[31]

Overcoming Consumers' Lack of Trust

Lack of trust in online sellers is one of the most frequently cited reasons that some consumers are not willing to purchase online. Can they be sure that the company or person with which they are dealing is legitimate and will send the item(s) they purchase? What if there is a problem with the product or service when it is received: for example, if it does not match the description on the Web site, is the wrong size or wrong color, is damaged during the delivery process, or does not work as advertised?

Online marketers must create specific trust-building strategies for their Web sites by analyzing their customers, products, and services. A perception of trustworthiness can be created by implementing one or more of the following strategies:

- Demonstrate a strong desire to build an ongoing relationship with customers by giving first-time price incentives, offering loyalty programs, or eliciting and sharing customer feedback.
- Demonstrate that the company has been in business for a long time.
- Make it clear that considerable investment has been made in the Web site.
- Provide brand endorsements from well-known experts or well-respected individuals.
- Demonstrate participation in appropriate regulatory programs or industry associations.
- Display Web site accreditation by the Better Business Bureau Online or TRUSTe programs.

Here are some tips to help online shoppers avoid problems:

- Only buy from a well-known Web site you can trust—one that advertises on national media, is recommended by a friend, or receives strong ratings in the media.

- Look for a seal of approval from organizations such as the Better Business Bureau Online or TRUSTe. See Figure 8.4.

FIGURE 8.4

Seals of approval

To avoid problems when shopping online, look on the Web site for a seal of approval from organizations such as the Better Business Bureau Online or TRUSTe.

- Review the Web site's privacy policy to be sure that you are comfortable with its conditions before you provide personal information.
- Determine what the Web site policy is for return of products purchased.
- Be wary if you must enter any personal information other than what's required to complete the purchase (name, credit card number, address, and telephone number).
- Do not, under any conditions, ever provide information such as your Social Security number, bank account numbers, or your mother's maiden name.
- When you open the Web page where you enter credit card information or other personal data, make sure that the Web address begins with "https," and check to see if a locked padlock icon appears in the Address bar or status bar, as shown in Figure 8.5.
- Consider using virtual credit cards, which expire after one use, when doing business.
- Before downloading music, change your browser's advanced settings to disable access to all computer areas that contain personal information.

FIGURE 8.5

Web site security

Web site that uses "https" in the address and a secure site lock icon.

Overcoming Global Issues

E-commerce and m-commerce offer enormous opportunities by allowing manufacturers to buy supplies at a low cost worldwide. They also offer enterprises the chance to sell to a global market right from the start. Moreover, they offer great promise for developing countries, helping them to enter the prosperous global marketplace, which helps to reduce the gap between rich and poor countries. People and companies can get products and services from around the world, instead of around the corner or across town. These opportunities, however, come with numerous obstacles and issues, first identified in Chapter 1 as challenges associated with all global systems:

- **Cultural challenges**. Great care must be taken to ensure that a Web site is appealing, easy to use, and inoffensive to people around the world.
- **Language challenges**. Language differences can make it difficult to understand the information and directions posted on a Web site.
- **Time and distance challenges**. Significant time differences make it difficult for some people to be able to speak to customer services representatives or to get technical support during regular waking hours.
- **Infrastructure challenges**. The Web site must support access by customers using a wide variety of hardware and software devices.

- **Currency challenges**. The Web site must be able to state prices and accept payment in a variety of currencies.
- **State, regional, and national law challenges**. The Web site must operate in conformance to a wide variety of laws that cover a variety of issues, including the protection of trademarks and patents, the sale of copyrighted material, the collection and safeguarding of personal or financial data, the payment of sales taxes and fees, and much more.

ELECTRONIC AND MOBILE COMMERCE APPLICATIONS

E-commerce and m-commerce are being used in innovative and exciting ways. This section examines a few of the many B2B, B2C, C2C, and m-commerce applications in retail and wholesale, manufacturing, marketing, advertising, bartering, retargeting, price comparison, couponing, investment and finance, banking, and e-boutiques. As with any new technology, m-commerce will succeed only if it provides users with real benefits. Companies involved in e-commerce and m-commerce must think through their strategies carefully and ensure that they provide services that truly meet customers' needs.

Retail and Wholesale

electronic retailing (e-tailing): The direct sale of products or services by businesses to consumers through electronic storefronts, typically designed around the familiar electronic catalog and shopping cart model.

cybermall: A single Web site that offers many products and services at one Internet location.

E-commerce is being used extensively in retailing and wholesaling. **Electronic retailing**, sometimes called *e-tailing*, is the direct sale of products or services by businesses to consumers through electronic storefronts, which are typically designed around the familiar electronic catalog and shopping cart model. Companies such as Office Depot, Walmart, and many others have used the same model to sell wholesale goods to employees of corporations. Tens of thousands of electronic retail Web sites sell everything from soup to nuts.

Cybermalls are another means to support retail shopping. A **cybermall** is a single Web site that offers many products and services at one Internet location—similar to a regular shopping mall. An Internet cybermall pulls multiple buyers and sellers into one virtual place, easily reachable through a Web browser. For example, the Intl Super Cyber Mall (*www.applaudwomen.com /IntlSuperCyberMallatApplaudWomen.html*) provides direct links to over 150 stores representing 34 different categories of products from businesses such as Auto Zone, Best Buy, Foot Locker, Old Navy, Pandora, Dr. Wayne Dyer, The Great Courses, and dozens of other online shopping sites.[32]

A key sector of wholesale e-commerce is spending on manufacturing, repair, and operations (MRO) goods and services—from simple office supplies to mission-critical equipment, such as the motors, pumps, compressors, and instruments that keep manufacturing facilities running smoothly. MRO purchases often approach 40 percent of a manufacturing company's total revenues, but the purchasing system can be haphazard, without automated controls. In addition to these external purchase costs, companies face significant internal costs resulting from outdated and cumbersome MRO management processes. For example, studies show that a high percentage of manufacturing downtime is often caused by not having the right part at the right time in the right place. The result is lost productivity and capacity. E-commerce software for plant operations provides powerful comparative searching capabilities to enable managers to identify functionally equivalent items, helping them spot opportunities to combine purchases for cost savings. Comparing various suppliers, coupled with consolidating more spending with fewer suppliers, leads to decreased costs. In addition, automated workflows are typically based on industry best practices, which can streamline processes.

Industrial Parts House provides access to over 1 million MRO parts and supplies with a 99 percent fill rate on all customer orders. It provides 24-hour shipping with each order received by 3 pm shipped out the same day.[33]

Manufacturing

One approach taken by many manufacturers to raise profitability and improve customer service is to move their supply chain operations onto the Internet. Here, they can form an **electronic exchange**, an electronic forum where manufacturers, suppliers, and competitors buy and sell goods, trade market information, and run back-office operations, such as inventory control, as shown in Figure 8.6. This approach has greatly speeded up the movement of raw materials and finished products among all members of the business community and has reduced the amount of inventory that must be maintained. It has also led to a much more competitive marketplace and lower prices.

electronic exchange: An electronic forum where manufacturers, suppliers, and competitors buy and sell goods, trade market information, and run back-office operations.

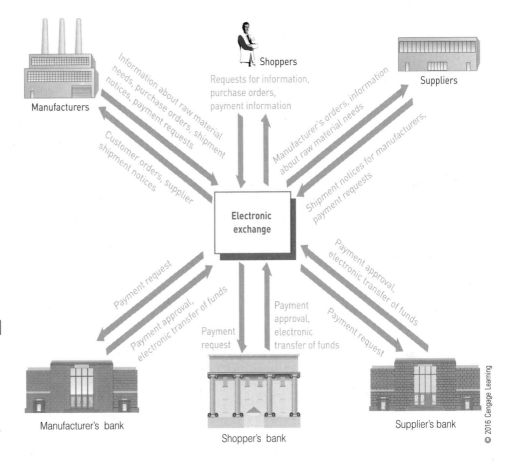

FIGURE 8.6

Model of an electronic exchange

An electronic exchange is an electronic forum where manufacturers, suppliers, and competitors buy and sell goods, trade market information, and run back-office operations.

© 2016 Cengage Learning

Companies can join one of three types of exchanges based on who operates the exchange. Private exchanges are owned and operated by a single company. The owner uses the exchange to trade exclusively with established business partners. Walmart's Retail Link is such an exchange. Consortium-operated exchanges are run by a group of traditionally competing companies with common procurement needs. For example, Covisint was developed to serve the needs of the big three auto makers. Independent exchanges are open to any set of buyers and sellers within a given market. They provide services and a common technology platform to their members and are open, usually for a fee, to any company that wants to use them. For example, Tinypass is a flexible e-commerce platform that enables content publishers to choose from a variety of payment models to sell access to their media. Publishers can offer limited previews to readers before they subscribe, ask for payment to view each video or article, or allow the audience to pay what they believe the content is worth. Content is defined by the publisher and can be any sort of digital media: an article, a movie, a blog post, a PDF, access to a forum, or access to an entire Web site.[34]

Several strategic and competitive issues are associated with the use of exchanges. Many companies distrust their corporate rivals and fear they might lose trade secrets through participation in such exchanges. Suppliers worry that online marketplaces will drive down the prices of goods and favor buyers. Suppliers also can spend a great deal of money setting up to participate in multiple exchanges. For example, more than a dozen new exchanges have appeared in the oil industry, and the printing industry has more than 20 online marketplaces. Until a clear winner emerges in particular industries, suppliers are more or less forced to sign on to several or all of them. Yet another issue is potential government scrutiny of exchange participants: When competitors get together to share information, it raises questions of collusion or antitrust behavior.

Many companies that already use the Internet for their private exchanges have no desire to share their expertise with competitors. At Walmart, the world's number-one retail chain, executives turned down several invitations to join exchanges in the retail and consumer goods industries. Walmart is pleased with its in-house exchange, Retail Link, which connects the company to 7,000 worldwide suppliers that sell everything from toothpaste to furniture. Through Retail Link, Walmart has created a supplier-managed inventory system where it lets each supplier decide where to put SKUs (stock keeping units) and how to ship through to stores. It empowers suppliers to make these decisions by providing them with inventory and sales data by SKU by hour, by store. This in turn makes Walmart more profitable, because it can hold each supplier accountable to maximize margin, with the lowest inventory possible, to produce the greatest return on investment in inventory.[35]

Marketing

The nature of the Web enables firms to gather more information about customer behavior and preferences as customers and potential customers gather their own information and make their purchase decisions. Analysis of this data is complicated because of the Web's interactivity and because each visitor voluntarily provides or refuses to provide personal data such as name, address, email address, telephone number, and demographic data. Internet advertisers use the data to identify specific markets and target them with tailored advertising messages. This practice, called **market segmentation**, divides the pool of potential customers into subgroups usually defined in terms of demographic characteristics, such as age, gender, marital status, income level, and geographic location.

market segmentation: The identification of specific markets to target them with tailored advertising messages.

In the past, market segmentation has been difficult for B2B marketers because firmographic data (addresses, financials, number of employees, and industry classification code) was difficult to obtain. Now, however, Nielsen, the marketing and media information company, has developed its Business-Facts database, which includes critical information such as contact names, locations, addresses, number of employees, annual sales, and Standard Industry Code (SIC) and North American Industry Classification System (NAICS) Industry classification codes for more than 14 million U.S. businesses. See Figure 8.7. Using this data, analysts can estimate potential sales for each business and rank the business against all other prospects and customers.[36]

Advertising

Mobile ad networks distribute mobile ads to publishers such as mobile Web sites, application developers, and mobile operators. Mobile ad impressions are generally bought at a cost per thousand (CPM), cost per click (CPC), or cost per action (CPA), in which the advertiser pays only if the customer clicks through and then buys the product or service. The main measures of success are the number of users reached, click through rate (CTR), and the number

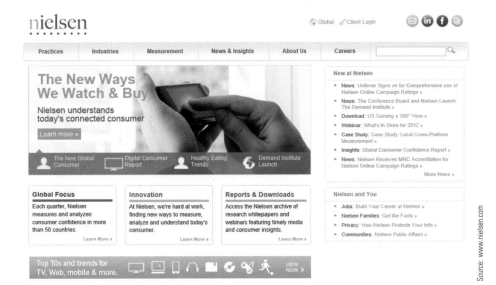

FIGURE 8.7

Nielsen marketing company

Nielsen is a major marketing company that measures and analyzes how consumers acquire information, consume media, and buy goods and services.

of actions users take, such as the number of downloads prompted by the ad. The advertiser is keenly interested in this data to measure the effectiveness of its advertising spending and may pay extra to purchase the data from the mobile ad network or a third party. Generally, there are three types of mobile ad networks—blind, premium blind, and premium networks—though no clear lines separate them. The characteristics of these mobile advertising networks are summarized in Table 8.5.

TABLE 8.5 Characteristics of three types of mobile advertising networks

Characteristic	Blind Networks	Premium Blind Networks	Premium Networks
Degree to which advertisers can specify where ads are run	An advertiser can specify country and content channel (e.g., news, sports, or entertainment) on which the ad will run but not a specific Web site.	Most advertising is blind, but for an additional charge, the advertiser can buy a specific spot on a Web site of its choice.	Big brand advertisers can secure elite locations on top-tier destinations.
Predominant pricing model and typical rate	CPC ($0.01 per click)	CPM ($20 per thousand impressions)	CPM ($40 per thousand impressions)
Examples	Admoda/Adultmoda AdMob BuzzCity InMobi	Jumptap Madhouse Millennial Media Quattro Wireless	Advertising.com/AOL Hands Microsoft Mobile Advertising Nokia Interactive Advertising Pudding Media YOC Group

AdMob is a mobile advertising provider that serves up ads for display on mobile devices and in applications like those that run on the Android and iPhone. With AdMob (part of Google), smartphone application developers can connect with more than a million Google advertisers and show relevant ads in their app. As users engage with the ads, the app developer earns money. App developers can also advertise their app in other apps to increase downloads. In this manner, app developers can distribute their apps for free and recover their costs over time through payments from advertisers.[37]

Because m-commerce devices usually have a single user, they are ideal for accessing personal information and receiving targeted messages for a particular consumer. Through m-commerce, companies can reach individual consumers to establish one-to-one marketing relationships and communicate whenever it is convenient—in short, anytime and anywhere. See Figure 8.8.

FIGURE 8.8

M-commerce is convenient and personal

Consumers are increasingly using mobile phones to purchase goods and perform other transactions online.

Bartering

During the recent economic downturn, many people and businesses turned to bartering as a means of gaining goods and services. A number of Web sites have been created to support this activity, as shown in Table 8.6. Businesses are willing to barter to reduce excess inventory, gain new customers, or avoid paying cash for necessary raw materials or services. Cash-strapped customers find bartering to be an attractive alternative to paying scarce dollars. Generally, bartering transactions have tax-reporting, accounting, and other record-keeping responsibilities associated with them. Indeed, the IRS hosts a Bartering Tax Center Web site that provides details about the tax laws and responsibilities for bartering transactions.

Retargeting

An average of 67.75 percent of all online shopping carts are abandoned, amounting to over $9 billion in lost sales for 2011.[38] "Retargeting" is a technique used by advertisers to recapture these shoppers by using targeted and personalized ads to direct shoppers back to a retailer's site. For example, a visitor who viewed the men's clothing portion of a retailer's Web site and

TABLE **8.6** Popular bartering Web sites

Web Site	Purpose
Craiglist.org	Includes a section where users can request an item in exchange for services or exchange services for services.
Goozez.com	Allows users to exchange video games and movies.
Swapagift.com	Enables users to buy, sell, or swap merchant gift cards.
SwapHog.com	Bartering site that offers a third-party service that first receives all items and inspects them before finalizing the transaction to eliminate fraud and ensure a successful transaction.
Swapstyle.com	Users can swap, sell, or buy women's accessories, clothes, cosmetics, and shoes.
Swaptree.com	Users trade books, CDs, DVDs, and video games on a one-for-one basis.
TradeAway.com	Enables users to exchange a wide variety of new or used items, services, or real estate.

then abandoned the Web site would be targeted with banner ads showing various men's clothing items from that retailer. The banner ads might even display the exact items the visitor viewed, such as men's casual slacks. The retargeting could be even further enhanced to include comments and recommendations from other consumers who purchased the same items. Thus, retargeting ensures that potential consumers see relevant, targeted ads for products they've already expressed interest in.

Price Comparison

An increasing number of companies provide mobile phone apps that enable shoppers to compare prices and products on the Web. Amazon's Price Check and Google's Shopper enable shoppers to do a quick price comparison by simply scanning the product's barcode or by taking a picture of a book, DVD, CD, or video game cover. Barcode Scanner allows shoppers to scan UPC or Quick Response codes to perform a price comparison and read the latest reviews.[39]

Couponing

During 2013, more than 287 billion free-standing insert coupons were distributed in North America with a total value of $467 billion, or an average of $1.67 per coupon.[40] Surprisingly, only 0.95 percent of those coupons were redeemed even during tough economic times for many people.[41]

Many manufacturers and retailers now send mobile coupons directly to consumers' smartphones. Unfortunately, the standard red laser scanners used at checkout stands have difficulty reading information displayed on a smartphone without special smartphone apps. Therefore, for many shoppers, current technology requires that the consumer print out the coupon, have it scanned, and present it to the clerk to enter the numbers from the coupon manually.

Procter and Gamble, the world's largest consumer products company, and mobeam piloted a new approach to enable mobile coupons to be read directly by the standard bar code scanners at the checkout counter. This will enable consumers to receive electronic coupons, sort and organize them on their smartphone, and bring them to the store where they can be scanned directly. The mobeam approach converts the barcode into a beam of light that can be read by the typical barcode scanner. The mobeam application must be loaded onto the smartphone before scanning.[42] The estimated number of mobile coupon redeemers is expected to increase due to the integration of couponing into social networks, along with an increase in smartphone and tablet users, new mobile apps, and location-based deals.[43] See Figure 8.9.

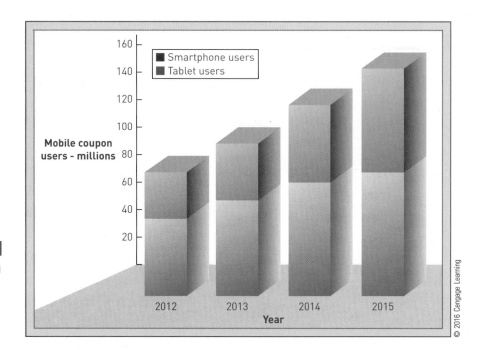

FIGURE 8.9

Growth in U.S. mobile coupon users

The number of mobile coupon redeemers is increasing significantly.

Groupon is an innovative approach to couponing. Discount coupons for consumers are valid only if a predetermined minimum number of people sign up for them. Merchants do not pay any money up front to participate in Groupon but must pay Groupon half of whatever the customer pays for the coupon.

Investment and Finance

The Internet has revolutionized the world of investment and finance. Perhaps the changes have been so significant because this industry had so many built-in inefficiencies and so much opportunity for improvement.

The brokerage business adapted to the Internet faster than any other arm of finance. See Figure 8.10. The allure of online trading that enables investors to do quick, thorough research and then buy shares in any company in a few seconds and at a fraction of the cost of a full-commission firm has brought many investors to the Web. TD Ameritrade offers a mobile trading app for investors to monitor their investments, view streaming quotes, access multiple chat rooms and data feeds to communicate live with other traders, interact with over 300 charts and indicators, access streaming news from CNBC, generate investment ideas from research and analysts' opinions, and execute trades from their Apple, Blackberry, or Android mobile devices.[44]

Banking

Online banking customers can check balances of their savings, checking, and loan accounts; transfer money among accounts; and pay their bills. These customers enjoy the convenience of not writing checks by hand, of tracking their current balances, and of reducing expenditures on envelopes and stamps. In addition, paying bills online is good for the environment because it reduces the amount of paper used, thus saving trees and reducing greenhouse gases.

FIGURE 8.10

Mobile investment and finance

Investment firms provide mobile trading apps to support clients on the go.

All of the major banks and many smaller ones in the United States enable their customers to pay bills online; many support bill payment via cell phone or other wireless device. Banks are eager to gain more customers who pay bills online because such customers tend to stay with the bank longer, have higher cash balances, and use more of the bank's products and services. To encourage the use of this service, many banks have eliminated all fees associated with online bill payment.

Consumers who have enrolled in mobile banking and downloaded the mobile application to their cell phones can check their credit card balances before making major purchases and can avoid credit rejections. They can also transfer funds from savings to checking accounts to avoid an overdraft.

M-Pesa (M for mobile, Pesa for money in Swahili) with some 20 million users worldwide is considered by many to be the most developed mobile payment system in the world. The service is operated by Safaricom and Vodacom, the largest mobile network operators in Kenya and Tanzania. M-Pesa enables users with a national ID card or passport to deposit, withdraw, and transfer money easily with a mobile device. Its services have expanded from a basic mobile money transfer scheme to include loans and savings products, bill pay, and salary disbursements.[45]

E-Boutiques

An increasing number of Web sites offer personalized shopping consultations for shoppers interested in upscale, contemporary clothing—dresses, sportswear, denim clothing, handbags, jewelry, shoes, and gifts. Key to the success of Web sites such as Charm Boutique and ShopLaTiDa is a philosophy of high customer service and strong, personal client relationships. Online boutique shoppers complete a personal shopping profile by answering questions about body measurements, profession, interests, preferred designers, and areas of shopping where they would welcome assistance. Shoppers are then given suggestions on what styles and designers might work best and where they can be found—online or in brick-and-mortar shops.

Quintessentially Gifts is a luxury gifts and shopping service whose researchers and editorial stylists can find the rarest and most exquisite gifts for the affluent shopper. See Figure 8.11. From a McQueen Luxury Dive Toy's underwater scooter to a Hermes Birkin handbag sans the usual two-year wait, the gift team can get it for you.[46]

FIGURE **8.11**

Luxury gifts online

Quintessentially Gifts is an online shopping service that features unusual luxury gifts.

STRATEGIES FOR SUCCESSFUL E-COMMERCE AND M-COMMERCE

With all the constraints to e-commerce just covered, a company must develop an effective Web site, one that is easy to use and accomplishes the goals of the company yet is safe, secure, and affordable to set up and maintain. The next sections examine several issues for a successful e-commerce site.

Defining an Effective E-Commerce Model and Strategy

The first major challenge is for the company to define an effective e-commerce model and strategy. Although companies can select from a number of approaches, the most successful e-commerce models include three basic components: community, content, and commerce, as shown in Figure 8.12. Message boards and chat rooms can build a loyal *community* of people who are interested in and enthusiastic about the company and its products and services. Providing useful, accurate, and timely *content*, such as industry and economic news and stock quotes, is a sound approach to encourage people to return to your Web site time and again. *Commerce* involves consumers and businesses paying to purchase physical goods, information, or services that are posted or advertised online.

FIGURE **8.12**

Content, commerce, and community

A successful e-commerce model includes three basic components.

Defining the Web Site Functions

When building a Web site, you should first decide which tasks the site must accomplish. Most people agree that an effective Web site is one that creates an attractive presence and that meets the needs of its visitors, as with the following:

- Obtaining general information about the organization
- Obtaining financial information for making an investment decision in the organization
- Learning the organization's position on social issues
- Learning about the products or services that the organization sells
- Buying the products or services that the company offers
- Checking the status of an order
- Getting advice or help on effective use of the products
- Registering a complaint about the organization's products
- Registering a complaint concerning the organization's position on social issues
- Providing a product testimonial or an idea for product improvement or a new product
- Obtaining information about warranties or service and repair policies for products
- Obtaining contact information for a person or department in the organization

After a company determines which objectives its site should accomplish, it can proceed to the details of developing the site.

As the number of e-commerce shoppers increases and they become more comfortable—and more selective—making online purchases, a company might need to redefine the basic business model of its site to capture new business opportunities. For example, consider the major travel sites such as Expedia, Travelocity, CheapTickets, Orbitz, and Priceline. These sites used to specialize in one area of travel—inexpensive airline tickets. Now they offer a full range of travel products, including airline tickets, auto rentals, hotel rooms, tours, and last-minute trip packages. Expedia provides in-depth hotel details to help comparison shoppers and even offers 360-degree visual tours and expanded photo displays. It also entices flexible travelers to search for rates, compare airfares, and configure hotel and air prices at the same time. Expedia has developed numerous hotel partnerships to reduce costs and help secure great values for consumers. Meanwhile, Orbitz has launched a special full-service program for corporate business travelers.

Establishing a Web Site

Companies large and small can establish Web sites. Some companies elect to develop their sites in-house, but this decision requires learning HTML, Java, and Web design software. Many firms, especially those with few or no experienced Web developers, have decided that to outsource the building of their Web sites gets the Web sites up and running faster and cheaper than doing the job themselves. Web site hosting companies such as Hostway and Broad-Spire make it possible to set up a Web page and conduct e-commerce within a matter of days and with little up-front cost.

These companies can also provide free hosting for your store, but to allow visitors to pay for merchandise with credit cards, you need a merchant account with a bank. If your company doesn't already have one, it must establish one.

Web development firms can provide organizations with prebuilt templates and Web site builder tools to enable customers to construct their own Web sites. Businesses can custom design a new Web site or redesign an existing Web site. Such firms have worked with thousands of customers to help them get their Web sites up and running.

storefront broker: A company that acts as an intermediary between your Web site and online merchants who have the products and retail expertise.

Another model for setting up a Web site is the use of a storefront broker, a business that serves as an intermediary between your Web site and online merchants who have the actual products and retail expertise. The storefront broker deals with the details of the transactions, including who gets paid for what, and is responsible for bringing together merchants and reseller sites. The storefront broker is similar to a distributor in standard retail operations, but in this case, no product moves—only electronic data flows back and forth. Products are ordered by a customer at your site, orders are processed through a user interface provided by the storefront broker, and the product is shipped by the merchant.

Shopify is a Canadian-based firm that helps retailers create their own online store without all the technical work involved in developing their own Web site or the huge expense of contracting someone else to build it. Clients can select a stylish e-commerce Web site template, customize it to meet their unique needs, upload product information, and then start taking orders and accepting payments. Thousands of online retailers, including General Electric, CrossFit, Tesla Motors, Encyclopaedia Britannica, Foo Fighters, and GitHub built their Web sites with help from Shopify.[47]

Building Traffic to Your Web Site

The Internet includes hundreds of thousands of e-commerce Web sites. With all those potential competitors, a company must take strong measures to ensure that the customers it wants to attract can find its Web site. The first step is to obtain and register a domain name, which should say something about your business. For instance, stuff4u might seem to be a good catchall, but it doesn't describe the nature of the business—it could be anything. If you want to sell soccer uniforms and equipment, then you'd try to get a domain name such as *www.soccerstuff4u.com*, *www.soccerequipment.com*, or *www.stuff4soccercoaches.com*. The more specific the Web address, the better.

The next step to attracting customers is to make your site search-engine friendly by improving its rankings. Following are several ideas on how to accomplish this goal:

meta tag: An HTML code, not visible on the displayed Web page, that contains keywords representing your site's content, which search engines use to build indexes pointing to your Web site.

- Include a meta tag in your store's home page. A meta tag is an HTML code, not visible on the displayed Web page, that contains keywords representing your site's content. Search engines use these keywords to build indexes pointing to your Web site. Again, keywords are critical to attracting customers, so they should be chosen carefully. They should clearly define the scope of the products or services you offer.
- Use Web site traffic data analysis software to turn the data captured in the Web log file into useful information. This data can tell you the URLs from which your site is being accessed, the search engines and keywords that find your site, and other useful information. Using this data can help you identify search engines to which you need to market your Web site, allowing you to submit your Web pages to them for inclusion in the search engine's index.
- Provide quality, keyword-rich content. Be careful not to use too many keywords, as search engines often ban sites that do this. Judiciously place keywords throughout your site, ensuring that the Web content is sensible and easy to read by humans as well as search engines.
- Add new content to the Web site on a regular basis. Again, this makes the site attractive to humans as well as search engines.
- Acquire links to your site from other reputable Web sites that are popular and related to your Web site. Avoid the use of low-quality links, as they can actually hurt your Web site's rating.

The use of the Internet is growing rapidly in markets throughout Europe, Asia, and Latin America. Obviously, companies that want to succeed on the

Web cannot ignore this global shift. A company must be aware that consumers outside the United States will access sites with a variety of devices, and the firm should modify its site design accordingly. In Europe, for example, closed-system iDTVs (integrated digital televisions) are becoming popular for accessing online content, with more than 50 percent of the population now using them. Because such devices have better resolution and more screen space than the PC monitors that U.S. consumers use to access the Internet, iDTV users expect more ambitious graphics. Successful global firms operate with a portfolio of sites designed for each market, with shared sourcing and infrastructure to support the network of stores and with local marketing and business development teams to take advantage of local opportunities. Service providers continue to emerge to solve the cross-border logistics, payments, and customer service needs of these global retailers.

Maintaining and Improving Your Web Site

Web site operators must constantly monitor the traffic to their sites and the response times experienced by visitors. AMR Research, a Boston-based independent research analysis firm, reports that Internet shoppers expect service to be better than or equal to their in-store experience.

Nothing will drive potential customers away faster than experiencing unreasonable delays while trying to view or order products or services. To keep pace with technology and increasing traffic, it might be necessary to modify the software, databases, or hardware on which the Web site runs to ensure acceptable response times.

Toys 'R' Us recently launched a redesigned Web site with the goal of making it easier for shoppers to find gifts. According to Fred Argir, senior vice president, chief digital officer: "We wanted new ways for shoppers to engage with each other and be inspired by ideas on the site." The Web site lets shoppers place items in Pinterest-like "boards" and shows trending products on the site. The new home page highlights "hot sellers" and personalized product recommendations. Shoppers can also move between the ToysRUs.com and BabiesRUs.com sites via a tab in the upper-left corner of each Web page and check out once using a single shopping cart to buy items from the two sites.[48]

personalization: The process of tailoring Web pages to specifically target individual consumers.

Web site operators must also continually be alert to new trends and developments in the area of e-commerce and be prepared to take advantage of new opportunities. For example, recent studies show that customers more frequently visit Web sites they can customize. **Personalization** is the process of tailoring Web pages to specifically target individual consumers. The goal is to meet the customer's needs more effectively, make interactions faster and easier, and consequently, increase customer satisfaction and the likelihood of repeat visits. Building a better understanding of customer preferences can also aid in cross-selling related products and more expensive products. The most basic form of personalization involves using the consumer's name in an email campaign or in a greeting on the Web page. Amazon uses a more advanced form of personalization in which the Web site greets each repeat customer by name and recommends a list of new products based on the customer's previous purchases.

Businesses use two types of personalization techniques to capture data and build customer profiles. *Implicit personalization* techniques capture data from actual customer Web sessions—primarily based on which pages were viewed and which weren't. *Explicit personalization* techniques capture user-provided information, such as information from warranties, surveys, user registrations, and contest-entry forms completed online. Data can also be gathered through access to other data sources such as the Bureau of Motor Vehicles, Bureau of Vital Statistics, and marketing affiliates (firms that share marketing data). Marketing firms aggregate this information to build databases containing a huge amount of consumer behavioral data. During each customer interaction, powerful algorithms analyze both types of data in real time to predict the consumer's needs and interests. This analysis makes it possible to deliver new, targeted information before the customer leaves the site. Because personalization depends on gathering and using personal user information, privacy issues are a major concern.

ExactTarget's iGoDigital is a sales data program used by Amazon, Best Buy, Dell, Sears, Walmart, and many other e-commerce retailers. The software recommends items to Web site visitors that might interest them based on their purchases and Web-browsing habits. iGoDigital collects information about individual shoppers such as what items they searched for, placed in their shopping basket, or purchased. This data is then stored in a central personalization engine and is used to make shopping recommendations to individual consumers on any Web site they visit that uses the software.[49]

These tips and suggestions are only a few ideas that can help a company set up and maintain an effective e-commerce site. With technology and competition changing constantly, managers should read articles in print and on the Web to keep up to date on ever-evolving issues.

TECHNOLOGY INFRASTRUCTURE REQUIRED TO SUPPORT E-COMMERCE AND M-COMMERCE

Now that we've examined how to establish e-commerce effectively, let's look at some of the technical issues related to e-commerce systems and the technology that makes it possible. Successful implementation of e-business requires significant changes to existing business processes and substantial investment in IS technology. These technology components must be chosen carefully and be integrated to support a large volume of transactions with customers, suppliers, and other business partners worldwide. Online consumers complain that poor Web site performance (e.g., slow response time, inadequate customer support, and lost orders) drives them to abandon some e-commerce sites in favor of those with better, more reliable performance. This section provides a brief overview of the key technology infrastructure components. See Figure 8.13.

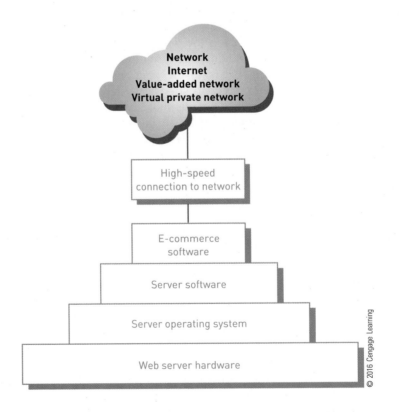

FIGURE 8.13

Key technology infrastructure components

E-commerce systems require specific kinds of hardware and software to be successful.

© 2016 Cengage Learning

Hardware

A Web server hardware platform complete with the appropriate software is a key ingredient to e-commerce infrastructure. The amount of storage capacity and computing power required of the Web server depends primarily on two things: the software that must run on the server and the volume of e-commerce transactions that must be processed. The most successful e-commerce solutions are designed to be highly scalable so that they can be upgraded to meet unexpected user traffic.

Key Web site performance measures include response time, transaction success rate, and system availability. Table 8.7 shows the values for the key measures for four popular online retailers for one week.

TABLE **8.7** Key performance measures for popular retail Web sites

Retail Apparel Firm	Response Time (seconds)	Success Rate	Outage Time During One Week
Abercrombie	4.64	98.6%	1 hour
Macy's	6.81	99.5%	0 hours
Sears	12.90	99.1%	1 hour
J Crew	7.89	97.7%	1 hour
Saks Fifth Avenue	10.59	95.7%	2 hours

Source: "Keynote Online Retail Transaction Indices," *e-Commerce Times, www.ecommercetimes.com/web-perfor mance*, February 15, 2014.

© 2016 Cengage Learning

A key decision facing a new e-commerce company is whether to host its own Web site or to let someone else do it. Many companies decide that using a third-party Web service provider is the best way to meet initial e-commerce needs. The third-party company rents space on its computer system and provides a high-speed connection to the Internet, thus minimizing the initial out-of-pocket costs for e-commerce start-up. The third party can also provide personnel trained to operate, troubleshoot, and manage the Web server.

Web Server Software

In addition to the Web server operating system, each e-commerce Web site must have Web server software to perform fundamental services, including security and identification, retrieval and sending of Web pages, Web site tracking, Web site development, and Web page development. The two most widely used Web server software packages are Apache HTTP Server and Microsoft Internet Information Services.

E-Commerce Software

After you have located or built a host server, including the hardware, operating system, and Web server software, you can begin to investigate and install e-commerce software to support five core tasks: catalog management to create and update the product catalog, product configuration to help customers select the necessary components and options, shopping cart facilities to track the items selected for purchase (see Figure 8.14), e-commerce transaction processing, and Web traffic data analysis to provide details to adjust the operations of the Web site.

Mobile Commerce Hardware and Software

For m-commerce to work effectively, the interface between the wireless, handheld device and its user must improve to the point that it is nearly as

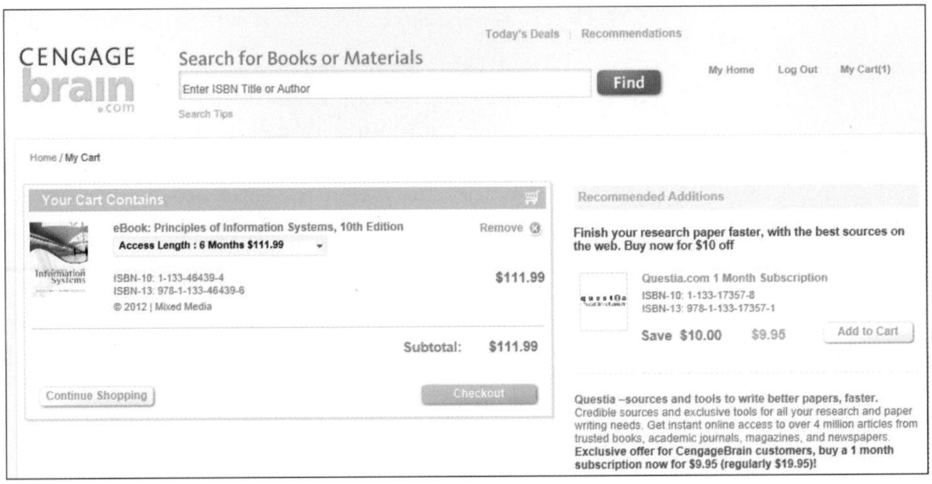

FIGURE 8.14

Electronic shopping cart

An electronic shopping cart allows online shoppers to view their selections and add or remove items.

easy to purchase an item on a wireless device as it is to purchase it on a PC. In addition, network speed must improve so that users do not become frustrated. Security is also a major concern, particularly in two areas: the security of the transmission itself and the trust that the transaction is being made with the intended party. Encryption can provide secure transmission. Digital certificates, discussed later in this chapter, can ensure that transactions are made between the intended parties.

The handheld devices used for m-commerce have several limitations that complicate their use. Their screens are small, perhaps no more than a few square inches, and might be able to display only a few lines of text. Their input capabilities are limited to a few buttons, so entering data can be tedious and error prone. They also have less processing power and less bandwidth than desktop or laptop computers, which are usually connected to a high-speed LAN. They also operate on limited-life batteries. For these reasons, it is currently impossible to directly access many Web sites with a handheld device. Web developers must rewrite Web applications so that users with handheld devices can access them.

To address the limitations of wireless devices, the industry has undertaken a standardization effort for their Internet communications. The Wireless Application Protocol (WAP) is a standard set of specifications for Internet applications that run on handheld, wireless devices. It effectively serves as a Web browser for such devices.

Electronic Payment Systems

Electronic payment systems are a key component of the e-commerce infrastructure. Current e-commerce technology relies on user identification and encryption to safeguard business transactions. Actual payments are made in a variety of ways, including electronic cash, electronic wallets, and smart, credit, charge, and debit cards. Web sites that accept multiple payment types convert more visitors to purchasing customers than merchants who offer only a single payment method.

Authentication technologies are used by many organizations to confirm the identity of a user requesting access to information or assets. A digital certificate is an attachment to an email message or data embedded in a Web site that verifies the identity of a sender or Web site. A certificate authority (CA) is a trusted third-party organization or company that issues digital certificates. The CA is responsible for guaranteeing that the people or organizations granted these unique certificates are in fact who they claim to be. Digital certificates thus create a trust chain throughout the transaction, verifying both purchaser and supplier identities.

digital certificate: An attachment to an email message or data embedded in a Web site that verifies the identity of a sender or Web site.

certificate authority (CA): A trusted third-party organization or company that issues digital certificates.

Many organizations that accept credit cards to pay for items purchased via e-commerce have adopted the Payment Card Industry (PCI) security standard. This standard spells out measures and security procedures to safeguard the card issuer, the cardholder, and the merchant. Some of the measures include installing and maintaining a firewall configuration to control access to computers and data, never using software or hardware vendor-supplier defaults for system passwords, and requiring merchants to protect stored data, encrypt transmission of cardholder information across public networks, use and regularly update antivirus software, and restrict access to sensitive data on a need-to-know basis.

Various measures are being implemented to increase the security associated with the use of credit cards at the time of purchase. The Address Verification System is a check built into the payment authorization request that compares the address on file with the card issuer to the billing address provided by the cardholder. The Card Verification Number technique is a check of the additional digits printed on the back of the card. Visa has Advanced Authorization, a Visa-patented process that provides an instantaneous rating of that transaction's potential for fraud to the financial institution that issued the card. The card issuer can then send an immediate response to the merchant regarding whether to accept or decline the transaction. The technology is now being applied to every Visa credit and check card purchase today. Visa estimates that this technique will reduce fraudulent credit card charges by 40 percent.

The Federal Financial Institutions Examination Council has developed a new set of guidelines called "Authentication in an Internet Banking Environment," which recommend two-factor authorization. This approach adds another identity check along with the password system. A number of multifactor authentication schemes can be used, such as biometrics, one-time passwords, or hardware tokens that plug into a USB port on the computer and generate a password that matches the ones used by a bank's security system. Currently, the use of biometric technology to secure online transactions is rare for both cost and privacy reasons. It can be expensive to outfit every merchant with a biometric scanner, and it is difficult to convince consumers to supply something as personal and distinguishing as a fingerprint. In spite of these problems, a growing number of financial service firms from large (e.g., Citibank) to small (e.g., Purdue Employees Federal Credit Union) are considering biometric systems.

Voice biometrics is used to combat the rising occurrence of fraud in contact centers resulting from attacks by sophisticated fraudsters. These criminals use information from social networks and identity theft of personal identification information in an attempt to dupe customer service agents and bypass traditional caller verification techniques. The system identifies fraudulent calls and as a result saves an organization tens of thousands of dollars in fraud losses each day.[50]

Secure Sockets Layer

Secure Sockets Layer (SSL): A communications protocol used to secure sensitive data during e-commerce.

All online shoppers fear the theft of credit card numbers and banking information. To help prevent this type of identity theft, the Secure Sockets Layer (SSL) communications protocol is used to secure sensitive data. The SSL communications protocol includes a handshake stage, which authenticates the server (and the client, if needed), determines the encryption and hashing algorithms to be used, and exchanges encryption keys. Following the handshake stage, data might be transferred. The data is always encrypted, ensuring that your transactions are not subject to interception or "sniffing" by a third party. Although SSL handles the encryption part of a secure e-commerce transaction, a digital certificate is necessary to provide server identification.

Electronic Cash

Electronic cash is an amount of money that is computerized, stored, and used as cash for e-commerce transactions. Typically, consumers must open an account with an electronic cash service provider by providing identification information. When the consumers want to withdraw electronic cash to make a purchase, they access the service provider via the Internet and present proof of identity—a digital certificate issued by a certification authority or a username and password. After verifying a consumer's identity, the system debits the consumer's account and credits the seller's account with the amount of the purchase. PayPal, BillMeLater, MoneyZap, and TeleCheck are four popular forms of electronic cash.

PayPal enables any person or business with an email address to securely, easily, and quickly send and receive payments online. To send money, you enter the recipient's email address and the amount you want to send. You can pay with a credit card, debit card, or funds from a checking account. The recipient gets an email message that says, "You've Got Cash!" Recipients can then collect their money by clicking a link in the email message that takes them to *www.paypal.com*. To receive the money, the user also must have a credit card or checking account to accept fund transfers. To request money for an auction, invoice a customer, or send a personal bill, you enter the recipient's email address and the amount you are requesting. The recipient gets an email message and instructions on how to pay you using PayPal. Today over 140 million Internet users use PayPal to send money and some 90 percent of eBay purchases go through PayPal.[51]

PayPal is rolling out Beacon, a hardware device for merchants that uses Bluetooth technology to improve the shopper's experience. Consumers must download the PayPal app to their smartphone and opt in to the service to use Beacon for hands-free check-in and payments. Beacon can communicate with compatible point-of-sale systems from Erply, Leaf, Leapset, Micros, NCR, ShopKeep, or Vend. When Beacon consumers walk into a store, Beacon will trigger a vibration or sound to confirm a successful check-in and their photo will appear on the screen of the merchant's point-of-sale system so they can be identified. Payment requires only a verbal confirmation and a receipt is emailed to the consumer. Using Beacon, a drugstore could fill your prescriptions or your name could be added to a wait list for tables at a restaurant simply by walking into the establishment.[52]

Credit, Charge, Debit, and Smart Cards

Many online shoppers use credit and charge cards for most of their Internet purchases. A credit card, such as Visa or MasterCard, has a preset spending limit based on the user's credit history, and each month the user can pay all or part of the amount owed. Interest is charged on the unpaid amount. A charge card, such as American Express, carries no preset spending limit, and the entire amount charged to the card is due at the end of the billing period. Charge cards do not involve lines of credit and do not accumulate interest charges. American Express became the first company to offer disposable credit card numbers in 2000. Other banks, such as Citibank, protect the consumer by providing a unique number for each transaction. Debit cards look like credit cards, but they operate like cash or a personal check. Credit, charge, and debit cards currently store limited information about you on a magnetic strip. This information is read each time the card is swiped to make a purchase. All credit card customers are protected by law from paying more than $50 for fraudulent transactions.

The **smart card** is a credit card–sized device with an embedded microchip to provide electronic memory and processing capability. Smart cards can be used for a variety of purposes, including storing a user's financial facts, health insurance data, credit card numbers, and network identification codes and passwords. They can also store monetary values for spending.

Smart cards are better protected from misuse than conventional credit, charge, and debit cards because the smart-card information is encrypted. Conventional credit, charge, and debit cards clearly show your account number on the face of the card. The card number, along with a forged signature, is all that a thief needs to purchase items and charge them against your card. A smart card makes credit theft practically impossible because a key to unlock the encrypted information is required, and there is no external number that a thief can identify and no physical signature a thief can forge. Table 8.8 compares various types of payment systems.

TABLE **8.8** Comparison of payment systems

Payment System	Description	Advantages	Disadvantages
Credit card	Carries preset spending limit based on the user's credit history	Each month the user can pay all or part of the amount owed	Unpaid balance accumulates interest charges—often at a high rate of interest
Charge card	Looks like a credit card but carries no preset spending limit	Does not involve lines of credit and does not accumulate interest charges	The entire amount charged to the card is due at the end of the billing period
Debit card	Looks like a credit card or automated teller machine (ATM) card	Operates like cash or a personal check	Money is immediately deducted from user's account balance
Smart card	Is a credit card device with embedded microchip capable of storing facts about cardholder	Better protected from misuse than conventional credit, charge, and debit cards because the smart card information is encrypted	Not widely used in the United States

© 2016 Cengage Learning

P-Card

p-card (procurement card or purchasing card): A credit card used to streamline the traditional purchase order and invoice payment processes.

A p-card (procurement card or purchasing card) is a credit card used to streamline the traditional purchase order and invoice payment processes. The p-card is typically issued to selected employees who must follow company rules and guidelines that may include a single purchase limit, a monthly spending limit, or merchant category code restrictions. Due to an increased risk of unauthorized purchases, each p-card holder's spending activity is reviewed periodically by someone independent of the cardholder to ensure adherence to the guidelines. Spending on p-cards has increased from $196 billion in 2012 to $229 billion in 2013.[53]

Payments Using Cell Phones

The use of cell phones has become commonplace to make purchases and transfer funds between consumers. Two options are available: payments linked to your bank account and payments added to your phone bill. The goals are to make the payment process as simple and secure as possible and for it to work on many different phones and through many different cell phone service providers—not simple tasks. Fortunately, the intelligence built into the iPhone and other smartphones can make this all possible.

You can use several services (e.g., Phone Transact iMerchant Pro, Square, RoamPay, and PayWare Mobile) to plug a credit card reader device into the headphone jack on a cell phone to accept credit card payments. Intuit's GoPayment service does not require a credit card reader but provides software that lets you enter the credit card number.

With Xipwire, consumers can text someone with a special code to place a purchase on their monthly phone bill and bypass any credit card system altogether. A free Starbucks Card Mobile app that runs on iPhones, iPod Touches, and some BlackBerry smartphones enables customers to pay for their java by holding their mobile device in front of a scanner that reads the app's on-screen barcode. Registered customers link their credit card information to their Starbucks.com account.

SUMMARY

Principle:

Electronic and mobile commerce are evolving, providing new ways of conducting business that present both potential benefits and problems.

Electronic commerce is the conducting of business activities (e.g., distribution, buying, selling, marketing, and servicing of products or services) electronically over computer networks. Business-to-business (B2B) e-commerce allows manufacturers to buy at a low cost worldwide, and offers enterprises the chance to sell to a global market. B2B e-commerce is currently the type of e-commerce with the greatest dollar volume of sales. Business-to-consumer (B2C) e-commerce enables organizations to sell directly to consumers, eliminating intermediaries. In many cases, this practice squeezes costs and inefficiencies out of the supply chain and can lead to higher profits and lower prices for consumers. Consumer-to-consumer (C2C) e-commerce involves consumers selling directly to other consumers. Online auctions are the chief method by which C2C e-commerce is currently conducted. e-Government involves the use of information and communications technology to simplify the sharing of information, speed formerly paper-based processes, and improve the relationship between citizens and government.

A successful e-commerce system must address the many stages consumers experience in the sales life cycle. At the heart of any e-commerce system is the ability of the user to search for and identify items for sale; select those items; negotiate prices, terms of payment, and delivery date; send an order to the vendor to purchase the items; pay for the product or service; obtain product delivery; and receive after-sales support.

From the perspective of the provider of goods or services, an effective e-commerce system must be able to support the activities associated with supply chain management and customer relationship management.

A firm must overcome three key challenges to convert its business processes from the traditional form to e-commerce processes: (1) it must deal effectively with consumer privacy concerns, (2) it must successfully overcome consumers' lack of trust, and (3) overcome global issues.

Mobile commerce is the use of wireless devices such as cell phones and smartphones to facilitate the sale of goods or services—anytime and anywhere. The market for m-commerce in North America is expected to mature much later than in Western Europe and Japan. Numerous retailers have established special Web sites for users of mobile devices.

Principle:

E-commerce and m-commerce can be used in many innovative ways to improve the operations of an organization.

Electronic retailing (e-tailing) is the direct sale from a business to consumers through electronic storefronts designed around an electronic catalog and shopping cart model.

A cybermall is a single Web site that offers many products and services at one Internet location.

Manufacturers are joining electronic exchanges, where they can work with competitors and suppliers to use computers and Web sites to buy and sell goods, trade market information, and run back-office operations, such as inventory control. They are also using e-commerce to improve the efficiency of the selling process by moving customer queries about product availability and prices online.

The Web allows firms to gather much more information about customer behavior and preferences than they could using other marketing approaches. This new technology has greatly enhanced the practice of market segmentation and enabled companies to establish closer relationships with their customers.

The Internet has revolutionized the world of investment and finance, especially online stock trading and online banking. The Internet has also created many options for electronic auctions, where geographically dispersed buyers and sellers can come together.

The numerous m-commerce applications include advertising, bartering, retargeting, price comparison, couponing, investment and finance, banking, and e-boutiques.

Principle:

E-commerce and m-commerce offer many advantages yet raise many challenges.

Businesses and people use e-commerce and m-commerce to reduce transaction costs, speed the flow of goods and information, improve the level of customer service, and enable the close coordination of actions among manufacturers, suppliers, and customers.

E-commerce and m-commerce also enable consumers and companies to gain access to worldwide markets. They offer great promise for developing countries, enabling them to enter the prosperous global marketplace and hence helping to reduce the gap between rich and poor countries.

Because e-commerce and m-commerce are global systems, they face cultural, language, time and distance, infrastructure, currency, product and service, and state, regional, and national law challenges.

Principle:

Organizations must define and execute a strategy to be successful in e-commerce and m-commerce.

Most people agree that an effective Web site is one that creates an attractive presence and meets the needs of its visitors. E-commerce start-ups must decide whether they will build and operate the Web site themselves or outsource this function. Web site hosting services and storefront brokers provide alternatives to building your own Web site.

To build traffic to your Web site, you should register a domain name that is relevant to your business, make your site search-engine friendly by including a meta tag in your home page, use Web site traffic data analysis software to attract additional customers, and modify your Web site so that it supports global commerce. Web site operators must constantly monitor the traffic and response times associated with their sites and adjust software, databases, and hardware to ensure that visitors have a good experience when they visit.

Principle:

E-commerce and m-commerce require the careful planning and integration of a number of technology infrastructure components.

A number of infrastructure components must be chosen and integrated to support a large volume of transactions with customers, suppliers, and other business partners worldwide. These components include hardware, Web server software, and e-commerce software.

M-commerce presents additional infrastructure challenges, including improving the ease of use of wireless devices, addressing the security of wireless transactions, and improving network speed. The Wireless Application Protocol (WAP) is a standard set of specifications to enable development of m-commerce software for wireless devices. The development of WAP and its derivatives addresses many m-commerce issues.

Electronic payment systems are a key component of the e-commerce infrastructure. A digital certificate is an attachment to an email message or data embedded in a Web page that verifies the identity of a sender or a Web site. To help prevent the theft of credit card numbers and banking information, the Secure Sockets Layer (SSL) communications protocol is used to secure all sensitive data. Several electronic cash alternatives require the purchaser to open an account with an electronic cash service provider and to present proof of identity whenever payments are to be made. Payments can also be made by credit, charge, debit, smart cards, and p-cards. Retail and banking industries are developing means to enable payments using the cell phone like a credit card.

KEY TERMS

electronic commerce (e-commerce)

business-to-business (B2B) e-commerce

business-to-consumer (B2C) e-commerce

consumer-to-consumer (C2C) e-commerce

e-government

identity theft

electronic retailing (e-tailing)

cybermall

electronic exchange

market segmentation

storefront broker

meta tag

personalization

digital certificate

certificate authority (CA)

Secure Sockets Layer (SSL)

electronic cash

smart card

p-card (procurement card or purchasing card)

CHAPTER 8: SELF-ASSESSMENT TEST

Electronic and mobile commerce are evolving, providing new ways of conducting business that present both potential benefits and problems.

1. _____ e-commerce activities include identifying and comparing competitive suppliers and products, negotiating and establishing prices and terms, ordering and tracking shipments, and steering organizational buyers to preferred suppliers and products.

2. _____ involves conducting business activities (e.g., distribution, buying, selling, marketing, and servicing of products or services) electronically over computer networks.
   a. B2B
   b. C2C
   c. B2C
   d. E-commerce

3. The average order size for B2C commerce is greater than B2B. True or False?

4. The largest B2C retailer in the United States is _____.
   a. Amazon
   b. Staples
   c. Apple
   d. Walmart

5. _____ of total retail sales is sold online.
   a. Around 2 percent
   b. Roughly 5 percent
   c. More than 10 percent
   d. Nearly 20 percent

E-commerce and m-commerce can be used in many innovative ways to improve the operations of an organization.

6. The Web has greatly enhanced the practice of market segmentation and enabled companies to establish closer relationships with their customers. True or False?

7. _____ is *not* a key challenge for e-commerce.
   a. Dealing with consumer privacy concerns
   b. Training customers on how to access and use e-commerce Web sites
   c. Overcoming consumers' lack of trust
   d. Overcoming global issues

8. The Internet Corporation for Assigned Names and Numbers (ICANN) created a domain called _____ to attract mobile users to the Web.

E-commerce and m-commerce offer many advantages yet raise many challenges.

9. A(n) _____ is an electronic forum where manufacturers, suppliers, and competitors buy and sell goods, trade market information, and run back-office operations, such as inventory control.
   a. B2B e-commerce Web site
   b. electronic exchange
   c. electronic storefront
   d. e-tailer

10. _____ is the direct sale of products or services by businesses to consumers through electronic storefronts, which are typically designed around the familiar electronic catalog and shopping cart model.

11. An average of 75 percent of all online shopping carts were abandoned, amounting to over $12 billion in lost sales for 2011. True or False?

12. Businesses are willing to _____ as a means to reduce excess inventory, gain new customers, or avoid paying cash for necessary raw materials or services.

13. The _____ security standard spells out measures and security procedures to safeguard the card issuer, the cardholder, and the merchant.

Organizations must define and execute a strategy to be successful in e-commerce and m-commerce.

14. Although companies can select from a number of approaches, the most successful e-commerce models include three basic components: community, content, and _____.

15. Web site hosting companies make it possible to set up a Web page and conduct e-commerce within a matter of days and with few up-front costs. True or False?

E-commerce and m-commerce require the careful planning and integration of a number of technology infrastructure components.

16. The amount of storage capacity and computing power required of a Web server depends primarily on _____.
   a. the geographical location of the server and number of different products sold
   b. the software that must run on the server and the volume of e-commerce transactions
   c. the size of the business organization and the location of its customers
   d. the number of potential customers and average dollar value of each transaction

17. Key Web site performance measures include response time, transaction success rate, and system availability. True or False?

CHAPTER 8: SELF-ASSESSMENT TEST ANSWERS

1. Buy-side
2. d.
3. False
4. a.
5. b.
6. True
7. b.
8. .mobi
9. b.
10. Electronic retailing or e-tailing
11. False
12. barter
13. Payment Card Industry or PCI
14. commerce
15. True
16. b.
17. True

REVIEW QUESTIONS

1. Briefly define the term electronic commerce, and identify five forms of electronic commerce based on the parties involved in the transactions.

2. How does the dollar volume of U.S. B2B e-commerce compare to the volume of B2C e-commerce?

3. Identify three top IS priorities related to e-commerce.

4. What region in the world has the greatest B2C sales? Which country has the greatest B2C sales?

5. What tools are available to help shoppers compare prices, features, and values and check other shoppers' opinions?

6. What are Web-influenced sales?
7. Identify the six stages consumers experience in the sales life cycle that must be supported by a successful e-commerce system.
8. Identify three key challenges that an organization faces in creating a successful e-commerce operation.
9. Outline at least three specific trust-building strategies for an organization to gain the trust of consumers.
10. What is electronic couponing and how does it work? What are some of the issues with electronic couponing?

11. What is an electronic exchange? Identify and briefly describe three types of exchanges based on who operates the exchange.
12. What is the two-step authentication process associated with items purchased via e-commerce?
13. Why is it necessary to continue to maintain and improve an existing Web site?
14. Identify the key elements of the technology infrastructure required to successfully implement e-commerce within an organization.

DISCUSSION QUESTIONS

1. Briefly discuss three models for selling mobile ad impressions. What are the primary measures for the success of mobile advertising?
2. Discuss—Should Congress implement a national solution for collecting sales tax on e-commerce purchases? Support your position with three sound arguments.
3. Why are many manufacturers and retailers outsourcing the physical logistics of delivering merchandise to shoppers? What advantages does such a strategy offer? What are the potential issues or disadvantages?
4. What is retargeting? What are some strategies used to retarget Web site visitors?
5. What are some of the privacy concerns that shoppers have with e-commerce?

6. Identify three specific actions an organization can take to overcome consumers' lack of trust.
7. Identify and briefly discuss three reasons for the steady growth in B2C e-commerce.
8. Identify and briefly describe three m-commerce applications you have used.
9. Discuss the use of e-commerce to improve spending on manufacturing, repair, and operations (MRO) of goods and services.
10. Outline the key steps in developing a corporate global e-commerce strategy.
11. Identify three kinds of business organizations that would have difficulty in becoming successful e-commerce organizations.
12. Identify five major global issues that deter the spread of e-commerce. What steps can an organization take to overcome these barriers?

PROBLEM-SOLVING EXERCISES

1. Use PowerPoint or some other presentation preparation software to produce a presentation of the key steps that an organization must take to avoid a data breach.
2. Develop a set of criteria you would use to evaluate various business-to-consumer Web sites based on factors such as ease of use, response time, availability, protection of consumer data, and security of payment process. Develop a simple spreadsheet containing these criteria. Evaluate three popular Web sites using the criteria you developed. Draft a recommendation of specific

changes that you recommend to the Web developer of the site that scored lowest.
3. Your refrigerator just gave out and must be replaced within the week! Use your Web-enabled smartphone (or borrow a friend's) to perform a price and product comparison to identify the manufacturer and model that best meets your needs and the retailer with the lowest delivered cost. Obtain peer input to validate your choice. Write a brief summary of your experience, and identify the Web sites you found most useful.

TEAM ACTIVITIES

1. Imagine that your team has been hired as consultants to a large organization that has just suffered a major public relations setback due to a large-scale

data breach that it handled poorly. Identify three key things that the organization must not do if it wishes to regain consumer confidence.

2. As a team, develop a set of criteria that you would use to evaluate the effectiveness of a mobile advertising campaign to boost the popularity of a candidate for an elected state government position. Identify the measures you would use and the data that must be gathered.

WEB EXERCISES

1. Do research to capture data on the growth of B2C e-commerce and retail sales over the past 10 years. Use the charting capability of your spreadsheet software to plot the growth of B2C e-commerce and retail sales and predict the year that B2C e-commerce will exceed 10 percent of retail sales. Document any assumptions you make.

2. Do research on the Web to find a dozen Web sites that offer mobile coupons. Separate the sites into two groups: those that provide coupons for a single retailer and those that aggregate coupons for multiple retailers. Produce a table that summarizes your results and shows the approximate number of coupons available at each site.

CAREER EXERCISES

1. Do research to identify three top organizations for developing and operating e-commerce Web sites for their clients. Visit their Web sites and identify current job openings. What sort of responsibilities are associated with these positions? What experience and education requirements are needed to fill these positions? Do any of these positions appeal to you?

2. For your chosen career field, describe how you might use or be involved with e-commerce. If you have not chosen a career yet, answer this question for someone in marketing, finance, or human resources.

CASE STUDIES

Case One

MobiKash: Bringing Financial Services to Rural Africa

Full participation in the twenty-first century economy requires access to financial services. However, this access is a luxury for many citizens of African nations. Due to the long distances between bank branches and the lack of rapid, cost-effective transportation to the urban areas in which banks are typically found, fewer than 10 percent of Africans participate in formal banking. Those who do often face time-consuming inefficiencies.

A new company, MobiKash Afrika, hopes to change this by empowering people in Africa with a secure and independent mobile commerce system that is easy to use. In planning its system, MobiKash established several standards:

- The service must be independent of specific mobile telephone operators.
- The service must be independent of specific banks or financial institutions.
- The service must work with all bill issuers.
- The service must not require smartphones or high-end feature phones.

MobiKash offers its members five services, all accessible from a mobile phone: loading money into their MobiKash account from any bank account, paying bills, sending money to any other mobile phone user or bank account, managing a bank or MobiKash account, and obtaining or depositing cash. Only the last pair of services requires members to visit a physical location where cash can be handled, but that site doesn't have to be a bank. MobiKash agents in market towns, convenient to rural areas, can handle transactions that require cash. Approximately 3,000 MobiKash agents operate in Kenya. Account holders don't even need to visit a bank to set up their MobiKash accounts: in fact, anyone with a mobile phone to whom a MobiKash user sends money becomes a MobiKash user automatically.

MobiKash charges for some services. Withdrawing cash costs 25 to 75 Kenya shillings (KShs) (about U.S. $0.30 to $0.90), for withdrawals up to KShs 10,000 (about U.S. $20), with higher fees for larger withdrawals. Paying bills from a mobile phone incurs a fixed fee of KShs 25, no matter how large the bill is. The largest fee that MobiKash charges is KShs 350 (about U.S. $4), for cash withdrawals in excess of KShs 75,000 (about U.S. $900). This fee schedule is consistent with the financial resources of MobiKash users and the value those users place on each financial service.

The MobiKash system is based on Sybase 365 mCommerce software. Several factors contributed to this choice, including the local presence of Sybase in Africa with experience in similar applications, its understanding of how to integrate with African financial institutions, and the system's ability to work with any mobile telephone. It operates from an existing Sybase data center in Frankfurt, Germany.

MobiKash services expects to expand in east, west, and southern Africa, starting with Zimbabwe. It is working with Masary, an Egyptian e-wallet firm, to cover northern Africa as well. Work is also under way to support intercontinental fund transfers to and from North America, Europe, and the Middle East. As for the future, CEO Duncan Otieno said, "We see

MobiKash in the next five years playing with the international or global mobile commerce space in at least 40 countries. The plans for building this network are already in progress."

Discussion Questions

1. Firms can base m-commerce systems on commercially available software, as MobiKash did here. Alternatively, they can write their own software. List three pros and cons of each approach. Do you think MobiKash made the right choice?

2. What companies or industries might be more likely to use commercially available software to meet their main goals? What companies or industries would be less likely?

Critical Thinking Questions

1. What challenges does a company like MobiKash face when they try to penetrate different national markets in developing countries? Why might Kenya be a good choice for the launch of m-commerce operations in Africa?

2. Contrast your m-commerce needs with those of a typical rural African. Would you find the MobiKash offering attractive in full, in part (which parts?), or not at all?

SOURCES: Masary Web site, *www.e-masary.com*, accessed March 1, 2012; MobiKash Afrika, "The First Intra-region Mobile Network and Bank Agnostic Mobile Commerce Solution," *Computerworld* case study, *www.eiseverywhere.com/file_uploads/e1bfbec2f385506b3890cbd7e b7e9dd9_MobiKash_Afrika_-_The_First_Intra-region_Mobile_Network_ and_Bank_Agnostic_Mobile_Commerce_Solution.pdf*, accessed March 1, 2012; MobiKash Africa Web site, *www.mobikash.com*, accessed March 1, 2012; "Reaching the Unbanked in a MobiKash World," interview with CEO Duncan Otieno, *MobileWorld, www.mobileworldmag.com/reaching-the -unbanked-in-a-mobikash-world/*, December 28, 2011; Sybase, "MobiKash Africa: Customer Case Study," *www.sybase.com/files/Success_Stories /Mobikash-CS.pdf*, accessed March 1, 2012.

Case Two

Kramp Group, A Million Spare Parts—and Counting

Kramp Group is Europe's largest distributor of accessories and parts for motorized equipment, agriculture, and construction machines. That may not sound glamorous, but as IT manager Robert Varga explains, "Modern agriculture is highly mechanized: it is impossible to run a farm successfully without tractors, harvesters and other machinery. If a critical component fails and puts one of our customers' machines out of action, the loss of productivity can cost them serious amounts of money. We have a catalogue of more than 700,000 spare parts which can be delivered within a single working day from any of our European warehouses to their nearest dealership, helping them get back up and running as quickly as possible."

Kramp Group CEO Eddie Perdok says, "We believe in the future and the power of e-commerce. Compared to other sales channels, the Internet gives us significant cost advantages."

Yet, to Kramp's customers, using the Internet isn't automatic. Kramp takes more than 50,000 customer orders every day from various channels. Prior to 2010, "nearly 40 percent of our customers still placed their orders by phone, which meant that our call center staff had to spend a lot of time on basic order-processing," says Varga. To reduce that figure, Kramp had to make its online store easier to use—but their existing store, which had been developed in-house, did not have the flexibility to achieve this goal.

Kramp turned to software packages from IBM and German software firm Heiler AG to modernize its e-commerce systems. Hans Scholten, a member of Kramp Group's executive board, says, "We deliberately opt for the 'best of breed' solution for all packages. That means we choose the best available software for different applications." That philosophy helped determine the packages the company chose.

From IBM, the firm obtained WebSphere Commerce for the customer-facing side of its system. This software's multilanguage capability was important: Operating throughout Europe as Kramp does, being able to have one site that can operate in any of 10 languages was crucial. Nevertheless, Kramp had to translate the content into all the languages, because in 2012 even the best automatic translation software couldn't replace a skilled person. However, the advantage was that the company didn't have to develop and support different sites.

Kramp also uses Heiler Software's Product Information Management (PIM) solution. That software manages product data in the catalog behind WebSphere Commerce. Kramp wants to expand its deliverable stock to over 1 million items and couldn't do so without PIM. Expanding to more than 1 million stocked items is crucial to Kramp's "long tail" strategy: the concept that each of the slow-selling items may not account for much revenue but that the total of all slow-selling items is large enough to make a difference to Kramp's success.

Finally, though Kramp has the in-house capability to manage its e-commerce system, it turned to CDC Software to help integrate the pieces. Doing so itself would have required the company to hire additional staff, which it wouldn't need when the project was done.

The result was that after Kramp's new system had been online, 90 percent of their customers chose to order online via the WebSphere Commerce solution. As a result, the company saw a significant reduction in the average cost per transaction." Varga reported, "Our call center staff now has more time to help customers solve complex problems, which improves customer service. Better service and lower operational costs are helping Kramp Group achieve 10 to 12 percent annual growth, so the solution is making a real contribution to the success of our business."

Discussion Questions

1. How do other types of e-commerce, such as business-to-consumer (B2C), differ from Kramp Group's business-to-business (B2B) e-commerce?

2. Kramp sees e-commerce as a complement to its call center operations. In this light, what risks did Kramp

need to accommodate when creating the IT infrastructure they now possess?

Critical Thinking Questions

1. What is Kramp's "long tail" strategy and why has it been effective?
2. What other types businesses and industries might benefit from the use of a "long tail" strategy?

SOURCES: "Kramp Focuses on Long Tail and Efficient Customer Response in Its E-Commerce Strategy," Heiler Software AG, *www .informatica.com/Images/02547_kramp-longtail-ecommerce_cs_en -US.pdf*, August 11, 2011; "Kramp Group Cuts Transaction Costs and Enhances Customer Service," IBM Commerce case study *www14.software.ibm.com/webapp/iwm/web/signup.do?source=swg -smartercommerce&S_PKG=500007153&S_CMP=web_ibm_ws_ comm_cntrmid_b2b* (free registration required), accessed March 1, 2012; Kramp Group Web site (English), *www.kramp.com/shop/action /start_60_-1*, accessed March 1, 2012; "Aptean Implemented a Flexible System for Order Fulfillment to Manage Distribution of 600,000 Parts across Europe," Aptean Web site, *www.aptean.com/en/Resource -Library/Customer-Success/Kramp-Group*, accessed February 23, 2014. "Grene and Kramp Join Forces to Become Europe's Largest Agro-Wholesaler," *Shouw+Co*, August 28, 2013, *www.schouw.dk/All -news.554.aspx?recordid554=204.*

Questions for Web Case

See the Web site for this book to read about the Altitude Online case for this chapter. The following are questions concerning this Web case.

Altitude Online: Electronic and Mobile Commerce

Discussion Questions

1. How does Altitude Online's Web site contribute to the company's commerce?
2. How will the new ERP system impact Altitude Online's Web presence?

Critical Thinking Questions

1. How can companies like Altitude Online, which sell services rather than physical products, use e-commerce to attract customers and streamline operations?
2. Consider a company like Fluid by reviewing its site, *www.fluid.com*. Fluid is similar to Altitude Online in the services it offers. What site features do you think are effective for e-commerce? How might you design the site differently?

NOTES

Sources for the opening vignette: Dhawan, Sugandh, "10 Reasons Why Mobile Commerce in India May Get Bigger than Online Commerce," iamwire, October 25, 2013, *www .iamwire.com/2013/10/10-reasons-mobile-commerce-india -bigger-online-commerce*; Mitra, Moinak and Sachitanand, Rahul, "Mobile Devices Will Redefine How E-Commerce Companies Do Business," *The Economic Times*, December 20, 2013, *http://articles.economictimes.indiatimes.com/2013 -12-30/news/45711181_1_airtel-money-pizza-india-bharti -airtel*; Bharti Airtel Web site, *www.airtel.in/about-bharti /about-bharti-airtel*.

1. "Building a World-Class B2B eCommerce Business," *Forrester Research*, January 7, 2013, *www.forrester.com /Building+A+WorldClass+B2B+eCommerce+Business /fulltext/-/-E-RES89642?objectid=RES89642*.
2. Davis, Don, "Signs Point Up for B2B e-Commerce," *Internet Retailer*, November 21, 2013, *www.internetre tailer.com/2013/11/21/signs-point-b2b-e-commerce*.
3. "2013 B2B Commerce Trends," *Oracle*, April 2013, *www.oracle.com/us/products/applications/atg/2013 -b2b-commerce-trends-1939002.pdf*.
4. "Grainger Reports Record Results for the Year Ended December 31, 2013," *Grainger Press Release*, January 24, 2014, *http://pressroom.grainger.com/phoenix.zhtml? c=194987&p=irol-newsArticle&ID=1893406&highlight=*.
5. It's here. The New Grainger iPad App, *www.grainger .com/content/mobile-features?cm_re=Section2-_-iPad Launch_20131122-_-Global*, accessed February 7, 2014.
6. Davis, Don, "Signs Point Up for B2B e-Commerce," *Internet Retailer*, November 21, 2013, *www.internetre tailer.com/2013/11/21/signs-point-b2b-e-commerce*.

7. "Global B2C E-Commerce Trends Report 2013," *CNBC*, October 2, 2013, *www.cnbc.com/id/101080838*.
8. "Global B2C E-Commerce Sales & Shares Report 2013," *CNBC*, October 2, 2013, *www.cnbc.com/id/101080838*.
9. "Brooks Brothers Is Getting into the Online Custom Business," *Women's Wear Daily*, January 15, 2013, *www.fluidretail.com/brooks-brothers-bringing-custom -business-online/*.
10. Sara, "5 B2C Pinteresting Marketing Lessons from Nordstrom, Williams-Sonoma, Barney's, Neiman Marcus & Vera Bradley," *Top Rank Blog*, *www.toprankblog .com/2012/06/5-b2c-marketing-lessons-pinterest/*, accessed February 9, 2014.
11. "About Shopycat," *www.facebook.com/Shopycat/info*, accessed February 9, 2014.
12. "At the #NRF13: Web-Influenced Purchases Drive Retail Sales (Both Online and Offline)," *Review Trackers*, January 13, 2013, *www.reviewtrackers.com/nrf13-web -influenced-purchases-drive-retail-sales-both-online-off line/*.
13. Barnes, Robert, "Supreme Court Declines Case on Making Online Retailers Collect Sales Taxes," *Washington Post*, December 2, 2013, *washingtonpost.com/Politics /Supreme-Court-Declines-Case-On-Making-Online -Retailers-Collect-Sales-Taxes/2013/12/02/E430ec8c -55f5-11e3-835d-E7173847c7cc_Story.html*.
14. Luo, Michael, McIntire, Mike, and Palmre, Griff, "Seeking Gun or Selling One, Web Is a Land of Few Rules," *The New York Times*, April 17, 2013, *www .nytimes.com/2013/04/17/us/seeking-gun-or-selling -one-web-is-a-land-of-few-rules.html?pagewanted= all&_r=0*.

15. Nussbaum, Alex, "Accenture Wins U.S. Contract for Obamacare Enrollment Website," *Bloomberg*, January 12, 2014, *www.bloomberg.com/news/2014-01-12 /accenture-wins-u-s-contract-for-obamacare-enrollment -website.html*.

16. "Oregon e-Government Program," *www.oregon.gov /DAS/ETS/EGOV/pages/ecommerce.aspx*, accessed February 10, 2014.

17. "Global B2C e-Commerce Trends Report 2013," *CNBC*, October 2, 2013, *www.cnbc.com/id/101080838*.

18. Jones, Chuck, "Ecommerce Is Growing Nicely while Mcommerce Is on A Tear," *Forbes*, October 2, 2013, *www.forbes.com/sites/chuckjones/2013/10/02/ecom merce-is-growing-nicely-while-mcommerce-is-on-a-tear/*.

19. Kennedy, John, "Retailer Harry Corry Invests Stg£10k In E-Commerce And Digital Marketing," Silicon Republic, March 27, 2013, *www.siliconrepublic.com/business /item/32044-retailer-harry-corry-invest*.

20. "Reducing Shipping Costs for Low-Volume Merchants," *Practical eCommerce*, February 1, 2012, *www.practical ecommerce.com/articles/3333-Reducing-Shipping -Costs-for-Low-Volume-Merchants*.

21. Brewster, Polly, "Need a Beer? These Ballpark Apps Are Changing How You Get One," *Entrepreneur*, May 22, 2013, *www.entrepreneur.com/article/226770*.

22. "Progressive Automotive Systems Expands e-Commerce Offerings by Integrating Its R.O. Writer Software with DST TurboParts," *AutoChannel*, January 20, 2012, *www.theautochannel.com/news/2012/01/18/021456 -progressive-automotive-systems-inc-expands-e-com merce-offerings-by-integrating.html*.

23. Morphy, Erika, "T-Mobile Gives Customers No-fee Checking," *Commerce Times*, January 23, 2014, *www .ecommercetimes.com/story/79846.html#sthash .QHXivufY.dpuf*.

24. Wahba, Phil, "Borders Files for Bankruptcy, to Close Stores," *The Huffington Post*, February 16, 2011, *www .huffingtonpost.com/2011/02/16/borders-files-for-bank ruptcy_n_823889.html*.

25. Leger, Donna Leinwand, "Target Data Breach under Close Investigative Scrutiny," *USA Today*, January 13, 2014, *www.usatoday.com/story/news/nation/2014 /01/10/target-data-breach-investigations-continue /4421345/*.

26. Westervelt, Robert, "The 10 Biggest Data Breaches of 2013 (So Far)," *CRN*, July 31, 2013, *www.crn.com/slide -shows/security/240159149/the-10-biggest-data -breaches-of-2013-so-far.htm*.

27. Ibid.

28. Harris, Elizabeth A., Perlroth, Nicole, and Popperjan, Nathaniel, "Neiman Marcus Data Breach Worse than First Said," *The New York Times*, January 23, 2014, *www.nytimes.com/2014/01/24/business/neiman -marcus-breach-affected-1-1-million-cards.html?_r=0*.

29. "What Is Identity Theft," *www.consumer.ftc.gov/arti cles/pdf-0014-identity-theft.pdf*, accessed February 10, 2014.

30. "Target Debit and Credit Card Breach Lawsuit," *LawyersandSettlements.com*, *www.lawyersandsettle ments.com/lawsuit/data-breach.html#.Uvom26-A1Ms*, accessed February 11, 2014.

31. "Secure Computing Solutions: Regulatory Compliance," *McAfee Secure Computing*, *www.securecomputing .com/compliance/#hipaa*, accessed February 10, 2014.

32. Intl Super Cybermall at Applaud Women, *www .applaudwomen.com/IntlSuperCyberMallatApplaud Women.html*, accessed February 10, 2014.

33. Industrial Parts House, *http://www.industrialparts house.com/about_us*, accessed February 17, 2014.

34. "Tinypass in Ruby,"*Tinypass Press Releases*, *www.tiny pass.com/blog/category/press-releases/*, accessed February 11, 2014.

35. Petersen, Chris, "Walmart's Secret Sauce: How the Largest Survives and Thrives," *RetailCustomer Experience.com*, March 27, 2013, *www.retailcustomer experience.com/blog/10111/Walmart-s-secret-sauce -How-the-largest-survives-and-thrives*.

36. "Nielsen Business Point Source and Methodology," *www.claritas.com/MyBestMarkets2/Default.jsp? ID=53&SubID=50&title=yes*, accessed February 11, 2014.

37. "Build a Great App Business with Admob," *www.google .com/ads/admob/*, accessed February 11, 2014.

38. Walker, Tommy, "Shopping Cart Abandonment: Why It Happens & How to Recover Baskets of Money," *Conversion XL*, July 19, 2013, *http://conversionxl.com /shopping-cart-abandonment-how-to-recover-baskets -of-money/#*.

39. "Barcode Scanner," February 4, 2014, *https://play .google.com/store/apps/details?id=com.google.zxing .client.android*.

40. "Kantar Media Reports Free Standing Insert (FSI) Coupon Activity Is Up 4.5% In 2013," *Kantar Media*, January 9, 2014, *www.kantarmediana.com/marx/press /kantar-media-reports-free-standing-insert-fsi-coupon -activity-45-2013#sthash.az9YixMo.dpuf*.

41. Dunn, Amy, "Coupon Use Plummets, and Some Wonder Whether It's the End of An Era," *NewsObserver.com*, March 9, 2013, *www.newsobserver.com/2013/03/09 /2735590/coupon-use-plummets-and-some-wonder .html#storylink=cpy*.

42. Ownby, Josh, "Mobeam Barcode Technology Could Replace NFC Payment Systems & Revolutionize Mobile Coupons," *Mad Mobile News*, March 9, 2013, *http:// madmobilenews.com/mobeam-barcode-technology -could-replace-nfc-payment-systems-revolutionize -mobile-coupons-1150/#.Uv0zkK-A3IU*.

43. Donovan, Fred, "Mobile Couponers to Fuel 11% Growth in Digital Coupon Use This Year," *FierceMobileIT*, October 21, 2013, *www.fiercemobileit.Com/Story /Mobile-Couponers-Fuel-11ex-Growth-Digital-Coupon -Use-Year/2013-10-21#Ixzz2teth8gu8*.

44. "TD Ameritrade Mobile Trader," *www.tdameritrade .com/tools-and-platforms/mobile-trading/td-ameritrade -mobile-trader.page*, accessed February 14, 2014.

45. Perez, Sarah, "How T-Mobile's New Mobile Banking Service Compares with Simple and Amex Serve," *Tech Crunch*, January 22, 2014, *http://Techcrunch.Com /2014/01/22/How-T-Mobiles-New-Mobile-Banking -Service-Compares-With-Simple-And-Amex-Serve/*.

46. "About Us," *Quintessentially Gifts Web site, www.quin tessentiallygifts.com/about-us*, accessed February 14, 2014.

47. "About Us," *Shopify* Web site, *www.shopify.com/about*, accessed February 14, 2014.

48. Stambor, Zak, "Toys 'R' Us Gives Its E-Commerce Site a Social Revamp," *Internet Retailer*, November 15, 2013, *www.internetretailer.Com/2013/11/15/Toys-R-Us-Gives -Its-E-Commerce-Site-Social-Revamp*.

49. Duda, Jessica, "Personalizing Retail's Online Experiences with iGoDigital, DegDigital," January 3, 2014, *www.degdigital.com/blog/Personalizing-Retails -Online-Experiences-With-iGoDigital*.

50. "Leading Financial Institution Uses NICE Contact Center Fraud Prevention Solution to Protect Customers and Reduce Fraud Losses," *PRNewswire*, September 11, 2013, *http://finance.yahoo.com/news/leading-financial -institution-uses-nice-110000609.html*.

51. Gil, Paul, "PayPal 101: How PayPal Works 2014," *http:// netforbeginners.about.com/od/ebay101/ss/paypal101 .htm*, accessed February 15, 2014.

52. Rao, Leena, "Paypal Debuts Its Newest Hardware, Beacon, a Bluetooth LE Enabled Device for Hands-Free Check Ins and Payments," *Tech Crunch*, September 9, 2013, *http://Techcrunch.Com/2013/09/09/Paypal -Debuts-Its-Newest-Hardware-Beacon-A-Bluetooth-Le -Enabled-Device-For-Hands-Free-Check-Ins-And -Payments/*.

53. "Purchasing Cards: Working to Simplify the Procure-to-Pay Process," *Pay Stream Advisers, http:// 8c12cf0ca0d6cec91f49-3bebbe33c01fdefb20da b8ed73fa2504.r68.cf2.rackcdn.com/2013%20Purchas ing%20Card%20Report%20-%20PayStream% 20Advisors.pdf*.

9 Enterprise Systems

Principles	Learning Objectives
• An organization must have information systems that support routine, day-to-day activities and that help a company add value to its products and services.	• Identify the basic activities and business objectives common to all transaction processing systems. • Describe the transaction processing systems associated with the order processing, purchasing, and accounting business functions.
• An organization that implements an enterprise system is creating a highly integrated set of systems, which can lead to many business benefits.	• Identify the basic functions performed and the benefits derived from the implementation of an enterprise resource planning system, customer resource management, and product lifecycle management system. • Describe the hosted software model for enterprise systems and explain why this approach is so appealing to SMEs. • Identify the challenges that organizations face in planning, building, and operating their enterprise systems. • Identify tips for avoiding many of the common causes for failed enterprise system implementations.

Information Systems in the Global Economy
BRONTO SKYLIFT, FINLAND

Aiming Higher with New Product Lifecycle Management Software

Bronto Skylift Oy Ab

Based in Finland, Bronto Skylift is the global leader in the design and manufacturing of truck mounted hydraulic platforms. Rescue workers and construction crews make use of these aerial ladder platforms and telescopic platforms. Telescopic platforms feature ladders with extendable sections; some can be insulated for maintenance crews working on live transmission lines. Bronto's aerial platforms help firefighters climb as high as 112 meters.

Over the past 50 years, Bronto Skylift has designed and manufactured more than 6,400 platforms for contractors, large fire departments, and equipment rental companies located in 120 countries around the world. The challenge for the clients is to choose from the dizzying array of customized platforms available. The company offers 50 models with advanced modularity that allow for thousands of variations. The challenge for Bronto Skylift is to manage the development of so many unique production projects simultaneously.

"We have about 100 projects going on at any one time," explains Jarmo Rajala, computer-aided design/product data management (CAD/PDM) administrator.

Bronto Skylift needed a comprehensive solution for managing product information and process-related data on a centralized system. The company chose to implement a product lifecycle management (PLM) system from Siemens. A PLM system provides a means for managing all the data associated with the product development, engineering design, production, support, and disposal of manufactured products. As products advance through these stages, product data is generated and distributed to various groups, both within and outside the manufacturing firm.

Bronto Skylift's PLM system keeps track of the thousands of part names and numbers, the product structures and 3D CAD models, and the documentation for each part. The system allows designers, producers, and managers working in Finland, Germany, Sweden, Switzerland, and the United States to access a centralized repository for product and business process information as each unique hydraulic platform is ordered, designed, and manufactured.

The system enhanced Bronto Skylift's internal communication and increased knowledge about standardized best practices. As a result, the company was not only able to operate more efficiently and cut costs, but it could plan for and accommodate future growth. With the PLM system in place, Bronto Skylift can introduce even more sophisticated products and manage their development.

As you read this chapter, consider the following:

- What advantages do PLM and other integrated enterprise systems offer an organization?
- What factors should companies consider when adopting these systems to support their business processes and plan for the future?

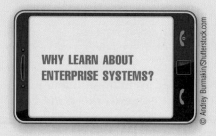

WHY LEARN ABOUT ENTERPRISE SYSTEMS?

Individuals and organizations today are moving from a collection of nonintegrated transaction processing systems to highly integrated enterprise systems to perform routine business processes and to maintain records about them. These systems support a wide range of business activities associated with supply chain management, customer relationship management, and product lifecycle management. Although they were initially thought to be cost effective only for very large companies, even small and midsized companies are now implementing these systems to reduce costs, speed time to market, and improve service.

In our service-oriented economy, outstanding customer service has become a goal of virtually all companies. To provide good customer service, employees who work directly with customers—whether in sales, customer service, or marketing—require high-quality and timely data to make good decisions. Such workers might use an enterprise system to check the inventory status of ordered items, view the production planning schedule to tell the customer when the item will be in stock, or enter data to schedule a delivery to the customer.

No matter what your role, it is very likely that you will provide input to or use the output from your organization's enterprise systems. Your effective use of these systems will be essential to raise the productivity of your firm, improve customer service, and enable better decision making. Thus, it is important that you understand how these systems work and what their capabilities and limitations are.

This chapter begins with an overview of the individual transaction processing systems that support the fundamental operations of many organizations. Their processing methods, objectives, and primary activities are covered. Then enterprise systems, collections of integrated information systems that share a common database, are discussed. Enterprise systems ensure that data can be shared across all business functions and all levels of management to support the operational and management decision making needed to run the organization. The basic functions and benefits of these systems as well as the challenges of successfully implementing them are discussed.

TRANSACTION PROCESSING SYSTEMS

Many organizations employ transaction processing systems (TPSs), which capture and process the detailed data necessary to update records about the fundamental business operations of the organization. These systems include order entry, inventory control, payroll, accounts payable, accounts receivable, and the general ledger, to name just a few. The input to these systems includes basic business transactions, such as customer orders, purchase orders, receipts, time cards, invoices, and customer payments. The processing activities include data collection, data editing, data correction, data processing, data storage, and document production. The result of processing business transactions is that the organization's records are updated to reflect the status of the operation at the time of the last processed transaction.

A TPS also provides valuable input to management information systems, decision support systems, and knowledge management systems. Indeed transaction processing systems serve as the foundation for these other systems. See Figure 9.1.

Transaction processing systems support routine operations associated with business processes, such as customer ordering and billing, shipping, employee payroll, purchasing, and accounting. TPSs use a large amount of input and output data to update the official records of the company about orders, sales, customers, and so on. TPSs, however, don't provide much support for decision making.

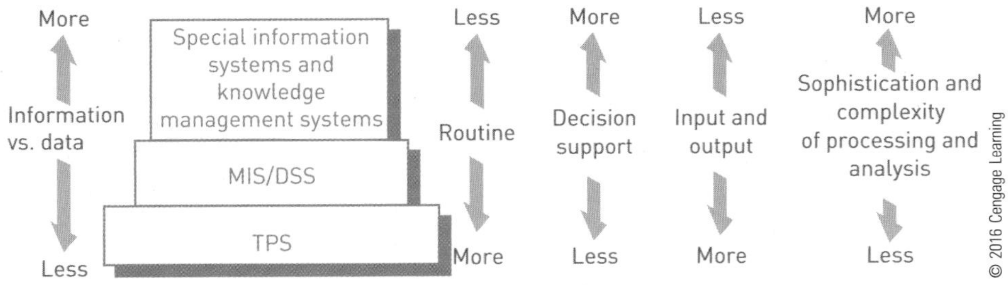

FIGURE 9.1

TPS, MIS/DSS, and special information systems in perspective

A TPS provides valuable input to MIS, DSS, and KM systems.

Independent Liquor Group (ILG) is a member owned organization serving over 1,100 hotels, liquor stores, pubs, and restaurants in Australia. The organization implemented a Web-based order transaction processing system that enables members to place orders online. The system consolidates multiple orders so that each member receives just one delivery and one invoice. The resulting delivery efficiency has enabled ILG to reduce costs by $0.50 per case on an annual volume of 2.5 million cases.[1]

Policy Bazaar is an Indian organization that provides online life insurance comparisons. The firm employs 800 workers and is growing rapidly. Policy Bazaar moved from an Excel and paper-based payroll to a fully automated payroll transaction processing system. As a result, the accuracy of payroll processing has been improved, the total cost has been reduced, and the firm is able to provide an employee self-service portal to support special reimbursements and tax return filings.[2]

Because TPSs often perform activities related to customer contacts—such as order processing and invoicing—these information systems play a critical role in providing value to the customer. For example, by capturing and tracking the movement of each package, shippers such as FedEx and DHL Express can provide timely and accurate data on the exact location of a package. Shippers and receivers can access an online database and, by providing the tracking number of a package, find the package's current location. If the package has been delivered, they can see who signed for it (a service that is especially useful in large companies where packages can become "lost" in internal distribution systems and mailrooms). Such a system provides the basis for added value through improved customer service.

Traditional Transaction Processing Methods and Objectives

With **batch processing systems**, business transactions are accumulated over a period of time and prepared for processing as a single unit or batch. See Figure 9.2a. Transactions are accumulated for as long as necessary to meet the needs of the users of that system. For example, it might be important to process invoices and customer payments for the accounts receivable system daily. On the other hand, the payroll system might receive time cards and process them biweekly to create checks, update employee earnings records, and distribute labor costs. The essential characteristic of a batch processing system is the delay between an event and the eventual processing of the related transaction to update the organization's records. For many applications, batch processing is an appropriate and cost effective approach. Payroll transactions and billing are typically done via batch processing.

Automatic Data Processing (ADP) is a major provider of business outsourcing solutions for payroll administration for 620,000 organizations in more than 125 countries. It uses a batch processing system to prepare the paychecks of one out of six Americans.[3]

Spectrum Family Medical is a five-provider practice in Maryland that employs a batch processing billing system. The practice averages 1,200 patient visits per month, but sends claims to medical insurance companies within two days and sends bills to patients within one day.[4]

batch processing system: A form of data processing whereby business transactions are accumulated over a period of time and prepared for processing as a single unit or batch.

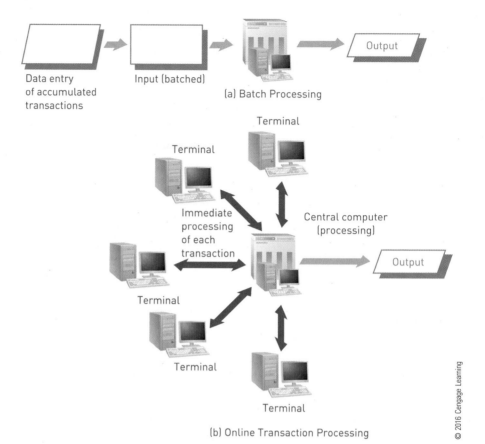

Data entry
of accumulated
transactions

Input (batched)

(a) Batch Processing

Output

Terminal

Terminal

Immediate
processing
of each
transaction

Central computer
(processing)

Output

Terminal

Terminal

Terminal

(b) Online Transaction Processing

© 2016 Cengage Learning

FIGURE **9.2**

**Batch versus online
transaction processing**

(a) Batch processing inputs and
processes data in groups. (b) In
online processing, transactions are
completed as they occur.

**online transaction processing
(OLTP):** A form of data processing
where each transaction is processed
immediately without the delay of accumulating transactions into a batch.

With **online transaction processing (OLTP)**, each transaction is processed immediately without the delay of accumulating transactions into a
batch, as shown in Figure 9.2b. Consequently, at any time, the data in an
online system reflects the current status. This type of processing is essential
for businesses that require access to current data such as airlines, ticket agencies, and stock investment firms. Many companies find that OLTP helps them
provide faster, more efficient service—one way to add value to their activities
in the eyes of the customer. See Figure 9.3.

PayPal provides a fast, secure method of payment between any two people in the world that have email accounts. With over 143 million active
accounts around the world, PayPal employs a massive OLTP system to process some 9 million payments every day (over 100 payment transactions per
second).[5]

The specific business needs and goals of the organization define the
method of transaction processing best suited for the various applications of
the company. Increasingly, the need for current data for decision making is
driving many organizations to move from batch processing systems to online
transaction processing systems when it is economically feasible. For example,
the State of Wisconsin Department of Health Services (DHS) runs the Women,
Infants, and Children (WIC) program. WIC's goal is to support and sustain the
health and well-being of nutritionally at-risk pregnant, breastfeeding, and
postpartum women, as well as their infants and children. DHS employed a
batch processing system to manage this program, and processed the WIC
data in a batch at the end of the day. This practice created a built-in delay in
obtaining information needed for decision-making and government-reporting
requirements. However, DHS needs up-to-date data to avoid dual participation incidents, such as a client or caregiver receiving more WIC checks than
allowed for one month, or receiving WIC checks and the Commodity

FIGURE 9.3

Example of OLTP system

Hospitality companies such as
ResortCom International can use an
OLTP system to manage timeshare
payments and other financial
transactions.

Supplemental Food Program (CSFP) payments at the same time. DHS moved
to an online transaction processing system to ensure that all data is now available on a current basis. The system is Web-based and WIC staff needs only a
Web browser and secure Internet access to work with the data.[6]

Figure 9.4 shows the traditional flow of key pieces of information from
one TPS to another for a typical manufacturing organization. When transactions entered into one system are processed, they create new transactions that
flow into another system.

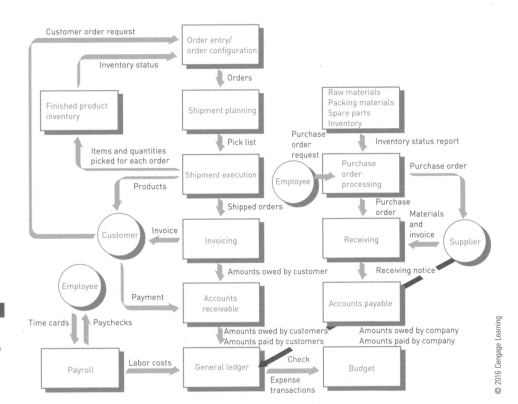

FIGURE 9.4

Integration of a firm's TPS

When transactions entered into one
system are processed, they create
new transactions that flow into
another system.

Because of the importance of transaction processing, organizations expect their TPSs to accomplish a number of specific objectives, including the following:

- Capture, process, and update databases of business data required to support routine business activities
- Ensure that the data is processed accurately and completely
- Avoid processing fraudulent transactions
- Produce timely user responses and reports
- Reduce clerical and other labor requirements
- Help improve customer service
- Achieve significant business benefits

A TPS typically includes the following types of systems:

- **Order processing systems.** Running these systems efficiently and reliably is so critical that the order processing system is sometimes referred to as the lifeblood of the organization. The processing flow begins with the receipt of a customer order. The finished product inventory is checked to see if sufficient inventory is on hand to fill the order. If sufficient inventory is available, the customer shipment is planned to meet the customer's desired receipt date. A product pick list is printed at the warehouse from which the order is to be filled on the day the order is planned to be shipped. At the warehouse, workers gather the items needed to fill the order and enter the item identifier and quantity for each item to update the finished product inventory. When the order is complete and sent on its way, a customer invoice is created with a copy included in the customer shipment.

- **Purchasing systems.** The traditional transaction processing systems that support the purchasing business function include inventory control, purchase order processing, receiving, and accounts payable. Employees place purchase order requests in response to shortages identified in inventory control reports. Purchase order information flows to the receiving system and accounts payable systems. A record is created upon receipt of the items ordered. When the invoice arrives from the supplier, it is matched to the original order and the receiving report, and a check is generated if all data is complete and consistent.

- **Accounting systems.** The accounting systems must track the flow of data related to all the cash flows that affect the organization. As mentioned earlier, the order processing system generates an invoice for customer orders to include with the shipment. This information is also sent to the accounts receivable system to update the customer's account. When the customer pays the invoice, the payment information is also used to update the customer's account. The necessary accounting transactions are sent to the general ledger system to keep track of amounts owed and amounts paid. Similarly, as the purchasing systems generate purchase orders and those items are received, information is sent to the accounts payable system to manage the amounts owed by the company. Data about amounts owed and paid by customers to the company and from the company to vendors and others are sent to the general ledger system, which records and reports all financial transactions for the company.

In the past, organizations knitted together a hodgepodge of systems to accomplish the transaction processing activities shown in Figure 9.4. Some of the systems might have been applications developed using in-house resources, some may have been developed by outside contractors, and others may have been off-the-shelf software packages. Much customization and modification of this diverse software was necessary for all the applications to work together efficiently. In some cases, it was necessary to print data from one system and then manually reenter it into other systems. Of course, this increased the amount of effort required and increased the likelihood of processing delays and errors.

The approach taken today by many organizations is to implement an integrated set of transaction processing systems from a single or limited number of software vendors that handle most or all of the transaction processing activities shown in Figure 9.4. The data flows automatically from one application to another with no delay or need to reenter data. For example, Zoës Kitchen is a chain of Mediterranean-influenced casual food restaurants with 16 locations in Alabama and neighboring states. The firm implemented a set of integrated systems across its multiple locations to manage food and labor costs, improve cash management, perform weekly reconciliation of cash and credit cards, and simplify the weekly bank reconciliation.[7]

Table 9.1 summarizes some of the ways that companies can use transaction processing systems to achieve significant business benefits.

TABLE 9.1 Examples of TPSs yielding significant benefits

Competitive Advantage	Example
Better relationship with suppliers	Internet marketplace to allow the company to purchase products from suppliers at discounted prices
Costs dramatically reduced	Warehouse management system employing RFID technology to reduce labor hours and improve inventory accuracy
Customer loyalty increased	Customer interaction system to monitor and track each customer interaction with the company
Inventory levels reduced	Collaborative planning, forecasting, and replenishing to ensure the right amount of inventory is in stores
Superior information gathering	Order configuration system to ensure that products ordered will meet customer's objectives
Superior service provided to customers	Tracking systems that customers can access to determine shipping status

© 2016 Cengage Learning

Depending on the specific nature and goals of the organization, any of the objectives in Table 9.1 might be more important than others. By meeting these objectives, TPSs can support corporate goals such as reducing costs; increasing productivity, quality, and customer satisfaction; and running more efficient and effective operations.

Transaction Processing Systems for Entrepreneurs and Small and Medium-Sized Enterprises

Many software packages provide integrated transaction processing system solutions for small and medium-sized enterprises (SMEs), wherein SME is a legally independent enterprise with no more than 500 employees. Integrated transaction processing systems for SMEs are typically easy to install and operate and usually have a low total cost of ownership, with an initial cost of a few hundred to a few thousand dollars. Such solutions are highly attractive to firms that have outgrown their current software but cannot afford a complex, high-end integrated system solution. Table 9.2 presents some of the dozens of such software solutions available.

QuickBooks is accounting software from Intuit that SMEs use to easily maintain their accounting records. In India, hundreds of companies are subsidiaries of much larger foreign companies. Quite often, these subsidiaries

TABLE **9.2** Sample of integrated TPS solutions for SMEs

Vendor	Software	Type of TPS Offered	Target Customers
AccuFund	AccuFund	Financial reporting and accounting	Nonprofit, municipal, and government organizations
OpenPro	OpenPro	Complete ERP solution, including financials, supply chain management, e-commerce, customer relationship management, and retail POS system	Manufacturers, distributors, and retailers
Intuit	QuickBooks	Financial reporting and accounting	Manufacturers, professional services, contractors, nonprofits, and retailers
Sage	Timberline	Financial reporting, accounting, and operations	Contractors, real estate developers, and residential builders
Redwing	TurningPoint	Financial reporting and accounting	Professional services, banks, and retailers

adopt QuickBooks to maintain all their accounts in an accurate and consistent manner. Users can maintain a customer database and record customer payments as well as keep track of current balances. The software makes it easy to create a supplier database and write checks to pay for goods and services.[8]

Qvinci.web allows companies to collect QuickBooks data from many locations and format that data into the company's standardized chart of accounts. Financial managers at various SMEs, such as Anytime Fitness, Christian Brothers Automotive, Dairy Queen, Sunoco Oil & Gas, The UPS Store, and Wellness Center use QuickBooks to create predefined financial reports.[9]

TRANSACTION PROCESSING ACTIVITIES

Along with having common characteristics, all TPSs perform a common set of basic data-processing activities. TPSs capture and process data that describes fundamental business transactions. This data is used to update databases and to produce a variety of reports for people both within and outside the enterprise. The business data goes through a transaction processing cycle that includes data collection, data editing, data correction, data processing, data storage, and document production. See Figure 9.5.

Data Collection

transaction processing cycle:
The process of data collection, data editing, data correction, data processing, data storage, and document production.

data collection: Capturing and gathering all data necessary to complete the processing of transactions.

source data automation:
Capturing data at its source and recording it accurately in a timely fashion with minimal manual effort and in an electronic or digital form so that it can be directly entered into the computer.

Capturing and gathering all data necessary to complete the processing of transactions is called data collection. In some cases, it can be done manually, such as by collecting handwritten sales orders or changes to inventory. In other cases, data collection is automated via special input devices such as scanners, point-of-sale (POS) devices, and terminals.

Data collection begins with a transaction (e.g., taking a customer order) and results in data that serves as input to the TPS. Data should be captured at its source and recorded accurately in a timely fashion with minimal manual effort and in an electronic or digital form that can be directly entered into the computer. This approach is called source data automation. An example of source data automation is an automated device at a retail store that speeds the checkout process—either UPC codes read by a scanner or RFID signals picked up when the items approach the checkout stand. Using UPC bar codes or RFID tags is quicker and more accurate than having a clerk enter codes manually at the cash register. The product ID for each item is determined automatically, and its price retrieved from the item database. The point-of-sale TPS uses the price data to determine the customer's bill. The store's inventory and purchase databases record the number of units of an

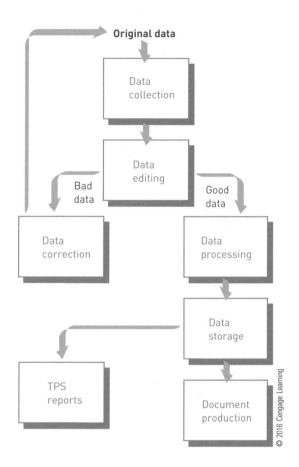

FIGURE 9.5

Transaction processing activities

A transaction processing cycle includes data collection, data editing, data correction, data processing, data storage, and document production.

item purchased, along with the price and the date and time of the purchase. The inventory database generates a management report notifying the store manager to reorder items that have fallen below the reorder quantity. The detailed purchases database can be used by the store or sold to marketing research firms or manufacturers for detailed sales analysis. See Figure 9.6.

Many grocery stores combine point-of-sale scanners and coupon printers. The systems are programmed so that each time a specific product—for

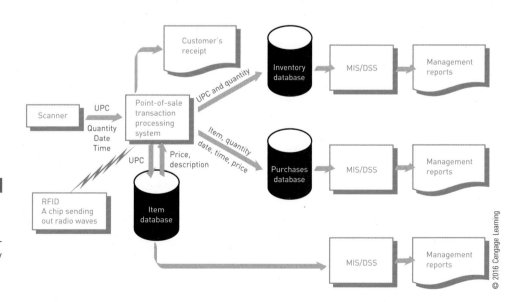

FIGURE 9.6

Point-of-sale transaction processing system

The purchase of items at the checkout stand updates a store's inventory database and its database of purchases.

example, a box of cereal—crosses a checkout scanner, an appropriate coupon, perhaps a milk coupon, is printed. Companies can pay to be promoted through the system, which is then reprogrammed to print those companies' coupons if the customer buys a competitive brand. These TPSs help grocery stores increase profits by improving their repeat sales and bringing in revenue from other businesses.

Many mobile POS systems operate on iPads, iPhones, and iPod Touch devices. Some mobile POS systems include marketing tools that SMEs can use to thank first-time customers and send automated emails to longtime customers that have not visited recently. The owner of the China Baroque jewelry store implemented a mobile POS that provides a reporting feature to enable her to see exactly what jewelry is selling the most and in which store location the sales were made. This enables her to make better production and buying decisions.[10]

Cloud-based POS systems provide a range of capabilities, including advanced integration with digital loyalty programs, various accounting tools, and the ability to generate gift cards and coupons. An SME can implement such a system for a few thousand dollars compared to more traditional cash register-based POS systems that can costs tens of thousands.[11]

Data Editing

data editing: Checking data for validity and completeness to detect any problems.

An important step in processing transaction data is to check data for validity and completeness to detect any problems, a task called data editing. For example, quantity and cost data must be numeric, and names must be alphabetic; otherwise, the data is not valid. Often, the codes associated with an individual transaction are edited against a database containing valid codes. If any code entered (or scanned) is not present in the database, the transaction is rejected.

Data Correction

data correction: Reentering data that was not typed or scanned properly.

It is not enough simply to reject invalid data. The system should also provide error messages that alert those responsible for editing the data. Error messages must specify the problem so proper corrections can be made. A data correction involves reentering data that was not typed or scanned properly. For example, a scanned UPC code must match a code in a master table of valid UPCs. If the code is misread or does not exist in the table, the checkout clerk is given an instruction to rescan the item or type the information manually.

Data Processing

data processing: Performing calculations and other data transformations related to business transactions.

Another major activity of a TPS is data processing, performing calculations and other data transformations related to business transactions. Data manipulation can include classifying data, sorting data into categories, performing calculations, summarizing results, and storing data in the organization's database for further processing. In a payroll TPS, for example, data processing includes multiplying an employee's hours worked by the hourly pay rate. Overtime pay, federal and state tax withholdings, and deductions are also calculated.

Data Storage

data storage: Updating one or more databases with new transactions.

Data storage involves updating one or more databases with new transactions. After being updated, this data can be further processed by other systems so that it is available for management reporting and decision making. Thus, although transaction databases can be considered a by-product of transaction processing, they have a pronounced effect on nearly all other information systems and decision-making processes in an organization.

Document Production

document production: Generating output records, documents, and reports.

Document production involves generating output records, documents, and reports. These can be hard-copy paper reports or displays on computer screens (sometimes referred to as soft copy). Printed paychecks, for example, are hard-copy documents produced by a payroll TPS, whereas an outstanding balance report for invoices might be a soft-copy report displayed by an accounts receivable TPS. Often, as shown earlier in Figure 9.6, results from one TPS flow downstream to become input to other systems, which might use the results of updating the inventory database to create the stock exception report, a type of management report showing items with inventory levels below the reorder point.

In addition to major documents such as checks and invoices, most TPSs provide other useful management information, such as printed or on-screen reports that help managers and employees perform various activities. A report showing current inventory is one example; another might be a document listing items ordered from a supplier to help a receiving clerk check the order for completeness when it arrives. A TPS can also produce reports required by local, state, and federal agencies, such as statements of tax withholding and quarterly income statements.

ENTERPRISE SYSTEMS

enterprise system: A system central to the organization that ensures information can be shared across all business functions and all levels of management to support the running and managing of a business.

An enterprise system is central to individuals and organizations of all sizes and ensures that information can be shared across all business functions and all levels of management to support the running and managing of a business. Enterprise systems employ a database of key operational and planning data that can be shared by all. This eliminates the problems of missing information and inconsistent information caused by multiple transaction processing systems that support only one business function or one department in an organization. Examples of enterprise systems include enterprise resource planning systems that support supply chain processes, such as order processing, inventory management, and purchasing, and customer relationship management systems that support sales, marketing, and customer service-related processes.

Businesses rely on enterprise systems to perform many of their daily activities in areas such as product supply, distribution, sales, marketing, human resources, manufacturing, accounting, and taxation so that work is performed quickly without waste or mistakes. Without such systems, recording and processing business transactions would consume huge amounts of an organization's resources. This collection of processed transactions also forms a storehouse of data invaluable to decision making. The ultimate goal is to satisfy customers and provide significant benefits by reducing costs and improving service.

Enterprise Resource Planning

Enterprise resource planning (ERP) is a set of integrated programs that manage a company's vital business operations for an entire organization, even a complex, multisite, global organization. Recall that a business process is a set of coordinated and related activities that takes one or more types of input and creates an output of value to the customer of that process. The customer might be a traditional external business customer who buys goods or services from the firm. An example of such a process is capturing a sales order, which takes customer input and generates an order. The customer of a business process might also be an internal customer, such as a worker in another department of the firm. For example, the shipment process generates the internal documents workers need in the warehouse and shipping departments to pick, pack, and ship orders. At the core of the ERP system is a database that is shared by all users so that all business functions have access to current and consistent data for operational decision making and planning, as shown in Figure 9.7.

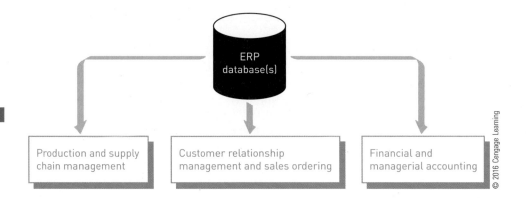

FIGURE 9.7

Enterprise resource planning system

An ERP integrates business processes and the ERP database.

ERP systems evolved from materials requirement planning (MRP) systems developed in the 1970s. These systems tied together the production planning, inventory control, and purchasing business functions for manufacturing organizations. During the late 1980s and early 1990s, many organizations recognized that their legacy TPSs lacked the integration needed to coordinate activities and share valuable information across all the business functions of the firm. As a result, costs were higher and customer service was poorer than desired. Large organizations, specifically members of the *Fortune* 1000, were the first to take on the challenge of implementing ERP. As they did, they uncovered many advantages as well as some disadvantages summarized in the following sections.

Advantages of ERP

Increased global competition, new needs of executives for control over the total cost and product flow through their enterprises, and ever more numerous customer interactions drive the demand for enterprise-wide access to real-time information. ERP offers integrated software from a single vendor to help meet those needs. The primary benefits of implementing ERP include improved access to quality data for operational decision making, elimination of inefficient or outdated systems, improvement of work processes, and technology standardization. ERP vendors have also developed specialized systems that provide effective solutions for specific industries and market segments.

Improved Access to Quality Data for Operational Decision Making

ERP systems operate via an integrated database, using one set of data to support all business functions. For example, the systems can support decisions on optimal sourcing or cost accounting for the entire enterprise or business units from the start rather than gathering data from multiple business functions and then trying to coordinate that information manually or reconciling data with another application. The result is an organization that looks seamless, not only to the outside world but also to the decision makers who are deploying resources within the organization. The data is integrated to facilitate operational decision making and allows companies to provide greater customer service and support, strengthen customer and supplier relationships, and generate new business opportunities. It is essential that the data used for decision making is of high quality.

Amrit Feeds is one of India's largest producers of chicken feed, poultry, and dairy products. It employs 2,100 workers and generates an annual revenue of 25,000 million rupees ($409 million). Until recently, the firm deployed separate sales teams with disparate order entry methods across India, making it difficult to capture current customer demand data. Amrit recognized that using nonstandard methods and multiple, poorly integrated systems was causing problems in production planning with frequent stockouts and unfilled sales orders. Over a period of time, Amrit worked with an experienced consulting firm to implement an ERP system whose scope includes sales ordering, demand forecasting, and production planning. The successful implementation and training of workers in the use of the ERP system has provided the firm with access to quality data to improve key decision making. As a result, the firm has increased production output by 2.5 percent, cut stockout of finished products by 16 percent, and increased its order fulfillment rate by 9 percent.[12]

Elimination of Costly, Inflexible Legacy Systems

Adoption of an ERP system enables an organization to eliminate dozens or even hundreds of separate systems and replace them with a single integrated set of applications for the entire enterprise. In many cases, these systems are decades old, the original developers are long gone, and the systems are poorly documented. As a result, the systems are extremely difficult to fix when they break, and adapting them to meet new business needs takes too long. They become an anchor around the organization that keeps it from moving ahead and remaining competitive. An ERP system helps match the capabilities of an organization's information systems to its business needs— even as these needs evolve.

Network Rail runs, maintains, and develops Britain's rail tracks, signaling, bridges, tunnels, level crossings, viaducts, and 17 key stations. It also ensures all current or potential future train operators, whether they carry passengers or freight, are treated fairly when they use or seek to use the railway. It employs an ERP system to support order management, logistics planning, and customer interactions. At one time, the system ran on a few powerful servers, an arrangement that made it difficult to add computing capacity as business demands increased. Network Rail migrated to a new setup with the ERP system running on more and smaller servers. This increased the organization's ability to expand the capacity of the system in small, relatively inexpensive increments to meet evolving business needs. It also improved system reliability in the event of a disaster—if one server should fail, many others can take up the workload.[13]

Improvement of Work Processes

Competition requires companies to structure their business processes to be as effective and customer oriented as possible. ERP vendors do considerable research to define the best business processes. They gather requirements of leading companies within the same industry and combine them with findings from research institutions and consultants. The individual application modules included in the ERP system are then designed to support these best practices, the most efficient and effective ways to complete a business process. Thus, implementation of an ERP system ensures good work processes based on best practices. For example, for managing customer payments, the ERP system's finance module can be configured to reflect the most efficient practices of leading companies in an industry. This increased efficiency ensures that everyday business operations follow the optimal chain of activities, with all users supplied the information and tools they need to complete each step.

The chemical division of an integrated petroleum company built on the successful implementation of its ERP system to capture best practices and support a program of continuous improvement with a goal of optimizing its supply chain. In the first wave of continuous improvement changes, project teams worked across business functions to reduce the number of suppliers and improve purchase pricing and services. In the next phase, the continuous improvement teams worked to increase cross functional collaboration and significantly advance internal processes. In the third wave of changes, project teams redesigned and redefined organizational roles, job skills, management

best practices: The most efficient and effective ways to complete a business process.

systems, and company culture and behaviors to increase efficiency and improve customer interactions and order fulfillment. The net effect of all these changes was to reduce overall supply chain costs by 12 percent and increase order satisfaction from 76 percent to 91 percent.[14]

Upgrade of Technology Infrastructure

When implementing an ERP system, an organization has an opportunity to upgrade the information technology (such as hardware, operating systems, and databases) that it uses. While centralizing and formalizing these decisions, the organization can eliminate the hodgepodge of multiple hardware platforms, operating systems, and databases it is currently using—most likely from a variety of vendors. Standardizing on fewer technologies and vendors reduces ongoing maintenance and support costs as well as the training load for those who must support the infrastructure.

DuPont with headquarters in Geneva, Switzerland, is recognized as one of the world's most innovative companies. It employs over 60,000 workers in 70 countries to provide a variety of products and services for customers in the agriculture, electronics, transportation, and apparel industries. Each DuPont strategic business unit had its own information systems operations group and strategy, creating a hodgepodge of applications, technology, and vendors. The support of all this diverse technology was costly and time consuming. The DuPont management team initiated the Legacy Application Migration Programme (LAMP) with a goal of migrating the business units to a single, integrated ERP environment. The scope of this effort included legal, corporate, and business reporting, inter-company processes, and price management. The project was successful and has resulted in elimination of costly-to-maintain legacy applications, a simpler infrastructure that is easier and less expensive to manage, and improved productivity.[15]

Leading ERP Systems

ERP systems are commonly used in manufacturing companies, colleges and universities, professional service organizations, retailers, and healthcare organizations. The business needs for each of these types of organizations varies greatly. In addition, the needs of a large multinational organization are far different from the needs of a small, local organization. Thus, no one ERP software solution from a single vendor is "best" for all organizations. To help simplify comparisons, ERP vendors are classified as Tier I, II, or III according to the type of customers they target.[16]

- Tier I vendors target large multinational firms with multiple geographic locations and annual revenues in excess of $1 billion. Tier I ERP system solutions are highly complex and expensive to implement and support. Implementation across multiple locations can take years. The primary Tier I vendors are Oracle and SAP.
- Tier II vendors target medium-sized firms with annual revenues in the $50 million to $1 billion range operating out of one or more locations. Tier II solutions are much less complex and less expensive to implement and support. There are two dozen or more Tier II vendors, including Oracle, SAP, Microsoft, Infor, Epicor, and Lawson.
- Tier III vendors target smaller firms with annual revenues in the $10 million to $50 million range that typically operate out of a single location. Tier III solutions are comparatively easy and inexpensive to implement and support. There are dozens of Tier III vendors, including ABAS, Bluebee Software, Cincom Systems, Compiere, ESP Technologies, Frontier Software, GCS Software, Microsoft, Netsuite, PDS, Plex, and Syspro. See Figure 9.8. Many of the Tier I and Tier II vendors also offer solutions for smaller firms.

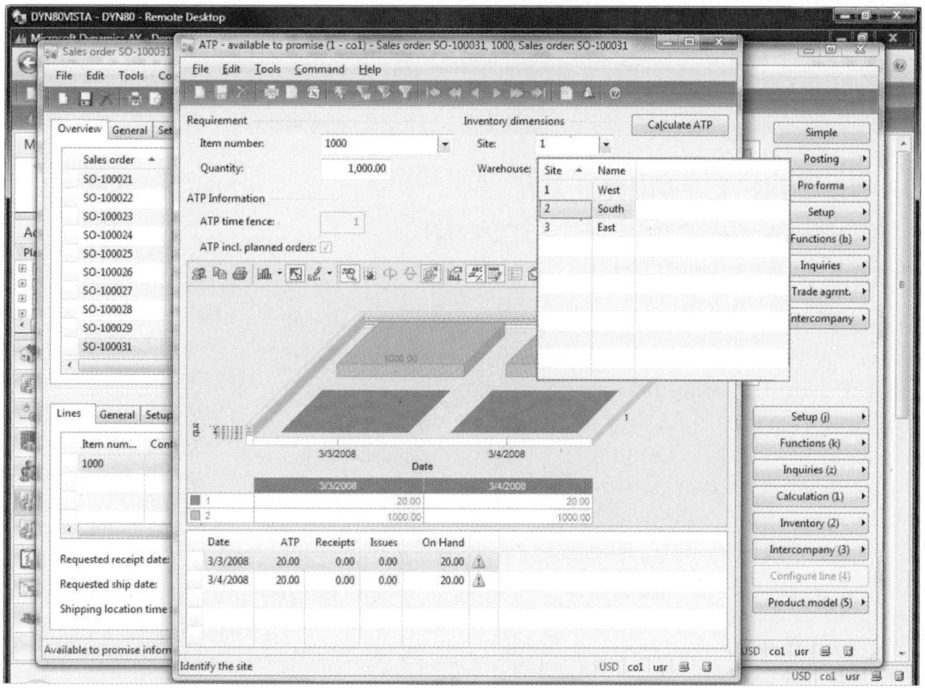

FIGURE 9.8

ERP software

Microsoft Dynamics is an ERP solution that is very popular among small businesses.

Large organizations were the leaders in adopting ERP systems as only they could afford the associated large hardware and software costs and dedicate sufficient people resources to the implementation and support of these systems. Many large company implementations occurred in the 2000s and involved installing the ERP software on the organizations' large mainframe computers. In many cases, this required upgrading the hardware at a cost of millions of dollars.

Smaller organizations moved to ERP systems about 10 years after larger organizations did. The smaller firms simply could not afford the investment required in hardware, software, and people to implement and support ERP. However, ERP software vendors created new ERP solutions with much lower start-up costs and faster, easier implementations. Some ERP vendors introduced cloud-based solutions, which further reduced the start-up costs by avoiding the need to purchase expensive ERP software and make major hardware upgrades. Instead, with a cloud-based solution, organizations could rent the software and run it on the vendor's hardware. Plex and NetSuite are two of the many cloud-based ERP solutions that enable users to access the ERP application using a Web browser and avoid paying for and maintaining high-cost hardware.

As an alternative, many organizations elect to implement open-source ERP systems from vendors such as Compiere. With open-source software, organizations can see and modify the source code to customize it to meet their needs. Such systems are much less costly to acquire and are relatively easy to modify to meet business needs.

Organizations frequently need to customize the vendor's ERP software to integrate other business systems, to add data fields or change field sizes from those in the standard system, or to meet regulatory requirements. A wide range of software service organizations can perform the system development and maintenance.

Supply Chain Management (SCM)

supply chain management (SCM): A system that includes planning, executing, and controlling all activities involved in raw material sourcing and procurement, converting raw materials to finished products, and warehousing and delivering finished products to customers.

An organization can use an ERP system within a manufacturing organization to support what is known as **supply chain management (SCM)**, which includes planning, executing, and controlling all activities involved in raw

INFORMATION SYSTEMS @ WORK

Using ERP Systems to Accommodate Rapid Growth in the Meat Industry

Founded in 1976 as a series butcher shops in the small village of Moygashel in County Tyrone in Northern Ireland, Dunbia today is one of Europe's leading red meat manufacturers for the retail and commercial markets. Since 2001, Dunbia has rapidly acquired an impressive list of competitors or related companies across the United Kingdom. They acquired Oriel Jones & Sons in Wales in 2001, Kepak Preston in the Republic of Ireland, Rhinds of Elgin in Scotland in 2007, Stevenson's & Co pork facility in Northern Ireland in 2009, and Heathfield Foods in England in 2011. In 2013 and 2014, Dunbia bought three additional companies in Wales, Scotland, and England. Meanwhile, Dunbia has been building new plants to debone meat, produce sausages, and package meats. In 2013, the company also revamped one of its Welsh meat plants, turning it into one of the most modern facilities of its kind in the world.

With each new acquisition, Dunbia inherited new information systems, workplace procedures, and decision-making processes. By 2011, Dunbia found itself with five different enterprise resource planning (ERP) systems. Moving to a single ERP solution not only offered Dunbia a chance to rid itself of the abundance of licensing and maintenance fees, but also to develop one ERP system that would standardize its existing systems and implement best practices.

Dunbia chose to deploy its existing meat industry factory-floor system, Emydex, in each of its 10 operating plants. The Emydex system is designed for the meat and fish industry, and provides customizable data collection and production management. Next, Dunbia integrated Emydex with other modules within the Microsoft Dynamic AX platform. The Microsoft Dynamic ERP system provides a wide range of modules that support administrative and operational processes: financial management, human capital management, manufacturing, supply chain management, project

management and accounting, retail, and business intelligence and reporting. Moreover, because Dunbia already used numerous Microsoft products, including its SQL Server database, the integration of these new ERP modules was likely to proceed smoothly.

One of the most important features of Dunbia's ERP system is that it accommodates the rapid growth the company has experienced and anticipates for the future. Moreover, due to inconsistencies in the five separate systems, the company could not make the most out of the business intelligence it was generating. Dunbia is now using the new ERP's business intelligence module to enforce group reporting requirements.

The company rolled out the new system in 2014, starting at its state-of-the-art facility in Wales and adding another plant into the system every couple of months. It's an aggressive, innovative plan, but one that makes the estimated return on investment worth the risk.

Discussion Questions

1. What are the advantages of deploying a single ERP across all of Dunbia's facilities?
2. What factors should a company consider when adopting an ERP system? How can it avoid outgrowing the system?

Critical Thinking Questions

1. How might Dunbia use its new ERP system to change work processes in the companies it has acquired?
2. What challenges might Dunbia face when its employees begin to use the new system?

SOURCES: "Dunbia's £12m meat plant revamp safeguards 600 jobs in Llanybydde," BBC, June 7, 2013, *www.bbc.com/news/uk-wales-22813800*; "Our History," Dunbia Web site, *www.dunbia.com/Discover-Dunbia/Our -History*; "Dunbia Powering Growth with Columbus Manufacturing," Columbus Food Web site, *www.columbusglobal.com/en-GB/Food/Client -cases/Dunbia*; "New from Microsoft Dynamics AX," Microsoft Web site, *www.microsoft.com/en-us/dynamics/erp-ax-overview.aspx*.

material sourcing and procurement, converting raw materials to finished products, and warehousing and delivering finished product to customers. The goal of SCM is to reduce costs and improve customer service, while at the same time reducing the overall investment in inventory in the supply chain.

Another way to think about SCM is that it manages materials, information, and finances as they move from supplier to manufacturer to wholesaler to retailer to consumer. The materials flow includes the inbound movement of raw materials from supplier to manufacturer as well as the outbound movement of finished product from manufacturer to wholesaler, retailer, and customer. The information flow involves capturing and transmitting orders and invoices among suppliers, manufacturers, wholesalers, retailers, and customers. The financial flow consists of payment transactions among suppliers, manufacturers, wholesalers, retailers, customers, and their financial institutions.

Kidrobot is a creator and retailer of limited-edition art toys, apparel, and accessories. The firm implemented a global supply chain management system with the flexibility to serve its toy, apparel, and accessory businesses. The system supports a complex domestic and international sales distribution strategy that encompasses multiple channels of distribution, including retail stores, wholesale customers, Web-based B2B, and e-Commerce B2C.[17]

The ERP system for a manufacturing organization typically encompasses SCM activities and manages the flow of materials, information, and finances. Manufacturing ERP systems follow a systematic process for developing a production plan that draws on the information available in the ERP system database.

The process starts with *sales forecasting* to develop an estimate of future customer demand. This initial forecast is at a fairly high level, with estimates made by product group rather than by each product item. The sales forecast extends for months into the future; it might be developed using an ERP software module or produced by other means using specialized software and techniques. Many organizations are moving to a collaborative process with major customers to plan future inventory levels and production rather than relying on an internally generated sales forecast.

The *sales and operations plan (S&OP)* takes demand and current inventory levels into account and determines the specific product items that need to be produced as well as when to meet the forecast future demand. Production capacity and any seasonal variability in demand must also be considered.

Demand management refines the production plan by determining the amount of weekly or daily production needed to meet the demand for individual products. The output of the demand management process is the master production schedule, which is a production plan for all finished goods.

Detailed scheduling uses the production plan defined by the demand management process to develop a detailed production schedule specifying production scheduling details, such as which item to produce first and when production should be switched from one item to another. A key decision is how long to make the production runs for each product. Longer production runs reduce the number of machine setups required, thus reducing production costs. Shorter production runs generate less finished product inventory and reduce inventory holding costs.

Materials requirement planning (MRP) determines the amount and timing for placing raw material orders with suppliers. The types and amounts of raw materials required to support the planned production schedule are determined by the existing raw material inventory and the bill of materials (BOM), which serves as a recipe of ingredients needed to make each item. The quantity of raw materials to order also depends on the lead time and lot sizing. *Lead time* is the amount of time it takes from the placement of a purchase order until the raw materials arrive at the production facility. *Lot size* has to do with discrete quantities that the supplier will ship and the amount that is economical for the producer to receive or store. For example, a supplier might ship a certain raw material in units of 80,000-pound rail cars. The producer might need 95,000 pounds of the raw material. A decision must be made to order one or two rail cars of the raw material.

Purchasing uses the information from MRP to place purchase orders for raw materials with qualified suppliers. Typically, purchase orders are released so that raw materials arrive just in time to be used in production and to minimize warehouse and storage costs. Often, producers will allow suppliers to tap into data via an extranet that enables them to determine what raw materials the producer needs, minimizing the effort and lead time to place and fill purchase orders.

Production uses the high-level production schedule to plan the details of running and staffing the production operation. This more detailed schedule takes into account employee, equipment, and raw material availability along with detailed customer demand data.

Sales ordering is the set of activities that must be performed to capture a customer sales order. A few of the essential steps include recording the items to be purchased, setting the sales price, recording the order quantity, determining the total cost of the order including delivery costs, and confirming the customer's available credit. If the item(s) the customer wants to order are out of stock, the sales order process should communicate this fact and suggest other items to substitute for the customer's initial choice. Setting sales prices can be quite complicated and can include quantity discounts, promotions, and incentives. After the total cost of the order is determined, a company must check the customer's available credit to see if this order is within the credit limit. Figure 9.9 shows a sales order entry window in SAP business software.

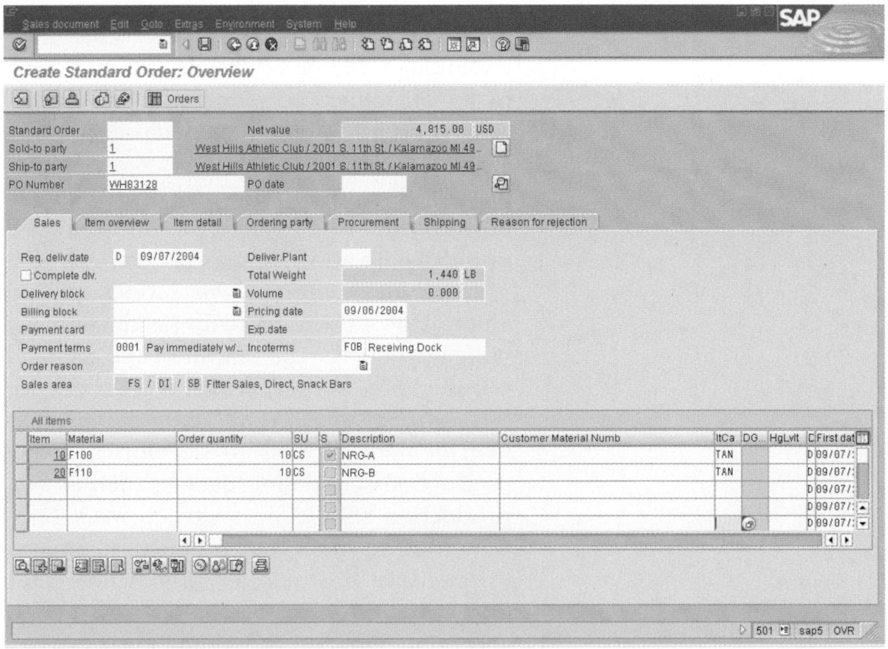

FIGURE 9.9

Sales order entry window

Sales ordering is the set of activities that must be performed to capture a customer sales order.

Source: SAP AG

ERP systems do not work directly with manufacturing machines on the production floor, so they need a way to capture information about what was produced. This data must be passed to the ERP accounting modules to keep an accurate count of finished product inventory. Many companies have personal computers on the production floor that count the number of cases of each product item by scanning a UPC code on the packing cases used to ship the material. Other approaches for capturing production quantities include using RFID chips and manually entering the data via a handheld computer.

Separately, production quality data can be added based on the results of quality tests run on a sample of the product for each batch of product produced. Typically, this data includes the batch identification number, which identifies the production run and the results of various product quality tests.

Retailers as well as manufacturers use demand forecasting to match production to consumer demand and to allocate products to stores. Oberto

Sausage Company is a leading manufacturer of meat snacks and sausage products whose brands include Oh Boy! Oberto, Lowrey's Meat Snacks, Pacific Gold Meat Snacks, and Smokecraft Real Smokehouse Snacks. The firm sells its products directly to mass merchandisers and major supermarket chains. Over the years, Oberto has developed a multi-step demand forecasting process that relies on demand forecasting software, historical sales and promotion data, and causal data about major customers. The process is executed by a team of individuals, including the demand manager, customer service reps, and sales forecast analysts. Each group contributes input to creating the final forecast. Once the forecast is completed, it is fed into the ERP system where it drives procurement, production planning, production scheduling, and plant execution.[18]

Customer Relationship Management

customer relationship management (CRM) system: A system that helps a company manage all aspects of customer encounters, including marketing, sales, distribution, accounting, and customer service.

A **customer relationship management (CRM) system** helps a company manage all aspects of customer encounters, including marketing, sales, distribution, accounting, and customer service. See Figure 9.10. A simplistic way to think about a CRM system is to imagine an address book with a historical record of all the organization's interactions with each customer. The goal of CRM is to understand and anticipate the needs of current and potential customers to increase customer retention and loyalty while optimizing the way that products and services are sold. CRM is used primarily by people in the sales, marketing, distribution, accounting, and service organizations to capture and view data about customers and to improve communications. Businesses implementing CRM systems report benefits such as improved customer satisfaction, increased customer retention, reduced operating costs, and the ability to meet customer demand.

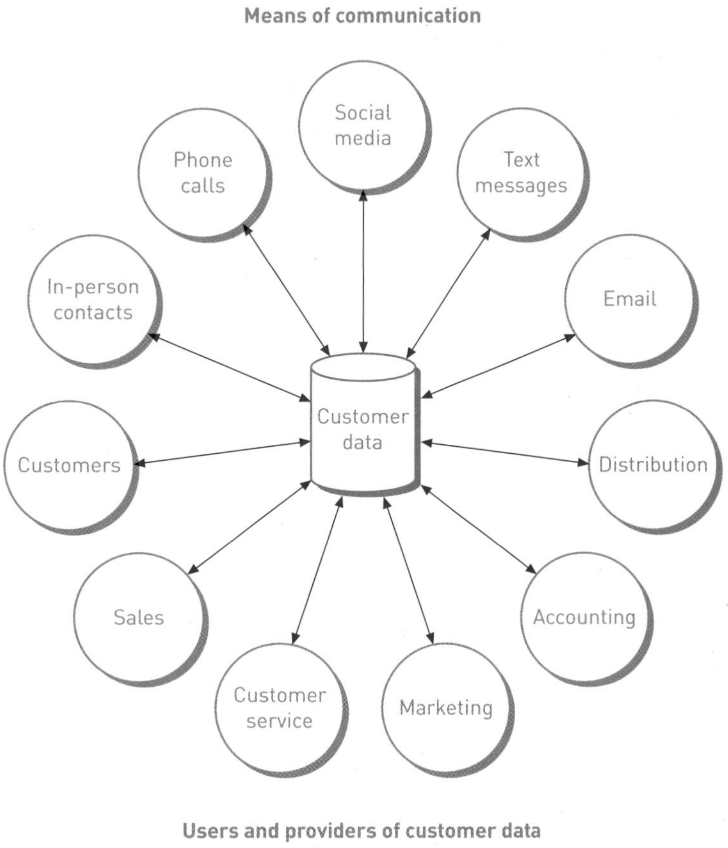

Means of communication

Users and providers of customer data

FIGURE **9.10**

Customer relationship management system

A CRM system provides a central repository of customer data used by the organization.

© 2016 Cengage Learning

CRM software automates and integrates the functions of sales, marketing, and service in an organization. The objective is to capture data about every contact a company has with a customer through every channel and to store it in the CRM system so that the company can truly understand customer actions. CRM software helps an organization build a database about its customers that describes relationships in sufficient detail so that management, salespeople, customer service providers, and even customers can access information to match customer needs with product plans and offerings, remind them of service requirements, and report on the other products the customers have purchased.

Small, medium, and large organizations in a wide variety of industries choose to implement CRM for many reasons, depending on their needs. Consider the following examples:

- Air Animal Pet Movers is a small company based in Tampa, Florida, that coordinates the moving of pets both nationally and internationally. Pet owners are nervous about their pet's move and expect responsive, attentive service throughout the process. Air Animal implemented a CRM system that not only tracks every interaction with its clients but also updates its sales and invoicing processes. Customers can complete an online form to provide details of their needs. This process generates an estimate for services and a new customer contact record. The system then captures details required to complete each step in the move, including flight information, pet boarding, and required international documents. The system then provides reminder alerts to ensure that each step is completed.[19]

- Phillips is a Dutch diversified technology company whose primary business units are focused on health care, consumer lifestyle, and lighting. It employs some 122,000 people across more than 60 countries. The company uses a cloud-based CRM system called Salesforce to provide its employees with real-time customer insights to make every customer interaction more meaningful. "We want to connect sales, service, marketing, and anyone that's customer-facing with Salesforce so we can share best practices and pockets of excellence. We also want to give our R&D, supply chain, and product groups insight into evolving customer needs and opportunities."[20]

- CSX is in the railroad transportation business and operates 21,000 miles of railway in 23 states across the United States. As part of its CRM implementation project, CSX wanted to improve its local operations service. This required a team effort with participation from trainmasters, sales, and marketing to gather key data about some 5,000 customer work sites. The data includes the customer's site location in CSX's GIS maps, track infrastructure characteristics, service challenges, operational improvement opportunities, and the customer's operational behaviors. Loading this data into its CRM system enables CSX employees to better manage their sales efforts, more closely meet customers' needs, and enhance communications with customers.[21]

The key features of a CRM system include the following:

- **Contact management.** The ability to track data on individual customers and sales leads and then access that data from any part of the organization. See Figure 9.11, which shows the SAP Contact Manager.
- **Sales management.** The ability to organize data about customers and sales leads and then to prioritize the potential sales opportunities and identify appropriate next steps.
- **Customer support.** The ability to support customer service representatives so that they can quickly, thoroughly, and appropriately address customer requests and resolve customer issues while collecting and storing data about those interactions.

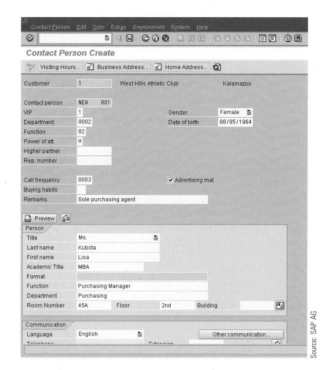

FIGURE **9.11**

SAP Contact Manager

Contact management involves tracking data on individual customers and sales leads and accessing that data from any part of the organization.

- **Marketing automation.** The ability to capture and analyze all customer interactions, generate appropriate responses, and gather data to create and build effective and efficient marketing campaigns.
- **Analysis.** The ability to analyze customer data to identify ways to increase revenue and decrease costs, identify the firm's "best customers," and determine how to retain and find more of them.
- **Social networking.** The ability to create and join sites such as Facebook, where salespeople can make contacts with potential customers.
- **Access by smartphones.** The ability to access Web-based customer relationship management software by devices such as the BlackBerry or Apple iPhone.
- **Import contact data.** The ability for users to import contact data from various data service providers such as Jigsaw, which offers company-level contact data that can be downloaded for free directly into the CRM application.

The focus of CRM involves much more than installing new software. Moving from a culture of simply selling products to placing the customer first is essential to a successful CRM deployment. Before any software is loaded onto a computer, a company must retrain employees. Who handles customer issues and when must be clearly defined, and computer systems need to be integrated so that all pertinent information is available immediately, whether a customer calls a sales representative or a customer service representative.

LEVIEV Extraordinary Diamonds has exclusive access to some of the world's most unique stones and sells large, rare, and colored diamonds through its boutiques in Dubai, London, New York, and Singapore. While caret, clarity, color, and cut are the factors that determine the value of a diamond, a one-of-a-kind diamond does not sell unless the customer has trust in the brand. Indeed LEVIEV CEO Paul Raps states: "Our relationships with customers are the most important part of our business." To that end, LEVIEV implemented a CRM system to ensure those relationships are formed and maintained. Its CRM system stores a photograph of every LEVIEV stone and piece of jewelry each customer has purchased, as along with any items the customer is creating with the company's designers plus a wish list of future purchases. This data can only be accessed by the customer and his or her sales associate. The CRM system not only keeps track of customers' birthdays and anniversaries but also where they vacation during the summer and winter. The goal is to help the sales associates plan the relationship-building activities necessary to sustain and increase the business.[22]

Table 9.3 lists the highest-rated CRM systems.[23]

TABLE 9.3 Highest-rated CRM systems, 2014

Rank	Vendor	Select Customers	Pricing Starts at
1	Salesforce Sales Cloud	Dell Dr. Pepper Snapple	$5 per user/month
2	OnContact CRM 7	Prudential Carfax	$50 per user/month
3	Sage Software CRM	Panasonic Lockheed Martin	$39 per user/month
4	Prophet CRM	AT&T Century 21	$24 per user/month

Due to the popularity of mobile devices, shoppers can easily compare products and prices on their mobile phones and instantly tweet their experiences with a brand to dozens of friends. Savvy retailers today use their CRM systems to stay on top of what these customers are saying on social networks. Wells Fargo Bank uses social media to hear what its customers are saying and then responds quickly to their issues and questions to improve customer satisfaction.[24]

Most CRM systems can now be accessed via smartphones to enable employees to see the most current customer information even while on the move. However, in a recent survey, just under 25 percent of salespeople who have a smartphone use it to access their firm's CRM system. Another 10 percent of salespeople worked for a company whose CRM system did not allow mobile access.[25]

Product Lifecycle Management (PLM)

product lifecycle management (PLM): An enterprise business strategy that creates a common repository of product information and processes to support the collaborative creation, management, dissemination, and use of product and packaging definition information.

product lifecycle management (PLM) software: Software that provides a means for managing the data and processes associated with the various phases of the lifecycle of a product, including sales and marketing, research and development, concept development, product design, prototyping and testing, process design, production and assembly, delivery and product installation, service and support, and product retirement and replacement.

computer-aided design (CAD): The use of software to assist in the creation, analysis, and modification of the design of a component or product.

Product lifecycle management (PLM) is an enterprise business strategy that creates a common repository of product information and processes to support the collaborative creation, management, dissemination, and use of product and packaging definition information.

Product lifecycle management (PLM) software provides a means for managing the data and processes associated with the various phases of the lifecycle of a product, including sales and marketing, research and development, concept development, product design, prototyping and testing, manufacturing process design, production and assembly, delivery and product installation, service and support, and product retirement and replacement. See Figure 9.12. As products advance through these stages, product data is generated and distributed to various groups both within and outside the manufacturing firm. This data includes design and process documents, bill of material definitions, product attributes, product formulations, and documents needed for FDA and environmental compliance. PLM software provides support for the key functions of configuration management, document management, engineering change management, release management, and collaboration with suppliers and original equipment manufacturers (OEMs).

The scope of PLM software may include computer-aided design, computer-aided engineering, and computer-aided manufacturing. **Computer-aided design (CAD)** is the use of software to assist in the creation, analysis, and modification of the design of a component or product. Its use can increase the productivity of the designer, improve the quality of design, and create a

Online Fundraising Supports Research into Rare Genetic Disorder

Prader-Willi Syndrome (PWS) is a rare genetic disorder that occurs about once in 15,000 children. It leads to life-threatening childhood obesity and other conditions, in part because the brain is convinced that the body is in a perpetual state of starvation. PWS has historically received little attention or support from medical researchers. The Foundation for Prader-Willi Research (FPWR) sought to change that situation.

FPWR was established in 2003 by 40 families to fund research into PWS. In 2005, the organization's $100,000 income came from a few large donors. The founders realized that increasing donations substantially required changing the way FPWR operated. In particular, the foundation had to establish an online presence. However, the organization had few information technology resources, limited financial resources, and no experience with the Web.

Online giving is a chancy process at best. Research has found that nearly half of the people who visit a charity's Web site, intending to make a donation, don't follow through. What's more, the fraction of visitors who don't donate varies a great deal from site to site. Simon Norris, CEO of consulting firm Nomensa, suggests that "Nonprofits should take a lesson from successful e-commerce brands to understand and deliver an optimal donation experience."

The key to this experience is creating a relationship between the charity and the donor. The FPWR founders understood this principle. They knew, as you learned in this chapter, that CRM systems can "help a company manage all aspects of customer encounters." Replace "customer" by "donor," and that help was exactly what the foundation needed: software to manage its donor relationships to strengthen the donors' connection to FPWR.

Fortunately, FPWR could choose from many available CRM packages—even if the C in CRM is taken as Constituent rather than Customer, as is more appropriate when donors are part of the picture. Unfortunately, the very abundance of CRM packages makes it difficult to choose one. FPWR's limited budget was a critical factor in selecting a CRM package. When the foundation learned of CiviCRM, designed specifically for charitable organizations and available at no charge, that system became the obvious answer.

CiviCRM is designed specifically for donor tracking. It can record contributions of cash, items or services of value (in-kind), and volunteer time. It can handle one-time gifts, recurring gifts, pledges of future gifts, and more. It can track offline gifts to provide a complete picture of a donor's contributions through all channels. The system also differentiates grants (which obligate FPWR to do something in return) from contributions (which don't). It tracks household and workplace affiliations to indicate who is connected to whom. It also lets the organization manage volunteers by skills and availability and create membership levels with various criteria and benefits.

Three people from FPWR plus a hired developer set up CiviCRM, and FPWR now takes in over $700,000 annually through online donations.

FPWR used CiviCRM to launch its OneSmallStep (OSS) for Research initiative. This initiative brought together over 500 fundraisers in 53 cities around the world to raise money for PWS research. OSS organizers in each city used CiviCRM to establish their campaigns and recruit fundraisers who, in turn, solicited donations. CiviCRM handles multiple currencies, languages, and payment processors as well as manages the legal donation tracking requirements of different countries.

The foundation has now awarded over $3 million in research grants to scientists working on possible cures. Without CiviCRM, this achievement would not have been possible.

Discussion Questions

1. How did FPWR leverage CiviCRM to grow its donor base?
2. Your university almost certainly solicits donations from its graduates. How do its donor management requirements differ from those of FPWR? How are they similar?

Critical Thinking Questions

1. What features does CiviCRM share with other CRM systems? What features are unique?
2. What difference would you expect to see between CiviCRM and a CRM designed to support a company in private industries, such as telecommunications or pharmacology?

SOURCES: CiviCRM Web site, *civicrm.org*, accessed March 29, 2014; Foundation for Prader-Willi Research Web site, *www.fpwr.org*, accessed May 2, 2012; Nomensa Web site, *www.nomensa.com*, accessed April 11, 2014; Norris, S. and Potts, J., "Designing the Perfect Donation Experience," Nomensa Ltd., *www.nomensa.com/insights/designing-perfect-donation-process-part-1* (requires free registration), October 2011; Sheridan, A., "Getting to Know You: CRM for the Charity Sector," Fundraising, *www.civilsociety.co.uk/fundraising/opinion/content/8759/getting_to_know_you_crm_for_the_sector*, April 6, 2011.

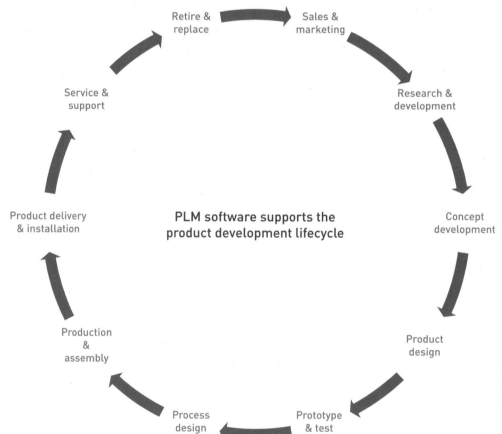

FIGURE 9.12

Scope of PLM software

Using PLM software, you can manage the data and processes associated with the various phases of the lifecycle of a product.

computer-aided engineering (CAE): The use of software to analyze the robustness and performance of components and assemblies.

computer-aided manufacturing (CAM): The use of software to control machine tools and related machinery in the manufacture of components and products.

database that describes the item. This data can be shared with others or used in the machining of the part or in other manufacturing operations. **Computer-aided engineering (CAE)** is the use of software to analyze the robustness and performance of components and assemblies. The software supports the simulation, validation, and optimization of products and manufacturing tools. CAE is extremely useful to design teams in evaluating and decision making. **Computer-aided manufacturing (CAM)** is the use of software to control machine tools and related machinery in the manufacture of components and products. The model generated in CAD and verified in CAE can be input into CAM software, which then controls the machine tool. See Figure 9.13.

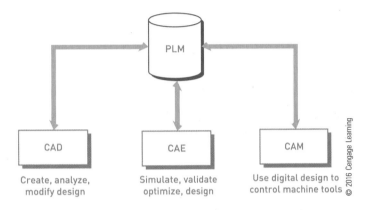

FIGURE 9.13

CAD, CAE, and CAM software

In manufacturing, the model generated in CAD and verified in CAE can be entered into CAM software, which then controls the machine tool.

Some organizations elect to implement a single, integrated PLM system that encompasses all the phases of the product lifecycle with which it is most concerned. Other organizations choose to implement multiple, separate PLM software components from different vendors over time. This piecemeal approach enables an organization to choose the software that best meets it needs for a particular phase in the product lifecycle. It also allows for incremental investment in the PLM strategy. However, it may be difficult to link all the various components together in such a manner that a single comprehensive database of product and process data is created.

Use of an effective PLM system enables global organizations to work as a single team to design, produce, support, and retire products, while capturing best practices and lessons learned along the way.[26] PLM powers innovation and improves productivity by connecting people across global product development and manufacturing organizations with the product and process knowledge they need to succeed. See Figure 9.14.

PLM software and its data are used by both internal and external users. Internal users include engineering, operations and manufacturing, procurement and sourcing, manufacturing, marketing, quality assurance, customer service, regulatory, and others. External users include the manufacturer's design partners, packaging suppliers, raw material suppliers, and contract manufacturers. These users must collaborate to define, maintain, update, and securely share product information throughout the lifecycle of the product. Frequently, these external users are asked to sign nondisclosure agreements to reduce the risk of proprietary information being shared with competitors.

The Flovel Group is a supplier of hydropower equipment and valves for turbines. Its headquarters and manufacturing plant are located about 50 km apart in the state of Haryana in northern India. The firm's strategy for success is to beat its competitors in the quick delivery of products for small- and medium-sized hydropower projects. To this end, it implemented PLM technology. This has enabled Flovel to speed up the release of customized, innovative products to market; improve collaboration and information reuse across all business units involved in the product development lifecycle; and

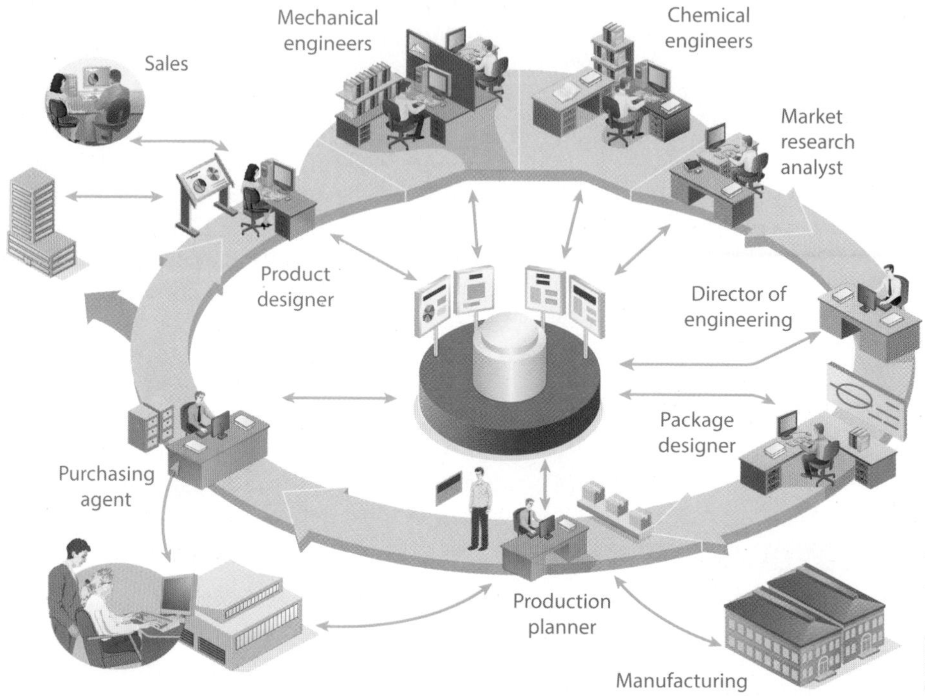

FIGURE 9.14

PLM business strategy

PLM powers innovation and improves productivity.

overcome the physical separation between its design center and manufacturing plant.[27]

Table 9.4 presents a list of some of the top-rated PLM software products (in alphabetic order) according to a 2013 report by Business-Software.com.[28]

TABLE 9.4 Top-rated PLM software products

Organization	Primary PLM Software Product	Technology Model	Select Customers
Arena	Cloud PLM	Cloud-based solution	SiriusXM, SunLink
Infor	Optiva	On-premise solution	Henkel, Sypris
Integware	Enovia Collaborative PLM	On-premise solution	Cummins, Steelcase
PTC	Windchill	SaaS solution	Medco Equipment, InterComm
SAP	PLM	On-premise solution	Porsche, Anadarko Petroleum
Siemens	Teamcenter	On-premise solution	Procter & Gamble, BAE Systems
Softech	ProductCenter PLM	SaaS solution	Hayward Tyler Motors, Monarch Hydraulics
Sopheon	Accolade	Cloud-based solution	PepsiCo, ConAgra

discrete manufacturing: The production of distinct items such as autos, airplanes, furniture, or toys that can be decomposed into their basic components.

process manufacturing: The production of products that are the result of a chemical process such as soda, laundry detergent, gasoline, and pharmaceutical drugs that cannot be easily decomposed into its basic components.

PLM software is created for two broad categories of manufacturing: discrete manufacturing and process manufacturing. **Discrete manufacturing** is the production of distinct items such as autos, airplanes, furniture, or toys that can be decomposed back into their basic components. **Process manufacturing** is the production of products that are the result of a chemical process such as soda, laundry detergent, gasoline, and pharmaceutical drugs that cannot be easily decomposed back into its basic components. Within those broad categories, some PLM software manufacturers specialize on specific industries such as aircraft manufacturing, consumer goods manufacturing, or drug manufacturing.

Table 9.5 outlines the benefits a business can realize when using a PLM system effectively.

Unilever produces and sells 14 categories of home, personal care, and food products with recent worldwide sales of just under €50 billion (about $70

TABLE **9.5** Benefits of a PLM system

Benefit	How Achieved
Reduce time to market	By connecting design, research and development, procurement, manufacturing, and customer service seamlessly through a flexible collaboration environment
	By improving collaboration among the organization and its suppliers, contract manufacturers, and OEMs
Reduce costs	By reducing prototyping costs through the use of software simulation
	By reducing scrap and rework through improved processes
	By reducing the number of product components through standardization
Ensure regulatory compliance	By providing a secure repository, tracking and audit trails, change and document management controls, workflow and communications, and improved security

billion). For over a decade, Unilever has partnered with Siemens to create a global specification management system to develop, configure, and manage all product specifications (e.g., raw materials, intermediate and finished products, and packaging materials). Such a system stores all product specifications in a single, controlled data repository and is a key function of an organization's PLM system. Development of this capability has been important to Unilever as it struggles to innovate in the face of mounting raw material costs. Use of the system has enabled an order of magnitude reduction in the number of specifications used in the organization. This in turn has led to purchasing fewer materials in greater quantities, enabling Unilever to negotiate better deals with suppliers. In addition, it takes a certain amount of R&D time to develop, manage, and maintain any individual specification. So by reducing the number of specifications, Unilever has been able to free R&D time that can be reinvested elsewhere.[29]

Overcoming Challenges in Implementing Enterprise Systems

Implementing an enterprise system, particularly for a large organization, is extremely challenging and requires tremendous amounts of resources, the best IS and businesspeople, and plenty of management support. In spite of all this, many enterprise system implementations fail, and problems with an enterprise system implementation can require expensive solutions. The following is a sample of major enterprise system implementation project failures:

- The United States Air Force wasted $1 billion in a failed attempt to implement an enterprise system to replace over 200 legacy systems involved with the global supply chain that ensures its men and women are well supported and provisioned. The scope of the system included product lifecycle management, planning and scheduling, repair and maintenance, and distribution and transportation.[30]
- Avon expended over $100 million on a new order management system that never was rolled out because it wreaked havoc on normal operations. The system was so difficult to use that sales reps quit the company rather than be forced to struggle with a "user-unfriendly" system.[31]
- The California state controller sued the enterprise software vendor of an integrated payroll and benefits program for $50 million. The software continued to generate significant errors even after an 8-month pilot testing period.[32]

Half of nearly 200 ERP implementations worldwide evaluated by Panorama, an ERP consulting firm, were judged to be failures. Table 9.6 lists and describes the most significant challenges to successful implementation of an enterprise system.[33]

TABLE **9.6** Challenges to successful enterprise system implementation

Challenge	Description
Cost and disruption of upgrades	Most companies have other systems that must be integrated with the enterprise system, such as financial analysis programs, e-commerce operations, and other applications that communicate with suppliers, customers, distributors, and other business partners. This integration takes even more effort and time.
Cost and long implementation lead time	The average ERP implementation cost is $5.5 million with an average project duration of just over 14 months.
Difficulty in managing change	Companies often must radically change how they operate to conform to the enterprise work processes. These changes can be so drastic to longtime employees that they depart rather than adapt to the change, leaving the firm short of experienced workers.
Management of software customization	The base enterprise system may need to be modified to meet mandatory business requirements. This modification can become extremely expensive and further delay implementation.
User frustration with the new system	Effective use of an enterprise system requires changes in work processes and in the details of how work gets done. Many users initially balk at these changes and require much training and encouragement.

© 2016 Cengage Learning

The following list provides tips for avoiding many common causes for failed enterprise system implementations:

- Assign a full-time executive to manage the project.
- Appoint an experienced, independent resource to provide project oversight and to verify and validate system performance.
- Allow sufficient time for transition from the old way of doing things to the new system and new processes.
- Plan to spend considerable time and money training people; many project managers recommend that 30–60 days per employee be budgeted for training of personnel.
- Define metrics to assess project progress and to identify project-related risks.
- Keep the scope of the project well defined and contained to essential business processes.
- Be wary of modifying the enterprise system software to conform to your firm's business practices.

Hosted Software Model for Enterprise Software

Many business application software vendors are pushing the use of the hosted software model for SMEs. The goal is to help customers acquire, use, and benefit from the new technology while avoiding much of the associated complexity and high start-up costs. Applicor, Intacct, NetSuite, SAP, and Workday are among the software vendors who offer hosted versions of their enterprise software at a cost of $50 to $200 per month per user.

This pay-as-you-go approach is appealing to SMEs because they can experiment with powerful software capabilities without making a major financial investment. Organizations can then dispose of the software without large investments if the software fails to provide value or otherwise misses expectations. Also, using the hosted software model means the small business firm does not need to employ a full-time IT person to maintain key business applications. The small business firm can expect additional savings from reduced hardware costs and costs associated with maintaining an appropriate computer environment (such as air conditioning, power, and an uninterruptible power supply).

Table 9.7 lists the advantages and disadvantages of hosted software.

TABLE 9.7 Advantages and disadvantages of hosted software model

Advantages	Disadvantages
Decreased total cost of ownership	Potential availability and reliability issues
Faster system start-up	Potential data security issues
Lower implementation risk	Potential problems integrating the hosted products of different vendors
Management of systems outsourced to experts	Savings anticipated from outsourcing may be offset by increased effort to manage vendor

© 2016 Cengage Learning

A corset is an item of apparel worn to hold and shape the upper body into a desired shape for aesthetic or medical purposes. Corset Story is one of the world's biggest corset retailers with hundreds of styles, designs, and fabrics from which its demanding customers may choose. The firm needed a PLM system to support the development of its complex product line. It decided to implement a cloud-based PLM system because of the speed at which it could be deployed. It took just five weeks from initial implementation to the time its people were trained and ready to use the system to support the design, development, material management, approvals, and critical path management activities associated with the development of its product line for each new fashion season.[34]

SUMMARY

Principle:

An organization must have information systems that support routine, day-to-day activities and that help a company add value to its products and services.

Transaction processing systems (TPSs) are at the heart of most information systems in businesses today. A TPS is an organized collection of people, procedures, software, databases, and devices used to capture fundamental data about events that affect the organization (transactions) and that use that data to update the official records of the organization.

The methods of TPSs include batch and online processing. Batch processing involves the collection of transactions into batches, which are entered into the system at regular intervals as a group. Online transaction processing (OLTP) allows transactions to be entered as they occur.

Order processing systems capture and process customer order data from the receipt of the order through creation of a customer invoice.

Accounting systems track the flow of data related to all the cash flows that affect the organization.

Purchasing systems support the inventory control, purchase order processing, receiving, and accounts payable business functions.

Organizations today, including SMEs, typically implement an integrated set of TPSs from a single or limited number of software vendors to meet their transaction processing needs.

Organizations expect TPSs to accomplish a number of specific objectives, including processing data generated by and about transactions, maintaining a high degree of accuracy and information integrity, compiling accurate and timely reports and documents, increasing labor efficiency, helping provide increased and enhanced service, and building and maintaining customer loyalty. In some situations, an effective TPS can help an organization gain significant business benefits.

All TPSs perform the following basic activities: data collection, which involves the capture of source data to complete a set of transactions; data editing, which checks for data validity and completeness; data correction, which involves providing feedback of a potential problem and enabling users to change the data; data processing, which is the performance of calculations, sorting, categorizing, summarizing, and storing data for further processing; data storage, which involves placing transaction data into one or more databases; and document production, which involves outputting records and reports.

Principle:

An organization that implements an enterprise system is creating a highly integrated set of systems, which can lead to many business benefits.

Enterprise resource planning (ERP) software supports the efficient operation of business processes by integrating activities throughout a business, including sales, marketing, manufacturing, logistics, accounting, and staffing.

Implementing an ERP system can provide many advantages, including allowing access to data for operational decision making; eliminating costly, inflexible legacy systems; providing improved work processes; and creating the opportunity to upgrade technology infrastructure.

Some of the disadvantages associated with ERP systems are that they are time consuming, difficult, and expensive to implement; they can also be difficult to integrate with other systems.

No one ERP software solution is "best" for all organizations. SAP, Oracle, Infor, and Microsoft are among the leading ERP suppliers.

Although the scope of ERP implementation can vary, most manufacturing organizations use ERP to support the supply chain management activities of planning, executing, and controlling all tasks involved in raw material sourcing and procurement, converting raw materials to finished products, warehousing the finished product, and delivering it to customers.

The production and supply chain management process starts with sales forecasting to develop an estimate of future customer demand. This initial forecast is at a fairly high level, with estimates made by product group rather than by individual product item. The sales and operations plan takes demand and current inventory levels into account and determines the specific product items that need to be produced as well as when to meet the forecast future demand. Demand management refines the production plan by determining the amount of weekly or daily production needed to meet the demand for individual products. Detailed scheduling uses the production plan defined by the demand management process to develop a detailed production schedule specifying details, such as which item to produce first and when production should be switched from one item to another. Materials requirement planning determines the amount and timing for placing raw material orders with suppliers. Purchasing uses the information from materials requirement planning to place purchase orders for raw materials and transmit them to qualified suppliers. Production uses the detailed schedule to plan the logistics of running and staffing the production operation. The individual application modules included in the ERP system are designed to support best practices, the most efficient and effective ways to complete a business process.

Organizations are implementing CRM systems to manage all aspects of customer encounters, including marketing, sales, distribution, accounting, and customer service. The goal of CRM is to understand and anticipate the needs of current and potential customers to increase customer retention and loyalty while optimizing the way products and services are sold.

Manufacturing organizations are implementing product lifecycle management (PLM) software to manage the data and processes associated with the various phases of the product lifecycle, including sales and marketing, research and development, concept development, product design, prototyping and testing, manufacturing process design, production and assembly, delivery and product installation, service and support, and product retirement and replacement. These systems are used by both internal and external users to enable them to collaborate and capture best practices and lessons learned along the way.

The most significant challenges to successful implementation of an enterprise system include the cost and disruption of upgrades, the cost and long implementation lead time, the difficulty in managing change, the management of software customization, and user frustration with the new system.

Business application software vendors are experimenting with the hosted software model to see if the approach meets customer needs and is likely to generate significant revenue. This approach is especially appealing to SMEs due to the low initial cost, which makes it possible to experiment with powerful software capabilities.

KEY TERMS

batch processing system

best practices

computer-aided design (CAD)

computer-aided engineering (CAE)

computer-aided manufacturing (CAM)

customer relationship management (CRM) system

data collection

data correction

data editing

data processing

data storage

discrete manufacturing

document production

enterprise system

online transaction processing (OLTP)

process manufacturing

product lifecycle management (PLM)

product lifecycle management (PLM) software

source data automation

supply chain management (SCM)

transaction processing cycle

CHAPTER 9: SELF-ASSESSMENT TEST

An organization must have information systems that support routine, day-to-day activities and that help a company add value to its products and services.

1. Transaction processing systems capture and process the detailed data necessary to update _____ about the fundamental business operations of the organization.

2. The essential characteristic of a batch processing system is that there is some _____ between an event occurring and the eventual processing of the related transaction.

3. Which of the following is *not* one of the basic components of a TPS?
   a. databases
   b. networks
   c. procedures
   d. analytical models

4. OLTP stands for _____.
   a. only last time processed
   b. one last transaction to process
   c. online transaction processing
   d. only temporary processing

5. The specific business needs and goals of the organization define the method of transaction processing best suited for the various application of the company. True or False?

6. Which of the following is not an objective of an organization's transaction processing system?
   a. Capture, process, and update databases of business data required to support routine business activities
   b. Ensure that data is processed immediately upon occurrence of a business transaction
   c. Avoid processing fraudulent transactions
   d. Produce timely user responses and reports

7. Business data goes through a cycle that includes data collection, data _____, data correction, data processing, data storage, and documentation production.

8. Unfortunately, there are few choices for software packages that provide integrated transaction processing system solutions for small and medium-sized enterprises. True or False?

9. Capturing and gathering all the data necessary to complete the processing of transactions is called _____.

An organization that implements an enterprise system is creating a highly integrated set of systems, which can lead to many business benefits.

10. Small organizations were among the first to adopt ERP systems because of the relative simplicity of implementing these systems in such an environment. True or False?

11. The individual application modules included in an ERP system are designed to sup-

port _____, the most efficient and effective ways to complete a business process.

12. _____ software helps a customer manage all aspects of customer encounters, including marketing, sales, distribution, accounting, and customer service.

13. The hosted software model for enterprise software helps customers acquire, use, and benefit from new technology while avoiding much of the associated complexity and high start-up costs. True or False?

14. _____ is software used to analyze the robustness and performance of components and assemblies.
   a. PLM
   b. CAD
   c. CAE
   d. CAM

15. Many multinational companies roll out standard IS applications for all to use. However, standard applications often don't account for all the differences among business partners and employees operating in other parts of the world. Which of the following is a frequent modification that is needed for standard software?
   a. Software might need to be designed with local language interfaces to ensure the successful implementation of a new IS.
   b. Customization might be needed to handle date fields correctly.
   c. Users might also have to implement manual processes and overrides to enable systems to function correctly.
   d. All of the above

CHAPTER 9: SELF-ASSESSMENT TEST ANSWERS

1. records
2. delay
3. d
4. c
5. True
6. b
7. editing
8. False

9. data collection
10. False
11. best practices
12. Customer relationship management
13. True
14. c
15. d

REVIEW QUESTIONS

1. Identify and briefly describe six basic transaction processing activities performed by all transaction processing systems.
2. Provide a data processing example for which the use of a batch processing system to handle transactions is appropriate. Provide an example

for which the use of online transaction processing is appropriate.
3. What is an enterprise system? Identify and briefly discuss the goals of three types of enterprise systems.
4. What are best practices?
5. Define supply chain management.

6. What is a Tier I ERP software vendor?
7. Identify and discuss some of the benefits that are common to the use of an ERP, CRM, or PLM enterprise system, whether it be for an SME or a large multinational organization.
8. How does materials requirement planning support the purchasing process in an ERP environment? What are some of the issues and complications that arise in materials requirement planning?
9. Identify and briefly describe at least four key business capabilities provided by the use of a CRM system.
10. Identify the basic business processes included within the scope of product lifecycle management.
11. Discuss the difference between discrete and process manufacturing.
12. What is source data automation? What benefits can it be expected to deliver?

DISCUSSION QUESTIONS

1. Identify and briefly discuss five challenges to the successful implementation of an enterprise system. Provide several tips to overcome these challenges.
2. Assume that you are the owner of a small bicycle sales and repair shop serving hundreds of customers in your area. Identify the kinds of customer information you would like your firm's CRM system to capture. How might this information be used to provide better service or increase revenue? Identify where or how you might capture this data.
3. Why were SMEs slow to adopt ERP software? What changed to make ERP software more attractive for SMEs?
4. Briefly describe the hosted software model for enterprise software and discuss its primary appeal for SMEs.
5. Explain how CAD, CAE, and CAM software can work together to support the product development lifecycle.
6. In what ways is the implementation of a CRM system simpler and less risky for an SME than for a large multinational corporation?
7. You are a member of the engineering organization for an aircraft parts manufacturer. The firm is considering the implementation of a PLM system. Make a convincing argument for selecting a system whose scope includes CAD, CAE, and CAM software.
8. What benefits should the suppliers and customers of a firm that has successfully implemented an ERP system expect to see? How might an ERP implementation affect an organization's suppliers?
9. Many organizations are moving to a collaborative process with their major suppliers to get their input on designing and planning future product modification or new products. Explain how a PLM system might enhance such a process. What issues and concerns might a manufacturer have in sharing product data?

PROBLEM-SOLVING EXERCISES

1. Imagine that you are a new employee in the engineering organization of a large camping equipment and outdoor furniture manufacturing firm. The company is considering implementing a PLM system to better manage the design and manufacture of its products. You have been invited to a meeting to share your thoughts on how such a system might be used and what capabilities are most important. How would you prepare for this meeting? What points would you make? Develop a presentation containing three or four slides that summarize your thoughts.
2. In a spreadsheet program, enter the ingredients and quantity required to make your favorite homemade cookie. This represents a simple bill of materials (BOM). Add a column to show the cost for each ingredient. Now "explode" the BOM to show the quantity and cost of each ingredient required to make 10,000 cookies.

TEAM ACTIVITIES

1. With your team members, interview several business managers at a firm that has implemented an enterprise system (ERP, CRM, or PLM system). Interview them to document the scope, cost, and schedule for the overall project. Find out why the organization decided it was time to implement the enterprise system? Make a list of what they see as the primary benefits of the

implementation. What were the biggest hurdles they had to overcome? Are there any remaining issues that must be resolved before the project can be deemed a success? What are they? With the benefit of 20–20 hindsight, is there anything they would have done differently to have made the project go more smoothly?

2. As a team, develop a list of seven key criteria that a nonprofit charitable organization should consider in selecting a CRM system. Discuss each criterion and assign a weight representing the relative importance of that criterion. Develop a simple spreadsheet to use in scoring various CRM alternatives in terms of how well they meet these criteria on a scale of 0 to 4. Do research on the Web to identify three candidate CRM software packages. Based on information presented on their Web site, score each alternative using your set of criteria. Which candidate CRM software does your team select?

WEB EXERCISES

1. Do research on the Web to find several sources that discuss the challenges associated with the implementation of an enterprise system. Is there general agreement among the sources as to the most significant challenges? What advice is offered as to the most effective way to overcome these challenges? Develop your own list of the five most significant challenges and five most effective tactics for overcoming these challenges.

2. Using the Web, identify several software services firms that offer consulting services to help organizations implement enterprise systems. Gain an understanding of what sort of services they offer and become familiar with several of their success stories. If you had to choose one of the software services firms to assist your SME organization, which one would you choose and why?

CAREER EXERCISES

1. Enterprise system software vendors need business systems analysts who understand both information systems and business processes. Make a list of six or more specific qualifications needed to be a strong business systems analyst who supports the implementation and conversion to an enterprise system within an SME. Are there additional qualifications needed for someone who is doing similar work but for a large multinational organization?

2. Imagine that you are a commercial solar heating salesperson for a manufacturing and installation firm. You make frequent sales calls on potential customers in a three-state area. The purpose of these sales calls is to acquaint the firms with your company's products and get them to consider purchase of your products. Describe the basic functionality you would want in your organization's CRM system for it to help identify potential new customers and to support you in preparing and making presentations to these people.

CASE STUDIES

Case One

From Stand-Alone to Integrated Applications

YIOULA Group is the largest glass manufacturer in the Balkans, producing over 625,000 glass containers annually as well as over 30,000 tons of tableware. Starting in the 1990s in Greece, the company expanded by acquiring other glassmaking firms in Romania, Bulgaria, and Ukraine. The company has seven factories in four countries, about 2,100 employees, and net annual sales of about €180 million (about U.S. $240 million).

As a result of its growth through acquisition, YIOULA Group found itself with a confusing variety of information systems. The group was unable to compare production costs for the same item across factories, could not improve efficiencies by coordinating purchasing and financial management across all its plants, and was not positioned for continued growth or expansion into new market areas. Clearly, its legacy stand-alone applications needed to be replaced.

YIOULA Group CIO Zacharias Maridakis had previous experience using integrated enterprise software when he worked at Mobil Oil's Greek subsidiary, Mobil Oil Hellas S.A., in the 1990s. Therefore, he was well acquainted with the advantages of such software. Under his direction, YIOULA Group investigated various software packages. They selected JD Edwards EnterpriseOne, named for a company that had become part of Oracle Corporation in 2005. Part of the reason for this choice was that most other ERP packages, including the SAP software with which Maridakis had worked at Mobil, are designed primarily for much larger organizations. EnterpriseOne was always intended for medium-sized firms.

Because YIOULA Group had little experience with EnterpriseOne, it enlisted the help of Oracle partner Softecon to help configure the software to the company's needs, meet the legal requirements of each region in which it operates, and manage implementation in each area. Support for the Greek language (as well as English and eighteen others) is a standard JD Edwards EnterpriseOne capability available from Oracle; Softecon added the other languages that YIOULA Group needed to the user interface. YIOULA Group also added a specialized cost comparison module from Softecon to the basic EnterpriseOne package. This module helps the group choose the lowest-cost facility to manufacture a product.

The conversion to a single enterprise package gave YIOULA Group the expected benefits. Time from order to invoice, delivery time, and cash collection have all been accelerated. Financial data is now available two weeks after the end of a period versus one month previously. A consolidated view of inventory across all plants has enabled the group to manage inventory more efficiently and comprehensively and to use just-in-time purchasing methods.

Perhaps even more importantly, YIOULA Group is now positioned to grow. As Maridakis puts it, "Oracle's JD Edwards EnterpriseOne is a key enabler of our strategy to enhance market leadership in the Balkans, grow our business in the Ukraine, and continue to improve productivity, efficiency, and profitability as we expand into new markets."

Discussion Questions

1. What problems had the YIOULA Group's stand-alone legacy software created for the company?
2. What are the advantages of ERP systems over stand-alone software packages?

Critical Thinking Questions

1. What immediate and long-term needs did EnterpriseOne fill for the YIOULA Group?
2. The YIOULA group adopted a general ERP system that was not industry specific. What are the advantages and disadvantages of general ERP systems and industry-specific systems?

SOURCES: "Oracle Corporation," JD Edwards EnterpriseOne Web site, *www.oracle.com/us/products/applications/jd-edwards-enterpriseone /index.html*, accessed April 11, 2014; "YIOULA Group Builds Scalable Platform for Sustained Growth, Profitability, and Market Leadership," Oracle Corporation, *http://www.oracle.com/us/corporate/customers /jde-oow-2012-booklet-1842754.pdf*, September 2012; Softecon Enterprise Web site (English), *www.softecon.com/site/en*, accessed April 11, 2014; YIOULA Group Web site, *www.yioula.com*, accessed March 29, 2014.

Case Two

Kerry Group Is on Your Table

In business, sourcing is the set of activities involved in finding, evaluating, and then engaging suppliers of goods or services. Before a business can start to manage its supply chain, as described in this chapter, it must complete a sourcing process.

Ireland's Kerry Group, a supplier of food ingredients and flavors to the worldwide food industry and of consumer food products to the British Isles, requires a wide range of raw materials from many suppliers. With annual revenue of €5.8 billion (about U.S. $10 billion) in 2013, it needs a lot of those materials. With plants in 24 countries and 40 percent of revenue from outside Europe, it is impossible for the people in one plant to know about all possible suppliers worldwide,

but making local sourcing decisions would reduce economies of scale. With the thin profit margins of the food industry, good sourcing decisions are vital to Kerry Group's profitability. Software to manage the sourcing process is one way to help make those decisions.

Kerry Group was already a SAP customer when it chose SAP Sourcing OnDemand, having used SAP ERP systems since 2009. The advantage of obtaining a new system from its existing ERP supplier is assured compatibility with applications the company already uses. "What we needed was an intuitive sourcing system that would be completely integrated with our SAP back-office for an end-to-end procurement process," said Peter Fotios, Kerry Group's director of e-procurement services.

SAP Sourcing OnDemand uses the cloud computing concept. As its OnDemand name suggests, customers do not have to dedicate computing resources to the software. They use SAP resources on demand as their needs require, paying on a per-user, per-month subscription basis. Meanwhile, SAP is responsible for administrative tasks such as data backup and, if necessary, restoration.

Kerry Group implemented SAP Sourcing OnDemand by beginning with a pilot plant. "We rolled it out smoothly in Ireland first, then England and then throughout our global operations in 23 countries," explains Fotios. If any problems appeared in Ireland, the pilot site, Kerry Group could have focused all its problem-solving resources on that location. Fortunately, no major issues arose.

Another thing that Kerry Group did right at implementation time was training. Recognizing that it had competent in-house trainers and competent technical professionals, but few if any who were both, the firm engaged SAP's Irish training partner Olas to assist with that end of the project. Olas brought SAP expertise to the training team, completing the required set of capabilities.

Moving forward, Kerry Group has project plans extending into 2016 for the full roll-out of all its planned SAP ERP capabilities. The smoothness of its Sourcing OnDemand implementation, which took a total of four weeks elapsed time because the software was already running in the cloud when they began, is a good indication that the rest of the project (which is in many ways more complex) will probably go well. If Kerry Group is to carry out its mission statement, which includes being "the world leader in food ingredients and flavors serving the food and beverage industry," the roll-out will have to be smooth.

Discussion Questions

1. What needs did the Kerry Group's new ERP system meet?
2. Kerry Group is taking a slow and methodical approach to implementing the parts of SAP ERP software. What does the company gain and what does it lose by taking its time in this way?

Critical Thinking Questions

1. Why should Kerry Group standardize on one ERP package? Wouldn't it be simpler and less expensive to let each plant and sales operation choose its own software, as long as it can report its financial results to headquarters in a standard form?

2. What are the advantages and disadvantages to using a third-party vendor like Olas to deploy a new ERP system? What steps can companies take to overcome the disadvantages of relying on third-party vendors when deploying enterprise-wide systems?

SOURCES: Kerry Group Web site, *www.kerrygroup.com*, accessed April 11, 2014; Staff, "Kerry's SAP Transformation Measures Up to Their L&D Beliefs," Olas, *olas.ie*, May 18, 2011; Staff, "Kerry Group Transforms Its Global Procurement Group in Weeks With SAP Sourcing OnDemand Solution," SAP, *www.sap.com/news-reader/index.epx?pressid=18809*, May 1, 2012.

Questions for Web Case

See the Web site for this book to read about the Altitude Online case for this chapter. Following are questions concerning this Web case.

Altitude Online: Enterprise Systems Considerations
Discussion Questions

1. Judging from the ERP features, how important is an ERP to the functioning of a business? Explain.
2. What consideration do you think led Altitude Online to decide to host the ERP on its own servers rather than using SaaS? What are the benefits and drawbacks of both approaches?

Critical Thinking Questions

1. What challenges lay ahead for Altitude Online as it rolls out its new ERP system?
2. How might the ERP affect Altitude Online's future growth and success?

NOTES

Sources for the opening vignette: Bronto Skylift Web site, *www.bronto.fi/sivu.aspx?taso=0&id=10*; "Hydraulic Platform Maker Gets Lift from Design Data Management," Siemens Web site, *www.plm.automation.siemens.com/en_us /about_us/success/case_study.cfm?Component=219780& ComponentTemplate=1481*.

1. "ILG Independent Liquor Group," Solentive Software, *www.solentivesoftware.com.au/our-clients/ilg-indepen dent-liquor-group*, accessed March 2, 2014.
2. "Payroll Excel to Automation Drives Productivity for Growing Policy Bazaar," *www.payrollinsights.com/wp -content/uploads/policy-bazaar-case-study.pdf*, accessed March 2, 2014.
3. "Who We Are ADP," *www.adp.com/about-us.aspx*, accessed March 3, 2014.
4. "Spectrum Family Medicine," *eClinical Works*, January 7, 2014, *www.eclinicalworks.com/Collateral /Documents/English-US/Spectrum_Family_Medicine _CaseStudy_2014_January7.pdf*.
5. "About PayPal," *www.paypal-media.com/about*, accessed March 5, 2014.
6. "Ciber Case Study: Wisconsin Department of Health Services—WIC," *www.ciber.com/tasks/render/file /?whitepaper=wisconsin-department-of-health -services-wic-program&fileID=2BEF3900-A42E-F37F -92DD52E2C5F22E4A*, accessed March 3, 2014.
7. "Customer Success Story: Zoës Goes Chef's Kitchen To Streamline Operations," *www.kianoff.com/casestudies /ZoesKitchen.pdf*, accessed March 6, 2014.
8. Chawla, Mehak, "Accounting for SMEs," *Computer Financial Express*, January 18, 2013, *http://computer .financialexpress.com/sections/news-analysis/1117 -accounting-for-smes*.
9. "Qvinci Clients," *www.qvinci.com/Clients*, accessed March 8, 2014.
10. "Customer Stories: China Baroque," *www.ncrsilver.com /customer-stories.html*, accessed March 8, 2014.
11. Miles, Stephanie, "7 Cloud-Based POS Systems for SMBs," Street Fight, February 4, 2013, *http://streetfight mag.com/2013/02/04/7-cloud-based-pos-systems-for -smbs/*.

12. "IBM Case Studies: Amrit Feeds Solves Complex Sales Order Forecasting with SAP ERP and IBM Global Business Services," April 17, 2013, *www-01.ibm.com /software/success/cssdb.nsf/CS/STRD-96UKRN?Open Document&Site=default&cty=en_us*.
13. "Network Rail's ERP System is Fit for the Future," CSC Success Stories, *http://assets1.csc.com/uk/downloads /Network_Rail_ERP_case_study.pdf*, accessed March 8, 2014.
14. "Petroleum Company Optimizes Supply Chain," CSC Success Stories, *http://www.csc.com/success_stories /flxwd/78768-case_study?article=http://www.csc.com /management_consulting/success_stories/70174-csc _drives_supply_chain_optimization_for_petroleum _client.js&searched=ERP+best practices*, accessed March 12, 2014.
15. "DuPont: CSC Creates Single Backbone to Update, Integrate Global Systems," CSC Case Study, *www.csc .com/success_stories/flxwd/78768-case_study?article =http://www.csc.com/chemical/success_stories/39058 -dupont_csc_creates_single_backbone_to_update _integrate_global_systems.js&searched=erp*, accessed March 12, 2014.
16. "Top Ten Enterprise Resource Planning (ERP) Vendors," Compare Business Products, *http://resources.idgenter prise.com/original/AST-0067016_Top_10_ERP _Vendors.pdf*, accessed March 7, 2014.
17. "A Supply Chain Management Success Story: Kidrobot," *www.simparel.com/customers/success-stories/kidrobot .html*, accessed March 10, 2014.
18. "Oberto Sausage Finds the Right Recipe for Forecasting," ForecastPro success story, *www.forecast pro.com/pdfs/Success%20Story-Oberto%20Sausage %20Co.pdf*, accessed March 10, 2014.
19. "Air Animal," *http://info.airanimal.com/aw01/?gclid= CKO1mYSVj70CFYc7Ogod7WkAFw*, accessed March 13, 2014.
20. "Salesforce Helps Philips Stay Light Years Ahead of the Competition," *www.salesforce.com/customers/stories /philips.jsp*, accessed March 13, 2014.
21. "Know Your Customers: How a Premier US Railway Company Takes Charge with CRM," *www.microsoft*

.com/en-us/dynamics/customer-success-stories-detail
.aspx?casestudyid=395000000081, accessed March 13,
2014.

22. "LEVIEV Success Story," *Salesforce.com, www.sales
force.com/customers/stories/leviev.jsp*, accessed
March 10, 2014.

23. "CRM Software Review 2014," *http://crm-software
-review.toptenreviews.com*, accessed March 13,
2014, and "2014 Edition Top 40 CRM Software
Report," *Business-Software.com*, accessed March 13,
2014.

24. "Wells Fargo Bank," Salesforce.com Success Story,
www.salesforce.com/customers/stories/wells-fargo.jsp,
accessed March 14, 2014.

25. Chipman, Steve, "2014 Smartphone CRM Access by
Salespeople," *CRM Switch*, February 11, 2014, *www
.crmswitch.com/mobile-crm/2014-crm-smartphone
-salesperson-access/*.

26. "What is PLM Software?" Siemens, *www.plm.automa
tion.siemens.com/en_us/plm/*, accessed March 1, 2014.

27. "Leader in Hydropower Equipment Seeks World-Class
Advantage," *www.plm.automation.siemens.com/fr_fr
/about_us/success/case_study.cfm?Component=
119952&ComponentTemplate=1481*, accessed
March 16, 2014.

28. 2013 Edition Top 10 Product Lifecycle Management
(PLM) Software Report, Business-Software.com *http:*

//ptccreo.files.wordpress.com/2013/10/top_10_plm
_report.pdf accessed March 1, 2014.

29. "Creating Perceptible Differences That Drive Top-Line
Growth," Siemens Case Study, *http://www.plm.automa
tion.siemens.com/CaseStudyWeb/dispatch/viewRe
source.html?resourceId=14529*, accessed March 1, 2014.

30. Charette, Robert N., "The U.S. Air Force Explains Its
$1 Billion ECCS Bonfire," *IEEE Spectrum*, December 6,
2013, *http://spectrum.ieee.org/riskfactor/aerospace
/military/the-us-air-force-explains-its-billion-ecss
-bonfire*.

31. Kepes, Ben, "UPDATED-Avon's Failed SAP
Implementation a Perfect Example of the Enterprise IT
Revolution," *Forbes*, December 17, 2013, *www.forbes
.com/sites/benkepes/2013/12/17/avons-failed-sap
-implementation-a-perfect-example-of-enterprise-it
-revolution/*.

32. Kanaracus, Chris, "California Sues SAP Over Failed
Payroll Software Project," *Computerworld*,
November 22, 2013, *www.computerworld.com/s/article
/9244287/California_sues_SAP_over_failed_payroll
_software_project*.

33. Jutras, Cindy, "2011 ERP Solution Study Highlights,"
Epicor, September 2011.

34. "Corset Story Chooses WFX Cloud PLM," *http://1970i
.com/corset-story-chooses-wfx-cloud-plm/*, accessed
March 15, 2014.

10 Information and Decision Support Systems

Principles	Learning Objectives
• Good decision-making and problem-solving skills are the key to developing effective information and decision support systems.	• Define the stages of decision making. • Discuss the importance of implementation and monitoring in problem solving.
• The management information system (MIS) must provide the right information to the right person in the right format at the right time.	• Explain the uses of MISs and describe their inputs and outputs. • Discuss information systems in the functional areas of business organizations.
• The focus of a decision support system (DSS) is on decision-making effectiveness when faced with unstructured or semistructured problems.	• List and discuss important characteristics of DSSs that give them the potential to be effective management support tools. • Identify and describe the basic components of a DSS.
• A group decision support system (GSS) uses the overall approach of a DSS to improve the decision-making process of a group.	• State the goals of a GSS and identify the characteristics that distinguish it from a DSS.

Information Systems in the Global Economy
UTTARAKHAND POWER CORPORATION LTD., INDIA

Lighting Up India with Management Information Systems

© TheYok/Shutterstock.com

Uttarakhand, a state in northeast India located along the foothills of the Himalayan mountains, has one of the fastest growing economies in the nation, reporting a 10 percent growth in its gross domestic product in recent years. With a rapidly developing economy, the state faces a sharply rising demand for electricity as businesses expand and as rural villages are added to the power grid. Uttarakhand Power Corporation Ltd. (UPCL) manages the distribution of electricity to 1.69 million consumers throughout the state. Until recently, however, UPCL lacked access to data that it needed to assess the performance of its power system. UPCL relied on an outside vendor that tracked electricity usage by manual methods.

"In the past, we would send out meter readers to manually record meter data and forward it to private agencies, who then used the information to create bills and send them to our customers," explains UPCL Superintending Engineer JMS Rauthan. "Customers would frequently file complaints about inaccurate charges, forcing bills to be revised, a time-consuming and costly process."

The company also lacked the ability to pinpoint faults in the power grid because they did not have an automated system of tracking outages and interruptions in service. Furthermore, UPCL did not have the ability to monitor power usage to improve efficiency of the grid and observe spikes in usage that would help the company detect incidents of electricity theft.

As a result, UPCL decided to adopt the IBM mPower Smart Utility Suite, a management information system (MIS) that handles meter-to-cash and customer care. A geographic information system (GIS) and a metrics dashboard are integrated into the system. The GIS allows UPCL managers to track outage and interruptions in service, so that they can schedule repairs to target weaknesses in the grid and establish a more efficient routine maintenance schedule. The system also reads the location of each meter and identifies defective meters. Technicians use handheld computers and terminals to record meter readings electronically rather than on paper that can be lost. Managers have used this information to improve UPCL's billing system, increasing customer satisfaction.

To meet the growing energy demands of the state, UPCL is expected to report how many customer service requests it receives and how many it addresses. Prior to implementing the new MIS, UPCL had incurred substantial financial penalties for failing to show that it was meeting expanding service levels. With service request and response now automated, UPCL is generating reports for the state's electricity regulatory commission and avoiding such fines.

Finally, the system automatically calculates and reports electrical consumption. When consumption rises or falls 10 to 15 percent above average rates, the system flags the spikes or drop in usage and sends an email to the vigilance department. Members of this department then investigate potential theft.

Deploying the new MIS system solved many problems for UPCL. Now the company is ready to begin its next big task: developing hydroelectric power to support increasing energy demands of the rapidly developing state.

As you read this chapter, consider the following:

- What types of information and decision support systems are used in different industries and organizations?
- What purposes do they serve, and how can they be used to support innovation and development?

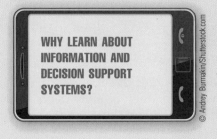

WHY LEARN ABOUT INFORMATION AND DECISION SUPPORT SYSTEMS?

You have seen throughout this book how information systems can make you more efficient and effective through the use of database systems, the Internet, e-commerce, enterprise systems, and many other technologies. The true potential of information systems, however, is in helping you and your coworkers make more informed decisions. This chapter shows you how to slash costs, increase profits, and uncover new opportunities for your company using management information and decision support systems. A financial planner can use management information and decision support systems to find the best investments for clients. A loan committee at a bank or credit union can use a group support system to help determine who should receive loans. Store managers can use decision support systems to help them decide what and how much inventory to order to meet customer needs and increase profits. An entrepreneur who owns and operates a temporary storage company can use vacancy reports to help determine what price to charge for new storage units. Everyone can become a better problem solver and decision maker. This chapter shows you how information systems can help. It begins with an overview of decision making and problem solving.

As shown in the opening vignette, information and decision support are the lifeblood of today's organizations. Thanks to information and decision support systems, managers and employees can obtain useful information in real time. Transaction processing systems and enterprise systems capture a wealth of data. When this data is filtered and manipulated, it can provide powerful support for managers and employees. The ultimate goal of management information and decision support systems is to help managers and executives at all levels make better decisions and solve important problems. The result can be increased revenues, reduced costs, and the realization of corporate goals. No matter what type of information and decision support system you use, its primary goal should be to help you and others become better decision makers and problem solvers.

DECISION MAKING AND PROBLEM SOLVING

Every organization needs effective decision makers. In most cases, strategic planning and the overall goals of the organization set the course for decision making, helping employees and business units achieve their objectives and goals. Often, information systems also assist with problem solving, helping people make better decisions and meet corporate goals as discussed in the opening vignette.

Baosteel is a leading steel manufacturer in China that, until recently, relied on simple manual methods to support its supply chain-related decision making. Unfortunately, these methods were time consuming and inefficient, resulting in frequent out-of-stock positions on key items as well as high inventory and production costs. Over a period of six years, Baosteel gradually upgraded its decision-making processes to include the use of information systems employing creative optimization techniques. Its new decision-making processes led to increased plant productivity and reduced consumption of energy and resources. Management estimates that the improved decision making led to a total cost savings of over $76 million.[1]

Decision Making as a Component of Problem Solving

Problem solving is a critical activity for any business organization. It is generally accepted that problem solving ability differs dramatically from one person to the next with some people having good problem-solving skills, while others do not. In business, one of the highest compliments you can receive is

decision-making phase: The first part of problem solving, including three stages: intelligence, design, and choice.

to be recognized by your colleagues and peers as a "real problem solver." A well-known model developed by Herbert Simon divides the decision-making phase of the problem-solving process into three stages: intelligence, design, and choice.[2] This model was later incorporated by George Huber into an expanded model of the entire problem-solving process.[3] See Figure 10.1.

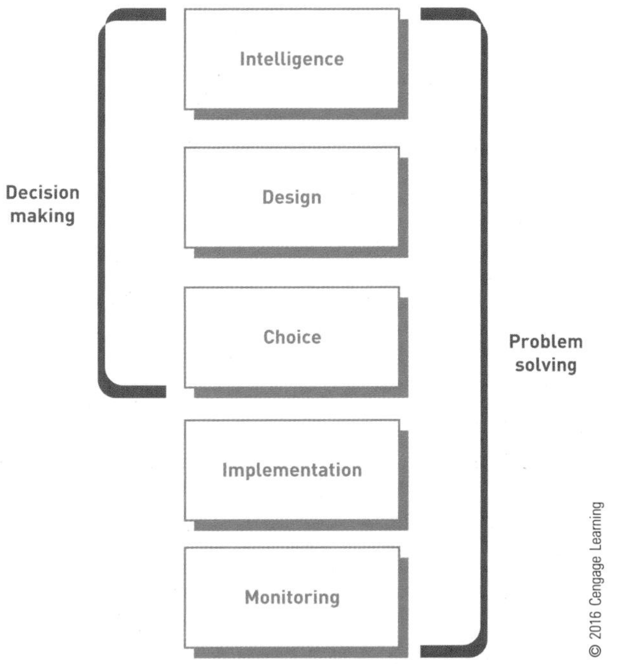

FIGURE 10.1

How decision making relates to problem solving

The three stages of decision making—intelligence, design, and choice—are augmented by implementation and monitoring to result in problem solving.

intelligence stage: The first stage of decision making in which you identify and define potential problems or opportunities.

The first stage in the problem-solving process is the intelligence stage. During this stage, you identify and define potential problems or opportunities. You also investigate resource and environmental constraints. For example, flood control is a critical issue for the Netherlands with over 50 percent of this densely populated country below sea-level and subject to flooding. Natural sand dunes, human-made dikes, dams, and floodgates are all employed to protect the Dutch against storm surges from the sea. In addition, river dikes are needed to prevent flooding from water flowing into the country from the Rhine and Meuse rivers. The Second State Delta Committee, commissioned by the Dutch Secretary of Public Works and Water Management, was deeply troubled by the dike failures in New Orleans when it was hit by Hurricane Katrina. As a result of this and other factors, the committee recommended that measures be taken to raise flood protection levels in all diked areas and set a budget of 1 percent of gross national product, or about €1.2 billion to €1.6 billion, per year until 2050 to implement the necessary measures. Historical data was gathered and new sea water level forecasts were generated for use in developing new flood risk assessments.[4] This completed the intelligence stage for this problem and clearly framed the issue—how should this large sum of money be allocated across 3,500 km of dikes?

design stage: The second stage of decision making in which you develop alternative solutions to the problem and evaluate their feasibility.

In the design stage, you develop alternative solutions to the problem and evaluate their feasibility. In the Dutch flooding problem, a new methodology was developed for making flood risk assessments based on cost benefit analysis. Multiple flood risk assessments were made based on the historical data and new sea level forecasts gathered during the intelligence stage. Mixed integer nonlinear programming techniques were used to generate optimal strategies for all areas of the country protected by the dikes.[5]

choice stage: The third stage of decision making, which requires selecting a course of action.

The last stage of the decision-making phase, the choice stage, requires selecting a course of action. In the Dutch flooding example, the various strategies were analyzed and a decision was made to implement a set of economically efficient flood protection standards for different parts of the Netherlands that varied greatly from the existing standards. The new cost/benefit analysis showed that it was necessary and economically efficient to raise protection standards along the Rhine and Meuse rivers and two other areas of the country. Meanwhile, for many areas in the coastal region, the existing legal flood protection standards were judged to be more than adequate. There was no need to increase the legal flood protection standards for all flood-prone areas in the Netherlands by a factor 10, as was originally recommended.[6]

problem solving: A process that goes beyond decision making to include the implementation stage.

Problem solving includes and goes beyond decision making. It also includes the **implementation stage** when the solution is put into effect. This would include making the recommended changes to each individual dike in the Dutch flooding example. The final stage of the problem-solving process is the **monitoring stage**. In this stage, decision makers evaluate the implementation to determine whether the anticipated results were achieved and to modify the implementation if needed. For example, should flooding occur due to unusually high sea levels or other unexpected weather conditions, or should dike modification prove more expensive than anticipated, the implementation would be modified appropriately.

implementation stage: A stage of problem solving in which a solution is put into effect.

monitoring stage: The final stage of the problem-solving process in which decision makers evaluate the implementation.

Programmed versus Nonprogrammed Decisions

In the choice stage, various factors influence the decision maker's selection of a solution. One factor is whether the decision can be programmed. **Programmed decisions** are routine and repetitive decisions. Often a rule, procedure, or quantitative method is employed to make these kinds of decisions. For example, to determine that a stock keeping unit should be reordered when the inventory level drops below the reorder point is a programmed decision because it adheres to a rule. Programmed decisions are easy to implement using traditional information systems.

programmed decision: A decision made using a rule, procedure, or quantitative method.

Kraft is a global leader in the food and beverage industry with its popular brands in the beverage, cheese, and refrigerated meals categories found in nearly every North American household. It operates a large, complex supply chain with operations in some 72 countries and more than 150 manufacturing and processing locations worldwide. Many of the Kraft stock keeping units are seasonal products with a short shelf-life. The firm also offers frequent new product introductions and sales promotions. All this makes it critical for Kraft to manage its inventory in a highly efficient and cost-effective manner. To this end, Kraft implemented a sophisticated inventory management system that controls its inventory levels using programmed decisions based on preprogrammed reorder points and safety stock targets. See Figure 10.2. The programmed decision-making process has improved forecasting accuracy and reduced the possibility of manufacturing the wrong types of inventory, which has saved money and preserved cash reserves.[7]

nonprogrammed decision: A decision that deals with unusual or exceptional situations.

Nonprogrammed decisions are typically one-time decisions that in many cases are difficult to quantify. Determining the appropriate training program for a new employee, deciding whether to develop a new type of product line, and weighing the benefits and drawbacks of installing an upgraded pollution control system are examples. Each decision contains unique characteristics, and standard rules or procedures might not apply to them.

Structured, Semistructured, and Unstructured Decisions

structured decisions: Decisions where the variables that comprise the decision are known and can be measured quantitatively.

Anthony Gorry and Michael Scott Morton developed a framework that became the foundation of much of the research done on decision support systems.[8] Their work classified decisions based on their degree of structure. **Structured decisions** are ones where the variables that comprise the decision are known

FIGURE **10.2**

Programmed decisions

Kraft controls its inventory levels using programmed decisions embedded into its computer systems.

unstructured decisions:
Decisions where the variables that affect the decision cannot be measured quantitatively.

semistructured decisions:
Decisions where only some of the variables can be measured quantitatively.

and can be measured quantitatively. **Unstructured decisions** are ones where the variables that affect the decision cannot be measured quantitatively. **Semistructured decisions** are ones where only some of the variables can be measured quantitatively. Most business decisions are semistructured. All three types of decisions can be encountered at each level of the organization—operational, tactical, and strategic. Table 10.1 identifies examples of each type of decision.

TABLE 10.1 Gorry-Morton framework

	Operational Control	**Management Control**	**Strategic Control**
Structured	Accounts receivable	Budget analysis	Tanker fleet mix
	Order entry	Short-term forecasting	Warehouse and factory location
	Inventory control		
Semistructured	Production scheduling	Budget variance analysis	Mergers and acquisitions
Unstructured	Critical path scheduling	Sales and production	Research and development planning

Gorry and Morton believed that decision support systems helped solve many nonprogrammed decisions in which the problem is not routine and rules and relationships are not well defined (unstructured or semistructured problems). These problems can include deciding on the best location for a manufacturing plant or whether to rebuild a hospital that was severely damaged from a hurricane or tornado.

Optimization, Satisficing, and Heuristic Approaches

In general, computerized decision support systems can either optimize or satisfice. An **optimization model** finds the best solution, the one that will best help the organization meet its goals. Optimization models use problem constraints. A limit on the number of available work hours in a manufacturing facility is an example of a problem constraint.

Südzucker AG operates 29 sugar factories and 3 refineries in 11 European countries that produce more than 5 million tons of sugar annually. The sugar is converted into more than 2,000 products that are distributed to thousands of customers across Europe. In an effort to support its growth plans, the company

optimization model: A process to find the best solution, the one that will best help the organization meet its goals.

developed a sophisticated model to analyze trade-offs between production, warehousing, transportation costs, and service requirements. For example, Südzucker can accurately determine the financial value of moving the production of specific sugar products to a facility in Belgium versus opening new warehouse locations in Austria. The model enables the quick generation and evaluation of options for a given set of assumptions and constraints (such as labor costs, factory production capacity, and storage costs) from which the optimal option can be determined.[9]

Some spreadsheet programs, such as Excel, have optimizing features, as shown in Figure 10.3. Optimization software also allows decision makers to explore various alternatives.

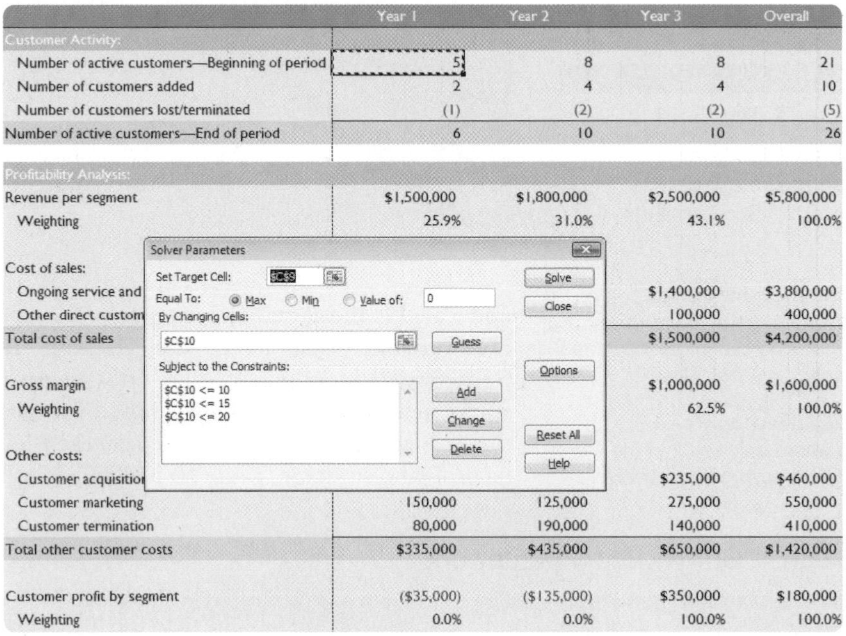

FIGURE 10.3

Optimization software

Some spreadsheet programs, such as Microsoft Excel, have optimizing routines. This figure shows Solver, which can find an optimal solution given certain constraints.

satisficing model: A model that will find a good—but not necessarily the best—solution to a problem.

A **satisficing model** is one that finds a good—but not necessarily the best—solution to a problem. Satisficing is used when modeling the problem properly to get an optimal decision would be too difficult, complex, or costly. Satisficing normally does not look at all possible solutions but only at those likely to give good results.

For example, the traveling salesman problem is a classic problem that seeks to find the answer to the question: Given a set of destinations, what is the shortest route that allows the salesperson to visit every destination and return to the starting place? The solution of the problem has an obvious application to the routing of delivery trucks. It also has practical applications to solving other problems such as drilling holes in circuit boards, scheduling tasks on a computer, and ordering features of a genome. As it turns out, no general algorithm guarantees an optimal solution to this problem when the number of destinations is large. For a small number of destinations, the problem can be easily solved by computing every round-trip route to find the shortest one. But as the number of destinations increases, the number of possible routes grows exponentially—for 15 destinations, the number of possible routes exceeds 87 billion.[10]

UPS relies on a route optimization tool called ORION (On-Road Integrated Optimization and Navigation) to recommend a delivery route for each of its 55,000 drivers who make some 16 million deliveries each day. The tool must incorporate promised delivery times into its calculations. While ORION cannot possibly optimize each route, it must develop a solution that is close to the optimal as the stakes are high. The cost to UPS per year if each driver drives just one more mile each day than necessary is $30 million.[11]

heuristics: Commonly accepted guidelines or procedures that usually find a good solution.

Heuristics, also known as "rules of thumb," are commonly accepted guidelines or procedures that experience has shown usually leads to a good solution. These rule-of-thumb strategies shorten decision-making time and enable people to function without constantly deliberating over what course of action to take. While heuristics are helpful in many situations, they can also lead to biases and place too much emphasis on the past.

A heuristic that baseball team managers use is to place batters most likely to get on base at the top of the lineup, followed by the power hitters who can drive them in to score. An example of a heuristic that an organization might use to manage its assets is "Don't allow total accounts payable to exceed cash on hand by more than 50 percent."

ESET is a Slovakia-based IT security company that develops leading-edge security solutions against cyber threats. Its products provide the ability to detect unknown malware (such as a virus, worm, or Trojan horse) based on the use of advanced heuristics. This approach looks for certain instructions or commands within a program that are not found in typical application programs. As a result, it is able to detect potentially malicious functionality in new, previously unexamined, malware.[12]

Benefits of Information and Decision Support Systems

The information and decision support systems covered in this chapter and the next help individuals, groups, and organizations make better decisions, solve problems, and achieve their goals. These systems include management information systems, decision support systems, group support systems, executive support systems, knowledge management systems, and a variety of special-purpose systems. As shown in Figure 10.4, the benefits of these systems are a measure of increased performance of the systems versus the cost to deliver them. The plus sign (+) by the arrow from *performance* to *benefits* indicates that increased performance has a positive impact on benefits. The minus sign (−) from *cost* to *benefits* indicates that increased cost has a negative impact on benefits.

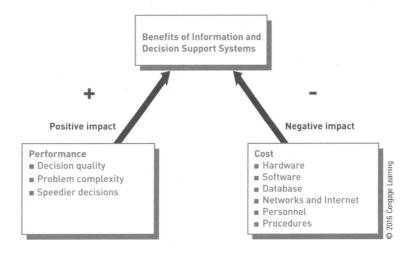

FIGURE 10.4

Benefits of information and decision support systems

The benefits are increased performance of the information and decision support systems compared to the cost to deliver them.

The performance of these systems is typically a function of decision quality, problem complexity, and decision-making speed. Decision quality can result in increased effectiveness, increased efficiency, higher productivity, and many other measures. Problem complexity depends on how hard the problem is to solve and implement. Speed of decision making is improved, resulting in quicker implementation of a solution. The costs of delivering these systems are the expenditures of the information technology components, including hardware, software, databases, networks and the Internet, people, and procedures. But how do these systems actually deliver benefits to the individuals, groups, and organizations that use them? It depends on the system. We begin our discussion with traditional management information systems.

AN OVERVIEW OF MANAGEMENT INFORMATION SYSTEMS

A management information system (MIS) is an integrated collection of people, procedures, databases, and devices that provides managers and decision makers with information to help achieve organizational goals. MISs can often give companies and other organizations a competitive advantage by providing the right information to the right people in the right format and at the right time.

Management Information Systems in Perspective

The primary purpose of an MIS is to help an organization achieve its goals by providing managers with insight into the regular operations of the organization so that they can control, organize, and plan more effectively. One important role of the MIS is to provide the right information to the right person in the right format at the right time. In short, an MIS provides managers with information, typically in reports, that supports effective decision making and provides feedback on daily operations. Figure 10.5 shows the role of MISs within the flow of an organization's information. Note that business transactions can enter the organization via traditional methods, via the Internet, or via an extranet connecting customers and suppliers to the firm's ERP or transaction processing systems. The use of MISs spans all levels of management; that is, they provide support to and are used by employees throughout the organization.

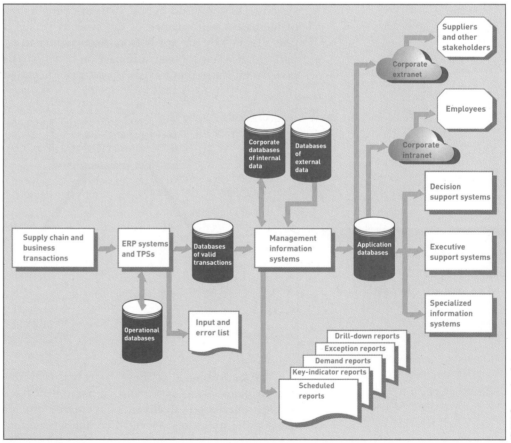

© 2016 Cengage Learning

FIGURE 10.5

Sources of managerial information

The MIS is just one of many sources of managerial information. Decision support systems, executive support systems, and expert systems also assist in decision making.

Inputs to a Management Information System

As shown in Figure 10.5, data that enters an MIS originates from both internal and external sources, including a company's supply chain. The most significant internal data sources for an MIS are the organization's various TPS and ERP systems and related databases. External sources of data can include customers, suppliers, competitors, and stockholders, whose data is not already captured by the TPS and enterprise systems, as well as other sources, such as the Internet. Companies also use data warehouses and data marts to store valuable business information that can be used across the organization.

Outputs of a Management Information System

The output of most MISs is a collection of reports that are distributed to managers. Many MIS reports are generated using the data in an organization's databases. These reports can be tailored for each user and can be delivered in a timely fashion.

Aarogyasri Health Care Trust is a not-for-profit project for the Andhra Pradesh state of India. It provides healthcare coverage for millions of low income families connected to over 340 network hospitals through primary care centers and medical camps. The Trust worked with Tata Consultancy Services to create a database of critical patient, hospital, and insurance information to provide services and monitor operations. Hundreds of doctors and staff at the network hospitals and over 1,000 users from third-party insurance companies use a reporting software tool to access this database and deliver information to make better informed and quicker decisions.[13] Many reporting systems can also create an **executive dashboard** that presents a set of key performance indicators about the state of a process at a specific point in time to enable managers make better real-time decisions. For example, a dashboard like that shown in Figure 10.6 can provide hospital bed managers a real-time view of bed availability and discharge status including:

- Occupied and available beds across the system and by unit
- Number of critical and telemetry beds available
- Number of observation patients
- Length of stay (LOS) and discharge statistics from time a discharge order is written until the patient actually leaves the room
- Key hospital support service performance relative to bed turns, such as Environmental Services: stat turnaround, clean next bed turnaround, last bed on the unit turnaround, and routine turnaround

executive dashboard: A diagram that presents a set of key performance indicators about the state of a process at a specific point in time to enable managers make better real-time decisions.

FIGURE 10.6

Executive dashboard

Reporting software tools can create executive dashboards that present a set of key performance indicators about the state of a process at a specific point.

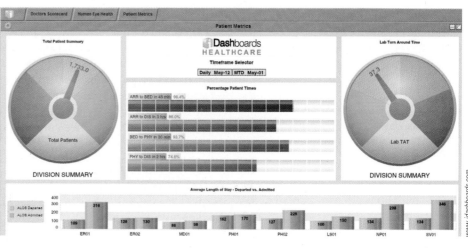

Management reports can come from various company databases, data warehouses, and other sources. These reports include scheduled reports, key-indicator reports, demand reports, exception reports, and drill-down reports in addition to executive dashboards. See Figure 10.7.

(a) Scheduled Report

Daily Sales Detail Report

Prepared: 08/10/16

Order #	Customer ID	Salesperson ID	Planned Ship Date	Quantity	Item #	Amount
P12453	C89321	CAR	08/12/16	144	P1234	$3,214
P12453	C89321	CAR	08/12/16	288	P3214	$5,660
P12454	C03214	GWA	08/13/16	12	P4902	$1,224
P12455	C52313	SAK	08/12/16	24	P4012	$2,448
P12456	C34123	JMW	08/13/16	144	P3214	$720
....	....	....	....	......	......	....

(b) Key-Indicator Report

Daily Sales Key-Indicator Report

	This Month	Last Month	Last Year
Total Orders Month to Date	$1,808	$1,694	$1,914
Forecasted Sales for the Month	$2,406	$2,224	$2,608

(c) Demand Report

Daily Sales by Salesperson Summary Report

Prepared: 08/10/16

Salesperson ID	Amount
CAR	$42,345
GWA	$38,950
SAK	$22,100
JWN	$12,350
....	....
....	....

(d) Exception Report

Daily Sales Exception Report—Orders Over $10,000

Prepared: 08/10/16

Order #	Customer ID	Salesperson ID	Planned Ship Date	Quantity	Item #	Amount
P12345	C89321	GWA	08/12/16	576	P1234	$12,856
P22153	C00453	CAR	08/12/16	288	P2314	$28,800
P23023	C32832	JMN	08/11/16	144	P2323	$14,400
....	....	....	....	......	......	....

(e) First-Level Drill-Down Report

Earnings by Quarter (Millions)

		Actual	Forecast	Variance
2nd Qtr.	2016	$12.6	$11.8	6.8%
1st Qtr.	2016	$10.8	$10.7	0.9%
4th Qtr.	2016	$14.3	$14.5	-1.4%
3rd Qtr.	2016	$12.8	$13.3	-3.8%

(f) Second-Level Drill-Down Report

Sales and Expenses (Millions)

Qtr: 2nd Qtr. 2016	Actual	Forecast	Variance
Gross Sales	$110.9	$108.3	2.4%
Expenses	$ 98.3	$ 96.5	1.9%
Profit	$ 12.6	$ 11.8	6.8%

(g) Third-Level Drill-Down Report

Sales by Division (Millions)

Qtr: 2nd Qtr. 2016	Actual	Forecast	Variance
Beauty Care	$ 34.5	$ 33.9	1.8%
Health Care	$ 30.0	$ 28.0	7.1%
Soap	$ 22.8	$ 23.0	-0.9%
Snacks	$ 12.1	$ 12.5	-3.2%
Electronics	$ 11.5	$ 10.9	5.5%
Total	$110.9	$108.3	2.4%

(h) Fourth-Level Drill-Down Report

Sales by Product Category (Millions)

Qtr: 2nd Qtr. 2016 Division: Health Care	Actual	Forecast	Variance
Toothpaste	$12.4	$10.5	18.1%
Mouthwash	$ 8.6	$ 8.8	-2.3%
Over-the-Counter Drugs	$ 5.8	$ 5.3	9.4%
Skin Care Products	$ 3.2	$ 3.4	-5.9%
Total	$30.0	$28.0	7.1%

FIGURE 10.7

Reports generated by an MIS

The types of reports are (a) scheduled, (b) key-indicator, (c) demand, (d) exception, and (e–h) drill down.

© 2016 Cengage Learning

Scheduled Reports

scheduled report: A report produced periodically, such as daily, weekly, or monthly.

Scheduled reports are produced periodically, such as daily, weekly, or monthly. For example, a production manager might use a weekly scheduled report that lists total payroll costs to monitor and control labor and job costs. Other scheduled reports can help managers control customer credit, monitor the performance of sales representatives, check inventory levels, and more.

key-indicator report: A summary of the previous day's critical activities, typically available at the beginning of each workday.

A **key-indicator report** summarizes the previous day's critical activities and is typically available at the beginning of each workday. These reports can summarize inventory levels, production activity, sales volume, and the like. Key-indicator reports are used by managers and executives to take quick, corrective action on significant aspects of the business.

The North Carolina Community College System serves over 800,000 students. Each year it produces a report called "Performance Measures for Student Success," based on data compiled from the previous year. The report informs colleges and the public on the performance of its 58 community colleges. The following eight key performance indicators are included:[14]

- Basic Skills Student Progress
- Developmental Student Success Rate in College–Level English Courses
- First Year Progression
- Licensure and Certification Passing Rate
- GED Diploma Passing Rate
- Developmental Student Success Rate in College–Level Math Courses
- Curriculum Student Completion
- College Transfer Performance

Demand Reports

demand report: A report developed to give certain information at someone's request rather than on a schedule.

Demand reports are developed to provide certain information upon request. In other words, these reports are produced on demand rather than on a schedule. Like other reports discussed in this section, they often come from an organization's database system. For example, an executive might want to know the production status of a particular item. A demand report can be generated to provide the requested information by querying the company's database. Suppliers and customers can also use demand reports. FedEx, for example, provides demand reports on its Web site to allow customers to track packages from their source to their final destination.

Exception Reports

exception report: A report automatically produced when a situation is unusual or requires management action.

Exception reports are reports automatically produced when a situation is unusual or requires management action. For example, a manager might set a parameter that generates a report of all inventory items with fewer than the equivalent of five days of sales on hand. This unusual situation requires prompt action to avoid running out of stock on the item. The exception report generated by this parameter would contain only items with fewer than five days of sales in inventory.

Capital One 360 is a large savings bank whose customers conduct most of their transactions online. The bank closely monitors several critical data files throughout the course of its operations. For example, one file holds data about payments that are scheduled to be sent overnight to other banks and financial institutions. There is a cut-off time when this file can no longer be modified. If a change is requested after the cut-off time, an exception report is generated. The report identifies when the change was requested and by whom. Then an employee manually checks the report to make sure that all changes were properly authorized and conducted correctly. The report ensures that no data has been tampered or transactions interfered with.[15]

As with key-indicator reports, exception reports are most often used to monitor aspects important to an organization's success. In general, when an exception report is produced, a manager or executive takes action. Parameters, or *trigger points*, should be set carefully for an exception report. Trigger points that are set too low might result in too many exception reports; trigger points that are too high could mean that problems requiring action are overlooked. For example, if the purchasing manager of a large manufacturing company wants an exception report that shows all purchases of raw materials over $100, the system might retrieve almost every purchase. The $100 trigger point is probably too low. A trigger point of $10,000 might be more appropriate.

Drill-Down Reports

drill-down report: A report providing increasingly detailed data about a situation.

Drill-down reports provide increasingly detailed data about a situation. Using these reports, analysts can see data at a high level first (such as sales for the entire company), then at a more detailed level (such as the sales for one department of the company), and then a very detailed level (such as sales for one sales representative). Companies and organizations of all sizes and types use drill-down reports.

Characteristics of a Management Information System

Dashboard, scheduled, key-indicator, demand, exception, and drill-down reports have all helped managers and executives make better, more timely decisions. In general, MISs perform the following functions:

- Provide reports with fixed and standard formats.
- Produce hard-copy and soft-copy reports.
- Use internal data stored in the computer system.
- Allow users to develop custom reports.
- Require user requests for reports developed by systems personnel.

FUNCTIONAL ASPECTS OF THE MIS

Most organizations are structured along functional areas such as finance, manufacturing, marketing, human resources, and other specialized areas of the business. The MIS can also be divided along those functional lines to produce reports tailored to the individual functions. See Figure 10.8.

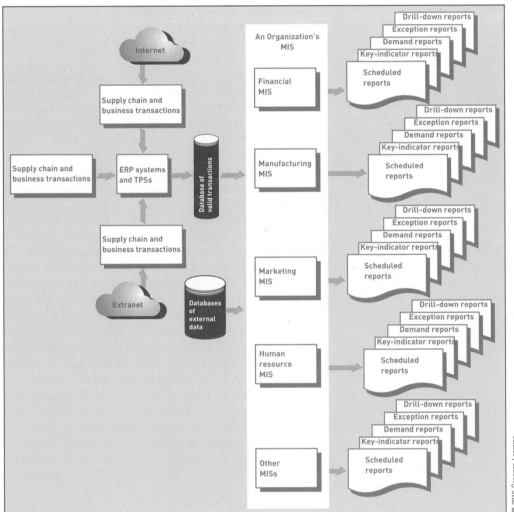

FIGURE 10.8

An organization's MIS

The MIS is an integrated collection of functional information systems, each supporting particular functional areas.

Financial Management Information Systems

financial MIS: An information system that provides financial information for workers who need to make better decisions on a daily basis.

A **financial MIS** provides financial information for workers who need to make better decisions on a daily basis. Most financial MISs perform the following functions:

- Integrate financial and operational information from multiple sources, including the Internet, into a single system.
- Provide easy access to data for both financial and nonfinancial users, often through the use of a corporate intranet to access corporate Web pages of financial data and information.
- Make financial data immediately available to shorten analysis turnaround time.
- Enable analysis of financial data along multiple dimensions—time, geography, product, plant, and customer.
- Analyze historical and current financial activity.
- Monitor and control the use of funds over time.

The general ledger defines the accounting categories of a business and is a key component of the financial MIS. It is often divided into categories, including assets, liabilities, revenue, expenses, and equity. These categories, in turn, are subdivided into subledgers to capture details such as cash, accounts payable, and accounts receivable. The business processes required to capture and report these accounting details are essential to the operation of any organization. Input to the general ledger occurs simultaneously with the input of a business transaction to a specific module. The following are several examples of how this process occurs:

- An order clerk records a sale generating an accounts receivable entry indicating that a customer owes money for goods received.
- A buyer enters a purchase order, generating an accounts payable entry in the general ledger registering that the company has an obligation to pay for goods that will be received at some time in the future.
- A dock worker enters a receipt of purchased materials from a supplier generating a general ledger entry to increase the value of inventory on hand.
- A production worker withdraws raw materials from inventory to support production generating a record to reduce the value of inventory on hand.

Transaction processing systems or enterprise systems capture transactions entered by workers in all functional areas of the business. These systems then create the associated general ledger records to track the financial impact of the transaction. This set of records is an extremely valuable resource that companies can use to support financial and managerial accounting.

Financial accounting consists of capturing and recording all the transactions that affect a company's financial state and then using these documented transactions to prepare financial statements to external decision makers, such as stockholders, suppliers, banks, and government agencies. These financial statements include the income statement, balance sheet, and cash-flow statement. See Table 10.2. They must be prepared in strict accordance to rules and guidelines of agencies such as the Securities and Exchange Commission, the Internal Revenue Service, and the Financial Accounting Standards Board. Data gathered for financial accounting can also form the basis for tax accounting because it involves external reporting of a firm's activities to the local, state, and federal tax agencies.

Managerial accounting involves using both historical and estimated data in providing information that management needs to conduct daily operations, plan future operations, and develop overall business strategies. Managerial accounting provides data to enable the firm's managers to assess the

TABLE **10.2** Income statement

An income statement shows an organization's business results, including revenues and costs including taxes.

Pinnacle Peak Manufacturing Income Statement			
Date Prepared: July 3, 2017			
Fiscal year	2016	2015	2014
Total Revenue	$28,365,000	$25,296,000	$22,956,000
Cost of Goods Sold	$5,191,000	$3,455,000	$3,002,000
Gross Profit	$23,174,000	$21,841,000	$$19,954,000
Operating Expense			
Research and Development	$4,307,000	$4,379,000	$3,775,000
Selling, General, and Administrative Expenses	$6,957,000	$5,742,000	$5,242,000
Operating Income			
Operating Income	$11,910,000	$11,720,000	$10,937,000
Total Other Income and Expenses Net	($397,000)	($195,000)	$3,338,000
Earnings Before Interest and Taxes	$11,513,000	$11,525,000	$14,275,000
Interest Expense	N/A	N/A	N/A
Income Before Taxes	$11,513,000	$11,525,000	$14,275,000
Income Tax Expense	$3,684,000	$3,804,000	$4,854,000
Net Income	$7,829,000	$7,721,000	$9,421,000

profitability of a given product line or specific product, identify underperforming sales regions, establish budgets, make profit forecasts, and measure the effectiveness of marketing campaigns.

All transactions that affect the financial state of the firm are captured and recorded in the financial MIS. This data is used to prepare the statements required by various constituencies. The data can also be used in the managerial accounting modules of the MIS system along with various assumptions and forecasts to perform different analyses such as generating a forecasted profit-and-loss statement to assess the firm's future profitability. The use of an MIS to perform financial and managerial accounting can contribute significantly to a company's success.

BMW developed a financial MIS to plan the volume and profitability of its future business. The results of these analyses were integrated into an enterprise-wide reporting system while meeting the requirements of regulatory agencies and reducing the manual effort of its financial managers.[16]

Figure 10.9 shows typical inputs, function-specific subsystems, and outputs of a financial MIS, including profit and loss, auditing, and uses and management of funds.

Some of the financial MIS subsystems and outputs include:

profit center: An independent business unit that is treated as a distinct entity enabling its revenues and expenses to be determined and its profitability to be measured.

revenue center: An organizational unit that gains revenue from the sale of products or services.

- **Profit/loss and cost systems**. A profit center is an independent business unit that is treated as a distinct entity enabling its revenues and expenses to be determined and its profitability to be measured. Profit centers are separated for accounting purposes so that the management can monitor how much profit each center makes and compare their relative effectiveness and profit. The manager of a profit center is held accountable for both revenue and costs. The investment division of a large insurance company and the service department of an auto dealer are examples of profit centers. A revenue center is an organizational unit

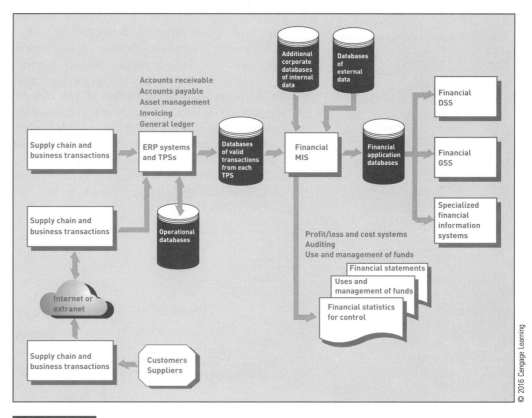

FIGURE 10.9

Overview of a financial MIS

A financial MIS shows profit and loss, auditing, and uses and management of funds.

that gains revenue from the sale of products or services. The manager of a revenue center is responsible for revenue generation only. Still other organizational units, such as manufacturing or research and development, can be cost centers, which are divisions within a company that do not directly generate revenue. Information systems are used to compute revenues, costs, and profits.

cost center: A division within a company that does not directly generate revenue.

- **Auditing**. Auditing provides an objective appraisal of the accounting, financial, and operational procedures and information of an organization. Several types of audits may be conducted. A financial audit is a thorough assessment of the reliability and integrity of the organization's financial information and the methods used to process it. An operational audit is an assessment of how well management uses the resources of the organization and how effectively organizational plans are being executed. Internal auditing is performed by individuals within the organization. For example, the finance department of a corporation might use a team of employees to perform an audit of its accounts payable operation to ensure that it is adhering to company standards and policies. External auditing is performed by an outside group, usually an accounting firm such as PricewaterhouseCoopers, Deloitte & Touche, or another major international accounting firm. Computer systems are used in all aspects of internal and external auditing. An audit of the New York State Common Retirement Fund (CRF) revealed several information system problems at the Office of the State Comptroller (OSC). If left unmitigated, these problems could lead to a disaster for New Yorkers who rely on OSC to administer and distribute their retirement savings. The audit by the Department of Financial Services (DFS) revealed that the mainframe

auditing: Provides an objective appraisal of the accounting, financial, and operational procedures and information of an organization.

financial audit: A thorough assessment of the reliability and integrity of the organization's financial information and the methods used to process it.

operational audit: An assessment of how well management uses the resources of the organization and how effectively organizational plans are being executed.

internal auditing: Auditing performed by individuals within the organization.

external auditing: Auditing performed by an outside group.

computer that processes pension transactions is over 25 years old and uses a computer language from the 1950s in which few programmers are still trained. To make matters even worse, key software used for the pension fund is no longer supported by its manufacturer so that it is not updated with security patches to protect against new security threats.[17]

- **Uses and management of funds**. Internal uses of funds include purchasing additional inventory, updating plants and equipment, hiring new employees, acquiring other companies, buying new computer systems, increasing marketing and advertising, purchasing raw materials or land, investing in new products, and increasing research and development. Personal finance software can also help you manage your expenditures and financial decisions. See Figure 10.10.

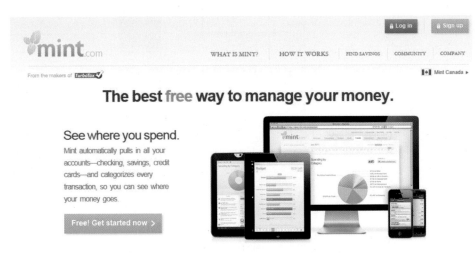

mint.com

FIGURE 10.10

Mint personal finance software

Mint helps you organize and categorize your spending so you know where every dime goes and helps you to be comfortable with your financial decisions.

Manufacturing Management Information Systems

Without question, advances in information systems have revolutionized manufacturing. As a result, many manufacturing operations have been dramatically improved over the last decade. The use of computerized systems is emphasized at all levels of manufacturing—from the shop floor to the executive suite.

The Daimler Group produces Mercedes-Benz cars, Daimler trucks, Mercedes-Benz vans, and Daimler buses. Daimler produces 10,000 cylinder heads per day at its light-metal foundry in Stuttgart, Germany. If the cylinder heads do not pass exacting standards, they must be rejected, melted down, and then remanufactured. The firm uses a manufacturing MIS to gather over 500 factors related to production that enables workers to monitor and control the manufacturing process. The use of this system has increased productivity by over 25 percent.[18] Figure 10.11 gives an overview of some of the manufacturing MIS inputs, subsystems, and outputs.

The manufacturing MIS subsystems and outputs are used to monitor and control the flow of materials, products, and services through the organization. As raw materials are converted to finished goods, the manufacturing MIS monitors the process at every stage. The success of an organization can depend on the manufacturing function. Some common information subsystems and outputs used in manufacturing are provided in the following list:

- **Design and engineering**. Manufacturing companies often use computer-assisted design (CAD) with new or existing products. For example, The Boeing Company employs 3D CAD/CAM (computer-aided

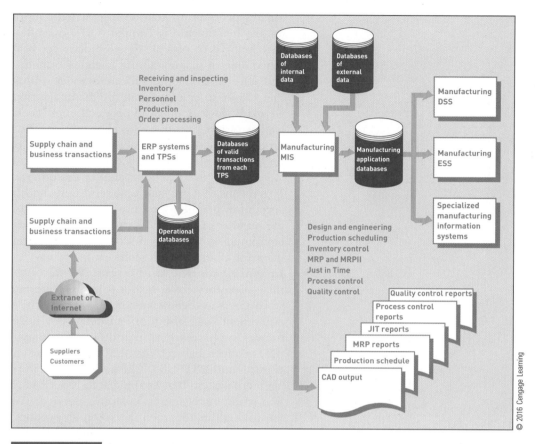

FIGURE **10.11**

Overview of a manufacturing MIS

Manufacturing MIS subsystems and outputs are used to monitor and control the flow of materials, products, and services through the organization.

design/computer-aided manufacturing) technology to model airplane parts as 3D solids in a CATIA (computer-aided three-dimensional interactive application) system. See Figure 10.12. This system, along with several Boeing proprietary applications, enabled Boeing engineers to simulate the geometry of an airplane design and avoid the need for the costly and time-consuming effort to create physical mock-ups.[19]

FIGURE **10.12**

Design and engineering

Boeing uses computer-assisted design (CAD) and computer-aided manufacturing (CAM) in the development and design of its aircraft.

- **Master production scheduling**. Scheduling production is a critical activity for any manufacturing company. The overall objective of master production scheduling is to provide detailed plans for both short-term and long-range scheduling of manufacturing facilities. Sumida AG designs, manufactures and sells electronic parts for automotive, industrial, and consumer use. The 175 or so employees in the manufacturing department at its Lehesten, Germany, factory must fill production orders to meet long-term contracts as well as orders that arrive on short notice. The factory implemented a new production scheduling system to improve its manufacturing planning process. Now, instead of considering the production order as a whole, the new system plans every process step of the order in the production schedule. This means that the start time, end time, and processing time are taken into account in planning production. The system is also capable of optimizing the number of units to be produced based on the availability of staff and equipment. A production schedule is generated for each piece of equipment for all three work shifts.

- **Inventory control**. Most inventory control techniques are used to minimize inventory costs. Fisher Scientific International, Inc., provides researchers and clinicians in labs around the world with the instruments, equipment, and laboratory supplies they need. It serves over 350,000 customers in pharmaceutical and biotech companies, colleges and universities, medical research institutions, hospitals, and quality control, process control, and R&D labs.[20] Fisher Scientific implemented an inventory management system that enabled it to reduce its overall inventory by $5 million while increasing its customer service. This was accomplished by improving the alignment between its product inventory and customer demand. Inventory control techniques determine when to restock and how much inventory to order. One method of determining the amount of inventory to order is called the economic order quantity (EOQ). This quantity is calculated to minimize the total inventory costs. The "when to order" question is based on inventory usage over time. Typically, the question is answered in terms of a reorder point (ROP), which is a critical inventory quantity level. When the inventory level for a particular item falls to the reorder point, or critical level, the system generates a report so that an order is immediately placed for the EOQ of the product.

- **Just-in-time (JIT) inventory** and manufacturing is an approach that maintains inventory at the lowest levels without sacrificing the availability of finished products. With this approach, inventory and materials are delivered just before they are used in a product. At one time, Harley Davidson was a highly inefficient manufacturer that avoided production problems by carrying an excessive amount of inventory to avoid stock outs. However, the investment in inventory led to excessive storage and handling costs plus tied up a lot of capital. The firm implemented JIT and became an agile manufacturer able to meet customer demand and provide short lead times to produce products. Use of JIT enabled Harley Davidson to increase productivity and reduce its inventory levels by 75 percent.

- **Process control**. Managers can use a number of technologies to control and streamline the manufacturing process. Computers can directly control manufacturing equipment using computer-aided manufacturing (CAM) systems to control drilling machines, assembly lines, and more. See Figure 10.13. Computer-integrated manufacturing (CIM) uses computers to link the components of the production process into an effective system. CIM's goal is to tie together all aspects of production, including order processing, product design, manufacturing, inspection and quality control, and shipping. A flexible manufacturing system (FMS) is an approach that allows manufacturing facilities to rapidly and efficiently change from making one product to another. In the middle of a production run, for example,

economic order quantity (EOQ): The quantity that should be reordered to minimize total inventory costs.

reorder point (ROP): A critical inventory quantity level.

just-in-time (JIT) inventory: An inventory management approach in which inventory and materials are delivered just before they are used in manufacturing a product.

computer-integrated manufacturing (CIM): Using computers to link the components of the production process into an effective system.

flexible manufacturing system (FMS): An approach that allows manufacturing facilities to rapidly and efficiently change from making one product to making another.

FIGURE 10.13

Computer-aided manufacturing

Computer-assisted manufacturing systems control complex processes on the assembly line and provide users with instant access to information.

the production process can be changed to make a different product or to switch manufacturing materials. By using an FMS, the time and cost to change manufacturing jobs can be substantially reduced, and companies can react quickly to market needs and competition. The Willi Elbe Group, based in Germany, produces steering modules and steering components for passenger cars and commercial vehicles. The firm implemented a flexible manufacturing system that includes five horizontal machining centers. The centers are loaded and unloaded by robots and connected to a parts-cleaning system by a custom feed belt. The work pieces from these centers are automatically integrated into the later process stages.

- **Quality control and testing**. With increased pressure from consumers and a general concern for productivity and high quality, today's manufacturing organizations are placing more emphasis on quality control, a process that ensures that the finished product meets the customers' needs. Information systems are used to monitor quality and take corrective steps to eliminate possible quality problems.

quality control: A process that ensures that the finished product meets the customers' needs.

Marketing Management Information Systems

Marketing is the process of determining the needs and wants of consumers and creating, communicating, and delivering products that satisfy those needs and wants. Marketing covers a broad range of activities including:

marketing: The process of determining the needs and wants of consumers and creating, communicating, and delivering products that satisfy those needs and wants.

- Performing market research to determine the needs and wants of consumers
- Designing a product or service that will appeal to consumers
- Setting a price that will be attractive to the consumer and profitable to the organization
- Determining the various media to be used to inform potential customers about your product or service
- Advertising using the selected forms of media
- Deciding on the chain of businesses and/or intermediaries through which the product or service will travel to reach the consumer (channels of distribution)
- Determining the handling, movement, and storage of goods from the point of origin to the point of consumption (physical distribution)

marketing MIS: A system that uses data gathered from both internal and external sources to provide reporting and aid decision making in all areas of marketing (market research, product design, pricing, media selection, advertising, selling, channel distribution, and product distribution).

A marketing MIS is a system that uses data gathered from both internal and external sources to provide reporting and aid decision making in all areas of marketing.

Figure 10.14 shows the inputs, subsystems, and outputs of a typical marketing MIS. The subsystems for the marketing MIS and their outputs help marketing managers and executives increase sales, reduce marketing expenses, and develop plans for future products and services to meet the changing needs of customers. These subsystems include market research, product design, pricing, media selection, advertising, selling, and channel distribution.

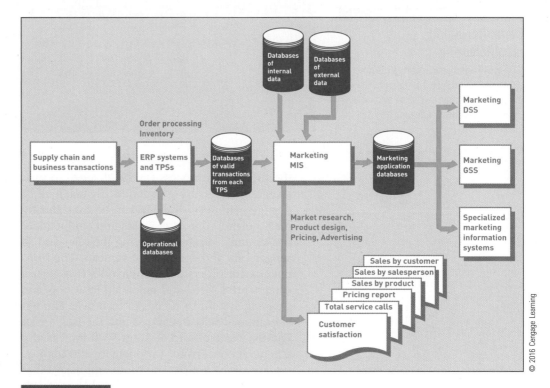

© 2016 Cengage Learning

FIGURE 10.14

Overview of a marketing MIS

A marketing MIS helps marketing managers and executives increase sales, reduce marketing expenses, and develop plans for future products and services to meet the changing needs of customers.

- **Market research**. The purpose of market research is to analyze the market to identify threats, opportunities, and customer needs and wants. Companies use the Internet as an important source of market research data by browsing social media Web sites to find postings about their organization and products, requesting site visitors to fill out an online questionnaire, and gathering online feedback forms from customers. Marketing MIS systems are used to summarize and report the results of surveys, questionnaires, pilot studies, consumer panels, and interviews. People who place messages on social networks such as Facebook may be surprised to discover that what they post is used in market research to provide input to design new or improved products and to develop more effective ads. An Internet marketing firm did market research with the help of the National Hot Rod Association (NHRA) to raise attendance at race tracks. Together they gathered data to build a marketing MIS that included a database of racing ticket buyers and NHRA members that held data about their attendance at races and the types of tickets purchased. This data was used to launch an email marketing campaign that helped NHRA-member tracks sell more tickets.[21]

- **Product design**. Product design is the process of generating a new product or service to be sold by an organization to its customers. The product may be entirely new or it may be a revised version of an existing product. The design process begins with the identification of customer needs and desires and requires a clear understanding of the functions and the performance expected of that product. Much of this data is stored within the marketing MIS. In addition, the product designer's role has been aided by digital tools that enable designers to visualize, analyze, communicate, and produce new product ideas in a manner that would have taken greater effort and elapsed time than in the past.

- **Pricing**. Product pricing is another key marketing function that involves setting the retail price, wholesale price, and price discounts. Marketing MIS systems are often used to store data showing the relationship between prices and consumer purchasing behavior. Nestle's used Decision Insight's proprietary online virtual shopping platform called SimuShop with the roll out of a new ice cream novelty product. Shoppers were recruited online to participate in a virtual shopping experience that was closely monitored to determine alternate shelf placements and prices for the product.[22] Companies try to develop pricing policies that will maximize total sales revenues. Some companies use *Internet behavioral pricing*, where the price customers pay online depends on what they are willing to pay based on large databases of personal information that reveal individual shopping behaviors and practices. Other companies resort to attracting customers as they walk by the store. Shopkick, Inc., for example, makes smartphone applications that offer discounts and rewards to customers simply for entering a store. See Figure 10.15. Over 6 million people use this application when shopping at Best Buy, Crate & Barrel, Macy's, Old Navy, Target, and other retailers.[23]

- **Media selection**. Media mix is the combination of various advertising channels (radio, TV, billboard, Internet, or newspaper) used to meet the objectives of a marketing program. The goal of media selection is to determine the best mix of media that will meet the objective of the campaign (e.g., raise brand awareness of the firm among the 18–24 age group, send prospects to a retail store, or generate more traffic to the organization Web site) at minimal cost. The marketing MIS can store the data necessary to make media selection trade-offs. Most marketing organizations choose a combination of both Internet and offline media to achieve their marketing goal. However, with an estimated 85 percent of buyers going online to research their purchases, the Internet is becoming an increasingly important component of the media mix.[24] The Internet media channel includes several components—one can choose from among dozens of highly popular social media Web sites (page or group), email, blog, or organizational Web site. Each Internet channel has its strengths and weaknesses depending on the goal of the marketing campaign. Some 43 percent of surveyed small business owners spend six or more hours per week on social media marketing by posting their messages to Facebook, Google +, Instagram, LinkedIn, Pinterest, Twitter, and YouTube. The owner of Daily Melt in midtown Miami brands his store as a restaurant that sells comfort through its delicious sandwich melts, laid-back atmosphere, and pleasant workers. The owner hired a social media

Get free rewards for visiting stores.

shopkick.com

FIGURE **10.15**

Shopkick

Shopkick makes smartphone applications that offer discounts and rewards to customers simply for entering a store.

marketing firm to engage his customers online with photos of weekly specials and a cheery message.[25]

- **Advertising**. One of the most important functions of any marketing effort is promotion and advertising. Product success is a direct function of the types of advertising and sales promotion done. Increasingly, organizations are using the Internet, smartphones, and other mobile devices to advertise and sell products and services. See Figure 10.16. Many small businesses are effectively advertising their products and services using Internet sites such as Groupon. With Groupon, users receive a daily advertisement for a deal from a local company, which can be as much as a 50 percent discount over normal prices.[26] Many companies promote their products on games and other applications for the Apple iPhone and other devices. In some cases, the advertising is hidden within free gaming applications. When you download and start playing the game, the advertising pops up on the screen. However, some people are not happy with Internet advertising. They complain that popular Internet search programs often display ads for completely unrelated searches. Some physicians and dentists, for example, claim that ads for their services are displayed to people searching for taxicab companies, barbers, and hair stylists, or other unrelated services.

- **Selling**. The marketing MIS can produce reports that identify products, sales personnel, and customers who contribute to profits and those who do not. This analysis can be done for sales and ads that help generate sales. Engagement ratings, for example, show how ads convert to sales. Several reports can be generated to help marketing managers make good sales decisions. See Figure 10.17.

FIGURE **10.16**

Internet advertising

The Internet is an important component of advertising for many organizations. Corporate marketing departments use social networking sites, such as Facebook (*www.facebook.com*) to advertise their products and perform market research.

The sales-by-product report lists all major products and their sales for a specified period of time. This report shows which products are doing well and which need improvement or should be discarded altogether. The sales-by-salesperson report lists total sales for each salesperson for each week or month. This report can also be subdivided by product to show which products are being sold by each salesperson. The sales-by-customer report is a tool that can be used to identify high- and low-volume customers. Swedbank is a large financial institution operating in Scandinavia and the Baltic states of Estonia, Latvia, and Lithuania. The bank employs 16,000 people and serves over 4 million customers in Sweden alone. Over the course of about a year, the bank developed a Customer Analysis tool to analyze

FIGURE **10.17**

Reports generated to help marketing managers make good decisions

(a) This sales-by-product report lists all major products and their sales for the period from August to December. (b) This sales-by-salesperson report lists total sales for each salesperson for the same time period. (c) This sales-by-customer report lists sales for each customer for the period. Like all MIS reports, totals are provided automatically by the system to show managers at a glance the information they need to make good decisions.

(a) Sales by Product						
Product	**August**	**September**	**October**	**November**	**December**	**Total**
Product 1	34	32	32	21	33	152
Product 2	156	162	177	163	122	780
Product 3	202	145	122	98	66	633
Product 4	345	365	352	341	288	1,691

(b) Sales by Salesperson						
Salesperson	**August**	**September**	**October**	**November**	**December**	**Total**
Jones	24	42	42	11	43	162
Kline	166	155	156	122	133	732
Lane	166	155	104	99	106	630
Miller	245	225	305	291	301	1,367

(c) Sales by Customer						
Customer	**August**	**September**	**October**	**November**	**December**	**Total**
Ang	234	334	432	411	301	1,712
Braswell	56	62	77	61	21	277
Celec	1,202	1,445	1,322	998	667	5,634
Jung	45	65	55	34	88	287

customers for cross-selling opportunities and planning marketing campaigns. Customer advisers and branch managers use the tool to plan which customers to meet, when, and for what purpose.[27]

- **Channel distribution**. Distribution channel optimization involves defining the chain of intermediary organizations through which a product flows to reach the final consumer. Distribution channel participants can include wholesalers, retailers, distributors, and the Internet. A direct distribution channel is one that enables the consumer to buy the product directly from the manufacturer. Distribution partners enable manufacturers to provide goods and services to customers and often offer some forms of customer service that the manufacturer does not (e.g., financing, maintenance, or training). Distribution channel optimization is a key factor in reaching customers where they prefer to buy as well as expanding sales into new markets and regions. There are three phases to distribution channel optimization: 1) evaluation of current channel partner effectiveness, 2) identification of new, high-growth opportunities and selection of appropriate partners to capture these opportunities, and 3) ongoing assessment and support of the performance of distribution partners.[28] An organization's marketing MIS can contain much data about existing and potential distribution partners as well as data about marketing opportunities to support channel optimization. Canadian Blood Services (CBS) is responsible for the collection, testing, manufacturing, procurement, and distribution of safe blood and blood products for patient care in Canada. The organization recognized that many in the general public wanted to give blood but simply were not following through and donating. So CBS decided to use an online distribution channel to nudge these intenders into action. The organization created an online community called Operation LifeBlood with the goal of alleviating potential donors' apprehensions and educating them about the donor process. It also built a social network Web site where donors and potential donors could share their experiences and engage in discussions. The program raised the conversion rate for potential donors to 16 percent, well above the goal of 10 percent.[29]

- **Product distribution**. Product distribution involves determining the best way to get products to customers. Organizations use their marketing MIS in an attempt to minimize distribution costs while still meeting customer time for delivery requirements. Grocery stores (e.g., Target, Walmart, and Meijer) allow shoppers to order products online and then pick them up or have them delivered at an agreed time. Mabe is a Mexican-owned, Mexico-based company that designs, produces, and distributes 15 brands of appliances to more than 70 countries around the world. A serious concern was drop and impact damage to its products as they traveled over the firm's distribution network from production floor to multiple warehouses via multiple freight carriers to the customer. Mabe decided to reapply the same computer-aided engineering tools used to design its appliances to the optimization of product packaging. The firm developed a new package design that minimized potential damage while reducing material costs and packaging weight.[30] Some organizations (such as The Apple Store, The Microsoft Store, shop411, Newegg, and VioSoftware) use the Internet to serve as their primary channel of distribution and employ digital distribution to send audio, video, software, video games, and books to their customers.

Human Resource Management Information Systems

human resource MIS (HRMIS): An information system that is concerned with activities related to previous, current, and potential employees of an organization, also called a personnel MIS.

A **human resource MIS (HRMIS)** is concerned with activities related to previous, current, and potential employees of the organization. The complexity of the human resource management function has increased dramatically over the last decade primarily due to the need to conform with new laws and regulations. The HRMIS is being used more and more to oversee and manage part-time employees, virtual work teams, and job sharing in addition to traditional job titles and duties. Because the human resource function relates to all other functional areas in the business, the HRMIS plays a valuable role in ensuring organizational success. Some of the activities performed by this important MIS include workforce analysis and planning, hiring, training, job and task assignment, and many other personnel-related issues. An effective HRMIS allows a company to keep personnel costs at a minimum while serving the required business processes needed to achieve corporate goals. Although traditional human resource information systems focus on cost reduction, many of today's HR systems concentrate on hiring and managing existing employees to get the total potential of the human talent in the organization. Figure 10.18 shows some of the inputs, subsystems, and outputs of the human resource MIS.

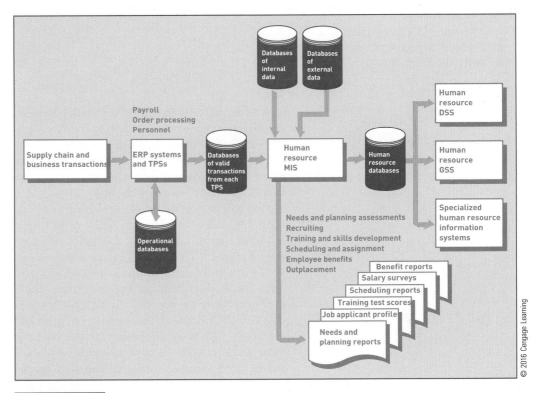

FIGURE **10.18**

Overview of a human resource MIS

A human resource MIS (HRMIS) helps to determine human resource needs and hiring through retirement and outplacement.

Human resource subsystems and outputs range from the determination of human resource needs and hiring through retirement and outplacement. Most medium and large organizations have computer systems to assist with human resource planning, hiring, training and skills inventorying, and wage and salary administration. See Figure 10.19. Outputs of the HRMIS include reports, such as human resource planning reports, job application review profiles, skills inventory reports, and salary surveys. Most human resource departments start with planning, discussed next.

- **Human resource planning.** One of the first aspects of any human resource MIS is determining the human resources required to meet the organization's goals and developing strategies to meet those needs. The overall purpose of this MIS subsystem is to place the right number and

FIGURE 10.19

Users of an HRMIS

Human resource MIS subsystems help to determine personnel needs and match employees to jobs.

type of employees in the right jobs when needed, including internal employees who work exclusively for the organization and outside workers who are hired when they are needed. Determining the best use of existing employees is a key component of human resource planning. Surprisingly, many companies and industries face serious shortages of workers due to lack of human resource planning. Landscape companies employ some 40,000 workers in Colorado and contribute around $2 billion to the state's economy, but many firms say they must turn down jobs because they do not have enough workers.[31] United States airlines are facing a critical shortage of pilots.[32] The oil and gas production industry has a labor shortage.[33] Well-managed organizations are looking ahead and planning how their work force needs will change over time. They then develop plans to meet these changing needs. The Tualatin Valley Water District (TVWD) provides water to the people of Beaverton, Oregon. TVWD needed additional workers to keep up with the growth in demand for water; however, 10 percent of its workers were eligible to retire within the next five years. The organization faced some serious challenges of succession planning, personnel selection and recruiting, training, and job placement. Human resource planning enabled TVWD to identify these issues well before they created a staffing crisis. TVWD was able to develop a timely solution that allowed a smooth transition to meet its staffing needs.[34]

- **Personnel selection and recruiting**. If the human resource plan reveals that additional personnel are required, the next logical step is recruiting and selecting personnel. Companies seeking new employees often use computers to schedule recruiting efforts and trips and to test potential employees' skills. Most companies now use the Internet to advertise open positions and screen for job applicants. Applicants use a template to load their résumés onto the Internet site. HR managers can then access these résumés and identify applicants they are interested in interviewing.

- **Training and skills inventory**. Some jobs, such as programming, equipment repair, and tax preparation, require very specific training for new employees. Other jobs may require general training about the organizational culture, company orientation, norms for interacting with other employees and customers, and expectations of the organization. When training is complete, employees often take computer-scored tests to evaluate their mastery of skills and new material. TTI Success Insights, based in

Scottsdale, Arizona, has developed a sophisticated online talent profiling system that evaluates job candidates based on several measures of superior performance: personal behaviors, motivators, acumen (a person's keenness and depth of perception), competencies in 25 personal skills directly related to the business environment, and emotional intelligence. The system was used by a national retailer to help complete the management team for a new chain of stores. Job benchmarks were created for assistant manager, general manager, and district manager positions. Candidates were evaluated against the benchmark as well as current employees. Development programs for current employees were defined based on gaps uncovered in the benchmark process.

- **Scheduling and job placement.** Schedules are developed for each employee, showing job assignments over the next week or month. Job placements are often determined based on skills inventory reports showing which employee might be best suited to a particular job. Sophisticated scheduling programs are often used in the airline industry, the military, and many other areas to get the right people assigned to the right jobs at the right time. Queen Anne's County DES EMS in Centerville, Maryland, employs more than 40 full-time people on rotation plus additional part-time people to fill in for vacationing employees and special events. Scheduling for this many people to ensure around-the-clock coverage is challenging. Scheduling became especially difficult when someone called in sick, needed time off, or requested overtime. Queen Anne's implemented on an online, Web-based scheduling system and trained the entire staff. Each member of the EMS can view their schedule and initiate their own trades when they need time off. The system enforces company rules on scheduling and ensures that sufficient numbers of workers are always available. All this happens with no supervisor intervention.

- **Wage and salary administration.** Another human resource MIS subsystem involves determining wages, salaries, and benefits, including medical payments, savings plans, and retirement accounts. Wage data, such as industry averages for positions, can be taken from the corporate database and manipulated by the HRMIS to provide wage information and reports to higher levels of management. Most organizations provide a self-service Web-based system component to their HRMIS. This enables employees to enter their timesheets, make changes to their W-4 withholding data, change their selection of various company benefit programs, and request W-2 statements or a printout of their paycheck.

- **Outplacement.** Employees leave a company for a variety of reasons. Outplacement services are offered by many companies to help employees make the transition. *Outplacement* can include job counseling and training, job and executive search, retirement and financial planning, and a variety of severance packages and options. Many employees use the Internet to plan their future retirement or to find new jobs, using job sites such as *www.monster.com* and *www.linkedin.com*.

Other Management Information Systems

In addition to finance, manufacturing, marketing, and human resource MISs, some companies have other functional management information systems. For example, most successful companies have well-developed accounting functions and a supporting accounting MIS. Also, many companies use geographic information systems for presenting data in a useful form.

Accounting MISs

accounting MIS: An information system that provides aggregate information on accounts payable, accounts receivable, payroll, and many other applications.

In some cases, accounting works closely with financial management. An accounting MIS performs a number of important activities, providing aggregate information on accounts payable, accounts receivable, payroll, and many other applications. The organization's enterprise resource planning and transaction processing system captures accounting data, which is also used by most other functional information systems.

Some smaller companies hire outside accounting firms to assist them with their accounting functions. These outside companies produce reports for the firm using raw accounting data. In addition, many excellent integrated accounting programs are available for personal computers in small companies. Depending on the needs of the small organization and its staff's computer experience, using these computerized accounting systems can be a very cost-effective approach to managing information.

Geographic Information Systems

geographic information system (GIS): A computer system capable of assembling, storing, manipulating, and displaying geographic information, that is, data identified according to its location.

Increasingly, managers want to see data presented in graphical form. A **geographic information system (GIS)** is a computer system capable of assembling, storing, manipulating, and displaying geographically referenced information; that is, data identified according to its location. The US Department of Housing and Urban Development (HUD) grants funds to state and local governments to provide people with decent housing. These funding decisions are based on an evaluation of needs and market conditions in each grantee's jurisdiction. The Office of Community Planning and Development (CPD) Maps is a geospatial application that provides data and maps to help grantees understand how to target aid based on where needs are greatest. For example, grantees can now see concentrated poverty on the map. See Figure 10.20.

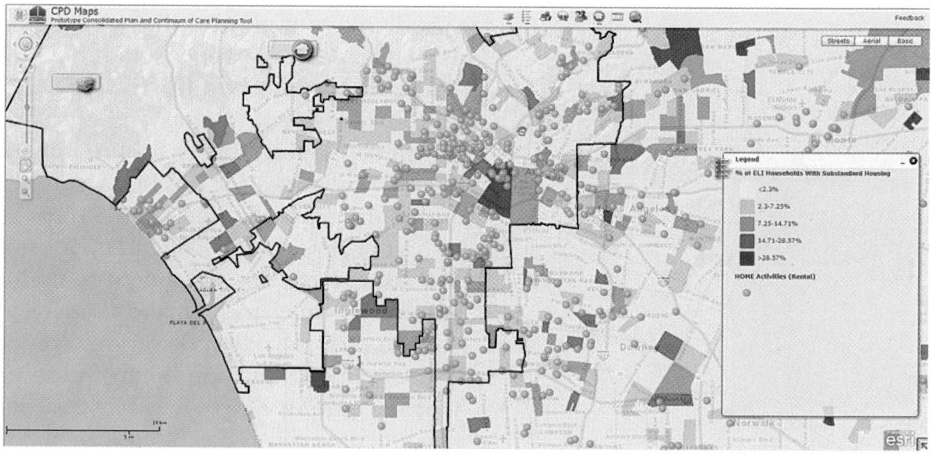

FIGURE **10.20**

CPD Maps

CPD Maps is a tool in the HUD eCon Planning Suite, a GIS application used to make affordable housing and community development planning decisions.

Loopt's mobile application and website (*http://looptworks.com*) enable its users to tap into local intelligence about places that make it easy to find friends and the locations of stores with the best deals. WHERE is another mobile app that helps you search and discover what's nearby with real-time information on the local news and weather plus recommendations on restaurants, movies, and places to shop.

AN OVERVIEW OF DECISION SUPPORT SYSTEMS

A decision support system (DSS) is an organized collection of people, procedures, software, databases, and devices used to help make decisions that solve problems. The focus of a DSS is on decision-making effectiveness when faced with unstructured or semistructured business problems. Decision support systems offer the potential to generate higher profits, lower costs, and better products and services. Decision support systems, although skewed

ETHICAL& SOCIETAL ISSUES

You Want to Put That *Where*?

Land use is often a contentious topic. Everyone wants the benefits that airports, electricity-generating plants, prisons, and all-night railroad freight car classification yards bring to society. Still, few people want to live next door to one of these operations.

Fortunately, geographic information systems (GISs) can help sort out the issues involved with siting these and other operations. In fact, the government of Queensland, Australia, used a GIS to figure out the best locations for poultry farms in the southern part of that state.

As background, chicken is the most popular form of meat for Australians. Queensland has about 22 percent of Australia's population and produces about 20 percent of its chicken. Chicken farming is split between two major centers: near the town of Mareeba in the north and near the capital city of Brisbane in the south. Owing to the larger number of competing land uses near Brisbane, the government of Queensland needed to develop objective ways to allocate this scarce resource.

Poultry farms are not nearly as objectionable as some other operations that modern society finds necessary, but many factors still determine the best places to put them. William Mortimer, senior spatial analyst at Queensland Government, writes that "Geographic information systems and spatial analysis tools enable the departmental decision makers to visualize and understand complex issues on a site specific and regional scale basis." Among these issues are what he calls *primary constraints*. The location of a poultry farm *may* not be:

- Too close (under 1 km, about 0.6 miles) to another poultry farm
- In a key mineral resource extraction area
- In an urban or residential area (a 2 km buffer, about 1.2 miles, is desirable)
- In an area of high ecological significance
- In a low-lying, flood-prone area
- In a koala conservation area
- In a designated water catchment area
- Within the Royal Australian Air Force base at Amberley

As secondary constraints, a poultry farm *should* not be:

- On land that is too steep (over 10 percent slope)
- Next to a watercourse
- On good quality agricultural land
- On land suitable for strategic crops
- In a national park or other protected area
- On an oil or gas pipeline
- On acid sulphate soil

Conversely, it is desirable for a poultry farm to be:

- Near poultry processing plants
- Near paved roads
- Near a reliable supply of clean water
- Near a supply of electricity
- Near poultry feed mills

Using these constraints and ESRI's ArcGIS software, the Queensland government was able to produce maps of the southern part of Queensland, showing areas that were suitable for new poultry farms, calculating automatically the amount of land available in each of them, and showing areas of different sizes in different colors. This mapping provides a good basis for future planning—both for the poultry industry and for those affected by it.

Discussion Questions

1. How could this approach be used to help choose locations for new wind farms? What primary constraints would have to be changed? What could stay essentially the same?
2. When considering where to locate public resources such as power plants, prisons, and public schools, who should have say in defining the primary constraints for choosing the location?

Critical Thinking Questions

1. Is the Queensland decision regarding where to locate chicken farms an example of a satisficing model? Why or why not?
2. How can GIS be used to facilitate the siting of public and private facilities and to resolve disputes over zoning? What other types of technologies can help resolve these contentious issues?

SOURCES: Australia Chicken Meat Federation Web site, *www.chicken.org.au*, accessed June 4, 2014; Department of Local Government and Planning, Queensland Government, "Rural Planning: The Identification and Constraint Mapping of Potential Poultry Farming Industry Locations within Southern Queensland," OZRI 2011 conference, *www10.giscafe.com/link/Esri-Australia-Rural -Planning-identification-constraint-mapping-potential-poultry-farming-industry-locations-within -Southern-Queensland./36838/view.html*, October 14, 2011; Queensland Government Web site, *www.qld.gov.au*, accessed June 4, 2014; ESRI ArcGIS software Web site, *www.esri.com/software /arcgis*, accessed June 4, 2014.

somewhat toward the top levels of management, can be used at all levels. DSSs are also used in a wide range of applications in business, sports, government, law enforcement, and nonprofit organizations. See Figure 10.21. TDX is a debt liquidation organization with headquarters in the United Kingdom. It provides banking, utility, and government creditors with technology, data, and advisory solutions to optimize returns from their debt portfolios. It has £8.4 billion (slightly over $14 billion) of debt under management and works

FIGURE 10.21

Decision support systems

Decision support systems are used by government and law enforcement professionals in many settings.

© Graham Taylor/Shutterstock.com

with over 200 clients.[35] One service that TDX provides is to advise its clients which debt collection agency it should use for each of its various debts. TDX employs a decision support system to optimize the choice of collection agency to maximize the net return (amount received from the debtor minus debt collection agency fees) to the creditor.[36]

Characteristics of a Decision Support System

Decision support systems have many characteristics that allow them to be effective management support tools. Of course, not all DSSs work the same. The following list shows some important characteristics of a DSS:

- Provide rapid access to information. Handle large amounts of data from different sources. Harrah's Entertainment, Inc., gathers data from more than 19 million customers across its 21 casinos as input to a DSS that helps target its marketing campaigns and offer tailor-made packages to clients based on their individual gaming preferences.[37]
- Provide report and presentation flexibility.
- Offer both textual and graphical orientation.
- Support drill-down analysis. Canopius Managing Agents Unlimited, a division of a specialist underwriting business and insurer, deployed a DSS with drill-down analysis capability to over 100 underwriting, claims, actuarial, and senior management users. The system enables users to view data at their preferred level of granularity—from summary level down to the details of individual policies and claims.[38]
- Perform complex, sophisticated analyses and comparisons using advanced software packages. A number of sophisticated clinical decision support systems are under development to improve a clinician's ability to distinguish among a variety of complex diagnoses and avoid prescribing medicines that may cause a bad drug-to-drug or allergic interaction.[39]
- Support optimization, satisficing, and heuristic approaches. See Figure 10.22.

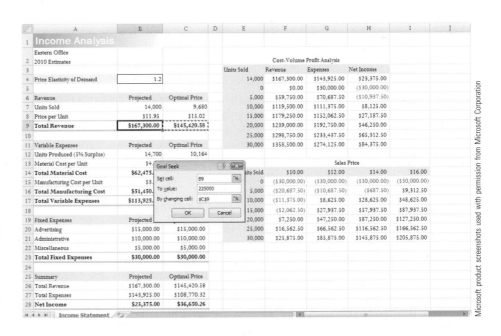

FIGURE **10.22**

Spreadsheet as a DSS tool

With a spreadsheet program, a manager can enter a goal, and the spreadsheet will determine the input needed to achieve the goal.

- Perform simulation analysis. A DSS has the ability to duplicate the features of a real system, where probability or uncertainty is involved. Anyone who wants to offer fishing and sailing charters, drive a dive boat, run sightseeing tours, or captain a large ocean-going cruise ship must first earn an appropriate license. However, it is extremely difficult for non-licensed mariners to get "practice time" on an actual ship. Thus many mariner schools use a computer-based simulation to engage students in real-life situations. The system enables the candidates to demonstrate their ability to handle different situations to obtain credentials for licenses and helps them in applying for new jobs or assignments.

- Forecast a future opportunity or problem. Staples uses a decision support system to reduce customer attrition. The system tracks millions of customers' purchases and, if spending for regular customers drops, it sends personalized offers to bring them back.[40]

Capabilities of a Decision Support System

Developers of decision support systems strive to make them more flexible than management information systems and to give them the potential to assist decision makers in a variety of situations. Warathas Rugby is the professional rugby team of the Australian state of New South Wales. Rugby is not a game for the meek. It is physically demanding and during the course of a match, a player is typically involved in 20 to 40 violent collisions. Over the course of a season, roughly 25 percent of the players on a team will be injured to the extent that they cannot participate in one or more matches. Warathas piloted the use of a decision support system to identify those players likely to be injured. The system was fed performance statistics, medical data, and data from sensors attached to the players during training sessions and matches. The system was able to detect early warning signs of injury and was successful in identifying three players who sustained an injury in the following weeks. With the accuracy of the system proven, the coaching staff will now use the system to prevent injuries by modifying an individual player's training regime or resting them during a match.[41]

In addition to being flexible, DSSs can assist with all or most problem-solving phases, decision frequencies, and varying degrees of problem structure. DSS approaches can also help at all levels of the decision-making process. A single DSS, however, might provide only a few of these capabilities, depending on its uses and scope.

Support for Problem-Solving Phases

The objective of most decision support systems is to assist decision makers during the phases of problem solving. As previously discussed, these phases include intelligence, design, choice, implementation, and monitoring. A specific DSS might support only one or a few phases. By supporting all types of decision-making approaches, a DSS gives the decision maker a great deal of flexibility in getting computer support for decision-making activities.

Support for Various Decision Frequencies

Decisions can range on a continuum from one-of-a-kind to repetitive decisions. One-of-a-kind decisions are typically handled by an ad hoc DSS. An **ad hoc DSS** is concerned with situations or decisions that come up only a few times during the life of the organization; in small businesses, they might happen only once. For example, a company might need to decide whether to build a new manufacturing facility in another area of the country. Repetitive decisions are addressed by an institutional DSS. An **institutional DSS** handles situations or decisions that occur more than once, usually several times per year or more. It is used repeatedly and refined over the years. Examples of institutional DSSs include systems that support portfolio and investment decisions and production scheduling. These decisions might require decision support numerous times during the year. Between these two extremes are decisions that managers make several times but not routinely.

ad hoc DSS: A DSS concerned with situations or decisions that come up only a few times during the life of the organization.

institutional DSS: A DSS that handles situations or decisions that occur more than once, usually several times per year or more. It is used repeatedly and refined over the years.

Support for Various Decision-Making Levels

Decision support systems can provide help for managers at various levels within an organization. Operational managers can get assistance with daily and routine decision making. Tactical decision makers can use analysis tools to ensure proper planning and control. At the strategic level, DSSs can help managers by providing analysis for long-term decisions requiring both internal and external information. See Figure 10.23.

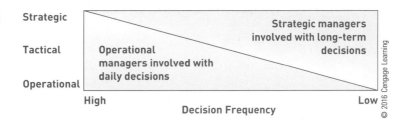

A Comparison of DSS and MIS

A DSS differs from an MIS in numerous ways, including the type of problems solved, the support given to users, the decision emphasis and approach, and the type, speed, output, and development of the system used. Table 10.3 lists brief descriptions of these differences.

TABLE 10.3 Comparison of DSSs and MISs

Factor	DSS	MIS
Approach	Serves as a direct support system that provides interactive reports on computer screens.	Typically serves as an indirect support system that uses regularly produced reports.
Development	Has users who are usually more directly involved in its development. User involvement usually means better systems that provide superior support. For all systems, user involvement is the most important factor for the development of a successful system.	Is frequently several years old and often was developed for people who are no longer performing the work supported by the MIS.
Emphasis	Emphasizes actual decisions and decision-making styles.	Usually emphasizes information only.
Output	Produces reports that are usually screen oriented, with the ability to generate reports on a printer.	Is oriented toward printed reports and documents.
Problem type	Can handle unstructured problems that cannot be easily programmed.	Normally used only with structured problems.
Speed	Is flexible and can be implemented by users, so it usually takes less time to develop and is better able to respond to user requests.	Provides response time usually longer than a DSS.
Support	Supports all aspects and phases of decision making; it does not replace the decision maker—people still make the decisions.	In some cases, makes automatic decisions and replaces the decision maker.
System	Uses computer equipment that is usually online (directly connected to the computer system) and related to real time (providing immediate results). Computer terminals and display screens are examples—these devices can provide immediate information and answers to questions.	Uses printed reports that might be delivered to managers once per week, so it cannot provide immediate results.
Users	Supports individuals, small groups, and the entire organization. In the short run, users typically have more control over a DSS.	Primarily supports the organization. In the short run, users have less control over an MIS.

COMPONENTS OF A DECISION SUPPORT SYSTEM

dialogue manager: A user interface that allows decision makers to easily access and manipulate the DSS and to use common business terms and phrases.

At the core of a DSS are a database and a model base. In addition, a typical DSS contains a user interface, also called a **dialogue manager**, which allows decision makers to easily access and manipulate the DSS and to use common business terms and phrases. Finally, access to the Internet, networks, and other computer-based systems permits the DSS to tie into other powerful systems, including the TPS or function-specific subsystems. Figure 10.24 shows a conceptual model of a DSS, although specific DSSs might not have all the components shown in this figure.

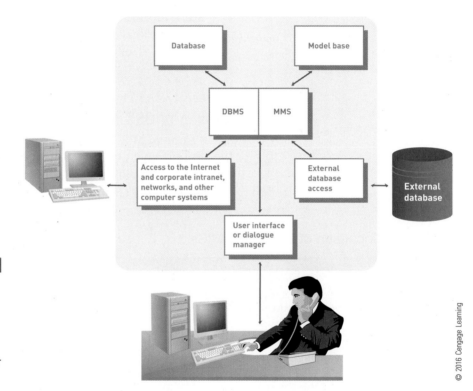

FIGURE 10.24

Conceptual model of a DSS

DSS components include a model base; database; external database access; access to the Internet and corporate intranet, networks, and other computer systems; and a user interface or dialogue manager.

The Database

The DSS database management system allows managers and decision makers to perform *qualitative analysis* on the company's vast stores of data in databases, data warehouses, and data marts, using data mining and business intelligence, introduced in Chapter 5. While business organizations frequently use a DSS, such systems are also used by governmental agencies and nonprofit organizations. Indeed, many city governments use the data they routinely collect to improve services.

Each year, about 1 percent of 330,000 inspectable buildings in New York City break out in a major fire. (One and two-family houses are not inspected.) The New York City Fire Department is piloting the use of data mining to predict which houses are most likely to catch fire. Analysts have identified some 60 characteristics (e.g., neighborhood income level, age of the building, the presence of sprinklers, and whether the building is vacant or occupied) that indicate which buildings are more likely to catch fire than others. The DSS uses this data and an algorithm to assign each building a risk score. Now when fire inspectors set out on their weekly inspections, the DSS provides a priority list of buildings ranked by their risk score to be inspected.[42]

The DSS database management system can also connect to external databases to give managers and decision makers even more information and decision support. External databases can include the Internet, libraries, and government databases, among others. Access to a combination of internal and external databases can improve the performance of DSS systems. For example, Twitter generates a lot of data with its millions of users publicly sending on the order of 500 million tweets. Many of these tweets are tagged with precise location and time data and, if processed properly, can become valuable input to DSS systems. For example, researchers have found that for 19 of the 25 crime types studied, the addition of Twitter data improves crime prediction performance.[43]

The Model Base

model base: Part of a DSS that allows managers and decision makers to perform quantitative analysis on both internal and external data.

The model base allows managers and decision makers to perform *quantitative analysis* on both internal and external data. Once large databases have been collected and stored, companies use models (analytics) to turn the data into future products, services, and profits. The model base gives decision makers access to a variety of models so that they can explore different scenarios and see their effects. Ultimately, it assists them in the decision-making process.

model management software (MMS): Software that coordinates the use of models in a DSS, including financial, statistical analysis, graphical, and project-management models.

Model management software (MMS) can coordinate the use of models in a DSS, including financial, statistical analysis, graphical, and project-management models. Depending on the needs of the decision maker, one or more of these models can be used. See Table 10.4. What is important is how the mathematical models are used, not the number of models that an organization has available. In fact, too many model-based tools can be a disadvantage. MMS can often help managers effectively use multiple models in a DSS.

TABLE **10.4** Model management software

Model Type	Description	Software
Financial	Provides cash flow, internal rate of return, and other investment analysis	Spreadsheet, such as Microsoft Excel
Statistical	Provides summary statistics, trend projections, hypothesis testing, and more	Statistical programs, such as SPSS or SAS
Graphical	Assists decision makers in designing, developing, and using graphic displays of data and information	Graphics programs, such as Microsoft PowerPoint
Project Management	Handles and coordinates large projects; also used to identify critical activities and tasks that could delay or jeopardize an entire project if they are not completed in a timely and cost-effective fashion	Project management software, such as Microsoft Project

© 2016 Cengage Learning

The User Interface, or Dialogue Manager

The user interface, or dialogue manager, allows users to interact with the DSS to obtain information. It assists with all aspects of communications between the user and the hardware and software that constitute the DSS. In a practical sense, to most DSS users, the user interface is the DSS. Upper-level decision makers are often less interested in where the information came from or how it was gathered than that the information is both understandable and accessible.

Nielsen provides its clients with data about what consumers watch and buy. The firm is testing a technology called the IBM Watson Engagement Advisor for supporting individuals at client organizations who are responsible for buying ads based on Nielsen ratings. These users can ask questions about how Nielsen compiles its results or ask for advice on how best to spend their advertising dollars. Software called Ask Watson provides an interface that allows clients to communicate with the technology via instant message, text message, email, Web chat, or a dedicated app on their mobile phone.[44]

GROUP DECISION SUPPORT SYSTEMS

group decision support system (GSS): Software application that consists of most of the elements in a DSS, plus software to provide effective support in group decision-making settings; also called *group support system* or *computerized collaborative work system*.

The DSS approach has resulted in better decision making for all levels of individual users. However, some DSS approaches and techniques are not suitable for a group decision-making environment. A group decision support system (GSS), also called a *group support system* and a *computerized collaborative work system*, consists of most of the elements in a DSS, plus software to provide effective support in group decision-making settings. See Figure 10.25.

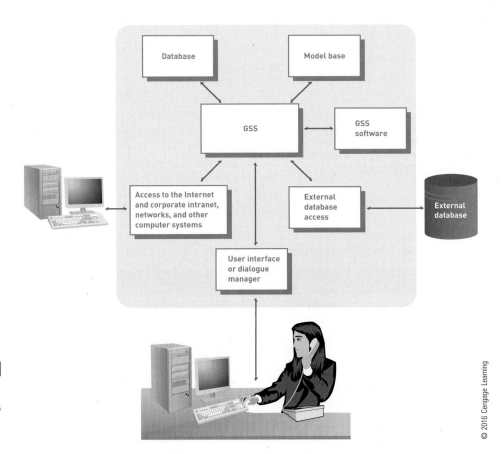

FIGURE **10.25**

Configuration of a GSS

A GSS contains most of the elements found in a DSS, plus software to support group decision making.

Group decision support systems are used in business organizations, nonprofits, government units, and the military. They are also used between companies when the firms are involved in the same supply chain, as first discussed in Chapter 2. For example, an organization might get raw materials and supplies from one company and use another company to distribute finished products to consumers. These separate companies involved in the same supply chain often use group decision support systems to coordinate joint forecasting, planning, and other activities critical to delivering finished products and services to customers.

Characteristics of a GSS That Enhance Decision Making

When it comes to decision making, a GSS's unique characteristics have the potential to result in better decisions. Developers of these systems try to build on the advantages of individual support systems while adding new approaches unique to group decision making. For example, some GSSs allow the exchange of information and expertise among people without direct face-to-face interaction, although some face-to-face meeting time is usually beneficial. The following sections describe characteristics that can improve and enhance decision making.

Special Design

The GSS approach acknowledges that special procedures, devices, and approaches are needed in group decision-making settings. These procedures must foster creative thinking, effective communications, and good group decision-making techniques.

Ease of Use

Like an individual DSS, a GSS must be easy to learn and use. Systems that are complex and hard to operate will seldom be used. Many groups have less tolerance than do individual decision makers for poorly developed systems.

Flexibility

Two or more decision makers working on the same problem might have different decision-making styles and preferences. Each manager makes decisions in a unique way, in part because of different experiences and cognitive styles. An effective GSS not only has to support the approaches that managers use to make decisions but also must find a means to integrate their different perspectives into a common view of the task at hand. GSS flexibility is also important with customers and outside companies.

Decision-Making Support

delphi approach: A structured, interactive, iterative decision-making method that relies on input from a panel of experts.

A GSS can support different decision-making approaches, including the **delphi approach**, a structured, interactive, iterative decision-making method that relies on input from a panel of experts. Its purpose is to solicit responses from a panel of experts regarding a particular problem or situation and hopefully converge on a "correct" answer. The experts are provided a questionnaire stating the problem and soliciting their opinion. A facilitator collects the responses and provides an anonymous summary of the experts' forecasts as well as the basis for their judgments. The experts are then encouraged to revise their earlier answers in light of the replies of the other members of the panel of experts. This process is repeated until a predefined number of rounds is completed or the group has achieved a consensus. Typically the range of the answers will decrease and the group will converge toward a common answer. The technique had its genesis at the Rand Corporation in the early 1950s where it was used to forecast the impact of technology on warfare.

brainstorming: A decision-making approach that consists of members offering ideas "off the top of their heads," fostering creativity and free thinking.

In another approach, called **brainstorming**, members offer ideas "off the top of their heads," fostering creativity and free thinking. How2Media is a twenty-first century television production company whose award winning programming includes "World's Greatest ...... (fill in the blank)." The company frequently employs brainstorming to come up with new ideas for its programming.[45]

group consensus approach: A group decision-making process that seeks the consent of all participants.

The **group consensus approach** is a group decision-making process that seeks the *consent* of the participants. Giving consent does not mean that the solution being considered is a participant's first choice. Group members can vote their consent to a proposal because they choose to work with the group to accomplish some result, rather than insist on their personal preference. A group must decide on the level of agreement necessary to finalize a decision—unanimous agreement, unanimous consent, super majority (two-thirds is common), or simple majority. The group must also decide which members of the group can vote on the decision (such as all or executive committee members only). The Shuttle Project Engineering Office at the Kennedy Space Center has used the Consensus-Ranking Organizational-Support System (CROSS) to evaluate space projects in a group setting. See Figure 10.26.

FIGURE 10.26

Using the GSS approach

NASA engineers use the Consensus-Ranking Organizational-Support System (CROSS) to evaluate space projects in a group setting.

nominal group technique (NGT): A structured method for group brainstorming that encourages contributions from everyone.

The group consensus approach analyzes the benefits of various projects and their probabilities of success. CROSS is used to evaluate and prioritize advanced space projects.

The **nominal group technique (NGT)** is a structured method for group brainstorming that encourages contributions from everyone. It has several advantages over simple brainstorming. It avoids the domination of discussion by a single person and gets all participants involved in making suggestions. It reduces the likelihood of heated discussions to "defend" ideas not accepted by others. Participants feel more "ownership" in the solution. It results in a set of prioritized solutions or recommendations. The steps involved in the nominal group technique are as follow:

1. The facilitator states the subject of the brainstorming session and works to clarify the problem statement until everyone understands it.
2. Each participant silently identifies and writes down as many ideas as possible in a set period of time.
3. The facilitator then calls on each participant in turn to state aloud *one* of his or her ideas. The facilitator records the idea on a flipchart or whiteboard for all to see. Ideas may be discussed to add clarity or answer questions, but no attempt is made to evaluate the idea or reject it. Duplicate ideas are discarded. Wording may be changed to add clarity.
4. The facilitator continues to poll each participant until all participants' ideas have been recorded. The participants then prioritize the ideas using multivoting.

multivoting: Any one of a number of voting processes used to reduce the number of options to be considered.

Multivoting is any one of a number of voting processes used to reduce the number of options to be considered. For example, following the first four steps of a nominal group technique session, the group may have identified 14 options for consideration. One multivoting approach is to allow each participant to vote for half the identified options. On a cue from the facilitator, the participants go to the flipchart or whiteboard and place one vote next to each of the seven options they think are best. The facilitator then adds the votes for each option. The seven options that received the most votes are used to create a reduced list of options. Again, the ideas are discussed to add clarity or answer questions and the voting process is repeated. This process continues until the number of options remaining is acceptable to the group.

Anonymous Input

Many GSSs allow anonymous input, where the person giving the input is not known to other group members. For example, some organizations use a GSS to help rank the performance of managers. Anonymous input allows the group decision makers to concentrate on the merits of the input without considering who gave it. In other words, input given by a top-level manager is given the same consideration as input from employees or other members of the group. Some studies have shown that groups using anonymous input can make better decisions and have superior results compared with groups that do not use anonymous input.

Reduction of Negative Group Behavior

One key characteristic of any GSS is the ability to suppress or eliminate group behavior that is counterproductive or harmful to effective decision making. In some group settings, dominant individuals can take over the discussion, thereby preventing other members of the group from participating. In other cases, one or two group members can sidetrack or subvert the group into areas that are nonproductive and do not help solve the problem at hand. At other times, members of a group might assume they have made the right decision without examining alternatives—a phenomenon called *groupthink*. If group sessions are poorly planned and executed, the result can be a tremendous waste of time. Today, many GSS designers are developing software and hardware systems to reduce these types of problems. Procedures for effectively planning and managing group meetings can be incorporated into the GSS approach. A trained meeting facilitator is often employed to help lead the group decision-making process and to avoid groupthink. See Figure 10.27.

FIGURE 10.27

Importance of a trained facilitator

A trained meeting facilitator can help lead the group decision-making process and avoid groupthink.

© iStockphoto.com/Golden KB

Parallel and Unified Communication

With traditional group meetings, people must take turns addressing various issues. One person normally talks at a time. With a GSS, every group member can address issues or make comments at the same time by entering text messages to the GSS. These comments and issues are displayed for every group member to see immediately. *Parallel communication* can speed meeting times and result in better decisions. Organizations are using unified communications to support group decision making. *Unified communications* ties together and integrates various communication systems, including traditional phones, cell phones, email, text messages, and the Internet. With unified communications, members of a group decision-making team use a wide range of communications methods to help them collaborate and make better decisions.

Automated Record Keeping

Most GSSs can automatically keep detailed records of a meeting. Each comment that is entered by a group member can be recorded. In some cases, literally hundreds of comments can be stored for future review and analysis. In addition, most GSS packages have automatic voting and ranking features. After group members vote, the GSS records each vote and makes the appropriate rankings.

GSS Hardware and Software Tools

Today, executives and corporate managers are collaborating with smartphones and tablet computers to a greater extent. GSS software, often called *groupware* or *workgroup software*, helps with joint workgroup scheduling, communication, and management. One popular package, IBM Lotus Notes, can capture, store, manipulate, and distribute memos and communications that are developed during group projects. Some companies standardize on messaging and collaboration software, such as Lotus Notes. Lotus Connections is a feature of Lotus Notes that allows people to post documents and information on the Internet. The feature is similar to popular social networking sites such as Facebook and LinkedIn, but it is designed for business use. Microsoft has invested billions of dollars in GSS software to incorporate collaborative features into its Office suite and related products. Office Communicator, for example, is a Microsoft product developed to allow better and faster collaboration. Other GSS software packages include Collabnet, OpenMind, and TeamWare. All of these tools can aid in group decision making. *Shared electronic calendars* can be used to coordinate meetings and schedules for decision-making teams. Using electronic calendars, team leaders can block out time for all members of the decision-making team.

A number of additional collaborative tools are available. SharePoint (*www.microsoft.com*), WebEx WebOffice (*www.weboffice.com*), and Base-Camp (*www.basecamp.com*) are just a few examples. Fuze (*www.fuze.com*) provides video collaboration tools on the Internet. The service can automatically bring participants into a live chat, allow workers to share information on their computer screens, and broadcast video content in high definition. Twitter (*www.twitter.com*) and Google+ (*plus.google.com*) are Internet sites that some organizations use to help people and groups stay connected and coordinate work schedules. Yammer (*www.yammer.com*) is a Web site that helps companies provide short answers to frequently asked questions. See Figure 10.28. Managers and employees must first log into their private company network on Yammer to get their questions answered. Teamspace (*www.teamspace.com*) is yet another collaborative software package that assists teams to successfully complete projects. Many of these Internet packages embrace the use of Web 2.0 technologies. Some executives, however, worry about security and corporate compliance issues with any new technology.

GSS Alternatives

Group support systems can take on a number of network configurations, depending on the needs of the group, the decision to be supported, and the geographic location of group members. GSS can be used to improve both the speed and quality of decision making. GSS alternatives include a combination

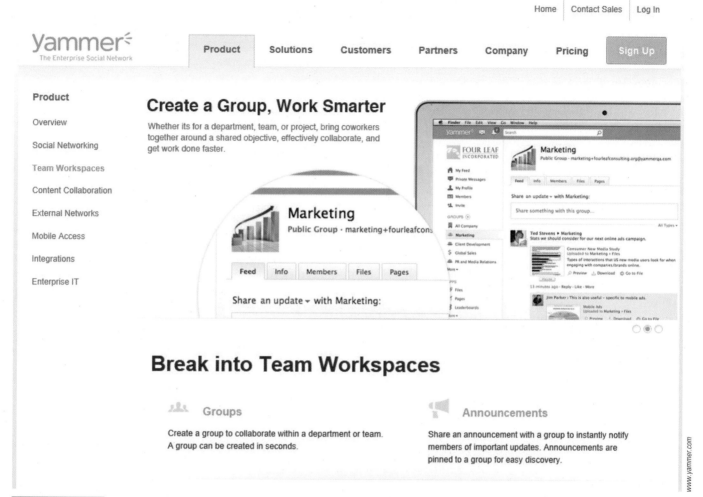

FIGURE 10.28

Yammer

Yammer helps organizations provide short answers to frequently asked questions.

of decision rooms, local area networks, teleconferencing, and wide area networks:

decision room: A room that supports decision making, with the decision makers in the same building, and that combines face-to-face verbal interaction with technology to make the meeting more effective and efficient.

- The **decision room** is a room that supports decision making, includes decision makers in the same building, and combines face-to-face verbal interaction with technology to make the meeting more effective and efficient. It is ideal for situations in which decision makers are located in the same building or geographic area, and the decision makers are occasional users of the GSS approach. A typical decision room is shown in Figure 10.29.
- The *local area decision network* can be used when group members are located in the same building or geographic area and under conditions in which group decision making is frequent. In these cases, the technology and equipment for the GSS approach is placed directly into the offices of the group members.
- *Teleconferencing* is used when the decision frequency is low and the location of group members is distant. These distant and occasional group meetings can tie together multiple GSS decision-making rooms across the country or around the world. The video game creator Activision Publishing

INFORMATION SYSTEMS @ WORK

Flaws in Group Support Systems

At 11:38 am on January 28, 1986, the shuttle orbiter Challenger launched from Cape Canaveral, Florida. Less than a second later, gray smoke streamed out from a hot flare burning in the rocket motor. The flare ignited liquid hydrogen and nitrogen inside the fuel tank, which exploded 73 seconds after liftoff. As the Challenger was torn apart, all seven astronauts on board were killed.

In the days and weeks that followed the disaster, it became clear that two O-rings designed to separate the sections of the rocket booster had failed. Engineers working for the space agency had warned of just such a failure. They had expressed concerns that the O-ring seals could fail when outside temperatures dropped below 53 degrees Fahrenheit. On the morning of January 28, the temperature was 36 degrees. The launch pad was covered with solid ice.

Group support systems facilitate communication and data exchange between employees making important decisions. In fact, NASA had just such a system in place to coordinate its work with engineers at Morton Thiokol, the manufacturer of the shuttle's solid rocket motor, which included the faulty O-rings.

On the evening of January 27, 1986, Morton Thiokol engineers expressed concerns about launching the shuttle under such abnormally cold weather conditions. The data provided by their group decision support system indicated that the O-ring seals would withstand such low temperatures. However, the engineers doubted the accuracy of the database analysis. They recommended that NASA wait to launch until the temperature outside reached 53 degrees. One NASA manager asked, "My God, Thiokol, when do you want me to launch, next April?" That NASA manager then asked a second NASA manager to intervene. The second NASA manager responded that he was "appalled at Thiokol's recommendation but would not launch over the contractor's objection." The NASA manager continued to maintain that the arguments presented by the Thiokol engineers were inconclusive. Thiokol managers then requested to have five minutes offline to discuss the issue with their engineers. When Thiokol representatives logged back into the system, they supported the decision to launch and NASA welcomed this decision.

After the disaster, the president ordered a commission to investigate the disaster and find out what went wrong. The commission interviewed those involved in the decision-making process and looked over documentation, such as that recorded by the group support system.

One of the Thiokol engineers explained to the presidential commission investigating the data that the engineers just didn't have enough data to determine whether the O-rings could seal properly at lower temperatures. Unlike other Thiokol managers, however, one engineer did not sign the launch recommendation on that fateful evening of January 27. As a result, he stayed with the company and was put in charge of redesigning the solid rocket motor. The redesign was used in 110 successful shuttle mission launches.

Discussion Questions

1. The group support system recorded the interaction between the Thiokol and NASA teams. What was this recorded interaction used for?
2. In what other ways can tracking individual contributions to a GSS be used to support the goals of an organization?

Critical Thinking Questions

1. The Thiokol engineers doubted the reliability of the analyses they ran on the data in their system. Why do you think Thiokol and NASA managers found it so hard to believe that the engineers might be right and the system output might be wrong?
2. What lessons can be learned from the Challenger disaster that can be applied to the implementation of other group decision support systems?

SOURCES: Oberg, James, "7 Myths about the Challenger Shuttle Disaster," NBC News, January 25, 2011, *www.nbcnews.com/id /11031097/ns/technology_and_science-space/t/myths-about-challenger -shuttle-disaster/#.U2AsylFdUrU*, accessed April 29, 2014; "Engineer Who Opposed Challenger Launch Offers Personal Look at Tragedy," Researcher News, NASA Web site, October 5, 2012, *www.nasa.gov /centers/langley/news/researchernews/rn_Colloquium1012.html*, accessed April 29, 2014; Challenger Disaster, History Channel, *www .history.com/topics/challenger-disaster*, accessed April 29, 2014; "Failure as a Design Criteria: Human Systems Interaction > Flawed Decision Making: Challenger Space Shuttle," *www.tech.plym.ac.uk /sme/interactive_resources/tutorials/failurecases/hs1.html*, accessed April 29, 2014.

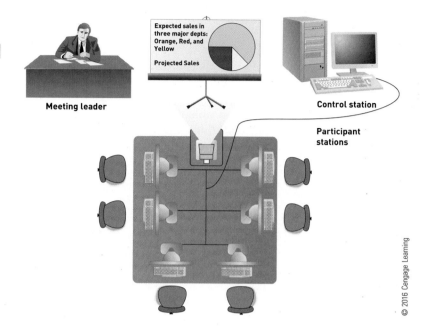

© 2016 Cengage Learning

FIGURE **10.29**

GSS decision room

For group members who are in the same location, the decision room is an optimal GSS alternative. This approach can use both face-to-face and computer-mediated communication. By using networked computers and computer devices, such as project screens and printers, the meeting leader can pose questions to the group, instantly collect members' feedback, and with the help of the governing software loaded on the control station, process this feedback into meaningful information to aid in the decision-making process.

virtual workgroups: Teams of people located around the world working on common problems.

uses video conferencing and collaboration tools to bring its developers together to solve the problems of video game design. The use of this technology has dramatically speeded up the time it takes to create new games.

• The *wide area decision network* is used when the decision frequency is high and the location of group members is distant. In this case, the decision makers require frequent or constant use of the GSS approach. This GSS alternative allows people to work in **virtual workgroups**, where teams of people located around the world can work on common problems.

SUMMARY

Principle:

Good decision-making and problem-solving skills are the key to developing effective information and decision support systems.

Every organization needs effective decision making and problem solving to reach its objectives and goals. Problem solving begins with decision making. A well-known model developed by Herbert Simon divides the decision-making phase of the problem-solving process into three stages: intelligence, design, and choice.

Decision making is a component of problem solving. In addition to the intelligence, design, and choice steps of decision making, problem solving also includes implementation and monitoring. Implementation places the solution into effect. After a decision has been implemented, it is monitored and modified if necessary.

Decisions can be programmed or nonprogrammed. Programmed decisions are made using a rule, procedure, or quantitative method. Ordering more inventory when the level drops below the reorder point is an example of a programmed decision. A nonprogrammed decision deals with unusual or exceptional situations. Determining the best training program for a new employee is an example of a nonprogrammed decision.

Structured decisions are ones where the variables that affect the decision are known and they can be measured. Unstructured decisions are ones where the variables that affect the decision cannot be measured. Semistructured decisions are ones where only some of the variables can be measured.

Decisions can use optimization, satisficing, or heuristic approaches. Optimization finds the best solution. Optimization problems often have an objective such as maximizing profits given production and material constraints. When a problem is too complex for optimization, satisficing is often used. Satisficing finds a good, although not necessarily the best, decision. Finally, a heuristic is a "rule of thumb" or common guideline or procedure used to find a good decision.

Principle:

The management information system (MIS) must provide the right information to the right person in the right format at the right time.

A management information system is an integrated collection of people, procedures, databases, and devices that provides managers and decision makers with information to help achieve organizational goals. An MIS can help an organization achieve its goals by providing managers with insight into the regular operations of the organization so that they can control, organize, and plan more effectively and efficiently. The primary difference between the reports generated by the TPS and ERP systems and those generated by the MIS is that MIS reports support managerial decision making at the higher levels of management.

Data that enters the MIS originates from both internal and external sources. The most significant internal sources of data for the MIS are an organization's various TPSs and ERP systems. Data warehouses and data marts also provide important input data for the MIS. External sources of data for the MIS include extranets, customers, suppliers, competitors, and stockholders.

The output of most MISs is a collection of reports that are distributed to managers. These reports include executive dashboards, scheduled reports, key-indicator reports, demand reports, exception reports, and drill-down reports. Executive dashboards present a set of key performance indicators about the state of a process at a specific point in time to enable managers to make better real-time decisions. Scheduled reports are produced periodically, such as daily, weekly, or monthly. A key-indicator report is a special type of scheduled report. Demand reports are developed to provide certain information at a manager's request. Exception reports are automatically produced when a situation is unusual or requires management action. Drill-down reports provide increasingly detailed data about situations.

More and more MIS reports are being delivered over the Internet and through mobile devices, such as cell phones.

Most MISs are organized along the functional lines of an organization. Typical functional management information systems include financial, manufacturing, marketing, human resources, and other specialized systems. Each system is composed of inputs, processing subsystems, and outputs. The primary sources of input to functional MISs include the corporate strategic plan, data from the ERP system and TPS, information from supply chain and business transactions, and external sources including the Internet and extranets. The primary outputs of these functional MISs are summary reports that assist in managerial decision making.

A geographic information system (GIS) is a computer system capable of assembling, storing, manipulating, and displaying geographically referenced information, that is, data identified according to its location.

Principle:

The focus of a decision support system is on decision-making effectiveness when faced with unstructured or semistructured business problems.

A decision support system (DSS) is an organized collection of people, procedures, software, databases, and devices working to support managerial decision making. DSS characteristics include the ability to handle large amounts of data; obtain and process data from a variety of sources; provide report and presentation flexibility; support drill-down analysis; perform complex statistical analysis; offer textual and graphical orientations; support optimization, satisficing, and heuristic approaches.

DSSs provide support assistance through all phases of the problem-solving process. Different decision frequencies also require DSS support. An ad hoc DSS addresses unique, infrequent decision situations, and an institutional DSS handles routine decisions. Highly structured problems, semistructured problems, and unstructured problems can be supported by a DSS. A DSS can also support different managerial levels, including strategic, tactical, and operational managers. A common database is often the link that ties together a company's TPS, MIS, and DSS.

The components of a DSS are the database, model base, user interface or dialogue manager, and a link to external databases, the Internet, the corporate intranet, extranets, networks, and other systems. The database can use data warehouses and data marts. A data-driven DSS primarily performs qualitative analysis based on the company's databases. Data-driven DSSs tap into vast stores of information contained in the corporate database, retrieving information on inventory, sales, personnel, production, finance, accounting, and other areas. Data mining is often used in a data-driven DSS. The model base contains the models used by the decision maker, such as financial, statistical, graphical, and project-management models. A model-driven DSS primarily performs mathematical or quantitative analysis. Model management software (MMS) is often used to coordinate the use of models in a DSS. The user interface provides a dialogue management facility to assist in communications between the system and the user. Access to other computer-based systems permits the DSS to tie into other powerful systems, including the TPS or function-specific subsystems.

Principle:

A group decision support system (GSS) uses the overall approach of a DSS to improve the decision-making process of a group.

A group decision support system (GSS), also called a group support system and computerized collaborative work system, consists of most of the elements in a DSS, plus software to provide effective support in group decision-making settings. GSSs are typically easy to learn and use and can offer specific or general decision-making support. GSS software, also called groupware, is specially designed to help generate lists of decision alternatives and perform data analysis. These packages let people work on joint documents and files over a network. Text messages and the Internet are also commonly used in a GSS.

The frequency of GSS use and the location of the decision makers will influence the GSS alternative chosen. The decision room alternative supports users in a single location who meet infrequently. Local area decision networks can be used when group members are located in the same geographic area and users meet regularly. Teleconferencing is used when decision frequency is low and the location of group members is distant. A wide area network is used when the decision frequency is high and the location of group members is distant.

KEY TERMS

accounting MIS

ad hoc DSS

auditing

brainstorming

choice stage

computer-integrated manufacturing (CIM)

cost center

decision room

decision-making phase

delphi approach

demand report

design stage

dialogue manager

drill-down report

economic order quantity (EOQ)

exception report

executive dashboard

external auditing

financial audit

financial MIS

flexible manufacturing system (FMS)

geographic information system (GIS)

group consensus approach

group decision support system (GSS)

heuristics

human resource MIS

implementation stage

institutional DSS

intelligence stage

internal auditing

just-in-time (JIT) inventory

key-indicator report

marketing

marketing MIS

model base

model management software (MMS)

monitoring stage

multivoting

nominal group technique (NGT)

nonprogrammed decision

operational audit

optimization model

problem solving

profit center

programmed decision

quality control

reorder point (ROP)

revenue center

satisficing model

scheduled report

semistructured decision

structured decision

unstructured decision

virtual workgroups

CHAPTER 10: SELF-ASSESSMENT TEST

Good decision-making and problem-solving skills are the key to developing effective information and decision support systems.

1. During which stage of the problem-solving process do you identify and define potential problems as well as investigate resource and environmental constraints?
   a. initiation stage
   b. intelligence stage
   c. design stage
   d. choice stage

2. The three stages of decision making are augmented by implementation and monitoring to result in problem solving. True or False?

3. _____ decisions deal with typically one-time decisions that in many cases are difficult to quantify.
   a. Structured
   b. Unstructured
   c. Programmed
   d. Nonprogrammed

4. A decision that inventory should be ordered when inventory levels drop below the reorder point is an example of a(n) _____.
   a. semistructured decision
   b. asynchronous decision
   c. nonprogrammed decision
   d. programmed decision

5. A satisfying model is one that will find a good problem solution, although not necessarily the best problem solution. True or False?

The management information system (MIS) must provide the right information to the right person in the right format at the right time.

6. A(n) _____ presents a set of key performance indicators about the state of a process at a specific point in time to enable managers to make better real-time decisions.
   a. key-indicator report
   b. demand report
   c. exception report
   d. executive dashboard

7. The _____ defines the accounting categories of a business and is a key component of the financial MIS.

8. Financial accounting and managerial accounting are basically the same thing. True or False?

9. _____ is an independent business unit that is treated as a distinct entity enabling its revenue and expenses to be determined and its profitability to be measured.
   a. Profit center
   b. Revenue center
   c. Cost center
   d. Sales center

The focus of a decision support system is on decision-making effectiveness when faced with unstructured or semistructured business problems.

10. Decision support systems are designed solely for use by the top levels of management. True or False?

11. What component of a decision support system allows decision makers to easily access and manipulate the DSS and to use common business terms and phrases?
    a. the knowledge base
    b. the model base
    c. the user interface or dialogue manager
    d. the model management software

A group decision support system (GSS) uses the overall approach of a DSS to improve the decision-making process of a group.

12. The _____ approach is a structured, interactive, iterative decision-making method that relies on input from a panel of experts.

13. The _____ is a structured method for brainstorming that encourages contributions from everyone.

14. There are several multivoting processes that can be used to reduce the number of options to be considered. True or False?

CHAPTER 10: SELF-ASSESSMENT TEST ANSWERS

1. b
2. True
3. d
4. d
5. True
6. d
7. general ledger

8. False
9. a
10. False
11. c
12. Delphi
13. nominal group technique
14. True

REVIEW QUESTIONS

1. What is the difference between decision making and problem solving?
2. What is a satisfying model? What is an optimization model? Describe a situation where each should be used.
3. Identify and briefly describe the three stages of decision making.
4. What is the difference between a structured and an unstructured decision? Give several examples of each.
5. Give several examples of heuristics that you use in decision making.
6. Identify and briefly describe the basic kinds of reports produced by an MIS.

7. Describe the difference between a profit center, revenue center, and cost center.
8. How can a social networking site be used in a DSS?
9. What are the primary activities supported by a marketing MIS?
10. Describe the functions of a human resource MIS.
11. What is a geographic information system? Give an example of such a system.
12. How can location analysis be used in a marketing research MIS?
13. List some software tools used in group support systems.

14. Identify and briefly describe the primary components of a decision support system.
15. State the objective of a group support system (GSS) and identify three characteristics that distinguish it from a DSS.
16. Identify and briefly describe five decision-making approaches frequently used with GSS.
17. What is a decision room and when might one be used?

DISCUSSION QUESTIONS

1. Think of an important problem you had to solve during the last few months. Describe how you used the problem-solving steps discussed in this chapter to resolve the problem. Did you elect to get others involved in helping solve this problem? What sources of data did you employ to help reach a decision?
2. Identify a problem that would benefit from using data from a social networking site as input to a decision support system. What difficulties might be encountered in capturing and trying to use this data?
3. Describe the key features of a human resource MIS for a management consulting firm. What are the primary inputs and outputs? What are the subsystems?
4. Why is auditing so important in a financial MIS? Give an example of an audit that failed to disclose the true nature of the financial position of a firm. What was the result?
5. Describe two industries where a marketing MIS is critical to sales and success.

6. Pick a company and research its human resource management information system. Describe how the system works. What improvements could be made to the company's human resource MIS?
7. Under what conditions and for what types of problems would you recommend the use of a group decision support system over the use of a single user decision support system?
8. What functions do DSSs support in business organizations? How does a DSS differ from a TPS and an MIS?
9. How is decision making in a group environment different from individual decision making, and why are information systems that assist in the group environment different? What are the advantages and disadvantages of making decisions as a group?
10. You have been hired to develop group support software for your university. Describe the features you would include in your new GSS software.

PROBLEM-SOLVING EXERCISES

1. Use the Internet to identify two GSS software solutions that can be used to facilitate group decision making. Use a spreadsheet program to show a side-by-side comparison of the key features and capabilities as well as the hardware required of each software solution. Develop a set of slides using a graphics program to deliver a presentation comparing the two solutions.
2. Review the summarized consolidated statement of income for the manufacturing company whose data is shown in Table 10.5. Use graphics software to prepare a set of bar charts that shows the data for this year compared with the data for last year.

   a. This year, operating revenues increased by 1.5 percent, while operating expenses increased 1.0 percent.
   b. Other income and expenses decreased to $12,000.
   c. Interest and other charges increased to $285,000.

TABLE 10.5 Operating results for a manufacturing firm

Operating results (in millions)	Amount
Operating Revenues	$2,924,100
Operating Expenses (including taxes)	$2,483,600
Operating Income	$440,500
Other Income and Expenses	$13,400
Income before Interest and Other Charges	$453,900
Interest and Other Charges	$262,800
Net Income	$191,100
Average Common Shares Outstanding	145,000
Earnings per Share	$1.32

© 2016 Cengage Learning

If you were a financial analyst tracking this company, what additional data might you need to perform a more complete financial analysis? Write a brief memo summarizing your data needs.

3. As the head buyer for a major supermarket chain, you are constantly being asked by manufacturers and distributors to stock their new products. Over 50 new items are introduced each week. Many times, these products are launched with national advertising campaigns and special promotional allowances to retailers. To add new products, the amount of linear shelf space allocated to existing products must be reduced or items must be eliminated altogether. Develop a simple spreadsheet DSS program that you can use to estimate the change in profits from adding or deleting an item from inventory. Your analysis should include input such as estimated weekly sales in units, the amount of linear shelf space allocated to stock an item (measured in inches), total cost per unit, and sales price per unit. Your analysis should calculate total annual profit by item and then sort the rows in descending order based on total annual profit.

TEAM ACTIVITIES

1. Use the Internet to identify three GSS software solutions that can be used to facilitate group decision making. As a group, come to a decision on which of the three software solutions is the best for use by small teams like yours. Document your decision and the process you followed to reach a decision.

2. Have your team make a group decision to identify ways to improve their grade in this course. Secretly appoint one or two members of the team to disrupt the meeting with negative group behavior. After the meeting, have your team describe how to prevent this negative group behavior. What GSS software features would you suggest to prevent the negative group behavior your team observed?

3. Have your team design a human resource MIS for a medium-sized retail store. Describe the features and characteristics of your human resource MIS. How could you achieve a competitive advantage over a similar retail store with your superior human resource MIS?

WEB EXERCISES

1. Do research on the Web to find an example of an external audit that uncovered serious problems at an organization. Briefly summarize the findings of the audits. What recommendations were made to correct those problems?

2. Use the Internet to explore applications for smartphones and tablet computers that can be used in decision making. You might be asked to develop a report or send an email message to your instructor about what you found.

3. Software, such as Microsoft Excel, is often used to find an optimal solution to maximize profits or minimize costs. Search the Internet using Yahoo!, Google, or another search engine to find other software packages that offer optimization features. Write a report describing one or two of the optimization software packages. What are some of the features of the packages?

CAREER EXERCISES

1. What decisions are critical for success in a career that interests you? What specific types of reports could help you make better decisions on the job? Give three specific examples.

2. Describe the features of a decision support system that you would want, assuming you are a brand assistant in a consumer products company in charge of the marketing for one of your company's brands.

CASE STUDIES

Case One

DSS Dashboards Spur Business Growth at Irish Life

Irish Life, founded in 1939, is Ireland's largest life insurer and provider of employee benefit solutions for both the private and public sector. In addition, the company also handles pensions for 595,000 Irish workers and is Ireland's largest investment manager.

However, Irish Life had a problem. It collected vast amounts of data. It had lots of software to help analyze all this data, but that software wasn't doing the job. Paul Egan, IT manager at Irish Life, explains that "a lot of the tools were only IT tools and only IT people could use them, but [with those tools] we could never keep up with the appetite the business had for this." Irish Life needed software that its business managers could use in their decision making without having to become technical specialists.

After looking at the available DSS packages from its incumbent supplier and other software vendors, Irish Life sought advice from consultants at the Gartner Group. The life insurance provider then chose software from Tableau Software of Seattle, Washington, and engaged Tableau partner MXI Computing to help implement that software.

Using the Tableau software, Irish Life could represent data graphically across the organization, mapping patterns and trends more clearly than it could before the company began to use it. It originally made Tableau dashboards available to about 300 users. These users were able to build their own dashboards, to publish on the Web, or distribute on mobile devices running Android or iOS software. The net result, Irish Life believes, was improved decision making because of better availability of data and better insight into the data. The Intelligence and Design stages of decision making are especially well positioned to benefit from this insight.

For example, Irish Life releases the Personal Lifestyle Strategy program for customized retirement planning within the framework of a corporate pension plan. Making the decisions that were involved in developing this program required detailed analysis of workforce data—exactly what data visualization is suited for.

"Managers can come up with their own dashboards based on the numbers they know they need. There's less work for IT in the front end: IT now only have to worry about the data warehouse, which is where we can add value. We don't have to worry about the visuals as much," added Egan. Insights from the DSS tool have already led to Irish Life moving its management team's focus in certain cases to product lines or customer accounts that needed closer attention.

The results are that Irish Life has been able to offer improved products and services. Customers can speak with better informed financial experts or they can go online and access their own pension information and estimate what financial resources they will have in the future depending on their own pension choices. As a result, Irish Life has almost tripled its customer base since it first adopted the system.

Discussion Questions

1. Irish Life had business software that was only accessible to the members of the IT department. Why was this a problem?

2. What steps can companies take to make sure that the users of a DSS system are able to use it effectively?

Critical Thinking Questions

1. What data do financial experts at a company like Irish Life have to analyze and present to clients? What analyses must the DSS system provide the experts so they can help customers?

2. Irish Life is now offering online tools that enable customers to access pension information themselves. What are the advantages of providing these online tools to the customers? What advantages do financial experts with access to the more sophisticated DSS tools offer above and beyond these online tools?

SOURCES: Irish Life Web site, *www.irishlife.ie*, accessed April 29, 2014; Savvas, A., "Irish Life Deploys New BI System," *Computerworld UK*, *www.computerworlduk.com/news/applications/3321944/irish-life-deploys-new-bi-system*, November 30, 2011; Smith, G., "Irish Life Chooses Tableau to Deliver Business Intelligence Dashboards," *Silicon Republic*, *www.siliconrepublic.com/strategy/item/25782-irish-life-chooses-tableau*, February 14, 2012; Tableau Software Web site, *www.tableausoftware.com*, accessed June 4, 2014.

Case Two

Mando: Streaming Inventory Management for Growth

Mando Corporation is South Korea's largest manufacturer of automobile steering, brake, and suspension components. Originally a division of automobile manufacturer Hyundai, it is now separate, though both are in the same *chaebol* (conglomerate). Mando supplies many other automobile firms as well, including Chinese auto makers and GM. Its 2014 annual revenue was about U.S. $7 billion. With plants in China, India, Malaysia, Turkey, Poland, and Brazil as well as South Korea and with a wide range of mechanical and electronic products, inventory management is critical to its success.

With inventory management (and more) in mind, Mando chose Oracle's E-Business Suite as an integrated ERP system to connect all its divisions. Using a single enterprise-wide database reduced errors. For example, it enabled Mando to standardize on a common numbering system, eliminating inventory-tracking errors because of part number differences when applying design changes.

As you read in this chapter, inventory management decisions use a variety of reports. Therefore, if you saw "Mando Achieves 99.9% Accuracy in Inventory Tracking," you'd probably assume that management information systems and their reports were part of the reason. You'd be right. The E-Business Suite software can produce a wide variety of reports of all types.

Tracking inventory, or knowing what you have, is only part of the answer. You have to have the *right* inventory, which is often specified in reports. Inventory management decisions depend on reports as well.

Some inventory management decisions can be programmed. When stock drops to the reorder point, an order is placed for the reorder quantity. In this instance, management uses reports to make sure the programmed procedures are operating properly and meet the organization's needs.

Other inventory management decisions are less structured. New products have no usage history on which to base reorder points or quantities. Inventory of products being replaced must be managed to ensure proper phase-out. Management doesn't want to be left with a stock of parts that have no current use or run out of a key component before production ends. The transition from mechanical to electronic controls involves more than just replacing one part with a slightly different one. In making these inventory decisions, reports must be used along with sales forecasts and careful analysis to ensure that the right amounts of the right items are on hand.

In addition to reports, Mando used the capabilities of Oracle Business Intelligence software to create a real-time decision-making environment. Inventory information and other data are presented to senior managers through a dashboard on a daily and monthly basis. The dashboards deliver key information in an easy-to-view format and help managers determine business trends.

Park ByoungOk, Mando's CIO, is pleased with these software capabilities. He says, "The [ERP] system enabled us to standardize more than 200 processes globally, which gave senior managers an integrated, enterprise-wide view of sales, financials, inventory, and quality management." Giving managers an overview of the company is, in the final analysis, the purpose of any management information system.

Discussion Questions

1. As a manager, you must choose between two inventory management software packages. One is a stand-alone package that only manages inventory. It allows users to define their own reports without much training. The other requires a professional programmer for new reports, but it is part of an ERP system that can handle much more than inventory management. Describe how you would choose between the two packages.

2. As a manager of a Mando factory, you might be faced with making inventory decisions about new products. Describe what steps you would take to transition smoothly from mechanical to electronic control of the inventory system? Once in place, what follow-up steps would you have to take to monitor the electronic inventory system?

Critical Thinking Questions

1. Managers at Mando receive daily and monthly reports. Describe the types of reports managers need to review daily and the types they need to review monthly?

2. Explain why it would be more difficult for Mando to manage its inventory if the databases for all its factories were different and used different numbers for the same part. Give a specific example of a problem that could arise.

SOURCES: "Mando: New Orders Are Winning Over Investors," KDB Daewoo Securities, downloaded from *www.kdbdw.com/bbs/download /82746.pdf?attachmentId=82746*, December 20, 2011; Mando Corporation English Web site, *www.mando.com/200909_mando/eng /main.asp*, accessed April 15, 2012; "Mando Corporation Achieves 99.9% Accuracy in Inventory Tracking," Oracle Corporation, *Information for Success*, p. 50, downloaded from *innovative.com.br/wp-content /uploads/2011/06/ebsr12referencebooklet-354227.pdf*, March 2011; Mando Corp (060980.KS) Financials, Reuters Web site, *www.reuters .com/finance/stocks/financialHighlights?symbol=060980.KS*; accessed April 29, 2014.

Questions for Web Case

See the Web site for this book to read about the Altitude Online case for this chapter. Following are questions concerning this Web case.

Altitude Online: Information and Decision Support Systems Considerations

Discussion Questions

1. What functional areas of Altitude Online are supported by MISs?

2. How do MISs and DSSs provide a value add to Altitude Online's products?

Critical Thinking Questions

1. How do you think MISs and DSSs assist Altitude Online's top executives in guiding the direction of the company?

2. How can the quality of information systems affect Altitude Online's ability to compete in the online marketing industry?

NOTES

Sources for the opening vignette: Directorate of Economics and Statistics, Government of Uttarakhand, "Uttarakhand at a Glance (2012–2013)" and "Uttarakhand at a Glance (2010–2011)," *http://uk.gov.in/files/pdf/Uttarakhand_at_a_glance _in_english_2012-13.pdf*, accessed April 30, 2014; Uttarakhand Power Corporation Ltd. Web site, *www.upcl.org*, accessed April 30, 2014; "Uttarakhand Power Corporation Ltd. powers up a smarter network (USEN)," IBM Systems and Technology Smarter Computing Web site, *www-01.ibm.com /common/ssi/cgi-bin/ssialias?subtype=AB&infotype=PM& appname=STGE_OI_OI_USEN&htmlfid=OIC03038USEN& attachment=OIC03038USEN.PDF*, accessed April 30, 2014.

1. "O.R. Transforms Baosteel's Operations," *www.informs .org/Sites/Getting-Started-With-Analytics/Analytics -Success-Stories/Case-Studies/Baosteel*, accessed March 23, 2014.

2. Simon, Herbert, *Administrative Behavior: A Study of Decision-Making Processes in Administrative Organizations*, 4th ed., New York: The Free Press, 1997.

3. Huber, G.P., *Managerial Decision Making*, Glenview, Illinois:Scott, Foresman and Co, 1980.

4. Macrabrey, Jean-Marie, "The Dutch Strive to Make Their Country 'Climate Proof'," *New York Times*, June 1, 2009, *www.nytimes.com/cwire/2009/06/01/01climatewire -the-dutch-strive-to-make-their-country-clima-44710 .html?pagewanted=all*.

5. "Dutch Delta Commissioners Use Economically Efficient Standards to Protect the Netherlands against Flooding,"

www.informs.org/Sites/Getting-Started-With-Analytics /Analytics-Success-Stories/Case-Studies/Dutch-Delta -Commissioners, accessed March 24, 2014.

6. Ibid.

7. "Success Stories: Kraft," Logility Web site, *www.logility .com/library/success-stories/kraft,* accessed March 25, 2014.

8. Gorry, A. and Morton, Scott M., "A Framework for Management Information Systems," *Sloan Management Review*, pages 55–70, Fall 1971.

9. "Südzucker," IBM Success Story, July, 2012, *https://www.ibm.com/developerworks/community /blogs/sca/resource/Sudzuckerfinal7-30.pdf?lang=en.*

10. Wohlsen, Marcus, "The Astronomical Math behind UPS' New Tool to Deliver Packages Faster", *Wired*, June 13, 2013, *www.wired.com/2013/06/ups-astronomical -math/.*

11. Ibid

12. ESET Technology Web page, *www.eset.com/int/about /technology/,* accessed March 26, 2014.

13. "IntelliView Success Story: Aarogyasri Health Care Trust," *www.synaptris.com/pdf/Synaptris_IntelliVIEW _Success-Story_Aarogyasri.pdf*, accessed March 29, 2014.

14. "2013 North Carolina Community College Creating Success," *www.nccommunitycolleges.edu/Publications /docs/Publications/2013%20Performance%20Measures %20Report.pdf*, accessed March 29, 2014.

15. "VARONIS Case Study: ING Direct," *http://info.varonis .com/hs-fs/hub/142972/file-566784889-pdf/docs/case _studies/en/Case_Study_-_ING_DIRECT.pdf*, accessed March 29, 2014.

16. BMW Financial Services, February 21, 2014, *www-01.ibm.com/software/success/cssdb.nsf/CS/STRD -9GHF45?OpenDocument&Site=corp&cty=en_us.*

17. Anderson, Matt, "DFS Audit Uncovers Serious Information Technology Problems at State Pension Fund That Put Retirees and Taxpayers at Risk," Department of Financial Services Press Release, August 20, 2013, *www.dfs.ny.gov/about/press2013/pr1308201 .htm.*

18. "Automotive Manufacturer Increases Productivity for Cylinder-Head Production by 25 Percent," February 21, 2014, *http://www-01.ibm.com/common/ssi/cgi-bin /ssialias?infotype=PM&subtype=AB&htmlfid=YTC 03659WWEN.*

19. "Computing & Design/Build Processes Help Develop the 777," *www.boeing.com/boeing/commercial /777family/compute/compute2.page*, accessed April 3, 2014.

20. Fisher Scientific Corporate Profile, *www.fishersci.ca /aboutus.aspx?id=61*, accessed April 3, 2014.

21. "Client Success Stories: Automotive Market Research and Marketing," *http://hedgescompany.com /market-research-and-client-work*, accessed April 6, 2014.

22. "Nestlé's Merchandising Location Strategy Wins with Retailers," *www.decisioninsight.com/content/pdf/Nestle -Dreyers.pdf*, accessed April 6, 2014.

23. "About Shopkick," *www.shopkick.com/about*, accessed April 6, 2014.

24. Goodman, Cindy Krischer, "Tweet Success: Small Businesses Turn to Social Media Marketing to Build Brands," *Miami Herald*, January 26, 2014, *www .miamiherald.com/2014/01/26/3891535/tweet-success -small-businesses.html.*

25. Ibid.

26. "Groupon Launches Elite Deal Series," Groupon Press Release, April 1, 2014, *http://investor.groupon.com /releasedetail.cfm?ReleaseID=836857.*

27. "Swedbank Empowers 5,000+ Users with Customers Analysis Tool Using Qlikview," *www.qlik.com/us /explore/solutions/industries/financial-services /banking*, accessed April 9, 2014.

28. "Growth Process Toolkit: Distribution Channel Optimization," Frost & Sullivan, *www.frost.com/prod /servlet/cpo/189738462*, accessed April 8, 2014.

29. "More Than Just Collecting Blood," *www.delvinia.com /expertise/success-stories/canadian-blood-services -operation-lifeblood/*, accessed April 9, 2014.

30. "Improving the Protection of Appliances for Global Distribution with Packaging Optimization," Altair Product Design Success Story, *http://resources.altair .com/pdd/images/en-US/CaseStudy/Mabe-Improving-the -Protection-of-Appliances-with-Packaging -Optimization.pdf*, accessed May 13, 2014.

31. Lofholm, Nancy, "Colorado Landscapers Face a Shortage of Workers," *The Denver Post*, February 24, 2014, *www.denverpost.com/news/ci_25219697 /colorado-landscapers-face-shortage-workers.*

32. Brancatelli, Joe, "How Miserly Airlines Created Their Own Pilot Shortage," *The Business Journals*, February 20, 2014, *www.bizjournals.com/bizjournals/blog /seat2B/2014/02/commuter-airlines-face-pilot-shortage .html?page=all.*

33. Peixe, Joao, "Oil and Gas Projects Face Labor Shortage," *OilPrice.com*, February 17, 2014, *http://oilprice.com /Latest-Energy-News/World-News/Oil-and-Gas-Projects -Face-Labor-Shortage.html.*

34. "Tualatin Valley Water District, OR," *www.ema-inc.com /success-stories/people-workforce/tualatin-valley-water -district-workforce-succession-planning*, accessed April 9, 2014.

35. "About TDX," *www.tdxgroup.com/images/Press% 20releases/PP%20win.pdf*, accessed April 19, 2014.

36. "TDX Builds a Flexible Platform for Automated Decision-Making," IBM Success Story, February 12, 2013, *www-01.ibm.com/software/success/cssdb.nsf/CS /STRD-94UMRZ?OpenDocument&Site=corp&cty=en_us.*

37. "Harrah's Entertainment Confirms Cognos BI Solution," *www.tgc.com/dsstar/01/0417/102928.html*, accessed April 19, 2014.

38. "QlikView Customer Success Story: Canopius Improves Performance Analysis across Syndicates with Qlikview," *www.qlik.com*, accessed April 19, 2014.

39. Cerrato, Paul, "Clinical Decision Support Needs to Get Smarter," *InformationWeek*, January 9, 2014, *www .informationweek.com/healthcare/analytics/clinical -decision-support-needs-to-get-smarter/d/d-id/1113365? print=yes.*

40. "Boosting Profits, Loyalty Through Better Marketing," SAS Customer Stories, *www.sas.com/en_us/customers*

/staples-marketing-automation.html, accessed May 13, 2014.

41. Masters, Haydn, "How Predictive Analytics is Helping New South Wales Rugby Sideline Injuries," *A Smarter Planet* (blog), February 3, 2014, *http://asmarterplanet .com/blog/2014/02/smarter-analytics.html.*

42. Dwoskin, Elizabeth, "How New York's Fire Department Uses Data Mining," *New York Times*, January 24, 2014, *http://blogs.wsj.com/digits/2014/01/24/how-new -yorks-fire-department-uses-data-mining/.*

43. Gerber, Matthew S., "Predicting Crime Using Twitter and Kernel Density Estimation," Decision Support Systems, Volume 61, May 2014, Pages 115–125, *www .sciencedirect.com/science/article/pii/S016792361 4000268.*

44. Klie, Leonard, "IBM's Watson Boosts Customer Engagement," Sci Tech Today, April 2, 2014, *www.sci -tech-today.com/story.xhtml?story_id=0100011 K1Q6K.*

45. Babcock, Liza, "Ideas To Go Featured on 'World's Greatest!...' TV Series," *IdeasToGo* (blog), March 25, 2014, *www.ideastogo.com/itg-on-worlds-greatest.*

11 Knowledge Management and Specialized Information Systems

Principles	Learning Objectives
• Knowledge management allows organizations to share knowledge and experience among its workers.	• Discuss the differences between data, information, and knowledge. • Describe the role of the chief knowledge officer (CKO). • List some of the tools and techniques used in knowledge management.
• Artificial intelligence systems form a broad and diverse set of systems that can replicate human decision making for certain types of well-defined problems.	• Define the term *artificial intelligence* and state the objective of developing artificial intelligence systems. • List the characteristics of intelligent behavior and compare the performance of natural and artificial intelligence systems for each of these characteristics. • Identify the major components of the artificial intelligence field and provide one example of each type of system.
• Expert systems can enable a novice to perform at the level of an expert but must be developed and maintained very carefully.	• List the characteristics and basic components of expert systems. • Outline and briefly explain the steps for developing an expert system. • Identify the benefits associated with the use of expert systems.
• Multimedia and virtual reality systems can reshape the interface between people and information technology by offering new ways to communicate information, visualize processes, and express ideas creatively.	• Discuss the use of multimedia in a business setting. • Define the term *virtual reality* and *augmented reality* and provide three examples of these applications.
• Specialized systems can help organizations and individuals achieve their goals.	• Discuss examples of specialized systems for organizational and individual use.

Revolutionizing Spinal Surgery with Robotics

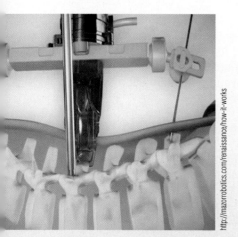

http://mazorrobotics.com/renaissance/how-it-works

In Jerusalem, in Moscow, and even in Jacksonville, Florida, Mazor Robotics Renaissance™ Guidance System is revolutionizing the accuracy and improving the outcome of spinal surgery across the globe. Renaissance Robot serves as a sidekick to surgeons, locating with precision the points of incision along the spines of patients suffering from mild spinal instabilities such as scoliosis to other complex spinal deformities.

Here's how it works. A few days prior to the operation, a CT scan of the patient's spine is done to create a 3D model of the spine. Because the spine shifts and is not in the exact same position as it was during the CT scan, technicians feed live X-rays of the spine into the robot's software as the patient lies on the operating table to obtain a real-time 3D image. The robot is mounted on the patient's back and comes to a rest at the point of incision. The surgeon then implants a screw at that location. The screw serves to connect or reposition the vertebrae to stabilize the spine. Once implanted, the robot moves to the next point of incision.

Without the aid of the Renaissance Robot, a spinal surgeon risks cutting into the spinal cord or nerve canals. As a result, some 10 percent of patients wind up with misplaced implanted screws and half of those suffer long-term neurological damage. In the first 4,000 operations conducted using the Renaissance Robot, not a single patient suffered long-term damage to the nervous system.

The guidance system has other advantages. Studies show that the average length of hospital stays is reduced by 27 percent and complication rates are reduced by 48 percent. Patients are exposed to much less than the standard X-ray radiation that is used during surgery to create static models of the spine. Finally, the guidance system can reduce the intrusiveness for many surgical procedures.

As a result, Mazor Robotics has rocketed to success, named by Fast Company as the fourth most innovative robotic company in the world. The Mazor Robotics has offices in United States and Germany and sends employees around the world to train surgeons in the use of the Renaissance Robot. As a start-up, the company had originally planned to develop robotic solutions for hip, knee, and other surgeries, but expense forced them to narrow their focus. Now, thanks to the large infusion of capital made possible by their recent listing on the NASDAQ, the company is expanding development. It is now working on a robotic guidance system for brain surgery.

As you read this chapter, consider the following:

- How can specialized IT systems and devices provide expertise superior to that which can be obtained through human effort?
- What are the many uses for IT systems designed to collect knowledge and provide expertise?

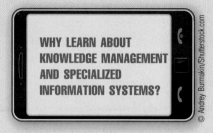

WHY LEARN ABOUT KNOWLEDGE MANAGEMENT AND SPECIALIZED INFORMATION SYSTEMS?

Knowledge management and specialized information systems are used in almost every industry. As a manager, you might use a knowledge management system to obtain advice on how to approach a problem that others in your organization have already encountered. As line manager of an automotive company, you might oversee robots that attach windshields to cars or paint body panels. As a young stock trader, you might use a special system called a *neural network* to uncover patterns and make millions of dollars trading stocks and stock options. As a marketing manager for a PC manufacturer, you might use virtual reality on a Web site to show customers your latest laptop and tablet computers. As a member of the military, you might use computer simulation as a training tool to prepare you for combat. As an employee of a petroleum company, you might use an expert system to determine where to drill for oil and gas. You will see many additional examples of using these specialized information systems throughout this chapter. Learning about these systems will help you discover new ways to use information systems in your day-to-day work.

Like other aspects of an information system, the overall goal of knowledge management and the specialized systems discussed in this chapter is to help people and organizations achieve their goals. In this chapter, we explore knowledge management, artificial intelligence, and many other specialized information systems, including expert systems, robotics, vision systems, natural language processing, learning systems, neural networks, genetic algorithms, intelligent agents, multimedia, virtual reality, and augmented reality.

KNOWLEDGE MANAGEMENT SYSTEMS

Chapter 1 defines and discusses data, information, and knowledge. Recall that *data* consists of raw facts, such as an employee number, number of hours worked in a week, inventory part numbers, or sales orders. A list of the quantity available for all items in inventory is an example of data. When these facts are organized or arranged in a meaningful manner, they become information. You may recall from Chapter 1 that *information* is a collection of facts organized so that it has additional value beyond the value of the facts themselves. An exception report of inventory items that might be out of stock in a week because of high demand is an example of information. *Knowledge* is the awareness and understanding of a set of information and the ways that information can be made useful to support a specific task or reach a decision. Knowing the procedures for ordering more inventory to avoid running out is an example of knowledge. In a sense, information tells you what the current situation is (some items have low inventory levels), while knowledge tells you what action is needed to address the situation (make phone calls to the right people to get the needed inventory shipped overnight). See Figure 11.1.

FIGURE **11.1**

Differences between data, information, and knowledge

Data consists of raw facts, information explains the current situation, and knowledge identifies the action needed to address the situation.

Data	There are 20 PCs in stock at the retail store.
Information	The store will run out of inventory in a week unless more is ordered today.
Knowledge	Call 800-555-2222 to order more inventory.

A *knowledge management system (KMS)* is an organized collection of people, procedures, software, databases, and devices used to create, store, share, and use the organization's knowledge and experience. KMSs cover a wide range of systems, from software that contains some KMS components to dedicated systems designed specifically to capture, store, and use knowledge.

Overview of Knowledge Management Systems

An effective KMS enables an organization to make better use of its gathered knowledge. This avoids wasted time to find valuable information and prevents reinventing the wheel, or duplicating work or a process that has already been performed successfully. The use of a KMS can reduce wasted resources, improve customer satisfaction, raise an organization's competitiveness in the marketplace, and increase the success of its planning processes. AstraZeneca, the biopharmaceutical company, implemented a KMS to index some 200 million documents so that scientists in its global R&D organization can find relevant information concerning drugs, diseases, and genes.[1]

For many organizations, KM can mean providing better customer service or providing special services to people and groups. See Figure 11.2. Legato Support Systems (recently acquired by EMC) engages in the development, marketing, and support of storage software products and services worldwide. The firm implemented a KMS to enable customers to obtain self-service and reduce by 25 percent the number of calls that had to be handled by the support staff.

FIGURE 11.2

Knowledge management software

Advent Software uses a knowledge management system to help its employees find critical investment information.

Knowledge can be of two types—explicit and tacit knowledge. *Explicit knowledge* is objective and can be measured and documented in reports, papers, and rules. For example, knowing the best road to take to minimize driving time from home to the office when a major highway is closed is explicit knowledge. It can be documented in a report or a rule, as in "If I-70 is closed, take Highway 6 to the office." *Tacit knowledge*, on the other hand, is hard to measure and document and typically is not objective or formalized. Knowing the best way to negotiate with a foreign government about nuclear disarmament or a volatile hostage situation often requires a lifetime of experience and a high level of skill. These are examples of tacit knowledge. It is difficult to write a detailed report or a set of rules that would always work in every hostage situation. Many organizations actively attempt to convert tacit knowledge to explicit knowledge to make the knowledge easier to measure, document, and share with others.

Data and Knowledge Management Workers and Communities of Practice

The personnel involved in a KMS include *knowledge workers* (a term first coined by management guru Peter Drucker),[2] people who earn their living by creating, using, and disseminating knowledge. This covers a wide range of today's workers. See Figure 11.3. "There are 615 million knowledge workers in the world but 2.1 billion workers who are not 'knowledge workers,'" according to Jim Patterson, the co-founder and CEO of Cotap, a messaging software start-up firm.

FIGURE 11.3

Knowledge workers

Knowledge workers are people who create, use, and disseminate knowledge and include professionals in science, engineering, business, and other areas.

chief knowledge officer (CKO):
The individual who presents the organization's knowledge management vision with clarity and effectiveness, strives mightily to achieve that vision, provides executive level leadership to implement and sustain KM, and is the ultimate focal point for knowledge creation, sharing, and application.

The **chief knowledge officer (CKO)** is the individual who represents the organization's knowledge management vision with clarity and effectiveness, strives mightily to achieve that vision, provides executive level leadership to implement and sustain KM, and is the ultimate focal point for knowledge creation, sharing, and application. The CKO is responsible for the organization's KMS and typically works with other executives and vice presidents, including the chief executive officer (CEO) and chief financial officer (CFO), among others.

Each NASA center has been directed to appoint a chief knowledge officer and implement a KM program. Dr. Edward Hoffman (NASA-overall CKO) and Dr. Edward Rogers (NASA-Goddard CKO) were two of the first appointed CKOs. Dr. Rogers is a recognized NASA expert on the use of institutional learning case studies and has helped develop over 50 case studies to make mission knowledge attractive and engaging.[3]

community of practice (COP):
A group of people with common interests who come together to create, store, and share knowledge of a specific topic.

Some organizations and professions use **communities of practice (COP)**, which are groups of people with common interests who come together to create, store, and share knowledge on a specific topic. A group of oceanographers investigating climate change or a team of medical researchers looking for new ways to treat lung cancer are examples of COPs. COPs often connect people who might not otherwise have an opportunity to interact, either frequently or perhaps not at all. Thus an effective COP can lead to a quantum leap in collaboration among people with common interests. COPs help individuals enhance their area of expertise by providing a forum to share information, stories, personal experiences, and solutions to common problems.

Companies in the oil and gas industry have been among the leaders in establishing COPs. Members of a COP come together to share and learn from one another on a specific topic. Two early communities of practice were exploration and production. Eventually additional communities of practice formed on such topics as health and safety, energy efficiency, and process engineering. Chevron Texaco has over 100 active communities of practice.[4]

Obtaining, Storing, Sharing, and Using Knowledge

Obtaining, storing, sharing, and using knowledge is the key to any KMS. The Directorate-General for Competition is responsible for establishing and implementing a clear competition policy for the European Union. In this role, the Directorate-General must review all proposed mergers and acquisitions for potential antitrust violations. It also verifies suspected abuse of a dominant market position or illicit cartels. The Directorate-General must reach decisions quickly to minimize any adverse effects on consumers and affected competitors. Each case may involve the review of thousands of documents and contemplation of intricate legal issues. The Directorate-General implemented a KMS to help it discover all relevant information and to keep track of key information related to each case.[5]

Using a KMS often leads to additional knowledge creation, storage, sharing, and usage. Drug companies and medical researchers invest billions of dollars in creating knowledge on cures for diseases. Knowledge management systems can also diminish the reliance on paper reports and thus reduce costs and help protect the environment. Although knowledge workers can act alone, they often work in teams to create or obtain knowledge. See Figure 11.4.

FIGURE 11.4

Knowledge management system

Obtaining, storing, sharing, and using knowledge is the key to any KMS.

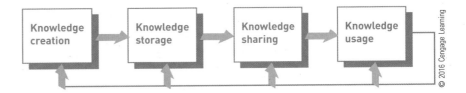

After knowledge is created, it is often stored in a *knowledge repository* that includes documents, reports, files, and databases. The knowledge repository can be located both inside the organization and outside. Bio-Botanica manufactures cosmetic, personal care, and pharmaceutical products that require much regulatory data, R&D documentation, and specification data. The firm must be able to prove that it is managing all this data and associated workflow processes according to standards defined by the Federal Drug Administration and others. Bio-Botanica collects this data from numerous sources within the company and stores it in a knowledge repository managed by its KMS.[6]

Some types of software can store and share knowledge contained in documents and reports. Adobe portable document format (PDF) files, for example, allow you to store corporate reports, tax returns, and other documents and send them to others over the Internet. The publisher and the authors of this book used PDF files to store, share, and edit each chapter. Traditional databases, data warehouses, and data marts often store the organization's knowledge. Specialized knowledge bases in expert systems, discussed later in this chapter, can also be used.

Because knowledge workers often work in groups or teams, they can use collaborative work software and group support systems to share knowledge, such as groupware, meeting software, and collaboration tools. Intranets and password-protected Internet sites also provide ways to share knowledge. Many businesses, however, use patents, copyrights, trade secrets, Internet firewalls, and other measures to keep prying eyes from seeing important knowledge that is expensive and hard to create.

Using a knowledge management system begins with locating the organization's knowledge. This procedure is often done using a *knowledge map* or directory that points the knowledge worker to the needed knowledge. Medical researchers, university professors, and even textbook authors use Lexis-Nexis to locate important knowledge. Corporations often use the Internet or corporate Web portals to help their knowledge workers find knowledge stored in documents and reports.

Technology to Support Knowledge Management

KMSs use a number of tools discussed throughout the book. In Chapter 2, for example, we explored the importance of *organizational learning* and *organizational change*. An effective KMS is based on learning new knowledge and changing procedures and approaches as a result. A manufacturing company, for example, might learn new ways to program robots on the factory floor to improve accuracy and reduce defective parts. The new knowledge will likely cause the manufacturing company to change how it programs and uses its robots. In Chapter 5, we investigated the use of *data mining* and *business intelligence*. These powerful tools can be important in capturing and using knowledge. Enterprise resource planning tools, such as SAP, include knowledge management features. In Chapter 10, we showed how *groupware* can improve group decision-making and collaboration. Groupware can also be used to help capture, store, and use knowledge. Of course, hardware, software, databases, telecommunications, and the Internet, discussed in Part 2, are important technologies used to support most knowledge management systems.

Hundreds of organizations provide specific KM products and services. See Figure 11.5. In addition, researchers at colleges and universities have developed tools and technologies to support knowledge management. American companies spend billions of dollars on knowledge management technology every year. Companies such as IBM have many knowledge management tools

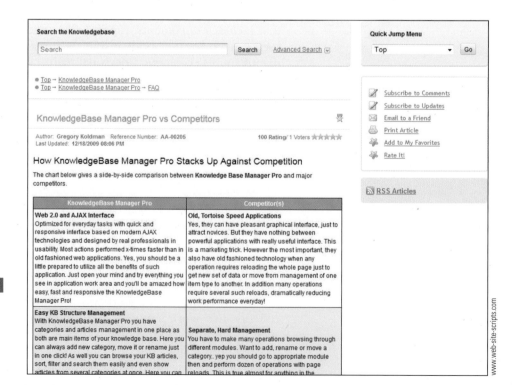

FIGURE 11.5

Knowledge management technology

Knowledgebase Manager Pro is designed for helping organizations create knowledge bases.

in a variety of products, including IBM Lotus Notes (now known as IBM Connections Mail), discussed in Chapter 10. Hughes Christensen is an oil and gas-drilling tool provider whose engineers had acquired a depth and breadth of drilling expertise. The organization built a knowledge-sharing tool it dubbed "Drilling Performance Guidelines" based on IBM Domino/Notes. The tool enables experts within the firm to publish and share their knowledge and experience with others within the firm as well as outside clients. Hughes Christensen has been highly successful in attracting new clients who need advice on difficult drilling projects. One client, oil-drilling specialist BP Norge, was able to save nearly $7 million on a drilling project in Norway.[7]

Microsoft offers a number of knowledge management tools, including Digital Dashboard, which is based on the Microsoft Office suite. Digital Dashboard integrates information from a variety of sources, including personal, group, enterprise, and external information and documents. Other tools from Microsoft include Web Store Technology, which uses wireless technology to deliver knowledge to any location at any time; Access Workflow Designer, which helps database developers create effective systems to process transactions and keep work flowing through the organization; and related products.

Some smaller, lesser-known software firms provide knowledge management software tools that make it easy to build a knowledge base and make it possible for employees and customers to find the right knowledge, answers, and information that they need. Examples of such knowledge management software solutions are summarized in Table 11.1.

TABLE **11.1** Knowledge management software

Software	Vendor	Select Customers
Bloomfire	Bloomfire	Toyota Dannon
Communifire	Axero Solutions	Electronic Music Alliance Together.in
Intelligence Bank	Intelligence Bank	Deloitte SunCorp Bank
Moxie Knowledgebase	Moxie Software	Student Loans Company Infusionsoft
Oxcyon	Oxcyon CentralPoint CMS	Tanner Health VCA Antech
Smart Support	Safe Harbor Knowledge Solutions	SunTrust Bank Audi AG

© 2016 Cengage Learning

OVERVIEW OF ARTIFICIAL INTELLIGENCE

At a Dartmouth College conference in 1956, John McCarthy proposed the use of the term *artificial intelligence (AI)* to describe computers with the ability to mimic or duplicate the functions of the human brain. A paper was presented at the conference proposing a study of AI based on the conjecture that "every aspect of learning or any other feature of intelligence can in principle be so precisely described that a machine can be made to simulate it."[8] Many AI pioneers attended this first conference; a few predicted that computers would be as "smart" as people by the 1960s. The prediction has not yet been realized, but many applications of artificial intelligence can be seen today, and research continues.

Watson, a supercomputer developed by IBM with artificial intelligence capabilities, was able to soundly defeat two prior champions of the popular

INFORMATION SYSTEMS @ WORK

Knowledge Management Improves Customer Support at Canon

Millions of U.S. consumers own Canon digital cameras, copiers, printers, binoculars, fax machines, camcorders, and calculators. Canon Information Technology Services (CITS) in Chesapeake, Virginia, fields support requests at a current rate of 200,000 calls, 50,000 emails, and 1,000 letters per month: a total of about three million contacts per year. CITS employs over 500 people to handle these contacts.

Canon's problem is that, until recently, they had no central knowledge repository. Product information was scattered over a CITS intranet, the Canon USA Web site, hard-copy manuals, and an internally developed knowledge system. CITS could not ensure that all of the content was correct and did not conflict with the manuals or another system. Customers could use only the knowledge system, which was not searchable. Support agents needed to check multiple sources of information on any product. This process was cumbersome, annoyed the agents, and wasted valuable time.

To address this problem, Canon installed Consona's Knowledge-Driven Support (KDS). KDS integrates knowledge management with case management software, a type of Customer Relationship Management software that you studied in Chapter 9.

As an example of integration, KDS supports *in-process authoring*. A representative who has just written a customer a long, complex explanation of how to solve a problem can enter that explanation directly into the knowledge base without having to re-create it or even copy and paste it. Agents don't have to take time after a call to create new knowledge when they could be improving their performance reports by taking another call. As Consona puts it, "knowledge isn't something that you do in addition to solving problems—it becomes the way you solve problems."

The results are that, during the first six months that the system was in full use, the fraction of customer questions resolved online without a phone call increased from 51 to 71 percent. This saved agent time while providing customers with better service. Another measure of the need for follow-up, email escalation rate, dropped 47 percent from the same period of the previous year. Overall customer satisfaction scores were up from 6.5 to 7.1 on a scale of 1 to 10, and customer resolution rates rose from 50 to 60 percent.

"The Consona CRM knowledge base has been a great help to our service agents and to our customers. It lets the customers get the answers to the 'easy' questions themselves, while freeing up the agents to focus on the more difficult problems," says Jay Lucado, CITS assistant director of knowledge management and delivery.

CITS also leveraged the knowledge base to improve agent training. Its new training curriculum focuses on teaching agents to find the answers in the system rather than how to fix any problem a customer might have. In addition, system-based training is remotely available, which works well with CITS's work-at-home program. Agents work from their homes four days each week and are able to complete their training remotely as well.

Discussion Questions

1. Discuss two reasons the cost/benefit ratio of a knowledge management system such as KDS goes up as the company using it gets larger. Which of these reasons apply to other applications besides knowledge management?
2. What other industries could benefit from searchable knowledge management systems that allow easy access to the content within user manuals and other documentation?

Critical Thinking Questions

1. How could making a searchable knowledge management system accessible to Canon's customers online affect CITS's call volume and customer satisfaction?
2. How would the need for a system such as KDS change if each of Canon's product lines (including cameras and printers) was sold by a different company?

SOURCES: Briggs, M., "New Consona Report Uncovers Best Practices for Easier and More Effective Knowledge Management," Consona press release, August 4, 2011, *www.prweb.com/releases/Consona/Knowledge -Management/prweb8697920.htm*; Canon ITS Web site, *www.cits .canon.com*, accessed May 19, 2014; Canon USA Web site, *www.usa .canon.com/cusa/home*, accessed February 11, 2012; Consona, Inc., Knowledge-Driven Support Web site, *crm.consona.com/software /products/knowledge-driven-support.aspx*, accessed June 4, 2014; Johnson, S., "Canon Information Technology Services, Inc./Consona Knowledge Management," *Office Product News*, October 24, 2011, *www.officeproductnews.net/case_studies/canon_information _technology_services_inc_consona_knowledge_management*.

TV game show, *Jeopardy!* See Figure 11.6. The artificial intelligence computer could process human speech, search its vast databases for possible responses, and reply in a human voice. Now a new cloud-based Watson system will be used by oncologists to fight glioblastoma, an aggressive brain cancer that kills over 13,000 people in the United States each year. The system will correlate data from the DNA associated with each patient's disease to the latest findings from medical journals, new studies, and clinical records to develop a highly personalized treatment regimen. The goal is for Watson to increase the number of patients who can benefit from care options uniquely tailored to their disease's DNA. Watson will continually learn and improve as it deals with each new patient scenario and new medical research becomes available.

CAROLINE SEIDEL/EPA/Landov

FIGURE **11.6**

IBM Watson

Watson is an AI system that can answer questions posed in natural language over a nearly unlimited range of knowledge.

artificial intelligence system:
The people, procedures, hardware, software, data, and knowledge needed to develop computer systems and machines that can simulate human intelligence processes, including learning (the acquisition of information and rules for using the information), reasoning (using rules to reach conclusions), and self-correction (using the outcome from one scenario to improve its performance on future scenarios).

Artificial Intelligence in Perspective

Computers were originally designed to perform simple mathematical operations, using fixed programmed rules and eventually operating at millions of computations per second. When it comes to performing mathematical operations quickly and accurately, computers beat humans hands down. However, computers have trouble recognizing patterns, adapting to new situations, and drawing conclusions when not provided complete information—all activities that humans can perform quite well. Artificial intelligence systems tackle these sorts of problems. Artificial intelligence systems include the people, procedures, hardware, software, data, and knowledge needed to develop computer systems and machines that can simulate human intelligence processes, including learning (the acquisition of information and rules for using the information), reasoning (using rules to reach conclusions), and self-correction (using the outcome from one scenario to improve its performance on future scenarios).

AI is a complex and interdisciplinary field that involves several specialties, including biology, computer science, linguistics, mathematics, neuroscience, philosophy, and psychology. The study of AI systems causes one to ponder philosophical issues such as the nature of the human mind and the ethics of creating objects gifted with human-like intelligence. Today artificial intelligence systems are used in many industries and applications. Researchers, scientists, and experts on how human beings think are often involved in developing these systems.

Nature of Intelligence

From the early AI pioneering stage, the research emphasis has been on developing machines with the ability to "learn" from experiences and apply knowledge acquired from those experiences; to handle complex situations; to solve problems when important information is missing; to determine what is important and to react quickly and correctly to a new situation; to understand visual images, process and manipulate symbols, be creative and imaginative; and to use heuristics, which together is considered intelligent behavior.

The *Turing Test* was designed by Alan Turing, a British mathematician. It attempts to determine whether a computer can successfully impersonate a human. Human judges are connected to the computer and to another human via an instant messaging system and the only information flowing between the contestants and judges is text. The judges pose questions on any topic from the arts to zoology, even questions about personal history and social relationships. To pass the test, the computer must communicate via this medium so competently that the judges cannot tell the difference between the computer's responses and the human's responses.[9] No computer has yet passed the Turing Test, although many computer scientists believe that it may happen in the next few years.[10] The Loebner Prize is an annual competition in artificial intelligence that awards prizes to the computer system designed to simulate an intelligent conversation that is considered by the judges to be the most human-like. After many years of failure by various software developers, a computer program created by a team based in Russia succeeded in passing the test in June 2014.[11]

Some of the specific characteristics of intelligent behavior include the ability to do the following:

- **Learn from experience and apply the knowledge acquired from experience**. Learning from past situations and events is a key component of intelligent behavior and is a natural ability of humans, who learn by trial and error. This ability, however, must be carefully programmed into a computer system. Today, researchers are developing systems that can "learn" from experience. The 20 questions (20Q) Web site, *www.20q.net* (see Figure 11.7), is an example of a system that learns.[12] The Web site is an artificial intelligence game that learns as people play.

intelligent behavior: The ability to learn from experiences and apply knowledge acquired from those experiences; to handle complex situations; to solve problems when important information is missing; to determine what is important and to react quickly and correctly to a new situation; to understand visual images, process and manipulate symbols, be creative and imaginative; and to use heuristics.

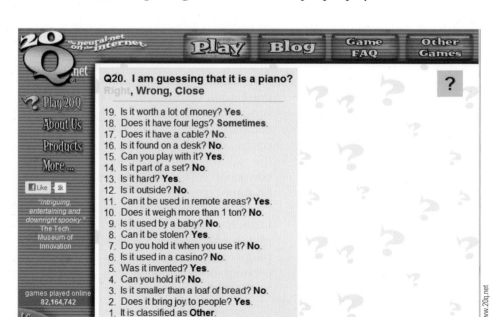

FIGURE **11.7**

20Q

20Q is an online game where users play the popular game, 20 Questions, against an artificial intelligence foe.

- **Handle complex situations**. In a business setting, top-level managers and executives must handle a complex market, challenging competitors, intricate government regulations, and a demanding workforce. Even human experts make mistakes in dealing with these matters. Very careful planning and elaborate computer programming are necessary to develop systems that can handle complex situations.

- **Solve problems when important information is missing**. An integral part of decision making is dealing with uncertainty. Often, decisions must be made with little or inaccurate information because obtaining complete information is too costly or impossible. Today, AI systems can make important calculations, comparisons, and decisions even when information is missing.

- **Determine what is important**. Knowing what is truly important is the mark of a good decision maker. Developing programs and approaches to allow computer systems and machines to identify important information is not a simple task.

- **React quickly and correctly to a new situation**. A small child, for example, can look over an edge and know not to venture too close. The child reacts quickly and correctly to a new situation. Computers, on the other hand, do not have this ability without complex programming.

- **Understand visual images**. Interpreting visual images can be extremely difficult, even for sophisticated computers. Moving through a room of chairs, tables, and other objects can be trivial for people but extremely complex for machines, robots, and computers. Such machines require an extension of understanding visual images, called a perceptive system. Having a perceptive system allows a machine to approximate the way a person sees, hears, and feels objects.

- **Process and manipulate symbols**. People see, manipulate, and process symbols every day. Visual images provide a constant stream of information to our brains. By contrast, computers have difficulty handling symbolic processing and reasoning. Although computers excel at numerical calculations, they aren't as good at dealing with symbols and three-dimensional objects. Recent developments in machine-vision hardware and software, however, allow some computers to process and manipulate some symbols.

- **Be creative and imaginative**. Throughout history, some people have turned difficult situations into advantages by being creative and imaginative. For instance, when defective mints with holes in the middle arrived at a candy factory, an enterprising entrepreneur decided to market these new mints as LifeSavers instead of returning them to the manufacturer. Ice cream cones were invented at the St. Louis World's Fair when an imaginative store owner decided to wrap ice cream with a waffle from his grill for portability. Developing new products and services from an existing (perhaps negative) situation is a human characteristic. While software has been developed to enable a computer to write short stories, few computers can be imaginative or creative in this way.

- **Use heuristics**. For some decisions, people use heuristics (rules of thumb arising from experience) or even guesses. In searching for a job, you might rank the companies you are considering according to profits per employee. Today, some computer systems, given the right programs, obtain good solutions that use approximations instead of trying to search for an optimal solution, which would be technically difficult or too time consuming.

This list of traits only partially defines intelligence. Another challenge is linking a human brain to a computer.

perceptive system: A system that approximates the way a person sees, hears, and feels objects.

Brain Computer Interface

Developing a link between the human brain and the computer is another exciting area that touches all aspects of artificial intelligence. Called *Brain Computer Interface (BCI)*, the idea is to directly connect the human brain to a computer and have human thought control computer activities. One example is BrainGate, which can be used to connect a human brain to a computer. If successful, the BCI experiment could allow people to control computers and artificial arms and legs through thought alone. The objective is to give people without the ability to speak or move (called Locked-in Syndrome) the capability to communicate and move artificial limbs using advanced BCI technologies. Honda Motors has developed a BCI system that allows a person to complete certain operations, such as bending a leg, with 90 percent accuracy. See Figure 11.8. The new system uses a special helmet that can measure and transmit brain activity to a computer.

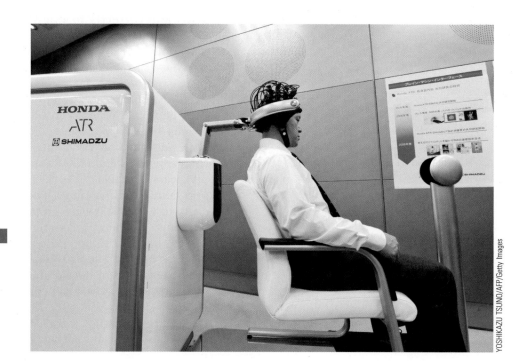

FIGURE **11.8**

Brain-machine interface

Honda Motors has developed a brain-machine interface that measures electrical current and blood flow change in the brain and uses the data to control ASIMO, the Honda robot.

Major Branches of Artificial Intelligence

AI is a broad field that includes several specialty areas, such as expert systems, robotics, vision systems, natural language processing, learning systems, and neural networks. See Figure 11.9. Many of these areas are related; advances in one can occur simultaneously with or result in advances in others.

Expert Systems

An expert system consists of hardware and software that stores knowledge and makes inferences, enabling a novice to perform at the level of an expert. Because of their many business applications, expert systems are discussed a little later in this chapter.

Robotics

robotics: Mechanical or computer devices that perform tasks requiring a high degree of precision or that are tedious or hazardous for humans.

Robotics involves developing mechanical or computer devices that can paint cars, make precision welds, and perform other tasks that require a high

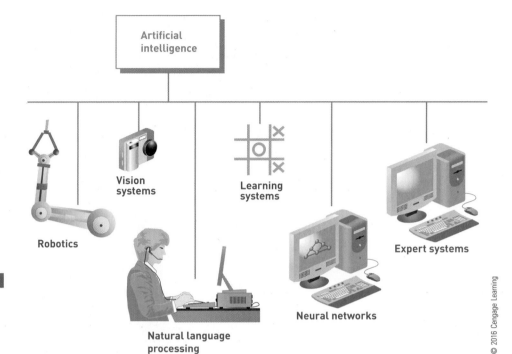

FIGURE 11.9

Conceptual model of artificial intelligence

AI is a broad field that includes several specialty areas.

© 2016 Cengage Learning

degree of precision or are tedious or hazardous for human beings. Karel Capek introduced the word "robot" in his 1921 play, *R.U.R.* (an abbreviation of Rostrum's Universal Robots). The play was about an island factory that produced artificial people called "robots" who are consigned to do drudgery work and eventually rebel and overthrow their creators, causing the extinction of human beings.[13] Organizations today do indeed use robots to perform dull, dirty, and/or dangerous jobs. They are often used to lift and move heavy pallets in warehouses, perform welding operations, and provide a way to view radioactively contaminated areas of power plants inaccessible by people.

However, the use of robots has expanded and is likely to continue to grow in the future. Robots are increasingly being used in surgical procedures from prostrate removal to open-heart surgery. See Figure 11.10. Robots can provide doctors with enhanced precision, improved dexterity, and better visualization. The U.S. Navy's Bluefin 21 robotic submarine made several trips below the Indian Ocean's surface to scan the seabed for any trace of the missing Malaysia Airlines Flight 370. iRobot (*www.irobot.com*) is a company that builds a variety of robots, including the Roomba Floorvac for vacuuming floors, the Looj for cleaning gutters, and the PackBot, an unmanned vehicle used to assist and protect soldiers.[14]

Some robots, such as the ER series by Intelitek, can be used for training or entertainment.[15] Play-i is a start-up firm that created robots Bo and Yana to help young children (ages 5+) to learn programming concepts and creative problem solving.[16] See Figure 11.11.

Some people fear that robots will increasingly take jobs from human employees. For example, Chapter 1 discussed that once governments have created the policy and developed the infrastructure needed to accommodate the use of autonomous vehicles, some or all of the almost six million truck drivers, chauffeurs, and cab drivers on the road today may find themselves without work.

vision system: The hardware and software that permit computers to capture, store, and manipulate visual images.

Vision Systems

Another area of AI involves vision systems. **Vision systems** include hardware and software that permit computers to capture, store, and process visual

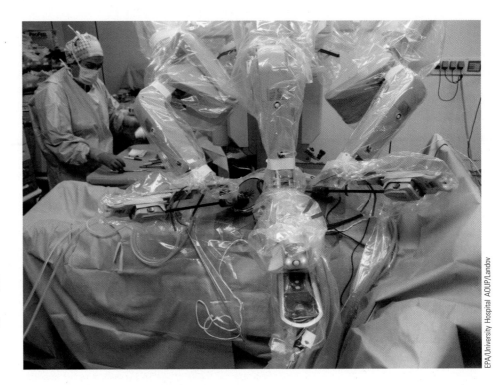

EPA/University Hospital AOUP/Landov

FIGURE **11.10**

Robotic surgery

The arms of the Da Vinci robot assist in a kidney transplant. A surgeon controls the robot remotely from a corner of the operating room.

https://www.play-i.com

FIGURE **11.11**

Play-i educational robots Bo and Yana

Play-i creates robots to help young children learn programming concepts and develop creative problem-solving skills.

images. 3D machine vision systems are used to increase the accuracy and speed of industrial inspections of parts. Automated fruit-picking machines use a unique vacuum-gripper combined with a vision system to pick fruit. Facebook is developing a new AI vision system it calls DeepFace, which creates 3D models of the faces in photos. The technology represents a vast improvement over current facial recognition software. DeepFace can correctly tell if two photos show the same person with 97.25 percent accuracy. This nearly matches humans who are correct 97.53 percent of the time.[17]

Next Generation Identification Database

The Federal Bureau of Investigation (FBI) is developing and deploying Next Generation Identification (NGI), the largest biometric database on the planet. In 2015, the system is capable of querying up to 52 million photos and over 100 million prints, including fingerprints, palm prints, and retina scans. The system will build on and improve the FBI's Automated Fingerprint Identification System (IAFIS) services. The goals of NGI are to ensure public safety and national security, provide biometric leadership in cooperation with state and local governments, improve the efficiency of biometric data retrieval and analysis, ensure privacy and data protection, and allow smooth transitions between existing systems. One astounding new capability, for example, is a search engine that queries photographs to identify individuals based on tattoos, scars, and other marks. In addition, NGI provides advanced facial recognition technology.

The NGI has also significantly improved on IAFIS's capacity to store and share data. Enhancing the interstate photo system, cities and states are able to directly upload photos and prints into the system. So, for example, the New York Police Department has been scanning the irises of arrestees since 2010. Their collection is now part of NGI.

The system's faster response time will have a positive impact on the criminal justice system. The time it takes to obtain a fingerprint match for a criminal suspect has been reduced from two hours using the IAFIS system to ten minutes using NGI. Moreover, the NGI lets agents and police specify whether the search is urgent, routine, or non-urgent. Urgent requests can be met within 10 minutes, while non-urgent requests allow the system to respond within a week. NGI has also implemented a quality check automation. With IAFIS, as many as 98 percent of print matches required a manual review. With NGI, that number is reduced to 15 percent.

Privacy groups, however, are up in arms. Of the 52 million photos, only 46 million are criminal images and only an additional 215,000 come from the Repository of Individuals of Special Concern. About 4.3 million are images collected by state and local government during criminal proceedings. Privacy advocates want to know the origins of the approximately 1.5 million remaining photos. Some groups, like the Electronic Privacy Information Center (EPIC), also worry about the potential to connect the system to driver license photos and live feeds and recordings from closed circuit television (CCTV) surveillance cameras. The Department of Homeland Security has worked with state and local governments to install approximately 30 million CCTVs across the country. EPIC is also concerned that the FBI is relying on private companies to develop the system, potentially giving them access to the database.

The purpose of NGI is to allow law enforcement to decrease crime and prevent terrorist attacks. The United States cannot wage a conventional war against terrorist organizations because they are international non-governmental bodies. The collection and sharing of intelligence is vital to the prevention of terrorist attacks. The question the American public must consider then is how to balance the need to fight crime and terrorism with the protection of privacy rights.

Discussion Questions

1. Lockheed Martin, IBM, and Accenture are among those private contractors that are helping develop and implement NGI. What privacy concerns does their involvement in the project raise?

2. Some privacy advocates fear that the system will lead to the identification of "false positives"—implicating innocent civilians in criminal or terrorist activities. What steps could the FBI take to reduce the likelihood of mistaking individuals' identity?

Critical Thinking Question

1. NGI uses facial recognition software that could allow CCTV cameras to identify people within a crowd. What privacy concerns does this usage raise?
2. What advantages would such a system have? Do the benefits outweigh costs? Why or why not?

SOURCES: "EPIC v. FBI - Next Generation Identification," Epic Web site, *http://epic.org/foia/fbi/ngi*, accessed May 20, 2014; "Next Generation Identification," FBI Web site, *www.fbi.gov/about-us/cjis /fingerprints_biometrics/ngi*, accessed May 20, 2014; Love, Dylan, "The FBI's Facial Recognition System Is a Privacy Nightmare That Collects Your Data Even if You've Never Broken the Law," *Business Insider*, April 15, 2014, *www.businessinsider.com/fbi-ngi-facial-recognition-system-2014 -4#ixzz30fPWcusH*.

Natural Language Processing and Voice Recognition

natural language processing:
Involves the computer understanding, analyzing, manipulating, and/or generating "natural" languages such as English.

Natural language processing involves the computer understanding, analyzing, manipulating, and/or generating "natural" languages such as English. Many companies provide natural language-processing help over the phone. When you call the help phone number, you are typically given a menu of options and asked to speak your responses. Many people, however, become easily frustrated talking to a machine instead of a human. Dragon Systems' Naturally Speaking uses continuous voice recognition, or natural speech, that allows the user to speak to the computer at a normal pace without pausing between words. The spoken words are transcribed immediately onto the computer screen. See Figure 11.12.

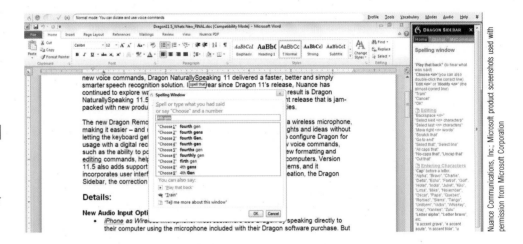

FIGURE 11.12

Voice-recognition software

With the Naturally Speaking application from Dragon Systems, computer users can speak commands or text to transcribe into software such as Microsoft Word.

In some cases, voice recognition is used with natural language processing. *Voice recognition* involves converting sound waves into words. After converting sounds into words, natural language-processing systems react to the words or commands by performing a variety of tasks. Brokerage services are a perfect fit for voice recognition and natural language-processing technology to replace the existing "press 1 to buy or sell a stock" touchpad telephone menu system. Using voice recognition to convert recordings into text is also possible. Some companies claim that voice recognition and natural language-processing software is so good that customers forget they are talking to a computer and start discussing the weather or sports scores.

Learning Systems

learning systems: A combination of software and hardware that allows a computer to change how it functions or how it reacts to situations based on feedback it receives.

Another part of AI deals with learning systems, a combination of software and hardware that allows a computer to change how it functions or how it reacts to situations based on feedback it receives. For example, some computerized games have learning abilities. If the computer does not win a game, it remembers not to make the same moves under the same conditions again. *Reinforcement learning* is a learning system involving sequential decisions with learning taking place between each decision. Reinforcement learning often involves sophisticated computer programming and optimization techniques, first discussed in Chapter 10. The computer makes a decision, analyzes the results, and then makes a better decision based on the analysis. The process, often called *dynamic programming*, is repeated until it is impossible to make improvements in the decision.

Learning systems software requires feedback on the results of actions or decisions. At a minimum, the feedback needs to indicate whether the results are desirable (winning a game) or undesirable (losing a game). The feedback is then used to alter what the system will do in the future.

Google combined natural language processing with learning systems in its Android smartphone operating system to reduce word errors by 25 percent.[18] With this combined technology, the voice assistant asks questions to clarify what you are looking for.

Neural Networks

neural network: A computer system that can recognize and act on patterns or trends that it detects in large sets of data.

An increasingly important aspect of AI involves neural networks, also called neural nets. A neural network is a computer system that can recognize and act on patterns or trends that it detects in large sets of data. A neural network employs massively parallel processors in an architecture that is based on the human brain's own meshlike structure. As a result, neural networks can process many pieces of data at the same time and learn to recognize patterns.

AI Trilogy, available from the Ward Systems Group (*www.wardsystems .com*), is a neural network software program that can run on a standard PC. The software can make predictions with NeuroShell Predictor and classify information with NeuroShell Classifier. See Figure 11.13. The software package also contains GeneHunter, which uses a special type of algorithm called a genetic algorithm to get the best result from the neural network system. (Genetic algorithms are discussed next.) Some pattern recognition software uses neural networks to make credit lending decisions by predicting the likelihood a new borrower will pay back a loan. Neural networks are also used to identify bank or credit card transactions likely to be fraudulent. Large call centers use neural networks to create staffing strategies by predicting call volumes.

Dr. José R. Iglesias-Rozas at the Katharinen hospital in Stuttgart, Germany, is a leader in researching the use of neural networks to diagnose the degree of malignancy of tumors. In his early research, microscopic sections of 786 different human brain tumors were collected. A neural network tool called NeuralTools was then used to predict the degree of malignancy based on the presence of 10 histological characteristics. The neural network accurately predicted over 95 percent of the sample cases. Dr. Iglesias-Rozas plans to expand his research to analyze over 30 years of data from more than 8,000 patients with brain tumors.[19]

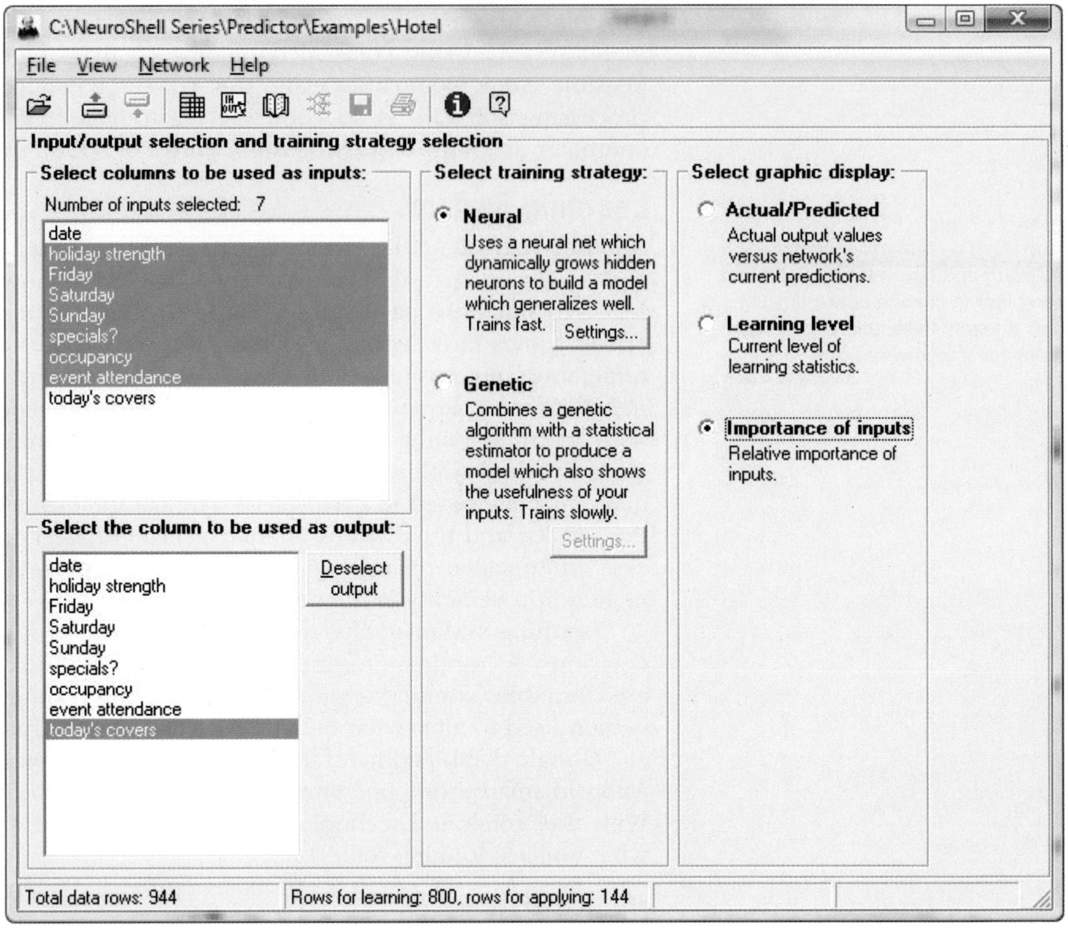

FIGURE 11.13

Neural network software

NeuroShell Predictor uses recognized forecasting methods to look for future trends in data.

Other Artificial Intelligence Applications

genetic algorithm: An approach to solving problems based on the theory of evolution and the survival of the fit-test as a problem-solving strategy.

A few other artificial intelligence applications have been developed in addition to those just discussed. A **genetic algorithm** is an approach to solving problems based on the theory of evolution that uses the survival of the fittest concept as a problem-solving strategy. The genetic algorithm uses a fitness function that quantitatively evaluates a set of initial candidate solutions. The highest scoring candidate solutions are allowed to "reproduce" with random changes introduced to create new candidate solutions. These digital offspring are subjected to a second round of fitness evaluation. Again, the most promising candidate solutions are selected and used to create a new generation with random changes, and the process repeats for hundreds or even thousands of rounds. The expectation is that the average fitness of the population will increase each round, and that eventually very good solutions to the problem will be discovered.

Genetic algorithms have been used to solve large, complex scheduling problems such as scheduling airline crews to meet flight requirements while minimizing total costs and not violating federal guidelines on maximum crew flight hours and minimum hours of rest. Genetic algorithms have also been used to design mirrors to funnel sunlight to a solar collection panel and focus signals to a radio antenna.

intelligent agent: Programs and a knowledge base used to perform a specific task for a person, a process, or another program; also called an *intelligent robot* or *bot*.

An **intelligent agent** (also called an *intelligent robot* or *bot*) consists of programs and a knowledge base used to perform a specific task for a person, a process, or another program. Like a sports agent who searches for the best endorsement deals for a top athlete, an intelligent agent often searches to find the best price, schedule, or solution to a problem. The programs used by an intelligent agent can search large amounts of data as the knowledge base refines the search or accommodates user preferences. Often used to search the vast resources of the Internet, intelligent agents can help people find information on any topic, such as the best price for a new digital camera or used car.

OVERVIEW OF EXPERT SYSTEMS

As mentioned earlier, an expert system enables a novice to perform at the level of a human expert in a particular field. Like human experts, computerized expert systems use heuristics, or rules of thumb, to arrive at conclusions or make suggestions. Since expert systems can be difficult, expensive, and time consuming to develop, they should be developed when there is a high potential payoff or when they significantly reduce downside risk and the organization wants to capture and preserve irreplaceable human expertise.

Colossus is an expert system employed by 25 percent of the top 100 U.S. insurers to assist their claims handlers to accurately and consistently handle personal injury claims. The claims handler is the key individual you deal with should you have an accident. The claims handler investigates, assesses, and negotiates your claim, based on personal knowledge and experience with many previous claims to achieve a fair settlement. As the claims handler enters details about your injury, Colossus steers the data entry process with a series of questions determined by defined business rules to ensure accurate and complete capture of all pertinent data. Once all claim details have been entered, Colossus evaluates your claim based on relevant medical treatment information and suggests to the claims handler a range of settlement amounts suitable to the injury and circumstances. The claims handler uses the suggested amounts to negotiate with you the amount to be paid. Because so many insurers use the same system, the variance in payouts on similar bodily injury claims is reduced and customers are treated more consistently.[20]

Components of Expert Systems

An expert system consists of a collection of integrated and related components, including a knowledge base, an inference engine, an explanation facility, a knowledge base acquisition facility, and a user interface. A diagram of a typical expert system is shown in Figure 11.14. In this figure, the user interacts with the interface, which interacts with the inference engine. The inference engine interacts with the other expert system components. These components must work together to provide expertise. This figure also shows the inference engine coordinating the flow of knowledge to other components of the expert system. Note that knowledge can flow in different ways, depending on what the expert system is doing and on the specific expert system involved.

Knowledge Base

The knowledge base stores all relevant information, data, rules, cases, and relationships that the expert system uses. As shown in Figure 11.15, a knowledge base is a natural extension of a database (presented in Chapter 5) and an information and decision support system (presented in Chapter 10). A knowledge base must be developed for each unique application. For example, a medical expert system contains facts about diseases and symptoms. Rules and cases are frequently used to create a knowledge base.

A **rule** is a conditional statement that links conditions to actions or outcomes. In many instances, these rules are stored as **IF-THEN statements**,

rule: A conditional statement that links conditions to actions or outcomes.

IF-THEN statement: A rule that suggests certain conclusions.

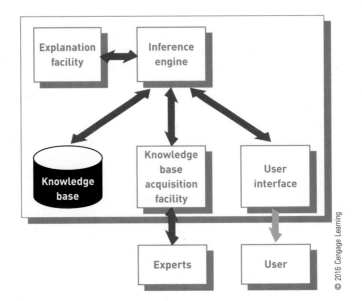

FIGURE **11.14**

Components of an expert system

An expert system includes a knowledge base, an inference engine, an explanation facility, a knowledge base acquisition facility, and a user interface.

FIGURE **11.15**

Relationships between data, information, and knowledge

A knowledge base stores all relevant information, data, rules, cases, and relationships that an expert system uses.

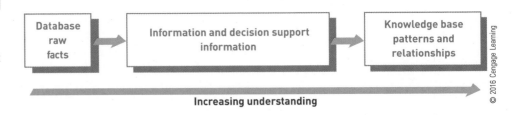

which are rules that suggest certain conclusions. The American Express Authorizer's Assistant rules-based expert system was developed in 1988 and is still in use today. It is used to process credit requests, deciding whether to authorize or reject, and involves some 35,000 rules.[21] Figure 11.16 shows how to use expert system rules in determining whether a person should receive a mortgage loan from a bank. These rules can be placed in almost any standard programming language (discussed in Chapter 4) using IF-THEN statements or into special expert systems shells and products, discussed later in the chapter. In general, as the number of rules that an expert system knows increases, the precision of the expert system also increases.

An expert system can also use cases in developing a solution to a current problem or situation. Each case typically contains a description of the problem, plus a solution and/or the outcome. The case-based solution process involves (1) finding cases stored in the knowledge base that are similar to the problem or situation at hand, (2) reusing the case in an attempt to solve the problem at hand, (3) revising the proposed solution if necessary, and (4) retaining the new solution as part of a new case. A washing machine repair man who fixes a washer recalling another washer that presented similar symptoms is using case-based reasoning. So is the lawyer who advocates a particular outcome in a trial based on legal precedents. A company might use a case-based expert system to determine the best location for a new service facility in the state of New Mexico. The expert system might identify two previous cases involving the location of a service facility where labor and transportation costs were important—one in the state of Colorado and the other in the state of Nevada. The expert system can modify the solution to these two cases to determine the best location for a new facility in New Mexico.

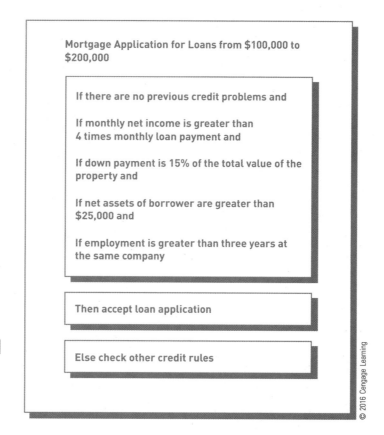

Mortgage Application for Loans from $100,000 to $200,000

If there are no previous credit problems and

If monthly net income is greater than 4 times monthly loan payment and

If down payment is 15% of the total value of the property and

If net assets of borrower are greater than $25,000 and

If employment is greater than three years at the same company

Then accept loan application

Else check other credit rules

© 2016 Cengage Learning

FIGURE 11.16

Rules for a credit application

Expert system rules can determine whether a person should receive a mortgage loan from a bank.

Inference Engine

inference engine: Part of the expert system that seeks information and relationships from the knowledge base and provides answers, predictions, and suggestions similar to the way a human expert would.

The overall purpose of an inference engine is to seek information and relationships from the knowledge base and to provide answers, predictions, and suggestions similar to the way a human expert would. In other words, the inference engine is the component that delivers the expert advice. Consider the expert system that forecasts future sales for a product. One approach is to start with a fact such as "The demand for the product last month was 20,000 units." The expert system searches for rules that contain a reference to product demand. For example, "IF product demand is over 15,000 units, THEN check the demand for competing products." As a result of this process, the expert system might use information on the demand for competitive products. Next, after searching additional rules, the expert system might use information on personal income or national inflation rates. This process continues until the expert system can reach a conclusion using the data supplied by the user and the rules that apply in the knowledge base.

Explanation Facility

explanation facility: Component of an expert system that allows a user or decision maker to understand how the expert system arrived at certain conclusions or results.

An important part of an expert system is the explanation facility, which allows a user or decision maker to understand how the expert system arrived at certain conclusions or results. A medical expert system, for example, might reach the conclusion that a patient has a defective heart valve given certain symptoms and the results of tests on the patient. The explanation facility allows a doctor to find out the logic or rationale of the diagnosis made by the expert system. The expert system, using the explanation facility, can indicate all the facts and rules that were used in reaching the conclusion, which the doctors can look at to determine whether the expert system is processing the data and information correctly and logically.

Knowledge Acquisition Facility

A difficult task in developing an expert system is the process of creating and updating the knowledge base. In the past, when more traditional programming languages were used, developing a knowledge base was tedious and time consuming. Each fact, relationship, and rule had to be programmed into the knowledge base. In most cases, an experienced programmer had to create and update the knowledge base.

Today, specialized software allows users and decision makers to create and modify their own knowledge bases through the knowledge acquisition facility, as shown in Figure 11.17. The purpose of the knowledge acquisition facility is to provide a convenient and efficient means of capturing and storing all components of the knowledge base. Knowledge acquisition software can present users and decision makers with easy-to-use menus. After entering the appropriate attributes, the knowledge acquisition facility correctly stores information and relationships in the knowledge base, making the knowledge base easier and less expensive to set up and maintain.

knowledge acquisition facility:
Part of the expert system that provides a convenient and efficient means of capturing and storing all the components of the knowledge base.

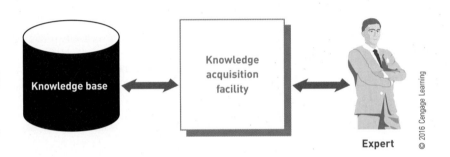

© 2016 Cengage Learning

FIGURE 11.17

Knowledge acquisition facility

The knowledge acquisition facility acts as an interface between experts and the knowledge base.

User Interface

The main purpose of the user interface is to make an expert system easier for users and decision makers to develop and use. At one time, skilled computer personnel created and operated most expert systems; today, the user interface permits decision makers to develop and use their own expert systems. A typical user interface between a user and the expert system for the credit application shown in Figure 11.16 follows:

EXPERT SYSTEM: Are there any previous credit problems?

USER: No.

EXPERT SYSTEM: Is the applicant's net income greater than four times the monthly loan payment?

USER: Yes.

EXPERT SYSTEM: Is the down payment greater than 15 percent of the property value?

USER: Yes.

EXPERT SYSTEM: Are the net assets of the borrower greater than $25,000?

USER: Yes.

EXPERT SYSTEM: Has the borrower worked more than three years at the same company?

USER: Yes.

EXPERT SYSTEM: Accept the loan application.

Participants in Developing and Using Expert Systems

Typically, several people are involved in developing and using an expert system. See Figure 11.18.

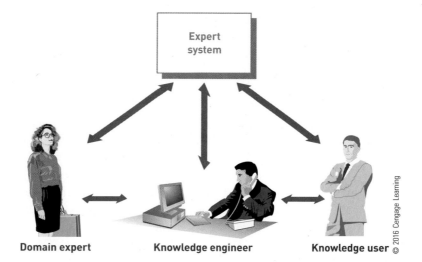

Domain expert   Knowledge engineer   Knowledge user

FIGURE 11.18

Participants in expert systems development and use

A domain expert, knowledge engineer, and knowledge user work with an expert system.

domain expert: The person or group with the expertise or knowledge the expert system is trying to capture (domain).

knowledge engineer: A person who has training or experience in the design, development, implementation, and maintenance of an expert system.

knowledge user: The person or group who uses and benefits from the expert system.

The **domain expert** is the person or group with the expertise or knowledge the expert system is trying to capture (domain). In most cases, the domain expert is a group of human experts. Research has shown that good domain experts can increase the overall quality of an expert system. A **knowledge engineer** is a person who has training or experience in the design, development, implementation, and maintenance of an expert system, including training or experience with expert system shells. Knowledge engineers can help transfer the knowledge from the expert system to the knowledge user. The **knowledge user** is the person or group who uses and benefits from the expert system. Knowledge users do not need any previous training in computers or expert systems.

Expert Systems Development Tools and Techniques

Theoretically, expert systems can be developed using any programming language. Since the introduction of computer systems, programming languages have become easier to use, more powerful, and better able to handle specialized requirements. In the early days of expert systems development, traditional languages, including Pascal, FORTRAN, and COBOL, were used. LISP was one of the first special languages developed and used for artificial intelligence applications, and PROLOG was also developed for AI applications. Since the 1990s, however, other expert system products (such as shells) have become available that remove the burden of programming, allowing nonprogrammers to develop and benefit from the use of expert systems.

Pharmaceutical, biotechnology, medical device, and contract research organizations use Oracle Clinical software to conduct their clinical trials. The software enables such organizations to better manage their critical clinical trial activities by providing a single application for management of all clinical trial data in a single system, thus improving data accuracy and data visibility.[22] iHelp is an interactive and configurable user guide that comes with Siebel Clinical. iHelp employs expert system technology to walk users through tasks step by step while they are using the system.[23]

Expert System Shells and Products

An *expert system shell* is a suite of software that allows construction of a knowledge base and interaction with this knowledge base through use of an inference engine. Expert system shells are available for both personal computers and mainframe systems, with some shells being inexpensive, costing less than $500. In addition, off-the-shelf expert system shells are complete and ready to run. The user enters the appropriate data or parameters, and the expert system provides output to the problem or situation. Table 11.2 lists a few expert system products.

TABLE **11.2** Popular expert system products

Name of Product	Application and Capabilities
Clips	A tool for building expert systems on PCs.
Cogito	Software by Expert System Semantic Intelligence helps an organization extract knowledge from text in email messages, articles, Web sites, documents, and other unstructured information.
Exsys Corvid	An expert system tool that simulates a conversation with a human expert from Exsys (*www.exsys.com*).
ESTA (Expert System Shell for Text Animation)	An expert system shell that provides all necessary components except the knowledge base.
Imprint Business Systems	An expert system that helps printing and packaging companies manage their businesses.
Lantek Expert System	Software that helps metal fabricators reduce waste and increase profits.
OpenExpert	An expert system tool mainly for developing legal expert systems.
Prolog Expert System	Free software for building an expert system knowledge base.

MULTIMEDIA AND VIRTUAL REALITY

The use of multimedia and virtual reality has helped many companies achieve a competitive advantage and increase profits. The approach and technology used in multimedia is often the foundation of virtual reality systems, discussed later in this section. While these specialized information systems are not used by all organizations, they can play a key role for many. We begin with a discussion of multimedia.

Overview of Multimedia

multimedia: Text, graphics, video, animation, audio, and other media that can be used to help an organization efficiently and effectively achieve its goals.

Multimedia is text, graphics, video, animation, audio, and other media that can be used to help an organization efficiently and effectively achieve its goals. Multimedia can be used to create stunning brochures, presentations, reports, and documents. Many companies use multimedia approaches to develop exciting cartoons and video games to help advertise products and services. For example, insurance company Geico uses animation in some of its TV ads. Animation Internet sites, such as Xtranormal and GoAnimate, can help individuals and corporations develop these types of animations. Although not all organizations use the full capabilities of multimedia, most use text and graphics capabilities.

Text and Graphics

All large organizations and most small and medium-sized ones use text and graphics to develop reports, financial statements, advertising pieces, and other documents used internally and externally. Internally, organizations use text and graphics to communicate policies, guidelines, and much more to managers and employees. Externally, they use text and graphics to communicate to suppliers, customers, federal and state groups, and a variety of other stakeholders. Text can have different sizes, fonts, and colors, and graphics can include photographs, illustrations, drawings, a variety of charts, and other still images. Graphic images can be stored in a variety of formats, including JPEG (Joint Photographic Experts Group format) and GIF (Graphics Interchange Format).

While standard word-processing programs are an inexpensive and simple way to develop documents and reports that require text and graphics, most organizations use specialized software. See Figure 11.19. Adobe Illustrator, for example, can be used to create attractive and informative charts, illustrations, and brochures. The software can also be used to develop digital art, reference manuals, profit and loss statements, and a variety of reports required by state and federal governments. Adobe Photoshop is a sophisticated and popular software package that can be used to edit photographs and other visual images. Once created, these documents and reports can be saved in an Adobe PDF file and sent over the Internet or saved on a CD or similar storage device.

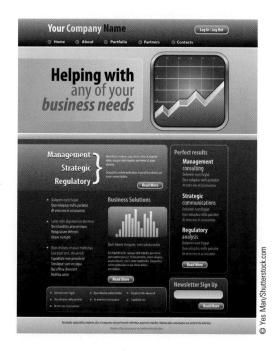

FIGURE **11.19**

Digital graphics

Businesses create graphics such as charts, illustrations, and brochures using software such as Adobe Photoshop or Adobe Illustrator.

Microsoft Silverlight is a powerful development tool for creating engaging, interactive user experiences for Web and mobile applications. easyJet is one of Europe's leading low cost airlines and operates over 600 routes across more than 30 countries with a fleet of more than 200 Airbus aircraft.[24] It uses the Internet as its primary ticket distribution channel. easyJet used Microsoft Silverlight to design its travel Web site in an attempt to offer customers the most intuitive site they have ever experienced. The company hopes that this unique Web site will draw large numbers of new customers, and greatly increase the number of reservations with easyJet.[25]

PowerPoint, also by Microsoft, can be used to develop a presentation that is displayed on a large viewing screen with sound and animation. Other graphics programs include Paint and PhotoDraw by Microsoft and CorelDraw by Corel Corporation.

Many graphics programs can also create 3D images. James Cameron's movie *Avatar* used sophisticated computers and 3D imaging to create one of the most profitable movies in history. Once used primarily in movies, 3D technology can be employed by companies to design products, such as motorcycles, jet engines, and bridges. Autodesk, for example, makes exciting 3D software that companies can use to design everything from fruit-packing machines for Sunkist[26] to large skyscrapers and other buildings for architectural firms. The technology used to produce 3D movies will also be available with some TV programs. Nintendo developed the Nintendo 3DS, one of the first portable gaming devices that displays images in 3D.

Audio

Audio includes music, human voices, recorded sounds, and a variety of computer-generated sounds. It can be stored in a variety of file formats, including MP3 (Motion Picture Experts Group Audio Layer 3), WAV (wave format), and MIDI (Musical Instrument Digital Interface). When audio files are played while they are being downloaded from the Internet, it's called *streaming audio*.

Input to audio software includes audio recording devices: microphones, imported music or sound from CDs or audio files, MIDI instruments that can create music and sounds directly, and other audio sources. Once stored, audio files can be edited and augmented using audio software, including Apple QuickTime, Microsoft Sound Recorder, Adobe Audition, and Source-Forge Audacity. See Figure 11.20. Once edited, audio files can also be used to enhance presentations, create music, broadcast satellite radio signals, develop audio books, record podcasts for iPods and other audio players, provide realism to movies, and enhance video and animation (discussed next).

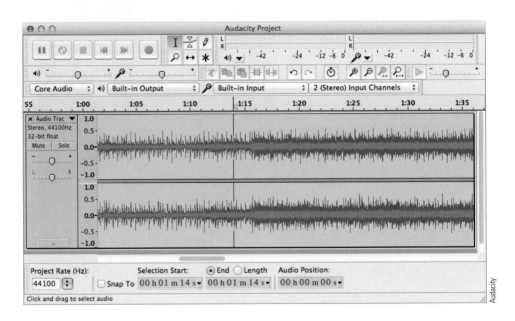

FIGURE 11.20

Audio-editing software

Audacity provides tools for editing and producing audio files in a variety of formats.

Video and Animation

The moving images of video and animation are typically created by rapidly displaying one still image after another. Video and animation can be stored in AVI (Audio Video Interleave) files used with many Microsoft applications, MPEG (Motion Picture Experts Group format) files, and MOV (QuickTime format) files used with many Apple applications. When video files are played while they are being downloaded from the Internet, it's called *streaming video*. For example, Netflix, which allows people to stream movies and TV programs to their PC, is becoming a popular alternative to renting DVDs at a video store. On the Internet, Java applets (small downloadable programs) and animated GIF files can be used to animate or create "moving" images.

A number of video and animation software products can be used to create and edit video and animation files. Many video and animation programs can create realistic 3D moving images. Adobe's Premiere and After Effects and Apple's Final Cut Pro can be used to edit video images taken from cameras and other sources. Final Cut Pro, for example, has been used to edit and produce full-length motion pictures shown in movie theaters. Adobe Flash and LiveMotion can be used to add motion and animation to Web pages.

Video and animation have many business uses. Companies that develop computer-based or Internet training materials often use video and audio software. An information kiosk at an airport or shopping mall can use animation to help customers check-in for a flight or to get information.

Visual effects involve the integration of live action footage and generated imagery to create settings that look completely lifelike, but would be dangerous or extremely expensive to capture on film. RenderMan is Pixar's technical specification for a standard communications interface between 3D computer graphics programs and rendering programs. (Rendering is the final step in the animation process and provides the final appearance to the animation with visual effects such as shading, texture-mapping, shadows, reflections, and motion blurs). RenderMan software is used everywhere to create outstanding graphics for feature films and broadcast television. Indeed, it has been used on every Visual Effects Academy Award Winner of the past 15 years.[27] See Figure 11.21.

FIGURE **11.21**

Creating animation for Pixar

Pixar uses sophisticated proprietary animation software called RenderMan to create cutting-edge 3D movies such as *Brave*.

File Conversion and Compression

Most multimedia applications are created, edited, and distributed in a digital file format, such as the ones discussed earlier. Older inputs to these applications, however, can be in an analog format from old home movies, magnetic tapes, vinyl records, or similar sources. In addition, some older digital formats are no longer popular or used. In these cases, the analog and older digital formats must be converted into a newer digital format before they can be edited and processed by today's multimedia software. This conversion can be done with a program or specialized hardware. Some of the multimedia software discussed earlier, such as Adobe Premium, Adobe Audition, and many others, have this analog-to-digital conversion capability. Standalone software and specialized hardware can also be used. Grass Valley, for example, is a hardware device that can be used to convert analog video to digital video or digital video to analog video. With this device, you can convert old VHS tapes to digital video files or digital video files to an analog format.

Because multimedia files can be large, it's sometimes necessary to compress files to make them easier to download from the Internet or send as email attachments. Many of the multimedia software programs discussed earlier can be used to compress multimedia files. In addition, standalone file conversion programs, such as WinZip, can be used to compress many file formats.

Designing a Multimedia Application

Designing multimedia applications requires careful thought and a systematic approach. The overall approach to modifying any existing application or developing a new one is discussed in the next chapters on systems development. However, developing a multimedia application involves additional considerations. Multimedia applications can be printed on beautiful brochures, placed into attractive corporate reports, uploaded to the Internet, or displayed on large screens for viewing. Because these applications are typically more expensive than preparing documents and files in a word-processing program, it is important to spend time designing the best possible multimedia application. Designing a multimedia application requires that the end use of the document or file be carefully considered. For example, some text styles and fonts are designed for Internet display. Because different computers and Web browsers display information differently, it is a good idea to select styles, fonts, and presentations based on computers and browsers that are likely to display the multimedia application. Because large files can take much longer to load into a Web page, smaller files are usually preferred for Web-based multimedia applications.

Overview of Virtual Reality

The term *virtual reality* was initially coined in 1989 by Jaron Lanier, founder of VPL Research. Originally, the term referred to *immersive virtual reality* in which the user becomes fully immersed in an artificial, 3D world that is completely generated by a computer. Through immersion, the user can gain a deeper understanding of the virtual world's behavior and functionality. The Media Grid at Boston College supports a wide range of virtual reality-based applications such as immersive education; real-time visualization of complex data (e.g., engineering, medical, weather); telemedicine (e.g., drug design, medical imaging, remote surgery); immersive multiplayer games; and vehicle and aircraft design and simulation.[27]

virtual reality system: A system that enables one or more users to move and react in a computer-simulated environment.

A **virtual reality system** enables one or more users to move and react in a computer-simulated environment. Virtual reality simulations require special interface devices that transmit the sights, sounds, and sensations of the simulated world to the user. These devices can also record and send the speech and movements of the participants to the simulation program, enabling users to sense and manipulate virtual objects much as they would real objects. This natural style of interaction gives the participants the feeling that they are immersed in the simulated world. For example, an auto manufacturer can use virtual reality to help it simulate and design factories.

In justifying Facebook's $2 billion acquisition of virtual reality company Oculus VR, Mark Zuckerberg said that "while mobile is the key platform for today, virtual reality will be one of the major platforms for tomorrow. Imagine enjoying a courtside seat at a game, studying in a classroom of students and teachers all over the world or consulting with a doctor face-to-face, just by putting on goggles in your home."[29]

Interface Devices

To see in a virtual world, the user often wears a head-mounted display (HMD) with screens directed at each eye. The HMD also contains a position tracker to monitor the location of the user's head and the direction in which the user is looking. Employing this information, a computer generates images of the virtual world—a slightly different view for each eye—to match the direction in which the user is looking and displays these images on the HMD. Many companies sell or rent virtual reality interface devices, including Virtual Realities (*www.vrealities.com*), Amusitronix (*www.amusitronix.com*), and I-O Display Systems (*www.i-glassesstore.com*), among others.

The Electronic Visualization Laboratory (EVL) at the University of Illinois at Chicago introduced a room constructed of large screens on three walls and a floor on which the graphics are projected. The CAVE, as this room is called, provides the illusion of immersion by projecting stereo images on the walls and floor of a room-sized cube (*www.evl.uic.edu*). Several persons wearing lightweight stereo glasses can enter and walk freely inside the CAVE. A head-tracking system continuously adjusts the stereo projection to the current position of the leading viewer. The most recent version of the CAVE is called CAVE2, and features realistic high-resolution graphics that respond to user interactions. See Figure 11.22.

FIGURE 11.22

Large-scale virtual reality environment

The CAVE2 virtual reality system has 72 stereoscopic LCD panels encircling the viewer 320 degrees and creates a 3D environment that can simulate the bridge of the Starship U.S.S. Enterprise, a flyover of the planet Mars, or a journey through the blood vessels of the brain.

AP Images/Charles Rex Arbogast

Users hear sounds in the virtual world through earphones, with information reported by the position tracker also being used to update audio signals. When a sound source in virtual space is not directly in front of or behind the user, the computer transmits sounds to arrive at one ear a little earlier or later than at the other and to be a little louder or softer and slightly different in pitch.

The *haptic* interface, which relays the sense of touch and other physical sensations in the virtual world, is the least developed and perhaps the most challenging to create. One virtual reality company has developed a haptic interface device that can be placed on a person's fingertips to give an accurate feel for game players, surgeons, and others. Currently, with the use of a glove and position tracker, the computer locates the user's hand and measures finger movements. The user can reach into the virtual world and handle objects; still, it is difficult to generate the sensations of a person tapping a hard surface, picking up an object, or running a finger across a textured surface. Touch sensations also have to be synchronized with the sights and sounds users experience. Today, some virtual reality developers are even trying to incorporate taste and smell into virtual reality applications.

Forms of Virtual Reality

Aside from immersive virtual reality, virtual reality can also refer to applications that are not fully immersive, such as mouse-controlled navigation through a 3D environment on a graphics monitor, stereo viewing from the monitor via stereo glasses, and stereo projection systems. *Augmented reality*, a newer form of virtual reality, has the potential to superimpose digital data over real photos or images. Augmented reality is being used in a variety of settings. Some luxury car manufacturers, for example, display dashboard information, such as speed and remaining fuel, on windshields. The application is used in some military aircraft and is often called heads-up display. First down yellow lines displayed on TV screens during football games is another example of augmented reality, where computer-generated yellow lines are superimposed onto real images of a football field. GPS maps can be combined with real pictures of stores and streets to help you locate your position or find your way to a new destination. Using augmented reality, you can point a smartphone camera at a historic landmark, such as a castle, museum, or other building, and have information about the landmark appear on your screen, including a brief description of the landmark, admission price, and hours of operation. Although still in its early phases of implementation, augmented reality has the potential to become an important feature of tomorrow's smartphones and similar mobile devices. See Figure 11.23.

FIGURE 11.23

Augmented reality

Augmented reality technology shows additional information when it captures images through a camera on devices such as a smartphone.

Kyodo/Landov

Virtual Reality Applications

You can find thousands of applications of virtual reality, with more being developed as the cost of hardware and software declines and as people's imaginations are opened to the potential of virtual reality. Virtual reality applications are being used in medicine, education and training, business, and entertainment, among other fields.

Medicine

Virtual reality has been successful in treating children with autism by helping them pick up on social cues, refine their motor skills, and learn real life lessons such as looking both ways before crossing the street. It seems that children with autism interact well with technology because of its predictability,

I sit very still for him

LIPO CHING/MCT/Landov

FIGURE 11.24

Treating children with autism

The Model Me Going Places app helps autistic children learn appropriate behaviors in various settings, such as a barber shop.

controllability, and incredible patience. See Figure 11.24. Virtual reality has also been used to help train medical students with simulations for many forms of surgery from brain surgery to delivery of a baby.[30]

Education and Training

Virtual environments are used in education to bring exciting new resources into the classroom. Thousands of administrators, faculty, researchers, staff, and students are members of the Immersive Education Initiative, a nonprofit international partnership of colleges, companies, research institutes, and universities working together to define and develop open standards, best practices, platforms, and communities of support for virtual reality and game-based learning and training systems. The following is the current curriculum of fully immersive courses offered through the Woods College of Advancing Studies at Boston College:[31]

- MT 35101 Discovering Computer Graphics
- MT 35801 Video Games and Virtual Reality
- MT 38101 Independent Study in Immersive Education and Virtual Reality
- MT 34101 Web 2.0: New Era of Web Technology
- MT 34801 Information Systems: Applications Overview
- MT 34901 Information Systems: Collaborative Computing

Virtual technology has also been used to train members of the military. To help with aircraft maintenance, a virtual reality system has been developed to simulate an aircraft and give a user a sense of touch, while computer graphics provide a sense of sight and sound. The user sees, touches, and manipulates the various parts of the virtual aircraft during training. Also, the Pentagon is using a virtual reality training lab to prepare for a military crisis. The virtual reality system simulates various war scenarios.

Business and Commerce

Virtual reality is being used in business for many purposes—to provide virtual tours of plants and buildings, enable 360-degree viewing of a product or machine, and train employees. Ford uses virtual reality technology to refine its auto designs. Elizabeth Baron, virtual reality and advanced visualization technical specialist at the company states: "We want to be able to see the cars and our designs, and experience them before we have actually produced them." Perhaps 30 to 40 people from the design and engineering departments might participate in a portion of a typical virtual reality session lasting up to a few hours. Workers are able to scrutinize the interior and exterior of a car design. If they wish, they can even dissect a particular component, say the side mirror or front bumper, and see exactly how it is designed. This is possible because the virtual reality technology is tied directly into Ford's Autodesk computer aided design (CAD) system.[32]

Pepsi Max used augmented virtual reality to turn a London bus shelter into a fake window through which flying saucers, a giant sea monster, a tiger, and other improbable subjects appeared to be moving down the street. Waiting bus riders were fascinated by what they saw and watched the action unfold all the way to the final scene, which showed the Pepsi logo and the words, "Pepsi Max maximum taste, no sugar UNBELIEVABLE."[33]

Microsoft is developing a virtual reality headset for enterprise workers to interact with office productivity software.[34] With this headset and associated software, users can see Microsoft Excel PivotTables that actually pivot in 3D, send weekly status reports that appear in a fully immersive environment, and generate PowerPoint presentations that support full positional head tracking and provide a 3D stereo sound sensation for the listener. Virtual reality headsets such as those by Oculus Rift can be used to walk through the simulated environment. See Figure 11.25.

FIGURE 11.25

Virtual reality headset

A British creative agency developed an immersive walkthrough of a grocery store using the Oculus Rift VR headset to enhance online shopping.

figuredigital.com/Rex Features

OTHER SPECIALIZED SYSTEMS

In addition to artificial intelligence, expert systems, and virtual reality, other interesting specialized systems have appeared, including assistive technology systems, game theory, and informatics. These will now be discussed.

assistive technology systems:
A wide range of assistive, adaptive, and rehabilitative devices to help people with disabilities perform tasks that they were formerly unable to accomplish or had great difficulty accomplishing.

Assistive Technology Systems

Assistive technology systems includes a wide range of assistive, adaptive, and rehabilitative devices to help people with disabilities perform tasks that they were formerly unable to accomplish or had great difficulty accomplishing.

Many assistive technology products are designed to enhance the human-computer interface. Electronic pointing devices are available that enable users to control the pointer on the screen without the use of hands using ultrasound, infrared beams, eye movements, and even nerve signals and brain waves. Sip-and-puff systems are activated by inhaling or exhaling. Braille embossers can translate text into embossed Braille output. Screen readers can be used to speak everything displayed on the computer screen, including text, graphics, control buttons, and menus. Speech recognition software enables users to give commands and enter data using their voices rather than a mouse or keyboard. Text-to-speech synthesizers can "speak" all data entered to the computer to allow users who are visually impaired or who have learning difficulties to hear what they are typing.[35] Stephen Hawking is an English theoretical physicist and cosmologist considered by many to be the most intelligent man alive today. Hawking is almost entirely paralyzed and uses assistive technology systems to communicate his thoughts and to interact with computers. See Figure 11.26.

FIGURE 11.26

Stephen Hawking

Stephen Hawking employs a number of assistive technology systems to support his activities.

Personal assistive listening devices help people understand speech in difficult situations. They separate the speech that a person wants to hear from background noise by improving what is known as the "speech to noise ratio." While there are several different solutions, each personal assistive learning device has at least three components: a microphone, a transmission technology, and a device for receiving the signal and bringing the sound to the ear. Depending on the technology, you just need a headset to connect to the device.[36]

Personal emergency response systems use electronic sensors connected to an alarm system to help maintain security, independence, and peace of mind for anyone who is living alone, at risk for falls, or recuperating from an illness or surgery. These systems include fall detectors, heart monitors, and unlit gas sensors. When an alert is triggered, a message is sent to a caregiver or contact center who can respond appropriately.

game theory: A mathematical theory for developing strategies that maximize gains and minimize losses while adhering to a given set of rules and constraints.

Game Theory

Game theory is a mathematical theory for developing strategies that maximize gains and minimize losses while adhering to a given set of rules and constraints. Game theory is frequently applied to solve various decision-making problems where two or more participants are faced with choices of action, by which each may gain or lose, depending on what others choose to do or not to do. Thus the final outcome of a game is determined jointly by the strategies chosen by all participants. Such decisions involve a degree of uncertainty because no participant knows for sure what course of action the other participants will take. In zero-sum games, the fortunes of the players are inversely related so that one participant's gain is the other participant's loss. In non-zero-sum games, it wise for the participants to cooperate so that the action taken by one participant may benefit both participants. Two-person zero-sum games are used by military strategists. Many-person non-zero-sum games are used in many business decision-making settings. Game theory Explorer and Gambit are collections of software tools for building, analyzing, and exploring game models.[37]

In the TV game show *Jeopardy!*, contestants typically select a single category and progressively move down from the top question (easiest and lowest dollar value) to the bottom (hardest and highest dollar value). This provides the contestants and viewers with an easy-to-understand escalation of difficulty. But recently one player developed a much different strategy employing the fundamentals of game theory. This player seeks out the hidden Daily Double questions, which are usually the three highest-paying and most difficult questions in the categories. Thus rather than selecting a single category and increasing the degree of difficulty, he begins with the two most difficult questions in the category. Once the two most difficult questions have been taken off the board in one category, he skips to another category in search of the Daily Doubles. This strategy has proven to be highly successful.[38]

The United States Coast Guard employs a game theory system called PROTECT (Port Resiliency for Operational/Tactical Enforcement to Combat Terrorism) to randomize patrols while still achieving a very high level of security that provides maximum deterrence. There are insufficient resources to provide full security coverage around the clock at all high-value potential targets in the 361 shipping ports in the United States. This means that enemies can observe patrol and monitor activities and take actions in an attempt to avoid patrols. PROTECT generates patrol and monitoring schedules that take into account the importance of different targets at each port, and the enemy's likely surveillance and anticipated reaction to those patrols.[39]

Informatics

informatics: The combination of information technology with traditional disciplines such as medicine or science while considering the impact on individuals, organizations, and society.

Informatics is the combination of information technology with traditional disciplines such as medicine or science while considering the impact on individuals, organizations, and society. Informatics places a strong emphasis on the interaction between humans and technology with the goal of engineering information systems that provide users with the best possible user experience. Indeed, informatics represents the intersection of people, information, and technology. See Figure 11.27. The field of informatics has great breadth and encompasses many individual specializations such as biomedical, health, nursing, medical, and pharmacy informatics. Those who study informatics learn how to build new computing tools and applications. They gain an understanding of how people interact with information technology and how information technology shapes our relationships, our organizations, and our world.

Biomedical informatics (or bioinformatics) develops, studies, and applies theories, methods, and processes for the generation, storage, retrieval, use, and sharing of biomedical data, information, and knowledge. Bioinformatics has been used to help map the human genome and conduct research on biological organisms. Using sophisticated databases and artificial intelligence, bioinformatics helps unlock the secrets of the human genome, which could

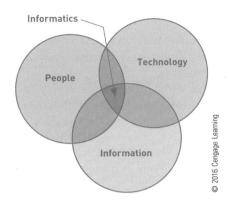

FIGURE 11.27

Informatics

Informatics represents the intersection of people, information, and technology.

© 2016 Cengage Learning

eventually prevent diseases and save lives. Some universities have courses on bioinformatics and offer bioinformatics certification.

Health informatics is the science of how to use data, information, and technology to improve human health and the delivery of healthcare services. Health informatics applies principles of computer and information science to the advancement of patient care, life sciences research, health professional education, and public health. Journals, such as Healthcare Informatics, report current research on applying computer systems and technology to reduce medical errors and improve health care.

New Jersey hospitals participating in a nationwide quality and patient safety program prevented 9,206 adverse events for patients and reduced related healthcare costs by over $100 million in 2013. Data collection played a key role in identifying 13 hospital-acquired conditions to be targeted by this quality improvement process.[40]

SUMMARY

Principle:

Knowledge management allows organizations to share knowledge and experience among its workers.

Knowledge is an awareness and understanding of a set of information and the ways that information can be made useful to support a specific task or reach a decision. A knowledge management system (KMS) is an organized collection of people, procedures, software, databases, and devices used to create, store, share, and use the organization's knowledge and experience. Explicit knowledge is objective and can be measured and documented in reports, papers, and rules. Tacit knowledge is hard to measure and document and is typically not objective or formalized.

Knowledge workers are people who create, use, and disseminate knowledge and include a wide range of workers. The chief knowledge officer (CKO) is the individual who represents the organization's knowledge management vision with clarity and effectiveness, strives mightily to achieve that vision, provides executive-level leadership to implement and sustain KM, and is the ultimate focal point for knowledge creation, sharing and application. Some organizations and professions use communities of practice (COP), which are groups of people with common interests who come together to create, store, and share knowledge on a specific topic.

Obtaining, storing, sharing, and using knowledge is the key to any KMS, with the employment of a KMS often leading to additional knowledge creation, storage, sharing, and usage. Many tools and techniques can be used to create, store, and use knowledge.

Principle:

Artificial intelligence systems form a broad and diverse set of systems that can replicate human decision making for certain types of well-defined problems.

The term *artificial intelligence* is used to describe computers with the ability to mimic or duplicate the functions of the human brain. The objective of building AI systems is not to replace human decision making but to replicate it for certain types of well-defined problems.

Intelligent behavior encompasses several characteristics, including the abilities to learn from experience and apply this knowledge to new experiences, handle complex situations and solve problems for which pieces of information might be missing, determine relevant information in a given situation, think in a logical and rational manner and give a quick and correct response, and understand visual images and process symbols. Computers are better than people at transferring information, making a series of calculations rapidly and accurately, and making complex calculations, but human beings are better than computers at all other attributes of intelligence.

Artificial intelligence is a broad field that includes several key components, such as expert systems, robotics, vision systems, natural language processing, learning systems, and neural networks. An expert system consists of the hardware and software used to produce systems that behave as a human expert would in a specialized field or area (e.g., credit analysis). Robotics uses mechanical or computer devices to perform tasks that require a high degree of precision or are tedious or hazardous for humans (e.g., stacking cartons on a pallet). Robots are increasingly being used in surgical procedures. Vision systems include hardware and software that permit computers to capture, store, and manipulate images and pictures (e.g., face-recognition software). Natural language processing allows the computer to understand and react to statements and commands made in a "natural" language, such as English. Learning systems use a combination of software and hardware to allow a computer to change how it functions or reacts to situations based on feedback it receives (e.g., a computerized chess game). A neural network is a computer system that can recognize and act on patterns or trends that it detects in large sets of data. A genetic algorithm is an approach to solving problems based on the theory of evolution and the concept of survival of the fittest. Intelligent agents consist of programs and a knowledge base used to perform a specific task for a person, a process, or another program.

Principle:

Expert systems can enable a novice to perform at the level of an expert but must be developed and maintained very carefully.

An expert system consists of a collection of integrated and related components, including a knowledge base, an inference engine, an explanation facility, a knowledge acquisition facility, and a user interface. The knowledge base is an extension of a database and an information and decision support system. It contains all the relevant data, rules, and relationships used in the expert system. The rules are often composed of IF-THEN statements, which are used for drawing conclusions.

The inference engine processes the rules, data, and relationships stored in the knowledge base to provide answers, predictions, and suggestions similar to the way a human expert would. The explanation facility of an expert system allows the user to understand what rules were used in arriving at a decision. The knowledge acquisition facility helps the user add or update knowledge in the knowledge base. The user interface makes it easier to develop and use the expert system.

The people involved in the development of an expert system include the domain expert, the knowledge engineer, and the knowledge user. The domain expert is the person or group who has the expertise or knowledge being captured for the system. The knowledge engineer is the developer whose job is to extract the expertise from the domain expert. The knowledge user is the person who benefits from the use of the developed system.

Expert systems can be implemented in several ways. Traditionally, languages including Pascal, FORTRAN, and COBOL were used. LISP and PROLOG are two languages specifically developed for creating expert systems from scratch. A faster and less expensive way to acquire an expert system is to purchase an expert system shell or existing package. The shell program is a collection of software packages and tools used to design, develop, implement, and maintain expert systems.

Principle:

Multimedia and virtual reality systems can reshape the interface between people and information technology by offering new ways to communicate information, visualize processes, and express ideas creatively.

Multimedia is text, graphics, video, animation, audio, and other media that can be used to help an organization efficiently and effectively achieve its goals. Multimedia can be used to create stunning brochures, presentations, reports, and documents. Although not all organizations use the full capabilities of multimedia, most use text and graphics capabilities. Other applications of multimedia include audio, video, and animation. File compression and conversion are often needed in multimedia applications to import or export analog files and to reduce file size when storing multimedia files and sending them to others. Designing a multimedia application requires careful thought to get the best results and achieve corporate goals.

A virtual reality system enables one or more users to move and react in a computer-simulated environment. Virtual reality simulations require special interface devices that transmit the sights, sounds, and sensations of the simulated world to the user. These devices can also record and send the speech and movements of the participants to the simulation program. Thus, users can sense and manipulate virtual objects much as they would real objects. This natural style of interaction gives the participants the feeling that they are immersed in the simulated world.

Virtual reality can also refer to applications that are not fully immersive, such as mouse-controlled navigation through a three-dimensional environment on a graphics monitor, stereo viewing from the monitor via stereo glasses, and stereo projection systems. Some virtual reality applications allow views of real environments with superimposed virtual objects. Augmented reality, a newer form of virtual reality, can superimpose digital data over real photos or images. Virtual reality applications are found in medicine, education and training, real estate and tourism, and entertainment.

Principle:

Specialized systems can help organizations and individuals achieve their goals.

A number of specialized systems have recently appeared to assist organizations and individuals in new and exciting ways. Assistive technology systems include a wide range of assistive, adaptive, and rehabilitative devices to help people with disabilities perform tasks that they were formerly unable to accomplish or had great difficulty accomplishing. Game theory is a mathematical theory that helps to develop strategies for maximizing gains and minimizing losses while adhering to a given set of rules and constraints. Informatics is the combination of information technology with traditional disciplines such as medicine or science while considering the impact on individuals, organizations, and society. It represents the intersection of people, information, and technology.

KEY TERMS

artificial intelligence system

assistive technology system

chief knowledge officer (CKO)

community of practice (COP)

domain expert

explanation facility

game theory

genetic algorithm

IF-THEN statement

inference engine

informatics

intelligent agent

intelligent behavior

knowledge acquisition facility

knowledge engineer

knowledge user

learning systems

multimedia

natural language processing

neural network

perceptive system

robotics

rule

virtual reality system

vision system

CHAPTER 11: SELF-ASSESSMENT TEST

Knowledge management allows organizations to share knowledge and experience among its workers.

1. _____ knowledge is hard to measure and document and typically is not objective or formalized.

2. What type of person creates, uses, and disseminates knowledge?
   a. information worker
   b. knowledge worker
   c. domain expert
   d. knowledge engineer

3. Representing the organization's knowledge management vision is a key role for the _____ of an organization.
   a. CEO
   b. CKO
   c. CFO
   d. CTO

4. The number of knowledge workers in the world far exceed the number of non-knowledge workers. True or False?

Artificial intelligence systems form a broad and diverse set of systems that can replicate human decision making for certain types of well-defined problems.

5. The Turing Test attempts to determine whether a computer can defeat a human at games that require logic and reasoning such as chess or checkers. True or False?

6. _____ are rules of thumb arising from experience or even guesses.

7. _____ is *not* an important characteristic of intelligent behavior.
   a. The ability to receive input from sensors
   b. The ability to learn from experience
   c. The ability to determine what is important
   d. The ability to react quickly and correctly to a new situation

8. A(n) _____ system approximates the way a person sees, hears, and feels objects.

9. Researchers are exploring the possibility of directly connecting the brain to a computer and have human thought control computer activities. True or False?

10. A(n) _____ is a computer system that can recognize and act on patterns or trends in data.

Expert systems can enable a novice to perform at the level of an expert but must be developed and maintained very carefully.

11. Rules and cases are often used to build the knowledge base for an expert system. True or False?
12. A(n) _____ is a collection of software packages and tools used to develop expert systems that can be implemented on most popular PC platforms to reduce the time and costs required to develop an expert system.
13. The overall purpose of a(n) _____ is to seek information and relationships from the knowledge base and to provide answers, predications, and suggestions similar to the way a human expert would.
    a. domain expert
    b. explanation facility
    c. knowledge acquisition facility
    d. inference engine
14. What stores all relevant information, data, rules, cases, and relationships used by the expert system?
    a. the explanation facility
    b. the knowledge base
    c. the inference engine
    d. the acquisition facility
15. The _____ is the person with the expertise or knowledge that the expert system is trying to capture.
16. Which component of an expert system enables the user or decision maker to understand how the system arrived at a certain conclusion or result?
    a. the domain expert
    b. the inference engine
    c. the explanation facility
    d. the knowledge base
17. The purpose of the _____ is to provide a convenient and efficient means of capturing and storing all components of the knowledge base.

18. A(n) _____ is a person who has training and experience in the design, implementation, and maintenance of an expert system.
    a. chief knowledge officer
    b. domain expert
    c. knowledge engineer
    d. knowledge user

Multimedia and virtual reality systems can reshape the interface between people and information technology by offering new ways to communicate information, visualize processes, and express ideas creatively.

19. _____ has the potential to superimpose digital data over real photos or images.
20. _____ is a file format frequently used to store graphic images.
    a. GIF, JPEG
    b. MP3, WAV, MIDI
    c. AVI, MPEG, MOV
    d. DOC, DOCX
21. What type of virtual reality is used to make human beings feel as though they are in a 3D setting, such as a building, an archaeological excavation site, the human anatomy, a sculpture, or a crime scene reconstruction?
    a. cloud
    b. relative
    c. immersive
    d. visual

Specialized systems can help organizations and individuals achieve their goals.

22. _____ include a wide range of devices that help people with disabilities to perform tasks that they were formerly unable to accomplish or had great difficulty accomplishing.
23. _____ involves the use of information systems to develop competitive strategies for people, organizations, or even countries.

CHAPTER 11: SELF-ASSESSMENT TEST ANSWERS

1. tacit
2. b
3. b
4. False
5. False
6. Heuristics
7. a
8. perceptive
9. True
10. neural network
11. True
12. expert system shell
13. d
14. b
15. domain expert
16. c
17. knowledge acquisition facility
18. c
19. Augmented reality
20. a
21. c
22. Assistive technology systems
23. Game theory

REVIEW QUESTIONS

1. Briefly explain the difference between data, information, and knowledge.
2. Briefly explain the difference between explicit and tacit knowledge. Give an example of each.
3. What is the role of the chief knowledge officer?
4. What is a community of practice? Give an example of a COP. What are some of the advantages of participating in a COP?
5. What is a knowledge repository?
6. What is the Turing Test?
7. How would you define artificial intelligence?
8. Identify several specific characteristics of intelligent behavior.
9. Identify six major branches of artificial intelligence.
10. What is a genetic algorithm? Give an example of the use of a genetic algorithm.
11. Identify and briefly describe the five components of an expert system.
12. Identify and briefly describe two approaches for defining a knowledge base.
13. What is a domain expert? What role do they have in the development of an expert system?
14. What is a knowledge engineer?
15. What is an expert system shell?
16. Identify and briefly describe five forms of media that can be used to help an organization achieve its goals.
17. What is a virtual reality system? Identify four areas of virtual reality application.
18. What is an assistive technology system?
19. What is game theory? Identify two applications of game theory.
20. What is informatics?

DISCUSSION QUESTIONS

1. What are the requirements for a computer to exhibit human-level intelligence? How long will it be before we have the technology to design such computers? Do you think we should push to accelerate such a development? Why or why not?
2. You work on the customer software support desk of a large software manufacturing firm as an entry-level manager. The software support specialists need both explicit and tacit knowledge. Describe the types of explicit and tacit knowledge that would be useful to such workers. How would you capture each type of knowledge?
3. Many of us use heuristics each day in completing ordinary activities such as planning our meals, executing our workout routine, or determining what route to drive to school or work. Imagine that you are developing the rules for an expert system to help you in a specific activity. What rules or heuristics would you include?
4. How could you use a community of practice to help you in your work or studies? How would you go about identifying who to invite to join the COP?
5. What are some of the tasks at which robots excel? Which human tasks are difficult for robots to master? What fields of AI are required to develop a truly perceptive robot?
6. Describe how natural language processing could be used in a medical office setting.
7. Discuss the similarities and differences between learning systems and neural systems. Give an example of how each technology might be used.
8. What is the relationship between a database and a knowledge base?
9. Describe how game theory might be used in a business setting.
10. Describe how augmented reality can be used in a classroom. How could it be used in a work setting?
11. Describe how assistive living systems might benefit the residents of a nursing home.

PROBLEM-SOLVING EXERCISES

1. You are investigating the use of an automated fruit-picking machine to reduce the labor costs on your 600-acre Valencia orange grove that yields about 240,000 pounds of fruit (roughly 80,000 oranges) per season. You currently employ a crew of 10 migrant workers to hand-pick the fruit over a three-day period and pay them $8/hour. The fruit-picking machine costs $25,000 and requires two people to operate it. It is capable of picking oranges right off the tree at the rate of one orange per 10 seconds. The machine is quite sophisticated and employs a vacuum-gripper combined with a vision system to pluck ripe fruit from a tree. Does it make economic sense to purchase the automated fruit-picking machine?

2. Consider an expert system to suggest what clothes you should wear based on the previous night's weather forecast. Use a word-processing

program to list and describe the IF-THEN rules or cases that you would use.

3. Use a graphics program, such as PowerPoint, to develop a brochure for a small restaurant. Contrast your brochure to one that could have been developed using a specialized multimedia application used to develop brochures. Write a report using a word-processing application on the advantages of a multimedia application compared to a graphics program.

TEAM ACTIVITIES

1. Do research with your team to identify several instances where robots are taking jobs away from human employees. Does your team believe that the government should encourage or discourage the increasing use of robots? Why? Write a one-page summary of your findings and opinions.
2. Work with your team to design an expert system to predict how many years it will take a typical student to graduate from your college or university. Some factors to consider include the major

the student selects, the student's SAT score, the number of courses taken each semester, and the number of parties or social activities the student attends each month. Identify six other factors that should be considered. Develop six IF-THEN rules or cases to be used in the expert system.
3. Have your team members explore the use of assistive technology systems by recent war veterans. Write a short paper summarizing your findings and the advantages and disadvantages of these type systems.

WEB EXERCISES

1. Use the Internet to identify several applications of neural networks. Write a brief summary of these applications.
2. Do research to find information about the acceptance (or lack thereof) of natural language

processing systems. In your opinion, have these systems gained broad acceptance?
3. Use the Internet to find information about current applications of expert systems. Write a report about what you found.

CAREER EXERCISES

1. Develop three rules of thumb that individuals can use to select a career that is right for them. Develop three rules individuals can use to identify a career that is *not* right for them.
2. Imagine that you are forming a community of practice to deal with the issues of how to select a

career. Identify people from your experience and others you may know of who you would like to include as members. Identify three key topics you would like the community to deal with.

CASE STUDIES

Case One

Knowledge Management Facilitates Energy Innovation

Repsol is a Spanish oil and gas company with 2013 revenues of over U.S. $76 billion. Repsol's business ranges from exploration, refining, and chemical manufacturing to retail marketing at over 7,000 service stations.

Repsol recognizes that "the key assets in an R&D organization like Repsol are the researchers and technologists, who have the training, experience, knowledge, creativity, and motivation: the necessary ingredients for discovering, improving, and assimilating new technologies." Without such *knowledge workers*, every stage in Repsol's value chain would dry up.

The value of such people is in what they know. China's Hilong Group, a supplier to the energy industry, lists many examples: geologists and geophysicists who use their knowledge to determine what rocks are beneath the earth's surface that can contain oil or gas, drilling engineers who plan well locations for efficient oil extraction, platform designers who must reduce costs to improve the efficiency of drilling platforms, and others. All of these people are in professions that call for specialized knowledge. Ideally, that knowledge should be available to anyone in the company who needs it.

Consider oil exploration, one of Repsol's core objectives. Geologists set off vibrations at one point and record them at another. They measure how strong the vibrations are at the receiving end, how long it takes the vibrations to get there, and how strength and delay vary with vibration frequency. From those measurements, the geologists infer how much oil is beneath the surface and how hard extracting it will be. Oil companies use their conclusions to decide how much to bid for the rights to drill in an area. Companies that understand these measurements well can make reasonable predictions of how much oil will come from an area, will create accurate bids, and will be profitable. Companies that do not understand the measurements will bid too much for a barren oil field and lose money, or they will not bid enough for a rich field and be outbid by others who figure out its true value.

Knowing how to interpret these measurements—or how to do specialized work in any other field—comes from years of study and experience. Even the best expert has knowledge gaps: the expert might not know a fact or process, for example, while someone else at the company probably does. That's where knowledge management (KM) comes in. With a KM system, experts throughout the company can tap into what their colleagues know, no matter where they or those colleagues happen to be.

Before 2011, knowledge management at Repsol was haphazard; it depended on each person's knowing who else might know something plus a few localized knowledge repositories. In 2011, Repsol chose IDOL and Virage software from Autonomy (Cambridge, U.K.) to underpin its corporate knowledge management efforts. The company explains that "Autonomy's enterprise search enable[s] Repsol employees to search across different departments and operating systems, geographic locations and languages, to find timely, relevant information, regardless of data type or format. [It can] deliver personalized information through Agents that understand users' interests and monitor business-critical information to provide automated alerts [to help] Repsol work more efficiently and quickly identify market trends, risks, or opportunities."

Repsol's new KM system and innovative approach to technology has helped fuel its success. Over the past five years, Repsol has made over 40 oil discoveries, including eight of the biggest in the world. It has used its revenue to prepare for the future, investing heavily in research and development not only in oil and gas, but in new energy and sustainability.

Discussion Questions

1. What types of knowledge did Repsol employees need to access?
2. What sort of knowledge do people use in your chosen career field? How can a knowledge management system help your employer make full use of everyone's knowledge?

Critical Thinking Questions

1. How do knowledge management systems, such as the one Repsol uses, differ from other types of information systems you have read about in this book?
2. Repsol has operations located in 50 different countries. How can KM systems help overcome language and other barriers that complicate the interchange of knowledge?

SOURCES: "Financials Information for Repsol S.A.," Hoovers Web site, *www.hoovers.com/company-information/cs/revenue-financial. Repsol__SA.9bc3284ea358226f.html*, accessed May 19, 2014; "Company Profile—An Overview," *www.repsol.com/es_en/corporacion/conocer -repsol/como-somos/perfil-compania/default.aspx*, accessed May 19, 2014; Hilong Group, "Why Do So Many Oil Companies Walk in the Forefront of Knowledge Management?" *www.bilonggroup.net/en/news /showNews.aspx?classid=144959613005987840&id=68*, February 18, 2011; Orton, E., "Autonomy Selected by Repsol to Transform Knowledge Management System," *www.prnewswire.com/news-releases/autonomy -selected-by-repsol-to-transform-knowledge-management-system -125795713.html*, July 19, 2011; Savvas, A., "Repsol Deploys Knowledge Management," *Computerworld UK*; July 23, 2011, *www.computer worlduk.com/news/it-business/3292947/repsol-deploys-knowledge -management*; Repsol Web site, *www.repsol.com/es_en*, accessed February 3, 2012; Repsol Knowledge Management, *www.repsol.com /es_en/corporacion/conocer-repsol/canal-tecnologia/ctr_investigadores /gestion-conocimiento*, accessed June 4, 2014.

Case Two

Vision Technologies Automate Urban Inspections

More than 4 million miles (6.5 million km) of roads cross the United States, with millions more in other countries. Proper maintenance is essential to ensure the safety of the users of these roads. Frequent repaving to completely prevent problems is too expensive, but word of mouth, resident complaints, and spot checks are not a dependable basis for planning repair work. As a result, systematic inspection of all roads is necessary—but that's expensive, too. To make things worse, systematic inspection needs to be done on a regular basis with the changes tracked and analyzed over time to predict when road repair will be necessary and to schedule the work in advance. Cash-strapped city and regional governments, therefore, need an inexpensive way to manage ongoing road maintenance and repair.

Fortunately, vision systems are coming to the rescue. City, town, and regional governments use vision systems to help municipalities maintain their share of the world's roadways. Allied Vision Technologies (AVT) is a leading manufacturer of high-performance vision cameras. According to AVT's Web site, vision systems can "collect field data and assess the condition of all roadway and pavement features such as longitudinal cracks, transverse cracks, alligator cracks, edge cracks, potholes, and rutting. Image-based systems offer a less labor-intensive and more reliable solution than traditional manual surveys, and allow the data to be stored for future referencing."

A system developed by AVT and used in the state of Florida incorporates two cameras from AVT and software from NorPix Inc. The cameras, mounted on the roof of a vehicle with one facing forward and one to the rear, capture images of the roadway every 5 to 10 feet (1.5 to 3 meters) as the vehicle drives over it, for a total of up to 180,000 images per day. GPS data is linked to the images to reference them to their actual locations. Images are geometrically flattened to eliminate perspective distortion from the angle of the photograph, superimposed on a map for analysis, and compared with images of the same location from previous years to determine the rate of change. The AVT system still relies on people for the final data interpretation, though its image-processing capability simplifies their task.

Other vision systems can analyze the pavement as well. Pavemetrics Systems of Québec, Canada, offers systems that use lasers and high-speed cameras with custom optics to detect cracks, ruts, and surface deterioration, at speeds of over 60 mph (100 km/hr), day or night, on all types of road surfaces. Pavemetrics systems classify cracks into three categories and evaluate their severity. The systems can also measure and report on the condition of lane markings.

The use of vision systems in pavement inspection is expected to become more widespread in next few years. However, pavement inspection imposes unique challenges on vision systems. Inspection must take place quickly so that the inspecting vehicle won't obstruct traffic. The system must be able to tell the difference between a crack and other surface imperfections such as oil stains under conditions of low contrast. All in all, vision systems in pavement inspection have a tall order, but filling it saves government agencies a great deal of money by making road repairs at the right time—not too early, not too late—and on a planned rather than an emergency basis.

Vision systems are evolving rapidly. Improvements to the underlying hardware and software technologies, combined with research into the use of those components in a variety of vision-based applications, contribute to better acquisition, storage, and analysis of images.

Discussion Questions

1. What other routine inspections do city, state, and national governments perform? How could vision technologies, combined with knowledge management systems, improve efficiency?
2. How could vision systems, combined with knowledge management systems improve government account-ability and help citizens keep track of government performance?

Critical Thinking Questions

1. You work for a city highway department. Your job is to drive over its roads, noting their condition to deter-mine which must be repaired, which must be moni-tored, and which can be left alone for a while. Your mayor suggests that the city should buy a vision system and asks for your opinion. Options include (a) no new system, (b) a system such as the AVT system men-tioned earlier, and (c) at higher cost, a system such as the Pavemetrics system. Write a memo to the mayor making and justifying your recommendation.

2. A van equipped with a pavement inspection system costs about as much as a full-time highway department employee for a year. The highway department employee can use a car that the department already has. In addition, there are ongoing costs for using and maintaining the inspection system. Compare, as best you can from the available information, the costs of a pavement inspection system with its possible benefits.

SOURCES: Allied Vision Technologies, "Mobile Machine Vision System Featuring AVT GigE Cameras Surveys Pavement Condition," *www .alliedvisiontec.com/emea/products/applications/application-case -study/article/mobile-machine-vision-system-featuring-avt-gige -cameras-surveys-pavement-condition.html*, accessed May 18, 2014; Allied Vision Technologies, GC 1350 camera information, *www.allied visiontec.com/emea/products/cameras/gigabit-ethernet/prosilica-gc /gc1350.html*, accessed May 18, 2014; Chambon, S. and Moliard, J.-M., "Automatic Road Pavement Assessment with Image Processing: Review and Comparison," *International Journal of Geophysics, www. hindawi.com/journals/ijgp/2011/989354*, June, 2011; Norpix Web site, *www.norpix.com*, accessed May 18, 2014; Pavemetrics Systems, Inc., "LCMS—Laser Crack Measurement System," *www.pavemetrics.com/en /lcms.html*, accessed May 18, 2014; Salari, E. and Bao, G., "Automated Pavement Distress Inspection Based on 2D and 3D Information," 2011 IEEE International Conference on Electro/Information Technology, Mankato, MN, May 15–17, 2011; SSMC, "Pavement Mapping/Condition Assessment," *www.southeasternsurveying.com/pavement_mapping .html*, accessed May 18, 2014.

Questions for Web Case

See the Web site for this book to read about the Altitude Online case for this chapter. Following are questions concerning this Web case.

Altitude Online: Knowledge Management and Specialized Information Systems

Discussion Questions

1. Why do you think it is a good idea for Altitude Online to maintain records of all advertising projects?
2. How can social networks and blogs serve as knowl-edge management systems?

Critical Thinking Questions

1. What challenges lie in filling a wiki with information provided by employees?
2. What other tools could Altitude Online use to capture employee knowledge, build community, and reward productive employees?

NOTES

Sources for the opening vignette: Mazor Robotics Web site, *http://mazorrobotics.com*, accessed May 19, 2014; Sofge, Erik, "The World's Top 10 Most Innovative Companies in Robotics," FastCompany.com, *www.fastcompany.com/most -innovative-companies/2013/industry/robotics*, accessed May 19, 2014; Keighley, Paul Sanchez, "Mazor Robotics: Revolutionizing The World of Surgery with Robot

Side-Kicks," *NoCamels*, June 7, 2013, *http://nocamels.com /2013/06/mazor-robotics-revolutionizing-the-world-of -surgery-with-robot-side-kicks*, accessed May 18, 2014.

1. "Search Solution Supports R&D," *KMWorld*, February 24, 2014, *www.kmworld.com/Articles/News/KM-In -Practice/Search-solution-supports-RandD-94993.aspx*.

2. Drucker, Peter, *The Landmarks of Tomorrow*, New York: Harper and Row, 1959, p. 122.

3. "NASA Sponsors JPL KM Sessions," JPL Knowledge Management Newsletter, Issue 1-Spring 2014.

4. Grant, Robert M., "The Development of Knowledge Management in the Oil and Gas Industry," Universia Business Review, Cuarto Trimestre 2013, *http://ubr.universia.net/pdfs_revistas/articulo_352_1381330 772384.pdf*.

5. "Improving Management of Competition Cases," *KM World*, October 2, 2013, *www.kmworld.com/Articles /News/KM-In-Practice/Improving-management-of -competition-cases-92385.aspx*.

6. "Botanical Manufacturer Enhances Product Documentation Processes," Knowledge Management, August 26, 2013, *www.kmworld.com/Articles/News/KM-In-Practice /Botanical-manufacturer-enhances-product- documentation-processes-91571.aspx*.

7. "Case study: Drilling for Success and Hitting Knowledge-Management Gold for Baker Hughes," *Transition, www.transition.co.uk/clients/baker-hughes*.

8. McCarthy, J.,Minsky, M.L., Rochester, N., Shannon, C.E., "A Proposal for the Dartmouth Summer Research Project on Artificial Intelligence," August 31, 1955, *www-formal.stanford.edu/jmc/history/dartmouth /dartmouth.html*.

9. "By 2029 No Computer—or 'Machine Intelligence'—Will Have Passed the Turing Test," *http://longbets.org/1/*, accessed May 2, 2014.

10. Griffin, Andrew, "Turing Test Breakthrough as Super-computer Becomes First to Convince Us It's Human," The *Independent*, June 8, 2014, *www.independent.co. uk/life-style/gadgets-and-tech/computer-becomes-first -to-pass-turing-test-in-artificial-intelligence-milestone -but-academics-warn-of-dangerous-future-9508370 .html*.

11. Gee, Sue, "Mitsuku Wins Loebner Prize 2013," I-Programmer, September 15, 2013, *www.i -programmer.info/news/105-artificial-intelligence /6382-mitsuku-wins-loebner-prize-2013.html*.

12. 20 Q Web site, *www.20q.net*, accessed May 2, 2014.

13. Capek, Karel, "Beyond the Robots," Legacy.com, *www .legacy.com/news/legends-and-legacies/karel-capek —beyond-the-robots/302/#sthash.RQyp1B1R*, accessed May 3, 2014.

14. iRobot Web page, *www.irobot.com/us/learn/home.aspx*, accessed May 3, 2014.

15. "Robotics Engineering Curriculum," *www.intelitek.com /engineering/robotics/rec-for-cortex-robotics -engineering-curriculum*, accessed May 3, 2014.

16. Gupta, Vikas, "A Look at Play-i's Successful Crowd-funding Campaign," *TechCrunch*, April 26, 2014, *http://techcrunch.com/2014/04/26/how-to-run-a -successful-crowdfunding-campaign/*.

17. "Facebook's New Face Recognition Knows You from the Side," CNN Money, April 4, 2014, *http://money.cnn .com/2014/04/04/technology/innovation/facebook -facial-recognition/*.

18. D'Orazio, Dante, "Google Now and Speech Recognition Get Big Updates in Android 4.4 Kitkat," *The Verge*, October 31, 2013, *www.theverge.com/2013/10 /31/5051458/android-kit-kat-bring-big-updates-to -google-now-and-speech-recognition*.

19. "Neural Tools Used for Tumor Diagnosis," Palisade Case Studies, *www.palisade.com/cases/katherinenhospital .asp?caseNav=byIndustry*, accessed May 3, 2014.

20. "Motor Insurers' Bureau Gets Consistent Claims with Colossus," *www.csc.com/success_stories/flxwd/78768 -case_study?article=http://www.csc.com/p_and _c_general_insurance/success_stories/87826 -motor_insurers_bureau_gets_consistent_claims _with_colossus.js&searched=expert system*, accessed May 3, 2014.

21. "Reasoning Systems Rules Based Systems," University of Stirling, *www.cs.stir.ac.uk/courses/ITNP60/lectures/2% 20Decision%20Support/1%20-%20Rule%20Based% 20Systems.pdf*, accessed June 5, 2014.

22. "Powering Clinical Studies with Oracle Clinical," *www .oracle.com/us/industries/life-sciences/045788.pdf*, accessed May 5, 2014.

23. "Products: Siebel Clinical iHelp Package," *www .biopharm.com/products/ascend/siebel-clinical -ihelp-package.aspx*, accessed May 5, 2014.

24. "About Us," EasyJet PLC, *http://corporate.easyjet.com /about-easyjet.aspx?sc_lang=en*, accessed May 6, 2014.

25. "EasyJet," *http://download.microsoft.com/documents /uk/government/80593_v7-SQL-Server-Cust-Stories.pdf*, accessed May 6, 2014.

26. "KEITV Customer Success Stories—Sunkist Growers," *http://ketiv.com/company/customer-success-stories /sunkist*, accessed May 6, 2014.

27. Seymour, Mike, "Pixar's RenderMan Turns 25 (Exclusive)," *fx Guide*, July 25, 2013, *www.fxguide.com /featured/pixars-renderman-turns-25/*.

28. "About the Media Grid," *www.mediagrid.org*, accessed May 7, 2014.

29. King, Leo, "Facebook, Oculus, and Businesses' Thirst for Virtual Reality," *Forbes*, March 30, 2014, *www.for bes.com/sites/leoking/2014/03/30/facebook-oculus -and-businesses-thirst-for-virtual-reality*.

30. Casti, Taylor, "6 Ways Virtual Reality Is Already Changing the World (No Facebook Required)," *Huffington Post*, March 28, 2014, *www.huffingtonpost.com/2014 /03/28/virtual-reality-uses-medicine-autism-ptsd-burn -amputee-victims_n_5045111.html*.

31. "Immersive Education @Boston College," *http://im mersiveeducation.org/@/bc*, accessed May 7, 2014.

32. King, Leo, "Ford, Where Virtual Reality Is Already Manufacturing Reality," *Forbes*, May 3, 2014, *www.forbes.com/sites/leoking/2014/05/03/ford -where-virtual-reality-is-already-manufacturing -reality/*.

33. Kastrenakes, Jacob, "Pepsi's Bus Stop Ad in London Might Be the Best Use of Augmented Reality Yet," *The Verge*, March 25, 2014, *www.theverge.com/2014 /3/25/5545842/pepsi-bus-stop-ad-augmented -reality*.

34. Hart, Brian, "Microsoft Targets Enterprise Virtual Reality with Business Oriented VR Headset," *Road to VR*, April 1, 2014, *www.roadtovr.com/microsoft-enterprise-virtual -reality-business-vr-headset/*.

35. "Microsoft Accessibility—Types of Assistive Technology Products," *www.microsoft.com/enable/at/types.aspx*, accessed May 12, 2014.

36. "Assistive Listening Systems and Devices," *http://nad .org/issues/technology/assistive-listening/systems-and -devices,* accessed May 12, 2014.

37. Savani, Rahul and von Stengel, Bernhard, "Game Theory Explorer – Software for the Applied Game Theorist," March 16, 2014, *www.maths.lse.ac.uk /Personal/stengel/TEXTE/largeongte.pdf.*

38. Levenson, Eric, "Jeopardy's New Game-Theory Devotee Is One to Keep an Eye on," *The Wire,* Jan 31, 2014, *www.thewire.com/entertainment/2014/01/jeopardys -newest-star-proves-optimal-strategy-really-unfriendly /357609/.*

39. "Port Resilience Operational / Tactical Enforcement to Combat Terrorism (PROTECT) Model for the United States Coast Guard," *http://teamcore.usc.edu/projects /coastguard/,* accessed May 13, 2014.

40. DeGaspari, John, "N.J. Hospital Quality Effort Averts 9,206 Adverse Events and $100 Million in Costs in 2013," *Healthcare Informatics,* May 13, 2014, *www .healthcare-informatics.com/news-item/nj-hospital -quality-effort-averts-9206-adverse-events-and -100-million-costs-2013.*

Systems Development

CHAPTERS

© Meder Lorant/Shutterstock.com

12 Systems Development: Investigation, Analysis, and Design

Principles	Learning Objectives
• Effective systems development requires a team effort from stakeholders, users, managers, systems development specialists, and various support personnel, and it starts with building an information systems plan.	• Identify the key participants in the systems development process and discuss their roles in ensuring project success. • Discuss the importance of information systems planning and outline the steps of this process.
• Systems investigation is needed to gain a clear understanding of the specifics of the problem to be solved or the opportunity to be addressed and to determine if the opportunity is worth pursuing.	• Outline the steps associated with systems investigation. • Discuss some of the tools and techniques used in this phase of systems development. • Define feasibility analysis and describe technical, economic, legal, operational, and schedule feasibility.
• Systems analysis is needed to define what the information system must do to solve the problem.	• Outline the steps associated with systems analysis. • Discuss some of the tools and techniques used in this phase of systems development. • Discuss the importance of the make-versus-buy decision and outline a process for performing this activity.
• Systems design is needed to define exactly how the information system will solve a problem.	• Outline the steps associated with systems design. • Discuss some of the tools and techniques used in this phase of systems development.

Fighting to Hold Back the Water

© Wil Tilroe-Otte/Shutterstock.com

In the Netherlands, 55 percent of the population lives in areas prone to large-scale flooding. Much of the country—20 percent—is located below sea level and a total of 50 percent of its land mass is no more than 1 meter above sea level. Today, the government spends approximately $9.5 billion annually on water management. With rising sea levels, extended droughts, heavier rains, and less water pouring in from rivers, the Netherlands faces future challenges that are predicted to increase its already hefty water budget by as much as $3 billion per year.

Many private companies, educational institutions, and government agencies are involved in flood prevention, water quality management, and water-related research. The Digital Delta project aims to improve communication and cooperation between all these groups by sharing information through a cloud-based water data management system. Each group collects tens of terabytes of data from dike sensors, pumping stations, radar and weather forecasts, water run-off level monitors, and other devices. The Dike Data Service Center collects 2 petabytes of data annually. The questions the IT system developers face are first, how can smart combinations and analytics of this data produce improved water management, and second, how can dashboards and other tools make this data easier for stakeholders to access so that Dutch authorities can respond more quickly and effectively to floods, droughts, and threats to water quality? The developers must answer these questions before they can design and develop the new system that will be based on the IBM Intelligent Operations for Water and the Smarter Water Resource Management solution.

During its first year, Digital Delta is starting with small projects to find answers. One of its first steps is to figure out how to facilitate cooperation between Rijkswaterstaat, the Dutch government agency responsible for the maintenance of waterways and water systems, and 25 other local water authorities. The water level is optimized in each district, even though the actions of one district affect the others. Water districts respond reactively to the decisions of others, and if they want to receive information from another district, they do so by phone or email. Digital Delta is providing a mechanism to share real-time data to bring the districts together not only to optimize the discharge of water and save 40 percent in energy costs, but also to improve water containment during dry spells and prevent sea-water salt from damaging agriculture.

Digital Delta is working with each stakeholder to find business processes that will overcome barriers to communication. In doing so, the project's participants hope to eventually gain the ability to discharge water at sea at just the right moment, predict when tunnels will flood, prevent sewage overflow, improve water-level forecasting, and monitor river depth more accurately for shipping transportation.

As you read this chapter, consider the following:

- What steps do IT systems developers need to take before they begin to design a new product?
- What role should users and stakeholders play in the development of new systems like Digital Delta?

WHY LEARN ABOUT SYSTEMS INVESTIGATION, ANALYSIS, AND DESIGN?

Throughout this book, you have seen many examples of the use of information systems in a variety of careers. But where do you start to acquire these systems or have them developed? How can you work with IS personnel, such as systems analysts and computer programmers, to get what you need to succeed on the job or in your own business? This chapter, the first of two chapters on systems development, provides the answers to these questions. You will see how you can initiate the systems development process, analyze your needs with the help of IS personnel, and design how the new system must work to meet the defined business needs. Systems investigation, systems analysis, and systems design are the first three steps of the systems development process. This chapter provides specific examples of how new or modified systems are initiated, analyzed, and designed in a number of industries. In this chapter, you will learn how your project can be planned, aligned with corporate goals, analyzed, designed, and approved by senior management. We start with an overview of the systems development process.

When an organization needs to accomplish a new task or change a work process, how does it proceed? Often it must develop a new system or modify an existing one. Systems development is the activity of creating new systems or modifying existing systems. It refers to all aspects of the process—from identifying problems to solve or opportunities to exploit to implementing and refining the chosen solution. Gartner, the U.S. information technology and advisory firm, forecasts that annual worldwide IT spending will grow from $3.8 trillion in 2014 to $4.4 trillion in 2018. Roughly two-thirds of this spending will be on software and IS services.[1] As a result, systems development expenditures are expected to continue at a high level over the next few years. Many IS departments and systems developers will concentrate on creating more mobile applications for their businesses and organizations.

AN OVERVIEW OF SYSTEMS DEVELOPMENT

In today's businesses, managers and employees in all functional areas work together and use business information systems. As a result, they are expected to help and even lead systems development teams. Users might request that a systems development team determine whether they should purchase new mobile computing devices or create an attractive Web site. In another case, an entrepreneur might use systems development to build a mobile application to compete with large corporations. This chapter and the next provide you with a deeper appreciation of the systems development process.

Corporations and nonprofit organizations often use the systems development process to build information systems to achieve their goals. The Cincinnati Zoo developed an information system that pools data from ticketing and point-of-sale systems throughout the zoo with membership information and geographical data grouped by the zip codes of all visitors. The system generates reports and dashboards that summarize this data so that managers and staff can take actions to improve the overall customer experience and eliminate ineffective promotions. Together these actions are credited with saving the zoo more than $100,000 in promotional expenses and boosting attendance by over 50,000 in just one year.[2]

The Standish Group has been tracking the success rate of projects for over 20 years. Although the rate has increased over time with improved methods, training, and tools, the number of failed and challenged projects (those that are late, over budget, or lacking required features) stands at 61 percent.[3] This chapter and the next will help you avoid failed and challenged systems development projects.

Participants in Systems Development

Effective systems development requires a team effort. The development team consists of stakeholders, users, managers, systems development specialists, and various support personnel. The team is responsible for determining the objectives of the information system and delivering a system that meets these objectives. Selecting a strong team for the systems development project is critical to project success.

project manager: The person assigned by the organization to do the work of the project and achieve the project objectives.

The **project manager** is the person assigned by the organization to do the work of the project and achieve the project objectives. The project manager coordinates all people and resources required to complete the project successfully. Project managers need technical, business, and people skills. See Figure 12.1. In addition to completing the project on time and within the specified budget, the project manager is usually responsible for controlling project scope, ensuring project quality, training personnel, facilitating communications, managing risks, and acquiring any necessary equipment, including office supplies and sophisticated computer hardware and software systems. The project manager often delegates some of these tasks to various members of the team.

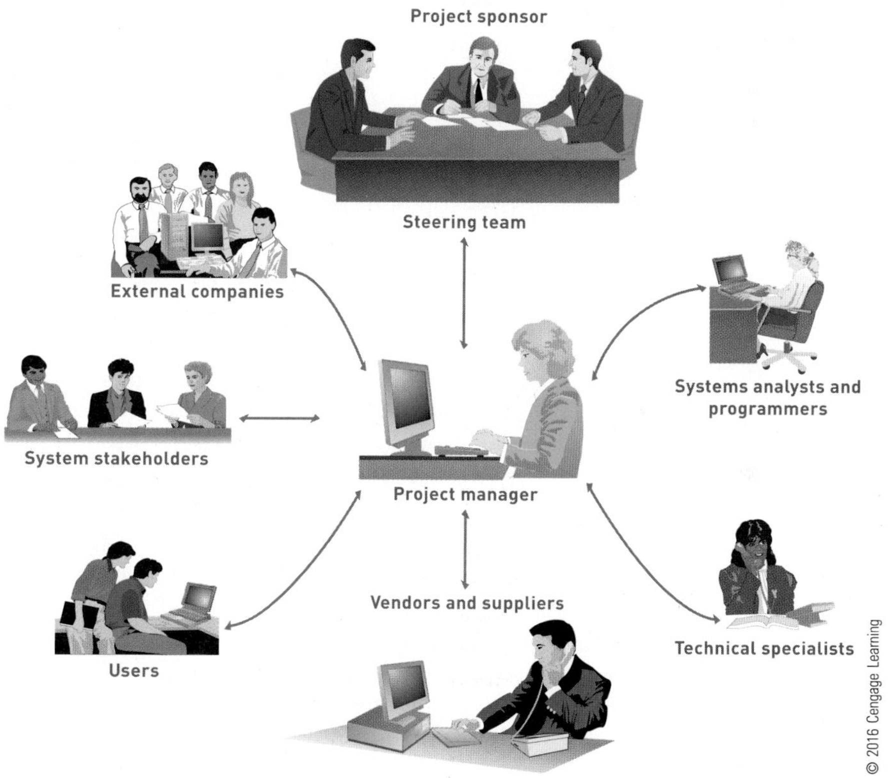

FIGURE 12.1

Role of the project manager

The project manager plays a key role in the systems development project.

stakeholders: People who ultimately will be affected (for better or worse) by the systems development project.

users: People who will regularly interact with the system.

systems analyst: A professional who specializes in analyzing and designing business systems.

In the context of systems development, **stakeholders** are people who will ultimately be affected (for better or worse) by the systems development project. **Users** are the people who will regularly interact with the system as they complete their work. They can be employees or nonemployees such as customers, suppliers, or others outside the organization.

An information systems development team also includes systems analysts and programmers, among others. A **systems analyst** is a professional who specializes in analyzing and designing business systems. Systems analysts play various roles while interacting with the stakeholders and users, management, vendors and suppliers, external companies, programmers, and other IS support personnel. Like an architect developing blueprints for a new building, a systems analyst develops detailed plans for the new or modified system.

programmer: A specialist responsible for modifying or developing programs to satisfy user requirements.

The programmer is responsible for modifying or developing programs to satisfy user requirements. Like a contractor constructing a new building or renovating an existing one based on an architect's drawings, the programmer takes the system design from the systems analysis team and builds or modifies the necessary software.

Other members of the development team may include technical specialists, such as database and telecommunications experts, hardware engineers, and software or hardware supplier representatives. The various members of the project may come and go depending on the phase of the project and its needs for certain specialists.

For small businesses, the development team might consist only of a systems analyst and the business owner as the primary stakeholder. In contrast, multinational organizations often form virtual project teams with a team of stakeholders, users, systems analysts, programmers, and other IS personnel from around the globe.

steering team: A small group of senior managers representing the business and IS organizations that provide guidance and support to the project.

In addition to the development team, each project should have a steering team of senior managers representing the business and IS organizations that provide guidance and support to the project. The number of members on the steering team should be limited (three to five) to simplify the decision-making process and ease the effort to schedule a quorum of these busy executives. The project manager and select members of the development team meet with the steering team on an as needed basis, typically at the end of each project phase or every few months.

project sponsor: A key member and leader of the steering team who plays such a critical role that lack of this essential individual raises the distinct probability of project failure.

The project sponsor is a key member and leader of the steering team who plays such a critical role that lack of this essential individual raises the probability of project failure. Following are the sponsor's responsibilities.

- Aligns project goals and objectives with organizational goals and objectives
- Obtains budget, people, and other necessary resources for the project
- Acts as a vocal and visible champion for the project to gain the support of others
- Identifies and removes barriers to project success
- Resolves any issues outside the control of the project manager
- Provides advice and counsel to the project team
- Keeps informed of major project activities and developments
- Has final approval of all requests for changes in project scope, budget, and schedule
- Signs off on approvals to proceed to each succeeding project phase

Information Systems Planning

information systems planning: The identification of those information systems development initiatives needed to support organizational strategic goals.

Information systems planning identifies those information systems development initiatives needed to support organizational strategic goals. Systems development initiatives arise from all levels of an organization and are both planned and unplanned. Organizations initiate systems development projects for many reasons, as shown in Figure 12.2.

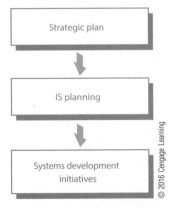

FIGURE 12.2

Information systems planning

Information systems planning transforms organizational goals outlined in the strategic plan into specific systems development activities.

Long-range IS planning ensures that the project meets strategic goals and that the organization gains the best value from its IS resources. The IS plan should guide development of the entire IS infrastructure over time. Though the IS plan provides a broad framework for future success, it can also stimulate specific systems development initiatives. The steps of IS planning are shown in Figure 12.3.

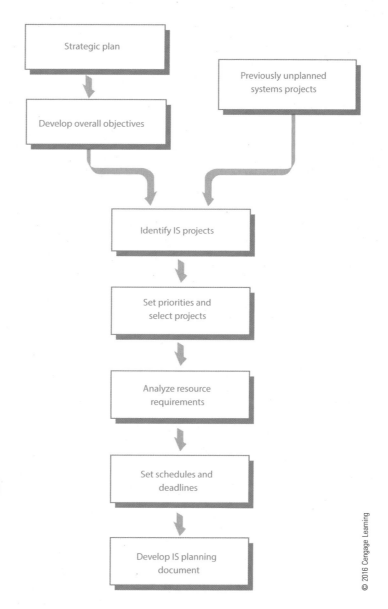

FIGURE 12.3

Steps of information systems planning

IS initiatives flow from the organizational strategic plan and are prioritized by how well they support organizational goals and objectives.

critical success factors (CSFs): Factors that are essential to the success of a functional area of an organization.

An organization's goals define a system's objectives. A manufacturing plant, for example, might determine that it must minimize the total cost of owning and operating its equipment so it can meet production and profit goals. **Critical success factors (CSFs)** are factors that are essential to the success of certain functional areas of an organization. The CSF for manufacturing—minimizing equipment maintenance and operating costs—would be converted into specific objectives for a proposed system. One specific objective might be to alert maintenance planners when a piece of equipment is due for routine preventive maintenance (e.g., cleaning and lubrication). Another objective might be to alert the maintenance planners when the necessary cleaning materials, lubrication oils, or spare parts inventory levels are below specified limits. These objectives could be accomplished either through automatic stock replenishment via electronic data interchange or through the use of exception reports.

Opportunities and problems that frequently trigger the initiation of an information system project include the following:

- The availability of new technology that creates an opportunity to improve an existing business process or to reach new customers. A New England restoration company transitioned from outdated paper-based processing to a mobile app that runs on smartphones. The new system greatly speeds up the ability to respond to customers, a critical consideration when dealing with a home or business that has been damaged by smoke and fire and has floors covered by inches of water.[4]
- Mergers and acquisitions require organizations to integrate systems, people, and procedures into a single IS function. When United and Continental Airlines merged, combining their reservation systems and data led to flight delays and lost loyalty plan data. Indeed, United Continental's chief revenue officer James Compton claimed that recurrent IS integration issues had "put a great deal of stress on our operation and our people" and harmed the company's performance.[5]
- New laws and regulations can also encourage new systems development projects in the public and private sectors. The American Taxpayer Relief Act (ATRA) contained a provision that allowed small businesses to expense the entire cost of new software in year one rather than depreciating the expense over three years.[6] Such tax relief was an encouragement to many small firms to invest in computer software.

Failure to align information systems goals to the needs of the business can have disastrous consequences. Gregg Steinhafel stepped down from the CEO position at Target following a massive data breach that affected perhaps 110 million customers and damaged the firm's reputation. Steinhafel "held himself personally responsible" for the breach.[7] Steinhafel's resignation followed the resignation of Target CIO Beth Jacob two months earlier. In an effort to better align IS effort to corporate goals, Target elevated the priority assigned to information security and compliance structure and practices. The firm conducted an external search for a new CIO, chief information security officer, and chief compliance officer.[8] Target also is replacing all its existing RED cards with new cards using the MasterCard-branded chip-and-PIN technology.[9]

TRADITIONAL SYSTEMS DEVELOPMENT LIFE CYCLE

The systems development process is also called a *systems development life cycle (SDLC)* because the activities associated with it are ongoing. As each system is built, the project has timelines and deadlines until at last the system is installed and accepted. The later an error is detected in the SDLC, the more expensive it is to correct. One reason for the mounting costs is that if an error is found in a later phase of the SDLC, the previous phases must be reworked to some extent. Thus, experienced systems developers prefer an approach that detects and removes errors early in the project life cycle.

Common systems development life cycles include traditional, prototyping, agile, object-oriented, and individual development. With some companies, these approaches are formalized and documented so that systems developers have a well-defined process to follow; other companies use less formalized, undocumented (ad hoc) approaches. This chapter covers the first three phases of the traditional systems development life cycle and the next chapter will discuss the remaining phases of the traditional system development life cycle as well as prototyping, agile, object-oriented, and individual development life cycles.

The **traditional systems development life cycle** is a sequential multi-stage process where work on the next stage cannot begin until the results of the previous stage are reviewed and approved or modified as necessary. The phases of the traditional systems development life cycle might vary from one company to the next, but many organizations use an approach with six phases: investigation, analysis, design, construction, integration and testing, and implementation. Once the system is built, organizations complete the additional steps of operation and maintenance and disposition. See Figure 12.4.

traditional systems development life cycle:
A sequential multistage process where work on the next stage cannot begin until the results of the previous stage are reviewed and approved or modified as necessary.

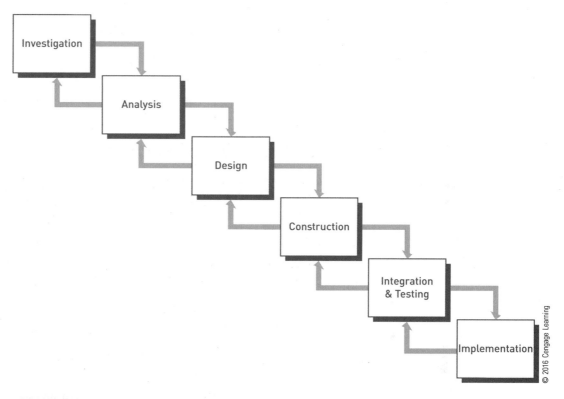

FIGURE 12.4

Traditional systems development life cycle

The traditional systems development life cycle is also known as the waterfall approach.

As shown in Figure 12.4, a system under development moves from one phase of the traditional SDLC to the next. At the end of each phase, a review is conducted to ensure that all tasks and deliverables associated with that phase were produced and that they are of good quality. In addition, the overall project scope, costs, schedule, and benefits associated with the project are reviewed to ensure that the project is still attractive. As a result, the traditional SDLC allows for a high degree of management control. However, a major problem is that users do not interact with the solution until the integration and testing phase when the system is nearly complete. Table 12.1 lists additional advantages and disadvantages of the traditional SDLC.

An information system project for the California Department of Motor Vehicles (DMV) following the traditional SDLC was canceled after seven years of effort and an expenditure of $50 million. This project obviously would have benefitted from closer review earlier in the effort.[10]

TABLE 12.1 Advantages and disadvantages of traditional SDLC

Advantages	Disadvantages
Formal review at the end of each phase allows maximum management control.	Users get a system that meets the needs as understood by the developers; this might not be what the users really needed.
This approach requires creation of considerable system documentation.	Documentation is expensive and time consuming to create. It is also difficult to keep current.
Formal documentation ensures that system requirements can be traced back to stated business needs.	Often, user needs go unstated or are miscommunicated or misunderstood.
Approach produces many intermediate products that can be reviewed to see whether they meet the users' needs and conform to standards.	Users can't easily review intermediate products and evaluate whether a particular product (e.g., a data-flow diagram) meets their business requirements.

© 2016 Cengage Learning

SYSTEMS INVESTIGATION

Systems investigation is the first phase in the traditional SDLC of a new or modified business information system. The purpose is to gain a clear understanding of the specifics of the problem to solve or the opportunity to address. What is the scope of the problem? Who is affected and how? How often does this occur? After gaining a good understanding of the problem, the next question is, "Is the problem worth addressing?" Given that organizations have limited resources—people and money—this question deserves careful attention. What are the potential costs, both the one-time initial costs and recurring, ongoing costs? What risks are associated with the project? If successful, what benefits, both tangible (measurable) and intangible (not easily measured) will the system provide? The steps of the investigation phase are outlined next and discussed on the following pages.

1. Review systems investigation request
2. Identify and recruit team leader and team members
3. Develop budget and schedule for investigation
4. Perform investigation
5. Perform preliminary feasibility analysis
6. Prepare draft of investigation report
7. Review results of investigation with steering team

Review Systems Investigation Request

systems investigation request: A document filled out by someone who wants the IS department to initiate a systems investigation.

Because systems development requests can require considerable time and effort to investigate, many organizations have adopted a formal procedure for initiating a systems investigation. A systems investigation request is completed, ideally by members of the organization that will be most affected by the potential new or modified system. This request typically includes the following information:

- A preliminary statement of the problem or opportunity to be addressed (this will be refined during the course of the investigation)
- A brief discussion of how this effort aligns with previously defined company and organization objectives, goals, and strategies
- Identification of the general areas of the business and business processes to be included in the scope of the study (e.g., the handling of customer discounts in the order-processing system)

The information in the systems request helps senior management to rationalize and prioritize the activities of the IS department and decide which investigation projects should be staffed. Based on the overall IS plan, the organization's needs and goals, and the estimated value and priority of the proposed projects, managers make decisions regarding the initiation of each systems investigation for such projects.

Identify and Recruit Team Leader and Team Members

After managers grant approval to initiate systems investigation, the next step is to identify and recruit the leader for the investigation phase, followed by the other members of the investigation team. The members of the investigation team are responsible for gathering and analyzing data, preparing an investigation phase report, and presenting the results to the project steering team. The systems investigation team can be quite diverse, often with members located around the world. Business knowledge of the areas under study, communication, and collaboration are characteristics of successful investigation teams. Members of the development team change from phase to phase depending on the knowledge, experience, and skills required.

Develop Budget and Schedule for Investigation

After identifying the leader and members, the team develops a list of specific objectives and activities to accomplish during systems investigation along with a schedule for completing this work. The team establishes major milestones to help monitor progress and determine whether problems or delays occur in performing the systems investigation. The group also prepares a budget to complete the investigation including any travel required and funds necessary to cover the use of any outside resources or consultants.

Perform Investigation

The major tasks to perform during investigation include refining the initial problem definition and scope described in the systems investigation request, identifying the high-level business requirements the system must meet, and identifying any issues or risks associated with the project.

Joint Application Development (JAD)

joint application development (JAD): A structured meeting process that can accelerate and improve the efficiency and effectiveness of the investigation, analysis, and design phases of a systems development project.

Joint application development (JAD) is a structured meeting process that can accelerate and improve the efficiency and effectiveness of not only the investigation phase, but also the analysis and design phases of a systems development project. JAD involves carefully planned and designed meetings in which users, stakeholders, and IS professionals work together to analyze existing systems, define problems, identify solution requirements, and propose and evaluate possible solutions including costs and benefits. See Figure 12.5. The JAD process has proven to be extremely effective and efficient at accomplishing these tasks. In addition, the highly participative nature of the sessions goes a long way to helping ensure stakeholders and users buy into the results. With today's technology such as group decision support systems and video conferencing, it is possible to conduct effective live JAD sessions with people located in many different places without the need for expensive travel.

The success or failure of a JAD session depends on how well the JAD facilitator plans and manages the session. It is not unusual for the facilitator to spend three hours planning and preparing for the JAD session for each hour the JAD session lasts. In addition, the participants of a JAD session must be carefully chosen to include users of the system as well as people from other organizations who will likely be affected by, provide input for, or receive output from the system. Ideally, people from the operational level as well as the executive level will attend. Table 12.2 identifies the JAD session participants as well as their role and qualifications.

FIGURE **12.5**

JAD session

JAD can accelerate and improve the efficiency and effectiveness of the investigation, analysis, and design phases of a systems development project.

TABLE 12.2 JAD participants and their role

Role	Responsibilities	Qualifications
Facilitator	• Determines JAD session objectives • Plans JAD session to meet objectives • Leads JAD session • Encourages everyone to participate	• Excellent meeting facilitator • Unbiased and does not take sides
Decision makers	• Resolve conflicts • Avoid gridlock	• Stakeholders selected by project sponsor to make decisions • Have the authority and willingness to make decisions
Users	• Describe business as it is and as it should be • Provide business expertise • Define problems, identify potential benefits, analyze existing system, define requirements of a new system, and propose and evaluate possible solutions	• Represent all major areas affected • Expert in their area of the business
System developers	• Observe carefully • Offer technical opinion on cost or feasibility, if requested • Gain deep understanding of customers' needs and desires	• Member of system development team
Scribe	• Participate in discussion to clarify points and capture them accurately • Document key points, issues, next steps, and decisions throughout the JAD session • Publish results of JAD session and solicit feedback	• Excellent listening skills • Experience in using software engineering tools to document requirements and create system models

The consulting firm Liquid Mercury Solutions uses JAD in working with its clients to develop information system solutions.[11] The firm used JAD in working with the USDA Biotechnology Regulatory Services branch to streamline work processes and implement systems to eliminate a large backlog of petitions to deregulate various genetically engineered organisms.[12]

Functional Decomposition

functional decomposition:
A technique used during the investigation, analysis, and design phases to define the business processes included within the scope of the system.

Functional decomposition is a technique used primarily during the investigation phase to define the business processes included within the scope of the system. Recall from Chapter 1 that a process is a set of logically related tasks performed to achieve a defined outcome. A process is usually initiated in response to a specific event and requires input that it processes to create output. Often feedback is generated that is used to monitor and refine the process.

To create the functional decomposition chart (see Figure 12.6), begin with the name of the system, and then identify the highest-level processes to be performed. Each process should have a two word "verb-subject" name that clearly defines the process. Next, break those high-level processes down into lower-level subprocesses. For the systems investigation phase, three or four levels of decomposition are usually sufficient to define the scope of the system.

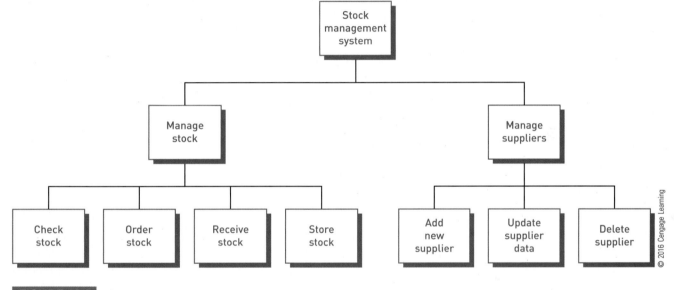

© 2016 Cengage Learning

FIGURE **12.6**

Functional decomposition chart

Functional decomposition is used to define the scope of the system.

Perform Preliminary Feasibility Analysis

feasibility analysis: Assessment of the technical, economic, legal, operational, and schedule feasibility of a project.

A major step of the systems investigation phase is feasibility analysis, which assesses technical, economic, legal, operational, and schedule feasibility. See Figure 12.7. At this stage in the systems development process, this is a preliminary analysis that will be repeated with more accuracy during the analysis and design phases when more details about the system and its requirements are known.

technical feasibility: Examines if the project is feasible within the current limits of available technology.

Technical feasibility examines whether the project is feasible within the current limits of available technology. Determining the technical feasibility is critical when new technology is first being considered for use within an organization, prior to its widespread use. The Neo4j graph database is a new technology that is being evaluated in the medical community for patient management, drug research, clinical trials, and genomics. In many cases, these applications require such demanding computations and data searches that they would simply be infeasible using traditional relational database technology. Organizations evaluating this software include Curaspan Health Group, Good Start Genetics, SharePractice, and Janssen Pharmaceuticals.[13]

economic feasibility: The determination of whether the project makes financial sense and whether predicted benefits offset the cost and time needed to obtain them.

Economic feasibility determines whether the expected benefits associated with the project outweigh the expected costs sufficiently to make the project financially attractive. Cost and benefit estimates should be made for

FIGURE 12.7

Feasibility analysis

The feasibility analysis examines the technical, economic, legal, operational, and schedule feasibility of a proposed system.

© Carballo/Shutterstock.com

multiple years to allow for calculation of the internal rate of return or net present value of the project as discussed in Chapter 2. It is important to recognize that at this early stage of the development process, the cost and benefit amounts are rough estimates and subject to change should the project continue. So while the mathematics involved may make it appear that the results are precise, in actuality, the result is no more accurate than the cash flow estimates, which are often no more than refined guesses. Table 12.3 lists some of the typical costs and benefits that need to be considered.

Organizations must guard against spending more than is appropriate as the success or failure of the systems development effort will, at least to some degree, be measured against meeting the project budget. The United Kingdom Ministry of Defence wasted millions of pounds on a planned £1.3 billion (approximately $2.2 billion) information system to enable the army to recruit online. One benefit to be derived from the project was to increase recruitment levels above historic levels. This goal has not been achieved.[14]

legal feasibility: The determination of whether laws or regulations may prevent or limit a systems development project.

Legal feasibility determines whether laws or regulations may prevent or limit a systems development project. Legal feasibility involves an analysis of existing and future laws to determine the likelihood of legal action against the systems development project and the possible consequences of such action. Nearly every country in Europe and many in Latin America, Asia, and Africa have implemented data protection laws that prohibit the disclosure or misuse of information held on private individuals. These laws make it possible for the Human Resources departments of multinational companies to share personal employee data across country borders only in limited circumstances.

operational feasibility: Concerned with how the system will be accepted by people and how well it will meet various system performance expectations.

Operational feasibility is concerned with how the system will be accepted by people and how well it will meet various system performance expectations. It takes into consideration people issues such as overcoming employee resistance to change, gaining managerial support for the system, providing sufficient motivation and training, and rationalizing any conflicts with organizational norms and policies. In other words, if the system is developed, will it be used? Operational feasibility also takes into account the need to meet certain system performance requirements (e.g., response time for frequent online transactions, number of concurrent users it must support, reliability, and ease of use) that are considered important to system users and stakeholders.

schedule feasibility: The determination of whether the project can be completed in a reasonable amount of time.

Schedule feasibility determines whether the project can be completed in a reasonable amount of time. This process involves balancing the time and resource requirements of the project with other projects. Many projects that involve delivering a new financial information system have a desired start-up date at the beginning of the organization's fiscal year. Unfortunately, it is not

TABLE **12.3** Cost/benefit table

Costs	Year 1	Year 2	Year ..	Year N
Costs to analyze, design, construct, integrate and test, and implement system				
Employees				
Vendor				
Software package purchase and customization				
Travel				
Hardware costs				
Software costs				
Other costs				
Initial costs to establish system				
Software license fees				
New hardware costs				
Cost to upgrade existing hardware				
Cost to upgrade network				
User training				
Purchase of any necessary data				
Cost to migrate existing data to new system				
Other costs				
Ongoing operations costs				
Software lease or rental fees				
Hardware lease or rental fees				
Network usage fees				
System operations and support staff				
User training				
Increased electric and other utilities				
Costs associated with disaster recovery				
Other costs				
Tangible benefits (can be quantified in dollars)				
Reduction in current costs				
Reduction in current staff				
Reduction in inventory levels				
Reduction in computer hardware costs				
Reduction in software costs				
Other reduced costs				
Increase in revenue				
Increase in sales from reaching new customers				
Increase in sales from charging more				
Acceleration in cash flow				
Other increases in revenue				
Intangible benefits (difficult to quantify in dollars)				
Improved customer service				
Improved employee morale				

always possible to meet this date and so a compromise must be made—deliver part of the system at the start of the fiscal year or wait another year to deliver the full system.

Prepare Draft of Investigation Report

systems investigation report:
A summary of the results of the systems investigation with a recommendation of a course of action.

The systems investigation ends with production of a **systems investigation report** that summarizes the results of the systems investigation and recommends a course of action: continue on into systems analysis, modify the project in some manner and perhaps repeat the systems investigation, or drop the project altogether. See Figure 12.8. A typical table of contents for the systems investigation report is shown in Figure 12.9.

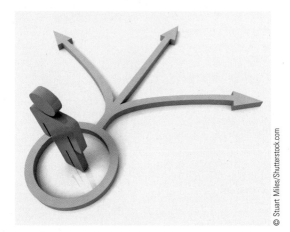

© Stuart Miles/Shutterstock.com

FIGURE 12.8

Systems investigation recommendation

Continue on into systems analysis, modify the project in some manner and perhaps repeat the systems investigation, or drop the project altogether.

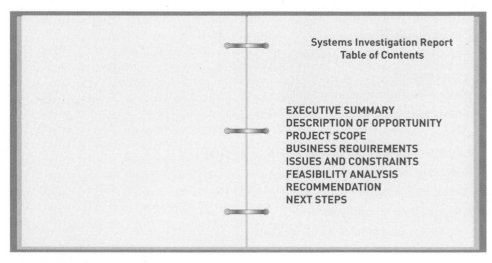

**Systems Investigation Report
Table of Contents**

**EXECUTIVE SUMMARY
DESCRIPTION OF OPPORTUNITY
PROJECT SCOPE
BUSINESS REQUIREMENTS
ISSUES AND CONSTRAINTS
FEASIBILITY ANALYSIS
RECOMMENDATION
NEXT STEPS**

© 2016 Cengage Learning

FIGURE 12.9

Table of contents for systems investigation report

A typical systems investigation report begins with an executive summary and ends with a list of next steps.

Review Results of Investigation with Steering Team

The systems investigation report is reviewed with the steering team to gain their input and counsel. Typically the written report is shared in advance and then the project manager and selected members of the team meet with the steering team to present their recommendations.

After the project review, the steering team might agree with the recommendations of the systems development team, or it might suggest a change in

INFORMATION SYSTEMS @ WORK

Queensland Health Payroll Debacle

On August 7, 2013, Queensland, the second largest state in Australia, banned IS giant IBM from entering into any new contracts with the state government. The government claims that IBM rolled out a flawed payroll system for Queensland's healthcare system that resulted in thousands of payroll errors over a period of months. Scrambling to fix the problem, Queensland Health eventually set up a system of work processes that requires over 1,000 employees to process data. The Queensland government estimates that this new system will cost the government $1.2 billion AUD (approximately $1.12 USD) to implement over the next eight years.

Queensland's problems, however, did not begin with IBM. In 2003, the government established its Shared Services Initiative to coordinate and improve the efficiency of information services across its many departments and agencies. The government turned to a company called CorpTech to deliver human resource and payroll services. CorpTech, however, made little progress. It employed a wide range of contractors, and only one company, Logistica, succeeded in deploying financial services to 12 agencies and payroll services to one department, Housing. As a result, the government decided to award a contract to one prime contractor who would oversee the entire Shared Services Initiative. By the time IBM won the contract in 2007, the development of a new Health payroll system had become an urgent priority. The company maintaining its legacy system, LATTICE, stated that it would no longer service or update the system after June 30, 2008. By October 2008, according a Queensland inquiry, IBM had not achieved any of its Shared Service goals. Having been paid about $32 million of its $98 million contract, the company forecasted that the true cost to achieve the goals of the contract would run up to $181 million AUD (approximately $170 million USD). The government decided to abandon its Shared Service goals and focus only on building a new payroll system for Queensland Health.

What went wrong? The Queensland Health Payroll System Commission of Inquiry issued a 264-page report outlining the missteps in what it deemed to be one of the worst public administration failures in Australia. The first problem arose in defining the scope of the project. The Queensland government admitted that Queensland Health did not adequately communicate the business requirements for the new system. While IBM was documenting system requirements, the government pressured IBM to begin designing and developing the system. IBM issued a notice in its statement of work that the scope of the project would likely need to be redefined during development. Queensland also involved a large and ever-changing number of parties and individuals in the governance and oversight of the project. A formal report based on the Queensland inquiry noted "an unhealthy willingness to establish bureaucratic bodies to govern the Project" with no clear governance processes. Meanwhile, the miscommunication over business requirements led to a staggering 220 change orders to the original contract and a delay that meant that the system took three times longer to develop than anticipated. Finally, the new system was ready to be tested. User acceptance testing (UAT) found thousands of defects, and the UAT director warned Queensland not to go live with the program. The state ignored his advice and implemented the program in 2010. As the debacle came to public attention, the parties opted to execute manual "workarounds" to improve the system. The problem, however, was that not all the defects in the program had been identified.

In attempting to remedy the errors, Queensland insisted that IBM fix "the bugs" in the program. IBM responded that the program contained no "programming" errors and as such, IBM was not responsible for its failure. In November 2011, TechCorp assumed responsibility for the project, now called the "Payroll Stabilization Project." Queensland hired additional employees to support the new payroll system. Since the stabilization project began, the payroll staff increased from 650 to 1,010.

In response to Queensland's actions, an IBM spokesperson said, "As the prime contractor on a complex project, IBM must accept some responsibility for the issues experienced when the system went live in 2010. However, as acknowledged by the Commission's report, the successful delivery of the project was rendered near impossible by the State failing to properly articulate its requirements or commit to a fixed scope. IBM operated in a complex governance structure to deliver a technically sound system. When the system went live it was hindered primarily through business process and data migration issues outside of IBM's contractual, and practical, control."

Queensland took the issue of blame to court in December 2013, hoping to place some of the cost for the system's failures upon IBM. The suit, however, may well be settled out of court as both parties find some means of compromising.

Discussion Questions

1. Only four companies applied for the Queensland Health payroll project and one withdrew during the bidding process. What management practices in the Queensland government should have raised red flags for IBM both before and after it accepted the contract?
2. Which party bears more responsibility for the failure of the IS project? Why?

Critical Thinking Questions

1. Identify the mistakes made at each stage of the software development process.

2. What could IBM have done to prevent the release of its defective payroll system?

SOURCES: Chesterman, The Honourable Richard N., "Queensland Health Payroll System Commission of Inquiry," The Government of Queensland Web site, July 31, 2013, *www.healthpayrollinquiry.qld .gov.au/__data/assets/pdf_file/0014/207203/Queensland-Health -Payroll-System-Commission-of-Inquiry-Report-31-July-2013.pdf*; Sharwood, Simon, "Australian State to Sue IBM over $AUD1bn Project Blowout," *The Register*, December 6, 2013, *www.theregister.co.uk /2013/12/06/australian_state_to_sue_ibm_over_aud1bn_project _blowout/*; Charette, Robert N., "Queensland Government Bans IBM from IT Contracts," *IEEE Spectrum*, August 7, 2013, *http://spectrum .ieee.org/riskfactor/computing/it/queensland-government-bans-ibm -from-it-contracts.*

project focus to concentrate more directly on meeting a specific company objective. Another alternative is that everyone might decide that the project is not feasible and thus cancel the effort. This input is used to finalize the systems investigation report.

SYSTEMS ANALYSIS

After a project has completed the investigation phase and been approved for further study, the next step is to answer the question, "What must the information system do to solve the problem?" The overall emphasis of analysis is gathering data on the existing system, determining the requirements for the new system, considering alternatives within identified constraints, and investigating the feasibility of alternative solutions. The primary outcome of systems analysis is a prioritized list of systems requirements and a recommendation of how to proceed with the project. The steps in the systems analysis phase are outlined next and discussed in the following pages. Note that many of the steps were also performed during systems investigation.

1. Identify and recruit team leader and team members
2. Develop budget and schedule for systems analysis activities
3. Study existing system
4. Develop prioritized set of requirements
5. Perform preliminary make-versus-buy analysis
6. Identify and evaluate alternative solutions
7. Perform feasibility analysis
8. Prepare draft of systems analysis report
9. Review results of systems analysis with steering team

The British firm Think IS offers B2B solutions that provide its customers with the tools and control needed to promote and grow their business. The company recognized an opportunity to create a new system product targeted at financial institutions that would enable them to adapt their products to the personal profile of each customer and to identify profitable Web traffic. A systems analysis team was formed to identify the business requirements and specify functions that it must perform. The system was eventually built at a cost of just over $1 million.[15]

Identify and Recruit Team Leader and Team Members

In many cases, there is some personnel turnover when moving from the systems investigation to the systems analysis phase. Some players may no longer be available to participate in the project and new members with a different set of skills and knowledge may be required. So the first step in systems analysis is to identify and recruit the team leader and members. Ideally, some members of the original investigation team will participate in the systems analysis to provide project continuity.

Develop Budget and Schedule for Systems Analysis Activities

After the participants in the systems analysis phase are determined, this group develops a list of specific objectives and activities required to complete the systems analysis. They also establish a schedule complete with major milestones to track project progress. The group also prepares a budget of the resources required to complete the systems analysis including any travel required and funds to cover the use of outside resources.

Study Existing System

The purpose of studying the system is to identify the strengths and weaknesses of the existing system and examine current inputs, outputs, processes, security and controls, and system performance. While analysis of the existing system is important to understanding the current situation, the study team must recognize that after a point of diminishing returns, further study of the existing system will fail to yield additional useful information.

Many useful sources of information about the existing system are available, as shown in Figure 12.10. JAD sessions (already discussed), direct observation, and surveys are often used to uncover pertinent information.

Internal Sources	External Sources
Users, stakeholders, and managers	Customers
Organization charts	Suppliers
Forms and documents	Stockholders
Procedure manuals and policies	Government agencies
Financial reports	Competitors
IS manuals	Outside groups
Other measures of business process	Journals, etc.
	Consultants

© 2016 Cengage Learning

FIGURE 12.10

Internal and external sources of data for systems analysis

JAD sessions, direct observation, and surveys are often used to uncover data for systems analysis.

Direct Observation

direct observation: Directly observing the existing system in action by one or more members of the analysis team.

With **direct observation**, one or more members of the analysis team directly observe the existing system in action. This approach provides excellent insight into how things work and can reveal important problems and opportunities that would be difficult to obtain using other data collection methods. In addition, it provides an opportunity for users to state their concerns and express their ideas for improvement. An example would be observing the work procedures, reports, and computer screens associated with an accounts payable system being considered for replacement. See Figure 12.11.

FIGURE 12.11

Direct observation

Direct observation is a method of data collection. One or more members of the analysis team directly observe the existing system in action.

Surveys

When many system users and stakeholders are spread over a wide geographic area, the use of a survey might be the best method to obtain their input on a set of standard questions. Typically, a limited sample survey with a few select users is first conducted to fine-tune the survey before it is widely distributed.

Develop Prioritized Set of Requirements

The purpose of this step is to determine user, stakeholder, and organizational needs for the new or modified system. A set of requirements must be determined for system processes (including inputs, processing, outputs, and feedback), databases, security and controls, and system performance. See Figure 12.12. As requirements are identified, an attempt is made to prioritize them into one of the following categories:

- **Critical**—Almost all users agree that the system is simply not acceptable unless it performs this function or provides this capability. Lack of this feature or capability would cause users to call a halt to the project.
- **Medium priority**—While highly desirable, most users agree that although their work will be somewhat impaired, the system will still be effective without this feature or capability. Some users may argue strongly for this feature or capability but in the end would want the project to continue.
- **Low priority**—Most users agree that their ability to use the system to accomplish their work will only be minimally impaired by lack of this feature or capability although it would be "nice to have." Almost no user will argue strongly for this feature or capability.

Identifying, confirming, and prioritizing system requirements is perhaps the single most critical step in the entire traditional system development life cycle. When following the traditional system development process, failure to identify a requirement or an incorrect definition of a requirement may not be

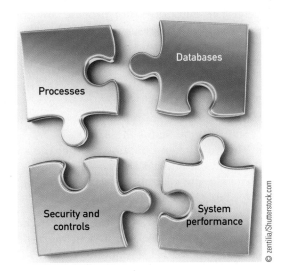

FIGURE 12.12

Defining system requirements

System requirements must be checked for consistency so that they all fit together.

discovered until much later in the project, causing much rework, additional costs, and delay in the systems effort.

JAD sessions with a cross section of users and stakeholders in the project is an effective way to define system requirements. A technique often used in a JAD session is to ask managers and decision makers to list only the factors that are critical to the success of their areas of the organization. A CSF for a production manager might be adequate raw materials from suppliers, while a CSF for a sales representative could be a list of customers currently buying a certain type of product. Starting from these CSFs, the processes, databases, security and control, and performance requirements associated with each CSF can be identified.

Processes

The functional decomposition performed during the investigation phase has identified the majority of the processes included within the scope of the system. Now the processes must be further defined so that they will be practical, efficient, economical, accurate, and timely to avoid delays. In addition, the individuals or organizations responsible for completing each step in the process must be identified.

A process requires input that it uses to create output. Often feedback is generated. The questions that need to be answered during system analysis are: what data entities are required, where will this data come from, what methods will be used to collect and enter the data, who is responsible for data input, and what edits should be performed on the input data to ensure that it is accurate and complete? Another important consideration is the creation of an audit trail that records the source of each data item, when it entered the system, and who entered it. The audit trail may also need to capture when the data is accessed or changed and by whom.

Because the success of a new system is highly dependent upon the acceptability of its output, the identification of common system outputs such as printed reports, screens, and files is critical to developing a complete set of system requirements.

Data-Flow Diagram

data-flow diagram (DFD): A diagram used during both the analysis and design phases to document the processes of the current system or to provide a model of a proposed new system.

A **data-flow diagram (DFD)** is a diagram used during both the analysis and design phases to document the processes of the current system or to provide a model of a proposed new system. It shows not only the various processes within the system but also where the data needed for each process comes from, where the output of each process will be sent, and what data will be stored and where. The DFD does not provide any information about the process timing (e.g., whether the various processes happen in sequence or are parallel).

DFDs are easy to develop and easily understood by nontechnical people. Data-flow diagrams use four primary symbols:

data-flow line: A line that includes arrows showing the direction of data movement.

process symbol: A symbol that identifies the function being performed.

entity symbol: A symbol that shows either the source or destination of the data.

data store symbol: A symbol that reveals a storage location for data.

1. The data-flow line includes arrows that show the direction of data movement
2. The process symbol identifies the function being performed (e.g., Check Status, Issue Status Message)
3. The entity symbol shows either the source or destination of the data (e.g., Customer, Warehouse)
4. A data store symbol reveals a storage location for data (e.g., Pending Orders, Accounts Receivable)

Figure 12.13 shows a level 1 DFD. Each of the processes shown in this diagram could be documented in more detail to show the subprocesses and create a level 2 DFD. Frequently, level 3 DFD diagrams are created and used in the analysis and design phases.

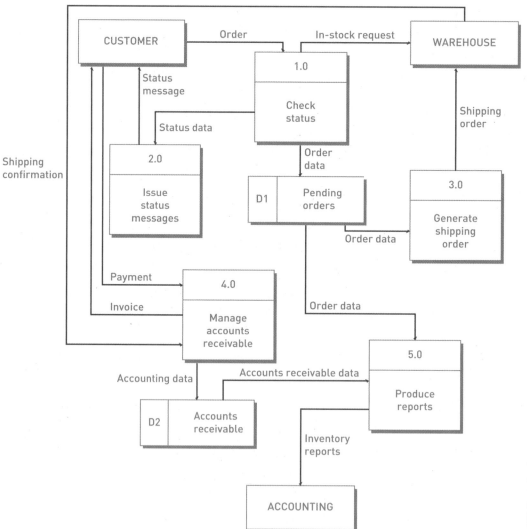

FIGURE 12.13

Data-flow diagram

A data-flow diagram documents the processes of the current system or provides a model of a proposed new system.

Databases

Data modeling is defining the databases that the system will draw data from as well as any new databases that it will create. Entity-relationship diagrams is one technique that is frequently used for this purpose.

Entity-Relationship (ER) Diagrams

Recall from Chapter 5 that an ER diagram is used to show logical relationships among data entities such as in Figure 12.14. An ER diagram (or any other modeling tool) cannot by itself fully describe a business problem or solution because it lacks descriptions of the related activities. It is, however, a good place to start because it describes entity types and attributes about which data might need to be collected for processing.

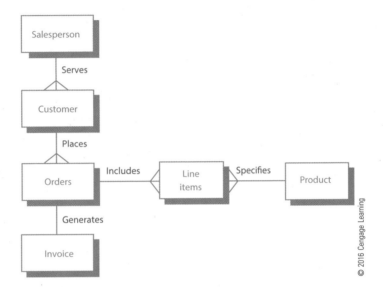

FIGURE 12.14

Entity-relationship (ER) diagram for a customer order database

Development of ER diagrams helps ensure that the logical structure of application programs is consistent with the data relationships in the database.

© 2016 Cengage Learning

Computer-Aided Software Engineering (CASE)

Many systems development teams use computer-aided software engineering (CASE) software to document both the existing systems and proposed solutions. Most CASE tools have generalized graphics programs that can generate a variety of diagrams and figures. Entity-relationship diagrams, data-flow diagrams, and other diagrams can be developed using CASE tools to help describe the existing system.

As requirements are developed and agreed on, entity-relationship diagrams, data-flow diagrams, screen and report layout forms, and other types of documentation are stored in a CASE repository. These documents can be used later as a reference during the rest of systems development or even for a different, but related systems development project.

Security and Control

Security and control considerations need to be an integral part of the entire system development process. Unfortunately, they are often treated as an afterthought, after system requirements have been defined and system design is well underway. This approach usually leads to problems that become security vulnerabilities, which can cause major security breaches resulting in significant legal and system modification expenses. A more effective and less costly approach is to define security and control requirements when other system requirements are being identified. The following list outlines areas where requirements need to be defined:[16]

- Access controls including controls to authenticate and permit access only to authorized individuals

- Encryption of electronic customer information, including while in transit or in storage on networks or systems to which unauthorized individuals may have access
- Dual control procedures, segregation of duties, and employee background checks for employees with responsibilities for or access to customer, employee, or organization-sensitive information
- Monitoring systems and procedures to detect actual and attempted attacks on or intrusions into information systems
- Measures to protect against destruction, loss, or damage of customer, employee, or organization-sensitive data due to potential environmental hazards, such as fire and water damage, technological failures, or disasters such as hurricanes and terrorism
- Business resumption procedures to get the system up and running with no major business disruption and with no loss of data in the event of a disaster (e.g., fire, hurricane, terrorism)

People with a special interest in security and control include the organization's internal auditors and members of senior management. They should provide input and advice during the systems analysis and design phases.

System security and control requirements need to be defined in the context of the organization's existing policies, standards, and guidelines. See Figure 12.15. For example, the Gramm-Leach-Bliley Act requires companies legally defined as financial institutions to ensure the security and confidentiality of customer information. Thus, financial institutions have established policies, standards, and guidelines to which any new information system must adhere.

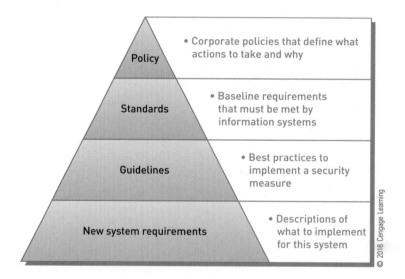

FIGURE 12.15

Context for new system security and control requirements

New system security and control requirements must be developed within the organization's existing policies, standards, and guidelines.

© 2016 Cengage Learning

System Performance

How well a system performs can be measured through its performance requirements. Failure to meet these system performance requirements results in unproductive workers, dissatisfied customers, and missed opportunities to deliver outstanding business results. System performance is usually determined by factors such as the following:

- **Timeliness of output.** Is the system generating output in time to meet organizational goals and operational objectives? Since GEICO began advertising that you can save 15 percent on auto insurance in just 15 minutes, speed has become a major factor in selecting an insurance company. Nationwide touts its online tool as the fastest path to a quick car insurance quote. The General auto insurance boasts, "Give us two minutes and we'll give you an auto insurance quote."

- **Ease of use.** Developing applications that managers and employees can easily learn and use is essential to ensure that people will work with the applications productively.
- **Scalability.** A scalable information system can handle business growth and increased business volume without a noticeable degradation in performance.
- **System response time.** The average response time for frequent online transactions is an important factor in determining worker productivity and customer service.
- **Availability.** Availability measures the hours per month the system is scheduled to be available for use. Systems typically must be unavailable a few hours a week to allow for software upgrades and maintenance.
- **Reliability.** Reliability is the hours the system is actually available for use divided by the hours the system is scheduled to be available and is expressed as a percentage. Worker productivity decreases and customer dissatisfaction increases as system reliability decreases.

Perform Preliminary Make-Versus-Buy Analysis

Today, most organizations purchase or rent the software they need rather than make it—simply because it costs too much and takes too long to build a quality information system. Organizations elect to build proprietary systems only when its information system requirements are unique. This may be because of the nature of the business or because the organization is attempting to build an information system that will provide it with a strategic competitive advantage.

A software application can vary from an unmodified, commercial off-the-shelf (COTS) software package at one extreme to a custom, written-from-scratch program at the other extreme. See Figure 12.16. Between those two extremes is a range of options based on the degree of customization. The greater the amount of customization, the greater is the cost to implement. A comparison of the two extreme approaches is shown in Table 12.4. One question to answer during systems analysis is: which solution approach is best for this particular system? This decision is often called the **make-versus-buy decision**.

The analysis team should assess the software marketplace to determine whether existing packages can meet the organization's needs. The primary tool

make-versus-buy decision: The decision regarding whether to obtain the necessary software from internal or external sources.

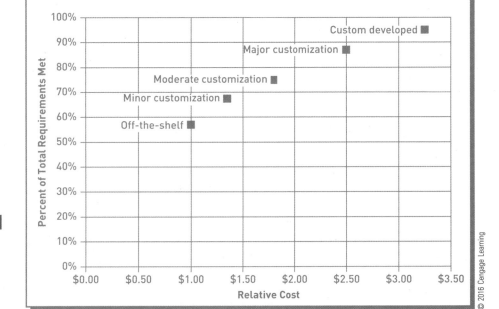

Relative cost of custom software

The more customization in software, the greater is the cost to implement it.

TABLE **12.4** Comparison of developed and off-the-shelf software

Factor	Develop (Make)	Off-the-Shelf (Buy)
Cost	The cost to build the system can be difficult to estimate accurately and is frequently higher than off-the-shelf	The true cost to implement an off-the-shelf solution is also difficult to estimate accurately but is likely to be less than a custom software solution
Needs	Custom software is more likely to satisfy your needs	Might not get exactly what you need
Process improvement	Tend to automate existing business processes even if they are poor	Adoption of a package may simplify or streamline a poor existing business process
Quality	Quality can vary depending on the development team	Can assess the quality before buying
Speed	Can take years to develop	Can acquire it now
Staffing and support	Requires in-house skilled resources to build and support a custom-built solution	Requires paying the vendor for support
Competitive advantage	Can develop a competitive advantage with good software	Other organizations can have the same software and same advantage

© 2016 Cengage Learning

request for proposal (RFP):
A formal document that outlines an organization's hardware or software needs and requests vendors to develop a detailed proposal of how they would meet those needs and at what cost.

for doing this is the **request for proposal (RFP)**, a formal document that outlines an organization's hardware or software needs and requests vendors to develop a detailed proposal of how they would meet those needs and at what cost. See Figure 12.17. The RFP outlines the desired system and its requirements. It also identifies the pieces of data that the software vendor must include in the proposal. Insisting that all vendors provide the same data in a consistent manner reduces the time and effort to compare vendor proposals. The RFP is sent to vendors who are capable of providing the desired software.

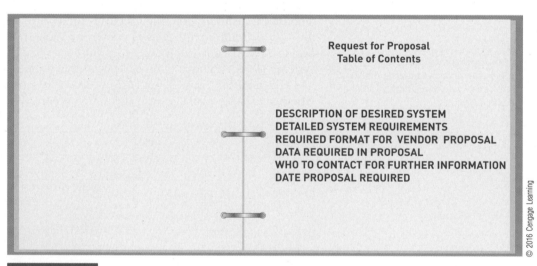

Request for Proposal
Table of Contents

DESCRIPTION OF DESIRED SYSTEM
DETAILED SYSTEM REQUIREMENTS
REQUIRED FORMAT FOR VENDOR PROPOSAL
DATA REQUIRED IN PROPOSAL
WHO TO CONTACT FOR FURTHER INFORMATION
DATE PROPOSAL REQUIRED

© 2016 Cengage Learning

FIGURE 12.17

Recommended table of contents for a request for proposal
The RFP outlines the desired system and its requirements, identifying the pieces of data that the software vendor must include in the proposal.

Before sending out the RFP, the team should ask the organization's purchasing and legal departments whether any vendor under consideration should be excluded because of their financial standing, credit worthiness, reputation within the software industry, or involvement in disputes with customers or governments.

The systems analysis team will evaluate the vendor proposals and narrow their choice down to the most promising two or three solutions as alternatives for further evaluation. Often this may require a visit to the vendor's place of business to meet managers and observe a demo of the vendor's system.

Identify and Evaluate Alternative Solutions

The analysis team must think creatively and consider several system solution options. By looking at the problem in new or different ways, questioning current assumptions and the way things are done today, and removing current constraints and barriers, the team is free to identify highly creative and effective information system solutions. Such critical analysis requires unbiased and careful questioning of whether system elements are related in the most effective ways, considering new or different relationships among system elements, and possibly introducing new elements into the system. Critical analysis also involves challenging users about their needs and determining which are truly critical requirements rather than "nice to have" features.

Pareto principle (80–20 rule): An observation that for many events, roughly 80 percent of the effects come from 20 percent of the causes.

The Pareto principle (also known as the 80–20 rule) is a rule of thumb used in business that helps people focus on the vital 20 percent that generate 80 percent of the results. This principle means that implementing 20 percent of the system requirements can achieve 80 percent of the desired system benefits. An 80–20 option will have a low cost and quick completion schedule relative to other potential options. However, this option may not be an ideal solution and may not even be acceptable to the users, stakeholders, and the steering team who may be expecting more. Additional candidate solutions can be defined that implement all or most of the critical priority system requirements and team-selected subsets of the medium and low-priority requirements. Table 12.5 illustrates some of the many potential candidates the analysis team may want to evaluate.

TABLE 12.5 Additional candidates for systems analysis

Scope of system	Build system	Customize software package
Build system that meets all critical requirements, but no medium or low priority requirements	Option #1	
Modify package so that it meets all critical requirements, but no medium or low priority requirements		Option #2
Build system that meets 20% of all requirements that will provide 80% of the system benefits	Option #3	
Modify package so that it meets 20% of all requirements that will provide 80% of the system benefits		Option #4
Implement software package just as is with no customization to enable it to meet unique requirements		Option #5

© 2016 Cengage Learning

Perform Feasibility Analysis

At this stage in the system development process, the project team has identified several promising solutions based on implementing all or most of the critical requirements and various subsets of the medium and low-priority requirements. The feasibility analysis conducted during the investigation phase is repeated for each of these candidate solutions the team wants to consider. This time, the analysis can be more in-depth because more is known about the system and its requirements as well as the costs and benefits of the various options.

Prepare Draft of Systems Analysis Report

Systems analysis concludes with a formal systems analysis report summarizing the findings of this phase of the project. The table of contents for the systems analysis report is shown in Figure 12.18. This report is a more complete and detailed version of the systems investigation report. At this phase of the project, the costs and benefits of the project should be fairly accurate, certainly more accurate than at the end of the investigation phase. The team should also recommend whether to build the system or purchase or rent a software package (although the final vendor may not yet be selected).

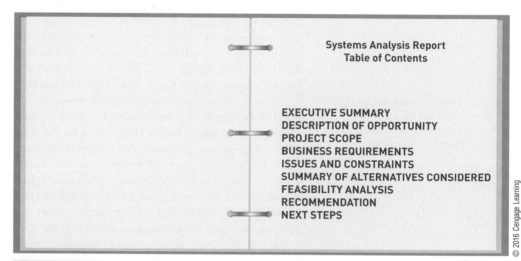

Systems Analysis Report
Table of Contents

EXECUTIVE SUMMARY
DESCRIPTION OF OPPORTUNITY
PROJECT SCOPE
BUSINESS REQUIREMENTS
ISSUES AND CONSTRAINTS
SUMMARY OF ALTERNATIVES CONSIDERED
FEASIBILITY ANALYSIS
RECOMMENDATION
NEXT STEPS

© 2016 Cengage Learning

FIGURE 12.18

Typical table of contents for a report on an existing system

The systems analysis report is a more complete and detailed version of the systems investigation report.

Review Results of Systems Analysis with Steering Team

The systems analysis report is presented to the project steering team with a recommendation to stop, revise, or go forward with the systems development project. Following the steering team meeting, the project team incorporates the recommendations and suggested changes into the final report. It is not unusual to need to request a change in the project scope, budget, benefits, or schedule based on the findings from the analysis phase. However, the project sponsor and the steering team must formally approve of any changes.

SYSTEMS DESIGN

systems design: The stage of systems development that answers the question, "How will the information system solve a problem?"

The purpose of systems design is to answer the question, "How will the information system solve this problem?" The primary result of the systems design phase is a technical design that details system outputs, inputs, controls, and user interfaces; specifies hardware, software, databases, telecommunications, personnel, and procedures; and shows how these components are interrelated. In other words, systems design creates a complete set of technical specifications that can be used to construct the information system. The steps in the systems design phase are outlined next and discussed in the following pages. Again, note that many of the steps were performed in the investigation and systems analysis phase but are now repeated with more current and complete information.

1. Identify and recruit team leader and team members
2. Develop schedule and budget for systems design activities

3. Design user interface
4. Design system security and controls
5. Design disaster recovery plan
6. Design database
7. Perform feasibility analysis
8. Prepare draft of systems design report
9. Review results of systems design with steering team
10. Finalize contract

Identify and Recruit Team Leader and Team Members

Because some personnel turnover is likely when moving from the systems analysis to the systems design phase, the first step in systems design is to identify and recruit the team leader and members. Ideally, some members of the systems analysis team will participate in the systems design to ensure project continuity.

Develop Schedule and Budget for Systems Design Activities

The systems design team begins by developing a list of specific objectives and activities required to complete the systems design. It also establishes a schedule complete with major milestones to track project progress. Some tasks may involve working with the steering team to resolve issues and questions raised during the review of the systems analysis phase. For example, if the systems analysis recommendation is to purchase or rent a software package, the systems design team must choose a vendor from the remaining contenders. The group also prepares a budget for completing the systems design, including any travel required and funds to cover the use of outside resources.

Design User Interface

How the user experiences the information system determines whether the system will be accepted and used. In speaking about the importance of user interface design for Apple software products, Jef Raskin, an interface expert, once said, "As far as the customer is concerned, the interface is the product."[17]

User interface design integrates concepts and methods from computer science, graphics design, and psychology to build interfaces that are accessible, easy to use, and efficient. Over the years, various authors have identified user interface design principles, including those listed in Table 12.6.[18,19]

TABLE 12.6 Principles of good user interface design

Principle	How to Apply
Strive for consistency	Consistent sequences of actions should be required in similar situations; identical terminology should be used in prompts, menus, and help screens; and consistent commands should be employed throughout.
Offer informative feedback	For every user action, there should be some system feedback. For frequent and minor actions, the response can be modest, while for infrequent and major actions, the response should be more substantial.
Offer simple error handling	As much as possible, design the system so the user cannot make a serious error. If an error is made, the system should be able to detect the error and offer simple, comprehensible instructions for handling the error.
One primary action per screen	Every screen should support a single action of real value to the user.
Provide progressive disclosure	Show only what is necessary on each screen. If the user is making a choice, show enough information to allow the user to choose, and then display details on a subsequent screen.
Strive for aesthetic integrity	The graphic design elements used in an interface should be simple and clean, pleasant to look at, and easy to understand.

User interface design must consider a number of components. Most systems provide a *sign-on procedure* that requires identification numbers, passwords, and other safeguards to improve security and prevent unauthorized use. With a *menu-driven system,* users select what they want to do from a list of alternatives. Most people can easily operate these types of systems. In addition, many designers incorporate a *help facility* into the system or program. When users want to know more about a program or feature or what type of response is expected, they can activate the help facility. Systems often use *lookup tables* to simplify and shorten data entry. For example, if you are entering a sales order for a company, you can type its abbreviation, such as ABCO. The program searches the customer table, normally stored on a disk, the Internet, or other storage device, and looks up the information you need to complete the sales order for the company abbreviated as ABCO.

Using screen painter software, an analyst can efficiently design the features, layout, and format of the user interface screens. See Figure 12.19. Several screens can be linked together to simulate how the user can move from screen to screen to accomplish tasks. Conducting an interactive screen design session with a few users at a time is an effective process for defining the system user interface.

© Pressmaster/Shutterstock.com

FIGURE 12.19

User interface design

Analysts can develop screen mock-ups and simulate how the user moves from screen to screen.

Design System Security and Controls

The systems analysis phase identified areas where system security and controls need to be defined. During the design phase, designers must develop specific system security and controls for all aspects of the information system, including hardware, software, database systems, telecommunications, and Internet operations as shown in Table 12.7. Security considerations involve error prevention, detection, and correction; disaster planning and recovery; and systems controls. The goal is to ensure secure systems without burdening users with many identification numbers and passwords for different applications.

After developing controls, they should be documented in standards manuals that indicate how to implement the controls. The controls should then be implemented and frequently reviewed. It is common practice to measure how much control techniques are used and to take action if the controls have not been implemented. Organizations often have *compliance departments* to make sure the IS department is adhering to its systems controls along with all local, state, and federal laws and regulations. See Figure 12.20.

TABLE **12.7** Using systems controls to enhance security

Controls	Description
Input controls	Maintain input integrity and security. Their purpose is to reduce errors while protecting the computer system against improper or fraudulent input. Input controls range from using standardized input forms to eliminating data-entry errors and using tight password and identification controls.
Processing controls	Deal with all aspects of processing and storage. The use of passwords and identification numbers, backup copies of data, and storage rooms that have tight security systems are examples of processing and storage controls.
Output controls	Ensure that output is handled correctly. In many cases, output generated from the computer system is recorded in a file that indicates the reports and documents that were generated, the time they were generated, and their final destinations.
Database controls	Deal with ensuring an efficient and effective database system. These controls include the use of identification numbers and passwords, without which a user is denied access to certain data and information. Many of these controls are provided by database management systems.
Telecommunications controls	Provide accurate and reliable data and information transfer among systems. Telecommunications controls include firewalls and encryption to ensure correct communication while eliminating the potential for fraud and crime.
Personnel controls	Make sure that only authorized personnel have access to certain systems to help prevent computer-related mistakes and crime. Personnel controls can involve the use of identification numbers and passwords that allow only certain people access to particular data and information. ID badges and other security devices (such as smart cards) can prevent unauthorized people from entering strategic areas in the information systems facility.

© 2016 Cengage Learning

FIGURE 12.20

Compliance department

The compliance department ensures that the information system adheres to all appropriate systems controls including local, state, and federal laws and regulations as well as pertinent industry standards.

© iStockphoto.com/GlobalStock

ETHICAL& SOCIETAL ISSUES

Hydro One: A Leader in Privacy Protection

It's not hard to get managers to agree that an information system should protect privacy. It's harder to make privacy a priority so that the system meets all its privacy requirements.

Hydro One, a Toronto-based supplier of electricity to the Canadian province of Ontario, faced this problem in developing its Advanced Distribution System (ADS) pilot project. As a smart solution, the ADS senses problems and reroutes power automatically to avoid outages and reduce the length of outages, reduces greenhouse gas emissions by facilitating the connection to renewable energy sources, and provides the company's 1.2 million customers with real-time data so that they can better manage their own energy consumption. In addition, Hydro One decided to adopt the principles of Privacy by Design (PbD).

The PbD approach is based on seven principles covering information systems, business practices, and infrastructure. A development team begins to apply these principles in the first stages of system development, where respect for privacy is a core foundational requirement, and continues through the stages of system development covered in this chapter and the next. The PbD idea is that it is not necessary to sacrifice privacy to design an effective information system; rather, organizations can and should design a system that provides both privacy and effectiveness. In 2010, the 32nd International Conference of Data Protection and Privacy Commissioners approved resolutions that recommended organizations adopt PbD principles as a fundamental concept and encouraged governments to incorporate those principles into future privacy policies and legislation in their respective countries. The Federal Trade Commission in the United States followed suit in 2012, urging U.S. companies to incorporate PbD practices.

Hydro One's ADS had four business objectives when it was conceived: to optimize power distribution, optimize network planning, improve distribution reliability, and optimize outage restoration. Early in the systems analysis stage, the analysts broke those four objectives into 30 specific capabilities that ADS must have to support 30 business processes, such as maintenance reporting and outage-related customer communications. The processes communicated, to varying degrees, with shareholders, customers, suppliers, and regulatory authorities. In these interfaces, privacy requirements were most at risk. For example, the grid domain will not retain any data about an individual customer's identity.

To make sure privacy requirements weren't violated, Hydro One adopted 12 security design principles such as "Compartmentalize elements with common security and privacy requirements." The company also looked at 60 threat scenarios, ranking each for seriousness (insignificant to catastrophic) and likelihood (rare to almost certain), to see if the design principles would protect against them. These scenarios included malicious code threats, physical threats, problems with identification and authentication, flawed implementation, eavesdropping, and cryptographic threats. The likelihood of a threat was based on three factors: motive, means, and opportunity. If all three are low, the likelihood is *rare*. If all are high, it is *almost certain*. Other combinations lead to *unlikely*, *possible*, and *likely*.

The team then came up with 28 privacy requirements. The ADS controls and monitors remote access into its information system. It records the data for each event: the type of event, the location within the system, the user or subject identity that initiated the event, and the outcome. The system detects unauthorized changes to the software. It also used real-time alarms and surveillance equipment to respond to physical intrusions at remote or unmanned facilities. Within the project lifecycle, ADS is scheduled for regular internal private assessments and audits. Hydro One had to take special precautions when collecting metering data from distributed generation devices owned by private individuals. The company ensured that no data regarding customer identity remains on any device running between the meter and the ADS system. Hydro One implemented measures so that an unauthorized recipient of data could not tie a transaction to a location or an individual.

The design process imposed requirements for the system's three business domains: the grid, services, and customers. This meant the company had to work hard to ensure the cooperation of groups and individuals interfacing with the system. However, by making sure that system design conformed to these privacy requirements, Hydro One today stands at the forefront of privacy practices.

Discussion Questions

1. What were the goals of the new Advanced Distribution System (ADS)? What steps did Hydro One take in the first stage of development of their ADS?
2. Think of four threats to the information system of a hospital emergency room. Evaluate their likelihood for the three factors in the case (motive, means, and opportunity) as low, medium, or high. For each threat, unless it scored low on all three, suggest a way to reduce at least one factor that you rated as medium or high.

Critical Thinking Questions

1. Why was developing and implementing Privacy by Design a challenge for systems like ADS?
2. What added costs are involved in implementing a standard like Privacy by Design? Should companies bear these costs? What advantages does developing a system that provides privacy protection provide for the company?

SOURCES: Dougherty, S., "Privacy by Design: From Resolution to Reality," IBM case study, *www.cio.gov.bc.ca/local/cio/informationsecurity/documents/PS_2011_PDFs/Dougherty_Steven-WorkshopF.pdf*, accessed June 17, 2014; Hydro One Web site, *www.hydroone.com*, accessed June 17, 2014; Hill, K., "Why Privacy by Design Is the New Corporate Hotness," *Forbes, www.forbes.com/sites/kashmirhill/2011/07/28/why-privacy-by-design-is-the-new-corporate-hotness*, July 28, 2011; Cavoukian, A., "About PbD," Privacy by Design Web site, *www.privacybydesign.ca*, accessed January 23, 2012; FTC Report, "Protecting Consumer Privacy in an Era of Rapid Change: Recommendations for Businesses and Policymakers," March 2012, *www.ftc.gov/sites/default/files/documents/reports/federal-trade-commission-report-protecting-consumer-privacy-era-rapid-change-recommendations/120326privacyreport.pdf*; accessed June 17, 2014; "Hydro One Showcases Distribution System Modernization," Hydro One News Release, March 6, 2012, *www.hydroone.com/OurCompany/Media Centre/Documents/NewsReleases2012/03_06_2012_Distribution_System_Modernization.pdf*.

Design Disaster Recovery Plan

disaster recovery plan:
A documented process to recover an organization's business information system assets including hardware, software, data, networks, and facilities in the event of a disaster.

A **disaster recovery plan** is a documented process to recover an organization's business information system assets including hardware, software, data, networks, and facilities in the event of a disaster. It is a component of the organization's overall business continuity plan, which also includes occupant emergency plan, continuity of operations plan, and an incident management plan. The disaster recovery plan focuses on technology recovery and identifies the people or the teams responsible to take action in the event of a disaster, what exactly these people will do when a disaster strikes, and the information system resources required to support critical business processes.

Disasters can be natural or manmade as shown in Table 12.8. In performing disaster recovery planning, organizations should think in terms of not being able to gain access to their normal place of business for an extended period of time, such as several months. See Figure 12.21.

TABLE 12.8 Various disasters can disrupt business operations

Intentional Man Made Disasters	Accidental Man Made Disasters	Natural Disasters
Sabotage	Auto accident knocks down power lines to data center	Flood
Terrorism	Backhoe digs up a telecommunications line	Tsunami
Civil unrest	Operator error	Hurricane/cyclone
	Fire	Earthquake
		Volcanic eruption

© 2016 Cengage Learning

FIGURE 12.21

Disaster recovery planning

Disasters can hit unexpectedly and affect operations for months.

© Petrov Stanislav/Shutterstock.com

mission-critical processes:
Processes that play a pivotal role in an organization's continued operations and goal attainment.

As part of defining the business continuity plan, organizations conduct a business impact analysis to identify critical business processes and the resources that support them. The recovery time for an information system resource should match the recovery time objective for the most critical business processes that depend on that resource. Some business processes are more pivotal to continued operations and goal attainment than others. These processes are called **mission-critical processes**. An order-processing system, for example, is usually considered mission-critical. Without it, the sales organization cannot continue its daily activities that generate the cash flow needed to keep the business operating.

For some companies, personnel backup can be critical. Without the right number of trained employees, the business process can't function. For information system hardware, hot and cold sites can be used as backups. A duplicate, operational hardware system that is ready for use (or immediate access to one through a specialized vendor) is an example of a hot site. If the primary computer has problems, the hot site can be used immediately as a backup. However, the hot site must be situated so that it will not be affected by the same disaster. Another approach is to use a cold site, which is a computer environment that includes rooms, electrical service, telecommunications links, data storage devices, and similar equipment. If the primary computer site has problems, backup computer hardware is brought into the cold site, and the complete system is made operational.

Cloud computing has added another dimension to disaster recovery planning. If your organization is hit by a disaster, information systems that are running on the cloud are likely to be operational and accessible by workers from anywhere they can access the Internet. Data is also stored safely and securely at the site of the cloud-computing service provider, which could be hundreds of miles from the organization. On the other hand, if the cloud service provider is hit by a disaster, it may cause a serious business disruption for your organization even though it is otherwise unaffected by a distant disaster. Thus, part of the evaluation of a cloud service provider must include analysis of the provider's disaster recovery plans.

Files and databases can be protected by making a copy of all files and databases changed during the last few days or the last week, a technique called incremental backup. This approach to backup uses an image log, which is a separate file that contains only changes to applications. Whenever an application is run, an image log is created that contains all changes made to all files. If a problem occurs with a database, an old database with the last full backup of the data, along with the image log, can be used to re-create the current database.

Organizations can also hire outside companies to help them perform disaster planning and recovery. EMC, for example, offers data backup in its Recover-Point product.[20] For individuals and some applications, backup copies of important files can be placed on the Internet. *Failover* is another approach to backup. When a server, network, or database fails or is no longer functioning, failover automatically switches applications and other programs to a redundant or replicated server, network, or database to prevent an interruption of service. SteelEye's LifeKeeper[21] and Application Continuous Availability by NeverFail[22] are examples of failover software. Failover is especially important for applications that must be operational at all times. See Figure 12.22.

Design Database

As discussed in Chapter 5, the database provides a user view of data and makes it possible to add and modify data, store and retrieve data, manipulate the data, and generate reports. One of the steps in designing a database involves "telling" the DBMS the logical and physical structure of the data and the relationships among the data for each user. This description is called a schema and is entered into the DBMS using a data definition language. A data definition language (DDL) is a collection of instructions and commands that define and describe data and relationships in a specific database.

Another important step designing the database is to establish a data dictionary, a detailed description of all data used in the database. A data dictionary is valuable in maintaining an efficient database that stores reliable information with no redundancy and makes it easy to modify the database when necessary. Data dictionaries also help computer and system programmers who require a detailed description of data elements stored in a database to create the code to access the data.

hot site: A duplicate, operational hardware system or immediate access to one through a specialized vendor.

cold site: A computer environment that includes rooms, electrical service, telecommunications links, data storage devices, and the like.

incremental backup: A backup copy of all files changed during the last few days or the last week.

image log: A separate file that contains only changes to applications.

schema: A description of the logical and physical structure of data and the relationships among the data for each user.

data definition language (DDL): A collection of instructions and commands that define and describe data and relationships in a specific database.

data dictionary: A detailed description of all data used in the database.

FIGURE **12.22**

Disaster recovery service

Companies that suffer a disaster can employ a disaster recovery service, which can back up critical data and provide a facility from which to operate and communications equipment to stay in touch with customers.

preliminary evaluation: An evaluation that begins during systems analysis and identifies the two or three strongest contenders.

final evaluation: An evaluation that begins with a detailed investigation of the contenders' proposals as well as discussions with two or three customers of each vendor.

performance evaluation test: A comparison of vendor options conducted in a computing environment (e.g., computing hardware, operating system software, database management system) and with a workload (e.g., number of concurrent users, database size, and number of transactions) that matches its intended operating conditions.

Adhering to the standards defined in the data dictionary also makes it easy to share data among various organizations without the need for extensive data scrubbing and translation.

Choose Vendor

A **preliminary evaluation** of software packages and vendors began during systems analysis when the two or three strongest contenders were identified. The **final evaluation** begins with a detailed investigation of the contenders' proposals as well as discussions with two or three customers of each vendor.

The vendors should be asked to make a final presentation and to fully demonstrate their solution using a **performance evaluation test** conducted in a computing environment (e.g., computing hardware, operating system software, database management system) and with a workload (e.g., number of concurrent users, database size, and number of transactions) that matches the intended operating conditions. Such a test can help measure system performance attributes such as ease of use and response time.

At this point, the design team should be in a good position for the make-versus-buy decision and, if the decision is to buy, to select the best vendor. Selecting a vendor solution involves weighing the following factors:

- How well the vendor's solution matches the needs of the users and business
- Results of the performance evaluation test
- Relative costs and benefits associated with each alternative
- The technical, economic, legal, operational, and schedule feasibility
- Input from your legal and purchasing resources
- Feedback from customers of each vendor

Perform Feasibility Analysis

When implementing information systems hardware and software, several choices are available, including purchase, lease, or rent. Cost objectives and constraints set for the system play a significant role in the choice, as do the advantages and disadvantages of each. In addition, traditional financial tools, including net present value and internal rate of return, can be used. Table 12.9 summarizes the advantages and disadvantages of these financial options.

TABLE 12.9 Advantages and disadvantages of acquisition options

Renting (e.g., Software as a Service or cloud computing)	
Advantages	**Disadvantages**
No risk of obsolescence	No ownership of equipment
No long-term financial investment	High monthly costs
No initial investment of funds	Restrictive rental agreements
Maintenance usually included	Data security and disaster recovery concerns

Leasing (intermediate to long-term option)	
Advantages	**Disadvantages**
No risk of obsolescence	High cost of canceling lease
No long-term financial investment	Longer time commitment than renting
No initial investment of funds	No ownership of equipment
Less expensive than renting	Data security and disaster recovery concerns

Purchasing (long-term option)	
Advantages	**Disadvantages**
Total control over equipment	High initial investment
Can sell equipment at any time	Additional cost of maintenance
Can depreciate equipment	Possibility of obsolescence
Low cost if owned for a number of years	Cost of data security and disaster recovery

Prepare Draft of Systems Design Report

Systems design concludes with a formal systems design report summarizing the findings of this phase of the project. Any changes from the systems analysis findings are highlighted and explained. The table of contents for the systems design report is shown in Figure 12.23. This report is a more complete and detailed version of the systems investigation report.

Review Results of Systems Design with Steering Team

The systems design report is presented to the project steering team with a recommendation to stop, revise, or go forward with the systems development project. The steering team carefully reviews the recommendations because if the decision is to proceed, considerable human and financial resources will be committed and legally binding vendor contracts will be signed. Following the steering team meeting, the project team incorporates the recommendations and changes suggested into the final report.

At the end of the design phase, organizations employing the traditional systems development life cycle freeze the scope and the user and business requirements. Any potential changes that are identified or suggested after this point must go through a formal scope change process. This process requires the organization to assess how the proposed changes affect the project feasibility, cost, and schedule. It may be necessary to rerun net present value and return on investment calculations. Next, the proposed changes are presented to the project steering team along with their associated costs and schedule impact.

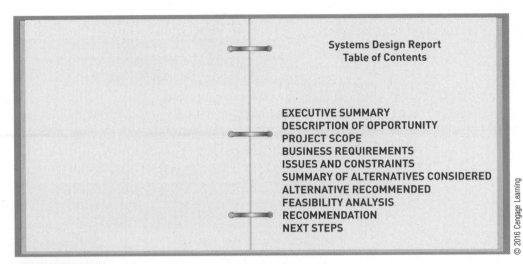

Systems Design Report
Table of Contents

EXECUTIVE SUMMARY
DESCRIPTION OF OPPORTUNITY
PROJECT SCOPE
BUSINESS REQUIREMENTS
ISSUES AND CONSTRAINTS
SUMMARY OF ALTERNATIVES CONSIDERED
ALTERNATIVE RECOMMENDED
FEASIBILITY ANALYSIS
RECOMMENDATION
NEXT STEPS

© 2016 Cengage Learning

FIGURE 12.23

Typical table of contents for a systems design report
The systems design report is a more complete and detailed version of the systems investigation report.

The steering team must approve the changes before the project team can begin work to incorporate them into the current design. Frequently, the steering team disapproves changes to ensure that the project is completed without exceeding the current budget and schedule. If the steering team approves the changes, however, the project team might need to repeat portions of the systems analysis and design phases to incorporate the changes.

Finalize Contract

Develop a fair contract when acquiring new computer hardware or software. Although the vendor may insist that everyone signs their standard contract, do not do so without review by experienced members of your legal and purchasing departments. Recognize that the standard contract is written from the vendor's perspective and protects its interests, not yours. Request a copy of each contending vendor's standard contract at the start of the design phase and allow at least two months for review and negotiation of a final contract.

Organizations that elect to use the cloud-computing or software-as-a-service approach need to take special precautions in signing contracts with the service provider. The contract should clarify how the provider ensures data privacy, handles discovery if there is a lawsuit, resolves service level problems, and manages disaster recovery, and where the cloud-computing servers and computers are located. Organizations should confirm this information in discussions with other customers of the service provider and by a visit to the service provider's facilities.

A contract covering the modification of a software package should have provisions for monitoring systems development progress, ownership and property rights of the new or modified system, contingency provisions in case something doesn't work as expected, and dispute resolution if something goes wrong.

The next chapter covers the remaining phases of the traditional system development life cycle. It will also discuss alternative system development life cycles, including the prototype, agile, object-oriented, and individual development. In addition, critical project management considerations will be addressed.

SUMMARY

Principle:

Effective systems development requires a team effort from stakeholders, users, managers, systems development specialists, and various support personnel, and it starts with building an information systems plan.

The systems development team consists of stakeholders, users, systems development specialists, and various support personnel. The development team determines the objectives of the information system and delivers to the organization a system that meets its objectives.

Stakeholders are people who, either themselves or through the area of the organization they represent, ultimately benefit from the systems development project.

Users are people who will interact with the system regularly. They can be employees, managers, customers, or suppliers.

The project manager is the person assigned by the organization doing the work of the project to achieve the project objectives.

A systems analyst is a professional who specializes in analyzing and designing business systems.

The programmer is responsible for modifying or developing programs to satisfy user requirements.

Other support personnel on the development team include technical specialists, either employees from the IS department or outside consultants.

In addition to the development team, each project should have a steering team of senior managers representing the business and IS organizations that provide guidance and support to the project.

The project sponsor is a key member and leader of the steering team who plays such a critical role that lack of this essential individual raises the probability of project failure.

Information systems planning involves the translation of strategic and organizational goals into systems development initiatives. Benefits of IS planning include a long-range view of information technology use and better use of IS resources.

Critical success factors (CSFs) can identify important system development objectives, which can include performance goals (quality and usefulness of the output and the speed at which output is generated) and cost objectives (development costs, fixed costs, and ongoing investment costs).

Systems development projects are initiated for many reasons, including the availability of new technology, in response to mergers and acquisitions, and because of new laws and regulations.

Failure to align information system project goals to the needs of the business can have disastrous consequences.

The systems development process is also called a systems development life cycle (SDLC) because the activities associated with it are ongoing. Common systems development life cycles include traditional, prototyping, agile, object-oriented, and individual development.

The traditional SDLC provides for maximum management control, creates considerable system documentation, ensures that system requirements can be traced back to stated business needs, and produces many intermediate products for review. However, following this approach means that users may get a system that meets the needs as understood by the developers, expensive and difficult to maintain documentation is generated, users' needs go unstated or might not be met, and users can't easily review the many intermediate products produced.

Principle:

Systems investigation is needed to gain a clear understanding of the specifics of the problem to be solved or the opportunity to be addressed and to determine if the opportunity is worth pursuing.

In most organizations, a systems request form initiates the investigation process.

Participants in systems investigation can include stakeholders, users, managers, employees, analysts, and programmers.

The systems investigation is designed to assess the technical, economic, legal, operational, and schedule feasibility of implementing solutions for business problems.

Joint application development (JAD) has proven extremely efficient and effective at analyzing existing systems, defining problems, identifying solution requirements, and proposing and evaluating possible solutions including costs and benefits.

Functional decomposition is used to define the business processes included with the scope of the new system.

As the final step in the investigation process, a systems investigation report should be prepared to document relevant findings and the project team should present their recommendations to the project steering team.

Principle:

Systems analysis is needed to define what the information system must do to solve the problem.

Systems analysis involves the examination of existing systems to further understand the system's weaknesses and examine inputs, outputs, processes, security and controls, and system performance.

Data is frequently gathered using JAD sessions, direct observation, and surveys.

Perhaps the single most critical step in the entire traditional system development life cycle is the identification, confirmation, and prioritization (critical, medium, low) of system requirements.

Data-flow diagrams are used to document the processes of the current system or to provide a model of a proposed new system.

Entity-relationship diagrams are used to show logical relationships among the data entities included in the scope of the system.

CASE tools are used to document both the existing system and proposed new solutions.

It is extremely important to define security and control requirements at the same time as other system requirements are being identified. Leaving them as an afterthought will lead to problems that translate into security vulnerabilities.

System performance requirements in terms of timeliness of output, ease of use, scalability, response time, availability, and reliability must also be defined.

Most organizations buy or rent the software they need rather than build it. Thus, it is important to perform a preliminary make-versus-buy analysis during the analysis phase. The primary tool for doing this is the request for proposal.

Several solution options should be identified and a feasibility analysis performed to identify a candidate solution to recommend to the project steering team.

As the final steps in the analysis phase, a systems analysis report is prepared to document relevant findings and the project team presents their recommendations to the project steering team.

Principle:

Systems design is needed to define exactly how the information system will solve a problem.

User interface design integrates concepts and methods from computer science, graphics design, and psychology to build interfaces that are accessible, easy to use, and efficient. Over the years, numerous sets of good design principles have been identified.

Designers develop specific system security and controls for all aspects of the information system, including hardware, software, database systems, telecommunications, and Internet operations.

A disaster recovery plan is a documented process to recover an organization's business information system assets including hardware, software, data, networks, and facilities in the event of a disaster. The recovery time for an information system resource should match the recovery time objective for the business processes that depend on that information system resource. Files and databases can be protected using incremental backups and image logs.

Evaluating and selecting the best design involves achieving a balance of system objectives that will best support organizational goals.

Vendor software and hardware options can be compared using a performance evaluation test.

The scope and the user and business requirements are frozen at the end of the design phase of the traditional systems development life cycle. Any potential changes that are identified or suggested after this point must be approved by a formal scope change process before any work on them can begin.

As the final step in the design phase, a systems design report is prepared to document relevant findings and the project team presents their recommendations to the project steering team.

KEY TERMS

cold site

critical success factor (CSF)

data definition language (DDL)

data dictionary

data-flow diagram

data-flow line

direct observation

disaster recovery plan

economic feasibility

entity symbol

feasibility analysis

final evaluation

functional decomposition

hot site

image log

incremental backup

information systems planning

joint application development (JAD)

legal feasibility

make-versus-buy decision

mission-critical process

operational feasibility

Pareto principle

performance evaluation test

preliminary evaluation

process symbol

programmer

project manager

project sponsor

request for proposal (RFP)

schedule feasibility

schema

stakeholder

steering team

systems investigation request

systems analyst

systems design

systems investigation report

systems investigation request

technical feasibility

traditional system development life cycle

users

CHAPTER 12: SELF-ASSESSMENT TEST

Effective systems development requires a team effort from stakeholders, users, managers, systems development specialists, and various support personnel, and it starts with building an information systems plan.

1. According to the Standish Group, _____ of all projects fail or are challenged.
   a. around 25%
   b. anywhere from 25% to 50%
   c. 61%
   d. over 70%
2. _____ is the activity of creating or modifying existing business systems. It refers to all aspects of the process—from identifying problems to be solved or opportunities to be exploited to the implementation and refinement of the chosen solution.
3. Which of the following people ultimately benefit from a systems development project?
   a. computer programmers
   b. systems analysts
   c. stakeholders
   d. senior-level manager
4. The _____ is a key member and the leader of the steering team who plays such a critical role that lack of this essential individual raises the possibility of project failure.
5. The term _____ refers to the translation of strategic and organizational goals into systems development initiatives.
6. Traditional systems development encourages end users to constantly change the system requirements throughout the entire system development process. True or False?

Systems investigation is needed to gain a clear understanding of the specifics of the problem to be solved or the opportunity to be addressed and to determine if the opportunity is worth pursuing.

7. The systems investigation phase follows information systems planning and immediately precedes systems design. True or False?
8. During systems investigation, the feasibility of implementing a solution to a business problem is determined and includes the technical, economic, operational, schedule, and _____ feasibility.
9. _____ is a technique used during the systems investigation phase to identify the processes included within the scope of the system.

Systems analysis is needed to define what the information system must do to solve the problem.

10. The individual who plans and leads a JAD session is called the _____.
    a. JAD facilitator
    b. project manager
    c. JAD scribe
    d. project sponsor
11. Feasibility analysis is typically done during which systems development stage?
    a. investigation
    b. analysis
    c. design
    d. all of the above
12. Data modeling is most often accomplished through the use of a(n)_____.
    a. entity-relationship diagram
    b. data-flow diagram
    c. functional decomposition diagram
    d. activity diagram

Systems design is needed to define exactly how the information system will solve a problem.

13. Good user interface design integrates concepts and methods from computer science, graphics design, and psychology. True or False?
14. The _____ objective for an information system resource should match the recovery time objective for the business processes that depend on that information system resource.
15. Any potential change in system requirements that are identified or suggested after the design phase must _____.
    a. go through a formal scope change process before work on them begins
    b. be evaluated in terms of how they might affect system performance
    c. require feasibility analysis
    d. all of the above

CHAPTER 12: SELF-ASSESSMENT TEST ANSWERS

1. c
2. Systems development
3. c
4. project sponsor
5. information systems planning
6. False
7. False
8. legal
9. Functional decomposition
10. a
11. d
12. a
13. True
14. recovery time
15. d

REVIEW QUESTIONS

1. Distinguish between project stakeholders and system users.
2. What is the purpose of a project steering team? Who are members of the team? What is the role of the project sponsor?
3. What is the purpose of IS planning? What are the benefits of performing IS planning?
4. Identify three typical reasons to initiate a systems development effort.
5. Identify three advantages and three disadvantages associated with the traditional system development life cycle.
6. Describe what is involved in feasibility analysis.
7. What is the purpose of systems analysis? Identify the major steps of this phase.
8. Define the different types of feasibility that the systems development team must consider.

9. What is the result or outcome of systems analysis? What happens next?
10. What is a data-flow diagram? How is it used in the system development process?
11. Identify and briefly describe five system performance factors.
12. What is the make-versus-buy decision? Briefly explain how this decision is made.
13. What is the Pareto principle and how does it apply to defining system requirements?
14. What is the role of the compliance department?
15. Explain the purpose of a hot site. What is the difference between a hot site and cold site?
16. What is a performance evaluation test? How is it used in the system development process?

DISCUSSION QUESTIONS

1. What personality characteristics should an effective project sponsor possess?
2. You have been selected to participate on the systems investigation team for a new system in your area of the business. How can you contribute to the success of the effort? How might you use critical success factors to identify important system requirements?
3. You have been appointed to a special team to identify the causes for your organization's biggest IT project failure ever. Where would you start and who would you speak with?
4. You must approach one of the mid-level line managers in your organization and convince her to assign one of her key people to lead the system investigation phase of an important project. This phase of the project is expected to last three months and the individual will be needed full time during the investigation. What resistance do you expect from this manager? What counterpoints can you offer to convince her to assign this person?
5. Why is it important for business managers to have a basic understanding of the systems development process?
6. Your company wants to develop or acquire a new customer relationship management system to help sales representatives identify potential new customers. Describe what factors you would consider in deciding whether to develop the application in-house or buy a software package to fulfill this need.

7. Assume that you work for a financial services company. Describe three applications that would be critical for your clients. What systems development tools and techniques might be used to develop these applications?
8. How important are communications skills to the IS members of a systems development team? Consider this statement: "IS personnel need a combination of skills—one-third technical skills, one-third business skills, and one-third communications skills." Do you think this is true? How might this affect the selection and training of IS personnel?
9. You have been hired to perform systems investigation for an Indian restaurant owner in a large metropolitan area. She is thinking of opening a new restaurant with a state-of-the-art computer system that would allow customers to place orders on the Internet or at kiosks at restaurant tables. Describe how you would determine the technical, economic, legal, operational, and schedule feasibility for the restaurant and its proposed computer system.
10. Discuss three reasons why aligning overall business goals with IS goals is important.
11. You are the chief information officer for a medium-sized retail store and would like to develop a Web site to allow your loyal customers to see and buy your products on the Internet. Describe how you would determine the requirements for the new system.

PROBLEM-SOLVING EXERCISES

1. For a business of your choice, use a graphics program to develop a data-flow diagram of one of its main processes and an entity-relationship diagram showing the data within the scope of the system.
2. Use a word processing program to develop an agenda for a JAD session to identify the security and control requirements for a new employee time-recording system for your place of work or your school. Identify the participants you would like to attend. Briefly describe the process you would use to help these participants define their requirements.

TEAM ACTIVITIES

1. Have your team interview people involved in a systems development project at a local business or at your college or university. Identify each team member and document their role on the project. Solicit their feedback on how the project is going and how they feel about their participation. With the benefit of 20–20 hindsight, is there anything they would like to change?
2. Your team has been hired to determine the feasibility of a new Web site that contains information about upcoming entertainment, sports, and other events for students at your college or university. Use a word processing program to describe your conclusions for the different types of feasibility and your final recommendations for the new Internet site.
3. Your team has been hired to perform systems investigation for a new billing program for a small heating and air conditioning company. Perform a functional decomposition to define the scope of the system.

WEB EXERCISES

1. Find and read the latest CHAOS report available from the Standish Group. Find and read at least one other report that disagrees with the CHAOS report. After reading these two reports, briefly summarize your major findings into a series of half a dozen or so slides. State your conclusion as to whether the success rate of information systems projects is improving or getting worse. Be prepared to make a brief presentation to your class and defend your position.
2. Using the Internet, explore the most useful mobile applications for a business or industry of your choice. Also explore mobile applications for this business or industry that are not currently available. Write a report describing what you found.

CAREER EXERCISES

1. Pick a career that you are considering. Identify an information system frequently employed by people in that career field. Discuss how you might be involved as a user or stakeholder in the development of such a system for your future company. Identify three things that you could do that would greatly improve the success of such a project. Identify three things that you could do (or fail to do) that could greatly reduce the probability of success of such a project.
2. Using the Internet, research career opportunities in which you would develop applications for new tablet computers. Describe two individuals or companies that have successfully developed applications for tablet computers.

CASE STUDIES

Case One

Establishing Information System Governance in Higher Education

You read in this chapter that each project should have a steering team of senior managers representing the business and IS organizations that provide guidance and support to the project. This is an important aspect of *information systems governance*: oversight of how the organization uses information systems to further its business objectives.

Nottingham Trent University (NTU) in Nottingham, England, was formed in the 1990s by a merger of several other institutions, some dating to the mid-nineteenth century. As a result, it had to deal with many information systems and technology platforms. In 2004, NTU brought its resources together into a central IS department. When this centralization was followed by the departure of their IS director in 2006, the stage was set to rethink NTU's approach to managing information resources.

Richard Eade, an information technology software manager at NTU, writes that, "Balancing risks and opportunities [was] the major driver for the introduction of IT governance at NTU. One significant risk identified is associated with the university culture, … a perception that IT staff can 'do what they like.' This has arisen from poor management. Consequently, IT governance has been introduced to bring in systems of control, without repressing initiative and enthusiasm."

Anarchy, while it sounds attractive to those who can do as they please, does not yield the best information systems or the best use of resources. NTU's challenge was to get control of its IS efforts in ways that faculty and staff would accept. In addition, the university wanted to move from spending 80 percent of its time operating existing systems, with only the remaining 20 percent of its efforts going to developing new ones, to a 50:50 ratio.

Achieving these goals was a big task. Eade says NTU approached it the same way one approaches eating an elephant: "One bite at a time."

Managing new system development was not the first area NTU addressed. Some top-priority areas had to be tackled first, including risk analysis, financial audits, security, and legal issues such as data protection. Once those urgent matters were taken care of, though, NTU could address project priorities and approval. In the long run, getting control of development priorities would have a greater payoff.

To improve the IS department's focus on meaningful projects, NTU created the position of *business relationship manager*. The person in this position was the IS department's "eyes and ears" to the rest of the university. This manager's role was to provide communication links in both directions.

Next, the department strengthened its steering team. Previously, it had focused on the allocation of capital funding but had no controls to ensure the money was spent as the steering team specified. Now, both a sponsor and a statement of business benefits were required for all new projects.

Finally, NTU recognized that project management was vital to project success. The goals of the IS department were to deliver projects on time, on budget, and at an agreed-upon quality level. In the past, all three goals were missed consistently. NTU now trained project managers in the PRINCE2 project management methodology. This methodology provides proven processes for every project, from start to finish. It defines the required competencies, duties, and behaviors of eight types of people involved in a project. In sum, it changes project management from a "seat of the pants" activity to a systematic one. It helps projects stay on track and ensures that scope changes are well documented and properly agreed upon, and it provides evidence that risks and issues are well managed. NTU uses project boards (committees) for high-level control, with weekly or monthly highlight reports circulated to the IS management team.

Eade summarized NTU's new governance with, "Ensuring that IT systems are fit for the purpose, are well managed, and can be relied upon means that we must undertake more effective measures to identify that appropriate strategies, policies, procedures, and controls are in place to bring risks and problems to our attention. NTU senior managers have identified the role the IT systems play —and will continue to play—in taking the university forward. They now expect the principles of IT governance to be in place to ensure that IT remains strong."

Discussion Questions

1. How can NTU's use of formal IS governance help it achieve its goal of redirecting about 30 percent of its resources from operations to development?
2. What lessons can other higher education institutions take from NTU?

Critical Thinking Questions

1. What procedures did NTU take to implement IS governance?
2. Suppose NTU, instead of arising from a recent merger, had been one institution for over a century but had the same problems, how might that difference affect its approach to information systems governance?

SOURCES: Eade, R., "IT Governance: How We Are Making It Work," UCISA (Universities and Colleges Information Systems Association) 2011 conference, March 23, 2011, *www.ucisa.ac.uk/events/2011/conference 2011/~/media/Files/events/ucisa2011/presentations/richard_eade.ashx*, accessed January 23, 2012; Eade, R., "Making IT Governance Work," ECAR Research Bulletin, no. 20, October 5, 2010; *www.educause.edu /Resources/MakingITGovernanceWork/214687*, accessed July 3, 2014; Nottingham Trent University Web site, *www.ntu.ac.uk*, accessed July 3, 2014; Prince2 Methodology Web site, *www.prince-officialsite.com*, accessed July 3, 2014.

Case Two

Improving Requirements Implementation at Honeywell

As you read in this chapter, determining system requirements is a vital part of the development of any information system. Complex information systems have many sets of requirements. It is, therefore, essential to have a systematic way to determine them.

Honeywell Technology Solutions Lab (HTSL), through its IT Services and Solutions business unit, develops software solutions for other parts of Honeywell Inc. HTSL is based in Bengaluru (Bangalore), India, with centers in Beijing (China), Brno (Czech Republic), Hyderabad (India), Madurai (India), and Shanghai (China).

In 2010, the company identified a problem: At HTSL, various groups such as requirement writers and development, quality assurance (QA), and project management teams worked independently in separate "silos." It was difficult to track project requirements and the status of their implementation. HTSL needed a system to manage the requirements and their relationships to each other.

Beyond managing the requirements, HTSL needed an application that could coordinate test cases, design elements, and defects. Requirement writers would create the requirements for software, and HTSL customers (other Honeywell divisions) would review and approve these requirements. Once approved, the development team would implement them, and the QA team would generate test cases based on them. Any defects found in executing the test cases would also be tracked.

HTSL had a great deal of experience in developing software for aerospace, automation and control, specialty materials, and transportation systems. However, they had no experience in developing software to manage the development process itself. The company recognized this deficit and turned to specialists.

Kovair, of Santa Clara, California, is such a specialist. Its Application Lifecycle Management (ALM) package is for "implementing a software development life cycle (SDLC) process, collaborating on the entire development cycle and tracing implementations back to original specs. [It] ensures that all developers are working from the same playbook … and that there are no costly last minute surprises."

One ALM module is Requirements Management. Using it, HTSL can gather requirements, rank them, manage their changes, and coordinate them with system test cases. The Requirements Management module can also produce a variety of reports, including formatted requirements specifications and reports showing the distribution of requirements by type, criticality, source, or any other descriptor.

Honeywell already had a formal development process called "Review, Approval, Baseline, Technical Design, Test Design, Implementation and Testing." Kovair's ALM solution was customized to fit into this process. When a requirement is entered into ALM, it is marked "Submitted," and the review process begins. ALM generates Review tasks for stakeholders, ensuring that they will give their views on the new requirement. When they approve it, perhaps after changes, its status is changed to "Approved," and a task is entered for its owner to add it to the baseline system design. When this step is completed, two new tasks are created: one for the development team to develop technical specifications and then the software and one for the quality assurance team to develop test cases. Development can then continue.

What were the results? HTSL reduced rework due to incorrect requirements and speeded up development. Development team productivity was improved by about 20 percent, and requirements-related defects were reduced by at least 1 percent.

Discussion Questions

1. Why did Honeywell turn to Kovair for help? What goals did Kovair help Honeywell meet?

2. The ALM software is intended to help companies manage the steps of software development. Software development is only one of the processes that businesses use every day. What are the characteristics of a process that make a software package like ALM useful?

Critical Thinking Questions

1. Honeywell reported that it increased team productivity by 20 percent and reduced requirement errors by 1 percent. What functionalities of ALM may have enabled Honeywell to accomplish this?

2. This case is based in part on information from Kovair. Many organizations need to track software development projects, so other companies besides Kovair offer packages to do that. Suppose you were given the job of choosing such a package, list at least four criteria you would use in comparing different packages. Rank the items on your list from most to least important.

SOURCES: Kovair, Inc., "Requirements Management Case Study for Honeywell," *www.kovair.com/whitepapers/Requirements-Management-Case-Study-for-Honeywell.pdf*, August 2011, accessed July 14, 2014; HTSL Web site, *http://aerospace.honeywell.com/services/maintenance-and-monitoring/depot-partnerships/life-cycle-management*, accessed July 3, 2014; Kovair ALM Web site, *www.kovair.com/alm/application-lifecycle-management-description.aspx*, accessed July 3, 2014.

Questions for Web Case

See the Web site for this book to read about the Altitude Online case for this chapter. The following are questions concerning this Web case.

Altitude Online: Systems Development: Investigation, Analysis, and Design

Discussion Questions

1. What important activities did Jon's team engage in during the systems investigation stage of the systems development life cycle?

2. Why are all forms of feasibility considerations especially important for an ERP development project?

Critical Thinking Questions

1. Why is the quality of the systems analysis report crucial to the successful continuation of the project?

2. Why do you think Jon felt the need to travel to communicate with Altitude Online colleagues rather than using email or phone conferencing? What benefit does face-to-face communication provide in this scenario?

NOTES

Sources for the opening vignette: Feron, Raymond, "Digital Delta: Integrated Operations for Water Management," September 2013, *www.slideshare.net/RaymondFeron/digital-delta-eng-sept-2013*; Wolpe, Toby, "Big Data Deluge: How Dutch Water Is Trying to Turn the Tide," ZDNet, October 1, 2013, *www.zdnet.com/big-data-deluge-how-dutch-water-is-trying-to-turn-the-tide-7000021385/*; "Digital Delta Transforms Dutch Water System Using Big Data," IBM Smarter Cities, November 21, 2013, *https://www.youtube.com/watch?v=O8gsNsgFYBo*.

1. "Gartner Worldwide IT Spending Forecast," *www.gartner.com/technology/research/it-spending-forecast/*, accessed May 19, 2014.

2. "Cincinnati Zoo Transforms Customer Experience and Boosts Profits," IBM Case Study *http://public.dhe.ibm .com/common/ssi/ecm/en/ytc03380usen/YTC03380 USEN.PDF*, accessed May 22, 2014.

3. "CHAOS Manifesto 2013, Think Big, Act Small," The Standish Group International, *www.versionone.com /assets/img/files/CHAOSManifesto2013.pdf*, accessed June 11, 2014.

4. Gatto, Joe, "Cleaning and Restoration Company Deploys Mobile Apps on iPhone and BlackBerry Using Canvas," *Canvas*, May 14, 2014, *www.gocanvas.com/content /blog/post/cleaning-and-restoration-company-deploys -mobile-apps-on-iphone-and-blackber*.

5. Schectman, Joel, "Airline Merger Glitches Inevitable 'Cost of Doing Business'," *CIO Journal*, February 19, 2013, *http://blogs.wsj.com/cio/2013/02/19/airline -merger-glitches-inevitable-cost-of-doing-business/*.

6. Suelzer, Marcia Richards, "Extended Bonus Depreciation, Expensing and Tax Credits Aim to Stimulate Business Growth," Business Owner Toolkit, January 3, 2013, *www.bizfilings.com/toolkit/news/tax-info/bonus -depreciation-expensing-credits-fiscal-cliff.aspx*.

7. Dignan, Larry, "Target CEO Departure Watershed for IT, Business Alignment," *ZDNet*, May 5, 2014, *www.zdnet .com/target-ceo-departure-watershed-for-it-business -alignment-7000029069/*.

8. Dignan, Larry, "Target CIO Jacob Resigns Following Data Breach," *ZDNet*, March 5, 2014, *www.zdnet.com /target-cio-jacob-resigns-following-data-breach -7000027020/*.

9. Jayakumar, Amrita, "Target Names New Chief Information Officer, Announces Partnership with Mastercard," *The Washington Post*, April 29, 2014, *www.washingtonpost.com/business/economy/target -names-new-chief-information-officer-announces -partnership-with-mastercard/2014/04/29 /ae56d80e-cfa0-11e3-a6b1-45c4dffb85a6_story.html*.

10. Wood, Collin, "California DMV Cancels IT Modernization Project Contract," *Government Technology*, February 14, 2014, *www.govtech.com /e-government/DMV-IT-Modernization-Project.html*.

11. "Joint Application Development," Liquid Mercury Solutions Web site, *www.liquidmercurysolutions.com /whatwedo/spdev/Pages/Joint-Application-Development. aspx*, accessed June 1, 2014.

12. "Liquid Mercury Solutions Modernizes Business Critical Petition Process for the U.S. Department of Agriculture Using SharePoint with AgilePoint BPMS," AgilePoint Web site, *http://agilepoint.com/solutions/liquid -mercury-solutions/*, accessed June 2, 2014.

13. Jackson, Joab, "Graph Databases Find Answers for the Sick and Their Healers," *Computerworld*, June 6, 2014, *www.computerworld.com/s/article/9248929/Graph _databases_find_answers_for_the_sick_and_their _healers*.

14. "Ministry of Defence 'Wasted Millions on Failed Computer System'," *The Guardian*, January 13, 2014, *www.theguardian.com/uk-news/2014/jan/14/ministry -of-defence-failed-computer-system*.

15. "Think IS," *www.comm-it.com/wp-content/uploads /2011/09/Think_IS-en.pdf*, accessed June 2, 2014.

16. "Interagency Guidelines Establishing Information Security Standards," Board of Governors of the Federal Reserve System, *www.federalreserve.gov/bankinforeg /interagencyguidelines.htm*, accessed June 9, 2014.

17. Ward, Brian, "The Importance of Good Interface Design," *heehaw.digital* (blog), February 27, 2013, *http://blog.heehaw.co.uk/2013/02/the-importance-of -good-interface-design/*, accessed July 14, 2014.

18. Shneiderman, Ben and Plaisant, Catherine, *Designing the User Interface: Strategies for Effective Human- Computer Interaction*, Fifth edition, 2009, Pearson: New York.

19. Porter, Joshua, "Principles of User Interface Design," *http://bokardo.com/principles-of-user-interface-design/*, accessed July 3, 2014.

20. EMC RecoverPoint, *www.emc.com/storage/recoverpoint /recoverpoint.htm*, accessed June 16, 2014.

21. SteelEye LifeKeeper, *www.ha-cc.org/high_availability /components/application_availability/cluster/high _availability_cluster/steeleye_lifekeeper/*, accessed June 16, 2014.

22. "NeverFail Application Continuous Availability," *www .virtualizationadmin.com/software/High-Availability /Neverfail-for-VMware-VirtualCenter-.html*, accessed June 16, 2014.

13 Systems Development: Construction, Integration and Testing, Implementation, Operation and Maintenance, and Disposal

Principles	Learning Objectives
• The goal of systems construction, integration and testing, and implementation is to put into operation an information system that provides real value to the organization.	• State the purpose of systems construction, integration and testing, and implementation. • Discuss the primary activities associated with these phases of systems development.
• System operation and maintenance add to the useful life of a system but can consume large amounts of resources. These activities can benefit from the same rigorous methods and project management techniques applied to systems development.	• State the importance of system operation and maintenance. • Identify and discuss some of the activities required to keep a system operating effectively. • Describe the systems review process.
• The systems development team must select the appropriate systems development approach to match the needs of the project.	• Identify and discuss the advantages and disadvantages of the prototyping and agile development as compared to the traditional system development life cycle. • Discuss key aspects of object-oriented, mobile, and end-user system development.
• The systems development team must take measures to avoid the common pitfalls to project success.	• Identify the most common causes of information system project failure. • Identify project management tools used to track and monitor system development projects.

Information Systems in the Global Economy
BRITISH TELECOM, UNITED KINGDOM

Spreading Agile Development Across the Globe

AP Images/Anthony Upton/REX/FEREX

In 2005, British Telecom (BT) took a big risk: the company dropped its traditional systems development cycle and embraced agile development. Previously, BT had outsourced the gathering of system requirements to a third-company, which would take three to nine months to meet with customers and stakeholders and create a requirements list. Next, the project would move back to BT where programmers struggled to interpret the requirements and then develop and test the system within 18 months—although some projects needed more time. In late 2005, BT took only 90 days to roll out a new Web-based system that monitored phone traffic. The system allowed traffic managers to change switches and other physical devices more quickly to handle shifts in load along BT's telecommunications network. The success of this initial project reverberated throughout the IT world, as BT became the first telecommunications giant to adopt agile development—sometimes developing products in three 30-day iterative cycles.

The new systems development approach had other advantages, too: programmers and customers communicated closely; and teams from different locations around the world, initially the UK and India, worked together to develop the system. To overcome customer doubts, BT invited them to development "hot houses" to see how the agile development process worked. Many customers became such ardent believers that they adopted the agile approach themselves. In 2010, BT used its new systems development process to create the 21st Century Next Generation Access Network process, which enjoyed an 80 percent return on its initial investment within its first year. Today, BT deploys agile development to service its customers across the globe.

In 2014, for example, BT applied the agile approach to deploy telepresence solutions for the international energy and chemical producer Sasol, a company with over 34,000 employees based in 37 countries. To oversee its operations and interact with clients, senior managers based in South Africa were traveling millions of miles each year, which was not good for the managers, the company's budget, or the planet. BT installed telepresence suites across South Africa and in Houston, London, Calgary, and Hamburg. Sasol achieved a 100 percent usage rate at each of these suites, and BT secured a five-year contract to provide continued support.

BT had one major concern about agile development: previously, the company had conducted 16 or 17 types of tests before deploying a new system. Many feared that a shorter life cycle meant compromising on quality assurance. However, BT now continues testing with customers after system setup and finds that testing the product with customer involvement has significant advantages.

"The main advantage I see is that you spend more time working on the right [system] features by talking to customers all the time and working on it," says Kerry Buckley, a software developer who worked on the initial phone-traffic monitoring system. Moreover, software engineers working at BT are excited about working on customer-facing live applications. As one engineer notes, "All your work matters and will be released to the public." Agile development at BT has taken systems developers out of their isolated bubble, inspiring them, and proving to the IT world that agile development can work.

As you read this chapter, consider the following:

- What risks are involved with adopting new methods of systems development?
- What are the different approaches to testing? Are some approaches more suited to different types of software systems or industries than others?

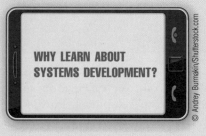

WHY LEARN ABOUT SYSTEMS DEVELOPMENT?

A manager at a hotel chain can use an information system to look up guest preferences. An accountant at a manufacturing company can use an information system to analyze the costs of a new production line. A sales representative for a shoe store can use an information system to determine which shoes to order and which to discount because they are not selling. A computer engineer can use an information system to help determine why a computer system is running slowly. Information systems have been designed and implemented for almost every career and industry. An individual can use systems design and implementation to create applications for smartphones for profit or enjoyment. Information systems are designed and implemented for employees and managers every day. This chapter shows how you can be involved in the construction, integration and testing, and implementation of an information system that will directly benefit you on the job. It also outlines alternative software development life cycles and provides advice on when each approach should be used. This chapter starts with a discussion of the remaining phases of the traditional software development life cycle.

TRADITIONAL SYSTEMS DEVELOPMENT LIFE CYCLE—CONTINUED

Like investigation, analysis, and design covered in Chapter 12, the construction, integration and testing, implementation, operation and maintenance, and disposal phases covered in this chapter strive to put in place an information system that provides real value to the organization by reducing costs, increasing profits, or improving customer service. We begin this chapter with a discussion of systems construction.

CONSTRUCTION

system construction: The phase of systems development that converts the system design into an operational system by acquiring and installing hardware and software, coding and testing software programs, creating and loading data into databases, and performing initial program testing.

The system construction phase follows the completion of the system design phase when the project steering team approves of proceeding with the project. System construction converts the system design into an operational system by acquiring and installing hardware and software, coding and testing software programs, creating and loading data into databases, and performing initial program testing. These steps are outlined next and are discussed in the following pages.

1. Acquire and install hardware
2. Acquire and install software
3. Code software components
4. Create and load data
5. Perform unit testing

Acquire and Install Hardware

Organizations can purchase, lease, or rent computer hardware and other resources from an IS vendor or service provider to acquire the hardware needed for an information system. Types of IS vendors include general computer manufacturers (such as IBM and Hewlett-Packard), small computer manufacturers (such as Dell and Sony), peripheral equipment manufacturers (such as Epson and SanDisk), computer dealers and distributors (such as The Computer Shack and Best Buy), and chip makers (such as Intel and AMD). Some of the most successful vendors include IBM (hardware and other services), Oracle (databases), Apple (personal and tablet computers), Microsoft (software), and Accenture (IS consulting).

Determining the specific equipment needed, ordering the equipment, and receiving the equipment can require a long lead time, as much as several months.

Many companies employ multiple hardware vendors, but managing them can be difficult. Vendors first compete against each other to earn a contract with an organization, and then they must coordinate their efforts to develop an effective information system at a good price. Open communication among the vendors is critical. Some CIOs assemble vendor teams that work together to solve current and future problems for the organization. See Figure 13.1.

FIGURE 13.1

IS vendors

IBM is an IS vendor that offers hardware, software, and IS personnel.

ODD ANDERSEN/AFP/Getty Images

In addition to buying, leasing, or renting computer hardware, companies can pay only for the computing services that they use. Called "pay-as-you-go," "on-demand," or "utility" computing, this approach requires an organization to pay only for the computer power it uses, just as it would pay for a utility such as electricity. Companies such as IBM and Hewlett-Packard offer their clients an on-demand computing service in which organizations pay according to the computer resources actually used, including processors, storage devices, and network facilities.

Many organizations use virtual servers and other computers to make the most of their computing resources. Virtualization has had a profound impact on the acquisition of information system hardware. Adways Inc. is a global Internet company with headquarters in Tokyo, Japan. It provides various online services, including affiliate advertising, mobile content, multiplayer games, and smartphone applications. The firm implemented an on-demand information system infrastructure using VMWare virtualization tools to accommodate its rapid growth. When Adways rolled out a new mobile service and received almost six million logins per day, 15 times the original estimate of users, the firm could quickly increase its capacity to meet the extra demand with no service outage.[1]

Many organizations are also employing cloud-based services rather than acquiring their own computer hardware. For example, the IT Infrastructure Services division of Tata Consultancy Services enables hundreds of Indian organizations to access computing power, data storage devices, software, and other resources from the cloud. With this service, Tata can cut customer costs by 30 percent, startup new customers in just 20 days, and provide 99.5 percent service availability.[2]

Acquire and Install Software

A company planning to purchase or lease software from an outside company has many options. It can use commercial off-the-shelf software or combine software from multiple vendors to create a finished system. In many cases, the company's programmers need to write some original software from scratch and integrate it with purchased or leased software. For example, a company can purchase or lease software from several software vendors and combine it into a single information system.

As mentioned in Chapter 4, *Software as a Service* (*SaaS*) allows businesses to subscribe to Web-delivered application software by paying a monthly service charge or a per-use fee. Instead of acquiring software from a traditional software vendor and installing it on the organization's computers, SaaS allows individuals and organizations to access software applications over the Internet. This practice avoids the time and expense of purchasing and installing new software.

RamSoft provides patient information systems to healthcare organizations such as ambulatory and acute care practices, imaging facilities, and radiology centers. However, small organizations typically cannot afford to purchase their software or hire IS specialists to support the software users. RamSoft decided to offer these customers a hosted software solution, or SaaS. With this service, a radiologist can produce a report and deliver it to the referring and attending physicians along with critical findings, and emergency room physicians can view the images and reports—all without requiring the healthcare organization to form or hire an IS department.[3]

Companies such as Google are using the cloud-computing approach to deliver word-processing, spreadsheet, and other software over the Internet.

Code Software Components

Another option to acquire the software an organization needs is to write the program source code itself. As discussed in Chapter 12, this approach usually takes longer, is more costly, and introduces more risk than implementing a software package. However, it can provide an organization with custom code that meets its unique business needs or provides it with a potential competitive advantage.

Software code must be written according to defined design specifications so that the system meets user and business needs and operates in the manner the user expects. Most software development organizations use a variety of software tools to generate program source code that conforms to those specifications.

Developers can use CASE tools to design an application and have the computer generate the code to create it. This process reduces costs as well as development time, and ensures the code is consistent with the design specifications.

Some template-driven code generators can create source code automatically. CodeSmith Generator is an example of a template-driven code generator that automates the creation of common application source code for several languages (e.g., C#, Java, VB, PHP, ASP.NET, SQL). The templates are designed to create typical types of business programs. You can modify a template or create one of your own to generate the code you need.[4]

The purpose of screen painters is to design new data entry screens for software applications. This easy-to-use environment allows developers to create screens by "painting" them and then use "dialogue boxes" to define the characteristics of the data that goes in each field.

Menu-creation software allows users to develop and format menus with features such as color palettes, graphics characters, automatically generated boxes, headings, and system variables.

Report generator software captures an image of a desired report and generates the code to produce that report based on the database and database schema you are using. In many cases, users can design and code reports with this software.

One organization that decided to code software components is the Arizona court system, which includes the State Supreme Court, 15 Superior Courts, 85 Municipal, and 76 Limited Jurisdiction courts. All the courts must coordinate scheduling of court dates, keep track of state-issued citations, and track adults and juveniles on probation. Over time, the Arizona courts developed a number of systems using various programming languages, making it difficult to modify programs to keep up with changes in the law. The court system is now rewriting many of its applications and standardizing on the Microsoft .NET architecture. The courts are using a software code generator called Visible Developer to generate 85 to 90 percent of the code.[5]

technical documentation: Written details used by computer operators to execute the program and by analysts and programmers to solve problems or modify the program.

An organization also needs useful software documentation to accompany the software code. Technical documentation includes written details that computer operators follow to execute the program and that analysts and programmers use to solve problems or modify the program. Technical documentation explains the purpose of every major piece of computer code. It also identifies and describes key variables.

user documentation: Written descriptions developed for people who use a program; in easy-to-understand language, it shows how the program can and should be used to meet the needs of its various users.

User documentation is developed for the people who use the system. In easy-to-understand language, this type of documentation shows how the program can and should be used to perform user tasks. Linx Software produces LinxCRM, a customer relationship management system. The company implemented special software to help it create high-quality user documentation including annotated screen shots from the system. Linx also created a video to help train users.[6]

Create and Load Data

This step involves making sure that all files and databases are populated and ready to be used with the new information system. Data for the initial loading of a new database may come from several sources—the old files or database of the system being replaced, from files of other systems used in the organization, or from data sources purchased from an outside organization. In any case, it may be necessary to write at least one new program to read the old data from these sources, reformat the data into a format compatible with the database design of the new system, and merge these data sources together. Another program may be needed to edit the merged data for accuracy and completeness and to add new entities, attributes, and/or relationships. For example, if an organization is installing a new customer relationship management program, a program might need to read the old customer contact data and convert it to a format that the new system can use. However, if the old customer contact data does not contain the same data, such as a separate "bill to" and "ship to" address for existing customers, this data may need to be added manually. The "bill to" address may be used to calculate to which of the organization's sales regions the customer belongs for sales reporting and accounting purposes. Considerable

ETHICAL& SOCIETAL ISSUES

Raspberry Pi and Building a Programming Society

In this chapter, you read about computer programming as a professional activity. The great majority of the programs you use or interact with every day are produced by professional programmers. Your computer's operating system, the word processor you use to write term papers, the spreadsheet program you use to track your expenses, and the browser you use to surf the Web—all of these were written by pros.

What, however, would be the impact on society if everyone could develop his or her own apps? What if children were taught to program? Would it help their creativity, their career prospects, or anything else? Professor John Naughton teaches public understanding of technology at the U.K.'s Open University. He writes, "Starting in primary school, children from all backgrounds and every part of the UK should have the opportunity to learn some of the key ideas of computer science, understand computational thinking, learn to program, and have the opportunity to progress to the next level of excellence in these activities." He concludes, "If we don't act now, we will be short-changing our children…. They will grow up as passive consumers of closed devices and services, leading lives that are increasingly circumscribed by technologies created by elites working for huge corporations such as Google, Facebook, and the like. We will, in effect, be breeding generations of hamsters for the glittering wheels of cages built by Mark Zuckerberg and his kind." Is Professor Naughton right, or would computing become just another topic to stuff into school curricula, already overloaded with too much content and suffering from insufficient budgets?

While there may not yet be definitive answers to these questions, efforts to find those answers are under way. Many people and organizations are devoted to the cause of teaching children to program in the belief that children and society overall will benefit.

Being able to program requires a computer. Not all schools have enough computers for students in a classroom, let alone to ensure that children have them for homework. The Raspberry Pi project can provide a $35 credit-card sized computer to anyone who wants one. The project's single-board computer runs a Linux operating system and connects to a TV set as a display and to any keyboard. Storage comes in the form of inexpensive SD cards, which are used in most digital cameras. The SD cards that serious photographers discard as too small and outdated are more than sufficient.

The next requirement is for software. Programming needs a programming language. While children could in principle be taught a professional language such as C++, they need to devote many hours of study before they can create an interesting program. This makes learning a professional programming language unsuited to all but the most highly motivated students. Instead, educators have designed languages such as Logo (the first such language), Simple, Kodu, and Scratch for this purpose. A pro wouldn't use these languages to code a word processor or a CRM application, but children can use them to quickly develop simple games and animations. The languages teach, without the pupils realizing what's happening, the mental discipline of breaking a process down into logical components, planning the sequence of operations, and figuring out what data the program needs to accomplish its purpose.

Web sites such as CNET.com now abound with projects that school children can complete with Raspberry Pi computers and educational programming languages. Students can program these microcomputers to serve as arcade game machines, Web servers, or wearable computer sunglasses. Even if the project does not produce a generation of Mark Zuckerbergs, it has certainly sparked the imaginations of many.

Discussion Questions

1. Software companies are continually improving programming languages. Would learning a programming language in grade school provide you with skills that you would need more than a decade later when you enter the workforce? Why or why not?
2. Suppose a large school district decides to add programming to its elementary school curriculum. Few teachers can program. How could a school district deal with that problem? Would school districts with more money fare better with these projects than school districts with fewer financial resources?

Critical Thinking Questions

1. What type of computer and media skills and ethics should be taught in schools?
2. Do you agree with John Naughton that tomorrow's educated person will know how to program a computer?

SOURCES: Turtle Logo Web site, Codeplex, *logo.codeplex.com*, accessed July 23, 2014; Scratch Web site, Massachusetts Institute of Technology, *scratch.mit.edu*, accessed July 23, 2014; Kodu, Microsoft Research, *www.kodugamelab.com/*, accessed July 23, 2014; Naughton, J., "Why All Our Kids Should Be Taught How to Code," *The Guardian, www.guardian.co.uk/education/2012/mar/31/why-kids -should-be-taught-code*, March 31, 2012; Raspberry Pi Web site, *www.raspberrypi.org*, accessed July 23, 2014; Simple Web site, *www.simplecodeworks.com/website.html*, accessed July 23, 2014; Watters, A., "5 Tools to Introduce Programming to Kids," *MindShift* (blog), KQED, *blogs.kqed.org/mindshift/2011/05/5-tools-to-introduce-programming-to-kids*, May 16, 2011; Wayner, P., "Programming for Children, Minus Cryptic Syntax," *The New York Times, www.nytimes. com/2011/11/10/technology/personaltech/computer-programming-for-children-minus-cryptic-syntax .html*, November 9, 2011; Obscura, Audrey, Raspberry Pi Projects, Instructables Web site, June 20, 2014, *www.instructables.com/id/Raspberry-Pi-Projects/*.

time and effort can be expended in creating and loading the new database. See Figure 13.2.

Perform Unit Testing

unit testing: Testing that ideally forces an individual program to execute all of its various functions and user features.

With the programs written and the database available, it is now possible for the developers to do initial testing of code components. This process is called **unit testing**, which involves testing individual components of code (subroutines, modules, and programs) to verify that each unit performs as designed. Unit testing is accomplished by developing test data that ideally will force an individual component to execute all of its various functions and user features. In addition, each program is tested with abnormal input to determine how it will handle erroneous input. As testers find problems, they modify the programs to work correctly. A good set of unit tests can be saved and rerun each time any code is changed to quickly detect any new defects.

INTEGRATION AND TESTING

Several types of testing must be conducted before a new or modified information system is ready to be put into production. These tests are outlined next and discussed in the following sections.

- Integration testing
- System testing
- Volume testing
- User acceptance testing

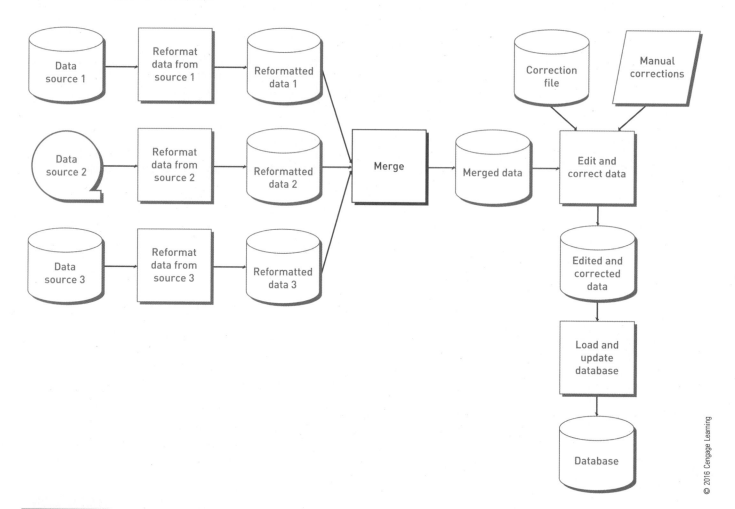

FIGURE 13.2

Database preparation tasks

Creating and loading a new database can take considerable resources.

Integration Testing

integration testing: Testing that involves linking all of the individual components together and testing them as a group to uncover any defects between individual components.

Integration testing (sometimes called integration and testing, I & T) involves linking individual components together and testing them as a group to uncover any defects in the interface between one component and another (e.g., component 1 fails to pass a key parameter to component 2). Even if unit testing is successful, developers cannot assume they can combine individual components into a working system without any problems. Unfortunately, one component that functions incorrectly can affect another component and, if these problems go undetected, can cause serious trouble later.

System Testing

system testing: Testing the complete, integrated system (hardware, software, databases, people, and procedures) to validate that the information system meets all specified requirements.

System testing involves testing the complete, integrated system (hardware, software, databases, people, and procedures) to validate that the information system meets all specified requirements. System testing is often done by independent testers who were not involved in developing program code. They attempt to make the system fail. They frequently employ testing called black box testing because it requires no specific knowledge of the application's code and internal logic. In other words, the system tester is aware of what the software is supposed to do but is not aware of how it does it.

INFORMATION SYSTEMS @ WORK

System Testing Reveals Problems in the Kill Vehicle Program

On June 23, 2014, the U.S. Missile Defense Agency reported long-awaited good news. Its Exoatmospheric Kill Vehicle (EKV) Capability Enhanced II kill vehicle successfully intercepted a missile fired from the Marshall Islands. The kill vehicle, a warhead launched from the Vandenberg Air Force Base in California, hit the intercontinental ballistic missile in midcourse, that is, after it had been launched and prior to its reaching the target. Although the engineers at the air force base left little to chance by programming the exact coordinates of its target into the kill vehicle, the test was considered an important success. The three previous attempts, all executed between 2008 and 2014, had failed. In fact, of the 17 tests of the Ground-based Midcourse Defense (GMD) system, only eight had hit their targets, giving the project—which will cost American taxpayers $40 billion by 2017—a 47 percent success rate.

In 1983, President Ronald Reagan first backed the idea of creating missile defense technology that would render nuclear weapons obsolete. The Strategic Defense Initiative (SDI), popularly known as Star Wars, cost taxpayers approximately $30 billion before the project was abandoned. In 1999, however, the U.S. Congress decided that it would begin development of the GMD system to protect the United States against a nuclear missile launched by a rogue nation. In 2006, communist North Korea had launched its first successful test of a nuclear missile, and both Iran and Iraq had made efforts to obtain nuclear technology. Congress set no date for the completion of the GMD system, but simply specified that it should be deployed as soon as it was technologically feasible.

However, terrorists attacked the Twin Towers and the Pentagon on September 11, 2001. On December 16, 2002, President George W. Bush issued a directive to deploy the GMD system by 2004, although two tests of the system had failed a week earlier. Rather than continuing work on the prototype and test the system, the Missile Defense Agency began deploying missiles in silos. Approximately 38 percent of the kill vehicles' software had not been validated through flight testing. The political pressure to deploy in the wake of the 9/11 attacks overrode concerns about faults in the software and other components. In 2004 and 2005, however, the Missile Defense Agency aborted tests of the GMD system when the missiles remained stuck in their silos due to software failures. In 2010, a test failed because

the sea-based radar system the kill vehicle used to calculate the trajectory of the transcontinental ballistic missile became confused by pieces of metal that tore away from the missile as it approached the kill vehicle. Before each new test, engineers redesigned the defective component. However, the Missile Defense Agency has stopped short of a total redesign and carefully planned systems development of a new prototype.

In February 2013, Frank Kendall, the undersecretary of Defense for acquisition, technology, and logistics, became the first to admit to the inherently failed development process when he announced, "The root cause was a desire to field these things very quickly and very cheaply.... We are seeing a lot of bad engineering, frankly, and it was because there was a rush."

Clearly, if the kill vehicles can only hit the missiles when they are given the coordinates in advance, these warheads will likely fail to bring down a nuclear missile fired by a rogue nation when both the launch time and position of the missile is unknown. The question remains as to whether the United States will be able to develop a functional GMD system before a rogue nation or terrorist organization becomes capable of launching a nuclear missile.

Discussion Questions

1. What error did the Missile Defense Agency make in the development of the GMD system?
2. How do the factors that pushed the agency to release the GMD compare to those that rush the development of business software?

Critical Thinking Questions

1. What steps can businesses take to ensure that engineers report all potential problems that arise during development?
2. What steps can IT professionals take to make business managers aware of the importance of following the complete systems development process?

SOURCES: "First in 6 Years: Troubled US Missile Defense System Hits Test Target," *RT Network*, June 23, 2014, *http://rt.com/usa/167728-gmd-launch-successful-failure/*; Willman, David, "$40-Billion Missile Defense System Proves Unreliable," *LA Times*, June 15, 2014, *www.latimes.com/nation/la-na-missile-defense-20140615-story.html#page=1*; "Timeline on North Korea's Nuclear Program," *New York Times*, August 6, 2013, *www.nytimes.com/interactive/2013/02/05/world/asia/northkorea-timeline.html?_r=0#/#time238_7085*.

Volume Testing

volume testing: Testing to evaluate the performance of the information system under varying yet realistic work volume and operating conditions to determine the work load at which systems performance begins to degrade and to identify and eliminate any issues that prevent the system from reaching its required service-level performance.

Volume testing involves evaluating the performance of the information system under varying yet realistic work volume and operating conditions (e.g., database size, number of concurrent users, number of transactions, and number of queries). The goals of volume testing are to determine the work load at which systems performance begins to degrade and to identify and eliminate any issues that prevent the system from reaching its required system-level performance.

User Acceptance Testing

user acceptance testing: Testing performed by trained system users to verify that the system can complete required tasks in a real-world operating environment and perform according to the system design specifications.

During **user acceptance testing (UAT)**, trained users test the information system to verify that it can complete required tasks in a real-world operating environment and perform according to the system design specifications. UAT is also known as beta testing, application testing, and end-user testing. Unlike system testing, which ensures that the system itself works, UAT determines whether the system meets its intended business needs.

UAT is a critical activity that must be completed successfully before newly developed software can be rolled out to the market. In the case of implementing a software package or software developed by an outside organization, the customer performs user acceptance testing before accepting transfer of ownership. UAT involves the following steps:

- The UAT test team is selected from the set of likely users.
- The UAT test team is trained using the currently available training material.
- The overall UAT strategy and schedule is defined.
- The UAT team designs test cases to exercise the functions and features of the information system.
- The test cases are documented in a clear and simple step-by-step manner to make the tests easy to execute.
- The UAT team executes the defined test cases and documents the results of each test.
- The software development team reviews the test results and makes any required changes to the code so it meets the design specifications.
- The UAT team retests the information system until all defects have been fixed or it is agreed that certain defects will not be fixed.
- The UAT team indicates its acceptance or nonacceptance of the information system. If accepted, the information system is ready to be fully implemented.
- The UAT team provides feedback on the user training material to allow this to be updated and improved.

Prior to releasing a new software package or a major revision of an existing package, commercial software development organizations conduct alpha and beta testing. Alpha testing is a limited internal acceptance test where employees of the software development organization and a limited number of other "friendlies" use the software and provide feedback. After fixing problems uncovered in alpha testing, the developer makes a beta test version of the software available to potential users outside the organization. For example, Microsoft might make a free beta test version of software available on the Internet to increase the amount of user feedback.

user acceptance document: A formal agreement that the user signs stating that a phase of the installation or the complete system is approved.

Most software manufacturers and third-party software developers have a **user acceptance document**—a formal agreement the user signs stating that a phase of the installation or the complete system is approved. This is a legal document that usually removes or reduces the IS vendor's liability for problems that occur after the user acceptance document has been signed.

Because this document is so important, many companies get legal assistance before they sign it.

Table 13.1 summarizes five types of testing: user acceptance, volume, system, integration, and unit testing.

TABLE 13.1 Tests conducted on an information system

Form of Test	What Is Tested	Purpose of Test	Who Does It
User Acceptance	Test the complete, integrated system (hardware, software, databases, people, and procedures).	Verify the information system can complete required tasks in a real-world operating environment and do this according to the system design specifications.	Trained users of the system
Volume	Evaluate the performance of the information system under realistic and varying work volume and operating conditions.	Determine the work load at which systems performance begins to degrade and identify and eliminate any issues that prevent the system from reaching its required service-level performance.	System development team and members of the operations organization
System	Test the complete, integrated system (hardware, software, databases, people, and procedures).	Validate that the information system meets all specified requirements.	Independent test team separate from the software development team
Integration	Test all of the individual units of the information system linked together.	Uncover any defects between individual components of the information system.	Software developers or independent software testers using black box testing measures
Unit	Test individual units of the system.	Verify that each unit performs as designed.	Software developers

© 2016 Cengage Learning

IMPLEMENTATION

A number of steps are involved in system implementation. These are outlined next and discussed in the following sections.

- User preparation
- Site preparation
- Installation
- Cutover

User Preparation

user preparation: The process of readying managers, decision makers, employees, other users, and stakeholders to accept and use the new system.

User preparation is the process of readying managers, decision makers, employees, system users, and other stakeholders to accept and use the new system. Ideally, user preparation begins in the early stages of systems investigation and continues through implementation.

As discussed in Chapter 2, the major challenges to successful implementation of an information system are often more behavioral than technical. Successfully introducing an information system into an organization requires a mix of organizational change skills and technical skills. Strong, effective leadership is required to overcome the behavioral resistance to change and achieve a smooth and successful system introduction. Chapter 2 also introduced several change management models that can prove useful in user preparation.

The dynamics of how change is implemented can be viewed in terms of the Lewin and Schein three-stage approach for change of ceasing old habits and creating a climate that is receptive to change; learning new work methods, behaviors, and systems; and reinforcing changes to make the new process second nature, accepted, and part of the job.

Leavitt's Diamond proposes that every organizational system is made up of people, tasks, structure, and technology with an interaction among the four components so that any change in one of these elements will necessitate a change in the other three elements. Thus, to successfully implement a new information system, appropriate changes must be made to the people, structure, and tasks affected by the new system. People must be convinced to take a positive attitude to the change and be willing to exhibit new behaviors consistent with the change. Management might need to modify the reward system to recognize those who exhibit the desired new behaviors. Training in any required new skills is also necessary. See Figure 13.3.

FIGURE 13.3

User preparation

Providing users with proper training can help ensure that the information system is used correctly, efficiently, and effectively.

The technology acceptance model (TAM) specifies the factors that can lead to better attitudes about the use of a new information system, along with its higher acceptance and usage. Perceived usefulness and perceived ease of use strongly influence whether someone will use an information system. Management can improve that perception by demonstrating that others have used the system effectively and by providing user training and support.

The diffusion of innovation theory cautions that adoption of any innovation does not happen all at once for all members of the targeted population; rather, it is a drawn out process with some people quicker to adopt the innovation than others. Rogers' diffusion of innovation theory defined five categories of adopters, each with different attitudes toward innovation. When promoting an innovation to a target population, first understand the characteristics of the target population that will help or hinder adoption of the innovation and then apply the appropriate strategy. This theory can be useful in planning the rollout of a new information system.

Because user training is so important, some companies employ a variety of training approaches including in-house, software, video, Internet, and other training approaches. The material used to train the UAT team can serve as a starting point with updates and changes based on feedback from the test team.

The eventual success of any system depends not only on how users work with it, but how well the IS personnel within the organization can operate and support it. The IS personnel should also attend training sessions similar to those for the users, although their sessions can provide more technical details. Effective training will help IS personnel use the new system to perform their jobs and support other users in the organization. IBM and many other companies are using online and simulated training programs to cut training costs and improve effectiveness.

Site Preparation

site preparation: Preparation of the location of a new system.

A location for the hardware associated with the new system needs to be prepared, a process called **site preparation**. For a small system, site preparation can be as simple as rearranging the furniture in an office to make room for a computer. The computer and associated hardware in a larger system might require special wiring, air conditioning, or construction. A special floor, for example, might have to be built and cables placed under it to connect the various computer components, and a new security system might be needed to protect the equipment. The project team needs to consider the amount of site preparation that may be necessary and build sufficient lead time into the schedule to allow for it. See Figure 13.4.

FIGURE **13.4**

Site preparation

Site preparation may be relatively inexpensive and easy or expensive and complex, requiring significant lead time.

© Cynthia Farmer/Shutterstock.com

Today, organizations want to develop IS sites that are energy efficient and secure. One company, for example, installed special security kiosks that let visitors log on and request a meeting with a company employee. The employee can see the visitor on his or her computer screen and accept or reject the visitor. If the visitor is accepted, the kiosk prints a visitor pass.

M&T Bank is the largest deposit-holder in western New York with head-quarters in Buffalo. The bank invested around $60 million in data centers over a three-year period to meet current business needs and strengthen its backup systems in case of disasters.[7]

Installation

Installation: The process of physically placing the computer equipment on the site and making it operational.

Installation is the process of physically placing the computer equipment on the site and making it operational. See Figure 13.5. Although normally the manufacturer is responsible for installing computer equipment, someone from the organization (usually the project manager) should oversee the process, making sure that all equipment specified in the contract is installed at the proper location. After the system is installed, the manufacturer performs several tests to ensure that the equipment is operating as it should.

FIGURE **13.5**

Installation

After preparing users and a site for a new system, the manufacturer typically installs the system and prepares it for regular use.

Cutover

cutover: The process of switching from an old information system to a replacement system.

Cutover is the process of switching from an old information system to a replacement system. Cutover is critical to the success of the organization because, if not done properly, the results can be disastrous.

Hershey's, the largest chocolate manufacturer in North America, provides a classic example of a failed system cutover. The firm planned to upgrade a mix of legacy information systems into an integrated environment of the latest software from leading vendors, including SAP for ERP functionality, Manugistics for supply chain management, and Siebel for customer relationship management. The cutover was targeted for July, one of the company's busiest months when it was shipping orders for Halloween and Christmas. Unfortunately, Hershey's was not well prepared and the cutover was a fiasco. As a result, Hershey was unable to process over $100 million worth of orders. The resulting operational paralysis led to nearly a 20 percent drop in quarterly profits and an 8 percent decline in share price.

Organizations can follow one of several cutover strategies. See Figure 13.6. **Direct conversion** (also called *plunge* or *direct cutover*) involves stopping the old system and starting the new system on a given date. Direct conversion is high-risk approach because of the potential for problems and errors when the old system is shut off and the new system is turned on at the same instant.

direct conversion: Stopping the old system and starting the new system on a given date; also called *plunge* or *direct cutover*.

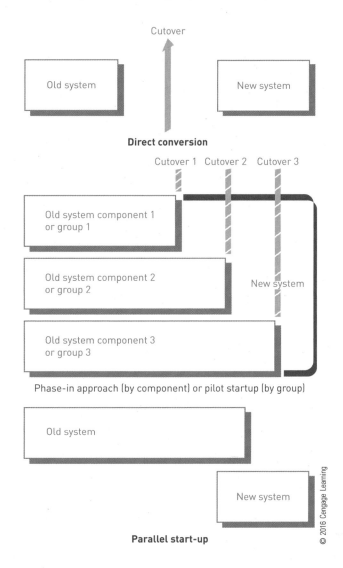

FIGURE 13.6

System cutover strategies
Cutover can be through direct conversion, phase-in approach, or parallel startup.

Shell is one of the largest corporations in the world with recent annual revenues exceeding $450 billion. One of Shell's major business subdivisions is called Downstream, an organization that converts crude oil into a range of refined products, which are moved and marketed around the world for domestic, industrial, and transport use.[8] The 37,000 workers in 36 countries in the Downstream business rely on SAP-based software to complete their work, making it a mission-critical application. A few years ago, Shell decided to upgrade to a new version of the Downstream software to access new functions and support services. The organization began planning the world's largest SAP upgrade in October 2011, which culminated with a direct cutover on a weekend in February 2013—18 months later. Shell had many tasks to accomplish before the cutover, including updating several databases, installing new application servers, replacing hardware, and expanding storage capacity by 30 percent. Despite its huge complexity and the high risk associated with such a major cutover, the upgrade was a success.[9]

Many organizations follow a **phase-in approach** where components of the new system are slowly phased in while components of the old one are slowly phased out. When everyone is confident that all components of the new system are performing as expected, the old system is completely phased out. This gradual replacement is repeated for each component until the new system has fully replaced the old system. In some cases, the phase-in approach, also called a *piecemeal approach*, can take several months.

phase-in approach: Slowly replacing components of the old system with those of the new one; this process is repeated for each application until the new system is running every application and performing as expected; it is also called a *piecemeal approach*.

pilot start-up: Running the complete new system for one group of users rather than all users.

parallel start-up: Running both the old and new systems for a period of time and closely comparing the output of the new system with the output of the old system; any differences are reconciled. When users are comfortable that the new system is working correctly, the old system is eliminated.

Pilot start-up involves running the complete new system for one group of users rather than all users. For example, a manufacturing company with many retail outlets throughout the country could use the pilot start-up approach and install a new inventory control system at one of its retail outlets. When this pilot retail outlet runs without problems, the new inventory control system can then be implemented at other retail outlets one by one. The next retail outlet can then benefit from the experience and learnings gained from the previous outlet.

Parallel start-up involves running both the old and new systems for a period of time. The performance and output of the new system are compared closely with the performance and output of the old system, and any differences are reconciled. When users are comfortable that the new system is working correctly, the old system is eliminated.

SYSTEMS OPERATION AND MAINTENANCE

The steps involved in systems operation and maintenance are outlined next and discussed in the following sections.

- Operation
- Maintenance
- Disposal

Operation

systems operation: Use of a new or modified system under all kinds of operating conditions.

Systems operation involves using the new or modified system under all kinds of operating conditions. Getting the most out of a new or modified system during its operation is the most important aspect of systems operations for many organizations. To provide adequate user support, many companies establish a formal help desk for their employees and customers. A *help desk* consists of computer systems, manuals, people with technical expertise, and other resources needed to solve problems and give accurate answers to questions. If you are having trouble accessing or using one of your organization's information systems, you can call the help desk for support.

monitoring: Tracking the number of errors encountered, the amount of memory required, the amount of processing or CPU time needed, and other performance indicators.

Monitoring involves measuring system performance by tracking the number of errors encountered, the amount of memory required, the amount of processing or CPU time needed, and other performance indicators. If a particular system is not performing as expected, it should be modified, or a new system should be developed or acquired.

System performance products can measure all components of an information system, including hardware, software, database, telecommunications, and network systems. Microsoft Visual Studio, for example, has features that allow systems developers to monitor and review how applications are running and performing, permitting developers to make changes if needed. IBM Tivoli OMEGAMON XE is a software family of performance monitors for analysis of IBM mainframe operating systems, such as z/OS and z/VM and various subsystems, such as CICS, DB2, and IMS. Precise Software Solutions has system performance products that provide around-the-clock performance monitoring for ERP systems, Oracle database applications, and other programs.[10] HP also offers a software tool called Business Technology Optimization (BTO) to help companies analyze the performance of their computer systems, diagnose potential problems, and take corrective action if needed. When properly used, system performance products can quickly and efficiently locate actual or potential problems.

Allscripts is a $2 billion publicly traded company that provides practice management, electronic healthcare records, and financial software to hundreds of physician practices, hospitals, and other healthcare organizations. Its customers typically have between 7 and 20 servers running Allscripts applications at all times. Keeping the software running without interruption is a major challenge. To solve this problem, Allscripts has its customers install eG performance monitoring software to monitor the network, operating system, and applications on its servers. This enables Allscripts to constantly monitor the software to identify and fix problems before they affect users.[11]

systems review: The process of analyzing systems to make sure they are operating as intended.

Systems review is the process of analyzing systems to make sure they are operating as intended. Systems review often compares the performance and benefits of the system as it was designed with the actual performance and benefits of the system in operation.

U.S. citizens were alarmed and dismayed when an audit of 731 Veterans Affairs (VA) hospitals and clinics found that some 57,000 veterans nationwide experienced wait times of 90 days or longer for their first medical appointments. An additional 64,000 veterans were not even on the VA electronic waiting list for doctor appointments that they had requested. Shockingly, 13 percent of VA employees interviewed were told to falsify records so that wait times would appear shorter.[12] In a separate audit of its information systems, the Veterans Affairs (VA) inspector reported that the agency had continuing problems protecting its mission-critical systems. The audit found that although the VA had made progress developing security policies and procedures, it still suffered from "significant deficiencies related to access controls, configuration management controls, continuous monitoring controls, and service continuity practices designed to protect mission-critical systems."[13] It is not clear to what degree these system shortcomings contributed to the incorrect reporting of wait times.

Internal employees, external consultants, or both can perform systems review. An organization's billing application, for example, might be reviewed for errors, inefficiencies, and opportunities to reduce operating costs. In addition, the billing application might be redone if corporations merge, if one or more new managers require different information or reports, or if federal laws on bill collecting and privacy change. This is an event-driven approach.

Maintenance

systems maintenance: A stage of systems development that involves changing and enhancing the system to make it more useful in achieving user and organizational goals.

Systems maintenance is a stage of systems development that involves changing and enhancing the system to make it more useful in achieving user and organizational goals. Some of the reasons for program maintenance are the following:

- Poor system performance such as slow response time for frequent transactions
- Changes in business processes
- Changes in the needs of system stakeholders, users, and managers
- Bugs or errors in the program
- Technical and hardware problems
- Corporate mergers and acquisitions
- Changes in government regulations
- Changes in the operating system or hardware on which the application runs

Organizations can perform systems maintenance in-house, or they can hire outside companies to perform maintenance for them. Many companies that use information systems from Oracle or SAP, for example, often hire these companies to maintain their systems. Systems maintenance is important for individuals, groups, and organizations. Individuals, for example, can use the Internet, computer vendors, and independent maintenance companies, including YourTechOnline.com (*www.yourtechonline.com*), Geek Squad (*www.geek squad.com*), and PC Pinpoint (*www.pcpinpoint.com*). Organizations often have personnel dedicated to maintenance. Software maintenance for purchased software can cost 20 percent or more of the purchase price annually.

The maintenance process can be especially difficult for older software. A *legacy system* is an old system that might have cost millions of dollars to develop and patch or modify repeatedly over the years. The maintenance costs for legacy systems can become quite expensive and, at some point, it becomes more cost effective to switch to new programs and applications than to repair and maintain the legacy system.

Royal Bank of Scotland (RBS) and National Westminster Bank (NatWest) are two of the United Kingdom's largest and most established banks. However, customers of these banks have been blocked from using ATMs or debit cards due to problems with legacy banking systems. Some of their systems are over 30 years old and were originally designed to handle simple branch banking. Over the years, the banks have had to make changes to support ATMs, online banking, and mobile banking as well as changes to accommodate new regulatory requirements. These changes were implemented using different programming languages running on different computers and operating systems by different development teams. It is impossible for one person or team to fully comprehend the entire system.[14] The banks recently announced that they will be spending £1 billion (approximately $1.7 billion USD) to improve their personal and small business banking services to make it easier for customers on the move.[15]

Four generally accepted categories signify the amount of change involved in maintenance. A slipstream upgrade is a minor upgrade—typically a code adjustment or minor bug fix. Many companies don't announce to users that a slipstream upgrade has been made. Because a slipstream upgrade usually requires recompiling all the code, it can create entirely new bugs. This maintenance practice explains why the same computers sometimes work differently with what is supposedly the same software. A patch is a minor change to correct a problem or make a small enhancement. It is usually patched into an existing program; that is, the programming code representing the system enhancement is usually added to the existing code. Although slipstream upgrades and patches are minor changes, they can cause users and support personnel big problems if the programs do not run as before. Many patches come from off-the-shelf software vendors. A new release is a significant program change that often requires changes in the documentation of the software. Finally, a new version is a major program change, typically encompassing many new features. Figure 13.7 shows the relative amount of change and effort associated to test and implement these four categories of maintenance.

slipstream upgrade: A minor upgrade—typically a code adjustment or minor bug fix—not worth announcing. It usually requires recompiling all the code, and in so doing, it can create entirely new bugs.

patch: A minor change to correct a problem or make a small enhancement. It is usually an addition to an existing program.

release: A significant program change that often requires changes in the documentation of the software.

version: A major program change, typically encompassing many new features.

FIGURE **13.7**

System maintenance efforts

This chart shows the relative amount of change and effort associated to test and implement slipstream upgrades, patches, releases, and versions.

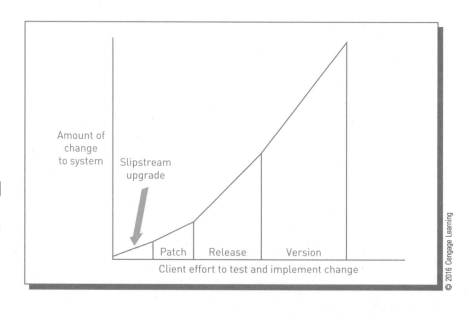

© 2016 Cengage Learning

request for maintenance form:
A form authorizing modification of programs.

Because of the amount of effort that can be spent on maintenance, many organizations require a request for maintenance form to be completed and approved before authorizing the modification of an information system. This form is usually signed by a business manager who documents the need for the change and identifies the priority of the change relative to other work that has been requested. The IS group reviews the form and identifies the programs to change, determines the people to assign to the project, estimates the expected completion date, and develops a technical description of the change. A cost/benefit analysis might be required if the change requires substantial resources. The completed change request is then reviewed and prioritized relative to the other change requests that have been made.

Disposal

At some point, an existing information system may become obsolete, uneconomical to operate and/or maintain, or unrepairable. Information systems typically evolve to this stage in the life cycle because the system can no longer be modified to keep up with changing user and business requirements, outdated technology causes the system to run slowly or unreliably, or key vendors are no longer able or willing to continue to provide necessary service or support.

system disposal: Those activities that ensure the orderly dissolution of the system, including disposing of all equipment in an environmentally friendly manner, closing out contracts, and safely migrating information from the system to another system or archiving it in accordance with applicable records management policies.

System disposal involves those activities that ensure the orderly dissolution of the system, including disposing of all equipment in an environmentally friendly manner, closing out contracts, and safely migrating information from the system to another system or archiving it in accordance with applicable records management policies. The steps involved in system disposal are outlined and discussed in the following sections.

1. Communicate intent
2. Terminate contracts
3. Make backups of data
4. Delete sensitive data
5. Dispose of hardware

Communicate Intent

A memo communicating the intent to terminate the information system should be distributed to all key stakeholders months in advance of the actual shutdown. This ensures that everyone is aware of the shutdown and allows time for them to convert to the new system or process replacing the terminated system. For example, the Microsoft Windows XP operating system was released in 2001. Microsoft announced in September 2007 that it would end support of this popular operating system in April 2014. Despite the end-of-life announcement, an estimated 25 percent of consumers and businesses including 75 percent of ATMs in the United States had not converted to a replacement operating system by early 2014.[16]

Terminate Contracts

The various vendors who provide hardware, software, or services associated with the information system must be notified well in advance to avoid any penalty fees associated with abrupt termination of a contract.

Make Backups of Data

Prior to deleting files associated with the system, make any backup copies of data according to your organization's records management policies.

Delete Sensitive Data

Extreme care must be taken to remove customer, employee, financial, and company-sensitive data from all computer hardware and storage devices before disposing of it. Otherwise, your discarded equipment could become a treasure trove to identity thieves or your competition. Remember, when you delete a file, the bits and pieces of the file physically stay on your computer until they are overwritten, and they can be retrieved with a data recovery program. To remove data from a hard drive permanently, the hard drive needs to be wiped clean. Utility programs to perform this task are available online or in computer stores. Select a program that overwrites or wipes the hard drive several times to ensure that the data is truly deleted. An alternative is to remove the hard drive and physically destroy it.

Dispose of Hardware

After backing up and then removing data from drives, members of the project team can dispose of obsolete or damaged computer hardware. Governments, environmental agencies, and leading hardware manufacturers are attempting to reduce hazardous materials in electronic products. However, some hardware components still contain materials that are toxic to the environment. Responsible disposal techniques should be used regardless of whether the hardware is sold, given away, or discarded. As mentioned in Chapter 3, many computer hardware manufacturers including Dell and HP have developed programs to assist their customers in disposing of old equipment.

ALTERNATE SYSTEMS DEVELOPMENT LIFE CYCLES AND APPROACHES

Now that we have covered all the phases of the traditional systems development life cycle, we will discuss alternate system development life cycles, including prototyping, agile, object-oriented, mobile, and end-user development.

Prototyping

prototype: A working model of a system developed to enable users to interact with the system and provide feedback so developers can better understand what is needed.

A software **prototype** is a working model of a system developed to enable users to interact with it and provide feedback so developers can better understand what is needed. Building and using a prototype enables developers and users to test concepts and evaluate alternatives before expending a major effort to implement the system. Prototypes can be classified as throw-away prototypes or working prototypes.[17]

prototyping: An iterative software development approach based on the use of software prototypes.

Prototyping is an iterative software development approach based on the use of software prototypes as shown in Figure 13.8. The advantages and disadvantages of prototyping are summarized in Table 13.2.[18]

throw-away prototype: A prototype that is used to help define the software solution but does not become part of the final solution.

A **throw-away prototype** is one that is used to help define the software solution but does not become part of the final solution. Throw-away prototypes provide a highly effective way for developers to demonstrate their understanding of how the system should work to the client or users. The feedback generated during the demo identifies misunderstood or overlooked user requirements. The demo also provides the users with an opportunity to change their mind once they see the prototype system in action.[19]

working prototype: A prototype that starts with an initial prototype that undergoes a series of iterations of demo, feedback, and refinement and eventually evolves into the final software solution.

A **working prototype** starts with an initial prototype that undergoes a series of iterations of demo, feedback, and refinement and eventually evolves into the final software solution. The client or users are deeply involved throughout the development process by providing continuous feedback. With each iteration, the working prototype moves further from the initial prototype and closer to a working system that meets the needs of its users.

Rational Unified Process (RUP): An iterative systems development approach developed by IBM that includes a number of tools and techniques that are typically tailored to fit the needs of a specific company or organization.

The **Rational Unified Process (RUP)** is an iterative systems development approach developed by IBM that includes a number of tools and techniques that are typically tailored to fit the needs of a specific company or organization. RUP stresses quality as the software is changed and updated over time. Many companies have used RUP to their advantage.[20]

Agile Development

agile development: An iterative system development process that develops the system in "sprint" increments lasting from two weeks to two months.

Agile development is an iterative system development process that develops the system in "sprint" increments lasting from two weeks to two months.

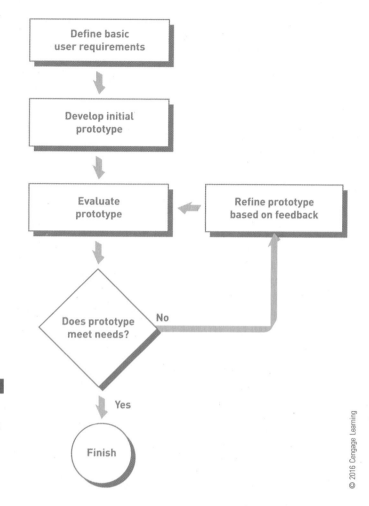

FIGURE **13.8**

Prototyping

Prototyping is an iterative approach to systems development. Each generation of prototype is a refinement of the previous generation based on user feedback.

TABLE **13.2** Advantages and disadvantages of prototyping

Advantages	Disadvantages
Users can try the system and provide constructive feedback during development.	Each iteration builds on the previous one. The final solution might be only incrementally better than the initial solution.
A throw-away prototype can be produced in days.	Formal end-of-phase reviews might not occur. Thus, it is very difficult to contain the scope of the prototype, and the project never seems to end.
As solutions emerge, users become more positive about the process and the results.	System documentation is often absent or incomplete because the primary focus is on development of the prototype.
Prototyping enables early detection of errors and omissions.	System backup and recovery, performance, and security issues can be overlooked in the haste to develop a prototype.

Unlike the traditional system development process, agile development accepts the fact that system requirements are evolving and cannot be fully understood or defined at the start of the project. Agile development concentrates instead on maximizing the team's ability to deliver quickly and respond to emerging requirements—hence the name agile. When a team stops and reevaluates the system every two weeks to two months, it has ample opportunity to identify and implement new or changed system requirements.[21]

Scrum is a method employed to keep the agile system development effort focused and moving quickly. A **scrum master** is the person who coordinates all scrum activities, and a scrum team consists of a dozen or fewer people who perform all systems development activities from investigation to testing.

scrum: A method employed to keep the agile system development effort focused and moving quickly.

Scrum master: The person who coordinates all scrum activities.

Thus there is less personnel turnover on a typical agile project than when using the traditional system development process. The scrum master does not fill the role of a traditional project manager and has no people management responsibilities. Instead, the primary responsibility of the scrum master is to anticipate and remove barriers to the project team producing its deliverables and meeting the project schedule.[22]

product owner: A person who represents the project stakeholders and is responsible for communicating and aligning project priorities between the stakeholders and development team.

The product owner is a person who represents the project stakeholders and is responsible for communicating and aligning project priorities between the stakeholders and development team.

Using the scrum method, the product owner works with the stakeholders and team to create a prioritized list of project requirements called a product backlog. Next, a sprint planning session is held during which the team selects the highest priority requirements from the top of the product backlog to create the sprint backlog and decide how to implement those requirements. The team sets a certain amount of time—typically two to eight weeks—to complete its work. During the sprint, each day at the same time, the team meets briefly (15 minutes at most) to share information necessary for coordination. At this meeting, team members describe what they completed the previous day and identify any obstacles that stand in their way of completing the day's activities. The sprint is complete when the team presents a working system that incorporates the new requirements and that can be used and evaluated. During the sprint review meeting, the team shares what it learned from the current sprint iteration so that knowledge can be applied in the next sprint iteration. See Figure 13.9. Along the way, the scrum master keeps the team focused on its goals.[23]

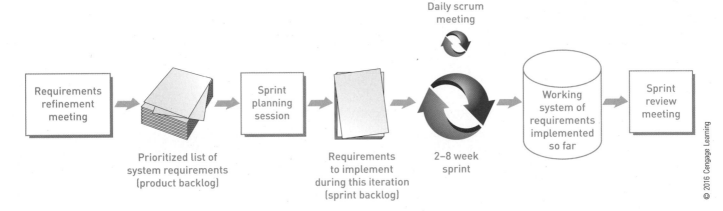

© 2016 Cengage Learning

FIGURE 13.9

Agile system development life cycle

The agile approach aims to develop a system in sprint increments lasting from two weeks to two months.

Agile development requires cooperation and frequent face-to-face meetings with all participants, including systems developers and users, as they modify, refine, and test the system's capabilities and how it meets users' needs. Organizations are using agile development to a greater extent today to improve the results of systems development, including global projects requiring IS resources distributed in many locations. Agile is better suited for developing smaller information systems than larger ones. During an agile project, the level of participation of stakeholders and users is much higher than in other approaches. Table 13.3 lists advantages and disadvantages of agile development.[24]

extreme programming (XP): An approach to writing code that promotes incremental development of a system using short development cycles to improve productivity and to accommodate new customer requirements.

Extreme programming (XP) is an approach to writing code that promotes incremental development of a system using short development cycles to improve productivity and to accommodate new customer requirements. Other essentials of extreme programming include programming in pairs, performing extensive code review, unit testing of all code, putting off the

TABLE 13.3 Advantages and disadvantages of agile development

Advantages	Disadvantages
For appropriate projects, this approach puts an application into production sooner than any other approach.	This intense SDLC can burn out systems developers and other project participants.
Documentation is produced as a by-product of completing project tasks.	This approach requires systems analysts and users to be skilled in agile systems development tools and agile techniques.
Agile forces teamwork and lots of interaction between users and stakeholders.	Agile requires a larger percentage of stakeholders' and users' time than other approaches.

© 2016 Cengage Learning

programming of system features until they are actually needed, use of a flat project management structure, simplicity and clarity in code, expecting changes in system requirements as the project progresses and the desired solution is better understood, and frequent communication with the customer and among programmers. These qualities make extreme programming compatible with agile software development.[25]

Table 13.4 compares the key features of the agile, prototype, and traditional system development lifecycles.

TABLE 13.4 Comparison of system development life cycles

Characteristic	System Development Life Cycle		
	Agile	Prototype	Traditional
Description	An iterative process that develops the system in sprint increments lasting 2–8 weeks; each increment focuses on implementing the highest priority requirements that can be completed in the allotted time	An iterative process that constructs prototypes or uses application frameworks	A sequential multistage process where work on the next stage cannot begin until the results of the previous stage are reviewed and approved or modified as necessary
Basic assumption	System requirements cannot be fully defined at start of project	System requirements cannot be fully defined at start of project	All critical system requirements can be fully defined at start of project
How requirements and design are defined	Users interacting with systems analysts and working software	Users interacting with systems analysts and prototypes	Users interacting with systems analysts and system documentation and/or models
Associated processes	Scrum	Rapid application development	Structured systems analysis and design

© 2016 Cengage Learning

Object-Oriented Systems Development

As discussed in Chapter 4, an object consists of data and the actions that can be performed on the data. The object containing the data, instructions, and procedures is a programming building block. An object can relate to data on a product, an input routine, or an order-processing routine. The object-oriented (OO) approach is frequently used in the investigation, analysis, and design phases of system development.

Consider a kayak rental business in Maui, Hawaii, where the owners want to computerize their operations, including renting kayaks to customers and adding new kayaks into the rental program. See Figure 13.10. As shown in

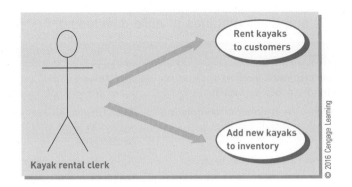

FIGURE 13.10

Use case diagram for a kayak rental application

The kayak rental clerk is an actor that interacts with the use cases, which are the actions in the ovals.

the figure, the kayak rental clerk rents kayaks to customers and adds new kayaks to the current inventory available for rent. The stick figure is an example of an *actor*, and the ovals each represent an event, called a *use case*. In this example, the actor (the kayak rental clerk) interacts with two use cases (rent kayaks to customers and add new kayaks to inventory). The use case diagram is part of the Unified Modeling Language (UML) used in object-oriented systems development.

The object-oriented approach can also be used during systems analysis. Like traditional analysis, problems or potential opportunities are examined and key participants and essential data are identified during object-oriented analysis. Instead of analyzing the existing system using data-flow diagrams, the team uses an object-oriented approach.

A more detailed analysis of the kayak rental business reveals that there are two classes of kayaks: single kayaks for one person and tandem kayaks that can accommodate two people. With the OO approach, classes are used to describe different types of objects, such as single and tandem kayaks. The classes of kayaks can be shown in a generalization/specialization hierarchy diagram as in Figure 13.11. KayakItem is an object that will store the kayak identification number (ID) and the date the kayak was purchased (datePurchased).

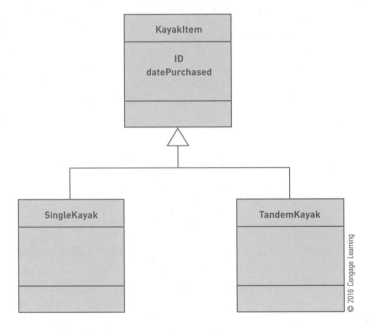

FIGURE 13.11

Generalization/specialization hierarchy diagram

This generalization/specialization hierarchy diagram describes single and tandem kayak classes.

Of course, the system could have subclasses of customers, life vests, paddles, and other items. For example, price discounts for kayak rentals could be given to seniors and students. Thus, the Customer class could be divided into regular, senior, and student customer subclasses.

The object-oriented approach can be used during the design phase to design key objects and classes of objects in the new or updated system. This process includes considering the problem domain, the operating environment, and the user interface. The problem domain involves the classes of objects related to solving a problem or realizing an opportunity. In our example of the kayak rental shop, KayakItem in Figure 13.11 is an example of a problem domain object that will store information on kayaks in the rental program. The operating environment for the rental shop's system includes objects that interact with printers, system software, and other software and hardware devices. The user interface for the system includes objects that users interact with, such as buttons and scroll bars in a Windows program.

During the design phase, you also need to consider the sequence of events that must happen for the system to function correctly. For example, you might want to design the sequence of events for adding a new kayak to the rental program. The event sequence is often called a *scenario*, and it can be diagrammed in a sequence diagram. See Figure 13.12.

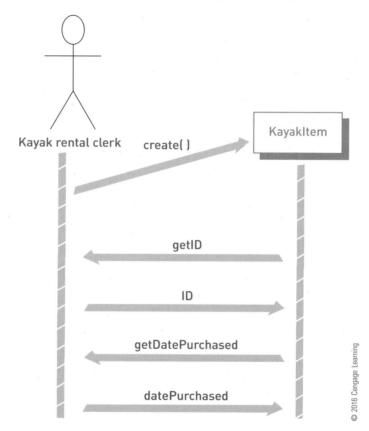

© 2016 Cengage Learning

FIGURE **13.12**

Sequence diagram

This sequence diagram adds a new KayakItem scenario.

You read a sequence diagram starting at the top and moving down:

1. The Create arrow at the top is a message from the kayak rental clerk to the KayakItem object to create information on a new kayak to be placed into the rental program.
2. The KayakItem object knows that it needs the ID for the kayak and sends a message to the clerk requesting the information (see the getID arrow).
3. The clerk then types the ID into the computer. This action is shown with the ID arrow. The data is stored in the KayakItem object.
4. Next, KayakItem requests the purchase date. This is shown in the getDatePurchased arrow.
5. Finally, the clerk types the purchase date into the computer. The data is also transferred to KayakItem object, as shown in the datePurchased arrow at the bottom of Figure 13.12.

This scenario is only one example of a sequence of events. Other scenarios might include entering information about life jackets, paddles, suntan lotion, and other accessories. The same types of use case and generalization/specialization hierarchy diagrams can be created for each event, and additional sequence diagrams will also be needed.

Mobile Application Development

Today, many organizations are developing or buying mobile applications for their managers and workers. Demand for mobile application developers is on the rise with demand moving from B2C apps to B2B apps. Ideally, these applications should work on a variety of devices, including iPhones, Android phones, BlackBerry phones, tablet computers, and other mobile devices. To create successful mobile apps, developers should consider who will use the app and what their goals are. This means developers must gain input from the users before the app is developed.[26]

While the overall approach of systems development is similar to mobile devices compared to traditional systems development projects, there are some important differences. The user interface is not the typical graphical user interface discussed in Chapter 4. Instead, most mobile devices use a touch user interface, called a *natural user interface (NUI)*, or multitouch interface by some. The systems development teams for mobile devices are typically smaller, allowing them to be more flexible and agile. It can also be difficult to find IS personnel with the skills and experience to develop good mobile applications. Having the application communicate with the Internet or corporate computers is another issue that must be resolved. How to handle phone calls in the middle of running an application also needs to be considered.

Some systems development tools available for mobile applications are shown in Table 13.5.[27]

TABLE 13.5 Application development tools for mobile environment

Tool	Target Environment
Alpha Anywhere	iOS, Android, Windows Phone
App Press	iPhone, iPad, Android
iBuildApp	iPhone, iPad, Android
Mobile Chrome Development Kit	iOS, Android, Chrome
Salesforce1	iOS, Android
ViziApps	iOS, Android

Ethan Nicholas is legendary among independent iPhone app developers. His tank artillery game iShoot was not an immediate success, so Nicholas decided to develop a free version of the app—iShoot Lite—inside which he advertised the $3 full version of iShoot. The free version was downloaded 2.4 million times from the Apple Store in just a few weeks and led to 320,000 iShoot Lite players paying for iShoot.[28] In addition to the Apple Store, Google has the Google Play store and BlackBerry has App World. Although most people purchase individual applications from authorized Web sites, unauthorized application stores that are not supported by the smartphone or cellular company can also be used to purchase or acquire useful applications.

In addition to developing innovative applications, organizations are using innovative approaches to deliver these applications to workers and managers. Some CIOs, for example, are investigating the use of application stores to deliver corporate information and applications to workers and executives. As with users of smartphones, tablet computers, and other mobile devices, workers and executives could go to a corporate applications store and download the latest programs, decision support systems, or other work-related applications. See Figure 13.13.

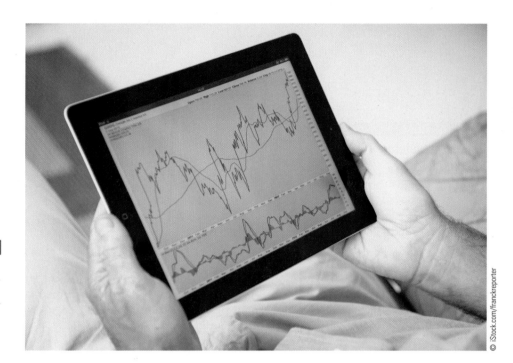

FIGURE 13.13

Mobile application development

Some organizations are using application stores to deliver corporate information and applications to workers and executives.

User Systems Development

For decades, professional software developers have been unable to keep up with the nearly insatiable appetite of today's workers, managers, and executives for more and more information, more and more reports, and more and more analysis. Users have grown weary of lengthy software development processes that all too frequently lead to implementation of systems that cost too much yet do not meet their expectations. As a result, users are increasingly doing their own software development and are now building over 25 percent of new business applications.[29]

end-user systems development: The creation, modification, or extension of software by people who are nonprofessional software developers.

End-user systems development is the creation, modification, or extension of software by people who are nonprofessional software developers. See Figure 13.14. Creating spreadsheets by tens of millions of people worldwide is perhaps the most common example of user development. Users also work with high-level programming languages such as Cognos BI, Crystal Reports, Focus, and SaS to create reports, dashboards, and graphs. Users also work with simple scripting languages such as ASP, JavaScript, Perl, PHP, Python, Ruby, and Tcl to add functionality to Web pages. They use software such as Visual Basic for Applications to extend and add capabilities to Microsoft Office programs.[30]

Programming by example (PbE or PbD for programming by demonstration) involves teaching an information system or a robot to perform in a certain manner by demonstrating the new behavior instead of by programming it using machine commands. The system records the user actions and infers a generalized program that can then be used with new examples. The students and professors at the MIT Media Lab (*web.media.mit.edu/~lieber/PBE/*) are experimenting with PbE languages such as Cocoa, Eager, Pygmalion, and Mondrian for potential use by systems users.[31]

FIGURE 13.14

End-user systems development

Many users are demonstrating their systems development capability by designing and implementing their own PC-based systems.

User-developed systems are subject to the same reliability, performance, and quality issues as software developed by professionals. Care must be exercised to perform careful checking of user-developed software code including rigorous code review and testing.

TIPS TO AVOID PROJECT FAILURE

Successful systems development means delivering a system that meets user and organizational needs—on time and within budget. However, as discussed in Chapter 12, the number of failed and challenged projects (those that are late, over budget, or lacking required features) stands at 61 percent.[32] Another study found that half of all large information system software development projects costing more than $15 million run 66 percent over budget and disappoint their stakeholders by delivering 17 percent less value than expected.[33]

Following are the major reasons projects fail:

- Executives fail to provide leadership and direction
- Project scope is unclear
- Expectations are poorly managed
- Insufficient user involvement
- Organization is not prepared for change
- Poor planning

See Figure 13.15. These factors are discussed and summarized in Table 13.6.

Executives Fail to Provide Leadership and Direction

The appointment of a steering team of senior managers representing the business and IS organizations to provide guidance and support to the project is absolutely essential to the success of any project. However, business executives are extremely busy addressing many priorities competing for their attention. They must be shown how a potential information system project is clearly aligned to the business strategy and will help achieve important organizational goals. Failure to do so means they will have no interest and no time available to provide leadership and support for the project.

The system investigation team must work hard to ensure that the problem or opportunity is aligned with business strategy and worth working on;

FIGURE 13.15

Project failure

Projects fail for six major reasons: insufficient executive leadership, unclear project scope, poor management of expectations, insufficient user involvement, organization not properly prepared, and poor planning.

TABLE 13.6 Factors in project failure

Factors	Potential Reason(s)	Countermeasures
Business executives fail to provide leadership and direction to project team	Project is not aligned with business strategy or addresses the wrong problem or opportunity Correct business sponsor is not identified or recruited to provide leadership	System investigation team must work hard to ensure that the problem or opportunity is aligned with business strategy and worth working on Project manager must insist that project steering team be appointed including the correct business sponsor
Scope of the project is unclear	The root cause of the problem to be solved or opportunity to be addressed has not been well defined	System investigation team must work with stakeholders to correctly define scope of the project using techniques such as functional decomposition Narrow the project focus to address only the most important business opportunities
Expectations are poorly managed	Project manager incorrectly assumes that the initial statement of stakeholder and end-user expectations is complete and unchanging	Project manager must meet with stakeholders and end users on a regular basis to discuss expectations, document project success criteria, and share project results and status
Insufficient user involvement	Users are busy and do not see value in their participation	Key users should be part of the project team and have an ongoing role in ensuring that their needs and the needs of the business are met Use of prototyping
Organization not prepared for change	Project team focuses on technical aspects of project	Project steering team should assist in preparing organization to accept change
Poor planning	Project team unable to define schedule for complex project	Use project management tools to determine and document who needs to do what and when

otherwise, they cannot expect future management support of the effort. Indeed, if the project is not aligned with business strategy, it should be terminated.

Occasionally, the wrong senior managers are appointed to the steering team. This can happen when a large project will have a major impact on one portion of the organization and a lesser impact on other portions of the organization. The correct manager for the steering team is the one whose portion of the organization will be affected the most. Thus the investigation team should confirm that the correct managers have been appointed to the steering team. It is not unusual for the project team to suggest some changes to the steering team at the end of the investigation phase.

Project Scope Is Unclear or Not Managed

Without a clear definition of the problem to be solved, a good solution is unlikely. The system investigation team must work with stakeholders and users to correctly define the scope of the project using techniques such as functional decomposition.

Even after the initial scope is defined, the project team should strive to narrow the project focus to address only the most important business opportunities. Narrowing the scope of a project helps the development team concentrate on the 20 percent of the project requirements that will deliver 80 percent of the benefits. This approach reduces project cost and shortens the schedule. Reduced scope also decreases project complexity and can greatly increase the probability of a successful project.

scope creep: The temptation to add more features and functionality to the original scope of the system.

As the project evolves, team members are often tempted to expand the scope of the project (this is called scope creep) to add more features and functionality. Scope creep is one of the most dangerous developments in a project. If not handled properly, it can lead to cost and schedule overrun. The scope of the project should be carefully managed with the formal approval of the steering committee necessary to allow a scope change.

Expectations Are Poorly Managed

Project stakeholders and users, in the absence of clear, complete, current information from the development team, will form their own expectations about the information system project, such as what it will deliver, when it will be ready for use, how easy it will be to convert from the old system to the new system, and what level of support will be provided.

Even if the project manager met with stakeholders and users during the system investigation phase to define expectations, it is naive to assume this initial statement of expectations is complete and unchanging. Things change as the project progresses.

The project manager must meet with stakeholders and users on a regular basis to discuss expectations, document project success criteria, and share project results and status. Failure to do so sets up stakeholders and users for frustration when project progress differs from their expectations and disappointment with when and how the system is finally implemented. Effective and continuous communications should be one of a project manager's most important tasks. While formal meetings and status reports are necessary, useful information can also be conveyed informally by meeting for coffee or lunch with a group of users. Such meetings also help build rapport and trust.

Insufficient User Involvement

Users are busy and often do not understand the value of their participation in what they view as a purely technical project. The development team should explain that user involvement is necessary to the success of the project.

In addition, users must be shown that their input is necessary in determining the project schedule. Users must be available to complete tasks such as providing feedback on prototypes, user acceptance testing, user training, and system cutover. Furthermore, such activities should be scheduled to avoid peaks in business volume and activities.

Key users should be part of the project team and have an ongoing role in ensuring that their needs and the needs of the business are met. The use of prototyping and agile system development methods are effective in increasing user involvement.

Organization Not Prepared for Change

The organization should recognize the concerns and needs of users and deal with them before they become a threat to the success of the new or modified system. This means that all members of the organization are prepared for and motivated to change from the old way of doing things to the new way. Members of the project steering team can help the organization prepare by communicating a compelling need for change. Managers can also make it clear that use of the new information system is not optional and that users are expected to modify their behaviors according to the new way of completing tasks. Often incentives need to be put in place to motivate users to adopt the new behaviors and procedures.

Many larger projects will assign a change management specialist from the Human Resources department to the project team. Some organizations hire professional trainers to develop user training materials and design and deliver training courses.

Poor Planning

The bigger the project, the more likely that poor planning will lead to significant problems. Well-managed projects use effective planning tools and techniques, including schedules, milestones, and deadlines.

A **project schedule** is a detailed description of when project activities are performed. The schedule includes each project activity, the use of personnel and other resources, and expected completion dates. A **project milestone** is a critical date for completing a major part of the project, such as program design, coding, testing, and cutover. The **project deadline** is the date the entire project should be completed and operational—when the organization can expect to begin to reap the benefits of the project.

In systems development, each activity has an earliest start time, earliest finish time, and slack time, which is the amount of time an activity can be delayed without delaying the entire project. The **critical path** consists of all activities that, if delayed, would delay the entire project. These activities have zero slack time. Any problems with critical path activities will cause problems for the entire project. To ensure that critical path activities are completed on time, project managers use certain approaches and tools such as Microsoft Project to help compute these critical project attributes.

Although the steps of systems development seem straightforward, larger projects can become complex, requiring hundreds or thousands of separate activities. For these systems development efforts, formal project management methods and tools are essential. A formalized approach called **Program Evaluation and Review Technique (PERT)** creates three time estimates for an activity: shortest possible time, most likely time, and longest possible time. A formula is then applied to determine a single PERT time estimate. A **Gantt chart** is a graphical tool used for planning, monitoring, and coordinating projects; it is essentially a grid that lists activities and deadlines. Each time a task is completed, a marker such as a darkened line is placed in the proper grid cell to indicate the completion of a task. See Figure 13.16.

project schedule: A detailed description of when project activities are performed.

project milestone: A critical date for the completion of a major part of the project.

project deadline: The date the entire project should be completed and operational.

critical path: Activities that, if delayed, would delay the entire project.

Program Evaluation and Review Technique (PERT): A formalized approach for developing a project schedule that creates three time estimates for an activity.

Gantt chart: A graphical tool used for planning, monitoring, and coordinating projects.

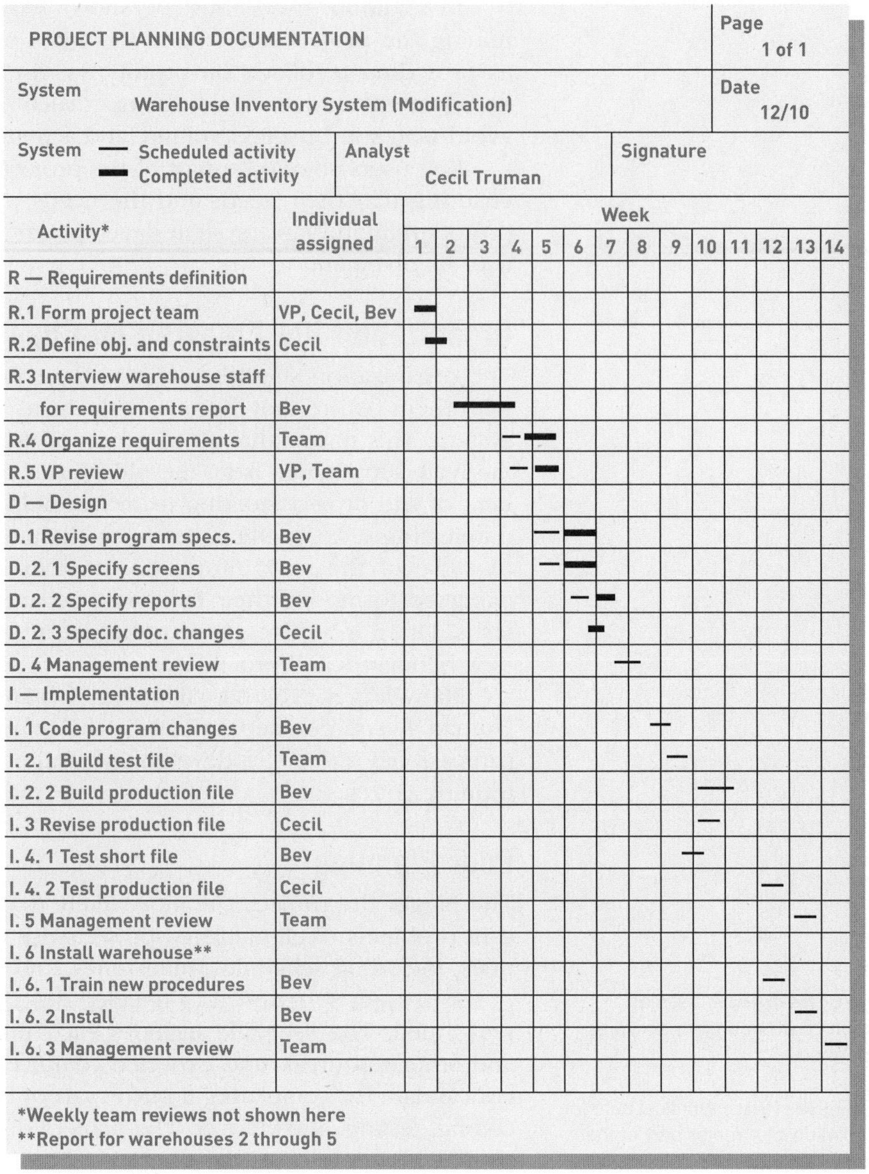

PROJECT PLANNING DOCUMENTATION															Page 1 of 1	

System	Warehouse Inventory System (Modification)														Date 12/10	

| System ── Scheduled activity ▬ Completed activity | Analyst Cecil Truman | | | | | | | | Signature | | | | | | | |

Activity*	Individual assigned	|1	2	3	4	5	6	7	8	9	10	11	12	13	14
R — Requirements definition															
R.1 Form project team	VP, Cecil, Bev	▬													
R.2 Define obj. and constraints	Cecil		▬												
R.3 Interview warehouse staff															
for requirements report	Bev			▬	▬										
R.4 Organize requirements	Team					─▬									
R.5 VP review	VP, Team					─	▬								
D — Design															
D.1 Revise program specs.	Bev						─▬								
D. 2. 1 Specify screens	Bev						─								
D. 2. 2 Specify reports	Bev						─▬								
D. 2. 3 Specify doc. changes	Cecil							▬							
D. 4 Management review	Team								─						
I — Implementation															
I. 1 Code program changes	Bev									─					
I. 2. 1 Build test file	Team									─					
I. 2. 2 Build production file	Bev										─				
I. 3 Revise production file	Cecil										─				
I. 4. 1 Test short file	Bev									─					
I. 4. 2 Test production file	Cecil												─		
I. 5 Management review	Team												─		
I. 6 Install warehouse**															
I. 6. 1 Train new procedures	Bev											─			
I. 6. 2 Install	Bev												─		
I. 6. 3 Management review	Team														─

*Weekly team reviews not shown here
**Report for warehouses 2 through 5

FIGURE 13.16

Sample Gantt chart

A Gantt chart shows progress through systems development activities by putting a bar through appropriate cells.

Both PERT and Gantt techniques can be automated using project management software. Project management software helps managers determine the best way to reduce project completion time at the least cost. Popular software packages include OpenPlan by Deltek, Microsoft Project, and Unifier by Skire.

SUMMARY

Principle:

The goal of systems construction, integration and testing, and implementation is to put into operation an information system that provides real value to the organization.

Systems construction converts the system design into an operational system by acquiring and installing hardware and software, coding and testing software components, creating and loading data into databases, and performing initial program testing.

The ordering and receiving of hardware can require a long lead time, as much as several months.

In addition to buying, leasing, or renting computer hardware, a company can pay only for the computing services that it uses with on-demand computing. Virtualization has had a profound impact on the acquisition of information system hardware. Many organizations are also employing cloud-based services rather than acquiring their own computer hardware.

A company planning to purchase or lease software from an outside company has many options. Commercial off-the-shelf development is often used. Sometimes software from multiple vendors are combined to create a finished system. In many cases, it is necessary to write some original software from scratch and integrate it with purchased or leased software.

Software as a Service (SaaS) allows businesses to subscribe to Web-delivered application software by paying a monthly service charge or a per-use fee.

Software code must be written according to the defined design specifications so that the system meets user and business needs and operates in the manner the user expects. Most software development organizations use a variety of software tools to generate program source code that conforms to those specifications.

Unit testing involves testing individual components of the system to verify that each component performs as designed using test data that forces an individual component to execute all of its various functions and user features.

Technical documentation includes written details used by computer operators to execute the program and by analysts and programmers to solve problems or modify the information system.

User documentation is developed for the people who use the system.

In the traditional systems development life cycle, the create-and-load data step involves making sure that all files and databases are populated and ready to be used with the new information system. Data for the initial loading of the new database may come from several sources.

Several types of testing must be conducted before an information system is ready to be put into production. Integration testing involves linking all of the individual components together and testing them as a group to uncover any defects between individual components. System testing involves testing the complete, integrated system (hardware, software, databases, people, and procedures) to validate that the information system meets all specified requirements. Volume testing involves evaluating the performance of the information system under varying work volume and operating conditions. During user acceptance testing (UAT), trained system users test the information system to verify that it can complete required tasks in a real-world operating environment and do this in a manner consistent with the system design specifications.

User preparation is the process of readying managers, decision makers, employees, system users, and other stakeholders to use the new system.

The eventual success of any system depends on how it is used not only by the users but how well it can be operated and supported by the IS personnel within the organization.

For a small system, site preparation can be as simple as rearranging the furniture in an office to make room for a computer. With a larger system, this process is not as straightforward because the computer and associated hardware can require special wiring and air conditioning.

Installation is physically placing the computer equipment on the site and making it operational.

System cutover is switching from an old information system to a replacement system. Cutover can be critical to the success of the organization because, if not done properly, the results can be disastrous.

Organizations can use several system cutover strategies. Direct conversion stops the old system and starts the new system on a given date. Direct conversion is a high-risk approach because of the potential for problems and errors when the old system is shut off and the new system is turned on at the same instant. With the phase-in approach, components of the new system are slowly phased in while components of the old one are slowly phased out. A pilot start-up involves running the new system for one group of users rather than all users. Parallel start-up involves running both the old and new systems for a period of time. The output of the new system is compared closely with the output of the old system, and any differences are reconciled. When users are comfortable that the new system is working correctly, the old system is eliminated.

Principle:

System operation and maintenance add to the useful life of a system but can consume large amounts of resources. These activities can benefit from the same rigorous methods and project management techniques applied to systems development.

System operation involves using the new or modified system under all kinds of operating conditions. Getting the most out of a new or modified system during its operation is the most important aspect of systems operations for many organizations.

Systems review is the process of analyzing systems to make sure that they are operating as intended. The systems review process often compares the performance and benefits of the system as it was designed with the actual performance and benefits of the system in operation.

Systems review also often involves monitoring the system, called system performance measurement. The number of errors encountered, the amount of memory required, the amount of processing or CPU time needed, and other performance measures should be closely observed.

Systems maintenance involves changing and enhancing the system to make it more useful in achieving user and organizational goals.

A legacy system is an old system that might have cost millions of dollars to develop and patch or modify repeatedly over the years.

The maintenance costs for legacy systems can become quite expensive and, at some point, it becomes more cost effective to switch to new programs and applications than to repair and maintain the legacy system.

Four generally accepted categories that signify the amount of change involved in maintenance are slipstream upgrade, patch, release, and version.

At some point, an existing information system may become obsolete, uneconomical to operate or maintain, or unrepairable.

System disposal involves ensuring the orderly dissolution of the system, including disposing of all equipment in an environmentally friendly manner, closing out any contracts in place, and safely migrating information from the system to another system or archiving it in accordance with applicable records management policies.

Organizations must take effective measures to remove customer, employee, financial, and company-sensitive data from all computer hardware and storage devices before disposal. Otherwise, discarded equipment could become a treasure trove to identity thieves or your competition.

Principle:

The systems development team must select the appropriate systems development approach to match the needs of the project.

A prototype is a working model of a system developed to enable users to interact with the system and provide feedback so developers can better understand what is needed. Prototypes can be classified as throw-away or working prototypes.

The Rational Unified Process (RUP) is an iterative systems development approach that was developed by IBM and includes a number of tools and techniques that are typically tailored to fit the needs of a specific company or organization.

Agile development is an iterative process that develops the system in "sprint" increments lasting from two weeks to two months. Unlike the traditional system development process, agile development accepts the fact that system requirements are evolving and cannot be fully understood or defined at the start of the project.

Scrum keeps the agile system development effort focused and moving quickly. Scrum components include a scrum master who coordinates all scrum activities, the scrum team consisting of a dozen or fewer people who perform all systems development activities from investigation to testing, and the product owner who represents the project stakeholders and is responsible for communicating and aligning project priorities between the stakeholders and development team.

Agile development requires cooperation and frequent face-to-face meetings with all participants, including systems developers and users, as they modify, refine, and test the system's capabilities and how it meets users' needs.

Extreme programming (XP) is an approach to writing code that promotes incremental development of a system using short development cycles to improve productivity and allow for the introduction of new customer requirements.

The object-oriented approach is frequently used in the investigation, analysis, and design phases of system development.

Creating successful mobile apps requires developers to consider who will be using the app and what their end goals may be.

While the overall approach of systems development is similar for mobile devices compared to traditional systems development projects, there are some important differences.

Systems development tools are available for mobile applications.

User systems development is the creation, modification, or extension of software by people who are nonprofessional software developers. User-developed systems are subject to the same reliability, performance, and quality issues as software developed by professionals. User-developed software code must be checked carefully through rigorous code review and testing.

Principle:

The systems development team must take measures to avoid the common pitfalls to project success.

The main reasons projects fail are: 1) executives fail to provide leadership and direction, 2) the project scope is unclear, 3) project expectations are poorly managed, 4) user involvement is insufficient, 5) the organization is not prepared for the change, and 6) project planning is poor.

KEY TERMS

agile development

critical path

cutover

direct conversion

end-user systems development

extreme programming (XP)

Gantt chart

installation

integration testing

monitoring

parallel start-up

patch

phase-in approach

pilot start-up

Program Evaluation and Review Technique (PERT)

product owner

project deadline

project schedule

project milestone

prototype

prototyping

Rational Unified Process (RUP)

release

request for maintenance form

scope creep

scrum

scrum master

site preparation

slipstream upgrade

system construction

system disposal

system testing

systems maintenance

systems operation

systems review

technical documentation

throw-away prototype

unit testing

user acceptance document

user acceptance testing (UAT)

user documentation

user preparation

version

volume testing

working prototype

CHAPTER 13: SELF-ASSESSMENT TEST

The goal of systems construction, integration and testing, and implementation is to put into operation an information system that provides real value to the organization.

1. _____ includes written details used by computer operators to execute the program and by analysts and programmers to solve problems or modify the information system.

2. The _____ is an example of a systems development task that can take months to complete.
   a. ordering and receiving of hardware
   b. site preparation
   c. negotiation of final contracts with hardware and software vendors
   d. All of the above

3. _____ is a form of testing that involves linking all of the individual components together and testing them as a group to uncover any defects between individual components.
   a. Unit testing
   b. System testing
   c. Integration testing
   d. Volume testing

4. _____ allows businesses to subscribe to Web-delivered application software by paying a monthly service charge or a per-use fee.
   a. On-demand computing
   b. Software-as-a-service

   c. Virtualization
   d. None of the above

5. During user acceptance testing (UAT), the system development team tests the information system to verify that it can complete required tasks in a real-world operating environment and do this in a manner consistent with the system design specifications. True or False?

6. _____ is the process of physically placing the computer equipment on the site and making it operational.

7. _____ is a form of system conversion that involves stopping the old system and starting the new system on a given date.
   a. Parallel conversion
   b. Direct conversion
   c. Pilot conversion
   d. Phase-in conversion

System operation and maintenance add to the useful life of a system but can consume large amounts of resources. These activities can benefit from the same rigorous methods and project management techniques applied to systems development.

8. A _____ is a significant program change that often requires changes in the documentation of the software.

a. patch
b. new version
c. slipstream upgrade
d. new release

9. _____ is the process of analyzing systems to make sure they are operating as intended and comparing the performance and benefits of the system as it was designed with the actual performance and benefits of the system in operation.

10. The maintenance costs for legacy systems can become so expensive it becomes more cost effective to switch to new programs than to repair and maintain a legacy system. True or False?

11. _____ consists of computer systems, manuals, people with technical expertise, and other resources needed to solve problems and give accurate answers to questions.

The systems development team must select the appropriate systems development approach to match the needs of the project.

12. A(n) _____ is a working model of a system developed to enable users to interact with the system and provide feedback so developers can better understand what is needed.

13. _____ is an iterative systems development approach developed by IBM.
a. Agile
b. Scrum
c. Prototype
d. Rational Unified Process

14. _____ is an iterative system development process that develops the system in "sprint" increments lasting from two weeks to two months.
a. Agile
b. Scrum
c. Prototype
d. Rational Unified Process

15. User-developed systems are subject to the same reliability, performance, and quality issues as software developed by professionals. True or False?

The systems development team must take careful measures to avoid the common pitfalls to project success.

16. It is necessary to show alignment with strategic business objectives and goals to motivate senior executives to join a steering team for an information system project. True or False?

17. The _____ consists of all activities that, if delayed, would delay the entire project.

CHAPTER 13: SELF-ASSESSMENT TEST ANSWERS

1. Technical documentation
2. d
3. c
4. b
5. False
6. System installation
7. b
8. d
9. System review

10. True
11. A help desk
12. prototype
13. d
14. Agile
15. True
16. True
17. Critical path

REVIEW QUESTIONS

1. Identify and briefly discuss the five steps of system construction.
2. Identify five approaches an organization can take to obtain the computing hardware it needs to run an information system.
3. Briefly describe unit, integration, system, volume, and user acceptance testing—who performs each type of test, and what is the goal of each type of test?
4. Distinguish between technical documentation and user documentation.
5. Identify three potential sources for the initial loading of data into a database.
6. Briefly describe what is involved in site preparation.
7. Identify and briefly discuss four system cutover strategies.
8. How is system operation different from system maintenance?
9. What is system review? What is its purpose?

10. What are the key activities associated with system disposal?
11. What is the primary difference in approach between the traditional system development process and the prototyping or agile development processes?
12. Briefly discuss the key features of extreme programming as an approach to writing code.
13. How is systems performance measurement related to the systems review?
14. Identify six primary reasons for failure for information system development projects. What countermeasures can be taken to avoid these pitfalls?

DISCUSSION QUESTIONS

1. Identify the participants in the systems implementation phase. How do these participants compare with the participants of systems investigation?
2. Describe how you would create systems and security controls for smartphones and tablet computers for a medium-sized business.
3. You have been hired to develop a billing system for a small start-up business. Describe how you could use prototyping to ensure that you capture all user requirements accurately and completely.
4. Identify and briefly describe the similarities and differences between the prototyping and agile system development processes.
5. Discuss the relationship between maintenance and systems design.
6. Assume that you are the CIO of a medium-sized music company. The company president wants you to develop a Web site to advertise and sell the music the company produces. Describe the procedures you would use to hire several IS personnel to help you develop the needed Web site. What types of training would you make available to the new and existing IS personnel to help you in creating the needed Web site?
7. What are the advantages and disadvantages of the traditional systems development process when building a small information system using in-house resources? How do these advantages and disadvantages change if you are building a large information system using third-party resources?
8. You have been hired to oversee a major systems development effort to purchase a new accounting software package. Describe what is important to include in the contract with the software vendor.
9. You have been hired to implement a new customer resource management software package for a medium-sized business. The system will be installed and operated on existing servers belonging to the business. Describe how you would start up the new system and place it into operation.
10. Identify the various forms of testing. Why are there so many different types of tests?
11. What is the goal of conducting a systems review? What factors need to be considered during systems review?
12. Identify some specialists who would be assigned to help successfully implement a major multimillion dollar information system and who would probably not participate on a small project to install a $200 software package to be used by three people. What role would these specialists play? At what phase of the project should they be introduced as members of the team?
13. Assume that you have a personal computer that is several years old. Describe the steps you would use to perform systems review to determine whether you should acquire a new PC.

PROBLEM-SOLVING EXERCISES

1. Go to the computer lab and gain access to a project scheduling software package such as Microsoft Project, part of the Microsoft Office software suite. Use the software to enter the tasks, their durations, and the dependencies associated with the systems analysis tasks discussed in Chapter 12. To keep it simple, for duration, enter any amount of time between two days and two weeks. Request a printout of a Gantt chart and the critical path for this phase of a project.

2. A project team has estimated the costs associated with the development and maintenance of a new system. One approach requires a more complete design and will result in a slightly higher design and implementation cost but a lower maintenance cost over the life of the system. The second approach cuts the design effort, saving some dollars but with a likely increase in maintenance cost.

   a. Enter the following data in the spreadsheet. Print the result.

Benefits of good design

	Good Design	Poor Design
Design costs	$14,000	$10,000
Implementation cost	$42,000	$35,000
Annual maintenance cost	$32,000	$40,000

© 2016 Cengage Learning

b. Create a stacked bar chart that shows the total cost, including the design, implementation, and maintenance costs over an expected system life of seven years. Be sure that the chart has a title and that the costs are labeled on the chart.

c. Use your word-processing software to write a paragraph that recommends an approach to take and explains why.

3. Assume you have just started a campus bicycle rental business. Use a word-processing program to describe the logical and physical design of a computer application to purchase new bicycles for the rental program and another application to rent bicycles to students. Use a graphics program to develop one or more sequence diagrams to buy new bicycles and to rent them to students.

TEAM ACTIVITIES

1. As a team, find two or three project managers and do a group interview on the topic of causes for project failures. Identify and prioritize their top causes for project failure. How does their list of causes compare to the causes presented in this chapter?

2. Your team has been hired by the owner of a new restaurant to explore word-processing, graphics, database, and spreadsheet capabilities. The new owner has heard about cloud computing, SaaS, and DaaS. Your team should prepare a report on the advantages and disadvantages of using a traditional office suite from a company such as Microsoft as compared to other approaches.

3. Your team has been asked to monitor the disposal of your school's 10-year old student registration system. Develop a schedule for the activities that must be performed. Which activities are of most concern?

WEB EXERCISES

1. HealthCare.gov is a health insurance exchange Website operated by the U.S. federal government. It is intended to support citizens who want to sign up to receive benefits under the Patient Protection and Affordable Care Act. The Web site was implemented to serve the residents of the 36 states that elected to not build their own state exchanges. The Web site enables the sale of private health insurance plans, offers subsidies to low-income citizens, and assists those persons who are eligible to sign up for Medicaid.

   The launch of the Healthcare.gov Web site occurred on October 1, 2013. Do research on the Web to identify specific problems that users encountered. With the benefit of 20–20 hindsight, identify steps that could have been taken to ensure a smoother system start-up. What measures are being used to track the performance of this important Web site?

2. Using the Web, search for examples of organizations that provide system performance monitoring software. Identify two organizations that seem to provide the most comprehensive software and services. Perform a side-by-side comparison of the two offerings. Which one would you choose to monitor the performance of your school's information systems and why?

CAREER EXERCISES

1. Do research on the role of project manager. What personal characteristics, education, and work experiences are usually associated with a project manager? Are project manager certifications available? What is the need for project managers in business? What is the starting salary range for project managers?

2. Research possible careers in developing applications for smartphones, tablet computers, and other portable devices. Write a report that describes these opportunities. Include in your report a description of a few applications that aren't currently available that you would find useful.

Case One

Data Lifecycle Management: A Big Challenge for Big Data

Over 90 percent of the world's data was generated in the last two years. Two years from now, the volume of data will double. Most companies are singularly aware of big data and the potential to leverage it to gain strategic advantages in their markets. However, the cost of data storage saps about 10 percent of the total IT budget, and this has made many companies look toward data lifecycle management solutions. In fact, data lifecycle management tools abound from IBM's Infosphere to SAP's Netweaver Information Lifecycle Management to Solix's Enterprise Data Management Suite that contain modules to archive databases and retire applications. Companies use these tools to relocate the high volume of information coming in so that it does not clog their data pipelines and slow the performance of their main systems. The tools move data to cheaper storage devices and reduce redundancy. For example, Rediff.com used Solix's suite to reduce its storage requirement by 75 percent, improve the performance of its backup and recovery systems, and ensure data growth doesn't impair the functioning or efficiency of its applications in the future. Yet in the study released about the project, no mention is made of the disposal of data—only the elimination of redundant copies of data.

In fact, some IT analysts complain that business managers view the management of the data lifecycle (including data disposal) and information governance in general as an IT responsibility. These analysts observe that companies rarely integrate information governance of data warehouses into their business processes. They ignore requests by IT professionals to set up processes for handling aging data.

Information governance, however, is becoming a major challenge that many organizations and businesses can no longer ignore. Hanging onto sensitive data increases risks over time. In general, business executives, IT professionals, and citizens concerned about their privacy all agree that whatever data does not need to be retained for business or regulatory purposes should be deleted. Moreover, in the United States, 30 states have data disposal laws, 29 of which apply to digital data disposal. Intended to protect individuals from identity theft and breaches of privacy, many of these laws, however, are fairly vague. For example, North Carolina stipulates that any company "that conducts business in North Carolina and any business that maintains or otherwise possesses personal information of a resident of North Carolina must take reasonable measures to protect against unauthorized access to or use of the information in connection with or after its disposal." With no clear directives from the state legislature, the state court system is left to determine what these "reasonable measures" are, which can vary from case to case.

In contrast to these data disposal laws, many federal regulations mandate that businesses hang onto sensitive data. The Internal Revenue Service requires that businesses and individuals keep bank statements for two years, federal tax returns for at least three years, and investment forms for at least seven years. The Department of Labor requires that employers maintain payroll records for three years. The U.S. Securities and Exchange Commission (SEC) requires that financial institutions retain data for seven years.

Banks and other financial institutions are required to archive data to facilitate e-discovery. Lawyers once combed through mountains of physical documents to present evidence at trial. Today, through e-discovery regulations, lawyers can use search engines to find documents and then request that the bank put a hold on these and all related documents. Each country has different laws about the retention of each type of data. Hence, managing the data lifecycle is complicated.

Litigation against banks and investigations into banking activities, such as issuing mortgages, has increased in recent years. IT and business units must work together to develop data governance processes and policies that dispose of all possible data to minimize risk while complying with each country's regulations. Perhaps these financial institutions can lead the way to incorporate responsible disposal of the mountains of data businesses and other organizations are collecting each day.

Discussion Questions

1. How do laws affect data retention and disposal?
2. How is data disposal similar to and different from retiring information systems?

Critical Thinking Questions

1. What are the disadvantages of leaving data disposal entirely to IT?
2. What data governance guidelines do you use in maintaining and disposing of your own digital data? Why are the policies and strategies financial institutions must use to manage data lifecycles so complicated?

SOURCES: White, Andrew, "Information Governance on the Data Warehouse—Does It Exist?" Gartner Web site, October 18, 2013, *http://blogs.gartner.com/andrew_white/2013/10/18/information -governance-on-or-in-the-data-warehouse-does-it-exist/*; Data Lifecycle Management, IBM Web site, *www-01.ibm.com/software/data/lifecycle -management/*, accessed July 7, 2014; Reddiff.com case study, Solix Web site, *www.solix.com/rediff.htm*; accessed July 7, 2014; "Comply with Regulations for Data Retention and Destruction—with Information Lifecycle Management," SAP Web site, *www.sap.com/pc/tech/enterprise -information-management/software/information-lifecycle/index.html*; accessed July 7, 2014; Waxman, Andrew, "The Discipline of Information Lifecycle Management," *Wall Street and Technology*, July 1, 2014, *www .wallstreetandtech.com/data-management/the-discipline-of-information -lifecycle-management/a/d-id/1278993*; Data Disposal Laws, National Conference of State Legislatures, December 26, 2013, *www.ncsl.org /research/telecommunications-and-information-technology/data-dis posal-laws.aspx*; "Data Retention: Selected Requirements by Data Type," Miller School of Medicine, University of Miami, *http://it.med.miami.edu /x1312.xml*; accessed July 8, 2014; North Carolina Legislature Web site, Enacted Legislation, *www.ncleg.net/EnactedLegislation/Statutes/HTML /BySection/Chapter_75/GS_75-64.html*; accessed July 9, 2014.

Case Two

Using CAST to Track Programmer Productivity

As you read in this chapter, computer programs are written by people. As with any type of work, some people are better at programming than others. Employers need a fair, objective way to find out who the excellent programmers are so as to recognize their superior work, to figure out what will help the others improve, and to learn what makes the excellent programmers better so the employers can try to duplicate this "secret sauce" throughout their workforce.

Superior programming is a composite of several measures. One is productivity: how much code a programmer produces. Another is quality: how error-free that code is. Other measures include the performance and security of the resulting program and its clarity for future modifications by people who were not involved in writing it.

Because it is difficult to measure these factors, most managers end up measuring the process by which software is built and the effort put into that process rather than its outcomes. As Jitendra Subramanyam, director of research at CAST, Inc., writes, "It's as if Michael Phelps tracks his time in the gym, the time it takes him to eat his meals, the time he spends on his Xbox, time walking his dog … but bizarrely, not the time it takes him to swim the 100 meter butterfly!"

IBM recognizes the need to focus on people and their output. "At the end of the day, people are in the middle of application development," says Pat Howard, vice president and cloud leader in IBM's global business services division. "It's really important to have great investments, great energy focused around the talent."

Howard's department uses the Application Intelligence Platform from French software firm CAST to quantify performance. "Essentially it permitted our people to walk around with a scorecard. They could begin to earn points, based on the results or the value they were driving for the business," Howard says.

The program also helps identify performance shortfalls and skill deficiencies. "We use it to identify where more training is needed," Howard says. Training budgets are tight, so "when you spend it, you've got to spend it really smartly, aim it at the right place."

Bank of New York Mellon is another CAST user. The bank uses CAST to control the quality of the software produced by offshore contract software developers. Vice president for systems and technology Robert-Michel Lejeune says, "You provide specifications, the offshorer has a process in place, but when they deliver, you don't know the level of quality. Using an automated tool provides you with facts and figures on the go."

A system such as this can never be the entire answer to employee or contractor performance evaluation. Systems cannot measure important employee efforts such as contributing ideas in team meetings, mentoring junior employees, and willingly taking on jobs that nobody else wants. However, CAST or something like it will be part of the answer at more and more companies in the future.

Discussion Questions

1. As a business manager, would you choose to use CAST to measure programmer productivity? Why or why not?
2. How would you feel as a programmer if your company announced that it was going to start using the CAST Application Intelligence Platform to measure your productivity and that of your colleagues?

Critical Thinking Questions

1. Are there any drawbacks to using a programmer productivity measurement tool such as CAST's Application Intelligence Platform? If there are, what are they?
2. What elements of programming and software development cannot be measured by CAST? How important are these elements?

SOURCES: Bednarz, A., "How IBM Started Grading Its Developers' Productivity," *Computerworld, www.computerworld.com/s/article /9221566/How_IBM_started_grading_its_developers_productivity*, November 7, 2011; CAST Web site, *www.castsoftware.com*, accessed July 25, 2014; Lejeune, R.-M., "Bank of New York Mellon Interview" (video), *www.youtube.com/watch?v=zLb7pCwA4rE*, February 7, 2012; Subramanyam, J., "5 Requirements for Measuring Application Quality," *Network World, www.networkworld.com/news/tech/2011/061611 -application-quality.html*, June 7, 2011.

Questions for Web Case

See the Web site for this book to read about the Whitmann Price Consulting case for this chapter. Following are questions concerning this Web case.

Altitude Online: Systems Development: Construction, Integration and Testing, Implementation, Operation and Maintenance, and Disposal

Discussion Questions

1. How did Jon's team coordinate with the vendor in the implementation stage of the systems development project?
2. What did Jon's team do in advance of contacting SAP that made the design and implementation systems proceed as smoothly as possible?

Critical Thinking Questions

1. What risks were involved in the systems development project?
2. What benefits were gained from this systems development project? Was it worth the risks?

NOTES

Sources for the opening vignette: Hoffman, Thomas, "BT: A Case Study In Agile Programming," *InfoWorld*, March 11, 2009, *www.infoworld.com/d/developer-world/bt-case-study -in-agile-programming-112?page=0,0*; "BT Switches to Agile Techniques to Create New Products," *ComputerWeekly.com*, January 29, 2010, *www.computerweekly.com/news/128009 1969/BT-switches-to-agile-techniques-to-create-new-products*; Sasol Company Profile, Overview, Sasol Web site, *www*

.sasol.com/about-sasol/company-profile/business-overview; accessed July 8, 2014; 'Turning a Far-Flung Organisation into a Single Community," Let's Talk, BT Web site, July 9, 2014, *http://letstalk.globalservices.bt.com/en/*; Software Engineer, IVR at BT (British Telecom), The JobCrowd, April 23, 2014, *www.thejobcrowd.com/employer/bt -british-telecom/reviews/software-engineer-ivr-at-bt-british -telecom.*

1. "VMware SDDC Architecture Gives Adways the Flexibility to Accelerate Global Growth," VMWare Case Study, *www.vmware.com/files/jp/pdf/customers/VMware-Adways-13Q4-EN-Case-Study.pdf?src=WWW_customers_VMware-Adways-13Q4-EN-Case-Study.pdf*, accessed July 1, 2014.

2. "SAP and VMware Virtualization," VMWare, Tata Consultancy, *www.vmware.com/business-critical-apps/sap-virtualization/customer-success.html*, accessed June 29, 2014.

3. "SAAS Success Story: RamSoft," *www.hostway.com/resources/media/ramsoft-case-study.pdf*, accessed July 1, 2014.

4. "CodeSmith Generator," *www.codesmithtools.com/product/generator*, accessed July 1, 2014.

5. "The Arizona Supreme Court Creates the Ultimate Outsource and Insource Simultaneously," Visible, *www.visible.com/News/arizona.htm*, accessed July 2, 2014.

6. Dr. Explain Web site, *www.drexplain.com/what-do-users-say/*, accessed July 14, 2014.

7. Kline, Allissa, "M&T To Invest $20M, Upgrade Data Center," *Buffalo Business First*, March 10, 2014, *www.bizjournals.com/buffalo/news/2014/03/10/m-t-to-invest-20m-in-data-center-upgrade.html*.

8. "Shell Businesses in the U.S.," About Us, *www.shell.us/aboutshell/shell-businesses.html*, accessed July 8, 2014.

9. "A Record-Breaking Feat," T-Systems, February 2013, *www.t-systems.com/news-media/shell-pulls-off-the-largest-sap-upgrade-in-history-now-its-mobile-collaboration-tools-are-delivered-from-a-private-cloud-t-systems/1100966*.

10. Precise Web site, *www.precise.com*, accessed July 14, 2014.

11. "Allscripts," *www.eginnovations.com/news/Allscripts_Case_study_letter_12914.pdf*, accessed July 14, 2014.

12. "VA Scandal Audit: 120,000 Veterans Experience Long Waits for Care," Azcentral, June 9, 2014, *www.azcentral.com/story/news/arizona/investigations/2014/06/09/va-scandal-audit-veterans-delayed-care/10234881/*.

13. Brewin, Bob, "VA Failed to Protect Critical Computer Systems, Audit Finds," Nextgov, May 29, 2014, *www.nextgov.com/defense/whats-brewin/2014/05/va-failed-protect-critical-computer-systems-audit-finds/85429/*.

14. Osborne, Hilary, "Why Do Bank IT Systems Keep Failing?" The Guardian, January 27, 2014, *www.theguardian.com/money/2014/jan/27/bank-it-systems-keep-failing-lloyds-rbs-natwest*.

15. "More than £1bn Committed to Improve Banking Services," June 27, 2014, *www.rbs.com/news/2014/06/more-than-p1bn-committed-to-improve-banking-services.html*.

16. "End of Windows XP Support Will Be Trouble for Businesses and Consumers," CBS Evening News, April 8, 2014, *www.cbsnews.com/videos/end-of-windows-xp-support-will-be-trouble-for-businesses-consumers/*.

17. Nickols, Fred, "Prototyping: Systems Development in Record Time," Distance Consulting LLC, 2012, *www.nickols.us/prototyping.htm*, accessed August 11, 2014.

18. Janus, Marion A. and Smith, Douglas L., "Prototyping for Systems Development: A Critical Appraisal," MIS Quarterly Review, 1985, *http://misq.org/prototying-for-systems-development-a-critical-appraisal.html?SID=v72ecviamkepsgsebt7nitrrd5*, accessed August 11, 2014.

19. Vennapoosa, Venna, "Throwaway Prototyping Model," Exforsys, Inc., January 14, 2013, *www.exforsys.com/career-center/project-management-life-cycle/throwaway-prototyping-model.html*.

20. "Rational Unified Process: Best Practices for Software Development Teams," *www.exforsys.com/career-center/project-management-life-cycle/throwaway-prototyping-model.html*, accessed August 3, 2014.

21. "What is Agile?" Agile Methodology, *http://agilemethodology.org/*, accessed August 3, 2014.

22. "Why Scrum?" Scrum Alliance, *www.scrumalliance.org/why-scrum*, accessed August 3, 2014.

23. "Scrum Methodology," *http://scrummethodology.com/*, accessed August 3, 2014. *www.my-project-management-expert.com/the-advantages-and-disadvantages-of-agile-software-development.html*, accessed August 3, 2014.

24. De Sousa, Susan, "The Advantages and Disadvantages of Agile Development," My PM Expert, *www.my-project-management-expert.com/the-advantages-and-disadvantages-of-agile-software-development.html*, accessed August 3, 2014.

25. "The Rules of Extreme Programming," *www.extremeprogramming.org/rules.html*, accessed August 3, 2014.

26. Kapustka, Paul, "Four Pitfalls Hindering Mobile App Success," *http://resources.idgenterprise.com/original/AST-0121105_OutSystems_Four_Pitfalls_Hindering_Mobile_App_Success.pdf*, accessed July 25, 2014.

27. Heller, Martin, "10 Simple Tools for Building Mobile Apps Fast," *InfoWorld*, March 20, 2014, *www.infoworld.com/slideshow/144802/10-simple-tools-building-mobile-apps-fast-238653*.

28. Chen, Brian X., "Coder's Half-Million Dollar Baby Proves iPhone Gold Rush Is Still On," *Wired*, February 12, 2009, *www.wired.com/2009/02/shoot-is-iphone/*.

29. Paternò, Fabio, "End User Development: Survey of an Emerging Field for Empowering People," Hindawi Publishing Corporation, ISRN Software Engineering, Volume 2013, Article ID 532659, *www.hindawi.com/journals/isrn.software.engineering/2013/532659/*.

30. Burnett, Margaret M. and Scaffidi, Christopher, "End-User Development," Interactive Design Foundation, *www.interaction-design.org/encyclopedia/end-user_development.html*, accessed August 3, 2014.

31. "What is Programming by Example?", *web.media.mit.edu/~lieber/PBE/*, accessed August 3, 2014.

32. "CHAOS Manifesto 2013, Think Big, Act Small," *www.versionone.com/assets/img/files/CHAOSManifesto2013.pdf*, accessed June 11, 2014.

33. Bloch, Michael, Blumberg, Sven, and Laartz, Jürgen, "Delivering Large-Scale IT Projects on Time, On Budget, and On Value," McKinsey & Company, October 2012, *www.mckinsey.com/insights/business_technology/delivering_large-scale_it_projects_on_time_on_budget_and_on_value*.

PART 1   PART 2   PART 3   PART 4   PART 5

Information Systems in Business and Society

CHAPTER

© Mediel Lorant/Shutterstock.com

14 The Personal and Social Impact of Computers

Principles	Learning Objectives
• Policies and procedures must be established to avoid waste and mistakes associated with computer usage.	• Describe some examples of waste and mistakes in an IS environment, their causes, and possible solutions. • Identify policies and procedures useful in eliminating waste and mistakes.
• Computer crime is a serious and rapidly growing area of concern requiring management attention.	• Explain the types of computer crime and their effects. • Identify specific measures to prevent computer crime.
• Privacy is an important social issue related to information systems.	• Discuss the principles and limits of an individual's right to privacy.
• Jobs, equipment, and working conditions must be designed to avoid negative health effects from computers.	• List the important negative effects of computers on the work environment. • Identify specific actions that must be taken to ensure the health and safety of employees.
• Practitioners in many professions subscribe to a code of ethics that states the principles and core values that are essential to their work.	• Outline criteria for the ethical use of information systems.

MT. GOX, JAPAN

Millions in Bitcoins Go Missing

© 123dartist/Shutterstock.com

In the wake of the 2008 and 2009 global financial crisis, an entirely new type of currency called a "bitcoin" emerged in the online marketplace. Similar to the use of cigarettes as currency in prisoner-of-war camps, the completely digital currency made use of the peer-to-peer (P2P) technology, with only a small group of individuals and companies trading bitcoins among themselves at first. As more currency was generated and released into circulation, a fast-growing pool of online and real-world merchants began to accept them as payment.

"The mission," says Gavin Andresen, chief scientist of the Bitcoin Foundation, "is really to create a stable worldwide currency for the Internet. And to let people all over the world transact with each other as easily as people all over the world send email to each other."

As the number of bitcoins on the market increased, people began purchasing them on bitcoin exchanges. Mt. Gox, a leading exchange in Tokyo, Japan, became an early leader, capturing almost 80 percent of the market.

Although people can buy bitcoins using credit cards or cash transfers, many simply go to a local bitcoin exchange, located in thousands of cities around the world, and use their country's currency to buy bitcoins. People can then transfer bitcoins to a family member's or a merchant's wallet over the Internet.

Bitcoin exchanges allow individuals to transfer money across the globe or make international payments, which are cheaper because the Bitcoin cuts out the middle men, the banks, and credit card companies. Unlike credit card transactions, neither the consumer nor the business needs to pay a transaction fee, and all purchases are as anonymous as a cash payment. These exchanges can service people without access to bank accounts, including aspiring entrepreneurs in developing economies. The downside is that like cash, bitcoins are not insured and can be lost, stolen by hackers, or destroyed by viruses.

These disadvantages proved overwhelming for the Mt. Gox exchange. On February 10, 2014, the company issued a press release that Mt. Gox had lost 850,000 bitcoins, valued at $827 apiece. Of these, 750,000 belonged to customers. The company claimed that it had been the victim of a malleability bug, and that hackers had fooled the company into making it think that bitcoin transfers had failed when they had not, so that Mt. Gox had transferred the money twice.

Computer scientists, who had been monitoring the bitcoin network for these types of fraudulent transactions, argued that the number of fraudulent transactions could not possibly account for the amount Mt. Gox claimed to have lost. Mt. Gox insiders leaked that the company was very badly managed. In fact, a little over a month later, the company happily reported that it had found 200 of the missing bitcoins in an old bitcoin wallet on a hard drive. Eventually, however, Mt. Gox was forced to file for bankruptcy, and some $473 million of bitcoins remain "lost."

At first, in early 2014, the value of the bitcoin fell. However, SecondMarket, Inc. began to buy the currency. Soon, other exchanges such as London-based Bitstamp were grabbing a greater share of the bitcoin market. The digital currency proved more resilient than anyone would have expected.

As you read this chapter, consider the following:

- How can new technologies, like Bitcoin, change societies and economies?
- What actions should governments take, if any, to ensure that new technologies help, rather than hurt, consumers?

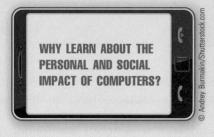

WHY LEARN ABOUT THE PERSONAL AND SOCIAL IMPACT OF COMPUTERS?

Both opportunities and threats surround a wide range of nontechnical issues associated with the use of information systems and the Internet. The issues span the full spectrum—from preventing computer waste and mistakes, to avoiding violations of privacy, to complying with laws on collecting data about customers, and to monitoring employees. If you become a member of a human resources, an information systems, or a legal department within an organization, you will likely be charged with leading the organization in dealing with these and other issues covered in this chapter. Also, as a user of information systems and the Internet, it is in your own self-interest to become well versed on these issues. You need to know about the topics in this chapter to help avoid becoming a victim of crime, fraud, privacy invasion, and other potential problems. This chapter begins with a discussion of preventing computer waste and mistakes.

Earlier chapters detailed the significant benefits of computer-based information systems in business, including increased profits, superior goods and services, and higher quality of work life. Computers have become such valuable tools that today's businesspeople have difficulty imagining work without them. Yet, the information age has also brought the following potential problems for workers, companies, and society in general:

- Computer waste and mistakes
- Computer crime
- Privacy issues
- Work environment problems
- Ethical issues

This chapter discusses some of the social and ethical issues as a reminder of these important considerations underlying the design, building, and use of computer-based information systems. No business organization, and hence no information system, operates in a vacuum. All IS professionals, business managers, and users have a responsibility to see that the potential consequences of IS use are fully considered. Even entrepreneurs, especially those who use computers and the Internet, must be aware of the potential personal and social impact of computers.

COMPUTER WASTE AND MISTAKES

Computer-related waste and mistakes are major causes of computer problems, contributing to unnecessarily high costs and lost profits. Examples of computer-related waste include organizations operating unintegrated information systems, acquiring redundant systems, and wasting information system resources. Computer-related mistakes refer to errors, failures, and other computer problems that make computer output incorrect or not useful; most of these are caused by human error. This section explores the damage that can be done as a result of computer waste and mistakes.

Computer Waste

Some organizations continue to operate their businesses using unintegrated information systems, which make it difficult for decisions makers to collaborate and share information. This practice leads to missed opportunities, increased costs, and lost sales. For example, local health departments use a combination of state-provided and locally implemented information systems for patient data collection, management, and reporting. Users report system inefficiencies, difficulties in generating reports, and limited data accessibility, necessitating the need for system workarounds. In addition, the use of a "shadow system" to maintain a duplicate set of information is common.[1] Such inefficient systems add to the growth in healthcare costs.

Many organizations unknowingly waste money to acquire systems in different organizational units that perform nearly the same functions. Implementation of such duplicate systems unnecessarily increases hardware and software costs. The U.S. government spends billions of dollars on information systems each year, with $80 billion spent in fiscal year 2013 alone. Some of this spending goes toward providing information systems that provide similar functions across the various branches and agencies of the government. The Government Accounting Office (GAO) conducted a check of the three federal departments with the largest IT budgets—the Defense Department, Department of Homeland Security, and Department of Health and Human Services. It uncovered a total of $321 million spent in the six-year period from 2008 to 2013 on projects that duplicated other efforts within those same agencies.[2]

A less dramatic, yet still relevant, example of waste is the amount of company time and money employees can spend playing computer games, sending personal email, surfing the Web, buying items online, liking a new picture on Instagram, and checking their status on LinkedIn. Some 60 percent of workers check their Facebook page daily and Nielsen found that 25 percent of working adults admit to viewing pornography on a computer while at work.[3] As a result, many companies, including Cintas, General Electric Aviation, Kroger, Procter & Gamble, and TriHealth have all found it necessary to limit employee access to nonwork-related Web sites.[4]

Computer-Related Mistakes

Despite many people's distrust of them, computers rarely make mistakes. If users do not follow proper procedures, however, even the most sophisticated hardware cannot produce meaningful output. Mistakes can be caused by unclear expectations coupled with inadequate training and a lack of feedback. A programmer might also develop a program that contains errors, or a data-entry clerk might enter the wrong data. Unless errors are caught early and corrected, the speed of computers can intensify mistakes. As information technology becomes faster, more complex, and more powerful, organizations and computer users face increased risks of experiencing the results of computer-related mistakes. Consider these recent examples of computer-related mistakes:

- Federal agencies reported an estimated $106 billion in improper payments for 2013. This includes payments that should not have been made, payments made in the wrong amount, or payments not supported by sufficient documentation. The payments came from 84 programs spread across 18 agencies.[5] See Figure 14.1.
- The Florida Comprehensive Assessment Test (FCAT) for students in grades 3 to 11 can have a tremendous impact on students, teachers, and schools. Poor test scores can hold back a student. Test scores are also a major factor in teacher evaluations. Those schools that produce low test scores are forced to undergo major changes or may even be closed. A series of widespread computer glitches prevented thousands of students across the state from signing into their computers and taking the test. At the same time, many students who had begun the test were interrupted. Some questioned whether the results from testing will be reliable and whether the tests should be retaken by all students.[6]
- The flight of a U-2 spy plane uncovered a design problem in the U.S. air traffic control system that temporarily shut down the system and grounded or delayed hundreds of Los Angeles area flights. The $2.4 billion En Route Automation Modernization system built by Lockheed Martin Corporation failed because it limits how much data each plane can send to the system. Most commercial planes have simple flight plans, so they

FIGURE **14.1**

Computer-related mistakes

Federal agencies recently reported an estimated $106 billion in improper payments.

do not approach that limit. However, the U-2 operates at high altitude, and that day had a complex flight plan that put it over the system's limit. Fortunately, no accidents or injuries were reported from the failure, though numerous flights were delayed or canceled.[7]

- The U.S. Centers for Medicare and Medicaid Services (CMS) is the lead agency responsible for implementing the Patient Protection and Affordable Care Act. The agency is working to help some 22,000 Americans fix enrollment mistakes that led to excessive charges, enrolled them in the wrong health plan, or denied them coverage altogether.[8]

PREVENTING COMPUTER-RELATED WASTE AND MISTAKES

To remain profitable in a competitive environment, organizations must use all resources wisely. To employ IS resources efficiently and effectively, employees and managers alike should strive to minimize waste and mistakes. This effort involves establishing, implementing, monitoring, and reviewing effective policies and procedures.

Establishing Policies and Procedures

The first step to prevent computer-related waste is to establish policies and procedures regarding efficient acquisition, use, and disposal of systems and devices. Computers permeate organizations today, and it is critical for organizations to ensure that systems are used to their full potential. As a result, most companies have implemented stringent policies on the acquisition of computer systems and equipment, including requiring a formal justification statement before computer equipment is purchased, definition of standard computing platforms (operating system, type of computer chip, minimum amount of RAM, etc.), and the use of preferred vendors for all acquisitions.

Prevention of computer-related mistakes begins by identifying the most common types of errors, of which there are surprisingly few. See Figure 14.2. Types of computer-related mistakes include the following:

- Data-entry or data-capture errors
- Errors in computer programs
- Errors in handling files, including formatting a disk by mistake, copying an old file over a newer one, and deleting a file by mistake
- Mishandling of computer output
- Inadequate planning for and control of equipment malfunctions
- Inadequate planning for and control of environmental difficulties (e.g., electrical and humidity problems)
- Installing computing capacity inadequate for the level of activity
- Failure to provide access to the most current information by not adding new Web links and not deleting old links

FIGURE 14.2

Preventing common computer errors

Preventing computer-related mistakes begins by identifying the most common types of errors.

© stockyimages/Shutterstock.com

To control and prevent potential problems caused by computer-related mistakes, companies have developed policies and procedures that cover the acquisition and use of computers. Training programs for individuals and work groups as well as manuals and documents covering the use and maintenance of computer systems also help prevent problems. The Error Prevention Institute offers online training on preventing human errors that explains the underlying reasons that humans make mistakes and how these mistakes can be prevented.[9] Other preventive measures include approval of certain systems and applications before they are implemented and used to ensure compatibility and cost effectiveness and a requirement that documentation and descriptions of certain applications, including all cell formulas for spreadsheets and a description of all data elements and relationships in a database system be filed or submitted to a central office. Such standardization can ease access and use for all personnel.

Many organizations have established strong policies to prevent employees from wasting time using computers inappropriately at work. See Figure 14.3.

FIGURE **14.3**

Computer usage policies

Organizations establish polices to keep employees from wasting time.

After companies plan and develop policies and procedures, they must consider how best to implement them. In some cases, violating these policies can lead to termination.

Genius is an iPhone app that allows users to provide annotations and interpretations of song lyrics, news stories, poetry, and other forms of text. Mahbod Moghadam, Genius's cofounder, allegedly was asked to leave the company after he annotated the 141-page manifesto left by Elliot Rodger with some strange comments. Rodger was the 22-year-old man who went on a shooting spree in Santa Barbara, California, killing six people and then committing suicide.[10]

Implementing Policies and Procedures

Implementing policies and procedures to minimize waste and mistakes varies according to the business conducted. Most companies develop such policies and procedures with advice from the firm's internal auditing group or its external auditing firm. The policies often focus on the implementation of source data automation, the use of data editing to ensure data accuracy and completeness, and the assignment of clear responsibility for data accuracy within each information system. Some useful policies to minimize waste and mistakes include the following:

- Changes to critical tables, HTML, and URLs should be tightly controlled, with all changes documented and authorized by responsible owners.
- A user manual should be available covering operating procedures and documenting the management and control of the application.
- Each system report should indicate its general content in its title and specify the time period covered.
- The system should have controls to prevent invalid and unreasonable data entry.
- Controls should exist to ensure that data input, HTML, and URLs are valid, applicable, and posted in the right time frame.
- Users should implement proper procedures to ensure correct input data.

Training is another key aspect of implementation. Many users are not properly trained in using applications, and their mistakes can be very costly. Because more and more people use computers in their daily work, they should understand how to use them. Training is often the key to acceptance and implementation of policies and procedures. See Figure 14.4. Because of the importance of maintaining accurate data and of people understanding their responsibilities, companies converting to ERP and e-commerce systems invest weeks of training for key users of the system's various modules.

FIGURE 14.4

Computer training

Training helps to ensure acceptance and implementation of policies and procedures.

Monitoring Policies and Procedures

To ensure that users throughout an organization are following established procedures, the next step is to monitor routine practices and take corrective action if necessary. By understanding what is happening in day-to-day activities, organizations can make adjustments or develop new procedures. Many organizations perform audits to measure actual results against established goals, such as percentage of end-user reports produced on time, percentage of data-input errors detected, number of input transactions entered per eight-hour shift, and so on.

When accounting firm KPMG audited the Boston Redevelopment Authority, it found that the agency failed to collect millions of dollars in lease payments and fees owed by developers for affordable housing. The agency keeps most of its records on paper and lacks adequate systems for monitoring and enforcing agreements with developers to improve roads and parks in exchange for city approval of their projects and collecting rents on public property.[11]

Reviewing Policies and Procedures

The final step is to review existing policies and procedures and determine whether they are adequate. During review, people should ask the following questions:

- Do current policies cover existing practices adequately? Were any problems or opportunities uncovered during monitoring?
- Does the organization plan any new activities in the future? If so, does it need new policies or procedures addressing who will handle them and what must be done?
- Are contingencies and disasters covered?

This review and planning allows companies to take a proactive approach to problem solving, which can enhance a company's performance, such as increasing productivity and improving customer service. During such a review, companies are alerted to upcoming changes in information systems that could have a profound effect on many business activities.

The results of failing to review and plan changes in policies and procedures can lead to disastrous consequences. For example, Walmart has one of the most sophisticated supply chain management systems in the consumer packaged goods industry. It employs an automated replenishment system so that as goods are purchased nationwide, computers in its headquarters create resupply orders to ensure that everything from Bounty paper towels to tomatoes are delivered to stores with amazing efficiency. Walmart needs workers who use pallet jacks and hand trucks to move the goods from Walmart back rooms to the store shelves. However, the company recently decided to slash operating costs by $740 million, largely by reducing the number of these workers.[12] These changes in policy and procedures have had a negative impact on the firm. Walmart was recently rated at the bottom among department and discount stores in the American Customer Satisfaction Index. Walmart customers' complaints about empty shelves and poor customer service are increasing. See Figure 14.5.[13]

FIGURE 14.5

Evaluating policies and procedures

Walmart's reduction of operating costs has had a negative impact on customer service.

Information systems professionals and users still need to be aware of the misuse of resources throughout an organization. Preventing errors and mistakes is one way to do so. Another is implementing in-house security measures and legal protections to detect and prevent a dangerous type of misuse: computer crime.

COMPUTER CRIME

Even good IS policies might not be able to predict or prevent computer crime. A computer's ability to process millions of pieces of data in less than one second makes it possible for a thief to steal data worth millions of dollars. Compared with the physical dangers of robbing a bank or retail store with a gun, computer crime is less dangerous as a computer criminal with the right equipment and know-how can steal large amounts of money without leaving his or her home.

Internet Crime Computer Center (IC3): An alliance between the White Collar Crime Center and the Federal Bureau of Investigation that provides a central site for Internet crime victims to report and to alert appropriate agencies of crimes committed.

The **Internet Crime Computer Center (IC3)** is an alliance between the White Collar Crime Center and the Federal Bureau of Investigation (FBI) and was formed in 2000. It provides a central site for Internet crime victims to report and to alert appropriate agencies of crimes committed. By May 2014, the IC3 had received 3 million consumer Internet crime complaints. Over the past five years, an average of 25,000 complaints were received per month. In 2013 alone, the verifiable dollar loss of complaints submitted to the IC3 totaled nearly $800 million. See Figure 14.6.[14]

© dean bertoncelj/Shutterstock.com

FIGURE 14.6

Computer crime

Computer crime is a serious and growing global concern.

Unfortunately, these numbers represent only a small fraction of total computer-related crimes, as many crimes go unreported because companies don't want the bad publicity or don't think that law enforcement can help. Such lack of publicity makes the job even tougher for law enforcement. Additionally, most companies that have been electronically attacked won't talk to the press. A big concern is loss of public trust and image—not to mention the fear of encouraging copycat hackers.

Today, computer criminals are a new breed—bolder and more creative than ever. With the increased use of the Internet, computer crime is now global. It's not just on U.S. shores that law enforcement has to battle cyber-criminals. Regardless of its nonviolent image, computer crime is different only because a computer is used. It is still a crime. Part of what makes computer crime unique and difficult to combat is its dual nature—the computer can be both the tool used to commit a crime and the object of that crime.

THE COMPUTER AS A TOOL TO COMMIT CRIME

A computer can be used as a tool to gain access to valuable information and as the means to steal millions of dollars. It is, perhaps, a question of motivation—many people who commit computer-related crime claim they do it for the challenge, not for the money. Credit card fraud—whereby a criminal illegally gains access to another's line of credit with stolen credit card numbers—is a major concern for today's banks and financial institutions. In general, criminals need two capabilities to commit most computer crimes. First, the criminal needs to know how to gain access to the computer system. Sometimes, obtaining access requires knowledge of an identification number and a password. Second, the criminal must know how to manipulate the system to produce the desired result. Frequently, a critical computer password has been talked out of a person, a practice called social engineering. Social engineering attacks are often conducted by phone with the hacker imitating someone in a position of authority and attempting to gradually draw information out of the user. Often the hacker claims to be a member of the help desk of the victim's organization or ISP service provider. Following is a brief list of tips to avoid becoming a victim of social engineering.

- Never provide information such as your user name, logon ID, password, Social Security number, account numbers, or answers to security questions (e.g., the name of the street where your best friend lives).
- Be highly suspicious of anyone who proactively contacts you about a problem with your computer or computer services.
- Ask for proof of identity if someone calls claiming to be from a different office in your company or from one of your suppliers and asks for sensitive information. For example, ask for an extension number so that you can call back. If they claim to be from a law enforcement agency, ask for a badge number.

Think no one would ever stoop so low as to hunt through your trash in search of bills that you already paid? Wrong! A dumpster can be an excellent source of information for an identity thief. Data from discarded bills, credit card approval letters, or financial statements can provide all the information needed to rob you of your identity. Sometimes the attackers simply go through the trash—dumpster diving—for important pieces of information that can help crack the computers or convince someone at the company to give them more access. See Figure 14.7. In addition, over 2,000 Web sites offer the digital tools—often without charge—that let people snoop, crash computers, hijack control of a machine, or retrieve a copy of every keystroke. While some of the tools were intended for legitimate use to provide remote technical support or monitor computer usage, hackers take advantage of them to gain unauthorized access to computers or data.

social engineering: Using social skills to get computer users to provide information that allows a hacker to access an information system or its data.

dumpster diving: Going through the trash of an organization to find secret or confidential information, including information needed to access an information system or its data.

FIGURE **14.7**

Dumpster diving

Identity thieves are not above searching an organization's trash to find confidential information.

Cyberterrorism

cyberterrorism: The intimidation of government or civilian population by using information technology to disable critical national infrastructures (e.g., energy, transportation, telecommunications, banking and finance, law enforcement, and emergency response) to achieve political, religious, or ideological goals.

Cyberterrorism is the intimidation of government or civilian population by using information technology to disable critical national infrastructures (e.g., energy, transportation, financial, law enforcement, emergency response) to achieve political, religious, or ideological goals. Cyberterrorism is an increasing concern for countries and organizations around the globe.

The U.S. government considered the potential threat of cyberterrorism serious enough that in February 1998 it established the National Infrastructure Protection Center. This function was later transferred to the Homeland Security Department's Information Analysis and Infrastructure Protection Directorate to serve as a focal point for threat assessment of, warning of, investigation of, and response to threats or attacks against the country's critical infrastructure, which provides telecommunications, energy, banking and finance, water systems, government operations, and emergency services. Successful cyberattacks against the facilities that provide these services could cause widespread and massive disruptions to the normal function of American society. See Figure 14.8.

FIGURE 14.8

Cyberterrorism

Cyberterrorism includes threats or attacks against a country's critical infrastructure, such as the air traffic control system.

cyberterrorist: Someone who intimidates or coerces a government or organization to advance his or her political or social objectives by launching computer-based attacks against computers, networks, and the information stored on them.

A **cyberterrorist** is someone who intimidates or coerces a government or organization to advance his or her political or social objectives by launching computer-based attacks against computers, networks, and the information stored on them. Following are a few recent examples of attacks by cyberterrorists from around the world:

- The United States and Israeli governments collaborated to develop Stuxnet, computer malware designed to attack industrial Programmable Logic Controllers (PLCs) that regulate industrial machinery. The Stuxnet malware was used to infect the computers that controlled the centrifuges for separating nuclear material for Iran's nuclear program. Government estimates have stated that the Stuxnet attacks set back the Iranian nuclear program by as much as two years, although outside experts are skeptical of that claim.[15]
- Russian hackers broke into the networks of at least three manufacturers of industrial control software and inserted malware into their product software. The software is used by many companies in the oil and energy

industry to enable their employees to access industrial control systems remotely. It is estimated that some 250 companies unknowingly downloaded malware-infected software. While there is no indication that the hackers intended to commit an act of cyberterrorism such as to blow up an oil rig or refinery, the potential for sabotage exists.[16]

- Ellie Mae, Inc. provides end-to-end business automation software for the residential mortgage industry. Roughly 20 percent of all mortgage obligations flow through its system. On March 31 and April 1, 2014, a critical end-of-the-month processing period, the loan origination system was unable to run, and lenders were unable to finish closing their loans. The outage was suspicious and raised speculation of a cyberattack designed to test the defenses of critical banking systems.[17]

Identity Theft

identify theft: A crime in which an imposter obtains key pieces of personal identification information, such as Social Security or driver's license numbers, to impersonate someone else.

Identity theft is a crime in which an imposter obtains key pieces of personal identification information, such as Social Security or driver's license numbers, to impersonate someone else. The information is then used to obtain credit, merchandise, or services in the name of the victim or to provide the thief with false credentials. More than 13 million U.S. adults fell victim to identity fraud in 2013, an increase of 500,000 from 2012. See Figure 14.9.[18]

FIGURE 14.9

Identity theft

More than 13 million U.S. adults fell victim to identity fraud in 2013.

The perpetrators of these crimes employ such an extensive range of methods that investigating them is difficult. One method of gaining personal identity information is from hackers gaining unauthorized access to the employee and customer records of organizations. From 2005, when the Identity Theft Resource Center began tracking security breaches, until July 2014, 4,652 total breaches have been recorded, affecting 633 million individuals. (Some individuals were affected multiple times, some were fortunate and were unaffected.)[19]

The number of U.S. taxpayers affected by identity theft has increased sixfold from 270,000 in 2010 to over 1.6 million in 2013. These thefts have resulted in billions of dollars in potentially fraudulent refunds. For example, a Florida mother of three pleaded guilty to using stolen identities to cheat the IRS out of $3 million, but only after she bought a $92,000 Audi, proclaimed herself a millionaire, and foolishly announced on her Facebook page that she was "the queen of IRS tax fraud."[20]

Another rapidly growing area of identity theft involves child identity theft. A recent survey found that 2.5 percent of U.S. households with children under age 18 experienced child identity fraud at some point during their child's lifetime.[21] Children's Social Security numbers are considered "clean," and their theft may not be detected for years. Signs of potential child identity theft include collection calls to the child, difficulty opening a bank account in the child's name, receiving bills or bank statements for the child, and teenagers that are denied an ID card or driver's license due to one already having been issued. Parents should request credit reports for their children to ensure that nothing is amiss.

In some cases, the identity thief uses personal information to open new credit accounts, establish a cellular phone service, or open a new checking account to obtain blank checks. In other cases, the identity thief uses personal information to gain access to the person's existing accounts. Typically, the thief changes the mailing address on an account and runs up a huge bill before the person whose identity has been stolen realizes there is a problem. The Internet has made it easier for an identity thief to use the stolen information because transactions can be made without any personal interaction.

Computer Theft

The number of bank robberies has been reduced by 60 percent since their peak in 1991, with robberies down 23 percent just between 2011 and 2012. The classic bank robbery is being replaced by ATM-skimming and other cybercrimes.[22] Ploutus (also called "Plotos") is malware designed to steal money directly from ATM machines. See Figure 14.10. The malware is uploaded to the ATM on a CD-ROM after picking a lock on the machine to access the CD-ROM drive. The thief can send a command to the malware using the ATM keypad interface to dispense cash. Use of the malware was first detected in Mexico in September 2013 when Mexican police arrested two Venezuelan men suspected of using the malware.[23]

FIGURE 14.10

Computer theft

Ploutus malware is designed to steal money directly from ATM machines.

© Matthew Ennis/Shutterstock.com

Financial institutions are also concerned about the potential for a "brick attack," where hackers infect the servers that store customer data and render them completely useless, unable to be turned on. The National Security Agency (NSA) reported that it thwarted such a brick attack directed at computers across the United States at the end of 2013.[24]

THE COMPUTER AS A TOOL TO FIGHT CRIME

The computer is also used as a tool to fight computer crime. Information systems are used to fight crime in many ways, including helping recover stolen property, monitoring sex offenders, and helping to better understand and diminish crime risks.

Recovery of Stolen Property

The LeadsOnline Web-based service system is one of several information systems used by law enforcement to recover stolen property. The system contains hundreds of millions of records in its database. Over 680 million transactions have been entered into the system from pawn brokers, second-hand dealers, and salvage yards. In some areas, state or local laws require that all such businesses register (with no charge to business owners) with LeadsOnline. The system allows law enforcement officers to search the database by item serial number or by individual. It even has a partnership with eBay that makes it possible to locate possible stolen merchandise that has been listed for sale or sold online.

The LeadsOnline system has frequently helped to catch criminals and return stolen property to its rightful owners. A police officer was assigned a theft case involving stolen aluminum coils and chain link fencing. To search LeadsOnline, he used a possible suspect name provided by the victim and found that the suspect had recently scrapped a large amount of metal at a local scrap yard. The police officer followed up at the scrap yard and obtained photos of the suspect and the items that he scrapped. The items were positively identified by the victim. Charges are pending in this case.[25]

Monitoring Criminals

JusticeXchange is a Web-based data sharing system that places millions of nationwide booking records at the fingertips of law enforcement officials. The system makes it easy to collaborate with other law enforcement professionals to locate persons of interest.

The system receives data from agencies that book and house offenders through interfaces to their existing jail management systems. Users can search for historical and current information about prisoners, create a "watch" so that they are notified of a specific offender's booking or release by email, and add behavioral information about currently incarcerated offenders to the database.[26]

Watch Systems is a technology partner and consultant to law enforcement organizations nationwide. Its Offender Watch program is a sex offender management and community notification solution for law enforcement. Some 4,500 local, county, and state agencies use it to manage 60 percent of the nation's sex offenders. This Web-based system stores the registered offender's address, physical description, and vehicle information. The public can access the information at *www.communitynotification.com*. The information available varies depending on the county and state. For example, in Hamilton County, Ohio, the data is provided by the sheriff's department and allows the user to search for registered sex offenders by township, school district, zip code, or within one mile of an entered address. The information displayed includes a photo of all registered sex offenders, their description, and current addresses. Law enforcement agencies can search the database based on full or partial license plate number or vehicle description.[27]

Assessing Crime Risk for a Given Area

The ready availability of personal computers, coupled with the development of mapping and analysis software, has led law enforcement agencies to use crime-related data, powerful analysis techniques, and geographic information systems (GIS) to better understand and even diminish crime risks. The use of such software enables law enforcement agencies, members of an organization's security department, and individuals to gain a quick overview of crime risk at a given address or in a given locale, as shown in Figure 14.11.

Map Scale

0 miles   2.75   5.5

2012 CAP Index Contours
□ 0 – 99 □ 100 – 199 ▨ 200 – 399 ▨ 400 – 799 ■ 800 – 2000

© Copyright 2014 CAP Index Inc.

FIGURE 14.11

Mapping crime risk

A GIS helps law enforcement agencies track and even diminish crime risks.

CAP Index Inc.'s CRIMECAST Reports provide a quick and thorough overview of the crime risk at any given location in the United States, Canada, and the United Kingdom. A detailed map and spreadsheet of risk scores isolate and identify crime-related issues in the vicinity of a specific site. Figure 14.11 shows Dallas, Texas. CRIMECAST clients include more than 80 percent of FORTUNE 100 companies, including Bank of America, Cabela's, Kraft, Lowe's, Nationwide, and Marriott. Companies and government organizations use CRIMECAST data to assess crime risk levels at their facilities, for selection of new sites, for allocation of security resources, and to defend against litigation related to premises security.[28]

With GIS tools, law enforcement agencies can analyze crime data relative to other factors, including the locations of common crime scenes (e.g., convenience stores and gas stations) and certain demographic data (e.g., age and income distribution). Common GIS systems include the following:

- The National Equipment Registry maps mobile equipment thefts in areas where peak equipment thefts have occurred so that police and equipment owners can take appropriate action. It includes more than 15 million ownership records for construction and farm equipment.[29]
- The CompStat (short for computer statistics) program uses GIS software to map crime and identify problem precincts. The program has a proven track record of reducing crime in Boston, Los Angeles, Miami, Newark, New Orleans, New York, and Philadelphia. Other cities are exploring its use, including San Francisco.[30]
- CargoNet is a national database that helps law enforcement and the transportation industry track cargo crimes, identify cargo theft patterns, and improve stolen property recovery rates. The database can be accessed by traditional desktop and laptop computers, tablet computers, and even smartphones.

THE COMPUTER AS THE OBJECT OF CRIME

A computer can also be the object of a crime rather than the tool for committing it. Tens of millions of dollars' worth of computer time and resources are stolen every year. Each time system access is illegally obtained, data or computer equipment is stolen or destroyed, or software is illegally copied, the computer becomes the object of crime. These crimes fall into several categories: illegal access and use, data alteration and destruction, information and equipment theft, software and Internet piracy, computer-related scams, and international computer crime. See Table 14.1.

TABLE 14.1 Common methods used to commit computer crimes

Methods	Examples
Add, delete, or change inputs to the computer system.	Delete records of absences from class in a student's school records.
Modify or develop computer programs that commit the crime.	Change a bank's program for calculating interest so it deposits rounded amounts in the criminal's account.
Alter or modify the data files used by the computer system.	Change a student's grade from C to A.
Operate the computer system in such a way as to commit computer crime.	Access a restricted government computer system.
Divert or misuse valid output from the computer system.	Steal discarded printouts of customer records from a company trash bin.
Steal computer resources, including hardware, software, and time on computer equipment.	Make illegal copies of a software program without paying for its use.
Offer worthless products for sale over the Internet.	Send emails requesting money for worthless hair growth product.
Blackmail executives to prevent release of harmful information.	Eavesdrop on organization's wireless network to capture competitive data or scandalous information.
Blackmail company to prevent loss of computer-based information.	Plant a logic bomb and send a letter threatening to set it off unless paid a considerable sum.

© 2016 Cengage Learning

Illegal Access and Use

Crimes involving illegal system access and use of computer services are a concern to both government and business. Since the outset of information technology, computers have been plagued by criminal hackers. Originally, a **hacker** was a person who enjoyed computer technology and spent time learning and using computer systems. A **criminal hacker**, also called a **cracker**, is a computer-savvy person who attempts to gain unauthorized or illegal access to computer systems to steal passwords, corrupt files and programs, or even transfer money. In many cases, criminal hackers are people who are looking for excitement—the challenge of beating the system. Today, many people use the term "hacker" and "cracker" interchangeably. **Script bunnies** is a derogatory term for inexperienced hackers who download programs called "scripts" that automate the job of breaking into computers. **Insiders** are employees, disgruntled or otherwise, working solo or in concert with outsiders to compromise corporate systems. The biggest threat for many companies is not external hackers but their own employees. Insiders have extra knowledge that makes them especially dangerous—they know logon IDs, passwords, and company procedures that help them evade detection.

Malaysia Airlines Flight 370 disappeared somewhere over the Indian Ocean in March 2014 with 239 passengers and crew on board. See Figure 14.12. The investigation of the disappearance has raised suspicions that an insider (one of

hacker: A person who enjoys computer technology and spends time learning and using computer systems.

criminal hacker (cracker): A computer-savvy person who attempts to gain unauthorized or illegal access to computer systems to steal passwords, corrupt files and programs, or even transfer money.

script bunny: A derogatory term for inexperienced hackers who download programs called "scripts" that automate the job of breaking into computers.

insider: An employee, disgruntled or otherwise, working solo or in concert with outsiders to compromise corporate systems.

FIGURE 14.12

Insider threats

The loss of Malaysia Airlines Flight 370 may have been an inside crime.

the pilots) was responsible for disabling the transponder that signals to ground controllers the location and speed of the aircraft and for reprogramming the aircraft's flight management system to cause the jetliner to deviate from its intended flight path.[31]

Catching and convicting criminal hackers remains a difficult task. The method behind these crimes is often hard to determine, even if the method is known, and tracking down the criminals can take a lot of time.

Because contractors often must be trusted with logon names and passwords and access to secure information systems to complete their job assignment, they can also be considered an insider threat. A man who served 10 years of a 20-year sentence on a murder conviction slipped through the screening process and was hired as a contractor to work at the Chicago O'Hara airport. He subsequently was caught on surveillance video stealing two laptops from a footlocker.[32]

Data and information are valuable corporate assets. The intentional use of illegal and destructive programs to alter or destroy data is as much a crime as destroying tangible goods. The most common of these programs are viruses and worms, which are software programs that, when loaded into a computer system, will destroy, interrupt, or cause errors in processing. Such programs are also called **malware**, and the growth rate for such programs is epidemic. It is estimated that hundreds of previously unknown viruses and worms emerge each day. Table 14.2 describes the most common types of malware.

In some cases, a virus or a worm can completely halt the operation of a computer system or network for days until the problem is found and repaired. In other cases, a virus or a worm can destroy important data and programs. If backups are inadequate, the data and programs might never be fully functional again. The costs include the effort required to identify and neutralize the virus or worm and to restore computer files and data as well as the value of business lost because of unscheduled computer downtime.

The Trojan horse program Pandemiya monitors its host's input and output data streams looking for user names and passwords for banking and financial accounts. It also scans for Social Security numbers, credit card details, and other data useful to identity thieves. All data of interest is forwarded to the computer of a cybercriminal who then packages the data for resale to other cybercrooks.[33]

malware: Software programs that when loaded into a computer system will destroy, interrupt, or cause errors in processing.

TABLE **14.2** Common types of computer malware

Type of Malware	Description
Logic Bomb	A type of Trojan horse that executes when specific conditions occur. Triggers for logic bombs can include a change in a file by a particular series of keystrokes or at a specific time or date.
Rootkit	A set of programs that enables its user to gain administrator level access to a computer or network. Once installed, the attacker can gain full control of the system and even obscure the presence of the rootkit from legitimate system administrators.
Trojan Horse	A malicious program that disguises itself as a useful application or game and purposefully does something the user does not expect.
Variant	A modified version of a virus that is produced by the virus's author or another person by amending the original virus code.
Virus	A malicious program that copies itself and infects a computer, spreading from one file to another, and then from one computer to another when the files are copied or shared. Most viruses attach themselves to executable files, but some can target a master boot record, autorun scripts, or Microsoft Office macros.
Worm	A malicious program that spreads from computer to computer, but unlike a virus, it can spread without any human action. For example, a worm can send a copy of itself to everyone listed in your email address book.

© 2016 Cengage Learning

Hackers have recently turned their attention to smartphones—especially ones running the popular Android operating system—for a couple of reasons. First, people have smartphones to be able to download an almost limitless array of apps; however, seemingly innocent programs can provide hackers with easy access to your phone. In addition, few smartphones have much security and antimalware protection, creating a situation ripe for exploitation. Malware creators can access email and contacts lists, monitor personal communications, and capture vital data such as the password used to access a mobile banking app.

One smartphone-hacking technique is taking a popular app such as Jetpack Joyride or 4 Pics, 1 Word, inserting a string of malicious commands into its code, and then relisting it on a third-party app site that doesn't have the same stringent application process as Google Play or the Apple Store. When a user downloads the app from the third-party app store for what they think is a bargain price, they instead get problems.[34]

The Star N9500, a cheap Android-powered smartphone made in China, ships with more than an 8-megapixel camera and quad-core processor, according G Data, a Germany cybersecurity company. The company says it has discovered malicious software—which could be used to track the phone's user and manipulate the device remotely—embedded in the device.[35]

Spyware

spyware: Software that is installed on a personal computer to intercept or take partial control of the user's interaction with the computer without the knowledge or permission of the user.

Spyware is software installed on a personal computer to intercept or take partial control of the user's interaction with the computer without the knowledge or permission of the user. Some forms of spyware secretly log keystrokes so that user names and passwords may be captured. Other forms of spyware record information about the user's Internet surfing habits and sites that have been visited. Still other forms of spyware change personal computer settings so that the user experiences slow connection speeds or is redirected to Web pages other than those expected. Spyware is similar to a Trojan horse in that users unknowingly install it when they download freeware or shareware from the Internet.

The Hacking Team is an Italian computer spyware firm whose software allegedly has been used by foreign governments to snoop on dissidents and journalists. Its software can filch documents from hard drives, eavesdrop on video chats, scan emails, steal contact lists, and remotely turn on cameras and microphones to spy on a computer's unsuspecting user. Victims include a human rights activist in Dubai, a group of journalists in Morocco critical of the government, and an Ethiopian journalist in the United States. All were hacked and had their email read without their knowledge. Many fear that in the wrong hands, the Hacking Team software can become a highly intrusive tool placing dissidents and activists at risk.[36] Such software also can be used by industrial spies and those who are suspicious of their significant other.

Information and Equipment Theft

Data and information are assets or goods that can also be stolen. People who illegally access systems often do so to steal data and information. To obtain illegal access, criminal hackers require identification numbers and passwords. Some criminals try various identification numbers and passwords until they find ones that work. Using password sniffers is another approach. A password sniffer is a small program hidden in a network or a computer system that records identification numbers and passwords. In a few days, a password sniffer can record hundreds or thousands of identification numbers and passwords. Using a password sniffer, a criminal hacker can gain access to computers and networks to steal data and information, invade privacy, plant viruses, and disrupt computer operations.

The Mask is a collection of malware that infects computers running the Windows, OS X, and Linux operating systems. It is considered to be the most sophisticated malware-driven espionage campaign uncovered to date. The malware captures key strokes, Skype conversations, and other forms of sensitive data. The Mask is aimed at specific people or organizations that possess unique data or capabilities with strategic national or business value. Its primary targets appear to be activists, energy companies, government agencies and embassies, private equity firms, and research institutions. Given its targets and degree of sophistication, experts believe that the Mask is the product of hackers sponsored by a well-financed nation-state.[37]

In addition to theft of data and software, all types of computer systems and equipment have been stolen from homes, offices, schools, and vehicles. Software is available to enable you to locate your laptop in the event it is lost or stolen. For example, MyTheftProtection enables you to track, trace, and monitor your computer using GPS technology and Google Maps. You can even get pictures of the thief via the webcam as well as communicate with the thief or user.[38]

In many cases, the data and information stored in these systems are more valuable than the equipment. Personal data can be used in identity theft. In addition, the victim organization receives a tremendous amount of negative publicity that can cause it to lose existing and potential future customers. Often, the victim organization offers to pay for credit-monitoring services for those people affected in an attempt to restore customer goodwill and avoid law suits.

password sniffer: A small program hidden in a network or a computer system that records identification numbers and passwords.

ghassem khosrownia/Getty Images

FIGURE 14.13

Protecting computers

To fight computer crime, many companies use devices that disable the disk drive or lock the computer to the desk.

Patent and Copyright Violations

Works of the mind, such as art, books, films, formulas, inventions, music, and processes that are distinct and "owned" or created by a single person or group, are called "intellectual property." Copyright law protects authored works such as art, books, film, and music. Patent laws protect processes, machines, objects made by humans or machines, compositions of matter, and new uses of these items. Software is considered intellectual property and may be protected by copyright or patent law.

Software piracy is the act of unauthorized copying, downloading, sharing, selling, or installing of software. When you purchase software, you are purchasing a license to use it; you do not own the actual software. The license states how many times you can install the software. If you make more copies of the software than the license permits, you are pirating.

The Business Software Alliance (BSA) has become a prominent software antipiracy organization. Software companies, including Adobe, Apple, Hewlett-Packard, IBM, Intel, and Microsoft contribute funds to the operation of BSA. The BSA estimates that the global rate of unlicensed PC software use was 43 percent in 2013 with a global commercial value of $62.7 billion. The region with the lowest overall rate of unlicensed software was North America at 19 percent, and the region with highest overall rate of unlicensed software was the Asia-Pacific region at 62 per cent.[39]

Digital rights management (DRM) refers to the use of any of several technologies to enforce policies for controlling access to digital media, such as movies, music, and software. Many digital content publishers state that DRM technologies are needed to prevent revenue loss due to illegal duplication of their copyrighted works. While the costs of movie piracy can only be estimated imprecisely, the Motion Picture Association of America (MPAA) estimates that 29 million U.S. adults have watched illegal copies of movies or TV shows. It is estimated that over 300 million users use BitTorrent, a commonly used peer-to-peer file-sharing service, to download free content each month.[40] On the other hand, many digital content users argue that DRM and associated technologies lead to a loss of user rights. For example, users can purchase a music track online for less than a dollar through Apple's iTunes music store. They can then burn that song to a CD and transfer it to an iPod. However, the purchased music files are encoded in the AAC format supported by iPods and protected by FairPlay, a DRM technology developed by Apple. To the consternation of music lovers, most music devices are not compatible with the AAC format and cannot play iTunes' protected files. See Figure 14.14.

Penalties for software piracy can be severe. If the copyright owner brings a civil action against someone, the owner can seek to stop the person from using its software immediately and can also request monetary damages. The copyright owner can then choose between compensation for actual damages—which includes the amount lost because of the person's infringement as well as any profits attributable to the infringement—and statutory damages, which can be as much as $150,000 for each program copied. In addition, the government can prosecute software pirates in criminal court for copyright infringement. If convicted, they could be fined up to $250,000 or sentenced to jail for up to five years or both.

Project Options Ltd, an engineering design company in the United Kingdom, was found to be using several unlicensed copies of Autodesk software for computer-aided design (CAD). The firm was ordered to pay £33,000 (over $55,000) in related fines. The software piracy was brought to the attention of the BSA from a confidential online report filed through their Web site. The BSA encourages the reporting of software piracy by promising a cash reward for anonymous reports.[41]

software piracy: The act of unauthorized copying, downloading, sharing, selling, or installing of copyrighted software.

digital rights management (DRM): Refers to the use of any of several technologies to enforce policies for controlling access to digital media, such as movies, music, and software.

FIGURE 14.14

Digital rights management

Due to digital rights management (DRM) technology, music files that iTunes members purchase and download play only on iPods and other AAC-compatible devices.

Another major issue in regards to copyright infringement is the downloading of copyright-protected music. Estimates vary widely as to how much music piracy is costing the recording industry. In the decade since peer-to-peer (p2p) file-sharing site Napster emerged in 1999, music sales in the United States dropped 47 percent, from $14.6 billion to $7.7 billion. The Institute for Policy Innovation estimates that the U.S. global recording industry loses about $12.5 billion in revenue from music piracy every year. It is projected that this results in 71,000 lost jobs and $2.7 billion in lost wages for U.S. workers.[42]

A Louisiana man was sentenced to two years in federal prison for manufacturing and distributing pirated movies and music albums. The individual duplicated copyrighted motion pictures and music using a home DVD/CD burner and then sold these illegal copies for $10 from his parked car. During a search of his home, investigators seized over 1,000 pirated DVDs and CDs with an estimated retail value of more than $12,000.[43]

Patent infringement is also a major problem for computer software and hardware manufacturers. It occurs when someone makes unauthorized use of another's patent. If a court determines that a patent infringement is intentional, it can award up to three times the amount of damages claimed by the patent holder. It is not unusual to see patent infringement awards in excess of $10 million.

Apple and Samsung are involved in a series of patent infringement legal battles regarding the design of smartphones and tablet computers. The problems began in spring 2010, when Samsung launched the Galaxy S, a new entry into the smartphone market. Apple designers thought the overall appearance of the Galaxy S, its screen, its icons, and even its box closely resembled the iPhone. See Figure 14.15. In addition, Apple alleged that many of its patented features such as "pinch to zoom" were copied in the Galaxy S. Samsung, in turn, claimed that Apple had violated over 22 of its patents. By October 2011, Apple and Samsung were litigating 19 ongoing cases in 10 countries. To date, the two companies have litigation costs exceeding $1 billion.[44]

To obtain a patent or to determine if a patent exists in an area a company seeks to exploit requires a search by the U.S. Patent Office; these can last longer than 25 months. Indeed, the patent process is so controversial that manufacturing firms, the financial community, consumer and public interest groups, and government leaders are demanding patent reform.

Samsung Galaxy S   Apple iPhone

FIGURE 14.15

Patent infringement

Apple and Samsung are involved in a series of patent infringement legal battles regarding the design of smartphones and tablet computers.

Computer-Related Scams

People have lost hundreds of thousands of dollars to real estate, travel, stock, and other business scams. Today, many of these scams are being perpetrated with computers. Using the Internet, scam artists offer get-rich-quick schemes involving bogus real estate deals, tout "free" vacations with huge hidden costs, commit bank fraud, offer fake telephone lotteries, sell worthless penny stocks, and promote illegal tax-avoidance schemes.

Many cases of Internet fraud involve nondelivery of automobiles advertised for sale on the Internet. The hoaxer posts photos and a description of a vehicle offered for sale. When an interested buyer responds, the victim is told that the vehicle is located overseas. The fraudster then tells the victim to send a deposit via a wire transfer to initiate the shipping process. Once that transfer is done, the buyer hears nothing further from the fraudster. In a devious variation on this scam, the hoaxer advises the victim about a problem with the initial wire transfer. To correct the problem, the hoaxer sends the victim a cashier's check (counterfeit) and tells the victim to cash the check and resend a second wire to a different account. The victim is unaware that the cashier's check is counterfeit and follows the directions, getting stung a second time.[45]

Another common complaint involves romance scams in which scammers target individuals searching for companionship or romance online. The fraudsters often use a stolen identity to appear reputable and begin to "friend" potential victims trying to develop an online relationship with their victims. Victims believe they are "dating" a good and honest person without ever physically meeting them. As the relationship grows, the fraudsters reveal that they are in a predicament and need cash. Perhaps they are overseas on urgent business and a family member has fallen ill. They need money to get home. Victims end up wiring funds (sometimes repeatedly) to the fraudster, believing they are involved in a genuine relationship.[46]

Over the past few years, credit card customers of various banks have been targeted by scam artists trying to get personal information needed to use their credit cards. The scam works by sending customers an email including a link that seems to direct users to their bank's Web site. At the site, they are greeted with a pop-up box asking them for their full credit card numbers, their personal

phishing: A form of computer scam that attempts to get users to gain access to a customer's private information through a fake Web site.

identification numbers, and their credit card expiration dates. The problem is that the Web site is fake, operated by someone trying to gain access to customers' private information, a form of computer scam called phishing.

Phishing attacks worldwide have been increasing and set a record in the first quarter of 2014 when 125,215 attacks were observed. The fraudsters attacking the Web sites of payment services accounted for 47 percent of the targets, financial services firms were the target in 20 percent of the attacks, and retail/service firms were targeted 11 percent of the time.[47]

The current round of phishing scams are so sophisticated that they look like emails you would expect to receive from a major bank. Messages display a familiar bank logo and clicking it takes you to the real bank's Web site. The email uses a real no-reply email address from the bank itself rather than a clearly fake Yahoo or Hotmail address. However, the messages inform recipients that because the bank found a serious problem with their account, they must complete a form and provide account numbers, personal identification numbers, and other key information scammers need to impersonate you. See Figure 14.16. Phishing has become such a serious problem that the Bank of America, Facebook, Fidelity Investments, Google, JP Morgan Chase & Company, LinkedIn, Microsoft, PayPal, Yahoo, and other organizations have formed the Domain-based Message Authentication, Reporting, and Conformance (DMARC) group to provide improved email security and protection from phishing.[48]

FIGURE 14.16

Sample phishing email message

Phishing attacks worldwide have been increasing.

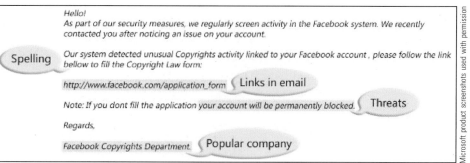

Microsoft product screenshots used with permission from Microsoft Corporation.

vishing: A scam that attempts to steal an individual's private information by having them call a phone number and enter personal data.

Vishing is similar to phishing. However, instead of using the victim's computer, it uses the victim's phone. The victim is typically sent a notice or message to call to verify account information. If the victim returns the message, the caller asks for personal information, such as a credit card account number or name and address. The information gained can be used in identity theft to acquire and use credit cards in the victim's name. Vishing criminals can even use the Spoof Card, sold online for less than $5 dollars for 25 calls. It causes phones to display a caller ID number specified by the caller rather than the actual number of the caller.[49]

smishing: A scam that attempts to steal an individual's private information by having them respond to a text message.

Smishing is similar to phishing and vishing. It is text-message fraud that occurs when criminals, posing as financial institutions, attempt to dupe mobile-phone users into giving personal information through text messages, calling a telephone number, or visiting a fraudulent Web site.

International Computer Crime

Computer crime becomes more complex when it crosses borders. Money laundering is the practice of disguising illegally gained funds so that they seem legal. With the increase in electronic cash and funds transfer, some are concerned that terrorists, international drug dealers, and other criminals are using information systems to launder illegally obtained funds.

Federal prosecutors indicted four Russians and a Ukrainian in what is one of the largest computer crimes in U.S. history. The five conspired in a worldwide scheme that targeted major corporate networks, stole more than 160 million

INFORMATION SYSTEMS @ WORK

The United States Charges the Chinese People's Liberation Army with Stealing Trade Secrets

In May, 2014, the United States Department of Justice (DOJ) charged five members of the Unit 61398 of the China's army, the Chinese People's Liberation Army (PLA), with 31 counts of cyber espionage. The charges accuse Gu Chunhui, Wang Dong, Sun Kailiang, Wen Xinyu, and Huang Zhenyu, members of PLA Unit 61398, of stealing trade secrets pertaining to Westinghouse AP1000 nuclear power plant technology, nabbing manufacturing plans and costs from SolarWorld, swiping the network credentials for every single Allegheny Technologies Incorporated (ATI) employee, and intercepting emails at Alcoa.

The information looted from U.S. corporations through these and the many other misdeeds listed in the indictment provide significant advantages to government-owned Chinese competitors. First, by illegally obtaining the plans to the Westinghouse technology, the Chinese nuclear companies gain both time and money they would have had to invest in the research and development necessary to develop the system themselves. Second, SolarWorld's manufacturing costs and plans will aid Chinese companies in their current campaign to undercut U.S. and other Western solar firms by flooding the market with cheaper solar technologies. Finally, the attacks on steel giants, ATI and Alcoa, aim at stealing the manufacturing secrets Chinese companies need to make high-quality steel so that they may gain a wider hold in the international marketplace.

The legal motion marked a new approach of the U.S. government toward government-sponsored Chinese espionage. "In the past, when we brought concerns such as these to Chinese government officials, they responded by publicly challenging us to provide hard evidence of their hacking that could stand up in court," explained John Carlin, director of DOJ's national security division. This time, the U.S. government turned to cyber defense company Mandiant, which issued a lengthy report based on an investigation it had conducted.

According to Mandiant, PLA Unit 61398 is located in a nondescript 12-floor building in Shanghai's Pudong District—a building that can house a maximum of 2,000 cyber spies. The unit may have other locations, as it controls over 1,000 servers. Since 2006, Mandiant estimates that Unit 61398 has stolen hundreds of terabytes of data from 141 companies, 115 of which were based in the United States. The unit's high-tech fiber-optic communications infrastructure is provided by state-owned China Telecom.

What is unclear, however, is whether legal action taken in a U.S. court can counter the Chinese threat. According to Mandiant, PLA Unit 61398 is only one of 20 Chinese cyberattack groups. Moreover, PLA Unit 61398 besides hacking into IT systems, has installed malware. Hackers could potentially break into a company's system and sabotage a factory's machines right before an important delivery deadline.

Even more frightening, perhaps, is that the PLA Unit 61398 and other Chinese hackers have not only breached the systems of strategic American industries, including aerospace, telecommunications, satellite, and IT, they have breached the IT systems of federal agencies, including those dedicated to defense. In July 2014, the U.S. DOJ charged Chinese national Su Bin with stealing 65 gigabytes of information related to Boeing fighter jets. In August 2014, well-known security expert Brian Krebs reported that PLA Unit 61398 had stolen 700 documents from three defense contractors that had developed Israel's missile defense system, the Iron Dome.

There's no question that these Chinese-government-sponsored hackers present a serious threat both economically and militarily. The question that remains open is what the U. S. government can do about it.

Discussion Questions

1. What is PLA Unit 61398 and what type of crimes are they charged with?
2. What can and should the United States do to stop PLA Unit 61398 and similar groups?

Critical Thinking Questions

1. What impact will the crimes PLA Unit 61398 have on Westinghouse, SolarWorld, Alcoa, ATI, and other victims of the group?
2. What are the potential military threats that PLA Unit 61398 poses to the U.S. and other Western nations?

SOURCES: "US Justice Department Charges Chinese with Hacking," *BBC News*, May 19, 2014, *www.bbc.com/news/world-us-canada-27475324*; Pagliery, Jose, "What Were China's Hacker Spies After?" *CNN Money*, May 19, 2014, *http://money.cnn.com/2014/05/19/technology/security /china-hackers/*; Li, Zoe, "What We Know about the Chinese Army's Alleged Cyber Spying Unit," *CNN World*, May 20, 2014, *www.cnn.com /2014/05/20/world/asia/china-unit-61398/*; Musil, Steven, "US Charges Chinese Executive with Hacking Military Data," *CNET*, *www.cnet.com*, July 13, 2014; Ghoshal, Debalina, "China Hacking Iron Dome, Arrow Missile Defense Systems," Gatestone Institute International Policy Council, August 5, 2014, *www.gatestoneinstitute.org/4578/china-hacking-missile-defense*.

credit card numbers, and resulted in hundreds of millions of dollars in losses.[50] The hacked companies included the French firm Carrefour SA, and several U.S.-based firms including JCPenney, JetBlue Airways, Nasdaq, and Visa. Two of the criminals hacked into networks; one mined data to steal user names and passwords, personal identification data, and credit and debit card numbers; one provided anonymous Web-hosting services to conceal the actions of the group; and another sold the stolen data and distributed the profits.[51]

PREVENTING COMPUTER-RELATED CRIME

Because of increased computer use today, greater emphasis is placed on the prevention and detection of computer crime. Although all states have passed computer crime legislation, some believe that these laws are not effective because companies do not always actively detect and pursue computer crime, security is inadequate, and convicted criminals are not severely punished. However, all over the United States, private users, companies, employees, and public officials are making individual and group efforts to curb computer crime, and recent efforts have met with some success.

Crime Prevention by State and Federal Agencies

State and federal agencies have begun aggressive attacks on computer criminals, including criminal hackers of all ages. In 1986, Congress enacted the Computer Fraud and Abuse Act, which mandates punishment based on the victim's dollar loss.

United States Computer Emergency Readiness Team (US-CERT): Part of the Department of Homeland Security that leads U.S. efforts to improve the nation's cyber-security posture, coordinate cyber information sharing, and proactively manage cyber risks to the nation.

United States Computer Emergency Readiness Team (US-CERT) is part of the Department of Homeland Security. US-CERT leads U.S. efforts to improve the nation's cybersecurity posture, coordinate cyber information sharing, and proactively manage cyber risks to the nation. It attempts to do all this while protecting the constitutional rights of Americans. US-CERT partners with private sector critical infrastructure owners and operators, academia, federal agencies, Information Sharing and Analysis Centers (ISACs), state and local partners, and domestic and international organizations to enhance the country's cybersecurity position.[52]

Advice for providing good computer and network security as well as a complete listing of computer-related legislation by state can be found at the US-CERT Web site at *https://www.us-cert.gov/ncas* and at the Online Security Web site at *www.onlinesecurity.com/forum/article46.php*. Recent court cases and police reports involving computer crime show that lawmakers are ready to introduce newer and tougher computer crime legislation.

Crime Prevention by Organizations

Public and private organizations are also taking crime-fighting efforts seriously. Many businesses have designed procedures and specialized hardware and software to protect their corporate data and systems. Specialized hardware and software, such as encryption devices, can be used to encode data and information to help prevent unauthorized use. Encryption is the process of converting an original electronic message into a form that can be understood only by the intended recipients. A key is a variable value that is applied using an algorithm to a string or block of unencrypted text to produce encrypted text or to decrypt encrypted text. Encryption methods rely on the limitations of computing power for their effectiveness: If breaking a code requires too much computing power, even the most determined code crackers will not be successful. The length of the key used to encode and decode messages partially determines the strength of the encryption algorithm.

Over 75 percent of U.S. organizations view data protection activities as a key component of enterprise risk management. Thus, the use of encryption to protect data stored on backup files and laptops and data transmitted externally is increasing. The primary justification for implementing encryption is to protect an organization's brand or reputation from the damage that would result from a serious data breach.

As a consequence of the Affordable Care Act, the government is now enforcing the healthcare data security laws, with major fines being imposed on noncompliant organizations. For example, when a laptop computer carrying the health information of 441 patients was stolen from the Hospice of North Idaho, the organization was fined over $50,000 by the Department of Health and Human Services.[53]

A class-action lawsuit was filed against the Maricopa County Community College District over a computer security breach that exposed the personal information of more than 2.4 million current and former students, employees, and vendors going back some 30 years. Banking information, Social Security numbers, and academic information were exposed. The lawsuit alleges that the district was negligent by not protecting the personal information of these people. The district has budgeted $17 million to deal with the incident including $10 million for credit-monitoring expenses for those affected.[54]

As employees move from one position to another in a company, they can build up access to multiple systems if inadequate security procedures fail to revoke access privileges. It is clearly not appropriate for people who have changed positions and responsibilities to still have access to systems that they no longer use. To avoid this problem, many organizations create role-based system access lists so that only people filling a particular role (e.g., invoice approver) can access a specific system.

Hackers sometimes gain access to systems by exploiting inactive user accounts. It is critical that accounts of employees or contractors who have left the company or who are on extended disability be terminated. A fired, former campaign manager for New Mexico's governor pleaded guilty to two felony counts of intercepting her email. Prosecutors alleged that he used her password and username information to change the computer account for the governor's 2010 campaign organization after she took office as governor. As a result, messages sent through the campaign email system by the governor and her aides were directed to a computer account controlled by the man.[55]

In addition, a fundamental concept of good internal controls is the careful separation of duties associated with a key process so that they must be performed by more than one person. Separation of duties is essential for any process that involves the handling of financial transactions so that fraud requires the collusion of two or more parties. When designing an accounts receivable information system, for instance, separation of duties dictates that you separate responsibility for the receipt of customer payments, approving write-offs, depositing cash, and reconciling bank statements.

separation of duties: The careful division of the tasks and responsibilities associated with a key process so that they must be performed by more than one person.

Proper separation of duties is frequently reviewed during any audit. A deputy in a county clerk's office was suspended for five days after using the county's server to work on his boss's re-election campaign. In addition, the county clerk himself used the county server to do campaign work. The state's campaign disclosure law requires a separation of duties so that candidates and those working on their campaigns cannot use taxpayer resources for political purposes.[56]

Crime-fighting procedures usually require additional controls on the information system. Before designing and implementing controls, organizations must consider the types of computer-related crime that might occur, the consequences of these crimes, and the cost and complexity of needed controls. In most cases, organizations conclude that the trade-off between crime and the additional cost and complexity weighs in favor of better system controls. Having knowledge of some of the methods used to commit crime is also helpful in preventing, detecting, and developing systems resistant to computer crime. Some companies actually hire former criminals to thwart other criminals.

Many current and proposed biometric ID systems have been designed to prevent crime. For example, fingerprint authentication devices provide security in the PC environment by using fingerprint recognition instead of passwords. Laptop computers from Lenovo, Toshiba, and others have built-in fingerprint readers used to log on and gain access to the computer system and its data. In addition, many new biometric ID systems are being considered for use with smartphones. Indeed, it is predicted that 619 million people will be using biometrics on their mobile devices by the end of 2015. See Figure 14.17. As smartphones become more and more valuable to us, the need for secure phone access becomes vital.[57]

FIGURE 14.17

Biometric smartphone

Many new biometric ID systems are being considered for use with smartphones.

The following list provides a set of useful guidelines to protect corporate computers from criminal hackers:

- Install strong user authentication and encryption capabilities on the corporate firewall.
- Install the latest security patches, which are often available at the vendor's Internet site.
- Disable guest accounts and null user accounts that let intruders access the network without a password.
- Do not provide overfriendly sign-in procedures for remote users (e.g., an organization that used the word "welcome" on its initial logon screen found it had difficulty prosecuting a criminal hacker).
- Restrict physical access to the server and configure it so that breaking into one server won't compromise the whole network.
- Dedicate one server to each application (email, File Transfer Protocol, and domain name server). Turn audit trails on.
- Install a corporate firewall between your corporate network and the Internet.
- Install antivirus software on all computers and regularly download vendor updates.
- Conduct regular IS security audits.
- Verify and exercise frequent data backups for critical data.

Using Intrusion Detection System

intrusion detection system (IDS): Monitors system and network resources and traffic and notifies network security personnel when it senses a possible intrusion.

An **intrusion detection system (IDS)** monitors system and network resources and traffic and notifies network security personnel when it senses a possible intrusion. Examples of suspicious activities include repeated failed logon attempts, attempts to download a program to a server, and access to a system at unusual hours. Such activities generate alarms that are captured on log files. When they detect an apparent attack, intrusion detection systems send an alarm, often by email or pager, to network security personnel. Unfortunately, many IDSs frequently provide false alarms that result in wasted effort. If the attack is real, network security personnel must make a decision about what to do to resist the attack. Any delay in response increases the probability of damage. Use of an IDS provides another layer of protection in case an intruder gets past the outer security layers—passwords, security procedures, and corporate firewall.

Metro Madrid is the public rail transportation system for Madrid, Spain. See Figure 14.18. With 175 miles of track, 300 stations, and over one billion passengers a year, it is one of the largest metropolitan rail systems in the world. Devices on its information system and control networks manage everything from automated ticketing machines to back office business systems to turnstiles and track management systems. Ensuring the security of these networks is essential for Metro Madrid to deliver safe, efficient, and reliable services. Metro Madrid implemented an intrusion detection system to monitor its tens of thousands of devices and application servers and protect from unwanted hackers.[58]

FIGURE 14.18

Metro Madrid

Metro Madrid uses an intrusion detection system to monitor the devices and application servers on its network and protect them from hackers.

Security Dashboard

security dashboard: Software that provides a comprehensive display on a single computer screen of all the vital data related to an organization's security defenses, including threats, exposures, policy compliance and incident alerts.

Many organizations use **security dashboard** software to provide a comprehensive display on a single computer screen of all the vital data related to an organization's security defenses, including threats, exposures, policy compliance, and incident alerts. The goal is to reduce the effort required for monitoring and to identify threats in time. Data comes from a variety of sources, including firewalls, applications, servers, and other software and hardware devices. See Figure 14.19.

McKesson Corporation is the largest pharmaceutical company in the world with recent annual sales of $137 billion, 50 global offices, and over 37,000 employees.[59] The firm implemented a security dashboard to gain a

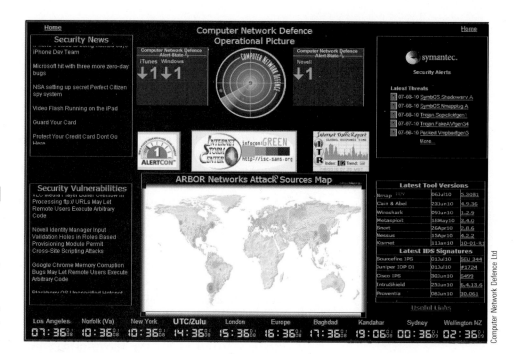

FIGURE 14.19

Computer Network Defence Internet Operational Picture

The Computer Network Defence Internet Operational Picture, a security dashboard designed for the United Kingdom government and military networks, displays near real-time information on new and emerging cyber threats.

clear enterprise-wide view of its network vulnerability status. The dashboard provides actionable information to enable the security team to prioritize known and emerging vulnerabilities on its global network.[60]

Using Managed Security Service Providers

Keeping up with computer criminals—and with new regulations—can be daunting for organizations. Criminal hackers are constantly poking and prodding, trying to breach the security defenses of companies. Also, such legislation as HIPAA, Sarbanes-Oxley, and the USA Patriot Act requires businesses to prove that they are securing their data. For most small and mid-sized organizations, the level of in-house network security expertise needed to protect their business operations can be quite costly to acquire and maintain. As a result, many are outsourcing their network security operations to **managed security service providers (MSSPs)**, such as AT&T, Computer Sciences Corporation (CSC), Dell SecureWorks, IBM, Symantec, and Verizon. MSSPs monitor, manage, and maintain network security for both hardware and software. These companies provide a valuable service for IS departments drowning in reams of alerts and false alarms coming from virtual private networks (VPNs); antivirus, firewall, and intrusion detection systems; and other security-monitoring systems. In addition, some provide vulnerability scanning and Web blocking and filtering capabilities.

OnCue Express operates over 50 gas and convenience stores in the Midwest. Nearly 10 million credit card transactions traverse its network annually. The firm must comply with the Payment Card Industry Data Security Standards (PCI DSS), which require it to achieve minimal levels of information security or face significant fines for noncompliance. In addition, OnCue would incur at least a $12,000 per hour loss in revenue if its network were disrupted. Facing these serious risks, OnCue decided to engage an MSSP to assess its network security and provide recommendations to improve it. OnCue now produces PCI Scanning reports of externally facing systems, such as point of sale (POS) servers, to identify and remediate any vulnerabilities detected. With the help of the MSSP, OnCue was able to upgrade its network security without an increase in staff.[61]

managed security service providers (MSSPs): Organizations that monitor, manage, and maintain network security for both hardware and software for other organizations.

Guarding against Theft of Equipment and Data

Organizations need to take strong measures to guard against the theft of computer hardware and the data stored on it. Here are a few measures to be considered:

- Set clear guidelines on what kind of data (and how much of it) can be stored on vulnerable laptops. In many cases, private data or confidential company data may not be downloaded to laptops that leave the office.
- Require that data stored on laptops be encrypted and do spot checks to ensure that this policy is followed.
- Require that all laptops be secured using a lock and chain device so that they cannot be easily removed from an office area.
- Provide training to employees and contractors on the need for safe handling of laptops and their data. For example, laptops should never be left in a position where they can be viewed by the public, such as on the front seat of an automobile.
- Consider installing tracking software on laptops. The software sends messages via a wireless network to the specified email address, pinpointing its location and including a picture of the thief (for those computers with an integrated Web cam).

Crime Prevention for Individuals and Employees

This section outlines actions that individuals can take to prevent becoming a victim of computer crime, including identity theft, malware attacks, theft of equipment and data, and computer scams.

Identity Theft

The U.S. Congress passed the Identity Theft and Assumption Deterrence Act of 1998 to fight identity theft. Under this act, the Federal Trade Commission (FTC) is assigned responsibility to help victims restore their credit and erase the impact of the imposter. It also makes identity theft a federal felony punishable by a prison term ranging from 3 to 25 years.

Consumers can protect themselves from identity theft by regularly checking their credit reports with major credit bureaus, following up with creditors if their bills do not arrive on time, not revealing any personal information in response to unsolicited email or phone calls (especially Social Security numbers and credit card account numbers), and shredding bills and other documents that contain sensitive information.

Some consumers contract with a service company that provides fraud-monitoring services, helps file required reports, and disputes unauthorized transactions in accounts. Some services even offer identity theft guarantees of up to $1 million. Some of the more popular services include TrustedID, Life-Lock, ProtectMyID, IDWatchdog, and Identity Guard. These services cost between $6 and $20 per month.

Malware Attacks

The number of personal computers infected with malware (viruses, worms, spyware, etc.) has reached epidemic proportions. As a result of the increasing threat of malware, most computer users and organizations have installed antivirus programs on their computers. See Figure 14.20. Such software runs in the background to protect your computer from dangers lurking on the Internet and other possible sources of infected files. The latest virus definitions are downloaded automatically when you connect to the Internet, ensuring that your PC's protection is current. To safeguard your PC and prevent it from spreading malware to your friends and coworkers, some antivirus software scans and cleans both incoming and outgoing email messages. Table 14.3 lists the top-rated antivirus software for 2014.[62,63,64]

antivirus program: Software that runs in the background to protect your computer from dangers lurking on the Internet and other possible sources of infected files.

TABLE 14.3 Top-rated antivirus software

For Windows systems	For Mac systems
Webroot Secure Anywhere Antivirus ($19.99)	Kromtech MacKeeper ($59.95)
Norton Antivirus ($49.99)	Intego Mac Internet Security ($39.95)
Bitdefender Antivirus Plus ($39.95)	Kaspersky Internet Security for Mac ($39.95)
Kaspersky Antivirus ($34.95)	Norton Antivirus (free)
AVG Antivirus (free)	Avira Free MacSecurity (free)
Malwarebytes Anti-Malware 2.0 (free)	

© 2016 Cengage Learning

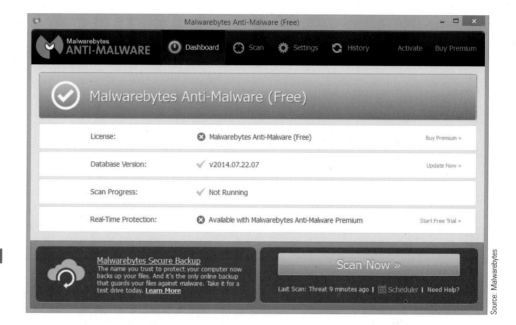

FIGURE 14.20

Antivirus software

Antivirus software should be used and updated often.

Source: Malwarebytes

Proper use of antivirus software requires the following steps:

1. **Install antivirus software and run it often.** Many of these programs automatically check for viruses each time you boot up your computer or insert a disk or CD, and some even monitor all email, file transmissions, and copying operations.
2. **Update antivirus software often.** New viruses are created all the time, and antivirus software suppliers are constantly updating their software to detect and take action against these new viruses.
3. **Scan all removable media, including CDs, before copying or running programs from them.** Hiding on disks or CDs, viruses often move between systems. If you carry document or program files on removable media between computers at school or work and your home system, always scan them.
4. **Install software only from a sealed package or secure Web site of a known software company.** Even software publishers can unknowingly distribute viruses on their program disks or software downloads. Most scan their own systems, but viruses might still remain.
5. **Follow careful downloading practices.** If you download software from the Internet or a bulletin board, check your computer for viruses immediately after completing the transmission.
6. **If you detect a virus, take immediate action.** Early detection often allows you to remove a virus before it does any serious damage.

Many email services and ISP providers offer free antivirus protection. For example, AOL and MWEB (one of South Africa's leading ISPs) offer free antivirus software from McAfee.

Computer Scams

The following is a list of tips to help you avoid becoming a victim of a computer scam:

- Don't agree to anything in a high-pressure meeting or seminar. Insist on having time to think it over and to discuss your decision with someone you trust. If a company won't give you the time you need to check out an offer and think things over, you don't want to do business with it. A good deal now will be a good deal tomorrow; the only reason for rushing you is if the company has something to hide.
- Don't judge a company based on appearances. Flashy Web sites can be created and published in a matter of days. After a few weeks of taking money, a site can vanish without a trace in just a few minutes. You might find that the perfect money-making opportunity offered on a Web site was a money maker for the crook and a money loser for you.
- Avoid any plan that pays commissions simply for recruiting additional distributors. Your primary source of income should be your own product sales. If the earnings are not made primarily by sales of goods or services to consumers or sales by distributors under you, you might be dealing with an illegal pyramid scheme.
- Beware of shills—people paid by a company to lie about how much they've earned and how easy the plan was to operate. Check with an independent source to make sure that the company and its offers are valid.
- Beware of a company's claim that it can set you up in a profitable home-based business but that you must first pay up front to attend a seminar and buy expensive materials. Frequently, seminars are high-pressure sales pitches, and the material is so general that it is worthless.
- If you are interested in starting a home-based business, get a complete description of the work involved before you send any money. You might find that what you are asked to do after you pay is far different from what was stated in the ad. You should never have to pay for a job description or for needed materials.
- Get in writing the refund, buy-back, and cancellation policies of any company you deal with. Do not depend on oral promises.
- Do your homework. Check with the Better Business Bureau, your state attorney general, and the National Fraud Information Center (NFIC) before getting involved, especially when the claims about a product or potential earnings seem too good to be true.

If you need advice about an Internet or online solicitation, or if you want to report a possible scam, use the Online Reporting Form or Online Question & Suggestion Form features on the Web site for the National Fraud Information Center at *http://fraud.org* or call the NFIC hotline at 1-800-876-7060.

PRIVACY ISSUES

Privacy is an important social issue related to information systems. In 1890, U.S. Supreme Court Justice Louis Brandeis stated that the "right to be left alone" is one of the most "comprehensive of rights and the most valued by civilized man." Basically, the issue of privacy deals with this right to be left alone or to be withdrawn from public view. With information systems, privacy deals with the collection and use or misuse of data. Data is constantly being collected and stored on each of us. This data is often distributed over easily accessed networks and without our knowledge or consent. Concerns of privacy regarding this data must be addressed. A difficult question to answer is "Who owns this information and knowledge?" If a public or private organization spends time and resources to obtain data on you, does the organization own the data, and can it use the data in any way it desires? Government legislation answers these questions to some extent for federal agencies, but the questions remain unanswered for private organizations. Today, many businesses have to handle many requests from law enforcement agencies for information about its employees, customers, and suppliers. Indeed, some phone and Internet companies have employees whose full-time role it is to deal with information requests from local, state, and federal law enforcement agencies.

Privacy and the Federal Government

The federal government has implemented many laws addressing personal privacy, which are summarized in Table 14.4. However, a number of recent revelations of previously clandestine federal government data collection programs have raised concerns and debate between those who favor data collection as a means to increased security and those who view such programs as a violation of rights guaranteed by the Constitution and Bill of Rights.

TABLE **14.4** Key federal privacy laws and their provisions

Law	Provisions
Fair Credit Reporting Act of 1970 (FCRA)	Regulates operations of credit-reporting bureaus, including how they collect, store, and use credit information
Family Education Privacy Act of 1974	Restricts collection and use of data by federally funded educational institutions, including specifications for the type of data collected, access by parents and students to the data, and limitations on disclosure
Tax Reform Act of 1976	Restricts collection and use of certain information by the Internal Revenue Service
Right to Financial Privacy Act of 1978	Restricts government access to certain records held by financial institutions
Foreign Intelligence Surveillance Act of 1978	Defines procedures to request judicial authorization for electronic surveillance of persons engaged in espionage or international terrorism against the United States on behalf of a foreign power
Electronic Communications Privacy Act of 1986	Defines provisions for the access, use, disclosure, interception, and privacy protections of electronic communications
Computer Matching and Privacy Act of 1988	Regulates cross-references between federal agencies' computer files (e.g. to verify eligibility for federal programs)
Cable Act of 1992	Regulates companies and organizations that provide wireless communications services, including cellular phones
Gramm-Leach-Bliley Act of 1999	Requires all financial institutions to protect and secure customers' nonpublic data from unauthorized access or use
USA Patriot Act of 2001	Requires Internet service providers and telephone companies to turn over customer information, including numbers called, without a court order, if the FBI claims that the records are relevant to a terrorism investigation
E-Government Act of 2002	Requires federal agencies to post machine-readable privacy policies on their Web sites and to perform privacy impact assessments on all new collections of data of ten or more people
Fair and Accurate Credit Transactions Act of 2003	Designed to combat the growing crime of identity theft; allows consumers to get free credit reports from each of the three major consumer credit-reporting agencies every 12 months and to place alerts on their credit histories under certain circumstances
Foreign Intelligence Surveillance Act Amendments Act of 2008	Renews the U.S. government's authority to monitor electronic communications of foreigners abroad and authorizes foreign surveillance programs by the NSA like PRISM and some earlier data collection activities

- The NSA began the collection of metadata (the phone numbers of the parties involved in the call, call duration, call location, time and date of the call, and other data) from millions of telephone calls soon after the September 11, 2001 attacks on the United States. The data enables the NSA to create a network of associations for every caller. A provision known as Section 215 of the Patriot Act provided all the legal justification needed for many proponents of data gathering. That the data was being used to help the government "connect the dots" between overseas terrorists and coconspirators within the United States provided them with sufficient moral justification. See Figure 14.21.[65]

FIGURE 14.21

NSA Data Center in Utah

This data center, code-named Bumblehive, is the first Intelligence Community Comprehensive National Cybersecurity Initiative (IC CNCI) data center designed to support the intelligence community's efforts to monitor, strengthen, and protect the nation. The data center is designed to cope with the vast increases in digital data that have accompanied the rise of the global network.

- PRISM is a tool used by the NSA and the FBI to collect private electronic data belonging to users of major Internet services such as AOL, Apple, Facebook, Google, Microsoft, Skype, Yahoo!, YouTube, and others. PRISM enables the NSA to access the servers of these organizations to collect material, including search history, the content of email messages, videos, photos, file transfers, and live chats. Unlike the collection of telephone call records, this surveillance includes the content of communications and not just the metadata. With PRISM, the NSA can obtain targeted communications without having to request them from the service providers and without having to obtain individual court orders.[66]
- Another NSA program called MYSTIC is used to intercept and record all telephone conversations in Afghanistan, the Bahamas, Mexico, Kenya, and the Philippines.[67, 68] Because there is no practical way to exclude them, the conversations include those of Americans who make calls to or from the targeted countries.[69]

Privacy at Work

The right to privacy at work is also an important issue. Employers are using technology and corporate policies to manage worker productivity and protect the use of IS resources. Employers are mostly concerned about inappropriate Web surfing, with over half of employers monitoring the Web activity of their employees. Organizations also monitor employees' email, with more than half retaining and reviewing messages. Statistics such as these have raised employee privacy concerns. In many cases, workers claim their right to privacy trumps their companies' rights to monitor employee use of IS resources. However, most employers today have a policy that explicitly eliminates any expectation of privacy when an employee uses any company-owned computer, server, or email system. The courts have ruled that, without a reasonable expectation of privacy, there is no Fourth Amendment protection for the employee. A California appeals court ruled in *Holmes v Petrovich Development Company* that emails sent by an employee to her attorney on the employer's computer were not "confidential communications between a client and lawyer." An Ohio federal district court in *Moore v University Hospital Cleveland Medical Center* ruled that an employee could be terminated for showing coworkers sexually explicit photos on his employer's computer. The court stated that the employee could have no expectation of privacy when accessing a hospital computer situated in the middle of a hospital floor within easy view of both patients and staff.[70]

The European Union (EU) has developed strict regulations to enforce data privacy standards across all members of the organization. Under these regulations, personal data can only be gathered legally under strict conditions and only for reasonable purposes. Furthermore, persons or organizations that collect and manage individuals' personal information must protect it from misuse and must respect certain rights of the data owners, which are guaranteed by EU law. These regulations affect virtually any company doing business in Europe.[71]

Privacy and Email

Email also raises some interesting issues about work privacy. See Figure 14.22. Federal law permits employers to monitor email sent and received by employees. Furthermore, email messages that have been erased from hard disks can be retrieved and used in lawsuits because the laws of discovery demand that companies produce all relevant business documents. On the other hand, the use of email among public officials might violate "open meeting" laws. These laws, which apply to many local, state, and federal agencies, prevent public officials from meeting in private about matters that affect the state or local area.

FIGURE 14.22

Email and work privacy

Email has changed how workers and managers communicate in the same building or around the world. Email, however, can be monitored and intercepted. As with other services, such as cell phones, the convenience of email must be balanced with the potential of privacy invasion.

In July 2013, the city council in Glendale, Arizona, voted to approve a complicated, $225 million-dollar deal that pays the Phoenix Coyotes hockey team to stay at Jobing.com Arena for at least five years.[72] However, a year later, allegations arose that some council members may have violated Arizona's Open Meeting Law and if proven, could potentially void Glendale's deal with the team. It is alleged that prior to the vote, some council members met separately, held cell phone discussions, and circulated an email discussing arena parking, tax-exempt municipal bonds, and an escape clause that would allow the city to evict the Coyotes.[73]

Privacy and Instant Messaging

Using instant messaging (IM) to send and receive messages, files, and images introduces the same privacy issues associated with email. As with email, federal law permits employers to monitor instant messages sent and received by employees. Employers' major concern involves IMs sent by employees over their employer's IM network or using employer-provided phones. To protect your privacy and your employer's property, do not send personal or private IMs at work. The following are a few other tips:

- Choose a nonrevealing, nongender-specific, unprovocative IM screen name (Sweet Sixteen, 2hot4u, UCLAMBA, all fail this test).
- Don't send messages you would be embarrassed to have your family members, colleagues, or friends read.
- Do not open files or click links in messages from people you do not know.
- Never send sensitive personal data such as credit card numbers, bank account numbers, or passwords via IM.

Privacy and Personal Sensing Devices

RFID tags, essentially microchips with antenna, are embedded in many of the products we buy, from medicine containers, clothing, and books to computer printers, car keys, and tires. RFID tags generate radio transmissions that, if appropriate measures are not taken, can lead to potential privacy concerns. Once these tags are associated with the individual who purchased the item, someone can potentially track individuals by the unique identifier associated with the RFID chip.

A handful of states have reacted to the potential for abuse of RFID tags by passing legislation prohibiting the implantation of RFID chips under people's skin without their approval. Still, advocates for RFID chip implantation argue their potential value in tracking children or criminals and their value in carrying an individual's medical records.

Mobile crowd sensing (MCS) is a means to acquire data (i.e., location, noise level, traffic conditions, and pollution levels) through sensor-enhanced mobile devices and share this data with individuals, healthcare providers, utility firms, and local, state, and federal government agencies for decision making.

Privacy and the Internet

Some people assume that there is no privacy on the Internet and that you use it at your own risk. Others believe that companies with Web sites should have strict privacy procedures and be held accountable for privacy invasion. Regardless of your view, the potential for privacy invasion on the Internet is huge. People wanting to invade your privacy could be anyone from criminal hackers to marketing companies to corporate bosses. Your personal and professional information can be seized on the Internet without your knowledge or consent. Email is a prime target, as discussed previously. Sending an email message is like having an open conversation in a large room—people can listen to your messages. When you visit a Web site on the Internet, information about you and your computer can be captured. When this information is combined with other information, companies can find out what you read, what products you buy, and what your interests are.

Most people who buy products on the Web say it's very important for a site to have a policy explaining how personal information is used, and the policy statement must make people feel comfortable and be extremely clear about what information is collected and what will and will not be done with it. However, many Web sites still do not prominently display their privacy policy or implement practices completely consistent with that policy. The real issue that Internet users need to be concerned with is what do content providers want to do with that personal information? If a site requests that you provide your name and address, you have every right to know why and what will be done with it. If you buy something and provide a shipping address, will it be sold to other retailers? Will your email address be sold on a list of active Internet shoppers? And if so, you should realize that this email list is no different from the lists compiled from the orders you place with catalog retailers. You have the right to be taken off any mailing list.

The Children's Online Privacy Protection Act (COPPA) was passed by Congress in October 1998. This act was directed at Web sites catering to children, requiring site owners to post comprehensive privacy policies and to obtain parental consent before they collect any personal information from children under 13 years of age. Web site operators who violate the rule could be liable for civil penalties of up to $11,000 per violation. COPPA has made an impact in the design and operations of Web sites that cater to children. For example, the Web site Skid-e-kids violated the act by collecting personal information from some 5,600 children without obtaining prior parental consent. The Federal Trade Commission, responsible for enforcing the act, required that the information be deleted.[74]

A social network service employs the Web and software to connect people for whatever purpose. There are thousands of such networks, which have become popular among teenagers. Some of the more popular social networking Web sites include Facebook, Twitter, LinkedIn, Pinterest, Google Plus, Tumblr, and Instagram—all have over 100 million unique monthly visitors.[75] Most of these sites allow you to easily create a user profile that provides personal details, photos, and even videos that can be viewed by other visitors. Some of the sites have age restrictions or require that a parent register his or her preteen by providing a credit card to validate the parent's identity. Teens can provide information about where they live, go to school, their favorite music, and their interests in hopes of meeting new friends. Unfortunately, they can also meet ill-intentioned strangers at these sites. Many documented encounters involve adults masquerading as teens attempting to meet young people for illicit purposes. Parents are advised to discuss potential dangers, check their children's profiles, and monitor their activities at such Web sites.

Facebook holds a startling amount of information about its more than 900 million members. In addition, many members are not discrete and reveal such information as their health conditions and treatments; where they will be on a certain day (helpful to potential burglars); personal details of members of their family; their sexual, racial, religious, and political affiliations and preferences; and other personal information about their friends and family. Facebook receives a notice every time you visit a Web site with a "Like" button whether or not you click the "Like" button, log on to Facebook, or are a Facebook user. Users and observers have raised concerns about how Facebook treats this sometimes very personal information. For example, should law enforcement officials file a subpoena for your Facebook information, they could obtain all these details as well as records of your postings, photos you have uploaded, photos in which you have been tagged, and a list of all your Facebook friends. Under what conditions can Facebook provide this information to third parties for marketing or other purposes?

Privacy and Internet Libel Concerns

Libel involves publishing an intentionally false written statement that is damaging to a person's or organization's reputation. Examples of Internet libel include an ex-husband posting lies about his wife on a blog, a disgruntled former employee posting lies about a company on a message board, and a jilted girlfriend posting false statements to her former boyfriend's Facebook account. A Hong Kong court even ruled that a local billionaire can sue Google for libel over its autocomplete search results, which suggest that he is connected to organized crime. The tycoon filed the lawsuit after Google refused to remove autocomplete suggestions, such as "triad" (in China, this is another name for an organized crime gang), which appear with searches on his name. The billionaire maintains that his reputation has been "gravely injured" and wants recompense.[76]

Individuals can post information on the Internet using anonymous email accounts or screen names. This anonymity makes it more difficult, but not impossible, to identify the libeler. The offended party can file what is known as a John Doe lawsuit and use the subpoena power it grants to force the ISP to provide whatever information it has about the anonymous poster, including IP address, name, and street address. (Under Section 230 of the Communications Decency Act, ISPs are not usually held accountable for the bad behavior of their subscribers.)

Brian Burke, the current general manager (GM) and president of the National Hockey League's (NHL) Calgary Flames, and former GM of several other NHL teams filed a lawsuit in the Supreme Court of British Columbia against 18 individuals who allegedly made defamatory statements regarding Burke on various Internet message boards and blogs.[77]

Privacy and Fairness in Information Use

Selling information to other companies can be so lucrative that many companies will continue to store and sell the data they collect on customers, employees, and others. When is this information storage and use fair and reasonable to the people whose data is stored and sold? Do people have a right to know about data stored about them and to decide what data is stored and used? As shown in Table 14.5, these questions can be broken down into four issues that should be addressed: knowledge, control, notice, and consent.

TABLE **14.5** The right to know and the ability to decide federal privacy laws and regulations

Fairness Issues	Database Storage	Database Usage
The right to know	Knowledge	Notice
The ability to decide	Control	Consent

Knowledge. Should people know what data is stored about them? In some cases, people are informed that information about them is stored in a corporate database. In others, they do not know that their personal information is stored in corporate databases.

Control. Should people be able to correct errors in corporate database systems? This ability is possible with most organizations, although it can be difficult in some cases.

Notice. Should an organization that uses personal data for a purpose other than the original purpose notify individuals in advance? Most companies don't do this.

Consent. If information on people is to be used for other purposes, should these people be asked to give their consent before data on them is used? Many companies do not give people the ability to decide if such information will be sold or used for other purposes.

Privacy and Filtering and Classifying Internet Content

filtering software: Software that screens Internet content.

To help parents control what their children see on the Internet, some companies provide filtering software to help screen Internet content. Many of these screening programs also prevent children from sending personal information over email or through chat groups. These programs stop children from broadcasting their name, address, phone number, or other personal information over the Internet. The 2014 top-rated Internet filtering software for both Windows and Mac systems is presented in Table 14.6.[78, 79]

TABLE **14.6** Top-rated Internet filters

Windows Systems	Mac Systems
NetNanny ($28.99)	Net Nanny ($29.99)
McAfee Family Protection ($49.99)	Safe Eyes ($49.95)
PureSight PC ($59.90)	Spector Pro ($99.95)

© 2016 Cengage Learning

Organizations also implement filtering software to prevent employees from visiting Web sites not related to work, particularly those involving gambling and those containing pornographic or other offensive material. Before implementing Web site blocking, the users must be informed about the company's policies and why they exist. To increase compliance, it is best if the organization's Internet users, management, and IS organization work together to define the policy to be implemented. The policy should be clear about the repercussions to employees who attempt to circumvent the blocking measures.

The U.S. Congress has made several attempts to limit children's exposure to online pornography, including the Communications Decency Act (enacted 1996) and the Child Online Protection Act (enacted 1998). Within two years of being enacted, the U.S. Supreme Court found that both these acts violated the First Amendment (freedom of speech) and ruled them to be unconstitutional. The Children's Internet Protection Act (CIPA) was signed into law in 2000 and later upheld by the Supreme Court in 2003. Under CIPA, schools and libraries subject to CIPA do not receive the discounts offered by the E-Rate program unless they certify that they have certain Internet safety measures in place to block or filter "visual depictions that are obscene, child pornography, or are harmful to minors." (The E-Rate program provides many schools and libraries support to purchase Internet access and computers.)

In the past few decades, significant laws have been passed regarding a person's right to privacy. Others relate to business privacy rights and the fair use of data and information. The following sections briefly discuss corporate privacy policies and individual efforts to protect privacy.

Corporate Privacy Policies

Even though privacy laws for private organizations are not very restrictive, most organizations are sensitive to privacy issues and fairness. They realize that invasions of privacy can hurt their business, turn away customers, and dramatically reduce revenues and profits. Consider a major international credit card company. If the company sold confidential financial information on millions of customers to other companies, the results could be disastrous. In a matter of days, the firm's business and revenues could be reduced dramatically. Therefore, most organizations maintain privacy policies, even though they are not required by law. Some companies even have a privacy bill of rights that specifies how the privacy of employees, clients, and customers will be protected. Corporate privacy policies should address a customer's knowledge, control, notice, and consent over the storage and use of information. They can also cover who has access to private data and when it can be used.

The BBB Code of Business Practices (BBB Accreditation Standards) requires that BBB-accredited businesses have some sort of privacy notice on

ETHICAL& SOCIETAL ISSUES

IT Companies Leading Green Initiatives

In 1972, before the idea of corporate social responsibility (CSR) had gained traction, the IT giant IBM established a program of sustainability. In response to environmental disasters during the late 1960s, IBM instituted a program of hazardous waste management for itself and its contractors. In 1976, the Love Canal disaster created national concern when babies born nearby had birth defects and chromosomal disorders, and people developed leukemia. An area of 900 houses had to be abandoned due to chemical pollution.

At that time, IBM produced mainframe computers, adding machines, typewriters, telephone routing systems, and most of the advanced information technology of the age. They were the one of the largest corporations in the world. However, their component manufacturing processes produce large amounts of benzene-based materials that tend to be carcinogenic. In an effort to take the lead in corporate responsibility, they established one of the first environmental programs of its kind.

The three-pronged program attempted to track waste from creation to disposal and to reduce both its reliance on toxic chemicals and the amount of toxic waste released during the manufacturing process. IBM incrementally reduced toxic waste. In 1987, the company produced 220,500 tons in toxic waste. By 2011, the company was down to 7,700 metric tons—a gargantuan achievement. IBM accomplished this in part by the recycling of 44 percent of the hazardous chemicals used in the manufacturing process. They have also changed manufacturing processes and substituted nonhazardous materials for toxic chemicals.

Throughout the late 20th century, IBM proactively identified potential environmental problems and took the lead in ameliorating them. In the 1980s, scientists noticed a hole in the ozone layer of the stratosphere over Antarctica during the summer months. This layer protects the earth from harmful ultraviolet radiation. In 1989, IBM led the IT world in its repudiation of the use of ozone-depleting chemicals, such as chlorofluorocarbons.

Today, the corporation has expanded its initiative beyond toxic waste management. Its programs now seek to reduce energy use, conserve water resources, create energy efficient products, spearhead safety in the use of nanotechnology, and combat climate change. IBM has also devoted itself to the use of environmentally preferable substances and materials. IBM continues to attempt to reduce or eliminate reliance on heavy metals and carcinogens. The company recently reduced greenhouse gas emissions by 3.2 percent.

Other large IT companies have followed suit, launching green initiatives. HP, for example, has a product return and recycling program in 70 countries and territories. The company recycles more than 75 percent of their ink cartridges and 24 percent of their laser toner cartridges. The company also runs a remanufacturing program for servers, storage, networking products, and other IT hardware to reduce the waste from the disposal of outdated products. With remanufacturing, used HP products are fully restored to like-new standards by trained and qualified remanufacturing teams in factories owned and managed by HP. HP also offers trade-in and return-for-cash programs that have allowed them to recover 3.8 billion pounds of HP product since 1987.

Dell also has a major green initiative that has achieved noteworthy results. It has recovered 230.9 million pounds of used electronics and is on track to reach a goal of 2 billion pounds by 2020. Dell has been able to reduce the average energy intensity of its product line by 23 percent compared to 2012. Operational emissions have been reduced by 10 percent. Dell has used more than 10 million pounds of post-consumer recycled plastics in its products.

Discussion Questions

1. Why did IBM instigate its sustainability programs in the 1970s?
2. What goals should IT companies and large corporations include in their green initiatives?

Critical Thinking Questions

1. What major achievements have IBM, HP, and Dell made with their green initiatives?
2. What impact has IBM had on other companies both inside and outside of the IT industry?

SOURCES: "IBM and the Environment Report," *www.ibm.com/ibm/environment/annual/IBMEnv Report_2013.pdf*, accessed August 28, 2014; "Corporate Responsibility Summary," *IBM, www.ibm .com/ibm/responsibility/2013/*, access August 28, 2014; "Product Return and Recycling," *HP* Web site, *www8.hp.com/us/en/hp-information/environment/product-recycling.html#.U_TbsMVdUrU*, accessed August 20, 2014; "Environment," *Dell* Web site, *www.dell.com/learn/us/en/uscorp1/dell -environment*, accessed August 21, 2014.

their Web site. See Figure 14.23. BBB recommends that a privacy notice includes the following elements:[80]

- **Policy** (what personal information is being collected on the site)
- **Choice** (what options the customer has about how/whether his or her data is collected and used)
- **Access** (how a customer can see what data has been collected and change/correct it if necessary)
- **Security** (state how any data that is collected is stored/protected)
- **Redress** (what a customer can do if the privacy policy is not met)
- **Updates** (how policy changes will be communicated)

Multinational companies face an extremely difficult challenge in implementing data collection and dissemination processes and policies because of the multitude of differing country or regional statutes. For example, Australia requires companies to destroy customer data (including backup files) or make it anonymous after it's no longer needed. Firms that transfer customer and personnel data out of Europe must comply with European privacy laws that allow customers and employees to access data about themselves and let them determine how that information can be used.

Web sites for a few corporate privacy policies are shown in Table 14.7.

A good database design practice is to assign a single unique identifier to each customer so each has a single record describing all relationships with the company across all its business units. That way, the organization can apply customer privacy preferences consistently throughout all databases. Failure to do so can expose the organization to legal risks—aside from upsetting customers who opted out of some collection practices. Again, the 1999 Gramm-Leach-Bliley Financial Services Modernization Act requires all financial service institutions to communicate their data privacy rules and honor customer preferences.

Individual Efforts to Protect Privacy

Although numerous state and federal laws deal with privacy, the laws do not completely protect individual privacy. In addition, not all companies have privacy policies. As a result, many people are taking steps to increase their own

Privacy Notice

This privacy notice discloses the privacy practices for (Web site address). This privacy notice applies solely to information collected by this web site. It will notify you of the following:

1. What personally identifiable information is collected from you through the web site, how it is used and with whom it may be shared.
2. What choices are available to you regarding the use of your data.
3. The security procedures in place to protect the misuse of your information.
4. How you can correct any inaccuracies in the information.

Information Collection, Use, and Sharing
We are the sole owners of the information collected on this site. We only have access to/collect information that you voluntarily give us via email or other direct contact from you. We will not sell or rent this information to anyone.

We will use your information to respond to you, regarding the reason you contacted us. We will not share your information with any third party outside of our organization, other than as necessary to fulfill your request, e.g. to ship an order.

Unless you ask us not to, we may contact you via email in the future to tell you about specials, new products or services, or changes to this privacy policy.

Your Access to and Control Over Information
You may opt out of any future contacts from us at any time. You can do the following at any time by contacting us via the email address or phone number given on our Web site:

- See what data we have about you, if any.
- Change/correct any data we have about you.
- Have us delete any data we have about you.
- Express any concern you have about our use of your data.

Security
We take precautions to protect your information. When you submit sensitive information via the Web site, your information is protected both online and offline.

Wherever we collect sensitive information (such as credit card data), that information is encrypted and transmitted to us in a secure way. You can verify this by looking for a closed lock icon at the bottom of your web browser, or looking for "https" at the beginning of the address of the web page.

While we use encryption to protect sensitive information transmitted online, we also protect your information offline. Only employees who need the information to perform a specific job (for example, billing or customer service) are granted access to personally identifiable information. The computers/servers in which we store personally identifiable information are kept in a secure environment.

If you feel that we are not abiding by this privacy policy, you should contact us immediately via telephone at XXX YYY-ZZZZ or via email.

Source: The Better Business Bureau

FIGURE 14.23

Sample privacy notice
The BBB provides this sample privacy notice as a guide to businesses to post on their Web sites.

TABLE 14.7 Corporate privacy policies

Company	URL
Intel	www.intel.com/sites/sitewide/en_US/privacy/privacy.htm
Starwood Hotels & Resorts	www.starwoodhotels.com/corporate/privacy_policy.html
TransUnion	www.transunion.com/corporate/privacyPolicy.page
United Parcel Service	www.ups.com/content/corp/privacy_policy.html
Visa	http://usa.visa.com/legal/privacy-policy/index.jsp
Walt Disney Internet Group	https://disneyprivacycenter.com/

© 2016 Cengage Learning

privacy protection. Some of the steps that you can take to protect personal privacy include the following:

- **Find out what is stored about you in existing databases**. Call the major credit bureaus to get a copy of your credit report. You are entitled to a free credit report every 12 months (see *www.freecreditreport.com*). You can also obtain a free report if you have been denied credit in the last 60 days. The major companies are Equifax (800–685-1111, *www.equifax .com*), TransUnion (800–916-8800, *www.transunion.com*), and Experian (888–397-3742, *www.experian.com*). You can also submit a Freedom of Information Act request to a federal agency that you suspect might have information stored on you.

- **Be careful when you share information about yourself**. Don't share information unless it is absolutely necessary. Every time you give information about yourself through an 800, 888, or 900 call, your privacy is at risk. Be vigilant in insisting that your doctor, bank, or financial institution not share information about you with others without your written consent.

- **Be proactive to protect your privacy**. You can get an unlisted phone number and ask the phone company to block caller ID systems from reading your phone number. If you change your address, don't fill out a change-of-address form with the U.S. Postal Service; you can notify the people and companies that you want to have your new address. Destroy copies of your charge card bills and shred monthly statements before disposing of them in the garbage. Be careful about sending personal email messages over a corporate email system. You can also get help in avoiding junk mail and telemarketing calls by visiting the Direct Marketing Association Web site at *www.thedma.org*. Go to the site and look under Consumer Help-Remove Name from Lists.

- **Take extra care when purchasing anything from a Web site.** Make sure that you safeguard your credit card numbers, passwords, and personal information. Do not do business with a site unless you know that it handles credit card information securely. (Look for a seal of approval from organizations such as the Better Business Bureau Online or TRUSTe. When you open the Web page where you enter credit card information or other personal data, make sure that the Web address begins with *https* and check to see if a locked padlock icon appears in the Address bar or status bar). Do not provide personal information without reviewing the site's data privacy policy. Many credit card companies issue single-use credit card numbers on request. Charges appear on your usual bill, but the number is destroyed after a single use, eliminating the risk of stolen credit card numbers.

WORK ENVIRONMENT

The use of computer-based information systems has changed the makeup of the workforce. Jobs that require IS literacy have increased, and many less-skilled positions have been eliminated. Corporate programs, such as reengineering and continuous improvement, bring with them the concern that, as business processes are restructured and information systems are integrated within them, the people involved in these processes will be removed. Even the simplest tasks have been aided by computers, making customer checkout faster, streamlining order processing, and allowing people with disabilities to participate more actively in the workforce. As computers and other IS components drop in cost and become easier to use, more workers will benefit from the increased productivity and efficiency provided by computers. Yet, despite these increases in productivity and efficiency, information systems can raise other concerns.

Health Concerns

Organizations can increase employee productivity by paying attention to the health concerns in today's work environment. For some people, working with computers can cause occupational stress. Anxieties about job insecurity, loss of control, incompetence, and demotion are just a few of the fears workers might experience. In some cases, the stress can become so severe that workers avoid taking training to learn how to use new computer systems and equipment. Monitoring employee stress can alert companies to potential problems. Training and counseling can often help the employee and deter problems.

Heavy computer use can affect one's physical health as well. A job that requires sitting at a desk and using a computer for many hours a day qualifies as a sedentary job. Such work can double the risk of seated immobility thromboembolism (SIT), the formation of blood clots in the legs or lungs. People leading a sedentary lifestyle are also likely to experience an undesirable weight gain, which can lead to increased fatigue and greater risk of type 2 diabetes, heart problems, and other serious ailments.

Repetitive strain injury (RSI) is an injury or disorder of the muscles, nerves, tendons, ligaments, or joints caused by repetitive motion. RSI is a very common job-related injury. Tendonitis is inflammation of a tendon due to repetitive motion on that tendon. Carpal tunnel syndrome (CTS) is an inflammation of the nerve that connects the forearm to the palm of the wrist. CTS involves wrist pain, a feeling of tingling and numbness, and difficulty grasping and holding objects.

Avoiding Health and Environmental Problems

Two primary causes of computer-related health problems are a poorly designed work environment and failure to take regular breaks to stretch the muscles and rest the eyes. The computer screen can be hard to read because of glare and poor contrast. Desks and chairs can also be uncomfortable. Keyboards and computer screens might be fixed in place or difficult to move. The hazardous activities associated with these unfavorable conditions are collectively referred to as *work stressors*. Although these problems might not be of major concern to casual users of computer systems, continued stressors such as repetitive motion, awkward posture, and eye strain can cause more serious and long-term injuries. If nothing else, these problems can severely limit productivity and performance.

ergonomics: The science of designing machines, products, and systems to maximize the safety, comfort, and efficiency of the people who use them.

The science of designing machines, products, and systems to maximize the safety, comfort, and efficiency of the people who use them, called **ergonomics**, has suggested some approaches to reducing these health problems. Ergonomic experts carefully study the slope of the keyboard, the positioning and design of display screens, and the placement and design of computer tables and chairs. Flexibility is a major component of ergonomics and an important feature of computer devices. People come in many sizes, have differing preferences, and require different positioning of equipment for best results. Some people, for example, want to place the keyboard in their laps; others prefer it on a solid table. Because of these individual differences, computer designers are attempting to develop systems that provide a great deal of flexibility. See Figure 14.24.

It is never too soon to stop unhealthy computer work habits. Prolonged computer use under poor working conditions can lead to carpal tunnel

FIGURE **14.24**

Ergonomics

Developing certain ergonomically correct habits can reduce the risk of adverse health effects when using a computer.

syndrome, bursitis, headaches, and permanent eye damage. Strain and poor office conditions cannot be left unchecked. Unfortunately, at times, we are all distracted by pressing issues such as the organization's need to raise productivity, improve quality, meet deadlines, and cut costs. We become complacent and fail to pay attention to the importance of healthy working conditions. Table 14.8 lists some common remedies for heavy computer users.

TABLE **14.8** Avoiding common discomforts associated with heavy use of computers

Common Discomforts Associated with Heavy Use of Computers	Preventative Action
Red, dry, itchy eyes	Change your focus away from the screen every 20 or 30 minutes by looking into the distance and focusing on an object for 20 to 30 seconds
	Make a conscious effort to blink more often
	Consider the use of artificial tears
	Use an LCD screen that provides a much better viewing experience for your eyes by virtually eliminating flicker while still being bright without harsh incandescence.
Neck and shoulder pain	Use proper posture when working at the computer
	Stand up, stretch, and walk around for a few minutes every hour
	Shrug and rotate your shoulders occasionally
Pain, numbness, or tingling sensation in hands	Use proper posture when working at the computer
	Do not rest your elbows on hard surfaces
	Place a wrist rest between your computer keyboard and the edge of your desk.
	Take an occasional break and spread fingers apart while keeping your wrists straight
	Taken an occasional break with your arms resting at your sides and gently shake your hands

Source: Pekker, Michael, "Long Hours at Computer: Health Risks and Prevention Tips," *http://webfreebies4u.blogspot.com/2011/01/long-hours-at-computer-health-risks-and.html*, January 4, 2011.

The following is a useful checklist to help you determine if you are properly seated at a correctly positioned keyboard:[81]

- Your elbows are near your body in an open angle to allow circulation to the lower arms and hands
- Your arms are nearly perpendicular to the floor
- Your wrists are nearly straight
- The height of the surface holding your keyboard and mouse is 1 or 2 inches above your thighs
- Center the keyboard in front of your body.
- The monitor is about one arm's length (20 to 26 inches) away
- The top of your monitor is at eye level
- Your chair has a backrest that supports the curve of your lower (lumbar) back

ETHICAL ISSUES IN INFORMATION SYSTEMS

code of ethics: A code that states the principles and core values that are essential to a set of people and that, therefore, govern these people's behavior.

As you've seen throughout this book in the "Ethical and Societal Issues" boxes, ethical issues deal with what is generally considered right or wrong. Laws do not provide a complete guide to ethical behavior. Just because an activity is defined as legal does not mean that it is ethical. As a result, practitioners in many professions subscribe to a code of ethics that states the principles and core values that are essential to their work and, therefore, govern their behavior. The code can become a reference point for weighing what is legal and what is ethical. For example, doctors adhere to varying versions of the 2000-year-old Hippocratic Oath, which medical schools offer as an affirmation to their graduating classes.

Some IS professionals believe that their field offers many opportunities for unethical behavior. They also believe that unethical behavior can be reduced by top-level managers developing, discussing, and enforcing codes of ethics. Various IS-related organizations and associations promote ethically responsible use of information systems and have developed useful codes of ethics. Founded in 1947, the Association for Computing Machinery (ACM) is the oldest computing society and boasts more than 100,000 members in more than 100 countries.[82] The ACM has a code of ethics and professional conduct that includes eight general moral imperatives that can be used to help guide the actions of IS professionals. These guidelines can also be used for those who employ or hire IS professionals to monitor and guide their work. These imperatives are outlined in the following list:[83] As an ACM member I will ...

1. contribute to society and human well-being.
2. avoid harm to others.
3. be honest and trustworthy.
4. be fair and take action not to discriminate.
5. honor property rights including copyrights and patents.
6. give proper credit for intellectual property.
7. respect the privacy of others.
8. honor confidentiality.

The mishandling of the social issues discussed in this chapter—including waste and mistakes, crime, privacy, health, and ethics—can devastate an organization. The prevention of these problems and recovery from them are important aspects of managing information and information systems as critical corporate assets. More organizations are recognizing that people are the most important component of a computer-based information system and that long-term competitive advantage can be found in a well-trained, motivated, and knowledgeable workforce that adheres to a set of principles and core values that help guide that workforce's actions.

Principle:

Policies and procedures must be established to avoid waste and mistakes associated with computer usage.

Computer waste is the inappropriate use of computer technology and resources in both the public and private sectors. Computer mistakes relate to errors, failures, and other problems that result in output that is incorrect and without value. At the corporate level, computer waste and mistakes impose unnecessarily high costs for an information system and drag down profits. Waste often results from poor integration of IS components, leading to duplication of efforts and overcapacity. Inefficient procedures also waste IS resources, as do thoughtless disposal of useful resources and misuse of computer time for games and personal use. Inappropriate processing instructions, inaccurate data entry, mishandling of IS output, and poor systems design all cause computer mistakes.

Preventing waste and mistakes involves establishing, implementing, monitoring, and reviewing effective policies and procedures. Companies should develop manuals and training programs to avoid waste and mistakes. Changes to critical tables, HTML, and URLs should be tightly controlled.

Principle:

Computer crime is a serious and rapidly growing area of concern requiring management attention.

Some crimes use computers as tools. For example, a criminal can use a computer to manipulate records, counterfeit money and documents, commit fraud via telecommunications networks, and make unauthorized electronic transfers of money.

Criminals can gain pieces of information to help break into computer systems by dumpster diving and social engineering techniques.

A cyberterrorist is someone who intimidates or coerces a government or organization to advance his political or social objectives by launching computer-based attacks against computers, networks, and the information stored on them.

Identity theft is a crime in which an imposter obtains key pieces of personal identification information to impersonate someone else. The information is then used to obtain credit, merchandise, and services in the name of the victim or to provide the thief with false credentials.

The computer is also used as a tool to fight crime. The LeadsOnline Web-based system helps law enforcement officers recover stolen property. JusticeXchange provides law enforcement officials with fast, easy access to information about former and current offenders held in participating jails. Offender Watch tracks registered sex offenders. Law enforcement agencies use GPS tracking devices and software to monitor the movement of registered sex offenders. Law enforcement agencies use crime-related data and powerful analysis techniques, coupled with GIS systems, to better understand and even diminish crime risks.

A criminal hacker, also called a "cracker," is a computer-savvy person who attempts to gain unauthorized or illegal access to computer systems to steal passwords, corrupt files and programs, and even transfer money. Script bunnies are crackers with little technical savvy. Insiders are employees, disgruntled or otherwise, working solo or in concert with outsiders to compromise corporate systems. The greatest fear of many organizations is the potential harm that can be done by insiders who know system logon IDs, passwords, and company procedures.

Computer crimes target computer systems and include illegal access to computer systems by criminal hackers, alteration and destruction of data and programs by viruses, and simple theft of computer resources.

"Malware" is a general term for software that is harmful or destructive. There are many forms of malware, including viruses, variants, worms, Trojan horses, logic bombs, and rootkits. Spyware is software installed on a personal computer to intercept or take partial control over the user's interactions with the computer without knowledge or permission of the user. A password sniffer is a small program hidden in a network or computer system that records identification numbers and passwords.

Digital rights management refers to the use of any of several technologies to enforce policies for controlling access to digital media.

Software piracy might represent the most common computer crime. Patent infringement is also a major problem for computer software and hardware manufacturers.

Computer-related scams, including phishing, vishing, and smishing, have cost people and companies thousands of dollars. Computer crime is an international issue.

A fundamental concept of good internal controls is the careful separation of duties associated with key processes so that they are spread among more than one person.

Use of an intrusion detection system (IDS) provides another layer of protection in the event that an intruder gets past the outer security layers—passwords, security procedures, and corporate firewall. An IDS monitors system and network resources and notifies network security personnel when it senses a possible intrusion. Many small and mid-sized organizations are outsourcing their network security operations to managed security service providers (MSSPs), which monitor, manage, and maintain network security hardware and software.

Security measures, such as using passwords, identification numbers, and data encryption, help to guard against illegal computer access, especially when supported by effective control procedures. Virus-scanning software identifies and removes damaging computer programs. Organizations can use a security dashboard to provide a comprehensive display of vital data related to its security defenses and threats. Organizations and individuals can use antivirus software to detect the presence of all sorts of malware.

Principle:

Privacy is an important social issue related to information systems.

Balancing the right to privacy versus the need for additional monitoring to protect against terrorism and cyberattacks is an especially challenging problem.

Privacy issues are a concern with email, instant messaging, and personal sensing devices.

The federal government has implemented many laws addressing personal privacy; however, data collection programs have raised concerns and debate between those who favor data collection as a means to increased security and those who view such programs as a violation of their rights.

Employers use technology and corporate policies to manage worker productivity and protect the use of IS resources. This activity includes monitoring of employees' Web surfing, email, and instant messaging. Most employers today have a policy that explicitly eliminates any expectation of privacy when an employee uses any company-owned computer, server, or email system.

A business should develop a clear and thorough policy about privacy rights for customers, including database access. That policy should also address the rights of employees, including electronic monitoring systems and email. Fairness in information use for privacy rights emphasizes knowledge, control, notice, and consent for people profiled in databases. People should know the data that is stored about them and be able to correct errors in corporate database systems. If information on people is to be used for other purposes, individuals should be asked to give their consent beforehand. Each person has the right to know and to decide.

Principle:

Jobs, equipment, and working conditions must be designed to avoid negative health effects from computers.

Jobs that involve heavy use of computers contribute to a sedentary lifestyle, which increases the risk of health problems. Some critics blame computer systems for emissions of ozone and electromagnetic radiation.

The study of designing and positioning computer equipment, called "ergonomics," has suggested some approaches to reducing these health problems. Ergonomic design principles help to reduce harmful effects and increase the efficiency of an information system. RSI (repetitive strain injury) prevention includes keeping good posture, not ignoring pain or problems, performing stretching and strengthening exercises, and seeking proper treatment.

Principle:

Practitioners in many professions subscribe to a code of ethics that states the principles and core values that are essential to their work.

A code of ethics states the principles and core values that are essential to the members of a profession or organization. Ethical computer users define acceptable practices more strictly than just refraining from committing crimes; they also consider the effects of their IS activities, including Internet usage, on other people and organizations. The Association for Computing Machinery developed guidelines and a code of ethics. Many IS professionals join computer-related associations and agree to abide by detailed ethical codes.

KEY TERMS

antivirus programs

code of ethics

cracker

criminal hacker

cyberterrorism

cyberterrorist

digital rights management (DRM)

dumpster diving

ergonomics

filtering software

hacker

identity theft

insiders

Internet Crime Computer Center (IC3)

intrusion detection system (IDS)

malware

managed security service providers (MSSPs)

password sniffer

phishing

script bunnies

security dashboard

separation of duties

smishing

social engineering

software piracy

spyware

United States Computer Emergency Readiness Team (US-CERT)

vishing

CHAPTER 14: SELF-ASSESSMENT TEST

Policies and procedures must be established to avoid waste and mistakes associated with computer usage.

1. The Government Accounting Office (GAO) found a total of _____ spent in a six-year period on information system projects that duplicated other efforts.
   a. $80 billion
   b. $3.2 billion
   c. $320 million
   d. $80 million
2. Preventing waste and mistakes involves establishing, implementing, monitoring, and _____ policies and procedures.
3. Few companies have found it necessary to limit employee access to nonwork-related Web sites. True or False?

Computer crime is a serious and rapidly growing area of concern requiring management attention.

4. The _____ is an alliance between the White Collar Crime Center and the Federal Bureau of Investigation that provides a central site for Internet crime victims to report and to alert appropriate agencies of crimes committed.
5. Convincing someone to divulge his or her logon name and critical computer password is an example of _____.
6. It is thought that the United States and _____ collaborated to develop Stuxnet, computer malware designed to attack industrial Programmable Logic Controllers.
   a. IBM
   b. Israel
   c. British Secret Intelligence Service (also known as MI6)
   d. Turkey
7. Child identity theft is a rapidly growing area of computer crime. True or False?
8. It is estimated that over _____ U.S. taxpayers were affected by identity theft in 2013.
   a. 16 million
   b. 160,000
   c. 160 million
   d. 1.6 million

9. The LeadsOnline Web-based service uses Geographic Information System software to map crime and identify problem precincts. True or False?
10. _____ is a type of Trojan horse that executes when specific conditions occur.
11. _____ refers to the use of any of several technologies to enforce policies for controlling access to digital media.
    a. Software piracy
    b. Digital rights management
    c. Copyright
    d. Patent
12. The _____ is a fundamental concept of good internal controls that ensures that the responsibility for the key steps in a process is spread among more than one person.

Privacy is an important social issue related to information systems.

13. As opposed to the European Union, the United States has implemented few laws addressing personal privacy. True or False?
14. _____ is a tool used by the NSA and FBI to access the servers of major Internet services such as Facebook, Google, YouTube, and others to collect the content of emails, video, photos, file transfers, and live chats.

Jobs, equipment, and working conditions must be designed to avoid negative health effects from computers.

15. Heavy computer use can negatively affect one's physical health. True or False?
16. The study of designing and positioning computer equipment is called _____.

Practitioners in many professions subscribe to a code of ethics that states the principles and core values that are essential to their work.

17. Just because an activity is defined as legal does not mean that it is ethical. True or False?
18. Founded in 1977, the Association for Computing Machinery (ACM) is the oldest computing society and boasts more than 200,000 members in more than 120 countries. True or False?

CHAPTER 14: SELF-ASSESSMENT TEST ANSWERS

1. c
2. reviewing
3. False
4. Internet Crime Computer Center
5. social engineering
6. b
7. True
8. d
9. False
10. Logic bomb

11. b
12. separation of duties
13. False
14. PRISM

15. True
16. ergonomics
17. True
18. False

REVIEW QUESTIONS

1. What issues and problems are raised by the use of unintegrated information systems?
2. What is US-CERT and what does it do?
3. Define the term "cyberterrorism." For how long has the threat of cyberterrorism been considered serious by the U.S. government?
4. What is a managed security service provider? What sort of services does such an organization provide?
5. What is social engineering? What is dumpster diving?
6. Why might some people consider a contractor to be a serious threat to their organization's information systems?
7. Give two reasons that smartphones are such a ripe target for hackers.
8. How do you distinguish between a hacker and a criminal hacker?
9. What measures can you take to avoid becoming a victim of identity theft?
10. What is a security dashboard? How is it used?
11. What is smishing? What actions can you take to reduce the likelihood that you will be a victim of this crime?
12. What is filtering software? Why would organizations use such software? What objections might be raised against the use of this software?
13. What does intrusion detection software do? What are some of the issues with the use of this software?
14. What is ergonomics? How can it be applied to office workers?
15. What is digital rights management?
16. What is a code of ethics? Give an example.

DISCUSSION QUESTIONS

1. Identify and briefly discuss several measures that a private organization might take to reduce the amount of company resources and time employees waste in nonproductive use of information system resources.
2. Identify and briefly discuss four specific information systems that are used to fight crime.
3. Briefly discuss software piracy. What is it, how widespread is it, and who is harmed by it?
4. Imagine that you are starting a dating Web site to help match compatible couples. What sort of personal data might you need to gather? What measures might need to be taken to protect this sensitive data? What key statements might potential users wish to see in the privacy statement of this Web site?
5. Outline an approach, including specific techniques (e.g., dumpster diving, phishing, social engineering) that you could employ to gain personal data about the members of your class.
6. Your 12-year-old niece shows you a dozen or so innocent photos of herself and a brief biography, including address and cell phone number that she plans to post on Facebook. What advice might you offer her about posting personal information and photos?
7. What measures can you suggest to beef up the security of ATM machines to insulate them from malware?
8. Briefly discuss the potential for cyberterrorism to cause a major disruption in your daily life. What are some likely targets of a cyberterrorist? What sort of action could a cyberterrorist take against these targets?
9. What is meant by the separation of duties? When does this concept come into play? Provide a business situation where separation of duties is important.
10. What measures must one take to avoid being a victim of a smartphone hacker?
11. Do you think that there is a difference between acting ethically and acting legally? Explain.

PROBLEM-SOLVING EXERCISES

1. Do research to identify the latest findings on the negative effects of sitting for long hours working at a computer. Prepare a brief presentation that summarizes your findings and identifies what can be done to offset these negative effects.
2. Access the Web site for the Motion Picture Association of America (MPAA) and other Web sites to find estimates of the dollar amount of movie piracy worldwide for at least the past five years. Use spreadsheet software and appropriate

forecasting methods and assumptions to develop a forecast for the amount of movie piracy for the next three years. Document any assumptions you make in developing your forecast.

3. Visit the Internet Crime Complaint Center at *www .ic3.gov/default.aspx*. Develop a brief presentation that identifies and briefly describes the most frequently encountered Internet computer crimes.

TEAM ACTIVITIES

1. Imagine that your team has been hired to conduct a review of the information system policies and procedures at your school or university. Develop a list of at least 10 specific questions that your team would use to assess the effectiveness of these policies and procedures in reducing waste and costs.

2. Have each member of your team access six different Web sites and summarize their findings in terms of the existence of data privacy policy statements. Did each site have such a policy? Was it easy to find? Did it seem complete and easy to understand? Does it adequately cover any concerns you might have as a visitor to that site?

WEB EXERCISES

1. Do research on the Web to find recent examples of cyberterrorism around the world. Is it your opinion that cyberterrorism has reached the level of a serious international problem? Why or why not? Prepare a brief report summarizing your findings and conclusions.

2. Visit the Web site of the Electronic Frontier Foundation (EFF) at *https://www.eff.org/* and learn about its purpose. Do research to document its position on the NSA's collection of phone call and Internet communications data. Do you agree with EFF's position? Why or why not? Prepare a set of slides that documents your position and that of the EFF.

3. Request a current copy of your credit report from TransUnion, Equifax, or Experian. (This should be available for free.) Review the report carefully for any inaccuracies. Follow the necessary steps to remove these inaccuracies.

CAREER EXERCISES

1. You have been approached by the NSA to work in an information systems group that will use high-powered computers and advanced analytic techniques to study phone call metadata and other data in an attempt to identify terrorists and stop impending terrorist acts. Obviously, you will not be able to talk to anyone about your work; however, your total compensation will be more than 10 percent greater than any position for which you have applied. Would you accept this position? Why or why not?

2. Do research to find any professional organization or code of ethics associated with your current or desired future career. What might be the benefits of joining such a professional organization? How might a code of ethics help guide you in career-related decision making?

CASE STUDIES

Case One

Net Neutrality in the EU and the United States

On April 3, 2014, the European Parliament voted to unequivocally support net neutrality, the principle that all data streaming across the Internet is treated equally regardless of content, user, site, platform, or mode of communication. In the past, Internet service providers (ISPs) had blocked or slowed down Skype and Netflix data as it flowed across their pipeline, affecting approximately 100 million users. The new European Union (EU) regulation only allows ISPs to slow down or block pipelines when they are protecting network security, relieving temporary congestion, or adhering to a court order.

Advocates of net neutrality share numerous concerns. If ISPs and telecommunications companies are allowed to block or interfere with data transmission at will, they could potentially block competition, hike up prices, and hurt both consumers and the free market. Some people, however, oppose net neutrality, or at least they object to placing tough limits on charging third parties for faster network access.

In 2007, Comcast—today the largest broadband provider—blocked Internet content coming from file-sharing networks, such as BitTorrent. Although the company served as a means for users to share copyrighted movies and music, BitTorrent also provided a way to disseminate illegal content. When users tried to upload or download files, Comcast sent a message to each PC that looked like it came from the other PC and that the users could not see. The message commanded the other PC to stop communicating. Comcast likely took this step to prevent this peer-to-peer technology from slowing down its network. Some criticized Comcast's decision as a breach of net neutrality, and Comcast voluntarily ended the practice. Comcast, however, has argued against placing too many restrictions on telecommunications companies. The company points out that unfair legal restrictions might deter IT companies from investing in infrastructure to increase speed, extend services, and improve efficiency.

In 2011, however, when Comcast merged with media content conglomerate NBC Universal, many people worried that the merger would destroy the online video market. They feared the giant Comcast-NBC Universal company would be tempted to block content or favor its own content. By the early months of 2014, indeed, Netflix saw streaming speeds for its online video rentals decline by 27 percent. The company reluctantly agreed to sign a "mutually beneficial interconnection agreement" with Comcast. Netflix had wanted to connect to Comcast's broadband network without compensating the company for the heavy traffic level generated by Netflix users.

The EU law would not bar such agreements, as it allows ISPs to offer a short list of specialized services at a higher price. But these services are limited to video on-demand, data-intensive cloud applications, and other high-load activities. Many hope that the EU decision will reverberate across the Atlantic where the Federal Communications Commission (FCC) is reformulating its net neutrality rules. The EU legislation demands that any interference to relieve temporary network congestion must be "transparent, nondiscriminatory and proportionate." As a result, a telecommunications giant such as Comcast would have to come out in the open about slowing down data transmitted from a particular site or application. The intent of the EU legislation is to allow the Internet to continue to drive economic growth, technological innovation, and social development.

Discussion Questions

1. What is net neutrality, and what does it mean for Internet users, small start-ups, and large telecommunications companies?
2. What does net neutrality mean for governments? Which types of governments would you expect to embrace net neutrality and which would not?

Critical Thinking Questions

1. Is the agreement of Comcast and Netflix in the best interest of consumers? Why or why not?
2. Is Comcast's purported practice of surreptitiously slowing or stopping the flow of data to sites that hog bandwidth ethnical? Why or why not?

SOURCES: Svensson, Peter, "Comcast Blocks Some Internet Traffic," *NBC News*, November 19, 2007, *www.nbcnews.com/id/21376597/#.U-Uc4eN*

dUrU; Reardon, Marguerite, "What the Comcast-NBC Deal Means to You (FAQ)," *CNET*, January 11, 2011, *www.cnet.com/news/what-the-comcast-nbc-deal-means-to-you-faq/*; Musil, Steven, "Netflix Reaches Streaming Traffic Agreement with Comcast," *CNET*, February 23, 2014, *http://www.cnet.com/news/netflix-reaches-streaming-traffic-agreement-with-comcast/*; McCullagh, Declan, "FCC Formally Rules Comcast's Throttling of BitTorrent Was Illegal," *CNET*, August 1, 2008, *www.cnet.com/news/fcc-formally-rules-comcasts-throttling-of-bittorrent-was-illegal/*.

Case Two

Protecting Health Care Privacy

The U.S. Health Insurance Portability and Accountability Act (HIPAA) addresses (among other things) the privacy of health information. Its Title 2 regulates the use and disclosure of protected health information (PHI), such as billing services, by healthcare providers, insurance carriers, employers, and business associates.

Email is often the best way for a hospital to communicate with off-site specialists and insurance carriers about a patient. Unfortunately, standard email is insecure. It allows eavesdropping, later retrieval of messages from unprotected backups, message modification before it is received, invasion of the sender's privacy by providing access to information about the identity and location of the sending computer, and more. Since healthcare provider email often carries PHI, healthcare facilities must be sure their email systems meet HIPAA privacy and security requirements.

Children's National Medical Center (CNMC) of Washington, D.C., "The Nation's Children's Hospital," is especially aware of privacy concerns because all such concerns are heightened with children. CNMC did what many organizations do when faced with a specialized problem: rather than try to become specialists or hire specialists for whom the hospital has no long-term full-time need, it turned to a specialist firm.

CNMC chose Proofpoint of Sunnyvale, California, for its Security as a Service (SaaS) email privacy protection service. Matt Johnston, senior security analyst at CNMC, says that children are "the highest target for identity theft. A small kid's record is worth its weight in gold on the black market. It's not the doctor's job to protect that information. It's *my* job."

Johnston explains that he likes several things about the Proofpoint service:

- "I don't have to worry about backups." Proofpoint handles those.
- "I don't have to worry about if a server goes down. [If it was a CNMC server, I would have to] get my staff ramped up and bring up another server. Proofpoint does that for us. It's one less headache."
- "We had a product in-house before. It required several servers which took a full FTE [full-time employee] just to manage this product. It took out too much time."
- "Spam has been on the rise. Since Proofpoint came in, we've seen a dramatic decrease in spam. It takes care of itself. The end user is given a digest daily."
- Email can be encrypted or not, according to rules that the end user need not be personally concerned with.
- "Their tech support has been great."

Proofpoint is not the only company that provides healthcare providers with email security services. LuxSci of

Cambridge, Massachusetts, also offers HIPAA-compliant email hosting services, as do several other firms. They all provide the same basic features: user authentication, transmission security (encryption), logging, and audit. Software that runs on the provider's computers can also deliver media control and backup. Software that runs on a user organization's server necessarily relies on that organization to manage storage; for example, deleting messages from the server after four weeks as HIPAA requires.

As people become more aware of the privacy risks associated with standard email, the use of secure solutions such as these will undoubtedly become more common in the future.

Discussion Questions

1. What privacy concerns does transmitting healthcare information via email raise?
2. What requirement does HIPAA institute to safeguard patient privacy?

Critical Thinking Questions

1. Universities use email to communicate private information. For example, an instructor might send you an email explaining what you must do to raise your grade. The regulations about protecting that information under the Family Educational Rights and Privacy Act (FERPA) are not as strict as those under HIPAA. Do you think they should be as strict as HIPAA's requirements? Why or why not?

2. How does Proofpoint safeguard patient privacy? Could Proofpoint do the same for university and corporate emails? Why or why not?

SOURCES: Children's National Medical Center Web site, *www.childrens national.org*, accessed August 28, 2014; LuxSci Web site, *www.luxsci .com*, accessed August 28, 2014; Proofpoint Web site, *www.proofpoint .com*, accessed August 28, 2014; Staff, "HIPAA Email Security Case Study: Children's National Medical Center," Proofpoint, *www.youtube.com /watch?v=RVaBaNvwkQE*, accessed August 7, 2014.

Questions for Web Case

See the Web site for this book to read about the Altitude Online case for this chapter. Following are questions concerning this Web case.

Altitude Online: The Personal and Social Impact of Computers

Discussion Questions

1. Why do you think extending access to a corporate network beyond the business's walls dramatically elevates the risk to information security?
2. What tools and policies can be used to minimize that risk?

Critical Thinking Questions

1. Why does information security usually come at the cost of user convenience?
2. How do proper security measures help ensure information privacy?

NOTES

Sources for the opening vignette: "What is Bitcoin?" CNN Money, *http://money.cnn.com/infographic/technology/what -is-bitcoin/*, accessed August 11, 2014; Bosker, Bianca and Andresen, Gavin, "Bitcoin Architect: Meet the Man Bringing You Bitcoin (And Getting Paid in It)," *Huffington Post*, April 16, 2013, *www.huffingtonpost.com/2013/04/16/gavin -andresen-bitcoin_n_3093316.html*; Bustillos, Maria, "The Bitcoin Boom," April 1, 2013, *www.newyorker.com/tech /elements/the-bitcoin-boom*; "The Troubling Holes in MtGox's Account of How It Lost $600 Million in Bitcoins," *MIT Technology Review*, April 4, 2014, *www.technologyreview .com/view/526161/the-troubling-holes-in-mtgoxs-account-of -how-it-lost-600-million-in-bitcoins/*; Dougherty, Carter, "Bitcoin Price Plunges as Mt. Gox Exchange Halts Activity," *Bloomberg.com*, February 7, 2010, *www.bloomberg.com /news/2014-02-07/bitcoin-price-falls-as-mt-gox-exchange -halts-activity.html*; Durden, Tyler, "Mt Gox Files for Bankruptcy after $473 Million in Bitcoins 'Disappeared'," *Zero Hedge* (blog), February 28, 2014, *www.zerohedge.com /news/2014-02-28/mt-gox-files-bankruptcy-after-473-million -bitcoins-disappeared*.

1. Vest, Joshua R., Issel, L. Michele, and Lee, Sean, "Experience of Using Information Systems in Public Health Practice: Findings from a Qualitative Study," *www.ncbi .nlm.nih.gov/pmc/articles/PMC3959909/*.
2. Gallagher, Sean, "De-Dupe Time: GAO Finds $321 Million in Redundant Government IT Spending," *Ars Technica*, September 17, 2013, *http://arstechnica.com/information -technology/2013/09/de-dupe-time-gao-finds-321-million -in-redundant-government-it-spending/*.
3. Conner, Cheryl, "Who Wastes the Most Time at Work?" *Forbes*, September 7, 2013, *www.forbes.com/sites/chery lsnappconner/2013/09/07/who-wastes-the-most-time-at -work/*.
4. Holthaus, David, "P&G Tries to Close Online Pandora's Box," *The Cincinnati Enquirer*, April 3, 2012, p. A1.
5. "Improper Payments," GAO-14-737T, July 9, 2014, *www.gao.gov/products/GAO-14-737T*.
6. Vasquez, Michael, Smiley, David, and McGrory, Kathleen, "FCAT Computer Glitches Halt Testing for Thousands of Students," *Miami Herald*, April 22, 2014, *www.miamiherald.com/2014/04/22/4073816/fcat -computer-glitches-halts-testing.html*.
7. Scott, Alwyn and Menn, Joseph, "Glitch in Air Traffic Control System Caused by Computer Memory Shortage, U-2 Spy Plane," *Huffington Post*, July 11, 2014, *www .huffingtonpost.com/2014/05/12/glitch-in-air-traffic -control-system_n_5307552.html*.
8. Morgan, David and Cornwell, Susan, "Obamacare Computers Still Can't Correct Previous Errors: Report," *Huffington Post*, April 5, 2014, *www.huffingtonpost .com/2014/02/03/obamacare-computers-broken_n _4714928.html*.
9. "Corporate E-Learning," Error Prevention Institute, *smartpeopledumbthings.com/e-learning/corporate -training/*, accessed July 21, 2014.

10. Levy, Karyne, "Rap Genius' Cofounder Has Been Fired after Comments about California Shooter," *Business Insider*, May 26, 2014, *www.businessinsider.com/rap-genius-cofounder-fired-2014-5#ixzz386mJPcFZ*.

11. Ross, Casey, "BRA Left Millions in Fees Untaken, Audit Says," *Boston Globe*, July 17, 2014, *www.bostonglobe.com/business/2014/07/16/bra/uTnJ8ySWs47QAeKJxOKDjO/story.html*.

12. Saporito, Bill, "The Trouble Lurking on Walmart's Empty Shelves," *Time*, April 9, 2013, *http://business.time.com/2013/04/09/the-trouble-lurking-on-walmarts-empty-shelves/*.

13. Chesser, Paul, "Walmart Prefers Political Correctness to Profitability," National Legal and Policy Center, October 22, 2013, *http://nlpc.org/stories/2013/10/22/walmart-continues-stumble-focus-remains-political-correctness*.

14. "The Internet Crime Complaint Center Receives 3 Millionth Complaint," May 19, 2014, *www.ic3.gov/media/2014/140519.aspx*.

15. "Obama Administration Sped Up Cyberattacks on Iran after Stuxnet Disclosure," *Info Security*, June 4, 2012, *www.infosecurity-magazine.com/view/26138/obama-administration-sped-up-cyberattacks-on-iran-after-stuxnet-disclosure*.

16. Perlroth, Nicole, "Russian Hackers Targeting Oil and Gas Companies," *New York Times*, June 30, 2014, *www.nytimes.com/2014/07/01/technology/energy-sector-faces-attacks-from-hackers-in-russia.html?_r=0*.

17. Swanson, Brenda, "Was Ellie Mae Attack the Work of Cyberterrorists?" *Housingwire*, April 4, 2014, *www.elliemae.com/about-us/company-overview/*.

18. "Annual Identity Fraud Report Finds More than 13 Million Consumers Were Victims in 2013," *PRWeb*, February 5, 2014, *www.prweb.com/releases/2014/02/prweb11556963.htm*.

19. Identity Theft Resource Center, *www.idtheftcenter.org/id-theft/data-breaches.html*, accessed July 29, 2014.

20. Kranish, Michael, "IRS Is Overwhelmed by Identity Theft Fraud," *The Boston Globe*, February 16, 2014, *www.bostonglobe.com/news/nation/2014/02/16/identity-theft-taxpayer-information-major-problem-for-irs/7SC0BarZMDvy07bbhDXwvN/story.html*.

21. "2012 Child Identity Fraud Report," Identity Theft Center, *www.identitytheftassistance.org/pageview.php?cateid=47#childIDfraudReport*, accessed July 29, 2014.

22. Glassberg, Jason, "The Future of Crime: 8 Cyber-Crimes to Expect in Next 20 Years," *FOX Business*, May 14, 2014, *www.foxbusiness.com/personal-finance/2014/05/14/future-crime-8-cyber-crimes-to-expect-in-next-20-years/*.

23. "Ploutus/Plotos," Kaspersky Labs, *http://go.kaspersky.com/rs/kaspersky1/images/Ploutos_and_ploutus.pdf*, accessed July 23, 2014.

24. Glassberg, Jason, "The Future of Crime: 8 Cyber-Crimes to Expect in Next 20 Years," *FOX Business*, May 14, 2014, *www.foxbusiness.com/personal-finance/2014/05/14/future-crime-8-cyber-crimes-to-expect-in-next-20-years/*.

25. "LeadsOnline Identifies Ohio Suspect Selling Stolen Scrap Metal," *www.leadsonline.com/main/success/metal-theft.php*, accessed July 29, 2014.

26. "Justice Xchange," *www.appriss.com/justicexchange.html*, accessed July 29, 2014.

27. "Community Notification," *www.communitynotification.com/*, accessed July 31, 2014.

28. "Client Testimonials," CAP Index, *www.capindex.com/Testimonials/Testimonials.aspx*, accessed July 30, 2014.

29. NER Web site, *www.ner.net/*, accessed July 30, 2014.

30. COMPSTAT, *www.lapdonline.org/crime_mapping_and_compstat/content_basic_view/6363*, accessed July 30, 2014.

31. Chabrow, Eric, "370 Investigation: Cyber Ties," *Bank Info Security*, March 22, 2014, *www.bankinfosecurity.com/blogs/flight-370-investigation-cyber-ties-p-1641*.

32. Schmadeke, Steve, "O'Hare Worker Charged with Stealing from Military Footlockers," *Chicago Tribune*, July 25, 2014, *www.chicagotribune.com/news/local/breaking/chi-ohare-military-theft-20140725,0,7023986.story*.

33. Rankin, Bob, "Pandemiya: The New Trojan Horse," *http://askbobrankin.com/pandemiya_the_new_trojan_horse.html*, accessed July 30, 2014.

34. Mayer, Andre, "Smartphones Becoming Prime Target for Criminal Hackers," *CBC News*, March 6, 2014, *www.cbc.ca/news/technology/smartphones-becoming-prime-target-for-criminal-hackers-1.2561126*.

35. Dorner, Stephan, "Chinese-Made Smartphone Comes with Spyware, Security Firm Says," *Wall Street Journal*, June 17, 2014, *http://blogs.wsj.com/digits/2014/06/17/chinese-made-smartphone-comes-with-spyware-security-firm-says/*.

36. Nakashima, Ellen and Soltani, Ashkan, "Italian Spyware Firm Relies on U.S. Internet Servers," *Washington Post*, March 3, 2014, *www.washingtonpost.com/world/national-security/italian-spyware-firm-relies-on-us-internet-servers/2014/03/03/25f94f12-9f00-11e3-b8d8-94577ff66b28_story.html*.

37. Goodin, Dan, "Meet Mask, Possibly the Most Sophisticated Malware Campaign Ever Seen," *Ars Technica*, February 10, 2014, *http://arstechnica.com/security/2014/02/meet-mask-possibly-the-most-sophisticated-malware-campaign-ever-seen/*.

38. "MyTheftProtection," *www.mysecuritycenter.com/products/my-theft-protection*, accessed July 31, 2014.

39. "The Compliance Gap: BSA Global Software Survey," June 2014, *http://globalstudy.bsa.org/2013/downloads/studies/2013GlobalSurvey_Study_en.pdf*.

40. Ruen, Chris, "Bored with Hollywood Blockbusters? Blame Digital Piracy," *New Republic*, July 25, 2014, *www.newrepublic.com/article/118858/digital-piracy-ruining-pop-culture*.

41. Paulson, Matt, "Software Piracy 'Bytes' Back: Engineering Design Company Fined over $55k," *Software Licensing Report*, June 13, 2014, *www.softwarelicensingreport.com/articles/381253-software-piracy-bytes-back-engineering-design-company-fined.htm*.

42. "For Students Doing Reports," RIAA, *www.riaa.com/faq.php*, accessed August 1, 2014.

43. News release, "Louisiana Man Gets 2 Years in Prison for Selling Pirated Movies, Music," September 20, 2013, *www.ice.gov/news/releases/1309/130920neworleans.htm*.

44. Eichenwald, Kurt, "The Great Smartphone War," *Vanity Fair*, June 2014, *www.vanityfair.com/business/2014/06/apple-samsung-smartphone-patent-war*.

45. "2013 Internet Crime Report," Federal Bureau of Investigation and the Internet Crime Complaint Center, *www.ic3.gov/media/annualreport/2013_IC3Report.pdf*.

46. Ibid.

47. Rapport, Marc, "Phishing in 2014 Upswing," *Credit Union Times*, July 8, 2014, *www.cutimes.com/2014/07/08/phishing-in-2014-upswing*.

48. "DMARC—What Is It?" *www.dmarc.org/*, accessed August 4, 2014.

49. "SpoofCard," *https://www.spoofcard.com/*, accessed August 4, 2014.

50. Voreacos, David, "5 Hackers Charged in Largest Data-Breach Scheme in U.S.," *Bloomberg*, July 26, 2013, *www.bloomberg.com/news/2013-07-25/5-hackers-charged-in-largest-data-breach-scheme-in-u-s-.html*.

51. Post, Ashley, "Five Hackers Charged in Biggest Cyber Crime Case in U.S. History," *Inside Counsel*, July 26, 2013, *www.insidecounsel.com/2013/07/26/five-hackers-charged-in-biggest-cyber-crime-case-i*.

52. "US-CERT," *www.us-cert.gov/about-us*, accessed August 14, 2014.

53. Maliyil, Tim, "Why Encryption Is Crucial to Your Organization," *Healthcare IT Times*, July 8, 2014, *www.healthcareitnews.com/blog/why-encryption-crucial-your-organization*.

54. Faller, Mary Beth, "Lawsuit Filed over Maricopa District's Security Breach," *Arizona Republic*, May 2, 2014, *www.azcentral.com/story/news/local/phoenix/2014/05/02/lawsuit-filed-maricopa-districts-security-breach/8619189/*.

55. Contreras, Russell, "Guilty Plea in Gov. Susana Martinez Hacked Email Case," *The Washington Times*, June 16, 2014, *www.washingtontimes.com/news/2014/jun/16/hearing-set-in-governors-hacked-email-case/*.

56. Schory, Brenda, "Cunningham Used County Email Address for Campaign: 'I Was Wrong'" May 6, 2014, *Kane County Chronicle*, *www.kcchronicle.com/2014/05/06/cunningham-used-county-email-address-for-campaign-i-was-wrong/abruk63/*.

57. Bhatia, Pooja, "Biometric Identification That Goes Beyond Fingerprints," *USA Today*, April 19, 2014, *www.usatoday.com/story/news/world/2014/04/19/ozy-biometric-identification/7904685/*.

58. "AlienVault Unified Security Management Platform Protects Metro Madrid's Public Rail System," *www.alienvault.com/docs/case-studies/MetroMadrid_CaseStudy.pdf*, accessed August 5, 2014.

59. "McKesson Key Facts," *www.mckesson.com/about-mckesson/key-facts/*, accessed August 5, 2014.

60. "McKesson: Empowering Healthcare," *www.tenable.com/case-studies/mckesson*, accessed August 5, 2014.

61. "Retailer Delivers on Customer Promise with Dell Secureworks PCI Services," *www.secureworks.com/assets/pdf-store/white-papers/OnCue_Case_Study_April_2014.pdf*, accessed August 5, 2014.

62. Rubenking, Neil J., "The Best Antivirus for 2014," *PC Magazine*, April 21, 2014.

63. Sutherland, Randall, "Mac Antivirus Software Review," *Top Ten Reviews*, March 14, 2014.

64. Rubenking, Neil J., "12 Antivirus Apps for the Mac," *PC Magazine*, April 7, 2013.

65. Rampton, Rebecca, "Obama to Propose Ending NSA Bulk Collection of Phone Records: Official," *Reuters*, March 24, 2014, *www.reuters.com/article/2014/03/25/us-usa-security-obama-nsa-idUSBREA2O03O20140325*.

66. "NSA Prism Program Taps into User Data of Apple, Google and Others," *The Guardian*, June 6, 2013, *www.theguardian.com/world/2013/jun/06/us-tech-giants-nsa-data*.

67. "NSA Reportedly Recording All Phone Calls in a Foreign Country," *Associated Press*, March 19, 2014, *www.foxnews.com/politics/2014/03/19/nsa-reportedly-recording-all-phone-calls-in-foreign-country/*.

68. Makarechi, Kia, "Julian Assange Goes Where Glenn Greenwald Wouldn't," *Vanity Fair*, May 19, 2014, *www.vanityfair.com/online/daily/2014/05/julian-assange-glenn-greenwald-nsa-afghanistan*.

69. "NSA Reportedly Recording All Phone Calls in a Foreign Country," *Associated Press*, March 19, 2014, *www.foxnews.com/politics/2014/03/19/nsa-reportedly-recording-all-phone-calls-in-foreign-country/*.

70. Miller, Ron, "Employees Have No Reasonable Expectation to Privacy for Material Viewed or Stored on Employer-Owned Computers or Servers," Wolters Kluwer, November 24, 2011, *www.employmentlawdaily.com/index.php/2011/11/24/employees-have-no-reasonable-expectation-to-privacy-for-materials-viewed-or-stored-on-employer-owned-computers-or-servers/*, access August 28, 2014.

71. "Protection of Personal Data," *http://ec.europa.eu/justice/data-protection/*, accessed August 17, 2014.

72. Giblin, Paul, "Glendale Approves Deal That Will Keep Coyotes in Town," *USA Today*, July 3, 2013, *www.usatoday.com/story/sports/nhl/coyotes/2013/07/03/phoenix-coyotes-glendale-city-council-vote/2485295/*.

73. Corbett, Peter, "Glendale Mayor: Council Members Violated Open Meeting Law," *The Republic*, July 22, 2014, *www.azcentral.com/story/news/local/glendale/2014/07/21/glendale-mayor-council-members-violated-open-meeting-law/12956523/*.

74. "COPPA—Children's Online Privacy Protection Act," *www.coppa.org/coppa.htm*, accessed August 7, 2014.

75. "Top 15 Most Popular Social Networking Sites | August 2014," *www.ebizmba.com/articles/social-networking-websites*, accessed August 7, 2014.

76. Worstall, Tim, "Now Google Autocomplete Could Be Found Guilty of Libel in Hong Kong," *Forbes*, August 6, 2014, *www.forbes.com/sites/timworstall/2014/08/06/now-google-autocomplete-could-be-found-guilty-of-libel-in-hong-kong/*.

77. Matthew, Lee, "Defamation, Celebrities, and the Internet," *Harvard Journal on Sports and Entertainment Law*, April 17, 2014, *http://harvardjsel.com/2014/04/defamation-internet/*.

78. "Internet Filter Software Review," *http://internet-filter-review.toptenreviews.com/*, accessed August 13, 2014.

79. "2014 Mac Internet Filter Software Product Comparisons," *http://internet-filter-review.toptenreviews.com/mac-internet-filter-software/*, accessed August 13, 2014.

80. "BBB Sample Privacy Policy," *www.bbb.org/dallas/for -businesses/bbb-sample-privacy-policy1/*, accessed August 14, 2014.

81. "How to Sit at a Computer," American Academy of Orthopedic Surgeons, *http://orthoinfo.aaos.org/topic .cfm?topic=a00261*, accessed August 14, 2014.

82. "What Is ACM?" *www.acm.org/about*, accessed August 14, 2014.

83. "ACM Code of Ethics and Professional Conduct," *www .acm.org/about/code-of-ethics*, accessed August 14, 2014.

Glossary

A

accounting MIS An information system that provides aggregate information on accounts payable, accounts receivable, payroll, and many other applications.

ad hoc DSS A DSS concerned with situations or decisions that come up only a few times during the life of the organization.

agile development An iterative system development process that develops the system in "sprint" increments lasting from two weeks to two months.

antivirus program Software that runs in the background to protect your computer from dangers lurking on the Internet and other possible sources of infected files.

application programming interface (API) A set of programming instructions and standards for one software program to access and use the services of another software program.

application service provider (ASP) A company that provides the software, support, and computer hardware on which to run the software from the user's facilities over a network.

arithmetic/logic unit (ALU) The part of the CPU that performs mathematical calculations and makes logical comparisons.

ARPANET A project started by the U.S. Department of Defense (DoD) in 1969 as both an experiment in reliable networking and a means to link the DoD and military research contractors, including many universities doing military-funded research.

artificial intelligence (AI) A field in which the computer system takes on the characteristics of human intelligence.

artificial intelligence system The people, procedures, hardware, software, data, and knowledge needed to develop computer systems and machines that can simulate human intelligence processes, including learning (the acquisition of information and rules for using the information), reasoning (using rules to reach conclusions), and self-correction (using the outcome from one scenario to improve its performance on future scenarios).

assistive technology systems A wide range of assistive, adaptive, and rehabilitative devices to help people with disabilities perform tasks that they were formerly unable to accomplish or had great difficulty accomplishing.

attribute A characteristic of an entity.

auditing Provides an objective appraisal of the accounting, financial, and operational procedures and information of an organization.

B

backbone One of the Internet's high-speed, long-distance communications links.

batch processing system A form of data processing whereby business transactions are accumulated over a period of time and prepared for processing as a single unit or batch.

best practices The most efficient and effective ways to complete a business process.

big data The term used to describe data collections that are so large and complex that traditional data management software, hardware, and analysis processes are incapable of dealing with them.

blade server A server that houses many individual computer motherboards that include one or more processors, computer memory, computer storage, and computer network connections.

Bluetooth A wireless communications specification that describes how cell phones, computers, faxes, personal digital assistants, printers, and other electronic devices can be interconnected over distances of 10 to 30 feet at a rate of about 2 Mbps.

brainstorming A decision-making approach that consists of members offering ideas "off the top of their heads," fostering creativity and free thinking.

broadband communications A relative term but it generally means a telecommunications system that can transmit data very quickly.

bus A set of physical connections (cables, printed circuits, etc.) that can be shared by multiple hardware components so they can communicate with one another.

bus network A network in which all network devices are connected to a common backbone that serves as a shared communications medium.

business intelligence (BI) A broad range of technologies and applications that enable an organization to transform mostly structured data obtained from information systems to perform analysis, generate information, and improve the decision making of the organization.

business-to-business (B2B) e-commerce A subset of e-commerce in which all the participants are organizations.

business-to-consumer (B2C) e-commerce A form of e-commerce in which customers deal directly with an organization and avoid intermediaries.

byte (B) Eight bits that together represent a single character of data.

C

cache memory A type of highspeed memory that a processor can access more rapidly than main memory.

Cascading Style Sheets (CSS) A markup language for defining the visual design of a Web page or group of pages.

cash flow Takes into account all the increases and decreases in cash flow associated with the project.

central processing unit (CPU) The part of the computer that consists of three associated elements: the arithmetic/logic unit, the control unit, and the register areas.

centralized processing An approach to processing wherein all processing occurs in a single location or facility.

certificate authority (CA) A trusted third-party organization or company that issues digital certificates.

certification A process for testing skills and knowledge, which results in a statement by the certifying authority that confirms an individual is capable of performing particular tasks.

change model A representation of change theories that identifies the phases of change and the best way to implement them.

channel bandwidth The rate at which data is exchanged, usually measured in bps.

character A basic building block of most information, consisting of uppercase letters, lowercase letters, numeric digits, or special symbols.

chief knowledge officer (CKO) The individual who presents the organization's knowledge management vision with clarity and effectiveness, strives mightily to achieve that vision, provides executive level leadership to implement and sustain KM, and is the ultimate focal point for knowledge creation, sharing, and application.

choice stage The third stage of decision making, which requires selecting a course of action.

circuit-switching network A network that sets up a circuit between the sender and receiver before any communications can occur; this circuit is maintained for the duration of the communication and cannot be used to support any other communications until the circuit is released and a new connection is set up.

client/server architecture An approach to computing wherein multiple computer platforms are dedicated to special functions, such as database management, printing, communications, and program execution.

clock speed A series of electronic pulses produced at a predetermined rate that affects machine cycle time.

cloud computing A computing environment where software and storage are provided as an Internet service and are accessed with a Web browser.

code of ethics A code that states the principles and core values that are essential to a set of people and that, therefore, govern these people's behavior.

cold site A computer environment that includes rooms, electrical service, telecommunications links, data storage devices, and the like.

command-based user interface A user interface that requires you to give text commands to the computer to perform basic activities.

community of practice (COP) A group of people with common interests who come together to create, store, and share knowledge of a specific topic.

compact disc read-only memory (CD-ROM) A common form of optical disc on which data cannot be modified once it has been recorded.

competitive advantage A significant and ideally long-term benefit to a company over its competition.

competitive intelligence One aspect of business intelligence and encompasses information about competitors and the ways that knowledge affects strategy, tactics, and operations.

compiler A special software program that converts the programmer's source code into the machine-language instructions, which consist of binary digits.

computer-aided design (CAD) The use of software to assist in the creation, analysis, and modification of the design of a component or product.

computer-aided engineering (CAE) The use of software to analyze the robustness and performance of components and assemblies.

computer-aided manufacturing (CAM) The use of software to control machine tools and related machinery in the manufacture of components and products.

computer-based information system (CBIS) A single set of hardware, software, databases, telecommunications, people, and procedures that are configured to collect, manipulate, store, and process data into information.

computer graphics card A component of a computer that takes binary data from the CPU and translates it into an image you see on your display device.

computer-integrated manufacturing (CIM) Using computers to link the components of the production process into an effective system.

computer literacy The knowledge and ability to use computers and related technology effectively.

computer network The communications media, devices, and software needed to connect two or more computer systems or devices.

computer program A sequence of instructions for the computer.

concurrency control A method of dealing with a situation in which two or more users or applications need to access the same record at the same time.

consumer-to-consumer (C2C) e-commerce A subset of e-commerce that involves electronic transactions between consumers using a third party to facilitate the process.

contactless payment card A card with an embedded chip that only needs to be held close to a terminal to transfer its data; no PIN number needs to be entered.

content streaming A method for transferring large media files over the Internet so that the data stream of voice and pictures

plays more or less continuously as the file is being downloaded.

continuous improvement Constantly seeking ways to improve business processes and add value to products and services.

control unit The part of the CPU that sequentially accesses program instructions, decodes them, and coordinates the flow of data in and out of the ALU, the registers, the primary storage, and even secondary storage and various output devices.

coprocessor The part of the computer that speeds processing by executing specific types of instructions while the CPU works on another processing activity.

cost center A division within a company that does not directly generate revenue.

counterintelligence The steps an organization takes to protect information sought by "hostile" intelligence gatherers.

criminal hacker (cracker) A computer-savvy person who attempts to gain unauthorized or illegal access to computer systems to steal passwords, corrupt files and programs, or even transfer money.

critical path Activities that, if delayed, would delay the entire project.

critical success factors (CSFs) Factors that are essential to the success of a functional area of an organization.

culture A set of major understandings and assumptions shared by a group, such as within an ethnic group or a country.

customer relationship management (CRM) system A system that helps a company manage all aspects of customer encounters, including marketing, sales, distribution, accounting, and customer service.

cutover The process of switching from an old information system to a replacement system.

cybermall A single Web site that offers many products and services at one Internet location.

cyberterrorism The intimidation of government or civilian population by using information technology to disable critical national infrastructures (e.g., energy, transportation, telecommunications, banking and finance, law enforcement, and emergency response) to achieve political, religious, or ideological goals.

cyberterrorist Someone who intimidates or coerces a government or organization to advance his or her political or social objectives by launching computer-based attacks against computers, networks, and the information stored on them.

D

dashboard A data visualization tool that displays the current status of the key performance indicators (KPIs) for an organization.

data Raw facts, such as an employee number, total hours worked in a week, inventory part numbers, or the number of units produced on a production line.

data administrator A nontechnical position responsible for defining and implementing consistent principles for a variety of data issues.

data center A climate-and-access-controlled building or a set of buildings that houses the computer hardware that delivers an organization's data and information services.

data cleansing (data cleaning or data scrubbing) The process of detecting and then correcting or deleting incomplete, incorrect, inaccurate, irrelevant records that reside in a database.

data collection Capturing and gathering all data necessary to complete the processing of transactions.

data correction Reentering data that was not typed or scanned properly.

data definition language (DDL) A collection of instructions and commands that define and describe data and relationships in a specific database.

data dictionary A detailed description of all the data used in the database.

data editing Checking data for validity and completeness to detect any problems.

data entry Converting human-readable data into a machine-readable form.

data-flow diagram (DFD) A diagram used during both the analysis and design phases to document the processes of the current system or to provide a model of a proposed new system.

data-flow line A line that includes arrows showing the direction of data movement.

data input Transferring machine-readable data into the system.

data item The specific value of an attribute.

data manipulation language (DML) A specific language, provided with a DBMS, which allows users to access and modify the data, to make queries, and to generate reports.

data mart A subset of a data warehouse that is used by small- and medium-sized businesses and departments within large companies to support decision making.

data mining An information-analysis tool that involves the automated discovery of patterns and relationships in a data warehouse.

data model A diagram of data entities and their relationships.

data processing Performing calculations and other data transformations related to business transactions.

data storage Updating one or more databases with new transactions.

data store symbol A symbol that reveals a storage location for data.

data warehouse A large database that collects business information from many sources in the enterprise, covering all aspects of the company's processes, products, and customers, in support of management decision making.

database An organized collection of facts and information, typically consisting of two or more related data files.

database administrators (DBAs) Skilled and trained IS professionals who hold discussions with users to define their data needs; apply database programming languages to craft a set of databases to meet those needs; test and evaluate databases; implement changes to improve their performance; and assure that data is secure from unauthorized access.

database approach to data management An approach to data management where multiple information systems share a pool of related data.

database management system (DBMS) A group of programs that manipulate the database and provide an interface between the database and the user of the database and other application programs.

decentralized processing An approach to processing wherein processing devices are placed at various remote locations.

decision room A room that supports decision making, with the decision makers in the same building, and that combines face-to-face verbal interaction with technology to make the meeting more effective and efficient.

decision-making phase The first part of problem solving, including three stages: intelligence, design, and choice.

decision support system (DSS) An organized collection of people, procedures, software, databases, and devices used to support problem-specific decision making.

delphi approach A structured, interactive, iterative decision-making method that relies on input from a panel of experts.

demand report A report developed to give certain information at someone's request rather than on a schedule.

design stage The second stage of decision making in which you develop alternative solutions to the problem and evaluate their feasibility.

desktop computer A nonportable computer that fits on a desktop and provides sufficient computing power, memory, and storage for most business computing tasks.

dialogue manager A user interface that allows decision makers to easily access and manipulate the DSS and to use common business terms and phrases.

diffusion of innovation theory A theory developed by E.M. Rogers to explain how a new idea or product gains acceptance and diffuses (or spreads) through a specific population or subset of an organization.

digital audio player A device that can store, organize, and play digital music files.

digital camera An input device used with a PC to record and store images and video in digital form.

digital certificate An attachment to an email message or data embedded in a Web site that verifies the identity of a sender or Web site.

digital rights management (DRM) Refers to the use of any of several technologies to enforce policies for controlling access to digital media, such as movies, music, and software.

digital subscriber line (DSL) A telecommunications service that delivers high-speed Internet access to homes and small businesses over the existing phone lines of the local telephone network.

digital video disc (DVD) A secondary storage device that looks similar to a CD ROM but with greater storage capacity and faster data transfer rate.

direct access A retrieval method in which data can be retrieved without the need to read and discard other data.

direct access storage device (DASD) A device used for direct access of secondary storage data.

direct conversion Stopping the old system and starting the new system on a given date; also called plunge or direct cutover.

direct observation Directly observing the existing system in action by one or more members of the analysis team.

disaster recovery plan A documented process to recover an organization's business information system assets including hardware, software, data, networks, and facilities in the event of a disaster.

discrete manufacturing The production of distinct items such as autos, airplanes, furniture, or toys that can be decomposed into their basic components.

disk mirroring A process of storing data that provides an exact copy that protects users fully in the event of data loss.

distributed processing An approach to processing wherein processing devices are placed at remote locations but are connected to each other via a network.

document production Generating output records, documents, and reports.

documentation Text that describes a program's functions to help the user operate the computer system.

domain The range of allowable values for a data attribute.

domain expert The person or group with the expertise or knowledge the expert system is trying to capture (domain).

downsizing Reducing the number of employees to cut costs.

drill-down report A report providing increasingly detailed data about a situation.

dumpster diving Going through the trash of an organization to find secret or confidential information, including information needed to access an information system or its data.

E

economic feasibility The determination of whether the project makes financial sense and whether predicted benefits offset the cost and time needed to obtain them.

economic order quantity (EOQ) The quantity that should be reordered to minimize total inventory costs.

e-Government The use of information and communications technology to simplify the sharing of information, speed formerly paper-based processes, and improve the relationship between citizens and government.

electronic business (e-business) Using information systems and the Internet to perform all business-related tasks and functions.

electronic cash An amount of money that is computerized, stored, and used as cash for e-commerce transactions.

electronic commerce (e-commerce) Any business transaction executed electronically between companies (business-to-business), companies and consumers (business-to-consumer), consumers and other consumers (consumer-to-consumer), business and the public sector, and consumers and the public sector; conducting business activities (e.g., distribution, buying, selling, marketing, and servicing of products or services) electronically over computer networks.

electronic document distribution A process that enables the sending and receiving of documents in a digital form without being printed (although printing is possible).

electronic exchange An electronic forum where manufacturers, suppliers, and competitors buy and sell goods, trade market information, and run back-office operations.

electronic product environmental assessment tool (EPEAT) A system that enables purchasers to evaluate, compare, and select electronic products based on a total of 51 environmental criteria.

electronic retailing (e-tailing) The direct sale of products or services by businesses to consumers through electronic storefronts, typically designed around the familiar electronic catalog and shopping cart model.

empowerment Giving employees and their managers more responsibility and authority to make decisions, take action, and have more control over their jobs.

encryption The process of converting an original message into a form that can be understood only by the intended receiver.

encryption key A variable value that is applied (using an algorithm) to a set of unencrypted text to produce encrypted text (ciphertext) or to decrypt encrypted text.

end-user systems development The creation, modification, or extension of software by people who are nonprofessional software developers.

enterprise application integration (EAI) The systematic tying together of disparate applications so that they can communicate.

enterprise data modeling Data modeling done at the level of the entire enterprise.

enterprise resource planning (ERP) system A set of integrated programs that manages the vital business operations for an entire multisite, global organization.

enterprise sphere of influence The sphere of influence that serves the needs of the firm in its interaction with its environment.

enterprise system A system central to the organization that ensures information can be shared across all business functions and all levels of management to support the running and managing of a business.

entity A person, place, or thing for which data is collected, stored, and maintained.

entity-relationship (ER) diagrams Data models that use basic graphical symbols to show the organization of and relationships between data.

entity symbol A symbol that shows either the source or destination of the data.

ergonomics The science of designing machines, products, and systems to maximize the safety, comfort, and efficiency of the people who use them.

European Union's restriction of hazardous substances directive A directive that restricts the use of many hazardous materials in computer manufacturing and requires manufacturers to use at least 65 percent reusable or recyclable components, implement a plan to manage products at the end of their life cycle in an environmentally safe manner, and reduce or eliminate toxic material in their packaging.

exception report A report automatically produced when a situation is unusual or requires management action.

execution time (E-time) The time it takes to execute an instruction and store the results.

executive dashboard A diagram that presents a set of key performance indicators about the state of a process at a specific point in time to enable managers make better real-time decisions.

expert system A system that gives a computer the ability to make suggestions and function like an expert in a particular field.

explanation facility Component of an expert system that allows a user or decision maker to understand how the expert system arrived at certain conclusions or results.

Extensible Markup Language (XML) The markup language designed to transport and store data on the Web.

external auditing Auditing performed by an outside group.

extranet A network based on Web technologies that allows selected outsiders, such as business partners and customers, to access authorized resources of a company's intranet; A web technology that links selected resources of a company's intranet with its customers, suppliers, or other business partners.

extreme programming (XP) An approach to writing code that promotes incremental development of a system using short development cycles to improve productivity and to accommodate new customer requirements.

F

feasibility analysis Assessment of the technical, economic, legal, operational, and schedule feasibility of a project.

feedback Information from the system that is used to make changes to input or processing activities.

field Typically a name, number, or combination of characters that describes an aspect of a business object or activity.

file A collection of related records.

File Transfer Protocol (FTP) A protocol that provides a file transfer process between a host and a remote computer and allows users to copy files from one computer to another.

filtering software Software that screens Internet content.

final evaluation An evaluation that begins with a detailed investigation of the contenders' proposals as well as discussions with two or three customers of each vendor.

financial audit A thorough assessment of the reliability and integrity of the organization's financial information and the methods used to process it.

financial MIS An information system that provides financial information for workers who need to make better decisions on a daily basis.

five-forces model A widely accepted model that identifies five key factors that can lead to attainment of competitive advantage, including (1) the rivalry among existing competitors, (2) the threat of new entrants, (3) the threat of substitute products and services, (4) the bargaining power of buyers, and (5) the bargaining power of suppliers.

flat organizational structure An organizational structure with a reduced number of management layers.

flexible manufacturing system (FMS) An approach that allows manufacturing facilities to rapidly and efficiently change from making one product to making another.

forecasting Predicting future events to avoid problems.

full-duplex channel A communications channel that permits data transmission in both directions at the same time; a full-duplex channel is like two simplex channels.

functional decomposition A technique used during the investigation, analysis, and design phases to define the business processes included within the scope of the system.

G

game theory A mathematical theory for developing strategies that maximize gains and minimize losses while adhering to a given set of rules and constraints.

Gantt chart A graphical tool used for planning, monitoring, and coordinating projects.

gateway A telecommunications device that serves as an entrance to another network.

genetic algorithm An approach to solving problems based on the theory of evolution and the survival of the fittest as a problem-solving strategy.

geographic information system (GIS) A computer system capable of assembling, storing, manipulating, and displaying geographic information, that is, data identified according to its location.

gigahertz (GHz) Billions of cycles per second, a measure of clock speed.

graphical user interface (GUI) An interface that displays pictures (icons) and menus that people use to send commands to the computer system.

graphics processing unit (GPU) A powerful processing chip that renders images on the screen display.

green computing A program concerned with the efficient and environmentally responsible design, manufacture, operation, and disposal of IS-related products.

grid computing The use of a collection of computers, often owned by multiple individuals or organizations, to work in a coordinated manner to solve a common problem.

group consensus approach A group decision-making process that seeks the consent of all participants.

group decision support system (GSS) Software application that consists of most of the elements in a DSS, plus software to provide effective support in group decision-making settings; also called group support system or computerized collaborative work system.

H

hacker A person who enjoys computer technology and spends time learning and using computer systems.

half-duplex channel A communications channel that can transmit data in either direction but not simultaneously.

handheld computer A compact-sized computing device that is small enough to hold comfortably in one hand, and typically includes a display screen with stylus and/or touch screen input along with a compact keyboard or numeric keypad.

hard disk drive (HDD) A direct access storage device used to store and retrieve data from rapidly rotating disks coated with magnetic material.

hardware Computer equipment used to perform input, processing, storage, and output activities.

heuristics Commonly accepted guidelines or procedures that usually find a good solution.

hierarchy of data Bits, characters, fields, records, files, and databases.

hot site A duplicate, operational hardware system or immediate access to one through a specialized vendor.

human resource MIS (HRMIS) An information system that is concerned with activities related to previous, current, and potential employees of an organization, also called a personnel MIS.

hyperlink Highlighted text or graphics in a Web document that, when clicked, opens a new Web page containing related content.

Hypertext Markup Language (HTML) The standard page description language for Web pages.

I

identify theft A crime in which an imposter obtains key pieces of personal identification information, such as Social Security or driver's license numbers, to impersonate someone else; someone using your personal identification information without your permission to commit fraud or other crimes.

IF-THEN statement A rule that suggests certain conclusions.

image log A separate file that contains only changes to applications.

implementation stage A stage of problem solving in which a solution is put into effect.

incremental backup A backup copy of all files changed during the last few days or the last week.

inference engine Part of the expert system that seeks information and relationships from the knowledge base and provides answers, predictions, and suggestions similar to the way a human expert would.

informatics The combination of information technology with traditional disciplines such as medicine or science while considering the impact on individuals, organizations, and society.

information A collection of data organized and processed so that it has additional value beyond the value of the individual facts.

information literacy The ability to recognize a need for additional information, and then to find, access, evaluate, and effectively use that information to deal with the issue or problem at hand.

information system (IS) A set of interrelated components that collect, process, store, and disseminate data and information and provide a feedback mechanism to meet an objective.

information systems literacy Knowledge of how data and information are used by individuals, groups, and organizations.

information systems planning The identification of those information systems development initiatives needed to support organizational strategic goals.

infrared transmission A form of communications that sends signals at a frequency of 300 GHz and above—higher than those of microwaves but lower than those of visible light.

Infrastructure as a Service (IaaS) A computing model in which an organization outsources the equipment used to support its business operations, including storage, hardware, servers, and networking components, and the service provider owns the equipment and is responsible for housing, running, and maintaining it.

in-memory database A database management system that stores the entire database in random access memory (RAM).

input The activity of gathering and capturing raw data.

insider An employee, disgruntled or otherwise, working solo or in concert with outsiders to compromise corporate systems.

installation The process of physically placing the computer equipment on the site and making it operational.

instant messaging A method that allows two or more people to communicate online in real time using the Internet.

institutional DSS A DSS that handles situations or decisions that occur more than once, usually several times per year or more. It is used repeatedly and refined over the years.

instruction time (I-time) The time it takes to perform the fetch instruction and decode instruction steps of the instruction phase.

integration testing Testing that involves linking all of the individual components together and testing them as a group to uncover any defects between individual components.

intelligence stage The first stage of decision making in which you identify and define potential problems or opportunities.

intelligent agent Programs and a knowledge base used to perform a specific task for a person, a process, or another program; also called an intelligent robot or bot.

intelligent behavior The ability to learn from experiences and apply knowledge acquired from those experiences; to handle complex situations; to solve problems when important information is missing; to determine what is important and to react quickly and correctly to a new situation; to understand visual images, process and manipulate symbols, be creative and imaginative; and to use heuristics.

internal auditing Auditing performed by individuals within the organization.

internal rate of return The rate of return that makes the net present value of all cash flows (benefits and costs) generated by a project equal to zero.

Internet The world's largest computer network, consisting of thousands of interconnected networks, all freely exchanging information.

Internet censorship The control or suppression of the publishing or accessing of information on the Internet.

Internet Crime Complaint Center (IC3) An alliance between the White Collar Crime Center and the Federal Bureau of Investigation that provides a central site for Internet crime victims to report and to alert appropriate agencies of crimes committed.

Internet Protocol (IP) A communication standard that enables computers to route communications traffic from one network to another as needed.

Internet service provider (ISP) Any organization that provides Internet access to people.

intranet An internal network based on Web technologies that allows people within an organization to exchange information and work on projects.

intrusion detection system (IDS) Monitors system and network resources and traffic and notifies network security personnel when it senses a possible intrusion.

IP address A 64-bit number that identifies a computer on the Internet.

J

Java An object-oriented programming language from Sun Microsystems based on the C++ programming language, which allows applets to be embedded within an HTML document.

joining Manipulating data to combine two or more tables.

joint application development (JAD) A structured meeting process that can accelerate and improve the efficiency and effectiveness of the investigation, analysis, and design phases of a systems development project.

just-in-time (JIT) inventory An inventory management approach in which inventory and materials are delivered just before they are used in manufacturing a product.

K

kernel The heart of the operating system and controls its most critical processes.

key-indicator report A summary of the previous day's critical activities, typically available at the beginning of each workday.

key performance indicators (KPIs) Quantifiable measurements that assess progress toward organizational goals and reflect the critical success factors of an organization.

knowledge The awareness and understanding of a set of information and the ways that information can be made useful to support a specific task or reach a decision.

knowledge acquisition facility Part of the expert system that provides a convenient and efficient means of capturing and storing all the components of the knowledge base.

knowledge base The collection of data, rules, procedures, and relationships that must be followed to achieve value or the proper outcome.

knowledge engineer A person who has training or experience in the design, development, implementation, and maintenance of an expert system.

knowledge user The person or group who uses and benefits from the expert system.

L

laptop computer A personal computer designed for use by mobile users, being small and light enough to sit comfortably on a user's lap.

lean enterprise management A philosophy that considers the use of resources for any purpose other than to create value for the customer to be wasteful and therefore a target for elimination.

learning systems A combination of software and hardware that allows a computer to change how it functions or how it reacts to situations based on feedback it receives.

Leavitt's diamond A theory that proposes that every organizational system is made up of four main components—people, tasks, structure, and technology—with an interaction among the four components so that any change in one of these elements will necessitate a change in the other three elements.

legal feasibility The determination of whether laws or regulations may prevent or limit a systems development project.

linking The ability to combine two or more tables through common data attributes to form a new table with only the unique data attributes.

local area network (LAN) A network that connects computer systems and devices within a small area, such as an office, home, or several floors in a building.

long term evolution (LTE) A standard for wireless communications for mobile phones based on packet switching.

M

machine cycle The instruction phase followed by the execution phase.

magnetic stripe card A type of card that stores a limited amount of data by modifying the magnetism of tiny iron-based particles contained in a band on the card.

magnetic tape A type of sequential secondary storage medium, now used primarily for storing backups of critical organizational data in the event of a disaster.

mainframe computer A large, powerful computer often shared by hundreds of concurrent users connected to the machine over a network.

make-versus-buy decision The decision regarding whether to obtain the necessary software from internal or external sources.

malware Software programs that when loaded into a computer system will destroy, interrupt, or cause errors in processing.

managed security service providers (MSSPs) Organizations that monitor, manage, and maintain network security for both hardware and software for other organizations.

management information system (MIS) An organized collection of people, procedures, software, databases, and devices that provides routine information to managers and decision makers.

market segmentation The identification of specific markets to target them with tailored advertising messages.

marketing The process of determining the needs and wants of consumers and creating, communicating, and delivering products that satisfy those needs and wants.

marketing MIS A system that uses data gathered from both internal and external sources to provide reporting and aid decision making in all areas of marketing (market research, product design, pricing, media selection, advertising, selling, channel distribution, and product distribution).

massively parallel processing system A system that speeds processing by linking hundreds or thousands of processors to operate at the same time, or in parallel, with each processor having its own bus, memory, disks, copy of the operating system, and applications.

matrix organization structure An organization structure in which an individual has two reporting superiors (managers)—one functional and one operational.

mesh network A network that uses multiple access points to link a series of devices that speak to each other to form a network connection across a large area.

meta tag An HTML code, not visible on the displayed Web page, that contains keywords representing your site's content, which search engines use to build indexes pointing to your Web site.

metropolitan area network (MAN) A telecommunications network that connects users and their computers in a geographical area that spans a campus or city.

middleware Software that allows various systems to communicate and exchange data.

MIPS Millions of instructions per second, a measure of machine cycle time.

mission-critical processes Processes that play a pivotal role in an organization's continued operations and goal attainment.

mobile commerce (m-commerce) The use of mobile, wireless devices to place orders and conduct business.

model base Part of a DSS that allows managers and decision makers to perform quantitative analysis on both internal and external data.

model management software (MMS) Software that coordinates the use of models in a DSS, including financial, statistical analysis, graphical, and project-management models.

modem A telecommunications hardware device that converts (modulates and demodulates) communications signals so they can be transmitted over the communication media.

monitoring Tracking the number of errors encountered, the amount of memory required, the amount of processing or CPU time needed, and other performance indicators.

monitoring stage The final stage of the problem-solving process in which decision makers evaluate the implementation.

Moore's Law A hypothesis stating that transistor densities on a single chip will double every two years.

motherboard The backbone of the computer, connecting all of its components including the CPU and primary storage and providing connectors for peripheral devices such as printers, external hard drives, sound cards, and video cards.

MP3 A standard format for compressing a sound sequence into a small file.

multicore microprocessor A microprocessor that combines two or more independent processors into a single computer so that they share the workload and improve processing speed.

multimedia Text, graphics, video, animation, audio, and other media that can be used to help an organization efficiently and effectively achieve its goals.

multiprocessing The simultaneous execution of two or more instructions at the same time.

multivoting Any one of a number of voting processes used to reduce the number of options to be considered.

N

natural language processing Involves the computer understanding, analyzing, manipulating, and/or generating "natural" languages such as English.

Near Field Communication (NFC) A very short-range wireless connectivity technology designed for consumer electronics, cell phones, and credit cards.

net present value A method of evaluating a project is the sum of the present value of the net cash flow for each time period.

nettop computer An inexpensive desktop computer designed to be smaller, lighter, and consume much less power than a traditional desktop computer.

network Computers and equipment that are connected in a building, around the country, or around the world to enable electronic communications.

network-attached storage (NAS) A hard disk drive storage device that is set up with its own network address and provides file-based storage services to other devices on the network.

network-management software Software that enables a manager on a networked desktop to monitor the use of individual computers and shared hardware (such as printers), scan for viruses, and ensure compliance with software licenses.

network operating system (NOS) Systems software that controls the computer systems and devices on a network and allows them to communicate with each other.

network topology A diagram that indicates how the communications links and hardware devices of the network are arranged.

networking protocol A set of rules, algorithms, messages, and other mechanisms that enable software and hardware in networked devices to communicate effectively.

neural network A computer system that can recognize and act on patterns or trends that it detects in large sets of data.

nominal group technique (NGT) A structured method for group brainstorming that encourages contributions from everyone.

nonprogrammed decision A decision that deals with unusual or exceptional situations.

NoSQL database A database designed to store and retrieve data in a manner that does not rigidly enforce the atomic conditions associated with the relational database model in order to provide faster performance and greater scalability.

O

offshore outsourcing (offshoring) An outsourcing arrangement where the organization providing the service is located in a country different than the firm obtaining the services.

off-the-shelf software Software mass-produced by software vendors to address needs that are common across businesses, organizations, or individuals.

online analytical processing (OLAP) A form of analysis that allows users to explore data from a number of perspectives, enabling a style of analysis known as "slicing and dicing."

online transaction processing (OLTP) A form of data processing where each transaction is processed immediately without the delay of accumulating transactions into a batch.

open-source software Software that is distributed, typically for free, with the source code also available so that it can be studied, changed, and improved

operating system (OS) A set of computer programs that controls the computer hardware and acts as an interface with applications.

operational audit An assessment of how well management uses the resources of the organization and how effectively organizational plans are being executed.

operational feasibility Concerned with how the system will be accepted by people and how well it will meet various system performance expectations.

optical storage device A form of data storage that uses lasers to read and write data.

optimization model A process to find the best solution, the one that will best help the organization meet its goals.

organization A group of people that is structured and managed to meet its mission or set of group goals.

organizational change How for-profit and nonprofit organizations plan for, implement, and handle change.

organizational culture The major understandings and assumptions for a business, corporation, or other organization.

organizational learning The adaptations and adjustments based on experience and ideas over time.

organizational structure Organizational subunits and the way they relate to the overall organization.

output Production of useful information, usually in the form of documents and reports.

outsourcing A long-term business arrangement in which a company contracts for services with an outside organization that has expertise in providing a specific function.

P

packet-switching network A network in which no fixed path is created between the communicating devices, and the data is broken into packets, with each packet transmitted individually and capable of taking various paths from sender to recipient.

parallel computing The simultaneous execution of the same task on multiple processors to obtain results faster.

parallel start-up Running both the old and new systems for a period of time and closely comparing the output of the new system with the output of the old system; any differences are reconciled. When users are comfortable that the new system is working correctly, the old system is eliminated.

Pareto principle (80–20 rule) An observation that for many events, roughly 80 percent of the effects come from 20 percent of the causes.

password sniffer A small program hidden in a network or a computer system that records identification numbers and passwords.

patch A minor change to correct a problem or make a small enhancement. It is usually an addition to an existing program.

payback period Takes into account all the increases and decreases in cash flow associated with the project.

p-card (procurement card or purchasing card) A credit card used to streamline the traditional purchase order and invoice payment processes.

perceptive system A system that approximates the way a person sees, hears, and feels objects.

performance evaluation test A comparison of vendor options conducted in a computing environment (e.g., computing hardware, operating system software, database management system) and with a workload (e.g., number of concurrent users, database size, and number of transactions) that matches its intended operating conditions.

personal area network (PAN) A network that supports the interconnection of information technology close to one person.

personal productivity software The software that enables users to improve their personal effectiveness, increasing the amount of work and quality of work they can do.

personal sphere of influence The sphere of influence that serves the needs of an individual user.

personalization The process of tailoring Web pages to specifically target individual consumers.

phase-in approach Slowly replacing components of the old system with those of the new one; this process is repeated for each application until the new system is running every application and performing as expected; it is also called a piecemeal approach.

phishing A form of computer scam that attempts to get users to gain access to a customer's private information through a fake Web site.

pilot start-up Running the complete new system for one group of users rather than all users.

pipelining A form of CPU operation in which multiple execution phases are performed in a single machine cycle.

point-of-sale (POS) device A terminal used to enter data into the computer system.

policy-based storage management Automation of storage using previously defined policies.

portable computer A computer small enough to carry easily.

predictive analysis (also called predictive analytics) A form of data mining that combines historical data with assumptions about future conditions to predict outcomes of events, such as future product sales or the probability that a customer will default on a loan.

preliminary evaluation An evaluation that begins during systems analysis and identifies the two or three strongest contenders.

primary key A field or set of fields that uniquely identifies the record.

primary storage (main memory; memory) The part of the computer that holds program instructions and data.

private branch exchange (PBX) A telephone switching exchange that serves a single organization.

problem solving A process that goes beyond decision making to include the implementation stage.

procedures The strategies, policies, methods, and rules for using a CBIS.

process A set of logically related tasks performed to achieve a defined outcome.

process manufacturing The production of products that are the result of a chemical process such as soda, laundry detergent, gasoline, and pharmaceutical drugs that cannot be easily decomposed into its basic components.

process symbol A symbol that identifies the function being performed.

processing Converting or transforming data into useful outputs.

product lifecycle management (PLM) An enterprise business strategy that creates a common repository of product information and processes to support the collaborative creation, management, dissemination, and use of product and packaging definition information.

product lifecycle management (PLM) software Software that provides a means for managing the data and processes associated with the various phases of the lifecycle of a product, including sales and marketing, research and development, concept development, product design, prototyping and testing, process design, production and assembly, delivery and product installation, service and support, and product retirement and replacement.

product owner A person who represents the project stakeholders and is responsible for communicating and aligning project priorities between the stakeholders and development team.

profit center An independent business unit that is treated as a distinct entity enabling its revenues and expenses to be determined and its profitability to be measured.

Program Evaluation and Review Technique (PERT) A formalized approach for developing a project schedule that creates three time estimates for an activity.

programmed decision A decision made using a rule, procedure, or quantitative method.

programmer A specialist responsible for modifying or developing programs to satisfy user requirements.

programming languages Sets of keywords, commands, symbols, and rules for constructing statements by which humans can communicate instructions to a computer.

project deadline The date the entire project should be completed and operational.

project manager The person assigned by the organization to do the work of the project and achieve the project objectives.

project milestone A critical date for the completion of a major part of the project.

project organizational structure A structure focused on major products or services, with program managers responsible for directing one or more projects.

project schedule A detailed description of when project activities are performed.

project sponsor A key member and leader of the steering team who plays such a critical role that lack of this essential individual raises the distinct probability of project failure.

projecting Manipulating data to eliminate columns in a table.

proprietary software One-of-a-kind software designed for a specific application and owned by the company, organization, or person that uses it.

prototype A working model of a system developed to enable users to interact with the system and provide feedback so developers can better understand what is needed.

prototyping An iterative software development approach based on the use of software prototypes.

Q

quality The ability of a product or service to meet or exceed customer expectations.

quality control A process that ensures that the finished product meets the customers' needs.

R

Radio Frequency Identification (RFID) A technology that employs a microchip with an antenna to broadcast its unique identifier and location to receivers.

random access memory (RAM) A form of memory in which instructions or data can be temporarily stored.

rational unified process (RUP) An iterative systems development approach developed by IBM that includes a number of tools and techniques that are typically tailored to fit the needs of a specific company or organization.

read-only memory (ROM) A non-volatile form of memory.

record A collection of data fields all related to one object, activity, or individual.

redundant array of independent/ inexpensive disks (RAID) A method of storing data that generates extra bits of data from existing data, allowing the system to create a "reconstruction map" so that if a hard drive fails, the system can rebuild lost data.

reengineering (process redesign) The radical redesign of business processes, organizational structures, information systems, and values of the organization to achieve a breakthrough in business results.

register A high-speed storage area in the CPU used to temporarily hold small units of program instructions and data immediately before, during, and after execution by the CPU.

relational model A simple but highly useful way to organize data into collections of two-dimensional tables called relations.

release A significant program change that often requires changes in the documentation of the software.

reorder point (ROP) A critical inventory quantity level.

request for maintenance form A form authorizing modification of programs.

request for proposal (RFP) A formal document that outlines an organization's hardware or software needs and requests vendors to develop a detailed proposal of how they would meet those needs and at what cost.

responsive Web design A means of providing custom layouts to devices based on the size of the browser window.

revenue center An organizational unit that gains revenue from the sale of products or services.

reverse 911 service A communications solution that delivers emergency notifications to users in a selected geographical area.

rich Internet application (RIA) Software that has the functionality and complexity of traditional application software but that does not require local installation and runs in a Web browser.

robotics Mechanical or computer devices that perform tasks requiring a high degree of precision or that are tedious or hazardous for humans.

router A telecommunications device that forwards data packets between computer networks.

rule A conditional statement that links conditions to actions or outcomes.

S

satisficing model A model that will find a good—but not necessarily the best—solution to a problem.

scalability The ability to increase the processing capability of a computer system so that it can handle more users, more data, or more transactions in a given period.

schedule feasibility The determination of whether the project can be completed in a reasonable amount of time.

scheduled report A report produced periodically, such as daily, weekly, or monthly.

schema A description of the logical and physical structure of data and the relationships among the data for each user; a description of an entire database.

scope creep The temptation to add more features and functionality to the original scope of the system.

script bunny A derogatory term for inexperienced hackers who download programs called "scripts" that automate the job of breaking into computers.

scrum A method employed to keep the agile system development effort focused and moving quickly.

scrum master The person who coordinates all scrum activities.

search engine A valuable tool that enables you to find information on the Web by specifying words that are key to a topic of interest, known as keywords.

secondary storage Devices that store large amounts of data, instructions, and information more permanently than allowed with main memory.

secure sockets layer (SSL) A communications protocol used to secure sensitive data during e-commerce.

security dashboard Software that provides a comprehensive display on a single computer screen of all the vital data related to an organization's security defenses, including threats, exposures, policy compliance and incident alerts.

selecting Manipulating data to eliminate rows according to certain criteria.

semistructured decisions Decisions where only some of the variables can be measured quantitatively.

separation of duties The careful division of the tasks and responsibilities associated with a key process so that they must be performed by more than one person.

sequential access A retrieval method in which data must be accessed in the order in which it is stored.

sequential access storage device (SASD) A device used to sequentially access secondary storage data.

server A computer employed by many users to perform a specific task, such as running network or Internet applications.

service-oriented architecture (SOA) A software design approach based on the use of discrete pieces of software (modules) to provide specific functions as services to other applications.

simplex channel A communications channel that can transmit data in only one direction and is seldom used for business telecommunications.

single-user license A software license that permits you to install the software on one or more computers, used by one person.

site preparation Preparation of the location of a new system.

Six Sigma A measurement-based strategy to improve processes and reduce variation through completion of Six Sigma projects.

slipstream upgrade A minor upgrade—typically a code adjustment or minor bug fix—not worth announcing. It usually requires recompiling all the code, and in so doing, it can create entirely new bugs.

small cell A miniature cellular base station designed to provide improved cellular coverage and capacity for homes and organizations and even metropolitan and rural public spaces.

smart card A credit card–sized device with an embedded microchip to provide electronic memory and processing capability; Credit cards embedded with computer chips containing key consumer and account data; cardholders must either enter their pin (chip-and-PIN) or sign (chip-and-sign) for each transaction to be approved.

smishing A scam that attempts to steal an individual's private information by having them respond to a text message.

social engineering Using social skills to get computer users to provide information that allows a hacker to access an information system or its data.

social graph analysis A data visualization technique in which data is represented as networks where the vertices are the individual data points (social network users) and the edges are the connections among them.

software The computer programs that govern the operation of the computer.

Software as a Service (SaaS) A service that allows businesses to subscribe to Web-delivered application software.

software defined networking An emerging approach to networking that allows network administrators to have programmable central control of the network via a controller without requiring physical access to all the network devices.

software piracy The act of unauthorized copying, downloading, sharing, selling, or installing of copyrighted software.

software suite A collection of programs packaged together in a bundle.

source data automation Capturing data at its source and recording it accurately in a timely fashion with minimal manual effort and in an electronic or digital form so that it can be directly entered into the computer.

speech-recognition technology Input devices that recognize human speech.

spyware Software that is installed on a personal computer to intercept or take partial control of the user's interaction with the computer without the knowledge or permission of the user.

stakeholders People who ultimately will be affected (for better or worse) by the systems development project.

star network A network in which all network devices connect to one another through a single central device called the hub node.

steering team A small group of senior managers representing the business and IS organizations that provide guidance and support to the project.

storage area network (SAN) A high-speed, special-purpose network that integrates different types of data storage devices (e.g., hard disk drives, magnetic tape, solid state secondary storage devices) into a single storage system and connects that to computing resources across an entire organization.

storage as a service Storage as a service is a data storage model where a data storage service provider rents space to individuals and organizations.

storefront broker A company that acts as an intermediary between your Web site and online merchants who have the products and retail expertise.

strategic alliance (or strategic partnership) An agreement between two or more companies that involves the joint production and distribution of goods and services.

structured decisions Decisions where the variables that comprise the decision are known and can be measured quantitatively.

supercomputer One of the most powerful computer systems with the fastest processing speed.

supply chain management (SCM) The management of all the activities required to get the right product into the right consumer's hands in the right quantity at the right time and at the right cost, from acquisition of raw materials through customer delivery; a system that includes planning, executing, and controlling all activities involved in raw material sourcing and procurement, converting raw materials to finished products, and warehousing and delivering finished products to customers.

switch A telecommunications device that contains ports to which all the devices on the network can connect and uses the physical device address in each incoming message to determine to which output port it should forward the message to reach its intended destination.

syntax A set of rules associated with a programming language.

system A set of elements or components that interact to accomplish goals.

system construction The phase of systems development that converts the system design into an operational system by acquiring and installing hardware and software, coding and testing software programs, creating and loading data into databases, and performing initial program testing.

system disposal Those activities that ensure the orderly dissolution of the system, including disposing of all equipment in an environmentally friendly manner, closing out contracts, and safely migrating information from the system to another system or archiving it in accordance with applicable records management policies.

system testing Testing the complete, integrated system (hardware, software, databases, people, and procedures) to validate that the information system meets all specified requirements.

systems analyst A professional who specializes in analyzing and designing business systems.

systems design The stage of systems development that answers the question, "How will the information system solve a problem?"

systems development The activity of creating or modifying information systems.

systems investigation report A summary of the results of the systems investigation with a recommendation of a course of action.

systems investigation request A document filled out by someone who wants the IS department to initiate a systems investigation.

systems maintenance A stage of systems development that involves changing and enhancing the system to make it more useful in achieving user and organizational goals.

systems operation Use of a new or modified system under all kinds of operating conditions.

systems review The process of analyzing systems to make sure they are operating as intended.

T

tablet computer A portable, lightweight computer with no keyboard that allows you to roam the office, home, or factory floor carrying the device like a clipboard.

tag Code that tells the Web browser how to format text—as a heading, as a list, or as body text—and whether images, sound, and other elements should be inserted.

technical documentation Written details used by computer operators to execute the program and by analysts and programmers to solve problems or modify the program.

technical feasibility Examines if the project is feasible within the current limits of available technology.

technology acceptance model (TAM) A model that specifies the factors that can lead to better attitudes about an information system, along with higher acceptance and usage of it.

technology infrastructure All the hardware, software, databases, telecommunications, people, and procedures that are configured to collect, manipulate, store, and process data into information.

telecommunications The electronic transmission of signals for communications that enables organizations to carry out their processes and tasks through effective computer networks.

telecommunications medium Any material substance that carries an electronic signal to support communications between a sending and a receiving device.

telecommuting The use of computing devices and networks so that employees can work effectively away from the office.

thin client A low-cost, centrally managed computer with no internal or external attached drives for data storage.

throw-away prototype A prototype that is used to help define the software solution but does not become part of the final solution.

time value of money Takes into account the fact that a dollar today is worth more than a dollar paid in the future.

total quality management A management approach to long-term organizational success through satisfying customer needs.

traditional approach to data management An approach to data management whereby each distinct operational system uses data files dedicated to that system.

traditional hierarchical organizational structure (functional structure) An organizational structure in which the hierarchy of decision making and authority flows from the strategic management at the top down to operational management and nonmanagement employees.

traditional systems development life cycle A sequential multistage process where work on the next stage cannot begin until the results of the previous stage are reviewed and approved or modified as necessary.

transaction Any business-related exchange such as payments to employees, sales to customers, and payments to suppliers.

transaction processing cycle The process of data collection, data editing, data correction, data processing, data storage, and document production.

transaction processing system (TPS) An organized collection of people, procedures, software, databases, and devices used to perform and record business transactions.

Transmission Control Protocol (TCP) The widely used transport layer protocol that most Internet applications use with IP.

tunnelling The process by which VPNs transfer information by encapsulating traffic in IP packets over the Internet.

U

ultra wideband (UWB) A form of short-range communications that employs extremely short electromagnetic pulses lasting just 50 to 1,000 picoseconds that are transmitted across a broad range of radio frequencies of several gigahertz.

Uniform Resource Locator (URL) A Web address that specifies the exact location of a Web page using letters and words that map to an IP address and a location on the host.

unit testing Testing that ideally forces an individual program to execute all of its various functions and user features.

United States Computer Emergency Readiness Team (US-CERT) Part of the Department of Homeland Security that leads U.S. efforts to improve the nation's cybersecurity posture, coordinate cyber information sharing, and proactively manage cyber risks to the nation.

unstructured decisions Decisions where the variables that affect the decision cannot be measured quantitatively.

user acceptance document A formal agreement that the user signs stating that a phase of the installation or the complete system is approved.

user acceptance testing Testing performed by trained system users to verify that the system can complete required tasks in a real-world operating environment and perform according to the system design specifications.

user documentation Written descriptions developed for people who use a program; in easy-to-understand language, it shows how the program can and should be used to meet the needs of its various users.

user interface The element of the operating system that allows people to access and interact with the computer system.

user preparation The process of readying managers, decision makers, employees, other users, and stakeholders to accept and use the new system.

users People who will regularly interact with the system.

utility program Program that helps to perform maintenance or correct problems with a computer system.

V

value chain A series (chain) of activities that an organization performs to transform inputs into outputs in such a way that the value of the input is increased.

version A major program change, typically encompassing many new features.

videoconferencing A set of interactive telecommunications technologies that enable people at multiple locations to communicate using simultaneous two-way video and audio transmissions.

virtual private network (VPN) A private network that uses a public network (usually the Internet) to connect multiple remote locations.

virtual reality An artificial three-dimensional environment created by hardware and software and experienced through sensory stimuli (primarily sight and sound, but sometimes through touch, taste, and smell) and within which an individual can interact to affect what happens in the environment.

virtual reality system A system that enables one or more users to move and react in a computer-simulated environment.

virtual server A method of logically dividing the resources of a single physical server to create multiple logical servers, each acting as its own dedicated machine.

virtual tape A storage device for less frequently needed data so that it appears to be stored entirely on tape cartridges, although some parts of it might actually be located on faster hard disks.

virtual team A group of individuals whose members are distributed geographically, but who work as a coherent unit through the use of information systems technology.

virtual workgroups Teams of people located around the world working on common problems.

vishing A scam that attempts to steal an individual's private information by having them call a phone number and enter personal data.

vision system The hardware and software that permit computers to capture, store, and manipulate visual images.

voice mail Technology that enables users to send, receive, and store verbal messages to and from other people around the world.

voice mail-to-text service A service that captures voice mail messages, converts them to text, and sends them to an email account.

volume testing Testing to evaluate the performance of the information system under varying yet realistic work volume and operating conditions to determine the work load at which systems performance begins to degrade and to identify and eliminate any issues that prevent the system from reaching its required service-level performance.

W

Web Server and client software, the Hypertext Transfer Protocol (HTTP), standards, and markup languages that combine to deliver information and services over the Internet.

Web 2.0 The Web as a computing platform that supports software applications and the sharing of information among users.

Web browser Web client software, such as Chrome, Firefox, Internet Explorer, Safari, and Opera, used to view Web pages.

Web design framework A collection of files and folders of standardized code (HTML, CSS, and Javascript documents), which can be used to support the development of Web sites.

Web log (blog) A Web site that people can create and use to write about their observations, experiences, and opinions on a wide range of topics.

Web portal A Web page that combines useful information and links and acts as an entry point to the Web; portals typically include a search engine, a subject directory, daily headlines, and other items of interest. Many people choose a Web portal as their browser's home page (the first page you open when you begin browsing the Web).

wide area network (WAN) A telecommunications network that connects large geographic regions.

Wi-Fi A medium-range wireless telecommunications technology brand owned by the Wi-Fi Alliance.

wireless access point A device that enables wireless devices to connect to a wired network using Wi-Fi, or other wireless network standards.

workgroup Two or more people who work together to achieve a common goal.

workgroup application software Software that supports teamwork, whether team members are in the same location or dispersed around the world.

workgroup sphere of influence The sphere of influence that helps workgroup members attain their common goals.

working prototype A prototype that starts with an initial prototype that undergoes a series of iterations of demo, feedback, and refinement and eventually evolves into the final software solution.

workstation A more powerful personal computer used for mathematical computing, computer-assisted design, and other high-end processing but still small enough to fit on a desktop.

Worldwide Interoperability for Microwave Access (WiMAX) A 4G alternative based on a set of IEEE 802.16 metropolitan area network standards that support various types of communications access.

Z

ZigBee A developing network wireless communications standard designed to carry small amounts of data at fairly low bandwidth of 20 Kbps to 250 Kbps over mid-range distances or 100 meters or so using very little power.

Subject Index

Note: A boldface page number indicates a key term and the location of its definition in the text.

A

Aakash, 139
ACA Correlator, 105
Access, 225, 230
Access Workflow Designer, 507
accounting management information system (MIS), **472**–473
accounting systems, 414
accredited domain name registrars, **312**
Accumulo, 244
ACD (automatic call distributor), 292–293
ACID properties, 230
ACM (Association for Computing Machinery), 684
Active Directory, 194
actors, **618**
ad hoc DSS, **478**
Adobe Audition, 526, 527
Adobe Buzzword, 316
Adobe ColdFusion, 324
Adobe Dreamweaver CC, 322
Adobe Flash, **320,** 527
Adobe Illustrator, 525
Adobe Photoshop, 525
Adobe Photoshop Express, 326
Adobe Premium, 527
ADS (Advanced Distribution System), 578–579
ADSL (asymmetric DSL), **290**
Advanced Distribution System (ADS), 578–579
Advanced Encryption Standard (AES), 286
advertising, 382–384, 468
  Internet, 324
AES (Advanced Encryption Standard), 286
Affordable Care Act, 185, 664
After Effects, 527
aggregator software, **338**
agile development, 595, **614**–617
agile information systems, 80
Aguirre, Viviana, 348
AI. *See* artificial intelligence (AI)

Airbnb, 321
Airtel Money, 363
AI Trilogy, 517
AIX, 177
Alfresco, 176
Alice, 200
alphanumeric data, 5
alpha testing, 604
ALU (arithmetic/logic unit), **107**
AmazonFresh Web site, 59
Amazon Instant, 340
Amazon Relational Database Service (Amazon RDS), 239
Amazon Web Services (AWS), 16, 187, 321
American Recovery and Reinvestment Act, 87
American Taxpayer Relief Act (ATRA), 554
analysis, 429
Andresen, Gavin, 639
Android Emulator, 202
Android operating system, 13, 167, 175, 194, 202
animation, 320, 526–527
anonymous input, 485
ANSYS, 176
antispyware software, 182
antivirus, 182, **668**–669
AOL Video, 340
Apache, 176
Apache HTTP Server, 393
Apatar, 245
AppEngine, 186
Apple App Store, 194, 656
Apple Computer operating systems (OS), 173–174
Apple Mail, 335
Apple Messages, 338
Apple Safari, 185, 317
AppleShare, 277
applets, **319**
Application Continuous Availability, 581
application programming interface (API), **171**

application service provider (ASP), **186**
application software, 13, 165–166, 184–197
  enterprise, 196–197
  information, decision support, and competitive advantage, 197
  mobile, 194–195
  off-the-shelf software, **185**–186
  overview of, 185–188
  personal, 188–194
  primary function of, 184
  proprietary software, **185**
  workgroup, **195**
apps (applications), 298
Apps for Business and Postini Archiving & Discovery, 195
Apps Run the World blog, 20
Architectural Digest, 248
Argir, Fred, 391
arithmetic/logic unit (ALU), **107**
ARM processors, 109
ARPANET, **309**
Ars Technica, 248
artificial intelligence (AI), 28–30, **507**
  Brain Computer Interface (BCI), **512**
  branches of, 512
  expert system, 512
  genetic algorithm, **518**
  intelligent agent, **518**–519
  learning systems, **517**
  natural language processing, 516–517
  nature of, 510–511
  neural networks, **517**
  perspective, 509–510
  robotics, **512**–513
  vision systems, **513**–514
  voice recognition, **516**–517
artificial intelligence systems, **509**
Asana, 196
Ash, Michael, 190
Ask, 330, 332
ASP, 621
ASP (application service provider), **186**
aspect ratio, 131

Company Index